Longman
Essential

Put Your Ideas Into Words

Longman

The publishers and editorial team would like to thank the many people who have contributed to the making of this dictionary, in particular the Linglex Dictionary and Corpus Advisory Committee who have reviewed and commented on the book at several stages from concept planning to final text:

Lord Quirk (chair), Professor Douglas Biber, Rod Bolitho, Professor Gillian Brown, Professor David Crystal, Professor Geoffrey Leech, Dr Paul Meara, Philip Scholfield, Professor Peter Trudgill, Professor Katie Wales, Professor John Wells

and also Professor Yoshihiko Ikegami and Professor Thomas Herbst.

Thanks also go to Yuri Komuro, and all the teachers and students throughout the world who have given us feedback and advice, as well as all those who have contributed to the Longman Learner's Corpus.

Publishers
Emma Campbell
Lizzie Warren

Managing Editor
Michael Rundell

Associate Lexicographers
Stella O'Shea
Sue Engineer

Senior Editors
Emma Campbell
Chris Fox
Ted Jackson

Lexicographers
Paula Biswas
Pat Bulhosen
Lucy Hollingworth
Jill Leatherbarrow
Joanna Leigh
Glennis Pye
and
Patrick Gillard
Fiona McIntosh
Elaine Pollard

American English
Karen Cleveland Marwick
Rebecca Campbell
Dileri Borunda Johnston
Carol Pomeroy Zhong

Pronunciation Editor
Dinah Jackson

Administrative Assistants
Sandra Rootsey
Helen Spencer
Jane Whittle
Liz Wrighton
Lee Hodder

Director
Della Summers

Editorial Director
Adam Gadsby

Grammar section
David Crystal

Project Manager
Alan Savill

Senior Production Editor
Alison Steadman

Production Editor
Claire Parkyns

Production Manager
Clive McKeough

Corpus development
Steve Crowdy
Denise Denney

Technical support
Trevor Satchell
Keith Mardell

Design
Jenny Fleet

Illustrators
Karen Donnelly
Angela Lumley
Pat Murray
Gillian Hunt

Keyboarder
Pauline Savill

Proofreader
Gerard Delaney

Pronunciation table

consonants

symbol	example word
b	**b**ack
d	**d**ay
ð	**th**en
dʒ	**j**ump
f	**f**at
g	**g**et
h	**h**ot
j	**y**ell
k	**k**ey
l	**l**ed
m	su**m**
n	su**n**
ŋ	su**ng**
p	**p**en
r	**r**ed
s	**s**oon
ʃ	**fish**ing
t	**t**ea
tʃ	**ch**eer
θ	**th**ing
v	**v**iew
w	**w**et
x	lo**ch**
z	**z**ero
ʒ	plea**s**ure

vowels

symbol	example word
iː	sh**ee**p
ɪ	sh**i**p
i	happ**y**
e	b**e**d
æ	b**a**d
ɑː	c**a**lm
ɒ	p**o**t
ɔː	c**au**ght
ʊ	p**u**t
u	act**u**ality
uː	b**oo**t
ʌ	c**u**t
ɜː	b**ir**d
ə	c**u**pb**oar**d
eɪ	m**a**ke
əʊ	n**o**te
aɪ	b**i**te
aʊ	n**ow**
ɔɪ	b**oy**
ɪə	h**ere**
iə	pec**u**l**iar**
eə	th**ere**
ʊə	p**oor**
uə	rit**ual**

special signs

‖	separates British and American pronunciations: British on the left, American on the right
/ˈ/	shows main stress
/ˌ/	shows secondary stress
/◄/	shows stress shift
/ʳ/	means that the /r/ sound is pronounced in American English, but usually not pronounced in British English, except at the end of a word when the word that follows begins with a vowel sound
/ɪ̯ə/	means that some speakers use /ɪ/ and others use /ə/
/ʊ̯ə/	means that some speakers use /ʊ/ and others use /ə/
/ə/	means that /ə/ may or may not be used

CONTENTS

How to use the Longman Essential Activator

The **Longman Essential Activator** will help you make your language more accurate, more varied, and more like that of a native speaker. For example, imagine you want to find a better word to use instead of 'very happy' in this sentence:

I was <u>very happy</u> to hear about your new job.

(Longman Learner's Corpus extract, intermediate level student.)

This is what you do:

1. Think of a word which expresses the basic meaning of what you want to say.

HAPPY

2. Find that word in the *Essential Activator,* and choose the most suitable section.

2 happy because something good has happened

3. Read the definitions of the words in that section, and decide which is the best one for you to use.

delighted /dɪˈlaɪtᵻd/ [*adj* not before noun] extremely happy because something very good has happened: *She has been offered a job in Japan, and she's delighted of course.*

4. Now use this word to improve your sentence.

I was <u>delighted</u> to hear about your new job.

You can also find help when you need to write about a particular subject or topic, by using the **Essential Word Banks.** For example, if you want to write an article about the environment, turn to **E** to look up **ENVIRONMENT**, where you will find vocabulary, information, and ideas related to this subject.

When you are dealing with real situations in English, such as apologizing, complaining, or having a conversation, use the **ESSENTIAL COMMUNICATION** section, like this:

1. Choose the type of situation you need to deal with in English.

SAYING GOODBYE

2. Decide which box best describes the situation you are in.

> saying goodbye to a friend you will see again soon

3. Read the options you are given and select the one which is most suitable...

> **See you soon**

4. ...and use this to communicate in English.

I must go, or I'll be late. See you soon!

If you need help with grammar, turn to the **ESSENTIAL GRAMMAR** section, where you will find help with all the major grammar problems.

Every word and phrase in the **Longman Essential Activator** also appears in the index at the back, so if you know which word you want, but need more information about it, you can see exactly where to find it:

The **Longman Essential Activator** is the essential one-stop resource for language production.

VOCABULARY IS DIVIDED INTO MEANING AREAS

GENUINELY HELPFUL CROSS-REFERENCES

NATURAL CORPUS-BASED EXAMPLES GIVE APPROPRIATE CONTEXT

MAXIMUM HELP WITH LANGUAGE PRODUCTION

BALANCED COVERAGE OF BOTH AMERICAN AND BRITISH ENGLISH

SPOKEN AS WELL AS WRITTEN EXAMPLES

IRREGULAR COMPARATIVES, SUPERLATIVES, AND INFLECTIONS ARE SPELLED OUT IN FULL

ANGRY

➡ if you mean 'not angry or upset' go to **CALM**

1 feeling angry

angry /'æŋgri/ [adj] if you are **angry**, you feel a strong emotion, for example about someone who has treated you badly or about something that you think is wrong or unfair: *I was so angry that I could hardly speak.* | *A crowd of angry demonstrators gathered outside the embassy.* | *After the programme, the TV station received hundreds of angry phone calls.*
+ with *She was angry with him because he had lied to her.*
+ about *Don't you feel angry about the way you've been treated?*
+ that *Local people are angry that they weren't consulted about plans to expand the airport.*
angry – angrier – angriest

⚠ Use **angry with** about people: *I was really angry with him.* Use **angry about** about things: *I was really angry about it.*

angrily [adv] *Rachel slammed the door angrily on her way out.*

mad /mæd/ [adj not before noun] INFORMAL, ESPECIALLY AMERICAN angry: *Tom will be real mad when he sees what you've done to his car.* **+ at** *She used to get mad at Harry because he was always changing his mind.* **+ about** *Come on, Maria – what are you so mad about?*

mad – madder – maddest

annoyed /ə'nɔɪd/ [adj not before noun] a little angry, but not very angry: *I'll be annoyed if he's forgotten to deliver my message.*
+ with *Joe was annoyed with her for making him miss the film.* | *I was annoyed with myself for playing so badly.*
+ at/by *Kay was clearly annoyed at John's remark.*

furious /'fjʊəriəs/ [adj] very angry: *I've never been so furious in all my life.* | *a furious argument* (=when people shout at each other in an angry way)

+ with *She'd be furious with me if she knew I was reading her diary.*
+ at/about *He came home furious at something his boss had said.*

⚠ Don't say 'very furious'. Say **absolutely furious.**

furiously [*adv*] *"Stop it," shouted Ralph furiously.*

livid /ˈlɪvᵻd/ [*adj*] so angry that it is difficult for you to speak properly or think clearly: *"Was he angry when you got in so late?" "Angry? He was livid!"* | *I know I shouldn't have spoken to her like that, but I was absolutely livid.*

⚠ Don't say 'very livid'. Say **absolutely livid** or just **livid.**

offended /əˈfendᵻd/ [*adj* not before noun] angry and upset because someone has said or done something rude or has insulted you: *A lot of Muslims were offended when the book came out.* | *I hope you won't be offended if I leave early.*
+ by *Many readers were offended by the newspaper's anti-Irish comments.*

🔍**cross** /krɒs‖krɔːs/ [*adj*] BRITISH, ESPECIALLY SPOKEN angry – used especially by children or when you are talking to children: *Do you think Dad will be cross when he finds out what happened?*
+ with *Are you cross with me?*

fed up with sth/sick of sth /ˌfed ˈʌp wɪð (sth), ˈsɪk ɒv (sth)/ INFORMAL to be annoyed because something bad has been happening for a long time and you want it to stop: *I'm really fed up with this awful weather.* | *Joe was getting sick of Carol's stupid comments.* | *I left the job because I got fed up with being treated like a servant.*

2 to become angry

get angry/get mad /ɡet ˈæŋɡri, ɡet ˈmæd/ to become angry: *He tends to get angry if he loses at tennis.*
+ at *Just calm down. There's no need to get mad at me.*

⚠ Don't say 'become angry' except in fairly formal written English. **Get angry** and **get mad** are the usual expressions.

COLLOCATING PREPOSITIONS AND GRAMMAR PATTERNS ARE HIGHLIGHTED AND ILLUSTRATED

POTENTIAL ERRORS ARE HIGHLIGHTED, AND AVOIDANCE STRATEGIES GIVEN – ALL INFORMATION BASED ON THE LONGMAN LEARNER'S CORPUS

EXTENSIVE COVERAGE OF SPOKEN ENGLISH

FORMALITY IS CLEARLY INDICATED

COMPREHENSIVE INFORMATION ABOUT FREQUENCY AND USAGE

A

ABOUT

➡ look here for ...
- about a person or subject
- not exact

➡ if you mean 'be about to', go to the **ESSENTIAL GRAMMAR** section 5

1 about a person or subject

about /ə'baʊt/ [preposition] concerned with a particular subject or person: *She talks about him all the time.* | *I'm reading a story about some children who get lost on a mountain.* | *I've been thinking about what you said, and I've decided that you're right.* | *Does anyone have any questions about tonight's homework?*
be about *"It's a really good film." "What's it about?" "It's about some students in New York."*

on /ɒn‖ɑːn, ɔːn/ [preposition] about a particular subject: *a book on 18th century European literature* | *Professor Dodd is giving a lecture on medieval history.*
opinions/ideas/views on *a survey of young people's opinions on marriage*
+ how/why/what etc *We would like to hear your views on how services could be improved.*

> ⚠ Don't use **on** to talk about books, films etc that tell stories. Use it about more serious subjects or opinions.

concerning/regarding /kən'sɜːrnɪŋ, rɪ'gɑːrdɪŋ/ [preposition] FORMAL about – use this to talk about information, ideas, questions, or discussions, not to talk about books, films, or stories: *The police have new information concerning the identity of the murder victim.* | *Thank you for your letter regarding my student loan.*

deal with sth /'diːl wɪð (sth)/ [phrasal verb T] if a book, film, play etc **deals with** a subject, it is about that subject: *The story deals with the problems of poverty and unemployment.* | *The earliest films made in India dealt with religious subjects.*
dealing – dealt – have dealt

> ⚠ Only use **deal with** about serious subjects or problems.

2 not an exact number or amount

about (also **around** ESPECIALLY AMERICAN) /ə'baʊt, ə'raʊnd/ [adv] a little more or a little less than a number, amount, distance, or time: *The church is about a mile away.* | *It's about 2 years since I last saw him.* | "What time would you like me to come?" "Oh, about 9 o'clock." | *The murder was committed at around noon on Friday.* | *It cost around $1500.*

approximately /ə'prɒksɨmɨtli‖ə'prɑːk-/ [adv] a little more or a little less than a number, amount, distance, or time: *Each disk can store approximately 144 pages of text.* | *Approximately 30% of the community is Polish.*

> ⚠ **Approximately** is more formal than **about** or **around**, and is mostly used in writing.

roughly /'rʌfli/ [adv] a little more or a little less than a number – use this when you are making a guess which you know is not at all exact: *A new computer like this one would cost roughly $2000.* | *There were roughly 50 people there.*

or so /ɔːr 'səʊ/ use this after a number or amount to show that it may be a little more or a little less: "How many people are coming?" "Oh, about a dozen or so." | *A month or so later, they heard that Blake was dead.*

give or take /ˌgɪv ɔːr 'teɪk/ **give or take a few days/miles/dollars etc** ESPECIALLY SPOKEN use this after a number, to show that it is not exact but it is nearly correct: *She's been working there for two years, give or take a few weeks.*

ACCEPT

➡ look here for ...
- accept an offer or gift
- accept an idea or suggestion
- accept a situation that you cannot change

1 to accept an offer, invitation, or request

➡ opposite **REFUSE**

➡ see also ⟐ **SAYING YES**, ⟐ **INVITATIONS**, ⟐ **OFFERS**

accept /ək'sept/ [v T] to say yes to an offer, an invitation, or a chance to do something: *I decided to accept the job.* | *The President has accepted an invitation to visit Beijing.* | *If they offered you a place on the course, would you accept it?*

> ⚠ Don't say 'I accepted to do it'. Say **I agreed to do it**

take /teɪk/ [v T] if you **take** an opportunity or a job that someone offers you, you accept it: *He says he'll take the job if the money's right.* | *This is a wonderful opportunity – I think you should take it.*
taking – took – have taken

> ⚠ **Take** is more informal than **accept**

Qsay yes /ˌseɪ 'jes/ ESPECIALLY SPOKEN to say you will do what someone has invited you to do or asked you to do: *We'd love you to come with us to France this summer. Please say yes!* | *He doesn't usually lend his CDs, so I was surprised when he said yes.*

agree /ə'griː/ [v I] to say you will do what someone has asked you to do, especially something that may be difficult, inconvenient etc: *They've asked me to attend the conference, and I've agreed.*
agree to do sth *I wish I had never agreed to teach him to drive.*
agreeing – agreed – have agreed

take sb up on sth/take up sb's offer /ˌteɪk (sb) 'ʌp ɒn (sth), ˌteɪk ʌp (sb's) 'ɒfəʳ‖-'ɔːf-/ to accept someone's offer to do something for you, especially some time after it was made: *"If you need a babysitter, give me a call." "Thanks – I may take you up on that some time!"* | *In the end he took up his parents' offer of a loan.*

2 to take money or a gift that someone offers you

➡ opposite **REFUSE**

take /teɪk/ [v T] to take something that someone offers you: *He gave us a lot of helpful advice, but refused to take any payment for it.*
take sth from sb *My mother always warned us never to take candy from strangers.*
Qtake it or leave it SPOKEN (used to tell someone that you will not change your offer) *I'm offering you $100 – take it or leave it.*

taking – took – have taken

accept /ək'sept/ [v T] to take money or a gift from someone: *We hope you'll accept this small gift.* | *The hotel accepts all major credit cards.*
accept sth from sb *The Director was accused of accepting bribes from oil companies.*

> ⚠ **Accept** is more formal than **take**.

3 to agree that a suggestion or idea is right

➡ opposite **DISAGREE, AGAINST**

➡ see also ⟐ **SAYING YES**, ⟐ **AGREEING**, ⟐ **SUGGESTIONS**

accept /ək'sept/ [v T] to agree that a suggestion or idea is right, especially when you did not previously think so: *People are beginning to accept the idea that higher taxes may be necessary.*
+ that *The judge accepted that Carter had not intended to harm anyone.*

agree /ə'griː/ [v I] to accept that a plan or suggestion is good, especially when you have the power to decide whether it will be allowed to happen: *I spoke to my boss yesterday about postponing the meeting, and she agreed.*
+ to *We want to have a big party, but I don't think my parents will agree to it.*
+ that *Everyone agreed that Dave should play at the school concert.*

welcome /'welkəm/ [v T] to think that a plan, suggestion, or decision is very good, and eagerly accept it: *Most companies have welcomed the idea of job-sharing.*
be warmly welcomed *These new proposals were warmly welcomed by the German Chancellor.*

4 to accept a situation which you do not like

accept /əkˈsept/ [v T] to accept a situation which you do not like but you cannot change: *There's nothing we can do – we have to accept the voters' decision.*
+ that *Local people have reluctantly accepted that the airport will have to be extended.*

put up with sth /ˌpʊt ˈʌp wɪð (sth)/ [phrasal verb T] to accept an annoying situation or someone's annoying behaviour, without trying to stop it or change it: *I don't know how you put up with all this noise day after day.* | *You see what I have to put up with – the kids never stop quarrelling.*

tolerate /ˈtɒləreɪt‖ˈtɑː-/ [v T] to accept an unpleasant situation, without trying to change it: *For years the workers have had to tolerate low wages and terrible working conditions.* | *I don't know why his mother tolerates his behaviour.*

> ⚠ **Tolerate** is more formal than **put up with sth.**

live with sth /ˈlɪv wɪð (sth)/ [phrasal verb T] to accept an unpleasant situation as a permanent part of your life which you cannot change: *You have to learn to live with stress.* | *We don't really like the new system, but I suppose we'll just have to live with it.*

be resigned to sth /biː rɪˈzaɪnd tuː (sth)/ to realize that you must accept an unpleasant situation, because you cannot prevent it or avoid it: *Joe is resigned to the fact that he will miss tomorrow's big race.* | *Pat knew her husband wasn't coming back and she was resigned to being alone.*

make the best of it /ˌmeɪk ðə ˈbest əv ɪt/ INFORMAL to accept a situation that you do not like, and try to enjoy it or make it less bad: *The school isn't the one I really wanted to go to, but I suppose I'll just have to make the best of it.*

5 to officially accept a new law or proposal

pass /pɑːs‖pæs/ [v T] if a parliament or

similar group **passes** a law or proposal, the members vote to accept it: *The State Assembly passed a law which banned smoking in public places.* | *The bill was passed by 197 votes to 50.*

approve /əˈpruːv/ [v T] to officially accept something that has been planned to happen: *The Medical Research Council said it could not approve the use of the new drug.* | *The deal has already been approved by shareholders.*

approval /əˈpruːvəl/ [n U] when a suggestion or plan is officially accepted: *The parking proposals have been given the mayor's approval.* (=he has approved them)

ACCIDENT

➡ if you mean 'by accident', go to
ACCIDENTALLY

HURT/INJURE   DAMAGE
KILL   see also   BREAK
PAIN   FALL
DRIVE   MEDICAL TREATMENT 6

1 at home, at work, when doing a sport etc

accident /ˈæksɪdənt/ [n C] when someone gets hurt or something gets damaged, without anyone intending them to be: *Jim was rushed to the hospital after an accident at work.*
have an accident *She had an accident while she was playing basketball and broke her arm.*
serious accident *The park is now closed following a serious accident last week.*
riding/climbing/skiing etc accident *Greg has been unable to walk since he was injured in a riding accident.*

2 in a car, train, plane etc

accident /ˈæksɪdənt/ [n C] when a car, train etc hits an object, a person, or another vehicle: *The accident was caused by someone driving too fast.*

have an accident *Sue won't be able to come tonight – she had an accident on the way home.*
bad/serious accident *There are delays on the main road into town following a serious accident.*
road/car accident *Road accidents are the biggest cause of death among young people.*

crash /kræʃ/ [n C] an accident in which a car, plane, train etc hits something and is badly damaged or destroyed: *Wearing a seat belt can save your life in a crash.*
plane/train/car crash *Her husband died in a plane crash in 1990.*
have a crash/be in a crash (=in a car) *He was in a car crash last week.*

crash /kræʃ/ [v I/T] to have an accident in a car, train etc by hitting something: *The plane crashed just after take-off.* | *Prost lost control on the first bend and crashed.* | *Someone stole my car and crashed it.*
+ into *The truck skidded across the road before crashing into a wall.*

⚠ Don't say 'crash with something'. Say **crash into something.**

wreck /rek/ [n C] AMERICAN an accident involving a car, plane, train etc: *The wreck caused a 5-mile traffic jam.*

collision /kə'lɪʒən/ [n C] an accident in which two or more cars, planes etc hit each other while they are moving: *Several cars were involved in a collision on the expressway this morning.*
+ with *A 25-year-old man was thrown from his motorcycle in a collision with a truck.*
+ between *a mid-air collision between two planes*
head-on collision (=between two cars etc moving directly towards each other)

pile-up /'paɪl ʌp/ [n C] INFORMAL a serious road accident in which a lot of cars hit each other: *The pile-up happened in thick fog.*

get run over /ˌget rʌn 'əʊvəʳ/ if someone **gets run over**, a car or other vehicle hits them, and they get hurt or killed: *Our last cat got run over by a car outside our house.* | *Don't run out into the road – you'll get run over.*

3 an extremely bad accident when people are killed

disaster /dɪ'zɑːstəʳ‖-'zæs-/ [n C] an extremely bad accident in which a lot of people are killed: *The Zeebrugge ferry disaster, in which a ship carrying hundreds of people sank was one of the worst in recenty history.* | *Could your hospitals cope with a major disaster like a train crash?*
natural disaster (=caused by wind, rain, or other natural forces) *Natural disasters such as earthquakes are common in this part of the world.*

catastrophe /kə'tæstrəfi/ [n C] a terrible event that causes death, damage, and destruction over a very large area: *The destruction of the ozone layer could lead to an environmental catastrophe.* | *fears of a possible nuclear catastrophe*

ACCIDENTALLY
when you do something that you did not intend to do

➡ opposite **DELIBERATELY**

accidentally/by accident /ˌæksɪ̩'dentli◄, baɪ 'æksɪ̩dənt/ [adv] if you do something **accidentally** or **by accident**, you do it even though you did not intend to: *I accidentally burnt a hole in her sofa with my cigarette.* | *Doctors discovered the new drug quite by accident, while they were researching something else.*

⚠ Word order: **accidentally** can come between the subject and the verb (*I accidentally broke it*), but **by accident** usually comes at the end of a sentence or clause (*I broke it by accident*).

unintentionally /ˌʌnɪnˈtenʃənəli/ [adv] ESPECIALLY WRITTEN if you do something **unintentionally**, especially something bad, you do it even though you did not intend to: *Some male science teachers unintentionally discourage the girls in their classes.*

by mistake /baɪ mɪˈsteɪk/ [adv] if you do something **by mistake**, you intend to do one thing but you make a mistake and do something else instead: *Gary wandered into the wrong hotel room by mistake.* | *Police believe Burton may have shot the woman by mistake.*

◯didn't mean to /ˌdɪdnt ˈmiːn tuː/ ESPECIALLY SPOKEN if you **didn't mean to** do something bad or wrong, you did not intend to do it
didn't mean to do sth *Sorry, I didn't mean to upset you.* | *I'm sure Rachel didn't mean to leave the door unlocked.*

⚠ You often say **I didn't mean to** when you are saying sorry to someone: *I'm sorry I shouted at you. I didn't mean to.*

accidental /ˌæksɪˈdentl◄/ [adj] use this about bad or dangerous things that happen, which no one intended to happen: *Gina took an accidental overdose of painkillers.* | *70% of accidental deaths are alcohol related.*

unintentional /ˌʌnɪnˈtenʃənəl◄/ [adj] ESPECIALLY WRITTEN said or done accidentally, especially when you were trying to say or do something completely different: *Any offence these remarks might have caused was wholly unintentional.*

◯it was an accident /ɪt wəz ən ˈæksɪdənt/ SPOKEN say this to tell someone that you did not intend to do something, for example when you have broken something or made a mistake, and someone is angry with you: *It was an accident – the handle just came off when I picked it up.*

When you see **EC**, go to the
ESSENTIAL COMMUNICATION section.

➡ see also **FILMS/MOVIES, THEATRE, TELEVISION AND RADIO**

1 someone who performs in plays or films

actor /ˈæktəʳ/ [n C] someone whose job is to perform in plays or films: *Keanu Reeves is my favourite actor.* | *The actor who played Macbeth was really good.*

actress /ˈæktrɪs/ [n C] a woman whose job is to perform in plays or films: *I've always wanted to be an actress.* | *actress and singer, Cher*

⚠ You can use **actor** about a man or a woman. Some women prefer to be called **actors** and do not like the word **actress**.

star /staːʳ/ [n C] a very famous actor, especially in films: *Hundreds of fans gathered to watch the stars arriving at the Oscar ceremony.*
film/movie star *Movie star Arnold Schwarzenegger has said he would like to enter politics.*

2 to be in a play or film

act /ækt/ [v I] to be an actor in plays or films, especially as a job: *I decided I wanted to act when I was twelve years old.* | *She always enjoyed acting.*

acting /ˈæktɪŋ/ [n U] the job or skill of being an actor: *Before he became famous, James Dean studied acting in New York.* | *a career in acting*

play /pleɪ/ [v T] to act as a particular character in a play or film
play Hamlet/Cleopatra/James Bond etc *Timothy Dalton was the fourth actor to play James Bond.* | *Mother Courage was played by Diana Rigg.*
play a part *We still need someone to play the part of the messenger.*

be in sth /biː ɪn (sth)/ [phrasal verb T] ESPECIALLY SPOKEN to act in a particular play or film: *You remember Larry Hagman – he used to be in 'Dallas'.*

perform /pəʳˈfɔːʳm/ [v T] if a group of actors **performs** a play, they act in it for people to watch: *The children perform a*

Christmas pantomime every year. | The group will be performing 'Cats' in the Open Air Theatre.

performance /pəˈfɔːrməns/ [n C] the way someone acts in a play or film – use this to talk about how good or bad someone's acting is: *Sean Penn's finest performance was in 'Dead Man Walking'.*
give a good/bad etc performance *Meryl Streep, playing the murdered baby's mother, gives a marvellous performance.*

3 to be the most important actor in a play or film

star /staər/ [v I/T] if an actor **stars** in a film or a play, he or she is one of the most important actors in it; if a film or play **stars** an actor, he or she plays one of the most important characters in it
+ in *Can you name the actress who starred in 'Gone with the Wind'?*
+ as *Bob Hoskins stars as a private detective.* | *'Heat' is a police drama starring Robert de Niro and Al Pacino.*
starring – starred – have starred

leading role/starring role /ˌliːdɪŋ ˈrəʊl, ˈstɑːrɪŋ ˈrəʊl/ [n C] the job of acting as the most important character in a film: *Judy Garland became famous after her starring role in 'The Wizard of Oz'.*
play the leading/starring role (=act as the most important character) *Michael Keaton played the leading role in the first two 'Batman' movies.*

lead /liːd/ [n C] the most important actor or character in a play or film
play the lead (=be the main actor) *She was given the chance to play the lead when Pamela Anderson became ill.*
lead part/role/actor etc *Kevin Costner has been given the lead role in a $50m movie about life after a nuclear war.*

4 the person that an actor pretends to be in a play or film

character /ˈkærəktər/ [n C] one of the people in the story of a play or film: *Demi Moore's character is a woman who has an affair with the local preacher.*

part /pɑːrt/ [n C] the job of acting as a particular character in a play or film: *She*

knew she wanted the part as soon as she read the movie script.
play the part of (=act as a particular character) *She played the part of the Wicked Stepmother in 'Snow White'.*

ADD

➡ see also **MORE, INCREASE, INCLUDE/ NOT INCLUDE**

1 to add a new part to something

add /æd/ [v T] to put a new part or piece onto or into something, especially in order to improve it: *The book would look a lot more attractive if they added a few colour pictures.*
add sth to sth *Adding fertilizer to the soil will help the plants to grow more quickly.* | *The fresh chillies add a spicy flavour to the sauce.*

add on /ˌæd ˈɒn‖-ˈɑːn/ [phrasal verb T] to add another part to something so that it becomes bigger
add on sth *We're having a bedroom added on at the back of the house.*

2 to put two or more numbers together

➡ see also **COUNT/CALCULATE**

add /æd/ [v T] to put two or more numbers together in order to calculate the total
add sth and sth/add sth to sth *"What do you get when you add 68 and 32?" "100."*

3 to add more to an amount or cost

add /æd/ [v I/T] to add more to an amount or to the cost of something: *The builder added an extra £150 for tax.*
add sth to sth *Watson's recent victory added $30,000 to his total prize money in 1996.*

put sth on sth /ˌpʊt (sth) ˈɒn (sth)‖-ˈɑːn/ [phrasal verb T] to add an amount of money or tax to the cost of something: *The new tax will put another ten cents on the price of gas.*

4 something that is added

addition /əˈdɪʃən/ [n C/U] something that is added to something else

+ to *The latest addition to the museum's collection is a picture by Salvador Dali.*

make an addition *Several helpful additions have been made to this piece of software in the new version.*

additive /ˈædɪ̯tɪv/ [n C] a chemical substance that is added to food in order to make it taste better or stay fresh longer: *This product contains no artificial additives.*

ADMIRE
to have a very good opinion of someone

1 to admire someone

admire /ədˈmaɪər/ [v T] to have a very good opinion of someone, either because they have achieved something special or because they have skills or qualities that you would like to have: *I admire the way she's brought up those children on her own.* | *Which world leader do you most admire?*

admire sb for sth *She had to admire him for the way he handled the situation.*

respect /rɪˈspekt/ [v T] to have a good opinion of someone, even if you do not agree with them or want to be like them, because they have high standards and good personal qualities: *Dr Watt was a rather strange man, but his colleagues all respected him.*

respect sb for doing sth *I don't agree with him, but I respect him for sticking to his principles.*

> ⚠ Don't say 'I respect to him'. Just say I **respect him**

look up to sb /ˌlʊk ˈʌp tuː (sb)/ [phrasal verb T] to admire and respect someone who is older than you or who has authority over you: *I always looked up to my older brothers.*

idolize (also **idolise** BRITISH) /ˈaɪdəl-aɪz/ [v T] to admire someone very much, especially a famous person, so that you think everything about them is perfect: *Marilyn Monroe was idolized by movie fans all over the world.*

2 the feeling of admiring someone

admiration /ˌædməˈreɪʃən/ [n U] the feeling that someone is very good, very clever etc, either because of something special they have achieved or because they have skills or qualities you would like to have

in/with admiration *We listened with admiration as she played the violin.*

+ for *The other players were full of admiration for him.*

respect /rɪˈspekt/ [n U] the feeling that someone is good because they have high standards and good personal qualities

+ for *My respect for my teacher grew as the months passed.*

great respect (=a lot of respect) *I have great respect for Tony's judgment.*

earn/win sb's respect (=make someone respect you) *She always managed to win the kids' respect.*

3 someone you admire

hero/heroine /ˈhɪərəʊ, ˈherəʊɪn/ [n C] your **hero** or **heroine** is a man or woman who you admire very much because of their achievements, skills, or personal qualities: *I used to love David Bowie – he was my hero.*

plural **heroes**

idol /ˈaɪdl/ [n C] a famous actor, actress, musician, or sports player that a lot of people admire: *Thousands of fans were at the airport to greet their idol.* | *ageing Hollywood idol, Marlon Brando*

ADMIT

➡ see also CRIME, MISTAKE, GUILTY/NOT GUILTY

1 to agree that you have done something wrong

admit /əd'mɪt/ [v T] to say that you have done something wrong or illegal, especially when someone asks or persuades you to do this
+ (that) *Blake finally admitted he had stolen the money.* | *She admitted that she had made a mistake.*
admit (to) doing sth *Many workers admit to taking time off work when they are not sick.*
admit responsibility *The hospital has refused to admit responsibility for his death.*
admitting – admitted – have admitted

confess /kən'fes/ [v I/T] to tell the police or someone in a position of authority that you have done something very bad, especially after they have persuaded you to do this: *After two days of questioning, he finally confessed.*
+ (that) *She confessed that she had killed her husband.*
confess to a robbery/murder/crime etc *People were forced to confess to crimes they had not committed.*
confess to doing sth *Edwards eventually confessed to being a spy.*

own up /ˌəʊn 'ʌp/ [phrasal verb I] to admit that you did something, especially something that is not very serious: *Unless the guilty person owns up, the whole class will be punished.*
own up to (doing) sth *No-one owned up to breaking the window.*

> ⚠ **Own up** is more informal than **admit** or **confess**.

2 a statement admitting something

confession /kən'feʃən/ [n C] an official statement that someone makes to the police, admitting that they have done something illegal and explaining what happened: *Sergeant Thompson wrote down Smith's confession and asked him to sign it.*
make a confession *At 3 a.m., Higgins broke down and made a full confession.*

admission /əd'mɪʃən/ [n C usually singular] when you admit that you were wrong or that you have done something bad or illegal: *You only married him for his money? What an admission!*

+ (that) *The Senator's admission that he had lied to Congress shocked many Americans.*
admission of guilt/failure/defeat (=when you admit that you are guilty, you have failed etc) *The court may assume that your silence is an admission of guilt.*

3 to agree that something is true, although you do not want to

admit /əd'mɪt/ [v T] to accept that something is true or that someone is right, although you do not want to accept it, or you feel embarrassed about accepting it: *"Yes, I was frightened," he admitted.*
+ (that) *I know you don't like her, but you have to admit that she's good at her job.*
admit (to) doing sth *Both men admitted to having admired Hitler during the 1930s.*
ᇬI must admit (that)/I have to admit (that) SPOKEN *I must admit I really enjoy watching soap operas.*
ᇬadmit it SPOKEN *You were wrong, weren't you? Come on, admit it!*
admitting – admitted – have admitted

ᇬadmittedly /əd'mɪtɪdli/ [adv] SPOKEN use this when you are admitting that something is true: *Admittedly, the questions were fairly easy, but you all did very well.* | *The treatment is painful, admittedly, but it is usually very successful.*

ADULT

➡ opposite **CHILD**
➡ see also **AGE, OLD, YOUNG**

1 not a child

adult /'ædʌlt, ə'dʌlt/ [n C] someone who is not a child – use this to talk about someone who is at least 18: *The cost of the trip is $59 for adults and $30 for children.* | *Some children find it difficult to talk to adults.*

> ⚠ You can also use **adult** before a noun, like an adjective: *The book is intended for adult readers.* | *adult education*

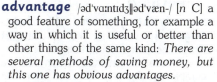

⚠ Don't say 'adult people'. Just say **adults**.

grown-up /ˌɡrəʊn ˈʌp◂/ [n C] an adult – used especially by children or when you are talking to children: *Grown-ups are so boring! All they ever do is talk!*
grown-up [adj] *Margaret has two grown-up sons.* | *Ryan felt very grown-up being allowed to stay up so late.*

full grown/fully grown /ˌfʊl ˈɡrəʊn◂, ˌfʊli ˈɡrəʊn◂/ [adj] a person, animal, or plant that is **full grown** or **fully grown** has reached its full adult size: *A fully grown blue whale may be up to 30m long.*

2 to become an adult

grow up /ˌɡrəʊ ˈʌp/ [phrasal verb I] to become an adult: *What do you want to do when you grow up?* | *We plan to go and live in Florida when the children have grown up.*

3 the time when you are an adult

adult life /ˌædʌlt ˈlaɪf, əˌdʌlt-/ [n U] the part of someone's life when they are an adult: *He has spent most of his adult life in the US.*

adulthood /ˈædʌlthʊd, əˈdʌlthʊd/ [n U] FORMAL the time when someone is an adult – use this especially to talk about people reaching this time: *Children with the disease have little chance of surviving to adulthood.*
reach adulthood (=become an adult) *By the time we reach adulthood our heart-rate has dropped to around 70 beats per minute.*

ADVANTAGE/ DISADVANTAGE

➡ look here for ...
• the good and bad points about something
• something that makes some people more successful than others
➡ see also **GOOD, BAD**

1 a good feature of something

advantage /ədˈvɑːntɪdʒ‖ədˈvæn-/ [n C] a good feature of something, for example a way in which it is useful or better than other things of the same kind: *There are several methods of saving money, but this one has obvious advantages.*
+ of *The advantage of cycling to work is that I get some exercise.*
big advantage *One of the biggest advantages of this course is that it gives students experience of working in a company.*

◔**the good thing about sth** /ðə ˈɡʊd θɪŋ əbaʊt (sth)/ SPOKEN use this when you are talking about one of the main advantages of something: *The good thing about this job is that I can work at home whenever I want.*

benefit /ˈbenɪ̩fɪt/ [n C/U] a feature of something that has a good effect on people's lives: *Tourism has brought many benefits to the area.*
+ of *the benefits of a healthy lifestyle* | *What are the benefits, for Britain, of belonging to the European Union?*

2 a bad feature of something

disadvantage /ˌdɪsədˈvɑːntɪdʒ‖-ədˈvæn-/ [n C] a bad feature of something, for example a way in which it causes problems or is worse than other things of the same kind
+ of *Nuclear power has a lot of disadvantages – for example what do you do with all the nuclear waste?* | *The main disadvantage of being a nurse is working irregular hours.*

drawback /ˈdrɔːbæk/ [n C] a disadvantage of something, which makes it seem less attractive – use this especially when something seems good in other ways: *It's a good-looking car – the only drawback is the price.*
+ of *One of the drawbacks of working for a large company is that you never know who is really in charge.* |
+ to *There are quite a lot of drawbacks to this method.*

A

3 when you compare what is good and bad about something

the advantages and disadvantages /ði əd,vɑːntɪdʒ̩z ən ˈdɪsədvɑːntɪdʒ̩z‖ -ˌvæn-/ the good and bad features of something – use this especially when you are comparing what is good and what is bad about something
+ of *We had to write about the advantages and disadvantages of living in the country.*

pros and cons /ˌprəʊz ən ˈkɒnz‖-ˈkɑːnz/ the advantages and disadvantages of something, which you need to think about in order to make a decision
+ of *Your doctor should explain the pros and cons of the different treatments available.*
weigh up the pros and cons (=think carefully about all the advantages and disadvantages) *I'm not sure if I'm going to take the job – I need more time to weigh up all the pros and cons.*

4 something that helps someone to be more successful than others

advantage /ədˈvɑːntɪdʒ/ədˈvæn-/ [n C] something that makes you more likely to succeed than other people
have an advantage *The American team seemed to have all the advantages – better training, better facilities, and much better financial support.*
give sb an advantage (=make them more likely to succeed)
+ over *I had already lived in France for a year, and this gave me a big advantage over the other students.*

privilege /ˈprɪvl̩ɪdʒ/ [n C] a special advantage or right that only a few people have, for example because their family is rich or because they have an important job: *Foreign diplomats have all kinds of special privileges – for example they can park their cars anywhere they like.*
the privilege of *Not everyone has the privilege of a private education.*
privileged [adj] having a lot of privileges: *At that time, the universities were only open to a privileged minority.*

5 something that makes it more difficult for someone to succeed

disadvantage /ˌdɪsədˈvɑːntɪdʒ‖-ədˈvæn-/ [n C] something that makes it more difficult for you to succeed or do what you want, especially as compared with other people
have a disadvantage *She has the same qualifications as the other candidates, but she has one big disadvantage – she lacks experience.*
be at a disadvantage (=have a disadvantage compared with other people) *In the basketball team, the smaller players are at a disadvantage.*

1 advertising

advertising /ˈædvərtaɪzɪŋ/ [n U] the business of persuading people to buy things, using pictures, words, songs etc on TV and radio, large public notices, and newspapers and magazines: *How much does Coca-Cola spend on advertising?* | *Cigarette advertising isn't allowed on TV any more.* | *Beth wants a job in advertising.* (=in a company that makes advertisements) | *How much do you think you are influenced by advertising?*
advertising campaign (=a planned series of advertisements for a new product) *Nissan is about to launch a nationwide advertising campaign for its new range of cars.*

publicity /pʌˈblɪsl̩ti/ [n U] the business of making sure that people know about a new product, a new film, a famous person etc, for example by talking about them on

TV or writing about them in magazines: *The show's organizers spent over $500,000 on publicity alone.*

good/bad publicity *The band appeared on the Larry King show, which was good publicity for their US tour.*

marketing /ˈmɑːrkɪtɪŋ/ [n U] the business of trying to sell a product by deciding which type of people are likely to buy it and making it attractive and interesting to them: *I'm looking for a job in marketing.* | *Good marketing has always been a major factor in the company's success.*

hype /haɪp/ [n U] INFORMAL attempts to make people interested in a product, entertainer, film etc, using television, radio, and newspapers – use this to show that you do not trust this kind of information: *Despite all the hype, I thought the film was pretty boring.*

2 an advertisement

advertisement /ədˈvɜːtɪsmənt‖ˌædvər-ˈtaɪz-/ [n C] something such as a large public notice, a short film on television, or a picture with words in a newspaper that is designed to persuade people to buy something: *Most car advertisements are aimed at men.*
+ for *In the autumn, the newspapers are full of advertisements for winter breaks.*

ad (also **advert** BRITISH) /æd, ˈædvɜːrt/ [n C] INFORMAL an advertisement: *He began his acting career by doing shampoo adverts on TV.*
+ for *I saw an ad for some cheap furniture in our local paper.*

commercial /kəˈmɜːrʃəl/ [n C] an advertisement on television or radio: *Have you seen the new Levi jeans commercial?*
commercial break (=when there are commercials in the middle of a programme) *We'll be right back with you after a short commercial break.*

slogan /ˈsləʊɡən/ [n C] a short clever phrase used in an advertisement: *a dry-cleaning company that used the slogan 'We know the meaning of cleaning'*

hoarding BRITISH **billboard** AMERICAN /ˈhɔːrdɪŋ, ˈbɪlbɔːrd/ [n C] a large flat board in a public place, where large printed advertisements are shown: *Beside the freeway was a huge billboard covered in ads for washing powder.*

3 to advertise something

advertise /ˈædvərtaɪz/ [v I/T] to use advertisements on television or radio, in newspapers etc, in order to try to persuade people to buy something: *There was a big poster advertising a well-known brand of cola.* | *a small company that can't afford to advertise on TV*
be advertised on TV/the radio *"How did you find out about the new software?" "It was advertised on TV."*
be advertised in a newspaper/magazine etc *The concert was advertised in all the national newspapers.*

> ⚠ Don't write 'advertize'. **Advertise** is never spelled with a 'z'.

promote /prəˈməʊt/ [v T] to try to make people buy a new product, see a new film etc, for example by selling it at a lower price or talking about it on television: *Meg Ryan is in Europe to promote her new movie.*
promote sth as sth *They're trying to promote Dubai as a tourist destination.*

ADVISE

ASK   TELL

see also

SUGGEST   WARN

🖙 ADVICE

1 to advise someone

advise /ədˈvaɪz/ [v T] to tell someone what you think they should do, especially when you have more knowledge or experience than they have
advise sb to do sth *I advise you to think very carefully before making a decision.* | *All US citizens in the area have been advised to return home.*
advise sb against doing sth (=advise them not to do it) *Her lawyers have advised her against saying anything to the newspapers.*

advise sb on/about sth *Your teacher will be able to advise you about what qualifications you will need.*

strongly advise *I'd strongly advise you to get medical insurance if you're going skiing.*

> ⚠ **Advise** is more formal than **say sb should do sth.**

> ⚠ Don't confuse 'advise' and 'advice'. **Advise** is a verb and **advice** is a noun.

say sb should do sth/say sb ought to do sth /ˌseɪ (sb) ʃʊd 'duː (sth), ˌseɪ (sb) ɔːt tə 'duː (sth)/ to give your personal opinion about what someone should do: *My friends keep saying I ought to learn to drive.* | *Her mother said she should call the police immediately.*

> ⚠ This is the most common way of saying 'to **advise** someone'.

tell /tel/ [v T] to tell someone that you think they should do something, especially in order to avoid problems

tell sb to do sth *I told him to go and see a doctor if he was worried.*

tell sb (that) they should do sth *Jimmy had told him he should keep away from the gang for the next couple of weeks.*

telling – told – have told

> ⚠ Use **tell** especially in spoken English or informal writing.

suggest /sə'dʒest‖səg-/ [v T] to tell someone your ideas about what they should do, where they should go etc: *"Why not ask Dad?" he suggested.*

+ (that) *Sarah suggested that I should apply for this job.*

give advice /ˌgɪv əd'vaɪs/ to advise someone about a problem or subject, especially something that they have asked you about: *The centre gives free advice to young people who have drug problems.*

give sb advice *Can you give me some advice? I'm thinking of buying an electronic organizer.*

> ⚠ Don't say 'give advices' or 'give an advice'. **Advice** is an uncountable noun.

2 to ask someone to advise you

ask sb's advice /ˌɑːsk (sb's) əd'vaɪs‖ˌæsk-/ to ask someone to advise you about something: *Can I ask your advice? I need to find somewhere to stay in London.*

+ on/about *I always ask my brother's advice about computers.*

consult /kən'sʌlt/ [v T] FORMAL to get advice from someone who is paid to advise people, for example a lawyer or a doctor: *If the symptoms persist, consult your doctor.* | *I want to consult my lawyer before I say anything.*

consult sb about sth *Tonight the President will consult his military advisers about the likelihood of an attack.*

3 to do what someone advises you to do

take sb's advice/follow sb's advice /ˌteɪk (sb's) əd'vaɪs, ˌfɒləʊ (sb's) əd'vaɪs‖ˌfɑː-/ to do what someone advises you to do: *I've decided to take your advice and go to art school.* | *If she had followed my advice, this would never have happened.*

listen to sb /'lɪsən tuː (sb)/ to do what someone advises you to do, especially because you respect them and trust their judgement: *You tell him, Dad – I'm sure he'll listen to you.* | *Bob warned us about this. I wish we'd listened to him.*

on sb's advice/on the advice of sb /ɒn (sb's) əd'vaɪs, ɒn ði əd'vaɪs ɒv (sb)/ if you do something **on someone's advice** or **on the advice of someone,** you do it because they have advised you to do it: *On her doctor's advice, she took a few days off work.* | *He decided not to take the exam, on the advice of his professor.*

4 someone's opinion about what you should do

advice /əd'vaɪs/ [n U] what someone advises you to do: *Get some advice from the people in the tourist office.*

+ on/about *For advice on AIDS, phone this free number.*

give sb advice *I decided to ask Emma what she thought I should do. She always gave me good advice.*

piece of advice (=some advice) *Years ago, my father gave me a piece of advice that I've never forgotten.*

medical/legal/professional advice *You should get legal advice before you sign the contract.*

⚠️ **Advice** is an uncountable noun, so don't say 'an advice' or 'some advices'. Say **a piece of advice** or **some advice**.

tip /tɪp/ [n C] a simple but useful piece of advice about how to do something more easily or more effectively: *Here's a good tip: if you spill red wine on a carpet, pour salt on it to get rid of the stain.*
+ on *a leaflet containing some tips on how to take better photos*

guidance /'gaɪdəns/ [n U] advice about what to do in your job, your education, or your private life – use this about advice you get from someone whose job is to advise and help people
give guidance on sth *Your teacher can give you guidance on choosing a career and writing a job application.*

counselling BRITISH **counseling** AMERICAN /'kaʊnsəlɪŋ/ [n U] advice and support given by an expert, to help someone who has personal problems or who has had a very unpleasant experience: *The college will provide counselling for students who have emotional problems.* | *Victims of violent crimes often need counseling.*

5 someone who advises people

adviser (also **advisor** AMERICAN) /əd'vaɪzər/ [n C] someone whose job is to give advice, especially in business, law, or politics
financial/legal/careers adviser *Talk to an independent financial adviser before you invest your money.*
+ on *the Prime Minister's personal adviser on economic affairs*
+ to *She's been appointed as scientific advisor to the President.*

AFTER

➡ opposite **BEFORE**
➡ see also **LATER/AT A LATER TIME**

1 after something happens or after someone does something

after /'ɑːftər‖'æf-/ [preposition/conjunction/ adv] after something happens or after someone does something: *After the party Jo stayed behind to help clean up the mess.* | *What are you going to do after you finish college?* | *Let's eat after the movie.*
after that *In the summer Joni left him, and after that he always looked sad.*
just after (=a short time after) *My mother died just after Mark was born.*
straight after/right after (=immediately after) *We'll be starting the class straight after lunch.*

⚠️ **After** can be used as an adverb, but only in expressions like **soon after** and **not long after**: *I left college when I was 21, and got married soon after.* Don't use **after** on its own as an adverb. Instead, use **then, after that,** or **afterwards** in sentences like this: *We had a game of tennis, and then/after that/ afterwards we went for a cup of coffee.* Don't use 'will' with **after**. Don't say 'after I will leave school, I am going to university'. Say **after I leave school ...**

afterwards (also **afterward** AMERICAN) /'ɑːftərwərd(z) ‖'æf-/ [adv] after an event or a time that you have just mentioned: *Afterwards, Nick said he'd never been so nervous in his life.* | *What's the point of going to the gym if you always eat a chocolate bar afterwards?*
two years/three months afterwards *A couple of years afterwards I met him by chance in the street.*
soon/shortly afterwards (=a short time later) *Her husband became ill and died soon afterwards.*

next /nekst/ [adv] after something happens or after someone does something – use this when you are describing a series of events in the order they happened: *Can you remember what happened next?* | *First we asked Jim what to do. Next we tried asking Dad.*

then /ðen/ [adv] after you have done something – use this when you are describing a series of things you did, or when you are giving instructions: *First we played tennis,*

A

and then we went swimming. | Add a cup of sugar. Then beat in three eggs.

2 after a particular time or date

after /'ɑːftər‖'æf-/ [*preposition*] after a particular time or date: *Could you call again after 6 o'clock? | After 1800, more and more people worked in factories.*
just after (=a short time after) *If they left just after twelve, they should be here soon.*

past /pɑːst‖pæst/ [*preposition*] **past 3 o'clock/ midnight/dinner time etc** ESPECIALLY BRITISH after 3 o'clock, midnight etc – use this especially when someone is late for something: *Wake up! It's past 9 o'clock! | We didn't get home till past midnight.*
way past INFORMAL (=a long time after) *Sorry, it's way past closing time.*

from/as from /frəm, 'æz frəm/ [*preposition*] use this to say that a new rule or arrangement will start at a particular time and will continue from then: *We will be at our new address from next week. | As from tomorrow, all accidents must be reported to me.*

from then on /frəm ˌðen 'ɒn/ use this to talk about something that started to happen at a time in the past, and continued from that time: *He went to his first football game when he was four, and from then on he was crazy about it.*

3 after a period of time has passed

after /'ɑːftər‖'æf-/ [*preposition*] **after a week/several hours/a long time etc** after a period of time has passed: *After half an hour we got tired of waiting and went home. | Jane was very shy, but after a while* (=after a short time) *she became more confident.*
after a week/a year etc of (doing) sth *The war ended after another six months of fighting.*

in /ɪn/ [*preposition*] **in a minute/a few hours/a month etc** a minute, a few hours etc after the present time: *I'll be with you in a minute. | Rosie should be home in a week or two. | He gets his test results in a couple of days.*

in an hour's time/a few minutes' time etc *In a few weeks' time I'll be off to university.*

⚠ Don't confuse **after** (use this about something that has happened in the past) and **in** (use this about something that will happen in the future).

within /wɪð'ɪn‖wɪð'ɪn, wɪθ'ɪn/ [*preposition*] **within a month/two weeks/a year etc** less than a month, two weeks etc after something happens, especially when this is an unusually short time: *One of the soldiers was bitten by a snake and was dead within three hours. | Within minutes the building was full of smoke.*
within a month/a few days etc of doing sth *The plane got into difficulties within a few minutes of taking off.*

later /'leɪtər/ [*adv*] some time after now or after the time you are talking about: *See you later. | Reagan later became Governor of California.*
three months/two years/ten days etc later *A couple of days later I saw her in a downtown bar.*
later on (=at a later time during the same day, event etc) *The first half of the movie is really boring, but it gets better later on.*
much later (=a long time afterwards) *Eventually he got married, but that was much later.*
later that day/month/year etc (=use this when telling stories or describing past events) *Later that month we got another letter, asking for more money.*
later in the morning/evening/day etc *Let's meet for dinner later in the week.*

⚠ Don't use **after** and **later** in the same sentence.

4 the next day/month/ year etc

next /nekst/ [*adj* only before noun] **the next day/week etc** the day, week etc that comes just after the one you were talking about: *I finished my classes on the 5th, and the next day I went home to Cleveland.*
next Monday/week/August etc (=the one after this Monday, this week, this August etc) *Next Thursday is my birthday.*

⚠️ Don't confuse **next week** and **the next week**. Use **next week, next Friday** etc (without **the**) to talk about the future: *See you next Saturday!* Use **the next week, the next day** etc to talk about the past: *She got married and spent the next five years in Boston.*

⚠️ Don't say 'on next Sunday'. Just say **next Sunday**.

⚠️ Don't say 'next Tuesday/Friday etc' when you are talking about a day in the present week. Say **this Tuesday/Friday** etc: *The concert's this Saturday, not next Saturday.*

after /ˈɑːftəʳ‖ˈæf-/ [adv/preposition/conjunction] **the day/Monday/month/year after** the day, Monday etc that comes after the time or event that you are talking about: *The party's not this Saturday but the Saturday after.* | *The weather changed the morning after we arrived.* | *I felt rather tired the day after the party.*

following /ˈfɒləʊɪŋ‖ˈfɑː-/ [adj only before noun] **the following day/month/year etc** the next day, month etc – use this especially in stories and descriptions, to talk about what happened in the past: *The following day she woke up with a splitting headache.* | *They agreed to meet the following week in the Café Rouge.*

5 to happen or exist after something else

come after /ˌkʌm ˈɑːftəʳ‖ˈæf-/ [phrasal verb T] to happen after something else and often as a result of something else: *The agreement came after six months of negotiations.*
come three weeks/five days etc after sth *My first chance to talk to her came three days after our quarrel.*

follow /ˈfɒləʊ‖ˈfɑː-/ [v I/T] if an event or period **follows** another event or period, it happens after it: *We saw each other a lot in the months that followed.* | *the long period of stability that followed the war*
be followed by sth *The wedding was followed by a big party at the Chelsea Hotel.*
be closely followed by sth (=come very soon after) *China's first nuclear test in*

October 1964 was closely followed by a second in May 1965.

6 the person, thing, or time that comes after the present one

next /nekst/ [adj/adv] the **next** person or thing is the one that comes just after the present one in a series, list etc: *Could you ask the next patient to come in, please?* | *Look at the diagram on the next page.* | *I'm afraid you'll have to wait for the next train.*
come next (=come immediately after something that has just been mentioned) *Kennedy, Johnson, Nixon ... who comes next?*
◯ **be next** (=be the next person or thing in a list, line etc) SPOKEN *Hey, I'm next! I was here before you!*

be after sth/come after sth /biː ˈɑːftəʳ (sth), ˌkʌm ˈɑːftəʳ (sth)‖ˈæf-/ [phrasal verb T] if someone or something **is after** or **comes after** another person or thing in a list, line etc, they are the one just after, with no others in between: *My name is after hers on the list.* | *In American addresses, the name of the city always comes after the name of the street.*

later /ˈleɪtəʳ/ [adj only before noun] happening some time later, not immediately afterwards
a later date/time/chapter/meeting etc *We can decide on the final details at a later stage.* | *This will be discussed more fully in a later chapter.*
in later years/months/centuries etc ESPECIALLY WRITTEN *In later years, he became a Buddhist.*

subsequent /ˈsʌbsɪkwənt/ [adj only before noun] FORMAL happening after something you have just mentioned: *Many of Marx's theories were disproved by subsequent events.* | *The first meeting will be in the City Hall, but all subsequent meetings will be held in the school.*

⚠️ **Subsequent** is often followed by a plural noun.

follow /ˈfɒləʊ‖ˈfɑː-/ [v I/T] to come after something in a book, series, or list: *Taylor*

explains his theory in the pages that follow.
be followed by sth In English the letter
Q is always followed by a U. | Each
chapter is followed by a set of exercises.

7 when several things happen one after another

in a row /ɪn ə ˈrəʊ/ **four days in a row/
three times in a row etc** when someone does something on four days, on three occasions etc, one after the other, with no other days etc in between: He won the competition five years in a row. | I was late for school four days in a row.

one after another /ˌwʌn ɑːftər əˈnʌðəʳ‖ -æf-/ if several things happen **one after another**, each thing happens immediately after the previous one: There were three loud explosions, one after another.

consecutive /kənˈsekjʊtɪv/ [adj only before noun] **consecutive** days, years, or occasions come one after the other, with no other days, years etc in between: If you miss work for more than three consecutive days, you need a letter from your doctor.
fourth/seventh etc consecutive It was their fourth consecutive win this season.

series /ˈsɪəriːz/ [n C] a **series** of events or actions is several of them that happen one after another
+ of She gave a series of talks at the university. | Harris finally resigned after a series of public scandals.
plural **series**

AGAIN

➡ if you mean 'say something again',
go to SAY

1 again

again /əˈgen, əˈgeɪn‖əˈgen/ [adv] Would you say that again? I didn't hear you. | Julie! It's your sister on the phone again. | Nice to see you again. | On no! Here comes that boy again. | I rang the bell again, but no-one answered.

> ⚠ **Again** usually comes at the end of a sentence or clause.

once again/once more /ˌwʌns əˈgen, ˌwʌns ˈmɔːʳ/ FORMAL again – use this about something very worrying, serious, or annoying that has happened before: Once again I must remind you of the seriousness of the problems we face. | The crops had failed, and once more famine threatened the region.

yet again /jet əˈgen/ again – use this when something has happened too many times before in a way that is very annoying: Yet again, Flora had changed her mind. | It seems that yet again the police have allowed a very dangerous man to escape.

one more time/once more /ˌwʌn mɔːʳ ˈtaɪm, wʌns ˈmɔːʳ/ again, and usually for the last time: He kissed her one more time before he left.
just one more time/just once more Can we practise that just once more?

back /bæk/ [adv] again – use this about telephoning or writing to someone again, or asking someone to come to your house again
call/write back I'll call back as soon as I have some news.
invite/ask sb back Her kids wrecked the house last time they were here – that's why I've never asked them back.

2 to do something again

do sth again /ˌduː (sth) əˈgen/ I'd like you to do this exercise again. | She spilled coffee on the application form and had to do it all again.

repeat /rɪˈpiːt/ [v T] to do something again, especially many times, in order to achieve something useful
repeat a test / experiment / exercise / process / performance In their training, they have to repeat the safety process again and again until they can do it in 30 seconds. | Repeat this exercise 20 times every day and you'll soon have firmer, more muscular arms.

over /ˈəʊvəʳ/ [adv] AMERICAN if you do something **over**, you do it again from the beginning: I'm afraid you'll have to do it over. | I'm sorry I messed it up – let's start over.

all over again /ɔːl ˌəʊvər əˈgen/ ESPECIALLY SPOKEN if you do something long or difficult **all over again**, you do it again from the beginning: *At the police station they asked me the same questions all over again.*

start (sth) all over again *The computer crashed and deleted all my work – I had to start the essay all over again.*

redo /riːˈduː/ [v T] to do a piece of work again: *I can't read a word of this – you'll have to redo it.*

redoing – redid – have redone

retake /riːˈteɪk/ [v T] to do a test again because you failed it: *She retook her driving test five times before she passed.*

retaking – retook – have retaken

3 to start again

start again /ˌstɑːrt əˈgen/ [phrasal verb I/T] to start doing something again, or to start happening again: *The drilling noise started again in the next room.*

start work/school etc again *After her vacation Trish really didn't feel like starting her classes again.*

start doing sth again *Have Jill and Larry started talking to each other again?*

start to do sth again *It's starting to snow again.*

bring back sth /ˌbrɪŋ ˈbæk (sth)/ [phrasal verb T] to start to use a law, method, or system again: *Do you think they should bring back the death penalty?*

revival /rɪˈvaɪvəl/ [n C] when something becomes popular or fashionable again – use this especially about ideas, customs, or styles in art or music: *a seventies revival* (=when things from the 1970s become fashionable again)

+ of *the recent revival of interest in astrology and faith healing*

go back to sth /ˌgəʊ ˈbæk tuː (sth)/ [phrasal verb T] to start doing a job or activity again after a period when you stopped it: *I wouldn't like to go back to full-time work again.*

go back to doing sth *Tim was determined he would never go back to using drugs.*

When you see **EC**, go to the **ESSENTIAL COMMUNICATION** section.

AGAINST

A

when you think that something is wrong and should not be allowed

➡ opposite SUPPORT
➡ see also DISAGREE, **EC** DISAGREEING, **EC** OPINIONS

1 to think something is wrong and try to prevent it

be against sth/be opposed to sth /biː əˈgenst (sth), biː əˈpəʊzd tuː (sth)/ to think that something is wrong and that it should not be allowed, especially because you think it is morally wrong: *I'm not against people eating meat, but I don't think people should kill animals for sport.* | *92% of the population is opposed to the use of nuclear weapons.*

be strongly opposed to sth *They are strongly opposed to any form of violence.*

object to sth /əbˈdʒekt tuː (sth)/ to believe that something is wrong, unfair, or unreasonable, especially when this makes you angry: *What I object to most is the way the book portrays women.*

strongly object to sth *Most of the students strongly object to the new rules.*

⚲not agree with sth /nɒt əˈgriː wɪð (sth)/ ESPECIALLY SPOKEN to be against something, for example because it is new or different and you do not like things to change: *I don't agree with all these new anti-smoking laws, do you?* | *My grandmother doesn't agree with divorce.*

not believe in sth /nɒt bɪˈliːv ɪn (sth)/ to be against something, especially because you think it is wrong or immoral: *She doesn't believe in sex before marriage.* | *I don't believe in hitting children for any reason.*

anti- /ˈæntɪˌˈænti, -taɪ/ [prefix] **anti-war/anti-smoking/anti-American etc** against war, smoking, America etc: *Anti-war demonstrators gathered on Capitol Hill.* | *anti-Communist propaganda*

2 someone who is against something

opponent /əˈpəʊnənt/ [n C] someone who thinks that a plan, type of behaviour etc is

A

wrong, and tries to prevent it: *a debate between an anti-abortion group and its opponents*
+ of *All opponents of the government are likely to be imprisoned.*
life-long opponent (=someone who has opposed something since they were young) *a life-long opponent of nuclear weapons*

3 things you say or do to show that you are against something

opposition /ˌɒpəˈzɪʃən‖ˌɑːp-/ [n U] things that people say or do in order to show that they are against something: *Plans to build the airport faced a lot of opposition from local people.*
+ to *Opposition to the war was growing rapidly.*
strong opposition *The new law was passed, despite strong opposition.*
widespread opposition (=when a lot of people are against something) *Widespread opposition to the military government led to rioting and violence on the streets.*

objection /əbˈdʒekʃən/ [n C] a reason that you give to explain why you are against something: *If anyone has any objections, please let us know as soon as possible.*
+ to *What were her father's objections to their marriage?*
have no objection (=not be against something) FORMAL *I'll give them your name as a witness, if you have no objection.*

AGE

YOUNG   BABY

OLD ← see also → ADULT

CHILD   DESCRIBING PEOPLE

1 how long someone has lived, or how long something has existed

age /eɪdʒ/ [n C/U] the number of years that someone has lived or something has existed
the age of sb/sth *The average age of the students is 18.* | *The amount you pay depends on the age of the car.*
sb's age *I tried to guess her age.* | *The children's ages range from three to 17.*
be sb's age (=be the same age as someone) *When I was your age I was already working.*
the same age as sb/sth *Their house is about the same age as ours.*
of my age/her age etc (=about the same age as me, her etc) *I'm surprised a girl of your age didn't know that!*
at the age of 10/20 etc WRITTEN (use this to say how old someone was when something happened) *He died in 1995 at the age of 73.*
over/under the age of (=older or younger than) *Anyone over the age of 14 had to pay the full fare.*
be small/tall etc for your age (=be small, tall etc compared with other people of the same age) *Jimmy's very tall for his age.* | *She's 86, but very fit for her age.*

> ⚠ Don't say 'His age is 49' or 'I'm at the age of 27'. Say **He is 49** or **I'm 27**.

> ⚠ Don't use **in** before **age**. Don't say 'children in my age'. Say **children of my age**. Don't say 'he died in the age of 25'. Say **he died at the age of 25**.

how old /haʊ ˈəʊld/ use this to ask or talk about the age of a person or thing: *"How old are you?" "I'm 24."* | *I'm not sure how old my grandfather is.* | *How old were you when you got married?* | *Archaeologists are trying to discover how old these buildings are.*

be /biː/ [v]
be 5/10/27 etc (only use this about people) *Julie will be 30 on her next birthday.*
be 5/10/27 years old (use this about people or things) *Simon's almost 15 years old.* | *The school is 100 years old next year.*
be 5/10/27 years of age FORMAL (only use this about people) *He appeared to be about 35 years of age.*

5-year-old/60-year-old etc [adj only before noun] use this to say how old someone or something is: *27-year-old Susan*

Walker is the new world champion. | *an eight-year-old car* | *a six-week-old baby*

⚠ Don't say 'a 14 years old boy'. Say **a 14-year-old boy** or **a boy of 14**.

a man of 50/a child of 5 etc a man aged 50, a child aged 5 etc: *If a man of 45 loses his job in this city he'll never get another.* | *This calculator is so simple a child of five could use it.*

in your 20s/in her 40s/in their 80s etc use this to say that someone is between the age of 20 and 29, 40 and 49, 80 and 89 etc: *I'm not sure how old she is – I think she's in her 50s.*
in your late 20s/30s/40s etc (=between 27 and 29, 37 and 39 etc) *Police say that the man is tall, has dark hair, and is in his late thirties.*
in your early 20s/30s/40s etc (=between 20 and 23, 30 and 33 etc) *He first visited Europe when he was in his early twenties.*
in your mid 20s/30s/40s etc (=between 24 and 26, 34 and 36 etc) *My grand-parents are both in their mid eighties.*

aged /eɪdʒd/ [*adj*] ESPECIALLY WRITTEN **aged 5/10/27 etc** use this to say how old someone is, usually when you are writing about them: *McIntosh died on April 25th, aged 67.* | *He wrote a song for his daughter Soraya, now aged six.* | *A man aged 20 has been arrested on suspicion of murder.*

2 people who are the same age

generation /ˌdʒenəˈreɪʃən/ [*n* C usually singular] all the people in a country or in a society who are about the same age: *preserving the environment for future generations* | *There was now a whole generation of people who had never experienced peace.*
of sb's generation *People of my father's generation aren't used to computers.* | *She was one of the best writers of her generation.*
the younger generation (=young people in general – used by older people) *There is not much interest in politics among the younger generation.*

age group /ˈeɪdʒ ɡruːp/ [*n* C] all the people who are between two particular ages –

use this to talk about the problems, behaviour, interests etc of people of a particular age: *Boys in this age group watch TV for an average of five hours a day.* | *a competition for the 11–15 age group*

the over-60s/under-5s etc /ði ˈəʊvəʳ (60s), ˈʌndəʳ (5s), etc/ ESPECIALLY BRITISH people who are older than 60, younger than 5 etc: *an aerobics class for the over-50s* | *She teaches young children, mostly the under-5s.*

AGREE

➡ look here for ...
- have the same opinion as someone else
- say you will do what someone else asks you

1 to have the same opinion as someone else
- opposite **DISAGREE 1**
- see also 🔲 **AGREEING**, 🔲 **OPINIONS**, **SUPPORT 1**

agree /əˈɡriː/ [*v* I/T] to have the same opinion: *I think it's too expensive. Do you agree?* | *"That's right," Richard agreed.*
+ with *Everyone agreed with Karen.*
+ on/about *I agree with you about the colour – it looks awful.* | *The one thing all the parties agreed on was the need for fair elections.*
+ that *Most experts agree that drugs like heroin can cause permanent brain damage.*

agreeing – agreed – have agreed

⚠ Don't say 'I am agreeing', 'he is agreeing etc'. Say **I agree, he agrees** etc.

⚠ If you want to say that two people agree with each other, you can just say 'they agree': *Jack and I agree about most things.*

⚠ Don't say 'I agree you' or 'I am agree you'. Say **I agree with you**

be in agreement /biː ɪn əˈɡriːmənt/ FORMAL if people **are in agreement**, they agree about something, especially after discussing it a lot and trying to agree: *No*

A

decision can be made until everybody is in agreement.

+ with *I found myself in agreement with the lawyer, for once.*

share sb's view /ˌʃeəʳ (sb's) 'vjuː/ FORMAL to agree with someone else's opinion, especially about something important, in politics, business, science etc: *Many people shared Davidson's view, and thought the plan should be stopped.*

share this/that view *This view is shared by many doctors.*

unanimous /juːˈnænɪ̯məs/ [adj] if a group of people is **unanimous**, everyone in the group agrees about something

unanimous decision/vote/verdict *Harvey was elected by a unanimous vote.* (=everyone voted for him) | *The committee reached a unanimous decision.*

+ that *The jury was unanimous that Simpson was not guilty.*

  unanimously [adv] *The members voted unanimously to appoint her as chairperson.*

2 to agree with someone else's plan or suggestion

➡ see also **LET 1, ⊞ SAYING YES, ⊞ SUGGESTIONS, ⊞ PERMISSION**

agree /əˈgriː/ [v I] to say yes to someone else's plan or suggestion: *Charles suggested going for a picnic, and we all agreed.*

agree to sth (=agree to allow something to happen) *The Council of Ministers would never agree to such a plan.*

agreeing – agreed – have agreed

go along with sth /ˌgəʊ əˈlɒŋ wɪð (sth) ‖ -əˈlɔːŋ-/ [phrasal verb T] to agree with someone else's plan or suggestion, even though you are not sure if it is the right thing to do: *We went along with Eva's idea, as no-one could think of a better one.* | *Often it was easier just to go along with him, rather than risk an argument.*

3 when people make a decision or plan after talking about it

➡ opposite **DISAGREE 2**

agree /əˈgriː/ [v I/T] if two or more people **agree**, they reach a decision about what to do, and they are all satisfied with it

+ on *We've finally agreed on a date for the party.*

agree to do sth *They agreed to meet again later in the week.*

+ that *In the end, everyone agreed that the best thing to do was to wait.*

it is agreed (=a group of people have agreed about something) *It was agreed that the price should be fixed at $200.*

 we are (all) agreed SPOKEN (say this when everyone in a group has agreed about something) *Right then, are we all agreed?*

agreeing – agreed – have agreed

reach an agreement /ˌriːtʃ ən əˈgriːmənt/ to finally agree on something, by discussing it until everyone is satisfied with the decision: *After two years of talks, the Russians and Americans finally reached an agreement.*

+ with *What will happen if the two sides fail to reach an agreement?*

compromise /ˈkɒmprəmaɪz‖ˈkɑːm-/ [v I] to reach an agreement with someone, by both of you accepting less than you really want: *The employers will have to be ready to compromise if they want to avoid a strike.*

+ on *Stalin refused to compromise on any of his demands.*

make a deal/do a deal /ˌmeɪk ə ˈdiːl, ˌduː ə ˈdiːl/ to make an agreement with someone so that you get what you want, and they get what they want

+ with *The government denied making a deal with the kidnappers.*

4 to tell someone you will do what they asked you to do

➡ opposite **REFUSE 1**

agree to do sth /əˌgriː tə ˈduː (sth)/ to say that you will do what someone has asked you to do, especially something that may be difficult, inconvenient etc: *I've agreed to look after Pat's children next weekend.* | *Why did I ever agree to teach him to drive?*

⚠ Don't use 'accept' in this meaning. Don't say 'he accepted to wait'. Say **he agreed to wait**.

5 something that has been agreed

agreement /ə'griːmənt/ [n C] an arrangement that is made when two or more people, countries, or organizations agree to do something

make an agreement They made a secret agreement not to tell anyone about their plans.

sign an agreement The US has signed a trade agreement with China.

under an agreement (=according to an agreement) Under the agreement, UN troops will remain in Bosnia for another year.

compromise /'kɒmprəmaɪz‖'kɑːm-/ [n C] an agreement in which both people or groups accept less than they really want

reach/find a compromise After several hours of discussions, they managed to reach a compromise.

+ between The treaty represented a compromise between the Communists and the Nationalists.

treaty /'triːti/ [n C] a written agreement between two or more countries, especially to end a war: The Treaty of Versailles ended the First World War.

sign a treaty A peace treaty was signed in 1975.

plural **treaties**

contract /'kɒntrækt‖'kɑːn-/ [n C] a written legal agreement with all the details of a job or business arrangement, for example what someone must do and how much they will be paid: My contract says I have to work 35 hours per week.

sign a contract (with sb) REM signed an 80 million dollar contract with Warner Brothers.

ALIVE

➡ opposite **DEAD**
➡ see also **EXIST, DIE, LIFE**

1 not dead

alive /ə'laɪv/ [adj not before noun] not dead: Are all your grandparents still alive? | He was badly injured, but at least he was alive.

alive and well (=alive and not injured or ill) The children were found alive and well after being missing for ten days.

living /'lɪvɪŋ/ [adj only before noun] still living now: Mary's brother is her only living relative, and he lives in Australia. | Seamus Heaney is Ireland's greatest living poet.

2 to continue to be alive

live /lɪv/ [v I] to continue to be alive: She's seriously ill, but the doctor thinks she'll live. | People are living longer these days.

live for 2 years/3 months/a long time etc He lived for five years after his heart operation. | Cats normally live for about 12 years.

stay alive /ˌsteɪ ə'laɪv/ to not die, even though you are in a dangerous situation: They were lost in the desert for several days, but managed to stay alive by eating insects.

keep sb alive /ˌkiːp (sb) ə'laɪv/ [phrasal verb T] to prevent someone from dying by giving them food, medicine etc: Doctors have a legal duty to keep a patient alive, whether the patient wants it or not.

survive /səˈvaɪv/ [v I/T] to not die in an accident or war, or from an illness or operation: The plane crashed into the sea, but over half of the passengers survived.

survive a war/crash/accident/operation My grandmother is too old to survive another operation.

survivor /səˈvaɪvəʳ/ [n C] someone who has not died in an accident or war: The survivors were rushed to the nearest hospital. | The ship hit an iceberg and sank. There were no survivors.

ALL

➡ if you mean 'all the time' (=through all of a period of time), go to **TIME 8**
➡ if you mean 'all the time' (=without stopping), go to **ALWAYS 4**
➡ see also **EVERYWHERE**

1 all things or all people

⚠ **All, all of,** and **every** mean the same thing: All the computers in the school were stolen = All of the computers in the school were stolen = Every computer in the school was stolen.

A

all /ɔːl/ [predeterminer/quantifier] all the things or people in a group: *There was no-one in the office – they were all having lunch.* | *The new government banned all political parties.*

we all/you all/them all *We all passed our English test.* | *He thanked us all for coming.* | *Have you all finished your dinner?* | *The Red Sox played three games and won them all.*

all the/these/their/my etc *All the teachers at my school are women.* | *Did you take all these photos yourself?* | *I invited all my friends to the party.*

all of *I invited all of my friends to the party.* | *Do we have to read all of the books on this list?* | *The Red Sox played three games and won all of them.*

almost/nearly all *Almost all my friends have computers.* | *The cups fell off the shelf and nearly all of them broke.*

all dogs/all cars/all children etc (=use this to make a general statement about things or people of the same kind) *All mammals are warm-blooded.* | *All cars over 5 years old must have a test certificate.*

⚠ Word order with auxiliary or modal verbs (like **have, will, can, should** etc): **all** goes after the auxiliary or modal verb, and before the main verb: *The new students will all arrive tomorrow.* | *You should all go and visit her in the hospital.*

⚠ Don't use 'all the …' to make general statements about people or things. Don't say 'all the dogs have four legs'. Say **all dogs have four legs.**

every /'evri/ [determiner] all – use this only with singular nouns: *Every room in the house was painted white.* | *The bank has branches in every city in France.* | *She bought presents for every member of her family.* | *Every teacher knows the problems that difficult children can cause.*

every single (used to emphasize that you really mean everyone or everything, especially when this is surprising) *It rained every single day of our vacation.* | *The police questioned every single passenger on the plane.*

⚠ Use **every** with a singular noun and a singular verb.

each /iːtʃ/ [determiner/pronoun] all – use this to emphasize that you mean every separate person or thing in a group: *The calendar has a different picture for each month of the year.* | *She had a ring on each finger of her right hand.* | *The president shook hands with each member of the team.*

each of *She gave each of them a plate of food.* | *Each of the bedrooms has its own shower.*

we each/they each/us each *My brother and I each have our own room.* | *She gave us each a pen and a piece of paper.*

in each/for each/to each etc *She dug several tiny holes in the soil, planting a seed in each.*

⚠ You can use **each** before a singular noun or after a plural pronoun: *Each child has a desk and a chair.* | *They each have a desk and a chair.* Use **each of** with a plural noun and a singular verb: *Each of the children has a desk and a chair.*

everything /'evriθɪŋ/ [pronoun] all the things in a group, or all the things that someone says or does: *Everything in the store costs less than $10.* | *I agree with everything she said.*

⚠ Use **everything** with a singular verb. Don't say 'everything were very expensive'. Say **everything was very expensive**.

⚠ Don't write this word as 'every thing'. The correct spelling is **everything**.

everyone/everybody /'evriwʌn, 'evribɒdi‖-bɑːdi/ [pronoun] all the people in a group: *I think everyone enjoyed the party.* | *If everybody is ready, I'll begin.* | *Has everyone gone home?*

⚠ Use **everyone** and **everybody** with a singular verb. Don't say 'everyone were late'. Say **everyone was late**.

⚠ You can also use **everyone** and **everybody** to talk about people in general: *Everyone knows that smoking is bad for your health.*

unanimous /juːˈnænɪməs/ [adj] if a group of people or a decision they make is **unanimous,** all the members of the

group agree about something: *Many party members agreed with their leader, but they certainly weren't unanimous.*
unanimous decision/agreement/verdict (=a decision that everyone in a group agrees on) *The committee made a unanimous decision to expel the three students.*

2 the whole of something

all /ɔːl/ [predeterminer/quantifier] all of something – use this especially with uncountable nouns
all the/this/that/my etc *He spends all his money on beer and cigarettes.* | *I've finished all my homework.* | *Did you eat all that bread?*
all of the/this/that/my etc *I enjoyed the book although I didn't understand all of it.*
it all *What's happened to the paint? Did you use it all?*
all day/week/year etc (=the whole of a period of time) *I spent all day cleaning the house.*

> ⚠ **All** and **all of** mean the same: *The children ate all the food* = *The children ate all of the food.*

whole /həʊl/ [adj/quantifier] all of something that is large or has a lot of parts, for example a large area of land, a long period of time, or a large group of people: *Police searched the whole area for the murder weapon.* | *She was so frightened, her whole body was shaking.* | *I didn't see her again for a whole year.*
the whole of *She spent the whole of the journey complaining about her boyfriend.* | *The Romans conquered almost the whole of western Europe.*

> ⚠ Don't use **the whole** directly before 'it' or before the name of a place or an organization. Use **the whole of**. Don't say 'the whole Mexico', say **the whole of Mexico**

complete /kʌmˈpliːt/ [adj] use this to say that something includes all the parts that it should have, with nothing missing: *They discovered the complete skeleton of a dinosaur.* | *He has a complete collection of all Elvis's records.*

full /fʊl/ [adj] all of something, with everything included – use **full** with these words:

name, address, details, set, report, statement, price, cost, amount, refund: *Please write your full name and address.* | *I used my student card, so I didn't have to pay the full price.*
a full refund (=when a shop or company gives you back all the money you paid for something)

entire /ɪnˈtaɪəʳ/ [adj only before noun] all of something – use this especially to show that you are annoyed or surprised by this: *I had to re-write the entire essay after my computer crashed.* | *A single CD-ROM can hold the entire text of a 20-volume encyclopedia.* | *We wasted an entire day waiting at the airport.*

3 any person or thing

any /ˈeni/ [determiner/pronoun] use this to talk about each one of the people or things in a group, when it is not important to say exactly which one: *Any student who wishes to go on the trip should sign this list.* | *You can buy the magazine at any good bookstore.*
any of the/these/my/them etc *You are welcome to borrow any of these books.* | *Will any of your friends be going to the same university?*

anything /ˈeniθɪŋ/ [pronoun] any object, action, idea etc: *I went shopping with Kathy, but we didn't buy anything.* | *There's plenty of food – take anything you want.* | *Do you know anything about network computers?* | *If anything goes wrong with the car, call a mechanic.*

anyone/anybody /ˈeniwʌn, ˈenibədi‖ -bɑːdi/ [pronoun] any person: *This would be an ideal job for anyone who speaks French and Italian.* | *Peter's more intelligent than anybody I know.* | *If anyone needs more information, come and see me after the class.*

> ⚠ **Anyone** and **anybody** are singular and take a singular verb: *Has anyone seen my keys?* But we usually use plural pronouns (**they, them,** and **their**) with these words: *If anyone phones me, tell them I'll be back later.* In more formal situations, you can say 'he or she', 'him or her' etc instead of 'they' or 'them': *If anyone wishes to speak to the Principal, he or she should make an appointment.*

whatever /wɒt'evə^r‖waɪt-/ [pronoun] anything at all – use this to emphasize that it does not matter which object, action, idea etc
whatever sb does/says/wants etc *They told me I could eat whatever I wanted from the fridge.* | *We'll do whatever we can to help.* | *It's best just to agree with whatever he says.*

whoever /huː'evə^r/ [pronoun] any person at all – use this to emphasize that it does not matter which one: *You can invite whoever you want to your party.* | *It seems that whoever is in charge of the team, we always lose.*

4 affecting everything or every part of a situation

total/complete /'təʊtl, kəm'pliːt/ [adj only before noun] affecting everything or every part of a situation: *They want a total ban on cigarette advertising.* | *My parents had complete control over my life.* | *the complete destruction of the rainforest*

ALMOST

1 almost

almost/nearly /'ɔːlməʊst, 'nɪə^rli/ [adv] use this to say that something is a little less than a number or amount, or to say that something almost happens or is almost true

> ⚠ You can use **almost** or **nearly** in these combinations: **with numbers:** *There were almost 200 people at the meeting.* **with verbs:** *I was laughing so much I almost fell off my chair.* | *She nearly died of her injuries.* **with:** all, every, everyone, everything, always: *She lost almost all her money.* | *We see each other nearly every day.* **with:** as + adjective + as: *She's almost as tall as her big sister.*

> ⚠ Don't say 'almost my friends came' or 'almost of my friends came'. Say **almost all my friends came** or **almost all of my friends came.**

> ⚠ In American English, **almost** is much more common than **nearly**, but in British English both words are common.

> ⚠ You can use 'very' with **nearly**, but you can't use it with **almost**. Don't say 'Brazil **very almost** lost the game', say **Brazil very nearly** lost the game.

practically/virtually /'præktɪkli, 'vɜː^r-tʃuəli/ [adv] almost completely: *Communism has virtually disappeared from Western Europe.*
+ full/empty/impossible/the same etc *The theatre was practically empty* | *It's virtually impossible for a woman to become president in this country.*
+ all/every/everyone (=very nearly all) *Tom knew practically everyone at the party.* | *Virtually all the children come to school by car.*

> ⚠ Don't use **practically** or **virtually** with numbers.

just about/more or less /ˌdʒʌst ə'baʊt, ˌmɔːr ɔː^r 'les◄/ ESPECIALLY SPOKEN not completely or exactly, but almost so that the difference is not important: *I had more or less convinced her that I was telling the truth.*
+ ready/finished/straight/the same etc *Dinner's just about ready.* | *All the rooms are more or less the same size.*
+ every / everyone / everything *She's invited just about everyone she knows.*

not quite /nɒt 'kwaɪt/ not completely, but almost – use this to say that something is not true or has not happened, but it is almost true or has almost happened: *She hasn't quite finished her homework yet.* | *This skirt isn't quite long enough.* | *Give me five minutes – I'm not quite ready.*
not quite as good/big/strong as *The female bird isn't quite as big as the male.*

> ⚠ Don't use **not quite** with numbers.

2 when something happens, but almost does not

just /dʒʌst/ [adv] use this to talk about something that does happen, but almost does not happen: *He just failed the examination – two more points and he would have passed.* | *I just managed to get there before the train left.*

only just These pants only just fit me. (=they are almost too small)
just big enough/old enough etc The tunnel is just wide enough for two trucks to pass each other.

hardly /ˈhɑːʳdli/ [adv] almost not: I hadn't seen him for 12 years, but he'd hardly changed at all.
can/could hardly do sth (=can only do it with difficulty) I was so tired I could hardly keep my eyes open.
hardly any/anyone/anything (=almost none, almost no-one, almost nothing) There's hardly any fuel left in the tank.
hardly ever (=almost never) She hardly ever goes to church.

⚠️ Be careful with the word order. **Hardly** goes before the verb: She hardly spoke to me all day. If there is a modal or auxiliary verb (like **have**, **will**, **should** etc), **hardly** goes after this and before the main verb: She had hardly spoken to me all day. I The writing was so small, I could hardly read it.

ALONE

➡ see also **INDEPENDENT**

1 when there are no other people with you

alone/on your own/by yourself
/əˈləʊn, ɒn jɔːʳ ˈəʊn, baɪ jɔːʳˈself/ [adj/adv] when you are in a place and no-one else is there with you: She was sitting alone on a park bench. I I don't really like walking home on my own at night. I Do you share the apartment, or do you live by yourself?
all alone/on your own/by yourself
(=completely alone) Wendy was frightened, all alone in that big old house.
leave sb alone/on their own/by themselves The first time his parents left him alone in the house, he set fire to the kitchen. I Mark's not well. I can't go out and leave him on his own.

⚠️ **On your own** and **by yourself** are more informal than **alone**. **Alone** is often used in written stories and descriptions.

⚠️ Don't confuse **alone** (=when no-one else is there) and **lonely** (=when you feel unhappy because you are alone).

2 when you do something without anyone else

on your own/by yourself /ɒn jɔːʳ ˈəʊn, baɪ jɔːʳˈself/ if you do something **on your own** or **by yourself**, you do it without anyone with you or helping you: I don't like going to restaurants on my own. I Surely he's old enough to get dressed by himself, isn't he?
all on your own/all by yourself (=when it is surprising that someone has done something without anyone's help) How did you manage to prepare so much food all on your own?

single-handed/single-handedly
/ˌsɪŋɡəl ˈhændɪd, ˌsɪŋɡəl ˈhændɪdli/ [adv] if you do something **single-handed** or **single-handedly**, especially something very difficult or impressive, you do it without any help from anyone else: Do you remember that part in the movie where Superman single-handedly saves the whole city from destruction? I In 1992, he rowed across the Atlantic single-handed.

solo /ˈsəʊləʊ/ [adv] if you do something **solo**, you do something alone that people often do in groups, for example playing music, climbing mountains, or sailing a boat: I flew solo for the first time this weekend.
go solo (=start to do something on your own instead of in a group) He played in a band for five years before going solo.
solo [adj only before noun] Her first solo album will be released next week.

3 alone and unhappy

lonely (also **lonesome** AMERICAN) /ˈləʊnli, ˈləʊnsəm/ [adj] unhappy because you are alone or you have no friends: Martha felt very lonely when she first arrived in New York. I a lonely old woman I I get so lonesome here with no-one to talk to.
loneliness [n U] the feeling you have when you are lonely: Many old people complain of loneliness.

isolated /'aɪsəleɪtd̩/ [adj] if you feel **iso-lated**, you feel that there is no-one who can talk to or have as a friend, because your situation makes it difficult for you to meet people: *Young single parents often feel isolated and forgotten.*
+ from *Children of very rich parents can grow up isolated from the rest of society.*

miss /mɪs/ [v T] to feel lonely because someone that you like very much is not with you: *When are you coming home? I miss you.* | *It was great living in Prague, but I really missed all my friends.*

4 someone who spends a lot of time alone

loner /'ləʊnər/ [n C] someone who likes to do things alone and does not have many friends: *Jo had always been a loner, happy to stay in at night with a good book.*

recluse /rɪ'kluːs‖'rekluːs/ [n C] someone who lives alone and avoids meeting other people – use this especially about rich or famous people: *an 80-year-old millionaire who had been a recluse for most of his life*

ALWAYS

➡ opposite **NEVER**
➡ if you mean 'continuing for a long time', go to **CONTINUE 5**
➡ see also **OFTEN, USUALLY, SOMETIMES**

> ⚠ Word order with **always**. Always goes between the subject and the verb: *I always play tennis on Saturdays.* The only time this does not happen is when the verb is **to be** when **always** comes after it: *He's always late for class.* If there is a modal or auxiliary verb (like **have, will, should** etc), **always** goes after this and before the main verb: *Karen had always wanted to visit Thailand.*

1 when someone always does something or something always happens

always /'ɔːlwz̩z, -weɪz/ [adv] *She was always ready to listen to my problems.* |

Why do you always blame me for everything? | *He always has sandwiches for his lunch.* | *We always meet at the station café.*

every time /,evri 'taɪm/ [adv/conjunction] on every occasion – use this to say that when one thing happens, something else always happens: *My neck hurts every time I move.* | *He jumped every time he heard a footstep outside.* | *The coach says we should go out on the field expecting to win every time.*

whenever /wen'evər/ [conjunction] every time that something happens: *He goes to visit Amy whenever he's in town.* | *You can use my computer whenever you like.*
whenever possible (=whenever you can) *Try to use public transport whenever possible.*

every /'evri/ [determiner] **every day/week/Monday etc** use this to say that something happens regularly on each day, each week etc: *We use the car almost every day.* | *Thousands of tourists visit Bali every year.*

nine times out of ten /,naɪn taɪmz aʊt əv 'ten/ ESPECIALLY SPOKEN almost always – use this to emphasize that something almost always happens in a particular way: *I often leave work early, and nine times out of ten no-one notices.*

2 always in the future

always /'ɔːlwz̩z, -weɪz/ [adv] *I'll always remember the first time I went to Paris.* | *She said she would always love him.* | *Don't worry! Things won't always seem this confusing!*

forever/for ever /fər'evər/ [adv] for all time in the future – use this to emphasize that something will continue for a very long time: *I'd like to stay here forever.* | *If you wait for Victor to make up his mind, you'll be waiting for ever.*

> ⚠ Use **forever** or **for ever** at the end of a sentence or clause.

permanent /'pɜːrmənənt/ [adj] something that is **permanent** will exist for all time in the future and cannot be changed or removed: *a disease which can cause permanent brain damage* | *a permanent ink stain*

permanently [adv] *The accident left him permanently disabled.*

for life /fə^r 'laɪf/ for the rest of your life: *There's no such thing as a job for life any more.* | *If you help me, I'll be your friend for life!*

be jailed for life (=be sent to prison for life) *She was jailed for life in 1965 for the murder of her husband and children.*

for good /fə^r 'gʊd/ if someone does something **for good**, they do something that causes a permanent change in their situation: *He said he was tired of boxing and was giving it up for good.* | *I'm leaving her, and this time it's for good.*

3 always in the past

always /'ɔːlwɪz, -weɪz/ [adv] *Have you always lived here?* | *He's always wanted to work in TV.* | *I always thought there was something strange about him.*

Qall along /ɔːl ə'lɒŋ‖-ə'lɔːŋ/ ESPECIALLY SPOKEN if something has been true **all along**, it has been true all the time but you did not know it: *He realized that she'd been right all along.* | *I spent three hours looking for my keys and they were in my purse all along!*

from the start /frəm ðə 'stɑː^rt/ always, from the time when something first began: *Their marriage was a disaster from the start.*

right from the start (=use this to emphasize that something has been happening or was true from when it first began) *They liked each other right from the start.*

4 all the time, without stopping

all the time /ɔːl ðə 'taɪm/ without stopping: *I seem to be tired all the time these days.* | *Do you wear your glasses all the time, or just for reading?* | *The situation is changing all the time.*

always /'ɔːlwɪz, -weɪz/ [adv] all the time – use this especially about something bad or annoying: *There's always loud music coming from the room upstairs.* | *As Jim is always telling us, things were different when he was a boy.*

Qthe whole time /ðə ˌhəʊl 'taɪm/ SPOKEN all the time while something is

happening – use this about something annoying or surprising: *He talked about himself the whole time I was with him.* | *We realized that Duncan had been standing there the whole time.*

constant /'kɒnstənt‖'kɑːn-/ [adj usually before noun] continuing all the time without ever changing or stopping: *His constant complaining is really beginning to annoy me.* | *a constant supply of fresh water*

constantly [adv] *We knew we were constantly in danger.*

permanent /'pɜː^rmənənt/ [adj] remaining the same for a very long time or for ever: *a country in a permanent state of crisis* | *He seems to have a permanent smile on his face.*

permanently [adv] *This door is kept permanently locked.*

AMOUNT/NUMBER

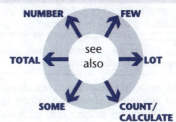

1 an amount of something such as money, food, time, or crime

amount /ə'maʊnt/ [n C]

the amount of sth *The amount of tax you pay depends on how much you earn.* | *Try to reduce the amount of fat in your diet.*

a small/tiny amount *The water here contains small amounts of calcium and other minerals.*

a large/enormous/considerable amount *He knows an enormous amount about Italian paintings.*

⚠ Don't say 'a big amount'.

how much /ˌhaʊ 'mʌtʃ/ use this to ask or talk about the size of an amount of money, time, food etc: *I'll get you some* paint if you'll tell me how much you need. | How much did your jeans cost? **how much time/money/food etc** How much money do I owe you? | Do you realize how much trouble you caused? | How much nitrogen is there in the air?

> ⚠ Only use **how much** with uncountable nouns like 'money' and 'time'.

> ⚠ Only say 'how much is ...' when you are asking about the cost of something: How much is this dress? Don't say 'how much is the temperature?' Say **what is the temperature?**

quantity /'kwɒntɪti‖'kwɑːn-/ [n C] use this, especially in written descriptions or instructions, to talk about amounts of food, liquid, or other substances that can be measured
+ of Make sure that you add the correct quantity of water. | Use equal quantities of flour and butter.
a large/small/enormous etc quantity An enormous quantity of chemical waste had been dumped in the river.

> ⚠ Don't use **quantity** to talk about amounts of money or time.

level /'levəl/ [n C] use this to talk about the exact amount of something at one time, even though this amount may go up or go down at other times
the level of sth a device that measures the level of carbon monoxide in the air | the rising level of crime in the inner-cities
a high/low level At that time Spain had a very high level of unemployment.

100 pounds' worth/ten dollars' worth etc /(£100 etc) wɜːᵗθ/ an amount of something that is worth £100, $10 etc:
+ of Over £10 million worth of heroin was seized in the raid. | The company owns millions of dollars' worth of real estate in downtown Tokyo.

extent /ɪk'stent/ [n C] use this to talk about how large and how serious a problem is
the extent of sth Government inspectors will assess the extent of the damage. | Considering the extent of his injuries, he's lucky to be alive.

sum /sʌm/ [n C] an amount of money
a large/enormous sum It cost over $25,000, which was an enormous sum in those days.
a sum of money She left a small sum of money to her two granddaughters.

> ⚠ **Sum** is more formal than **amount** and is usually used in written English.

volume /'vɒljuːm‖'vɑːljəm/ [n singular] use this to talk about amounts of business activity or amounts of traffic that are continually increasing or decreasing
the volume of trade/sales/traffic/business The volume of traffic on our roads has increased by 50% in the last three years. | After 1929, there was a rapid fall in the volume of trade.

2 a number of people or things

number /'nʌmbəʳ/ [n C]
the number of We need to know the number of students in each class. | The number of cars on our roads has doubled since 1970.
a large/small number A large number of reporters had gathered outside the house. | Thousands of men apply to join the Marines but only a small number are accepted.

> ⚠ Don't say 'a big number'. Say **a large number**.

> ⚠ **Number** is used with a plural verb: Only a small number of people were injured.

> ⚠ **Number** can be used in the plural with the same meaning: 'large numbers of people' means the same as 'a large number of people'.

how many /ˌhaʊ 'meni/ use this to talk about or ask about the number of people or things that there are
how many people/things/years etc How many cups of coffee do you have a day? | He wouldn't tell us how many girlfriends he'd had.
+ of How many of you can swim?

> ⚠ Only use **how many** with countable nouns.

quantity /'kwɒntˌʒti‖'kwɑːn-/ [n C] a number of things – use this especially to talk about things that are being sold, stored, or carried

a quantity of A man was loading a quantity of TV sets onto the back of a truck.
a large quantity Customs officers discovered a large quantity of cigarettes in his baggage.

⚠ Quantity can be used in the plural with the same meaning: 'large quantities of weapons' means the same as 'a large quantity of weapons'.

100 pounds' worth/ten dollars' worth etc /(£100 etc) wɜːrθ/ a number of things that together are worth £100, $10 etc: Police seized over a million pounds' worth of stolen diamonds at London Heathrow Airport yesterday.
+ of $100,000 worth of rugs were destroyed in the fire.

3 a number that is compared with another number

percentage /pər'sentɪdʒ/ [n C usually singular] a number or amount that is calculated as part of a total of 100, and is shown using a % sign
+ of The percentage of women students at the university has increased steadily. | a slight fall in the percentage of nitrogen in the air
a high/large percentage a country where a high percentage of the population lives in poverty.
a low/small percentage The disease is serious, and in a small percentage of cases it can be fatal.

proportion /prə'pɔːrʃən/ [n singular] the number or amount of something, compared with the whole number or amount that exists
+ of a program to increase the proportion of women and black people in the police service
a high/low/large/small proportion Part-time workers now make up a high proportion of jobs.

ratio /'reɪʃiəʊ‖'reɪʃəʊ/ [n singular] a set of numbers, such as '20:1' or '5:1', that shows how much larger one quantity is than another

the ratio of sth to sth a school where the ratio of students to teachers is about 5:1

⚠ Don't confuse ratio and rate.

rate /reɪt/ [n C] a measurement showing the number of times that something happens during a particular period, which is used especially for talking about social changes or problems
the crime/divorce/suicide/murder etc rate the city that has the highest murder rate in the US

fraction /'frækʃən/ [n singular] a very small part of an amount of number: Computers can now do the same job at a fraction of the cost. | The disease affects only a tiny fraction of the population.

ANGRY

➡ if you mean 'not angry or upset', go to CALM

1 feeling angry

angry /'æŋgri/ [adj] if you are **angry**, you feel a strong emotion, for example about someone who has treated you badly or about something that you think is wrong or unfair: I was so angry that I could hardly speak. | A crowd of angry demonstrators gathered outside the embassy. | After the programme, the TV station received hundreds of angry phone calls.
+ with She was angry with him because he had lied to her.
+ about Don't you feel angry about the way you've been treated?
+ that Local people are angry that they weren't consulted about plans to expand the airport.

⚠ Use **angry with** about people: I was really angry with him. Use **angry about** about things: I was really angry about it.

angry – angrier – angriest
  angrily [adv] Rachel slammed the door angrily on her way out.

mad /mæd/ [adj not before noun] INFORMAL, ESPECIALLY AMERICAN angry: Tom will be real mad when he sees what you've done to his car.

+ at *She used to get mad at Harry because he was always changing his mind.*
+ about *Come on, Maria – what are you so mad about?*

mad – madder – maddest

annoyed /əˈnɔɪd/ [adj not before noun] a little angry, but not very angry: *I'll be annoyed if he's forgotten to deliver my message.*
+ with *Joe was annoyed with her for making him miss the film.* | *I was annoyed with myself for playing so badly.*
+ at/by *Kay was clearly annoyed at John's remark.*

furious /ˈfjʊəriəs/ [adj] very angry: *I've never been so furious in all my life.* | *a furious argument* (=when people shout at each other in an angry way)
+ with *She'd be furious with me if she knew I was reading her diary.*
+ at/about *He came home furious at something his boss had said.*

> ⚠ Don't say 'very furious'. Say **absolutely furious.**

furiously [adv] *"Stop it," shouted Ralph furiously.*

livid /ˈlɪvɪd/ [adj] so angry that it is difficult for you to speak properly or think clearly: *"Was he angry when you got in so late?" "Angry? He was livid!"* | *I know I shouldn't have spoken to her like that, but I was absolutely livid.*

> ⚠ Don't say 'very livid'. Say **absolutely livid** or just **livid.**

offended /əˈfendɪd/ [adj not before noun] angry and upset because someone has said or done something rude or has insulted you: *A lot of Muslims were offended when the book came out.* | *I hope you won't be offended if I leave early.*
+ by *Many readers were offended by the newspaper's anti-Irish comments.*

Q cross /krɒs‖krɔːs/ [adj] BRITISH, ESPECIALLY SPOKEN angry – used especially by children or when you are talking to children: *Do you think Dad will be cross when he finds out what happened?*
+ with *Are you cross with me?*

fed up with sth/sick of sth /ˌfed ˈʌp wɪð (stʃ), ˈsɪk ɒv (stʃ)/ INFORMAL to be

annoyed because something bad has been happening for a long time and you want it to stop: *I'm really fed up with this awful weather.* | *Joe was getting sick of Carol's stupid comments.* | *I left the job because I got fed up with being treated like a servant.*

2 to become angry

get angry/get mad /get ˈæŋgri, get ˈmæd/ to become angry: *He tends to get angry if he loses at tennis.*
+ at *Just calm down. There's no need to get mad at me.*

> ⚠ Don't say 'become angry' except in fairly formal written English. **Get angry** and **get mad** are the usual expressions.

lose your temper /ˌluːz jɔːʳ ˈtempəʳ/ to suddenly become very angry, especially after you have been trying not to: *Donald doesn't have much patience – he often loses his temper.* | *"I've told you already," said Kathryn, trying hard not to lose her temper.*
+ with *Whatever you do, don't lose your temper with the students – you'll only make things worse.*

throw a tantrum /ˌθrəʊ ə ˈtæntrəm/ to shout and cry angrily, especially because you cannot have what you want – use this especially about children: *Josie threw a tantrum in the supermarket again today.*

3 behaving in an angry unfriendly way

bad-tempered /ˌbæd ˈtempəʳd◂/ [adj] someone who is **bad-tempered** behaves in an angry and unfriendly way: *Our teacher was a bad-tempered old woman.* | *Pressure at work was making her more and more bad-tempered.*

be in a bad mood /biː ɪn ə ˌbæd ˈmuːd/ if someone **is in a bad mood**, they are annoyed and upset about something, and this makes them behave in an unfriendly way: *Why's Jenny in such a bad mood this morning?*
put sb in a bad mood (=make someone annoyed) *I missed the bus, which put me in a bad mood for the rest of the day.*

grumpy/grouchy /'grʌmpi, 'graʊtʃi/ [adj] INFORMAL someone who is **grumpy** or **grouchy** is angry and unfriendly, and complains a lot: *a grumpy old man* | *Her illness made her grumpy and impatient.* | *Dan is always tired and grouchy in the mornings.*
grumpy – grumpier – grumpiest
grouchy – grouchier – grouchiest

moody /'muːdi/ [adj] someone who is **moody** often becomes annoyed or unhappy, even though there does not seem to be a good reason for feeling that way: *moody teenagers* | *Tara had been moody and difficult all day.*
moody – moodier – moodiest

irritable /'ɪrɪtəbəl/ [adj] someone who is **irritable** easily gets annoyed by things that are not important: *The heat was making me irritable.* | *Zoe hadn't had much sleep and was feeling tired and irritable.*

touchy /'tʌtʃi/ [adj] if someone is **touchy**, they easily get offended, so you have to be careful what you say to them: *She always gets a little touchy when you ask her about her parents.*
+ about *Don't say anything about his bald patch – he's a little touchy about it.*
touchy – touchier – touchiest

sulky /'sʌlki/ [adj] someone who is **sulky** has an angry, unhappy look on their face and does not talk much, especially because they think they have been treated unfairly: *a sulky little boy who refused to play with the other children*
sulky – sulkier – sulkiest
sulkily [adv] *She just sat in the corner and stared sulkily at the floor.*

4 someone or something that makes you angry

annoying /ə'nɔɪ-ɪŋ/ [adj] an **annoying** person, fact, or situation makes you feel annoyed or impatient: *Henry's the most annoying person I have ever met.* | *Just as I got into the shower the phone rang. It was so annoying.*

irritating /'ɪrɪteɪtɪŋ/ [adj] something that is **irritating** is very annoying and it keeps happening: *Steve has an irritating habit of leaving the fridge door open.* | *I do find it irritating when people keep interrupting me.*

frustrating /frʌ'streɪtɪŋ‖'frʌstreɪtɪŋ/ [adj] a **frustrating** situation makes you feel annoyed because it stops you from doing what you want to do: *It's so frustrating when you're in a hurry and the traffic isn't moving.* | *Learning a new language can be a frustrating experience.*

be a nuisance /biː ə 'njuːsəns‖-'nuː-/ ESPECIALLY SPOKEN someone or something that **is a nuisance** is annoying because they cause problems or inconvenience for you: *My car's broken down again. It's a nuisance, isn't it?*
what a nuisance! SPOKEN *She can't babysit tonight because she has to go and see her mother. What a nuisance!*

infuriating /ɪn'fjʊərieɪtɪŋ/ [adj] something that is **infuriating** makes you very angry, especially because there is nothing you can do to stop it: *He always pretends he doesn't understand what I'm saying. It's absolutely infuriating.* | *infuriating delays*

5 to make someone angry

make sb angry/make sb mad ESPECIALLY AMERICAN /ˌmeɪk (sb) 'æŋgri, ˌmeɪk (sb) ˌmæd/ *Sophie tried not to do anything that would make Henry angry.*
it makes sb angry/mad when *It always makes me mad when people drive up behind me and start flashing their lights.*

annoy /ə'nɔɪ/ [v T] to make someone feel annoyed: *The only reason she went out with him was to annoy her parents.* | *Are you doing that just to annoy me?*
it annoys sb that/when *It annoys me that Kim never returns the books she borrows.*

irritate /'ɪrɪteɪt/ [v T] to annoy someone – use this about things that keep happening or things that people keep doing: *That silly smile of hers always irritated him.* | *After a while, the loud ticking of the clock began to irritate me.*

offend /ə'fend/ [v T] to make someone feel angry and upset by doing or saying something rude or insulting: *I'm sorry if I offended you.* | *Some people were offended by Leary's racist jokes.*

get on sb's nerves /ˌget ɒn (sb's) ˈnɜːʳvz/ INFORMAL if someone or something **gets on your nerves**, they make you feel more and more annoyed, especially because they keep saying or doing something that you do not like: *The noise from the apartment upstairs was beginning to get on my nerves.* | *I hope Diane isn't going to be there – she really gets on my nerves.*

◯**drive sb crazy/drive sb mad** BRITISH /ˌdraɪv (sb) ˈkreɪzi, ˌdraɪv (sb) ˈmæd/ INFORMAL, ESPECIALLY SPOKEN if someone or something **drives you crazy** or **drives you mad**, they annoy you so much that you cannot feel calm or think clearly: *Turn that music down – it's driving me mad!* | *Being alone all day with three small kids is enough to drive anyone crazy.*

provoke /prəˈvəʊk/ [v T] to deliberately try to make someone angry: *She would never have hit you if you hadn't provoked her.*

provoke sb into doing sth *Charlie was trying to provoke him into losing his temper.*

6 angry feelings

anger /ˈæŋgəʳ/ [n U] an angry feeling: *He was finding it difficult to control his growing anger.* | *Her heart was filled with sadness more than anger.*

with anger (=because of anger) *His face went bright red with anger.*

rage /reɪdʒ/ [n U] a very strong feeling of anger that often makes you feel violent as well

with rage (=because of rage) *By now Samuel was white in the face and absolutely shaking with rage.*

a fit of rage (=when someone suddenly feels very angry) *Verlaine shot Rimbaud in a fit of jealous rage.*

frustration /frʌˈstreɪʃən/ [n U] a feeling of being annoyed and impatient because you cannot do what you want to do or you cannot change a bad situation

in/with frustration (=because of frustration) *Jess stared out of the window, almost crying with frustration.* | *Kay stamped her foot in frustration and marched out of the room.*

7 to talk angrily to someone because they have done something wrong

tell sb off /ˌtel (sb) ˈɒf‖-ˈɔːf/ [phrasal verb T] to talk to someone, especially a child, in an angry way because they have done something wrong: *She's always telling her kids off or shouting at them.*

+ for *He's upset because the teacher told him off for talking in class.*

◯**get told off** SPOKEN *I got told off by my dad when I got home.*

yell at sb /ˈjel æt (sb)/ [phrasal verb T] ESPECIALLY AMERICAN to shout or talk angrily to someone because they have done something wrong or annoying: *It was so embarrassing – he just started yelling at his wife.*

◯**get yelled at** SPOKEN *I got yelled at at school because I was wearing the wrong shirt.*

ANOTHER

one more of the same kind

➡ see also **MORE**

another /əˈnʌðəʳ/ [determiner, pronoun] use this to talk about one more person or thing that is similar to the one you already have: *"I've lost my pencil." "Don't worry, here's another."*

another person/thing/glass etc *Would you like another drink?* | *She got another chance to see him after the show.*

another one *"That was a good cup of coffee." "Would you like another one?"*

+ of *This is just another of his crazy ideas. Ignore it.*

> ⚠ Only use **another** with a singular countable noun. With uncountable nouns, use **more**. Compare *Would you like another glass of wine?* | *Would you like more wine?*
>
> ⚠ Don't say 'also another'. Just say **another**: *There's another way of doing this.* (not 'there's also another way'.)

one more /ˌwʌn ˈmɔːʳ/ another – use this when you mean that this will be the last one: *One more drink and then I really have to go.* | *I'll give you one more chance to tell the truth.*

extra /ˈekstrə/ [adj only before noun] in addition to the usual amount or number – use this about something useful that you may need: *Bring an extra set of clothes in case you decide to stay overnight.* | *Do you want to earn some extra cash?*

spare /speəʳ/ [adj only before noun] **spare room/key/tyre etc** another room, key, etc that you do not usually use but you can use if you need to: *I always leave a set of spare keys with my neighbour.* | *All cars have to carry a spare tyre by law.*

additional /əˈdɪʃənəl/ [adj only before noun] FORMAL more than the usual or expected amount: *There will be an additional charge for any extra baggage.* | *Additional security was provided for the President's visit.*

ANSWER

➡ see also **ASK**

1 to say something when someone asks a question or speaks to you

answer /ˈɑːnsəʳ‖ˈæn-/ [v I/T] to say something to someone when they have asked you a question or spoken to you: *Jamie thought carefully before answering.* | *I said hello to her, but she didn't answer.* | *"Why don't you just leave?" "I'd like to," she answered, "but I have nowhere else to go."*

answer a question *I had to answer a lot of questions about what I was doing that morning.*
+ that *Hugh answered that he knew nothing about the robbery.*
answer sb *Why don't you answer me?*

⚠ Don't say 'she didn't answer to me' or 'she didn't answer to my question'. Say **she refused to answer me** or **she didn't answer my question**

answer /ˈɑːnsəʳ‖ˈæn-/ [n C] something you say when someone asks you a question or

speaks to you: *I called out her name, but there was no answer.* | *Each time I ask him when the work will be done, I get a different answer.*

give sb an answer *I should be able to give you a definite answer tomorrow.*
the answer is (that) *Why don't people complain? The answer is that they are frightened of losing their jobs.*
+ to *These are important questions, and we want answers to them.*

reply /rɪˈplaɪ/ [v I/T] to answer someone when they have asked you a question or spoken to you – use this especially in written English to report what someone said: *"I'm so sorry," he replied.* | *Before she could reply, Grant put the phone down.*
+ that *Lisa replied that she didn't like playing tennis.*
reply to a question *The Senator refused to reply to any more questions.*

replying – replied – have replied

⚠ Don't say 'he replied me'. Say **he replied**.

reply /rɪˈplaɪ/ [n C] something you say when someone asks you a question or speaks to you – use this especially in written English to report what someone said: *"Yes, I think we should be going," was her reply.* | *Kathy murmured a reply, but I couldn't hear it.*
reply to a question/request/inquiry/accusation *He turned and left the room, without waiting for a reply to his question.*

plural **replies**

2 to answer a letter, invitation, or advertisement

write back /ˌraɪt ˈbæk/ [phrasal verb I] to write a letter to someone who has written a letter to you: *I wrote back and said that of course they could stay with us.*
+ to *You must write back to Amy and tell her all the news.*

reply /rɪˈplaɪ/ [v I] to write a letter to someone who has written to you, or to someone who has put an advertisement in a newspaper: *I wrote to Franca three weeks ago but she hasn't replied yet.*

When you see **EC** , go to the **ESSENTIAL COMMUNICATION** section.

reply to a letter/invitation/advertisement etc *Becky hasn't replied to our invitation so I assume she isn't coming.*

replying – replied – have replied

> ⚠ Don't say 'reply a letter', 'reply an advertisement' etc. Say **reply to a letter/ advertisement** etc: *If you want to reply to this ad, write to the above address.*

reply /rɪ'plaɪ/ [n C] a written answer to a letter, invitation, or advertisement: *Any customer who complains to the bank will receive a reply within 48 hours.*

+ to *We got over a hundred replies to our advertisement.*

plural **replies**

answer /'ɑːnsəʳ‖'æn-/ [v T] if you **answer** a letter or advertisement, you write a letter to the person who has written it: *He spent the morning answering letters in his study.* | *Paola got the job by answering an ad in the paper.*

> ⚠ Don't say 'answer to a letter', 'answer to an advertisement' etc. Say **answer a letter/advertisement** etc.

3 telephone/door

answer /'ɑːnsəʳ‖'æn-/ [v I/T] to pick up the telephone and speak when it rings, or go to the door and open it when someone knocks: *I knocked and knocked but no one answered.*

answer the phone/the door/a call *A strange man answered the phone.* | *He still isn't answering my calls.*

> ⚠ Don't say 'answer to the phone/door'. Say **answer the phone/door.**

get /get/ [v T] SPOKEN to answer the telephone, or go to the door when someone knocks: *"I think that's the phone." "It's OK – I'll get it."* | *Can someone get the door – I'm in the shower!*

getting – got – have got

there was no answer/there was no reply /ðeəʳ wɒz nəʊ 'ɑːnsəʳ, ðeəʳ wɒz nəʊ rɪ'plaɪ‖-'æn-/ BRITISH use this to say that no-one answered the telephone or the door: *She tapped on Mike's door but there was no answer.* | *I've been trying to call Cathy all morning and there's no reply.*

4 in a test or competition

answer /'ɑːnsəʳ‖'æn-/ [n C] an answer to a question in a test or competition: *Write your answers on a postcard and send it to this address.*

the answer (=the correct answer) *And the answer is ... Washington DC!*

+ to *What's the answer to question 4?*

the right/wrong answer *The first person to call us with the right answer will win 10 CDs of their choice.*

answer /'ɑːnsəʳ‖'æn-/ [v I/T] to give an answer to a question in a test or competition

answer a question *You have 20 minutes to answer all the questions.*

answer correctly/wrongly *If you answer correctly, you could win a video camera.*

solution /sə'luːʃən/ [n C] the correct answer to a complicated problem in a test or competition: *Have you worked out the solution yet?*

+ to *The solution to last week's crossword puzzle is on page 25.*

5 the answer to a problem

answer /'ɑːnsəʳ‖'æn-/ [n C] a way of dealing with a problem

+ to *There are no easy answers to today's environmental problems.*

the answer (=the best way of dealing with a problem) *Some people think cars should be banned from the city, but I don't think that's the answer.*

solution /sə'luːʃən/ [n C] a way of dealing with a problem, especially a complicated or difficult problem

+ to *Nuclear power can never be the only solution to our energy problems.*

find a solution/come up with a solution *So far, all attempts to find a solution have failed.*

solve /sɒlv‖sɑːlv, sɔːlv/ [v T] to successfully deal with a problem

solve a problem *The only way to solve the city's housing problems is to spend a lot more money on new homes.*

know what to do /nəʊ ˌwɒt tə 'duː/ to know what you should do in order to deal with a problem: *Go and ask Larry – he'll know what to do.*

+ about Carrie thought her boyfriend was seeing another girl, but she didn't know what to do about it.

AREA

a part of the world, a country, or a surface

➡ see also SPACE, PLACE, LAND AND SEA

1 an area of the world or of a country

area /ˈeəriə/ [n C] There will be sunshine in most areas tomorrow.
+ of A substantial area of Brazil is still covered by rainforest.
industrial/agricultural/rural area The news hadn't reached the rural areas yet.

region /ˈriːdʒən/ [n C] a large area that is part of a country or of the world: There have been reports of fighting throughout the region. | They finally settled in the north-west region.
+ of Wild dogs are rare, even in the remoter regions of Africa.

zone /zəʊn/ [n C] an area that is in some way special or different from the areas around it, for example because it has a particular type of problem: San Francisco and Tokyo are both located in earthquake zones. | They want the Pacific Ocean to become a nuclear-free zone.
war/battle zone UN troops are unwilling to enter the war zone.

2 an area in or around a town or city

area /ˈeəriə/ [n C] an area in or around a town or city
+ of They used to live in Mochfeld, an area of Duisburg.
poor/rich area Diego was brought up in a very poor area of Buenos Aires.
the surrounding area (=the area around a town or city) Police are searching Blickling and the surrounding area for the missing child.

district /ˈdɪstrɪkt/ [n C] part of a town or city that is either one of its officially fixed divisions or is a place where a particular group of people live or a particular activi-ty takes place: The financial district is in the centre of Manila.
+ of Their apartment is in the Chongwen district of Peking.

neighbourhood BRITISH **neighbor-hood** AMERICAN /ˈneɪbəʰhʊd/ [n C] one of the parts of a town or city where people live: Freddie and his family lived in a big house in a wealthy neighbourhood. | Everyone in the neighborhood seemed to have heard the news.

suburb /ˈsʌbɜːʰb/ [n C] an area away from the centre of a city, where people live, especially an area where there are houses with gardens
+ of Amy teaches at a school in a suburb of Boston.
the suburbs It took about an hour to drive through the suburbs.

block /blɒk‖blɑːk/ [n C] ESPECIALLY AMERICAN a group of buildings in a city, with four streets around it – often used as a way of talking about distances in the city: She lived three blocks away, on 32nd Street. | Most of the families on our block are Italian Americans.

precinct /ˈpriːsɪŋkt/ [n C] AMERICAN an area in an American town or city that has its own local government and police: the fourteenth precinct

3 an area that is a part of a surface

area /ˈeəriə/ [n C] a part of a surface that has a particular size and shape: There were several damp areas on the living room walls.
+ of The garden has a small area of grass, with a few fruit trees around it.

patch /pætʃ/ [n C] a small area that is different from the parts around it: a white kitten with black patches
damp/dirty/icy etc patch Icy patches on the road are making driving dangerous.
patch of dirt/damp/grease etc a patch of dirt in the middle of the rug
plural **patches**

When you see **EC**, go to the **ESSENTIAL COMMUNICATION** section.

ARGUE

➡ see also **DISAGREE, SHOUT,**
🔄 DISAGREEING

1 to argue

⚠️ You can use argue about anyone, but people who quarrel, squabble, or have a fight/have a row usually know each other well or belong to the same family.

argue /ˈɑːʳgjuː/ [v I] if people **argue**, they speak angrily to each other because they disagree about something: *Jim and Beth seem to spend all their time arguing.*
+ with *Don't argue with me, John. Just do what I tell you.*
+ about/over *Out in the street, a cab driver and his passenger were arguing about the fare.* | *A lot of time was spent arguing over the details of the contract.*

quarrel /ˈkwɒrəl‖ˈkwɔː-, ˈkwɑː-/ [v I] if two people **quarrel**, they argue angrily and may stop being friends with each other: *They haven't spoken to each other since they quarrelled.*
+ with *She left home after quarrelling with her parents.*
quarrel about/over sth *The two brothers had quarreled over ownership of the farm.*
quarrelling – quarrelled – have quarrelled (BRITISH)
quarreling – quarreled – have quarreled (AMERICAN)

have a fight (also **have a row** BRITISH) /hæv ə ˈfaɪt, hæv ə ˈraʊ/ INFORMAL if two people **have a fight** or **have a row**, they argue very angrily and noisily
+ with *I had a fight with my Mom last night – she wouldn't let me go out.*
+ about *Kelvin and his wife have endless rows about money.*

squabble /ˈskwɒbəl‖ˈskwɑː-/ [v I] to argue noisily about something that is not really important – use this especially about children or when you think someone is behaving like a child: *Oh, for goodness sake, stop squabbling, you two!*
+ about/over *The kids always squabble about who should do the dishes.*

fall out with sb /ˌfɔːl ˈaʊt wɪð (sb)/ [phrasal verb T] to stop having a friendly relationship with someone, because you have quarrelled with them: *I think she's fallen out with her boyfriend.*
+ about/over *I don't want to fall out with you over something so unimportant.*

2 an argument

➡ if you mean 'the reason that someone gives why something is right, wrong etc', go to REASON

argument /ˈɑːʳgjᵿmənt/ [n C] when people speak angrily to each other because they disagree about something
have an argument *My sister and I had a terrible argument last night.*
+ about/over *the usual family arguments about what time we should be home at night*
+ with *I could hear her on the phone, having an argument with someone from the bank.*
get into an argument (=start arguing, without intending to) *Phil got into an argument with a guy at the bar.*
start an argument (=to say something that makes someone argue with you) *I didn't want to start an argument, so I kept quiet.*

quarrel /ˈkwɒrəl‖ˈkwɔː-, ˈkwɑː-/ [n C] an angry argument between people who know each other well: *a family quarrel*
+ with *I was tired of these stupid quarrels with my parents.*
have a quarrel *They had some sort of quarrel years ago, and they haven't spoken to each other since.*

disagreement /ˌdɪsəˈɡriːmənt/ [n C] a situation in which people disagree with each other, but without shouting or getting angry
+ about/over *There were the occasional disagreements about money, but mostly we got on well.*
+ with *Ginny had left the company after a disagreement with her boss.*
+ between *a disagreement between the USA and China*

row /raʊ/ [n C] BRITISH an argument, when two people shout angrily at each other: *There were always rows when my dad got home.*

a blazing row (=a very angry, noisy argument) *The couple in the house next door were having a blazing row.*

squabble /ˈskwɒbəl‖ˈskwɑː-/ [n C] a noisy argument about something that is not important, especially between children: *Uncle Matt bought them a computer game to share, which led to endless squabbles.*
+ about/over *the usual squabbles over who should sit in the front of the car*

dispute /dɪˈspjuːt, ˈdɪspjuːt/ [n C] FORMAL when two people, organizations, or countries publicly disagree and argue with each other about something important
+ over/about *an international dispute over fishing rights*
+ with *Morris has been involved in a long legal dispute with his publisher.*
+ between *the bitter dispute between Clinton and the Republican leadership*
settle a dispute (=end it by agreement) *All efforts to settle the dispute have so far failed.*

3 someone who likes arguing

argumentative/quarrelsome /ˌɑːrgjʊˈmentətɪv, ˈkwɒrəlsəm‖ˈkwɔː-, ˈkwɑː-/ [adj] someone who is **argumentative** or **quarrelsome** seems to like arguing or starting arguments: *When he drinks too much, he becomes very argumentative.* | *She had had enough of all her quarrelsome relatives.*

4 to stop arguing

⌕**make up/make it up** /ˌmeɪk ʌp, ˌmeɪk ɪt ˈʌp/ [phrasal verb I] ESPECIALLY SPOKEN if two people who know each other well **make up** or **make it up**, they stop arguing and start being friendly to each other again: *I'm glad to see that you two have made up at last.*
+ with *Have you made it up with your sister yet?*

settle your differences /ˌsetl jɔːr ˈdɪfərənsɪz/ if two people or organizations **settle their differences**, they stop arguing and discuss things in a sensible way until they come to an agreement: *By the early 1970s, France and Britain had settled their differences over European trade.* |

Is it at all possible that you and your husband could settle your differences?

ARMY
WAR   WEAPON
PEACE   see also   SHOOT
ATTACK   EXPLODE
DEFEND   POSITION/RANK

1 the army, navy etc

army /ˈɑːrmi/ [n C] a large organized group of people trained to fight on land in a war: *the armies of Britain and France*
be in the army *Both my brothers are in the army.*
join the army/go into the army *He joined the army when he was seventeen.*
plural **armies**

> ⚠ You can also use **army** before a noun, like an adjective: *army officers* | *army uniform*

> ⚠ In British English, you can use **army** with a singular or plural verb: *The army has/have been heavily criticized.* In American English, always use a singular verb: *The army has been heavily criticized.*

the armed forces /ðiː ˌɑːrmd ˈfɔːrsɪz/ [n plural] FORMAL the army, navy, and air force of a country: *people who served in the armed forces during the war*

the military /ðə ˈmɪlɪtəri‖-teri/ [n singular] ESPECIALLY AMERICAN the army, navy, and air force of a country: *The company supplies electronic equipment to the US military.* | *In 1976 there was a coup and the military seized power.*

military /ˈmɪlɪtəri‖-teri/ [adj only before noun] use this about things or people that belong to or are connected with the armed forces
military power/aircraft/training/uniform etc *the supreme US military commander in Europe* | *The airport is used by civilian and military planes.*

A

2 someone who is in the army, navy etc

soldier /ˈsəʊldʒəʳ/ [n C] a member of an army, especially someone who is not an officer

troops /truːps/ [n plural] soldiers – use this especially to talk about soldiers taking part in a military attack: *Thousands of French troops died in the attack.* | *Troops were sent in to stop the riots.*

officer /ˈɒfɟsəʳ‖ˈɔː-, ˈɑː-/ [n C] a member of the army, navy etc who is in charge of a group of soldiers, sailors etc: *He's an officer in the US Marines.*

3 to join the army, navy etc

join /dʒɔɪn/ [v T] **join the army/navy/air force/marines** to become a member of the army, navy etc: *He wants to join the air force when he finishes school.*

join up /ˌdʒɔɪn ˈʌp/ [phrasal verb I] to join the armed forces during a war: *My dad joined up at the beginning of the war.*

enlist /ɪnˈlɪst/ [v I] to join the armed forces, either in peacetime or during a war: *By the end of 1915, over 700,000 men had enlisted.*
+ in *Frank enlisted in the Marines at the age of 19.*

> ⚠ Enlist is more formal than join or join up.

4 when people must join the army, navy etc

conscription (also **the draft** AMERICAN) /kənˈskrɪpʃən, ðə ˈdrɑːft‖-ˈdræft/ [n U] when people are officially ordered to join the armed forces, especially during a war: *When was conscription introduced in Britain?* | *Many young men went abroad to avoid the draft.*

military service /ˌmɪlɪtəri ˈsɜːrvɟs‖-teri-/ [n U] the system in which everyone has to be a member of the armed forces for a period of time: *All males between the ages of 18 and 30 were liable for military service.*
do military service (=be a member of the armed forces as part of this system) *Did you have to do military service?*

> ⚠ Don't say 'the military service', just say military service.

be called up BRITISH **be drafted** AMERICAN /biː ˌkɔːld ˈʌp, biː ˈdrɑːftɟd‖-ˈdræf-/ to be officially ordered to join the armed forces during a war: *I was called up three months after the war started.* | *Thousands of young Americans were drafted to fight in Vietnam.*

AROUND

➡ if you mean 'turn around', go to **TURN**

1 around someone or something

around (also **round** BRITISH) /(ə)ˈraʊnd/ [adv/prep] completely surrounding or enclosing someone or something: *A group of students sat around the table chatting.* | *She was wearing a silver chain round her neck.* | *a package with tape wrapped around it*
all around/all round *Enemy soldiers were now all around us.* | *a long garden with high walls all round*

be surrounded by /biː səˈraʊndɟd baɪ/ if someone or something **is surrounded by** people or things, those people or things are around them on every side: *The tops of the hills were surrounded by clouds.* | *Jill sat on the floor surrounded by boxes.*

on all sides /ɒn ˌɔːl ˈsaɪdz/ if something is around you **on all sides**, you see it everywhere and you may feel that you are unable to move or escape because of it: *Mountains rose steeply on all sides.*
from all sides *There was the sound of gunfire from all sides.*

> ⚠ Use on all sides especially when you are writing stories or descriptions.

2 to move into a position around someone or something

surround /səˈraʊnd/ [v T] to stand in a circle around someone or something, especially to prevent someone escaping: *Football fans ran onto the field and surrounded the referee.* | *Police officers moved to surround Evans as he came out of the courtroom.*

gather around (also **gather round** BRITISH) /ˌgæðəʳ (ə)ˈraʊnd/ [*phrasal verb* I/T] if a group of people **gathers around** someone or something, they move nearer to them in order to see or hear them: *A crowd of young boys had gathered round to admire the car.*
gather around sth *People were gathering around the TV to watch the game.*

crowd around (also **crowd round** BRITISH) /ˌkraʊd (ə)ˈraʊnd/ [*phrasal verb* I/T] if a group of people **crowds around** someone or something, they stand near them closely together, often pushing forward to see what is happening: *Fire officers asked the people who had crowded round to stand back.*
crowd around sb/sth *Dozens of journalists crowded around the Princess and started asking her questions.*

3 moving in a circle or moving around something

around (also **round** BRITISH) /(ə)ˈraʊnd/ [*adv/prep*] use this after verbs of movement, to show that someone or something is moving in a circle or moving around something
go/fly/travel/run etc around *The Earth goes around the Sun.* | *The helicopter flew round and round above us.*

in circles /ɪn ˈsɜːʳkəlz/ if someone or something moves **in circles**, they move around in a circle several times: *Birds flew in circles above the lake.* | *As the dog got more and more excited, it started running around us in circles.*

circle /ˈsɜːʳkəl/ [*v* I/T] ESPECIALLY WRITTEN to move around someone or something in a circle: *The plane circled the airport several times before landing.*
+ around/above *Seagulls were circling above the cliffs.*

orbit /ˈɔːʳbɪt/ [*v* T] to go around the Earth, the Moon, the Sun etc in a continuous circular movement: *a TV satellite that orbits the Earth every 48 hours*

ARRIVE

⇒ opposite **LEAVE**
⇒ see also **LATE/NOT LATE, EARLY**

1 to arrive somewhere

arrive /əˈraɪv/ [*v* I] to get to the place you were going to: *What time do you think we'll arrive?*
arrive at the house/hotel/airport etc *It was already dark by the time they arrived at their hotel.*
arrive in France/Tokyo etc *The British Prime Minister arrived in Tokyo today.*
arrive here/there/back/home *When I first arrived here none of the other students would talk to me.*
+ from *They were the first refugees to arrive from Bosnia.*

> ⚠ Don't say 'arrive to' a place. Say **arrive at** (a building or public place) or **arrive in** (a city or country).
>
> ⚠ Don't say 'arrive at home' or 'arrive to home'. Say **arrive home**.
>
> ⚠ **Arrive** is more formal than **get to**.

get to /ˈget tuː/ [*phrasal verb* T] to arrive at a place: *It'll take us about half an hour to get to the airport.*
get back to *I'll call her when I get back to Chicago.*
get there/here/home *What time do you usually get home in the evening?* | *I want to get there before the stores close.*

come /kʌm/ [*v* I] if someone or something **comes**, they arrive at the place where you are waiting for them: *When the visitors come, bring them up to my office.* | *Has the mail come yet?*
come home *What time is Dad coming home?*
coming – came – have come

reach /riːtʃ/ [*v* T] to arrive at a place, especially after a long or difficult journey: *It took them over three days to reach the top of the mountain.* | *On March 3rd the US 1st Army finally reached Cologne.*

> ⚠ Don't say 'reach to' or 'reach at'.

A

be here /biː ˈhɪəʳ/ SPOKEN you say someone **is here** when they have arrived at the place where you are waiting for them: *Susan, your friends are here.* | *Is Nick here yet?*

turn up/show up /ˌtɜːʳn ˈʌp, ˌʃəʊ ˈʌp/ [phrasal verb I] INFORMAL to arrive – use this about someone you are expecting to arrive, especially when they arrive late: *Steve turned up half an hour late as usual.* | *Some of the people I invited never showed up.*

2 a plane, ship, or train arrives

arrive /əˈraɪv/ [v I] *The plane arrived two hours late.*
+ **in/at/from** *a train arriving in Osaka at 5.30* | *Planes carrying military supplies have been arriving at the airbase.*

⚠️ Arrive is more formal than **get in**.

get in /ˌget ˈɪn/ [phrasal verb I] to arrive – use this when you are talking about the time when a train, ship, or plane arrives: *What time does your train get in?*
+ **to** *The ferry gets in to Milwaukee around noon.*

land /lænd/ [v I] if a plane **lands**, it arrives at an airport
+ **at** *When the plane landed at JFK, it was three hours late.*
+ **in** *What time do you land in Miami?*
come in to land (=go down slowly towards the ground at an airport) *There's a plane coming in to land now.*

⚠️ Planes **land at** an airport, or **land in** a city or country.

come in /ˌkʌm ˈɪn/ [phrasal verb I] if a plane, ship, or train **comes in**, it arrives in the place where you are waiting: *Crowds had gathered at the harbour to watch the ship come in.* | *Has the Air India flight come in yet?*

3 when someone or something arrives

arrival /əˈraɪvəl/ [n singular, U]
sb's arrival *Joe's sudden arrival spoiled all our plans.*

the arrival of sb/sth *We apologize for the late arrival of flight 605.*
+ **at/in** *TV crews filming President Mandela's arrival at the airport* | *the day after our arrival in Paris*
on arrival (=when someone arrives) *She was rushed to the hospital but was found to be dead on arrival.*

4 to arrive somewhere without intending to

end up /ˌend ˈʌp/ [phrasal verb I] to arrive in a place that you did not intend to go to
+ **in/at** *I fell asleep on the bus and ended up in Denver.* | *We had planned to go straight home, but we all ended up at Tom's place.*

come to sth /ˈkʌm tuː (sth)/ [phrasal verb T] to arrive at a place during a journey, without knowing that you would arrive there: *We were walking through the forest when we came to a waterfall.*

⚠️ Use **come to** especially when you are writing stories.

ART

FILMS/MOVIES
PAINT **OPINIONS**
PICTURE **THEATRE**
see also
MUSIC **DESIGN**
DECORATE **DRAW**
BOOKS/LITERATURE

1 something that an artist has produced

art /ɑːʳt/ [n U] a way of representing things or expressing ideas, using pictures, sculpture, and other objects that people can look at: *a book about German art in the 19th century* | *Is a pile of bricks in a gallery really art?* | *What kind of art do you like?*

work of art /ˌwɜːʳk əv ˈɑːʳt/ [n C] something produced by an artist, especially something that most people agree is of very high quality: *Several priceless works*

of art were badly damaged when the palace was bombed.
plural **works of art**

work /wɜːᵏk/ [n C] a picture, statue, sculpture etc – use this especially when you are also saying who the artist was: *David Hockney's latest work has just gone on display. | Her later works reflected her growing depression.*

masterpiece /ˈmaːstəᵣpiːs‖ˈmæs-/ [n C] a picture, statue etc that is of extremely high quality, especially one that is believed to be the best work of a particular artist: *one of the great Italian masterpieces | Many people regard this painting as Raphael's masterpiece.*

⚠️ You can use **work of art**, **work**, and **masterpiece** about any kind of art.

2 types of picture

painting /ˈpeɪntɪŋ/ [n C] a picture made using paint: *a 17th century Dutch painting*
+ of *a paiting of a woman lying on a bed*
+ by *a painting by Turner*
oil painting (=done using a special type of paint made with oil)

drawing /ˈdrɔːɪŋ/ [n C] a picture drawn with pencils or pens
+ of *a 16th century drawing of the canals in Venice*

photograph /ˈfəʊtəgrɑːf‖-græf/ [n C] a picture made using a camera

mosaic /məʊˈzeɪ-ɪk/ [n C] a picture made using very small pieces of glass or stone

collage /ˈkɒlaːʒ‖kəˈlaːʒ [n C] a picture made by sticking paper, cloth, or other pictures onto a surface

portrait

portrait /ˈpɔːᵣtrɪ̩t/ [n C] a picture of a person

watercolour BRITISH **watercolor** AMERICAN /ˈwɔːtəᵣˌkʌləᵣ‖ˈwɔː-, ˈwɑː-/ [n C] a picture painted using a special type of paint that is mixed with water, so the colours are pale

still life

still life /ˌstɪl ˈlaɪf◂/ [n C] a picture of an object or several objects, especially fruit or flowers

landscape

landscape /ˈlændskeɪp/ [n C] a picture of the countryside

seascape

seascape /ˈsiːskeɪp/ [n C] a picture of the sea

When you see **EC**, go to the **ESSENTIAL COMMUNICATION** section.

A **3** **other types of art**

sculpture /ˈskʌlptʃər/ [n C/U] a work of art made of materials such as stone, metal, or wood

statue

statue /ˈstætʃuː/ [n C] an image of a person or animal made from a hard material such as stone or metal

ceramics /sᵻˈræmɪks/ [n plural] pots, bowls etc made of clay

⚠ Ceramics is always used in the plural: *an exhibition of Japanese ceramics.* Don't use ceramics when you are talking about one bowl. Say 'a bowl', 'a plate' etc.

4 **the subject of a picture, painting etc**

of /ɒv‖ɑːv/ [preposition] use this to show what the subject of a picture, painting etc is: *a portrait of King Charles* | *a statue of a horse*

depict /dɪˈpɪkt/ [v T] FORMAL if a painting or other piece of art **depicts** something, that is what it shows or represents: *Her drawings depict life in an African village.*

5 **someone who draws, paints etc**

artist /ˈɑːrtᵻst/ [n C] someone who produces paintings, sculptures, or any kind of art: *an exhibition of work by young artists*

painter /ˈpeɪntər/ [n C] someone who produces paintings: *Pissarro was a famous French painter.*

sculptor /ˈskʌlptər/ [n C] someone who produces sculptures

photographer /fəˈtɒɡrəfər‖-ˈtɑː-/ [n C] someone who takes photographs

6 **to make drawings, pictures etc**

paint /peɪnt/ [v I/T] to make a picture using paint: *Botticelli painted 'The Birth of Venus'.*

draw /drɔː/ [v I/T] to make a picture using a pencil or pen: *The students were drawing a Chinese vase that stood on the table.* | *Where did you learn to draw like that?*

photograph /ˈfəʊtəɡrɑːf‖-ɡræf/ [v I/T] to take a photograph of someone or something: *Eve Arnold photographed Marilyn Monroe many times.*

⚠ Don't say 'I photographed my friends on the beach'. Say **I took a photo of my friends** or **I took a picture of my friends**. Only use the verb **photograph** about artists or professional photographers.

7 **a place where art is shown**

gallery also **art gallery** /ˈɡæləri, ˈɑːrt ˌɡæləri/ [n C] a building or room where you can go to look at paintings, sculptures etc: *the National Gallery* | *There's a small art gallery in the centre of the town.*

⚠ In American English **gallery** is only used about a room or a small building

museum /mjuːˈziːəm‖mjʊ-/ [n C] AMERICAN a large building where you can go to look at paintings, sculptures etc: *The Museum of Modern Art* | *The museum has a few of Van Gogh's early works.*

exhibition /ˌeksᵻˈbɪʃən/ [n C] a collection of paintings, sculptures etc, often the work of one particular artist, which you can go to see – use this especially when they are only being shown for a limited period of time: *Have you been to the Picasso exhibition yet?*

+ of *an exhibition of black and white photographs*

8 styles of art

classical

classical /'klæsɪkəl/ [adj] the main style of art in 18th century Europe, based on the styles of ancient Greece and Rome, often showing scenes and characters from the Christian religion

romantic

romantic /rəʊ'mæntɪk, -rə-/ [adj] a style of art popular in 19th century Europe, often showing the sea or the countryside, and usually expressing strong emotions

impressionist

impressionist /ɪm'preʃənˌɪst/ [adj] a style of art that was developed in France in the late 19th century, which uses colours to show the effects of light on people, objects, and places, and does not show small details

A

modern

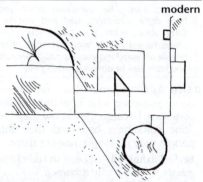

modern /'mɒdən‖'mɑːdərn/ [adj] the style of art in the 20th century that is deliberately different from art of the 18th and 19th centuries, and does not show people, objects, or places as they appear in real life

abstract

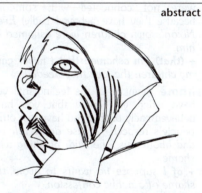

abstract /'æbstrækt/ [adj] a type of modern art that uses shapes, colours, and patterns to express ideas and feelings, rather than pictures that look like people, objects, or places

When you see **EC**, go to the **ESSENTIAL COMMUNICATION** section.

A

ASHAMED

➡ see also **EMBARRASSED, GUILTY/NOT GUILTY, SORRY**

⚠ Don't confuse ashamed and embarrassed. Use ashamed when you have done something bad and you feel sorry about what you have done. Use embarrassed when you feel that other people are watching you, especially because you have said or done something silly.

ashamed /ə'ʃeɪmd/ [adj not before noun] someone who is **ashamed** feels very sorry because they know they have done something bad, and they think people may no longer respect them

be/feel ashamed *I've been so rude to our guests – I feel really ashamed.*

ashamed of doing sth *Frank was ashamed of having lied to his mother.*

ashamed of yourself *You ought to be ashamed of yourself – coming home drunk like that!*

ashamed of sb (=when you wish you were not connected with someone because they have behaved badly) *Even Nixon's own children were ashamed of him.*

+ (that) *I'm ashamed that I never gave my children the love they needed.*

shame /ʃeɪm/ [n U] the feeling that you have when you know that you have behaved badly or that you have lost other people's respect: *"Please don't tell my dad about this," he said, blushing with shame.*

+ of *I suppose he wants to avoid the shame of a public confession.*

in shame (=because you are ashamed) *As Philip entered the courtroom, he hung his head in shame.*

⚠ Don't say 'I feel shame'. Say **I feel ashamed**.

disgrace /dɪs'greɪs/ [n U] when you have completely lost other people's respect because of something bad you have done

in disgrace *Browne was caught selling drugs, and was sent home from college in disgrace.*

+ of *Garton killed himself because he could not bear the disgrace of a public scandal.*

humiliating /hjuːˈmɪlieɪtɪŋ/ [adj] a **humiliating** experience makes you seem weak or stupid in a way that many other people can see: *I had to apologize in front of all the other students – it was so humiliating!*

ASK

➡ if you want to know how to form questions, go to the **ESSENTIAL GRAMMAR** section 1

1 **to ask questions**

ask /ɑːsk‖æsk/ [v I/T] to ask someone a question because you want to get information from them: *I knew there was something wrong, but I didn't like to ask.*

ask (sb) what/how/why etc *Ask Kim what she'd like for her birthday.* | *I asked why, but they wouldn't give a reason.*

ask (sb) if/whether *Let's ask dad if we can go to the movies.* | *He asked whether I was looking for accommodation.*

ask (sb) about sth *At the interview, they're sure to ask you about your work experience.*

ask (sb) a question *Would anyone like to ask me any questions?*

ask sb *If you need any more information, ask your doctor.*

⚠ Don't say 'ask to someone'. Say **ask someone**: *If you don't understand, ask your teacher.*

consult /kən'sʌlt/ [v T] FORMAL to ask for information or advice from someone, because it is their job to know about it

consult a doctor/lawyer/expert etc *Before starting any exercise programme, you should consult your doctor.*

consult sb about sth *He should have consulted his advisors about this before taking any action.*

question /ˈkwestʃən/ [v T] to ask someone a lot of questions, in order to get information or find out what they think: *Half of the people we questioned thought the President should resign.*
question sb about sth *The police have already questioned him about the missing $50,000.*

interrogate /ɪnˈterəgeɪt/ [v T] to keep asking someone a lot of questions for a long time, sometimes using threats, in order to get information – use this especially about the police: *Police officers interrogated him non-stop for 24 hours until he confessed.*

make inquiries (also **make enquiries** BRITISH) /ˌmeɪk ɪnˈkwaɪəriz/ to try to get information about something by asking several people, especially people whose job is to know about it: *We went to the French Embassy to make inquiries.*
+ about *A detective was here earlier, making inquiries about your friend Gary.*

2 to ask for something

ask /ɑːsk‖æsk/ [v I/T] to ask for something, or to ask someone to do something for you: *If you ever need any help, just ask.* | *I need some more money, but I don't dare ask my dad.*
ask (sb) for sth *A lot of people don't like asking for help.*
ask sb to do sth *Ask him to wait outside for a moment.*
ask to do sth (=ask to be allowed to do something) *She walked right in here and asked to speak to the manager.*

⚠ Don't say 'ask to someone'. Say **ask someone.**

order /ˈɔːrdər/ [v T] to ask for something that you are going to pay for – use this about asking for food or drink in restaurants, or asking companies to send you goods: *Have you ordered the wine yet?* | *Nina orders a lot of her clothes from mail-order catalogues.*

demand /dɪˈmɑːnd‖dɪˈmænd/ [v T] to ask for something, or ask someone to do something, in a firm or angry way that shows you expect them to do it: *This is outrageous! I demand an explanation.*

demand to do sth *He demanded to know what I was doing there.*

beg /beg/ [v I/T] to ask for something, or ask someone to do something, in an anxious way that shows you want it very much: *She begged and begged until finally they agreed to let her come.*
beg sb to do sth *I begged Greg not to tell Cindy about it.*
+ for *The prisoners were begging for mercy.*
begging – begged – have begged

nag /næg/ [v I/T] to keep asking someone to do something, in a very annoying way: *Oh, stop nagging – I'll do it later!*
nag sb to do sth *My parents keep nagging me to get my hair cut.*
nagging – nagged – have nagged

3 to ask for something officially

apply /əˈplaɪ/ [v I] to write to someone asking for something such as a job, an opportunity to study at a university, or permission to do something: *There was a job vacancy at the radio station, and 150 people applied.*
+ for *Why don't you apply for a loan?*
apply to do sth *In the 1960s, thousands of people applied to emigrate to South Africa.*
applying – applied – have applied

claim /kleɪm/ [v T] to ask for something, especially money, from a government, company etc, because you believe you have a legal right to have it: *Thousands of people who should get welfare payments never even bother to claim them.*
claim sth from sb *Ms Larkins believes she was unfairly dismissed, and is claiming compensation from her former employer.*

appeal /əˈpiːl/ [v I] to make a public request, for example on television or in the newspapers, for money, food, information etc, especially in order to help someone who is in a very bad situation
+ for *We are appealing for food and clothes for the refugees.*
appeal to sb for sth *Police appealed to the public for any information about the missing girl.*

request /rɪˈkwest/ [v T] FORMAL to officially ask someone for something or ask someone

A

to do something: *The pilot requested permission to land the plane at Rome airport.*

⚠ Don't say 'request for something'. Say **request something**.

4 to ask for money or food because you do not have any

beg (also **panhandle** AMERICAN) /beg, 'pæn-hændl/ [v I] to ask people in the street for money or food because you do not have any: *In London there are more and more homeless kids begging in the streets.* | *an old man panhandling outside the bus terminal*

begging – begged – have begged

5 something that you ask

question /'kwestʃən/ [n C] what you say or write when you are asking for information: *There were several questions she wanted to ask.* | *That's a difficult question.*
+ about *Does anyone have any questions about the timetable?*

request /rɪ'kwest/ [n C] a statement, letter etc in which you ask for something politely or formally
+ for *She refused all requests for an interview.*
on request (=when you can get something by formally asking for it) *Information about the test is available on request.*

demand /dɪ'mɑːnd‖dɪ'mænd/ [n C] a strong request saying very clearly what you want, especially when you are asking for something that someone does not want to give you: *The kidnappers sent a list of demands to a national newspaper.*
+ for *a demand for a 10% pay increase*

6 a set of questions that you ask in order to find out what people think

survey /'sɜːrveɪ/ [n C] an attempt to find out about people's opinions, the way they live, what they like and dislike etc, by asking a large number of people a set of questions: *A recent survey showed that 50% of 18–22-year-olds had tried drugs.*

carry out/conduct a survey *We are carrying out a survey into the effects of TV violence on children.*
+ of *a national survey of sexual behaviour among young people*

opinion poll /ə'pɪnjən ˌpəʊl/ [n C] an attempt to find out about people's political opinions, by asking many people how they intend to vote, which politicians they like etc: *Opinion polls show that the Democrats are way ahead.*

questionnaire /ˌkwestʃə'neər, ˌkes-/ [n C] a piece of paper with a set of questions on it, which is given to a large number of people to find out what they think
complete a questionnaire (=answer all the questions on it) *Complete our questionnaire and you might win a car!*

ATTACK

➡ opposite **DEFEND**

CRITICIZE
VIOLENT   CRIME
WAR   see   PROTECT
       also
ARMY   SUFFER
SHOOT   THREATEN

1 to attack a person

attack /ə'tæk/ [v T] to use violence against someone and try to hurt them: *She was attacked on her way to the station.* | *A big dog jumped out and attacked me.*
attack sb with sth *He'd been attacked with some kind of heavy object.*
attacker [n C] someone who attacks another person: *Could you give me a description of your attacker?*

mug /mʌg/ [v T usually in passive] to attack someone and take money from them in a public place such as a street: *He's been mugged twice since he moved to London.*
mugging – mugged – have mugged

ambush /'æmbʊʃ/ [v T] if a group of people **ambush** someone, they hide and wait for them and then suddenly attack them: *An armed gang ambushed a security vehicle and killed the driver.*

assault /əˈsɔːlt/ [v T] to attack and hurt someone – use this especially to talk about the crime of attacking someone: *Several police officers were assaulted by demonstrators.*

2 to attack a place or country

attack /əˈtæk/ [v I/T] to attack a place or country using weapons, aircraft, soldiers etc: *Enemy planes attacked the city throughout the night.* | *General McArthur gave the order to attack.*

invade /ɪnˈveɪd/ [v I/T] if a country's army **invades** another country, it enters it and tries to control it: *In the summer of 1968, Soviet troops invaded Czechoslovakia.*

raid /reɪd/ [v T] if a group of soldiers **raids** a place or town belonging to an enemy, they attack it suddenly and without any warning and cause a lot of damage in a short time: *Shortly after dawn a small group of commandos raided the enemy camp.*

3 to attack someone because they attacked you

retaliate /rɪˈtælieɪt/ [v I] to attack someone because they have attacked you first
retaliate by doing sth *When soldiers began shooting into the crowd, a few people retaliated by throwing stones.*
　retaliation /rɪˌtæliˈeɪʃən/ [n U] when you attack someone because they attacked you
　in retaliation for (=as retaliation when someone attacks you) *The rockets were fired in retaliation for Tuesday's bomb attack.*

counter-attack /ˈkaʊntərəˌtæk/ [n C] an attack that an army makes after it has been attacked by an enemy: *The British counter-attack forced the French back into their own territory.*
　counter-attack [v I] to attack an enemy after they have attacked you: *The General ordered two divisions to counter-attack.*

4 an attack against a person

attack /əˈtæk/ [n C] when someone uses violence against another person and tries

to hurt them: *The attack took place as Mr Owen was leaving his home.* | *Police are investigating a series of racial attacks in the city.*
+ on *a serious attack on a young Turkish worker in Germany yesterday*

mugging /ˈmʌɡɪŋ/ [n C] an attack on someone in a public place such as a street, in order to steal something from them: *Every year there are thousands of muggings on the subway.*

assault /əˈsɔːlt/ [n C/U] an attack on someone – use this especially to talk about the crime of attacking someone: *Reed was serving a 5-year jail sentence for burglary and assault.*
+ on *Statistics show an increase in the number of assaults on women.*

5 a military attack

attack /əˈtæk/ [n C] when a military force attacks a place or country, using weapons, aircraft, soldiers etc: *The attack began at dawn.* | *a terrorist attack*
+ on *a carefully planned attack on American air bases*
launch/mount an attack (=start an attack) *Troops launched an attack on the city in the early hours of the morning.*

invasion /ɪnˈveɪʒən/ [n C] when an army from one country enters another country and tries to control it: *Hundreds of civilians were killed while resisting the invasion.*
+ of *Mussolini's invasion of Abyssinia in 1935*
American/Russian/German etc invasion *the Russian invasion of Afghanistan*

raid /reɪd/ [n C] a short, quick attack by a group of soldiers, planes, or ships on a place that belongs to an enemy
+ on *Several raids were made on frontier villages.*
air raid (=when aircraft drop bombs on a place) *A series of air raids almost totally destroyed the ancient city centre.*

ambush /ˈæmbʊʃ/ [n C] a sudden attack by a group of soldiers who have been hiding and waiting for someone: *Several Red Cross workers were killed in an ambush only five miles outside the town.*
plural **ambushes**

6 a person or place that is attacked

victim /ˈvɪktɪm/ [n C] someone who has been attacked: *The man ran off when his victim called for help.*
be the victim of a crime/assault/attack etc *Saleem, aged 16, was the victim of a vicious racial attack yesterday evening.*

target /ˈtɑːrgɪt/ [n C] a person or place that someone decides to attack
+ for *Government buildings have recently been a target for terrorist attacks.*

AVAILABLE/ NOT AVAILABLE

➡ see also **GET**

1 available for someone to have or use

available /əˈveɪləbəl/ [adj] if something is **available**, you can get it, buy it, or use it: *Do you have any accommodation available? | There's no room for more books – we've used up all the available space. | This treatment is not available in all hospitals.*
+ to *Grants are available to students who have high grades.*
+ from *His latest book is available from all good bookstores.*
readily/freely available (=very easy to get) *Drugs like heroin are readily available on the streets.*
make sth available *These statistics are never sold or made available to the public.*

spare /speər/ [adj] something that is **spare** is not being used now, but it can be used if someone needs it: *There are some spare chairs in the next room if you need them. | I need 50 cents for the parking meter – do you have any spare change?*

free /friː/ [adj] a room or seat that is **free** is not being used by anyone now, and no-one has asked for it be kept for them to use later: *Is this seat free?*
have sth free *The hotel never has any rooms free over the Christmas period.*

2 not available

unavailable/unobtainable /ˌʌnə-ˈveɪləbəl, ˌʌnəbˈteɪnəbəl/ [adj not before noun] if something is **unavailable** or **unobtainable**, it is impossible to get it or buy it: *Fresh fruits were unavailable in winter. | Good apartments to rent had become almost unobtainable.*

AVOID

1 to make sure that something bad does not happen

avoid /əˈvɔɪd/ [v T] to make sure that something bad does not happen to you, either by doing something or by deliberately not doing something: *You can avoid a lot of problems if you use travellers cheques. | helping students to avoid common errors | businessmen who try to avoid taxes*
avoid doing sth (=not do something, in order to make sure that you do not have problems) *It's best to avoid going out in the strong midday sun. | You should avoid making up your mind before you know all the facts.*

⚠ Don't say 'avoid to do something'. Say **avoid doing sth.**

get out of sth /ˌget ˈaʊt ɒv (sth)/ [phrasal verb T] INFORMAL to avoid doing something that you should do or that you have promised to do: *I was supposed to stay at home with my baby sister today, but I'll try to get out of it.*
get out of doing sth *He always manages to get out of paying for the drinks.*

get around sth (also **get round sth** BRITISH) /ˌget (ə)ˈraʊnd (sth)/ [phrasal verb T] INFORMAL to find a way of avoiding a difficult or unpleasant situation, so that you do not have to deal with it: *There's no way of getting around it – you're going to have to tell her the truth. | Isn't there any way of getting round these regulations?*

When you see **EC**, go to the **ESSENTIAL COMMUNICATION** section.

2 **to keep away from a person or place**

avoid /əˈvɔɪd/ [v T] to keep away from a person, because you do not want to talk to them, or keep away from a place, because there are problems there: *I'm sure Sarah's been avoiding me recently.* | *Drivers are advised to avoid Elm Street, because traffic is heavy and there are long delays.*

avoid sb/sth like the plague INFORMAL (=try very hard to avoid them) *Except when they were filming, the two actors avoided each other like the plague.*

stay away/keep away /ˌsteɪ əˈweɪ, ˌkiːp əˈweɪ/ [phrasal verb I] to not go near a person or place, because they may be dangerous or may cause problems
+ from *That evening he received a note warning him to stay away from the camp.* | *Keep away from my children, or I'll call the police.*
stay/keep well away (=completely avoid) *She walked along the path, keeping well away from the cliff's edge.*

○**steer clear of sb/sth** /ˌstɪəʳ ˈklɪər ɒv (sb/sth)/ ESPECIALLY SPOKEN to make an effort to avoid a person or place, because there could be serious problems if you do not: *We were told to steer clear of the main roads, where we might be recognized.* | *She advised me to steer clear of Matthew – she said he couldn't be trusted.*

3 **to avoid a difficult question or subject**

avoid /əˈvɔɪd/ [v T] to **avoid** talking about a subject or answering a question, because you do not want to cause embarrassment or problems for yourself: *Try to avoid*

subjects like sex or religion that might offend people.* | *Typical politician! He just kept avoiding the question.*

evasive /ɪˈveɪsɪv/ [adj] someone who is **evasive** tries to avoid answering questions or explaining their plans, because they want to hide something: *All of the journalists' questions were met with vague, evasive answers.* | *When we asked him where his wife was, O'Hare suddenly became evasive.*

4 **to avoid being hit**

avoid /əˈvɔɪd/ [v T] to move so that you do not hit something or get hit by it: *I had to swerve to avoid the truck.*
avoid doing sth *Penny jumped out of the way to avoid being hit by the falling branch.*

get out of the way /get ˌaʊt əv ðə ˈweɪ/ to move quickly in order to avoid something dangerous that is moving towards you: *"Get out of the way!" he yelled, as the wall began to crumble.*
+ of *trying to get out of the way of the advancing fire*

duck /dʌk/ [v I] to move your head and the top part of your body down in order to avoid something: *I forgot to duck and hit my head on the low doorway.* | *Josie ducked and the vase smashed against the wall.*

dodge /dɒdʒ‖dɑːdʒ/ [v I/T] to avoid something or someone by quickly moving sideways: *We had to run across some open ground, dodging the bullets.* | *He almost caught me, but I dodged and ran across the road.*
+ behind/into/through *When Kevin saw the soldiers, he dodged into an alley.*

B

BABY

BORN ← MOTHER
CHILD ← see also → FATHER
YOUNG ← FAMILY

1 a baby

baby /'beɪbi/ [n C] a very young child who has not yet learned to speak or walk: *Who will look after the baby when you go back to work?*
new baby (=a baby that was born only recently) *Have you seen Rachel's new baby?*
newborn baby (=a baby that has just been born and is only a few hours old) *The average weight of a newborn baby is about seven pounds.*
baby boy/girl *a four-day-old baby boy*
baby son/daughter *Steve and Martha are proud to announce the birth of their baby daughter, Kate Louise.*
unborn baby (=a baby that is still growing inside its mother) *There are a lot of sounds that an unborn baby can hear.*
plural **babies**

child /tʃaɪld/ [n C] a baby – use this especially in writing or in formal speech: *They had their first child after ten years of marriage.*
unborn child (=a baby that is still growing inside its mother) *The rubella virus can seriously harm the unborn child.*
plural **children**

2 to be born

be born /biː 'bɔːʳn/ when a baby **is born**, it comes out of its mother's body and begins its life: *The baby was born two months early.* | *Where were you born?*

⚠ Don't say 'I borned'. Say **I was born**.

birth /bɜːʳθ/ [n C/U] the process of being born, or the time when someone is born
+ of *It's quite common for fathers to be present at the birth of their babies.*
at birth (=at the time when a baby is born) *He only weighed 1.5 kg at birth.*

premature /'premətʃəʳ, -tʃʊəʳ, ˌpremə-'tʃʊəʳǁˌpriːmə'tʃʊər/ [adj] a **premature** baby is born too early and is often small or weak: *Many premature babies have breathing problems.*
three months/seven weeks etc premature (=born three months etc before the normal time) *The baby was six weeks premature.*

3 have a baby

have a baby /ˌhæv ə 'beɪbi/ if a woman **has a baby**, it comes out of her body: *Helen had her baby at home.*
have a boy/girl *Val had a baby boy at 9 o'clock yesterday evening.*
have twins (=have two babies at the same time)

give birth /ˌgɪv 'bɜːʳθ/ if a woman **gives birth**, a baby comes out of her body: *An Italian woman has given birth at the age of 61.*
give birth to a boy/girl/son/daughter *Your wife has given birth to a lovely baby boy.*

⚠ **Give birth** is more formal than have a baby, and is not often used in conversation.

childbirth /'tʃaɪldbɜːʳθ/ [n U] the process during which a baby is coming out of its mother's body: *drugs that ease the pain of childbirth*
natural childbirth (=without drugs, medical operations etc)

in labour BRITISH **in labor** AMERICAN /ɪn 'leɪbəʳ/ a woman is **in labour** during the hours when her baby is being born: *She was in labour for over 16 hours with her first child.*
go into labour (=when labour starts) *Anna was at work when she went into labour.*

4 going to have a baby

pregnant /'pregnənt/ [adj] a **pregnant** woman has a baby growing inside her body: *Have you heard that Liz is pregnant?*

get pregnant (=become pregnant) *She got pregnant while she was only 15.*

twelve weeks/eight months etc pregnant *Helen's three months pregnant.*

⟲be going to have a baby /biː ˌɡəʊɪŋ tə hæv ə ˈbeɪbi/ ESPECIALLY SPOKEN to have a baby growing inside your body: *I've got something to tell you all: I'm going to have a baby!*

> ⚠ Use be going to have a baby especially when you are telling someone for the first time that you or someone else is going to have a baby.

pregnancy /ˈpreɡnənsi/ [n C/U] the time when a woman has a baby growing inside her body: *an increase in the number of teenage pregnancies* (=teenagers becoming pregnant) | *This drug should not be taken during pregnancy.*

plural **pregnancies**

maternity /məˈtɜːrnɪti/ [adj only before noun] intended or designed for women who are going to have a baby

maternity hospital/ward/unit (=a hospital or part of a hospital where women go to have their babies)

maternity clothes (=clothes specially designed for women who are going to have a baby)

maternity leave (=the period of time that a mother is allowed to spend away from work when she has a baby)

5 when a baby is not born alive

have a miscarriage /ˌhæv ə ˈmɪskærɪdʒ/ if a woman **has a miscarriage**, the baby is born dead and is only partly developed: *She was pregnant during her first marriage but had a miscarriage.*

lose the baby /ˌluːz ðə ˈbeɪbi/ if a woman **loses a baby**, it dies before it is born: *Patricia lost the baby after six months.*

abortion /əˈbɔːrʃən/ [n C/U] when a woman has a medical operation to remove a baby that is developing inside her, before the baby is ready to be born: *In Europe there are over 2 million abortions a year.* | *The Catholic Church remains strongly opposed to abortion.*

have an abortion *She had an abortion when she was only 15.*

6 a baby animal

kitten /ˈkɪtn/ [n C] a young cat

puppy /ˈpʌpi/ [n C] a young dog
plural **puppies**

lamb /læm/ [n C] a young sheep

piglet /ˈpɪɡlət/ [n C] a young pig

calf /kɑːf‖kæf/ [n C] a young cow
plural **calves**

foal /fəʊl/ [n C] a young horse

chick /tʃɪk/ [n C] a young bird

young /jʌŋ/ [n plural] an animal's baby or babies: *The mother bird will stay with her young until they are four weeks old.*

> ⚠ **Young** is used especially in written English and in descriptions of the way animals live and behave.

baby /ˈbeɪbi/ [adj only before noun] **baby rabbit/elephant/monkey etc** a very young animal: *The baby mónkey was following its mother.*

7 how animals and humans produce babies

breed /briːd/ [v I] if animals **breed**, they produce babies: *Rabbits breed very quickly.*

breeding – bred – have bred

reproduce /ˌriːprəˈdjuːs‖-ˈduːs/ [v I] FORMAL to produce babies: *Fish reproduce by laying eggs.*

reproduction /ˌriːprəˈdʌkʃən/ [n U] the process of producing babies, young animals, or young plants: *Reproduction is the main aim of almost all lifeforms.*

> ⚠ **Reproduce** is used when talking or writing about scientific subjects.

When you see EC, go to the ESSENTIAL COMMUNICATION section.

BAD

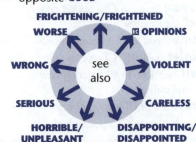

➡ opposite GOOD

FRIGHTENING/FRIGHTENED
WORSE · OPINIONS
WRONG · see also · VIOLENT
SERIOUS · CARELESS
HORRIBLE/UNPLEASANT · DISAPPOINTING/DISAPPOINTED

1 bad films/books/methods/plans/food

bad /bæd/ [adj] something that is **bad** is of a low standard, because it has been done badly, designed badly, performed badly etc: *The movie was so bad that we left halfway through.* | *This is the worst book she's ever written.* | *Opponents of the plan say it is a bad way of managing city traffic.* | *In the 1980s, their cars had a bad reputation for reliability.*

bad – worse – worst

○**no good** /nəʊ 'ɡʊd/ SPOKEN not good at all: *I wouldn't go there – the beer's no good.* | *The buses only run twice a day, which is no good at all.* | *I've tried that diet, and it's no good.*

awful/terrible/appalling /'ɔːfəl, 'terɪbəl, ə'pɔːlɪŋ/ [adj] very bad: *Tony said the food at their hotel was awful.* | *What a terrible performance!* | *Your handwriting is appalling!*

○**garbage** ESPECIALLY AMERICAN **rubbish** BRITISH /'ɡɑːʰbɪdʒ, 'rʌbɪʃ/ [n U] SPOKEN INFORMAL something that is very bad or very stupid, especially things people say or write: *I don't know why you're watching that programme. It's complete garbage.* | *I've never read such rubbish in my life!*

2 products that are badly made or of bad quality

poor quality/low quality /pʊəʰ 'kwɒl̩ti, ləʊ 'kwɒl̩ti‖-'kwɑː-/ **poor quality** products have been made badly: *Poor quality housing often leads to health problems.* | *low quality products*

be of poor/low quality *The cloth is cheap and of low quality.*

badly made /ˌbædli 'meɪd◄/ made without care or skill: *Her clothes looked cheap and badly made.* | *Badly made furniture like that doesn't last long.*

cheap /tʃiːp/ [adj] **cheap** furniture, jewellery, clothes etc look unattractive and badly made, and seem to have been produced using low quality materials: *The room was depressing, with a dim light and cheap furniture.* | *hungry-looking young men in cheap suits*

3 not very bad, but not very good

○**not very good** /nɒt veri 'ɡʊd/ ESPECIALLY SPOKEN not good – use this when you are disappointed because you were expecting something better: *"What was the movie like?" "Not very good, really."* | *He's been learning English for five years, but his pronunciation isn't very good.*

○**nothing special** /ˌnʌθɪŋ 'speʃəl/ SPOKEN not very bad, but not especially good: *The town's nice, but the beach is nothing special.* | *"Was the food good?" "It was okay, but nothing special."*

second-rate /ˌsekənd 'reɪt◄/ [adj] not as good as other things of the same kind: *a second-rate horror movie* | *It was a pretty awful speech, full of second-rate jokes.*

mediocre /ˌmiːdi'əʊkəʰ◄/ [adj] something that is **mediocre** is of a lower standard than it should be, and does not show much quality or skill: *The team gave another mediocre performance last night.* | *He was trying to sell his mediocre paintings.*

4 unpleasant events/experiences/weather

bad /bæd/ [adj] not at all pleasant, enjoyable, or successful: *If the weather's bad, we could go to the museum instead.* | *I'm afraid I have some bad news.* (=news of a bad event) | *bad housing conditions* | *Terry started shouting at me, which just made things worse.*

a bad day/year/time etc (=when a lot of unpleasant things happen) *It had been a bad day, and I just wanted to go home.* |

The company has had a very bad year, and profits have fallen dramatically.

bad – worse – worst

awful/terrible/horrible /ˈɔːfəl, ˈterɪbəl, ˈhɒrɪbəl‖-ˈhɑː-, -ˈhɑː-/ [adj] very bad: *I just burst into tears in front of everyone. It was awful! | That's terrible! Surely they can't just fire you for no reason. | She had a horrible nightmare that night.*

unpleasant /ʌnˈplezənt/ [adj] an **unpleasant** experience is one that you do not like or enjoy at all: *a drug with unpleasant side effects | The news came as an unpleasant shock. | It has an unpleasant taste and smell.*

> **unpleasantly** [adv] *The room was unpleasantly damp.*

appalling /əˈpɔːlɪŋ/ [adj] so bad that you are shocked: *the appalling suffering caused by the civil war | No ship could leave port in such appalling weather.*

5 a bad problem/ accident/illness

serious /ˈsɪəriəs/ [adj] use this about problems, accidents, or illnesses that are very bad, and that people are worried about: *There was a serious accident on the freeway. | serious head injuries | Youth unemployment is a serious problem in Britain.*

> **seriously** [adv] *Her father is seriously ill with pneumonia. | a legal case that seriously damaged her political career*

bad /bæd/ [adj] use this about something that causes a lot of pain, worry, or problems: *a bad car crash | "How are things at home?" "Bad!" | It was the worst mistake I ever made.*

a bad cold/headache etc *Jane's not at school today – she has a bad cold. | a bad attack of asthma*

bad – worse – worst

> **badly** [adv] *Several people were killed or badly injured. | The furniture was badly damaged in the fire.*

> ⚠️ Don't say 'her hands were burned badly'. Say **her hands were badly burned**. **Badly** comes before a past participle.

horrific /hɒˈrɪfɪk‖hɔː-/ [adj] use this about accidents or injuries that are extremely serious, and make you feel shocked or upset: *Diane has made a full recovery after a horrific riding accident last year. | a horrific attack on an innocent child*

nasty /ˈnɑːsti‖ˈnæsti/ [adj] ESPECIALLY SPOKEN use this about accidents, injuries, or illnesses that are not very serious, but are quiet unpleasant: *That cough sounds nasty – you ought to see a doctor. | He had a nasty cut on his head.*

nasty – nastier – nastiest

6 when a situation is so bad that you cannot bear it

can't stand sth/can't bear sth /ˌkɑːnt ˈstænd (sth), ˌkɑːnt ˈbeər (sth)‖-kænt-/ to be unable to accept an unpleasant situation: *Europeans never stay there for long. They can't stand the heat.*

can't stand/bear the thought of sth *She couldn't bear the thought of losing her children.*

can't bear to do sth *I couldn't bear to listen to her screams.*

can't take sth /ˌkɑːnt ˈteɪk (sth)‖ˌkænt-/ ESPECIALLY SPOKEN to be unable to accept an unpleasant situation without becoming angry or upset, especially when someone's behaviour is not fair or reasonable: *Careful what you say – he can't take criticism.*

can't take any more of sth *I can't take any more of this – she's always complaining about something.*

unbearable /ʌnˈbeərəbəl/ [adj] something that is **unbearable**, such as a pain or a bad situation, is too bad for you to deal with or live with: *The pain was unbearable. | Without him, life would be unbearable.*

7 a situation that is very bad

emergency /ɪˈmɜːrdʒənsi/ [n C] a very serious and dangerous situation that happens suddenly and needs to be dealt with immediately: *Lifeguards are trained to deal with any emergency.*

in an emergency *In an emergency dial 911 for the police, the fire department, or an ambulance.*

B

the emergency services BRITISH (=the organizations and people that come immediately to help you if there is an emergency) *The emergency services in this area simply couldn't cope if there was a major accident or a terrorist attack.*
plural **emergencies**

> ⚠ You can also use emergency before a noun, like an adjective: *emergency surgery* | *The plane made an emergency landing.*

crisis /'kraɪsɪs/ [n C] a very bad situation in which there is a risk that serious problems will become suddenly worse: *The Cuban missile crisis of 1960 was probably the closest we have been to nuclear war.* | *Their marriage was going through a crisis which almost ended in divorce.* | *an economic crisis*
plural **crises**

disaster /dɪˈzɑːstəʳ‖dɪˈzæ-/ [n C] a terrible event that causes a lot of damage or a lot of deaths: *a mining disaster in which 108 people lost their lives* | *the Chernobyl nuclear disaster*
natural disaster (=caused by storms, floods etc) *a fund set up to deal with natural disasters such as earthquakes or floods*
• see also ACCIDENT

8 bad people or bad behaviour

bad /bæd/ [adj] use this about behaviour that is morally wrong, or about people who do things that are morally wrong: *In spite of all the bad things he had done, I still loved him.* | *In most movies, the bad guy gets caught in the end.* | *Is there any crime worse than murdering a child?* | *He had a bad influence on his younger brother.*
bad – worse – worst

wrong /rɒŋ‖rɔːŋ/ [adj not before noun] use this about behaviour, actions, or situations that are not morally right: *He knew it was wrong, but he couldn't resist taking the money.*
it is wrong to do sth *It is wrong to tell lies.*
it is wrong that *It's wrong that so many people are starving, when there is plenty of food in the world.*

immoral /ɪˈmɒrəl‖ɪˈmɔː-/ [adj] use this about actions which you believe are morally wrong and unacceptable, even if they are not illegal: *Many people think that testing drugs on animals is immoral.* | *To spend £23 billion on nuclear weapons is immoral, and a terrible waste of money.*

> ⚠ Immoral is more formal than wrong. Don't say 'very immoral'. Say totally immoral or highly immoral.

evil/wicked /'iːvəl, 'wɪkɪd/ [adj] deliberately very bad and very cruel to other people: *Sutcliffe was an evil murderer.* | *Police described the woman's crime as wicked and inhuman.*

9 a bad child

naughty /'nɔːti‖'nɔːti, 'nɑːti/ [adj] a child who is **naughty** behaves badly, for example by being rude or by doing things that are not allowed: *I only smack the children if they're very naughty.* | *We've been looking for you everywhere, you naughty boy!*
naughty – naughtier – naughtiest

spoiled (also **spoilt** BRITISH) /spɔɪld, spɔɪlt/ [adj] children who are **spoiled** or **spoilt** behave badly because their parents always let them do what they want and have what they want: *You're a spoilt, ungrateful little girl!* | *Those kids are definitely spoiled – they need to learn some manners.*

mischievous /'mɪstʃɪvəs/ [adj] a child who is **mischievous** behaves badly, but in a way that makes people laugh rather than making them angry: *She was a mischievous little girl, who was always playing tricks on people.*
mischievously [adv] *Ben smiled mischievously.*

badly behaved /ˌbædli bɪˈheɪvd◄/ [adj] a **badly behaved** child behaves badly and causes a lot of trouble: *Two or three badly behaved children are causing all the problems in the class.*

brat /bræt/ [n C] INFORMAL a child that you do not like, who behaves badly and is rude: *The school is full of rich brats.*
spoiled/spoilt brat (=a child who behaves badly because they have always been allowed to do whatever they want)

10 **bad at doing something**

bad /bæd/ [adj] not able to do something well, for example a job, sport, or activity
bad teacher/driver/player etc *He's the worst driver I've ever seen.* | *The problem was caused by bad management.*
+ at *I was always bad at French!*
bad at doing sth *I'm very bad at remembering people's names.*
bad – worse – worst

⚠ Only use **bad** about other people if you want to criticize them strongly. If you want to be more polite, use **not very good** instead.

badly /'bædli/ [adv] if you do something **badly**, you do it carelessly, not skilfully, or you do it in the wrong way: *Kate plays the violin very badly.* | *The company had been badly managed from the start.*

⚠ Don't say 'I speak English very bad'. Say **I speak English very badly**. Remember that **bad** is an adjective and **badly** is an adverb.

◯**not very good** /nɒt veri 'gʊd/ ESPE-
CIALLY SPOKEN not able to do something well: *He's a nice guy, but he's not a very good actor.*
+ at *I'm afraid I'm not very good at algebra!*
not very good at doing sth *She's not very good at communicating with other people.*
not very well *"Do you play the piano?" "Not very well."*

◯**no good at sth** /ˌnəʊ 'gʊd æt (sth)/
SPOKEN very bad at a skill or activity: *I'm no good at tennis.*
no good at doing sth *He can drive quite well, but he's no good at parking.*

◯**terrible/useless/hopeless** /'terɪ-
bəl, 'juːsləs, 'həʊpləs/ [adj] ESPECIALLY SPOKEN very bad at doing something, or very badly done: *She's very intelligent but she's a hopeless cook.* | *That was a terrible shot – it missed the goal by a mile!*
+ at *I'm useless at spelling.*

incompetent /ɪn'kɒmpɪtənt‖-'kɑːm-/ [adj]
someone who is **incompetent** lacks the skills they need to do their job – use this to criticize someone who is very bad at

something and makes a lot of mistakes: *This government is totally incompetent.* | *incompetent management*

⚠ Don't say 'very incompetent'. Say **totally/completely incompetent**.

11 **in bad condition**

in bad condition /ɪn ˌbæd kən'dɪʃən/ if something is in **bad condition**, it is old, dirty, or not working well: *We got the furniture cheap because it was in very bad condition.* | *The machinery in the factory is in bad condition, and is probably dangerous.*

⚠ Don't say 'in a bad condition'. Say **in bad condition**.

◯**be falling apart** /biː ˌfɔːlɪŋ ə'pɑːrt/
ESPECIALLY SPOKEN if something **is falling apart**, it is gradually breaking into pieces, because it is old or it was not well made: *I need some new shoes. These are falling apart.*

battered /'bætərd/ [adj usually before noun]
something that is **battered** is old and in bad condition because it has been used a lot: *a battered old suitcase* | *Professor Dewey got out a battered copy of Shakespeare's plays.* | *a couple of battered wooden chairs*

rotten /'rɒtn‖'rɑːtn/ [adj] wood that is **rotten** has decayed and become very soft, so that it breaks easily: *The window frames were rotten, so we had to replace them.*

rusty /'rʌsti/ [adj] metal that is **rusty** is red-brown in colour, because it has been damaged by the effects of water: *A few rusty nails held the door in place.* | *The railings were old and rusty.*
rusty – rustier – rustiest
　　rust [n U] *You can't see it, but underneath the car is covered in rust.*

shabby /'ʃæbi/ [adj] clothes, furniture, or places that are **shabby** are no longer in good condition because they have been worn or used a lot: *Paul was wearing a shabby old suit.* | *Their hotel room was dark and shabby.*
shabby – shabbier – shabbiest

dilapidated /dɪ'læpɪdeɪtɪd/ [adj] a building that is **dilapidated** is in very bad condition, because it has not been looked after or repaired: *The warehouse is now empty and dilapidated.* | *an old dilapidated school with a leaky roof*

bad /bæd/ [adj] food that is **bad** is not good to eat, because it has started to decay: *I got really sick from eating bad seafood.* | *the smell of bad eggs*

⌒go off/go bad /gəʊ 'ɒf, gəʊ 'bæd/ ESPECIALLY SPOKEN if food **goes off** or **goes bad**, it starts to decay because it has been kept for too long: *In this heat, fish goes off very quickly.* | *The fruit went bad before we could eat it all.*

12 to think something or someone is bad or morally wrong

disapprove /ˌdɪsə'pruːv/ [v I] to think that a person or action is bad, morally wrong, or very stupid: *I wanted to become an actor but my parents disapproved.*
+ of *Debbie's father disapproves of her boyfriend.*
disapprove of sb doing sth *My friends disapprove of me smoking.*
strongly disapprove (=disapprove very much) *I strongly disapprove of any form of gambling.*

think sth is wrong /ˌθɪŋk (sth) ɪz 'rɒŋ‖ -'rɔːŋ/ to think that something is morally bad and should not happen: *Jane thinks sex before marriage is wrong.*
think it is wrong to do sth *I think it's wrong to hit a child, whatever the circumstances.*

disapproval /ˌdɪsə'pruːvəl/ [n U] how you feel when you think someone's ideas, behaviour, or actions are bad or morally wrong: *She looked at our clothes with obvious disapproval.*
sb's disapproval/the disapproval of sb *Peter was determined to go to art school, despite his parents' disapproval.*
+ of *They tried not to show any disapproval of Sandy's lifestyle.*

disapproving /ˌdɪsə'pruːvɪŋ‖/ [adj] if someone speaks to you or looks at you in a **disapproving** way, they show by the way they talk or look that they disapprove of you: *John gave me a disapproving look when I suggested another drink.* |

"Do you think you should be doing that?" he said, in a disapproving voice.

13 so bad that it makes you very angry

outrageous/disgraceful /aʊt'reɪdʒəs, dɪs'greɪsfəl/ [adj] use this about actions or situations that are very bad or very unfair and should not be allowed to happen: *an outrageous waste of public money* | *I thought their behaviour was disgraceful.*

⌒be a disgrace /biː ə dɪs'greɪs/ SPOKEN if you say that something **is a disgrace**, you are angry about it and think that it should not be allowed to happen: *The level of unemployment in this country is a disgrace.*
it's a disgrace that *It's an absolute disgrace that my wife had to wait five hours to see a doctor.*

BANKS

➡ see pages 58-60

BEAUTIFUL

➡ opposite **UGLY**
➡ see also **DESCRIBING PEOPLE**

1 women

beautiful /'bjuːtɪfəl/ [adj] use this about a woman who is extremely attractive in a way that is fairly unusual and special, so that people notice and admire her: *a beautiful woman with long black hair and green eyes* | *Karen was even more beautiful than I had remembered.* | *She has a beautiful smile.*

good-looking /ˌgʊd 'lʊkɪŋ‹/ [adj] use this about a woman who is nice to look at and has an attractive face and body: *Ginny was tall and good-looking.* | *A good-looking woman dressed in black came into the room.* | *She seems to get better-looking the older she gets.*
good-looking – better-looking – best-looking

pretty /'prɪti/ [adj] use this about a young woman or girl who has an attractive face and is good-looking, but not in an unusual way: *Maureen's really pretty, isn't she?* | *a pretty girl in white jeans* | *She has a pretty face.*

pretty – prettier – prettiest

attractive /ə'træktɪv/ [adj] use this about a woman who is good-looking in a way that makes people sexually interested in her: *Frances was a charming and attractive girl.* | *Your wife's a very attractive woman.*

find sb attractive *A lot of men find plump women attractive.*

○**nice-looking** /ˌnaɪs 'lʊkɪŋ◀/ [adj] ESPE-CIALLY SPOKEN use this about a woman who looks pleasant and friendly but is not extremely pretty: *A nice-looking girl was walking her dog in the park.*

cute /kjuːt/ [adj] INFORMAL, ESPECIALLY AMERICAN use this about a girl or young woman who is pretty and sexually attractive: *Do you like Jill Anderson? I think she's cute!*

○**gorgeous** /'gɔːʳdʒəs/ [adj] ESPECIALLY SPOKEN use this to emphasize that a woman is extremely attractive, in a sexual way: *That woman in 'Baywatch', I think she's gorgeous.*

look gorgeous *Ursula, you look absolutely gorgeous in that dress!*

glamorous /'glæmərəs/ [adj] use this about a woman who looks like a beautiful actress or film star, and has an attractive body and wears expensive clothes: *Princess Diana is still one of the world's most glamorous women.* | *The picture showed a glamorous young woman sitting in a sports car.*

stunning /'stʌnɪŋ/ [adj] use this about a woman who is extremely beautiful and sexually attractive, in a way that everyone notices and admires: *stunning French actress Juliette Binoche*

look stunning *Beth looked stunning in a beautiful green silk dress.*

elegant /'elɪgənt/ [adj] use this about a woman who is tall and attractive, and wears clothes that look good: *An elegant young woman sat at the next table, sipping a cocktail.*

look elegant *a woman in a well-cut navy coat who, despite the rain, still looked elegant*

2 men

good-looking /ˌgʊd 'lʊkɪŋ◀/ [adj] use this about a man who is nice to look at: *A tall good-looking man asked me if I wanted to dance.* | *She showed me a photo of a good-looking young soldier.*

good-looking – better-looking – best looking

attractive /ə'træktɪv/ [adj] use this about a man who is good-looking in a way that makes people sexually interested in him: *He was a tall attractive man in his mid-forties.*

find sb attractive *I don't find those body-builders with huge muscles attractive at all.*

cute /kjuːt/ [adj] INFORMAL, ESPECIALLY AMERI-CAN use this about a young man who looks nice and is sexually attractive: *I don't know why she won't go out with him. I think he's kind of cute.*

○**gorgeous** /'gɔːʳdʒəs/ [adj] ESPECIALLY SPOKEN use this to emphasize that a man is extremely attractive in a sexual way: *Look at that guy over there. Isn't he gorgeous?*

handsome /'hænsəm/ [adj] ESPECIALLY WRITTEN use this about a man who is good-looking, especially one who is tall and strong-looking: *Richard was a handsome man with a lot of charm.* | *My brother was two years older than me, taller, and more handsome.*

look handsome *He looks really handsome in his uniform, doesn't he?*

> ⚠ Use **handsome** especially in writing stories and descriptions.

○**nice-looking** /ˌnaɪs 'lʊkɪŋ◀/ [adj] ESPE-CIALLY SPOKEN use this about a man who looks pleasant and friendly but is not extremely attractive: *I suppose he's quite nice-looking, but he's not really my type.*

3 children

beautiful /'bjuːtɪfəl/ [adj] use this about a child who is so good-looking that everyone notices and admires him or her: *Parents always think their baby is the most beautiful baby in the world.* | *On her desk there was a photograph of two beautiful children.*

BEAUTIFUL continues on page 61

BANKS

WORD BANK

see also

OWE
PAY
BORROW
SPEND
SAVE
MONEY
LEND
EARN
☞ OPINIONS
BUY

❷ The bank gave him a **cheque book** and a **bank card**.

❶ When Kevin left school he opened a **bank account**.

❸ Kevin enjoyed himself a lot... but unfortunately, he wasn't very **good with money** and he **got into debt**.

vocabulary

ATM /ˌeɪ tiː 'em/ [n C] AMERICAN a machine in the wall of a bank, shop etc that lets you take money out of your bank account using a special card

bank account (also **account**) /ˈbæŋk əˌkaʊnt, əˈkaʊnt/ [n C] if you have a bank account with a particular bank, you keep your money there, and take some out when you need it
open a bank account (=start a new bank account)

bank card /ˈbæŋk kɑːʳd/ [n C] a small plastic card given to you by your bank, which you show when you write a cheque, and which also lets you get money out of a cashpoint or ATM. A bank card can often also be used as a debit card.

bank statement /ˈbæŋk ˌsteɪtmənt/ [n C] a printed list that your bank sends you regularly, which shows what money you have paid into and taken out of your bank account

borrow /ˈbɒrəʊǁbɑː-/ [v I/T] to use money that belongs to someone else which you must give back to them later: *I had to borrow $1000 to pay for the car.*
borrow $100/£50/£1000 etc from sb *He didn't have enough money for the air fare, so he borrowed $1000 from his parents.*

cashpoint /ˈkæʃpɔɪnt/ [n C] BRITISH a machine in the wall of a bank, shop etc that lets you take money out of your bank account using a special card

cash card BRITISH **ATM card** AMERICAN /ˈkæʃ kɑːʳd, ˌeɪ tiː 'em kɑːʳd/ [n C] a plastic card given to you by your bank, that you use to get money out of a cashpoint or ATM

cheque BRITISH **check** AMERICAN /tʃek/ [n C] a printed piece of paper that you get from your bank which you can write an amount on and use instead of money to pay for things. Your bank gives you several cheques in the form of a small book, called a **cheque book** or **check book**.

BANKS

4 One day he went to the **cashpoint**, and discovered that he couldn't **get** any **money out** because he was £100 **overdrawn**.

Oh no! I'll have to pay by cheque.

SORRY YOU HAVE INSUFFICIENT FUNDS

5 The bank agreed to give him an **overdraft**.

6 Soon Kevin had gone over his **overdraft limit** and couldn't **withdraw** any more money.

Oh no!

I'm sorry, sir...

7 And so he got a **credit card** with a £2000 **credit limit**...

+ for *a check for $300*
  pay by cheque/check *Can I pay by cheque?*
credit card /ˈkredɪt ˌkɑːʳd/ [n C] a plastic card that you can use to pay for things with money you borrow from a financial organization such as VISA or MasterCard. A **credit card** lets you pay for things, and then pay what you owe to the organization later: *We accept all major credit cards.* | *credit card fraud* (=dishonest use of credit cards)
credit limit /ˈkredɪt ˌlɪmɪt/ [n C] the largest amount of money that you can borrow using your credit card
debit card /ˈdebɪt ˌkɑːʳd/ [n U] a plastic card that you can use to pay for things, which allows the money to be taken directly from your bank account.
debts /dets/ [n plural] the amount of money that you owe to a person or a bank
  have debts *The company has debts of around $100 million.*

be in financial difficulties /biː ɪn fɪˌnænʃəl ˈdɪfɪkəl-tiz/ to have serious problems with money, because you have spent more money than you have, and you owe money to a person or the bank
get/go into debt /ˌget, ˌgəʊ ɪntə ˈdet/ to get into a situation in which you owe a lot of money
get money out /ˌget ˈmʌni aʊt/ to get money from your bank account by using a cashpoint or ATM, or by going into a bank
good with money /ˌgʊd wɪð ˈmʌni/ good at managing your money and making sure that you do not spend more than you can afford
  not very good with money (=not able to control the way you spend your money, so that you spend more money than you have)
lend /lend/ [v T] to give someone money, but only if they

BANKS continues on the next page

BANKS

8 and went off to the Caribbean.

9 Soon Kevin **was in** serious **financial difficulties**.

BANK STATEMENT

10 He had to **borrow** money from his mother...

*All right, I'll **lend** you £10, but I want it back. And don't forget you already **owe** me £20.*

11 ...and get a second job to help him **pay off** his **debts**.

---

agree to give it back to you at a later time
lend sb $40/£100 etc *The bank has already lent the company $50 million.* | *Can you lend me five pounds till tomorrow?*
overdraft /ˈəʊvəˈdrɑːft‖-dræft/ [n C] BRITISH an amount that you owe your bank, when you have spent more money than you have in your account
　have a £50/$300 overdraft (=when you owe the bank this amount of money) *I've got a £200 overdraft.*
　give sb an overdraft (=when a bank agrees to let someone have an overdraft) *The bank manager gave me an overdraft.*
overdraft limit /ˈəʊvəˈdrɑːft ˌlɪmɪt‖ -dræft/ [n C] the largest amount of money that the bank has agreed to lend you
　go over your overdraft limit (=spend more money

than the bank has agreed to lend you)
overdrawn /ˌəʊvəˈdrɔːn/ [adj not before noun] if you are **overdrawn**, you have spent more money than you have in your bank account, so that you owe the bank money
　be £300/$80 overdrawn (=owe the bank £300/$80)
owe /əʊ/ [v T] if you owe someone money, they have lent you money and you have not yet given it back to them
　owe sb £15/$50 etc *Kevin owes his mother £30.*
pay off /ˌpeɪ ˈɒf ‖ ˈɔːf/ [phrasal verb T] to pay all the money that you owe
　pay off your debts/overdraft/credit card *I've almost paid off my debts.*
withdraw /wɪðˈdrɔː, wɪθ-/ [v T] if you withdraw money, you get it out of your bank account
　withdraw £100/$200 etc *You can withdraw up to £100 a day.*

BEAUTIFUL continued from page 57

lovely /ˈlʌvli/ [adj] use this about a child who looks nice and has a pleasant, friendly character: *They've got three lovely kids.* | *Rosie's a lovely baby.*

look lovely *Don't the Schultz sisters look lovely?*

lovely – lovelier – loveliest

⚠ Don't say 'very lovely'. Just say **lovely**.

cute /kjuːt/ [adj] INFORMAL use this about a child who looks attractive and has a happy or amusing character: *He's really naughty, but he's so cute.* | *You were such a cute baby!*

look cute *Doesn't he look cute in that baseball cap!*

4 animals

beautiful /ˈbjuːtɪf̩fəl/ [adj] use this about animals that look extremely attractive and impressive

beautiful bird/horse/animal/feathers/fur etc *a beautiful bird with bright blue feathers* | *A beautiful grey horse trotted up to the gate.*

cute/sweet /kjuːt, swiːt/ [adj] use this about pets and baby animals that look nice in a way that makes people want to look after them

+ kitten/puppy/dog/baby bird etc *cute kittens* | *She has a funny little dog – he's really sweet!*

magnificent /mægˈnɪf̩sənt/ [adj] use this about animals and large birds that are very beautiful and impressive because they are large and strong or beautifully coloured: *The horse was a magnificent creature with a gleaming jet black coat.* | *a magnificent golden eagle* | *The Siberian Tiger is a magnificent animal.*

5 things/buildings

beautiful (also **lovely** ESPECIALLY BRITISH) /ˈbjuːtɪf̩fəl, ˈlʌvli/ [adj] use this about things or buildings that look extremely good, and give you a feeling of pleasure: *a beautiful painting* | *"Do you like the house?" "Like it? It's beautiful!"* | *Thanks for the flowers – they're lovely!* | *one of Europe's loveliest churches*

lovely – lovelier – loveliest

beautifully [adv] *a beautifully decorated house* | *The presents were all beautifully wrapped in pink tissue paper.*

pretty /ˈprɪti/ [adj] use this about objects that are small and delicate, or things in your home such as curtains and carpets: *pretty wallpaper with yellow flowers on it* | *What a pretty vase!*

pretty – prettier – prettiest

magnificent /mægˈnɪf̩sənt/ [adj] very beautiful and impressive – use this about large and impressive buildings or pieces of furniture, especially old ones: *The room is dominated by a magnificent four-poster bed.* | *a magnificent 15th century castle*

gorgeous /ˈɡɔːrdʒəs/ [adj] ESPECIALLY SPOKEN use this about beautiful things that you admire very much

gorgeous dress/coat/colour etc *I love your dress! It's such a gorgeous colour!* | *The apartment had been furnished in rich, deep colours and gorgeous fabrics.*

exquisite /ɪkˈskwɪzɪt, ˈekskwɪ-/ [adj] very beautiful – use this about jewellery or small things that have been designed with great care and made with a lot of skill: *an exquisite handcarved ivory brooch* | *There's a little courtyard with fountains and orange trees – it's really exquisite.*

elegant /ˈelɪ̩ɡənt/ [adj] use this about buildings, furniture, and clothes that are beautifully designed in a simple but usually expensive way: *We first met him at an elegant hotel in the uptown district of Manhattan.* | *an elegant rosewood dining table* | *She was wearing an elegant black suit.*

6 places/countryside/views

beautiful /ˈbjuːtɪf̩fəl/ [adj] use this about places that everyone admires and likes to visit: *Florence is such a beautiful city.* | *Cornwall has some of the most beautiful stretches of coastline in Britain.* | *a restaurant with beautiful views over Sorrento and the Gulf of Naples*

lovely /ˈlʌvli/ [adj] use this about places that are beautiful in a way that makes you feel relaxed and gives you a lot of pleasure: *The hills will be lovely at this time of year.* | *You are so lucky to live here with all this lovely countryside around you.* | *The garden was looking lovely.*

> ⚠ Don't say 'very lovely'. Just say **lovely**.

lovely – lovelier – loveliest

stunning/breathtaking /'stʌnɪŋ, 'breθ,teɪkɪŋ/ [adj] use this about views that are extremely beautiful and extremely impressive: *The view from the top of the mountain was stunning.* | *the breathtaking beauty of the Niagara Falls* | *breathtaking views of the Himalayas*

magnificent /mæg'nɪfɪsənt/ [adj] use this about areas where there are beautiful, large, and impressive mountains, valleys, rivers etc: *magnificent views across the valley* | *the magnificent mountains around Lake Titicaca*

picturesque /,pɪktʃə'resk◀/ [adj] use this about villages and towns that are pretty and old-fashioned: *We visited the picturesque fishing village of Lochinver.* | *He rents a small house in the picturesque old quarter of town.*

scenic /'siːnɪk/ [adj] use this about roads that go through beautiful countryside
scenic route/journey/drive/road *We travelled to the coast by a very scenic route.* | *a scenic road through the Welsh mountains*

7 the beautiful appearance of someone or something

beauty /'bjuːti/ [n U] the beautiful appearance of a place or person: *the beauty of the countryside in spring* | *He had written a poem about Sylvia, praising her charm and beauty.*
of great beauty (=very beautiful) FORMAL *There were ancient carvings of great beauty.*

good looks /,gʊd 'lʊks/ [n plural] someone's attractive appearance: *Although over 50 she had not lost her good looks.*

BECOME

1 with adjectives

> ⚠ Word choice - **become** and **get**:
> 1. **Become** is more formal than **get** and is used mainly in written English. **Get** is the usual word to use in conversation: say **it's**

getting cold, I'm getting hungry etc (not 'it's becoming cold'). 2. You can use **become** with most adjectives, but **get** can only be used with some adjectives: see the note at **get** for details.

become /bɪ'kʌm/ [v] if you **become** rich, famous, worried etc, you start to be rich, famous, worried etc: *Julian's book was a big success and he quickly became rich and famous.* | *The weather was becoming warmer.* | *It soon became clear that the fire was out of control.* | *After a while, my eyes became accustomed to the dark.*
becoming – became – have become

get /get/ [v] to become: *It normally gets dark at about 8.30 p.m.* | *The man got annoyed and started shouting at me.* | *The situation doesn't seem to be getting any better.* | *I'm getting too old for this kind of thing.*
getting – got – have got BRITISH **have gotten** AMERICAN

> ⚠ Don't use **get** with these words: **available, calm, clear, famous, happy, important, necessary, obvious, poor, powerful, proud, sad, silent, successful, useful**. But you can use **get** with comparatives, such as: **clearer, happier, more famous, more important**. You can also use **get** with past participles, such as: **annoyed, bored, damaged, lost, broken**.

grow /grəʊ/ [v] **grow old/tired/worse/larger** etc to slowly and gradually become old, tired etc: *As we grow old, we worry more about our health.* | *The sound of footsteps grew louder.* | *They had grown tired of waiting.* | *The children were late, and she was growing anxious.*
growing – grew – have grown

> ⚠ Use **grow** especially when you are writing stories or descriptions.

go /gəʊ/ [v] to become – only use **go** with these words
go grey/white/red/dark *Her face went bright red with embarrassment.*
go mad/wild/crazy *Your dad'll go crazy when he finds out.*
go quiet/silent *As soon as the band started playing, the crowd went quiet.*
go bad/sour/cold *My coffee's gone cold.*

turn /tɜːᵣn/ [v] **turn red/blue/white etc** to become a different colour because of a natural change: *My father's hair turned grey when he was only 40.* | *In autumn the leaves turn red and yellow.*

going – went – have gone

2 with nouns

⚠ Don't use **get** with nouns.

become /bɪˈkʌm/ [v] *In the 19th century, the city became a major trading centre.* | *Since she won all that money, she's become a very unpleasant person.*

become a doctor/writer/teacher etc *Theroux decided to give up teaching and become a writer.*

becoming – became – have become

⚠ You can also say 'I want to **be** a doctor/an actor etc when I leave college'.

change into sth/turn into sth /ˈtʃeɪndʒ ɪntuː (sth), ˈtɜːᵣn ɪntuː (sth)/ [phrasal verb T] to completely change and become something else, often in a surprising way: *The little brown caterpillar eventually changes into a beautiful butterfly.* | *During the brewing process, all the sugar turns into alcohol.*

develop into sth /dɪˈveləp ɪntuː (sth)/ [phrasal verb T] to gradually become something that is much better, bigger, more important, or more serious: *In 20 years, the company has developed into a huge multinational organization.* | *a minor illness which developed into a serious chest infection*

BEFORE

➡ opposite **AFTER**
➡ see also **EARLY**

1 before something happens, or before someone does something

before /bɪˈfɔːᵣ/ [preposition/conjunction/adv] before you do something or before an event happens: *The family left France just before the war.* | *Think carefully before*

you give your final answer. | *Before I could say anything Dave walked away.*

before doing sth *Before joining IBM Jack worked for Toshiba.* | *You should check the oil before starting a long drive.*

before this/that *We spent two years in America, and before that we lived in Japan.*

the night before/the day before/the week before etc *The night before the wedding she was really nervous.*

a week/2 days/5 years etc before *I was born just 11 months before my brother.*

⚠ **Before** can be used as an adverb, but only in expressions like **a week before** and **the day before**: *When we got there, we found out he had left the day before.* Don't use **before** on its own as an adverb – use **before this** or **before that**: *I had a job as a waiter, and before that I worked in a supermarket.*

⚠ Don't use 'will' with **before**. Don't say 'before I will leave England, I want to visit Cambridge'. Say **before I leave England ...**

beforehand (also **ahead of time** AMERICAN) /bɪˈfɔːᵣhænd, əˌhed əv ˈtaɪm/ [adv] if you do something **beforehand** or **ahead of time**, you do it before you do something else, especially in order to make a situation easier: *We had agreed beforehand not to tell anyone else about our plans.* | *Decide ahead of time whether you will keep the dog indoors or outside.*

in advance /ɪn ədˈvɑːns‖-ˈvæns/ if you do something **in advance**, you do it before another event happens, especially so that you will be well prepared: *This is a meal you can easily prepare in advance.*

tell/warn sb in advance (=warn them that something may happen) *I wish you'd told me in advance that you were going to be late.*

six months in advance/a year in advance etc *Preparations for the visit had been made months in advance.*

pre- /priː/ [prefix] **pre-war/pre-school/pre-Christmas etc** before the war, before starting school etc: *life in pre-war Britain* | *The government seems to have forgotten all its pre-election promises.*

2 before a particular time or date

before /bɪˈfɔːʳ/ [preposition] before a particular time or date: *Call me back before 4.30.*
just before *She was born just before Christmas.*

by /baɪ/ [preposition] **by 6 o'clock/Friday/next winter etc** at some time before 6 o'clock, Friday etc, and certainly not later than this: *I'll be home by 6, I promise. | Make sure you get the work done by Friday. | By 9 o'clock, all the guests had arrived.*

3 before now

before /bɪˈfɔːʳ/ [adv] before now: *I've never seen such a big dog before. | Stan's never been up in a plane before and he's feeling very nervous.*

ago /əˈgəʊ/ [adv] **five minutes/two weeks/20 years etc ago** five minutes, two weeks etc before now: *He went out half an hour ago, but he'll be back soon. | She died two months ago.*
a long time ago *"When did you live in Germany?" "Oh, it was a long time ago – in 1967."*
ages ago SPOKEN (=a very long time ago) *He wrote to me once, but that was ages ago.*

⚠ Use **ago**, not **before**, when you are saying how much time has passed since something happened. For example, don't say 'he died 10 years before'. Say **he died 10 years ago.**

⚠ Don't use **ago** with verbs in the present perfect. Don't say 'she has left 10 minutes ago'. Say **she left 10 minutes ago.**

earlier /ˈɜːʳliəʳ/ [adv] at some time, date, year etc before or before the time you are talking about: *Didn't I give you the key earlier?*
earlier in the day/year etc *I saw Barbara earlier in the day – she looked very upset.*
20 years earlier/10 minutes earlier/moments earlier etc *Three years earlier, he had been happily married with a good job. Things were different now.*

previously /ˈpriːviəsli/ [adv] before a time or event in the past: *She got the job two years ago, after previously working in another computer company. | The attack was carried out by a previously unknown group of terrorists.*
two days/three weeks/six months etc previously *A few weeks previously I had met Herr Mueller at a conference.*
previous [adj] *Jane had spent the previous summer working in Greece.*

formerly /ˈfɔːʳməʳli/ [adv] FORMAL during a period in the past but not now: *Watkins was formerly editor of a national newspaper. | Zimbabwe was formerly known as Rhodesia.*

4 someone or something that existed before, or that you had before

previous /ˈpriːviəs/ [adj only before noun] the **previous** person, thing, or time is the one that existed just before now or before the time you are talking about: *Please ignore my previous instructions. | In her previous job she'd been an accountant. | The car's previous owner was a doctor.*
previous day/week/year etc (=the day, week etc before the time in the past that you are talking about) *The previous day my father had looked perfectly healthy. | The weather that summer was much better than in previous years.*

last /lɑːst‖læst/ [adj only before noun] the **last** person or thing is the one that you had just before now, or the one that existed just before now: *The last apartment we lived in was much smaller than this one. | Clare broke up with her last boyfriend because he drank too much.*
last night/week/year etc (=the one before this one) *I couldn't sleep last night because of the heat.*

⚠ Don't say 'the last week/night/Tuesday'. Say **last week/night/Tuesday**: *What did you do last Saturday?*

ex- /eks/ [prefix] **ex-wife/ex-boyfriend/ex-policeman/ex-soldier etc** someone who used to be someone's wife, used to be a policeman etc, but is not any more: *Joe's father's an ex-policeman. | I wish you* *wouldn't keep talking about your ex-boyfriends.*

old /əʊld/ [adj only before noun] **sb's old job/car/girlfriend/boss etc** the job, car etc that someone had before the one they have now: *How much did you sell your old car for? | I tried to contact Jim, but I only have his old phone number. | We had a big family room in our old house.*

> ⚠ **Old** is less formal than **previous**, and you usually use it in conversation. You use it about things that you used to have, or people that you used to work with or have a relationship with.

the one before /ðə ˌwʌn bɪˈfɔːr/ the person or thing that existed before the one that you have just mentioned: *I didn't enjoy Spielberg's latest movie but I thought the one before was great.*

the day before/the week before/the year before etc (=the day, week etc before the time in the past that you are talking about) *We got married in 1992, but I met her the year before, while I was at university.*

former /ˈfɔːrmər/ [adj only before noun] FORMAL existing at some time in the past, but not now – use this especially to talk about someone who used to have a particular job or position: *former US President Jimmy Carter | Robert's former wife now lives in Switzerland. | the former Soviet Republic of Georgia*

predecessor /ˈpriːdɪˌsesər‖ˈpre-/ [n C] FORMAL someone's **predecessor** is the person who had the same job before them: *Sally's predecessor had warned her that the class could be very difficult. | Kennedy's predecessor, President Eisenhower*

5 when you do something before anyone else does it

first /fɜːrst/ [adv] if you do something **first**, go somewhere **first** etc, you do it, go there etc before anyone else: *We got here first – these seats are ours. | Let Michael read the magazine. He saw it first.*

be the first to do sth *My sister always said I would be the first to get married, but she was wrong.*

6 before something else in a list or series

before /bɪˈfɔːr/ [preposition] before something or someone else in a list, series, or set: *I think you were before me in line, weren't you? | The chapter before this one was about Jenny's family. | Harajuku station is one stop before Shibuya station on the Yamanote Line.*

in front of/ahead of /ɪn ˈfrʌnt ʊv, əˈhed ʊv/ [preposition] before another person in a group of people who are waiting to do something: *The man in front of me let me go first. | There were about fifty people ahead of us waiting for tickets.*

previous /ˈpriːviəs/ [adj only before noun] coming before the one that you are dealing with now: *In a previous chapter we considered how children learn language. | He played the part of Tommy in a previous series of the show.*

earlier /ˈɜːrliər/ [adj only before noun] coming at some time before the one you have just mentioned – use this especially about something that is very different from what is happening now: *These plays lack the wit and energy of his earlier work. | Harrison's latest remarks seems less confident than his earlier statement.*

the one before /ðə ˌwʌn bɪˈfɔːr/ the thing that comes before another in a series: *I don't like this song – the one before was much better. | In the series 2, 4, 8, 16, each number is twice as big as the one before.*

above /əˈbʌv/ [adj only before noun] FORMAL WRITTEN use this in formal written English to talk about a person or thing that was mentioned earlier: *Write to the above address for more information. | The above diagram shows a normal car engine.*

the above (=the people or things mentioned earlier) *Contact any of the above for more details.*

above [adv] *the organizations mentioned above*

BEGINNING

START   STOP

see
also

END   FINISH

FIRST

1 the beginning of something

the beginning /ðə bɪˈgɪnɪŋ/ [n singular] the first part of an event, period of time, story etc
+ of *It will be ready by the beginning of next week.* | *The beginning of the movie is very violent.*
at the beginning *There's always a spelling test at the beginning of each class.*
from the beginning (=all the time, from the beginning of a long period) *It was obvious from the beginning that his plan was going to fail.*

start /stɑːʳt/ [n singular] the beginning of something, or the way that something begins
the start of sth *The runners are now lining up for the start of the race.*
at the start *At the start, their relationship was very good.*
right from the start (=use this to emphasize that something has been true all the time from when it started) *We've had problems with this car right from the start.*
from start to finish (=from the beginning to the end) *a book that holds your attention from start to finish*
a good/bad start to sth *Well, first the car broke down – which wasn't a very good start to the vacation.*

origin /ˈɒrɪdʒɪn‖ˈɔː-, ˈɑː-/ [n C] the **origin** of something is where it came from or how it first started to exist: *AIDS became widespread in the 1980s, but no-one is certain of its origin.*
+ of *a dictionary that explains the origin of words*

starting point /ˈstɑːʳtɪŋ pɔɪnt/ [n C usually singular] the **starting point** of something is where it begins or develops from: *If you want to learn about working*

overseas this book would be a good starting point.
+ for/of *They took the present situation in South Africa as the starting point for their discussion.* | *The assassination of Archduke Ferdinand is seen as the starting point of the war.*

2 at the beginning

at the beginning/at the start /ət ðə bɪˈgɪnɪŋ, ət ðə ˈstɑːʳt/ *We agreed at the start that we would discuss any problems openly.*
+ of *Your rent is due at the beginning of every month.* | *The team was doing well at the start of the season.*

at first /ət ˈfɜːʳst/ at the beginning of an event or period, especially when the situation later gets worse or better: *Barney was shy at first, but gradually he became more confident.*

initially /ɪˈnɪʃəli/ [adv] at first – use this to say what happened at the beginning of a process or situation, especially when something different happened later: *They offered her the job, initially on a temporary basis but later as a full member of staff.* | *Initially, the President didn't support this proposal.*
  initial [adj only before noun] happening at first: *My initial impression of Sadie was that she was shy and a little unhappy.*

⚠️ **Initially** is more formal than **at first**, and is often used to talk about business or politics. **At first** can be used in any situation.

originally /əˈrɪdʒɪnəli, -dʒənəli/ [adv] at the beginning – use this to talk about the situation at the time when something first existed: *She's Canadian, but her family originally came from Scotland.* | *Originally, the book was published as a series of magazine articles.*
  original /əˈrɪdʒɪnəl, -dʒənəl/ [adj only before noun] existing at the beginning: *The original owner of the painting was a friend of the artist.*

early /ˈɜːʳli/ [adv] near the beginning of an event, story, or period: *I'll be seeing him early next week.*
early in the game/story/century etc *United scored early in the game.*
early – earlier – earliest

early [adj only before noun] *We're spending two weeks in Malaysia in early May. | a man in his early thirties (=between 30 and 33 years old) | the story of her early life in India.*

3 a speech or piece of writing that comes at the beginning

introduction /ˌɪntrəˈdʌkʃən/ [n C] a short part at the beginning of a book or speech, explaining what it is about: *You'll understand the poems better if you read the introduction first.*
+ to *Scott's introduction to his novel 'Ivanhoe'*

introductory /ˌɪntrəˈdʌktəri◀/ [adj] **intro-ductory remark / paragraph / sentence** things that someone says or writes at the beginning of a book, speech etc to explain what it is about: *Write an introductory paragraph giving the background to your research.*

BEHAVE

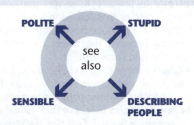

POLITE   STUPID

see
also

SENSIBLE   DESCRIBING PEOPLE

1 to behave in a particular way

behave /bɪˈheɪv/ [v I] the way someone **behaves** is the things that they do and say, and the effects these have on other people: *How does Sam behave at school?*
behave well/badly/unreasonably etc *I'm not going to talk to him until he starts behaving reasonably.*
behave as if *The next time I saw him, Frank behaved as if nothing had happened.*
behave like sb/sth *Oh, be quiet! You're behaving like a two-year-old.*
behave towards sb *William was behaving very strangely towards me.*

be /biː/ [v] **be rude/helpful/silly etc** to behave in a rude, helpful, or silly etc way: *Don't be so rude! | The waiter was really friendly and helpful. | Stop being silly! | Why is she being so nice to us?*

act /ækt/ [v I] to behave in a particular way, especially in a way that seems unusual, surprising, or annoying to other people
act strangely/stupidly/oddly etc *Tina's been acting very strangely lately.*
act like sb/sth *He has been accused of acting like a dictator.*
act as if *She acts as if she owns the place and we're her servants.*

react /riˈækt/ [v I] to say or do something because of what another person has said or done, or because of something that has happened: *How did she react when you told her the news?*
react angrily/violently/calmly *Parents reacted angrily when the school asked them to keep their children at home.*

treat /triːt/ [v T] to behave towards someone or deal with someone in a particular way
treat sb well/badly *Amy's treated him really badly – no wonder he's upset.*
treat sb like sb/sth *I'm sick of my parents treating me like a child.*
treat sb with respect/contempt/kindness *Douglas was treated with much more respect after his promotion.*

treatment /ˈtriːtmənt/ [n U] the way that a person, organization etc treats someone: *Harper described the treatment he had received in prison.*
+ of *We're shocked by the government's treatment of young homeless people.*
special/preferential treatment (=when one person is treated better than everyone else) *Although I was the boss's daughter, I didn't get preferential treatment.*

2 to behave well

behave /bɪˈheɪv/ [v I] ESPECIALLY SPOKEN to do what people tell you and not cause any trouble – use this especially about children: *If you two don't behave, I'm taking you straight home.*
behave yourself (=behave well) *Make sure you behave yourselves when we visit Grandma.*

good /ɡʊd/ a child who is **good** does not cause trouble and does what he or she is

B

told to do: *I was always very good at school.* | *He's a good little boy.* | *Bye now Jessie. Be good.*

well-behaved /ˌwel bɪˈheɪvd◄/ [adj] someone who is **well-behaved** does not cause any trouble and does what other people tell them to do – use this especially about children, pets, or large groups of people: *Can I bring my dog? She's very well-behaved.* | *The crowd was noisy but well-behaved.*

be on your best behaviour BRITISH **behavior** AMERICAN /biː ɒn jɔːʳ ˌbest bɪˈheɪvjəʳ/ to make a special effort to behave well by doing and saying the right things and being very polite, because you know other people are watching you: *Dinner was very formal, with everyone on their best behaviour.*

3 to behave badly

behave badly /bɪˌheɪv ˈbædli/ to be rude, unhelpful, or unpleasant and not do what you are told to do: *I knew I'd behaved very badly and I was sorry.* | *The kids behaved so badly that I was embarrassed.*

misbehave /ˌmɪsbɪˈheɪv/ [v I] if children **misbehave**, they deliberately behave badly by being noisy, fighting etc: *Kids often misbehave when they are bored or tired.* | *We never dared to misbehave in Miss Dill's classes.*

act up /ˌækt ˈʌp/ [phrasal verb I] INFORMAL to behave badly by being very active and noisy: *During his parents' divorce, Robert began acting up in class.*

4 the way someone behaves

behaviour BRITISH **behavior** AMERICAN /bɪˈheɪvjəʳ/ [n U] the way someone behaves: *His behaviour in school is beginning to improve.* | *That kind of behavior is not acceptable.*
+ towards *Eric's behaviour towards his family surprised me.*

⚠ Don't say 'behaviours' or 'a behaviour'. **Behaviour** is an uncountable noun.

manner /ˈmænəʳ/ [n singular] the way someone behaves when they are talking to or dealing with other people: *The driver's* manner was very unfriendly. | *She impressed everyone with her business-like manner.*

⚠ Don't confuse **manner** (=the way someone behaves when dealing with other people) and **manners** (=polite ways of behaving in social situations, for example knowing how to behave during a meal or when to say 'please' and 'thank you').

BELIEVE/ NOT BELIEVE

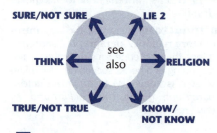

SURE/NOT SURE   LIE 2

THINK ← see also → RELIGION

TRUE/NOT TRUE   KNOW/ NOT KNOW

1 to believe something

believe /bɪˈliːv/ [v T] to be sure that something is true or that someone is telling the truth: *Did the police believe her story?* | *No-one believed me when I explained that the gun wasn't mine.*
+ (that) *People used to believe the Earth was flat.* | *The government believes that its campaign against drugs is working.*
believe in sth/sb (=believe that something or someone exists) *Do you believe in ghosts?* | *If you don't believe in God, why are you getting married in church?*
firmly/strongly believe *Within a few months, Kit firmly believed he had made the biggest mistake of his life.*

⚠ Don't say 'I am believing', 'he is believing' etc. Say **I believe, he believes**.

accept /əkˈsept/ [v T] to believe something because someone has persuaded you to believe it: *He seems to just accept everything they tell him, without questioning it.* | *I'm not sure whether your story would be accepted by a jury.*
+ that *I don't accept that he knew nothing about these payments until now.*

⚠️ Don't say 'I am accepting', 'he is accepting' etc. Say **I accept, he accepts**.

be taken in /biː ˌteɪkən ˈɪn/ to believe that someone is telling the truth, when in fact they are lying in order to trick you: *He told me that it was a genuine diamond, and I was completely taken in.*

+ by *Don't be taken in by products claiming to make you lose weight quickly.*

gullible /ˈɡʌlɪbəl/ [adj] too willing to believe what other people tell you, so that it is easy for people to cheat you: *I was so gullible – I thought he loved me! | cheap goods sold at high prices to gullible tourists*

2 something that someone believes

belief /bɪˈliːf/ [n C/U] something you believe to be true

religious/political beliefs *They were put in prison because of their religious beliefs.*

+ that *Their experiments were based on the belief that you could make gold from other metals.*

contrary to popular belief (=despite what most people believe) FORMAL *Contrary to popular belief, eating carrots does not improve your eyesight.*

superstition /ˌsuːpərˈstɪʃən, ˌsjuː-‖ˌsuː-/ [n C/U] a belief that some things are lucky and some are unlucky, even though there are no scientific reasons for believing this: *There is an old superstition that walking under a ladder is unlucky. | These people lived in an age of superstition and ignorance.*

3 when something seems to be true

convincing /kənˈvɪnsɪŋ/ [adj] a **convincing** explanation, argument, reason, etc seems likely to be true: *There is some convincing evidence that women are more intelligent than men. | I didn't find any of their arguments very convincing.*

plausible /ˈplɔːzɪbəl/ [adj] something that is **plausible** seems reasonable and likely to be true, even though it may actually be untrue – use this especially with these words: **explanation, excuse, answer,**

theory: *His explanation sounds fairly plausible to me. | I need to think of a plausible excuse for not going to the meeting.*

4 to not believe something

not believe /nɒt bɪˈliːv/ [v T] *Don't believe everything you read in the newspapers. | I told her I was sorry, but she didn't believe me.*

+ (that) *I can't believe he's only 25!*

🔵**not believe a word of it** (=not believe it at all) SPOKEN *They say they're going to send me the money, but I don't believe a word of it.*

⚠️ Don't say 'I am not believing', 'he is not believing' etc. Say **I don't believe, he doesn't believe**.

doubt /daʊt/ [v T] to think that something is probably not true: *Kim never doubted his story.*

+ if/whether *I doubt whether anyone really understood what I was trying to say.*

I doubt it *He may be the best person for the job, but I doubt it.*

doubt very much (=think something is almost certainly not true) *She says she'll leave him, but I doubt very much if she will.*

⚠️ Don't say 'I am doubting', 'he is doubting' etc. Say **I doubt, he doubts**.

sceptical BRITISH **skeptical** AMERICAN /ˈskeptɪkəl/ [adj] someone who is **sceptical** about something is not sure whether it is true, or does not really believe it: *When I started this investigation I was sceptical. | Russell's sceptical attitude towards the Christian religion*

+ about *I wish him luck, but I'm sceptical about his chances of success.*

cynical /ˈsɪnɪkəl/ [adj] someone who is **cynical** is not willing to believe that people have good or honest reasons for doing something: *I think movie stars just do charity work to get publicity – but maybe I'm too cynical. | an author with a cynical view of life*

+ about *Since her divorce, she's become very cynical about men.*

disbelief /ˌdɪsbᵻˈliːf/ [n U] the feeling that you have when you are very surprised by something and do not believe that it is true: *People's usual reaction to bad news is shock and disbelief.*

stare/watch in disbelief *I stared at him in disbelief. "You're not serious, surely?"*

5 what you say when you do not believe what someone is telling you

○**you're kidding/you're joking** /jɔːʳ ˈkɪdɪŋ, jɔːʳ ˈdʒəʊkɪŋ/ SPOKEN INFORMAL say this when you are very surprised by what someone has just said and cannot believe that it is true: *They got married! You're kidding!*

⚠ Only say this to friends and people who you know well.

○**come off it** /kʌm ˈɒf ɪt/ SPOKEN INFORMAL say this when you cannot believe what someone has said, and you think they do not really believe it themselves: *"I'm going to fail!" "Oh come off it, you couldn't possibly fail after all the work you've done."*

⚠ Only say this to friends and people who you know well. If you use **come off it** to people who you do not know well, it will seem rude.

BEND

➡ opposite **STRAIGHT**

1 to bend your body, or part of your body

bend /bend/ [v I/T] if you **bend**, you move the top part of your body forwards or down; if you **bend** your arm, leg, or knee, you move it so that it folds at the joint: *Bend your arms and then stretch them upwards.*
+ **forward/towards/across** *She bent towards me and whispered in my ear.*
bending – bent – have bent

bend over/bend down /ˌbend ˈəʊvəʳ, ˌbend ˈdaʊn/ [phrasal verb I] to bend the top part of your body down, for example to pick something up: *She bent over to*

bend down

He bent down to pick up the papers.

pick up the ball. | *I can't bend down because I've hurt my back.*

bow /baʊ/ [v I] to bend your head and the upper part of your body forward slightly, in order to show respect or as a formal greeting: *All the men turned and bowed as the Emperor passed.*

bow

crouch /kraʊtʃ/ [v I] to bend your legs under you and bring your body close to the ground: *I saw him crouching behind some bushes.*
crouch down *She crouched down to watch the spider.*

crouch

curl up

curl up /ˌkɜːʳl ˈʌp/ [phrasal verb I] to lie or sit with your arms and legs bent close to your body: *I just want to curl up in my chair and watch TV.*

2 to bend something

bend /bend/ [v T] to push or press something into a curved shape, or fold it to form an angle: *I hit the nail too hard and bent it a little.*
bend sth back/down/into *Bend the wire into an 'S' shape.*
bending – bent – have bent

twist /twɪst/ [v T] to bend and turn something, such as wire or rope, several times **twist sth around/through/into** *He twisted a coil of wire around the handle.* | *Her hair was twisted into a knot at the back of her head.*

3 easy to bend

flexible /'fleksɪ̥bəl/ [adj] something that is **flexible** is easy to bend: *shoes with flexible rubber soles* | *A long flexible hose is attached to the tap.*

4 not easy to bend

stiff /stɪf/ [adj] hard, and difficult to bend: *a sheet of stiff cardboard* | *The hairs on its back were stiff, as though it was frightened.*

rigid /'rɪdʒɪ̥d/ [adj] an object that is **rigid** cannot be bent at all: *The framework of the aircraft is rigid but light.* | *a rigid metal structure*

5 someone who finds it easy to bend their arms, back etc

supple /'sʌpəl/ [adj] someone who is **supple** can bend and stretch very easily and comfortably: *a supple young gymnast*

6 something that is not straight

bent /bent/ [adj] something that is **bent** is no longer flat or straight: *How did this spoon get bent?* | *The lid is bent and it won't shut.* | *Stand with your legs slightly bent.*

twisted /'twɪstɪ̥d/ [adj] something that is **twisted** is bent in many different directions: *The driver was dead, and the car was a heap of twisted metal.*

twisted

curved /kɜːʳvd/ [adj] something that is **curved** has a smooth round bend in it: *a sword with a curved blade*

wavy /'weɪvi/ [adj] **wavy** lines or hair have a lot of smooth curves in a regular pattern: *A series of wavy lines appeared on the screen.* | *She had long wavy brown hair.*

curved

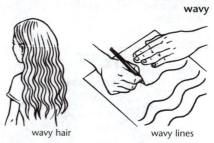
wavy

wavy hair   wavy lines

7 when a road, river, or path bends

bend /bend/ [n C] a place on a road, river, or path where it turns to go in a different direction: *Soon you come to a point where there's a bend in the river.* | *The car came round the bend too fast.*
a sharp bend (=one that turns suddenly) *After you've passed the church, you go around a sharp bend.*

curve /kɜːʳv/ [v I] a road, river, or path that **curves** has a long smooth bend in it, like part of a circle: *From here the railway curves away towards the town.* | *a sandy beach curving gently around the bay*
curving /'kɜːʳvɪŋ/ [adj only before noun] *a wide curving staircase*

wind /waɪnd/ [v I] a road, river, or path that **winds** has a lot of curved bends over a long distance
+ through/along/around *The trail winds through the forest, then descends towards the lake.*
winding /'waɪndɪŋ/ [adj only before noun] *a peaceful little town on the banks of a winding river*
winding – wound – have wound

zigzag /'zɪgzæg/ [v I] a road or path that **zigzags** keeps turning to the left and then the right with a lot of sharp bends
+ down/across/through *ski routes zigzagging down the mountainside*

B

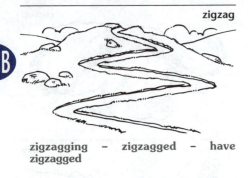

zigzag

zigzagging – zigzagged – have zigzagged

BEST

SUITABLE/UNSUITABLE

GOOD · PERFECT

see also

BETTER · PRAISE

CONVENIENT/ NOT CONVENIENT · FAVOURITE/ FAVORITE

1 better than all the others

best /best/ [adj usually before noun] better than anything or anyone else: *The best ice-cream in the world is made in Italy.* | *She got the award for 'Best Actress' for her part in the movie.* | *Two of their best players were injured.* | *What's the best way to cook sweet potatoes?*
the best (=someone or something that is better than all the others) *I chose a Japanese camera because I wanted to buy the best.*
the best in the country/the world/the class etc *Woods is the best player in the team.* | *Their heart surgery unit is the best in the country.*
by far the best (=much better than any others) *It was by far the best vacation I've ever had.*
the best thing to do *I think the best thing to do would be to call a doctor.*
best [adv] *I've tried a lot of shampoos but this is the one I like best.* | *Nadia is the best-dressed woman I know.*

greatest /ˈɡreɪtⁱst/ [adj] the best and most important that there has ever been – use this about artists, political leaders, sports players etc, or about paintings, books, music, achievements etc: *Picasso was one of the greatest artists of the 20th century.* | *Gorbachev's greatest achievement was ending the Cold War.* | *The First World War produced some of the greatest poetry ever written.*

finest /ˈfaɪnⁱst/ [adj] the best and most skilful, or the best and highest quality – use this about artists, writers, performances, or achievements, or about wines, foods, products, or materials: *Marlon Brando was perhaps the finest film actor of them all.* | *Many people regard Beethoven's Fifth Symphony as his finest work.* | *We use only the finest ingredients.*

top /tɒp‖tɑːp/ [adj only before noun] the most skilful, most successful, and most famous – use this about people such as sports players, lawyers, entertainers, photographers, or designers: *one of the world's top tennis players* | *Several top rock acts will be performing at the charity concert.* | *By the age of 18, she was already a top fashion model.*

star /stɑːʳ/ [adj only before noun] **star player/performer/student/pupil etc** the best player in a team, the best student in a class etc: *Their star player earned millions of dollars.* | *Bob Woodward, the Washington Post's star reporter*
star [n C] *They're a pretty good class, but Laura's undoubtedly the star.*

2 when you do something better than ever before

at your best /ət jɔːʳ ˈbest/ if you are **at your best**, you are performing at your highest level of skill: *At his best, Maradona was one of the most exciting players in the world.* | *The album shows Stephan Grappelli at his very best.*

be at your peak /biː ət jɔːʳ ˈpiːk/ to be at the time in your life when you are playing a sport, doing your job etc better than at any other time: *Long distance runners are usually at their peak in their mid-30s.* | *At his peak, McEnroe was one of the best tennis players of all time.*

When you see **EC**, go to the **ESSENTIAL COMMUNICATION** section.

3 the thing that you do best

best /best/ [adj only before noun] your **best** subject, sport etc is the one that you do better than anything else: *My best subject at school was history.* | *He's good at lots of sports but his best event is the high-jump.*

speciality BRITISH **specialty** AMERICAN /ˌspeʃiˈælᵻti, ˈspeʃəlti/ [n C] the thing that you do best and that you are the most skilful at: *She loved baking, and cakes were her speciality.* | *Christie also runs the 200 metres, but the 100 is his speciality.*
plural **specialities** BRITISH **specialties** AMERICAN

BETTER

➡ opposite **WORSE**

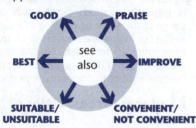

GOOD   **PRAISE**

BEST   see also   **IMPROVE**

SUITABLE/ UNSUITABLE   **CONVENIENT/ NOT CONVENIENT**

1 better than someone or something else

better /ˈbetər/ [adj] *A better job with a better salary – that's what I want.*
+ than *Your stereo's better than mine.*
better at sth (=able to do something better) *Paul's better at tennis than I am.* | *Here, let me do it – I'm better at drawing.*
it is better to do sth *I think it would be better to go tomorrow instead.*
much/far/a lot better *The sales figures are much better than we expected.*
  better [adv] *You can probably explain this better than I can.*

superior /suːˈpɪəriər, sjuː-‖suː-/ [adj] better – use this about people's skills, or about products or services that you can buy: *Sampras's superior technique meant that he won the game.*
+ to *Are French wines really superior to British ones?*

> ⚠ Superior is more formal than **better**, and is mostly used in writing.

preferably /ˈprefərəbli/ [adv] use this to say that something would be better or more suitable: *Come early next week – on Monday preferably.* | *We need well-qualified people, preferably with good computer skills.*

2 better than before

better /ˈbetər/ [adj] *I hope the weather's better next week.*
+ than *The food here's a lot better than it used to be.*
get better *His work got better after he changed schools.*
much/far/a lot better *I'm still not very good at Japanese, but I'm much better than I used to be.*

be an improvement /biː ən ɪmˈpruːvmənt/ to be better than something similar that you had or did before or that existed before
+ on *This new heating system is definitely a big improvement on the old one.*

improved /ɪmˈpruːvd/ [adj only before noun] better than before, because changes have been made: *the new improved Mark IV engine* | *improved relations between India and Pakistan*

Q that's more like it /ˌðæts mɔːr ˈlaɪk ɪt/ SPOKEN say this when a situation is better than before, or when someone starts to do something better: *Can't you walk faster – that's more like it.* | *He's reduced his price to $800. Now that's more like it!*

3 to do something better

do better /duː ˈbetər/ to do something better than you did before, or do something better than someone else: *You'd do better if you practised more often.*
+ than *John did better than most of the other students in the class.* | *Come on – you can do better than that!*

improve on sth /ɪmˈpruːv ɒn (sth)/ [phrasal verb T] to do something better than it was done before, especially by trying very hard: *We have improved on last year's results.* | *Smithson has 165* *points, and I don't think anyone will improve on that.*

outdo /aʊtˈduː/ [v T] to be more successful at something than someone else: *Clare is always trying to outdo her sister.*
outdoing – outdid – have outdone

4 better after an illness

better /ˈbetəʳ/ [adj not before noun] ESPECIALLY SPOKEN better after you have been ill: *Is Helen better yet?*
get better *I hope you get better soon. | He was getting better every day.*

well /wel/ [adj not before noun] when you are no longer ill: *As soon as you're well again, we'll go to Florida.*
get well soon SPOKEN (say this when someone is ill)

recover /rɪˈkʌvəʳ/ [v I] to get well again after you have had an illness or injury: *She had chickenpox, and it took her ten days to recover.*
+ from *Gascoigne is recovering from a knee injury.*
be fully recovered (=be completely well again) *Mitchell is fully recovered and will be taking part in the race.*

⚠ **Recover** is more formal than **get better**, and is usually used about serious illnesses or injuries.

BIG

➡ opposite **SMALL**
➡ if you want to know about word order with adjectives, go to the **ESSENTIAL GRAMMAR**, section 13

WIDE/NARROW
FAT **TALL**
see also
THICK **HIGH**
GROW **INCREASE**

1 things/groups/organizations

big/large /bɪg, lɑːʳdʒ/ [adj] *His car's really big. | A large package came in the mail*

next day. | That bag's too small – you'll need a bigger one. | Boeing is the world's largest commercial airplane manufacturer. | They say it's the biggest music festival since Woodstock.
big – bigger – biggest

⚠ **Big** and **large** mean the same thing. **Large** is a little more formal than **big**, so **large** is more common in written English, and **big** is more common in spoken English.

enormous/huge /ɪˈnɔːʳməs, hjuːdʒ/ [adj] very big and impressive: *In the corner of the room there was a huge desk. | a cathedral with an enormous tower | Huge crowds had gathered outside the embassy.*

⚠ Don't say 'very enormous' or 'very huge'. Just say **enormous** or **huge**.

gigantic /dʒaɪˈgæntɪk/ [adj] something that is **gigantic** is much bigger than other things of the same type, often in a slightly strange or frightening way: *Gigantic waves more than 40 feet high crashed against the boat. | These gigantic creatures became extinct in the Jurassic period.*

2 places/areas/cities/rooms

big/large /bɪg, lɑːʳdʒ/ [adj] *London is the biggest city in Europe. | I like the bedroom – it's really big. | Flooding has affected large areas of the country.*
big – bigger – biggest

⚠ You can usually use **big** and **large** in the same situations, but it is more usual to talk about **big** cities and towns and **large** areas.

enormous/huge /ɪˈnɔːʳməs, hjuːdʒ/ [adj] very big and impressive: *They have a huge garden. | The kitchen was enormous. | The Grosvenor family once owned huge areas of land.*

spacious /ˈspeɪʃəs/ [adj] use this about the inside of a room or building that has a lot of space: *a spacious apartment in Manhattan | Jenny's kitchen is spacious, light, and airy. | the company's spacious offices in Oxford*

vast /vɑːst‖væst/ [adj] use this about very large areas of land, sea, or space: *China is a vast country.* | *Whales can communicate across vast distances.*

3 people

➡ see also **TALL, FAT**

big/large /bɪg, lɑːrdʒ/ [adj] use this about someone who is tall and has a large body: *My father was a big man, with legs like tree trunks.* | *A large woman in her early 50s answered the door.*

> ⚠ **Large** is more formal than **big** and is used especially in written descriptions. It is not polite to tell a woman that she is **big** or **large**.

well-built /ˌwel ˈbɪlt◄/ [adj] use this about someone who is big and strong and has a lot of muscles: *He was handsome and well-built, like a Hollywood movie star.*

huge/enormous /hjuːdʒ, ɪˈnɔːrməs/ very big and tall, in a way that is impressive or frightening: *The other wrestler was enormous, and must have weighed over 250 pounds.* | *A huge policeman stood outside the gate.*

4 numbers/amounts

> ⚠ Don't use **big** to talk about numbers and amounts.

large /lɑːrdʒ/ [adj]
large amount/quantity/number *The thieves escaped with large amount of money.* | *Large quantities of nuclear waste have been dumped into the sea.*
a large sum (=a large amount of money) *She was offered a large sum of money for carrying drugs across the border.*
in large numbers *By the 1950s, women had begun attending university in large numbers.*

huge/massive/enormous /hjuːdʒ, ˈmæsɪv, ɪˈnɔːrməs/ [adj] very large, in a way that is impressive or shocking
+ amount/number/increase/reduction etc *The government spends huge amounts of money on health care.* | *There has been a massive increase in the number of people living below the poverty line.* | *job losses on an enormous scale* (=when a large number of people lose their jobs)

high /haɪ/ [adj] use this about prices and levels, especially when you think that something is too expensive or there is too much of it: *Many old people cannot afford the high cost of heating their homes.* | *The level of pollution is unacceptably high.* | *very high interest rates on bank loans*

> ⚠ Don't say 'high amount'. Say **large amount**.

5 problems/changes/differences/effects

> ⚠ Don't use **large** about problems, changes, differences, or effects.

big /bɪg/ [adj only before noun] *Our biggest problem is lack of money.* | *There will have to be some big changes around here.* | *Your clothes can make a big difference to the way you feel about yourself.*
big – bigger – biggest

huge/enormous /hjuːdʒ, ɪˈnɔːrməs/ [adj] very big, and very important, or serious: *Young people from poor families often have enormous difficulty in finding jobs.* | *Advances in technology have had a huge impact on the way people work.*

major /ˈmeɪdʒər/ [adj only before noun] use this about something that has serious and important effects on many people, many places etc
major difference/change/difficulty/problem *We have been told to expect major changes in the Earth's climate.* | *There is one major difference between these two systems of government.*

6 how big something is

size /saɪz/ [n C/U] *Once again, teachers are protesting about class sizes in schools.* | *It takes a cat two years to reach full adult size.*
+ of *The amount of tax you pay will depend on the size of your family.*
of this/that size (=as big as this) *There simply aren't the resources to support a population of this size.*
the size of sth (=the same size as something) *A whole library of information can be stored on a microchip the size of a fingernail.*

how big /ˌhaʊ ˈbɪg/ use this to talk about or ask about the size of something: *I'm not sure how big the apartment is.* | *How big do these fish grow?*

scale /skeɪl/ [n singular] the size of something such as a problem or a change, not of an object, vehicle etc

the scale of sth *Rescue workers are trying to assess the scale of the disaster.* | *Scientists are only just beginning to realize the scale of the problem.*

on a large/massive/huge scale (=when something very big happens) *The rainforest is being destroyed on a massive scale.*

7 to become bigger

➡ see also **GROW, INCREASE**

get bigger /ˌget ˈbɪgəʳ/ to become bigger: *The hole in the ozone layer is getting bigger every year* | *a problem that's getting bigger all the time*

get bigger and bigger (=continue to become bigger) *The waves were getting bigger and bigger as the wind grew stronger.*

grow /grəʊ/ [v I] to become bigger – use this especially about amounts, organizations, and places: *Mark's business grew rapidly in the first year.* | *Tandem's annual profits grew by 24% in 1990.* | *Tokyo has grown a lot over the last ten years.*

growing – grew – have grown

expand /ɪkˈspænd/ [v I] to become bigger and more successful – use this about businesses and other organizations: *Medical insurance companies expanded rapidly during the 1980s.* | *The sports and leisure market is expanding more quickly than ever before.*

swell up /ˌswel ˈʌp/ [phrasal verb I] use this about parts of your body that have become bigger because you are ill or injured: *Her face went blue and the veins in her neck swelled up.*

swelling up – swelled up – have swollen up

swollen [adj] *The boy's right knee was badly swollen.* (=it had become much bigger because he was injured)

stretch /stretʃ/ [v I] if something such as a piece of clothing **stretches**, it gets bigger and changes its shape because it is being pulled or pressed: *Don't worry if the boots are tight at first – they'll soon stretch when you wear them.*

8 to make something bigger

stretch /stretʃ/ [v T] to pull cloth, plastic, leather, etc so that it gets bigger and changes its shape: *Stretch the canvas so that it covers the whole frame.*

enlarge /ɪnˈlɑːʳdʒ/ [v T] to make a photograph, picture, or document bigger: *The photocopier can enlarge documents by up to 100%.*

have/get sth enlarged *That's a lovely photo of Amy. Why don't you get it enlarged?*

magnify /ˈmægnɪfaɪ/ [v T] to make something look bigger than it is, for example by using a microscope: *a picture of an insect, magnified 10 times*

magnifying – magnified – have magnified

extend /ɪkˈstend/ [v T] BRITISH to make a building bigger by adding more rooms or more space: *The hotel has been recently renovated and extended.* | *We're thinking of extending the kitchen.*

BITE

➡ see also **EAT, FOOD**

bite /baɪt/ [v I/T] to cut or crush something with your teeth: *She sat there nervously biting her fingernails.* | *Don't worry about the dog – he won't bite.*

bite

+ into/through *biting into a juicy apple* | *A shark had bitten right through our nets.*

bite sb on the hand/leg etc *The snake bit her on the ankle.*

bite sth off (=remove something by biting it) *He took a cigar and bit the end off.*

biting – bit – have bitten

When you see **EC**, go to the **ESSENTIAL COMMUNICATION** section.

have a bite/take a bite /ˌhæv ə ˈbaɪt, ˌteɪk ə ˈbaɪt/ to take a piece from some food by biting it: *"That looks good." "Here, have a bite."* | *Sandy picked up a doughnut and took an enormous bite.*
+ of *Can I have a bite of your candy bar?*

chew /tʃuː/ [v I/T] to keep biting something that is in your mouth: *Don't eat so quickly. Chew your food.* | *Helen sat chewing her pencil, trying to think what to write next.*

peck /pek/ [v I/T] if a bird **pecks** something, it makes quick movements with its beak to try to bite it: *A bird flew down and pecked my hand.*
+ at *Hens pecked at the corn on the ground.*

peck

BLAME

to say or think that someone is responsible for something bad that has happened

➡ see also **GUILTY/NOT GUILTY, CRITICIZE**

1 to blame someone

blame /bleɪm/ [v T] to say or think that someone is responsible for something bad that has happened: *He always blames someone else when things go wrong.* | *It's your idea – don't blame me if it doesn't work.*
blame sb for sth *At first, everyone blamed the pilot for the crash.*
blame sth on sb/sth *You can't blame everything on the government.*
blame yourself *For many years I blamed myself for her death.*

say sth is sb's fault /ˌseɪ (sth) ɪz (sb's) ˈfɔːlt/ ESPECIALLY SPOKEN to say that someone is responsible for something bad that has happened
+ (that) *How can you say it's my fault you lost your job?*

put the blame on sb /ˌpʊt ðə ˈbleɪm ɒn (sb)/ to say or think that someone is responsible for something bad that has happened, especially when this is unfair: *Don't try to put the blame on me!*

put the blame for sth on sb *Richard still puts the blame for the divorce on his wife.*

accuse /əˈkjuːz/ [v T] to say that someone is guilty of a crime or of doing something bad
accuse sb of doing sth *Are you accusing me of telling lies?*
be accused of murder/armed robbery etc *West has been accused of murder.*

2 to be blamed for something

get the blame /ˌget ðə ˈbleɪm/ to be blamed for something, especially something that you did not do: *The other kids all ran off, and I was the one who got the blame.*
+ for *I don't know why I always get the blame for everything.*

scapegoat /ˈskeɪpgəʊt/ [n C] someone who is blamed for something that someone else is much more responsible for, especially because people want someone to be punished: *He was just a scapegoat – the people who were really responsible were his bosses in London.*

3 to be responsible for something bad that has happened

be sb's fault /biː (sb's) ˈfɔːlt/ ESPECIALLY SPOKEN if something **is someone's fault**, they are responsible for it, especially because they made a mistake: *"The dog's gone." "It's your fault. You left the gate open."*
be sb's own fault (=when someone is responsible for something bad that happens to them) *It's her own fault – she just shouldn't have married him.*
+ (that) *I'm so sorry. It's my fault that we're so late.*

be to blame /biː tə ˈbleɪm/ if someone or something **is to blame** for a bad situation, they caused it, especially by doing something wrong: *It's not the teachers who are to blame, it's the parents.*
+ for *Some people think television is to blame for a lot of the problems in modern society.*

be responsible /biː rɪˈspɒnsɪbəl‖ -ˈspɑːn-/ if someone **is responsible** for an accident, a crime etc, they caused it and they should be punished for it

+ for *The police are trying to find out who was responsible for the attack.*

feel responsible (=think that something is your fault) *You mustn't feel responsible for his death. You did everything you could.*

> ⚠ Don't say 'be responsible of something'. Say **be responsible for something**: *The truck driver was responsible for the crash.*

4 to not be responsible for something bad that has happened

not be sb's fault /nɒt biː (sb's) ˈfɔːlt/ if something **is not someone's fault**, they did not make it happen and they should not be blamed for it: *Don't worry – it's not your fault.* | *She felt guilty, even though the accident wasn't her fault.*

+ (that) *It wasn't her husband's fault that she felt so bored.*

◯**sb can't help it** /(sb) ˌkɑːnt ˈhelp ɪt‖ ˌkæntɪ-/ ESPECIALLY SPOKEN if you say someone **can't help it**, you mean they should not be blamed because they cannot prevent something from happening: *"I wish you'd stop walking around like that!" "I can't help it – I'm really nervous."*

+ if *Dad can't help it if the car keeps breaking down.*

be not to blame /biː nɒt tə ˈbleɪm/ to not be responsible for something bad that happens – use this especially when other people think you might have done something to make it happen

+ for *Hospital workers were not to blame for a nine-year-old's death, a court decided yesterday.* | *The report said that no-one was to blame for the accident.*

5 to say that you are responsible for something bad that has happened

take the blame /ˌteɪk ðə ˈbleɪm/ to admit that you are responsible for something bad that has happened, especially when other people are responsible for it but they are not blamed: *It's not my fault and I don't see why I should take the blame.*

+ for *She refused to take the blame for something she didn't do.*

take full responsibility/accept full responsibility /teɪk ˌfʊl rɪˌspɒn-sɪˈbɪlɪti, əksept ˌfʊl rɪˌspɒnsɪˈbɪlɪti‖ -spɑːn-/ if you **take** or **accept full responsibility** for something bad that has happened, you admit that you are completely responsible for it – use this especially about managers and leaders admitting that they are responsible

+ for *The Chairman of the airline said he accepted full responsibility for the accident and immediately resigned.*

BODY

➡ if you mean 'dead body', go to DEAD

1 the body of a person or animal

body /ˈbɒdi‖ˈbɑːdi/ [n C] your **body** is your head, arms, chest, waist, legs, feet, and all the other physical parts of you: *My body ached all over, and I knew I was getting the flu.* | *The weight of your body will be partly supported by the water.* | *The cancer may have spread to other parts of her body.*

the human body (=the body of any person) *There are over 1000 muscles in the human body.*

plural **bodies**

> ⚠ You can also use **body** to talk about the main part of someone's body, not including the head, arms, or legs: *a spider with orange markings all over its body* | *The victim had bruises all over his face, neck, and body.*

2 the shape of someone's body

figure /ˈfɪgəʳ‖ˈfɪgjər/ [n C usually singular] the shape of a woman's body – use this especially to talk about a women whose body has an attractive shape: *She has a marvellous figure – she could be a model if she wanted to.*

body /ˈbɒdi‖ˈbɑːdi/ [n C] the shape, size, and appearance of someone's body: *Teenagers are often embarrassed about their bodies.*
have a good/wonderful/great body (=a very attractive body) *At the age of fifty, she still has a great body.*
plural **bodies**

physique /fɪˈziːk/ [n C usually singular] the shape and size of someone's body – use this especially to talk about the body of a man who is very strong and has a lot of muscles: *Brad had a superb physique and the looks of a young Marlon Brando.*

3 concerning your body

physical /ˈfɪzɪkəl/ [adj] concerning your body, not your mind: *Your son seems to be in good physical health.* | *During the war, people suffered terrible physical and emotional hardships.*
physically [adv] *At the end of the week I was physically and mentally exhausted.*

WORD BANK

BOOKS/ LITERATURE

STORY　　READ
EC OPINIONS　　　　WRITE
　　　see
　　　also
THEATRE　　　　ART
FREE TIME　　FILMS/MOVIES

1 a book

book /bʊk/ [n C]
+ by *a book by Charles Dickens*

+ about *I'm reading a book about a little girl who was a slave in 19th century Atlanta.*
book on sth (=a book giving information about a particular subject) *Do you have any books on astronomy?*

paperback /ˈpeɪpəʳbæk/ [n C] a book with a cover made of stiff paper

hardback /ˈhɑːʳdbæk/ [n C] a book with a hard cover

2 a book about imaginary people and events

novel /ˈnɒvəl‖ˈnɑː-/ [n C] a book about people and events that the writer has imagined: *a Jane Austen novel*
+ by *The movie is based on a novel by Anne Tyler.*
romantic novel (=about love)
historical novel (=about people and events in the past)

fiction /ˈfɪkʃən/ [n U] books about imaginary people and events: *His first novel won a prize for modern fiction.* | *I'm taking a class in Victorian fiction.*
romantic fiction (=about love)

literature /ˈlɪtərətʃəʳ‖-tʃʊər/ [n U] books, plays, and poems, especially famous ones that people think are important: *She's studying 19th century French literature.* | *the Nobel Prize for Literature*

science fiction /ˌsaɪəns ˈfɪkʃən/ [n U] stories about things that happen in the future or in other parts of the universe

detective story /dɪˈtektɪv ˌstɔːri/ [n C] a story in which someone tries to find who is responsible for a crime, especially a murder: *I like reading Sherlock Holmes and other detective stories.*

thriller /ˈθrɪləʳ/ [n C] an exciting story, for example about a crime or war, in which surprising events happen suddenly and you never know what will happen next: *Stephen King's new psychological thriller*

short story /ˌʃɔːʳt ˈstɔːri/ [n C] a short piece of writing in which the writer tells a story: *a collection of short stories by Henry James*

When you see **EC**, go to the **ESSENTIAL COMMUNICATION** section.

B

3 a book about real people, places, or events

non-fiction /ˌnɒn ˈfɪkʃən‖ˌnɑːn-/ [n U] books about real events, people, or places: *The books in the library are divided into fiction and non-fiction.*
   non-fiction [adj] *non-fiction books*

4 a book about someone's life

biography /baɪˈɒɡrəfi‖-ˈɑːɡ-/ [n C] a book about someone's life, written by another person: *Boswell's biography of Dr Johnson*
plural **biographies**

autobiography /ˌɔːtəbaɪˈɒɡrəfi‖-ˈɑːɡ-/ [n C] a book in which someone writes about their own life: *In her autobiography, Doris Lessing writes about her childhood in Zimbabwe.*
plural **autobiographies**

5 a book that gives you information about a subject

reference book /ˈrefərəns ˌbʊk/ [n C] a book that you look at in order to get information, especially a dictionary or encyclopedia: *Do not remove reference books from the library.*

encyclopedia /ɪnˌsaɪkləˈpiːdiə/ [n C] a large book or set of books containing facts about a lot of different subjects, usually arranged in alphabetical order: *"Does anyone know when Mozart was born?" "Look it up in the encyclopedia."* | *the Encyclopedia of Science*

textbook /ˈtekstbʊk/ [n C] a book that contains information and ideas about a subject, which you use when you are studying that subject: *a geography textbook* | *The school says it doesn't have enough money to buy textbooks for every student.*

dictionary /ˈdɪkʃənəri‖-neri/ [n C] a book that tells you the meaning of words and lists them in alphabetical order
plural **dictionaries**

atlas /ˈætləs/ [n C] a book of maps: *a road atlas of Great Britain*

6 someone who writes books

writer /ˈraɪtər/ [n C] someone who writes books, stories, or articles in magazines as a job: *When I was young I wanted to be a writer.* | *Have you read any books by American writers?* | *Greene was one of the finest writers of his generation.*

author /ˈɔːθər/ [n C] someone who writes books, or who wrote a particular book: *The prize was won by the German author, Heinrich Böll.* | *Balzac was one of her favourite authors.*
+ of *Who was the author of 'Catch 22'?*

novelist /ˈnɒvələst‖ˈnɑː-/ [n C] someone who writes books about imaginary people or events: *George Eliot was one of the greatest 19th century novelists.* | *romantic novelist Barbara Cartland*

7 what happens in a book

story /ˈstɔːri/ [n C] what happens in a book: *'The 39 Steps' is a spy story.* | *I like ghost stories best.*
   the story of *'Mud and Dust' is the story of her travels across Africa.*
   true story (=when the events in a book really happened) *I could hardly beieve it was a true story.*

plot /plɒt‖plɑːt/ [n C] the events that happen in a book, and the way in which these events are connected: *The plot was so complicated that I kept getting lost.* | *It was like the plot of a detective novel.*

ending /ˈendɪŋ/ [n C] what happens at the end of a book: *I thought the ending was a real disappointment.* | *a sad story with a happy ending*

8 the words in a book

narrative /ˈnærətɪv/ [n C/U] the series of events described in a story and the way that the writer describes them: *The pace of the narrative makes this book an exciting read.*

dialogue /ˈdaɪəlɒɡ‖-lɑːɡ/ [n C/U] the things that the people in a book say to each other: *The novel is mostly description, with very little dialogue.* | *a long dialogue between the main character and his mother*

quotation (also **quote** INFORMAL) /kwəʊ-
'teɪʃən, kwəʊt/ [n C] a sentence or phrase
from a book: *He started his speech with
a quotation from Shakespeare.* | *a
famous quotation about love*

descriptive passage /dɪˈskrɪptɪv
'pæsɪdʒ/ [n C] a piece of writing that
describes the way someone or something
looks, sounds, smells etc

style (also **style of writing**) /staɪl,
‚staɪl əv 'raɪtɪŋ/ [n C] the way in which a
writer uses words in order to express ideas
or tell a story: *Margaret Atwood's my
favourite author – I like her style.* | *a
very distinctive style of writing*

9 the people in a book

character /ˈkærˌktər/ [n C] a person in the
story of a book: *The main character is a
soldier in the First World War.* | *a char-
acter from Dickens.*

hero/heroine /ˈhɪərəʊ, ˈherəʊɪn/ [n C] the
most important man or woman in a book:
In the end the heroine dies. | *Paul
Morel is the hero of 'Sons and Lovers'.*

10 the ideas or subject of a book

be about /‚biː əˈbaʊt/ if a book **is about** a
person, idea, or event, that person, idea,
or event is the main subject of the book:
Her first novel is about her childhood. |
I want to buy a book about gardening.

be set in /‚biː 'set ɪn/ if a book **is set in** a
place or period of time, the story happens
in that place or during that time: *Aldous
Huxley's 'Brave New World' is set in the
future.* | *The story is set in Paris.*

be based on /‚biː 'beɪst ɒn/ if a book **is
based on** a story or event, the things that
happen in the book are very similar to the
things that really happened: *a novel based
on a true story* | *The book is based on
Hemingway's experiences in the
Spanish civil war.*

theme /θiːm/ [n C] one of the main ideas
that an author writes about in a book: *The
themes of 'Oliver Twist' are poverty and
crime.* | *Love is the main theme in all
his novels.*

11 poems

poem /ˈpəʊˌɪm/ [n C] a piece of writing
which is arranged in patterns of lines and
sounds: *a poem by Sylvia Plath* | *She
quoted a few lines from Eliot's famous
poem 'The Waste Land'.*

poetry /ˈpəʊtri/ [n U] poems in general: *a
book of modern poetry* | *Do you read
much poetry?*

poet /ˈpəʊˌɪt/ [n C] someone who writes
poems: *the French poet Rimbaud*

12 a place where you can get books

bookshop BRITISH **bookstore** AMERICAN
/ˈbʊkʃɒp, ˈbʊkstɔːr|-ʃɑːp-/ [n C] a shop that
sells books

library /ˈlaɪbrəri|-breri/ [n C] a place that
has a lot of books that you can borrow for
a short time, usually without paying
money: *the college library*

BORING/BORED

➡ opposite **INTERESTING/INTERESTED**

⚠ Don't confuse **boring** and **bored**.
If something is **boring**, it is not interesting.
If you feel **bored**, you are not interested
in something, or you have nothing
interesting to do.

1 boring jobs, books, films, activities etc

boring /ˈbɔːrɪŋ/ [adj] something that is **boring** is not interesting in any way and makes
you feel tired: *a boring job in an office* | *a
long boring lecture on economic plan-
ning* | *I thought the party was really
boring.* | *What a boring way to spend an
evening!*

⚠ Be careful not to say 'I am boring'
when you mean 'I am bored'.

not very interesting /nɒt veri
ˈɪntrˌstɪŋ/ ESPECIALLY SPOKEN very ordinary,
and not really interesting or enjoyable:
*Did you watch that TV show about
Prince Charles? It wasn't very interest-
ing, was it?* | *There was nothing very*

interesting in the local newspaper – just the usual stuff.

monotonous /məˈnɒtənəs‖məˈnɑː-/ [adj] something that is **monotonous** is boring because it always continues in the same way and it never changes

monotonous work/job/routine a monotonous factory job

monotonous sound/voice/rhythm The teacher's low monotonous voice almost sent me to sleep.

tedious /ˈtiːdiəs/ [adj] something that is **tedious** is boring and tiring because it continues for too long: a tedious journey | Doing all those calculations without a computer would be extremely tedious.

bore /bɔːʳ/ [v T] to make someone feel bored, for example by talking too much about the same thing: Am I boring you?

bore sb with sth He bores everyone with his constant talk about computers.

bore sb to death/to tears INFORMAL (=make someone very bored) Being alone with a baby all day bored her to tears.

2 boring people

boring /ˈbɔːrɪŋ/ [adj] someone who is **boring** never says or does anything interesting: He's so boring – all he ever talks about is football. | Diana's nice enough. A bit boring though.

dull /dʌl/ [adj] someone who is **dull** is not unpleasant, but their life and their conversation is never interesting or exciting: Our neighbours are OK, I suppose, but they're so dull! | I'm afraid I must seem very dull compared with all those interesting people you meet.

bore /bɔːʳ/ [n C usually singular] a boring person who talks too much about themselves and about the things that they are interested in: At parties she always gets stuck with some bore who wants to tell her the story of his life.

3 boring places

boring /ˈbɔːrɪŋ/ [adj] not at all interesting or exciting to live in: This is such a boring town – there is nothing to do in the evenings. | It's so boring here. I wish we lived in New York!

dead /ded/ [adj not before noun] a town that is **dead** is boring because nothing

exciting happens and there is nothing interesting to do: In summer we get a few visitors, but most of the time this place is dead. | It's absolutely dead here when all the students go away for the summer vacation.

○**nothing ever happens** /ˌnʌθɪŋ evəʳ ˈhæpənz/ SPOKEN if you say that **nothing ever happens** in a place, you mean that nothing interesting or exciting happens there: Nothing ever happens around here. Why can't we move to the city?

dreary /ˈdrɪəri/ [adj] a **dreary** place is one where there is nothing attractive or cheerful to see: I was sent to yet another dreary government office. | Laurie gazed out over a dreary landscape of factories and waste ground.

dreary – drearier – dreariest

> ⚠ Use **dreary** when you are writing stories and descriptions.

4 when you feel bored

bored /bɔːʳd/ [adj] tired and impatient, either because you are doing something that you are not interested in, or because you have nothing to do: Dad, can we go home now? I'm bored! | gangs of bored teenagers wandering around the streets

get bored She seems to get bored very easily.

bored with doing sth Julia soon got bored with lying on the beach.

+ with I'm bored with pasta and tomatoes – let's have something else for a change.

bored to tears/bored stiff INFORMAL (=extremely bored) There's nothing to do here – I'm bored stiff!

> ⚠ Be careful not to say 'I am boring' when you mean 'I am bored'.

○**fed up** /ˌfed ˈʌp/ ESPECIALLY SPOKEN bored and annoyed with something that has continued for too long: Her husband's out working all the time, and she's really fed up.

+ with We were getting the same computer problems every day, and we were all fed up with it.

fed up with doing sth *I'm fed up with listening to her complaints the whole time.*
get fed up *When you have to stay in and study every night you just get fed up with it.*

be tired of sth/be sick of sth /biː ˈtaɪəʳd ɒv (sth), biː ˈsɪk ɒv (sth)/ to feel very annoyed and impatient with a situation that has continued for too long, or with a person who has done something for too long: *We're always arguing, and I'm just tired of it. | I'm really sick of him – he's always criticizing.*

be tired/sick of doing sth *People are tired of hearing politicians make promises that they never keep. | Do it yourself – I'm sick of cleaning up after you!*
get tired/sick of sth *He couldn't make a decision, and I got tired of waiting.*

> ⚠ Don't say 'very tired of something' or 'very sick of something'. Say **really tired of something** or **really sick of something**.

have had enough /həv ˌhæd ɪˈnʌf/ to be so bored with something that has continued for a long time that you decide to leave, do something different, or change the situation: *After 10 years of teaching, Allan has had enough.*

have had enough of (doing) sth *I'd had enough of living abroad, and I wanted to go home to England.*

5 the feeling of being bored

boredom /ˈbɔːʳdəm/ [n U] the feeling you have when you are bored: *an unbearable feeling of loneliness and boredom*
out of boredom (=because of boredom) *She says she started having affairs with other men out of boredom.*
relieve the boredom (=make a situation less boring) *Sometimes, we would play cards, just to relieve the boredom.*

BORN

➡ see also **BABY**

1 to be born

be born /biː ˈbɔːʳn/ a baby **is born** when it comes out of its mother's body and begins its life: *Until recently most babies were born at home.*

born in July/in 1961 etc (=in a particular month or year) *James was born in 1984.*
born on February 8th/29th August etc (=on a particular day) *Katie was born on 23rd of May, 1992.*
born in Russia/Texas/Oxford etc *Jodie was born in a small town in Nebraska.*

> ⚠ Don't say 'I borned' or 'I have been born'. Say **I was born**.

come from/be from /ˈkʌm frɒm, biː frɒm/ [phrasal verb T] if you **come from** or **are from** a particular country, area, or town, you were born there or spent the early part of your life there: *We live in California now, but we're from Boston originally. | "Where do you come from?" "Bari, in southern Italy."*

2 the place where you were born

home town /ˌhəʊm ˈtaʊn/ [n C] the town where you were born or where you spent the early part of your life: *She left her home town of Glasgow at the age of 18, and never returned.*

place of birth /ˌpleɪs əv ˈbɜːʳθ/ WRITTEN the town where you were born – used especially in official documents: *Please write your name, address, and place of birth on the form.*

birthplace /ˈbɜːʳθpleɪs/ [n C] the place where a famous person was born
+ of *The city of Assisi is known as the birthplace of St Francis.*

BORROW

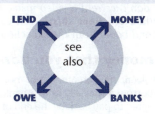

> ⚠ Be careful not to use **borrow** when you mean **lend**. You **lend** money, your car etc to someone (=you let them have it), but you **borrow** it from someone (=they let you have it). Don't say 'she borrowed me her car'. Say **she lent me her car.**

B

1 to borrow something

borrow /'bɒrəʊ‖'baː-, 'bɔː-/ [v I/T] if you **borrow** something from someone, they let you have it, and you agree to give it back to them later: *Can I borrow your calculator – I left mine at home.* | *She asked if she could borrow 50 cents to get a coffee.*
borrow sth from sb *I'm always borrowing books from the library and forgetting to return them.* | *Rwanda has applied to borrow $12 million from the World Bank.*
borrow heavily (=borrow a lot of money from a bank or financial organization) *Companies that borrowed heavily in the 80s are now having trouble paying their debts.*

2 to pay money to use someone else's car, house, equipment etc

rent /rent/ [v T] to pay money to use a house, office, shop etc that belongs to someone else
rent a house/apartment/building/office/room *They are renting an apartment near the park.* | *Marlowe rented a small office in downtown Los Angeles.*
rent sth from sb *When I was a student I rented a flat from an agency.*
  rented [adj] *During the shooting of the movie, Neeson stayed in a rented house in Beverley Hills.*

rent (also **hire** BRITISH) /rent, haɪəʳ/ [v T] to pay money to use a car, piece of equipment etc for a short period of time: *We hired a car at the airport and drove to our hotel.* | *I don't feel like going out – why don't we rent a video instead?*
rent/hire sth from sb/sth *You can hire skis and boots from the ski school.*

3 money that you borrow

loan /ləʊn/ [n C] an amount of money that you borrow, especially from a bank, which you agree to pay back by the end of a period of time: *If you need more money, we can arrange a loan.*
a £5000/$20,000 loan *The organization asked for a $2 million loan to plant new trees in the rainforest.*
take out a loan (=get a loan) *We took out a loan to buy a new car.*

pay off/repay a loan (=finish paying back what you borrowed) *It will take over three years to repay the loan.*
bank loan (=money you borrow from a bank)

mortgage /'mɔːʳgɪdʒ/ [n C] an amount of money that you borrow from a bank or a company in order to buy a house or apartment; **mortgages** are usually paid back by regular payments over a long period: *In 1994/5 the average mortgage was £35,000.*
pay the mortgage (=make regular payments to pay it back) *Some months we only just have enough to pay the mortgage.*
a mortgage on a house/apartment (=the money you have borrowed to buy it) *They have a large mortgage on their home in Central Park West.*
a £60,000/$85,000 mortgage (=the amount of money you have borrowed)
take out a mortgage (=get a mortgage) *I didn't want to take out a mortgage until I had a steady job.*

BRAVE/NOT BRAVE

➡ see also **DESCRIBING PEOPLE**

1 not afraid when you are in a dangerous or frightening situation

brave /breɪv/ [adj] someone who is **brave** does not show that they are afraid in a frightening situation or when they have to do something dangerous, painful, or unpleasant: *You have to be very brave to be a firefighter.* | *a brave rescue attempt* | *Your husband is a very brave man.*
ᐤbe brave (=behave bravely) SPOKEN *This may hurt a little, so be brave!*
it is brave of sb to do sth *It was very brave of you to tell her the truth.*
  bravely /'breɪvli/ [adv] *soldiers who fought bravely for their country*

courageous /kəˈreɪdʒəs/ [adj] ESPECIALLY WRITTEN someone who is **courageous** behaves very bravely, often for a long period, especially when they are fighting for something they believe in or suffering great pain: *Throughout his life, he was a courageous fighter for justice.* | *She died* *yesterday, after a long and courageous battle with cancer.*

   courageously [adv] *Slovo had courageously opposed apartheid for over 20 years.*

daring /'deərɪŋ/ [adj] someone who is **daring** is not afraid of taking risks, and seems to like doing dangerous things: *The daring Danish sailor, Bering, reached Alaska in 1741.* | *a daring attack on an enemy village*

hero /'hɪərəʊ/ [n C] a man who is remembered and admired for doing something very brave: *a famous war hero*
   plural **heroes**

heroine /'herəʊɪn/ [n C] a woman who is remembered and admired for doing something very brave: *a heroine of the resistance movement*

2 not afraid to do something new and different

daring /'deərɪŋ/ [adj] someone who is **daring** is not afraid of doing something new, unusual, or shocking, especially in areas such as art, fashion, and design: *Many architects copied Nash's new and daring style.* | *The more daring girls would wear short skirts and smoke cigarettes.*

bold /bəʊld/ [adj] not afraid of making big changes or taking difficult decisions: *The company needs a strong leader, who is bold enough to make some tough decisions.* | *bold new policies for reviving the inner-city areas*

3 to be brave enough to do something

dare /deər/ [v I] to be brave enough to do something that most people would be too frightened to do: *You can also go hang-gliding or bungee-jumping, if you dare.*
   dare to do sth *She was the only one who dared to stand up and ask questions.*

> ⚠ **Dare** is not usually used in positive sentences. Don't say 'he dared to tell them the truth'. It is more usual to say something like 'he wasn't afraid to tell them the truth', or 'he was brave enough to tell them the truth'.

have the guts/have the nerve

/ˌhæv ðə 'gʌts, ˌhæv ðə 'nɜːʳv/ INFORMAL to be brave enough to do something very difficult or unpleasant

   have the guts/nerve to do sth *OK, she made a mistake, but at least she had the guts to admit it!* | *Few of her colleagues would have had the nerve to contradict her.*

4 the ability to behave bravely

courage /'kʌrɪdʒ‖'kɜː-/ [n U] the ability to behave bravely and calmly in a situation where most people would be afraid or would lose confidence: *Martha showed great courage during her long illness.*

   have the courage to do sth *Not many people had the courage to speak out against Stalin.*

   it takes courage to do sth (=you need courage to do something) *It must have taken a lot of courage for her to admit that she had an alcohol problem.*

bravery /'breɪvəri/ [n U] when you behave bravely in a war or in a situation where your life is in danger: *Both sides fought with great bravery.* | *Two police officers received medals for bravery.*

guts /gʌts/ [n plural] INFORMAL someone who has **guts** is brave enough to do something difficult or dangerous, and you admire them for it: *You need guts and determination to succeed in motor racing.*

   it takes guts to do sth (=you need to be brave to do something) *It took a lot of guts to get up and speak in front of all those people.*

5 not brave

coward /'kaʊəʳd/ [n C] someone who is not brave enough to do something dangerous or unpleasant that they ought to do: *He wrote her a letter to say he was leaving – he was too much of a coward to tell her in person.* | *If you refused to fight, you were accused of being a coward.*

cowardly /'kaʊəʳdli/ [adj] not brave – use this especially when someone is not brave enough to accept the unpleasant results of a situation they have caused: *I really wanted to accept the new job, but I was too cowardly to tell my boss.* | *The* *bombing was described as 'a cowardly attack on completely innocent citizens'. | He was a weak, cowardly man.*

> ⚠ Remember that **coward** is a noun and **cowardly** is an adjective.

Qwimp /wɪmp/ [*n* C] SPOKEN INFORMAL someone that you do not respect because they are afraid to do something that is a little difficult or unpleasant: *Don't be such a wimp! Just tell her you want to go out with her.*

6 to not be brave enough to do something

not dare /nɒt ˈdeəʳ/ to not be brave enough to do something: *My sister used to steal things from the store, but I never dared.*

not dare to do sth/not dare do sth *I wouldn't dare do a parachute jump, would you? | We stood outside the old house, not daring to go in.*

hardly dare (=almost not dare) *The children were all frightened of Mrs Gates, and hardly dared even to speak to her.*

lose your nerve /ˌluːz jɔːʳ ˈnɜːʳv/ to suddenly lose the confidence that you need in order to do something difficult or dangerous: *At the top of the ski slope I lost my nerve. | Jane went to the police right away, before she lost her nerve.*

Qwimp out /ˌwɪmp ˈaʊt/ [*phrasal verb* I] SPOKEN INFORMAL to not be brave enough to do something you intended to do or said you would do: *We've come all this way to talk to her – you can't wimp out now.*

wimp out of (doing) sth *I bet he wimps out of giving that speech tomorrow.*

BREAK

BROKEN
DELIBERATELY
DAMAGE
see also
REPAIR
DESTROY
ACCIDENT
HURT/INJURE
ACCIDENTALLY

1 object/window/plate/cup etc

break /breɪk/ [*v* I/T] if something **breaks**, or if you **break** it, it separates into two or more pieces because it has been hit, dropped, or bent: *He dropped the vase and it broke. | I'm sorry, but I've broken one of your plates.*

get broken (=be broken accidentally) *A few of the cups got broken when we moved to the new house.*

break (sth) in two/break (sth) in half (=into two fairly equal pieces) *A tile came off the roof and broke in two as it hit the ground. | I broke the chocolate in half and gave a piece to my brother.*

breaking – broke – have broken

crack /kræk/ [*v* I/T] if a window, plate, cup etc **cracks**, or if you **crack** it, it becomes damaged and lines appear in its surface: *I put one of the wine glasses in hot water and it cracked. | A stone hit the car window and cracked it.*

smash /smæʃ/ [*v* I/T] if something **smashes**, or if you **smash** it, it breaks into pieces because it has been dropped, thrown, or hit, and it makes a loud noise: *I heard something smash in the kitchen. Dad must have dropped a dish or something. | They*

smash

He smashed two plates while washing up.

smashed the display window and grabbed $4000 worth of gold jewelry.

be smashed to pieces/bits *Their little boat hit the rocks and was smashed to bits.*

smash (sth) to pieces/bits *The bottle fell off the table and smashed to pieces on the floor.*

shatter

A stone bounced up and shattered the windscreen.

shatter /'ʃætər/ [v I/T] if a window, plate, mirror etc **shatters**, or if something **shatters** it, it breaks into very many small pieces, making a loud noise: *A big water jug slid off the table and shattered into a thousand pieces as it hit the floor.* | *The huge blast shattered office windows 500 metres away.*

2 machine/camera/ television etc

break /breɪk/ [v T] if you **break** a machine, camera etc, you damage it so that it does not work any more: *"Can I use your camera, Dad?" "OK, but be careful you don't break it."* | *If you turn the key too hard, you might break the lock.*

breaking – broke – have broken

3 paper/clothes/things made of cloth

⚠ Don't use **break** about paper, clothes, and things made of cloth.

tear /teər/ [v T] to pull paper or cloth apart, or to accidentally make a hole in it: *She unwrapped the present carefully, trying not to tear the paper.* | *Mark had torn his jacket climbing over a fence.*

tear

Crying bitterly, she tore up his letter.

tear up sth/tear sth up (=tear it into many pieces) *Crying bitterly, she tore up his letter.*
tear sth in half (=tear it into two pieces) *He took my ticket and tore it in half.*

tearing – tore – have torn

4 a bone in your body

break /breɪk/ [v T] to break or crack a bone in your body
break your arm/leg/ankle *Nicola broke her leg when she went skiing.*

breaking – broke – have broken

fracture /'fræktʃər/ [v T] to damage a bone in your body so that a line appears along it
fracture your skull/leg/ribs *The X-ray showed that he had fractured his skull.*

⚠ **Fracture** is the usual medical word that is used when someone breaks a bone in their body.

5 ball/tyre/water pipe etc

⚠ Don't use **break** about a ball, tyre, or water pipe.

burst /bɜːrst/ [v I] if a tyre, ball, pipe etc **bursts**, it breaks open, and air, gas, or liquid comes out: *One of the front tyres burst, causing the car to swerve and crash.* | *Thousands of gallons of oil flowed into the river when an oil pipeline burst.*

bursting – burst – have burst

blow /bləʊ/ [v I] AMERICAN if a tyre **blows**, it breaks open suddenly and all the air comes out of it: *One of the tires blew and we skidded off the freeway.*

6 when part of something is broken from the main part

break off /ˌbreɪk 'ɒf‖-'ɔːf/ [phrasal verb I/T] if something **breaks off**, or if you **break** it **off**, it becomes separated from the thing that it was fixed to, by being pulled very hard: *The wing of the plane broke off in the storm, and all 98 people on board were killed.* | *Don't turn the knob too far – you might break it off.*

come off /ˌkʌm 'ɒf‖-'ɔːf/ [phrasal verb I] if something **comes off**, it accidentally becomes separated from the thing that it is fixed to, because it is not fastened firmly enough: *Can you fix the door? The handle has come off.*
come off sth *Look, there's something in the road. It looks as if a wheel has come off a car.*

7 easily broken

fragile /'frædʒaɪl‖-dʒəl/ [adj] a **fragile** object is not strong, and can be easily broken or damaged: *Be careful with those glasses – they're fragile.* | *The package was marked FRAGILE – HANDLE WITH CARE.*

When you see **EC**, go to the **ESSENTIAL COMMUNICATION** section.

B

BREATHE

1 to breathe

breathe /briːð/ [v I] to take air into your lungs and send it out again through your nose or mouth: *The air was so smoky it was difficult to breathe.* | *The boy was unconscious, but he was still breathing.*
breathe deeply (=slowly take a lot of air into your lungs) *I want you to breathe deeply and relax.*

⚠️ Don't confuse **breathe** (verb) and **breath** (noun).

breathe in /ˌbriːð ˈɪn/ [phrasal verb I/T] to take air into your lungs, through your nose or mouth: *My chest hurts every time I breathe in.*
breathe in air/fumes etc *They stood on the cliff breathing in the fresh sea air.*

breathe out /ˌbriːð ˈaʊt/ [phrasal verb I] to send air out of your lungs, through your nose or mouth: *The doctor told him to breathe in, then breathe out slowly.*

blow /bləʊ/ [v I] to make air come out of your mouth quickly, with your lips close together: *I blew as hard as I could, but couldn't get a sound out of the trumpet.*
+ on/into *She blew on her coffee to cool it.*
blowing – blew – have blown

2 the action of breathing

breathing /ˈbriːðɪŋ/ [n U] when you breathe in and out – use this especially to talk about whether someone is breathing easily or with difficulty: *Breathing became more difficult as we got higher up the mountain.* | *She bent over the crib and listened to her baby's breathing.*

breath /breθ/ [n U] the air that you breathe out: *Their breath looked like smoke in the cold air.* | *I could feel the horse's breath on the back of my neck.*
hold your breath (=stop yourself from breathing for a short time) *I can swim underwater, but I can't hold my breath for very long.*
bad breath (=breath that smells unpleasant) *His teeth were rotten and he had bad breath.*

3 to breathe noisily

sniff /snɪf/ [v I] to breathe in noisily through your nose, especially because you have a cold or because you are crying: *Stop sniffing! Use your handkerchief.*
sniffing – sniffed – have sniffed

snore /snɔːr/ [v I] to breathe very noisily when you are asleep: *If you snore it's better not to sleep on your back.*
snoring [n U] when someone snores: *Does your partner's snoring keep you awake?*

sigh /saɪ/ [v I] to breathe in and out noisily, either because you are disappointed, tired, or sad, or because you can begin to relax after worrying about something
sigh deeply *My father put his head in his hands and sighed deeply.*
sigh with relief (=because you no longer have to worry) *"Thank God that's over," she said, sighing with relief.*

sigh /saɪ/ [n C] the action of sighing, or the sound you make when you sigh: *"Oh no!" he said with a sigh, "Not again!"*
breathe/give a sigh of relief *Irene closed the door behind her and breathed a big sigh of relief.*

gasp /ɡɑːsp‖ɡæsp/ [v I/T] to suddenly breathe in noisily, with your mouth open, because you are surprised, shocked, or in pain: *The crowd gasped as the plane burst into flames.*
gasp with amazement/shock/pain etc *One of the boys hit him in the face, and he gasped with pain.*

gasp /ɡɑːsp‖ɡæsp/ [n C] the sound you make when you gasp
gasp of astonishment/pain/admiration etc *There were gasps of astonishment from the audience.*

4 to breathe with difficulty

breathless/out of breath /ˈbreθləs, ˌaʊt əv ˈbreθ/ if you are **breathless** or **out of breath**, it is difficult to breathe, because you have just been running, climbing etc: *Do you get breathless going up and down stairs?* | *By the time we reached the top of the hill, we were all out of breath.*

pant /pænt/ [v I] to breathe loudly, with your mouth open, for example because you have been running: *Matt was still panting after his run.* | *The dog was panting in the heat.*

gasping for breath /ˌgɑːspɪŋ fəʳ ˈbreθ‖ˌgæsp-/ breathing very quickly and with great difficulty: *His mother was coughing and gasping for breath.*

5 to start to breathe normally again after running, playing sport etc

get your breath back /ˌget jɔːʳ ˈbreθ bæk/ to start to breathe normally again after you have been running, playing sport etc: *I need to stop a minute, just to get my breath back.* | *We'll wait till you've got your breath back.*

6 when you cannot breathe

can't breathe /ˌkɑːnt ˈbriːð‖ˌkænt-/ when you feel as though you cannot breathe: *I couldn't breathe in there – there were too many people.* | *The worst thing about asthma is the feeling that you can't breathe.*

choke /tʃəʊk/ [v I] if you **choke**, you cannot breathe because there is something in your throat that stops the air going into your lungs: *Do something – he's choking!* | *The car fumes made her choke.*
+ on *Scott died after choking on a chicken bone.*

suffocate /ˈsʌfəkeɪt/ [v I] to die because there is not enough air to breathe: *Many of the birds had suffocated in their boxes.* | *It was very hot inside the car, and I felt as though I was suffocating.*
suffocation /ˌsʌfəˈkeɪʃən/ [n U] when someone dies by suffocating: *Glue-sniffing carries the risk of suffocation.*

BRIGHT/ NOT BRIGHT

➡ for bright colours, go to
COLOUR/COLOR
➡ see also **SHINE, LIGHT, DARK**

1 bright light

bright /braɪt/ [adj] a **bright** light shines strongly: *From the top of the hill they could*

see the bright lights of the city below them. | *We set off in bright sunshine.*
brightly [adv] *The fire was burning brightly now.* | *a brightly lit hall*
brightness [n U] *She closed her eyes against the brightness of the sun.*

strong /strɒŋ‖strɔːŋ/ [adj] a **strong** light is very bright and it helps you to see things clearly: *The light from the flashlight wasn't strong enough to read by.* | *The colours had faded after years of being exposed to strong sunlight.*

blazing /ˈbleɪzɪŋ/ [adj only before noun] very bright – use this about the sun, or about lights that you can see from a long way away: *Tom went out to look for her in the blazing Mexican sun.* | *The blazing lights of the casino shone out across the bay.*

dazzling /ˈdæzəlɪŋ/ [adj] a **dazzling** light is so bright that it hurts your eyes: *We emerged from the cinema into dazzling sunshine.*

blinding /ˈblaɪndɪŋ/ [adj] a **blinding** light is so bright that you cannot see for a short time after you have looked at it: *There was a blinding flash and then a loud bang.*

2 a bright place

bright /braɪt/ [adj] a **bright** place is full of light, especially in a way that seems pleasant and attractive: *The kitchen was always bright and cheerful.* | *Claire had a nice bright bedroom which was decorated in yellow and white.*

well-lit /ˌwel ˈlɪt◄/ [adj] a **well-lit** place is bright because there are electric lights, so it is easy for you to see what you are doing: *She always tried to park in a well-lit area at night.* | *To avoid eye problems, make sure that your desk is well-lit.*

light /laɪt/ [adj] a **light** building or room has plenty of light in it, especially because it has big windows: *The kitchen is light and airy, with a fantastic view.*

3 not bright

dim /dɪm/ [adj] **dim** light is not very bright and makes it difficult for you to see: *I struggled to read by the dim light of the fire.*

dim – dimmer – dimmest

soft /sɒft‖sɔːft/ [adj only before noun] **soft** light is not too bright, in a way that is pleasant and relaxing: *In the soft evening light Sonia looked ten years younger.* | *The restaurant has a romantic atmosphere, with soft lights and background music.*

BROKEN

➡ opposite WORKING

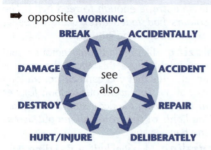

BREAK
ACCIDENTALLY
DAMAGE
see also
ACCIDENT
DESTROY
REPAIR
HURT/INJURE
DELIBERATELY

1 objects/cups/furniture/ clothes etc

broken /ˈbrəʊkən/ [adj] something that is **bro-ken** has become sepa-rated into pieces, for example by being hit or dropped: *The floor was covered in broken glass.* | *The old suit-case is no good – the handle's broken.* | *In the hut there was an old table and a couple of broken chairs.*

broken

cracked /krækt/ [adj] something that is **cracked** has a line on its surface where it is slightly damaged – use this especially about cups, plates, and things made of glass: *There was nothing in the cupboard except for a couple of old cracked cups.* | *The tiles were old and cracked.*

cracked

torn /tɔːrn/ [adj] **torn** paper, clothes, curtains etc have been damaged and have holes in them: *teenagers in torn jeans* | *a thick book with a torn green cover* | *The cover on the bed was torn in several places.*

torn

His jacket was old and torn.

2 broken bones

broken /ˈbrəʊkən/ [adj] a **broken** arm, leg etc has been damaged so that its main bone is cracked or has separated into two or more pieces; a **broken** bone has been cracked or separated into pieces: *One little boy had a broken arm.* | *I think my ankle's broken.*

fractured /ˈfræktʃərd/ [adj] a **fractured** bone has been cracked, but it has not completely separated: *The X-ray revealed that she had several fractured ribs.*

⚠ **Broken** is more common than **fractured**, which is the usual medical word.

3 buildings that are in bad condition

The old church is falling down.

be falling down /biː ˌfɔːlɪŋ ˈdaʊn/ if a building or wall **is falling down**, it is in very bad condition and many parts of it are broken: *The old church is falling down.*

crumbling /ˈkrʌmblɪŋ/ [adj] a **crumbling** building or wall has small pieces of stone, brick etc falling from it and it is in very bad condition, especially because it is very old: *the crumbling walls of a medieval castle*

4 machines, cars, phones etc that do not work

not working/doesn't work /nɒt ˈwɜːrkɪŋ, ˌdʌzənt ˈwɜːrk/ ESPECIALLY SPOKEN if a machine or piece of equipment is **not working** or **doesn't work**, it does not do the job it is supposed to do: *The dish-washer's not working.* | *Do you know your brake lights aren't working?* | *Take* the camera back to the store if it doesn't work.

⟨there's something wrong with /ðeərz ˌsʌmθɪŋ ˈrɒŋ wɪð‖-ˈrɔːŋ-/ ESPECIALLY SPOKEN if **there is something wrong with** a machine, car etc, it does not work properly, but you do not know exactly why: *There's something wrong with my car. I think it might be the battery.* | *There was something wrong with the photocopier, so we called in the service company.*

broken /ˈbrəʊkən/ [adj] not working – use this especially about small machines or equipment: *I think your doorbell's broken – I couldn't hear it ringing.* | *a broken watch*

out of order /ˌaʊt əv ˈɔːrdər/ not working – use this about machines in public places: *Every phone I tried was out of order.* | *The toilets were out of order.*

faulty /ˈfɔːlti/ [adj] something that is **faulty**, especially a piece of electrical equipment, is not working properly and may be dangerous: *Fires in the home are often caused by faulty electrical equipment.* | *Faulty traffic lights caused traffic jams on the A660 this morning.*

5 to stop working

His car broke down on the way to work.

break down /ˌbreɪk ˈdaʊn/ [phrasal verb I] if a car, bus, train, or large machine **breaks down**, it stops working completely: *I took the bus because my car broke down.* | *The escalators are always breaking down and it's hard work going up all those stairs.*

go wrong /ˌgəʊ ˈrɒŋ‖-ˈrɔːŋ/ to stop working normally – use this especially about complicated equipment, when you do not know what the problem is: *The television went wrong yesterday evening.* | *He said that if anything goes wrong, they'll send a repairman out.*

+ with *Something keeps going wrong with the heating system.*

crash /kræʃ/ [v I] if a computer **crashes**, it suddenly stops working, and information is often lost because of this: *The network crashed and we lost half a day's work.*

B

BUILD

➡ see also **DESIGN, HOUSES/WHERE PEOPLE LIVE**

1 to build something

build /bɪld/ [v T] **build a house/church/ school/road/bridge etc** to make a house, church etc using bricks, stone, wood, or other materials: *Our house was built in the early 1930s.* | *The Romans built roads all over Europe.* | *The cost of building the new football stadium was over £3 million.*
built of concrete/stone/wood etc *In those days most of the houses were built of wood, and were easily destroyed by fire.*
building – built – have built

building /ˈbɪldɪŋ/ [n C] something that has walls and a roof, for example a house, an office, or a church: *The church is one of the oldest buildings in the city.* | *a brand new office building in the centre of Tokyo*

builder /ˈbɪldər/ [n C] someone whose job is to build houses, offices etc: *The church roof is being repaired by a local builder.*

2 the design of buildings

architecture /ˈɑːrkɪtektʃər/ [n U] the way in which buildings are designed, or the work of designing buildings: *We spent the afternoon walking around Rome, admiring the architecture.* | *The City Hall is a fine example of Gothic architecture.* | *She studied architecture at university.*

architect /ˈɑːrkɪtekt/ [n C] someone whose job is to design buildings: *St Paul's Cathedral was designed by the famous architect, Sir Christopher Wren.*

When you see **EC**, go to the **ESSENTIAL COMMUNICATION** section.

BURN

FIRE
DESTROY   HOT

see
also

KILL   EXPLODE

HURT/INJURE   ACCIDENT

1 to burn something

burn /bɜːᵊn/ [v T] to damage or destroy something with fire or heat: *She lit a fire and burned his letters one by one.*
  badly burned *Their furniture was badly burned in the fire.*
  burn a hole in sth (=make a hole by burning it) *Someone had dropped a cigarette and burned a hole in the carpet.*
  burning – burned (also **burnt** BRITISH) – **have burned** (also **have burnt** BRITISH)
    burned/burnt [adj] *The cake is slightly burnt, I'm afraid.* | *The kitchen smelled of burned toast.*

> ⚠ Don't use **burn** when you want to say that someone destroys a building. Use **burn down**.

burn down /ˌbɜːᵊn ˈdaʊn/ [phrasal verb T] to completely destroy a building by burning it
  burn down sth *Police believe students were responsible for burning down the school.*
  burn sth down *Her ex-husband threatened to burn the house down with her and the kids inside.*

scorch /skɔːᵊtʃ/ [v T] to burn the surface of something and make a dark mark on it: *The stone walls were still scorched and blackened from the fire.* | *I scorched my shirt when I was ironing.*

2 to burn yourself

burn /bɜːᵊn/ [v T] if you **burn** yourself, you hurt yourself by accidentally touching something hot
  burn yourself *Don't touch the iron. You'll burn yourself.*
  burn your hand/leg/mouth etc *The soup was so hot it burnt my mouth.*

badly burned *Jerry was badly burned in the explosion.*
burning – burned (also **burnt** BRITISH) – **have burned** (also **have burnt** BRITISH)

scald /skɔːld/ [v T] to burn yourself with hot liquid
  scald yourself *Careful with the hot water – you'll scald yourself.*

burn /bɜːᵊn/ [n C usually plural] a mark on your skin where you have been burned
  severe/serious burns *Billy was taken to the hospital with severe burns.*
  minor burns (=not very serious)

3 to make something start burning

set fire to sth/set sth on fire /ˌset ˈfaɪəʳ tuː (sth), ˌset (sth) ɒn ˈfaɪəʳ/ to make something start to burn, so that it gets damaged: *Vandals set fire to an empty warehouse near the docks last night.* | *Don't put up the barbeque there – you might set fire to the trees.* | *Rioters set cars on fire and attacked the police.*

light /laɪt/ [v T] **light a cigarette/fire/candle** to make a cigarette, fire etc start to burn: *Ricky sat down and lit a cigarette.* | *We searched around for twigs and fallen branches, so we could light a fire.*
  lighting – lit – have lit

4 to make something stop burning

put out /ˌpʊt ˈaʊt/ [phrasal verb T] to make a fire stop burning, or make a cigarette, pipe etc stop burning
  put out the fire/the blaze *It took firefighters four hours to put out the blaze.*
  put out a cigarette/pipe *I put out my cigarette and went back into the house.*
  put sth out *She threw sand on the fire to put it out.*

extinguish /ɪkˈstɪŋgwɪʃ/ [v T] FORMAL to make a fire stop burning, or make a cigarette stop burning – used especially in official notices and requests: *Would all passengers please extinguish their cigarettes? Thank you.* | *He managed to extinguish the flames with his coat.*

blow out /ˌbləʊ ˈaʊt/ [phrasal verb T] to make a flame or fire stop burning by blowing on it

blow out a candle/a match/a fire *He blew out the candle and went to sleep.*
blow sth out *We tried to light a fire but the wind kept blowing it out.*

5 when something is burning

burn /bɜːʳn/ [v I] to produce flames and heat: *They could smell wood burning in the yard.* | *At one end of the room a coal fire burned brightly.*

burning – burned (also **burnt** BRITISH) –
have burned (also **have burnt** BRITISH)

    burning [adj only before noun] *He escaped by jumping from the fourth floor of a burning apartment block.*

be on fire /biː ɒn 'faɪəʳ/ if a building, vehicle, or piece of clothing **is on fire**, it is burning: *The whole house was on fire by the time the firefighters arrived.*

burn down /ˌbɜːʳn 'daʊn/ [phrasal verb I] if a building **burns down**, it is completely destroyed by fire: *The hotel burned down in 1990.*

blazing /'bleɪzɪŋ/ [adj only before noun] a **blazing** fire, building etc is producing a lot of flames and heat while it burns: *We sat in front of a blazing log fire.* | *An old woman was rescued from the blazing house by a neighbour.*

smoulder BRITISH **smolder** AMERICAN /'sməʊldəʳ/ [v I] to burn slowly, producing smoke but no flames: *A cigarette was smoldering in the ashtray.* | *The remains of the fire still smouldered in the grate.*

6 when something starts burning

catch fire /ˌkætʃ 'faɪəʳ/ to start burning accidentally: *Two farm workers died when a barn caught fire yesterday.* | *The car turned over, but luckily it didn't catch fire.*

burst into flames /ˌbɜːʳst ɪntə 'fleɪmz/ to suddenly start burning and produce a lot of flames that cause serious damage: *The plane burst into flames on the runway.*

go up in flames /ˌgəʊ ʌp ɪn 'fleɪmz/ if a building or vehicle **goes up in flames**, it starts burning and is destroyed by fire: *If*
the firefighters hadn't arrived when they did, the whole place might have gone up in flames.*

break out /ˌbreɪk 'aʊt/ [phrasal verb I] if a fire **breaks out**, it starts burning accidentally and spreads very quickly: *£200,000 worth of damage was caused when fire broke out in a hospital storeroom.*

7 something that burns easily

flammable /'flæməbəl/ [adj] **flammable** chemicals, gases, and other materials burn easily and quickly and are therefore dangerous: *Caution! Flammable substances.*
highly flammable (=extremely flammable) *Petrol is highly flammable.*

BUSINESS

1 the work that companies do

business /'bɪznɪs/ [n U] the work that companies do when they buy and sell goods and services: *Business in Europe has been badly affected by bad economic conditions.*
on business (=when someone goes somewhere for business reasons) *She'll be back next week – she's in Korea on business.*
the advertising/computer/insurance business (=the work of companies that are involved in advertising etc)

> ⚠ You can also use **business** before a noun, like an adjective: *a business meeting* | *studying at business school*

> ⚠ Don't confuse **business** [U] (=when you buy and sell goods) with a **business** [C] (=a company).

trade /treɪd/ [n U] the activity of buying and selling large quantities of goods, especially between one country and another: *the GATT agreement to encourage world trade*
+ with/between *During the war, trade between the two countries was suspended.* | *There used to be restrictions on trade with South Africa.*
the fur/arms/diamond trade (=the buying and selling of fur, weapons etc)
trade in rice/textiles/gold etc (=the buying and selling of rice, cloth etc)

⚠ You can also use **trade** before a noun, like an adjective: *a trade agreement between China and the US*

industry /ˈɪndəstri/ [n C/U] the production of goods to be sold, especially in factories: *The region has tried to attract new industry in order to reduce unemployment.*
steel/textile/automobile/manufacturing industry *the decline in Britain's iron and steel industries*
in industry (=in this area of work) *She left the nursing profession and got a job in industry.*
heavy industry (=the production of oil, metals, and coal, and of large goods such as cars and aircraft)
light industry (=the production of goods such as kitchen equipment, TVs, and computers)
plural **industries**
industrial /ɪnˈdʌstriəl/ [adj usually before noun] connected with industry: *industrial waste* | *industrial pollution*

⚠ Don't confuse **industry** (=the production of goods) with **factory** (=a place where goods are made) or **company** (=an organization that makes or sells goods and services).

⚠ Don't say 'the industry' when you mean all industries. Just say **industry**: *Industry is one of the main causes of pollution.*

commercial /kəˈmɜːrʃəl/ [adj only before noun] concerned with business: *Commercial pressures are forcing many companies to cut jobs.* | *The space shuttle is starting to be used for commercial purposes*

commercially [adv] concerned with whether something is successful and makes a profit: *Commercially, the movie was a disaster.*

2 a business agreement

deal /diːl/ [n C] a business agreement, especially when one company agrees to provide goods or services, and another company agrees to buy them: *The deal will give British Airways a 15% share in United Airlines.* | *Wicks lost a lot of money on property deals.*
+ with *a $55 million deal with a leading Japanese automobile company*
sign a deal *He recently signed a deal with a major record company worth over three million dollars.*

3 to take part in business activities

do business /ˌduː ˈbɪznɪs/ if a company **does business** with another company, it buys things from them or sells things to them: *STC is one of our regular customers – we've done business for years.*
+ with *They do a lot of business with Italian companies.*

be in business /biː ɪn ˈbɪznɪs/ if someone **is in business**, they own a company or shop, and they are involved in business activities: *Her father was in business in Korea.* | *They've been in business for 10 years, and are doing quite well.*

trade /treɪd/ [v I] if one country or company **trades** with another country or company, it buys things from them or sells things to them: *Slater's company continued to trade, even though it was in trouble.*
+ in *a French firm that trades in farm machinery*
+ with *For over 30 years, the US has refused to trade with Cuba.*
trading partner (=a country that regularly does business with another country) *Japan is one of our major trading partners.*

deal with sb /diːl wɪð (sb)/ [phrasal verb T] to buy goods from, or sell goods to, a particular person or company: *The firm deals directly with the manufacturers.* | *I've dealt with Bill Harrison for years and always found him very reliable.*

4 someone who works in business

businessman/businesswoman /ˈbɪz-nɪs̩mən, ˈbɪznɪs̩ˌwʊmən/ [n C] someone who works in business, especially as the manager or owner of a company: *Tim Knight is a highly successful businessman who runs his own electronics company.*

plural **businessmen – businesswomen**

entrepreneur /ˌɒntrəprəˈnɜːʳ‖ˌɑːm-/ [n C] someone who starts a new business or arranges new business deals, especially someone who is willing to risk their own money in order to make a profit: *Local entrepreneur Tony Ridley started his computer company five years ago and is now a millionaire.*

BUSY/NOT BUSY

➡ see also **FREE TIME, WORK**

1 a busy person

busy /ˈbɪzi/ [adj] if you are **busy**, you have a lot of things to do: *Sorry I haven't called you, but I've been really busy.* | *Not now Stephen, I'm busy.*

busy doing sth *He's busy trying to arrange our hotel rooms.*

+ with *Marion was busy with preparations for the wedding.*

keep sb busy (=make someone busy) *People liked our work, and we were kept busy all the time.*

busy – busier – busiest

⚠ Don't say 'she's busy with studying'. Say **she's busy studying** or **she's busy with her studies**.

have a lot to do /hæv ə ˌlɒt tə ˈduː‖ -ˌlɑːt-/ if you **have a lot to do**, you have to do a lot of things, and you need to hurry or work hard: *She had a lot to do before she could go home.*

be snowed under /biː ˌsnəʊd ˈʌndəʳ/ INFORMAL if you **are snowed under**, you have so much work that it is difficult for you to do it all: *Don't expect any help from John – he's completely snowed under at the moment.*

+ with *We've been snowed under with requests for help.*

be rushed off your feet /biː ˌrʌʃt ɒf jɔːʳ ˈfiːt/ INFORMAL, ESPECIALLY BRITISH to be very busy and always in a hurry, because you have a lot of things to do: *I've been rushed off my feet getting ready for the party.*

2 a busy place or time

➡ see also **CROWD**

busy /ˈbɪzi/ [adj] use this about places and times when a lot of people are travelling, shopping, or doing things: *By 10 o'clock the supermarket was really busy.* | *a busy main road* | *a doctor in a busy hospital* | *July and August are our busiest times.*

busy – busier – busiest

hectic /ˈhektɪk/ [adj] a **hectic** time or situation is very busy, so you are always in a hurry and you often feel worried or excited: *It was really hectic at work today.* | *The band had a hectic recording schedule.* | *When she lived in London she had a hectic social life.*

the rush hour /ðə ˈrʌʃ aʊəʳ/ [n singular] the time in the morning and evening when a lot of people are travelling to or from work: *In the rush hour the trains are always crowded.*

rush hour traffic *She got held up in rush hour traffic, and arrived 30 minutes late.*

the rush /ðə ˈrʌʃ/ [n singular] a time when a lot of people are shopping or travelling: *Sam got to the theatre early to avoid the rush.*

the Christmas/summer/weekend rush *Shop by mail and beat the Christmas rush!*

3 a person who is not busy

not busy /nɒt ˈbɪzi/ *Let's find a time when you're not so busy, and talk about this calmly.* | *Hopefully by March we won't be so busy.*

not have much to do /nɒt hæv ˌmʌtʃ tə ˈduː/ ESPECIALLY SPOKEN to not be busy – use this especially to say that you have enough time to do other things: *I could help if you want – I don't have much to do this weekend.*

free /friː/ [adj] not busy, because you have not arranged to do anything, or you do not have to go to work or school: *I'm busy all day today, but I'm free tomorrow morning.* | *Which days is she free next week?*

free time (=time when you do not have to work and you can do what you want) *What do you do in your free time?*

4 a place or time that is not busy

quiet /ˈkwaɪət/ [adj] a **quiet** place or time is one in which there is not much happening or not many people are travelling, shopping etc: *a quiet suburb of Seattle* | *I spent a quiet weekend at home.*

out of season BRITISH **in the off season** AMERICAN /aʊt əv ˈsiːzən◂, ɪn ðɪ ˈɒf ˌsiːzən‖-ˈɔːf-/ if you visit a tourist area **out of season**, you go there at a time of the year when there are not a lot of people: *It's much cheaper if you go there out of season.* | *Rooms, in the off season, are as cheap as $52 a night.*

BUY

EXPENSIVE   SPEND

CHEAP   see   MONEY
          also

FREE   COST

PAY   SHOP

1 to buy something

buy /baɪ/ [v T] to pay money so that you can have something: *He's just gone to buy some cigarettes.* | *The painting was bought by a museum in New York.*

buy sb sth *Let me buy you a drink.*

buy sth for sb/sth *The money was used to buy new equipment for the hospital.*

buy sth from sb/sth *Ella buys a lot of her clothes from second-hand stores.*

buy sth for $10/£50 etc *They bought their house for $200,000.*

buying – bought – have bought

When you see **EC**, go to the
ESSENTIAL COMMUNICATION section.

get /get/ [v T not in passive] ESPECIALLY SPOKEN to buy something, especially ordinary things such as food, clothes, or things for your house: *Did you remember to get some bread?*

get sb sth *I'm getting Dad a bottle of whiskey for his birthday.*

get sth for $10/£50 etc *She got that skirt for £10 in the market.*

getting – got – **have got** BRITISH
have gotten AMERICAN

purchase /ˈpɜːrtʃəs/ [v T] FORMAL to buy something, especially something large and expensive: *The cost of purchasing new equipment for the science laboratories was over £100,000.*

⚠ Purchase is used especially in business situations.

snap up /ˌsnæp ˈʌp/ [phrasal verb T] INFORMAL to buy something as soon as you see it, because it is very cheap or because you want it very much

snap up sth *I snapped up some real bargains in the sales.*

snap sth up *It was only $10, so I snapped it up.*

stock up /ˌstɒk ˈʌp‖ˌstɑːk-/ [phrasal verb I] to buy a lot of something in order to use it later: *The supermarkets are full of people stocking up for Christmas.*

+ on *We always stock up on cheap wine when we go to France.*

splash out on sth BRITISH **splurge on sth** AMERICAN /ˌsplæʃ ˈaʊt ɒn (sth), ˌsplɜːrdʒ ˈaʊt ɒn (sth)/ [phrasal verb T] INFORMAL to buy something expensive that you would not usually buy: *Why don't you splash out on a new dress for the party?* | *We splurged on a brand new sofa for the living room.*

2 to go to shops to buy things

go shopping /ˌgəʊ ˈʃɒpɪŋ‖-ˈʃɑː-/ to go to shops in order to look at things and buy things: *That afternoon, Jo and Emma went shopping in Oxford Street.*

⚠ Don't say 'go to shopping'. Say **go shopping**.

do the shopping /ˌduː ðə ˈʃɒpɪŋǁ-ˈʃɑː-/ to go to shops in order to buy the things that you need regularly, especially food: *I spent all day Saturday doing the shopping and cleaning the apartment.*

do your/my/his etc shopping *We do all our shopping at the local supermarket.*

go to the shops BRITISH **go to the store** AMERICAN /ˌgəʊ tə ðə ˈʃɒps, ˌgəʊ tə ðə ˈstɔːrǁ-ˈʃɑːps/ to go to the shops near your house in order to buy food or to buy one or two other small things that you need: *I'm just going to the shops for a newspaper – do you want anything?* | *If you go to the store could you get me some milk?*

shop /ʃɒpǁʃɑːp/ [v I] if you **shop** at a particular shop, you go there regularly to buy things

+ at *one of those rich women who always shop at Harrods*

shopping – shopped – have shopped

shop around /ˌʃɒp əˈraʊndǁˌʃɑːp-/ [phrasal verb I] to compare the price of something in several shops, before deciding where to buy it: *You could probably get the same camera cheaper if you shop around.*

window shopping /ˈwɪndəʊ ˌʃɒpɪŋǁ-ˌʃɑːp-/ [n U] when you look at things in shop windows without intending to buy anything: *We spent the morning window shopping in all the antique stores.*

3 someone who buys something

customer /ˈkʌstəmər/ [n C] someone who buys things from a shop or company, or who uses a restaurant, bar etc: *Several customers complained about how rude the waiters were.* | *We offer a 10% discount to regular customers.*

best/biggest customer (=someone who buys the most goods or services from a shop or company)

shoppers /ˈʃɒpərzǁˈʃɑːp-/ [n plural] the people in a shop or town who are buying things: *streets crowded with Christmas shoppers*

buyer /ˈbaɪər/ [n C] someone who buys something expensive such as a house or car: *Have you found a buyer for your house yet?* | *The advertisement is aimed at women car buyers.*

⚠ Don't use **buyer** about people buying things in shops.

consumers/the consumer /kənˈsjuːmərz, ðə kənˈsjuːmərǁ-ˈsuː-/ [n] all the people who buy and use goods and services: *Consumers are demanding more environmentally friendly products.* | *The consumer is interested in high quality goods, not just low prices.*

⚠ **Consumers/the consumer** is used especially by people who write about business.

C

CALM

not angry or upset, even in a difficult situation

ANGRY   RELAX

see also

WORRYING/   FRIGHTENING/
WORRIED   FRIGHTENED

1 calm

calm /kɑːm‖kɑːm, kɑːlm/ [adj] not getting angry or upset, even in a difficult situation: *Everyone praised Douglas for the calm way in which he handled the situation.* | *We'll talk about this when you're feeling calmer.*
keep calm *Keep calm and try not to panic.*
  calmly [adv] *The other kids were screaming, but Ellie calmly picked up the snake and threw it out of the window.*

relaxed /rɪˈlækst/ [adj] someone who is **relaxed** is very calm and does not seem to be worried about anything, and it is pleasant for other people to be with them: *George greeted us in his friendly relaxed way.* | *You seem much more relaxed since you changed jobs.*

stay cool/keep cool /ˌsteɪ ˈkuːl, ˌkiːp ˈkuːl/ to stay calm and not show your emotions, especially when other people are getting excited or angry: *Sampras is the kind of player who always manages to stay cool, even under pressure.*
keep your cool (=not become angry) *He managed to keep his cool and ignore her last comments.*
  coolly [adv] *She walked coolly to the front of the hall and picked up the microphone.*

keep your head /ˌkiːp jɔːʳ ˈhed/ to manage to stay calm and to behave in a sensible way when something is likely to make you feel frightened or worried: *Paul's good at keeping his head in a crisis.*

laid-back /ˌleɪd ˈbæk◄/ [adj] INFORMAL someone who is **laid-back** is always relaxed and never seems to worry about things that other people worry about: *Sue's always had a laid-back attitude to life.*

2 to become calm, or to make someone calm

calm down /ˌkɑːm ˈdaʊn‖ˌkɑːm-, ˌkɑːlm-/ [phrasal verb I/T] to become calm again after you have been angry or upset, or to make someone do this: *Once I'd calmed down, I realized he might be right.*
calm sb down *He put his arms around Christine and tried to calm her down.*

3 what you say to someone when you want them to be calm

○**calm down** /ˌkɑːm ˈdaʊn‖ˌkɑːm-, ˌkɑːlm-/ SPOKEN say this when someone is angry, upset, or excited and you want them to think calmly or speak calmly again: *Calm down! There's nothing whatever to worry about.*

○**relax** /rɪˈlæks/ SPOKEN say this to someone who is worried or frightened about something, in order to stop them worrying: *Relax! The injection won't hurt.*

○**take it easy** /ˌteɪk ɪt ˈiːzi/ SPOKEN INFORMAL say this when someone is angry or upset, and you want to stop them saying or doing anything stupid: *Hey, take it easy! Nobody's saying you're not good at your job.*

○**it's okay/it's all right** /ɪts əʊˈkeɪ, ɪts ˌɔːl ˈraɪt/ SPOKEN say this to someone to make them stop being worried: *It's okay, she's just phoning to say she'll be late.* | *It's alright, don't cry. Mummy's here.*

CAN/CAN'T

➡ look here for . . .
 • be able to do something
 • be allowed to do something
➡ if you want to know about modal verbs, go to the **ESSENTIAL GRAMMAR**, section 7
➡ see also ⬛ **REQUESTS**

⚠️ Don't say 'I can to come'. Say **I can come**.

⚠️ Past tense: If you just want to say that someone had the ability, money etc to do something at some time in the past, use **could**: *He could read by the time he was four.* | *He was a rich man who could afford to buy anything he wanted.* If you want to say that someone succeeded in doing something because they had the opportunity, ability, money etc, use **was able to do sth**: *When the rain stopped we were able to finish the game.*

⚠️ Future tense: Use **will be able to do sth** (often shortened to 'I'll be able', 'we'll be able', 'he'll be able' etc): *When everyone comes back from their vacations, we'll be able to get a lot more work done.* | *I'll be able to see my friends and family again very soon.* In spoken English you can use **can** to talk about tomorrow, next week etc: *I can come with you on Sunday.*

⚠️ Present perfect: Use **have been able to do sth** to mean that someone has succeeded in doing something: *Up to now no-one has been able to break the record set by Lewis.* Use **could have done sth** to mean that someone was able to do something but did not do it: *He could have become president, but he wasn't ambitious.*

⚠️ Infinitive: Use **to be able to do sth**: *He wants to be able to speak French.*

1 to have the ability, opportunity, time, or equipment that you need in order to do something

can /kən; *strong* kæn/ [modal verb] *"Can you speak Japanese?" "Yes, I can."*
can do sth *They've invented a computer that can talk.* | *Can you come for lunch on Saturday?* | *Adrian could read when he was four.* | *If we had a boat we could row across to the island.* | *The engine's making a funny noise – can you hear it?*

⚠️ Don't say 'I am able to see him' or 'they were not able to hear me'. Say **I can see him** and **they couldn't hear me**. Use **can**, not 'be able to', with verbs like 'see', 'hear', or 'feel'.

be able to do sth /biː ˌeɪbəl tə ˈduː (sth)/ use this especially about something that is difficult or that needs a lot of effort: *Will you be able to carry those bags on your own?* | *If you want to join this expedition, you must be able to speak English and swim.* | *Three weeks after the accident, she was able to walk and even exercise in the gym.*

be capable of sth /biː ˈkeɪpəbəl ɒv (sth)/ to have the power or ability to do something, especially something very difficult or unusual: *The 'sports' version is capable of a top speed of 170 mph.*
be capable of doing sth *a hard disk capable of holding 2 gigabytes of data*
be perfectly capable of doing sth (=be able to do something without anyone helping you) *Don't worry, she's perfectly capable of dealing with the situation.*

have the ability to do sth /hæv ði əˌbɪləti tə ˈduː (sth)/ to be able to do something, especially something that is unusual or that most people cannot do: *She seemed to have the ability to make people do anything she wanted.*

it is possible for sb to do sth /ɪt ɪz ˌpɒsɪbəl fər (sb) tə ˈduː (sth)‖-ˌpɑː-/ FORMAL use this especially when you are making an arrangement with someone, to ask or say what someone will be able to do: *Would it be possible for you to come to a meeting on Tuesday?* | *It might be possible for you to use the school library on Saturdays.*

⚠️ Don't use this when you are simply saying what you can do. Don't say 'it is possible for me to go'. Say **I can go**.

2 to be allowed to do something or have the power to do it
➡️ see also **🔲 PERMISSION, LET**

can /kən; *strong* kæn/ [modal verb] *If you want to come with us, you can.*
can do sth *It's my house and I can do what I want here.* | *Can I borrow your car?* | *Only the Supreme Court can change these laws.*

be able to do sth /biː ˌeɪbəl tə ˈduː (sth)/ use this especially when a law or rule makes it possible for someone to do something: *As senior students, we were able to attend some university classes.* | *You might be able to get a temporary passport.*

have the power to do sth /hæv ðə ˌpaʊəʳ tə ˈduː (sth)/ to be able to do something because your official position gives you the power to do it: *The judge has the power to order a witness to give evidence.* | *Each state had the power to make its own laws.*

3 the ability to do something

ability /əˈbɪlɪ̩ti/ [n C/U] something that you are able to do because you have the physical skill or intelligence to do it
ability to do sth *Our ability to think and speak makes us different from other animals.* | *the ability to understand what motivates other people*
have the ability *Are you confident he has the ability to do this job?*
plural **abilities**

> ⚠ Don't say 'ability of speaking'. Say **ability to speak**.

skill /skɪl/ [n C] a special ability that you need to learn in order to do a particular job or activity: *These exercises develop the student's reading and writing skills.* | *You need computing skills for most office jobs.*

4 to make someone able to do something

enable sb to do sth/allow sb to do sth /ɪnˌeɪbəl (sb) tə ˈduː (sth), əˌlaʊ (sb) tə ˈduː (sth)/ FORMAL to make it possible for someone to do something: *The money from my grandmother enabled us to buy the house.* | *This disk allows you to store larger quantities of data.* | *Having someone to help in the house allowed me to concentrate more on my work.*

> ⚠ **Enable sb to do sth** is more formal than **allow sb to do sth**.

make it possible /ˌmeɪk ɪt ˈpɒsɪ̩bəl‖ -ˈpɑː-/ if a situation, event, or change **makes it possible** for someone to do

something, they are able to do something that they could not do before
make it possible to do sth *The direct flight makes it possible to get from London to Tokyo in 12 hours.*
make it possible for sb to do sth *Changes in the law will make it possible for more fathers to stay at home and take care of their children.*

let sb do sth /ˌlet (sb) ˈduː (sth)/ [v T] if a machine, tool etc **lets someone do something,** it provides what you need to be able to do it
let sb do sth *The 'Moneymaster' program lets you control all your personal finances carefully and efficiently.*

5 to be unable to do something

can't/cannot /kɑːnt, ˈkænət, -nɒt‖kænt, ˈkænɑːt/ [modal verb] to be unable to do something, because you do not have the ability, time, equipment etc: *"Can you drive?" "No, I can't."*
can't/cannot do sth *Tom can't see anything without his glasses.* | *I packed so much into my suitcase that I couldn't lift it!* | *You can't do these sums without a calculator.*

> ⚠ **Cannot** is mostly used in written English: *Human beings cannot survive for long without water.* **Cannot** is always written as one word.

not be able to do sth /ˌnɒt biː ˌeɪbəl tə ˈduː (sth)/ *Unfortunately, I wasn't able to help them.* | *I'm afraid I won't be able to come to the meeting after all.* | *The doctor told Tina she wouldn't be able to have children.*

> ⚠ **Not be able to** is used mostly in past or future tenses. In the present tense, use **can't** or **cannot** instead. For example, don't say 'I am not able to drive'. Say I **can't drive**.

be unable to do sth /biː ʌnˌeɪbəl tə ˈduː (sth)/ WRITTEN to not be able to do something, especially something important that you want to do or need to do: *He lay awake all night, unable to sleep.* | *Many passengers were unable to reach the lifeboats in time.*

be incapable of doing sth/not be capable of doing sth /biː ɪnˌkeɪpəbəl əv ˈduːɪŋ (sth), nɒt biː ˌkeɪpəbəl əv ˈduːɪŋ (sth)/ to not have the physical strength or mental ability to do something: *Matthew seemed to be incapable of getting a job.* | *She's no longer capable of looking after herself.*

not be in a position to do sth /nɒt biː ɪn ə pəˌzɪʃən tə ˈduː (sth)/ FORMAL to not be able to do something, because you do not have enough money, knowledge, or authority: *I'm afraid I'm not in a position to answer your questions.* | *We are not in a position to publish the results of the survey yet.*

it is not possible for sb to do sth /ɪt ɪz nɒt ˌpɒsɪbəl fər (sb) tə ˈduː (sth)‖-ˌpɑː-/ FORMAL use this to explain to someone that the situation prevents you from doing what they want you to do: *I'm afraid it won't be possible for the Director to see you this morning.* | *Unfortunately, it wasn't possible for my daughter to come with me.*

inability to do sth /ɪnəˌbɪlɪ̥ti tə ˈduː (sth)/ when someone is not able to do something, especially something that you think they should be able to do: *Her actions show an inability to distinguish between fantasy and reality.*
sb's inability to do sth *their inability to understand even the simplest instructions*

6 to not be allowed to do something or not have the power to do it

can't/cannot /kɑːnt, ˈkænət, -nɒt‖kænt, ˈkænɑːt/ [modal verb] *"I want to see that film." "You can't, you're not old enough."* | *The President cannot change a law that has been approved by Congress.*
can't do sth *I'm sorry, you can't come in.* | *You can't get married until you're 16.*

⚠ Cannot is more formal than **can't**, and is used especially in written English: *Members of the public cannot enter the building without official permission.* Cannot is always written as one word.

not be able to do sth /ˌnɒt biː ˌeɪbəl tə ˈduː (sth)/ use this when a law or rule does not allow someone to do something: *If you don't have a library card, you won't be able to borrow any books.*

powerless /ˈpaʊərləs/ [adj not before noun] not able to control or stop something, because you do not have the power or legal right to do it
powerless to do sth *Although we all thought the decision was unfair, we were powerless to change it.*

CAREFUL

➡ opposite CARELESS

1 when you try to avoid danger or accidents

careful /ˈkeərfəl/ [adj] someone who is **careful** tries to avoid danger, risks, or accidents: *You should always be very careful when handling chemicals.* | *You'll be OK with Jane – she's a very careful driver.*
Q**careful!/be careful!** SPOKEN (=say this when you are warning someone that they must be careful) *That vase is very delicate. Be careful!*
+ with *Hey! Careful with that cigarette!*
careful to do sth *You must be careful not to trip over the wire.*
+ (that) *We had to be careful that we didn't fall off the raft.*
careful how/what/who etc *Be very careful how you handle those glasses!*
  carefully [adv] *Goodbye, Sarah – drive carefully!*

cautious /ˈkɔːʃəs/ [adj] someone who is **cautious** does not like taking risks and is always very careful to avoid them: *If we're too cautious, we might lose a good business opportunity.* | *My dad always goes really slowly – he's a very cautious driver.*
+ about *I've always been cautious about giving people my phone number.*
  cautiously [adv] *Slowly and cautiously, we made our way along the edge of the cliff.*

Q**watch out!/look out!** /ˌwɒtʃ ˈaʊt, ˌlʊk ˈaʊt‖ˌwɑːtʃ-, ˌwɔːtʃ-/ SPOKEN say this to warn someone that they are going to have an accident and they must do something quickly to avoid it: *Watch out – you're going to spill paint over my new carpet! | Look out, Phil – there's a car coming!*

with care/with caution /wɪð ˈkeə^r, wɪð ˈkɔːʃən/ if you do something **with care** or **with caution**, you are very careful to avoid accidents when you do it: *These antiques are fragile and must be handled with care. | Some roads may be icy and motorists are advised to drive with caution.*

⚠ With care and with caution are often used in instructions on bottles, packages etc that contain things that are dangerous or easy to break: *Toxic materials – handle with caution.*

be on your guard /biː ɒn jɔː^r ˈgɑːd/ to carefully watch and notice everything that is happening around you, in order to avoid problems or danger: *You need to be on your guard at the airport; there are a lot of pickpockets around.*

take no chances /ˌteɪk nəʊ ˈtʃɑːnsɪz‖ -ˈtʃæn-/ to organize something in a very careful way, because you want to avoid any possible risks: *This time we're taking no chances. Everything will be planned down to the last detail.*

2 when you try not to make mistakes or do things badly

careful /ˈkeə^rfəl/ [adj] someone who is **careful** tries not to make mistakes, and tries to do everything correctly: *She's a careful hard-working student.*
+ with *Try to be more careful with your punctuation.*
careful to do sth *They were careful not to touch anything until the police arrived.*
   carefully [adv] *Check your essay carefully for spelling mistakes.*

take care /ˌteɪk ˈkeə^r/ to do a piece of work carefully because you want it to be right, and you do not want to make mistakes: *Look at all these mistakes! Can't you take more care?*
+ with *Sally doesn't take enough care with her work.*
take care to do sth *Take care to label all the disks with the correct file names.*

thorough /ˈθʌrə‖ˈθʌrəʊ, ˈθʌrə/ [adj not usually before noun] someone who is **thorough** is careful that all the work they do is complete and correct: *Our mechanics will check everything; they're very thorough.*
   thoroughly [adv] *All the equipment had been thoroughly tested.*

conscientious /ˌkɒnʃiˈenʃəs◄‖ˌkɑːn-/ [adj] someone who is **conscientious** is very careful about their work or duties, and works hard to do everything that needs to be done: *Ryan has always been a conscientious worker. | a conscientious mother*
   conscientiously [adv] *The chairman carried out his duties conscientiously.*

meticulous /mɪˈtɪkjʊləs/ [adj] someone who is **meticulous** is very careful about every small detail, and always makes sure that everything is done correctly: *The jewellery was beautifully made, and was obviously the work of a meticulous craftsman.*
+ about *John's very meticulous about keeping accounts.*
   meticulously [adv] *Books and papers were meticulously arranged on his desk.*

pay attention to sth /ˌpeɪ əˈtenʃən tuː (sth)/ to be careful that a particular thing is done in the right way: *You need to pay more attention to your hair and make-up*

3 careful work/actions

careful /ˈkeə^rfəl/ [adj only before noun] a **careful** test, study, piece of work etc is done carefully and correctly, with a lot of attention to details: *A careful inspection showed cracks in the foundation of the building. | Her book is the result of years of careful research.*

thorough /ˈθʌrə‖ˈθʌrəʊ, ˈθʌrə/ [adj] a **thorough** search, check, examination etc is done carefully so that no detail is missed: *The police have made a thorough search of the area. | The doctor gave me a thorough check-up.*

systematic /ˌsɪstəˈmætɪk◄/ [adj] a **systematic** way of doing something uses a fixed plan, so that everything gets done thoroughly – use this especially about activities that are dishonest or harmful: *the* systematic destruction of the country's education system | Ex-prisoners talked of systematic cruelty within the jail.

systematically [adv] They went through the documents systematically, removing every reference to his former wife.

painstaking /'peɪnzˌteɪkɪŋ/ [adj] very careful and thorough, and taking a lot of time and effort: They began the long and painstaking task of compiling a bibliography.

   painstakingly [adv] The poet's house has been painstakingly restored.

CARELESS

➡ opposite **CAREFUL**

1 careless, so that accidents happen

careless /'keəʳləs/ [adj] someone who is **careless** does not take care to avoid accidents and is likely to damage something or hurt someone: a careless driver | the careless handling of explosives

+ about The airline was accused of being careless about security.

   carelessly [adv] Someone had carelessly dropped a lighted cigarette end into the wastebasket.

   carelessness [n U] injuries that were caused by someone else's carelessness

clumsy /'klʌmzi/ [adj] someone who is **clumsy** often drops things or breaks things because they move around in a careless way: I'm sorry about your vase – Rob's such a clumsy boy! | Paula always felt clumsy when she had to serve food to people. | a large man with big, clumsy hands

clumsy – clumsier – clumsiest

   clumsily [adv] I got up, clumsily knocking against the table.

irresponsible /ˌɪrɪ'spɒnsᵻbəl‖-'spɑːn-/ [adj] someone who is **irresponsible** does not do the things they should do, or does things they should not do, usually with harmful results: irresponsible parents who allow their teenage children to stay out all night | It was an irresponsible practical joke that might have caused serious injury.

reckless /'rekləs/ [adj] ESPECIALLY WRITTEN someone who is **reckless** does dangerous or stupid things without thinking that they or someone else might get hurt: The driver of the car was arrested for reckless driving. | a reckless disregard for human life

   recklessly [adv] young men recklessly risking their lives in a dangerous sport

negligence /'neglɪdʒəns/ [n U] when someone does not do an important job carefully enough, especially with the result that there is an accident and they are punished for causing it: a case of medical negligence in which a doctor has made some serious mistakes | You can claim compensation if your injury is a result of your employer's negligence.

   negligent [adj] The court said that the teacher had been negligent in not reporting the accident.

> ⚠ **Negligence** is a word used especially by lawyers.

2 careless, so that you make mistakes

careless /'keəʳləs/ [adj] someone who is **careless** makes mistakes because they do not think carefully enough about what they are doing: I made a few careless mistakes. | All the excitement had made him careless, and he left the house without locking the door.

it is careless of sb (to do sth) It was very careless of you to leave your purse lying on the desk.

   carelessly [adv] He had carelessly switched off his computer without saving the data.

   carelessness [n U] Most accidents are entirely due to carelessness.

sloppy /'slɒpi‖'slɑːpi/ [adj] done in a careless and lazy way – use this about someone's work or the way someone writes or speaks: *As a student, he was brilliant but sloppy.* | *The company's failure was blamed on sloppy management.*

sloppy – sloppier – sloppiest

3 when you decide too quickly

rash /ræʃ/ [adj] if you do something **rash**, you do not think carefully about the effect it will have, and you wish later you had not done it: *I'm sure she won't do anything rash – she's such a sensible girl.* | *Don't make any rash promises that you may regret later.*

> **rashly** [adv] *I rashly offered to lend her the money.*

hasty /ˈheɪsti/ [adj] too quick to do or say something, without taking time to think about it first: *I think I may have been a little hasty. I shouldn't have accused him of lying.* | *Don't make any hasty decisions.*

> **hastily** [adv] *He later admitted that he might have acted a little hastily.*

CARRY

➡ see also **TAKE/BRING, LIFT, HOLD**

1 to carry something or someone

carry /ˈkæri/ [v T] to take something from one place to another, by holding it in your hands, lifting it on your back etc: *A porter helped me carry my bags.*
carry sth to/out of/around etc *The women have to carry water from the well to the village.* | *I've been carrying this tape-recorder around with me all day.*

carrying – carried – have carried

> ⚠ Don't confuse **carry** (=take something somewhere by holding it in your hands) with **hold** (=have something in your hands) and **lift** (=move something that you are holding to a higher position).

> ⚠ Don't confuse **carry** and **take**. Don't say 'I carried him home in my car'. Say **I took him home in my car**.

be weighed down with sth/be loaded down with sth /biː ˌweɪd ˈdaʊn wɪð (sth), biː ˌləʊd̪d̪ ˈdaʊn wɪð (sth)/ to be carrying so many things that it is difficult for you to move: *She struggled back along the street, weighed down with shopping bags.*

be loaded with sth /biː ˈləʊd̪d̪ wɪð (sth)/ if a vehicle **is loaded with** something, it is carrying a lot of it: *A truck loaded with cement had crashed into the wall.*

2 easy to carry

portable /ˈpɔːtəbəl/ [adj usually before noun] **portable TV/computer/typewriter/heater etc** a television, computer etc that is fairly small and easy to carry around with you: *She has a small portable TV in the kitchen.* | *He still writes his novels on an old portable typewriter.*

CATCH

➡ look here for ...
- catch a ball
- catch someone after chasing them
- see someone doing something wrong
- catch an animal

1 to catch a ball or other moving object
➡ see also **THROW, SPORT**

catch /kætʃ/ [v T] to get hold of a ball or other object that is moving through the air: *I caught the ball with my left hand and threw it back to the pitcher.*

catch

Q catch! SPOKEN (say this when you throw something to someone) *Here's your lighter – catch!*

catching – caught – have caught

2 to catch someone who is trying to escape
➡ see also **RUN, FOLLOW, ESCAPE, PRISON**

catch /kætʃ/ [v T] to stop someone from escaping by running after them and

holding them: *The bigger boys ran while the little boys tried to catch them.* | *If the soldiers catch you, they will kill you.*
catching – caught – have caught

capture /'kæptʃər/ [v T] to catch an enemy, especially after defeating them in a war or battle: *The rebel leader was captured and publicly executed.* | *They captured twenty enemy soldiers.*

take sb prisoner /,teɪk (sb) 'prɪzənər/ to catch someone, especially in a war, and keep them as a prisoner: *6000 enemy soldiers were killed, and 4000 more were taken prisoner.*

3 when the police catch a criminal

➡ see also **POLICE, TELL 5**

catch /kætʃ/ [v T] if the police **catch** someone who has done something illegal, they find that person and stop them from escaping: *Police have so far failed to catch the murderer.* | *The thieves were never caught.*
catching – caught – have caught

arrest /ə'rest/ [v T] if the police **arrest** someone, they take them to a police station because they believe that person has done something illegal: *Police arrested nine men in a drugs raid.*
arrest sb for sth *Wayne was arrested for dangerous driving.*
> **arrest** [n C/U] when someone is arrested by the police: *His confessions led to the arrest of several well-known gangsters.*
make an arrest (=arrest someone) *Police made a number of arrests after a fight in a city bar.*

get /get/ [v T] INFORMAL to find the person who has done something illegal, and punish them: *They never actually got the man who did it.* | *Did the police get the people who stole your car?*
getting – got – have got

4 to catch someone while they are doing something wrong

catch /kætʃ/ [v T] to find or see someone while they are doing something wrong
catch sb doing sth *Monica caught her son stealing money from her purse.*

get caught *Be careful you don't get caught!*
be/get caught doing sth *Paul was caught cheating in a test.*
catch sb red-handed (=while they are in the process of doing something wrong, especially stealing) *"Are you sure Gavin took it?" "I caught him red-handed!"*
catching – caught – have caught

5 to catch an animal

catch /kætʃ/ [v T] to get an animal, for example by using a net or trap, and stop it from escaping: *Did you catch any fish?* | *a trap to catch mice*
catching – caught – have caught

trap /træp/ [v T] to catch an animal or bird using special equipment that will hold them so that they cannot escape: *Some of the birds had been shot, others trapped.*
trapping – trapped – have trapped

trap /træp/ [n C] a piece of equipment used to trap animals and birds: *The wolf had been caught in a trap.*

CAUSE

➡ see also **REASON**

1 to make something happen

cause /kɔːz/ [v T] to make something happen, especially something bad: *Smoking causes cancer.* | *The fire caused $30,000 worth of damage.* | *A lot of traffic accidents are caused by carelessness.*
cause sb embarrassment/anxiety/pain (=make someone feel embarrassed, anxious etc) *Robert's behaviour is causing his family a lot of anxiety.*
cause sth to do sth FORMAL *Inflation has caused fuel prices to rise sharply in recent months.*

⚠ The usual verb for saying that one thing makes another thing happen is **make**, not **cause**: *The smoke made my eyes sore.* **Cause**, followed by an infinitive, is used mostly in formal or technical writing: *This reaction causes the temperature to rise.*

C

> ⚠ Don't say 'cause that something happens'. Say **cause something to happen**.

make /meɪk/ [v T] to make someone do something or make something happen
make sb/sth do sth *Sarah's really funny – she always makes me laugh.* | *Petra's new hairstyle makes her look a lot younger.*
make sb angry/happy/nervous etc *Stop staring at me – you're making me nervous!*
make sth better/worse/easier etc *Senator Rawson's recent remarks seem to have made the situation worse.*
make it easy/difficult/impossible etc for sb to do sth *The new rail service should make it easier for commuters to get to work.*
making – made – have made

> ⚠ Don't say 'she made me to do it'. Say **she made me do it**.

be responsible for sth /biː rɪ'spɒnsəbəl fɔʳ (sth)‖-'spɑːn-/ if a person, or something that they do, **is responsible for** an accident, problem, mistake etc, it is their fault that it happens: *I felt partly responsible for the fact that her boyfriend left her.* | *Who is responsible for all this mess?*

> ⚠ Don't use 'of' with **responsible**.

bring about sth /ˌbrɪŋ ə'baʊt (sth)/ [phrasal verb T] to make something happen, especially a change or an improved situation: *The war brought about huge social and political changes.* | *improvements in public health that have been brought about by advances in medical science*

result in sth /rɪ'zʌlt ɪn (sth)/ [phrasal verb T] if an action or event **results in** something, it makes something happen: *a train crash that resulted in the deaths of all 52 passengers* | *All these changes in the rules have resulted in great confusion.*

lead to sth /'liːd tuː (sth)/ [phrasal verb T] if an action or event **leads to** something, it starts a process which finally makes something happen: *Their research eventually led to the development of nuclear power.* | *The bank has offered a reward for any information leading to the arrest of the robbers.*

trigger off sth /ˌtrɪɡər 'ɒf (sth)‖-'ɔːf-/ [phrasal verb T] if a small action or event **triggers off something** more serious, it makes it happen very quickly: *the events that triggered off World War I*

2 the thing that makes something else happen

cause /kɔːz/ [n C] the thing that makes something else happen, especially something bad: *The increase in violent crime has several causes.*
+ of *They still haven't found out the cause of the fire.*
root cause (=the true, basic cause, even if there are other causes that are easier to notice) *The root cause of Britain's economic problems is lack of investment.*

> ⚠ Don't say 'the cause for something'. Say **the cause of something**.

factor /'fæktəʳ/ [n C] one of several reasons that explain why something happens or why a situation exists: *The rise in crime is mainly due to factors such as unemployment.*
+ in *Wright's skill and experience has been an important factor in the team's success.*

CHANCE

➡ look here for ...
• the chance to do something interesting, exciting etc
• when something happens without being planned

1 when you have the chance to do something

chance /tʃɑːns‖tʃæns/ [n C] a situation in which it is possible for you to do something enjoyable or exciting, or something that you want to do
get the chance to do sth *I never got the chance to thank him for all his help.* | *It's a beautiful building – you should go and see it if you have the chance.*
give sb the chance to do sth *I wish he'd just give me the chance to explain.*
a second chance (=another chance after you have failed the first time) *Viewers will*

have a second chance to see Saturday's concert on Channel 4 tonight.

take the chance to do sth (=use a chance when you have it) *You should take the chance to travel while you're still young.*

sb's last chance (=when you will not have another chance) *It was her last chance to see him before she left town.*

miss a chance (=not use it when you have it) *Diane never misses the chance of a free meal.*

jump at the chance (of doing sth) (=eagerly when you get the chance to do something exciting) *You're so lucky. I'd jump at the chance of going to Hollywood.*

opportunity /ˌɒpə'tjuːnɪti‖ˌɑːpər'tuː-/ [n C] a chance to do something, especially something that is important or useful to you, or something that you want to do very much

have an opportunity to do sth *I've always wanted to visit Scotland, but I never had the opportunity till now.* | *He never had the opportunity to go to University when he was younger.*

opportunity for sb (to do sth) *Companies should provide more opportunities for women to go into senior management.*

miss an opportunity (to do sth) (=not use an opportunity when you have one)

career/job opportunities (=chances to find a job) *There are fewer and fewer career opportunities for young people.*

plural **opportunities**

2 when something happens for no reason or without being planned

➡ see also **LUCKY/UNLUCKY**

by chance /baɪ 'tʃɑːns‖-'tʃæns/ if something happens **by chance**, it is not deliberate or planned and you did not expect it to happen: *I met an old friend by chance on the train.*

quite/purely/entirely by chance (=completely by chance) *Quite by chance, a TV crew was filming in the area when the accident happened.*

coincidence /kəʊ'ɪnsɪdəns/ [n C/U] a surprising situation, when two similar things happen at the same time, or two or more people do the same thing, but no-one planned or intended this to happen

Qwhat a coincidence! SPOKEN *What a coincidence! I didn't know you were going to be in Geneva too.*

by coincidence *By coincidence, Jill was wearing the same dress as me.*

by a strange/curious/amazing coincidence *By a strange coincidence, all three girls had boyfriends called Simon.*

happen to do sth /ˌhæpən tə 'duː (sth)/ if you **happen to** meet someone, go somewhere, or see something, you do it by chance and not because you planned to do it: *A police car just happened to be driving past when the robbery took place.*

Qas it happens /əz ɪt 'hæpənz/ SPOKEN say **as it happens** when you are mentioning a fact that is connected, by chance, with what you have just been talking about: *"I'm thinking of selling my guitar." "Well, as it happens, I know someone who's thinking of buying one."*

luck /lʌk/ [n U] the way in which good or bad things happen to people by chance, not because they were planned or intended

it's a matter of luck/it's just luck (=it depends on luck) *There's no skill in roulette; it's all a matter of luck.*

fate /feɪt/ [n U] the power which some people believe controls what happens in everyone's lives: *It was fate that we should meet.*

by a twist of fate (=because fate made things happen in an unexpected way) *By a strange twist of fate, he died the day before his grandson was born.*

⚠ Use **fate** especially in stories.

CHANGE

➡ see also **DIFFERENT, SAME, BECOME**

1 to become different

change /tʃeɪndʒ/ [v I] to become different: *The city has changed a lot in recent years.* | *She's really changed since she went to college.* | *the changing role of women in society*

+ into *The caterpillar eventually changes into a beautiful butterfly.*

change from sth to/into sth *In the 18th century, Britain changed from a mainly agricultural society to an industrial one.*
change colour BRITISH **change color** AMERICAN *It was October, and the leaves on the trees were starting to change colour.*

alter /ˈɔːltəʳ/ [v I] to change – use this especially about someone's feelings or behaviour, or about a situation: *His mood suddenly altered and he seemed a little annoyed.* | *The situation altered dramatically in 1979 when Mrs Thatcher came to power.*

⚠ Alter is more formal than change, and is used mostly in written reports or stories.

vary /ˈveəri/ [v I] if something **varies**, it changes according to what the situation is: *Ticket prices to New York vary, depending on the time of year.*
vary considerably (=change a lot) *Her income varies considerably from one month to the next.*
varying – varied – have varied

turn into sth /ˈtɜːʳn ɪntuː (sth)/ [phrasal verb T] to become something completely different: *a story about a frog that turns into a prince* | *A trip to the beach turned into a nightmare for a local family yesterday.*

⟲go from ... to ... /ˈgəʊ frɒm ... tuː .../ ESPECIALLY SPOKEN to stop being one thing and start being something else, especially something very different: *In less than five years, he went from being a communist to being a member of the military government.* | *His face went from pink to bright red.*

2 to make someone or something different

change /tʃeɪndʒ/ [v T] to make someone or something different and usually better: *Unfortunately, there's nothing we can do to change the situation.* | *Being at college has changed her – she seems much more confident now.*

alter /ˈɔːltəʳ/ [v T] to change something so that it is better or more suitable: *The border was closed, and they were forced to alter their plans.* | *You can alter the colour and size of the image using a remote control.*

⚠ Alter is more formal than change.

make changes /ˌmeɪk ˈtʃeɪndʒɪz/ to change some parts of a system or the way something is done, but not all of it: *The new boss said he intended to make a few changes.*
+ to/in *The manufacturer has agreed to make one or two changes to the computer's design.*

reform /rɪˈfɔːʳm/ [v T] to change a law, system, or organization, so that it is fairer or more effective: *plans to reform the voting system* | *Many people think that the abortion laws should be reformed.*

adapt/modify /əˈdæpt, ˈmɒdɪfaɪ‖ˈmɑː-/ [v T] to change something slightly in order to improve it or make it suitable for a different purpose: *How much would it cost to adapt the existing equipment?* | *a modified version of the original computer program* | *You can adapt the recipe to suit your own requirements.*
adapt/modify sth for sth *The toilet facilities have been specially modified for use by people in wheelchairs.*
modifying – modified – have modified

3 to make something completely different

transform /trænsˈfɔːʳm/ [v T often in passive] to completely change something, especially so that it is much better: *When she smiled, her face was completely transformed.*
transform sth into sth *In the last 20 years, Korea has been transformed into a major industrial nation.*

turn sth into sth /ˈtɜːʳn (sth) ɪntuː (sth)/ [phrasal verb T] to make something become a completely different thing, for example because you want to use it for a different purpose: *We're planning to turn the study into an extra bedroom.* | *He turned Ajax into the most successful football team in Europe.*

revolutionize (also **revolutionise** BRITISH) /ˌrevəˈluːʃənaɪz/ [v T] to completely and permanently change the way people do something or think about something, especially because of a new idea or invention: *Computers have revolutionized the way we work.*

4 easy to change

flexible /ˈfleksɪbəl/ [adj] methods, systems, or rules that are **flexible** can easily be changed if necessary: *flexible working hours* | *Your schedule should be flexible enough to cope with interruptions or unexpected tasks.*

5 a change

change /tʃeɪndʒ/ [n C/U] when people or things become different: *She found it hard to get used to all the changes at home.* | *A lot of people are frightened of change.*
+ in *House plants are often sensitive to changes in the temperature.*
social/economic/political/technological change *1989 was a year of great political change in Eastern Europe.*
big/major change *There have been big changes in the way people learn languages.*
a change for the better/worse (=one that makes a situation better or worse) *For most ordinary workers, the new tax laws represent a change for the worse.*

alteration /ˌɔːltəˈreɪʃən/ [n C/U] a change, especially a small change – use this especially about changes in someone's feelings or behaviour, or about changes made to a plan or document
+ in *Did you notice any alteration in the patient's behaviour?*
make alterations (to sth) *We've made one or two small alterations, but the basic design remains the same.*
minor alteration (=small alteration) *After a few minor alterations, the proposal was accepted.*

reform /rɪˈfɔːrm/ [n C/U] a change that is made to a political or legal system in order to make it fairer or more effective
+ of *a reform of local government*
radical reform (=when things are changed very thoroughly) *The Socialists have promised a programme of radical social reform.*

revolution /ˌrevəˈluːʃən/ [n C] a complete and permanent change in the way people do things or think about things
+ in *Piaget's ideas caused a revolution in education.*

scientific/technological/social etc revolution *The 1970s saw the beginnings of a new technological revolution, based on microelectronics.*

upheaval /ʌpˈhiːvəl/ [n C/U] a big change in your life or in the way things are organized, especially when this causes problems and anxiety
+ for *Moving to a different school can be a major upheaval for young children.*
social/political/emotional etc upheaval *The recent civil war caused enormous social and economic upheaval.*

6 to change where you live, what you do etc

change /tʃeɪndʒ/ [v I/T] to change what you do or use, where you go etc, and start doing or using something else instead: *I'm thinking of changing my car.* (=selling it and getting another one)
change jobs/schools/doctors etc (=change your job, the school you go to, the doctor you go to etc) *Alex will be changing schools in September.*
change places/seats (=when two people sit in each other's seats) *Would you mind changing places so I can sit next to my girlfriend?*
change from sth to sth *Britain only recently changed from the old system of weights and measures to the metric system.*

move /muːv/ [v I/T] to go to live in a different house or city, or move the place where you work to a different office or city: *Karen doesn't live here any more – she's moved.*
move to (=go to another city or area) *We moved to Memphis when I was eight.*
move into (=go to another house or building) *The new offices should be ready for the company to move into very soon.*
move house/office BRITISH (=move from one house or office to another)

convert to sth /kənˈvɜːrt tuː (sth)/ [phrasal verb T] **convert to Christianity/ Islam/Judaism etc** to join a different religion from the one that you belonged to before: *She converted to Catholicism at the time of her marriage.*

When you see **EC**, go to the
ESSENTIAL COMMUNICATION section.

7 to change your plans, opinions, or decisions

change your mind /ˌtʃeɪndʒ jɔːʳ ˈmaɪnd/ to change your plans, opinions, or decisions: *Are you still coming out tonight, or have you changed your mind?*
+ about *I've changed my mind about Terry – he's actually a pretty nice guy.*

have second thoughts /hæv ˌsekənd ˈθɔːts/ to feel less sure about something that you intended to do, and start to wonder whether you really want to do it: *At first she was very interested in the idea, but then seemed to have second thoughts.*
+ about *Martin was having second thoughts about accepting the job.*

get cold feet /get ˌkəʊld ˈfiːt/ INFORMAL to suddenly feel that you are not brave enough to do something that you intended to do: *She's postponed the wedding – I wonder if she's getting cold feet.*

come around (also **come round** BRITISH) /ˌkʌm (ə)ˈraʊnd/ [phrasal verb I] to gradually change your mind and begin to agree with someone, although you did not agree with them before: *We had to work hard to persuade her, but she finally came around.*
come around to sb's point of view/come around to an idea *Give him time, and I'm sure he'll come round to your point of view.*

8 willing to change your ideas, opinions, or the way you do something

flexible /ˈfleksɪbəl/ [adj] willing to change your ideas, plans, or methods according to the situation: *Many employers say women are more flexible and better at team-work than men.*
+ about *Ken says he can be flexible about what time we start tomorrow.*

adaptable /əˈdæptəbəl/ [adj] someone who is **adaptable** does not get upset or annoyed if they have to change the way they do things, and easily gets used to a new situation: *Children are often more adaptable than adults.* | *I'm not sure Ken's adaptable enough to take a job abroad.*

9 not changing and always the same

permanent /ˈpɜːʳmənənt/ [adj] something that is **permanent** continues forever or for a very long time: *The accident left her with permanent brain damage.* | *a permanent job* | *We're hoping to find a permanent solution to the problem.*

fixed /fɪkst/ [adj] use this about amounts, prices, or times that cannot be changed: *Workers are paid a fixed rate per hour.* | *The classes begin and end at fixed times.*

constant /ˈkɒnstənt‖ˈkɑːn-/ [adj] use this about an amount or level that remains the same over a long period: *An animal's fur helps it to maintain a constant body temperature.* | *The noise level remained constant throughout the day.*

steady /ˈstedi/ [adj] use this about an amount that remains the same or a process that continues in the same way over a long period, especially when this is a good thing: *They drove along at a steady 80 kilometres per hour.* | *a steady improvement*
steady – steadier – steadiest
steadily [adv] *The standard of living has been rising steadily for 20 years.*

stable /ˈsteɪbəl/ [adj] use this about prices, amounts, or levels that are no longer changing, after a period when they were changing a lot: *Fuel prices have become more stable after several increases last year.* | *His temperature remained stable throughout the night.*

10 unwilling to change your ideas or opinions
➡ see also **DETERMINED**

stubborn /ˈstʌbəʳn/ [adj] someone who is **stubborn** refuses to change their ideas or opinions, even when other people think they are being unreasonable: *Mary didn't like admitting she was wrong – she could be very stubborn at times.*

be set in your ways /biː ˌset ɪn jɔːʳ ˈweɪz/ someone who **is set in their ways** does not want to change the way they do things, because they have done them in the same way for a long time: *He's too old and set in his ways to change now.*

11 changing a lot

changeable /'tʃeɪndʒəbəl/ [adj] something that is **changeable** changes often, so that you do not know what to expect next: *In the mountains the weather is very changeable.* | *Regular drug users often experience changeable moods and panic attacks.*

variable /'veəriəbəl/ [adj] changing according to the situation – use this about amounts, prices, speeds, temperatures etc: *The price of fruit tends to be very variable.*

CHEAP

➡ opposite **EXPENSIVE**

see also — SPEND, MONEY, COST, SHOP, BUY, PAY, FREE

1 not costing much money

cheap /tʃiːp/ [adj] something that is **cheap** costs very little money, or costs less than you expected: *My shoes were really cheap – they only cost $15.* | *The cheapest way to get to Chicago is to take the bus.*
it is cheap to do sth *It's cheaper to phone after six o'clock.*
relatively cheap (=cheap compared with other things) *These wooden houses are relatively cheap to build.*
get sth cheap (=buy something for a lower price than you expected) *The jacket was slightly damaged, so I got it cheap.*
cheaply [adv] *You can buy electronic diaries fairly cheaply nowadays.*

inexpensive /ˌɪnɪk'spensɪv◄/ [adj] not expensive – use this especially about things that are of good quality, even though they do not cost a lot: *The furniture is inexpensive but well-made.* | *a simple, inexpensive meal* | *Beans and lentils are an inexpensive source of protein.*

⚠ Use **inexpensive** especially in written English.

Ǫ not cost much /nɒt 'kɒst ˌmʌtʃ‖-'kɔːst-/ ESPECIALLY SPOKEN to not be expensive: *We had a very good meal and it didn't cost much.*
it doesn't cost much to do sth *It doesn't cost much to rent a TV.*

economical /ˌekə'nɒmɪkəl◄, ˌiː-‖-'nɑː-/ [adj] cheap to use or cheap to do – use this about cars, machines, or ways of doing things that do not waste any money, fuel etc: *We have a very economical heating system, so the bills aren't too high.*
be economical to use/run/operate *This is a well-designed car that is also very economical to run.*
it is more economical to do sth *It's more economical to buy the big packet – it's only 50p more than the small one.*

2 cheap but bad quality

cheap /tʃiːp/ [adj usually before noun] something that is **cheap** does not cost much, and is clearly of bad quality: *The tourist shops were full of cheap souvenirs.* | *an old woman smelling of cheap perfume*
cheap and nasty BRITISH (=cheap and unattractive because it is of very bad quality) *I wouldn't buy any of that jewellery – it's cheap and nasty.*

3 when you get something good for a low price

be good value /biː gʊd 'væljuː/ to be worth the price that you pay for it: *The meals at Charlie's Pizza are really good value.*
good value for money *There's a special ticket that means you can see six concerts, which is definitely good value for money.*

be a good buy /biː ə ˌgʊd 'baɪ/ something that **is a good buy** is worth the price you pay for it, because it is not expensive but is still good: *The Brazilian white wine is a good buy at only £2.99 a bottle.*

⚠ Use **a good buy** about goods or products, but not about services such as travel, entertainment, or meals.

bargain /ˈbɑːrgɨn/ [n C] something that costs a lot less than you expect or a lot less than it usually costs: *I got this shirt when I was in Thailand – it was a real bargain. | Did you get any bargains at the market?*

reasonable /ˈriːzənəbəl/ [adj] **reasonable** prices seem fair because they are not too high: *They sell good-quality hi-fi equipment at reasonable prices. | Only £15 a night? That's very reasonable!*

4 when the price has been reduced

sale /seɪl/ [n C] a time when a shop sells things more cheaply than usual: *The bookstore is having a closing-down sale.*
the sales BRITISH (=when a lot of shops sell things at reduced prices) *the January sales | I bought this coat half price in the sales.*

on sale /ɒn ˈseɪl/ AMERICAN something that is **on sale** is being sold at a specially low price in a shop: *"How much was your jacket?" "I got it on sale in Montgomery Wards for $45."*

reduced /rɪˈdjuːst‖-ˈduːst/ [adj not before noun] goods that are **reduced** are being sold at a lower price than usual: *Everything is reduced because the store's closing down next month.*
+ from ... to ... *These CDs were reduced from $10 to $5.*

£5/$20/10% etc off /(£5 etc) ˈɒf‖-ˈɔːf/ if there is **£5, $20, 10% etc off** something, its usual price has been reduced by that amount: *20% off all computers in Dixon's summer sale | We got $10 off the chair because it had a small mark on it.*

discount /ˈdɪskaʊnt/ [n C] a reduction in the price you pay for something, which is given for a special reason
get a discount (=pay less) *Do you get a discount if you pay in cash?*
30%/£50 etc discount *a 30% discount on all electrical goods*
+ on *Workers at the store get a discount on books and records.*
at a discount (=at a reduced price) *Air UK are currently offering tickets to students at a special discount.*

special offer /ˌspeʃəl ˈɒfər‖-ˈɔːf-/ [n C] a very low price that a shop sells something for, in order to persuade more people to buy things in that shop: *Today's special offer: melons at only 20p a kilo!*

CHEAT

1 to get money or possessions from someone dishonestly

cheat /tʃiːt/ [v T] to get money or possessions from someone dishonestly: *He always thinks that people in shops are trying to cheat him.*
cheat sb out of sth *She says she was cheated out of $10,000 she paid to a modeling agency.*

swindle /ˈswɪndl/ [v T] to get money from a person or organization by cheating them, especially using clever and complicated methods: *He was jailed in 1992 for attempting to swindle the insurance company he worked for.*
swindle sb out of sth *Investors have been swindled out of millions of pounds.*

con /kɒn‖kɑːn/ [v T] ESPECIALLY SPOKEN to persuade someone to buy something or to give you money by telling them lies
con sb out of sth *A man pretending to be a faith healer has conned around £20,000 out of desperate sick people.*
con sb into doing sth *They conned her into leaving a blank credit card slip as a deposit.*
conning – conned – have conned

fiddle /ˈfɪdl/ [v T] BRITISH INFORMAL to give false information or make dishonest changes in financial records, in order to get money or avoid paying money: *My boss thinks I've been fiddling my travel expenses.*

fiddle the books/fiddle the accounts
(=change a company's financial records)
*The company secretary has been fiddling
the books for years.*

2 to make someone pay too much money for something

overcharge /ˌəʊvəˈtʃɑːʳdʒ/ [v I/T] to
make someone pay too much for something in a shop, a restaurant, a taxi etc:
*Garage mechanics are twice as likely to
overcharge women car-owners than
men.*

overcharge sb for sth *The meal was
good, but we were overcharged for the
wine.*

◯**rip off** /ˌrɪp ˈɒf‖-ˈɔːf/ [phrasal verb T]
SPOKEN INFORMAL to make someone pay
much more than the usual price for something

rip sb off *They really ripped us off at
that hotel.*

rip off sb *The bars by the sea make huge
profits by ripping off tourists.*

◯**a rip-off** /ə ˈrɪp ɒf‖-ɔːf/ [n singular] SPOKEN
INFORMAL if something is **a rip-off**, it is
much too expensive and you think that
someone is trying to cheat you: *"It cost
£200 to get it fixed." "What a rip-off!"*

a complete/total rip-off *The meal cost
me $80 – it was a total rip-off.*

3 to cheat in an examination or game

cheat /tʃiːt/ [v I] to use dishonest methods
in order to pass an examination or win a
game: *Anyone caught cheating will automatically fail the exam.*

+ at *Jenny always cheats at cards.*

cheating [n U] when someone cheats in
an examination or game: *Cheating is
becoming fairly common in professional football.*

4 when people are dishonest in order to get money

fraud /frɔːd/ [n C/U] the crime of getting
money dishonestly from a big organization,
for example by giving false information or
changing documents, especially over a long
period: *Big losses due to theft and fraud*

forced the company to close. I *Credit
card fraud is very common.*

◯**scam** /skæm/ [n C] SPOKEN INFORMAL a
clever plan for dishonestly getting money or
advantages for yourself: *They set fire to
the house in order to get the insurance
money – it was all a big scam.*

a tax scam (=to avoid paying tax)

5 someone who cheats

cheat /tʃiːt/ [n C] someone who behaves
dishonestly, especially in an examination
or game: *Bergstrom accused his opponent of being a cheat.*

conman /ˈkɒnmæn‖ˈkɑːn-/ [n C] INFORMAL
someone who gets money by cheating
people or lying to them: *a handsome conman who charms women into giving him
money, then simply disappears from
their lives*

plural **conmen**

CHECK

LOOK AT 2   WRONG

see
also

RIGHT   SAFE

MISTAKE

1 to make sure that something is true or correct

check /tʃek/ [v I/T] to do something in
order to find out whether something is
really true or correct: *"Are you sure this
is the right phone number?" "Yes, I've
just checked."* I *Remember to check
your spellings in a dictionary.*

+ (that) *I'll just check I locked the
door.* I *Check that the meat is cooked
thoroughly before serving it.*

+ whether *She went back to the apartment to check whether he'd been home.*

make sure /ˌmeɪk ˈʃʊəʳ/ to check that a
situation really is the way you want or
expect it to be: *I don't think Sarah's back
yet, but you can knock on her door just
to make sure.*

+ (that) *I phoned the hotel to make sure that they had reserved a room for us.* | *Make sure there are no cars behind you before you drive off.*

double-check /ˌdʌbəl 'tʃek/ [v I/T] to check a second time, so that you are completely sure: *"Did you switch the heating off?" "Yes, I double-checked."* | *I can't have got it wrong! I checked and double-checked all my calculations.*

CHILD

1 a child

child /tʃaɪld/ [n C] a young person from the time they are born until they are aged about 14 or 15: *How many children are there in your class?* | *Children under 14 travel free.* | *Every child was given a present.*
plural **children**

⚠ You usually call a very young child that cannot walk or talk a **baby**.

kid /kɪd/ [n C] INFORMAL a child: *A gang of kids were playing in the yard.* | *I really enjoy working with kids.* | *Jamie's a bright kid.*

boy /bɔɪ/ [n C] a male child: *I used to live in Spain when I was a boy.* | *Harry teaches in a boys' school in Glasgow.*
little boy (=a very young boy) *Her best friend was a little boy called Sam.*

girl /gɜːrl/ [n C] a female child: *What's that girl's name?* | *More girls than ever before are choosing to study science.*
little girl (=a very young girl) *A little girl was sitting on the front doorstep.*

toddler /'tɒdlər‖'taːd-/ [n C] a very young child who has just learned to walk: *As a toddler, he was attacked and injured by the family's pet dog.*

2 someone's son or daughter

child /tʃaɪld/ [n C] someone's son or daughter, of any age: *She called her first child Katrin.* | *The house seems very quiet now all the children have left home.* | *One of her children lives in Australia now.*
only child (=a child who has no brothers or sisters)
plural **children**

kid /kɪd/ [n C] INFORMAL someone's son or daughter – use this about children aged up to 14 or 15: *All I ever wanted was to get married and have kids.* | *Could you look after the kids this evening?*

son /sʌn/ [n C] someone's male child: *We have two teenage sons.* | *Her son used to work in Scotland.*

daughter /'dɔːtər/ [n C] someone's female child: *Our eldest daughter has just left university.* | *My aunt had five daughters and three sons.*

little boy/little girl /ˌlɪtl 'bɔɪ, ˌlɪtl 'gɜːrl/ [n C] SPOKEN someone's young son or daughter: *Paula's had to go home – her little girl's sick.* | *"How old's your little boy?" "He's three."*

⚠ Use **little boy** or **little girl** when you are talking about very young children.

3 a child whose parents have died

orphan /'ɔːrfən/ [n C] a child whose parents have died: *Leila was an orphan whose parents had been killed in the war.*

4 the time when someone is a child

childhood /'tʃaɪldhʊd/ [n U] the time when someone is a child: *They've known each other since childhood.*
early childhood (=the time when you are very young) *I spent my early childhood living with my aunt and uncle.*

⚠ You can also use **childhood** before a noun, like an adjective: *childhood illnesses* | *He was deeply affected by those early childhood experiences.*

in infancy/during infancy /ɪn ˈɪnfən-si, ˌdjʊərɪŋ ˈɪnfənsi‖ˌdʊr-/ FORMAL while someone is a baby or a very young child – use this especially to talk about children dying or getting diseases: *Three of her children died in infancy.*

CHOOSE

➡ see also **DECIDE, VOTE, MUST**

1 to choose something

choose /tʃuːz/ [v I/T] to decide which one of several things or possibilities you want: *I can't decide what I want. You choose.* | *Will you help me choose a present for Warren?*
choose to do sth *Why do so few women choose to become engineers?*
+ whether/which/when etc *It took her three hours to choose which dress to wear.*
+ between (=choose one of two things) *We have to choose between doing geography or studying another language.*
+ from (=choose from among several things) *Viewers in Ireland can choose from up to 20 TV channels.*
choosing – chose – have chosen

pick /pɪk/ [v T] to choose something, especially without thinking carefully about it: *"Can I borrow a book to read?" "Yes, pick whatever you want."* | *Pick a number from one to five.*

⚠ **Pick** is more informal than **choose** or **select**.

select /sɪˈlekt/ [v T] FORMAL to choose something by carefully thinking about which is best or most suitable: *We asked Steve to help us select music for the wedding.* | *Our wines have been carefully selected from vineyards throughout Europe.*

decide on sth /dɪˈsaɪd ɒn (sth)‖-ɑːn-/ [phrasal verb T] to finally choose something, especially when making the decision has been difficult or has taken a long time: *Have you decided on a name for the baby yet?*

go for sth /ˈgəʊ fɔːr (sth)/ [phrasal verb T] SPOKEN INFORMAL to choose something

because you think it is the most attractive, interesting, or enjoyable: *She always goes for the most expensive thing on the menu.*

make a choice /ˌmeɪk ə ˈtʃɔɪs/ to make a decision, especially a difficult decision, about which thing to choose: *You have to make a choice now. Which of these two jobs do you want?*
make the right/wrong choice *He's decided to study law – I hope he's made the right choice.*

opt /ɒpt‖ɑːpt/ [v I] to choose something after thinking carefully about all the possibilities
+ for *More and more British drivers are opting for Japanese cars.*
opt to do sth *When her parents divorced, Mary Ann opted to live with her father.*

⚠ **Opt** is used especially in newspapers.

2 to choose someone for a job or a team

choose /tʃuːz/ [v T] to decide who is the best person for a job, team, prize etc: *Companies are now using computers to help them choose new workers.*
choose sb as sth *The judges have chosen Pat Barker as this year's Booker Prize winner.*
choose sb to do sth *Eventually, Jane was chosen to deliver the message.*
choosing – chose – have chosen

select /sɪˈlekt/ [v T] FORMAL to choose someone for a particular job, team, place at school etc, after considering a lot of different people who might be suitable: *The college selects only 12 students from the thousands who apply.*
select sb for sth *We selected four applicants for interview.*
select sb to do sth *Ernst has been selected to play in the game against Belgium.*

appoint /əˈpɔɪnt/ [v T] to officially choose someone to do an important job: *The company has appointed a new Sales Director.*
appoint sb as sth *They have appointed Jane Staller as their new East Coast manager.*

C

appoint sb to do sth *A committee was appointed to consider changes to the Prison Service.*

pick /pɪk/ [v T] to choose someone for a sports team or an important job: *Joe picked Steve and Terry to be on his team.* | *a change in the way the Conservative Party picks its leader*

⚠️ Pick is more informal than choose, select, or appoint

3 **the decision you make when you choose**

choice /tʃɔɪs/ [n C] *It was a difficult choice, but we finally decided that Hannah should have the prize.* | *These are the two designs that I like best. I'm leaving the final choice to you.*

4 **something or someone that has been chosen**

choice /tʃɔɪs/ [n singular] something or someone that has been chosen
first/second etc choice (=the thing you wanted most, the thing you wanted most after that etc) *Greece was our first choice for a vacation, but all the flights were full.*
sb's choice of sth (=the thing someone chooses) *I don't like his choice of friends.*

selection /sɪ'lekʃən/ [n C] a small group of the best things that have been chosen from a larger group
+ of *Kaori showed me a selection of her drawings.* | *a selection of songs from 'West Side Story'*

5 **the things or people that you can choose from**

choice /tʃɔɪs/ [n singular/U] all the different things or people that you can choose from
+ of *The school seems OK, but there isn't a great choice of courses.*
have a choice of (=be able to choose from several things) *You will have a choice of twelve questions in the exam.*
wide/good choice (=a lot of things to choose from) *There is a wide choice of hotels and hostels in the town.*

option /'ɒpʃən‖'ɑːp-/ [n C] one of the things that you can choose to do in a situation: *There were only two options: either we told Mr Greaves what we'd done, or said nothing and hope he didn't find out.*
keep your options open (=delay choosing so that you continue to have several things to choose from) *She hasn't decided which college to go to yet – she's keeping her options open.*

alternative /ɔːl'tɜːrnətɪv/ [n C] one of two or more ways of doing something: *Check out all the alternatives when deciding which class you want to go to.*
have no alternative (=to not have a choice about what to do or how to do it) *He says he doesn't want to see a doctor, but I'm afraid he has no alternative.*

selection /sɪ'lekʃən/ [n singular] a **selection** of cakes, wines, clothes, books etc is a lot of different cakes, wines etc for you to choose from, especially in a shop
+ of *A wonderful selection of cakes and pastries was displayed in the window.*
wide/large selection (=a lot of things to choose from) *The restaurant offers you a wide selection of local dishes.*

6 **someone who is very careful about choosing things**

choosy /'tʃuːzi/ [adj not before noun] INFORMAL someone who is **choosy** chooses things carefully and only wants the things that they think are the best: *I get offered a lot of work now, so I can be more choosy.*
+ about *She's very choosy about what airline she travels on.*

fussy/picky /'fʌsi, 'pɪki/ [adj] INFORMAL someone who is **picky** or **fussy** is difficult to please because they only like a few things and will only accept exactly what they want: *Don't be so picky! Eat what you are given.*
+ about *She was always very fussy about her clothes.*
picky/fussy eater (=someone who will only eat the few things they like)

selective /sɪ'lektɪv/ [adj not before noun] careful about what you choose, so that you only choose the best or most suitable things

+ about *People are becoming more and more selective about what foods they buy.*

⚠ Selective is more formal than choosy.

CLASS IN SOCIETY

social class based on your job, your family, how much you earn etc

➡ if you mean 'a class in a school', go to **EDUCATION**
➡ see also **POSITION/RANK**

1 someone's social class

class /klɑːs‖klæs/ [n C/U] the social group that you belong to because of your job, the type of family you come from, or the amount of money you have: *Success in this country seems to be based on class rather than on ability.* | *the professional and managerial classes*
the class system (=the system by which society is divided into classes) *The old class system is slowly disappearing.*
social class (=the class in society you come from) *There is a clear link between social class and educational achievement.*
plural **classes**

background /'bækgraʊnd/ [n C] the type of home and family that you come from, and its social class: *The school takes kids from all sorts of backgrounds.* | *We come from the same town and have a similar background.*
working-class/middle-class etc background *The organization helps children from working-class backgrounds to go to university.*

2 the highest class

upper-class /ˌʌpəʳ 'klɑːs◄‖-'klæs◄/ [adj] belonging to the class of people who originally had most of the money and power, especially families that own a lot of land: *Most senior politicians in the UK are from upper-class families.* | *He spoke with an upper-class accent.*
the upper class/the upper classes (=people who are upper class) *In South America, the upper classes tend to be European in origin.*

⚠ The upper classes means the same as the upper class.

Qposh /pɒʃ‖pɑːʃ/ [adj] BRITISH SPOKEN someone who is **posh** behaves and speaks in a way in which upper-class people usually behave or speak: *Will your posh university friends be coming tonight?*
posh school/hotel/restaurant etc (=one that is very expensive, that rich people go to) *She went to a posh girls' school in Switzerland.*

⚠ People often use the word posh when they are making fun of other people.

the aristocracy /ðɪ ˌærɪ'stɒkrəsi‖-'stɑː-/ [n singular] the people who belong to families that own a lot of land, and used to have a lot of power, and have special titles before their names, like 'Lord' or 'Lady' – used especially when you are talking about the past: *senior members of the British aristocracy* | *the French aristocracy*

3 the middle class

middle-class /ˌmɪdl 'klɑːs◄‖-'klæs◄/ [adj] belonging to the class of people who are usually well educated, fairly rich, and who work in jobs which they have trained for a long time to do; for example, doctors, lawyers, and managers are middle-class: *a newspaper whose readers are mostly middle-class* | *They live in a middle-class neighbourhood on the edge of town.*
the middle class/the middle classes (=people who are middle-class) *The government needs the support of the middle classes to win the next election.*

⚠ The middle classes means the same as the middle class.

white-collar /ˌwaɪt 'kɒləʳ◄‖-'kɑː-/ [adj only before noun] **white-collar worker/job/employee** someone who works in an office, not a factory, mine etc: *The economic recession has put many white-collar workers in danger of losing their jobs.*

4 the lowest class

working-class /ˌwɜːkɪŋ 'klɑːs◄‖-'klæs◄/ [adj] belonging to the class of people who do not have much money or power, and who have jobs where they do physical work; for example, factory workers, builders, and drivers are working-class: *Most of the people who live round here are working-class.* | *He's from a working-class background.*

the working class/the working classes (=people who are working class) *Cuts in welfare spending affect the working class most.*

⚠ **The working classes** means the same as **the working class**.

blue-collar /ˌbluː ˈkɒləʳ◀ǁ-ˈkɑː-/ [adj only before noun] **blue-collar worker/job/employee** someone who does physical work, for example in a factory or a mine, and does not work in an office: *His political support comes mainly from blue-collar workers.*

underclass /ˈʌndəʳklɑːsǁ-klæs/ [n singular] the lowest social class, who are very poor and may not have jobs, homes etc: *The government has created an underclass who do not feel they have any rights in society.*

5 someone who cares too much about social class

snob /snɒbǁsnɑːb/ [n C] someone who thinks that they are better than people from a lower social class, and does not want to talk to them or be friends with them: *My mother was such a snob she wouldn't let me play with the local children.*

snobbish /ˈsnɒbɪʃǁˈsnɑːb-/ [adj] someone who is **snobbish** thinks that they are better than people from a lower social class: *Snobbish home-owners are protesting about a refugee family moving into their street.*

CLEAN
not dirty

➡ opposite **DIRTY**
➡ see also **TIDY, SHINE, WASH**

⚠ Don't confuse **clean** (=not dirty) and **tidy** (=when everything is neatly arranged and is in the right place).

1 clean

clean /kliːn/ [adj] not dirty: *He changed into a clean shirt.* | *I'll put some clean sheets on the bed.* | *New houses are much easier to keep clean.*

nice and clean/lovely and clean BRITISH (=very clean) *Our hotel room was lovely and clean.*

clean water/air (=with no harmful substances in it) *What the villagers need most is a supply of clean drinking water.*

spotlessly clean/spotless /ˌspɒtləsli ˈkliːn, ˈspɒtləsǁˌspɑːt-/ [adj] completely clean – use this about clothes, rooms, or houses: *Nina keeps the kitchen absolutely spotless.* | *He was wearing a spotlessly clean white shirt.*

hygienic /haɪˈdʒiːnɪkǁ-ˈdʒe-, -ˈdʒiː-/ [adj] clean so that diseases cannot spread: *You shouldn't let the cat walk on the table. It's not hygienic.* | *Meat products must always be kept in hygienic conditions.*

2 to make something clean

clean /kliːn/ [v I/T] to make something clean by removing the dirt, dust etc: *I clean the windows every Saturday.* | *Tony was cleaning his car.* | *How often do you clean the kitchen?*

clean sth up/clean up sth (=remove dirt by cleaning, especially in a room, from a floor etc) *There was mud all over the carpet, and it took me a long time to clean it up.*

clean your teeth BRITISH *I always clean my teeth last thing at night.*

+ behind/under etc *Make sure you clean behind the stove.*

cleaning [n U] when you clean things, especially in a room, or a house: *I hate cleaning!*

do the cleaning *Her husband does most of the cleaning.*

⚠ You can also say **give something a clean** in British English. and it means the same as **clean something**: *I decided to give my bedroom a clean.*

spring-clean /ˌsprɪŋ ˈkliːn/ [v I/T] to clean your whole house very thoroughly, including things that you do not clean very often: *Barry spent the weekend spring-cleaning.* | *I want to spring-clean the whole apartment before Easter.*

3 to clean something with a cloth

wipe /waɪp/ [v T] to remove dirt or liquid from something using a slightly wet cloth: *The waiter was wiping the tables.*

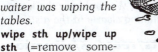
wipe

wipe sth up/wipe up sth (=remove something from a surface by wiping) *If you spill any paint, wipe it up immediately.*

dust /dʌst/ [v I/T] to remove dust from furniture, shelves etc using a soft cloth: *Take the ornaments off the shelf and dust them.*

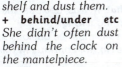
dust

+ behind/under etc *She didn't often dust behind the clock on the mantelpiece.*

polish /ˈpɒlɪʃ‖ˈpɑː-/ [v T] to make something clean and shiny, for example your shoes or a piece of furniture, by rubbing it with a cloth or brush: *She polished the piano until the wood shone.* | *a polished wooden floor*

4 to clean something with a brush

brush /brʌʃ/ [v T] to clean something with a brush: *You should brush your jacket – it's covered in dust.*

brush

brush sth off *I brushed the crumbs off the sofa.*
brush your teeth *Have you brushed your teeth yet?*

scrub /skrʌb/ [v T] to clean something by rubbing it hard with a brush and some water or soap: *I had a job in a restaurant, washing the dishes and scrubbing the floors.* | *Scrub*

scrub

the potatoes and boil them for 5-10 minutes.

scrubbing – scrubbed – have scrubbed

sweep /swiːp/ [v T] to clean the floor or the ground using a brush with a long handle: *When everyone had left, Ed swept the floor.*

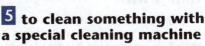
sweep

sweep up sth/sweep sth up (=remove something from a floor by sweeping) *Can you help me sweep up all the pieces of glass?*

sweeping – swept – have swept

5 to clean something with a special cleaning machine

vacuum (also **hoover** BRITISH) /ˈvækjuəm, -kjʊm, ˈhuːvər/ [v I/T] to clean something using a special machine that sucks dirt into a bag inside the machine: *Have you vacuumed all the carpets?*

vacuum

6 when you keep things clean to prevent disease

hygiene /ˈhaɪdʒiːn/ [n U] methods you use to make sure that everything is completely clean, especially in order to prevent disease: *Lack of hygiene attracted large numbers of rats.*

personal hygiene (=keeping your body clean) *Some kids just aren't interested in personal hygiene.*

disinfect /ˌdɪsɪnˈfekt/ [v T] to use chemicals to clean a place, a piece of equipment, or a wound, in order to prevent disease: *She cleaned and disinfected the cuts on his hands.* | *Disinfect the toilet regularly using bleach.*

sterilize (also **sterilise** BRITISH) /ˈsterəlaɪz/ [v T] to make something safe to use by heating it or using chemicals, in order to prevent disease – use this about medical or scientific equipment or babies' bottles: *Has the needle been sterilized?* | *Babies' bottles can be sterilized simply by boiling them in water.*

7 someone whose job is to clean things

cleaner /'kliːnər/ [n C] someone who is paid to clean a house or office: *We finish work at six, and then the cleaners come in.* | *a window cleaner*

cleaner's/dry cleaner's /'kliːnərz, ˌdraɪ 'kliːnərz/ [n C] a shop where you can take your clothes to be cleaned, especially with chemicals, not water: *My best suit is at the dry cleaner's.* | *Can you collect my dress from the cleaner's?*

8 what you use to clean things with

detergent /dɪ'tɜːrdʒənt/ [n C/U] a liquid or powder that you use to wash dishes or clothes: *What brand of detergent do you use?*

cleaner /'kliːnər/ [n C/U] **toilet/carpet/ oven etc cleaner** a substance that you use to clean toilets, carpets, ovens etc

disinfectant /ˌdɪsɪn'fektənt/ [n C/U] a chemical that you use for cleaning toilets, sinks etc, which helps prevent disease

bleach /bliːtʃ/ [n U] a strong chemical that you use to clean a place or surface completely, in order to prevent disease

CLEAR/NOT CLEAR

➡ look here for ...
- easy or difficult to see
- easy or difficult to understand

➡ if you mean 'something that you can see through', go to SEE 7

1 instructions/rules/ explanations etc

• see also **UNDERSTAND/NOT UNDERSTAND, EXPLAIN, INSTRUCTIONS**

clear /klɪər/ [adj] something that is **clear** is easy to understand because it is said or written in a simple way – use this especially about explanations, instructions, or rules: *Her article is a clear and readable introduction to the subject.*

+ about/on *The instructions aren't very clear on what you're supposed to do if there's a fire.*

+ to *The rules seem clear enough to me.*
make it clear (that) *Barlow made it very clear that he did not agree with us.*

clearly [adv] *The teacher explained everything to us very clearly.*

2 objects/views etc

clear /klɪər/ [adj] something that is **clear** is easy to see: *There was a clear view across the valley.*

clearly [adv] *We could see the harbour lights shining clearly in the distance.*

3 facts/reasons/situations etc

obvious /'ɒbviəs‖'ɑːb-/ [adj] something that is **obvious** is very easy to notice or understand: *There is an obvious connection between the two murders.* | *"Why is she leaving?" "Well, it's obvious, isn't it?"*

it is obvious that *It was obvious that there was something wrong.*

it is obvious to sb *It must be obvious to everyone that we cannot continue in this way.*

for obvious reasons (=when the reasons are so obvious that you do not need to say what they are) *For obvious reasons we have had to cancel tonight's performance.*

clear /klɪər/ [adj] if it is **clear** that something is true, it is easy to notice that it is true and you feel sure about it and have no doubts

it is clear that *It was clear that she was very upset by what had happened.*

it is clear to sb *It was clear to me that my father was dying.*

it becomes clear *It soon became clear that there were not enough police officers to deal with the situation.*

clear evidence/example/sign *There is clear evidence that some vitamins reduce your chances of getting cancer.*

obviously/clearly /'ɒbviəsli, 'klɪərli‖ 'ɑːb-/ [adv] use this to emphasize that it is easy to see that something is true: *We're obviously going to need more help.* | *Clearly, the situation is more complicated than we first thought.* | *"Is she pleased with the decision?" "Obviously not!"* | *The children were clearly upset.*

⚠ Don't say 'it is obviously that' or 'it is clearly that'. Say **it is obvious that** or **it is clear that**

⚠ **Obviously** is used in spoken and written English. **Clearly** is more formal, and is used mostly in written English.

can tell /kən ˈtel/ to know that something must be true because you can see signs that show this
+ (that) *I can tell that he isn't happy.* | *Even though it was dark, she could tell it was him.*
+ by *I could tell by the way she walked that her leg was still hurting.*

it is easy to see /ɪt ɪz ˌiːzi tə ˈsiː/ if **it is easy to see** that something is true, it is very easy for anyone to notice or understand that fact
+ (that) *It's easy to see that he isn't well.*
+ how/why/what *It's easy to see why this car is so popular.* | *It's easy to see how the mistake was made.*

noticeable /ˈnəʊtɪsəbəl/ [adj] a **noticeable** change, difference, or fact is easy to notice: *a noticeable difference in temperature*
it is noticeable that (=it is easy for people to notice something) *It was noticeable that she had invited everyone except Gail.*
  noticeably [adv] *When I showed him the letter, Simmons became noticeably nervous.*

blatant /ˈbleɪtənt/ [adj usually before noun] use this about something that someone does which is clearly bad, but which they do not seem to be ashamed of: *This is a lie, a blatant lie!* | *The company's refusal to hire him was a blatant act of discrimination.*
  blatantly [adv] *blatantly racist comments*

4 not easy to understand

unclear/not clear /ʌnˈklɪəʳ, nɒt ˈklɪəʳ/ [adj] use this about something that is difficult to understand because there is not enough information or it has not been explained well: *The reasons for his resignation are still unclear.*
+ whether/what/why etc *It's not clear why Parks didn't go straight to the police.* | *It is unclear whether the Princess will agree to the new arrangements.*

+ about *His ideas are good, but he's very unclear about how he's going to achieve them.*

ambiguous /æmˈbɪɡjuəs/ [adj] use this about something that someone says or writes that has more than one meaning and could be confusing: *The last part of her letter was deliberately ambiguous.*
  ambiguously [adv] *The contract was worded ambiguously.*

vague /veɪɡ/ [adj] use this about something that someone says or writes that is not clear because they do not give enough details: *Police say the warning about the bomb was too vague and too late.*
+ about *He was rather vague about the reasons why he never finished school.*
  vaguely [adv] *The man is vaguely described as 'medium build with brown hair'.*

confusing /kənˈfjuːzɪŋ/ [adj] a **confusing** situation, explanation, story etc is difficult to understand because there does not seem to be a clear pattern or order to it: *There are so many rules and regulations – it's all very confusing.* | *I found the book really confusing. I kept forgetting who the characters were.*

5 not easy to see or notice

faint /feɪnt/ [adj] a **faint** sound, smell, image etc is one you can only just hear, smell, or see: *His voice was so faint I could hardly hear it.* | *A faint smell of perfume wafted down the corridor.* | *the faint morning light*

subtle /ˈsʌtl/ [adj] a **subtle** change or difference is difficult to notice unless you look closely or think about it carefully: *The patterns look the same at first, but there are subtle differences between them.* | *subtle changes in his character* | *a subtle flavour*

blurred /blɜːʳd/ [adj] if a picture or image is **blurred**, you can see its general shape, but the edges are not clear: *The photographs were very blurred.* | *Everything looks blurred when I take my glasses off.*

When you see **EC** , go to the **ESSENTIAL COMMUNICATION** section.

CLIMB

➡ see also **UP, DOWN, LAND AND SEA**

1 to climb up something

climb /klaɪm/ [v I/T] to move up towards the top of a wall, mountain, tree etc, using your hands and feet: *Most kids love climbing trees.* | *Trying not to look down, Alan began to climb.*

climb

+ up/over/onto etc
Several fans climbed onto the roof of the arena to get a better view.

climb down (=go down a wall, tree etc using your hands and feet) *The prisoner had escaped by climbing down a drain-pipe.*

2 climbing hills or mountains as a sport

climbing /'klaɪmɪŋ/ [n U] the sport of climbing hills or mountains: *Eva's hobbies are horse-riding, climbing, and aerobics.* | *climbing boots*

rock climbing (=the sport of climbing up steep rocks and cliffs)

mountaineering /ˌmaʊntɪ'nɪərɪŋ/ [n U] the sport of climbing high mountains using special equipment: *Mountaineering can be a very dangerous sport.*

climber /'klaɪmər/ [n C] someone who climbs hills or rocks as a sport, especially using special equipment: *The search is continuing for a group of climbers reported missing in the Everest region.* | *an experienced climber*

When you see **EC**, go to the
ESSENTIAL COMMUNICATION section.

CLOTHES

FASHIONABLE/UNFASHIONABLE

TIGHT   MATERIAL 2

see also

LOOSE   DESIGN

FASTEN/   DESCRIBING
UNFASTEN   PEOPLE

1 clothes

clothes /kləʊðz, kləʊz/ [n plural] things that you wear, for example, coats, shirts, and dresses: *I need to buy some new clothes.* | *He was wearing summer clothes even though it was quite cold.* | *The other girls were all dressed up in their best clothes.* | *There are lots of good clothes shops in Covent Garden.*

⚠ Don't confuse **clothes** (=things you wear) and **cloth** (=the material that clothes are made from).

⚠ Don't say 'a nice clothes'. Just say **nice clothes**.

⚠ You can use **clothes** before a noun, like an adjective: *a clothes shop* | *a clothes line* (=for hanging wet clothes on)

clothing /'kləʊðɪŋ/ [n U] clothes in general – use this either to talk about a particular type of clothes, or to talk about a large quantity of clothes: *Charities have been delivering food and clothing to the disaster area.*

warm/light/protective/outdoor clothing *Make sure that you take plenty of warm clothing – it can be very cold up there.*

piece/item of clothing (=one thing that you wear, for example a shirt or a dress) FORMAL *There was nothing in the chest apart from a few items of clothing.*

⚠ Don't use **clothing** to talk about your own clothes or a particular person's clothes, except in very official situations: *I spilled coffee all over my clothes* (not 'my clothing'). | *The police said that some blood was found on the dead woman's clothing.*

⚠️ You can also use **clothing** before a noun, like an adjective: *the clothing industry*

○**something to wear** /ˌsʌmθɪŋ tə ˈweəʳ/ SPOKEN clothes, especially clothes that you can wear for a particular event or occasion: *I must buy something to wear for Julia's wedding.*

⚠️ In questions and negatives, say **anything to wear**: *I haven't got anything to wear to Jim's party.*

2 clothes that you wear together as a set

suit /suːt, sjuːt‖suːt/ [n C] a pair of trousers or a skirt, which you wear with a short coat made of the same material: *She wore a black suit for the interview.* | *Bob was wearing a business suit.*

outfit /ˈaʊtˌfɪt/ [n C] a set of clothes that look attractive together, which you wear for a special occasion: *I bought a new outfit for Kate's birthday party.* | *Natalie was wearing a blue and purple outfit.*

⚠️ Use **outfit** to describe clothes worn by women and children. Don't use it about men's clothes.

uniform /ˈjuːnɪˌfɔːʳm/ [n C/U] a set of clothes that are worn by all the people who belong to a particular organization, for example by soldiers, police officers, or schoolchildren: *Do you have to wear a uniform if you work at McDonald's?*
school uniform *I used to hate wearing school uniform.*
in uniform (=wearing uniform) *We saw two nurses in uniform.*

○**things** /θɪŋz/ [n plural] **swimming/ football/tennis etc things** SPOKEN the clothes that you wear for swimming, playing football etc: *Don't forget to bring your swimming things when we go to Brighton.*

costume /ˈkɒstjʊm‖ˈkɑːstuːm/ [n C/U] a set of clothes that you wear for acting in a play or performance: *The children were all wearing colourful costumes for the festival procession.* | *I didn't like the play much but the costumes were brilliant.*

national costume (=the traditional clothes of a country) *The dancers were dressed in Ukrainian national costume.*

3 to wear clothes

wear /weəʳ/ [v T] to have clothes, shoes, glasses, jewellery etc on your body: *She was wearing shorts and sandals.* | *Dave doesn't wear his wedding ring any more.*
wear black/red/green etc (=wear black clothes, red clothes etc) *I never wear black – it makes me look too pale.*
wearing – wore – have worn

⚠️ Be careful to use the right tense with **wear**. Say **he/she is wearing** when you are talking about what clothes someone is wearing now: *Catriona is wearing a green jacket and jeans.* Say **he/she wears** when talking about the clothes that someone usually wears: *Gina always wears a suit for work.*

in /ɪn/ [preposition] **in a suit/in a red dress etc** wearing a suit, a red dress etc: *There was a man in a linen suit standing at the bar.* | *a couple of girls in jeans and T-shirts*

have on /ˌhæv ˈɒn‖-ˈɑːn/ [phrasal verb T] to be wearing clothes, shoes, glasses, or jewellery: *She had on a red hat and a pair of matching shoes.*
have sth on *All the men had suits on.*

be dressed /biː ˈdrest/ to be wearing clothes: *We'll leave as soon as Stuart is dressed.*
+ in *They were all dressed in T-shirts and jeans.* | *a woman dressed in green*
be dressed as sb (=wearing clothes that make you look like someone else) *Some of the children were dressed as soldiers.*

4 to put on clothes

put on /ˌpʊt ˈɒn‖-ˈɑːn/ [phrasal verb T] to put on a piece of clothing
put sth on *Put your coat on if you're going out.*
put on sth *She put on her bathrobe and went downstairs.*

get dressed /ˌget ˈdrest/ to put on all your

put on

He put on his jumper.

clothes: *Go and get dressed – it's nearly time for school.* | *Sandra's in the bedroom getting dressed.*

try on /ˌtraɪ ˈɒn‖-ˈɑːn/ [phrasal verb T] to put on a piece of clothing, to see if it fits you and if it looks nice on you
try sth on *If you like the shoes, why don't you try them on?*
try on sth *I tried on a beautiful coat, but it was too big.*

dress up/get dressed up /ˌdres ˈʌp, get ˌdrest ˈʌp/ to put on clothes that are suitable for a special or formal occasion: *We always get dressed up for church.* | *It's an informal party, so you don't need to dress up.*

5 to take off clothes

take off /ˌteɪk ˈɒf‖-ˈɔːf/ [phrasal verb T] to remove a piece of clothing that you were wearing
take sth off *Why don't you take your coat off?* | *If I take my glasses off, I can hardly see anything.*

She took off her jumper.

take off sth *He took off his jacket and put it around my shoulders.*

⚠ Don't say 'he put off his clothes'. Say **he took off his clothes**.

get undressed /ˌget ʌnˈdrest/ to take off all your clothes, especially before going to bed: *She got undressed and went to bed.*

undress /ʌnˈdres/ [v I] WRITTEN to take off all your clothes, especially before going to bed: *Paul went into the bathroom to undress.*

get changed /ˌget ˈtʃeɪndʒd/ to take off your clothes and put on different clothes: *The first thing I do when I get home from school is get changed.* | *Are you going to get changed before the party?*

change /tʃeɪndʒ/ [v I/T] to take off all or some of your clothes and put some different clothes on: *I'll just change my shirt and I'll be with you in a minute.*
+ into *She changed into a sweater and some jeans.*

+ out of *Ed went upstairs to change out of his work clothes.*

6 describing people's clothes

tight /taɪt/ [adj] **tight** clothes fit your body very closely: *These jeans are too tight – I can't get them on.* | *a tight miniskirt*

loose /luːs/ [adj] **loose** clothes do not fit your body tightly, so you feel comfortable when you wear them: *She wore a loose sweater and leggings.* | *Loose clothes are best in summer.*

baggy /ˈbægi/ [adj] **baggy** trousers, shirts etc are designed to be big and loose and they hide the shape of your body: *He was wearing baggy jeans and a T-shirt.* | *a comfortable baggy sweater*

well-dressed /ˌwelˈdrest◄/ [adj] someone who is **well-dressed** is wearing good quality clothes and looks as if they have taken a lot of care about how they look: *The photograph showed a well-dressed man in his early 50s.*

fashionable /ˈfæʃənəbəl/ [adj] **fashionable** clothes are in a style that is popular at the moment: *Long skirts are very fashionable these days.* | *a pair of fashionable and expensive-looking trainers*

smart /smɑːʳt/ [adj] BRITISH if you look **smart** or your clothes are **smart**, you are dressed in an attractive way and you look very tidy: *a smart suit* | *You look really smart today, Paul. Have you got a job interview or something?*

casual /ˈkæʒuəl/ [adj] **casual** clothes are comfortable clothes that you wear when you are relaxing, not clothes that you wear on formal occasions: *a casual jacket*

scruffy /ˈskrʌfi/ [adj] people or clothes that are **scruffy** look dirty and untidy: *Change out of those scruffy jeans.* | *You look too scruffy to go out to a restaurant.*

match /mætʃ/ [v I/T] if clothes **match** each other, or if they **match**, they look good together, especially because they are a similar colour: *That shirt doesn't match your jacket.*
hat/scarf/tie to match (=the same colour as something else) *I've got some blue shoes – now I need a bag to match.*

suit /suːt, sjuːt‖suːt/ [v T] if a piece of clothing or a type of clothing **suits** you, it looks good on you: *Short skirts don't really suit me.*

fit /fɪt/ [v I/T] if clothes **fit**, they are the right size: *He's put on so much weight that his clothes don't fit any more.* | *Do those shoes still fit you?*
fitting – fitted (also **fit** AMERICAN) – **have fitted**

7 the way that clothes look

style /staɪl/ [n C] the way that clothes look and how they have been designed: *I like the colour, but I don't really like the style.* | *70s styles are coming back into fashion.*

8 wearing no clothes

○**have nothing on** /hæv ˌnʌθɪŋ ˈɒn/ ESPECIALLY SPOKEN to not be wearing any clothes: *Don't come in yet – I have nothing on!*
have nothing on your feet *I had nothing on my feet and some of the stones were really sharp.*

naked /ˈneɪkɪd/ [adj] wearing no clothes – use this especially when it is surprising that someone is not wearing clothes: *He was lying on the bed completely naked.* | *The magazine was full of pictures of naked men.*
stark naked (also **buck naked** AMERICAN) (=completely naked) *She was standing there stark naked.*

undressed /ʌnˈdrest/ [adj] wearing no clothes, because you have just taken them off, for example to have a bath or go to bed: *She went upstairs to make sure that the children were all undressed and ready for bed.*

bare /beəʳ/ [adj] a part of your body that is **bare** is not covered by any clothes: *My arms were bare and they got badly sunburned.* | *In summer all the kids go around in bare feet.*

COLD

➡ opposite **HOT**
➡ see also **WET, DRY, WEATHER**

1 weather

cold /kəʊld/ [adj] *a cold January morning* | *This is the coldest winter we've had for years.*
it's cold (=the weather is cold) *Put your gloves on – it's cold outside today!*
freezing cold (=extremely cold) *It gets freezing cold at night in the mountains.*
bitterly cold (=extremely cold and unpleasant) *a bitterly cold north wind*

the cold /ðə ˈkəʊld/ [n singular] cold weather – use this to emphasize how unpleasant and uncomfortable it is outside: *Come in. Don't stand out there in the cold!*

cool /kuːl/ [adj] cold in a pleasant way, especially after the weather has been hot: *a cool sea breeze*
it's cool (=the weather is cool) *Although the days are very hot, it's much cooler at night.*

chilly /ˈtʃɪli/ [adj] cold, but not extremely cold: *a chilly morning in April*
it's chilly (=the weather is chilly) *It's getting chilly – I think we'll go inside.*

frosty /ˈfrɒsti‖ˈfrɔːsti/ [adj] very cold, when everything is covered in a thin white layer of ice, and the sky is often very bright and clear: *a bright frosty morning*

freezing /ˈfriːzɪŋ/ [adj] extremely cold, so that rivers, streams etc turn to ice: *The freezing weather continued all through February.*
freezing cold (=the weather is extremely cold) *It was freezing cold outside.*
it's freezing *I'd never go on holiday there – it's always frezing.*

2 person

cold /kəʊld/ [adj] not before noun] feeling cold
be cold *Dad, I'm cold. Can I put the heater on?*
feel cold *He woke up in the middle of the night feeling cold.*
look cold *Come and sit by the fire. You look cold.*

○**freezing** /ˈfriːzɪŋ/ [adj] SPOKEN feeling very cold and uncomfortable: *"Are you warm enough?" "No, I'm absolutely freezing!"*

shiver /'ʃɪvəʳ/ [v I] to shake because you are cold: *I was shivering in my thin sleeping bag.*
shiver with cold *We stood in the doorway shivering with cold.*

have goosepimples BRITISH **have goosebumps** AMERICAN /hæv 'guːs-ˌpɪmpəlz, hæv 'guːsbʌmps/ to have small raised areas on your skin, because you are cold

3 place/room

cold /kəʊld/ [adj] *He waited an hour for the train on a cold platform.*
it's cold *Why is it always so cold in this office?*

cool /kuːl/ [adj] cold in a pleasant way, especially when the weather is hot: *Our hotel room was lovely and cool.*
it's cool *It's much cooler downstairs.*

chilly /'tʃɪli/ [adj] a little too cold for you to feel comfortable: *They have to get washed and dressed in a chilly bathroom.*
it's chilly *It's chilly in here – why don't you turn the heater on?*

draughty BRITISH **drafty** AMERICAN /'drɑːfti‖'dræfti/ [adj] a room that is **draughty** has cold air blowing into it from outside: *a cold, draughty apartment*

freezing /'friːzɪŋ/ [adj] extremely cold, so that you feel very uncomfortable: *The little children sat in rows in the freezing classroom.*
it's freezing *It's absolutely freezing outside.*

4 liquid/object/surface

cold /kəʊld/ [adj] *I wanted a bath but the water was cold.* | *We stood for hours on the cold stone floor.*

freezing /'friːzɪŋ/ [adj] extremely cold: *His friends pulled him from the freezing water.*
freezing cold *The river was freezing cold.*

cool /kuːl/ [adj] cold in a pleasant way, but not very cold: *Ruth put her cool hand on my burning forehead.*

5 food/drink

cold /kəʊld/ [adj] **cold** food has been

cooked, but is no longer hot: *a selection of cold meats* | *Serve the quiche hot or cold, with a fresh green salad.*

get cold/go cold (=become cold, especially when it should be hot) *Come and eat your dinner before it gets cold.*

stone cold (=completely cold when it should be hot) *By the time I'd finished on the phone my coffee was stone cold.*

cool /kuːl/ [adj] **cool** drinks are pleasantly cold, especially when the weather is warm: *She sat by the swimming pool with a cool glass of lemonade.*

chilled /tʃɪld/ [adj] **chilled** food or drink has been made very cold, especially by putting it on ice: *a bottle of chilled champagne* | *This soup is delicious served chilled.*

frozen /'frəʊzən/ [adj] **frozen** food is stored at a very low temperature so that you can keep it for a long time: *frozen peas* | *The only things I had in the freezer were a frozen chicken and a tub of ice-cream.*

ice-cold /ˌaɪs 'kəʊld◄/ [adj] very cold – use this about drinks that have been made very cold so that they are pleasant to drink in hot weather: *an ice-cold beer*

6 to become colder

get cold/get colder /get 'kəʊld, get 'kəʊldəʳ/ to become cold or colder: *It's got a lot colder recently.* (=the weather has become colder) | *Tell John his coffee's getting cold.*

cool down /ˌkuːl 'daʊn/ [phrasal verb I] to become colder after being hot: *Leave the bread on a wire tray to cool down.*

cool /kuːl/ [v I] use this about hot food or other hot substances that become colder: *As the metal cools, it will decrease in size.*

COLLECT

to keep things because you think they are attractive or interesting

collect /kə'lekt/ [v T] to get and keep things that are all of a similar kind, because you think they are attractive or interesting: *Do you collect stamps?* | *I've started collecting old bottles.*

collector /kəˈlektəʳ/ [n C] someone who collects things: *a coin collector* | *The auction room was full of art collectors and dealers.*

collection /kəˈlekʃən/ [n C] a group of things that someone has collected because they are attractive or interesting: *Her brother wanted to show me his postcard collection.*
+ of *The museum has one of the world's finest collections of impressionist paintings.*

set /set/ [n C] a complete group of one type of object that someone has collected: *I'm collecting American League baseball cards – I only need one more to have the set.*
+ of *For sale – 'The Guitarist' – complete set of magazines 1984–1992.*

COLOUR/COLOR

➡ if you mean 'colour of hair', go to
HAIR

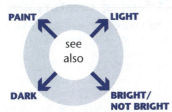

PAINT   LIGHT
see also
DARK   BRIGHT/NOT BRIGHT

1 a colour

colour BRITISH **color** AMERICAN /ˈkʌləʳ/ [n C/U] *Blue is my favorite color.* | *Why don't you paint it yellow? That's a nice bright colour.* | *Her hair was the same colour as mine.*
what colour is...? *"What color is your new car?" "Silver."*
change colour *In September the leaves start to change colour.*

shade /ʃeɪd/ [n C] a particular type of one colour, which is darker or lighter than other types of the same colour: *The pattern is available in three different shades: dark blue, pale green, and charcoal grey.*
shade of blue/green etc *Valerie's eyes are a beautiful shade of blue.*

colouring BRITISH **coloring** AMERICAN /ˈkʌlərɪŋ/ [n U] the colour of a person's or animal's hair, skin, or eyes: *This lipstick is perfect for your colouring.* | *He had his mother's looks and colouring.*

2 to be a particular colour

be /bi, *strong* biː/ [v]
be red/green/blue etc *Frogs are green, toads are brown – that's how you can tell the difference.* | *The Japanese flag is white with a red sun on it.*

⚠ Use **is, are** etc to talk about the colour of something: *My dad's car is red.* | *Her eyes were blue.* Don't use **have**, and don't use the word **colour** itself: *Her new bike is green.* (not 'Her bike has green.' or 'Her bike is green colour.') Only use **colour** when you are asking a question: *"What colour is your new bike?" "It's green."*

coloured BRITISH **colored** AMERICAN /ˈkʌləʳd/ [adj usually before noun] a **coloured** or **colored** object has one or more colours in it, but not black or white: *The town hall was decorated with hundreds of coloured ribbons.* | *panels of colored glass*

3 bright colours

bright /braɪt/ [adj] a **bright** colour is strong and very easy to notice: *an artist who loved bright colours* | *If you are cycling at night, always wear something bright.*
bright blue/red/yellow etc *The front door was painted bright red.* | *a bright yellow van*
brightly [adv] *a brightly painted boat* | *brightly coloured balloons*

colourful BRITISH **colorful** AMERICAN /ˈkʌləʳfəl/ [adj] something that is **colourful** or **colorful** has a lot of different colours in it, especially bright colours: *women in colourful summer dresses* | *Children's books need to have large clear letters and colorful pictures.*

brilliant /ˈbrɪljənt/ [adj usually before noun] **brilliant white/blue/green etc** so bright that it almost hurts your eyes to look at it: *a brilliant blue sky* | *The room was painted a brilliant white.*

C

4 light colours

light /laɪt/ [adj] **light** colours are closer to white than to black: *They both have brown hair, but Tina's is slightly lighter than Jan's.*
light blue/green/brown etc *The leaves are light green with small purple markings.*

pale /peɪl/ [adj] very light in colour: *her pale skin and dark hair*
pale blue/pink/yellow etc *a pale pink blouse* | *pale yellow wallpaper with a white daisy pattern*

pastel /'pæstl‖pæ'stel/ [adj only before noun] **pastel** colours, especially pink, yellow, green, or blue, are soft and light and not at all bright: *The bedrooms have all been designed in cool pastel shades.*

5 dark colours

dark /dɑːʳk/ [adj] **dark** colours are not at all light and are close to black: *Everyone at the funeral was dressed in dark colours, except for Rita, who wore a pink dress.*
dark blue/brown/green etc *She has beautiful dark brown hair.* | *a dark grey suit*

deep /diːp/ [adj only before noun] **deep** colours are strong, dark, and attractive: *a deep, rich shade of crimson*
deep blue/purple/red *A few stars began to appear in the deep blue sky.*

6 photograph/film/ television

colour BRITISH **color** AMERICAN /'kʌləʳ/ [adj] showing pictures in all colours, not just in black, white, and grey: *a delightful book containing 200 colour photographs of wild flowers* | *You need a color monitor to use this software.*
in colour (=showing all the colours) *All the pictures are in colour.*

black and white /ˌblæk ən 'waɪt◄/ showing pictures only in black, white, and grey: *an old black and white movie starring Charlie Chaplin*
in black and white (=showing only black, white, and grey) *Karsh's famous photographs of Churchill were all in black and white.*

7 to change colour or lose colour

dye /daɪ/ [v T] to change the colour of material or hair by using a special coloured liquid: *I bet she dyes her hair.*
dye sth blue/yellow etc *I'm going to dye this skirt dark blue.*
dyeing – dyed – have dyed

fade /feɪd/ [v I] if a colour or coloured material **fades**, its colour becomes paler, for example because it has been in sunlight for a long time: *Over the years the green curtains had faded.* | *Do not expose the paintings to strong sunlight, or the colours will fade.*
faded [adj] *faded blue jeans*

COMFORTABLE/ UNCOMFORTABLE

➡ see also **RELAX**

1 feeling comfortable

comfortable /'kʌmftəbəl, 'kʌmfət-‖'kʌmfərt-, 'kʌmft-/ [adj not before noun] feeling physically relaxed, for example because you are sitting on a soft chair or lying on a soft bed: *I was so warm and comfortable in bed I didn't want to get up.* | *Are you comfortable lying on the floor like that?*
make yourself comfortable *Sit down and make yourself comfortable.*
get comfortable (=get into a comfortable position) *My shoulder was hurting so I couldn't get comfortable.*
   comfortably [adv] *Brian was sitting comfortably in front of the television.*

comfy /'kʌmfi/ [adj not before noun] SPOKEN feeling comfortable: *"Comfy?" "Yes, thanks."*

snug /snʌg/ [adj not before noun] feeling comfortable, warm, and happy because you are in bed, wearing warm clothes etc: *She looks really snug under all those blankets.*

in comfort /ɪn 'kʌmfəʳt/ if you do something **in comfort**, you feel comfortable and relaxed while you are doing it: *Jardine sat down by the fire to enjoy his* whiskey in comfort. | Now that we have a bigger car, the whole family can travel in comfort.

2 comfortable furniture, clothes, places etc

comfortable /ˈkʌmftəbəl, ˈkʌmfət-‖ˈkʌmfərt-, ˈkʌmft-/ [adj] use this about clothes, furniture, or rooms that make you feel comfortable: *Our hotel room was very comfortable.* | *a comfortable leather armchair* | *Can you just wait a moment while I change into something more comfortable.*

comfortable to sit on/lie on/wear *Harder mattresses are often more comfortable to lie on*

  comfortably [adv] *a comfortably furnished apartment*

⊙comfy /ˈkʌmfi/ [adj] SPOKEN use **comfy** about clothes, furniture, or rooms that make you feel comfortable: *a comfy little cabin in the woods* | *a comfy chair*

cosy BRITISH **cozy** AMERICAN /ˈkəʊzi/ [adj] a **cosy** room or place is small, warm, and comfortable, and you feel relaxed and happy there: *a small cozy apartment* | *The bar looked lovely and cosy, with a log fire burning brightly.*

luxurious /lʌgˈzjʊəriəs, ləgˈʒʊəriəs‖ləgˈʒʊəriəs/ [adj] a **luxurious** house, hotel, ship etc makes you feel very comfortable because it has large rooms and expensive furniture, carpets etc: *a luxurious yacht, once owned by Aristotle Onassis* | *The hotel we stayed in was really luxurious.*

3 not comfortable

uncomfortable/not comfortable /ʌnˈkʌmftəbəl, nɒt ˈkʌmftəbəl, -ˈkʌmfət-‖ -ˈkʌmfərt-, -ˈkʌmft-/ [adj] not comfortable: *Come and sit here. You don't look very comfortable on that stool.* | *The heat was making us all feel very uncomfortable.* | *She was wearing very uncomfortable-looking shoes.*

4 something that makes you feel uncomfortable

cramped /kræmpt/ [adj] a **cramped** room, apartment, car etc is uncomfortable because there is not enough space: *cramped living conditions* | *They*

worked from cramped offices near the main station.

bumpy /ˈbʌmpi/ [adj] a **bumpy** journey in a car or plane is uncomfortable because the car or plane shakes a lot, as the result of bad roads or bad weather: *a bumpy ride up the mountainside in an old bus*

rough /rʌf/ [adj] a **rough** journey by sea is uncomfortable because the weather is bad and the boat goes up and down a lot: *We had a rough crossing and most of the passengers were seasick.* | *It'll be rough out there today with all this wind.*

COMPANY

BUSINESS
BUY
ADVERTISING
SELL
see also
MANAGER
WORK
MONEY
JOB
IN CHARGE OF
POSITION/RANK

1 different types of company

company /ˈkʌmpəni/ [n C] any organization, either large or small, that produces goods or provides services in order to make a profit: *The company employs over 10,000 people worldwide.*

oil/insurance/phone etc company *the second largest insurance company in Japan*

work for a company (=have a job there) *My father used to work for one of the big oil companies.*

join a company (=start to work there) *This year, we have had several new executives joining the company.*

set up/start a company *The company was set up in 1975.*

plural **companies**

⚠ You can also use **company** before a noun, like an adjective: *a company car* (=one that is provided for you by your company) | *Company profits have doubled in the last four years.*

firm /fɜːʳm/ [n C] a company, especially one that provides services rather than producing goods, often financial or legal services: *The firm employs about 15 full-time staff.*

law/electronics/building etc firm *She works for a law firm in Amsterdam.*

firm of lawyers/accountants etc *Ed's just got a job with a firm of accountants in Boston.*

join a firm (=start working for a firm) *Sara joined the firm when she was only 16.*

business /ˈbɪznɪs/ [n C] a company, shop, or factory that sells goods or provides services, especially one that employs only a small number of people or only one person: *Norm's a gardener – he has his own business.*

manage/run a business *She's running her own printing business now.*

set up/start a business *Profits have slowly increased since we started the business three years ago.*

small business (=one that employs only one person or very few people)

family business (=one that was started by and employs members of the same family)

corporation /ˌkɔːʳpəˈreɪʃən/ [n C] a large company that employs a lot of people, especially one that includes several different departments or several smaller companies: *IBM is one of the biggest corporations in the US.* | *the Coca-Cola Company*

multinational /ˌmʌltɪˈnæʃənəl◄/ [adj only before noun] **multinational company/corporation/business** a very large company that has offices or factories in many different countries: *Mitsubishi is a multinational company, whose head office is in Japan.*

multinational [n C] a very large company with offices and factories in many different countries: *the power of the big multinationals*

subsidiary /səbˈsɪdiəri‖-dieri/ [n C] a company that is owned and controlled by a larger company

+ of *The Isle of Man Bank is now a subsidiary of NatWest Bank plc.*

plural **subsidiaries**

employer /ɪmˈplɔɪəʳ/ [n C] a company – use this when you are talking about a company as something that provides jobs, not as something that produces and sells things: *Parker Plastics is the city's biggest employer, with about 3000 workers.* | *Your employer* (=the company you work for) *is responsible for ensuring safety in the workplace.*

2 abbreviations for different types of company

Ltd BRITISH **Inc.** AMERICAN the written abbreviations of 'Limited' and 'Incorporated' – used after the name of a large or small company to show that it is legally established and that its owners are legally responsible for only a limited amount of money if the company gets into debt: *Stevenson Securities Ltd* | *Syquest Technology Inc.*

Corp. the written abbreviation of 'Corporation' – used after the name of a large company, especially in the US: *Federal Express Corp.*

plc /ˌpiː el ˈsiː/ the abbreviation of 'Public Limited Company' – used in Britain after the name of a large company that ordinary people can buy shares in: *Marks & Spencer plc*

COMPARE

to think about two or more things or people, in order to see how similar or different they are

➡ see also **SAME, DIFFERENT**

1 to compare things

compare /kəmˈpeəʳ/ [v T] to think about two or more things or people, in order to see how similar or different they are: *We looked at a lot of computers before buying this one, in order to compare prices.*

compare sth/sb with sth/sb *If you compare rents in London with rents in Paris, you'll find they are about the same.* | *I hate the way you always compare me with your ex-boyfriend.*

⚠ **Compare sth/sb to sth/sb** usually means to say that someone or something is like another person or thing. For example:

a new young singer that some people have compared to Pavarotti (=they say he is as good as Pavarotti).

comparison /kəm'pær$_1$sən/ [n C] something that you say or write that shows how similar or different two things or people are
+ of/between *The students were asked to write a comparison between the two poems. | a comparison of the number of deaths from heart disease in Britain and America*
make a comparison *The documentary makes a comparison between working conditions before and after the war.*

2 when one thing is being compared with another

compared to/compared with /kəm'peə^{r}d tuː, kəm'peə^{r}d wɪð/ use this when you are comparing two or more things or people: *Their house seems like a palace compared to our small apartment. | Compared with some other EU countries, Britain has a low standard of living.*

in comparison/by comparison /ɪn kəm'pær$_1$sən, baɪ kəm'pær$_1$sən/ ESPECIALLY WRITTEN use this when you are comparing two or more things or people: *After months of living in a tropical climate, Spain seemed cool by comparison.*
+ with *In comparison with London, life in our small town was very quiet.*

⚠️ **In comparison** and **by comparison** are more formal than **compared to** and **compared with**, and are more common in written English.

in contrast/by contrast /ɪn 'kɒntrɑːst, baɪ 'kɒntrɑːst‖-'kɑːntræst/ use this when you are emphasizing the difference between two or more things or people: *Richard's small and slim. His father, by contrast, is tall and well-built.*
in contrast to/by contrast with *In contrast to his previous novels, his latest book is much more serious.*

relative /'relətɪv/ [adj] **relative importance/advantage/amount/size** the importance, advantage etc that one thing has when it is compared to other things: *the relative importance of money and job*

satisfaction | the relative advantages of different methods of transporting goods

COMPETITION

➡ look here for ...
• a game or sports event
• when people or companies are trying to be more successful than others
➡ see also **SPORT, TAKE PART**

1 a game or event in which people try to do better than each other

competition /ˌkɒmp$_1$'tɪʃən‖ˌkɑːm-/ [n C] an organized event in which people try to do an activity or sport better than other people, especially in order to win a prize: *He was awarded first prize in the National Poetry Competition.*
win a competition *A student from St Paul won the speechwriting competition.*
enter a competition (=be in a competition) *Enter our free competition and win a weekend in Paris.*
a competition to do sth *a competition to think of a name for the new building*

championship /'tʃæmpiənʃɪp/ [n C] an important sports event in which players or teams play against each other to decide who is the best in an area, the country, or the world: *the World Chess Championship*
win a championship *At 17, Becker was the youngest player to win the Men's Tennis Championship.*

tournament /'tʊənəmənt, 'tɔː-‖-'tɜːr-, 'tʊər-/ [n C] a competition in a sport or game in which each player or team plays a series of games until one person or team wins: *an international golf tournament*
win a tournament *Telford won the local five-a-side football tournament.*

⚠️ A **tournament** is usually not as important as a **championship**, and does not involve as many players or teams.

contest /'kɒntest‖'kɑːn-/ [n C] a competition in which a person or team does an activity, and a group of judges decide which of them is the best

win a contest *The singing contest was won by Sven from Sweden.*

beauty contest (=a contest in which judges decide who is the most beautiful woman)

⚠ **Contest** is not usually used about sports events.

2 someone who takes part in a competition

competitor /kəm'petɪtər/ [n C] someone who takes part in a competition: *Two of the competitors failed to turn up for the first race.*

contestant /kən'testənt/ [n C] someone who takes part in a contest, a TV game, test of knowledge etc: *The next contestant is Alice Jones from Vancouver. | Each contestant has to answer questions on a variety of subjects.*

3 to take part in a competition, sports event etc

compete /kəm'piːt/ [v I] to take part in a competition, sporting event etc
+ in *Athletes from 197 countries competed in the Olympic Games in Atlanta.*
+ against *Ten teams will compete against each other for the National Trophy.*

4 to try to do better than another person or organization

compete /kəm'piːt/ [v I] to try to do better than another person or organization, for example in business or politics
+ with *Nowadays we have to compete more and more with foreign companies.*
+ for (=in order to get something) *two little children competing for their mother's attention*
can't compete with (=not have enough skill, money etc to compete with another person, company etc) *Small British car companies just can't compete with giants like BMW and Volkswagen.*
compete to do sth *Fujitsu, Hitachi, and NEC are competing with US firms to build the world's fastest supercomputer.*

fight /faɪt/ [v I/T] to try extremely hard to get an important job or political position which other people are also trying to get
+ for *If you want the job, you'll have to fight for it.*
fight sb for sth *Williams fought several rivals for the leadership of the party.*
fighting – fought – have fought

5 a situation in which people try to do better than each other

competition /ˌkɒmpə'tɪʃən‖ˌkɑːm-/ [n U] when people or organizations try hard to get something that they all want but only one of them can get
+ for *Competition for these jobs is very tough – we've had over 200 applications.*
+ between *There's a lot of competition between the big supermarket chains.*
fierce/strong/tough competition (=when a lot of people are all trying very hard to get something) *There is fierce competition for places in the Olympic team.*

competitive /kəm'petɪtɪv/ [adj] a **competitive** situation is one in which people try hard to do better than each other, for example in business or at school: *Amanda hated working in advertising; it was so competitive.*
highly competitive (=very competitive) *The atmosphere at our school was highly competitive.*

rivalry /'raɪvəlri/ [n U] when two people, teams, or companies try to do better than each other, especially over a long period
+ between *Rivalry between brothers and sisters is quite normal. | the longstanding rivalry between Coca-Cola and Pepsi*
intense/fierce rivalry (=very strong rivalry) *There was intense rivalry between the Brazilian and Italian teams.*

battle /'bætl/ [n C] a situation in which people or organizations fight against each other to get power or control of something, and they are all very determined to win
+ for *The President's advisors were engaged in a battle for power.*

When you see **EC**, go to the **ESSENTIAL COMMUNICATION** section.

6 **people who are trying to do better than each other**

competitor /kəm'petɨtəʳ/ [n C] a person or company that tries to do better than another which offers similar goods or services: *Their major competitors are IBM and Sun Microsystems.*

rival /'raɪvəl/ [n C] a person, team, or company that tries to do better than another similar one, especially over a long period: *The two teams had always been rivals.*

⚠ You can also use **rival** before a noun, like an adjective: *A fight broke out between rival gangs in the city centre.* | *rival companies*

the competition /ðə ˌkɒmpɨ'tɪʃən‖ -ˌkɑːm-/ [n singular/U] all the people or groups that are trying to do better than you, especially in business or in a sport: *Our sales figures are 10% ahead of the competition.*
strong competition (=when the people you are competing against are very good) *The team overcame strong competition to gain their place in the finals.*

7 **someone who likes competing**

competitive /kəm'petɨtɪv/ [adj] someone who is **competitive** seems to enjoy competing and is always trying to do better than other people: *I hate playing tennis with her – she's so competitive.*

COMPLAIN

➡ see also 🔲 **COMPLAINING, SATISFIED/ DISSATISFIED**

1 **to complain**

complain /kəm'pleɪn/ [v I/T] to say that you are annoyed about something or not satisfied with something, for example because it is unfair or not as good as it should be: *We had to remove the advertisement because so many people complained.*
+ about *Local residents have complained about the noise from the club.*
+ that *Jenny's always complaining that her boss gives her too much work.*

+ to *If the hotel isn't satisfactory, you should complain to the Tourist Office.*

⚠ Don't say 'complain against' or 'complain for'. Say **complain about**.

make a complaint /ˌmeɪk ə kəm'pleɪnt/ to tell someone in an official position that you are not satisfied with something that they are responsible for: *Write to this address if you wish to make a complaint.*
+ to *Parents made a complaint to the principal about bullying in the school.*

protest /prə'test/ [v I/T] to complain about something that you think is wrong and should not be allowed to happen – use this especially about groups of people who meet in a public place to show that they do not approve of something
+ about/against/at *Workers protested angrily about job losses.*
protest sth AMERICAN *a large crowd protesting the war*

object /əb'dʒekt/ [v I] to say that you do not agree with something or you do not approve of it, because it annoys you or offends you: *The neighbours might object if you park your car in front of their house.*
+ to *Does anyone object to these proposals?*

2 **to complain a lot in an annoying way**

moan /məʊn/ [v I] INFORMAL, ESPECIALLY BRITISH to keep complaining in an annoying way – use this about someone who complains all the time, even about things that are not important: *I'm fed up with hearing you moaning the whole time!*
+ about *Why do people always moan about the weather?*

grumble /'grʌmbəl/ [v I] to keep complaining in a bad-tempered way, especially when you think you have been treated unfairly: *The old man turned away, grumbling as he went.*
+ about *She was grumbling about having to work so late.*

make a fuss /ˌmeɪk ə 'fʌs/ ESPECIALLY BRITISH to complain angrily and noisily about something, so that everyone hears you or notices you

+ about *The couple sitting next to us made a big fuss about their bill.*

3 something that you do or say when you complain

complaint /kəm'pleɪnt/ [n C/U] something that you say or write when you are complaining, especially to someone in an official position: *If you have any complaints, please contact our customer relations department.*
+ about *Channel 4 received hundreds of complaints about the show.*

protest /'prəʊtest/ [n C/U] a public complaint about something that people think is wrong or unfair and should not be allowed to happen: *Students' fees were increased, despite protests on all the college campuses.*
in protest (=as a way of making a protest) *When two members of the team were fired, the rest of them walked out in protest.*

outcry /'aʊtkraɪ/ [n C usually singular] an angry protest by a lot of people about something that they think is very wrong or unfair
+ about/over *the recent international outcry over French nuclear tests in the Pacific*
public outcry *The shooting of a teenager by police caused a public outcry.*

COMPLETELY

not partly, but in every way

➡ see also ALL
➡ for words meaning the opposite, go to **PARTLY**

completely /kəm'pliːtli/ [adv] not partly, but in every way: *The drug is completely safe.* | *Make sure that the tank is completely full.* | *I was fed up with school, and I felt like trying something completely different.*

complete /kəm'pliːt/ [adj only before noun]
complete success/failure/disaster (=when something is completely successful or unsuccessful) *Our first date was a complete disaster.*

make a complete recovery (=completely recover from an illness) *Doctors say he will make a complete recovery.*
a complete waste of time/money (=when something wastes time or money and is not useful at all) *The store was closed when I got there, so going down there was a complete waste of time.*

absolutely /'æbsəluːtli/ [adv] use this to show that you strongly agree with something or approve of something, or to emphasize strong adjectives
absolutely right/correct *You're absolutely right – we couldn't all fit in the car.*
absolutely marvellous/amazing/brilliant *That's an absolutely brilliant idea.*
absolutely certain/sure *Are you absolutely sure you don't mind?*
absolutely exhausted/soaked/ruined etc *By the end of the day, I was absolutely exhausted.*

> ⚠ Use **absolutely** especially with words that express a strong feeling or opinion, for example: *We had an absolutely fantastic time.* | *He was absolutely furious.* | *They don't let us wear T-shirts at school – it's absolutely crazy.*

fully /'fʊli/ [adv] use this especially to say that you have all the things you need, or all the information you need
fully understand/realize/appreciate *I fully appreciate your concern.*
fully aware/informed *Please keep me fully informed of any developments.*
fully furnished/equipped *The house is fully furnished, and has a dishwasher and a microwave.*

totally /'təʊtl-i/ [adv] use this especially to show that you strongly disagree with something or that you are very annoyed about it
totally refuse / ignore / reject / fail *He totally ignored my advice.*
totally impossible/unacceptable/ridiculous *The whole thing is totally ridiculous.*

entirely /ɪn'taɪəˈli/ [adv] in every possible way – use this especially in negative sentences, or with 'almost'

not entirely *I'm not entirely sure what he meant.* | *The reasons for his departure weren't entirely clear.*

almost entirely *The class consisted almost entirely of girls.*

utterly /'ʌtə^rli/ [adv] use this especially to describe things that are completely wrong, untrue, impossible etc

utterly ridiculous/impossible/useless etc *At first the idea sounded utterly ridiculous.* | *The map was utterly useless.*

> ⚠ **Utterly** is more formal than **totally**, and is mostly used in written or formal spoken English.

in every way /ɪn ˌevri 'weɪ/ use this to say that something is true in every detail or part: *The two drawings are the same in every way.* | *It was an excellent course in every way.*

⬡ **WORD BANK** # COMPUTERS

➡ see pages 136–139

CONFIDENT/ NOT CONFIDENT

PROUD   SHY

see also

INDEPENDENT   DESCRIBING PEOPLE

1 a confident person

confident /'kɒnfɪdənt‖'kɑːn-/ [adj] sure that you have the ability to do something well, and not worried about failing: *It's a difficult test, but she seems fairly confident.* | *He read his speech in a strong, confident voice.*

+ about *After living in France for a year I felt much more confident about my French.*

be/feel confident about (doing) sth *I don't feel very confident about going back to work.*

confidently [adv] *She answered each question confidently and competently.* | *smiling confidently*

> ⚠ Don't say 'confident of yourself' or 'confident about yourself'. Say **self-confident**.

self-confident /self 'kɒnfɪdənt‖-'kɑːn-/ [adj] someone who is **self-confident** is very confident about their own abilities, and is not shy or nervous in social situations: *Jess was only 12, but she was very self-confident.* | *When you have had more experience, you become more self-confident about speaking in front of groups of people.*

sure of yourself /'ʃʊər əv jɔː^rˌself/ very sure that what you do and think is right, even when other people do not agree with you: *He sounded so sure of himself that I didn't bother to argue.* | *Barnes looked older, and seemed less sure of himself.*

brash /bræʃ/ [adj] someone who is **brash** is very confident in an annoying way, for example because they talk too loudly and never listen to other people: *The hotel bar was full of brash, noisy journalists.* | *a brash young salesman from New York*

extrovert /'ekstrəvɜː^rt/ [n C] someone who enjoys being with other people, and getting a lot of attention from other people: *Most actors are natural extroverts.*

2 a confident feeling

confidence /'kɒnfɪdəns‖'kɑːn-/ [n U] the feeling that you have the ability to do things well, and to not make mistakes or be nervous in new situations

give sb confidence *If you understand the grammar, it will give you a lot more confidence.*

have the confidence to do sth (=be confident enough to do something) *In this job you have to have the confidence to make tough decisions.*

give sb the confidence to do sth *Going to college was good for me – it gave me the confidence to work on my own.*

full of confidence (=very confident) *I went into the test full of confidence, but it was more difficult than I had expected.*

CONFIDENT/NOT CONFIDENT continues on page 140

COMPUTERS

CD-ROM drive

screen/monitor

modem

printer

speaker

floppy disk drive

CD-ROMS

keyboard

floppy disk

mouse

mouse pad/mat

➡ see also **TECHNOLOGY, ▣ OPINIONS**

1 computers and computer equipment

IT/information technology /ˌaɪ ˈtiː, ˌɪnfəˈmeɪʃən tekˌnɒlədʒiǁ-ˌnɑː-/ the study or use of computers and other electronic equipment for storing, sending, and developing information: *She teaches IT at a local school.* | *the massive growth of information technology during the 1980s*

hardware /ˈhɑːˈdweəˈ/ [n U] computers and all the machinery and equipment connected with them

software /ˈsɒftweəˈǁˈsɑːf-/ [n U] the programs that you put into computers to make them do the job you want: *We supply software from games and electronic dictionaries to word-processing packages.* | *software companies such as Microsoft and IBM*

program /ˈprəʊɡræm/ [n C] a set of instructions that makes it possible for a computer to do a particular job: *a program designed to correct grammar*

hard disk /ˈhɑːˈd ˈdɪsk/ [n C] a part inside a computer that permanently stores information and instructions

floppy disk /ˌflɒpi ˈdɪsk/ [n C] a small flat thing that you can store information from a computer on, that you can remove and use in other computers

modem /ˈməʊdem/ [n C] a piece of electronic equipment that allows information to be sent from one computer to another

2 the Internet

the Internet/the net /ði ˈɪntəˈnet, ðə ˈnet/ a system that allows computer users around the world to send messages and information to each other

on the Internet *Are you on the Internet?* | *You might find some information on the net.*

surf the net (=look at the information on the Internet in order to find something that interests you)

World Wide Web/WWW/the Web /ˌwɜːˈld waɪd ˈweb/ the system that stores information for computer users around the world to use

online /ˈɒnlaɪn/ [adj] online services, conversations, games etc are those that take place or exist on the Internet: *an online romance*

online [adv] *Get online today!*

website /ˈwebsaɪt/ [n C] a place on the Internet that gives you information about a particular subject or product

home page /ˈhəʊm ˌpeɪdʒ/ [n C] the first page of a website

COMPUTERS

3 the advantages of computers

① Computers let you **access** a lot of information.

② Computers let you communicate very quickly, by **e-mail** or using the **Internet**.

③ Computers can do some jobs very quickly, for example sending out large numbers of letters or bills.

④ Computers make it possible to **work from home**.

I can access any information I need from the office using a modem.

⑤ **Word processors** make it easier to write letters and reports, and to do work for school or college.

BEFORE

AFTER

vocabulary

access /'ækses/ [v T] if you **access** information on a computer, you find it using a computer: *The new system made it easier to access patients' medical records.*

advance /əd'vɑːns‖-'væn-/ [v I] if technology **advances**, it develops and improves

bug /bʌg/ [n C] a small mistake in a computer program that stops it from working properly

CD-ROM /ˌsiːdiːˈrɒm‖-ˈrɑːm/ [n C/U] a small flat circular object on which large amounts of information can be stored to be used by a computer: *a new encyclopedia on CD-ROM*

computer game /kəmˈpjuːətʳ ɡeɪm/ [n C] a game that you play on a computer

crash /kræʃ/ [v I] if a computer **crashes**, it suddenly stops working: *My computer crashed, and I lost a*

whole afternoon's work.

database /'deɪtəbeɪs/ [n C] a large amount of information stored in a computer system so that you can find and use it easily: *Customers' names and addresses are stored on our database.*

e-mail /'iː meɪl/ [n C/U] a system that allows messages to be sent from one computer to another, or a message sent using this system

be on e-mail (=a computer that can send and receive e-mail messages)

send sb an e-mail: *"Does Glennis know about it?" "Yes, I sent her an e-mail."*

e-mail /'iː meɪl/ [v T] to send someone a message by e-mail: *Will you e-mail me about it?*

COMPUTERS continues on the next page

COMPUTERS

6 Children enjoy using computers, and **multimedia**, **interactive** software and **virtual reality** all make learning more exciting. Many books are now available on **CD-ROM**.

7 Large amounts of information can be stored on computer in a **database**.

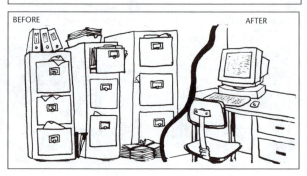

BEFORE

AFTER

4 the disadvantages of computers

1 Many people do not like using computers, and would prefer to deal with a person instead.

Good morning! How can I help you?

2 Computers can get **viruses**.

---

interactive /ˌɪntərˈæktɪv◄/ [adj] interactive programs and activities on a computer are those that you do not just read or look at, but which you can change and communicate with

lose work /ˌluːz ˈwɜːᵏk/ when the work that you have done on your computer disappears and you cannot get it back

multimedia /ˌmʌltiˈmiːdiə/ [adj] using a mixture of sound, pictures, film, and writing to give information on computers: *a new multimedia dictionary*

  multimedia [n U] *More and more schools are using multimedia as a teaching aid.*

obsolete /ˈɒbsəliːt‖-aːb-/ [adj] if a computer is **obsolete**, it has become old fashioned and you can now get much better ones: *You should expect your*

computer to become obsolete in only a few years.

police /pəˈliːs/ [v T] to control what people put on the Internet, and make sure that they do not use it to do anything illegal

virtual reality /ˌvɜːᵏtʃuəl riˈælɪti/ [n U] the effect produced by using computer images to make places or situations seem almost real when they are not

virus /ˈvaɪrəs/ [n C] a set of instructions secretly put into a computer that destroys the information stored in it, and stops it from working normally

work from home /ˌwɜːᵏk frəm ˈhəʊm/ to be employed by a company, but to work in your home and not in the company building

word processor /ˌwɜːᵏd ˈprəʊsesəᵏ/ [n C] a program or computer that you use to write letters, reports etc

COMPUTERS

③ Software often has **bugs**, and sometimes computers **crash**.

④ Some children spend too much time playing **computer games**, which can be very violent.

⑤ Anyone can put information or images on the Internet, so it can easily be used by criminals to communicate with each other, or to send pornography (pictures, film, or writing that show sexual acts). There are no laws to stop this yet, and it is extremely difficult to **police** the Internet.

⑥ Computers quickly become **obsolete**, so they soon need to be replaced.

⑦ If a computer is not working properly, most people do not know how to fix it, and this can be very annoying.

CONFIDENT/NOT CONFIDENT continued from page 135

self-confidence /self ˈkɒnfɪdəns‖-ˈkɑːn-/ [n U] a strong belief that you can do things well and that other people will like you, which means you behave confidently in most situations: *He's only 19 but he has plenty of self-confidence.*

morale /məˈrɑːl‖məˈræl/ [n U] the amount of confidence, satisfaction, and hope that people feel, especially a group of people who work together
low/high morale (=a low/high level of confidence) *We've had a lot of problems recently and the morale among the teachers is pretty low.*
keep up morale (=prevent people losing confidence) *They sang songs to keep up their morale until the rescuers arrived.*

3 not confident

shy /ʃaɪ/ [adj] someone who is **shy** feels nervous and embarrassed about talking to people, especially people they do not know: *She was very shy, and didn't like using the phone.* | *Five years ago, I was a shy, clumsy, overweight teenager.*
too shy to do sth *I wanted to ask a question, but I was too shy to say anything.*

lack confidence /ˌlæk ˈkɒnfɪdəns‖-ˈkɑːn-/ to not feel confident about your own abilities or about the way you look: *Francine lacks confidence and needs a lot of encouragement and support.*

lose confidence /ˌluːz ˈkɒnfɪdəns‖-ˈkɑːn-/ to stop feeling confident, especially after making a mistake: *"How was your driving test?" "Terrible – I made a small mistake, and then I just lost confidence."*

be unsure of yourself /biː ʌnˈʃʊər əv jɔːˌself/ to not be confident, especially because you are young or you do not have much experience of something: *He was only 21 and still very unsure of himself with women.*

insecure /ˌɪnsɪˈkjʊər/ [adj] not confident about making decisions, trying new experiences, or forming new relationships, especially because you are worried that you are not good enough: *Ben's parents' divorce left him lonely and insecure.*
+ about *Even though she's a model, she's very insecure about how she looks.*

CONFUSED

when you cannot understand something or you do not know what to do

➡ see also **UNDERSTAND/NOT UNDERSTAND**

1 confused

confused /kənˈfjuːzd/ [adj] unable to understand what is happening, what someone is saying etc, especially when this makes you feel worried: *I'm a little confused – could you explain it again?* | *She felt hurt and confused when her husband left her.*
+ about *Andrea is still confused about what happened on the night of the accident.*
get confused (=become confused) *Every time someone explains the Internet to me, I get even more confused.*

puzzled /ˈpʌzəld/ [adj] completely unable to understand why or how something happened: *The doctors are puzzled – they've never seen anything like this disease before.* | *She had a puzzled expression on her face.*
+ by/at *Mandy was puzzled by Bill's behaviour – why was he being so unfriendly?*

bewildered /bɪˈwɪldərd/ [adj] very confused and surprised when something unusual and unexpected happens to you: *He was bewildered to find three policemen at the front door.*
+ by *At first she was bewildered by all the noise and activity of the city.*

confusion /kənˈfjuːʒən/ [n U] the feeling you have when you feel confused, or a situation in which people are confused: *The new rules have caused a lot of confusion.*
+ about/over *There is some confusion about how the new law actually works.*

2 something that makes you feel confused

confusing /kənˈfjuːzɪŋ/ [adj] **confusing** instructions, explanations, situations etc make you feel confused, because it is not clear what they mean or what you should do: *The road signs were very confusing* and we ended up getting lost. | I found some of the questions really confusing.

puzzling /ˈpʌzəlɪŋ/ [adj] a **puzzling** action or situation makes you feel confused because you do not understand why or how it happened: *Jan's decision not to take part in the race was very puzzling.* | *I find it puzzling that no-one noticed them leave.*

bewildering /bɪˈwɪldərɪŋ/ [adj] a **bewildering** situation is very confusing, especially because it is strange or new, or because a lot of different things are happening at once: *Elderly people often find hospitals bewildering and frightening places.*
bewildering choice/variety/range (=so many things that it is difficult for you to choose) *There was a bewildering variety of styles to choose from.*

3 to make someone feel confused

confuse /kənˈfjuːz/ [v T] *You will confuse the students if you give them too much new information at once.*

4 to think one person or thing is another person or thing

confuse /kənˈfjuːz/ [v T] to wrongly think that one person or thing is someone or something else: *Try not to confuse 'your' and 'you're'.*
confuse sb with sb *I always confuse Anthea with her sister – they look so alike.*

mix up /ˌmɪks ˈʌp/ [phrasal verb T] to wrongly think one person or thing is someone or something else, especially because they are very similar
mix sth up/mix up sth *Children often mix up 'b' and 'd' when they're learning to write.*
get sb/sth mixed up *Which one's Jane and which one's Jen? I always get their names mixed up.*

⚠ Mix up is more informal than confuse

When you see **EC**, go to the **ESSENTIAL COMMUNICATION** section

CONNECTED/ NOT CONNECTED

when there is a relationship/no relationship between two things

➡ see also **JOIN, STICK**

1 to be connected with something

be connected/be related /biː kəˈnektɪd, biː rɪˈleɪtɪd/ if two things **are connected** with each other or **related** to each other, there is a relationship between them
be connected with sth *The police want to talk to people who saw anything that might be connected with the crime.*
be related to sth *Most of my problems were related to work.*
be closely connected/related *The two languages are closely related.* | *Achievement at school is closely connected with a child's home life.*

be linked /biː ˈlɪŋkt/ to be directly connected in some way – use this especially when there is one fact or cause that connects two things
be closely/strongly linked *Diet and health are strongly linked.*
+ to/with *Drug dealing has always been closely linked with organized crime.*

have/be something to do with /hæv, biː ˌsʌmθɪŋ tə ˈduː wɪð/ ESPECIALLY SPOKEN to be connected in a way that you do not understand clearly: *I don't know much about his job, but it has something to do with finance.* | *"What's wrong with your car?" "I'm not sure. I think it's something to do with the starter motor."*

2 something that connects two facts, events, or people

link/connection /lɪŋk, kəˈnekʃən/ [n C] something that connects two facts, events, or people with each other: *How can the weather affect the way people vote? I don't see any connection.*
+ between *The link between smoking and lung cancer has been definitely proved.* | *the connection between sports and gambling*

+ with *The firm has formed a trading link with Japan.* | *Do they think her murder has any connection with her political activities?*

relationship /rɪ'leɪʃənʃɪp/ [n C] the way in which two facts, events, or situations affect each other
+ between *the relationship between poverty and crime*

3 connected with the subject you are talking about

relevant /'relɪvənt/ [adj] directly connected with the subject you are talking about or considering: *Make sure that everything you write in your answer is relevant.* | *We can't make a decision until we have all the relevant information.*
+ to *I don't think your arguments are relevant to this discussion.*

4 not connected with someone or something

not connected/not related /nɒt kə'nektɪd, nɒt rɪ'leɪtɪd/ *The two diseases seem similar, but they are not related in any way.*
+ with *Is this group connected with any political party?*

⊂**have/be nothing to do with** /hæv, biː ,nʌθɪŋ tə 'duː wɪð/ ESPECIALLY SPOKEN to not be connected with something or someone in any way: *Those boxes are nothing to do with me. Sally left them there.* | *Your age has nothing to do with your ability to do the job.*

have no connection with sth /hæv ,nəʊ kə'nekʃən wɪð (sth)/ ESPECIALLY WRITTEN to not be connected with something in any way: *The first chapter of the book seems to have no connection with the main story.*

unrelated/unconnected /,ʌnrɪ'leɪtɪd◂, ,ʌnkə'nektɪd◂/ [adj] FORMAL not connected in any way: *The two robberies are said to be unconnected.*
unrelated to/unconnected with *Most of his books seem completely unrelated to real life.*

When you see **EC**, go to the
ESSENTIAL COMMUNICATION section.

5 not connected with the subject you are talking about

irrelevant /ɪ'relɪvənt/ [adj] *She kept asking irrelevant questions.* | *His age is irrelevant, as long as he can do the job.*
completely/totally irrelevant *What you are saying is true, but it's totally irrelevant.*

⊂**that's beside the point** /ðæts bɪ,saɪd ðə 'pɔɪnt/ SPOKEN say this when you think that what someone has said does not have any real connection with what you are talking about: *"Is she married or single?" "That's completely beside the point – the question is, will she make a good teacher?"*

⊂**what has that got to do with ...?** BRITISH SPOKEN **what does that have to do with ...?** AMERICAN SPOKEN /wɒt həz ,ðæt gɒt tə 'duː wɪð, wɒt dəz ,ðæt hæv tə 'duː wɪð‖-gɑːt-/ say this when someone has mentioned something and you cannot understand how it is connected with the subject you are talking about: *So your dad's ill? What's that got to do with our holiday plans?*

CONTAIN

1 to have something inside

contain /kən'teɪn/ [v T] to have something inside, or to have something as a part: *The bag contained a razor, some soap, and a towel.* | *Some paints contain lead, which can be poisonous.* | *Try to avoid foods that contain a lot of fat.*

⚠ Don't say 'the box is containing apples'. Say **the box contains apples**

have sth in it /'hæv (sth) ɪn ɪt/ if a container, room, or food or drink **has something in it**, something has been put into it: *Does this coffee have sugar in it?* | *She can't eat anything that has nuts in it.* | *The bedroom had a huge double bed in it.*

2 to be able to contain a particular amount

hold /həʊld/ [v T] if something **holds** 50 people, 10 litres etc, that is the largest amount that can go in it: *This jug holds about two litres.* | *The lecture theatre can hold up to 200 students.*

take /teɪk/ [v T not in passive] to have only enough space to contain a particular number or amount, but no more: *The car only takes five people, so the rest of you will have to take a taxi.* | *Our bookshelves won't take any more books.*

can carry /kən ˈkæri/ if a vehicle or ship **can carry** a particular amount of things or a particular number of people, it has enough space inside for them to go in it: *The new plane can carry up to 450 people.*

CONTINUE

➡ look here for ...
  • when something does not stop
  • when something starts again after stopping
➡ opposite **STOP**

1 when you continue to do something

continue /kənˈtɪnjuː/ [v I/T] to not stop doing something that you are already doing: *We will continue our struggle for independence.*

continue to do sth *She continued to live in the same room after Benny left.* | *Despite all the warnings, many people continue to smoke.*

continue doing sth *Senator Gramm continued speaking for another ten minutes.*

+ with *My teacher advised me to continue with my studies.*

go on/carry on /ˌgəʊ ˈɒn, ˌkæri ˈɒn‖-ˈɑːn/ [phrasal verb I] to continue to do something and not let anything stop you

go on/carry on doing sth *She ignored my question and carried on talking.* | *They obviously hate each other – I don't know why they go on living together.*

+ with *Don't stop. Carry on with your work.* | *They decided to go on with their meeting instead of going to lunch.*

⚠ Continue is more formal than **go on** or **carry on**

keep doing sth/keep on doing sth /ˌkiːp ˈduːɪŋ (sth), ˌkiːp ɒn ˈduːɪŋ (sth)/ to continue to do something for a long time, especially in order to get somewhere or achieve something: *Keep driving till you come to a crossroads.* | *We were all tired but we knew we had to keep moving.* | *If you keep on trying, I'm sure you'll get what you want.*

still /stɪl/ [adv] if someone is **still** doing something, they continue to do it – use this especially to show surprise: *He's 35 and he's still living with his parents.* | *You're not still working, are you?* | *Why are you still wearing your sweater? It's really hot in here.*

maintain /meɪnˈteɪn, mən-/ [v T] ESPECIALLY WRITTEN to make sure that something good continues to happen or continues to exist: *He always tried to maintain the old family traditions.* | *It is important that the US maintains its relationship with China.*

2 when something continues to happen

continue /kənˈtɪnjuː/ [v I] to continue happening: *The good weather seems likely to continue.* | *We don't know how long the strike will continue.*

continue for three months/several weeks/a long time etc *The war continued for another two months.*

continue happening/continue to happen *Several people have lost work, and this will continue to happen until we get the computer system fixed.*

last /lɑːst‖læst/ [v I] to continue – use this to say how long something continues

last two hours/six months/a long time etc *The concert lasted all day.* | *It's not certain how long the ceasefire will last.*

+ from/until *The meeting lasted until lunchtime.*

drag on /ˌdræg ˈɒn‖-ˈɑːn/ [phrasal verb I] if something that is happening **drags on**, it is boring and seems to continue for much longer than necessary: *The history lesson dragged on for another hour.*

When you see **EC**, go to the **ESSENTIAL COMMUNICATION** section.

go on /ˌgəʊ ˈɒn‖-ˈɑːn/ [phrasal verb I] to continue, especially for a long time: *How long does this TV show go on for?*
+ until/till *The party went on till three in the morning.*
go on and on (=continue for a very long time) *The noise went on and on – it was driving us crazy.*

⚠ Continue is more formal than **go on**.

3 to continue to be the same as before

stay /steɪ/ [v] **stay open/warm/calm etc** to continue to be open, warm etc: *The library stays open until 8pm on Fridays.* | *It will stay cold for the next few days.*

remain /rɪˈmeɪn/ [v] FORMAL **remain silent/calm/loyal etc** to continue to be silent, calm etc: *She remained calm and waited till he had finished shouting at her.* | *Would the audience please remain seated.*
remain a secret/mystery/problem etc *The details of his death remain a closely guarded secret.*
remain the same (=when someone or something does not change) *His doctors say that his condition remains the same.*
remain friends *They remained friends after their divorce.*

still /stɪl/ [adv] use this to emphasize that something or someone has not changed and continues to be the same: *At the age of 50, Marlene was still a beautiful woman.* | *She still has that rusty old car.* | *I'm still confused. Would you explain it again?*

4 to continue after stopping

continue /kənˈtɪnjuː/ [v I/T] to start again after stopping: *After a short time the rain stopped and the game continued.* | *Can we continue this discussion later?*
continue doing sth *When Andrew completed his military service, he continued writing his book.*

go on/carry on /ˌgəʊ ˈɒn, ˌkæri ˈɒn‖-ˈɑːn/ [phrasal verb I] to continue doing something or continue speaking, after a short pause: *It's one o'clock now – shall we carry on after lunch?* | *Go on, I'm listening.*

go on/carry on doing sth *The doctor looked up from her desk for a moment and then went on writing.*
+ with *As soon as Mr Saunders gets back we'll carry on with the meeting.* | *Do you want me to go on with my story?*

⚠ Continue is more formal than **go on/carry on**.

go back to sth /ˌgəʊ ˈbæk tuː (sth)/ [phrasal verb T] to start doing something again after a short period when you were doing something else: *Melanie made herself a cup of coffee and went back to her reading.*

5 continuing for a long time

continuous /kənˈtɪnjuəs/ [adj] continuing for a long time without stopping: *The north coast has had several days of continuous rain.* | *Education does not stop when you finish school – it's a continuous process.*
continuously [adv] *Radio Moscow played solemn music continuously throughout the day.*

constant /ˈkɒnstənt‖ˈkɑːn-/ [adj only before noun] use this about an unpleasant or worrying situation that seems as if it will never end: *He suffered constant pain in the months before his death.* | *The refugees live in constant fear of being attacked.*
constantly [adv] *We need to be constantly aware of the risk of accidents.*

non-stop /ˌnɒn ˈstɒp◂‖ˌnɑːn ˈstɑːp◂/ [adv] use this to emphasize that something happens continuously, and never stops even when you expect it to stop or want it to stop: *She talked non-stop for over an hour.*
non-stop [adj only before noun] *48 hours of non-stop rain*

steady /ˈstedi/ [adj only before noun] a **steady** change or improvement happens gradually, and continues without stopping or being interrupted: *There has been a steady increase in the number of students going to college.* | *a steady drop in road accidents*
steadily [adv] *The divorce rate has risen steadily since the 1950s.*
steady – steadier – steadiest

day after day/week after week etc /ˌdeɪ ɑːftəʳ ˈdeɪ, ˌwiːk ɑːftəʳ ˈwiːk (etc)‖-ˌæf-/ every day, every week etc for a long time: *The fighting went on week after week and there seemed no end to it.* | *She sits at home day after day, waiting for a message from her husband.*

day and night/around the clock /ˌdeɪ ən ˈnaɪt, əˌraʊnd ðə ˈklɒk‖-ˈklɑːk/ continuously, all day and all night without ever stopping: *Security guards watch the fence around the clock.* | *She nursed him day and night until he recovered.*

CONTROL

to make things happen in the way that you want, or make someone do what you want

➡ see also **POWER, LIMIT, IN CHARGE OF**

⚠ Don't confuse **control** (=make someone or something do what you want) with **check** or **inspect** (=look at something to see if it is correct or safe): *A guard got on the train and inspected our passports.* See LOOK AT.

1 to control what happens

control /kənˈtrəʊl/ [v T] to make things happen in the way that you want by using your power, skill, money etc: *The company used to control half of the world's oil trade.* | *Republican politicians now control the main congressional committees.* | *the parts of the brain that control the breathing process*
controlling – controlled – have controlled

be in control /ˌbiː ɪn kənˈtrəʊl/ to control a situation, organization, country etc – use this especially about someone who got their power by using force or by clever planning, but not by being elected: *The President has been arrested, and rebel forces are now in control.*
+ of *He is in control of over half the TV channels in the country.*

keep/get sth under control /ˌkiːp, ˌget (sth) ʌndəʳ kənˈtrəʊl/ to control a difficult or dangerous situation by doing every-thing that you can to stop it from getting any worse: *Firefighters struggled to keep the blaze under control.* | *We aim to be able to get the virus under control by 2005.*

2 to control a person

control /kənˈtrəʊl/ [v T] to make someone behave in the way that you want: *It was obvious that the teacher couldn't control the class.* | *Religion was just another way in which the country's rulers tried to control the people.*
controlling – controlled – have controlled

keep sb under control /ˌkiːp (sb) ʌndəʳ kənˈtrəʊl/ to prevent someone from causing trouble or problems: *Police were struggling to keep the demonstrators under control.* | *Can't you keep that dog under control?*

dominate /ˈdɒmɪneɪt‖ˈdɑː-/ [v T] if someone who has a strong character **dominates** another person, they have a very powerful effect on that person's mind and the way that they behave: *It was obvious that her husband completely dominated her.* | *his dominating manner*

manipulate /məˈnɪpjʊleɪt/ [v T] to make someone do what you want them to do by cleverly influencing them, especially when they do not realize what you are doing: *Maclaren skilfully manipulated the media, and the group quickly became as famous as the Beatles.*
manipulative /məˈnɪpjʊlətɪv‖-leɪ-/ [adj] clever at manipulating people: *Sweet as she was, there was a manipulative side to her character.*

3 to control the temperature, speed, or amount of something

control /kənˈtrəʊl/ [v T] to make the temperature, speed, or amount of something change in the way that you want or stay at the level you want: *This button controls the temperature in the building.* | *How do you control the speed of the drill?*
controlling – controlled – have controlled

keep sth under control /ˌkiːp (sth) ʌndəʳ kənˈtrəʊl/ to prevent the amount of something from becoming too great: *He's been trying for years to keep his drinking under control.* | *The administration has certainly succeeded in keeping inflation under control.*

regulate /'regjʊleɪt/ [v T] to keep the temperature, speed, or amount of something at exactly the right level: *Sweating helps you regulate your body temperature.*

4 to control your feelings

control /kən'trəʊl/ if you **control** yourself or **control** your feelings, you continue to behave calmly and sensibly and do not become too angry, excited, or upset
control yourself/himself etc *She was really annoying me, but I managed to control myself and not say anything.*
control your temper/anger *I wish he'd learn to control his temper.*
controlling – controlled – have controlled

self-control /,self kən'trəʊl/ [n U] the ability to behave calmly and sensibly and not become too angry, excited, or upset: *The German team showed amazing self-control throughout the game.*

5 unable to control your feelings

lose control /,luːz kən'trəʊl/ to become unable to control your feelings and become very angry or upset: *He made her so angry that she lost control and hit him.*

get carried away /get ,kærid ə'weɪ/ ESPECIALLY SPOKEN to feel so excited, interested etc that you cannot control what you are saying or doing: *It's easy to get carried away and buy a lot of things that you don't need.* | *Tony got a bit carried away on the dancefloor and started doing his Mick Jagger impersonation.*

6 to no longer be able to control a situation, vehicle, group of people etc

lose control /,luːz kən'trəʊl/ to no longer be able to control a situation, vehicle, group of people etc: *The car skidded on the ice, and I lost control.*
+ of *parents who lose control of their*

children | *O'Connor recently lost control of the company he had run for seven years.*

7 to get control of a situation, organization, country etc

take control /,teɪk kən'trəʊl/ to get control of a situation, organization, or place, often by using violent or illegal methods: *In 1949 the Chinese Communist Party took control.*
+ of *Troops were called in to take control of the prison.*

take over /,teɪk 'əʊvəʳ/ [phrasal verb I/T] to get control of a company or organization, or become the leader, president etc after someone else: *People are wondering who's going to take over when the old dictator dies.*
take over sth/take sth over *CBS records was taken over by Sony.*
+ from *She took over from Barton as Managing Director in 1994.*

8 difficult or impossible to control

uncontrollable /,ʌnkən'trəʊləbəl◂/ [adj] **uncontrollable** emotions or actions are difficult or impossible to control: *Barbara was shaking with uncontrollable laughter.* | *an uncontrollable rage*

out of control /,aʊt əv kən'trəʊl/ a situation that is **out of control** has got much worse and can no longer be controlled: *The fire was out of control.* | *Teenage crime was now out of control.*
get out of control (=become impossible to control) *It's easy to let spending on credit cards get out of control.*

CONVENIENT NOT CONVENIENT

➡ see also **SUITABLE/UNSUITABLE**

1 a suitable time to do something

convenient /kən'viːniənt/ [adj] a **convenient** time to do something is a time that does not cause you any problems, for example because you were not planning to do anything else: *I'd like to talk to the manager – can you suggest a convenient time?*

+ for *We need to arrange a meeting. Would 11 o'clock on Tuesday be convenient for you?*

a good time /ə gʊd 'taɪm/ ESPECIALLY SPOKEN a convenient time to do something: *"I'm too busy to talk to you now." "When would be a good time?"*

a good time to do sth *Now might be a good time to think about what you really want to do.*

+ for *I'm afraid Friday isn't a good time for me – I have to go to the dentist.*

suit /suːt, sjuːt‖suːt/ [v T] if a time or date **suits** you, it is convenient for you: *Let's go to see a movie next week. Which day would suit you best? | Finding a time that suits everyone is going to be difficult.*

be OK/be okay /biː ˌəʊˈkeɪ/ SPOKEN INFORMAL if a time or date **is OK** or **is okay**, it is convenient for you: *I'll drive over and get you. Is 10 o'clock OK?*

+ for *Friday's probably okay for me, but I'll check with Jean.*

fit in with sth /ˌfɪt ɪn wɪð (sth)/ [phrasal verb T] if something **fits in with** your plans, you do not need to change your plans in order to do it: *We'd like to go out for a meal on Thursday – does that fit in with what you're doing?*

2 a useful object, place, or method

• see also **NEAR**

convenient /kənˈviːniənt/ [adj] a **convenient** place or way of doing something is useful because it is quick, easy, and does not cause you any problems: *Credit cards are probably the most convenient way of paying for concert tickets.*

it is convenient to do sth *I could take the train, but it's more convenient to go in the car.*

convenient for the school/shops/station etc BRITISH (=near to the school etc, so it is easy to get there) *The hotel is very convenient for the station – it's only a two-minute walk.*

handy /ˈhændi/ [adj] INFORMAL a **handy** object, method, place etc is easy to use, easy to do, or easy to get to: *Many fruit juices are now available in handy little cartons. | It's a handy way of keeping a record of your spending.*

handy for the school/shops/station etc BRITISH (=near to the school etc, so it is easy to get there) *Our house is very handy for the shops.*

3 not convenient

inconvenient/not convenient /ˌɪn-kənˈviːniənt◄, nɒt kənˈviːniənt/ [adj] not convenient: *I'm afraid he's come at an inconvenient time.*

+ for *I can call you back later if it's not convenient for you to talk now. | The trouble with living in the country is that it's not very convenient for work.*

it is inconvenient to do sth *If you find it inconvenient to come to the office, we can mail the papers to you.*

a bad time /ə ˌbæd 'taɪm/ ESPECIALLY SPOKEN a time that is not convenient because you are busy or you have made other plans: *Sorry – have I come at a bad time?*

a bad time to do sth *It was definitely a bad time to ask Mr Field for more money.*

COOK

RESTAURANTS/EATING AND DRINKING

MEAL   DRINK

see also

EAT   MIX

FOOD   TASTE

1 to cook a meal or make something such as bread, soup etc

cook /kʊk/ [v I/T] to prepare food or a meal by heating it, boiling it, frying it etc: *I'm too tired to cook after school. | Prick the sausages with a fork before cooking them.*

cook lunch/supper/a meal etc *I usually cook lunch on Sunday.*

cook (sth) for sb (=cook a meal for someone) *The last time Lucy cooked a meal for us we both really enjoyed it.*

cooked [adj] *Mix the vegetables and the mayonnaise with the cooked rice. | Is that pasta cooked yet?*

make /meɪk/ [v T] to make a meal or dish or type of food, either by cooking it or by preparing it in some other way: *My mother used to make delicious strawberry jam. | I think I'll make fish pie for supper. | I'll make the salad.*

make lunch/dinner/supper etc *Martin was in the kitchen making lunch.*

make sb sth *I'll make you some sandwiches to take with you.*

making – made – have made

get /get/ [v T not in passive] SPOKEN to cook or prepare a meal

get breakfast/lunch/dinner *Sit down and let me get dinner.*

get sb their lunch/dinner etc *Joey was downstairs getting the kids their breakfast.*

getting – got – have got BRITISH

getting – got – have gotten AMERICAN

fix /fɪks/ [v T] ESPECIALLY AMERICAN to make a meal or dish – use this about meals you make quickly, not about big, formal meals

fix breakfast/lunch/dinner etc *I have to fix lunch now.*

fix sb sth *You're too late for supper but I can fix you some scrambled eggs.*

prepare /prɪ'peəʳ/ [v T] WRITTEN to make a meal or dish, especially something that needs time, effort, or skill: *Prepare a sauce with cream, lemon juice, and mustard. | Mrs Fujimoto had prepared a delicious meal for them when they got home.*

> ⚠ **Prepare** is more formal than **cook**

2 ways of cooking

boil /bɔɪl/ [v I/T] to cook food in very hot water: *Boil the potatoes until they are soft. | The beans should be boiled for at least 20 minutes.*

boiled [adj only before noun] *boiled eggs*

fry /fraɪ/ [v I/T] to cook food in hot oil, butter, or fat: *Fry the onions gently for five minutes. | Mushrooms are best when fried in olive oil.*

fried [adj only before noun] *fried bacon*

frying – fried – have fried

bake /beɪk/ [v I/T] to cook food in an oven, without any liquid or fat: *Put the cake into a hot oven and bake for 35 minutes. | Do you bake your own bread?*

baked [adj only before noun] *baked potatoes*

roast /rəʊst/ [v I/T] to cook meat or vegetables in an oven or over a fire using a small amount of fat: *Roast the chicken for three hours in a hot oven.*

roast [adj only before noun] *roast potatoes | There's some cold roast beef in the fridge.*

grill BRITISH **broil** AMERICAN /grɪl, brɔɪl/ [v I/T] to cook food, especially meat or fish, by putting it directly underneath a flame or a heated electric object: *Grill the steak for about five minutes on each side. | Brush the kebabs lightly with oil and broil them.*

grilled/broiled [adj only before noun] *grilled fish*

steam /stiːm/ [v I/T] to cook food in steam: *Steam the courgettes for 3–4 minutes.*

steamed [adj only before noun] *a steamed pudding*

3 ways of preparing food before you cook it

mix /mɪks/ [v I/T] to put two or more types of food together: *Add eggs to the flour and butter, and mix well.*

mix sth with sth *I usually make salad dressing by mixing olive oil with vinegar and adding a little mustard.*

mix sth together *Mix all the ingredients together in a large bowl.*

stir /stɜːʳ/ [v I/T] to mix things together by moving them slowly around with a spoon or fork: *She kept stirring the mixture until it was completely smooth. | Heat the soup in a pan, stirring constantly.*

stir in sth (=add an ingredient to a sauce or mixture and stir it) *When the sauce has cooled, stir in the grated cheese.*

stirring – stirred – have stirred

beat /biːt/ [v T] to mix eggs, cream etc together thoroughly with a fork or a special tool, using quick, strong movements: *Carry on beating the margarine and sugar until they are light and fluffy.*
beating – beat – have beaten

whisk /wɪsk/ [v T] to mix eggs, cream etc very quickly with a special tool or machine, so that they get air in them and become thicker: *My mother whisked the eggs and sugar in a large bowl.*

4 not cooked

raw /rɔː/ [adj] **raw** food has not been cooked: *a salad made with raw carrots, nuts, and raisins* | *Sushi consists of raw fish and rice.*

uncooked /ˌʌnˈkʊkt◀/ [adj only before noun] **uncooked** food has not yet been cooked, but must be cooked before it is eaten: *uncooked pastry* | *Uncooked meat should be stored separately.*

underdone/undercooked /ˌʌndərˈdʌn◀, ˌʌndərˈkʊkt◀/ [adj] not cooked enough: *It can be dangerous to eat undercooked pork.* | *The potatoes were underdone.*

5 cooked too much

overcooked/overdone /ˌəʊvərˈkʊkt◀, ˌəʊvərˈdʌn◀/ [adj] food that is **overcooked** or **overdone** has been cooked too much and does not taste nice: *This steak's a little overdone.* | *I hate overcooked vegetables.*

burn /bɜːrn/ [v T] to cook food for too long, or too close to the heat, so that it becomes black on the outside: *Oh no! I've burnt the turkey!*
burned/burnt [adj] *the smell of burnt toast*
burning – burned (also **burnt** BRITISH) – **have burned** (also **have burnt** BRITISH)

6 the activity of cooking

cooking /ˈkʊkɪŋ/ [n U] the activity of cooking: *His hobbies include cooking and cycling.*
do the cooking *Who does the cooking in your house?*
sb's cooking (=the way that someone cooks) *Stop criticizing my cooking!*

> ⚠ You can also use **cooking** before a noun, like an adjective: *Follow the cooking instructions carefully.* | *cooking utensils*

cookery /ˈkʊkəri/ [n U] ESPECIALLY BRITISH the activity or study of cooking: *My favourite subject at school was cookery.*

> ⚠ You can also use **cookery** before a noun, like an adjective: *cookery classes* | *a cookery book*

cuisine /kwɪˈziːn/ [n U] FORMAL the style of cooking of a particular country or place, especially when the food is very good: *The restaurant is famous for its excellent cuisine.*
French/Italian/Chinese cuisine (=the French etc style of cooking)

7 instructions for cooking

recipe /ˈresɪpi/ [n C] a set of instructions for cooking a particular dish or meal: *rabbit pie made to a traditional country recipe*
+ for *Could you give me the recipe for that chocolate cake?*

cookbook (also **recipe book** BRITISH) /ˈkʊkbʊk, ˈresɪpi bʊk/ [n C] a book that has instructions for preparing various dishes

8 someone who cooks

cook /kʊk/ [n C] someone who cooks food, either as their job or for pleasure: *Jane works as a cook in an Italian restaurant.*
a good/excellent/terrible cook (=someone who is very good or very bad at cooking)

chef /ʃef/ [n C] someone who has been trained to prepare and cook food, especially the most important cook in a hotel or restaurant: *Marco's a chef in a big hotel in Oxford.*

COPY

➡ look here for ...
• copy a document or photograph
• copy the way someone behaves

C

1 to copy a picture or piece of writing

copy /ˈkɒpi‖ˈkɑːpi/ [v T] to produce something that is the same as something else: *They were arrested for illegally copying video recordings.* | *Copy the graph on page 25, then answer the questions.*

copy sth from/into/onto sth *The drawings had been copied from photographs.* | *I copied her address onto a piece of paper.* | *We had to copy all our files onto floppy disks.*

copying – copied – have copied

make a copy /ˌmeɪk ə ˈkɒpi‖-ˈkɑːpi/ to copy something using a machine

+ of *I'll make a copy of my report for you.* | *Are you allowed to make copies of this software?*

photocopy (also **xerox** TRADEMARK, ESPECIALLY AMERICAN) /ˈfəʊtəkɒpi, ˈzɪərɒks‖-kɑːpi, -rɑːks/ [v T] to copy a piece of paper with writing or pictures on it, using a special machine that makes a photograph of the original: *I photocopied the letter before sending it off.* | *Where can I get these papers xeroxed?*

photocopying – photocopied – have photocopied

2 something that has been copied from something else

copy /ˈkɒpi‖ˈkɑːpi/ [n C] something that has been made to look exactly like something else

+ of *This statue is a copy of the one in the Louvre.* | *Using computer graphics, we can make an exact copy of the original design.*

plural **copies**

photocopy (also **xerox** TRADEMARK, ESPECIALLY AMERICAN) /ˈfəʊtəkɒpi, ˈzɪərɒks‖-kɑːpi, -rɑːks/ [n C] a copy of a document, letter, or picture etc, made by a machine that photographs the original

+ of *Please send a photocopy of your birth certificate.* | *xeroxes of the company's accounts*

plural **photocopies**

duplicate /ˈdjuːplɪkⁱt‖ˈduː-/ [adj only before noun] a **duplicate** key, bill etc is an exact copy of a key, bill etc and can be used in the same way, especially if the

original one is lost: *a duplicate set of keys* | *It's a good idea to keep duplicate files on floppy disk.*

model /ˈmɒdl‖ˈmɑːdl/ [n C] a small copy of a building, vehicle, or machine, made to look exactly like the original building, vehicle etc

+ of *We bought a little plastic model of the Eiffel Tower as a souvenir.*

model ship/airplane etc *There was a shelf in his bedroom full of model planes.*

replica /ˈreplɪkə/ [n C] a copy of a well-known vehicle, building, or weapon, especially one that is the same size as the original: *a replica gun*

+ of *You can now drive a perfect replica of this classic racing car.* | *The building is an exact replica of the original Globe theatre.*

reproduction /ˌriːprəˈdʌkʃən/ [n C] a copy of an old or valuable work of art or piece of furniture: *Of course this picture isn't the original – it's only a reproduction.* | *reproduction furniture*

+ of *a reproduction of a beautiful Ming vase*

3 to copy something without permission

copy /ˈkɒpi‖ˈkɑːpi/ [v I/T] to copy something and dishonestly pretend it is your own work: *Any student caught copying from someone else will be sent out.* | *She was furious when she discovered that another scientist had copied her ideas.*

copy sth from/out of sth *This isn't your own work. You copied it out of the book.*

copying – copied – have copied

forge /fɔːrdʒ/ [v T] to illegally copy something written or printed, such as a bank note or official document, for dishonest purposes: *The thief had forged my signature on a cheque.* | *He must have entered the country using a forged passport.*

4 an illegal copy

forgery /ˈfɔːrdʒəri/ [n C] an illegal copy of something such as a bank note or official document: *The passports were forgeries.* |

Further investigation showed that the so-called 'Hitler Diaries' were a forgery.

plural **forgeries**

counterfeit /ˈkaʊntəʳfɪt/ [adj] **counterfeit** money looks exactly like real money but has been produced illegally: *Police have warned stores to look out for counterfeit $50 bills.*

pirate /ˈpaɪərət/ [adj only before noun]
pirate copies/videos/CDs copies of books, records, films etc that have been made illegally and are sold without the permission of the people who originally produced them: *They were selling pirate copies of 'Windows 95'.*

5 to do the same as someone else

copy /ˈkɒpi‖ˈkɑːpi/ [v T] to do the same things that someone else does: *Many women copied the way Princess Diana dressed.* | *Billy started making rude noises, and of course the other kids copied him.*

copying – copied – have copied

imitate /ˈɪmɪteɪt/ [v T] to copy the way someone behaves, speaks, writes, or moves, especially because you admire them or want to be like them: *When children play, they frequently imitate adults.* | *A lot of writers have tried to imitate Lawrence's style.*

do what sb does /ˌduː wɒt (sb) ˈdʌz/ to do the same things as someone else, especially in order to learn from them: *Just watch the others and do what they do. You'll soon learn the job.*

follow sb's example /ˌfɒləʊ (sb's) ɪɡˈzɑːmpl‖ˌfɑːləʊ (sb's) ɪɡˈzæm-/ to do the same as someone else, especially because you admire them or because they have got good results by doing it: *Perhaps Britain should follow America's example and keep religion and education separate.*

6 to copy someone's behaviour or voice in order to make people laugh

imitate /ˈɪmɪteɪt/ [v T] to copy what someone says or does, in order to make people laugh: *She's really good at imitating our teacher's Scottish accent.*

do an impression of sb/do an impersonation of sb /ˌduː ən ɪmˈpreʃən ɒv (sb), ˌduː ən ɪmpɜːʳsəˈneɪʃən ɒv (sb)/ to copy the way a famous person speaks, walks, or behaves in order to make people laugh: *He did a pretty stupid impression of Charlie Chaplin.*

COST

CHEAP   BUY

EXPENSIVE   see also   SPEND

FREE   MONEY

PAY   SHOP

1 what you have to pay for something

cost /kɒst‖kɔːst/ [n C] the amount of money you must pay for services, activities, or things you need all the time like food and electricity
+ of *The cost of bread went up by 200%.* | *Many old people cannot afford the cost of heating their homes.*
high/low cost *the high cost of building land in Tokyo*
heating/transportation/legal etc costs *Delaney still owes his lawyer over £20,000 in legal costs.*
the cost of living (=the amount of money you need for things such as food, clothes, and rent)

⚠ Don't use 'cost' about things you buy in shops. Use **price**.

⚠ Don't say 'the cost is expensive'. Say **it is expensive**.

price /praɪs/ [n C] the amount of money you must pay to buy something that is for sale, especially in a shop: *There's a great new clothes store on Main Street, and the prices seem very reasonable.*
+ of *What's the price of a pack of cigarettes nowadays?*
half price (=half the usual price) *I bought these jeans half price in the sale.*
reduce/cut prices *Comet has reduced the prices of most electrical goods by 25%.*

rising prices (=prices that keep increasing) *Football fans have been complaining about rising ticket prices.*

oil/food/house etc prices *House prices have come down a lot in recent years.*

⚠ Don't say 'the price is expensive' or 'the price is cheap'. Say **it is expensive** or **it is cheap**.

⚠ You can also use **price** before a noun, like an adjective: *price increases | price controls*

fare /feə^r/ [n C] the cost of a journey on a bus, train, plane etc: *I'd like to visit my cousin in Canada, but I can't afford the fare.*

taxi/bus/plane etc fare *How much is the taxi fare home?*

rent /rent/ [n C/U] the amount of money that you must pay to live in or use a place that you do not own

pay rent *She pays £350 a month rent for a one-bedroomed apartment.*

high/low rent *Office rents are highest in the centre of town.*

put up the rent/raise the rent (=increase it) *Our landlord has just raised the rent again.*

charge /tʃɑː^rdʒ/ [n C/U] the amount of money that you must pay for a service or for being allowed to use something

bank/delivery/electricity etc charges *How much do you pay in bank charges a month?*

+ for *Is there an extra charge for using the swimming pool?*

fee /fiː/ [n C] the amount of money that you must pay to someone such as a doctor, lawyer, or teacher for a professional service: *My lawyer has increased his fee to $200 an hour.*

school/legal/medical etc fees *An accident on vacation can cost you a lot in medical fees.*

2 ways of saying or asking how much something costs

cost /kɒst‖kɔːst/ [v] if something **costs** £10, $100 etc, that is what you have to pay in order to buy it: *How much did that coat cost? | It only costs 50 cents.*

cost £10/$20/a lot etc *The holiday costs £600 per person.*

cost sb £10/$20 etc *That sofa cost me nearly $1000.*

cost a fortune INFORMAL (=cost a lot of money) *The car has cost a fortune to repair.*

it costs £10/$20/a lot etc to do sth *It costs about £500 to fly to America.*

costing – cost – have cost

⚠ Don't say 'it costs very expensive'. Say **it is expensive** or **it costs a lot**.

how much /haʊ 'mʌtʃ/ SPOKEN say **how much** to ask what the price or cost of something is: *How much is that table? | That's a beautiful ring – how much did you pay for it? | By the way, how much does it cost to use the swimming pool?*

⚠ Don't say 'how much costs this?' or 'how much cost was it?' Say **how much does this cost?** or **how much did it cost?**

be /biː/ [v] if something **is** £100, $1000 etc, that is how much it costs – use this especially when you are asking or replying to a question about the cost of something

be £5/$20/a lot of money etc *"That's a nice shirt – how much was it?" "It was only five pounds." | I can't remember how much it cost. I think it was around $400.*

3 how much something would cost if it was sold

value /'væljuː/ [n C/U] the amount of money that something expensive, rare, or old would cost if it was sold – use this to talk about things like houses, cars, jewellery, paintings, or furniture

+ of *The value of the painting was estimated at $500,000.*

increase/fall in value *Some fine wines increase in value as they get older.*

be worth /biː 'wɜː^rθ/ if something **is worth** £10, $100 etc, that is how much money it would cost if it was sold: *How much is your ring worth?*

be worth $500/£10 etc *I guess their house must be worth about £500,000. | That old piano can't be worth more than $200.*

4 to ask for a particular amount of money for something

charge /tʃɑːʳdʒ/ [v I/T] if someone **charges** an amount of money, that is how much you must pay them for providing a service or doing work for you

charge £10/$50 etc *He charges $200 an hour.* | *The engineer charged £70 for labour and £45 for parts.*

charge sb £10/$50 *How much are they charging you for the repairs?* | *The bank will charge its customers 6% interest from next week.*

ask /ɑːsk‖æsk/ [v T] to want an amount of money for something that you are selling, especially when other people think the price is too high

ask £100/$3000 etc for sth *I don't believe he's asking £2000 for that old car.*

◯ want /wɒnt‖wɑːnt/ [v T] ESPECIALLY SPOKEN to want an amount of money for something you are selling or for doing work for someone

want £20/$50 etc for sth *How much do you want for the video recorder?*

5 a statement that says how much something will probably cost

estimate /ˈestɪmɪt/ [n C] a statement that says how much money it will probably cost to build or repair something: *The final cost was £2000 higher than the original estimate.*

+ for *I've asked the builders to give us an estimate for fixing the roof.*

quotation also **quote** INFORMAL /kwəʊˈteɪʃən, kwəʊt/ [n C] a written statement of exactly how much money something will cost: *Get a few quotations from different firms so you can compare prices.*

When you see **EC**, go to the **ESSENTIAL COMMUNICATION** section.

NUMBER   TOTAL
see also
COST   AMOUNT/NUMBER

1 to count numbers, objects etc in order to find the total

count/count up /kaʊnt, ˌkaʊnt ˈʌp/ [v T] to find the total number of things or people in a group by counting them all: *Katherine counted her money. There was almost $50 left.* | *Count up the number of calories you have each day.* | *The teacher was counting the children as they got onto the bus.*

add up /ˌæd ˈʌp/ [phrasal verb T] to put several numbers or amounts together and calculate the total

add up sth *When we added up the receipts we realized we had spent too much.*

add sth up *The books cost quite a lot of money, when you added them all up.*

keep count /ˌkiːp ˈkaʊnt/ to keep a record, either on paper or in your memory, of numbers or amounts that increase over a period of time, so that you always know what the total is: *I don't know what the score was. I wasn't keeping count.*

+ of *She was trying to keep count of how many stations they'd passed.*

2 to calculate an amount or price

calculate /ˈkælkjʊleɪt/ [v T] to find out how much something will cost, how long something will take etc, by using numbers: *Their accountant calculated the total cost of the project.*

calculate how much/how many/how far etc *Try to calculate how long the fuel will last.*

+ that *Sally calculated that she needed $300 to pay all her bills.*

calculation /ˌkælkjʊˈleɪʃən/ [n C often plural] a process by which you calculate a total, price, time etc: *NASA calculations put the cost of the space program at $118 billion.*

Qwork out /ˌwɜːʳk ˈaʊt/ [phrasal verb T] ESPECIALLY SPOKEN to calculate an answer, amount, price, or value
work out sth *I always use a calculator to work out percentages.*
work sth out *"How much do I owe you?" "I haven't worked it out yet."*
work out how much/how many/how far etc *We need to work out how much food we'll need to take with us.*

estimate /ˈestɪmeɪt/ [v T] to guess an amount, price, or number, as exactly as you can
+ that *It's been estimated that the number of car-owners will increase by about 15%.*
estimate what/how many/how much etc *It is impossible to estimate how many illegal guns there are in circulation.*
estimate [n C] an amount that is guessed, not calculated exactly: *As a rough estimate, we currently recycle about 5% of the paper we use.*

3 to add one number to another

add /æd/ [v T] to put two or more numbers together and calculate the answer
add sth and sth *If you add 24 and 36 you get 60.*
add sth to sth *Add 10% to the total.*
addition [n U] when you add a number

Qplus /plʌs/ [preposition] SPOKEN use **plus** between numbers or amounts to show that you are adding one to another: *Eight plus six is fourteen.* | *The cost is £45 plus £5 for delivery.*

⚠ The written sign for **plus** is '+': $8 + 6 = 14$

4 to take one number from another

Qtake/take away /teɪk, ˌteɪk əˈweɪ/ [v T] ESPECIALLY SPOKEN to take one number from another and calculate the answer
take sth (away) from sth *If you take 17 from 100 you get 83.* | *Take 19 away from 48 and then add 15.*

subtract /səbˈtrækt/ [v T] to take one number from another and calculate the answer: *To convert the temperature into celsius, subtract 32, then multiply by 5 and divide by 9.*
subtract sth from sth *Subtract 12 from 32.*
subtraction [n U] when you subtract a number

⚠ **Subtract** is more formal than **take** or **take away**.

Qminus /ˈmaɪnəs/ [preposition] SPOKEN use **minus** between numbers or amounts to show that you are taking one from another: *30 minus 5 leaves 25.*

⚠ The written sign for **minus** is '−': $10 - 6 = 4$

5 to multiply one number by another

multiply /ˈmʌltɪplaɪ/ [v I/T] to add a number to itself a particular number of times
multiply sth by sth *If you multiply ten by seven you get seventy.*
+ by *To find the price in yen, you must multiply by 86.*
multiplied by *11 multiplied by 10 is 110.*
multiplying – multiplied – have multiplied
multiplication /ˌmʌltɪplɪˈkeɪʃən/ [n U] when you multiply a number: *Use your calculator for multiplication.*

⚠ The written sign for **multiplied by** is 'x': $6 \times 3 = 18$

Qtimes /taɪmz/ [preposition] SPOKEN use **times** between numbers or amounts to show that you are multiplying one by another: *Five times six equals thirty.* | *What's nine times eighteen?*

6 to divide one number by another

divide /dɪˈvaɪd/ [v I/T] to divide one number by another, usually smaller, number
+ by *It is easier to divide by 10 than by 12.*
divide sth by sth *If you divide thirty by five you get six.*

divided by 36 divided by 2 is 18.

division /dʒɪˈvɪʒən/ [n U] when you divide a number: We didn't learn division until we were older.

> ⚠ The written sign for **divided by** is '÷':
> 10 ÷ 2 = 5

COUNTRY

➡ if you mean 'land where there are trees and fields and not many buildings', go to **COUNTRYSIDE**
➡ see also **LAND AND SEA, WALK 2, 3, ENVIRONMENT**

1 country

country /ˈkʌntri/ [n C] an area of land with its own government, army etc, for example, France, Japan, or the USA: Brazil is one of the biggest countries in the world. | How many countries are there in Europe? | The northeast of the country was badly hit by the hurricane. | I've travelled all over the country. (=to a lot of places within a country)
the country (=all the people in a country) The explosion in Paris shocked the whole country.
plural **countries**

> ⚠ Don't say 'what is your country?'. Say **where are you from?** or **where do you come from?**

> ⚠ Don't call a country a 'land'. **Land** is mostly used in poetry or in stories about the past or about distant places. Long ago, in a land far away from here, there lived a wicked queen.

nation /ˈneɪʃən/ [n C] a country – use this especially to talk about a country's history, way of life, and social and economic conditions: Indonesia is the world's largest Muslim nation. | Representatives from the seven leading industrial nations will meet in Geneva this week. | The flag symbolizes a new united, democratic South African nation.
the nation (=all the people in a nation) The President will broadcast to the nation this evening. | a celebration that united the whole nation

state /steɪt/ [n C] a country – use this to talk about a country as a political organization with its own political system: In 1830 Greece became an independent state. | the member states of the European Union (=the countries that belong to the EU) | For more than 70 years the Soviet Union was a one-party state.

colony /ˈkɒləni ˈkɑː-/ [n C] a country that has no independent government of its own, but is controlled by another country, especially one that is a long way away: former British colonies in Africa
plural **colonies**

2 the country that you come from

be from/come from /biː ˈfrɒm, ˈkʌm frɒm/ [phrasal verb T] if you **are from** or **come from** a country, that is where you were born or is the place that you consider to be your home: Maya's father is from Sri Lanka and her mother is from Brazil. | "Where do you come from?" "Australia."

> ⚠ Don't say 'he is coming from Hong Kong'. Say **he comes from Hong Kong**.

home /həʊm/ [n U] the country that you consider to be your home, especially when you are living in a different country: I've lived abroad most of my life but I still think of England as my home.
◗**back home** SPOKEN (=in the country you come from) Back home we never had to lock our doors at night.
go/travel/fly home Air fares go up in December because everyone flies home for Christmas.

> ⚠ Don't say 'I'm going back to my country'. Say **I'm going home**

3 the line where one country ends and another begins

border /ˈbɔːrdər/ [n C] the official line that separates two countries
+ with The river runs along Mexico's border with the US.
the Brazilian border/Nigerian border etc (=the border where Brazil, Nigeria etc begins)

on the border *Jeumont is a small town on the French–Belgian border.*
cross the border *The refugees crossed the border at night.*

4 someone who has the right to live in a country

citizen /'sɪtˌzən/ [n C] a person from a particular country who has the legal right to vote, work, and live there: *He became a Dutch citizen after working there for eight years.* | *The US government is advising all American citizens in the war zone to come home.*

nationality /ˌnæʃə'nælˌti/ [n C/U] your **nationality** is the fact that you are American, Japanese, French etc: *We had to write our name and nationality on the form.* | *people of different nationalities*
plural **nationalities**

> ⚠ **Nationality** is a formal and official word. To tell someone where you come from, don't say 'my nationality is French'. Say **I am French** or **I come from France.**

citizenship /'sɪtˌzənʃɪp/ [n U] **US/Japanese etc citizenship** the legal right of being an American, Japanese etc citizen, especially when you were born in another country: *She married him so that she could get Swiss citizenship.*

5 existing in or happening in a country

national /'næʃənəl/ [adj usually before noun] use **national** about things that happen in or affect a whole country and not just a part of it: *Ice hockey is the national sport of Canada.* | *The Day of the Dead is a national holiday in Latin American countries.* | *national and local news*

> **nationally** [adv] *Nationally there was a 12% drop in crime last year.*

domestic /də'mestɪk/ [adj/adv usually before noun] use **domestic** about things that happen or exist within a county and do not affect any other country: *All domestic flights have been cancelled, but a few international flights are still running.* | *The factory produces cars mainly for the domestic market.*

6 existing in or happening in many countries

international /ˌɪntəᵣ'næʃənəl◄/ [adj usually before noun] use **international** about things that involve or affect people from several different countries: *an international conference on human rights* | *international trade agreements* | *Hal Hartley's latest movie has been an international success.*

multinational /ˌmʌlti'næʃənəl◄/ [adj only before noun] **multinational company/ bank/corporation** a large company that has offices or factories in many different countries: *His business has been bought by a huge multinational oil corporation.*

7 someone who loves their country

patriotic /ˌpætri'ɒtɪk◄, ˌpeɪ-‖ˌpeɪtri'ɑːtɪk◄/ [adj] someone who is **patriotic** loves their country and is very loyal to it: *We're just good, patriotic Americans ready to defend our freedom.* | *At school we had to raise the flag and sing patriotic songs every morning.*

> **patriotism** /'pætriətɪzəm, 'peɪ-‖'peɪ-/ [n U] love for your country

nationalistic /ˌnæʃənə'lɪstɪk◄/ [adj] someone who is **nationalistic** believes that their country is better than any other, and often has no respect for other countries: *As nationalistic feelings grew, life became increasingly difficult for immigrants.*

> **nationalism** /'næʃənəlɪzəm/ [n U] nationalistic feelings: *the rise of nationalism and military power that led to war in 1914*

8 people who want to form a separate country

nationalist /'næʃənəlˌst/ [n C] someone who wants a separate independent country for people of their own race, religion, or origin
Scottish/Welsh/Quebec etc nationalists *The Scottish nationalists won a record number of votes in the local elections.*

> **nationalist** [adj] *the nationalist campaign in French-speaking Canada*
> **nationalism** [n U] nationalist ideas and activities: *Basque nationalism*

C

COUNTRYSIDE

the parts of a country that are far from towns or cities

➡ see also **ENVIRONMENT**

countryside /'kʌntrɪsaɪd/ [n U] the parts of a country that are not near any big towns or cities, where there are farms, fields, villages etc: *a villa with wonderful views over the surrounding countryside*
the French/Sussex etc countryside *Cezanne's paintings of the French countryside*

the country /ðə 'kʌntri/ [n singular] an area that is not in or near a big town or city – use this when you are comparing this kind of area with towns and cities
in the country *I'd hate to live in the country – I'd get really bored.* | *They have an apartment in town and a cottage in the country.*

⚠ You can also use **country** before a noun, like an adjective: *a country house* (=a big house in the country) | *country people*

rural /'rʊərəl/ [adj only before noun] use **rural** about places and situations that exist far away from big towns and cities, especially when you are talking about employment, education, and social conditions: *poverty and unemployment in rural areas* | *rural health programs*
rural France/India etc *In many parts of rural India there is no electricity.*

nature /'neɪtʃər/ [n U] everything in the physical world that is not made or controlled by humans, such as wild plants and animals, rocks, and the weather: *Nature has an amazing power to heal.* | *the beauty of nature*
nature reserve (=an area where animals and plants are protected)

⚠ Don't use **nature** when you mean **countryside**. Don't say 'The nature around here is very beautiful'. Say **The countryside around here is very beautiful.**

When you see **EC**, go to the **ESSENTIAL COMMUNICATION** section.

WORD BANK COURT/TRIAL

➡ see pages 158–160

COVER

1 to put something over, on, or around something else

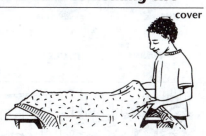

cover

cover /'kʌvər/ [v T] to put something over, on, or around something else, in order to hide it, protect it, or improve its appearance: *Prepare the salad, and cover it until it's time to serve.*
cover sth with sth *She covered her face with her hands and ran upstairs.*
cover up sth/cover sth up (=cover something completely) *They used special paint to cover up the cracks in the wall.*

put over /,pʊt 'əʊvər/ [phrasal verb T] to put a cloth or piece of material loosely over the top of something in order to cover it: *The stewardess gave him a blanket to put over his legs.*
put sth over sth *Before you paint the walls, put some old sheets over the furniture.*

wrap up

wrap up/wrap /,ræp 'ʌp, ræp/ [v T] to put paper, plastic, cloth etc tightly around something in order to protect it or decorate it: *Have you wrapped all your Christmas presents yet?*

COVER continues on page 161

COURT/TRIAL

WORD BANK

→ for the first part of this story, go to
POLICE

GUILTY/NOT GUILTY
CRIME
PRISON
KILL
see also
LAW
PUNISH
POLICE

C

❶ If someone is **arrested** by the police and **charged** with a crime, they have to go to **court** and stand **trial**. The trial takes place in a **courtroom** and the person who is on trial is called the **defendant**.
The defendant **pleads** either **guilty** or **not guilty**.

judge

defendant

vocabulary

arrest /əˈrest/ [v T] if the police **arrest** someone, they take them to a police station and keep them there, because they believe that person is guilty of a crime: *Police arrested 50 demonstrators outside the parliament building.*
arrest sb for sth *Bates was arrested for dangerous driving.*

charge /tʃɑːrdʒ/ [v T] if the police charge someone, they tell that person that they believe he or she is guilty of a crime, and that the person must appear in court so that it can be proved whether they are guilty or not
charge sb with murder/rape/theft etc *No-one has yet been charged with the murder.* | *Following last night's raid on a warehouse, police have charged three men with handling illegal drugs.*

client /ˈklaɪənt/ [n C] the person a lawyer is paid to work for during a trial. The lawyer tries to prove that his or her client is not guilty of a crime: *Your honour, my client and I would like some time to discuss the latest evidence.*

court /kɔːrt/ [n C/U] a building or room where all the information concerning a crime or legal problem is publicly and officially given, so that it can be legally judged: *A large group of photographers and reporters*
gathered outside the court. | *the American Supreme Court*

appear in court (=be in a court because the police think you have committed a crime or know something about a crime) *Fox appeared in court yesterday on three charges of assault.*

go to court (=officially ask to have a legal problem dealt with by a judge or jury in a court) *She says she will go to court to try to prove that she was unfairly dismissed from her job.*

commit /kəˈmɪt/ [v T] **commit a crime/offence** to do something illegal: *Can you be tried in this country for crimes that were committed abroad?* | *Since last year, he has committed at least three further offences.*

courtroom /ˈkɔːrtruːm, -rʊm/ [n C usually singular] the room where a trial takes place: *Simpson told a packed courtroom of the events that happened on the night of the murder.* | *A fight broke out in a London courtroom yesterday.*

defendant /dɪˈfendənt/ [n C] the person in a court who has been charged with a crime and is trying to prove that he or she did not do it: *The defendant pleaded not guilty.*

the defence BRITISH **the defense** AMERICAN /ðə dɪˈfens/ the lawyers in a court who try to prove that someone is

COURT/TRIAL

❷ The defendant is represented by **lawyers** who try to **prove** that he or she is **innocent**. These lawyers are known as **the defense**.

Your honor, *my client could not have* **committed** *this* **crime**

❸ The defense calls **witnesses** to give **evidence**.

He was at home with me all day. He didn't go out.

❹ The **prosecution** tries to prove that the defendant is guilty. They call witnesses who **give evidence against** him.

I saw that man coming out of the house carrying a television.

---

not guilty of a crime

defence lawyer/defense lawyer (=one of the members of the defence)

evidence /ˈevɪdəns/ [n U] all the information, objects, documents etc that are used in a law court to help to prove what really happened during a crime
piece of evidence *The most important piece of evidence, the murder weapon, had not been found.*
give evidence (=tell a court what you know about a crime or the people involved in it) *His former girlfriend was called to give evidence.*
give evidence against sb (=tell the court things that help to prove someone is guilty) *Husbands and wives cannot be forced to give evidence against each other.*

guilty /ˈgɪlti/ [adj] having done something that is a crime: *Do you think she's guilty?*
+ of *West was guilty of several robberies*
not guilty *He said that he was not guilty of any offence.*
find sb guilty/not guilty (=when a court officially decides that someone has or has not committed a crime) *She was found guilty of attempted murder.*

innocent /ˈɪnəsənt/ [adj] someone who is innocent has not committed a crime: *Throughout their imprisonment* (=when they were in prison), *the six men always insisted that they were innocent.*

judge /dʒʌdʒ/ [n C] the person in charge of a court, who knows a lot about the law, and who makes the official decision about what the punishment for a crime should be: *Everyone stood up as the judge entered the courtroom.* | *Judge Butler gave the defendant a six-month jail sentence.*

jury /ˈdʒʊəri/ [n C] a group of (usually 12) ordinary people, who listen to all the evidence about a crime, and then decide whether or not someone is guilty: *The jury was made up of seven women and five men.* | *Have you ever been on a jury?*

lawyer (also **attorney**) /ˈlɔːjəʳ/ [n C] someone who is trained in the law and who represents people in court: *You have to study for a long time to become a lawyer.* | *Everyone has the right to be represented in court by a lawyer.*

plead guilty/plead not guilty /ˌpliːd ˈgɪlti, ˌpliːd nɒt ˈgɪlti/ when the defendant in a trial **pleads guilty** or **pleads not guilty**, they officially tell a court at the beginning of a trial that they either did or did not commit a crime: *"How does the defendant plead?" "Not guilty, your honor."* | *If you plead guilty you might get a lighter sentence.* (=a punishment that is not as severe).

COURT/TRIAL continues on the next page

COURT/TRIAL

⑤ *Your honor, this man is obviously guilty...*

⑥ The **jury** listens to all the evidence, and decides whether the defendant is **guilty** or **not guilty**. They then give their **verdict**.

Guilty.

⑦ If the defendant is found guilty, the **judge** passes **sentence**.

I sentence you to one year in prison.

the prosecution /ðə ˌprɒsɪˈkjuːʃən‖ˌprɑː-/ the lawyers in a court who try to prove that someone is guilty of a crime

prove /pruːv/ [v T] to show that something is definitely true, so that there is no doubt

represent /ˌreprɪˈzent/ [v T] if a lawyer represents someone in a law court, they try to make sure that he or she gets a good result from a trial, for example by persuading the court that the person is not guilty of a crime

sentence /ˈsentəns/ [n C] the official punishment that someone is given by a judge when a court decides that they are guilty of a crime, especially a period of time in prison

a 7-year/6-month etc sentence (=when someone has to go to prison for 7 years, 6 months etc)

pass sentence (=when a judge says what the punishment will be) *Judge Evans will pass sentence on the three men tomorrow.*

life sentence (=when someone must go to prison for a very long time or for the rest of their life)

death sentence (=when the punishment is death)

sentence /ˈsentəns/ [v T] if a judge sentences someone, he or she says what the punishment for their crime will be

sentence sb to sth *Campbell was sentenced to 42*

days in jail. | *The judge sentenced him to 100 days' community service.* (=when you have to do something that will help the people in your local area)

trial /ˈtraɪəl/ [n C] an official and legal process in a law court, in which people try to prove whether or not someone is guilty of a crime: *The trial is due to take place next month at Wood Green Crown Court.*

be on trial (for sth) (=when a court is trying to decide whether or not someone is guilty of a crime) *A man from Seattle is on trial for the murder.*

stand trial (=to have to go to a trial in which the court tries to prove you are guilty of a crime) *The judge ruled that she was too ill to stand trial.*

verdict /ˈvɜːʳdɪkt/ [n C] the decision that the jury makes about whether someone is guilty of a crime or not: *What's the jury's verdict? Guilty or not guilty?*

return a verdict (=officially say whether someone is guilty or not)

witness /ˈwɪtnɪs/ [n C] someone who knows something about a crime, and tells the court what they know: *Would the first witness please stand up?*

call a witness (=officially ask a witness to answer questions about a crime in a court)

your honour BRITISH **your honor** AMERICAN /jɔːʳ ˈɒnəʳ‖-ˈɑːnəʳ/ the official name that people use in a court when they speak to the judge

COVER continued from page 157

cover · top · lid

C

wrap sth up/wrap up sth *I took the picture off the wall and wrapped it up in brown paper.*

wrap sth (up) in sth *He wrapped his muddy boots up in newspaper and threw them into a bag.*

coat /kəʊt/ [v T] to thinly cover the whole surface of something, especially food, with something soft or liquid

coat sth with/in sth *Coat the chicken with garlic butter and cook it at 200 °C.*

2 something that is used to cover something else

cover /ˈkʌvəʳ/ [n C] a piece of paper, plastic, cloth etc that is used to cover something: *I've bought some cushion covers to brighten up my room. | It's a good idea to buy a cover for your computer keyboard. | There were old record covers scattered all over the floor. | He removed the cover from the back of the TV.*

covering /ˈkʌvərɪŋ/ [n C] something that is used to cover a large flat area, especially in order to protect it from damage, dirt etc: *The prison cells have no electricity and no floor coverings. | The insect's shell gives it a tough protective covering.*

lid /lɪd/ [n C] a flat part that fits on top of a container, a pan, a box etc in order to close it: *a saucepan lid*

+ of *Sam lifted the lid of his desk and took out a calculator. | She was trying to unscrew the lid of a jar of honey.*

top /tɒp‖tɑːp/ [n C] a thing that fits on the top of a bottle, pen, or narrow container, which you press on or turn in order to close it: *Why don't you ever put the top back on the toothpaste? | I can't get the top off this bottle.*

wrapper /ˈræpəʳ/ [n C] a piece of paper, or very thin plastic or metal, that covers food, chocolate etc when you buy it: *The empty stadium was littered with burger wrappers and empty cans. | chewing-gum wrappers*

wrapper

3 a thin flat layer that covers a surface

layer /ˈleɪəʳ/ [n C] a thin flat quantity of something that covers the whole of a surface

+ of *A layer of dust covered everything in the room. | Sprinkle a layer of soil over the seeds.*

film /fɪlm/ [n C] a very thin clear layer, especially of something liquid, that has formed on a surface

a film of oil/grease/sweat/dust *A film of oil was floating on the surface of the water.*

coating /ˈkəʊtɪŋ/ [n C] a layer of a liquid or soft substance that has been put on the surface of something, for example in order to protect it or make it taste better: *Cassette tapes have a magnetic oxide coating.*

+ of *ice-cream with a thick coating of chocolate*

4 when an object or area has been covered with something

be covered in/with sth /biː ˈkʌvəʳd ɪn, wɪð (sth)/ if something is **covered in** or **covered with** something, it has that substance lying all over the top of it or spread all over it: *The ground was covered with snow.* | *Look at your clothes! They're covered in mud.* | *an ancient wall covered with ivy*

be coated in/with sth /biː ˈkəʊtˌd ɪn, wɪð (sth)/ if an object **is coated in** or **is coated with** a liquid or soft substance, it has a layer of that substance all over its surface: *Serve the chicken with new potatoes coated in butter.*

CRAZY

very strange and not at all sensible

➡ if you mean that someone has a mental illness, go to **MENTALLY ILL**

1 people

○**crazy** (also **mad** BRITISH) /ˈkreɪzi, mæd/ [adj] ESPECIALLY SPOKEN someone who is **crazy** or **mad** behaves in a strange or stupid way, as if there is something wrong with their mind: *My parents think I'm crazy, but I've always enjoyed dangerous sports.* | *You agreed to marry him? Are you mad?* | *crazy drivers who cause accidents*
go crazy/mad (=start to feel crazy) *I'll go crazy if I stay in this house much longer.*
drive sb crazy/mad (=make them start to feel crazy) *Stop that noise! You're driving me crazy.*
be crazy/mad to do sth *You must be crazy to lend him all that money!*
crazy – crazier – craziest
mad – madder – maddest

⚠ Don't say 'become crazy' or 'become mad'. Say **go crazy** or **go mad**.

⚠ Don't say 'very crazy' or 'very mad'. Say **completely crazy/mad** or **totally crazy/mad**: *Put that gun down! Are you totally crazy?*

○**insane/out of your mind** /ɪnˈseɪn, ˌaʊt əv jɔːr ˈmaɪnd/ [adj] ESPECIALLY SPOKEN you say someone is **insane** or **out of their mind** if they do something or intend to do something that is completely crazy: *Anyone who takes a boat out in this weather must be insane.* | *Tell the police? Are you out of your mind?*

○**be nuts** (also **be crackers** BRITISH) /biː ˈnʌts, biː ˈkrækəʳz/ SPOKEN INFORMAL to be crazy: *People will think you're crackers if you go around talking to yourself like that.* | *He's completely nuts, that guy! He goes camping in the middle of winter.*

○**maniac/lunatic** /ˈmeɪniæk, ˈluːnətɪk/ [n C] ESPECIALLY SPOKEN someone who behaves in a stupidly dangerous way: *He drives like a maniac.* | *Some lunatic threw paraffin on the fire.*

○**nutcase** /ˈnʌtkeɪs/ [n C] SPOKEN INFORMAL someone who behaves strangely and has very unusual ideas: *His sister's a real nutcase. She believes in fairies.*

2 things/ideas/situations

○**crazy** (also **mad** BRITISH) /ˈkreɪzi, mæd/ [adj] ESPECIALLY SPOKEN ideas, actions, or situations that are **crazy** or **mad** are not at all sensible and are likely to cause problems or danger: *You see drivers do some crazy things.* | *Jade wants to build a swimming pool in the garden. I think it's a mad idea.*
it's crazy *The farmers get more money from the government if they don't plant crops – it's crazy.*
crazy – crazier – craziest
mad – madder – maddest

⚠ Don't say 'very crazy' or 'very mad'. Say **absolutely crazy/mad** or **completely crazy/mad**: *How can we do all this work in one day? It's absolutely crazy.*

insane /ɪnˈseɪn/ [adj] an **insane** idea or plan is stupid or dangerous, and is very unlikely to succeed: *For some insane reason, he decided to do the whole drive in one day.*
it is insane to do sth *It would be insane to go out in the boat in weather like this.*

○**be lunacy** (also **be madness** BRITISH) /biː ˈluːnəsi, biː ˈmædnˌs/ [n U] ESPECIALLY SPOKEN you say that a situation or action **is lunacy** or **is madness** if you think it is completely crazy: *They can't close the hospital – it's madness!*
it is sheer lunacy/madness to do sth (=it is completely crazy to do it) *It would be sheer lunacy to try to cross the desert on your own.*

CRIME

THREATEN

TELL 5   KILL

POLICE   see also   DRUGS

LAW   STEAL

ATTACK   COURT/TRIAL

1 something that is not legal

crime /kraɪm/ [n C] an action that is against the law, such as stealing something, taking drugs, or deliberately hurting someone: *The number of crimes reported to the police has increased.*
commit a crime (=do something that is a crime) *We believe that the crime was committed around 7:30 p.m.*
+ against *Violent crimes against the elderly are on the increase.*
serious crime *The police say that 50% of serious crimes are drug-related.*
solve a crime (=find out who did it) *a terrible crime which was never solved*

⚠ Don't say 'he made a crime' or 'he did a crime'. Say **he committed a crime**.

offence BRITISH **offense** AMERICAN /əˈfens/ [n C] any action that can be punished by law: *Tarrant is now in jail for various offenses including rape.*
commit an offence (=do something that is an offence) *Bates is being tried for offences committed in the 1980s.*
criminal offence *Driving when drunk is a criminal offence.*
serious offence *The number of women convicted of serious offences is still relatively small.*
minor offence (=not very serious) *Hewson was arrested for a number of minor offences.*
speeding/parking offence *Speeding offenses are usually punishable by a fine.*

When you see **EC**, go to the **ESSENTIAL COMMUNICATION** section.

⚠ **Offence** is used especially in official situations by the police, judges, and lawyers. **Offence** can be used both for serious crimes like murder and robbery, and for less serious actions like parking your car in the wrong place or not paying your taxes.

⚠ Don't say 'do an offence'. Say **commit an offence**.

C

illegal /ɪˈliːɡəl/ [adj] not legal: *He was fined for selling illegal drugs.* | *There is a lot of illegal copying of computer software.*
it is illegal to do sth *In Britain, it is illegal to sell cigarettes to anyone under 16.*

be against the law /biː əˌɡenst ðə ˈlɔː/ if something **is against the law**, it is illegal to do it: *Drinking alcohol in a public place is against the law.*
it is against the law to do sth *In Sweden, it is against the law to hit a child.*

break the law /ˌbreɪk ðə ˈlɔː/ to do something that is illegal: *People who break the law must expect to be punished.* | *I didn't realize I was breaking the law.*

criminal /ˈkrɪmɪnəl/ [adj only before noun] connected with crimes: *James made around £100,000 from his criminal activities.*
criminal record (=a list of someone's crimes that is kept by the police) *It's very difficult to get a job if you have a criminal record.*
criminal charge (=an official statement by the police that someone has done something illegal) *West's wife faced serious criminal charges in connection with the murders.*

2 crimes in general

crime /kraɪm/ [n U] crimes in general – use this to talk generally about the reasons for crime, the problems it causes, and the number of crimes: *the growing problem of crime in the inner cities*
violent crime *Violent crime increased by 36% last year.*
serious crime *Victims of serious crime are often too scared to talk about their experiences.*

petty crime (=crime that is not very serious) *Leo became involved in petty crime at a very young age.*

⚠ You can also use **crime** before a noun, like an adjective: *an increase in the crime rate* (=the number of crimes that happen) | *crime prevention*

⚠ Don't say 'the crime' when you are talking about crimes in general: *People are worried about the increase in crime* (not 'in the crime').

3 someone who is guilty of a crime

criminal /ˈkrɪmɪnəl/ [n C] someone who is guilty of a serious crime or of several crimes: *The police are hunting for a dangerous criminal named Joseph DeCosta.*

offender /əˈfendəʳ/ [n C] someone who has broken the law and is being punished for doing this: *The courts should impose tougher punishments on offenders.*
young offender BRITISH **juvenile offender** AMERICAN (=under 18 years old) *The system for dealing with young offenders doesn't really work.*

⚠ **Offender** is used especially in official situations, for example by politicians or the police.

gang /gæn/ [n C] a group of criminals who work together: *Gangs of thieves used to hang around the station.*
armed gang (=with guns) *An armed gang robbed a warehouse in the south of the city.*

organized crime /ˌɔːrgənaɪzd ˈkraɪm/ [n U] large criminal organizations that plan and control serious crimes such as robbing banks and selling drugs: *Police need more resources to fight organized crime.*

CRITICIZE

⟳ COMPLAINING
⟳ OPINIONS   DISAGREE
see also
PRAISE   COMPLAIN
⟳ DISAGREEING   BLAME

1 to say what is bad about a person, plan, performance etc

criticize (also **criticise** BRITISH) /ˈkrɪtɪsaɪz/ [v I/T] to say what is bad about someone or something: *Stop criticizing my driving!* | *People are always criticizing the Royal family, but I think they do a good job.* | *It's easy to criticize, but managing a football team can be an extremely difficult job.*
criticize sb for doing sth *The United Nations was criticized for failing to react sooner to the crisis.*
criticize sb/sth as *The TV show was criticized as racist and inaccurate.*

attack /əˈtæk/ [v T] to strongly and publicly criticize a person, plan, or belief that you completely disagree with: *Several actors have attacked proposals to cut the theatre's budget.*
attack sb for (doing) sth *Critics attacked Roosevelt for not doing enough.*

be critical /biː ˈkrɪtɪkəl/ to strongly criticize a plan, system, or way of doing something, especially when you give detailed reasons why you think it is wrong: *Don't be so critical – we're doing our best.*
+ of *Miller was critical of the way the company was managed.*
be highly critical (=very critical) *The article is highly critical of US policies towards Central America.*

2 to criticize someone or something in an annoying, unfair, or unkind way

find fault with sth /ˌfaɪnd ˈfɔːlt wɪð (sth)/ to criticize things that are wrong with someone or something, especially small and unimportant things: *No-one enjoys working for a boss who always finds fault with their work.*

pick holes in sth /ˌpɪk ˈhəʊlz ɪn (sth)/ INFORMAL, ESPECIALLY BRITISH to criticize small details in someone's ideas or plan – use this about someone who seems to be looking for problems and mistakes: *As soon as she stopped talking, Janet's colleagues began to pick holes in the idea.*

talk about sb behind their back /ˌtɔːk əbaʊt (sb) bɪˌhaɪnd ðeəʳ ˈbæk/ to criticize someone when they are not there: *I was very upset when I found out that they'd all been talking about me behind my back.*   .

make fun of sb/poke fun at sb /ˌmeɪk ˈfʌn ɒv (sb), ˌpəʊk ˈfʌn æt (sb)/ to say unkind things about someone or about the things they do, in order to make them look silly: *The kids at school make fun of Jack because he's fat.* | *a comedian who pokes fun at TV celebrities and politicians*

3 to tell someone that they should not have done something

tell sb off /ˌtel (sb) ˈɒf‖-ˈɔːf/ [phrasal verb T] to tell someone that they should not have done something, and warn them that they must not do it again – use this especially about teachers and parents talking to children
+ for *When I got home my dad told me off for staying out so late.*
get told off (=be told off) *She was always getting told off by her teachers.*

chew sb out /ˌtʃuː (sb) ˈaʊt/ [phrasal verb T] AMERICAN INFORMAL to talk to someone angrily for a long time, and tell them that they should not have done something: *Diane was late for the third time that week, and the boss called her into his office and chewed her out.*
get chewed out *I was always getting chewed out for things I hadn't even done.*

When you see **EC**, go to the **ESSENTIAL COMMUNICATION** section.

4 something that you write or say in order to criticize

criticism /ˈkrɪtɪˌsɪzəm/ [n C/U] what you say or write when you criticize someone or something: *Bill's very sensitive to any kind of criticism.*
+ of *The report makes many criticisms of the nation's prison system.*
severe/strong criticism *There has been strong criticism of these proposals.*
come in for criticism (=be criticized) *Taylor has come in for a lot of criticism for his part in the affair.*

attack /əˈtæk/ [n C] a statement that criticizes someone publicly, especially in politics
+ on *The communist newspapers often contained attacks on the Church.*
come under attack from sb (=be criticized by someone) *Once again the oil companies have come under attack from environmentalists.*

critical /ˈkrɪtɪkəl/ [adj] a **critical** statement, report, or description criticizes someone or something: *She was offended whenever anyone made critical remarks about her acting ability.*
highly critical (=very critical) *The judge was highly critical of the Los Angeles Police Department.*

scathing /ˈskeɪðɪŋ/ [adj] criticizing someone or something very strongly, because you think they are completely wrong or of very low quality
scathing attack/comments etc *Her new book is a scathing attack on American imperialism in Central America.*
+ about *'The New York Times' was particularly scathing about his performance.*

5 someone who criticizes

critic /ˈkrɪtɪk/ [n C] someone who criticizes a person, such as a politician or business leader, or their plans or methods, especially in public: *The Prime Minister answered his critics in a televised speech.*
+ of *critics of nuclear power*

CROWD

➡ if you mean 'when there are a lot of people travelling, shopping etc', go to **BUSY/NOT BUSY**

1 a large number of people together in a public place

crowd /kraʊd/ [n C] a large number of people together in one place: *I don't often go to football games because I don't like big crowds.*
+ of *a crowd of angry protesters*
crowds of people/shoppers/tourists etc *The exhibition is expected to attract huge crowds of visitors.*

horde/hordes /hɔːˈd(z)/ [n] a large crowd of people who are behaving in a way that you disapprove of or that annoys you
+ of *A horde of screaming kids ran out of the building.* | *She was chased by hordes of reporters and camera crews.*

mob /mɒb‖mɑːb/ [n C] a crowd of noisy and violent people who are difficult to control: *The mob set fire to cars and buildings.*
+ of *A mob of 200 rioters caused millions of pounds worth of damage.*

2 when a place is full of people

crowded /ˈkraʊdᵻd/ [adj] so full of people that it is difficult to move or to find a place to sit or stand: *The train was really crowded.* | *James walked into the crowded bar.*
+ with *It was two weeks before Christmas and the mall was crowded with shoppers.*

packed /pækt/ [adj] INFORMAL so full of people that there is almost no space left: *The club is so popular that it's packed by 9 o'clock.* | *A bomb exploded this morning in a packed department store in the city centre.*
+ with *St Peter's Square was packed with tourists.*
jam-packed (=completely full) *The stadium was absolutely jam-packed.*

overcrowded /ˌəʊvəˈkraʊdᵻd◂/ [adj] a place that is **overcrowded** has too many people in it and is unpleasant and uncomfortable: *The buses were all filthy and overcrowded.* | *overcrowded prisons*

be swarming with /biː ˈswɔːˈmɪŋ wɪð/ if a place **is swarming with** people, it is so crowded with them that it is difficult to move or to go where you want to go – use this especially about people you disapprove of or when you are annoyed that a place is so crowded: *The place was swarming with noisy kids.*

3 when a crowd fills a place

crowd /kraʊd/ [v I/T] if people **crowd** a place, they fill it and move around in it: *Shoppers and tourists crowded the market square every day.*
+ around (also **round** BRITISH) *Fans crowded around the entrance, hoping to see the band as they arrived.*

fill /fɪl/ [v T] if a lot of people **fill** a place, there are so many of them that there is no room for any more: *An audience of over 50,000 had filled the arena.*

4 when people come together to make a crowd

gather /ˈgæðəˈ/ [v I] if people **gather**, they meet or come together and become a crowd: *By the time the President arrived, a large crowd had gathered.*
+ around/at/in etc *Angry workers were gathering around the steps of the City Hall.*

form /fɔːˈm/ [v I] if a crowd **forms**, more and more people join a group of people who are already watching or listening to something: *A crowd was beginning to form at the scene of the accident.*

congregate /ˈkɒŋgrᵻgeɪt‖ˈkɑːŋ-/ [v I] if people **congregate** in a place, a large number of them meet there, especially regularly in the same place, and at the same time
+ at/in/around etc *On Friday evening, teenagers would congregate outside the bars on the main street.*

5 when a crowd separates

disperse /dɪˈspɜːˈs/ [v I] if a crowd **disperses**, people begin to move away from it: *Once the ambulance left, the crowd began to disperse.*

break up /ˌbreɪk ˈʌp/ [*phrasal verb* I] if a crowd **breaks up**, people start to leave and move away in small groups: *When the police arrived, the crowd broke up very quickly.*

CRUEL

UNKIND   ATTACK

BAD 8   see also   VIOLENT

THREATEN   DESCRIBING PEOPLE

1 cruel people

cruel /ˈkruːəl/ [*adj*] someone who is **cruel** deliberately causes pain and does not care if other people suffer: *Children can sometimes be very cruel.*
it is cruel to do sth *I think it's cruel to keep dogs locked up inside all day.*
   cruelly [*adv*] *Women prisoners were treated especially cruelly.*
   cruel – crueller – cruellest BRITISH
   cruel – crueler – cruelest AMERICAN

ruthless /ˈruːθləs/ [*adj*] so determined to get what you want that you do not care how much other people suffer: *These men are ruthless terrorists and will kill anyone who tries to stop them.* | *the ruthless dictator, Joseph Stalin*
   ruthlessly [*adv*] *All political opponents were ruthlessly executed.*

sadist /ˈseɪdɪst/ [*n C*] someone who enjoys making people suffer: *Andrea's father was a real sadist. I'm not surprised that she hates him.*

sadistic /səˈdɪstɪk/ [*adj*] someone who is **sadistic** enjoys hurting people or being cruel to them: *He took a sadistic pleasure in embarrassing her in front of her friends.* | *The head teacher was a violent and sadistic man.*

2 cruel punishments/ behaviour

cruel /ˈkruːəl/ [*adj*] intended to upset someone or make them suffer: *Lyle was always playing cruel jokes on his little sister.* |

The electric chair is possibly the cruelest method of execution.
   cruel – crueller – cruellest BRITISH
   cruel – crueler – cruelest AMERICAN

barbaric /bɑːˈbærɪk/ [*adj*] extremely cruel, in a way that shocks people: *the barbaric treatment of civilians in the concentration camps* | *To most people, the custom of stoning criminals to death seems absolutely barbaric.*

cold-blooded /ˌkəʊld ˈblʌdɪd◂/ [*adj* only before noun] **cold-blooded murder/ killing/attack** a murder etc done without showing any feeling or pity for the person who is attacked: *The country has been shocked by the cold-blooded murder of the two girls.*

cruelty /ˈkruːəlti/ [*n U*] cruel treatment or behaviour: *Walter's wife left him because of his cruelty.*
+ to *She has campaigned against cruelty to farm animals for the past 20 years.*

abuse /əˈbjuːs/ [*n U*] deliberately cruel treatment of someone, especially someone in your family that you are supposed to care for: *a woman who had suffered abuse from her husband for many years*
child abuse (=cruel treatment of children) *There has been an increase in the number of cases of child abuse.*
sexual abuse (=when someone forces another person to take part in sexual activities) *a victim of sexual abuse*

3 to treat someone cruelly

be cruel to sb /biː ˈkruːəl tuː (sb)/ *Teachers at the school were often accused of being cruel to the children in their care.*

abuse /əˈbjuːz/ [*v T*] to treat someone in your family or someone that you are responsible for in a cruel way, especially violently or sexually: *My father abused us for years.* | *Erica runs a hostel for women who have been abused by their husbands.*
sexually abuse (=force someone to take part in sexual activities) *He was accused of sexually abusing five children.*

persecute /ˈpɜːrsɪkjuːt/ [*v T*] to be cruel to a person or group of people over a long period because of their race or their religious or political beliefs: *Countries all* over Europe have persecuted gypsies for centuries.

be persecuted *Jewish families were relentlessly persecuted.*

> **persecution** /ˌpɜːrsɪˈkjuːʃən/ [n U] *They left the country to escape persecution.*

bully /ˈbʊli/ [v T] to be cruel to someone who is smaller, younger, or weaker than you – use this especially about children being cruel to other children: *A group of girls would bully the younger kids, and force them to give them money.*

be bullied *He killed himself after being bullied at school.*

bullying – bullied – have bullied

> **bullying** [n U] when people are being bullied: *a campaign to put an end to bullying in schools*

CRY

➡ opposite **LAUGH**
➡ see also **SAD, WORRYING/WORRIED, SHOUT**

1 to cry

cry /kraɪ/ [v I] if you **cry**, tears come from your eyes, for example because you are sad or upset, or because you have hurt yourself: *I could hear the baby crying in the next room.* | *A little boy was crying because he'd fallen off his bike.* | *Don't cry. I'll be back soon.*

make sb cry *The film was so sad, it made me cry.*

cry and cry (=cry for a long time) *I sat at home that night and cried and cried.*

cry your eyes out (=cry a lot because you are very upset) *The poor kid's so miserable, he's upstairs crying his eyes out.*

cry with happiness/joy/relief *She cried with joy when she heard that the children were safe.*

crying – cried – have cried

weep /wiːp/ [v I] to cry a lot because you feel sad: *Caroline wept when she heard the news.* | *Weeping mourners followed the coffin into the churchyard.*

weep with emotion/grief/joy *Ivan wept with emotion as he waved goodbye to his family.*

weeping – wept – have wept

⚠ Use **weep** when you are writing stories and descriptions.

sob /sɒb‖sɑːb/ [v I] if you **sob**, you cry noisily and your body shakes, because you are very sad or because someone has upset you: *The sound of her sobbing kept them awake all night.* | *"Please don't leave me," she sobbed.*

sobbing – sobbed – have sobbed

⚠ Use **sob** when you are writing stories and descriptions.

in tears /ɪn ˈtɪərz/ crying because someone has upset you, or because a film, story etc is very sad: *Frank ran out of the room in tears.* | *Most of us were in tears by the time he'd finished his story.*

tear /tɪər/ [n C usually plural] a drop of water that comes from your eyes when you are crying: *Grandpa wiped the tears from his eyes.*

have tears in your eyes (=when you are nearly crying) *Ahmed had tears in his eyes, and I knew he was thinking of home.*

tears run down sb's face/cheeks (=they cry a lot) *Tears of joy ran down her face.*

be close to tears (=be almost crying) *Howell was close to tears as he told the court what had happened.*

sb's eyes water /(sb's) ˈaɪz ˌwɔːtər/ if your **eyes water**, they feel painful and you start to cry, for example when you are cutting onions or when there is a lot of smoke

make sb's eyes water *The cigarette smoke was making my eyes water.*

2 to start to cry

start to cry/start crying /ˌstɑːrt tə ˈkraɪ, ˌstɑːrt ˈkraɪ-ɪŋ/ *What should I do if the baby starts crying?* | *He started crying when I told him I wanted to end our relationship.*

burst into tears /ˌbɜːrst ɪntə ˈtɪərz/ to suddenly start to cry because you are very upset about something: *Janet burst into tears and ran out of the room.*

break down /ˌbreɪk ˈdaʊn/ [phrasal verb I] to suddenly start to cry a lot, after trying not to cry: *I broke down during the exam*

– *I just couldn't stand the pressure any more.*

break down and cry *As the funeral service began, Paolo broke down and cried.*
break down in tears *All the worry and anxiety had been too much for her, and she suddenly broke down in tears.*

CUT

➡ see also **SHARP/NOT SHARP, PIECE, HURT/INJURE**

1 with scissors or a knife

cut /kʌt/ [v I/T] to divide something into two or more pieces, using a knife or scissors: *You'll need a good pair of scissors to cut that fabric.* | *The woman had murdered her husband and cut his body up.* | *This knife doesn't cut very well.*
cut sth in two/cut sth in half *Mandy cut the paper in half and gave a piece to each child.*
cut sth up/cut up sth (=into several pieces) *Tommy sat on the floor, cutting up old magazines.*
cut sth open *Rescue workers had to use special equipment to cut the steel door open.*
cutting – cut – have cut

slit /slɪt/ [v T] to make a long narrow cut through something, especially skin or cloth: *He killed the sheep by slitting its throat.*
slit sth open *Diane slit the envelope open with a knife.*
slitting – slit – have slit

slash /slæʃ/ [v T] to cut something quickly and violently with a knife, because you want to damage it or cause injury: *Vandals got in and slashed the painting.* | *Maria was slashed across the face with a razor.*

2 to cut food

cut /kʌt/ [v T] to cut food: *Look! The bride and groom are going to cut the cake.*
cut sth into pieces/chunks *I'm going to cut the meat into four pieces.*
cutting – cut – have cut

chop/chop up /tʃɒp, ˌtʃɒp ˈʌp‖tʃɑːp-/ [v T] to cut something such as vegetables or meat into small pieces when you are preparing a meal: *Chop two onions for the stew.* | *Do you want me to chop up the vegetables?*
chop sth into pieces/chunks/cubes *Chop the eggplant into cubes.*
    chopped [adj only before noun] *Sprinkle some chopped walnuts on the salad.*
chopping – chopped – have chopped

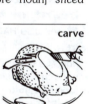
chop

slice /slaɪs/ [v T] to cut food such as bread, meat, or vegetables into thin flat pieces: *My grandmother sliced the carrots and put them in a saucepan of water.*
    sliced [adj only before noun] *sliced white bread*

slice

carve /kɑːrv/ [v T] to cut a large piece of cooked meat into pieces: *Who's going to carve the turkey?*

carve

mince BRITISH **grind** AMERICAN /mɪns, graɪnd/ [v T] to cut raw meat into very small pieces using a machine: *Will you ask the butcher to mince the lamb very finely?*
    minced/ground [adj only before noun] *minced meat* | *ground beef*
grinding – ground – have ground

grate /greɪt/ [v T] to cut cheese or vegetables into very small thin pieces by rubbing them against a metal surface with holes in it: *Grate some cheese over the potatoes before serving.*
    grated [adj] *grated orange peel*

grate

3 to cut part of your body
➡ see also **HURT/INJURE**

cut /kʌt/ [v T] to accidentally injure part of your body, so that it bleeds: *Be careful not to cut your finger on that can.*

cut yourself *Phil cut himself shaving this morning.*

cut [*n* C] a wound on your skin where it has been cut: *Several passengers were treated for cuts and bruises.*

cutting – cut – have cut

scratch /skrætʃ/ [*v* T] to cut part of your body very slightly, and not at all deeply: *The cat scratched me while I was playing with her.* | *I got scratched by the bushes trying to find that ball.*

scratch [*n* C] a slight cut that is not at all deep: *Don't cry, it's only a scratch.*

graze /greɪz/ [*v* T] to accidentally injure yourself by rubbing your skin against something hard and rough: *Tommy fell and grazed his knee in the yard.*

graze [*n* C] a slight wound on your skin where it has been rubbed against something hard and rough: *Cuts and grazes should be covered to keep out germs.*

4 to cut someone's hair, beard, or fingernails

➡ see also **HAIR**

cut /kʌt/ [*v* T] *My sister usually cuts my hair.* | *I wish you wouldn't cut your toenails in the living-room.*

have/get your hair cut (=pay someone to cut it for you) *Beth's at the hairdresser's having her hair cut.*

cut [*n* singular] *Your hair's too long. It needs a cut.*

cutting – cut – have cut

trim /trɪm/ [*v* T] to cut a small amount off someone's hair or beard, so that it looks tidier: *Could you just trim my hair at the back?*

trim [*n* singular] *Give my hair a trim, will you?*

trimming – trimmed – have trimmed

shave /ʃeɪv/ [*v* I/T] to cut the hair on your face or body, using a special blade, so that your skin feels smooth: *Have you shaved today?* | *I didn't have time to shave my legs.*

shave off sth/shave sth off *I wish you'd shave off that awful beard!*

shave [*n* singular] *He went upstairs and had a quick shave.*

5 to cut wood, plants, or grass

cut down/chop down /ˌkʌt ˈdaʊn, ˌtʃɒp ˈdaʊn‖ˌtʃɑːp-/ [*phrasal verb* T] to make trees or bushes fall down by cutting them

cut/chop down sth *Cutting down the rainforests has created serious ecological problems.*

cut/chop sth down *The old apple tree was dangerous so we had to chop it down.*

⚠ Don't use 'cut' on its own about trees. Don't say 'he cut the tree'. Say **he cut the tree down**

chop /tʃɒp‖tʃɑːp/ [*v* T] to cut wood into pieces using an axe (=a tool with a long handle and a sharp blade): *We soon got warm, chopping wood.*

chop sth up/chop up sth (=into several pieces) *I chopped the old fence up for firewood.*

chopping – chopped – have chopped

cut /kʌt/ [*v* T] to cut grass or cut off leaves, in order to make a place or plant look tidy: *She had to stand on a ladder to cut the top of the hedge.*

cutting – cut – have cut

mow /məʊ/ [*v* T] to cut grass using a special machine, in order to make it look tidy

mow the lawn/the grass *It took me two hours to mow the lawn.*

saw /sɔː/ [*v* T] to cut wood using a sharp tool that you push backwards and forwards across the surface of the wood: *Jane was in the basement, sawing wood.*

saw sth up/saw up sth (=into several pieces) *We had to saw it up to get it through the door.*

6 to cut something from something else

cut off /ˌkʌt ˈɒf‖-ˈɔːf/ [*phrasal verb* T] to cut part of something away from the rest of it

cut off sth *Van Gogh cut off his ear.*

cut sth off *Remove the cake from the oven and cut any burnt edges off.*

chop off /ˌtʃɒp ˈɒf‖ˌtʃɑːp ˈɔːf/ [*phrasal verb* T] to cut something off by hitting it hard or cutting it with a sharp tool

chop off sth *Chop off the tops of the carrots, and then peel them.*

chop sth off *Be careful you don't chop your fingers off!*

amputate /ˈæmpjʊteɪt/ [v T] to cut off someone's arm, leg, or foot as a medical operation: *He damaged his leg so badly that it had to be amputated.*

cut out /ˌkʌt ˈaʊt/ [phrasal verb T] to remove something from something else by cutting all around it

cut out sth *Did you cut out that photo of Tony in the newspaper?*

cut sth out *Wash the apples, and cut any bad parts out.*

D

DAMAGE

BREAK   ACCIDENTALLY

DESTROY   REPAIR

see also

SPOIL   BROKEN

MARK   HURT/INJURE

1 to damage objects, machines, buildings etc

damage /'dæmɪdʒ/ [v T] to cause physical harm to something, so that it no longer looks good or works properly: *The building was severely damaged by fire.* | *Don't put any hot pans on the table – you'll damage the surface.*

badly damaged *The goods hadn't been well packed, and were badly damaged when we received them.*

⚠ Don't use **damage** about people. Use **injure**: *The car was badly damaged and the driver was injured.*

break /breɪk/ [v T] to damage a machine or piece of equipment so that it does not work or cannot be used: *Leave that clock alone – you'll break it!* | *We used to have a remote-control thing for the TV, but my brother broke it.*

breaking – broke – have broken

scratch /skrætʃ/ [v T] to damage a painted or polished surface by making long thin marks on it with something sharp or rough: *Be careful not to scratch the table with those scissors.* | *I'm afraid I scratched your car when I came through the gate.*

vandalize (also **vandalise** BRITISH) /'vændəlaɪz/ [v T] to deliberately damage buildings, vehicles, or public property, just for fun: *All the public telephones in the area had been vandalized.*

vandal [n C] someone who vandalizes things: *Vandals broke into the school and wrecked two classrooms.*

vandalism [n U] the criminal activity of vandalizing things: *an increase in vandalism in inner-city areas*

smash up /ˌsmæʃ 'ʌp/ [phrasal verb T] to deliberately damage a room or building by breaking windows, furniture etc

smash sth up *Some of the soldiers got drunk and smashed the place up.*

smash up sth *Angry protesters broke shop windows and smashed up everything inside.*

trash /træʃ/ [v T] AMERICAN INFORMAL to cause a lot of damage to a thing or place, either deliberately or by using it carelessly: *That kid of yours just trashed my VCR.*

trash the place SPOKEN (=cause a lot of damage to a room or building) *Dad says it's OK to have the party here, so long as we don't trash the place.*

sabotage /'sæbətɑʒ/ [v T] to secretly damage machines or equipment so that they cannot be used, especially in order to harm an enemy: *The railway line had been sabotaged by enemy commandos.*

sabotage [n U] when people secretly damage machines or equipment: *terrorists carrying out acts of sabotage*

2 when things get gradually damaged over a long period

wear away /ˌweər ə'weɪ/ [phrasal verb T] if the wind, rain, sea etc **wears** something **away**, it makes it get gradually thinner until there is nothing left

wear away sth/wear sth away *places where the waves had worn away the cliff face* | *The cathedral steps were getting worn away by the tramping feet of thousands of visitors.*

wear out /ˌweər 'aʊt/ [phrasal verb T] to damage clothes, material, or equipment by wearing them or using them a lot

wear out sth/wear sth out *After only a month Terry had worn out the soles of his shoes.* | *The carpet on the stairs is getting worn out.*

erosion /ɪ'rəʊʒən/ [n U] the gradual process by which the weather, water, or air damages or destroys rocks, buildings, land etc: *soil erosion*

+ of *the erosion of the coastline*

3 to have a bad effect on something

harm/damage /hɑːrm, 'dæmɪdʒ/ [v T] to have a bad effect on something, in a way that makes it weaker, less effective, or less successful: *The scandal will damage the company's reputation.* | *Smoking can seriously damage your health.* | *If the peace talks fail, it will harm the President's chances of being re-elected.*

be bad for sth/have a bad effect on sth /biː 'bæd fɔːr (sth), hæv ə ˌbæd ɪ'fekt ɒn (sth)/ to change or affect something in a harmful way: *Losing her job had a bad effect on Patty's confidence.* | *An increase in interest rates at the present time would definitely be bad for business.*

hurt /hɜːrt/ [v T] ESPECIALLY AMERICAN to have a bad effect on an organization or activity, by making it less successful or effective: *new regulations that could hurt the farming industry*

hurting – hurt – have hurt

harmful /'hɑːrmfəl/ [adj] causing physical damage or serious problems – use this especially about things that harm the environment or are dangerous for people's health: *harmful ultra-violet rays* **+ to** *These chemicals are harmful to the ozone layer.*
harmful effects *the harmful effects of alcohol*

damaging /'dæmɪdʒɪŋ/ [adj] causing serious problems – use this especially about information, events, or situations that cause serious problems for a person or organization: *damaging rumors about the President's private life* **+ to** *If people found out about his divorce, it could be very damaging to his career.*

4 the physical damage caused by something

damage /'dæmɪdʒ/ [n U] physical damage that spoils the way something looks or the way it works: *It will take many years to repair the damage.*
cause/do damage (=damage something) *The explosion caused over $50,000 worth of damage.*
+ to *damage to the environment*

severe/serious damage *The pine forests of northern Europe have suffered severe damage from acid rain.*

harm/damage /hɑːrm, 'dæmɪdʒ/ [n U] the serious problems that something causes for a person, organization etc
do harm/damage *If you keep criticizing children, it can do a lot of harm.*
+ to *newspaper reports that resulted in serious damage to Captain Lee's career and reputation* | *The civil war did a lot of harm to the tourist trade.*

D

DANCE

1 to dance

dance /dɑːns‖dæns/ [v I] to move your body in time to music, for example at a social event or as part of a performance: *Everyone got up and danced.*
+ with *Will you dance with me?*
+ to *My parents were dancing to a sentimental old love song.*

dancing /'dɑːnsɪŋ‖'dæn-/ [n U] the activity of moving your feet and body to music: *My boyfriend doesn't like dancing.* | *There was music, Scottish dancing, and lots of food.*
go dancing (=go somewhere in order to dance) *We went dancing nearly every night.*

do /duː/ [v T] to do a particular kind of dance: *Can you do the twist?* | *She got up and did a little dance.*
doing – did – have done

2 different types of dance

dance /dɑːns‖dæns/ [n C] a set of movements that you do to a particular kind of music: *I prefer old-fashioned dances like the waltz and the tango.*
folk dance (=a traditional dance from a particular country or area) *Hungarian folk dances*

ballet /'bæleɪ‖bæ'leɪ, 'bæleɪ/ [n U] a serious artistic performance in which movement and dance are used to tell a story

disco /'dɪskəʊ/ [n U] a type of modern dancing done to loud popular music, in which there are no fixed movements

ballroom dancing /ˌbɔːlrʊm ˈdɑːnsɪŋ‖ -ˈdæn-/ [n U] a type of formal dancing in which people dance in pairs and do different, fixed movements to different types of music

country dancing BRITISH **square dancing** AMERICAN /ˌkʌntri ˈdɑːnsɪŋ, ˈskweəʳ ˌdɑːnsɪŋ‖-ˈdæn-/ [n U] traditional dancing in which pairs of dancers move in rows and circles

3 someone who dances

dancer /ˈdɑːnsəʳ‖ˈdæn-/ [n C] someone who dances, either because it is their job or for enjoyment: *As a child, Alice dreamed of becoming a ballet dancer.* | *I'm not a very good dancer.*

partner /ˈpɑːʳtnəʳ/ [n C] someone that you dance with: *When I saw her again, she was dancing with a different partner.* | *I kept stepping on my partner's toes.*

4 a social event where people dance

dance /dɑːns‖dæns/ [n C] an organized social event where people go to dance: *Later on, there was a dance in the school hall.*

club /klʌb/ [n C] a place where people pay to go at night to dance to loud popular music: *I met some friends at a party and then we went on to a club.*
go clubbing (=go to one or more clubs) *We always go clubbing on Saturday night.*

disco /ˈdɪskəʊ/ [n C] a place or fairly informal social event at which people dance to popular music: *Every Friday night, the kids went to a disco in town.*

ball /bɔːl/ [n C] a formal social event at which people dance and wear formal clothes: *The Summer Ball will be held at the end of June.*

prom /prɒm‖prɑːm/ [n C] a social event for high school students in the US where there is music and dancing, and which people usually go to with a partner: *Joey walked me home after the prom.*
high school prom *The band first played together at a high school prom.*

DANGEROUS

➡ opposite **SAFE**

RISK   WARN

see
also

HURT/   DAMAGE
INJURE

ACCIDENT

1 likely to cause death or serious harm

dangerous /ˈdeɪndʒərəs/ [adj] likely to cause death or serious harm: *Snow and ice are making driving conditions very dangerous.* | *dangerous drugs such as heroin* | *Motor-racing is a dangerous sport.*
highly/extremely dangerous (=very dangerous) *Police described the three escaped prisoners as highly dangerous.*
it is dangerous to do sth *It's dangerous to walk out on your own at night in this area.*
   dangerously [adv] *The plane was flying dangerously close to the mountain.*

risky /ˈrɪski/ [adj] if you do something **risky**, it is easy to make a mistake that might cause death or serious harm – use this about things that you decide to do although you know they may be dangerous: *He'll have to land the aircraft in a field. It's risky, but there's no alternative.* | *Doctors said that they could not operate now because it was too risky.*
risky – riskier – riskiest

poisonous /ˈpɔɪzənəs/ [adj] something that is **poisonous** will make you ill or kill you if you swallow it or breathe it: *The boy died after eating poisonous berries.* | *The river is full of poisonous chemicals.*

be a danger to sb/sth /biː ə ˈdeɪndʒəʳ tuː (sb/sth)/ to be likely to harm other people or things: *People who drink and drive are a danger to themselves and to others.* | *That man is a danger to the community.* | *sharp rocks that were a danger to the fishing boats*

hazard /'hæzəᵈdəs/ [n C] FORMAL something that may cause accidents or be dangerous to your health: *Signs warn drivers of hazards on the road ahead.* | *the potential hazards of using this machinery*
+ to *Polluted water sources are a hazard to wildlife.*
health hazard (=something that may damage your health)

2 to be in a situation in which you may be killed or injured

be in danger /biː ɪn 'deɪndʒəᵈ/ to be in a situation in which you may be killed or injured: *Mr and Mrs Watkins are worried that their daughter may be in danger.*
be in danger of stn (=be in a situation when it is possible you may be killed or injured by something dangerous) *Some of the children were in danger of starvation.*
sb's life is in danger *The lives of the crew were in danger and a helicopter had to lift them to safety.*

⚠ Don't say 'be in a danger'. Say **be in danger.**

be at risk /biː ət 'rɪsk/ if someone **is at risk**, they are in a dangerous situation, especially because they are weak and so they are likely to be harmed by disease or violence
+ from *Those most at risk from the flu epidemic are old people and very young children.* | *women who are at risk from violent husbands*

3 to do something that may hurt or kill you

risk your life /ˌrɪsk jɔːᵈ 'laɪf/ to do something very dangerous, especially in order to help someone: *Firemen risked their lives to save people from the flames.*

at your own risk /ət jɔːr ˌəʊn 'rɪsk/ if you do something **at your own risk**, you must accept that it is dangerous and that it is your own fault if you are injured or killed: *Anyone who swims in this part of the river does so at their own risk.*

⚠ **At your own risk** is used especially in official warnings.

4 danger of death or serious harm

danger /'deɪndʒəᵈ/ [n C/U] the possibility that someone or something will be harmed or killed: *Danger! Keep out.* | *I stood at the side of the road and waved my arms to warn other drivers of the danger.*
+ of *Many people are still not aware of the dangers of drugs such as Ecstasy.*

risk /rɪsk/ [n C/U] the possibility of serious harm if you do something dangerous – use this especially when you want to say how great the possibility is: *Doctor, how much risk is there with this kind of operation?* | *A lot of children start smoking without realizing what the risks are.*
+ of *Wearing a seat belt can reduce the risk of serious injury.*
+ to *The disease affects cats but there is no risk to humans.*

DARK

➡ look here for ...
• when there is not much light
• dark colour, skin, hair
➡ see also **COLOUR/COLOR, LIGHT, BRIGHT/NOT BRIGHT**

1 place/room

dark /dɑːᵈk/ [adj] if a place is **dark**, there is little or no light: *Thick curtains covered the windows and the room was very dark.* | *I hid in the darkest corner of the yard and prayed that the soldiers would not find me.* | *No, you can't play outside now – it's too dark.*
it gets dark (=night comes) *It was starting to get dark outside and lights were coming on all over the city.*
be pitch dark (=be completely dark) *It was pitch dark. She felt a small animal scuttle across her feet.*

⚠ Don't say 'it becomes dark' to talk about the time when night comes. Say **it gets dark.**

dimly-lit /ˌdɪmli 'lɪt◄/ [adj] a **dimly-lit** street, room, building etc is almost dark because the lights there are not bright: *a long dimly-lit corridor*

gloomy /ˈɡluːmi/ [adj] a **gloomy** place or room is not at all bright or cheerful – use this especially in stories or written descriptions: *Mr Casaubon would sit all day in his gloomy study.*

dingy /ˈdɪndʒi/ [adj] a building, room, office etc that is **dingy** is fairly dark and usually dirty and in bad condition: *He ate lunch in a dingy little café near the station.*

dingy – dingier – dingiest

the dark /ðə ˈdɑːʳk/ [n singular] when there is no light, especially in a room: *Most children are afraid of the dark.*

in the dark *Why are you sitting there in the dark? Put the light on.*

darkness /ˈdɑːʳknɪs/ [n U] a place or time where there is no light: *A voice came from out of the darkness, but she could see no-one.* | *There was a sudden flash of light, then darkness again.*

in complete/total darkness (=with no light at all) *The lights suddenly went out and we found ourselves in total darkness.*

2 colour/hair/skin

➡ see also **HAIR**

dark /dɑːʳk/ [adj] **dark** colours are close to black and are not at all bright or pale: *There was a dark stain on the carpet that looked like blood.* | *a boy with dark curly hair*

dark blue/green/brown etc *She had beautiful dark brown eyes.* | *a dark blue dress*

DEAD

➡ opposite **ALIVE**
➡ see also **DIE, EXIST**

1 no longer alive

dead /ded/ [adj] someone who is **dead** has stopped living: *She's stopped breathing – I think she's dead.* | *The dead man's wife was questioned by the police.* | *She was found dead in her apartment, with a bottle of sleeping pills beside her.*

late /leɪt/ [adj only before noun] ESPECIALLY WRITTEN use this as a polite way of talking about someone who has died, especially someone who died recently

sb's late husband/wife/mother/father *She set up the fund in memory of her late husband.*

the late President Marcos/John Lennon etc *He is the last surviving son of the late Indira Gandhi.*

the dead /ðə ˈded/ [n plural] ESPECIALLY WRITTEN people who have died – use this especially to talk about people who died in wars or accidents: *a religious service to commemorate the dead of two World Wars* | *Four of the dead had been travelling in the same car.*

⚠ When you are talking about a group of people who have died, don't say 'the dead people'. Say **the dead**.

2 the body of a dead person

body /ˈbɒdi‖ˈbɑːdi/ [n C] the body of someone who has died: *Police found the body of a young boy in Epping Forest last night.* | *The woman sat down beside her son's body and wept.*

plural **bodies**

⚠ We usually just say **body**, not 'dead body'. Only say 'dead body' if it is not clear from the rest of the sentence that the person is dead: *Have you ever seen a dead body?*

corpse /kɔːʳps/ [n C] the body of a dead person – use this when you are talking about the body as an object, not as a person: *A corpse was found floating in the river.*

remains /rɪˈmeɪnz/ [n plural] parts of a dead person's body, especially someone who has been dead for a long time

the remains of *They discovered the remains of a young woman hidden under the floorboards.*

sb's remains *His remains will be flown back to Ireland.*

ashes /ˈæʃɪz/ [n plural] the powder that is left after a body has been burned as part of a funeral ceremony

sb's ashes *His ashes were scattered over the Jumna river.*

DEAL WITH

to deal with a difficult problem or with things that need to be done

➡ see also **PROBLEM, ANSWER 5**

1 to do things that need doing

deal with sth /'diːl wɪð (sth)/ [phrasal verb T] to decide what needs to be done and make sure that it is done, especially when it is your job to do this: *Who is dealing with the accommodation arrangements for the conference?* | *I spend most of my working day dealing with customer inquiries.*

see to sth/attend to sth /'siː tuː (sth), ə'tend tuː (sth)/ [phrasal verb T] to deal with all the practical details of something that needs to be done or organized: *I'll join you later – there are a few things I have to see to at the office first.* | *Their mother was too upset to attend to the funeral arrangements.* | *You'd better get someone to see to that leaking pipe.*

take care of sth /ˌteɪk 'keər ɒv (sth)/ to make sure that arrangements are made or work is completed, especially when you do this for someone else so that they do not need to worry: *My secretary will take care of the details.* | *Don't worry about your passport and visa – it's all taken care of.*

◯**leave it to me** /ˌliːv ɪt tə 'miː/ SPOKEN say this to tell someone that you will be responsible for making arrangements or for doing something that needs doing: *"We need to make sure the others know where we'll be meeting." "Leave it to me. I'll phone them when I get home."*

2 to deal with a problem or difficult situation

tackle /'tækəl/ [v T] to begin to deal with a problem in a determined way, especially a big or complicated problem: *Many schools are now trying to tackle the problem of drug abuse.* | *new laws that are aimed at tackling unemployment*

handle /'hændl/ [v T] to deal with a problem or a difficult situation, especially in an

effective or confident way: *There were a few problems, but nothing I couldn't handle.* | *A lot of people find it difficult to handle criticism.*

handle sth well/badly *It's her first year as a doctor, but she is handling the pressures of the job very well.*

cope /kəʊp/ [v I] to succeed in dealing with difficult problems in your life, your job, or your relationships: *It's a tough job but I'm sure he'll cope.*
+ with *She has to cope with five children all on her own.*

sort out /ˌsɔːt 'aʊt/ [phrasal verb T] ESPECIALLY BRITISH to deal with all the small but difficult problems that are causing trouble or preventing you from doing something
sort out sth *I spent the weekend sorting out my tax affairs.*
sort sth out *We'll have to sort your immigration status out before we can offer you the job.*

get through sth /ˌget 'θruː (sth)/ [phrasal verb T] to live through an unhappy or unpleasant time in your life, and deal with the problems that it brings: *Her friends helped her to get through the first awful weeks after Bill died.*

3 when there are difficult problems that you must deal with

face /feɪs/ [v T] if you **face** a difficult problem, or if a difficult problem **faces** you, you must deal with it and you cannot ignore it: *The new administration faces the difficult task of rebuilding the country's economy.* | *One of the problems facing the management is the shortage of skilled workers.*
be faced with/by sth *I was faced with the awful job of breaking the bad news to the girl's family.*

4 to find the answer to a difficult problem

solve /sɒlv‖sɑːlv, sɔːlv/ [v T] to find a successful way of dealing with a problem: *They thought money would solve all their problems.* | *The two countries are meeting for talks in an attempt to solve the crisis.*

find a solution /ˌfaɪnd ə səˈluːʃən/ to think of a way to solve a problem, especially a complicated political or social problem: *Crime is rapidly increasing in our inner cities. We must find a solution.*
+ to *European governments are working together to find a solution to the problem of nuclear waste.*

DECIDE

➡ see also **DEPEND/IT DEPENDS, THINK**

1 to decide to do something

decide /dɪˈsaɪd/ [v I/T] to make a choice that you are going to do something
decide to do sth *She decided to tell her mother all about it that evening.*
decide not to do sth *If you decide not to accept our offer, let me know.*
+ (that) *I've decided that I really must stop smoking.*
decide what/how/when etc *Have you decided whether to apply for that job? | Martha took hours deciding which dress to wear.*
decide *I don't mind where we go. You decide.*
decide against sth (=decide not to do something) *Marlowe thought about using his gun, but decided against it.*

make up your mind /ˌmeɪk ʌp jɔːʳ ˈmaɪnd/ to finally decide that you will definitely do something, after thinking about it for a long time
make up your mind what/which/how etc *I couldn't make up my mind which college I wanted to go to.*
make your mind up *Haven't they made their minds up yet?*
make up your mind to do sth *John had made up his mind to forget the past and make a fresh start.*
+ (that) *He's made up his mind that he wants to study abroad.*

choose /tʃuːz/ [v T] to decide to do something because you want to, without worrying about what other people think
choose to do sth *More and more young couples are choosing not to get married. | I told him to drive more slowly, but he chose to ignore my advice.*

choosing – chose – have chosen

resolve /rɪˈzɒlv‖rɪˈzɑːlv, rɪˈzɔːlv/ [v T] FORMAL to decide that you will definitely do something and will not change your mind about it, especially because you have learned from your past experiences
resolve to do sth *After the divorce she resolved never to get married again. | I returned to Edinburgh, resolving to stay there until my book was finished.*

2 something that someone decides to do

decision /dɪˈsɪʒən/ [n C] *They're going to close the school, but I think that's the wrong decision.*
make/take a decision (=decide about something important) *As chief executive, I often have to take difficult decisions. | We don't have to make a decision right now. Let's talk about it tomorrow.*
decision to do sth *Brett's sudden decision to join the army surprised everyone.*
come to/reach a decision (=make a decision after thinking carefully or discussing it for a long time) *The jury took three days to reach a decision.*
big decision (=a difficult and important decision) *"Well, is he going to take the job or not?" "Give him more time – it's a big decision."*

3 to decide that something is true

decide /dɪˈsaɪd/ [v T] to think that something is true, after thinking about it, checking it, or looking at it
+ (that) *I decided he was probably telling the truth.*
decide whether/which/what etc *She couldn't decide whether the hat suited her or not.*

come to the conclusion that /ˌkʌm tə ðə kənˈkluːʒən ðət/ to decide that something is true after thinking carefully about all the facts: *I came to the conclusion that there was only one way of tackling the problem. | De Klerk eventually came to the conclusion that the apartheid system could not continue.*

jump to conclusions /ˌdʒʌmp tə kənˈkluːʒənz/ to decide too quickly that something is true, without considering all the facts: *We mustn't jump to conclusions. There may be a perfectly good explanation for him being so late.*

judge /dʒʌdʒ/ [v T] FORMAL to decide that something is true after examining a situation carefully and using your knowledge and experience

+ that *Kaldor judged that the moment was exactly right to call an election.*

judge whether/which/what etc *It's difficult to judge whether this is the right time to tell him.*

4 when someone has the right to decide

it is up to sb /ɪt ɪz ˈʌp tuː (sb)/ ESPECIALLY SPOKEN if you say **it is up to him / her / you etc,** you mean that that person should make the decision about something, and no one else: *"Should we finish the job now, or leave it till later?" "I don't know – it's up to you." | It's up to them what they do with the money.*

it is for sb to decide /ɪt ɪz fɔːr (sb) tə dɪˈsaɪd/ FORMAL use this when only one person or group has the official power to make a decision about something important: *We cannot say if he is guilty or not. That is for the court to decide.*

5 able to make decisions quickly and firmly

decisive /dɪˈsaɪsɪv/ [adj] someone who is **decisive** can make decisions firmly and confidently, without needing too much time to talk about them or think about them: *We're still waiting for Jim to make up his mind. I wish he'd be more decisive. | The country needs strong decisive leadership.*

decisively [adv] *The police responded to the crisis quickly and decisively.*

6 when someone cannot decide

can't decide /ˌkɑːnt dɪˈsaɪd‖ˌkænt-/ to not be able to make a decision: *"Are you going to take the job or not?" "I don't know; I can't decide."*

can't decide what/whether/how etc *I can't decide what to wear. | Lucinda couldn't decide whether she wanted to marry Jerry or not.*

indecisive /ˌɪndɪˈsaɪsɪv◄/ [adj] not good at making decisions quickly and firmly: *She'll never be a good manager – she's far too indecisive.*

dither /ˈdɪðər/ [v I] INFORMAL to keep changing your mind – use this when you think someone is weak or stupid because they cannot decide about something: *Stop dithering and make up your mind.*

DECORATE

to improve the way something looks, by painting it or adding something attractive to it

➡ see also **PAINT, DESIGN, PATTERN**

1 to decorate something

decorate

decorate /ˈdekəreɪt/ [v T] to improve the way something looks by painting it or adding something attractive to it: *The children always enjoy decorating the Christmas tree.*

be decorated with sth *The room was decorated with balloons and coloured ribbons. | a bowl decorated with patterns of ivy leaves and grape vines.*

decorated [adj] *On the table was an ancient book with a decorated cover.*

garnish /ˈgɑːrnɪʃ/ [v T] to make food look nice by adding a small amount of another type of food, usually of a different colour – used especially in cooking instructions

garnish sth with sth *Garnish the pasta with olives and basil.*

2 things that are used to decorate something

decorations /ˌdekəˈreɪʃənz/ [n plural] things that you use to decorate a place, object, piece of furniture etc, often for a special occasion: *Have you put up your Christmas* decorations yet? | *The bride's mother had made all the table decorations.*

decoration /ˌdekəˈreɪʃən/ [n U] designs and patterns used to decorate buildings, clothes, furniture, food etc: *The altar is a fine example of Baroque decoration.* | *These plants are grown mainly for decoration.*

decorative /ˈdekərətɪv‖ˈdekərə-, ˈdekəreɪ-/ [adj] something that is **decorative** is intended to make a place, object, piece of furniture etc look attractive – use this especially about designs and patterns: *There are decorative tiles around the fireplace, with pictures of birds and flowers on them.* | *Inside the church there are many interesting decorative features.*

ornamental /ˌɔːrnəˈmentl◂/ [adj usually before noun] something **ornamental**, especially in a garden or building, is intended to make a place look more attractive, and usually does not have a useful purpose: *Ornamental pots will brighten up your patio.* | *an ornamental pond*

3 something that has a lot of decoration

fancy /ˈfænsi/ [adj] **fancy** clothes, patterns etc have a lot of decoration or bright colours – use this especially when you think something has too much decoration: *a velvet jacket with fancy buttons* | *I don't like his designs – they're too fancy for me.*

fancy – fancier – fanciest

ornate /ɔːrˈneɪt/ [adj] an **ornate** object, picture, or part of a building has a lot of expensive or complicated decoration on it: *A pair of ornate gold candlesticks stood on the altar.* | *An ornate mirror hung above the fireplace.*

elaborate /ɪˈlæbərɪt/ [adj] carefully and skilfully decorated with a lot of small details and decorations: *Nick examined the elaborate carvings on the tomb.*

DEEP/NOT DEEP

➡ if you want to talk about solid objects made of wood, metal, stone etc, go to **THICK**
➡ if you mean 'a deep colour', go to **COLOUR/COLOR**

➡ if you mean 'a deep sound or voice', go to **LOW**

1 water/hole/snow/sand

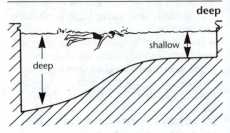

deep /diːp/ [adj] use this about water, holes, snow etc where the bottom is a long distance from the top: *Be careful! The water's quite deep here.* | *Someone had dug a deep hole in the middle of the field.* | *Larry had a deep cut on his left leg.*

get deeper (=become deeper) *The pond gets much deeper in the middle.*

> ⚠ Don't use **deep** to talk about materials such as wood, metal, or stone. Use **thick**

the depths /ðə ˈdepθs/ [n plural] **the depths** of the sea, the ocean, a lake etc are the very deepest parts of the sea, the ocean, or a large lake: *These strange creatures live in the depths of the ocean.*

> ⚠ Use **the depths** especially when you are writing stories and descriptions.

2 a long distance below the surface

deep /diːp/ [adv] a long distance below the surface of something
+ below/under/in *Earthquakes are caused by movements deep below the Earth's surface.*

3 how deep something is

how deep /haʊ ˈdiːp/ *How deep is the hole?* | *I wasn't sure how deep the water was and I didn't want to swim out too far.*

40 metres/100 feet etc deep /(40 metres etc) ˈdiːp/ use this to say exactly how deep something is: *The snow was over two metres deep.*

depth /depθ/ [n C/U] the distance from the surface to the bottom of a hole, river, sea etc: *"What's the depth of the pool?" "It's 12 feet at this end."*

4 not deep

not very deep /nɒt veri 'diːp/ when the bottom of a hole, river etc is not a long distance from the surface: *Come on in, the water isn't very deep.*

⚠ In spoken English, **not very deep** is much more common than **shallow**

shallow /'ʃæləʊ/ [adj] not very deep – use this especially about the water in a river, lake, swimming pool etc: *The river is too shallow for our boat.* | *The babies splashed around at the shallow end of the pool.*

DEFEND

what you say or do to protect yourself when someone is attacking you or criticizing you

1 to defend your country or yourself

defend /dɪ'fend/ [v T] to use physical or military force to protect a person or place that is being attacked: *Hundreds of soldiers died while defending the town.* | *US troops in Panama will only be used to defend the Canal.*

defend sth against/from *The castle was built in 1549 to defend the island against invaders.*

defend yourself *Mandel died trying to defend himself and his children.*

defence BRITISH **defense** AMERICAN /dɪ'fens/ [n U] all the weapons, soldiers, systems, or activities that a country uses to protect itself from attack by an enemy: *The amount spent on defence has risen by 10%.* | *Defense is expected to be a big issue during the next election.*

⚠ You can also use **defence** before a noun, like an adjective, especially to talk about the money a government spends on defence: *defence spending* | *massive cuts in the defense budget*

defensive /dɪ'fensɪv/ [adj] used only for protecting your country or group, not for attacking someone else: *Police officers claimed that their actions during the riots were purely defensive.*

defensive weapons/position/measures *According to the report, only defensive weapons had been supplied to Iran.*

self-defence BRITISH **self-defense** AMERICAN /,self dɪ'fens/ [n U] methods used by countries or people to stop themselves from being attacked or harmed: *All nations have the right to self-defence.* | *self-defence classes*

in self-defence (=in order to protect yourself) *She claims she shot him in self-defense.*

2 to defend your ideas or your rights

defend /dɪ'fend/ [v T] to say something to support an idea or person when other people are criticizing them or trying to take something away from them: *It's difficult to defend a sport that involves hurting animals.* | *a speech defending the workers' right to strike* | *The Fire Chief defended his staff, and said that they had done everything possible to save the girl's life.*

defend sb/sth against *She has repeatedly tried to defend her husband against hostile criticism in the press.*

defend yourself *She tried to defend herself by saying that she was only obeying orders.*

stand up for sb/sth /,stænd 'ʌp fɔːʳ (sb/sth)/ [phrasal verb T] to strongly defend someone who is being criticized, or strongly defend your ideas or your rights: *You have to be ready to stand up for what you believe in.* | *Didn't anyone* stand up for James and say it wasn't his fault?

stand up for yourself *Politics can be a very tough business, and you have to learn to stand up for yourself.*

stick up for sb /ˌstɪk ˈʌp fɔːr (sb)/ [phrasal verb T] SPOKEN to strongly defend someone who is being criticized, especially when no one else will defend them: *The only person who stuck up for me was Sarah.*

DELIBERATELY

when you do something because you intended to do it

➡ opposite **ACCIDENTALLY**

deliberately /dɪˈlɪbərətli/ [adv] if you do something **deliberately**, you do it because you want to do it, and you hope it will have a particular result or effect: *She left the letter there deliberately so that you'd see it.* | *Police believe the fire was started deliberately.* | *I think he was deliberately ignoring me.*

deliberate /dɪˈlɪbərət/ [adj] use this about things that you do or say deliberately: *a deliberate attempt to prevent the truth from being known* | *His rudeness was quite deliberate.*

on purpose /ɒn ˈpɜːrpəs/ [adv] ESPECIALLY SPOKEN if you do something **on purpose**, you do it deliberately, in order to annoy people or to get an advantage for yourself: *I spilled my drink on purpose – I needed an excuse to leave the room.* | *He always pronounces my name wrong. Do you think he does it on purpose?*

⚠ Don't use **on purpose** about crimes.

intentionally /ɪnˈtenʃənəli/ [adv] ESPECIALLY WRITTEN if you do something **intentionally**, you plan to do it and you hope it will have a particular result or effect: *The jury has to decide whether he killed John Bishop intentionally or whether it was an accident.* | *They arrived late intentionally, in order to avoid seeing him.*

⚠ **Intentionally** is more formal than **deliberately** or **on purpose** and is not common in spoken English.

intentional /ɪnˈtenʃənəl/ [adj] ESPECIALLY WRITTEN use this about things that you do or say deliberately in order to get a particular result or have a particular effect: *The damage was not intentional, but I was still annoyed.* | *If their advertisements are shocking, this is entirely intentional.*

⚠ **Intentional** is more formal than **deliberate** and is not common in spoken English.

intend to do sth /ɪnˌtend tə ˈduː (sth)/ if you **intend** to do something, you decide that you want to do it, and you plan to do it: *I intend to win this game.* | *She clearly intended to kill him, and nearly succeeded.*

DEPEND / IT DEPENDS

when the way something happens is influenced by other facts or events

➡ if you mean 'depend on someone', go to **TRUST/NOT TRUST**
➡ see also **DECIDE, THINK**

depend /dɪˈpend/ [v I] if something **depends** on a fact, result, decision etc, it is not fixed or decided because it will change if the fact, result, decision etc changes
+ on *The amount of tax you pay depends on how much you earn.*
it depends how/where/what etc *I might not be able to go to France – it depends how much it costs.*
depending on *I kept getting different answers, depending on who I asked.*

it depends/that depends SPOKEN (say this when you cannot give a definite answer, because your decision may change according to what happens) *"Are you going to apply for that job?" "Well, it depends."*

it all depends SPOKEN (say this to emphasize that you cannot be certain about something at all) *We still don't know whether we'll have to move to a new house or not – it all depends.*

⚠ Don't say 'it is depending'. Say **it depends**.

according to sth /əˈkɔːʳdɪŋ tuː (sth)/ if something is done **according to** particular facts or principles, these facts or principles are what affect the way it is done: *Telephone charges vary according to the time of day.* | *The students were grouped according to age and ability.*

DESCRIBE

➡ see also **DETAIL, DESCRIBING PEOPLE, HOUSES/WHERE PEOPLE LIVE**

1 to describe someone or something

describe /dɪˈskraɪb/ [v T] to talk or write about a person, place, event etc, saying what they are like and giving details about them: *Could you try and describe the man you saw?* | *In her book, she describes her journey across the Sahara.*
describe sb/sth as *Police described the attack as particularly violent.*
describe sb/sth to sb *I tried to describe the feeling to my doctor, but she didn't understand.*
describe how/what *It's difficult to describe how I felt.*

⚠ Don't say 'I described him the scenery'. Say **I described the scenery to him**

write about sb/sth /ˈraɪt əbaʊt (sb/sth)/ [phrasal verb T] to describe a person, place, or situation by writing about it: *Thomas Hardy wrote about life in the countryside in nineteenth-century England.*

give an account of sth /ˌgɪv ən əˈkaʊnt ɒv (sth)/ to describe something that happened, only giving the facts and not adding your own feelings or opinions: *Please give a brief account of your previous work experience.*

portray sb/sth as sth /pɔːʳˈtreɪ (sb/sth) æz (sth)/ [phrasal verb T] FORMAL to describe someone or something in a way that shows your opinion of them, especially when this is untrue or unfair: *In the book, Diana is portrayed as the victim of a loveless marriage.* | *The right-wing press portrayed the election as a major defeat for the Socialists.*

what sb/sth is like /wɒt (sb/sth) ɪz ˈlaɪk/ SPOKEN use this when you are asking someone to describe someone or something to you or when you are describing someone or something to them: *"I've just met Anna's new boyfriend." "What's he like?"* | *I'll try and explain to you what being in prison was like.*

2 a written or spoken description

description /dɪˈskrɪpʃən/ [n C] what you say or write when you are describing a person, place, thing etc
+ of *Write a description of someone you know well.*
give sb a description *Tom gave the police a description of his car.*
a full/detailed description (=containing all the important details) *The guidebook contains a full description of the church.*

report /rɪˈpɔːʳt/ [n C] a description of a situation or event, based on a study of the facts, which provides people with information about it and also tries to explain it: *The report is based on visits to schools in five cities.*
+ on *a government report on the effects of tobacco advertising*
newspaper/news/television report *News reports suggest that over 300 people may have died.*

account /əˈkaʊnt/ [n C] a written or spoken description of something that happened
+ of *The newspaper printed a detailed account of the trial.*
give an account *His book gives a fascinating account of this dangerous journey.*

commentary /ˈkɒməntəriˈkɑːmənteri/ [n C] a spoken description of a race or sports event on the radio or television, which is given while it is happening: *Don't miss tonight's game between the Bears and the Red Sox – commentary by Nick O'Ryan.*

+ **on** *Now let's go over to our London studio for commentary on the wrestling.*
plural **commentaries**

WORD BANK
DESCRIBING PEOPLE

➡ see pages 186–189

DESERVE

1 to deserve something good

deserve /dɪˈzɜːʳv/ [v T] if you **deserve** something, it is right that you should have it, because you have worked hard, done something well etc: *After all that hard work, you deserve a rest.*
deserve to do sth *Chang played better than Sampras, and he deserved to win.*
thoroughly deserve sth (=deserve something very much) *Jill was awarded first prize, and she thoroughly deserved it.*

well-deserved/well-earned /ˌwel dɪˈzɜːʳvd◄, ˌwel ˈɜːʳnd◄/ [adj usually before noun] a **well-deserved** or **well-earned** rest, win, drink etc is one that you deserve to have, because you have worked hard: *The game ended in a well-deserved victory for the German team. | At 9 o'clock, she settled down for a well-earned rest.*

2 to deserve something bad

deserve /dɪˈzɜːʳv/ [v T] if you think that someone **deserves** something bad that happens to them, you think it is fair that it happens because they have done something wrong or stupid
deserve to do sth *Anyone who drives like that deserves to lose their licence.*
deserve it (=deserve the bad things that happen) *"You really weren't very nice to her." "Well, she deserved it!"*
get what you deserve (=when something bad happens to you, and you deserve it) *In the end, the bully got what he deserved.*

thoroughly deserve sth *I can't help feeling sorry for him even though he thoroughly deserved to be fired.*

○**serve sb right** /ˌsɜːʳv (sb) ˈraɪt/ SPOKEN use this to say you think someone deserves something bad that happens to them, because they have been unkind or done something stupid
+ **for** *"I feel terrible." "Serves you right for drinking so much last night."*
it serves sb right *Her eyes filled with angry tears. "It'd serve them right if something did happen to me," she thought.*

DESIGN

the way that something has been planned to look or work

1 the design of something

design /dɪˈzaɪn/ [n C/U] the way that something has been planned and made, including its appearance and the way it works – use this about things like furniture, clothes, buildings, or machines: *Conran's furniture was based on simple, modern designs. | The success of the product was largely due to good design. | The problem was caused by a design fault.*
the design of sth *The basic design of the vehicle has been improved.*

2 to plan how something new will look or work

design /dɪˈzaɪn/ [v T] to make drawings or plans of something new that will be made or built: *Sally's amazing! She designs all her own clothes. | The car was designed and built in Korea.*
be well designed/badly designed *The offices weren't very well designed – the rooms are too small and it's much too hot in summer.*

plan /plæn/ [v T] to design a large space, such as a town or a park, and to decide how all the different parts should be arranged: *The campus was originally planned in the 1950s, when there weren't as many cars.*
planning – planned – have planned

3 someone whose job is designing things

designer /dɪˈzaɪnəʳ/ [n C] someone whose job is to design new machines, furniture, clothes etc: *De Lorean worked as a designer for the Ford Motor Company.*
fashion/furniture/software etc designer *The show features clothes by famous fashion designers like Jean-Paul Gaultier.*

architect /ˈɑːʳkɪˌtekt/ [n C] someone whose job is to design buildings: *The Imperial Hotel in Tokyo was designed by the famous architect Frank Lloyd Wright.*

DESTROY

to damage something so badly that it cannot be repaired

BREAK   DAMAGE

BROKEN   see also   EXPLODE

SPOIL   ENVIRONMENT

1 to destroy buildings, cities, trees etc

destroy /dɪˈstrɔɪ/ [v T] to damage something so badly that it cannot be repaired: *The earthquake destroyed much of the city.* | *In Brazil the rainforests are gradually being destroyed.* | *A force of 500 aircraft set out to destroy the US navy.* | *The factory was almost completely destroyed by fire.*

⚠️ Don't use **destroy** about clothes or cars.

devastate /ˈdevəsteɪt/ [v T] to cause so much damage over a large area that most of the buildings, trees, and crops there are

destroyed: *A huge explosion devastated the downtown area last night.* | *The country has been devastated by floods.*

be in ruins /biː ɪn ˈruːɪnz/ if a town or building **is in ruins**, it has been completely destroyed: *The village was in ruins. Nothing had survived.* | *Four days and nights of continuous bombing had left the city in ruins.*

wreck /rek/ [v T] to deliberately damage a building or room so badly that it cannot be used again: *A huge bomb wrecked the Opera House.* | *The bar was wrecked by a gang of drunks.*

destruction /dɪˈstrʌkʃən/ [n U] when something is destroyed: *The war caused widespread death and destruction.*
+ of *a campaign to halt the destruction of the Amazonian forest*

demolish /dɪˈmɒlɪʃ‖dɪˈmɑː-/ [v T] to destroy a building using special equipment, because it is old or not safe: *Eventually, in 1992, the apartment block was demolished.* | *When they demolished the church, a cave was discovered beneath it.*
> **demolition** /ˌdeməˈlɪʃən/ [[n U] when a building is demolished: *The plans involve the de-molition of some 18th century houses.*

knock down /ˌnɒk ˈdaʊn‖ˌnɑːk-/ [phrasal verb T] to destroy a building or part of a building in order to build something new
knock sth down *They'll have to knock these houses down when they build the new road.*
knock down sth *We knocked down the internal wall to make the room bigger.*

2 to completely destroy a car

wreck /rek/ [v T] to damage a car very badly in an accident: *They had stolen a car and wrecked it on the freeway.*
> **wrecked** [adj] *Wrecked vehicles lay abandoned at the roadside.*

write off /ˌraɪt ˈɒf‖-ˈɔːf/ [phrasal verb T] BRITISH to damage a car so badly in an accident that it cannot be repaired
write off sth/write sth off *She wrote off her mother's car the first time she drove it.*

DESTROY continues on page 190

DESCRIBING PEOPLE

WORD BANK

D

1 describing people's appearance

If you want to describe what someone looks like, you will find many useful words in other parts of this book. For example:

How big are they?
➡ go to **TALL, SHORT, FAT, THIN**

Are they good-looking?
➡ go to **BEAUTIFUL** or **UGLY**

How old are they?
➡ go to **AGE, YOUNG, OLD**

What is their hair like?
➡ go to **HAIR**

What are their clothes like?
➡ go to **CLOTHES, FASHIONABLE/ UNFASHIONABLE**

Do they have any other noticeable features? For example:

glasses /'glɑːsɪz‖'glæ-/ [n plural] two pieces of glass in a frame that people wear to help them see better: *She has blonde hair and she wears glasses.* | *I sat down next to a small man with glasses and a beard.*

freckles /'frekəlz/ [n plural] small brown spots on someone's face that are made darker by the sun: *Anna had pale skin and freckles.* | *a fair-haired boy with freckles*

    freckled [adj] *a girl with red hair and a freckled face*

wrinkles /'rɪŋkəlz/ [n plural] lines in the skin that people get when they get older: *His hair was almost white and there were wrinkles around his eyes and mouth.*

    wrinkled [adj] *a wrinkled face*

pierced ear /ˌpɪəʳst 'ɪəʳ/ [n C] when someone's ear has a small hole in it so that they can wear jewellery in it: *Nick's got long hair and a pierced ear.* | *Do you have pierced ears?*

tattoo /tə'tuː, tæ-/ [n C] a picture permanently marked on someone's skin with a needle and ink: *Ceri's got a tattoo of a butterfly on her shoulder.* | *a big man with tattoos all over his arms*

She was a slim, pretty woman in her mid-twenties. She had long, dark hair, and was wearing jeans and a t-shirt...

2 describing people's character

If you want to describe someone's character, you will find many useful words in other parts of this book. For example, **CALM, CONFIDENT/NOT CONFIDENT, DETERMINED, FRIENDLY/UNFRIENDLY, FUNNY, INTELLIGENT, INTERESTING, KIND/UNKIND**. Here are some general expressions that are useful for describing someone's character:

can be /'kæn biː, kən-/ if you say someone **can be** annoying, romantic, etc, you mean that sometimes they are annoying or romantic, but they are not like this most of the time

    can be quite/very/really *Mark can be quite bad-tempered when he's under*

DESCRIBING PEOPLE

pressure. | He can be really funny when he's had a few drinks.

can be a little ESPECIALLY AMERICAN **can be a bit** ESPECIALLY BRITISH Anna can be a little moody, but basically she's pretty nice.

can be ... at times Yes, he can be a bit annoying at times.

tend to be /'tend tə biː/ if someone **tends to be** rude, selfish etc, they are often rude or selfish

tend to be rather/quite/a little/a bit Small children tend to be rather selfish | Billy tended to be a bit impatient.

> ⚠ Only use **tend to be** about negative qualities.

🔍 **not very** /'nɒt veri/ ESPECIALLY SPOKEN if you say that someone is **not very** friendly, **not very** polite etc, you mean that they are unfriendly, rude etc. "What's he like?" "Not very nice. He's rather rude and arrogant."

> ⚠ People often use **not very**, especially in spoken English as a way of being less direct when they are saying something negative about someone: He's a nice boy, but not very bright (instead of 'he's a nice boy but stupid!').

always /'ɔːlwɪz, -weɪz/ [adv] if someone is **always** criticizing, **always** laughing etc, they do this very often, and it is an important part of their character: He's always complaining. | Margaret's really considerate – she's always helping people.

side /saɪd/ [n C usually singular] one of the parts of someone's character, especially a part that people do not often notice: Phil's always laughing and joking, but he does have a serious side too.

---

3 the signs of the zodiac

Some people believe that the time of year that you were born has an effect on your character because of the positions of the stars and the planets. They divide the year into 12 periods of time, and these are known as the 'signs of the zodiac'.

People born under different signs are thought to have different characteristics.

Aquarius

20 January - 18 February

People born under the sign of Aquarius are very **loyal**, but they can be a little **insensitive** at times.

Do you like my new dress?

Not really.

Aries

21 March - 19 April

People born under the sign of Aries are extremely **energetic** and **adventurous**. But they can also be **aggressive**.

Pisces

19 February - 20 March

People with the sign of Pisces can be very **romantic**, and are always **sympathetic** if you have a problem. But they can also be extremely **pessimistic**.

Taurus

20 April - 20 May

People with the sign of Taurus are always **calm** and **patient**, but also very **materialistic**.

DESCRIBING PEOPLE continues on the next page

DESCRIBING PEOPLE

D

Gemini

21 May - 20 June

People born under the sign of Gemini are very **witty**, but they tend to be a little **impatient**.

Cancer

21 June - 22 July

People with the sign of Cancer are very **kind** and **helpful**. But they can sometimes be very **moody**.

Leo

23 July - 22 August

People born under the sign of Leo are very **sociable**, but can often be **vain** as well.

Virgo

23 August - 22 September

People born under the sign of Virgo tend to be **hard-working**, but also a little **fussy** and very **critical**.

vocabulary

adventurous /ədˈventʃərəs/ [adj] always ready to try different and exciting things, even if they are dangerous: *For the more adventurous members of the group, there are activities such as rock-climbing and scuba diving.*

aggressive /əˈɡresɪv/ [adj] someone who is **aggressive** behaves in an angry way and seems to want to fight or argue: *Haynes suddenly became aggressive and started swearing at us.*

artistic /ɑːˈtɪstɪk/ [adj] good at painting and drawing, and at making and designing things using your skill and imagination: *She comes from a very artistic family – her mother's an interior designer and her brother's an architect.*

calm /kɑːm‖kɑːm, kɑːlm/ [adj] not getting angry or upset, even in a difficult situation: *Dr Weir answered their questions in a calm, professional manner.*
keep/stay calm *Meditation always helps me stay calm and relaxed.*

cheerful /ˈtʃɪəʳfəl/ [adj] always happy, smiling, and friendly: *Barbara greeted us with a cheerful smile. | The children managed to stay cheerful in spite of the bad weather.*

conceited /kənˈsiːtɪd/ [adj] too confident about your own abilities and achievements, in a way that annoys people: *Rupert and his wife are an awful couple – so snobbish and conceited.*

critical /ˈkrɪtɪkəl/ [adj] someone who is **critical** always says negative things about other people's work or the things they do and say: *Mrs Blake wasn't a popular teacher – she was too critical.*

cruel /kruːəl/ [adj] deliberately trying to hurt or upset people, and not caring if this makes them unhappy: *'How could anyone be so cruel!' she said and burst into tears.*
+ to *Kids can sometimes be very cruel to each other.*

energetic /ˌenəʳˈdʒetɪk◀/ [adj] very active and able to work hard and do a lot of things without getting tired: *If you're feeling energetic, we could go out for a run.*

fussy /ˈfʌsi/ [adj] someone who is **fussy** is difficult to please because they only like a few things and will only accept exactly what they want
+ about *Teenagers are often very fussy about what they eat.*

hard-working /ˌhɑːʳd ˈwɜːʳkɪŋ◀/ [adj] always working hard in your job or schoolwork: *Jane's teachers said she was a sensible hard-working girl.*

helpful /ˈhelpfəl/ [adj] always ready to help people, for example by giving them useful advice or information: *The staff at the museum were very helpful. | Thanks Sasha. You've been really helpful.*

impatient /ɪmˈpeɪʃənt/ [adj] someone who is **impatient** gets annoyed if they have to wait for something: *I'm coming – don't be so impatient!*

indecisive /ˌɪndɪˈsaɪsɪv◀/ [adj] someone who is indecisive is not good at making decisions quickly and keeps changing their mind about what they want to do: *The President's opponents described him as weak and indecisive.*

insensitive /ˌɪnˈsensɪtɪv/ [adj] not realizing that some of the things you say or do are likely to upset or offend people: *Carol's husband is an insensitive brute.*
+ to *She's insensitive to anyone's feelings but her own.*

kind /kaɪnd/ [adj] someone who is **kind** always tries to help people and make them happy or comfortable: *We'd like to thank all the doctors and nurses at St James's Hospital for being so kind. | She's one of the kindest, most considerate people I ever met.*
+ to *People at work were very kind to me when my mother died.*

loyal /ˈlɔɪəl/ [adj] always ready to help and support your friends, family etc, especially when other people criticize

DESCRIBING PEOPLE

Scorpio
23 October - 21 November

People born under the sign of Scorpio are often **passionate**, but sometimes a little **cruel**.

Sagittarius
22 November - 21 December

People born under the sign of Sagittarius are always **cheerful** and **optimistic**, but often tend to be **reckless**.

Libra
23 September - 22 October

People born under the sign of Libra are usually **artistic**. But also tend to be **indecisive**.

Capricorn
22 December - 19 January

People with the sign of Capricorn are **sensible** and **organized**, but are sometimes **conceited**.

---

or oppose them: *a loyal and devoted wife*
+ to *We'd like to thank all our fans who've been so loyal to the team.*

materialistic /məˌtɪəriəˈlɪstɪk◀/ [adj] thinking that money and possessions are more important than anything else: *A lot of young people nowadays are rebelling against the materialistic values of their parents.*

moody /ˈmuːdi/ [adj] often getting angry or annoyed, even though there seems to be no reason to feel like this: *What's wrong with Janet? She's not usually so moody.* | *After the accident, he had become increasingly moody and depressed.*

optimistic /ˌɒptɪ̯ˈmɪstɪk◀‖ˌɑːp/ [adj] someone who is **optimistic** always expects good things to happen, and believes that they will eventually get what they want: *Donna hasn't managed to find a job yet, but she is still very optimistic.*
+ about *How optimistic are you about your chances of winning a gold medal?*

organized /ˈɔːrgənaɪzd/ [adj] good at organizing your life and making plans, so you are always well prepared for the things you have to do: *You have to admire Helen - she's so organized.*

passionate /ˈpæʃənɪ̯t/ [adj] someone who is **passionate** has strong sexual or romantic feelings: *Todd put his arms around her and gave her a passionate kiss.*

patient /ˈpeɪʃənt/ [adj] able to wait calmly without becoming annoyed or bored: *"Are we going now Mum?" "No, not yet, you'll just have to be patient."*
+ with *Try and be patient with her – she's doing her best.*

pessimistic /ˌpesɪ̯ˈmɪstɪk◀/ [adj] someone who is **pessimistic** always expects bad things to happen, and thinks that if anything can go wrong it will go wrong: *I wish you'd stop being so pessimistic!*
+ about *Experts seem pessimistic about the chances of*

an economic recovery.

reckless /ˈrekləs/ [adj] behaving in an irresponsible or dangerous way, and not caring whether you harm yourself or other people: *A senior police officer blamed reckless motorists for the high number of deaths on the road.*

romantic /rəˈmæntɪk, rəʊ-/ [adj] someone who is **romantic** treats the person they love as someone very special, for example by buying them presents and giving them flowers: *"Phil's taking me to Paris for the weekend." "How romantic!"*

sensible /ˈsensɪ̯bəl/ [adj] always behaving in a responsible way, making good decisions, and not doing anything stupid or risky: *He was sensible enough to realize he wouldn't pass the exam without doing any work.* | *You can rely on Jill to take care of the car – she's a very sensible driver.*

sociable /ˈsəʊʃəbəl/ [adj] someone who is **sociable** is friendly, and enjoys being with other people and meeting new people: *Maria was a sociable and popular member of the class.*

sympathetic /ˌsɪmpəˈθetɪk◀/ [adj] ready to try to understand people's problems and to help them if you can: *Tell Frank how you feel – I'm sure he'll be sympathetic.*

> ⚠ Don't confuse **sympathetic** (=ready to understand and help people) and **nice** (=pleasant, friendly, and easy to talk to)

vain /veɪn/ [adj] very proud of yourself, especially because you think that you look very attractive or beautiful: *The girls at school used to tease her for being so vain.*

witty /ˈwɪti/ [adj] someone who is **witty** always says clever and amusing things: *Edberg's witty remarks kept us all amused.*

D

DESTROY continued from page 185

Qtotal /'təʊtl/ [v T] AMERICAN SPOKEN to damage a car so badly in an accident that it cannot be repaired: *It was a terrible accident. Both cars were totaled.*
totaling – totaled – have totaled

3 causing a lot of damage

destructive /dɪ'strʌktɪv/ [adj] something or someone that is **destructive** causes a lot of damage: *a wasteful and destructive war | Small children can be very destructive. | the destructive effects of mass tourism*

devastating /'devəsteɪtɪŋ/ [adj] causing very serious damage to all the buildings, trees, crops etc in an area: *The palace was rebuilt in 1832 after a devastating fire.*
have a devastating effect on *The oil spill had a devastating effect on sea birds and other wildlife.*

4 a place or thing that has been destroyed

wreckage /'rekɪdʒ/ [n U] the broken parts of a car, plane etc that has crashed: *Wreckage from the plane was scattered over a large area. | Passengers were trapped in the burning wreckage.*

ruins /'ruːɪnz/ [n plural] the parts of a building or town that remain after it has been destroyed
+ of *We visited the ruins of an ancient temple. | the ruins of a bombed-out office block*

wreck /rek/ [n C] a ship that has been sunk, or a car that has been badly damaged in a crash: *Divers went down to search the wreck. | The car was a complete wreck, but the driver escaped with minor injuries.*

write-off /'raɪt ɒf‖-ɔːf/ [n C] BRITISH a car that has been so badly damaged that it cannot be used again: *The car was a complete write-off – I was lucky I wasn't killed.*

5 be gradually destroyed by a natural process

rot/decay /rɒt, dɪ'keɪ‖raːt/ [v I] to be gradually destroyed by natural chemical changes – use this about dead plants or flesh, or about fruit or wood: *Peaches that had fallen from the trees were rotting on the ground. | the disgusting smell of rotting meat | Decaying vegetation blocked the stream.*
rot – rotting – have rotted

> ⚠ **Decay** is a more technical word than **rot.**

rust /rʌst/ [v I] if metal **rusts**, it becomes red-brown in colour because it has been damaged by the effects of water: *Your bike will rust if you leave it out in the rain.*

DETAIL

➡ see also **INFORMATION, DESCRIBE**

1 a specific piece of information

detail /'diːteɪl‖dɪ'teɪl/ [n C often plural] a single fact or piece of information about something: *The story's very complicated – I can't remember all the exact details.*
+ of *The student advice office provides details of all the university courses in the country. | Baker advises the President on the details of foreign policy.*
personal details (=information about someone, such as their age, their address, whether they are married etc) *To apply for a loan, first fill in the section marked 'Personal Details'.*

point /pɔɪnt/ [n C] a detail that you need to talk about when you are discussing a plan, statement, or written agreement: *There's one point in your letter that is not quite clear.*
small/minor point (=one that is not very important) *We only have a few small points left to discuss.*

Qthing /θɪŋ/ [n C] SPOKEN a detail in something such as a plan, statement, or written agreement: *There's one thing I'm not clear about, and that's how we are going to get to the airport. | I need to change a few things before I give the speech.*

the small print /ðə ˌsmɔːl 'prɪnt/ [n singular] the specific details in an agreement or document, which may be very important but which people do not always notice: *Be sure to read the small print before you sign anything.*

2 a specific feature of something you see

detail /ˈdiːteɪl‖dɪˈteɪl/ [n C/U] one of many specific features that you can see in something such as a picture, a building, or something that someone has made: *Look at all the tiny details in the background of the picture.* | *The cathedral has a carved ceiling which is full of interesting detail.*

3 with a lot of details

detailed /ˈdiːteɪld‖dɪˈteɪld/ [adj] a **detailed** description, explanation, picture etc contains a lot of details: *The police have issued a detailed description of the man they are looking for.* | *Do you have a more detailed map of the area?*

in detail /ɪn ˈdiːteɪl‖-dɪˈteɪl/ if you talk about or consider something **in detail**, you pay attention to all the details: *I haven't had time to look at the plans in detail yet.* | *This problem is discussed in more detail in Chapter 7.*

in great detail (=including a lot of detail) *Fortunately, she was able to describe her attacker in great detail.*

4 not containing many details

general /ˈdʒenərəl/ [adj only before noun] a general description or explanation of something contains the most basic information but does not include all the details: *The course is called 'A General Introduction to Computing'.*

a general idea (=basic knowledge) *This guidebook will give you a good general idea of the city.*

rough /rʌf/ [adj only before noun] **rough description/plan/outline etc** a description, plan etc that is not exact or complete, but has enough information to help you understand it: *We've drawn up a rough plan but we haven't worked out all the costs.*

a rough idea (=a basic explanation or understanding) *Give us a rough idea of what you're trying to do.*

vague /veɪg/ [adj] something that is **vague** is not clear because it does not provide enough details: *Dave's instructions were rather vague.* | *I had heard vague rumours that they were getting married.*

not go into detail /nɒt gəʊ ɪntə ˈdiːteɪl‖ -dɪˈteɪl/ if you do **not go into detail** when you are telling someone about something, you only give them the basic facts without any details: *It was only a quick explanation – he didn't really go into detail.*

DETERMINED

when you have definitely decided to do something, and you will not let anything stop you

➡ see also **DESCRIBING PEOPLE**

1 determined to do something

determined /dɪˈtɜːˠmɪ̩nd/ [adj] if you are **determined** to do something, you have decided that you are definitely going to do it, and you will not let anything stop you: *There's no point trying to stop her – it'll only make her more determined.*

determined to do sth *I was determined to be a professional dancer, and practised for hours every day.*

+ (that) *She was determined that her children should have the best possible education.*

be set on sth /biː ˈset ɒn (sth)/ to be determined to do something, especially something important that will affect your whole life, even if other people think you should not do it

be set on (doing) sth *Nina seems to be set on marrying him.*

be dead set on sth (=extremely determined to do something) *Bob's always been dead set on a career in advertising.*

2 someone who has a determined character

determined /dɪˈtɜːˠmɪ̩nd/ [adj] someone who is **determined** works very hard to achieve what they want to achieve, and will not let problems stop them: *Not many women went to university in those days,* *but Dorothy was a very determined woman.*

single-minded /ˌsɪŋgəl ˈmaɪndɪd◂/ [adj] someone who is **single-minded** works very hard in order to achieve one thing, and thinks that everything else is much less important: *You have to be tough and single-minded if you want a career in the movies.*

single-minded determination/ambition/ commitment *her single-minded commitment to improving the legal position of women*

3 determined to be successful in life or in your job

ambitious /æmˈbɪʃəs/ [adj] determined to become successful, rich, powerful, or famous: *John was very ambitious, and even at the age of 17 he began planning his career as a politician.* | *She had always been ambitious, and felt that marriage and children would damage her career.*

pushy /ˈpʊʃi/ [adj] INFORMAL someone who is **pushy** is so determined to do well and to get what they want that they behave in a way that is rude and annoying: *You have to be pushy to succeed in journalism.* | *Pushy parents can put their children under a lot of stress.*

pushy – pushier – pushiest

4 determined in a way that is annoying or silly

stubborn /ˈstʌbərn/ [adj] someone who is **stubborn** refuses to change their mind about something, even when people think they are wrong or are being unreasonable: *I told him it was a bad idea, but Dave's so stubborn that he just never listens.* | *The oil companies face stubborn opposition from environmentalists.*

stubbornly [adv] *My grandmother stubbornly refused to eat any 'foreign' foods.*

obstinate /ˈɒbstɪnɪt/ /ˈɑːb-/ [adj] someone who is **obstinate** always does what they want and refuses to change their mind, even when this is annoying and unreasonable: *How do you deal with an obstinate teenager who always says she isn't hungry?*

obstinately [adv] *She obstinately refused to admit she was wrong.*

pig-headed /ˌpɪg ˈhedɪd◂/ [adj] INFORMAL use this about someone who refuses to change their mind when you think that what they want to do is stupid: *We told him he was crazy to drive after drinking so much, but he's so pig-headed he just ignored us.*

5 so determined that you do not care who you harm

ruthless /ˈruːθləs/ [adj] someone who is **ruthless** is so determined to get what they want, especially in business or politics, that they do not care if they harm other people: *You should be careful of Allan – he can be pretty ruthless if anyone gets in his way.* | *With ruthless efficiency, the new management fired half the workforce to increase company profits.*

ruthlessly [adv] *Important evidence had been ruthlessly suppressed by the police.*

go to any lengths/stop at nothing /ˌgəʊ tʊ ˌeni ˈleŋθs, ˌstɒp ət ˈnʌθɪŋ/ /ˌstɑːp-/ to be willing to do anything, even if it is cruel, dishonest, or illegal, in order to get what you want: *He was prepared to go to any lengths to find the men who killed his daughter.* | *Lawrence would stop at nothing to achieve power and wealth.*

6 the ability to be determined

determination /dɪˌtɜːrmɪˈneɪʃən/ [n U] the ability to continue trying to achieve what you want, even when this is difficult: *After the accident, Bill learned to walk again through sheer hard work and determination.*

determination to do sth *A spokesman stressed the police's determination to find the girl's killer.*

ambition /æmˈbɪʃən/ [n U] determination to become successful, rich, powerful, or famous: *Eric wasn't particularly intelligent but he had plenty of ambition.*

willpower /ˈwɪlˌpaʊər/ [n U] the ability to control your mind and body in order to achieve whatever you decide to do: *It takes a lot of willpower to give up smoking.*

perseverance /ˌpɜːʳsɪˈvɪərəns/ [n U] the ability to keep on trying to achieve something over a long period, even when there are problems and difficulties: *You need patience and perseverance to learn a foreign language.*

DIE

➡ opposite **LIVE**
➡ see also **DEAD, ALIVE, EXIST**

1 to die because you are old or ill

die /daɪ/ [v I] to stop being alive, as a result of old age or illness: *I want to see Ireland again before I die.* | *Many people are worried about growing old and dying alone.*
+ of *Her youngest brother died of cancer when he was only thirteen.*
die young (=die when you are young) *His first wife had died young and he remarried at the age of 40.*
dying – died – have died

⚠ The usual preposition after **die** is **of**: *He died of a heart attack.* You can also use **from**, especially when someone dies as a result of being injured: *She was shot twice, and died later from her wounds.* But don't use **with** after **die**.

dying /ˈdaɪ-ɪŋ/ [adj] if someone is **dying**, they will die very soon because they are very ill or very badly injured: *He gave the dying man a drop of water from his flask.* | *Her aunt lay dying upstairs.*

death /deθ/ [n C/U] when someone dies:
the death of sb FORMAL (=when someone dies) *Over 100 years have passed since the death of Karl Marx.*
+ from *The number of deaths from AIDS is still increasing.*
on sb's death (=when they die) *Catherine will inherit a large sum of money on her father's death.*

pass away /ˌpɑːs əˈweɪ‖ˌpæs-/ [phrasal verb I] to die – use this when you want to avoid using the word 'die', because you think it might upset someone: *"Your mother passed away during the night,"* the doctor told him.

drop dead /ˌdrɒp ˈded‖ˌdrɑːp-/ SPOKEN if someone **drops dead**, they die very suddenly and unexpectedly, especially when they are in the middle of doing something: *Jim Fixx, the fitness guru, dropped dead while he was jogging.*

2 to die in an accident, war, fight etc

die/be killed /daɪ, biː ˈkɪld/ [v I] *Bob's parents died when their car was hit by a truck.*
die in an accident/explosion/the war etc *Two people were killed and four injured in a gas explosion this morning.*
die/be killed in action (=be killed while fighting in a war) *His brother was killed in action in Vietnam.*

death /deθ/ [n C/U] when someone dies in an accident or a war: *The number of deaths on Britain's roads continues to fall.*
the death of sb FORMAL (=when someone dies) *Police are investigating the mysterious deaths of two teenagers.*

to death /tə ˈdeθ/ **starve/freeze/bleed to death** to die because of having no food, being too cold, or losing blood: *The baby starved to death.* | *A young man was hit with a broken bottle and bled to death.*

lose your life /ˌluːz jɔːʳ ˈlaɪf/ to be killed in a terrible event – used especially in news reports and descriptions of past events: *Hundreds of people lost their lives when the ship overturned in a storm.* | *The Brazilian driver lost his life in an accident during a Formula One race in Germany.*

die for sth /ˈdaɪ fɔːʳ (sth)/ [phrasal verb T] to die for your country or because of something you believe in: *brave men who were ready to die for their country*

3 an illness or accident that you die from

fatal /ˈfeɪtl/ [adj] a **fatal** accident or medical condition kills the person who has it, usually immediately: *a fatal heart attack* | *Meyer's car was involved in a fatal accident on the A1.*
fatally [adv]
fatally injured/wounded *His father had been fatally injured in an explosion in the mine where he worked.*

terminal /ˈtɜːrmɪnəl/ [adj] a **terminal** illness cannot be cured, and the person who has it will soon die: *She was recently told she had terminal cancer.*

terminally [adv]
terminally ill *a ward for terminally ill patients*

4 when one of your relatives or friends dies

lose /luːz/ [v T] if you **lose** a friend or a close relative, they die: *Maya lost her mother when she was very young.* | *It's a terrible thing to lose someone very close to you.*

losing – lost – have lost

be widowed /biː ˈwɪdəʊd/ if you **are widowed**, your husband or wife dies: *Becky was widowed only ten months after her marriage.*

widowed [adj only before noun] *He's gone to stay with his widowed mother in Florida.*

be orphaned /biː ˈɔːrfənd/ if you **are orphaned**, both your parents die when you are still young: *Thousands of Rwandan children have been orphaned by the war.*

orphaned [adj only before noun] *a home for orphaned children*

5 when a type of animal or plant stops existing

die out /ˌdaɪ ˈaʊt/ [phrasal verb I] if a type of animal or plant **dies out**, fewer and fewer of them exist, until in the end there are no more left: *The dinosaurs died out long ago.* | *Many species of wildflower are dying out as a result of pollution.*

extinct /ɪkˈstɪŋkt/ [adj] a type of animal or plant that is **extinct** does not exist any more: *Animals such as the white rhino and the giant panda may soon be extinct.*
become extinct *Bears became extinct in this country over 100 years ago.*

6 places, ceremonies, etc connected with people who have died

funeral /ˈfjuːnərəl/ [n C] a religious ceremony when someone who has died is buried or burned

coffin (also **casket** AMERICAN) /ˈkɒfɪn, ˈkɑːskət‖ˈkɔː-, ˈkæs-/ [n C] the box in which a dead person's body is placed for their funeral

hearse /hɜːrs/ [n C] a large car used to carry a body in a coffin at a funeral

bury /ˈberi/ [v T] to put a dead person's body in a grave: *She was buried in the little churchyard, not far from the place where she was born.*

burying – buried – have buried

be cremated /biː krɪˈmeɪtɪd‖-ˈkriːmeɪtɪd/ when a dead person's body is burned, usually after a funeral

grave /greɪv/ [n C] a deep hole in the ground where a dead person's body is buried

graveyard /ˈgreɪvjɑːrd/ [n C] an area of land where dead people are buried; **graveyards** are usually smaller than **cemeteries**, and in Britain they are usually next to a church

cemetery /ˈsemətri‖-teri/ [n C] a large area of land where dead people are buried
war cemetery (=where soldiers killed in a war are buried)
plural **cemeteries**

DIFFERENT

➡ look here for ...
• different from someone or something else
• a different one, or not the same one

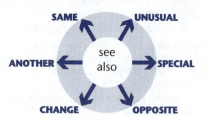

1 not like something or someone else

different /ˈdɪfərənt/ [adj] if something or someone is **different**, they are not like something or someone else, or they are not like they were before: *We've painted* *the door a different colour.* | *You look different. Have you had your hair cut?* | *Our two children are very different.*

different from sth/sb (also **different than sth/sb** AMERICAN) *This computer is different from the one I used in my last job.*

completely/totally different *The living-room looks totally different with those new curtains.*

differently [adv] *The two words sound the same, but they're spelled differently.*

> ⚠ If you want to say that two people or things are different from each other, you can just say **they are different**: *Rap music and reggae are different in lots of ways.*

not like /nɒt 'laɪk/ [preposition] different from – use this especially when two things or people are not at all similar: *You should remember that walking in the hills isn't like walking down the street – it can be very dangerous.*

not at all like/nothing like (=completely different from) *She's very shy – not at all like her sister.*

not look/sound like *The voice on the answering machine did not sound like Anna at all.*

not the same /nɒt ðə 'seɪm/ different – use this especially when two things are similar but not exactly like each other: *The two patterns are similar but not the same.*

+ as *I've tried Mexican food here in London, but it just isn't the same as in Mexico.*

vary /'veəri/ [v I] if things of the same type **vary**, they are all different from each other: *Methods of treatment vary according to the age and general health of the patient.*

vary considerably/greatly *Prices of video cameras vary considerably.*

vary in price/quality/size/flavour etc *The cheeses vary in flavour from mild to strong.*

varying – varied – have varied

differ /'dɪfər/ [v I] FORMAL if two things **differ**, they have different qualities or features

+ from *Scottish law has always differed from English law.*

differ in cost/size/appearance etc *The two drugs have the same effect, but they differ in certain important respects.*

differ greatly/widely *Opinions on the subject differ widely.*

2 completely different from anyone or anything else

unique /juːˈniːk/ [adj] something **unique** is so different, special, or unusual that it is the only one of its kind: *a musician with a unique style* | *a mental ability which makes the human race unique among animals*

special /'speʃəl/ [adj] designed for one particular purpose, and therefore different from other things of its type: *Bob's been on a special diet since his heart attack.* | *You need a special tool for this job.*

distinctive /dɪˈstɪŋktɪv/ [adj] something that is **distinctive** has a special quality or appearance that makes it different from other things, and makes it easy to recognize: *The distinctive taste of genuine malt whisky.* | *Sarah dressed in a very distinctive style.*

3 another one, not the same one as before

another /əˈnʌðər/ [determiner/pronoun] one more of the same kind of thing or person: *creatures from another planet* | *Louise has a house in New York, and another house in Florida.*

another one *I didn't like the dress I'd bought, so I changed it for another one.*

> ⚠ Don't say 'another countries'. Say **another country** or **other countries**. **Another** is not used before a plural or uncountable noun.

different /'dɪfərənt/ [adj only before noun] a **different** thing or person is not the same one that you have already mentioned: *The other portrait is by a different artist.* | *She used to be a teacher, but I think she's doing a different job now.*

new /njuː‖nuː/ [adj only before noun] use this about something or someone that replaces the one that was there before: *Have you met Keith's new girlfriend?* | *She's really enjoying her new job.*

else /els/ [adv] **something/somewhere/ someone else** another thing, place, or person instead of this one: *Go and play somewhere else. I'm trying to work.* | *Andrea's obsessed with money – she never talks about anything else.*

alternative /ɔːlˈtɜːrnətɪv‖ɔːl-, æl-/ [adj only before noun] an **alternative** plan, arrangement, or system can be used instead of the usual one: *The bridge is closed so we'll have to use an alternative route.* | *For vegetarian guests there is an alternative menu.*

4 several different things or people

different /ˈdɪfərənt/ [adj only before noun] use this about several people or things of the same general type, when you are comparing them with each other and noticing the differences between them: *Let's compare the prices of five different detergents.* | *a drug that affects different people in different ways*

various /ˈveəriəs/ [adj only before noun] of several different kinds, but the same general type: *I had to sign various documents before they would give me the package.* | *the advantages and disadvantages of the various teaching methods*

all sorts of/all kinds of /ɔːl ˈsɔːrts dv, ɔːl ˈkaɪndz dv/ ESPECIALLY SPOKEN a lot of people or things that are different from each other, but of the same general type: *I meet all sorts of people in my job.* | *The bureau provides advice on all kinds of housing problems.*

a variety of /ə vəˈraɪəti dv/ ESPECIALLY WRITTEN a lot of things that are different from each other, but of the same general type: *Children do badly at school for a variety of reasons.*
a wide variety of (=very many different things) *The college offers a wide variety of language courses.*

varied /ˈveərid/ [adj] including many different things or people, especially in a way that seems interesting: *I really enjoy the work here – it's very varied.* | *It is important that a child gets a varied diet.*

separate /ˈsepərɪt/ [adj only before noun] use this about two or more things of the same general type that are not connected with each other: *a word that has three separate meanings* | *She has been*

warned on a number of separate occasions.

5 the way in which two things are different

difference /ˈdɪfərəns/ [n C] what makes one thing or person different from another: *He's speaking Spanish, not Italian. Don't you know the difference?*
+ between *Try and spot the differences between these two pictures.*

contrast /ˈkɒntrɑːst‖ˈkɑːntræst/ [n singular] a very clear difference that you can easily see when you compare two things or people
+ between *The thing that surprised us was the contrast between the ancient temples and the ultra-modern office buildings.*

gap /gæp/ [n C] a big difference between two amounts, two ages, or two groups of people
+ between *There's a ten-year gap between Kay's two children.* | *The gap between rich and poor is getting wider.*

6 to notice that two things or people are different

can tell the difference /kən ˌtel ðə ˈdɪfərəns/ to be able to notice that two things or people are different, even though they are very similar: *It looked just like a real diamond – I couldn't tell the difference.*
+ between *Can you tell the difference between butter and margarine?*

can tell sb/sth apart /kən ˌtel (sb/sth) əˈpɑːrt/ to be able to see that two very similar people or things are different – use this especially in questions and negative statements: *The twins are identical – even their parents can't always tell them apart.*

distinguish /dɪˈstɪŋgwɪʃ/ [v I/T] to be able to see the difference between two or more similar things or people
+ between *Even an expert would find it hard to distinguish between the original painting and the copy.*
distinguish sb/sth from sb/sth *A tiny baby soon learns to distinguish its mother's face from other adults' faces.*

⚠ **Distinguish** is more formal than **can tell the difference**

7 when one statement makes a different one seem untrue

contradict /ˌkɒntrə'dɪkt‖ˌkɑːn-/ [v T] if one statement or fact **contradicts** another one, it is so different that it makes the other one seem untrue or impossible: *The two newspaper reports totally contradict each other.* | *Their theories have been contradicted by the results of recent experiments.*

DIFFICULT

➡ opposite **EASY**

1 difficult to do or understand

difficult/hard /'dɪfɪkəlt, hɑːrd/ [adj] not easy to do or understand: *The police have a difficult job to do.* | *Have you ever tried windsurfing? It's harder than it looks.*
difficult/hard to see/hear/read etc His handwriting is very difficult to read.
it is difficult/hard to do sth *It's difficult to explain these problems to a child.* | *It is hard to imagine what life was like in the 13th century.*
find it difficult/hard to do sth *People find it difficult to learn new skills as they get older.*
make it difficult/hard for sb to do sth *My mother's illness makes it very difficult for her to do a full-time job.*

⚠ **Difficult** is slightly more formal than **hard**

tough /tʌf/ [adj] very difficult to do or deal with – use this about jobs, decisions, questions, or problems: *People in government are always having to make tough decisions.* | *He'll have some pretty tough questions to answer in tonight's TV interview.*

complicated /'kɒmplɪˌkeɪtɪd‖'kɑːm-/ [adj] a **complicated** problem, situation, or system is difficult to understand because it consists of many different parts or details: *the complicated problem of bringing peace to the Middle East* | *a complicated set of instructions*

complex /'kɒmpleks‖kɑːm'pleks/ [adj] a **complex** process or system is difficult to understand because it has a lot of parts that are all connected in different ways: *The way humans think is a complex process that scientists cannot fully explain.* | *complex laws relating to sex discrimination*

⌐**it's easier said than done** /ɪts ˌiːziəʳ ˌsed ðən 'dʌn/ SPOKEN say this to tell someone that something is much more difficult than they think it is: *"You'll just have to find yourself a rich husband, won't you?" "Well, that's easier said than done!"*

2 something that needs a lot of skill, hard work, and determination

challenging /'tʃælɪndʒɪŋ/ [adj] a **challenging** job or activity needs a lot of hard work and skill, but you want to do it because you can achieve something good by doing it: *She finds working with handicapped children challenging but extremely rewarding.* | *The job wasn't challenging enough for me – I wanted something more creative.*

be a challenge /biː ə 'tʃælɪndʒ/ if a new job or activity **is a challenge**, it is difficult, but you are determined to do it because it is interesting and exciting: *You may find your first couple of months in the job quite a challenge.* | *We have to walk 60 kilometres in two days – it will be a real challenge.*

demanding /dɪ'mɑːndɪŋ‖dɪ'mæn-/ [adj] a **demanding** job or activity is very difficult and tiring, because it needs all your effort and skill and a lot of your time: *Being a nurse in a busy hospital is a demanding job, and you don't get much free time.*

daunting /'dɔːntɪŋ/ [adj] if something is **daunting**, it seems almost impossible, and the idea of doing it makes you feel nervous: *Climbing Everest was a daunting challenge for any mountaineer.*
daunting task *I was faced with the daunting task of learning the entire script in 24 hours.*

3 a situation that is difficult to deal with or talk about

difficult /'dɪfɪkəlt/ [adj] a **difficult** situation or subject is not easy to deal with or talk about, and it makes you feel nervous or unhappy: *Things at home have been very difficult since my father died.* | *Their relationship had been difficult from the start.*
in a difficult position (=when someone has problems that are difficult to deal with) *His ex-wife's accusations have put the President in a very difficult position.*

awkward /'ɔːkwəʳd/ [adj] an **awkward** situation or subject is difficult to deal with or talk about, especially because it might be embarrassing: *He's at the age when kids start asking awkward questions – like 'Where do babies come from?'*
feel awkward about *Many people feel awkward about discussing money, even with their partner.*

tricky /'trɪki/ [adj] a **tricky** situation is one that you have to deal with very carefully, because there are a lot of things that could easily go wrong: *Teachers often have to deal with tricky situations, such as interviews with angry parents.* | *Although I was his boss I was much younger than him, so things were rather tricky at first.*
tricky – trickier – trickiest

4 someone who is unhelpful and causes problems

difficult /'dɪfɪkəlt/ [adj] someone who is **difficult** is not easy to live with or work with because they do not behave in a helpful, friendly way, or they do not do what you want: *When Darren was a little boy, he was very difficult at times.* | *Campbell has the reputation of being difficult to work with.*

awkward /'ɔːkwəʳd/ [adj] someone who is **awkward** is deliberately unhelpful and unfriendly, and seems to like causing problems for people: *I don't think she's really too sick to come with us. She's just being awkward.*

Ọ**impossible** /ɪm'pɒsɪ̯bəl‖ɪm'pɑː-/ [adj not before noun] SPOKEN someone who is **impossible** makes you annoyed and

impatient, for example because they are never satisfied or they keep changing their mind: *Even when I offer to help her she always finds some reason to complain. She's impossible!*

5 a time when you have a lot of problems

difficult/hard/tough /'dɪfɪkəlt, hɑːʳd, tʌf/ [adj] use this about a period of time when you have a lot of problems or a lot of bad things happen to you: *The last few months have been especially difficult for her.* | *1996 was perhaps the hardest year we've faced so far.*
have a hard/difficult/tough time *Try to be nice to her. She's had a really tough time recently.*

6 to have problems when you are trying to do something

have difficulty /hæv 'dɪfɪkəlti/ if you **have difficulty** when you are trying to do something, you cannot do it easily
have difficulty doing sth *I noticed that she was having difficulty breathing.* | *Kelly was having difficulty controlling his temper.*
+ with *Do you have any difficulty with spelling?*

⚠ Don't say 'I had difficulty to walk'. Say **I had difficulty walking.**

find sth difficult /ˌfaɪnd (sth) 'dɪfɪkəlt/ to not be able to do something easily, especially because you do not have enough ability or skill: *I found the course difficult at first, but it gradually got easier.*
find it difficult to do sth *He's very shy, and finds it difficult to talk to people.*

with difficulty /wɪð 'dɪfɪkəlti/ ESPECIALLY WRITTEN if you do something **with difficulty**, you can do it, but only by using all your strength, all your determination etc: *With difficulty, the old man struggled up the stairs.* | *She spoke with difficulty, choking back her tears.*

can hardly /kən 'hɑːʳdli/ if you **can hardly** do something, you can only just do it, and it is very difficult: *He talks so fast, I can hardly understand what he's* *saying.* | *By the end of the day she could hardly walk.*

> ⚠ Don't say 'we can't hardly move'. Say **we can hardly move**.

◯**have a job doing sth** /hæv ə ˈdʒɒb duːɪŋ (sth)‖-ˈdʒɑːb-/ BRITISH SPOKEN if you **have a job doing something**, it takes a lot of time or a lot of effort, and you may not be able to do it: *You'll have a job persuading him to give you any more money.* | *There was some kind of festival going on, and we had a job finding somewhere to park the car.*

DIRECTION

➡ see also **WAY, ⬛ POSITION & DIRECTION**

1 the direction in which something or someone moves

direction /dɪˈrekʃən, daɪ-/ [n C usually singular] the direction that something or someone is moving towards or pointing towards
in sb's direction (=towards someone) *We crept past, hoping that the guard would not look in our direction.*
in the direction of sth (=towards something) *We carried on walking in the direction of the ocean.*
in the right/wrong direction *Are you sure we're going in the right direction?*
in the opposite direction *Bill marched off angrily in the opposite direction.*
from the direction of sth *Suddenly Anna heard a shout coming from the direction of the kitchen.*

way /weɪ/ [n C usually singular] the general direction that something or someone is moving towards or pointing towards: *"Which way does the garden face?" "South. It gets a lot of sun."*
this way/that way *The truck went that way – you can see its tracks in the snow.*
the right way/the wrong way *I think we're going the wrong way.*

> ⚠ **Way** and **direction** mean the same, but **way** is more common in spoken English and **direction** is more common in written English.

DIRTY

➡ opposite **CLEAN**
➡ see also **WASH, MARK**

1 dirty

dirty /ˈdɜːti/ [adj] not clean: *Look how dirty your hands are!* | *dirty clothes* | *The children had made dirty fingermarks on the wall.*
get dirty (=become dirty) *This carpet's getting very dirty – it needs cleaning.*
get sth dirty (=make it dirty) *I don't want to get my new shoes dirty.*
dirty – dirtier – dirtiest

filthy /ˈfɪlθi/ [adj] extremely dirty: *We didn't go swimming because the water looked filthy.* | *She put the cake into the filthiest, greasiest oven he had ever seen.*
absolutely filthy *You ought to wash your jeans – they're absolutely filthy.*
filthy – filthier – filthiest

muddy /ˈmʌdi/ [adj] covered in mud: *Take off your muddy boots.* | *She left a trail of muddy footprints behind her.* | *a muddy field*
muddy – muddier – muddiest

dusty /ˈdʌsti/ [adj] a **dusty** room, piece of furniture etc is covered in dust, especially because no-one has cleaned it for a long time: *The room was dark and dusty.* | *dusty shelves*
dusty – dustier – dustiest

greasy /ˈgriːsi, -zi/ [adj] something that is **greasy** looks dirty because it has an oily substance on it: *She had long greasy black hair.* | *He wiped his hands on a greasy cloth.*
greasy – greasier – greasiest

dingy /ˈdɪndʒi/ [adj] a **dingy** room, street, or building is dirty, dark, and in bad condition: *Marlowe's dingy little office was in a run-down block near the station.*
dingy – dingier – dingiest

2 dirty and bad for your health

➡ see also **ENVIRONMENT**

unhygienic /ˌʌnhaɪˈdʒiːnɪk◀‖-ˈdʒen-, -ˈdʒiːn-/ [adj] likely to cause disease – use this about dirty conditions in kitchens, restaurants, and hospitals: *It is unhygienic to store raw and cooked meats together.* | *Operations are carried out under the most unhygienic conditions.*

polluted /pə'luːt̬d/ [adj] water or air that is **polluted** has a lot of harmful waste or poisonous chemicals in it: *an effort to clean up Britain's polluted rivers*
+ with/by *Parts of the Mediterranean are polluted with toxic waste.*
heavily polluted (=very badly polluted) *The air is heavily polluted with exhaust fumes.*

contaminated /kən'tæmɪ̯neɪt̬d/ [adj] food, water, or land that is **contaminated** is not safe to use or be in because dangerous chemicals or bacteria have come into it: *contaminated drinking water*
+ with/by *Milk contaminated with lead has been on sale in the supermarkets.*
heavily contaminated (=very badly contaminated) *Crops cannot be grown in the heavily contaminated soil around Chernobyl.*

3 something that makes things dirty

dirt /dɜːʳt/ [n U] dust, mud, or anything else that makes things dirty: *She rubbed some dirt off the glass with her finger.* | *I've washed that shirt twice, but I can't get the dirt out.*

dust /dʌst/ [n U] dry powder that forms a layer on furniture, floors, clothes etc, especially when they have not been cleaned for a long time: *There was a thick layer of dust on the shelves.* | *Max brushed the dust off his coat.*

> ⚠ Don't say 'a lot of dusts'. Say **a lot of dust**. Dust has no plural form.

mud /mʌd/ [n U] very wet earth that sticks to your shoes, clothes, car, tyres etc: *Look! There's mud all over the carpet.* | *Hayley scraped the dried mud off her boots.*
be covered in mud *Their expensive riding jackets were covered in mud.*

pollution /pə'luːʃən/ [n U] the harmful effects on water, air, or land of chemicals and waste from factories, cars, modern farming methods etc: *Industrial pollution has killed all the fish in the river.* | *We*

moved to the country to get away from all the crime and pollution in Los Angeles.

DISABLED
when someone cannot use part of their body

1 disabled

disabled /dɪs'eɪbəld/ [adj] someone who is **disabled** cannot use part of their body normally, for example their legs or their arms: *David goes to a special school for disabled children.* | *Her son is disabled and she has to take care of him all the time.*
the disabled (=disabled people) *new laws to protect the rights of the disabled*
disabled toilets/parking etc (=special toilets, parking etc for disabled people)

handicapped /'hændɪkæpt/ [adj] someone who is **handicapped** has serious difficulty using part of their body or their mind, and this makes it difficult for them to have a normal life: *She works with handicapped teenagers.*
mentally handicapped (=handicapped in the mind) *a school for mentally handicapped children*
visually handicapped (=blind or partly blind)

special needs /ˌspeʃəl 'niːdz/ [n plural] people with **special needs** need different teaching methods, special equipment etc because they have physical or mental problems – used especially by people who work with children like this: *a school for children with special needs*
plural **disabilities**

disability /ˌdɪsə'bɪlɪ̯ti/ [n C/U] a problem with part of your body which makes it difficult for you to walk, talk, see etc: *There are special courses for people with disabilities.* | *His disability didn't stop him from becoming a world-class scientist.*

2 not disabled

able-bodied /ˌeɪbəl 'bɒdid◄-'bɑː-/ [adj] not disabled – use this when you are comparing disabled people with people who are not disabled: *Disabled students face different problems from their able-bodied friends.*

DISAGREE

➡ opposite **AGREE**

see also

OPINIONS · **ARGUE** · **SAYING NO** · **CRITICIZE** · **COMPLAIN** · **COMPLAINING** · **DISAGREEING**

1 to have a different opinion from someone else

disagree/not agree /ˌdɪsəˈɡriː, ˌnɒt əˈɡriː/ [v I] to have a different opinion from someone else: *This is what I'm suggesting. If you don't agree, just say so.* | *Anthea thought they should move to a bigger apartment, but Jim disagreed.*
+ with *You'll probably disagree with me, but I think we should sell the car.* | *They say the problem is caused by bad teaching, but I don't agree with that.*
+ about *Experts disagree about the effects of global warming.*

⚠ Don't say 'I am disagreeing', 'I am not agreeing etc'. Say **I disagree, I don't agree** etc.

⚠ If you want to say that two people disagree with each other, you can just say **they disagree** or **they don't agree**: *Bill and Larry disagreed about almost everything.*

⚠ Don't say 'I disagree to this idea' or 'I disagree this idea'. Say **I disagree with this idea.**

not see eye to eye /ˌnɒt siː ˌaɪ tʊ ˈaɪ/ ESPECIALLY SPOKEN if two people do **not see eye to eye** they have very different opinions and ideas, so that it is difficult for them to be friends or to work together
+ on/about *Unfortunately, Sally and I don't see eye to eye on money matters.*
+ with *She never saw eye to eye with her daughter-in-law.*

be divided/be split /biː dɪˈvaɪdɪd, biː ˈsplɪt/ if a group of people **is divided** or **is split** over something, some of them support one opinion and others support the opposite opinion
+ over/on *The country's leaders appear to be split on the question of tax cuts.* | *Voters are bitterly divided over the issue of gun control.*

contradict /ˌkɒntrəˈdɪkt, ˌkɑːn-/ [v T] to say that what someone has just said is wrong: *Don't contradict your father.* | *One of his students contradicted something he said, and he got really angry.*

2 a situation in which people disagree

disagreement /ˌdɪsəˈɡriːmənt/ [n C/U] when people disagree with each other
+ about/over *Disagreement over who should produce the next album caused the band to split.*
+ between/among *There is some disagreement among medical experts about the best treatment for back pain.*
have a disagreement with sb (=disagree and argue with them) *She had a disagreement with her boss – that's why she's upset.*

difference of opinion /ˌdɪfrəns əv əˈpɪnjən/ [n C] when people are unable to agree, especially about something important – use this as a way of avoiding more direct words like 'argument' and 'disagreement'
+ between/among *There were reports of a slight difference of opinion between the President and his advisers.*
+ about/over *Major differences of opinion over who should command the UN forces in Bosnia.*
plural **differences of opinion**

controversy /ˈkɒntrəvɜːsi, kənˈtrɒvəsi, ˈkɑːntrəˌvɜːrsi/ [n C/U] serious disagreement about a decision, plan, or action, which causes arguments for a long time in the newspapers, on television etc: *Controversy surrounds the TV show, which many consider to be racist, sexist, and homophobic.*
+ over *The controversy over the nuclear energy program is likely to continue.*
plural **controversies**

deadlock/stalemate /'dedlɒk, 'steɪl-meɪt‖-lɑːk/ [n U singular] a situation in which two groups disagree with each other, and no agreement is possible because each group refuses to change its mind: *After two weeks, the discussions reached complete deadlock.* | *The long-running dispute ended in a stalemate.*

> ⚠ **Deadlock** and **stalemate** are used especially in news reports and newspapers.

3 causing disagreement

controversial /ˌkɒntrə'vɜːrʃəl◀‖ˌkɑːn-/ [adj] something that is **controversial** causes a lot of disagreement and angry argument, especially in the newspapers, on television etc: *'Devil's Night' is a controversial new book about race relations in the city of Detroit.*

controversial issue (=a subject that many people disagree about) *Abortion is the most controversial issue in the US right now.*

DISAPPEAR

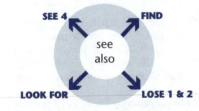

SEE 4   FIND

see also

LOOK FOR   LOSE 1 & 2

1 when you can't find someone or something

disappear /ˌdɪsə'pɪər/ [v I] if someone or something **disappears**, you cannot find them: *Where are my keys? They seem to have disappeared.*

+ from *The money had disappeared from the table.*

disappear without trace (=disappear and never be found again) *The plane disappeared without trace, and no survivors were ever found.*

> **disappearance** [n U] when someone or something disappears: *Her sudden disappearance was very worrying.*

> ⚠ Don't say 'he was disappeared', 'they are disappeared' etc. Say **he disappeared, they have disappeared** etc.

> ⚠ If you say that a person **has disappeared**, this can mean either that you do not know where they are at the moment, or that they have been taken away by someone and they may be in danger: *"Where's Tom?" "I don't know – he's disappeared."* | *A 12-year-old boy disappeared from his home in Kansas City last night.*

vanish /'vænɪʃ/ [v I] if someone or something **vanishes**, you suddenly cannot find them and you cannot understand what has happened to them: *When she returned, her car had vanished.*

vanish into thin air (=vanish in a way that seems impossible) *I don't know where my pen has gone. It seems to have vanished into thin air.*

go missing /ˌgəʊ 'mɪsɪŋ/ ESPECIALLY BRITISH if someone **goes missing**, they cannot be found anywhere, and they may be in danger: *Angela Priest went missing one year ago.*

+ from *The police were called after a six-year-old girl went missing from a playground near her home.*

2 to become impossible to see

disappear /ˌdɪsə'pɪər/ [v I] if someone or something **disappears**, you cannot see them any more

+ behind/under/into/over etc *The sun disappeared behind a cloud.* | *She watched the boat sail out to sea until it disappeared over the horizon.*

vanish /'vænɪʃ/ [v I] to disappear suddenly and in a way that cannot be explained: *Jake thought he saw a woman at the window, but when he looked again she had vanished.*

+ into/behind/under etc *A strange light appeared and then vanished again into the darkness.*

DISAPPOINTING/ DISAPPOINTED

unhappy because things did not happen in the way that you hoped

➡ see also **SATISFIED/DISSATISFIED**

1 disappointed

disappointed /ˌdɪsəˈpɔɪntɪd◄/ [adj] unhappy because things did not happen in the way you hoped they would, or were not as good as you expected them to be: *I felt a little disappointed when she didn't come to the party.* | *The hall was already full, and hundreds of disappointed fans were turned away at the door.*

+ with/by *Were you disappointed with the way you played today?*

+ that *The children were very disappointed that we couldn't go to the zoo.*

disappointed to find/learn/hear/see *We were disappointed to find that the museum was closed.*

bitterly disappointed (=very disappointed) *Backley was bitterly disappointed when an injury prevented him from competing in the Olympic Games.*

disappointment [n U] the feeling of being disappointed: *She couldn't hide her disappointment when David told her he wasn't coming.*

feel let down /fiːl ˌlet ˈdaʊn/ to feel disappointed because someone did not do what they promised to do, or did not help you when you needed them: *No wonder the nurses feel let down – they were promised a big pay increase, but nothing has happened.*

disillusioned /ˌdɪsɪˈluːʒənd◄/ [adj] you feel **disillusioned** when you realize that a person, belief, way of life etc is not as good as you thought they were: *Disillusioned voters are turning against the government.*

+ with *After three years of war, the army was becoming disillusioned with its leaders.*

2 something that makes you feel disappointed

disappointing /ˌdɪsəˈpɔɪntɪŋ◄/ [adj] something that is **disappointing** makes you feel slightly unhappy or dissatisfied, because it is not as good as you hoped it would be: *The team had a disappointing season.* | *Company profits this year have been very disappointing.*

be a disappointment /biː ə ˌdɪsəˈpɔɪntmənt/ something that **is a disappointment** does not happen in the way you hoped, or is not as good as you expected: *The holiday was a bit of a disappointment – it rained the whole time.*

+ to *Failing the test was a real disappointment to me.*

be a great disappointment *It was a great disappointment to my parents that I didn't go to university.*

not live up to expectations /nɒt lɪv ˌʌp tʊ ekspekˈteɪʃənz/ if an event or person **does not live up to expectations**, you expected them to be very good but in fact they are not: *I'm afraid as a husband I never really lived up to Kelly's expectations.*

be a letdown /biː ə ˈletdaʊn/ SPOKEN if something **is a letdown**, you do not enjoy it as much as you expected to: *The party was a real letdown.*

3 to make someone feel disappointed

disappoint /ˌdɪsəˈpɔɪnt/ [v T] to make someone feel disappointed: *I'm sorry to disappoint you, but there aren't any tickets left.*

let sb down /ˌlet (sb) ˈdaʊn/ [phrasal verb T] if someone **lets you down**, they do not do what they promised to do, or they do not behave as well as you expected them to: *I said I would help them – I can't let them down.*

let sb down badly *Many disabled soldiers feel the government has let them down very badly.*

DISHONEST

➡ opposite **HONEST**
➡ see also **CHEAT, LIE 2, TRICK/DECEIVE, TRUST/NOT TRUST**

D

1 dishonest

dishonest /dɪs'ɒnɪst‖-'ɑː-/ [adj] someone who is **dishonest** tells lies or tries to trick people or steal things: *a dishonest car salesman* | *dishonest practices among financial dealers* | *I'm sure you can trust Bob – he wouldn't do anything dishonest.*

dishonestly [adv] *He was accused of dishonestly obtaining an American passport.*

you can't trust sb /juː kɑːnt 'trʌst (sb)‖-kænt-/ SPOKEN say this about someone when you think that they may tell lies or try to trick you: *You can't trust the tobacco companies – they'll say anything to protect their business.*

unscrupulous /ʌn'skruːpjʊləs/ [adj] someone who is **unscrupulous** uses dishonest and unfair methods to get what they want, and does not care if they cause problems for other people: *Some unscrupulous employers hire illegal immigrants to work for very low wages.* | *unscrupulous landlords*

corrupt /kə'rʌpt/ [adj] a **corrupt** politician, official, or police officer uses their power in a dishonest way for their own advantage, for example by accepting money from people in return for helping them: *Corrupt customs officials allowed the drug trade to continue.*

devious /'diːviəs/ [adj] someone who is **devious** tries to get what they want by secretly using clever plans to trick people, so you can never be sure what their real intentions are: *a devious politician* | *one of Stalin's devious schemes*

suspicious /sə'spɪʃəs/ [adj] use this about behaviour or situations that make you think that someone is doing something dishonest: *It seems very suspicious to me. Where did he get all that money from?*

suspicious-looking *There was a suspicious-looking character standing in a doorway across the street.*

suspiciously [adv] *If you notice anyone behaving suspiciously, call the police.*

sneaky /'sniːki/ [adj] INFORMAL someone who is **sneaky** does things secretly and tricks people in order to get what they want: *the sneaky type of guy, who pretends to be nice and friendly just so he can steal all your ideas*

sneaky – sneakier – sneakiest

2 dishonest behaviour

dishonesty /dɪs'ɒnɪsti‖-'ɑː-/ [n U] dishonest behaviour: *Are you accusing me of dishonesty?* | *If a lawyer is suspected of dishonesty, he risks losing his job.*

corruption /kə'rʌpʃən/ [n U] when someone who works for the government, the police etc uses their power dishonestly to get money or gain an advantage: *The chief of police was forced to resign after allegations of corruption.*

bribery /'braɪbəri/ [n U] when someone offers money to a politician or government official in order to persuade them to do something: *US firms used bribery to win contracts.* | *a massive bribery scandal involving dozens of politicians*

bribery and corruption *The General promised to end bribery and corruption in the government.*

graft /ɡrɑːft‖ɡræft/ [n U] AMERICAN dishonest behaviour by politicians who accept money from companies in return for helping them: *Mayor Stevens was in court yesterday facing charges of graft and tax evasion.*

DO

➡ see also **REFUSE, AGREE 4, LET**

1 to do something

do /duː/ [v T] *"What are you doing?" "I'm trying to fix the television."*

do work/housework/homework *95% of housework is done by women.* | *I did a lot of work in the garden today.*

do the washing/cooking/shopping etc *His mother still does all his washing.*

do a test/exam/course etc *He's doing an art course at Wrexham College.*

do sth well/badly *She enjoys her job and she does it very well.*

doing – did – have done

achieve /əˈtʃiːv/ [v T] to succeed in doing something good or getting the result that you wanted, after trying hard for a long time: *At the age of 40, he felt he had achieved nothing in his life.* | *She was determined to become a pilot, and finally achieved her goal.*

carry out /ˌkæri ˈaʊt/ [phrasal verb T] to do something – use this only with these words:

carry out tests/research/a survey/a search (=do something that needs to be planned and organized) *Scientists are carrying out research into the effects of this drug.* | *Police carried out a thorough search of the building.*

carry out sb's orders / instructions / wishes (=do what someone told you to do) *The porter refused to let anyone into the building, but he was only carrying out orders.*

carry out a threat/promise (=do what you said you would do) *The terrorists carried out their threat and shot two of the hostages.*

commit /kəˈmɪt/ [v T] **commit a crime/murder/robbery etc** to do something that is a crime, especially a serious crime: *Women commit far fewer crimes than men.* | *The murder must have been committed between 7 and 10pm.*

committing – committed – have committed

perform /pərˈfɔːrm/ [v T] FORMAL **perform a duty/operation/task** to do a duty, operation, or piece of work: *The operation was performed by a team of surgeons at Addenbrookes Hospital.* | *Computers perform several tasks at the same time.*

⊙get on with sth /get ˈɒn wɪð (sth)‖ -ˈɑːn-/ [phrasal verb T] ESPECIALLY SPOKEN to start doing something that you should have started already, or that you have stopped doing for a short time: *Stop talking and get on with your work.*

get on with doing sth *As soon as the rain stops, I'll get on with painting the fence.*

⊙be up to something /biː ˈʌp tə ˌsʌmθɪn/ ESPECIALLY SPOKEN if someone **is up to something**, they are doing something but you do not know exactly what it is, and you think it is probably something bad: *There's a lot of whispering in the kitchen. I think the kids must be up to something.* | *I wish I knew what he was up to!*

2 to do something in order to deal with a bad situation

do something /ˈduː ˌsʌmθɪn/ to do something to deal with a problem, especially one that is urgent: *Quick, do something – there's water all over the floor!*

+ about *Street crime is becoming a real problem. It's time the police did something about it.*

intervene /ˌɪntərˈviːn/ [v I] to do something to try to stop people from fighting or quarrelling with each other: *After a few hours the police intervened to stop the rioting.*

+ in *The US finally intervened in the war in Bosnia.*

take action /ˌteɪk ˈækʃən/ to do something to stop a bad situation from happening or continuing – use this to talk about people in powerful positions, when they have a clear plan for dealing with a problem: *Unless governments take action soon, the Earth's atmosphere will be damaged forever.*

take action to do sth *Governments must take action to end the trade in rare and endangered animals.*

+ against *The school will take strong action against any students using illegal drugs.*

3 something that someone does

thing /θɪn/ [n C] something that someone does – always use this with the verb **do**: *The first thing you should do is connect the computer to the printer.*

a stupid/clever/difficult etc thing to do *You left your bag on the train? What a stupid thing to do!* | *It's a very dangerous thing to do.*

action /ˈækʃən/ [n C] FORMAL something that someone does: *Lavender's actions had been stupid, but he had not intended any harm.*

course of action (=something that you could do in order to deal with a situation) *There was only one possible course of action – he had to kill Siltz.*

⚠️ Don't use 'do' with **action**: *I think you did the right thing* (not 'action'). **Action** is rather formal, and it is more usual to say **thing** to talk about what someone does.

D

activities /ækˈtɪvɪtiz/ [n plural] things that people do, especially things people do as a group, for work or for pleasure: *Rebecca has always loved horse riding and other outdoor activities.* | *Police are investigating the company's business activities.*

leisure/social/cultural activities *The school arranges social activities for students to take part in at the weekends.*

achievement /əˈtʃiːvmənt/ [n C] something you succeed in doing after trying hard, especially something that is difficult to do and that other people admire: *We opened a bottle of champagne to celebrate our achievement.*

great / remarkable / tremendous achievement (=one that you admire a lot) *They sold over 20 million copies of their album in the US, which is a tremendous achievement.*

4 to not do something that you should do

not do sth /nɒt ˈduː (sth)/ *The translation? I'm sorry, I haven't done it yet.* | *She was terrified that he would hurt her if she didn't do what he said.*

fail to do sth /ˌfeɪl tə ˈduː (sth)/ FORMAL to not do something that you should do, especially when this has serious results: *The driver of the car failed to stop in time, and the boy was killed.*

do nothing/not do anything /ˌduː ˈnʌθɪŋ, nɒt duː ˈeniθɪŋ/ to not try to help someone or prevent a bad situation, even though you know it is happening: *He admitted he had seen the attack and done nothing.*

+ about *We told the police months ago, but they still haven't done anything about it.*

+ to help/stop/prevent sth *No-one in the company did anything to stop this disaster from happening.*

🗨**not bother** /nɒt ˈbɒðəʳ‖-ˈbɑː-/ ESPECIALLY SPOKEN to not do something because it does not seem important or necessary

don't bother *"Would you like me to wait for you?" "No, don't bother."*

not bother to do sth *He didn't even bother to tell me he was going to be late.*

leave /liːv/ [v T] to not do something now because you can do it later: *If you can't answer a question, leave it and go on to the next one.*

leave sth for now *Leave the details for now, we'll deal with them later.*

leave sth till later/tomorrow/next week etc *Can we leave the washing till tomorrow?*

leaving – left – have left

give sth a miss /ˌgɪv (sth) ə ˈmɪs/ BRITISH INFORMAL to decide not to do something that you had planned to do, for example because you are too tired: *I think I'll give my exercise class a miss tonight – I'm worn out.*

5 to not do anything

have nothing to do /hæv ˌnʌθɪŋ tə ˈduː/ if you **have nothing to do**, there is nothing interesting for you to do and you feel bored: *I get depressed if I have nothing to do.*

with nothing to do *She was sick of sitting around at home with nothing to do.*

sit around/stand around /ˌsɪt əˈraʊnd, ˌstænd əˈraʊnd/ [phrasal verb I] to sit or stand somewhere for a long time, feeling bored, when you are waiting for something to happen or when you are just being lazy: *I spent the whole morning sitting around waiting for news.* | *A group of teenagers were standing around outside the station.*

🗨**just sit there/just stand there** /dʒʌst ˈsɪt ðeəʳ, dʒʌst ˈstænd ðeəʳ/ SPOKEN to do nothing helpful or useful, especially when you should do something: *The rabbit's escaped! Don't just stand there – do something!* | *When the fire alarm went off she just sat there as if she hadn't heard a thing.*

DOCTOR

ILLNESS/DISEASE

ILL/SICK

MEDICAL TREATMENT

see also

PAIN

BETTER 4

MENTALLY ILL

HEALTHY/ UNHEALTHY

1 doctor

doctor /'dɒktər‖'dɑːk-/ [n C] someone who is trained to treat people who are ill: *Sylvia's met a really nice man – he's a doctor.*

see a doctor about sth *I think you should see a doctor about your cough.*

⚠ Don't say 'I want to be doctor' or 'he is doctor'. Say **I want to be a doctor** or **he is a doctor**.

⚠ The written abbreviation **Dr** is used before the name of a doctor: *Dr Anderson is an expert in tropical diseases.*

physician /fɪ'zɪʃən/ [n C] AMERICAN FORMAL a doctor: *My physician told me to stop smoking.* | *His parents are both physicians in a busy hospital.*

GP /ˌdʒiː 'piː/ [n C] BRITISH a doctor who is trained to treat all kinds of illnesses, and treats people who live in one local area: *I went to my GP and she prescribed antibiotics.*

⚠ GP is short for **General Practitioner**.

the medical profession /ðə 'medɪkəl prəˌfeʃən/ [n singular] FORMAL doctors, nurses, and other people who treat people who are ill

⚠ In British English, you can use **the medical profession** with a singular or plural verb: *The medical profession is unhappy/are unhappy about the changes.*

2 the place where you go to see a doctor

the doctor's BRITISH **the doctor's office** AMERICAN /ðə 'dɒktəz, ðə ˌdɒktəz 'ɒfɪs‖-'dɑːk-/ [n singular] SPOKEN the place

where a doctor works, where people who are ill can go at certain times to be examined: *You'd better go to the doctor's if your sore throat doesn't get any better.*

clinic /'klɪnɪk/ [n C] in the US, a place where several doctors have offices; in Britain, a place where people can go for advice about a specific medical condition: *a family-planning clinic* | *a clinic for people with alcohol problems*

health centre BRITISH **health center** AMERICAN /'helθ ˌsentər/ [n C] in Britain, a building where several doctors have offices and people can go to see them for treatment; in the US, a similar place in a college or university, where the students can go to see a doctor

surgery /'sɜːrdʒəri/ [n C] BRITISH the office where a doctor works, where people can go to be examined and treated: *The waiting room at the surgery was full of people with colds and flu.*

plural **surgeries**

3 a doctor with special knowledge of particular illnesses

specialist /'speʃəlɪst/ [n C] a doctor who has a lot of special knowledge about one type of illness or one part of the body: *His doctor sent him to see a specialist.*

heart/eye/skin etc specialist *a heart specialist*

surgeon /'sɜːrdʒən/ [n C] a doctor who does operations in a hospital: *Her operation was performed by a well-known surgeon.*

consultant /kən'sʌltənt/ [n C] BRITISH an important hospital doctor who has a lot of knowledge about one type of medical treatment: *The consultant told Jean that an operation was necessary to save her life.*

4 a doctor who treats people who have mental or emotional problems

psychiatrist /saɪ'kaɪətrɪst‖sə-/ [n C] a doctor who treats people who are mentally ill

analyst /'ænəlɪst/ [n C] ESPECIALLY AMERICAN a doctor who treats people with mental or emotional problems, by talking with them about their experiences and feelings

5 a doctor who treats people's teeth

dentist /'dentˌst/ [n C] someone who is trained to treat people's teeth: *I'm going to the dentist tomorrow, just for a check-up.*

6 a doctor who treats animals

vet /vet/ [n C] someone who is trained to give medical treatment to animals: *The cat's not well – I'll have to take her to the vet.*

DON'T CARE

when you do not care what happens or what someone does

1 to not care because something is not important to you

don't care /ˌdəʊnt 'keəʳ/ if you **don't care** about something, it is not important to you: *"What do you think I should do?" "I don't care. Do what you want."*
don't care what/whether/if etc *Just pay me the money by tomorrow – I don't care how you get it.* | *I like George, and I don't care what anyone else thinks about him.*
+ about *She doesn't care about anything except money.*

◯who cares?/so what? /ˌhuː 'keəʳz, ˌsəʊ 'wɒt/ SPOKEN INFORMAL say this when you do not care about something, because you do not think it is important at all: *"Phil was really mad when he heard what you'd done." "So what? It's none of his business."* | *I ought to be working really, but who cares?*

◯couldn't care less /ˌkʊdnt keəʳ 'les/ SPOKEN INFORMAL to not care at all about something. Say **I couldn't care less** when you feel annoyed. Say another person **couldn't care less** when you think they are behaving in a rude or unkind way: *"Do you know what Rita told me?" "I really couldn't care less."*

couldn't care less what/whether etc She does whatever she likes and couldn't care less what other people think.
+ about *To be honest, I couldn't care less about her stupid problems.*

◯it's not my problem /ˌɪts nɒt 'maɪ ˌprɒbləm‖-ˌprɑːb-/ SPOKEN INFORMAL say this when you do not care about a problem or difficult situation, because you will not have to deal with it: *"How am I going to explain this to my parents?" "Sorry, it's not my problem."*

2 to not care because you will be happy with whatever happens

don't mind /ˌdəʊnt 'maɪnd/ to not care because you will be happy with whatever happens or with whatever someone decides: *"What would you like to do tonight?" "I don't mind. You decide."*
don't mind where/what/how etc *Honestly, I don't mind whether Linda comes with us or not.* | *Bill was just happy to be with her, and he didn't mind where they went.*

> ⚠ Don't say 'I don't mind it'. Just say **I don't mind.**

◯it makes no difference to me /ɪt ˌmeɪks nəʊ ˌdɪfərəns tə 'miː/ SPOKEN say this when you do not mind what happens because it does not affect you or cause you any problems: *You can come on Thursday or Friday – it makes no difference to me.*

◯I'm easy /aɪm 'iːzi/ SPOKEN INFORMAL say this when someone asks you which of two things you would prefer and you want to say that you do not mind: *"Do you want to stay in, or go out for a meal?" "I'm easy – what do you want to do?"*

3 someone who does not seem to care

unconcerned /ˌʌnkən'sɜːʳnd/ [adj not before noun] not worried or not caring about something, especially when this is surprising: *They threatened to fire him from his job, but he seemed quite unconcerned.*
+ about *Many large companies remain completely unconcerned about the environment.*

indifferent /ɪnˈdɪfərənt/ [adj not before noun] not seeming to care about what is happening, especially about other people's problems or feelings: *My mother never cared about us. She was cold and indifferent.*
+ to *He's completely indifferent to her concerns about their baby's future.*

apathetic /ˌæpəˈθetɪk◄/ [adj] not interested in anything, or not caring about anything and not making any effort to change or improve things: *The students here aren't really apathetic – they just don't believe anyone will listen to what they say.*
+ about *Many young people have now become totally apathetic about politics.*

DOWN

➡ if you mean 'a price or number goes down', go to **LESS**
➡ if you want to know about other prepositions, go to ▣ **POSITION & DIRECTION**
➡ opposite **UP**

1 towards a lower position

down /daʊn/ [adv/prep] to a lower position or place: *Tears ran down his face.* | *I told you not to climb on the table. Get down!*
+ into/to/from/off *He's gone down to the basement to get some more beer.* | *The accident happened when we were coming down off the mountain.*
look/glance/gaze down *The doctor glanced down at the notepad on his desk.*

downwards ESPECIALLY BRITISH (also **downward** ESPECIALLY AMERICAN) /ˈdaʊn-wəʳd(z)/ [adv] moving, looking, or pointing towards a lower level or towards the ground: *a path winding downwards through the trees to the valley below* | *He was gazing downward into the pit.*
  downward [adj only before noun] *a gentle downward slope*

downhill /ˌdaʊnˈhɪl◄/ [adv] if you move, walk, or drive **downhill**, you go down a slope: *We set off downhill towards the lake.* | *After we get to the top, it'll be downhill all the way to Bakersfield.*

downstairs /ˌdaʊnˈsteəʳz◄/ [adv] down towards a lower floor of a building: *She said goodnight to the children and went downstairs.* | *Uncle Eric had fallen downstairs.*

2 to go down

go down /ˌgəʊ ˈdaʊn/ [phrasal verb I/T] to go down some stairs, a ladder, a slope etc: *You go down a steep slope, then turn left at the bottom of the hill.* | *Right, here's the ladder. Who's going down first?* | *I'll go down to the kitchen and get you a glass of water.*

fall /fɔːl/ [v I] to come down through the air from a higher place: *Don't stand on that ledge – you might fall.*
+ from/down/on etc *Leaves were falling from the tree.* | *Two bombs fell on the parliament building.*
falling – fell – have fallen

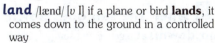
fall

land /lænd/ [v I] if a plane or bird **lands**, it comes down to the ground in a controlled way
+ in/on/at *We will be landing at Singapore airport at 3am local time.* | *A flock of geese landed on the river in front of us.*

⚠ Say that a plane **lands** when it reaches the ground in the normal way. If you say that a plane **came down** somewhere, you mean it crashed: *One of the aircraft came down in the ocean off the Florida Keys.*

descend /dɪˈsend/ [v I/T] WRITTEN to go down a slope, a mountain etc slowly and carefully: *We descended into the cave by a rope ladder.* | *Slowly the two climbers descended the cliff face.*

⚠ Use **descend** when you are writing stories or describing past events.

3 to go down under the water

sink

sink /sɪŋk/ [v I] to go down below the surface of water, mud, sand etc without being able to control or prevent it: *Hundreds of passengers tried to escape as the ferry started to sink.*

+ into *The heavy trucks were sinking deeper and deeper into the mud.*

sinking – sank – have sunk

> ⚠ Don't use **sink** about people who go down below the surface of the sea or a river. Use **drown** if they do this accidentally, or **dive** if they deliberately go down under the water.

dive /daɪv/ [v I] to jump head-first down into water: *She stood at the edge of the pool waiting to dive.*

dive

+ into/in *Ralph dived into the icy water.* | *A woman dived in to rescue the boy.*

diving – dived (also **dove** AMERICAN) **– have dived**

dive [n C] an act of diving: *She did a perfect dive from the top board.*

4 when the sun goes down

go down/set /ˌgəʊ ˈdaʊn, set/ [v I] if the sun **goes down** or **sets** at the end of the day, it moves downwards in the sky until it cannot be seen: *We sat on the balcony and watched the sun go down.* | *The sun was setting and the sky was red.*

setting – set – have set

sunset /ˈsʌnset/ [n C/U] the time when the sun goes down: *Everyone stopped work at sunset.* | *You get beautiful sunsets in Hawaii.*

5 to let something go down

drop /drɒp‖drɑːp/ [v T] if you **drop** something that you are holding, it suddenly falls from your hands: *You've dropped your handkerchief.* | *Be careful not to drop that bowl, it's very valuable.*

drop

dropping – dropped – have dropped

put down /ˌpʊt ˈdaʊn/ [phrasal verb T] to put something that you are holding down onto the ground or onto a surface

put down sth *Putting down her book, Sally stood up to greet us.*

put sth down *Put that gun down now!*

lower /ˈləʊəʳ/ [v T] to let something you are holding, or a part of your body, move slowly downwards: *The coffin was lowered slowly into the ground.*

lower your head/arms/body *Lowering its head, the bull charged at him.*

lower yourself into/onto sth (=move slowly and carefully downwards, using your hands for support) *The old man lowered himself wearily into his chair.*

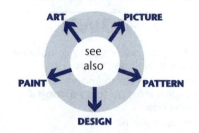

DRAW

ART PICTURE

see also

PAINT PATTERN

DESIGN

1 to draw a picture, pattern, line etc

draw /drɔː/ [v I/T] to make a picture, pattern, line etc using a pen or pencil: *What are you drawing?* | *She can draw really well.*

draw a picture of sb/sth *The teacher asked us to draw a picture of someone we know.*

draw a line/circle/square etc *Someone had drawn a line under my name.*

drawing – drew – have drawn

sketch /sketʃ/ [v I/T] to make a quick, simple drawing of a person, place etc, without many details: *Valerie sketched the view from her hotel window.* | *He sat by the river, sketching.*

doodle /ˈduːdl/ [v I] to draw shapes, lines, or patterns without thinking about what you are doing, while you are doing something else or when you feel bored: *I always doodle on my notepad while I'm on the phone.*

> When you see **EC**, go to the **ESSENTIAL COMMUNICATION** section.

2 something that you draw

drawing /'drɔːɪŋ/ [n C] a picture that you draw with a pen or pencil: *an original drawing by Pablo Picasso*
do a drawing of sb/sth *I did a drawing of the church.*

sketch /sketʃ/ [n C] a quick, simple drawing that does not show any details
do/draw a sketch *Phil drew a sketch to show us what the new school would look like.*
rough sketch (=a quick sketch that is not done very carefully)
plural **sketches**

DREAM

➡ see also **SLEEP, WAKE UP/GET UP, IMAGINE**

1 a dream

dream /driːm/ [n C] a series of thoughts, images, and experiences that come into your mind while you are asleep: *I can never remember my dreams when I wake up.*
have a dream *I had a strange dream last night – I was walking through the town with no clothes on.*
bad dream (=an unpleasant or frightening dream)

nightmare /'naɪtmeəʳ/ [n C] a very unpleasant and frightening dream: *I woke from the nightmare screaming.*
have a nightmare *Jim's been having nightmares about falling off a cliff.*

daydream /'deɪdriːm/ [n C] a series of pleasant thoughts and scenes that come into your mind while you are awake, so that you do not notice what is happening around you: *Neil seemed lost in a daydream and didn't hear what I said.*

2 to have a dream

have a dream /ˌhæv ə 'driːm/ to imagine something while you are asleep: *I had a dream that I was falling off a cliff.*

dream /driːm/ [v I/T] to have a dream or have dreams: *The dog must be dreaming – he keeps making funny noises!*

+ (that) *She often dreamt that she was back in India.*
+ about *I dreamt about you last night.*
dreaming – dreamt – have dreamt
ESPECIALLY BRITISH
dreaming – dreamed – have dreamed
ESPECIALLY AMERICAN

daydream /'deɪdriːm/ [v I] to think pleasant thoughts when you are awake, especially when you should be thinking about something else: *Stop daydreaming and pay attention to what I'm saying.*
+ about *Brian began to daydream about what he would do if he won the money.*

DRINK

1 to drink something

drink /drɪŋk/ [v I/T] to take liquid into your mount and swallow it: *Drink your coffee before it gets cold.* | *"What would you like to drink?" "Orange juice, please."*
drink from a cup/bottle *He didn't ask for a glass, he just drank straight from the bottle.*
drink up (=finish your drink) *Drink up your tea so that I can wash the cups.* | *Come on, drink up and we'll go home.*
drinking – drank – have drunk

> ⚠ We do not usually use the verb **drink** with objects like 'a cup of tea' or 'a glass of milk'. We usually say **have**: *After the class, we had a cup of coffee* (not 'we drank a cup of coffee').

have /hæv/ [v T] to have a drink of something
have a cup of tea/a glass of milk/a beer etc *I'm going to have a cup of coffee, do you want one?* | *I had a coke with my pizza.*

have a drink of sth *Can I have a drink of water please?*

having – had – have had

take /teɪk/ [v T] to drink a small amount or a single mouthful of something: *The patient still isn't well enough to eat, but he's taken a little water.*

take a sip/mouthful/gulp etc *He took a long swig (=drink) from the brandy bottle.*

sip /sɪp/ [v T] to drink something slowly, in very small amounts: *Sue sat at the bar sipping a Martini.*

sipping – sipped – have sipped

gulp down /ˌɡʌlp ˈdaʊn/ [phrasal verb T] to swallow a large amount of drink quickly

gulp down sth *'I'm coming,' said Mary, gulping down her tea.*

gulp sth down *He gulped his beer down and dashed out of the door.*

2 something that you drink

drink /drɪŋk/ [n C/U] something that you drink: *"Would you like a drink?" "Yes, I'll have some lemonade please."*

a drink of milk/water etc *Give the children a drink of milk and something to eat.*

food and drink(s) (=things to eat and drink) *You can bring your own food and drink to the picnic.*

○**something to drink** /ˌsʌmθɪŋ tə ˈdrɪŋk/ ESPECIALLY SPOKEN a drink: *I'm really thirsty. Let's stop for something to drink.*

3 when you need a drink

thirsty /ˈθɜːʳsti/ [adj not usually before noun] if you are **thirsty**, you feel that you want to drink something: *I'm really thirsty, let's have a drink.*

feel thirsty *The nuts were salty and they made me feel thirsty.*

thirsty – thirstier – thirstiest

thirst /θɜːʳst/ [n singular/U] the feeling you have when you want a drink very much: *The soldiers suffered constantly from hunger and thirst.*

4 to drink alcohol

have a drink /ˌhæv ə ˈdrɪŋk/ to drink something alcoholic: *We had a few drinks to celebrate.* | *I won't have another drink because I have to drive home.*

drink /drɪŋk/ [v I] to drink alcohol, especially regularly: *The doctor told him he had to stop drinking.* | *It was obvious that Jim had been drinking.*

drink and drive (=drink alcohol before driving your car) *People who drink and drive make me very angry.*

drink heavily (=regularly drink too much) *His uncle drank heavily and had problems with his liver.*

I don't drink (=used to say that you never drink alcohol) *"Would you like a glass of wine?" "No thanks, I don't drink. I'll have an orange juice."*

drinking – drank – have drunk

> ⚠ Don't say 'I don't drink alcohol'. Just say **I don't drink.**

5 drinks that contain alcohol

alcohol /ˈælkəhɒl‖-hɔːl/ [n U] drinks that contain alcohol – a word used especially in rules and warnings about alcoholic drinks: *We're not allowed to serve alcohol to people under 18.*

alcoholic /ˌælkəˈhɒlɪk◀‖-ˈhɔːl-/ [adj] containing alcohol: *You can't sell alcoholic drinks unless you have a licence.*

drink /drɪŋk/ [n C] a drink that contains alcohol: *"Can I offer you a drink?" "I'll have a gin and tonic please."* | *After a few drinks, I began to feel better.*

go (out) for a drink (=go somewhere such as a bar to drink alcohol) *Do you feel like going out for a drink tonight?*

> ⚠ In British English, **drink** can also be an uncountable noun, meaning alcoholic drinks in general: *An enormous amount of drink is consumed over the Christmas period.*

booze /buːz/ [n U] INFORMAL drinks that contain alcohol: *The doctor told Jimmy to stay off the booze for a while.*

liquor /ˈlɪkəʳ/ [n U] ESPECIALLY AMERICAN drinks that contain alcohol, especially strong alcoholic drinks: *Lambert spends all his money on liquor and gambling.* | *a liquor store*

hard liquor (=strong alcoholic drinks)

6 drinks that do not contain alcohol

soft drink /ˌsɒft ˈdrɪŋk‖ˌsɔːft-/ [n C] a cold drink, such as orange juice, which does not contain alcohol: *Do you want a beer, or would you prefer a soft drink?*

non-alcoholic /ˌnɒn ælkəˈhɒlɪk◄‖-ˈhɔː-/ [adj] a **non-alcoholic** drink does not contain alcohol: *I've bought some non-alcoholic drinks for the drivers.* | *non-alcoholic wine*

low-alcohol /ˌləʊ ˈælkəhɒl◄‖-hɔːl◄/ [adj only before noun] **low-alcohol** beer or wine contains very little alcohol: *There is a growing market for low-alcohol beers.*

7 drinks that contain gas or do not contain gas

fizzy ESPECIALLY BRITISH **carbonated** ESPECIALLY AMERICAN /ˈfɪzi, ˈkɑːrbəneɪt̬d/ [adj] **fizzy** drinks have gas in them: *fizzy lemonade* | *carbonated mineral water*

sparkling /ˈspɑːklɪŋ/ [adj only before noun] **sparkling** wine has gas in it: *Californian sparkling wine*

still BRITISH **uncarbonated** AMERICAN /stɪl, ʌnˈkɑːrbəneɪt̬d/ [adj] **still** drinks do not have gas in them: *Do you prefer still mineral water?*

flat /flæt/ [adj] if a drink that should contain gas is **flat**, there is no gas left in it
go flat (=become flat) *I opened this can of beer yesterday and now it's gone flat.*

8 what people say when they drink alcohol together

Q**cheers** /tʃɪərz/ SPOKEN say this as you raise your glass when you are drinking with someone: *Cheers, everyone!*

Q**here's to ....** /ˈhɪərz tuː/ SPOKEN say this when you want other people to drink with you to wish someone happiness or success: *Here's to Clare and Malcolm! May they have a long and happy married life!*

DRIVE

• see pages 215–217

DRUGS

dangerous or illegal drugs that people take to get pleasure

➡ if you mean 'drugs used to treat illnesses', go to **MEDICAL TREATMENT**
➡ see also **CRIME**, **DRINK**

1 drugs

drug /drʌg/ [n C] an illegal substance that people take for pleasure, or because they cannot stop taking it: *He was arrested for selling drugs.* | *a big advertising campaign to warn teenagers about the dangers of drugs*
hard drug (=a powerful illegal drug that can make you very ill or kill you) *hard drugs such as heroin and cocaine*
soft drug (=an illegal drug that is less dangerous than a hard drug) *Seven out of ten teenagers said they had tried soft drugs.*

> ⚠ You can also use **drug** before a noun, like an adjective: *Politicians who are demanding changes in the drug laws.* | *a clinic for people with drug problems*

narcotics /nɑːrˈkɒtɪks‖-ˈkɑː-/ [n plural] ESPECIALLY AMERICAN illegal drugs: *Laws governing the sale of narcotics vary from state to state.*

> ⚠ **Narcotics** is used especially by the police and in law courts in the US. You can also use **narcotics** before a noun, like an adjective: *The narcotics business is worth billions of dollars.*

2 to take drugs

take /teɪk/ [v T] to put an illegal drug into your body: *Scot admitted that he sometimes took ecstasy at parties.*
take drugs *I started taking drugs when I was 16.*

taking – took – have taken

be on sth /biː ˈɒn (sth)‖-ˈɑːn-/ [phrasal verb T] to take a drug regularly, especially because you cannot stop taking it: *How long has she been on heroin?*
be on drugs *My Dad thinks that all young people these days are on drugs.*

be high on sth /biː ˈhaɪ ɒn (sth)/ INFORMAL to behave or talk in a very excited or happy way because of the effect of a drug: *Paul was high on LSD.*

stoned /stəʊnd/ [adj] INFORMAL feeling very relaxed or happy and not able to behave normally because of the effect of a drug: *The guy playing lead guitar was completely stoned.*
get stoned (=take drugs and become stoned) *They get stoned most weekends.*

overdose /ˈəʊvədəʊs/ [n C] too much of a drug taken at one time, which makes you very ill or kills you: *Richards is recovering from a drug overdose.*
+ of *The cause of death was an overdose of heroin.*

overdose on sth /ˈəʊvərdəʊs ɒn (sth)/ [phrasal verb T] to take too much of a drug, especially when this causes death: *She overdosed on barbiturates.*

3 someone who often takes drugs and cannot stop

drug user /ˈdrʌg juːzəʳ/ [n C] someone who takes illegal drugs regularly: *It is estimated that there are over two million drug users in the UK.*

addict /ˈædɪkt/ [n C] someone who cannot stop taking illegal drugs: *Addicts often steal money to buy drugs.*
drug/heroin/crack addict *Heroin addicts run an increased risk of getting AIDS.*

addicted /əˈdɪkt‚d/ [adj not before noun] someone who is **addicted** cannot stop taking drugs and needs to take them regularly
+ to *By the age of 16, he was addicted to heroin.*
become addicted *I used to smoke dope occasionally but never became addicted.*

junkie /ˈdʒʌŋki/ [n C] INFORMAL someone who regularly takes dangerous illegal drugs and cannot stop taking them: *It's a scary part of town – there are thieves and junkies everywhere.*

hooked /hʊkt/ [adj not before noun] INFORMAL someone who is **hooked** cannot stop taking drugs and needs to take them regularly: *After my first cigarette, I was hooked!*
+ on *Celia got hooked on crack after her divorce.*

4 to stop taking drugs

come off sth /ˈkʌm ɒf (sth)/‖-ɔːf-/ [phrasal verb T] to gradually stop taking a drug that you have been taking for a long time: *It was ten years before she managed to come off morphine.*

be in rehab /ˌbiː ɪn ˈriːhæb/ AMERICAN if someone **is in rehab**, they are getting treatment to help them stop taking drugs or drinking too much alcohol: *He's been in rehab for over three months.*
rehab [adj only before noun] *a rehab center* | *a rehab counselor*

5 buying and selling drugs

drug trafficking /ˈdrʌg ˌtræfɪkɪŋ/ [n U] the illegal activity of carrying drugs from one country to another and selling them: *Drug trafficking is now big business.*
drug trafficker [n C] someone who carries drugs illegally from one country to another and sells them

drug dealer/dealer /ˈdrʌg ˌdiːləʳ, ˈdiːləʳ/ [n C] someone who sells illegal drugs: *Police arrested a dealer yesterday who was selling marijuana to 12-year-olds.*

pusher/drug pusher /ˈpʊʃəʳ, ˈdrʌg ˌpʊʃəʳ/ [n C] someone who sells illegal drugs, especially in order to encourage people to start taking drugs: *A pusher approached us, asking if we wanted to buy any crack.*

6 the problem of drugs

drug problem /ˈdrʌg ˌprɒbləm‖-ˌprɑː-/ [n singular] if a place has a **drug problem**, a lot of people take drugs there; if a person has a **drug problem**, they cannot stop taking drugs: *Glasgow's drug problem* | *If you think you have a drug problem, call our Helpline at this number.*

drug abuse /ˈdrʌg əˌbjuːs/ [n U] the illegal use of drugs: *the problem of drug abuse in schools*

addiction /əˈdɪkʃən/ [n C/U] when you cannot stop taking illegal drugs and you need to take them regularly
drug/heroin/morphine addiction *Drug addiction is now the biggest social problem in US cities.*
+ to *Evans struggled for years to overcome her addiction to heroin.*

DRIVE

1 to drive a car, train, or other vehicle

➡ see also **ACCIDENT, CONTROL, TRAVEL, TEST, ROAD/PATH**

drive /draɪv/ [v I/T] to drive a car, bus, train etc: *Drive carefully – the roads are icy.* | *They drive on the left in the UK.*
drive a car/bus/truck etc *We need someone to drive the school bus.* | *"What do you drive?" "A Fiat Brava."*

> ⚠ Don't say 'I'm learning to drive a car', 'can you drive a car?' etc. Say **I'm learning to drive, can you drive?** etc. The word 'car' is usually left out.

driving /'draɪvɪŋ/ [n U] the activity of driving a car or other road vehicle: *She was arrested for dangerous driving.* | *Driving in central London is pretty unpleasant.*

> ⚠ You can also use **driving** before a noun, like an adjective: *taking her driving test* | *a driving instructor* | *driving lessons*

joyriding /'dʒɔɪˌraɪdɪŋ/ [n U] when young people drive a stolen car very fast and dangerously for excitement: *Their night of joyriding ended in a child's death.*
joyrider [n C] someone who goes joyriding: *Police arrested two joyriders.*

2 to go somewhere in a car or other vehicle

drive /draɪv/ [v I] to go somewhere in a car
+ to/from/into/through etc *We drove to the airport, but couldn't find anywhere to park.* | *They drove home in silence.*
+ off/away (=leave somewhere in a car) *She drove off without saying goodbye.*
drive 50 kilometres/100 miles etc *We drove 50 miles north on Interstate 75.*
drive [n C] a journey in a car: *It's a two-hour drive to Hamilton from here.*

go by car/go by bike etc /gəʊ baɪ (car, etc)/ to go somewhere in a car, on a bicycle etc – use this especially when you are comparing different methods of travelling: *One group went by car and the others took a taxi.* | *I can get to work in about 20 minutes by bike.*

go for a drive (also **take a ride** AMERICAN) /ˌgəʊ fər ə 'draɪv, ˌteɪk ə 'raɪd/ to go somewhere in a car, for enjoyment: *Let's go for a nice long drive in the country.* | *We took a ride down to the ocean.*

3 to take someone somewhere in a car or other vehicle

take/drive sb somewhere /teɪk, draɪv (sb) 'sʌmweər/ *Could you take me to the station, please?* | *The President was driven away in a big black limousine.*

lift BRITISH **ride** AMERICAN /lɪft, raɪd/ [n C] if you give someone a **lift** or a **ride**, you take them somewhere in your car
give sb a lift/ride *Pedro stopped to give me a lift.*
+ to *Do you need a ride to school?*
a lift/ride home *I accepted her offer of a lift home.*

4 someone who drives a car, train, or other vehicle

driver /'draɪvər/ [n C] someone who drives a car, bus, train etc: *A car and a truck crashed into each other, but both drivers were unhurt.* | *accidents caused by drunk drivers*
a good/bad driver *Masahiro is an excellent driver.*
a bus/train/truck driver *Ask the bus driver where to get off.*

motorist /'məʊtərɪst/ [n C] someone who drives a car: *motorists who ignore speed limits*
motorists/the motorist (=all motorists, considered as a group) *Motorists will have to pay another £60 a year in tax.* | *Why should the countryside be destroyed for the benefit of the motorist?*

> ⚠ Use the word **motorist** when you are talking about laws, taxes, or prices that affect people who drive cars.

chauffeur /'ʃəʊfər, ʃəʊ'fɜːr/ [n C] someone whose job is to drive a car for a rich or important person: *Princess Diana's chauffeur held the door open for her.*

DRIVE

5 David takes his driving test

❶ David has just taken his **driving test**.

Well, Mr Perry, you made quite a few mistakes.

Did I pass?

❷ First, you drove all the way along the street without changing **gear**.

❸ Then, when you came to a **junction**, you **pulled out** without **signalling** or looking.

❻ ...and **overtook** a police car.

❼ Then I asked you to find a **parking space**. First, you tried to **park** in one that was too small and you **scraped** the side of the car.

Stop!

❽ Then you **reversed** into a tree and **dented** the back of the car.

vocabulary

accident /'æksɪdənt/ [n C] when a car, bus, train etc hits another vehicle or hits a person, tree, or building, causing damage or injuries
  have an accident *Ken had an accident when he was driving to work.*
  bad/serious/terrible accident *Highway Patrol reported a serious accident on Avenue 7.*
brake /breɪk/ [n C] the thing that you use to make a car go more slowly or to make it stop
  slam on your brakes (=press the brakes very hard to make your car stop suddenly)
brake [v I/T] to slow down or stop by using the brakes
crash into sth /kræʃ 'ɪntuː (sth)/ [phrasal verb T] if one vehicle **crashes into** another, or into a tree, building etc, it hits it hard and causes damage
dent /dent/ [v T] to cause slight damage to something, making a hollow area in its surface by hitting it: *Someone's dented my new car!*

driving licence BRITISH **driver's license** AMERICAN /'draɪvɪŋ ˌlaɪsəns, 'draɪvərz ˌlaɪsəns/ [n C] an official document which proves that you have the legal right to drive a car alone
driving test /'draɪvɪŋ ˌtest/ [n C] a test that you must pass before you can legally drive alone
  take your driving test (=do your driving test) *I'm taking my driving test on Friday – wish me luck!*
  pass/fail your driving test (=be successful or not)
examiner /ɪg'zæmɪnər/ [n C] the person who watches you drive when you take your test, and who decides whether you pass or fail
gear /gɪər/ [n C] a part of the system in a car that turns power from the engine into movement. Cars have several gears, which you can change as you go faster or more slowly: *The new Toyota has five gears.*
  first gear/second gear etc *The traffic was very slow, and we moved along in first gear.*
  change gear BRITISH **shift gear** AMERICAN (=move from one gear into another)

DRIVE

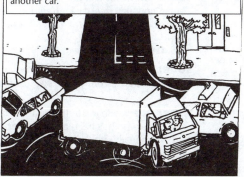

④ There was a **truck** behind us. The driver of the truck had to slam on his **brakes**. The car behind the truck **swerved, skidded,** and **crashed into** another car.

⑤ Then, you drove at 60 in an area where the **speed limit** is 40...

Slow down!

D

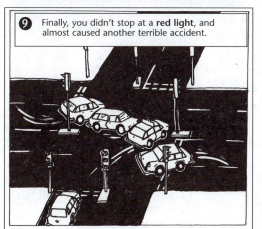

⑨ Finally, you didn't stop at a **red light**, and almost caused another terrible accident.

⑩

DRIVING SCHOOL

*So did I pass then? Do I get my **driving licence**?*

No!

---

junction /'dʒʌŋkʃən/ (also **intersection** /ˌɪntərsek-ʃən/ ESPECIALLY AMERICAN) [n C] a place where one road joins another: *Stop when you come to the junction.*

overtake /ˌəʊvərteɪk/ ESPECIALLY BRITISH **pass** /pɑːs/ ESPECIALLY AMERICAN [v I/T] to drive past another car and get in front of it: *Don't overtake now – there's a bend up ahead.*

park /pɑːrk/ [v I/T] to put your car in a place and leave it there for a period of time

parking space /'pɑːrkɪŋ ˌspeɪs/ [n C] a space where you can park your car

pull out /ˌpʊl 'aʊt/ [phrasal verb I] to drive your car from one road onto another road, or drive onto a road after stopping at the side: *Always look in your mirror before you pull out.*

red light /ˌred 'laɪt/ [n C] a light in a traffic light that is red and means you must stop: *He failed his test because he didn't stop at a red light.*

reverse /rɪ'vɜːrs/ (also **back** ESPECIALLY AMERICAN) [v I/T] to drive your car backwards

+ **up/along/into etc** *She reversed out of the drive-way.* | *Someone backed into my car* (=hit it when they reversed their car).

scrape /skreɪp/ [v T] if you **scrape** your car, you accidentally make it rub against a hard surface and damage the paint on it

signal /'sɪgnəl/ [v I] to show the direction that you are going to turn by using lights on the car

skid /skɪd/ [v I] if your car **skids**, it suddenly moves sideways or forwards and you cannot control it

slow down /ˌsləʊ 'daʊn/ [phrasal verb I] to drive more slowly: *Slow down as you approach the intersection.*

speed limit /'spiːd ˌlɪmɪt/ [n C] the fastest speed that you are allowed to drive at on a particular part of a road

swerve /swɜːrv/ [v I] to suddenly move sideways to avoid hitting something

truck /trʌk/ [n C] a large heavy vehicle used for carrying goods

DRUNK

when you have drunk too much alcohol

➡ see also **DRINK, RESTAURANTS/EATING AND DRINKING, ILL/SICK**

1 drunk

drunk /drʌŋk/ [adj not before noun] someone who is **drunk** has drunk too much alcohol and cannot think clearly: *She was so drunk, she could hardly stand up.* | *Gary was too drunk to remember what had happened that night.*
get drunk (=become drunk) *Everyone at the party got very drunk.*

⚠ Don't say 'drunken'.

have had too much to drink /həv hæd ˌtuː mʌtʃ tə ˈdrɪŋk/ to have drunk too much alcohol, so that you feel drunk or sick: *I'd better take Phil home – he's had too much to drink.*

tipsy /ˈtɪpsi/ [adj not before noun] INFORMAL a little drunk: *After the second glass of wine I was feeling a little tipsy.*

2 someone who is often drunk

alcoholic /ˌælkəˈhɒlɪk◄‖-ˈhɔː-/ [n C] someone who drinks too much alcohol every day and cannot stop: *Many alcoholics do not realise they have a problem until it is too late.*

drunk /drʌŋk/ [n C] someone who is drunk or who often gets drunk – use this especially to talk about a person you see in a public place such as a street or a bar: *A drunk came staggering down the street towards me.*

3 to drive while you are drunk

drink and drive /ˌdrɪŋk ən ˈdraɪv/ to drive after you have been drinking alcohol: *He was arrested for drinking and driving.*

drunk driver /ˌdrʌŋk ˈdraɪvər/ [n C] someone who drives when they have drunk too much alcohol

4 feeling ill the day after you have been drinking

hangover /ˈhæŋəʊvər/ [n C] the feeling you have the morning after you have drunk too much alcohol, when your head hurts and you feel sick: *Kevin woke up the next day with a terrible hangover.*

5 not drunk

sober /ˈsəʊbər/ [adj not before noun] not drunk: *I don't think I've ever seen Bill sober.*

sober up /ˌsəʊbər ˈʌp/ [phrasal verb I] if someone who has been drunk **sobers up**, they gradually become less drunk until they are not at all drunk: *He didn't sober up till he'd had a cup of strong coffee.*

DRY

➡ opposite **WET**
➡ see also **WEATHER**

1 not wet

dry /draɪ/ [adj] *The wood was dry and it burned easily.* | *You should change into some dry clothes.* | *The apples must be stored in a cool dry place.*
bone dry/dry as a bone (=completely dry and containing no water at all) *I forgot to water the plants and the soil has gone bone dry.*

dry – drier – driest

2 when there is not much rain

dry /draɪ/ [adj] if the weather is **dry**, there is not much rain: *It was a very dry summer.* | *Tunisia's hot, dry climate*

dry – drier – driest

dusty /ˈdʌsti/ [adj] a **dusty** road, town, track etc is dry and covered with dust, because the weather is hot and there is not much rain: *The road to Agra was long, hot, and dusty.* | *a small, dusty village on the edge of the desert*

dusty – dustier – dustiest

When you see **EC**, go to the **ESSENTIAL COMMUNICATION** section.

drought /draʊt/ [n C/U] a long period when there is little or no rain, so that people and animals do not have enough water and plants die: *Southern Africa is suffering its worst drought of the century.*

3 to become dry

dry /draɪ/ [v I] to become dry: *Wet clothes soon dry on a hot day.* | *Leave the dishes on the draining board to dry.*
hang sth out to dry (=hang clothes outside, so that they are dried by the sun or wind)
drying – dried – have dried

dry out /ˌdraɪ ˈaʊt/ [phrasal verb I] to become completely dry, on the inside and the outside: *Put your coat near the fire – it'll soon dry out.* | *Cover the pastry with a damp cloth to prevent it from drying out.*

dry up /ˌdraɪ ˈʌp/ [phrasal verb I] if a river or lake **dries up**, it becomes completely dry because there has not been any rain: *Last summer the river dried up and you could walk right across it.* | *The drought has made the reservoir dry up, and many homes are without water.*

shrivel up /ˌʃrɪvəl ˈʌp/ [phrasal verb I] if a plant or a fruit **shrivels up**, it becomes smaller and deep lines form on its surface, because it is so dry: *There was so little rain that most of the crops shrivelled up and died.*
shrivelling – shrivelled – have shrivelled BRITISH
shriveling – shriveled – have shriveled AMERICAN

4 to make something dry or make yourself dry

dry /draɪ/ [v T] to make something dry: *Could you wait ten minutes while I dry my hair?* | *We built a fire to get ourselves warm and dry our clothes.*
drying – dried – have dried

dry yourself off /ˌdraɪ jɔːˈself ˈɒf‖-ˈɔːf/ [phrasal verb T] to use a towel to make yourself dry, for example after a bath or a swim: *He got out of the pool and dried himself off.*

D

E

EARLY

➡ opposite **LATE**
➡ see also **SOON, BEGINNING, FIRST, TIME**

1 before the usual or expected time

early /'ɜːʳli/ [adj/adv] if something happens **early**, it happens before the usual time or the most suitable time; if someone is **early**, they arrive before the time they are expected to: *I finished work early today.* | *After an early lunch, we started the meeting at one o'clock.* | *If you plant the seeds too early, they won't grow.*

be early (=arrive early) *You're early – I wasn't expecting you till seven.*

seven months/three days etc early (=seven months/three days etc earlier than expected) *Our first child was born eight weeks early.*

far too early (=much too early) *We arrived far too early and had to wait outside for an hour.*

early – earlier – earliest

in good time /ɪn ˌgʊd 'taɪm/ early enough, so that you do not have to rush, or so that you have time to get ready: *If you want to make a left turn, reduce your speed and give a signal in good time.*

+ for *It is important to arrive in good time for your interview.*

with time to spare /wɪð ˌtaɪm tə 'speəʳ/ if you arrive somewhere or finish something **with time to spare**, you arrive or finish earlier than you need to: *We reached London with plenty of time to spare.*

with ten minutes/half an hour etc to spare *I finished the test with just two minutes to spare.* (=two minutes before the end)

premature /'premətʃəʳ, -tʃʊəʳ, ˌpremə-'tʃʊəʳ‖ˌpriːmə'tʃʊəʳ/ [adj] happening before the normal or natural time – use this especially about medical conditions

premature death/birth/ageing *Alcoholism is one of the major causes of premature death.*

premature baby (=a baby that is born too early) *Her baby was premature and weighed only 2kg.*

prematurely [adv] *Hannah's hair went prematurely grey when she was only 24.*

2 early in the morning

early /'ɜːʳli/ [adj/adv] early in the morning: *I always wake up early when the weather's warm.* | *Early the next day, Jamie received a call from his mother.*

bright and early (=when you get up or go somewhere early, because you are excited or eager to do something) *Daphne woke bright and early and went for a walk before the others got up.*

make an early start (=start an activity or journey early in the morning)

in the early hours (=very early in the morning) *The robbery took place in the early hours of Sunday morning.*

early – earlier – earliest

first thing /ˌfɜːʳst 'θɪŋ/ ESPECIALLY SPOKEN if you do something **first thing**, you do it immediately after you get up or as soon as you start work: *Don't worry – I'll phone her first thing.*

first thing tomorrow/Wednesday/in the morning *They promised to come and fix it first thing tomorrow.*

at the crack of dawn /ət ðə ˌkræk əv 'dɔːn/ INFORMAL use this to emphasize that something happens very early in the morning, when most people are still in bed: *My Dad used to get up at the crack of dawn every Sunday to go fishing.*

EARN

PAY → WORK

see also

MONEY → SPEND

1 to get money for your work

> ⚠ All these words mean 'to be paid money for working'. **Earn** is a little more formal than the others, so it is used less often in informal conversation. You use **make** or **get** when you are talking about the actual amount that someone earns, but **get** is more informal than **make**.

earn /ɜːʳn/ [*v* T] to be paid money for your work

earn £15,000 a year/£12 an hour etc *people earning more than $50,000 a year*

earn more than/less than/a few dollars etc *It's quite common for women to earn more than their husbands.* | *earning a few dollars playing in a bar*

earn a living/earn your living (=earn enough money to pay for the things you need) *It's difficult to earn a living as a writer.*

make /meɪk/ [*v* T] to earn money – use this when you are saying or asking how much someone earns: *In the first three months I made over $45,000.* | *How much do you think she makes?*

make $500 a week/£25,000 a year/a lot/a fortune etc *A supermodel can make millions of dollars a year.*

making – made – have made

get /get/ [*v* T] INFORMAL to earn money – use this when you are saying or asking how much someone earns

get £10 per hour/$350 a week etc *She gets £200 a day to run these training courses.*

get $25/£15 etc for doing sth *I got £5 for washing Nick's car.*

getting – got – have got

be paid/get paid /biː ˈpeɪd, get ˈpeɪd/ to earn money, when you work for an employer, and not for yourself

be paid £50/$200 etc *The cleaners are paid less than 1000 francs a week.*

2 earning a lot of money

highly paid/well-paid /ˌhaɪli ˈpeɪd◂, ˌwel ˈpeɪd◂/ [*adj*] earning a lot of money: *He's a lawyer, so he must be very well-paid.* | *highly paid and well-motivated workers*

well-paid job *She's a computer programmer. It's a really well-paid job.*

make a fortune /ˌmeɪk ə ˈfɔːʳtʃən/ to earn a lot of money, especially when you are in charge of your own business: *Some of these mechanics made an absolute fortune!*

make a fortune doing sth *Roger makes a fortune buying and selling yachts.*

3 not earning much money

low-paid/badly paid /ˌləʊ ˈpeɪd◂, ˌbædli ˈpeɪd◂/ [*adj*] earning less money than most people earn: *People who work in stores are usually very badly paid.*

low-paid job *Only low-paid temporary jobs were available.*

4 the money that you earn

pay /peɪ/ [*n* U] the money that you earn by working: *I'm looking for a job with better pay.* | *There have been complaints about the level of nurses' pay.*

sick pay (=pay that you get when you are ill and cannot work) *Joe's been receiving sick pay since the accident.*

> ⚠ You can also use **pay** before a noun, like an adjective: *a big pay increase* | *pay negotiations*

salary /ˈsæləri/ [*n* C] the money that someone is paid every month by their employer, especially someone who is in a profession, such as a teacher or a manager

a salary of £100,000/$10,000 etc *The university provided us with a salary of $2000 a month.*

be on a salary (=be earning a salary) *I joined the company in 1985, on a salary of $15,000 a year.* | *Please give details of your present salary.*

a good/high salary *She earns a good salary as an investment banker.*

plural **salaries**

wages /ˈweɪdʒɪ̇z/ [*n* plural] the money that someone is paid every week by their employer, especially someone who works in a factory, or in a shop etc: *We collect our wages on Friday mornings.* | *I was paying for bills, food, and everything from my wages.*

E

income /'ɪŋkʌm, 'ɪn-/ [n C/U] all the money that you receive regularly, for work or for any other reason: *Her annual income is just over $40,000.* | *We get some additonal income from an investment in an oil company.*

be on a low income (=receive very little money) *Families on low incomes get extra welfare payment.*

+ from *He has a comfortable income from his salary and his investments.*

fee /fiː/ [n C] the money paid to a lawyer, doctor, or similar skilled worker for a piece of work that they have done: *Our legal fees came to more than $200,000.* | *consultant's fees for the design work*

5 the person in a family who earns money

the breadwinner /ðə 'bredwɪnəʳ/ [n singular] the person in a family who earns most of the money that the family needs: *In the past it was always the husband who was expected to be the breadwinner.*

EASY

➡ opposite **DIFFICULT**

1 not difficult to do, use, or understand

easy /'iːzi/ [adj] not difficult to do, use, or understand: *The questions were really easy.* | *It's an easy journey – we just drive to the station, then take the direct train to Paris.*

be easy to read/use/learn etc (=when it is easy to read something, use something etc) *The machine is well-designed, and very easy to use.*

it is easy to do sth *It is easy to see why she didn't marry him.*

it is easy for sb to do sth *It wasn't easy for me to get a job.*

find sth easy (=when you have no difficulty doing something) *I can't operate the computer, but my children find it easy.*

easy – easier – easiest

easily /'iːzɪli/ [adv] if you can do something **easily**, you can do it without trying hard: *A burglar could easily climb*

through that window. | *When I went to college I made friends very easily.*

be easily recognized/damaged/done etc (=when something can be recognized, damaged etc easily) *These plates are easily damaged, so please be careful with them.*

not difficult /nɒt 'dɪfɪkəlt/ fairly easy: *"Did you make this pizza yourself?" "Yes, it's not difficult."*

it is not difficult to do sth *It's not difficult to see why she's unhappy all the time.*

simple /'sɪmpəl/ [adj] easy to use or understand, because it is not complicated – use this about things like explanations or instructions, or about machines or systems: *She drew us a simple map so that we wouldn't get lost.* | *Try this simple recipe for pasta sauce.*

be simple to use/make/prepare etc *The new photocopier is much simpler to use than the one we had before.*

straightforward /ˌstreɪt'fɔːʳwəʳd/ [adj] easy to understand and easy to do – use this especially about a method or process: *It's very straightforward – you just type the file name, then press 'Enter'.* | *There's a straightforward calculation for working out how much tax you have to pay.*

user-friendly /ˌjuːzəʳ 'frendli◄/ [adj] easy to use or understand – use this especially about computers or written instructions: *We are trying to develop software that is more user-friendly.*

2 what you say when you think something is very easy to do

it's easy /ɪts 'iːzi/ SPOKEN "*How do you print out files from your disk?*" "*It's easy. You just click on the 'Print' icon.*"

⚠ In informal spoken English, you can just say **easy** on it's own: "*How can we make sure she comes?*" "*Easy. Just tell her that Mark will be there.*"

there's nothing to it /ðeəʳz ˌnʌθɪŋ 'tuː ɪt/ SPOKEN say this when it is easy for you to do something, even though other people think it is difficult: *I fixed the washing machine – there was nothing to it.*

○**be a piece of cake** /biː ə ˌpiːs əv ˈkeɪk/ SPOKEN INFORMAL say this about something that is very easy for you to do, for example when compared with something more difficult: *If you can learn Japanese, learning French should be a piece of cake.*

3 to make something easier

make sth easier /ˌmeɪk (sth) ˈiːziəʳ/ to make it possible to do something more quickly and easily: *Large supermarkets have made shopping much easier.*
make it easier for sb to do sth *The Internet has made it easier for children to get access to pornography.*
make things/life easier *If the buses were more frequent it would make life a lot easier.*

simplify /ˈsɪmplɪfaɪ/ [v T] to make something easier to understand: *The whole procedure has been simplified.*
simplifying – simplified – have simplified

EAT

RESTAURANTS/EATING AND DRINKING

MEAL   DRINK

see also

COOK   TASTE

FOOD   HUNGRY

1 to eat

eat /iːt/ [v I/T] *Don't eat so fast – you'll get indigestion.* | *She was sitting on the wall, eating an apple.* | *Hey! – Someone's eaten all my chocolates.*
eating – ate – have eaten

have /hæv/ [v T] INFORMAL to eat a particular thing: *I wasn't very hungry, so I just had a sandwich.* | *I think I'll just have one more piece of cake.*
have sth for lunch/dinner/breakfast *What shall we have for dinner?* | *I usually just have fruit for breakfast.*
having – had – have had

chew /tʃuː/ [v I/T] to bite food several times and turn it around in your mouth: *I chewed the toffee slowly.* | *There was a cow in the field, slowly chewing a mouthful of grass*

swallow /ˈswɒləʊ/ˈswɑː-/ [v T] to make something go down your throat towards your stomach: *I threw a piece of meat to the dog, and he swallowed it in one go.* | *If you drink some water it will make the pills easier to swallow.*

lick /lɪk/ [v T] to eat something soft by moving your tongue across its surface: *The children sat licking their ice-creams.*
lick sth off sth *Nina licked the melted chocolate off her fingers.*

munch /mʌntʃ/ [v I/T] to eat something with continuous movements of your mouth, especially when you are enjoying your food: *Jamie came out of the store munching a bag of potato chips.*
+ on/at *We sipped black coffee and munched on homemade biscuits.*

nibble /ˈnɪbəl/ [v I/T] to eat something by biting very small pieces: *The horse lowered his head and began to nibble the grass.*
+ on/at *We stood around drinking wine and nibbling on little snacks.*

2 to have a meal

⚠ Don't say 'take dinner', 'take breakfast'. Say **have dinner, have breakfast**.

have /hæv/ [v T] to eat a meal
have breakfast/lunch/dinner *Make sure you have a good breakfast because lunch isn't until two o'clock.*
have a meal *We had an excellent meal in a Thai restaurant.*
○**have something to eat** ESPECIALLY SPOKEN (=eat a meal) *Let's stop here and have something to eat.*
having – had – have had

eat /iːt/ [v I/T] to eat a meal: *We usually eat at 7 o'clock.* | *I'm not hungry, thanks – I've already eaten.*
eat out (=eat a meal in a restaurant) *We eat out about once a month.*
eat lunch/dinner etc AMERICAN *We ate dinner at around six, then went out.*
eating – ate – have eaten

⚠ In British English, don't say 'eat breakfast', 'eat lunch' etc. Say **have breakfast, have lunch** etc.

3 to finish eating

finish /'fɪnɪʃ/ [v T] to finish eating something: *If you finish your pasta you can have some ice-cream.* | *Alice finished her lunch and took the dishes into the kitchen.*

4 to eat very little food or no food

diet /'daɪət/ [n C] when you eat less food because you want to get thinner: *I've tried lots of diets but none of them work.*
be on a diet (=be eating less food) *Do you want some dessert, or are you still on a diet?*
go on a diet (=start a diet) *As soon as Christmas is over, I'm going on a diet.*
   diet [v I] to eat less food in order to get thinner: *She first started dieting when she was only 12.*

fast /faːst‖fæst/ [v I] to stop eating food for a fixed period of time, especially for religious reasons: *Muslims fast during Ramadan.*
   fast [n C] *At the end of their fast, the people have a big party to celebrate.*

pick at sth /'pɪk æt (sth)/ [phrasal verb T] to eat only a small part of a meal, especially because you feel ill or unhappy: *I sat picking at my dinner, wishing I was somewhere else.*

hardly touch sth /ˌhaːrdli 'tʌtʃ (sth)/ to eat almost none of your meal: *Rachel hardly touched her dinner – is she okay?* | *Don't you like the pudding? You've hardly touched it.*

5 when you have eaten enough food

have had enough /həv ˌhæd ɪ'nʌf/ to have eaten enough food, so that you do not want any more: *"Would you like some dessert?" "No thanks, I've had enough."* | *Leave the rest if you've had enough.*

◯**be full** /biː 'fʊl/ SPOKEN if you **are full**, you have eaten so much food that you cannot eat any more: *"Would you like some more pie?" "No thanks, I'm full."*

6 someone who eats too much

greedy /'griːdi/ [adj] ESPECIALLY BRITISH someone who is **greedy** eats too much: *Don't be greedy – leave some cake for everyone else.*
greedy – greedier – greediest
   greedily [adv] *The children rushed to the table and started eating greedily.*

◯**pig** /pɪg/ [n C] SPOKEN INFORMAL a rude word for describing someone who eats too much: *What a pig! He ate that whole box of chocolates himself.*

EDGE

the part of something that is furthest from its centre

➡ see also SIDE, MIDDLE

edge /edʒ/ [n C] the part of something that is nearest to its outside or end: *The plates had blue lines around the edges.*
+ of *Don't go too near the edge of the water.*
on the edge (of) *They live in a little house on the edge of town.*

side /saɪd/ [n C] the part of an object that is near its left or right edge: *The stage was lit from the side.*
left-hand/right-hand side of sth (=on the left or right) *Roy's seat was on the left-hand side of the plane.*

⚠ The **edge** of an object is where it ends or begins. The **side** of an object is along one of its lengths.

⚠ Use **the edge of the road/pool/lake etc** about activities that happen near the road, pool, lake etc but not in it: *We stood at the edge of the lake and watched the sunset.* Use **the side of the road/pool/lake etc** about things that happen in the road, pool, lake etc, but close to the edge of it: *She swam to the side of the pool.*

When you see **EC** , go to the **ESSENTIAL COMMUNICATION** section.

the outskirts /ðiː ˈaʊtskɜːʳts/ [n plural] the areas of a city furthest away from the centre
+ of *By the time we reached the outskirts of the city it was already dark.*
on the outskirts (of) *Her parents lived in a big house on the outskirts of Seoul.*

boundary /ˈbaʊndəri/ [n C] the official line that marks the edge of an area of land, for example a farm or part of a country
+ of *She had never gone beyond the boundaries of the city.* | *The farmer put up a high fence to mark the boundary of his land.*
+ between *The Mississippi River forms the boundary between Tennessee and Arkansas.*
plural **boundaries**

margin /ˈmaːʳdʒən/ [n C] the part where nothing is written or printed at the side of a page: *Leave a two centimetre margin on the left side of the page.*

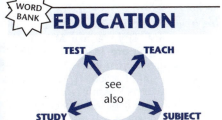

WORD BANK
EDUCATION

see also

TEST TEACH STUDY SUBJECT LEARN

⚠ Words like **school**, **nursery**, and **university** can be used as uncountable nouns, to mean the time that you spend there: *I missed a lot of school because of illness.* | *College starts next week.*

1 school

school /skuːl/ [n C/U] a place where children go to learn and be taught, up to the age of 18: *My mother is a teacher at the local school.* | *The nearest school was 10 miles away.* | *I hate school!*
to/from school *80% of parents take their children to school by car.*
state school BRITISH **public school** AMERICAN (=a school that is paid for by the government)

⚠ You can also use **school** before a noun, like an adjective: *the school bus* | *I got this book from the school library.*

⚠ Be careful with the phrase **public school**: in the US, this means a school that is paid for by the government and is available to all children; in Britain, it means one of a number of expensive private schools which parents must pay for.

2 schools for very young children

nursery BRITISH **nursery school** AMERICAN /ˈnɜːʳsəri, ˈnɜːʳsəri ˌskuːl/ [n C/U] a place where children aged between about two and five go for a few hours each day to play and do activities with other children
plural **nurseries**

kindergarten /ˈkɪndəʳgaːʳtən/ [n C/U] in American English, the name of the first year of school for children aged five; in British English, another name for a **nursery** for children aged four or five

pre-school /ˈpriː skuːl/ [n C/U] AMERICAN a school for children aged between about two and five: *a plan to provide pre-school for all children*

3 schools for children below the age of 12

primary school /ˈpraɪməri ˌskuːl/ [n C/U] in Britain, a school for children aged between five and eleven; **primary schools** are usually divided into the **infant school** or **the infants** (=for children aged five to seven) and the **junior school** or **the juniors** (=for children aged seven to eleven)

elementary school/grade school /elɪˈmentəri ˌskuːl, ˈgreɪd ˌskuːl/ [n C/U] in the US, a school for children aged between five and eleven

4 schools for older children

secondary school /ˈsekəndəri ˌskuːl‖ -deri-/ [n C/U] in Britain, a school for children aged between 11 and 18

junior high school /ˌdʒuːniəʳ ˈhaɪ skuːl/ [n C/U] in the US, a school for children aged between 12 and 13 or 14

E

high school /ˈhaɪ skuːl/ [n C/U] in the US, a school for children aged between 14 and 17

sixth form college /ˈsɪksθ fɔːˈm ˌkɒlɪdʒ‖ -ˌkɑː-/ [n C/U] in Britain, a college for students aged between 16 and 18

5 a place where people over 18 can study

university /ˌjuːnɪ̩ˈvɜːˈsɪ̩ti/ [n C/U] a place where students study one or two subjects at a high level, in order to get degrees: *There are many universities in Tokyo.* | *the University of Chicago*
be at university (=be a student at a university) *Both my sisters are at university.*
go to university (=become a student at a university) *She wants to go to university to study biology.*

> ⚠ You can also use **university** before a noun, like an adjective: *the university library* | *a big university campus*

> ⚠ In British English, always use the word **university** to talk about a place where students study to get degrees. But in American English, you can also use **school** or **college** to mean this.

plural **universities**

college /ˈkɒlɪdʒ‖ˈkɑː-/ [n C/U] in the US, a university; in Britain, a place where people can study academic subjects or practical skills after they leave secondary school, but which does not give degrees

> ⚠ You can also use **college** before a noun, like an adjective: *a college professor* | *the college football team*

school /skuːl/ [n C/U] AMERICAN INFORMAL a university or similar institution
go to school (=study at a college or university) *Phil gave up his job, and he's going back to school next year.*

law school/medical school/business school /ˈlɔː skuːl, ˈmedɪkəl skuːl, ˈbɪznɪ̩s skuːl/ [n C] a university or part of a university where you study law, medicine, or business

postgraduate BRITISH **graduate** AMERICAN /pəʊstˈgrædʒuɪ̩t, ˈgrædʒuɪ̩t/ [adj only before noun] use this about advanced education that takes place after a student has

finished a university degree, or about students who study at this level: *She got a degree in history last year, and now she's doing a postgraduate course.* | *postgraduate research* | *We met when we were both graduate students at Berkeley.*

higher education /ˌhaɪəˈ edjʊˈkeɪʃən‖ -edʒə-/ [n U] education at a university or similar institution: *a big increase in the numbers of students entering higher education*

adult education /ˌædʌlt edjʊˈkeɪʃən‖ -edʒə-/ [n U] special classes for adults, often in the evenings, either because they want to improve their skills or just for enjoyment

6 to go to a school or university to study

go to /ˈgəʊ tuː/ to go to a school or university to study: *"Which university did you go to?" "I went to Kyoto Women's University."* | *We both went to the same school.*

be at BRITISH **be in** AMERICAN /biː æt, biː ɪn/ [phrasal verb T] if you **are at school/college** or you **are in school/college** etc, you are studying there: *My younger brother is still at school.* | *Yes, I know Eileen – we were friendly when we were in college together.* | *Sara is at Oxford studying biology.*

> ⚠ **At school** (British) always means going to a school for children between 5 and 18 years old. **In school** (American) means attending a school, college, or university.

be educated /biː ˈedjʊkeɪtɪ̩d‖-ˈedʒə-/ to study at a particular school or university – use this especially in written descriptions of people's lives
+ at *He was born in South Wales in 1941, and was educated at the King's School, Canterbury.*
Harvard-educated/Oxford-educated etc *a Harvard-educated lawyer*

7 to finish school or university
➡ see also **LEAVE 9**

graduate /ˈgrædʒueɪt/ [v I] to successfully finish your studies – in Britain, you **graduate** from university, but in the US you

can graduate either from university or from high school: *Bobby left high school without graduating.*
+ from *He graduated from Yale in 1986.*

8 someone who studies at a school, university etc

schoolboy/schoolgirl /'skuːlbɔɪ, 'skuːl-gɜːʳl/ [n C] ESPECIALLY BRITISH a boy or girl who studies at school: *There was a group of schoolgirls waiting at the bus stop.*

schoolchildren /'skuːlˌtʃɪldrən/ [n plural] ESPECIALLY BRITISH children who are studying at school: *Only 10% of British school-children attend private schools.*

pupil /'pjuːpəl/ [n C] a child who studies at a particular school, especially in a school for children under the age of 12: *With over 2000 pupils, this is one of the biggest schools in London.*

> ⚠ **Pupil** is formal in American English, but not in British English.

student /'stjuːdənt‖'stuː-/ [n C] someone who studies at school, university, or college: *None of my students has ever failed this exam.*
high school/college etc student (=a student at high school or college)
English/history/art etc student (=someone who is studying English, history, art etc)

> ⚠ In American English, **student** can mean anyone who is studying at a school, college, or university. In British English, it usually means someone who is studying at a university or college, and children at school are usually called **schoolchildren** or **pupils**.

class /klɑːs‖klæs/ [n C] a group of students or schoolchildren who are taught together: *Everyone in the class passed the test.*
top/bottom of the class *At the end of the year I came top of the class in French.*

first year/second year etc /ˌfɜːʳst jɪəʳ, ˌsekənd jɪəʳ/ [n C] BRITISH someone who is in the first year, second year etc at a school or university: *The university only provides rooms for first years.*

freshman /'freʃmən/ [n C] AMERICAN some-one who is in the first year at university or high school

sophomore /'sɒfəmɔːʳ‖'sɑː-/ [n C] AMERICAN someone who is in the second year at university or high school

junior /'dʒuːniəʳ/ [n C] AMERICAN someone who is in the third year at university or high school

senior /'siːniəʳ/ [n C] AMERICAN someone who is in the fourth year at university or high school

postgraduate student BRITISH **graduate student** AMERICAN /ˌpəʊstˈgrædʒuːⁱt ˌstjuːdənt, ˈgrædʒuːⁱt ˌstjuːdənt‖-ˌstuː-/ [n C] someone who has already taken one degree and is studying for another, more advanced degree

9 what level you are at school, university etc

first/second etc grade /ˌfɜːʳst, ˌsekənd (etc) greɪd/ [n C] the first, second etc year of school in the US, starting from the first year of elementary school (aged six, after kindergarten): *Harry will be starting the third grade soon.*

first/second etc year /ˌfɜːʳst, ˌsekənd (etc) jɪəʳ/ [n C] the first, second etc year at university in Britain or the US, or the first, second etc year of school in Britain, starting from the first year of secondary school (aged 11): *I gave up German in the third year.*

year one/two etc /jɪəʳ ˈwʌn, ˈtuː/ [n C] the first, second etc year of school in Britain, starting from the first year of primary or infant school (aged five), and ending at year thirteen (aged 18): *By year eight, students should be able to understand what a noun is.*

> ⚠ The system starting from **year one** is more modern than the system starting from the **first year**.

10 one of the long periods into which the year is divided at school, university etc

term /tɜːʳm/ [n C] one of the three periods that the year is divided into at British schools and most British universities

autumn/spring/summer term *The main exams are at the end of the summer term.*

semester /sɪˈmestər/ [n C] one of the two periods that the year is divided into at American schools and most American universities
first/second semester *I took five classes in the first semester and three in the second.*

the school year/the academic year /ðə ˌskuːl ˈjɪər, ði ˌækədemɪk ˈjɪər/ [n singular] the period of the year when there are school or university classes: *In Japan the school year starts in April and ends in February or March.*

quarter /ˈkwɔːrtər/ [n C] one of the four main periods that the year is divided into at some American schools and universities

11 a short period in which students are taught a particular subject

class /klɑːs‖klæs/ [n C] a period of time, usually about 30 minutes to one hour, in which a teacher teaches a group of students: *Heidi fainted during the French class today!* | *Let's go – I have my first class in 10 minutes!*

lesson /ˈlesən/ [n C] a period in which someone teaches one person or a small number of people – use this especially about practical skills such as music, swimming, or driving: *Dominic will be having his first driving lesson this Thursday.* | *She gives English lessons to business people in the evenings.*

lecture /ˈlektʃər/ [n C] a long talk on a subject, given by a teacher at a college or university, and listened to by a large number of students
+ on *a lecture on the causes of the Russian Revolution*
give a lecture *Professor Blair is giving a series of lectures on Einstein's theories.*

seminar /ˈsemɪnɑːr/ [n C] a class, usually at a college or university, where a teacher and a small group of students discuss a subject
+ on *Every week we have a seminar on modern political theory.*

12 what you get when you finish a course successfully

qualification /ˌkwɒlɪfɪˈkeɪʃən‖ˌkwɑː-/ [n C often plural] you get a **qualification** when you finish a course and pass examinations at the end of it: *a two-year course, leading to a teaching qualification* | *He left school at 16, with no academic qualifications.*
sb's qualifications (=all the exams someone has passed) *List your qualifications in the space below.*

degree /dɪˈɡriː/ [n C] the qualification that you get when you successfully finish a course at university: *He has a degree in political science from the University of Chicago.*
do a degree/take a degree BRITISH (=study in order to get one) *Maggie is doing a degree in psychology.*

> ⚠ On its own, **degree** means the qualification you get when you do a 3- or 4-year course at university, usually when you are about 18-22 years old. **Degree** can also mean a more advanced qualification (=a **higher degree**), such as a **Master's degree** or a **PhD**.

Master's degree/Master's /ˈmɑːstərz dɪˈɡriː, ˈmɑːstərz‖ˈmæs-/ [n C] an advanced degree that you get by studying for one or two years after getting your first degree
+ in *To do this job, you need a Master's degree in Computer Science.*

doctorate/PhD /ˈdɒktərɪt, ˌpiː eɪtʃ ˈdiː‖ˈdɑːk-/ [n C] the most advanced type of degree, which you study for on your own for several years, doing work and writing a long report explaining what you have discovered
+ in *She has a PhD in industrial robotics.*

13 the process of studying and being taught

education /ˌedjʊˈkeɪʃən‖ˌedʒə-/ [n U] the whole process by which people learn and develop their minds in schools, colleges, and universities: *The government should spend more on education.* | *My parents wanted me to have a good education.* | *I spent all of my life from 5 to 18 in full-time education.*

private education (=paid for by parents, not provided by the government) *Only a minority of parents can afford private education for their children.*

educational /ˌedjuˈkeɪʃənəl‖ˌedʒə-/ [adj usually before noun] connected with education: *Different children have different educational needs.* | *We offer a wide range of educational and sporting activities.*

an educational institution (=a school, college, or university)

academic /ˌækəˈdemɪk◄/ [adj usually before noun] connected with education, especially at college or university level: *academic books* | *Jake was unemployed, and had no academic qualifications.*

EFFECT

a change caused by something that happens or by something that someone does

➡ see also **RESULT, CHANGE**

1 an effect

effect /ɪˈfekt/ [n C/U] a change that is caused by something that happens or by something that someone does

+ of *the harmful effects of smoking* | *Gail was still recovering from the effects of her operation.*

the effect of sth on sth *a study that is measuring the effect of fertilizers on the size of crops*

without much effect (=having almost no effect) *I tried using detergent to remove the stain, but without much effect.*

feel the effects of sth *By now we were feeling the effects of lack of sleep.*

side effects (=unwanted effects of a drug or medicine) *One of the possible side effects of the drug is loss of memory.*

> ⚠ Don't confuse **effect** (a noun) and **affect** (a verb – see Section 2).

impact /ˈɪmpækt/ [n singular/U] the big and permanent changes that happen as a result of something important

the impact of sth on sth *the impact of computers on people's lives*

have a great/enormous impact on sth *Einstein's work on relativity had an enormous impact on the way physics developed.*

have little impact on sth *At first, the revolution had little impact on the lives of ordinary people.*

influence /ˈɪnfluəns/ [n singular/U] the continuing effects that something has on the way that people think or behave, or on the way that things develop

+ of *The Chinese authorities were worried about the influence of western films and TV programmes.*

the influence of sth on sth *a book about the influence of feminist ideas on American society*

2 to have an effect on someone or something

have an effect /ˌhæv ən ɪˈfekt/ to make someone or something change in some way, for example by changing the way that things are done or by changing someone's attitudes: *For some patients, the treatment has an immediate effect.*

+ on *What you eat when you are pregnant can have an effect on your baby.*

have a good/bad/serious etc effect *The war had a very bad effect on the economy of Vietnam.*

have little/no effect *The tobacco companies say their advertisements have little effect on people's behaviour.*

have an influence /ˌhæv ən ˈɪnfluəns/ to have a continuing effect on the way that people think or behave, or on the way that things develop

+ on *Clearly, the cost of fuel has an influence on our energy policy.*

have a great/important/profound influence on sth *Descartes' ideas have had a profound influence on modern science.*

affect /əˈfekt/ [v T] to produce a change, for example in the way that something develops or in someone's situation: *The new tax law doesn't affect me because I'm a student.* | *The rate at which plants grow is affected by the amount of sunlight they receive.*

badly/seriously/severely affect *Playing video games too much could seriously affect children's eyesight.*

E

⚠️ Don't confuse **affect** (a verb) and **effect** (a noun – see Section 1).

influence /ˈɪnfluəns/ [v T] to affect someone's opinions or behaviour: *Don't let anything he says influence your decision.* | *How much does TV advertising influence what people buy?*

Q do sth to sth /ˈduː (sth) tuː (sth)/ [phrasal verb T] ESPECIALLY SPOKEN to affect someone or something in a harmful way: *Do you ever think about what those cigarettes must be doing to your lungs?* | *Look what the storm has done to the flowers.*

be good for/be bad for /biː ˈɡʊd fɔːr, biː ˈbæd fɔːr/ to have a good or bad effect on something or someone: *Eating plenty of fruit is good for your health.* | *Changing schools too often is bad for a child's development.*
it's good/bad for sb to do sth *It'll be good for her to meet some new people.* | *I think it's bad for children to always get what they want.*

EMBARRASSED

feeling uncomfortable and nervous about what people think of you

➡ see also **ASHAMED**

⚠️ Don't confuse **embarrassed** and **ashamed**. Use **embarrassed** when you worry about what other people think of you. Use **ashamed** when you feel guilty and bad about yourself, because you have done something that you know is wrong. **Ashamed** is a much stronger word.

1 embarrassed

embarrassed /ɪmˈbærəst/ [adj] feeling uncomfortable and worrying about what people think of you, for example because you have made a stupid mistake or because you have to talk about your feelings, about sex etc: *Tony spilled red wine all over their carpet. He was so embarrassed!* | *The teachers are supposed to teach us about 'safe sex', but most of them are too embarrassed.*

get embarrassed *She's a good singer, but she gets embarrassed if we ask her to sing.*
+ about *I got very drunk at the party, and I feel really embarrassed about it.*
+ by/at *Marlon was embarrassed by his lack of education.*

self-conscious /self ˈkɒnʃəs‖-ˈkɑːn-/ [adj] shy and embarrassed about your body, or about the way you look or talk: *I always feel really self-conscious in a bikini.*
+ about *Teenagers can feel very self-conscious about their appearance.*

uncomfortable /ʌnˈkʌmftəbəl, -ˈkʌmfət-‖ -ˈkʌmfərt-, -ˈkʌmft-/ [adj] feeling embarrassed because you cannot relax with the people around you: *All this talk about love and romance was making me uncomfortable.* | *Jim always felt uncomfortable on such formal occasions.* | *an uncomfortable silence*
  uncomfortably [adv] *Rhys shuffled his feet uncomfortably, trying to think of an excuse to leave.*

awkward /ˈɔːkwərd/ [adj] feeling so shy, nervous, and embarrassed that you cannot behave in a natural way: *I didn't know anyone at the party and I felt really awkward at first.*

2 to make someone feel embarrassed

embarrassing /ɪmˈbærəsɪŋ/ [adj] an **embarrassing** situation makes you feel embarrassed: *"She got locked in a public toilet and couldn't get out!" "How embarrassing!"* | *The doctor asked me a lot of embarrassing questions about my sex life.*

embarrass /ɪmˈbærəs/ [v T] to make someone feel embarrassed: *I hope I didn't embarrass you in front of your friends.* | *I chose my words carefully, in order to avoid embarrassing anyone.*

3 the feeling you have when you are embarrassed

embarrassment /ɪmˈbærəsmənt/ [n U] the feeling you have when you are embarrassed: *He looked down at the floor in an attempt to hide his embarrassment.*
Q die of embarrassment SPOKEN (a humorous way of saying you feel very

embarrassed about something) *She read my poem out to the whole class – I almost died of embarrassment!*

4 when your face goes red because you are embarrassed

blush/go red /blʌʃ, gəʊ 'red/ [v I] if you **blush** or **go red**, your face becomes red because you are embarrassed: *When he asked her to dance she just blushed and giggled.* | *David's really shy – he always goes red when the teacher asks him a question.*

EMPHASIZE

to say that you think that something is especially important

➡ see also **IMPORTANT/NOT IMPORTANT**

emphasize/stress /'emfəsaɪz, stres/ [v T] to say or show that you think something is especially important: *Mann stressed the need to educate people about the risks of AIDS.* | *She said smoking was not permitted anywhere in the school – emphasizing the word 'anywhere'.*

+ that *She emphasized that Bosnia would need international assistance to recover from the war.*

⚠ Don't say 'emphasize on something'. Say emphasize something.

⚠ In British English, emphasize can also be spelled emphasise.

overemphasize (also **overemphasise** BRITISH) /ˌəʊvər'emfəsaɪz/ [v T] to emphasize something too much: *I think the book overemphasizes the importance of religion in the history of the US.*

emphasis /'emfəsɪs/ [n U] special attention that is given to a particular activity, subject etc, because it is believed to be more important than other things

+ on *There is a greater emphasis on environmental issues nowadays.*

put emphasis on sth *The school puts a lot of emphasis on discipline and respect for authority.*

with the emphasis on sth *an exciting new French course for beginners, with the emphasis on fun as well as learning*

EMPTY

➡ opposite **FULL**

1 container/bottle/glass

empty /'empti/ [adj] a container, bottle, or glass that is **empty** has nothing inside it: *There were two empty bottles on the table.* | *I noticed her glass was empty, and offered her some more wine.* | *The box was empty – all the money was gone.*

2 place/room/seat

empty /'empti/ [adj] a room, building, town, or place that is **empty** has nothing or no-one in it: *It was Sunday, and the streets were empty.* | *My footsteps echoed across the empty room.*

free /friː/ [adj usually not before noun] a seat, space, or room that is **free** is not being used, and no-one has arranged to use it: *Is this seat free?* | *You'll have to wait till there's a meeting-room free.* | *I think there's a free table in the corner.*

bare /beər/ [adj] a room that is **bare** has very little furniture or other things in it; an area of land that is **bare** does not have much growing on it: *The little church was bare and cold.* | *We drove past mile after mile of bare fields.*

deserted /dɪ'zɜːrtɪd/ [adj] a place or building that is **deserted** is empty and quiet, because the people who are usually there have left: *The village seemed to be completely deserted.* | *We ran along the deserted beach.*

uninhabited /ˌʌnɪn'hæbɪtɪd◄/ [adj] an area or place that is **uninhabited** has no people living in it: *Most of the islands in Clear Bay are uninhabited.* | *The castle is now uninhabited.*

3 paper/tape/screen

blank /blæŋk/ [adj] a **blank** screen, tape, or piece of paper has nothing written or recorded on it: *I want to record the film.*

Do we have any blank video cassettes? |
Ian stared at the blank sheet of paper in front of him.

space /speɪs/ [n C] a place that has been left empty in a piece of writing, especially so that you can write something in it: *There's a space for you to sign your name.*

4 to make a place or container empty

empty /'empti/ [v T] to make something empty by removing what was in it: *The garbage cans are emptied once a week.* | *"See you," he called, emptying his glass and making for the door.*

emptying – emptied – have emptied

clear out /,klɪər 'aut/ [phrasal verb T] to empty a building, room, cupboard etc, especially because you no longer want the things that are in it
clear out sth *I found a pile of old letters while I was clearing out my desk.*
clear sth out *We must clear the garage out this weekend.*

END

➡ look here for ...
  • the end of a period of time, film, book etc
  • the end of an object, the street etc

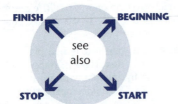

FINISH — BEGINNING

see also

STOP — START

1 the last part of a period, event, film, book etc

the end /ðɪ 'end/ [n singular] the last part of a period of time, an event, a film, a book etc
+ of *The end of the game was really exciting.*
at/before/until the end *Sam left New York at the end of December.* | *It was such a terrible movie, half of the audience walked out before the end.*

the very end (=the last moment, sentence etc) *You don't find out who the murderer is until the very end of the book.*

ending /'endɪŋ/ [n C] the things that happen at the end of a story or film: *In the Spanish version of this story, the ending is completely different.*
happy ending (=an ending in which everyone is happy) *I love those old Hollywood movies with happy endings.*

finale /fɪ'nɑːli‖fɪ'næli/ [n C usually singular] the exciting or impressive last part of a piece of music, show, ceremony etc
+ of *the finale of Beethoven's ninth symphony*
the grand finale (=the very impressive finale) *For the grand finale there was a marching band and fireworks.*

2 to end

end /end/ [v I] if an event, story, situation, or period of time **ends**, there is no more of it left: *World War II ended in 1945.* | *How does the story end?*
end in sth (=end in a particular way, especially a bad way) *Their marriage finally ended in divorce three years later.* | *a school trip that ended in tragedy when three children were killed in an accident*

finish /'fɪnɪʃ/ [v I] to end – use this especially to say what time something ends: *What time does your class finish?* | *The celebrations didn't finish till after midnight.*

> ⚠ **Finish** can often be used instead of **end**, but don't use it to talk about stories, films etc, or about periods of time. It is mostly used about organized events, such as a meeting, a class, or a party.

be over /biː 'əuvəʳ/ [phrasal verb I] if an event or activity **is over**, it has ended, and nothing more is going to happen: *By the time we arrived, the party was already over.*
be all over (=have completely finished) *The game should be all over by 5 o'clock.*

come to an end /,kʌm tu ən 'end/ to finally end – use this about a period of time, a situation, or an activity that has continued for a long time: *When this job comes to an end, I'll be unemployed again.* | *It was already September, and our stay in Zurich was coming to an end.*

3 happening at the end

at the end /ət ði 'end/ during the last part of an event or period of time: *The movie was really sad – at the end the little girl dies.*
+ of *There will be time for questions at the end of the meeting.*

> ⚠ Don't confuse **at the end** (=during the last part of something) and **in the end** (=after a period of time).

final /'faɪnl/ [adj only before noun] happening at the end of an event, book, or film: *the final stages of the project* | *the book's final chapter*

closing /'kləʊzɪŋ/ [adj only before noun] FORMAL **closing remarks/speech/ceremony etc** remarks etc which come at the end of an event, meeting, or book: *By the time he made his closing remarks, I was almost asleep.*

end with sth /'end wɪð (sth)/ [phrasal verb T] if an event, book, or film **ends with** something, that is what happens at the end of it: *The concert ended with a laser light show.* | *The advertisement ends with the usual appeal for people to give money.*

4 happening at the end of a long period of time

finally/eventually/in the end /'faɪnəli, ɪ'ventʃuəli, ɪn ði 'end/ [adv] a long period of time, especially after a lot of difficulties or after a long delay: *After a lot of questioning, James finally admitted he had broken the window.* | *The plane eventually arrived at 6:30 – over three hours late.* | *In the end, I decided that the best thing to do was to ask Billy for help.*

> ⚠ You can use **eventually** or **in the end** by itself to answer a question: *"Did you find the book you wanted?" "Yes, eventually."* Don't use **finally** like this.

at last /ət 'lɑːst‖-'læst/ use this when something good happens after you have waited for it for a long time: *I'm really glad that Ken's found a job at last.* | *At last the rain stopped and the players came back on the field.*

at long last (=after a very long time) *At long last he was able to see his family again.*

end up /ˌend 'ʌp/ [phrasal verb I] If you **end up** in a situation, you get into that situation at the end of a series of events which you did not plan: *Forbes ended up in a French prison for drug dealing.*
end up doing sth *We planned to go into town that night, but ended up staying in watching TV.*

5 the part or point at the end of an object

end /end/ [n C] the part at the end of something long and narrow: *Stop chewing the end of your pen!*
the end of the road/street/passage etc (=the furthest part at the end) *Go to the end of the street and turn left.*
at both ends/at one end *You need a long pole with a hook at one end.*

point /pɔɪnt/ [n C] the thin, sharp end of something such as a needle, stick, or sword
+ of *Colonel Bilby tapped the metal point of his umbrella on the wooden floor.* | *the point of a knife*

tip /tɪp/ [n C] the narrow part at the end of something such as a finger, a branch, or a piece of land
+ of *Dr Gordon felt my neck with the tips of his fingers.* | *The village is on the southern tip of the island.*

ENJOY

LOVE FREE TIME

see also

HATE LIKE/ NOT LIKE

ENTHUSIASTIC/UNENTHUSIASTIC

1 to get pleasure from doing something

enjoy /ɪn'dʒɔɪ/ [v T] to get pleasure from doing something: *Did you enjoy the party?*

enjoy doing sth *My father enjoys playing golf at weekends.*

enjoy yourself (=have fun and feel happy when you are doing something) *The park was full of people enjoying themselves in the sunshine.*

⚠ Don't say 'I enjoy to do it'. Say **I enjoy doing it**.

⚠ Don't say 'I very enjoy it'. Say **I enjoy it very much** or (in spoken English) **I really enjoy it**: *We enjoyed the meal very much – thanks for inviting us.*

like /laɪk/ [v T] to enjoy doing something, especially something that you do regularly or for a long time

like doing sth/like to do sth *I like to relax and read a book in the evenings.* | *Do you like travelling by train?*

⚠ Usually it doesn't matter whether you say **like doing sth** or **like to do sth**. But when you mean someone likes the situation or place they are in, you must use **like doing sth**: *I like living in London* (not 'I like to live in London').

⚠ Don't say 'I like very much watching TV'. Say **I really like watching TV**.

love /lʌv/ [v T] ESPECIALLY SPOKEN to enjoy doing something very much and get a lot of pleasure from it: *Cassie works in the theatre and she loves her work.*

love doing sth/love to do sth *She loved to sit in the park and feed the ducks.* | *I love going out in the snow.*

have a good time/have a great time /hæv ə ˌɡʊd 'taɪm, hæv ə ˌɡreɪt 'taɪm/ ESPECIALLY SPOKEN to enjoy yourself very much when you are doing something with other people: *We had a great time last night – you should have come.* | *Did you have a good time at the beach?*

have fun /ˌhæv 'fʌn/ to enjoy yourself with other people, for example by relaxing, talking, or laughing with them: *I was having so much fun I forgot how late it was.*

have fun doing sth *We had fun trying to guess who Mike's new girlfriend was.*

2 experiences and activities that you enjoy

enjoyable /ɪn'dʒɔɪəbəl/ [adj] an **enjoyable** activity, especially something you do with other people, is pleasant and interesting: *We spent an enjoyable evening playing cards.* | *I try to make my lessons more enjoyable by using games.*

fun /fʌn/ [n U] ESPECIALLY SPOKEN if something is **fun**, you enjoy it because you do interesting and exciting things: *"How was your weekend?" "It was fun."*

it is fun to do sth/it is fun doing sth *It's fun to play in the pool.* | *It'll be fun seeing all my old friends again.*

good fun (=very enjoyable) *Have you ever been windsurfing? It's really good fun.*

have fun (=enjoy something a lot) *I haven't had so much fun in years.*

⚠ Don't say 'it is a fun'. Say **it is fun**.

⚠ Don't confuse **fun** (something you enjoy) and **funny** (something that makes you laugh).

3 the feeling you get when you enjoy something

pleasure /'pleʒər/ [n U] the happy feeling you get when you are enjoying something

get pleasure from sth *My father always got a lot of pleasure from being with his grandchildren.*

do sth for pleasure (=because it gives you pleasure) *I don't very often read for pleasure.*

give/bring pleasure (=make people happy) *Her singing has given so much pleasure to so many people over the years.*

enjoyment /ɪn'dʒɔɪmənt/ [n U] the feeling you get when you enjoy doing something

get enjoyment out of sth *I get a lot of enjoyment out of working with young children.*

+ of *The bad weather didn't spoil our enjoyment of the vacation.*

When you see **EC**, go to the **ESSENTIAL COMMUNICATION** section.

4 someone that people enjoy being with

be good company /biː ˌgʊd ˈkʌmpəni/ if someone **is good company**, people enjoy spending time with them: *I like sharing a room with Kathy – she's good company.*

○**be fun** /biː ˈfʌn/ SPOKEN use this about people who are always cheerful, interesting, and amusing: *Let's invite Margy – she's always fun.*

5 to enjoy something that most people would not enjoy

revel in sth /ˈrevəl ɪn (sth)/ [phrasal verb T] to enjoy something that most people would not like: *Her job is very stressful, but she seems to revel in it.*
revelling – revelled – have revelled BRITISH
reveling – reveled – have reveled AMERICAN

take pleasure in doing sth /ˌteɪk ˈpleʒər ɪn duːɪŋ (sth)/ to enjoy doing something that upsets or annoys someone: *Her husband seemed to take pleasure in pointing out her mistakes.* | *Mr Broadbent took great pleasure in telling me I was fired.*

ENOUGH/ NOT ENOUGH

➡ see also **FULL**

1 when there is a large enough amount of something that you need

enough /ɪˈnʌf/ [quantifier] *Here's $20. Is that enough?* | *He wasn't making enough money, and so he closed the business.* | *Have you got enough drivers? I can help if you need me.*
enough money/space/work etc for *I made loads of food, so there should be enough for everyone.* | *Will there be enough room for Joey in the car?*

more than enough (=more than you need, but not too much or too many) *I've given you more than enough time to make up your mind.*
I've had enough BRITISH (=say this when you have eaten enough food) *"Would you like some more pizza?" "No thanks, I've had enough."*

> ⚠ Don't say 'the food wasn't enough'. Say **there wasn't enough food**. **Enough** usually goes before the noun.

plenty /ˈplenti/ [quantifier] more than enough – use this when you do not need any more of something: *"Do you need any more paper?" "Oh, no thanks. I have plenty here."*
+ of *There's plenty of food, so don't buy any more.* | *Don't worry, we've plenty of time.*

sufficient /səˈfɪʃənt/ [adj] FORMAL enough: *Does a vegetarian diet provide sufficient protein?*
+ for *Seven hours sleep is sufficient for most people.*

adequate /ˈædɪkwɪt/ [adj] FORMAL enough in amount, and good enough in quality: *None of his workers received adequate safety training.*
+ for *The computer has 16 megabytes of memory, which should be adequate for most users.*

last /lɑːst‖læst/ [v I] if an amount of food or money **lasts** for a period of time, there is enough of it for that period
+ until *I still have $100, but that won't last till the end of the vacation.*
last (sb) 2 years/3 days etc *We set off up the mountain, carrying equipment, tents, and enough food to last five days.*
last sb 4 years/3 months etc *£50? That won't last you a day in London!*

2 to have enough time or money to do what you want

have enough time/money /ˌhæv ɪnʌf ˈtaɪm, ˈmʌni/ to have enough time or enough money to do what you want: *I'll come and see you if I have enough time.*
have enough time/money to do sth *We didn't have enough money to go on vacation this year.*

E

have the time/have the money
/ˌhæv ðə ˈtaɪm, ˌhæv ðə ˈmʌni/ to have enough time or enough money to do something: *I know I should take some exercise, but I just never seem to have the time.*

have the time/money to do sth *Now that he's retired, he's got the time to travel.* | *If I had the money, I'd buy a car like that.*

can afford /kən əˈfɔːrd/ to have enough money to do something or to buy something: *I love the apartment, but I don't think we can afford the rent.*

can afford to do sth *They can afford to go on vacation in the Caribbean every year.*

⚠ Don't say 'can afford doing something'. Say **can afford to do something**.

3 big enough/old enough/ strong enough etc

enough /ɪˈnʌf/ [adv]
big enough/old enough/strong enough etc *Will that box be big enough?*
+ for *The road was just wide enough for the truck to get through.*
+ to do sth *Liz is smart enough to figure it out.*

⚠ Don't say 'she's enough old to drive a car'. Say **she's old enough to drive a car**. **Enough** comes after the adjective.

4 when you have done something enough or when it has happened enough

enough /ɪˈnʌf/ [adv] *I think we've talked about this enough.* | *If it rains enough this month, the harvest will be a good one.*

5 not enough

not enough /nɒt ɪˈnʌf/ not enough for what you need: *I gave her $200, but she said it wasn't enough.* | *There won't be enough chairs.* | *I don't think you're getting enough sleep.*
+ for *One bottle of wine won't be enough for everyone.*

not enough to do sth *There aren't enough people to make a full team.*

not have enough to do/eat/drink etc *They never give us enough to eat.*

not old/strong etc enough *She wanted to see the movie, but she wasn't old enough.* | *Could you get that book down for me? I'm not tall enough.*

too little/too few /tuː ˈlɪtl, tuː ˈfjuː/ [quantifier] less than you need or fewer than you need – use this especially when you are criticizing or complaining about something

too few roads/doctors/hotels etc *Too many patients and too few doctors – that's the problem!*

too little time/money/food etc *There's too little time to do everything that needs to be done.*

too little/too few to do sth *There were some police officers there, but too few to control the crowd.*

far too little/few (=much too little or few) *Far too little research has been done in this area.*

⚠ Use **too few** with countable nouns like books, shops, and students: *The school had to close because there were too few students.* Use **too little** with uncountable nouns like time, money, and food: *The government has paid too little attention to the needs of disabled people.*

⚠ In spoken English, it is more usual to say **not enough** than to say **too little** or **too few**.

shortage /ˈʃɔːrtɪdʒ/ [n C] a situation in which there is not enough of something very basic and important that people need in order to live or work

water/food/housing etc shortage *Parts of Britain are suffering water shortages after the unusually dry summer.*
+ of *There is a shortage of nurses and doctors in the area.*

acute/severe shortage (=a very bad shortage) *There is an acute shortage of housing in South Africa's urban areas.*

be short of /biː ˈʃɔːrt ɒv/ to not have enough of something basic that you need: *I was short of money, so I had to ask George for $20.*

scarce /skeə^rs/ [adj] if something is **scarce**, there is not enough of it, so it is very difficult to get or buy: *During the war, things like clothes and shoes were scarce.* | *Jobs are scarce, and a lot of people are unemployed.*

lack of /'læk ɒv/ [n singular] if there is a **lack of** something, there is not enough of it, or there is none of it at all
lack of sleep/time/money etc *Fernando's eyes were red through lack of sleep.* | *Most of our problems are caused by lack of money.*
lack of enthusiasm/confidence/interest etc *It's lack of confidence, not lack of ability, that makes most people fail.*

ENTER

➡ see also **LEAVE**

1 to enter a place

go in/go into /ˌgəʊ 'ɪn, ˌgəʊ 'ɪntuː/ [phrasal verb I/T] to go into a room, building etc: *It was getting cold, so we went in.* | *They won't let you go in unless you leave your bag outside.*
go into sth *Everyone showed their tickets as they went into the hall.*

enter /'entə^r/ [v T] FORMAL to go or come into a room, building, country etc: *The army entered the city from the north.* | *As soon as he entered the room, he knew there was something wrong.*

> ⚠ Don't say 'enter in a room' or 'enter to a room'. Say **enter a room**.

come in /ˌkʌm 'ɪn/ [phrasal verb I] if someone **comes in**, they enter a room or building that you are in: *As soon as Adrian came in, everyone stopped talking.* | *That must be Nina coming in right now.*
come into sth *Come into the house and get warm.*

get in /ˌget 'ɪn/ [phrasal verb I] to succeed in entering a room, building, or area that is difficult to enter, especially by finding an unusual way in: *How did you get in? I thought the door was locked.*
get into sth *The burglars got into the apartments by pretending to be electricians.*

burst in /ˌbɜː^rst 'ɪn/ [phrasal verb I] to suddenly enter a room making a lot of noise: *Two men with guns burst in and told us to lie on the floor.*
burst into sth *Lotty burst into the room waving a letter in the air.*

2 to use force to enter a place

force your way in /ˌfɔː^rs jɔː^r weɪ 'ɪn/ to enter a building or room by using force, especially when someone is trying to stop you: *They've blocked the door. We'll have to force our way in.*
force your way into sth *Police eventually forced their way into the building and arrested the gunman.*

break in /ˌbreɪk 'ɪn/ [phrasal verb I] to enter a building by using force, in order to steal something: *If anyone tries to break in, the alarm will go off.*
break into sth *Vandals broke into the school last night.*

3 to tell someone to enter your room or house

come in /ˌkʌm 'ɪn/ SPOKEN say **come in** when you want someone to come into your room, home, or office: *There was a knock at the door. 'Come in,' she called.* | *Come in and sit down. I'll be ready in a minute.*

ask sb in /ˌɑːsk (sb) 'ɪn‖ˌæsk-/ INFORMAL to ask someone if they want to come into your home: *Stella didn't know whether to ask him in or not.*

4 to allow someone to enter a place

let sb in /ˌlet (sb) 'ɪn/ [phrasal verb T] *Let me in! It's freezing out here.* | *There's Ryan at the door. Let him in, would you?*

5 to not allow someone to enter a place

keep out /ˌkiːp 'aʊt/ [phrasal verb T] to prevent someone from entering a room
keep sb out/keep out sb *His house has a complicated security system to keep out intruders.*

> When you see **EC**, go to the **ESSENTIAL COMMUNICATION** section.

E

keep sb out of sth *We've got to keep Bill out of the kitchen – his birthday present's in there!*

turn sb away /ˌtɜːʳn (sb) əˈweɪ/ [phrasal verb T] to refuse to let someone into a place where a public event is happening, especially because it is full: *The club's so popular we have to turn people away every night.* | *Hundreds of disappointed fans were turned away at the gates.*

lock sb out /ˌlɒk (sb) ˈaʊt‖ˌlɑːk-/ [phrasal verb T] to stop someone entering a room or building by locking the door: *My girlfriend locked me out of the house.*

6 a door or space that you use to enter a place

entrance (also **entry**) /ˈentrəns, ˈentri/ [n C] a door or space that you go through to enter a place: *Simpson used a side entrance to avoid the waiting reporters.*
+ to *the entrance to the exhibition*

way in /ˌweɪ ˈɪn/ [n C] the place where you can enter a large public building: *We walked all the way around the museum, looking for the way in.*

ENTHUSIASTIC/ UNENTHUSIASTIC

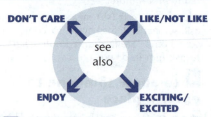

DON'T CARE   LIKE/NOT LIKE
see
also
ENJOY   EXCITING/ EXCITED

1 enthusiastic

enthusiastic /ɪnˌθjuːziˈæstɪk◀‖-ˌθuː-/ [adj] behaving in a way that shows how much you like, enjoy, or approve of something: *A small but enthusiastic crowd cheered as we ran onto the field.* | *Several enthusiastic young teachers have just started working at the school.*
+ about *He's still really enthusiastic about his new school.*

enthusiastically [adv] *The public has responded very enthusiastically to our appeal.*

keen /kiːn/ [adj] BRITISH very enthusiastic about an activity or job: *She hasn't much experience but she's very keen.*
+ on *Alex has always been keen on athletics.*
a keen golfer/photographer/gardener etc *Chris is a keen photographer – he's won several competitions.*
keen to do sth *Mark was keen to make a good impression on the new French teacher.*

eager /ˈiːgəʳ/ [adj] very enthusiastic and excited about something that is going to happen or about something that you are going to do: *A crowd of eager fans waited outside the hotel.*
eager to do sth *She hurried home from college, eager to hear Tom's news.*
eagerness [n U] very enthusiastic and excited feelings or behaviour
eagerness to do sth *He tripped over the cat in his eagerness to get to the phone.*

enthusiasm /ɪnˈθjuːziæzəm‖-ˈθuː-/ [n U] enthusiastic feelings or behaviour
+ for *I'd forgotten about Jim's enthusiasm for going on 20-mile walks.*
be full of enthusiasm (=be very enthusiastic) *Greta was full of enthusiasm for the plan.*

2 not enthusiastic

unenthusiastic/not enthusiastic /ˌʌnɪnθjuːziˈæstɪk, ˌnɒt ɪnˌθjuːziˈæstɪk‖-ˌθuː-/ [adj] *Are you sure you want to see the movie? You don't sound very enthusiastic.*
+ about *She had never been very enthusiastic about her job as a designer.* | *The teachers were distinctly unenthusiastic about the whole idea*

half-hearted /ˌhɑːf ˈhɑːʳtɪd◀‖ˈhæf-/ [adj] **half-hearted attempt/response/measure etc** an attempt etc that is made without much enthusiasm or effort: *Yves had made a half-hearted attempt to be friendly.*

WORD BANK # ENVIRONMENT

➡ see pages 240–243

EQUIPMENT

things you use for doing something

➡ see also **MACHINE, COMPUTERS**

equipment /ɪˈkwɪpmənt/ [n U] the special machines or tools that you use for doing something: *You should check all electrical equipment regularly.*
office/video/sports etc equipment *Thieves stole all the video equipment from the college.*
a piece of equipment *a special piece of equipment for checking tyres*

> ⚠ Don't say 'equipments' or 'an equipment'. **Equipment** is an uncountable noun.

◯**things** /θɪŋz/ [n plural] SPOKEN the special clothes and other equipment that you need for a sport or similar activity: *Now, have you got all your things ready?*
swimming/painting/sewing etc things *She keeps all her sewing things in a small basket.*

gear /ɡɪər/ [n U] INFORMAL the equipment and special clothes that you need to do something, especially an activity that you do in your free time: *Mike's crazy about photography – he's got all the gear.*
camping/fishing/skiing etc gear *Did you remember to pack your fishing gear?*

kit /kɪt/ [n C] **shaving/sewing/repair etc kit** a set of small things that you use to do something: *The sewing kit contained needles, pins, cotton, and a pair of scissors.*

◯**stuff** /stʌf/ [n U] SPOKEN INFORMAL the equipment that you use to do something
camping/cleaning/painting etc stuff *The cleaning stuff's in the cupboard under the stairs.*

> When you see **EC**, go to the **ESSENTIAL COMMUNICATION** section.

ESCAPE

1 from a place/person/prison/dangerous situation

escape /ɪˈskeɪp/ [v I] to succeed in leaving a dangerous place or situation, or a place that someone is trying to stop you from leaving: *Anyone trying to escape will be shot.* | *Only four people managed to escape before the roof collapsed.*
+ from *Josie managed to escape from her attacker and call the police.* | *Two men escaped from Durham Jail last night.*
+ over/into/through etc *Some refugees managed to escape over the border into Tanzania.*

get out /ˌɡet ˈaʊt/ [phrasal verb I] to escape from a place that is difficult to escape from, or where there is danger: *How could the dog get out when the gate was shut?*
+ of *No-one's gotten out of the Kansas county jail in 50 years.*
get out alive *We were lucky to get out alive – the whole building was on fire.*

> ⚠ **Get out** is more informal than **escape**.

get away /ˌɡet əˈweɪ/ [phrasal verb I] to escape from someone who is chasing you, so they do not catch you: *The gunmen got away in a stolen car.*
get away from *Thousands of civilians are trying to get away from the advancing army.*

run away/run off /ˌrʌn əˈweɪ, ˌrʌn ˈɒf‖ -ˈɔːf/ [phrasal verb I] to try to escape from someone by running away: *Don't run away – I'm not going to hurt you.*
+ into/down/across etc *He jumped out of the car and ran off into the woods.*
+ from *If you run away from the bull, it's almost certain to attack you.*

ESCAPE continues on page 244

ENVIRONMENT

WORD BANK

LAND AND SEA   TRANSPORT

PROBLEM   see also   DAMAGE

⚏ OPINIONS   DESTROY

PROTEST   PROTECT

POLLUTION
Pollution is damage to the air, sea, rivers, or land caused by chemicals, waste and harmful gases.
Pollutants include **toxic waste, pesticides,** and **fertilizers.**

E Many people believe that the way that we live our lives today is having an extremely bad effect on the environment. Here are some examples of environmental problems and solutions, and the vocabulary you need to talk about them.

1 environmental problems

CARS
The biggest **polluter** today is the car. Exhaust **fumes** are the main cause of bad **air quality**, which can make people feel ill and have difficulty breathing. This problem is especially bad in some cities where, on days when there is not much wind, a brown layer of **smog** hangs in the air. The number of cars is increasing every year, and this causes serious **congestion**. Governments then build new roads to try to improve the situation, but this means that they cut down trees and destroy more of the countryside.

vocabulary

acid rain /ˌæsɪd 'reɪn/ [n U] rain that is harmful to trees and buildings because it has become mixed with smoke from factories and power stations

air quality /'eəʳ ˌkwɒlᵻtiǁ-ˌkwɑː-/ [n U] how clean or dirty the air is in a particular town or place: *Sometimes the air quality is so bad that people have to stay indoors.*

alternative /ɔːl'tɜːʳnətɪv/ [adj] **alternative** methods are very different from the methods which have been used for a long time, and which people regard as normal, but they are usually less harmful: *Scientists are searching for alternative sources of energy.*

the atmosphere /ðɪ 'ætməsfɪəʳ/ [n singular] the mixture of air and gases that surrounds the Earth

car pool /'kɑːʳ puːl/ [n C] a group of car owners who agree to drive everyone in the group to work or school on different days, so that only one car is used at a time

CFCs also **chlorofluorocarbons** /ˌsiː ef 'siːz, ˌklɔːrəʊflʊərəʊ'kɑːʳbənz/ [n plural] chemicals that damage the ozone layer. CFCs are used especially in refrigerators and in some aerosols.

congestion /kən'dʒestʃən/ [n U] when there are too many cars on a road, so that the traffic moves very slowly: *If people lived closer to their jobs, there would be less congestion on the freeways.*

electric car /ɪˌlektrɪk 'kɑːʳ/ [n C] a car that uses special electric batteries, instead of petrol, as its source of power

endangered /ɪn'deɪndʒəʳd/ [adj] if a type of plant or animal is endangered, it may soon no longer exist
endangered species *The black rhino is an endangered species and is protected by law.*

the environment /ðɪ ɪn'vaɪərənmənt/ [n singular] the air, water, and land where people, animals, and plants live, and the way all these things depend on each other so that life can continue
harm/damage/destroy/pollute the environment *Local people are protesting because the planned new road will destroy the environment.*
protect the environment *New laws are being introduced to protect the environment from industrial gases that cause acid rain.*

environmental /ɪn'vaɪərən'mentl/ [adj] use this to talk about things that affect the environment, especially

ENVIRONMENT

THE GREENHOUSE EFFECT

The **greenhouse effect** is caused by harmful gases known as **greenhouse gases**. These gases are produced when we burn fuels, especially coal burned in **power stations** to make electricity.

greenhouse gases

heat

the Earth

These gases go up into the Earth's **atmosphere** and stop heat from leaving the Earth.

Because the heat cannot escape, the Earth is getting warmer. This is known as **global warming**.
Global warming may cause the ice at the North Pole and South Pole to melt and sea levels to rise, leading to serious flooding in many parts of the world. In other places, temperatures will rise and there will be less rain, turning more of the land into desert.

HOLES IN THE OZONE LAYER

The **ozone layer** is a layer of gases that protects us from **ultraviolet light** from the sun, which can have a harmful effect on animals, and causes **skin cancer** in humans.

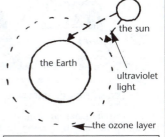

the sun

the Earth

ultraviolet light

the ozone layer

The ozone layer is being damaged by chemicals, especially **CFCs**, and when holes appear in the ozone layer, harmful light from the sun reaches the Earth.

---

problems and damage to the environment: *Public transportation systems can help to reduce environmental pollution.*

environmental group /ɪnˈvaɪərənˈmentl ˌgruːp/ [n C] a group of people that aims to protect the environment, for example by spreading information and trying to make governments change their policy

environmentally friendly /ɪnˈvaɪərənˈmentl-i ˈfrendli/ [adj] causing less harm to the environment

extinct /ɪkˈstɪŋkt/ [adj] if a type of plant or animal is extinct, it no longer exists

fertilizer /ˈfɜːtɪlaɪzə‖ˈfɜːrtl-aɪzər/ [n C] a mixture of chemicals used by farmers to help crops grow

flooding /ˈflʌdɪŋ/ [n U] when an area of land becomes covered with water

fumes /fjuːmz/ [n plural] harmful gas or smoke, for example from factories or cars, which damages the environment and people's health

exhaust fumes (=fumes from cars)

global warming /ˌgləʊbəl ˈwɔːmɪŋ/ the idea that the Earth's weather is gradually becoming warmer because of pollution

green /griːn/ [adj] use this to talk about things connected with protecting the environment, such as ideas and policies, or products you can buy that affect the environment

green issues (=ideas about the environment that are discussed in meetings, newspapers, on television etc) *People are becoming more aware of green issues, such as the need to reduce road traffic.*

green products (=that do not harm the environment) *They sell green products such as recycled paper and organic vegetables.*

greenhouse gas /ˈgriːnhaʊs ˌgæs/ [n C] a gas that forms a layer around the Earth and stops heat from leaving the atmosphere

the greenhouse effect /ðə ˈgriːnhaʊs ɪˌfekt/ [n singular] the gradual warming of the Earth caused by gases that stop heat from leaving the Earth's atmosphere

habitat /ˈhæbɪtæt/ [n C/U] the natural home of a plant or animal: *Cutting down the forest will destroy the habitat of thousands of birds and animals.*

natural habitat (=used especially when you are com-

ENVIRONMENT continues on the next page

ENVIRONMENT

ACID RAIN
Acid rain is rain that is harmful to the environment because it contains acid from factory smoke. Acid rain causes damage to trees, rivers, and buildings.

THE DESTRUCTION OF HABITATS
All over the world, **wildlife** is being **threatened** because **habitats** and **woodlands** are being destroyed. **Rainforest**s are being cut down so that people can use the land to grow crops. Many **species** of animal have become **extinct**, and many more are **endangered**.

2 some solutions

ALTERNATIVE FORMS OF TRANSPORT
One of the main problems with cars is that they cause a lot of pollution and often carry only one person. **Public transport** is more **environmentally friendly** because buses and trains can carry large numbers of people at the same time. **Car pools** are another way of reducing the number of cars on the roads. Even cleaner solutions are **electric cars**, and bicycles.

---

paring it with an unnatural habitat, such as a zoo) *This snake's natural habitat is the Amazonian jungle.*

organic /ɔːˈgænɪk/ [adj] **organic** fruit, meat, and vegetables have been produced without using chemicals

the ozone layer /ði ˈəʊzəʊn ˌleɪəʳ/ [n singular] a layer of gases around the Earth that protects us by stopping harmful light from the sun reaching the Earth

pesticide /ˈpestɪsaɪd/ [n C] a mixture of chemicals used by farmers to kill insects or small animals

pollutant /pəˈluːtənt/ [n C] a substance that pollutes the environment: *Scientists have discovered that the fish are being killed by pollutants in the water.*

polluter /pəˈluːtəʳ/ [n C] someone or something that damages the environment with harmful chemicals or waste

pollution /pəˈluːʃən/ [n U] damage caused to the environment by harmful chemicals or waste

power station /ˈpaʊəʳ ˌsteɪʃən/ [n C] a building where electricity is produced

protest /prəˈtest/ [v I/T] to publicly say or do something to show that you think something is wrong and you want it to be changed

protest against sth BRITISH **protest sth** AMERICAN *Environmental groups have organized a march to protest against government plans to build a road through the forest.*

protest /ˈprəʊtest/ [n C] when a group of people come together to show that they think something is wrong and they want it to be changed

protester /prəˈtestəʳ/ [n C] someone who protests against something

public transport BRITISH **public transportation** AMERICAN /ˌpʌblɪk ˈtrænspɔːt, ˌpʌblɪk ˌtrænspɔːˈteɪʃən‖-træn spɔr-/ [n U] bus and train services provided for everyone to use

rainforest /ˈreɪnˌfɒrɪst‖-fɔr-, -ˌfɑr-/ [n C] a tropical forest with tall trees that are very close together, growing in a part of the world where it rains a lot: *a campaign to stop the destruction of the rainforests*

recycle /riːˈsaɪkəl/ [v I/T] to take materials that have already been used, and to put them through a special process so that they can be used again

recycled /riːˈsaɪkəld/ [adj]
recycled paper/plastic/glass etc *All the bottles we*

ENVIRONMENT

RENEWABLE ENERGY SOURCES
Renewable energy sources such as **wind power**, **wave power**, and **solar power** do not pollute the environment. They are much cleaner than oil and coal.

wave turbine

solar panels

wind turbines

GREEN PRODUCTS
We can help the environment by choosing to buy **green** products. Examples of green products are **recycled** paper, wood from **sustainable sources**, and **organic** fruit and vegetables.

ORGANIC PRODUCE

RECYCLING
Recycling is when you use something again instead of throwing it away. Glass, cans, paper, and plastic can all be **recycled**.

PROTESTING
Many people try to protect the environment by joining **environmental groups** that inform people about **green** issues, and try to persuade governments to take more care of the environment, especially by organizing **protests**.

SAVE OUR FOREST

NO TO THE NEW ROAD

---

use are made from recycled glass

renewable energy /rɪˌnjuːəbəl ˈenərdʒɪ‖ˌnɪ.nuː-/ [n C] energy that is always replaced naturally after it has been used

renewable energy sources (=something that can provide renewable energy, eg the wind, waves, and the sun)

skin cancer /ˈskɪn ˌkænsər/ [n C/U] a skin disease that can kill people, caused by ultraviolet light

smog /smɒg‖smɔːg/ [n U] dirty brown air in cities that is a mixture of fog, smoke, and harmful gases

solar power /ˈsəʊlər ˌpaʊər/ [n U] energy from the sun, used to make electricity and to heat water

species /ˈspiːʃiːz/ [n C] a group of animals or plants of the same kind: *The coast is home to many species of birds.*

endangered species (=one that may soon no longer exist) *Wolves used to be common throughout Europe, but are now an endangered species.*

protected species (=one that is protected by laws, so that it is illegal to kill it or harm it)

sustainable source /səˌsteɪnəbəl ˈsɔːrs/ [n C] if wood is from a **sustainable source**, it is from a forest where

the trees can be replaced as quickly as they are cut down

threaten /ˈθretn/ [v T] if something **threatens** the environment or a type of plant or animal, it is damaging it and may eventually destroy it: *Economic development and rapid population growth threaten the entire planet.*

toxic waste /ˌtɒksɪk ˈweɪst‖ˌtɑːk-/ [n U] poisonous waste from industry

ultraviolet light /ˌʌltrəvaɪələt ˈlaɪt/ [n U] a part of sunlight that humans cannot see. It can be harmful but most of it does not normally reach the Earth

wave power /ˈweɪv ˌpaʊər/ [n U] energy from the movement of the sea, used to make electricity

wildlife /ˈwaɪldlaɪf/ [n U] animals and plants living and growing in natural conditions

wind power /ˈwɪnd ˌpaʊər/ [n U] energy from the wind, used to make electricity and to make machines work

woodland /ˈwʊdlənd/ [n C/U] an area covered with trees in the northern part of the world, especially Europe

ESCAPE continued from page 239

break out /ˌbreɪk 'aʊt/ [phrasal verb I] to escape from a prison: *Some of the men were planning to break out.*
+ of *breaking out of a maximum security prison*

on the run /ˌɒn ðə 'rʌn/ someone who is **on the run** is trying to hide or escape from someone who is chasing them, especially the police: *After the train robbery he spent three years on the run.*
+ from *Dean was a drug addict who was constantly on the run from the police.*

2 from a difficult/embarrassing/boring situation

escape/get away /ɪ'skeɪp, ˌget ə'weɪ/ [v I] to get out of a difficult, embarrassing, or boring situation: *He decided to tell me all about his trip to Majorca, and I just couldn't get away.* | *Let's see if we can escape before the speeches start.*

3 when someone escapes

escape /ɪ'skeɪp/ [n C] when someone escapes from prison, from danger, or from someone who is chasing them: *They had planned their escape very carefully.* | *Police described it as a very daring escape.*
+ from *It's the story of her escape from a group of kidnappers.*
make your escape (=succeed in escaping) *They made their escape in a small boat they had built themselves.*
a narrow escape (=when you only just escape from danger) *It was a narrow escape – a couple of minutes later the whole place went up in flames.*

4 unable to escape

can't escape/can't get out /ˌkɑːnt ɪ'skeɪp, ˌkɑːnt get 'aʊt‖ˌkænt-/ *I've locked all the doors and windows – he can't get out.* | *Two of the children couldn't escape, and died in the fire.*

trapped /træpt/ [adj] unable to escape from a dangerous place or an unpleasant situation: *The miners have been trapped underground for three days.* | *He was beginning to feel trapped in his job.*

be stuck /biː 'stʌk/ ESPECIALLY SPOKEN to be unable to escape from an unpleasant or boring situation
+ in/with/here *I don't want to be stuck in an office all my life.* | *I'm tired of being stuck here with the kids all day.*

ESPECIALLY

more than usual or more than others

especially/particularly /ɪ'speʃəli, pə'tɪkjʊlə'li/ [adv] use this to emphasize that something is more important or happens more with one particular thing than with any others: *This disease mostly affects women, particularly women over 50.* | *Paris is always full of tourists, especially during the summer months.* | *It's very worrying, especially if you have young children.*
especially good/important/difficult etc *This is a particularly good example of the problem we've been discussing.*

> ⚠ Don't use **especially** or **particularly** at the beginning of a sentence. Don't say 'Especially I like tennis'. Say **I like a lot of sports, especially tennis**.

in particular /ɪn pə'tɪkjʊlə'/ use **in particular** to mention one person or thing that is more important or more interesting than all similar things: *Mary loves most classical music, in particular Bach and Vivaldi.* | *We enjoyed visiting Britain and thought that Scotland in particular was very beautiful.*
anything/anyone/anywhere in particular *Was there anything in particular that you wanted to talk about?*

above all /əˌbʌv 'ɔːl/ use **above all** to emphasize that something is more important than all the other things you have mentioned: *Get plenty of sleep, eat lots of good food, and above all try to relax.* | *John felt sad, upset, and above all angry that his wife could treat him like this.*

special/particular /'speʃəl, pə'tɪkjʊlə'/ [adj only before noun] if you give **special** or **particular** care or attention to something, you give it more attention than usual, or more attention that you give anything else

+ care/attention *You should pay particular attention to spelling.* | *Take special care on the roads tonight – it's icy.*

EVERYWHERE

in or to every place

everywhere /'evriweə^r/ [adv] in every place, or in every part of a place: *I can't find my keys – I've looked everywhere for them.* | *There was water everywhere.* | *There are health clubs everywhere these days.* | *Poverty affects children everywhere – in Europe as well as places like Somalia and Ethiopia.*
everywhere else (=in every other place) *We deliver goods by 10 a.m. in the UK and by midday everywhere else.*

every place /'evri pleɪs/ [adv] AMERICAN INFORMAL everywhere: *They go every place together.*

all over /ɔːl 'əʊvə^r/ [preposition/adv] in every part of a place or surface
all over the world/country etc *a bank with branches all over the country* | *competing teams from all over the world*
all over the floor/wall/your face etc *Katie's toys were spread out all over the floor.* | *There was jam all over her face.*
all over *We had a great holiday in America – we travelled all over.* | *After a couple of hours of exercise, my body ached all over.*

wherever you go /weər,evə^r juː 'gəʊ/ if you see or do something **wherever you go**, you see it or do it in a lot of different places: *Wherever you go there are people asking for money.*

widespread /'waɪdspred/ [adj] happening in many places – use this especially about problems or bad situations that affect many areas or many countries: *There has been widespread flooding in Germany, and the rivers are still rising.* | *Diseases such as typhoid are widespread in the region.*

worldwide /,wɜː^rld'waɪd◂/ [adj only before noun] in every part of the world:

There has been a worldwide increase in cases of AIDS. | *Campaigners are calling for a worldwide ban on whale hunting.* | *a worldwide TV audience of over a billion people*
   worldwide [adv] *The company employs about 20,000 people worldwide.* | *On the Internet, people can communicate worldwide in seconds.*

nationwide /,neɪʃən'waɪd◂/ [adj only before noun] in every part of a country
nationwide strike/demonstration/campaign *Workers held nationwide strikes and demonstrations all over Spain.*
nationwide search/hunt/study/survey *A nationwide hunt was launched yesterday for the killer of 13-year-old Nicola Jones.*
   nationwide [adv] *We have a total of 96 stores nationwide.*

EXACT

1 an exact number/ amount/time

exact /ɪg'zækt/ [adj usually before noun] an **exact** number, amount, or time is completely correct and is no more and no less than it should be: *"Can you tell me the exact time?" "It's 6.37."* | *The exact weight of the baby at birth was 3.2 kg.*
to be exact (=used after a number when giving an exact answer, statement etc) *It took her about an hour – 58 minutes to be exact.*

exactly /ɪg'zæktli/ [adv] use this to emphasize that the number, amount, or time that you are mentioning is completely correct: *It's exactly 5 o'clock.* | *The bill came to exactly $1000.*

precise /prɪ'saɪs/ [adj usually before noun] **precise** information is based on clear and exact measurements, especially when it is important that no mistakes are made: *We need to know your precise location.* | *Each plane has to follow a precise route.*
be precise (=give precise information or figures) *It's difficult to be precise about the number of deaths caused by smoking.*
   precisely [adv] exactly – use this before or after a time: *At precisely 3 o'clock the ceremony began.*

on the dot /ɒn ðə ˈdɒt‖-ˈdɑːt/ INFORMAL if something happens at a particular time **on the dot**, it happens at exactly that time: *The doors of the museum closed at six o'clock on the dot.*

2 an exact description/ translation/copy

accurate /ˈækjɣrət/ [adj] **accurate** information, descriptions, reports etc are completely correct because all the details are true: *You must keep an accurate record of everything you eat for one day.* | *The witness tried to give an accurate description of what she had seen.*

exact /ɪgˈzækt/ [adj] an **exact** copy, model etc of something is like it in every possible way: *'Eavesdrop' means to listen secretly outside someone's door, but there is no exact equivalent in Spanish.* | *It's not an exact copy, but most people wouldn't notice the difference.*

literal /ˈlɪtərəl/ [adj only before noun] a **literal** translation gives the exact meaning of each single word instead of translating whole sentences in a natural way: *You can't give a literal translation of most poetry.*

    literally [adv] *'Vino di tavola' literally means 'table wine' in Italian.* | *The French word for 'bat' is 'chauve-souris', which literally means 'bald mouse'.*

word for word /ˌwɜːrd fər ˈwɜːrd/ if you repeat, copy, or translate something **word for word**, you use the exact words that are in it: *He asked me to repeat word for word the instructions he'd just given me.*

3 exactly how, what, where etc

exactly /ɪgˈzæktli/ [adv] use this when you are giving or asking for exact details or information: *Glue the pieces together, exactly as shown in the diagram.*

    exactly who/what/where etc *The police want to know exactly when you left the building.* | *The doctors can't say exactly what's wrong with my mother – we're very worried about her.*

    who/what/where exactly? *Where exactly are you from?* | *Who exactly did you want to see?*

precisely /prɪˈsaɪsli/ [adv] exactly – use this when it is important to describe something very carefully or to get very exact information

    precisely what/where/who etc *We need to know precisely how much this is going to cost.*

    where/what/who precisely? *What precisely do you mean by 'relativity'?*

4 exactly the right thing

exactly /ɪgˈzæktli/ [adv] use this to emphasize that something is the particular thing that you want or mean: *This is exactly the kind of job that computers are good at.*

    exactly what *The earrings are beautiful! They're exactly what I wanted.*

precisely /prɪˈsaɪsli/ [adv] exactly – use this to emphasize exactly what the situation is, exactly what happened, exactly what you meant etc: *"But none of us can speak French." "That's precisely the problem."* | *There have been a lot of burglaries, and we installed an alarm system for precisely this reason.*

5 not exact

➡ see also **ABOUT**

rough /rʌf/ [adj only before noun] not exact, or not containing exact details: *a rough estimate of the number of people without jobs* | *Tim drew me a rough plan of the farmhouse.*

approximate /əˈprɒksɪmət‖əˈprɑːk-/ [adj] FORMAL an **approximate** number, amount, or time is close to the true number, amount, or time but does not need to be completely correct: *Our approximate time of arrival will be 10:20.* | *Please state on the form the approximate value of all your household goods.*

EXAMPLE

1 a typical example of something

example /ɪgˈzɑːmpəl‖ɪgˈzæm-/ [n C] something that you mention because it is typical of the kind of thing that you are talking about: *There are many ways in which technology has changed our lives. The car is an obvious example.*

+ of *The church is an interesting example of the Gothic style.*

give an example *Attitude problems? Can you give me an example?*

good/typical example *This painting is a typical example of Picasso's work in his Blue Period.* | *Korea and Vietnam are good examples of the fast-growing economies of South-East Asia.*

case /keɪs/ [n C] an example of something that has happened, especially something bad

+ of *There have been some cases of women employees being fired because they are pregnant.*

in one case/in some cases/in every case *In one case a man was charged $2000 for a simple medical check-up.*

instance /ˈɪnstəns/ [n C] FORMAL an example of a particular kind of situation: *Some users of Ecstasy have actually died, but such instances are very rare.*

+ of *several instances of bad management that have led to serious problems*

2 what you say when you give an example

for example/for instance /fər ɪgˈzɑːmpəl, fər ˈɪnstəns‖-ˈzæm-/ use this when you are giving an example: *There are lots of famous buildings in Kyoto, for example the Golden Pavilion and Ryoanyi Temple.* | *Car prices can vary a lot. For example, in Belgium the VW Golf costs £1000 less than in Britain.*

eg/e.g. /ˌiː ˈdʒiː/ use this in written English when you are giving an example or a series of examples: *Make sure you eat foods that contain protein, e.g. meat, cheese, fish, milk, or eggs.* | *This course includes a study of basic language skills (e.g. speaking and listening).*

⚠ In British English, people usually write **eg**; in American English, people usually write **e.g.** Don't use **eg/e.g.** at the beginning of a sentence.

such as /ˈsʌtʃ æz/ [preposition] ESPECIALLY WRITTEN use this directly after a plural noun to give one or two examples of the things

you have just mentioned: *It is difficult to get even basic foods such as sugar and bread.* | *Clint Eastwood is most famous for his tough-guy police movies, such as 'Dirty Harry' and 'The Enforcer'.*

like /laɪk/ [preposition] ESPECIALLY SPOKEN use this when you are giving one or two examples: *We could cook something easy, like pasta.* | *There are a few problems we still haven't settled, like who is going to be in charge while I'm away.*

EXCEPT

➡ see also ⚙ **LINKING WORDS**

1 not including someone or something

except/except for /ɪkˈsept, ɪkˈsept fɔːr/ [preposition] not including the person or thing that you have mentioned: *Everyone's going except Donald.* | *The house was silent except for a clock chiming in the living room.*

⚠ Don't say 'except of' or 'except from'. Say **except** or **except for**.

⚠ At the beginning of a sentence, always use **except for**, not just the word **except** on its own: *Except for a couple of old chairs, the room was empty.*

except /ɪkˈsept/ [conjunction] use this when you say that something is true but then you want to introduce a fact that does not match what you have said

except (that) *Celia looks just like her sister, except that her sister has shorter hair.* | *It's similar to Paris, except the people look a lot poorer.*

except do sth *a computer that can do everything except talk* (=that is the only thing it cannot do)

⚠ Don't begin a sentence with **except**.

apart from (also **aside from** AMERICAN) /əˈpɑːrt frɒm, əˈsaɪd frɒm/ [preposition] use this when you mention one or two facts that do not fit into the main thing that you are saying: *This is an excellent piece of work, apart from a couple of spelling* mistakes. | *Aside from a toothbrush, she took no baggage with her.*

apart from doing sth *Apart from going swimming occasionally, I don't get much exercise.*

with the exception of /wɪð ði ɪkˈsepʃən ɒv/ FORMAL not including only one thing, person, or group: *The whole school, with the exception of the youngest class, had to attend the ceremony.*

with the possible exception of (=but possibly not that person or thing) *I think they should all pass the test, with the possible exception of Fauzi.*

2 someone or something that is not included

exception /ɪkˈsepʃən/ [n C] someone or something that is not included in a general rule, or does not do what most others in the same situation do: *Most of the students did well, though there were one or two exceptions.*

notable exception (=one that is very famous or special) *Women do not usually get to the top in politics, but there have been a few notable exceptions.*

major/minor exception (=an important/ not very important one) *With a few minor exceptions, the legal system in the two countries is very similar.*

EXCITING/EXCITED

➡ see also **ENTHUSIASTIC/ UNENTHUSIASTIC, HAPPY, ENJOY**

1 feeling excited about something

excited /ɪkˈsaɪtɪd/ [adj] feeling happy and full of energy, especially about something good that has happened or is going to happen: *Steve's coming home tomorrow – we're all really excited.* | *crowds of excited football fans*

+ about *How can you be so excited about a stupid computer game?*

get excited *Yes, I'm getting pretty excited about the tour of Eastern Europe. I'm getting a little nervous too.*

+ by *Doctors are very excited by the discovery.*

be excited to do sth *You must be really excited to be chosen out of all those other people.*

⚠ Be careful not to confuse **excited** (=when you feel excited) and **exciting** (=when something makes you feel excited) *We were all* **excited**. | *The movie was* **exciting**.

look forward to /lʊk ˈfɔːrwərd tuː/ [phrasal verb T] to feel excited about something good that is going to happen and to think about it a lot: *The kids are looking forward to their vacation – they've never been to California before.*

look forward to doing sth *She's really looking forward to getting her own flat.*

can't wait /ˌkɑːnt ˈweɪt‖ˌkænt-/ SPOKEN if you **can't wait** for something to happen, you want it to happen soon because you are very excited about it

+ for *I can't wait for him to walk in and find we're all already here.*

can't wait to do sth *He couldn't wait to get home and tell Dean the news.*

thrilled /θrɪld/ [adj not before noun] very excited, happy, and pleased

be thrilled to do sth *I'm thrilled to be back in this country again.*

+ with *Chester's absolutely thrilled with his baby daughter.*

+ at/by *Gemma's parents were thrilled by the enormous response to their appeal.*

thrilled to bits BRITISH SPOKEN **thrilled to pieces** AMERICAN SPOKEN (=very thrilled) *Julie won the competition – she's thrilled to bits.*

be on the edge of your seat /biː ɒn ði ˌedʒ əv jɔːr ˈsiːt/ to be excited and slightly nervous when you are watching something because you do not know what will happen next: *This is a movie that will keep you on the edge of your seat till the final seconds.*

2 when something makes you feel excited

exciting /ɪkˈsaɪtɪŋ/ [adj] making you feel excited: *I've got some exciting news for you.* | *Hockey is a fast, exciting game to watch.*

find sth exciting *Stuart found life in Paris enormously exciting.*

⚠ Be careful not to confuse **exciting** (=when something makes you feel excited) and **excited** (=when you feel excited) *The movie was very* **exciting**. | *We were all* **excited**.

thrilling /'θrɪlɪŋ/ [adj] making you feel very excited and slightly nervous: *The helicopter trip over the mountains was a thrilling end to a fantastic holiday.* | *a thrilling game won by a last-minute goal*

⚠ Don't say 'very thrilling'. Say **absolutely thrilling**.

gripping /'grɪpɪŋ/ [adj] use this about books or films that are so exciting that you cannot stop reading or watching them: *a gripping detective story*

exhilarating /ɪg'zɪləreɪtɪŋ/ [adj] an **exhilarating** experience or activity makes you feel excited and full of energy: *Surfing is a demanding and exhilarating sport.*

dramatic /drə'mætɪk/ [adj] a **dramatic** part of a story, film etc has a lot of exciting and unexpected things happening in it: *The movie starts with a dramatic car chase across the desert.*

3 feeling too excited

overexcited /ˌəʊvərɪk'saɪtɪd/ [adj] someone, especially a child, who is **overexcited** has become too excited to behave calmly: *The kids are getting overexcited and won't go to sleep.*

hysterical /hɪ'sterɪkəl/ [adj] unable to stop shouting, crying etc because you are extremely excited: *Hysterical fans tried to stop Damon's car at the airport.*
get/go hysterical (=become hysterical) *The crowd went hysterical as Juventus scored in the last minute of the game.*

4 the most exciting part of something

climax /'klaɪmæks/ [n C usually singular] the most exciting or important part of a story or event, usually near the end
+ of *A parade through the streets marks the climax of the festival.*
reach a climax *The opera reaches its climax with Violetta's death in the third act.*

highlight /'haɪlaɪt/ [n C] the part of an activity such as a holiday or game that is the most exciting or enjoyable
+ of *The week in New York was definitely the highlight of our trip.* | *Highlights of the ball game will be shown later.*

5 the feeling of being excited

excitement /ɪk'saɪtmənt/ [n U] the feeling of being excited: *If you're looking for excitement, you won't find it here.*
in/with excitement (=in an excited way) *Louise began jumping up and down in excitement.*
great/tremendous excitement (=a lot of excitement) *There's an atmosphere of tremendous excitement here in the stadium.*

thrill /θrɪl/ [n C usually singular] a sudden very strong feeling of excitement and sometimes fear: *Some people enjoy the thrill of hunting dangerous animals.*
get a thrill out of doing sth *I used to get a thrill out of riding a motorbike at high speed.*

exhilaration /ɪg,zɪlə'reɪʃən/ [n U] a feeling of excitement and energy that you get from an activity
the exhilaration of doing sth *the exhilaration of a gallop along the beach at dawn*

WORD BANK **EXERCISE**

➡ see pages 250–252

EXIST

➡ see also **ALIVE, DEAD**

1 to exist

exist /ɪg'zɪst/ [v I] to be something that is really present or living: *Do you think ghosts really exist?* | *The Earth has existed for more than four thousand million years.* | *Politicians who behave as if poverty didn't exist.*

EXIST continues on page 253

EXERCISE

WORD BANK

➡ see also **SPORT, HEALTHY/NOT HEALTHY**

E

❶ *You should get some* **exercise**. *Why don't you come to the* **sports centre** *with me one day?*

I'd really like to **get into shape** *and* **lose** *some* **weight**.

❷ I do quite a few **exercise classes**. I go to **aerobics** on Tuesdays and Thursdays. It's really **good for** your heart, and it helps you **tone up**.

❸ Or if you want something less **strenuous**, you could try **yoga**. Yoga **stretches** your body and makes it more **supple**.

yoga teacher

leggings

leotard

mat

vocabulary

aerobics /eə'rəʊbɪks/ [n U] a type of exercise where you do a lot of very active movements to music, usually in a class: *You should try aerobics – it's a great way of getting in shape.*
 do aerobics *She does a lot of aerobics – at least five classes a week.*
 go to aerobics (=go to a class and do aerobics)

exercise /'eksər'saɪz/ [n C/U] physical activities that you do in order to stay healthy and become stronger, such as running, cycling, or lifting weights. An **exercise** is also a particular movement that you repeat many times to make a part of your body stronger: *Regular exercise makes you feel a lot healthier.* | *This exercise is good for your back.* | *a book on diet and exercise*
 do/take exercise (=do exercise regularly) *I decided I should take more exercise, and went to join a gym.*
 do an exercise (=do a particular movement) *You should always do some exercises to warm up before you start dancing.*
 get some exercise (=do exercise when you do not

usually do any) *I'm not really in shape. I need to get some exercise.*

exercise /'eksər'saɪz/ [v I] to do sport, swim etc in order to stay healthy and become stronger: *If you exercise two or three times a week, you'll soon feel a lot healthier.*

exercise class /'eksər'saɪz ˌklɑːs‖-ˌklæs/ [n C] a class where a group of people do exercises: *There's an exercise class for beginners on Thursday evenings.*

good for you /'gʊd fər juː/ if a type of exercise is good for you, it makes you healthier and improves the condition of your body: *Yoga is really good for you – it helps you to relax.*
 good for your heart/back etc *Cycling is extremely good for your heart and lungs.*

gym /dʒɪm/ [n C] a place that has machines for doing exercises: *How often do you go to the gym?*
 join a gym (=pay money to a gym so that you go there and use it whenever you want)

in shape /ɪn 'ʃeɪp/ (also **fit** /fɪt/ BRITISH) if you are in

EXERCISE

4 Or you could join a **gym** and build up your **muscles**. I go **weight training** three times a week.

treadmill

weights

rowing machine

exercise bike

trainers BRITISH running shoes AMERICAN

5 I go **running** every day before breakfast.

6 Remember that it's important to **warm up** before doing any exercise.

---

shape or **fit**, your body is strong and healthy because you exercise regularly: *If you're a fire-fighter you have to be in shape.* | *Sandy's very fit – he runs about 30 miles a week.*

get into shape/get fit *People come to exercise classes to get in shape and reduce stress.*

keep in shape/keep fit (=stay strong and healthy) *I keep fit by swimming and going to the gym.*

lose weight /ˌluːz ˈweɪt/ to become thinner: *Kay's lost a lot of weight recently.*

muscle /ˈmʌsəl/ [n C/U] the parts of your body that connect your bones together, and that you use when you move: *I went to the gym, and my mus-cles were really aching the next day.*

arm/leg/stomach muscle *Use this exercise to build up your chest and arm muscles.*

build up a muscle (=make it bigger and stronger)

pull a muscle (=damage a muscle while you are exercising) *My leg hurts – I think I've pulled a muscle.*

press-up BRITISH **push-up** AMERICAN /ˈpres ʌp, ˈpʊʃ ʌp/ [n C] an exercise that makes your arms and chest stronger: *You lie on your stomach and use your arms to push your body up.*

do press-ups *Do 16 press-ups, then have a rest.*

running /ˈrʌnɪŋ/ [n U] when you run as a sport or for exercise: *She did a lot of running when she was at college.*

go running *I went running yesterday – it nearly killed me.*

sit-up /ˈsɪt ʌp/ [n C] an exercise that makes your stomach muscles stronger: *You lie on your back and use your stomach muscles to lift your head and shoulders off the floor.*

do sit-ups *Do sit ups every day for a flat stom-ach.*

sports centre /ˈspɔːrts sentər/ BRITISH [n C] a build-ing where you can do lots of different types of

EXERCISE continues on the next page

EXERCISE

7 I do exercises every night before I go to bed. I usually do 50 **press-ups**...

8 ...and 20 **sit-ups**.

9 But you don't have to **work out** every day – two or three times a week is enough.

sport, such as squash and basketball, as well as exercise classes and weight training

strenuous /'strenjuəs/ [adj] a **strenuous** activity needs a lot of effort and energy: We went for a strenuous hike through the hills. | The doctor advised him to avoid strenuous exercise for a while.

stretch /stretʃ/ [v I/T] to make a slow movement that straightens a part of your body so that it is at its full length: This is a good exercise for stretching your back.

supple /'sʌpəl/ [adj] someone who is **supple** can bend and move their body easily: Children are usually more supple than adults.

tone up /ˌtəʊn 'ʌp/ [phrasal verb I/T] to make your body or part of your body firmer: I'd like to tone up my hips, thighs, and stomach.

warm up /ˌwɔː'm 'ʌp/ [phrasal verb I] to move and stretch your body gently, so that your body is prepared for more active physical exercise

warm-up /ˌwɔː'm 'ʌp/ [n C] the part at the beginning of an exercise class when you warm up
do a warm up We'll do a ten-minute warm-up and then 20 minutes of aerobics.

weight training /'weɪt ˌtreɪnɪŋ/ [n U] a type of exercise where you lift specially shaped metal weights in order to strengthen your muscles
do weight training More and more women are doing weight training these days.

work out /ˌwɜː'k 'aʊt/ [v I] to exercise in a gym or in a class using all of the important muscles in your body, especially when you do this regularly: Conrad works out with weights twice a week.

yoga /'jəʊgə/ [n U] a type of exercise in which you slowly move your body into different positions to improve its condition and to relax your mind
do yoga She's started doing yoga, and she says she feels a lot calmer.
go to yoga (=go to a class and do yoga)

EXIST continued from page 249

⚠️ Don't say 'it is existing', 'they are existing' etc. Say **it exists/they exist** etc.

there is /ðeər ɪz/ if you say **there is** something, you mean that it exists: *Is there life on other planets?* | *There's no evidence to prove that Gray is the murderer.*

be found /bi: ˈfaʊnd/ FORMAL to exist in a particular place, or inside a particular thing: *Vitamin C is found in green vegetables and fresh fruit.* | *Otters are still found in some parts of Britain.*

⚠️ **Be found** is used especially in technical and scientific writing.

existence /ɪgˈzɪstəns/ [n U] when something exists
the existence of sth *For the first time she began to doubt the existence of God.*
be in existence (=exist at the moment) *The club has been in existence since 1990.*

2 to not exist

non-existent /ˌnɒn ɪgˈzɪstənt◄ˌnɑːn-/ [adj] something that is **non-existent** does not exist: *In rural parts of Japan, crime is virtually non-existent.*

there's no such thing /ðeəz ˌnəʊ sʌtʃ ˈθɪŋ/ SPOKEN use **there's no such thing** to tell someone that you are sure something does not exist: *I don't believe in witchcraft – there's no such thing.*
+ as *I've come to the conclusion that there's no such thing as perfect happiness.*

3 when something that used to exist no longer exists

extinct /ɪkˈstɪŋkt/ [adj] if a type of animal is **extinct**, none of them are alive any more: *The white rhino is now almost extinct.*
become extinct *Why did the dinosaurs become extinct?*

die out /ˌdaɪ ˈaʊt/ [phrasal verb I] if something such as a type of plant or animal **dies out**, there are fewer and fewer of them until finally there are none left:

Many of the old village traditions are dying out. | *Unless we do something now, hundreds of plant and animal species will die out.*

disappear /ˌdɪsəˈpɪəʳ/ [v I] if something **disappears**, it stops existing and can no longer be seen or felt: *Thousands of miles of rainforest are disappearing every year.* | *When I got my first job I felt as if all my worries had disappeared.*

⚠️ Don't say 'is disappeared' or 'was disappeared'. Say **has disappeared**.

EXPECT

➡ see also **HOPE, SURPRISING/SURPRISED**

1 to expect something

expect /ɪkˈspekt/ [v T] if you **expect** something to happen, you think it probably will happen: *I'm expecting a fax from Korea. Has anything arrived yet?* | *Drivers should expect long delays on all roads out of town today.*
expect to do sth *I expected to find him in the bar, but he wasn't there.*
expect sb/sth to do sth *No-one really expected the President to resign.* | *Economists expect the economy to grow by 5% next year.*
+ (that) *We all expected she'd get the job – it was a real shock when she didn't.*

⚠️ Don't confuse **expect** and **wait for**: *She stood outside the hotel, waiting for a taxi.* (=waiting until a taxi came past) | *I'm expecting a taxi.* (=I ordered one a while ago)

think /θɪŋk/ [v T] to believe that something is likely to happen
+ (that) *Do you think that she'll win an Oscar for the movie?* | *I never thought her business would do so well.*
think sth is likely *The builders said the job would be finished tomorrow, but I don't think that's likely.*

be due /bi: ˈdjuːǁ-ˈduː/ if something **is due** at a particular time, you expect it to happen or arrive at that time: *When's your baby due?*
be due in an hour/in three months/at 5 o'clock etc *The flight from New York is*

due at 10.30. | You'd better clean up this mess – Clarrie's due back in half an hour.

2 what you say when you expect something to happen

Q**I expect** /aɪ ɪk'spekt/ SPOKEN say this when you think something will probably happen: *Don't worry – they'll be here soon, I expect.*
+ (that) *I expect the tickets will be sold out by now.*
I expect so BRITISH (=used to say 'yes' when someone asks you if you think something is going to happen) *"Do you think he'll lend us the money?" "I expect so."*

Q**I bet** /aɪ 'bet/ SPOKEN INFORMAL say this when you are almost certain something will happen, because of what you know about a person or situation
+ (that) *I bet you'll miss your boyfriend when he goes to university.* | *She promised to arrive early, but I bet she doesn't.*

Q**I wouldn't be surprised** /aɪ ˌwʊdnt biː səˈpraɪzd/ SPOKEN say this when you think that something may happen, even though other people may think it is unlikely: *"Do you think they'll get married?" "I wouldn't be surprised."*
+ if *You know, I wouldn't be surprised if Warren ends up running the whole company.*

3 expecting something good to happen

optimistic /ˌɒptɪˈmɪstɪk◄ˌɑːp-/ [adj] someone who is **optimistic** expects good things to happen: *In spite of all her problems she manages to remain optimistic.* | *an optimistic economic forecast*
+ about *I'm pretty optimistic about our chances of winning here today.*
+ that *Are you still optimistic that the climbers can be rescued?*

optimist /ˈɒptɪmɪst‖ˈɑːp-/ [n C] someone who always expects good things to happen: *Optimists still believe we can resolve the problem without going to war.*

4 expecting something bad to happen

pessimistic /ˌpesɪˈmɪstɪk◄/ [adj] someone who is **pessimistic** always expects bad things to happen: *Don't be too pessimistic – we may still win the game.*
+ about *He's quite pessimistic about his chances of getting another job.*

pessimist /ˈpesɪmɪst/ [n C] someone who always expects bad things to happen: *Don't be such a pessimist – I'm sure you'll pass your driving test!*

5 when things happen in the way that you expected

as expected /əz ɪkˈspektɪd/ if something happens **as expected**, it happens in the way that you expected it to happen: *As expected, the Democrats won the majority of seats in Congress.* | *The parcel arrived the next day, as expected.*

it is no surprise /ɪt ɪz ˌnəʊ səˈpraɪz/ if something that happens **is no surprise**, it is exactly what you expected, so you are not surprised by it
+ that *It's no surprise that Jeff and his wife are getting divorced.*
it is no surprise to hear/discover/find etc *It was no surprise to hear that Joel had messed the whole thing up again.*

predictable /prɪˈdɪktəbəl/ [adj] happening exactly as you expect – use this especially about someone's behaviour, when you think they are boring or stupid because they always do exactly what you expect: *My dad's so predictable – every evening he comes home, has exactly two beers, and falls asleep in front of the TV.* | *a predictable speech about loyalty to one's country*
  predictably [sentence adverb] as you would expect: *Predictably, all the political parties are claiming the credit for rising living standards.*

6 when something happens that you did not expect

unexpected /ˌʌnɪkˈspektɪd◄/ [adj] something that is **unexpected** surprises you because you did not expect it: *There have* been unexpected delays on the freeway because of an accident.

completely/totally unexpected Bobby's decision to leave the band was totally unexpected.

unexpectedly [adv] He arrived unexpectedly at the camp one morning, along with an ancient-looking dog.

out of the blue /ˌaʊt əv ðə ˈbluː/ INFORMAL if something happens **out of the blue**, you did not expect it, and you are very surprised or shocked by it: One evening, Angela phoned me out of the blue and said she was in some kind of trouble.

EXPENSIVE

➔ opposite **CHEAP**

1 expensive

expensive /ɪkˈspensɪv/ [adj] something that is **expensive** costs a lot of money, more than other things of the same type: She spends most of her money on expensive clothes. | Things tend to be much more expensive in the cities.

expensive to make/run/buy etc Cadillacs are beautiful cars, but they're very expensive to run.

⚠ Don't say 'prices, costs, taxes etc are expensive'. Say **prices, costs etc are high**.

cost a lot /ˌkɒst ə ˈlɒt‖ˌkɔːst ə ˈlɑːt/ INFORMAL if something **costs a lot**, it is expensive: They had a big party at the Waldorf, and that must have cost a lot.

it costs a lot to do sth It costs a lot to get there by plane, but it's worth it.

high /haɪ/ [adj] if the price or cost of something is **high**, it costs a lot

high prices/costs/fees/rents The cost of living is higher in Denmark than in

Germany. | Rents in central London are very high.

cost a fortune /ˌkɒst ə ˈfɔːtʃən‖ˌkɔːst-/ INFORMAL, ESPECIALLY SPOKEN if something **costs a fortune**, it is very expensive

cost sb a fortune We had to eat out every night – it ended up costing us a fortune.

it costs a fortune to do sth It'll cost a fortune to get that old car of his repaired.

dear /dɪər/ [adj not before noun] BRITISH expensive – use this especially about things you buy in shops: The blue jacket is slightly dearer, but it's much better material.

E

2 expensive and fashionable

expensive /ɪkˈspensɪv/ [adj only before noun] an **expensive** hotel, restaurant, area etc is very fashionable and it is expensive to stay, eat, or live there: an expensive Chinese restaurant in town | The house is on West Boston Avenue, Detroit's most expensive residential area.

exclusive /ɪkˈskluːsɪv/ [adj] an **exclusive** area, school, shop, club etc is very expensive, and only a few very rich people have enough money to live there or use it: They live in Bel Air, an exclusive suburb of Los Angeles. | He's been invited to join the exclusive Millionaire's Club.

luxurious /lʌgˈzjʊəriəs, ləgˈʒʊəriəs‖ləgˈʒʊəriəs/ [adj] a **luxurious** building or room is large, very comfortable, and has expensive decorations and furniture: a room in a luxurious New York hotel | a small but luxurious bathroom

posh /pɒʃ‖pɑːʃ/ [adj] SPOKEN, ESPECIALLY BRITISH a **posh** restaurant, house, car etc is expensive and looks as if it is used or owned by rich people: When I'm famous I'm going to stay in a posh hotel and drink champagne all day. | She goes to a posh girls' school near Brighton.

fancy /ˈfænsi/ [adj] INFORMAL, ESPECIALLY AMERICAN a **fancy** house, car, hotel, restaurant etc is expensive and fashionable: eating in fancy restaurants

fancy – fancier – fanciest

3 too expensive

can't afford /ˌkɑːnt əˈfɔːrd‖ˌkænt-/ if you **can't afford** something, you do not have enough money to pay for it: *I really need a new coat, but I can't afford one.*
can't afford to do sth *We couldn't afford to go on vacation last year.*
can't afford it *Hiring a lawyer would be expensive, and she just couldn't afford it.*

exorbitant /ɪgˈzɔːrbɪtənt/ [adj] FORMAL **exorbitant** prices, charges, rents etc are very much higher than they should be and you think they are unfair: *The rents in this part of town are exorbitant.* | *They charge exorbitant prices for very ordinary food.*

a rip-off /ə ˈrɪp ɒf/ SPOKEN INFORMAL you say something is **a rip-off** when you think someone is unfairly charging too much money for it: *$80 for a pair of jeans? What a rip-off!*
a complete/total rip-off *Don't go to that new restaurant – it's a complete rip-off.*

4 worth a lot of money

valuable /ˈvæljuəbəl, -ljǧbəl/ [adj] use this about things that are expensive to replace such as jewellery or cameras, or things that are old and rare such as paintings, furniture, and books: *The museum has a valuable collection of old books and manuscripts.* | *a valuable porcelain vase*

be worth a lot /biː ˌwɜːrθ ə ˈlɒt‖-ˈlɑːt/ if something **is worth a lot**, you can get a lot of money if you sell it: *You should look after those old dolls – one day they could be worth a lot.*

be worth a fortune /biː ˌwɜːrθ ə ˈfɔːrtʃən/ INFORMAL if something **is worth a fortune**, it is worth a very large amount of money: *He was very poor when he died, but now his paintings are worth a fortune.*

precious /ˈpreʃəs/ [adj only before noun] **precious metal/stone** a metal such as gold or a jewel such as a diamond that is very valuable

priceless /ˈpraɪsləs/ [adj] worth so much money that it is impossible to calculate the price – use this about objects that are old and rare such as paintings, furniture, or jewellery: *The house was full of priceless antiques.* | *a priceless oil painting*

EXPERIENCE

➡ look here for ...
• something that happens to you
• when you know a lot about something

1 something that happens to you

experience /ɪkˈspɪəriəns/ [n C] something that happens to you or something that you do, especially something unusual or important that you remember and learn from: *Hannah later wrote a book about her experiences as a war reporter.*
+ of *Tonight on Channel 1, young people will be discussing their experiences of racism.*
have an experience *During her trip she had several frightening experiences.*
good/bad experience *Living alone has been a good experience for her.*

adventure /ədˈventʃər/ [n C/U] a situation in which exciting and dangerous things happen to you: *My grandfather used to tell us about his adventures as a sea captain during the war.* | *As a young man he went off to Africa, looking for adventure.*

2 something bad that happens to you

bad experience /bæd ɪkˈspɪəriəns/ [n C] something that happens to you that is unpleasant, frightening, or dangerous: *Don't let one bad experience put you off travelling altogether.* | *She described childbirth as the worst experience of her life.*

nightmare /ˈnaɪtmeər/ [n C usually singular] a very unpleasant or very frightening experience: *Starting school can be a real nightmare for some children.* | *She describes the war years as 'one long nightmare'.*

ordeal /ɔːrˈdiːl, ˈɔːrdiːl/ [n C] a painful, frightening, or worrying experience, especially one that continues for a long time: *The hostages have now been released, and are recovering from their ordeal in a military hospital.*

3 when something happens to you

happen to sb /'hæpən tuː (sb)/ [phrasal verb T] if something **happens to** you, it affects you and you are involved in it, but you did not do anything to make it happen: *The crash wasn't your fault. It could have happened to anyone.* | *Meeting Penny was the best thing that ever happened to me.*

experience /ɪkˈspɪəriəns/ [v T] if you **experience** something, especially an emotion, a physical feeling, or an unpleasant situation, it happens to you: *When you first tried a cigarette, you probably experienced a feeling of dizziness.* | *help for people who are experiencing unemployment problems* | *It was the first time she had ever experienced real poverty.*

go through sth /'gəʊ θruː (sth)/ [phrasal verb T] to live through a difficult or unhappy period: *Clare's been through a lot lately, so we should all try to help her.*
◯**go through hell** SPOKEN (=have a very unpleasant time) *He's been going through hell in the two years since his daughter died.*

4 when you know a lot about something because you have done it before
➡ see also **JOB, WORK, GOOD 5, 6**

experience /ɪkˈspɪəriəns/ [n U] the knowledge and skill you get from doing something, especially a job, for a long time
have experience *She's very bright and ambitious but she doesn't have much experience.*
experience of (doing) sth *She has plenty of experience of dealing with difficult situations.*
teaching/secretarial/political etc experience *Only people with five years' secretarial experience can apply for the job.*
previous experience (=experience you have gained already in a previous job) *Have you any previous experience of working in a restaurant?*
gain experience (=get experience) *Fran is gaining valuable experience working for her father's firm.*

⚠ Remember that in this meaning **experience** is uncountable. Don't say things like 'I have an experience as a teacher' or 'I have experiences as a teacher'.

experienced /ɪkˈspɪəriənst/ [adj] someone who is **experienced** knows a lot about a job or activity because they have done it for a long time: *Ms Carter is one of our most experienced teachers.*
experienced in (doing) sth *This job would suit someone experienced in dealing with the public.*
highly experienced (=very experienced) *Dr Blake is highly experienced in microsurgery.*

5 when you have not done something before

inexperienced /ˌɪnɪkˈspɪəriənst◄/ [adj] someone who is **inexperienced** does not know much about a job or activity, either because they have not done it at all or because they have done it for only a short time: *Inexperienced managers often have problems with their staff.* | *There are a lot of young, inexperienced players on the team.*

be new to sth /biː ˈnjuː tuː (sth)‖-ˈnuː-/ if you **are new to** a job or activity, you do not have much experience of doing it because you have only just started it: *As you are new to the job, we don't expect you to work as fast as the others.*

EXPLAIN

INSTRUCTIONS   **LEARN**

see also

TEACH   **CLEAR/ NOT CLEAR**

UNDERSTAND/NOT UNDERSTAND

1 to explain something

explain /ɪkˈspleɪn/ [v I/T] to give someone the information they need to understand something: *It's very simple really – I'll* *try to explain.* | *We listened carefully while Pam explained the process.*

explain sth to sb *Could you explain the rules of the game to me, please?* | *I'll explain it to you later.*

+ how/what/which etc *Can anyone really explain how the universe started?* | *The leaflet explains what drugs do to your body.*

⚠ Don't say 'explain me the rules' or 'I explained her the rules' etc. Say **explain the rules to me**.

⚠ Don't say 'explain me how/what etc'. Say **explain how/what** etc: *Can you explain what I need to do?*

◯**tell** /tel/ [v T] ESPECIALLY SPOKEN to explain to someone how something works or how to do something

tell sb how/what etc *Can you tell me how to log on to the computer?* | *The leaflet tells you what to do if you get malaria.*

⚠ Don't say 'tell to someone'. Say **tell someone**.

⚠ Don't say 'please teach me' when you are asking someone to explain something to you. Say **please tell me**.

telling – told – have told

show /ʃəʊ/ [v T] to explain to someone how to do something by doing it while they watch you

show sb how to do sth *Can you show me how to use your camera?*

show sb what to do *One of the other members of the class showed her what to do.*

show sb sth *The programme showed you the best way to cook asparagus.*

show sb *"How do you change the speed of the drill?" "Let me show you."*

demonstrate /ˈdemənstreɪt/ [v I/T] to show someone how to do something by doing it while they watch you, especially when it is your job to show people how to do things: *The ski instructor began by demonstrating the correct way to turn.*

+ how *A trainer came in to demonstrate how the new computer system worked.*

go through sth /ˌgəʊ ˈθruː (sth)/ [phrasal verb T] to explain all the details about something in the right order, to help someone understand it: *I'll go through the instructions once more in case you missed anything.*

2 what you say when you are going to explain something

◯**you see** /juː ˈsiː/ SPOKEN say this when you are explaining something to someone, and you want to check that they are listening and that they understand you: *This fits on here, you see, where the arrow is.* | *Simon's car broke down, you see, and neither of us knew how to fix it.*

in other words /ɪn ˌʌðər ˈwɜːrdz/ use this when you are saying something in a different way in order to explain it more clearly: *What we need is a more sustainable transport system, in other words, more buses and trains, and fewer cars.*

that is /ðæt ˈɪz/ ESPECIALLY WRITTEN use this when you are explaining the meaning of the previous word or phrase by giving more information about it: *The fare is reduced for children, that is, anyone under 16 years old.* | *Make sure you practise all four language skills, that is, reading, writing, listening, and speaking.*

◯**what I mean is** /wɒt aɪ ˈmiːn ɪz/ SPOKEN say this when you are explaining something that you have just said: *When I say Joe likes to win, what I mean is, I don't think he'll play for our team if we keep losing.*

◯**let me explain** /ˌlet miː ɪkˈspleɪn/ SPOKEN say this when you want to explain something to someone because you think they have not understood it: *I can see you're getting confused. Let me explain.*

3 the words you write or say to explain something

explanation /ˌekspləˈneɪʃən/ [n C] something that you say or write in order to make something clearer or to explain why something happened: *Each diagram is followed by a simple explanation.*

give (sb) an explanation *Can you give us a quick explanation of how it* *works?* | *He left suddenly, without giving any explanation.*

+ for *Did they give any explanation for their decision?*

instructions /ɪnˈstrʌkʃənz/ [n plural] written or spoken information that explains exactly how to do something: *The cooking instructions are on the back of the box.* | *Make sure you read the instructions carefully first.*

give (sb) instructions *They gave us detailed instructions explaining how to get to their house.*

follow instructions (=do what they tell you) *If you had followed my instructions, none of this would have happened.*

4 to explain why something happened

say why/tell sb why /ˌseɪ ˈwaɪ, ˌtel (sb) ˈwaɪ/ to tell someone the reasons why something happened: *Did he say why he needed the money?* | *My aunt never told us why she got divorced.*

explain /ɪkˈspleɪn/ [v I/T] to tell someone the reasons why something happened, so that they can understand the situation completely: *Don't get angry – I can explain everything.*

+ why *Can you explain why you're so late?*

EXPLODE

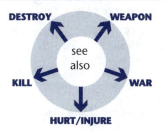

DESTROY   WEAPON

see also

KILL   WAR

HURT/INJURE

1 a bomb explodes

explode/go off /ɪkˈspləʊd, ˌgəʊ ˈɒfǁ-ˈɔːf/ [v I] if a bomb **explodes** or **goes off**, it bursts suddenly and violently with a loud noise, causing a lot of damage: *A bomb exploded in a crowded Metro station this morning, killing five people.* | *The bomb went off as people were still leaving the building.*

set off /ˌset ˈɒfǁ-ˈɔːf/ [phrasal verb T] to make a bomb explode, either deliberately or accidentally

set off sth *Any slight movement could have set off the device and blown us all up.*

set sth off *It was a car bomb – they must have used radio signals to set it off.*

detonate /ˈdetəneɪt/ [v T] to make a bomb explode, especially by using special equipment: *Army experts detonated the bomb safely in a nearby field.* | *The 200 kg bomb was detonated by terrorists using a remote-control device.*

> ⚠ **Detonate** is a more technical word than **set off**.

2 a building/plane etc explodes

blow up /ˌbləʊ ˈʌp/ [v I] if a building, car, plane etc **blows up**, it bursts suddenly and violently into pieces, causing a lot of damage: *The plane blew up in mid-air, killing all the passengers and crew.*

explode /ɪkˈspləʊd/ [v I] if a container of chemicals, oil, or gas **explodes**, it bursts suddenly and violently into pieces: *The car crashed and its fuel tank exploded a few seconds later.*

3 to destroy something using a bomb

blow up sth /ˌbləʊ ˈʌp (sth)/ [phrasal verb T] to destroy a building, car, plane etc using a bomb: *Terrorists blew up a government building in the city centre.* | *Two of the ships were blown up while they were still in the harbour.*

4 an explosion

explosion /ɪkˈspləʊʒən/ [n C] the loud noise and violent force that is produced when something explodes: *The noise of the explosion could be heard all over the city.*

blast /blɑːstǁblæst/ [n C] an explosion – used especially in news reports: *Twelve people were injured in a bomb blast in the city centre.* | *Every window in the building had been shattered by the force of the blast.*

F

FAIL

1 when you do not succeed
➡ opposite **SUCCEED**

fail /feɪl/ [v I] when you try to do something or achieve something, but you do not succeed: *We tried to make her change her mind, but we failed.*
fail to do sth *So far, scientists have failed to find a cure for the disease.*

not succeed /nɒt sək'siːd/ to fail to do something, or not be completely successful: *Simon had tried several times to get a job in TV, but he never succeeded.*
not succeed in doing sth *I didn't really succeed in convincing her that I was telling the truth.*

2 when a plan or attempt does not succeed
➡ opposite **SUCCEED**

fail /feɪl/ [v I] if a plan or attempt **fails**, it does not achieve what you want it to achieve: *Try changing the spark plugs, but if that fails take the car to a mechanic.* | *They said the latest space mission was bound to fail.*
fail to do sth *The investigation failed to establish the cause of the accident.*
  failure [n U] lack of success: *an attempt to climb Everest that ended in failure*
  + of *the failure of the peace negotiations*

unsuccessful /ˌʌnsək'sesfəl◄/ [adj] an **unsuccessful** attempt to do something does not have the result that you wanted: *The army made an unsuccessful attempt to end the rebellion.* | *I regret to inform you that your application was unsuccessful.*

be a failure /biː ə 'feɪljəʳ/ to be unsuccessful – use this especially about something that fails even though it was very carefully planned: *The government's expensive election campaign had been a failure.*
be a complete/total failure *There was a 5-year plan to modernize the economy, but it was a complete failure.*

go wrong /ˌgəʊ 'rɒŋ|-'rɔːŋ/ if something that you are trying to do **goes wrong**, it fails after it has started well: *The experiment went wrong when the chemicals combined to form a poisonous gas.*
go badly wrong (=fail completely) *a military campaign that went badly wrong*

not work /nɒt 'wɜːʳk/ if a method or attempt does **not work**, it fails because it is not suitable or not right for the situation you are in: *Teaching methods that work with adults do not always work with children.* | *I tried to fix it with glue, but that didn't work.*

3 when you fail an exam or test
➡ opposite **PASS**
➡ see also **TEST, DRIVE**

fail /feɪl/ [v I/T] to not succeed in an examination or test: *Jonathan failed his law exams at the end of the year.* | *If I fail my driving test again, I'm going to give up.* | *We expected her to pass easily, but she failed by 15 marks.*

⚠ Don't say 'he failed in the exam'. Say **he failed the exam** or just **he failed**.

flunk /flʌŋk/ [v I/T] AMERICAN INFORMAL to fail an examination or test: *Tony flunked chemistry.* | *I flunked, and had to do the test again.*

4 when something seems certain to fail

pointless /'pɔɪntləs/ [adj] something that is **pointless**, is unlikely to have a very useful or successful result, so it would be better not to do it or try it: *The argument was completely pointless.* | *a pointless waste of money*
it is pointless doing sth *It's pointless trying to speak to the boss – she's always too busy.*

there's no point/what's the point? /ˌðeəʳz ˌnəʊ 'pɔɪnt, ˌwɒts ðə 'pɔɪnt/ SPOKEN say this when you think that it is useless to do something because you will not achieve anything useful by doing it: *"Why don't you try to explain things to him?" "There's no point, he never listens to anything I say."*

there's no point (in) doing sth *There's no point in going shopping now – the stores will all be shut in half an hour.*

what's the point of doing sth? *What's the point of taking the exam if you know you're going to fail?*

◯**be a waste of time** /biː ə ˌweɪst əv ˈtaɪm/ ESPECIALLY SPOKEN something that is a **waste of time** is unlikely to achieve any useful result, so you would be wasting your time if you tried to do it

a complete waste of time *These meetings are a complete waste of time. Nothing ever gets decided.*

it is a waste of time doing sth *It's a waste of time going to the doctor – he'll just tell you to get plenty of rest.*

5 **when a company, shop, or business fails**

➡ opposite **SUCCEED 4**
➡ see also **BUSINESS, COMPANY, SHOP**

close down /ˌkləʊz ˈdaʊn/ [phrasal verb I] if a shop, factory, or business **closes down**, it stops making or selling things because it is no longer making a profit: *If the factory closes down, 600 people will lose their jobs.* | *A lot of small shops had to close down during the recession.*

go out of business /gəʊ ˌaʊt əv ˈbɪznɪs/ if a company **goes out of business**, it stops existing because it is no longer making a profit : *Many small farms are going out of business.*

go bankrupt /ˌgəʊ ˈbæŋkrʌpt/ if a person or company **goes bankrupt**, they cannot pay their debts, so they have to sell all their property and goods: *The family grocery business went bankrupt last year.*

FAIR/UNFAIR

➡ see also **CRUEL**

1 **fair**

fair /feəʳ/ [adj] treating everyone equally, or treating people in a way that most people think is right: *The old system of student funding seemed much fairer.* | *a fair way of dividing up the profits* | *a fair rent*

it is fair that *Do you think it's fair that she gets paid more money than me?*

◯**it's only fair** SPOKEN (=say this when you think that something would make a situation more fair) *Her husband should help take care of the baby – it's only fair.*

be fair to sb (=treat them in a fair way) *In order to be fair to everyone, ticket sales are limited to two for each person.*

◯**to be fair** SPOKEN (=say this when you are giving a reason why someone should not be criticized too strongly) *He really should have called you – though to be fair he's been very busy.*

fairly [adv] *Her job is to make sure that the money is distributed fairly.*

fairness [n U] *I wasn't sure about the fairness of the judge's decision.*

reasonable /ˈriːzənəbəl/ [adj] behaving fairly and sensibly, for example by not asking someone to do too much or not criticizing them unfairly: *I don't know why she reacted like that – it was a perfectly reasonable request.*

it is reasonable to do sth *Do you think it's reasonable to expect people to work more than 60 hours a week?*

2 **when all people have the same rights and are treated fairly**

equal /ˈiːkwəl/ [adj] people who are **equal** have the same rights as each other and are treated the same way as each other; if people get **equal** treatment, pay etc, they are all treated in the same way or get paid the same money: *Democracy is based on the idea that all members of society are equal.* | *The women are demanding equal pay.*

equal rights (=the idea that all types of people in society should have the same rights and should be treated fairly and equally) *Black protestors campaigned for equal rights throughout the 1960s.*

equally [adv] *People should be treated equally, regardless of their race or sex.*

equality /ɪˈkwɒlɪti‖ɪˈkwɑː-/ [n U] when all people have the same rights and opportunities in society and are treated equally: *Greater equality was one of the aims of the post-war government.*

racial/sexual equality *the movement towards sexual equality*

F

3 unfair

unfair/not fair /ʌnˈfeər◂, nɒt ˈfeər/ [adj]
not treating everyone equally, or not treating people in a way that most people think is right: *an unfair law* | *The present welfare system is very unfair.*

it's not fair SPOKEN *Why do I always have to do the laundry? It's not fair!*

it is unfair that/it is not fair that *It seems very unfair that she was blamed for the accident.*

it is unfair to do sth/it is not fair to do sth *It's not fair to keep pets locked up in the house all day.*

+ to *tax laws that are very unfair to young people without jobs*

unreasonable /ʌnˈriːzənəbəl/ [adj] behaving in a way that is not fair or sensible, especially by asking someone to do too much or criticizing them unfairly: *My parents say I should stay in and do homework every night – I think they're being very unreasonable.* | *an unreasonable demand*

it is unreasonable to do sth *It's unreasonable to expect people to pay for something they haven't even seen yet.*

biased /ˈbaɪəst/ [adj] treating one group in a way that shows you like them more or less than another group – use this for example about newspapers or reports, judges, or other people who you think should treat everyone fairly and equally: *accusations of biased reporting*

+ against *The Socialists claim that the newspapers are biased against them.*

biased in favour of sb (=unfairly treating someone better just because you like them better) *Do you think the law courts are biased in favour of white people?*

favouritism BRITISH **favoritism** AMERICAN /ˈfeɪvərˌtɪzəm/ [n U] when a teacher, parent, or manager treats one person in a much better way than the others because they like that person, not because that person deserves it: *If I give Paul the job, I'll be accused of favoritism.*

4 when people are treated unfairly because of their race, sex, age etc

discrimination /dɪˌskrɪmɪˈneɪʃən/ [n U]
when people are treated unfairly because of their race, sex, age etc

+ against *discrimination against women by male bosses*

racial discrimination (=because of someone's race) *tough new laws against racial discrimination*

sex discrimination (=because of someone's sex)

> ⚠ Don't say 'discriminations'. **Discrimination** is uncountable.

discriminate against sb /dɪˈskrɪmɪneɪt əˌgenst (sb)/ [phrasal verb T] to treat someone unfairly because of their race, sex, age etc – use this especially about companies, the police, judges etc: *Shaun says he has definitely been discriminated against because he's black.* | *Why do so many companies think that it's OK to discriminate against older people?*

prejudice /ˈpredʒʊdɪs/ [n C/U] when people do not like or trust someone who is different, for example because they belong to a different race, country, or religion

+ against *There's still a lot of prejudice against gay men.*

racial prejudice (=because of someone's race) *a training course to tackle the problem of racial prejudice in the police force.*

inequality /ˌɪnɪˈkwɒlɪtiǁ-ˈkwɑː-/ [n C/U]
when people do not have the same rights or opportunites in their education, their jobs etc, because of their sex, race, or social class: *The report looks at inequality in education.* | *There are still a lot of inequalities in society.*

social/sexual/racial inequality *Social inequality tended to increase rather than lessen in the 1980s.*

FALL

➡ look here for ...
- when someone or something falls
- when you make someone fall
- when you drop something

➡ see also **ACCIDENT, HURT/INJURE, STAND 2**

1 when someone falls accidentally

fall /fɔːl/ [v I] to accidentally fall onto the ground or towards the ground: *She was taken to the hospital after falling and hitting her head on the side of the table.*
+ off/out of/down *"How did you break your arm?" "I fell off my bike."* | *The police say he fell out of the window, but I think he was pushed.*
falling – fell – have fallen

fall over/fall down /ˌfɔːl 'əʊvəʳ, ˌfɔːl 'daʊn/ [phrasal verb I] to fall onto the ground from a standing position: *Don't run so fast – you'll fall over.* | *He tried to stand up, but immediately fell down again.*

trip/trip over /trɪp, ˌtrɪp 'əʊvəʳ/ [v I] to accidentally hit something with your foot when you are walking or running, so that you fall or nearly fall: *I didn't push him – he tripped.* | *She'd had quite a lot to drink and kept tripping over.*
trip over sth *Pick up that box – someone might trip over it.*
trip on sth *Gwen followed behind, tripping on the loose stones.*
tripping – tripped – have tripped

slip /slɪp/ [v I] to accidentally slide on a wet or smooth surface, so that you fall or nearly fall: *Be careful you don't slip – I've just washed the floor.*
+ on *She slipped on the icy sidewalk and grabbed Will's arm to steady herself.*
slipping – slipped – have slipped

stumble /'stʌmbəl/ [v I] to nearly fall down when you are walking or running, because you do not put your foot down carefully or because something is in the way: *In her hurry, Eva stumbled and dropped the tray she was carrying.*
+ on/over *Mason headed towards the house, stumbling on the rough ground.*

lose your balance /ˌluːz jɔːʳ 'bæləns/ to fall or nearly fall, when you are doing something that needs balance, for example standing on a ladder or riding a bicycle: *I tried to help Gina up, but I lost my balance and we both fell into the stream.*

2 when an object, building, wall etc falls

fall /fɔːl/ [v I] to fall from a higher place to a lower place
+ across/onto/on top of *A tree had fallen across the road and blocked it.*
+ off/out of/from *The days were getting shorter and the leaves had started falling from the trees.* | *I can't find my passport – it must have fallen out of my pocket.*
falling – fell – have fallen

fall over /ˌfɔːl 'əʊvəʳ/ [phrasal verb I] if a tall object **falls over**, it falls onto its side from an upright position: *That bookcase looks as if it's about to fall over.*

fall down /ˌfɔːl 'daʊn/ [phrasal verb I] if a building, wall, or fence **falls down**, part or all of it falls to the ground, because it is in bad condition or because it has been damaged: *A boy was injured yesterday when part of a wall fell down near to where he was playing.*

collapse /kə'læps/ [v I] if a building, wall etc **collapses**, it suddenly falls down, especially because of a sudden pressure: *Our tent collapsed in the middle of the night.* | *The building was badly damaged in the explosion, and rescue workers are worried that it may collapse.*

3 to make someone fall
➡ see also **HIT**

knock sb over/knock sb down /ˌnɒk (sb) 'əʊvəʳ, ˌnɒk (sb) 'daʊn‖ˌnɑːk-/ [phrasal verb T] to push or hit someone hard, so that they fall to the ground: *He was knocked down and kicked in the stomach by a gang of youths.* | *Careful where you're going! You nearly knocked me over!*

trip (also **trip up** BRITISH) /trɪp, ˌtrɪp 'ʌp/ [v T] to make someone fall or almost fall by putting your foot or another object in their way: *One of the athletes claimed she had been tripped.*

trip sb up *One man tripped me up and the other one grabbed my handbag.*

tripping – tripped – have tripped

4 to let something fall or make something fall

drop /drɒp‖drɑːp/ [v T] to stop holding something so that it falls, especially accidentally: *Watch you don't drop that box – it's very heavy.* | *Her hands shake constantly and she keeps dropping things.*

dropping – dropped – have dropped

knock over /ˌnɒk ˈəʊvəʳ‖ˌnɑːk-/ [phrasal verb T] to hit something so that it falls onto its side from an upright position, especially when you do this accidentally

knock sth over *Be careful or you'll knock the vase over.*

knock over sth *He bumped into the table and knocked over the candle.*

spill /spɪl/ [v T] to accidentally allow liquid or powder to fall onto a surface

spill sth down/all over/onto *"How was the party?" "OK, but some idiot spilled wine all over my new dress."*

spilling – spilt – have spilt BRITISH

spilling – spilled – have spilled AMERICAN

FALSE

NATURAL   CHEAT

see also

TRICK/   REAL
DECEIVE

TRUE/NOT TRUE

1 made to look real or natural

artificial /ˌɑːʳtɪˈfɪʃəl◂/ [adj] something that is **artificial** is not real or natural, but is made to look real or to do the job of something real: *It was hard to tell whether the flowers were real or artificial.* | *an electric fire with artificial logs*

artificial hip/leg/limb *My grandfather has an artificial hip.*

false /fɔːls/ [adj only before noun] not real – use this about teeth, nails, eyelashes, beards etc that are made to look real or do the job of a real part: *She was wearing a sixties-style wig and false eyelashes.* | *Nearly a third of adults in the UK have false teeth.* | *a false beard*

imitation /ˌɪmɪˈteɪʃən◂/ [adj usually before noun] use this about materials that look like something valuable, but are actually made of something less expensive

imitation leather/gold/diamonds/fur *an armchair made of imitation leather* | *She wore a woollen coat with an imitation fur collar.*

2 made to look real for dishonest purposes

false /fɔːls/ [adj only before noun] not real, but intended to seem real in order to trick someone or cheat them: *The man had given a false name and address.* | *Her suitcase had a false bottom, containing 2 kilos of heroin.*

fake /feɪk/ [adj only before noun] use this about objects or documents that are not real, but are intended to look like something more important or valuable: *They were selling fake Rolex watches on the market stall.* | *a fake driver's license*

fake [n C] a copy of a valuable object or painting that is intended to make people think it is real: *Is the vase a genuine antique or a fake?*

forged /fɔːʳdʒd/ [adj] a **forged** official document or bank note has been illegally made to look like a real one: *He came into the country using a forged visa.* | *a forged £50 note*

forgery /ˈfɔːʳdʒəri/ [n C] a copy of a document, painting, or bank note that is made to look real for dishonest purposes: *The painting, believed to be by Renoir, turned out to be a very clever forgery.*

plural **forgeries**

3 feelings or opinions that are not real

false /fɔːls/ [adj] emotions or feelings that are **false** are not real, and you are only pretending to feel them: *"Merry Christmas," she said with false cheerfulness.* | *The politician greeted them with a false smile.*

insincere /ˌɪnsɪnˈsɪəʳ◄/ [adj] pretending to like someone or to care about them when you do not really care: *"It's so good to see you again," she said, with an insincere smile.* | *an insincere compliment* | *He always praised everyone, so it was difficult to tell if he was being insincere or not.*

hypocritical /ˌhɪpəˈkrɪtɪkəl◄/ [adj] pretending to be morally good or to have beliefs that you do not really have: *I think it's a little hypocritical to get married in a church when you don't believe in God.* | *Politicians are so hypocritical – they preach about 'family values' while they all seem to be having affairs.*

> **hypocrite** /ˈhɪpəkrɪt/ [n C] someone who pretends to be morally good or to have beliefs that they do not really have: *My dad is such a hypocrite – he tells me off for smoking but he smokes 20 a day.*

FAMILY

CHILD   MOTHER

see also

BABY   FATHER

RELATIONSHIP

1 a group of people who are related to each other

family /ˈfæməli/ [n C] a group of people who are related to each other, especially a mother, father, and their children all living together: *He comes from a family of eight children.* | *A lot of the families living in this area are very poor.*

member of a family *Only members of the family were allowed in to see her.*

the Armstrong/Mitchell/Jones family (=the family with this name) *Various members of the Kennedy family were at the funeral.*

nuclear family (=a typical family consisting of a mother, a father, and their children)

extended family (=including cousins, grandparents etc as well as parents and children)

one-parent family (=a family in which there is only one parent)

plural **families**

> ⚠ In British English, you can use **family** with a singular or plural verb: *The family now lives/live in London.* In American English, always use a singular verb: *The family now lives in California.*

family tree

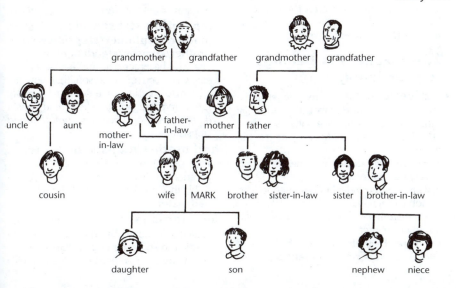

⚠ **Family** usually means a group of close relatives who live together: *The average family spends $120 a week on food.* But it can also mean all the other people you are related to, such as your cousins and grandparents: *It was a big wedding, and the whole family was there.*

⚠ Use **relatives** and **relations** to talk about members of your family who do not live with you in the same house. The people you live with (your parents, sisters etc) are your **family**, not your **relatives** or **relations**.

parents /'peərənts/ [n plural] someone's mother and father: *Do you get on well with your parents?* | *Parents are worried that their children may be taking drugs.*

background /'bækgraʊnd/ [n C] the kind of family and social class that you grew up in: *Most of his friends are from similar upper-class backgrounds.* | *The teachers try to know something about each child's background.*

2 things that happen in a family or belong to a family

family /'fæməli/ [adj only before noun] **family home/business/holiday/argument etc** something that belongs to a family or happens in a family: *Dino's family home is in Palm Springs.* | *I stopped going on family holidays when I was 15.* | *a big family celebration*

domestic /də'mestɪk/ [adj only before noun] **domestic violence/trouble/argument etc** fighting, arguments, or problems between members of the same family: *Victims of domestic violence are often too frightened to tell the police.* | *I'm worried about Jim – I think he has some sort of domestic trouble.*

3 someone that belongs to your family

relative/relation /'relətɪv, rɪ'leɪʃən/ [n C] someone who is a member of your family although they do not live with you: *Over 100 friends and relatives came to the funeral.*

close relative/relation (=someone who is closely related to you)

distant relative/relation (=someone who is not closely related to you) *We have some distant relations in Australia who we've never met.*

be a relative/relation of sb *She's a relative of the Queen, you know.*

4 to belong to the same family as someone

be related /biː rɪ'leɪtɪd/ if two people **are related**, they are both members of the same family – use this about cousins, grandparents etc, but not about your parents or your brothers and sisters: *"I didn't know you and Ted were related." "Yes, Ted's wife is my sister."*

+ to *John told me he was related to Mel Gibson – is it true?*

be descended from sb /biː dɪ'sendɪd frəm (sb)/ to be related to someone who lived a long time ago, especially someone famous or important: *She is descended from the Duke of Marlborough.*

5 people who are related to you because of marriage

mother-in-law/son-in-law etc [n C] someone who is related to you because someone in your family is married to them; for example, your **mother-in-law** is the mother of your wife or husband, and your **sister-in-law** is the sister of your wife or husband

plural **mothers-in-law, sons-in-law etc**

stepmother/stepson etc [n C] **stepmother/stepfather/stepsister/stepbrother/stepson/stepdaughter** someone who becomes your mother, sister, son etc when you or a person that you are related to marries for a second time: *My father married Jenny, who already has a daughter, so now I have a stepmother and stepsister.*

half-brother/half-sister /'hɑːf brʌðər, 'hɑːf sɪstər‖'hæf-/ [n C] if one of your parents marries a second time and has a child, that child is your **half-brother** or **half-sister**

by marriage /baɪ 'mærɪdʒ/ if you are related to someone **by marriage**, they are married to someone in your family or you are married to someone in their family:

John's my cousin by marriage. (=he is the cousin of my wife or husband)

in-laws /ˈɪn lɔːz/ [n plural] INFORMAL the parents of your husband or wife: *We lived with my in-laws until we had enough money to buy a house of our own.*

6 people who were in the same family as you a long time ago

ancestor /ˈænsəstə^r, -ses-‖-ses-/ [n C] a member of your family who lived a long time ago, especially hundreds of years ago: *My ancestors originally came from Ireland.* | *Tom's interested in finding out more about his ancestors.*

family /ˈfæməli/ [n C] people that you are related to who lived many years ago: *Her family came to America from Scotland in about 1750.*
plural **families**

descendant /dɪˈsendənt/ [n C] someone who is a relative of a person who lived and died a long time ago, especially a famous or important person
+ of *a descendant of King Charles I*

FAMOUS

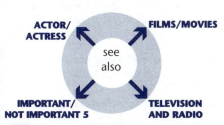

ACTOR/
ACTRESS

FILMS/MOVIES

see
also

IMPORTANT/
NOT IMPORTANT 5

TELEVISION
AND RADIO

1 famous

famous /ˈfeɪməs/ [adj] **famous** people, places, books etc are known about and talked about by many people in many places: *famous stars, like Keanu Reeves and Demi Moore* | *Sydney's famous Opera House* | *'David Copperfield' is one of Dickens' most famous books.*
+ for *Manchester is famous for its nightlife and for its football teams.*
world-famous (=famous all over the world) *Rio's world-famous carnival*
the rich and famous (=people who are

rich and famous) *a nightclub that is popular with the rich and famous*

well-known/well known /ˌwel ˈnəʊn◂/ [adj] fairly famous, especially in a particular place or among a particular group of people: *She works in local radio, and is quite well known in the Houston area.* | *a well-known engineering company*
best-known *one of the best-known names in the music business*
+ for *Hawking is well known for his work on the theory of black holes.*

well-known – better-known – best-known

legendary /ˈledʒəndəri‖-deri/ [adj] someone or something that is **legendary** is famous for being very special or interesting, and people like to talk or read about them: *The studio was owned by Sam Goldwyn, the legendary Hollywood producer.* | *the legendary wealth of John D Rockefeller* | *The album was recorded at the legendary Abbey Road studios.*

notorious /nəʊˈtɔːriəs/ [adj] well known because of something bad: *One of the country's most notorious criminals has escaped from prison.*
notoriously [adv] *a notoriously inefficient company*
+ for *a part of the city that is notorious for violence and prostitution*

fame /feɪm/ [n U] the success and attention people get when they are famous: *She came to Hollywood in search of fame.*
achieve fame/win fame (as) *Streisand first won fame as a singer before becoming an actress.*
at the height of your fame *The Beatles were at the height of their fame in 1965.*

2 to become famous

become famous /bɪˌkʌm ˈfeɪməs/ *She dreamed of becoming really famous.*
become famous overnight (=very suddenly) *With the success of their first record, they became famous overnight.*

make your name /ˌmeɪk jɔː^r ˈneɪm/ to become well known, especially as a result of hard work: *Clint Eastwood first made his name in the TV series 'Rawhide'.*
+ as *By the time he was 30, Evans had made his name as the editor of the 'Sunday Times'.*

F

make a name for yourself *She is beginning to make a name for herself as a fashion designer.*

3 a famous person

star /stɑːʳ/ [n C] a very famous and successful film actor, entertainer, or sports player: *Tilda's latest movie role could make her a big star.*

movie/rock/tennis star etc *Bruce Willis is one of my favourite movie stars.* | *She was once married to a well-known football star.*

celebrity /sɔ̩'lebrɔ̩ti/ [n C] someone who is well known, for example as an entertainer or sports player, and who is often seen on television or is written about in newspapers: *The event was attended by various golfing celebrities.*

TV/showbusiness/media celebrity *The club is popular with media celebrities and literary types.*

plural **celebrities**

superstar /'suːpəʳstɑːʳ, 'sjuː-‖'suː-/ [n C] an actor, musician, or sports player who is famous all over the world: *This was the movie that made Brando an international superstar.* | *tennis superstar Monica Seles*

4 not famous

unknown /ˌʌn'nəʊn◄/ [adj] not at all famous: *Gorbachev was virtually unknown in the West when he first came to power.* | *As an unknown author, it isn't easy to get your work published.*

a nobody /ə 'nəʊbədi/ [n singular] INFORMAL someone who is very ordinary and not at all famous or important: *Six months ago she was a nobody, and now she's a superstar.*

FAR

➡ opposite **NEAR**

1 a long distance

far /fɑːʳ/ [adv] a long distance – use this especially in negatives and questions: *Have you driven far?* | *Since I changed jobs, I have to travel farther to get to work.* | *Let's see who can jump the farthest.*

far away (=a very long way from where you are) *The ship was so far away that we could hardly see it.*

+ from *We were sitting too far from the stage to hear what the actors were saying.*

+ above/below/behind *They lay on the hillside with the sea far below them.*

far – farther – farthest or **far – further – furthest**

⚠ Don't say 'the school is far'. Say **the school is a long way away** or **it's a long way to the school**. **Far** is usually only used in questions and negative sentences.

⚠ You can use **farther/further** or **farthest/ furthest** in any kind of sentence, and you can use phrases such as **far away**, **far enough** or **too far** in any kind of sentence.

⚠ Don't say 'he lives far' or 'he lives 10 miles far from here'. Say **he lives far away/ a long way away** or **he lives 10 miles away**.

a long way /ə ˌlɒŋ 'weɪ‖-ˌlɔːŋ-/ a long distance: *You must be tired, you've come a long way.*

+ from *The farm is a long way from the highway.*

a long way away/a long way off (=a long way from where you are now or from the place you are talking about) *We could hear them shouting from a long way away.* | *From the map, it looked like the lake was still a long way off.*

+ ahead/below/behind etc *A long way below me, a man was riding his horse across the plain.*

miles /maɪlz/ [n plural] INFORMAL a very long way: *We walked miles yesterday.*

+ away *I don't see Jane much any more – she lives miles away.*

+ from *The hotel is miles from the station – I'll come and get you.*

miles from anywhere (=a long way from the nearest town) *They live up in the mountains, miles from anywhere.*

nowhere near /ˌnəʊweəʳ 'nɪəʳ/ [preposition] a very long way from somewhere, further than you expect to be, or further than someone else says you are: *West says he was nowhere near the cliff when his wife was killed.* | *After 8 hours' climbing, we were still nowhere near the top of the mountain.*

2 when something you can see or hear is far away

in the distance /ɪn ðə 'dɪstəns/ if you can see or hear something **in the distance**, it is a long way from where you are, so it looks small or does not sound loud: *In the distance, he could see the tall chimneys of the factory.* | *There was the sound of church bells in the distance.*

distant /'dɪstənt/ [adj only before noun] very far away, so that it looks small or sounds quiet: *distant thunder* | *By now, the plane was just a distant speck in the sky.*

> ⚠ Use **distant** when you are writing stories or descriptions.

on the horizon /ɒn ðə hə'raɪzən/ at the place far away where the land or sea seems to meet the sky: *Another ship appeared on the horizon.*

from a distance /frəm ə 'dɪstəns/ from a place that is a long way away: *From a distance, we could hear the faint sound of drums beating.* | *Until then I had only seen the castle from a distance.*

3 far away from other places

distant/far-off /'dɪstənt, 'fɑːr ɒf/ [adj only before noun] a **distant** or **far-off** town or country is far away from where you are: *The travellers told us stories about distant lands.* | *Many years ago, in a far-off city, there lived a wise old man.*

> ⚠ Use **distant** and **far-off** when you are writing stories or descriptions.

remote /rɪ'məʊt/ [adj] **remote** places are far away from other places or people, and very few people go there: *They moved to a remote farmhouse in North Wales.* | *The helicopter crashed in a remote desert area.*

in the middle of nowhere /ɪn ðə ˌmɪdl əv 'nəʊweər/ INFORMAL in a lonely place a long way from towns or villages, where you do not expect to find any houses: *Amazingly, we found a really nice motel in the middle of nowhere.*

4 how far

how far /ˌhaʊ 'fɑːr/ use this to ask what the distance is between where you are and another place: *"How far is it to Newark?" "It's about 200 miles."* | *God knows how far it is to the next gas station.*

from /frəm; *strong* frɒm‖frəm; *strong* frʌm, frɑːm/ [preposition] if one place is 10 kilometres/30 miles/20 minutes etc **from** another place, that is the distance between the two places, or the time it takes to get from one to the other: *Seattle is about 100 miles from the Canadian border.* | *The junior high school is five minutes from our house.* | *She was standing just a couple of metres from the edge of the cliff.*

away /ə'weɪ/ [adv] if a place or person is 10 kilometres/30 miles/20 minutes etc **away**, they are that distance from where you are, or it takes that amount of time to travel there: *The nearest village was about 20 miles away.* | *Toronto's only about an hour and a half away by car.*

distance /'dɪstəns/ [n C/U] how far it is from one place to another
distance from sth to sth *What is the distance from Freeport to Miami?*
the distance between sth and sth *Measure the distance between the window and the door.*

FASHIONABLE/ UNFASHIONABLE

➡ see also **CLOTHES, MUSIC**

1 fashionable

fashionable /'fæʃənəbəl/ [adj] clothes or styles that are **fashionable** are popular at the present time, but will probably only be popular for a short time: *The store sells fashionable clothes at prices you can afford.* | *a style of painting that was fashionable in the 1930s*
fashionable restaurant/school/resort etc (=a place that a lot of people want to go to, especially rich people, because it is fashionable) *a fashionable skiing resort*

F

trendy /'trendi/ [adj] very fashionable and exciting – use this about things people do, places they go etc in order to show how modern and fashionable they are: *a trendy street market in the centre of Paris* | *Parents and teachers are worried that some drugs are considered very trendy among teenagers.*

trendy – trendier – trendiest

stylish /'staɪlɪʃ/ [adj] well designed, and attractive in a fashionable way: *She was wearing a stylish black woollen dress.* | *stylish modern furniture*

designer /dɪ'zaɪnəʳ/ [adj only before noun] **designer jeans/watch/label/clothing etc** use this about clothes, watches etc that are made by a well-known and fashionable designer and are usually very expensive: *She was wearing a designer dress.*

2 fashionable people

fashionable /'fæʃənəbəl/ [adj] someone who is **fashionable** wears fashionable clothes, has fashionable things, and goes to fashionable places: *the style of hat worn by fashionable women in Milan*

trendy /'trendi/ [adj] INFORMAL someone who is **trendy** likes to show how fashionable and modern they are by the way they behave, dress, and decorate their home: *a trendy young photographer from Santa Monica* | *She only talks like that because she wants to sound trendy.*

trendy – trendier – trendiest

⚠️ **Trendy** is sometimes used in a negative way about people and their ideas, when you want to say that they are too easily influenced by the most modern ideas and methods: *The school's bad exam results are being blamed on trendy teaching methods.*

sophisticated /sə'fɪstɪkeɪtɪd/ [adj] someone who is **sophisticated** knows a lot about fashionable things and feels confident about being with fashionable people: *a sophisticated woman whose friends included many rich and famous people* | *a play that will appeal to a sophisticated audience*

When you see **EC**, go to the **ESSENTIAL COMMUNICATION** section.

3 a fashionable activity, product, style etc

fashion /'fæʃən/ [n C] a style of clothes, hair, behaviour etc that is fashionable **latest fashion** (=the newest styles of women's clothes) *the latest Paris fashions* **fashion in clothes/music etc** *changing fashions in popular music* **fashion for doing sth** *Who started this fashion for wearing old army clothes?*

trend /trend/ [n C] a way of doing something or a way of thinking that is becoming fashionable **+ in** *the latest trend in kitchen design* **set/start a trend for sth** *'Rambo' set the trend for a whole wave of violent action movies.*

craze/fad /kreɪz, fæd/ [n C] a fashion, activity, type of music etc that suddenly becomes very popular, but only remains popular for a short time: *The breakdancing craze soon passed, as most fads do.* | *a craze for wearing underwear outside your clothes*

4 the business of making and selling fashionable clothes

fashion /'fæʃən/ [n U] *He's one of the best-known designers in the world of fashion.*

⚠️ **Fashion** is usually used before a noun, like an adjective: *a top-selling fashion magazine* | *She works for a well-known fashion designer.* | *the fashion industry*

5 not fashionable

out of fashion /ˌaʊt əv 'fæʃən/ no longer fashionable – use this especially about clothes and music: *Shoulder pads are definitely out of fashion now, though lots of people wore them in the eighties.* **go out of fashion** *Rock'n'Roll began in the fifties and has never really gone out of fashion.*

unfashionable /ʌn'fæʃənəbəl/ [adj] not fashionable – use this especially about people's ideas, beliefs, and way of life: *formal language-teaching methods that were unfashionable in the 60s and 70s* |

She lived in an unfashionable part of West London.

FAST

➡ opposite **SLOW**
➡ see also **HURRY, RUN**

1 moving fast

⚠️ Fast and **quickly** both mean 'going at high speed', but you use **quickly** especially to talk about someone who is going only a short distance, especially because they are in a hurry.

fast /fɑːst‖fæst/ [adv] *Don't drive so fast – there's ice on the road.* | *The new fighter aircraft flies almost twice as fast as the old one.* | *Pat walked faster and faster as the footsteps behind her got closer.*
as fast as you can *He ran home as fast as he could.*
  fast [adj] able to go fast: *the fastest runner in the world* | *Dean always loved fast cars and expensive clothes.*

quickly /ˈkwɪkli/ [adv] moving fast for a short distance: *Richard ran quickly down the stairs.* | *If you hear the alarm, leave the building quickly and calmly.* | *Tell the doctor to come quickly.*

at high speed /ət ˌhaɪ ˈspiːd/ moving or working very fast – use this about cars, trains, machines etc: *Two cars raced past him at high speed.* | *a metal disc revolving at high speed*
  high-speed [adj only before noun] *You can travel by high-speed train from Paris to Brussels.* | *a high-speed drill*

at top speed /ət ˌtɒp ˈspiːd‖-ˌtɑːp-/ if someone is driving, running etc **at top speed**, they are moving as fast as they can: *Carson drove to the hospital at top speed.*

2 doing things quickly or happening quickly

quickly /ˈkwɪkli/ [adv] doing things quickly or happening quickly, without taking much time: *She undressed quickly and got into bed.* | *It's important to realize how quickly this disease can spread.* | *You fry the onions quickly, then add the meat.*

quick /kwɪk/ [adj] a **quick** movement or action is one that you do quickly or one that only takes a short time: *I'll just take a quick shower.* | *That was quick! Have you finished already?* | *I had to make a quick decision.*
be quick (=use this when you are telling someone to hurry) *You'll have to be quick – we don't have much time.*

fast /fɑːst‖fæst/ [adv] if you work, talk, or write **fast**, you do it quickly: *Don't talk so fast – I can't understand what you're saying.* | *We're working as fast as we can.*

rapid /ˈræpɪd/ [adj usually before noun] a **rapid** change, increase, or improvement is one that happens much more quickly than usual: *a rapid increase in the population* | *In China, it was a period of rapid change.* | *She made a rapid recovery after her operation.* (=she got better very quickly)
  rapidly [adv] *the rapidly changing world of computer technology*

prompt /prɒmpt‖prɑːmpt/ [adj] doing things quickly and without delay, especially when you have to deal with a problem
prompt action/reply/delivery *A major disaster was prevented by the prompt action of the police.* | *We guarantee prompt delivery of the goods you have ordered.*
  promptly [adv] *Sanders raised objections to the plan, and was promptly sacked.*

3 how fast

speed /spiːd/ [n C/U] how fast something or someone moves: *Police are advising drivers to reduce their speed because of thick fog.*
at a speed of 70 mph/40 kph etc *a truck travelling at a speed of 50 mph*
at a constant/steady speed (=keeping the same speed all the time) *The planet revolves at a constant speed.*

rate /reɪt/ [n C] how fast things happen, change, or develop
rate of growth / increase / change / development *China's economy is experiencing a very high rate of growth.*

at a faster / slower / different rate
Children learn to read at different
rates. | The population is increasing at a
faster rate than ever before.

pace /peɪs/ [n singular] how fast someone
walks or runs, or how fast they work or do
things
at a brisk/steady/gentle etc pace (=going
at a fast, regular, or slow speed) *soldiers
marching at a steady pace*
pace of work/life *The whole pace of life
seems a lot slower there.*

4 to go somewhere fast

⚠ All these verbs must be used with a
preposition (such as **to**, **across**, **through**, or
into), or with an *adverb* (such as **away**,
out, or **there**).

race /reɪs/ [v I] to go somewhere as fast as
you can, especially because you have to
deal with a dangerous situation
+ across/back/ahead etc *Hearing the
children's screams, she raced back into
the house. | A police car came racing
down the road.*

rush /rʌʃ/ [v I] to go somewhere very
quickly because you are in a hurry
+ out/around/into etc *Everyone rushed
out into the street to see what was hap-
pening. | People were rushing past me
on their way to work.*

dash /dæʃ/ [v I] to run somewhere very
fast, especially only a short distance
+ into/around/to etc *Pam dashed into
the store just as it was closing. | dash-
ing across the road to catch a bus*

speed /spiːd/ [v I] to move very fast – use
this about cars, trains, or buses, or about
people travelling in them
+ along/past/across etc *Soon we were
speeding across the desert. | An ambu-
lance sped past on its way to the accident.*
speeding – sped – have sped

5 to move or work faster

go faster /ˌgəʊ ˈfɑːstəʳ‖-ˈfæs-/
move/work etc faster *Could you go a
little faster? We don't want to miss our
plane. | You'll have to work a lot faster
than this.*

faster and faster (=more and more quickly)
*I could feel my heart beating faster and
faster.*

speed up /ˌspiːd ˈʌp/ [phrasal verb T] to
make something happen more quickly,
especially a job or process
speed up sth/speed sth up *Certain herbs
were thought to speed up the healing
process. | I'll phone the manager and
get them to speed things up.*

accelerate /əkˈseləreɪt/ [v I] to go faster –
use this about a car, bus etc, or about the
person driving it: *They were all thrown
backwards as Josef suddenly accelerated. |
The Ferrari Mondial can accelerate from
zero to 60 mph in 6.3 seconds.*

6 to move as fast as someone else

keep up with sb /ˌkiːp ˈʌp wɪð (sb)/
[phrasal verb T] to move as fast as someone
else who is walking, running, or driving in
the same direction: *Slow down, I can't keep
up with you. | She walked so fast that
Charlie had to run to keep up with her.*

FASTEN/UNFASTEN

**to join together the two sides of a
piece of clothing, bag, belt etc, so
that it is closed**

➡ see also **TIE/UNTIE, CLOTHES**

1 to fasten something

fasten

"Please fasten your seatbelts."

fasten /ˈfɑːsən‖ˈfæ-/ [v T] to join together the
two sides of a piece of clothing, bag, belt
etc, so that it is closed: *Fasten your coat –
it's cold outside. | We will shortly be
landing in Athens. Please fasten your
seatbelts. | I can't fasten my suitcase.
There's too much in it.*

fastened [adj not before noun] *Is your safety belt fastened?*

button/button up button

/ˈbʌtn, ˌbʌtn ˈʌp/ [v T] to fasten the buttons on a piece of clothing: *He began buttoning his shirt.*

button up sth/button sth up *He buttoned up his jacket and straightened his tie.* | *Button your coat up – it's raining.*

zip up zip up

/ˌzɪp ˈʌp/ [phrasal verb T] to fasten clothes, bags etc with a zip

zip up sth *I can't zip up these jeans – they're too tight!*

zip sth up *She took some money out of her purse and zipped it up again quickly.*

Q **do up** /ˌduː ˈʌp/ [phrasal verb T] ESPECIALLY SPOKEN to fasten clothes, or the buttons, zips etc on clothes

do up sth *Come on then, do up your coat and let's go.*

do sth up *I can't do this zip up – it's stuck.* | *Are your shoelaces done up properly?*

tie tie

/taɪ/ [v T] to fasten something by making a knot

tie shoelaces/a scarf etc *Don't forget to tie your shoelaces.* | *She tied a scarf around her head.*

tying – tied – have tied

She tied a scarf around her head.

2 to unfasten something

unfasten /ʌnˈfɑːsən‖-ˈfæ-/ [v T] to open the two sides of a piece of clothing, bag, belt etc: *It was hot in the waiting-room, so I unfastened my coat.* | *Jack unfastened his seatbelt and stepped out of the car.*

unfastened [adj not before noun] *The back of her dress was unfastened.*

undo /ʌnˈduː/ [v T] to unfasten clothes, or unfasten the buttons, zips etc on clothes: *My fingers were so cold that I couldn't undo the buttons.* | *Rosie undid the necklace and gave it back to him.*

undoing – undid – have undone

undone /ʌnˈdʌn/ [adj not before noun] *Your zip's undone!*

come undone (=become unfastened) *One of his shoelaces had come undone.*

unbutton /ʌnˈbʌtn/ [v T] to unfasten the buttons on a piece of clothing: *She unbuttoned her uniform and changed into her normal clothes.*

unbuttoned [adj not before noun] *His trousers were unbuttoned and his shirt was hanging out.*

unzip /ʌnˈzɪp/ [v T] to unfasten clothes, bags etc by unfastening a zip: *She unzipped the case and took out a thick file.*

unzipping – unzipped – have unzipped

untie /ʌnˈtaɪ/ [v T] to unfasten the knot that fastens shoes, a tie, a scarf etc: *Amy untied her apron and folded it neatly on the chair.*

untying – untied – have untied

loosen /ˈluːsən/ [v T] to unfasten clothes a little, in order to make yourself more comfortable: *I'd eaten so much that I had to loosen my belt.* | *Lay the patient on his side and loosen any tight clothing.*

FAT

➡ opposite **THIN**

BIG   THICK

see also

WIDE/
NARROW   DESCRIBING
PEOPLE

1 someone who is fat

fat /fæt/ [adj] *Do I look fat in this dress?* | *Clare's on a diet because she thinks she's too fat.*

get fat *I'm getting too fat for these jeans.*

fat – fatter – fattest

F

> ⚠ We usually use **fat** only to talk about ourselves. It is rude to say that someone else is **fat**. It is more polite to say that they are **large** or **overweight**, or that they **have put on weight**.

overweight /ˌəʊvəˈweɪt◂/ [adj not before noun] a little fatter than you should be: *Many teenagers are overweight because they don't get enough exercise.* | *He's not really fat – just a little overweight.*
5 kilos/10 pounds etc overweight *I was ten kilos overweight and smoked 40 cigarettes a day.*

plump /plʌmp/ [adj] fat in a pleasant, attractive way: *Her mother was a small, plump woman.*

chubby /ˈtʃʌbi/ [adj] a **chubby** child is a little fat in a pleasant, healthy-looking way: *a nice chubby baby* | *Who's that chubby little girl with dark hair?*
chubby – chubbier – chubbiest

large /lɑːʳdʒ/ [adj] use this as a polite way of saying that someone is fat: *fashionable clothes for the larger woman* | *I was squashed between two rather large men for most of the journey.*
large – larger – largest

obese /əʊˈbiːs/ [adj] much too fat, in a way that is dangerous to your health: *30% of the women on the island are obese.*
obesity [n U] the medical problem of being much too fat in a way that is dangerous to your health: *Doctors have recommended the diet as a treatment for obesity.*

> ⚠ **Obese** is used especially in medical writing.

2 part of the body

fat /fæt/ [adj] *I hate going swimming – I don't like people seeing my fat legs.*
fat – fatter – fattest

flabby /ˈflæbi/ [adj] covered in soft loose fat that looks very unattractive: *Her body was getting old and flabby.* | *John's flabby white thighs wobbled as he walked along the beach.*
flabby – flabbier – flabbiest

chubby /ˈtʃʌbi/ [adj] **chubby** arms, cheeks, legs etc are slightly fat in a pleasant, attractive way: *a little girl of about three, with blonde hair and chubby arms*
chubby – chubbier – chubbiest

thick /θɪk/ [adj] fat – use this about people's necks, ankles, wrists, or arms that have a lot of muscles or a lot of flesh on them: *a big heavy man with a thick neck and a broad red face*

3 to become fatter

get fatter /get ˈfætəʳ/ to become fatter: *Steve has got a lot fatter since I last saw him.*

put on weight /ˌpʊt ɒn ˈweɪt/ to become fatter: *John's put on a lot of weight recently, hasn't he?*
put on 5 kilos/2 pounds etc (=become 5 kilos/2 pounds etc heavier than you were before) *I put on several pounds over Christmas.*

> ⚠ It is more polite to say someone **has put on weight** than to say they **have got fatter**.

4 food that makes you fat

fattening /ˈfætnɪŋ/ [adj] food that is **fattening** makes you fat: *Try to avoid fattening foods.* | *Grilled fish tastes better and is less fattening than fried fish.*

FATHER

MOTHER BABY
see also
FAMILY CHILD
MAN

1 father

father /ˈfɑːðəʳ/ [n C] *My father's a doctor.* | *Like most fathers, I felt anxious when my son got his first motorcycle.* | *Larry Blake, a father of three children, was shot dead outside his home last night.*

dad /dæd/ [n C] a name you use to talk to your father or to talk about him or someone else's father: *Was your dad angry* when you got home? | Can I borrow your car, Dad? | My dad retired ten years ago.

daddy /'dædi/ [n C] a name for your father – used especially by young children or when you are talking to young children: Daddy, can I have a drink, please? | Go and ask Daddy if he'll play with you.

pop /pɒp‖pɑːp/ [n singular] AMERICAN a name you call your father: Pop and I went for a walk along the beach.

2 like a father

paternal /pə'tɜːᵣnl/ [adj] **paternal** feelings are like the feelings that a good father has for his children: Although he had no children of his own, he took a kind of paternal interest in Katie's progress at school.

FAVOURITE/ FAVORITE

the one you like better than any others

➡ see also **LIKE/NOT LIKE, BEST**

favourite BRITISH **favorite** AMERICAN /'feɪvərᵻt/ [adj only before noun] **sb's favourite colour/food/teacher etc** the colour, food etc that someone likes better than any other colour, food etc: My favourite colour is purple. | Who is your favorite singer? | We're going to her favourite restaurant for a meal.

◯like best /ˌlaɪk 'best/ ESPECIALLY SPOKEN to like something better than other things – use this especially when you are asking someone to choose or when you are choosing : Which of these dresses do you like best?
like sth best I think I like the red one best.

favourite BRITISH **favorite** AMERICAN /'feɪvərᵻt/ [n C] something that you like more than other things of the same kind: I like all her books, but this one's my favourite. | Oh great! Chocolate ice-cream – my favourite!

teacher's pet /ˌtiːtʃərz 'pet/ [n singular] INFORMAL someone who is their teacher's favourite student, and who the other students do not like because of this: Janice is a real teacher's pet and always sits at the front of the class.

FEEL

➡ see also **TOUCH**

1 to feel hot/tired/hungry etc

feel/be /fiːl, biː/ [v]
feel/be tired/hot/hungry etc I was very tired and I just wanted to sleep. | If you feel hungry between meals, have a piece of fruit. | Stop the car – Ben feels sick! | You'll be cold if you don't wear a coat.
feel well/better "How do you feel?" "I feel much better now I've had some sleep."
feeling – felt – have felt
being – was – have been

experience /ɪk'spɪəriəns/ [v T] FORMAL to have a feeling of pain, sickness etc: Most women experience some nausea when they are pregnant. | He said that he had never experienced such pain before.

sensitive /'sensᵻtɪv/ [adj] a part of your body that is **sensitive** feels pain, cold, heat etc more than is usual
sensitive to heat / light / cold etc Blue eyes tend to be more sensitive to light.
sensitive teeth / eyes / skin (=reacting strongly to cold, light, smoke etc) a special toothpaste for sensitive teeth

2 a physical feeling

feeling /'fiːlɪŋ/ [n C] a physical feeling of heat, cold, tiredness etc: When he woke up there was a horrible tight feeling in his chest.
+ of One symptom of this illness is a general feeling of ill-health and tiredness.

3 how something feels when you touch it

feel /fiːl/ [v] if something **feels** hot, soft, wet etc, this is the feeling it gives you when you touch it

F

feel hot/cold/soft etc *Your forehead feels very hot – let's check your temperature.* | *The marble felt cold and smooth against her cheek.*

feel like sth (=feel the same as) *The material feels just like silk.*

feeling – felt – have felt

4 when you cannot feel anything in part of your body

numb /nʌm/ [adj] if part of your body is **numb**, it does not feel anything, for example because it is very cold or because your blood is not reaching it: *My left hand was completely numb.*

go numb (=become numb) *It was so cold my fingers had gone numb.*

5 to feel happy/ frightened/bored etc

feel/be /fiːl, biː/ [v]

be happy/frightened/bored etc *A great many people are nervous about speaking to a large audience.*

feel happy/frightened/bored etc *I couldn't help feeling a little sad when he left.* | *You shouldn't feel guilty – it wasn't your fault.*

feeling – felt – have felt

being – was – have been

mood /muːd/ [n C] the way someone feels at a particular time, for example sad, happy, or angry: *She's a strange girl – her moods change very quickly.*

be in a good/bad mood (=be happy, angry etc at the present time) *Bill's in a good mood tonight, isn't he?*

put sb in a good/bad etc mood (=make someone feel happy, angry etc) *I was stuck in the traffic for hours, which put me in a bad mood all morning.*

state of mind /ˌsteɪt əv ˈmaɪnd/ [n singular] the way someone feels and thinks at a particular time, especially when they are upset or confused and this affects the way they behave: *Try to imagine this woman's state of mind at the time she committed the crime.*

6 a feeling of happiness, anger, fear etc

feeling /ˈfiːlɪŋ/ [n C] something that you feel, for example happiness, anger, or

fear: *It was a wonderful feeling to be home again.* | *Many men find it hard to express their feelings.*

a feeling of horror/sadness/rage etc *With a feeling of relief, I heard him coming home at last.* | *feelings of helplessness and terror*

emotion /ɪˈməʊʃən/ [n C/U] a strong feeling such as love, hate, or anger that is often difficult to control: *She stared at him, overcome by emotion.* | *Parents feel a mixture of emotions when their first child starts school.*

> ⚠ Don't say 'an emotion of anger/love etc'. Say **a feeling of anger/love etc.**

a sense of /ə ˈsens ɒv/ a good or bad feeling, for example of loneliness or peace, that stays with you for a long time: *Children need to be given a sense of security.* | *After his wife died, he had a terrible sense of emptiness.*

7 someone who has strong feelings

emotional /ɪˈməʊʃənəl/ [adj] someone who is **emotional** has strong feelings and is not afraid to show them: *George got very emotional when it was time for us to leave.* | *In an emotional speech, Nicky thanked everyone for helping her to win.*

passionate /ˈpæʃənɪt/ [adj] use this about people who express very strong feelings of sexual love, or about their behaviour and relationships: *a passionate and beautiful woman* | *He pulled her to him in a passionate embrace.* | *a passionate love affair*

passionately [adv] *She kissed him passionately.*

8 something that makes you have strong feelings

emotional /ɪˈməʊʃənəl/ [adj] an **emotional** situation or event makes people show strong feelings of sadness, happiness, anger etc: *There were emotional scenes as the hostages met their families for the first time in six years.*

moving /ˈmuːvɪŋ/ [adj] a **moving** experience or event makes you feel strong emotions such as sadness or sympathy: *She* told a moving story of life in the refugee camp. | I found the funeral ceremony very moving.

sentimental /ˌsentɪˈmentl◂/ [adj] a **sentimental** story, film, song etc is intended to make you feel emotions of love or sadness, but it is too emotional and seems silly and false: a sentimental children's story about a little orphan girl in 19th century London

9 to feel that you know something

feel /fiːl/ [v T] to feel that you know something, but without understanding why you feel this
+ (that) She felt that something terrible was about to happen. | "What do you mean?" he asked, feeling that she wasn't telling him the whole truth.
feeling – felt – have felt

instinct /ˈɪnstɪŋkt/ [n C/U] a natural ability to know what you should do without having to learn it or be told it: Some instinct told her that she couldn't trust him.
+ for Even a young animal has a strong instinct for self-preservation.

intuition /ˌɪntjuˈɪʃən‖-tu-, -tju-/ [n U] the ability to understand or know things by using your feelings instead of considering the facts: If you feel there's something odd about him you should trust your intuition.

feeling /ˈfiːlɪŋ/ [n C] if you have a **feeling** that something is true or that something will happen, you feel sure about it, even though you do not know why
have a feeling (that) I had a strange feeling that we would meet again.
gut feeling INFORMAL (=a feeling that you are sure is right, even though you cannot prove it) Her gut feeling was that he was lying.

WORD BANK

FESTIVALS AND SPECIAL DAYS

➡ see pages 278–290

FEW

➡ see also **LITTLE/NOT MUCH, ONLY, LOT**

1 a small number

a few /ə ˈfjuː/ [quantifier] a small number of people, things, or places etc: Most of the trees were destroyed by fire, but a few survived.
a few people/days/things/places etc She's gone to stay with her father for a few days. | At that time of night, there were only a few cars on the road. | I invited a few friends around on Saturday night.
a few of (=a small number from a larger group) I've read a few of his books. | Only a few of the students can afford computers.

⚠ Don't use **a few** with uncountable nouns like 'money', 'food', or 'water'. Use **a little**: Would you like a little milk in your coffee?

⚠ Don't confuse **few** (=a very small number) and **a few** (=a small number, not many): He was a horrible man and he had few friends. | Let's invite a few friends for dinner.

not many /nɒt ˈmeni/ [quantifier] a smaller number than you expect or want: "Were there many people in town?" "No, not many."
not many people / places etc There weren't many people at the party, but it was still fun. | Not many restaurants stay open after midnight.
+ of Not many of my friends play musical instruments.

one or two /ˌwʌn ɔːʳ ˈtuː◂/ [quantifier] ESPECIALLY SPOKEN a small number of people or things: "Do you have any R.E.M. records?" "Yes, one or two."
one or two people/places/questions etc We've had one or two problems with the car, but nothing serious. | There are one or two things I'd like to ask you about.
+ of One or two of the girls started arguing with the teacher.

FEW continues on page 281

FESTIVALS & SPECIAL DAYS

WORD BANK

➡ see also **HOLIDAY, FREE TIME, PARTY**

F

Christmas

Christmas Eve – 24th December
Christmas Day – 25th December

Christmas is one of the most important **festivals** of the year. It is the time when Christians celebrate the birth of Jesus Christ, and many people go to church on Christmas Eve or Christmas Day. But it is also a time when people have a holiday from school or work, give each other **presents**, and send each other **cards**.

The shops are always busy during the period before Christmas, when people buy presents and traditional Christmas food and drink.

People often spend Christmas with their families. They **decorate** their houses and usually have a **Christmas tree**, which they also decorate with coloured lights, shiny glass balls etc. On Christmas day they open their presents, and then they have a special meal. The **traditional** Christmas dinner is roast turkey, and in Britain this is followed by Christmas pudding.

New Year

New Year's Eve – 31st December
New Year's Day – 1st January

People **celebrate** the beginning of the New Year. On New Year's Eve, they often have a **party** with their family and friends, and when midnight comes, they sing a special song called 'Auld Lang Syne' and say 'Happy New Year' to each other.

The New Year is also seen as a time when people try to change their lives and 'make a new start', for example by promising to stop smoking or to take more exercise. These promises are called 'New Year resolutions'.

Happy New Year! Happy New Year!

Valentine's Day
14th February

On Valentine's day people send **cards** or give flowers or chocolates to the person they love.

Usually, a Valentine's card is not signed by the person who sends it, so the person who receives it has to guess who it is from.

Valentine's card

FESTIVALS & SPECIAL DAYS

Easter

A special time in the Christian religion, during March or April

Easter is a period of several days, when Christians celebrate their belief that Jesus Christ died and then returned to life. On Good Friday, they **remember** Christ's death on the cross, then two days later – on Easter Sunday – they celebrate his return to life. The following day, Easter Monday, is a holiday in Britain.

Easter is also the time when the Spring is just beginning. Adults give each other chocolates and flowers, and children are given Easter eggs (large eggs made of chocolate).

Easter eggs

Independence Day/ The Fourth of July

4th July

This is a national holiday when the people of the USA celebrate their **independence** with **parades**, picnics, and **fireworks**.

vocabulary

card /kɑːʳd/ [n C] a piece of stiff folded paper with a picture on it, which you write a message on and send to people on special days
Christmas card/Valentine's card/birthday card *Did you get any Valentine's cards?*
send sb a card *I must remember to send Amanda a Christmas card.*

celebrate /ˈselᵻbreɪt/ [v I/T] to show that an event or occasion is important by doing something special
celebrate Easter/Christmas etc *What are you going to do to celebrate New Year?*
celebrate Christmas/Easter by doing sth *Jewish people celebrate Hanukkah by giving each other gifts.*

Christmas tree /ˈkrɪsməs triː/ [n C] a real or artificial fir tree which people decorate and have in their houses at Christmas

decorate /ˈdekəreɪt/ [v T] to make a place, room, or thing look colourful and attractive by putting bright and pretty things everywhere
decorate sth with sth *We decorate the Christmas tree with tinsel and coloured lights.*

dress up /ˌdres ˈʌp/ [v I] to wear special clothes and make-up (=paint for your face), especially so that you look like someone or something else
+ as *Each year at the Carnival, the children dress up as butterflies and march through the town.*

festival /ˈfestᵻvəl/ [n C] a special occasion when people traditionally celebrate something such as an important religious event or an important event in the history of their country

fireworks /ˈfaɪəʳwɜːʳks/ [n plural] a thing that burns and explodes to produce coloured lights, noise, and smoke
firework display (=a special event where many fireworks are lit for people to look at and enjoy) *A quarter of a million people watched the firework display over Santa Monica Bay.*

the harvest /ðə ˈhɑːʳvᵻst/ [n singular] the time of year when the crops that people have grown are ready to be picked and eaten

independence /ˌɪndᵻˈpendəns/ [n U] the time when a country begins to govern itself after a period of being controlled by another country

FESTIVALS continues on the next page

FESTIVALS & SPECIAL DAYS

F

Halloween
31st October

In the past, people believed that the spirits of dead people appeared on this day.

Today children celebrate Halloween by **dressing up** as witches and ghosts, and going 'trick or treating'. They go out in groups and knock on people's doors, shouting 'Trick or treat!'. People usually give them sweets or small presents as a treat.

Guy Fawkes' Night/Bonfire Night
5th November

In Britain, people light bonfires and let off **fireworks** on 5th November. Traditionally, this is done to remember the time when Guy Fawkes tried (but failed) to destroy the British Houses of Parliament with gunpowder in the 17th century.

Thanksgiving
The fourth Thursday in November

Thanksgiving is a **national holiday** when people in the USA thank God for **the harvest**. Traditionally, Thanksgiving remembers the time in the 17th century when the first English people who came to live in America were taught to grow local crops by the Native American people, so they had enough food to live through the winter. People usually spend Thanksgiving with their families, and have a special meal of turkey and pumpkin pie.

national holiday/public holiday /ˌnæʃənəl ˈhɒlɪdi, ˌpʌblɪk ˈhɒlɪdi‖-ˈhɑːlədeɪ/ [n C] a special day when most people in a country do not have to go to work or school, because the country is celebrating an important religious or national event

parade /pəˈreɪd/ [n C] a big public celebration when people dress up, play music, and go along the street on foot or in decorated vehicles: *In New York they have a parade to celebrate St Patrick's Day.*

party /ˈpɑːti/ [n C] an occasion when people meet together to enjoy themselves by eating, drinking, and dancing
have a party *We're having a New Year party. Do you want to come?*
go to a party *I went to lots of parties last Christmas.*

present/gift /ˈprezənt, gɪft/ [n C] something that you give to someone on a special occasion
Christmas/birthday/wedding etc present *My mother wrapped the Christmas presents and put them under the tree.* | *a wedding gift*

remember /rɪˈmembəʳ/ [v T] to have a ceremony or do something special on a particular day because an important event happened on that day in the past: *On November 11th, we remember the end of the war, and think about those who died.*

traditional /trəˈdɪʃənəl/ [adj] traditional customs and ways of celebrating are what people have done in the same way for many years, sometimes hundreds of years

FEW continued from page 277

not common /nɒt 'kɒmən‖-'kɑː-/ [adj not before noun] fairly rare among a particular group of people or in a particular place: *A lot of people own guns in America but they're not so common in Britain.* | *This style of pottery is not at all common on the mainland.*

rare /reəʳ/ [adj] something that is **rare** is not common and not many of them exist: *The library contains some of the rarest books in Europe.* | *a new law to prevent the export of rare birds*

a minority /ə maɪˈnɒrɪ̩ti‖-mɪ̩ˈnɔː-/ [quantifier] a small number of the people who belong to a larger group
+ of *Nowadays only a minority of people leaving school have jobs to go to.*
a tiny/small minority *The Gaelic language is still spoken in Ireland, but only by a tiny minority.*

a couple /ə 'kʌpəl/ [quantifier] ESPE-CIALLY SPOKEN a small number, usually only two or three
+ of *A couple of kids were playing in the street.* | *I saw her a couple of days ago.*

⚠ In British English **a couple** usually means 'two', but in American English it can mean any small number.

2 a very small number

few/very few /fjuː, ˌveri 'fjuː/ [quantifier] a very small number of people, things, or places etc: *At that time, few people had televisions.* | *Very few companies have women directors.*
+ of *Very few of the students we asked said they were interested in politics.*

⚠ We usually say **very few** On its own, **few** is formal.

hardly any /ˌhɑːʳdli 'eni/ [quantifier] almost no people or things – use this especially to show that you are surprised or disappointed by how few there are
hardly any/anyone/anything etc *We thought there would be lots of places to see, but there were hardly any.* | *Hardly anyone came to my party.*
+ of *Hardly any of the people there even spoke to me.*

FIGHT

➡ look here for ...
- when people fight each other
- when you try hard to change something

1 when people hit each other

fight /faɪt/ [v I/T] if people **fight**, or if one person **fights** another, they hit or kick each other in order to hurt each other: *Two men were fighting in the street outside.* | *Grant fought the other boy and won.*
+ with *Billy had been fighting with some kids from another school.*
fight over sth (=fight because you dis-agree about something or because you both want to get something) *Two men in the bar began fighting over a game of cards.* | *The two boys were fighting over a toy car.*
fighting – fought – have fought

fight /faɪt/ [n C] when people fight each other: *There was a fight after school yesterday – one of my friends got badly hurt.*
have a fight (with sb) *I didn't want to have a fight with him – he was much bigger than me.*
be in a fight *You look terrible – have you been in a fight?*
get into a fight (=become involved in a fight, often without intending to) *David was always getting into fights at school.*
start a fight/pick a fight (with sb) (=deliberately try to make someone fight you, by arguing with them or insulting them) *I walked into a bar, and this drunk tried to pick a fight with me.*

fighting /'faɪtɪŋ/ [n U] when a lot of people fight each other in a public place: *There was fighting on the streets of Paris yesterday when police and demon-strators clashed.*

+ between *Fighting between rival gangs resulted in the death of a teenage boy.*

fighting breaks out (=it starts suddenly) *Fighting broke out between English and Dutch football fans after the game.*

riot /'raɪət/ [n C] a violent fight in a public place in which a lot of people attack the police and damage shops, cars etc, especially because they are angry with the government: *Their store got burned down in the LA riots.*

  rioting [n U] when there are riots happening, especially for a long period: *Days of rioting left the city in chaos.*

  rioter [n C] someone who takes part in a riot: *Police began shooting at the rioters.*

2 when people fight each other as a sport

fight /faɪt/ [v T] to take part in a sport in which you hit your opponent or try to throw him onto the ground: *Tyson fought Bruno for the World Heavyweight Championship.* | *The two wrestlers have fought each other many times before.*

fighting – fought – have fought

fight /faɪt/ [n C] a game in which two people hit each other or try to throw each other onto the ground: *Are you going to watch the big fight tonight?*

+ between *the fight between Joe Louis and Rocky Marciano*

boxing /'bɒksɪŋ‖'bɑːk-/ [n U] a sport in which two people wearing special thick gloves hit each other and try to make the other person fall onto the ground

  boxing match (=a game of boxing)

  boxer [n C] someone who does boxing

wrestling /'reslɪŋ/ [n U] a sport in which two people hold each other and try to throw each other onto the ground

  wrestling match (=a game of wrestling)

  wrestler [n C] someone who does wrestling

3 when soldiers try to kill other soldiers

• see also **WAR**

fight /faɪt/ [v I/T] if soldiers **fight**, they try to kill other soldiers in a war or battle

fight in a war/battle/campaign (=be a soldier in a war etc) *As a young man, he fought in the Spanish Civil War.*

fight for sb/sth (=fight to defend your country or ruler) *He died fighting for his country.*

+ against *Your grandfather fought against the Russians on the Eastern Front.*

fighting – fought – have fought

> ⚠ Only use **fight** as a transitive verb [v T] when talking about two countries or armies that fight each other: *The British and German armies fought each other in Northern France.*

fighting /'faɪtɪŋ/ [n U] when soldiers fight during a war or battle: *There has been fighting in the capital, and around 1000 people have been killed.* | *The road was full of refugees trying to escape the fighting in Bosnia.*

battle /'bætl/ [n C] a fight between two armies in one place: *After a long battle, the rebels were defeated.*

the Battle of Waterloo/Stalingrad etc *The Battle of the Somme started on the first of July, 1916.*

4 to try hard to stop something happening or to make something happen

fight /faɪt/ [v I/T] to try hard for a long time to stop something bad from happening or to make something good happen

fight sth (=fight to stop it from happening) *We are determined to fight drug abuse in schools.*

fight for freedom/independence/your rights etc (=fight in order to achieve something good) *Freedom of speech is something worth fighting for.*

fight to do sth *Local people have been fighting to save the forest.*

fight against terrorism/injustice/poverty (=fight to stop it from happening) *Amnesty is an organization that fights against torture and injustice.*

fighting – fought – have fought

campaign /kæm'peɪn/ [v I] to do things, such as writing to the government and organizing public meetings, because you want to change society or stop something bad from happening

+ against Greenpeace campaigned against nuclear weapons tests in the Pacific.

+ for Disabled people have been campaigning for equal rights for years.

campaign to do sth The animal rights movement is campaigning to stop experiments on live animals.

fight /faɪt/ [n singular] when people try hard for a long time to stop something bad from happening or to make something good happen

+ against New laws have been passed to help the police in their fight against organized crime.

+ for women's fight for equality

battle /'bætl/ [n C usually singular] when a person or group tries hard for a long time to change a bad situation, or deal with a problem in society

+ against her long battle against cancer | The President is fully committed to the battle against the drug traffickers.

struggle /'strʌgəl/ [n C usually singular] when people try for many years to get freedom, independence, or equal rights, and a lot of people suffer, are killed, or are put in prison

+ for Nkrumah led the people in their struggle for independence.

+ against He devoted his life to the struggle against fascism and oppression.

WORD BANK

FILMS/MOVIES

BOOKS/LITERATURE
MUSIC   FREE TIME

STORY   ACTOR/
                              ACTRESS
see
also
EC OPINIONS   FAMOUS

DANCE   VIOLENT
TELEVISION AND RADIO

1 films and going to see them

film ESPECIALLY BRITISH **movie** ESPECIALLY AMERICAN /fɪlm, 'muːvi/ [n C] a story that is told using sound and moving pictures

+ about a movie about the Vietnam War

see a film/movie Have you seen any good films lately? | I went to see 'Blue Velvet' last night.

⚠ You can also use **film** or **movie** before a noun, like an adjective: a film studio | movie stars

cinema BRITISH **movie theater** AMERICAN /'sɪnɪmə, 'muːvi ˌθɪətəʳ/ [n C] a building where you go to see films: the MGM cinema in Leicester Square | a movie theater built in the 1930s

go to the cinema BRITISH **go to the movies** AMERICAN /ˌgəʊ tə ðə 'sɪnɪmə, ˌgəʊ tə ðə 'muːviz/ to go to a cinema in order to see a film: Do you want to go the movies this weekend? | I haven't been to the cinema for ages.

be on ESPECIALLY BRITISH **be playing** ESPECIALLY AMERICAN /biː 'ɒn, biː 'pleɪ-ɪŋ/ if a film **is on** or **is playing**, it is being shown at a cinema: What's on at the cinema this weekend? | 'Diehard' is playing at the Majestic.

2 types of film

horror film

horror film/horror movie /'hɒrəʳ ˌfɪlm, 'hɒrəʳ ˌmuːvi‖'hɔː-, 'hɑː-/ [n C] a film that is intended to make you feel frightened, for example one in which people get attacked by strange creatures, or in which dead people come to life

comedy /'kɒmədi‖'kɑː-/ [n C] a film that is intended to make you laugh

When you see **EC**, go to the **ESSENTIAL COMMUNICATION** section.

F

science fiction film

road movie

science fiction film/science fiction movie /ˌsaɪəns ˈfɪkʃən fɪlm, ˌsaɪəns ˈfɪkʃən ˌmuːvi/ [n C] a film about life in the future, often with people or creatures who live in other parts of the universe

thriller /ˈθrɪləʳ/ [n C] a film that tells an exciting story about murder or crime

romantic comedy

romantic comedy /rəʊˌmæntɪk ˈkɒmədi‖ -ˈkɑː-/ [n C] a film that is intended to make you laugh, about two people who meet and have a romantic relationship

western

cartoon

western /ˈwestəʳn/ [n C] a film about cowboys and life in the 19th century in the American West

war film/war movie /ˈwɔːʳ fɪlm, ˈwɔːʳ ˌmuːvi/ [n C] a film about people fighting a war

action movie /ˈækʃən ˌmuːvi/ [n C] a film that has a lot of exciting events in it, for example people fighting or chasing each other in cars

road movie /ˈrəʊd ˌmuːvi/ [n C] a film about people who are on a long journey in a car, and the adventures they have while they are travelling

cartoon /kɑːʳˈtuːn/ [n C] a film made using photographs of models or drawings, which are put together to look as if they are moving

3 people in films

actor /ˈæktər/ [n C] someone who acts in films: *famous Hollywood actors* | *He began his career as an actor in the movie 'Gone with the Wind'.*

⚠ You can use **actor** about a man or a woman.

actress /ˈæktrɪs/ [n C] a woman who acts in films: *The part of Cathy will be played by the French actress Juliette Binoche.*

⚠ Some women prefer to be called **actors** and do not use the word **actress** .

star/film star/movie star /stɑːr, ˈfɪlm stɑːr, ˈmuːvi stɑːr/ [n C] a famous actor or actress in films

4 people who make films

director /dɪˈrektər, daɪ-/ [n C] the person who is in charge of making a film, and who tells the actors what to do: *The director was Martin Scorsese.*
  direct [v I/T] *'The Commitments' was directed by Alan Parker.*

producer /prəˈdjuːsər‖-ˈduː-/ [n C] the person who is in charge of organizing and making arrangements for a film, and who controls the money

film crew /ˈfɪlm kruː/ [n C] all the people who work to make a film, except the actors and actresses

5 to act in a film

play /pleɪ/ [v T] to act as a character in a film: *Kevin Kostner plays a bodyguard who falls in love with a singer.*

star /stɑːr/ [v T] if an actor **stars** in a film, or if a film **stars** an actor, he or she plays one of the most important characters in it: *a drama starring Demi Moore and Tom Cruise*
  + in *Elizabeth Taylor starred in 'National Velvet' when she was only ten.*
  + as *Daniel Day Lewis stars as the disabled writer, Christie Brown.*

performance /pərˈfɔːrməns/ [n C] the acting that is done by an actor in a film – use this especially to say how good or bad you think the acting is: *Alan Rickman's performance was outstanding.*

give a wonderful/superb/moving performance *She gave a moving performance, which had most of the audience in tears.*

be in /biː ɪn/ if someone **is in** a film, they play the part of one of the characters in it: *Have you heard? Simon's going to be in a film!* | *Was she the woman in 'Ghost'?*

6 the person that an actor pretends to be in a film

character /ˈkærɪktər/ [n C] a person in the story of a film: *I didn't think the characters were very realistic.* | *The main character is a female detective.*

part /pɑːrt/ [n C] the job of acting as a particular character in a film
  + in *She had always hoped to get a part in a movie.*
  play the part of *Lawrence Olivier played the part of the king.*
  big part (=an important part, with lots of words) *Judy Garland played Dorothy in 'The Wizard of Oz', which was a big part for such a young actor.*

7 what happens in a film

plot/story /plɒt, ˈstɔːri‖plɑːt-/ [n C] the things that happen in a film: *Tom Hanks was great, but I thought the plot was really boring.* | *It's basically a love story.*

scene /siːn/ [n C] one part of a film: *The first scene takes place on a beach.* | *a love scene* | *I love the scene where the alien comes out through John Hurt's chest.*

special effect /ˌspeʃəl ɪˈfekt/ [n C] an unusual image or sound that is produced artificially, in order to make something that is impossible look as if it is really happening: *The special effects were amazing – the dinosaurs looked as if they were alive.*

ending /ˈendɪŋ/ [n C] the way that the story in a film ends: *I like movies with a happy ending best.*

twist /twɪst/ [n C] something surprising that happens in a film, which you did not expect: *The film has a twist at the end, when we discover that the detective is the murderer.*

When you see **EC** , go to the
ESSENTIAL COMMUNICATION section.

⚠ People often use the present tense to describe the characters, events, or ideas in a film: *James Bond jumps out of the plane and parachutes to safety.* This makes the story seem more real.

8 the words and music in a film

soundtrack /ˈsaʊndtræk/ [n C] the music and sounds that are played during a film

script /skrɪpt/ [n C] the words that the actors say in a film

subtitles /ˈsʌbtaɪtlz/ [n plural] the words that appear on the screen to translate what the actors say in a film that is in a foreign language

dubbed /dʌbd/ [adj] if a film is **dubbed**, the words spoken by the actors have been changed into another language

9 the ideas or subject of a film

be about /biː əˈbaʊt/ if a film **is about** a person or idea, that person or idea is the main subject of the film: *'Back to the Future' is about a boy who travels back in time.*

be based on /biː ˈbeɪst ɒn/ if a film is **based on** a book, story, or real event, the things that happen in the film are very similar to the things that happened in the book, story etc: *Oliver Stone's movie 'Platoon' is based on his own experiences in the Vietnam War.* | *a film based on one of Jane Austen's novels*
be based on a true story (=be based on something that really happened) *It was supposed to be based on a true story, but it didn't seem possible to me.*

be set in /biː ˈset ɪn/ if a film **is set in** a place or period of time, the story happens in that place or during that time: *The film is set in France during the First World War.*

theme /θiːm/ [n C] one of the main subjects or ideas in a film: *The themes of the movie are power and revenge.*

When you see **EC**, go to the **ESSENTIAL COMMUNICATION** section.

FIND

➡ see also **LOOK FOR**

1 to find someone or something that is lost
➡ opposite **LOSE**

find /faɪnd/ [v T] to find someone or something that you have lost: *I've looked everywhere but I can't find my sunglasses.* | *Have you found your passport yet?* | *The murder weapon was found in bushes nearby.*

finding – found – have found

Ⓠturn up /ˌtɜːn ˈʌp/ [phrasal verb I] ESPECIALLY SPOKEN if something that is lost **turns up**, someone finds it later in a place where they did not expect it to be: *Don't worry about your earrings – I'm sure they'll turn up.* | *Have those files turned up yet?*

trace /treɪs/ [v T] to find someone or something by a careful process of asking a lot of people for information: *Police are anxious to trace the owner of a red Ford, which was seen near the crime scene.* | *Mr Philips is trying to trace his daughter, who has been missing for two months.*

2 to find something that you need or want
➡ opposite **LOSE 5**

find /faɪnd/ [v T] to find something that you need, such as a job or a place to live: *I'm only working here until I find something better to do.* | *It took us ages to find somewhere to park.* | *We need to find a new team coach.*
be easy/difficult/hard to find *Apartments like this one are hard to find.*
finding – found – have found

3 to find a place that you are trying to go to

find /faɪnd/ [v T] to find a place that you are trying to go to: *Did you manage to find the house OK?*
be difficult/easy/hard to find *The hotel is easy to find, and is situated right in the centre of the city.*
find your way (=find the right way to go) *The building was so big, I couldn't find*

my way out. | It was my first visit to New York, but I managed to find my way to the studio.

finding – found – have found

4 to find something new and important

find /faɪnd/ [v T] to find important information, or think of a new way of doing something, after trying to do this for a long time: Medical researchers are determined to find a cure for cancer. | They are trying to find cleaner ways of generating electricity.

finding – found – have found

discover /dɪsˈkʌvəʳ/ [v T] to find an object, a substance, a place, information etc, which is important and which no-one knew about before: The planet Pluto was discovered in 1930. | Australian researchers have discovered a substance in coffee that acts like morphine.

FIND OUT

to get information about something

➡ see also SECRET

1 to find out about something

find out /ˌfaɪnd ˈaʊt/ [phrasal verb I/T] to get information about something, either by chance or by deliberately trying to get it: "Do you have these shoes in a size 39?" "I'm not sure – I'll just go and find out."

find out what/where/whether etc I'll go and find out which platform the train leaves from. | Dad was really mad at me when he found out where I'd been.

+ about He's trying to find out about Japanese classes. | If she ever finds out about this, she'll kill me!

find out sth/find sth out Could you find out his address for me, please? | "John's been married twice." "How did you find that out?"

+ (that) She found out that her husband was having an affair.

discover /dɪsˈkʌvəʳ/ [v T] to find something out, especially something that is surprising or something that is difficult to find out: Fire officers are still trying to discover the cause of the fire.

+ (that) I began to learn the guitar, and discovered that I was pretty good at it. | She discovered there was over £1000 missing from the cash box.

discover how/why/what etc They never discovered who the murderer was.

> ⚠ **Discover** is more formal than **find out**

see /siː/ [v I/T] to get the information that you want by going somewhere to look, or by doing something and noticing what happens: "Is he ready yet?" "I don't know – I'll go and see."

see if/whether Sharon, see if there's any beer in the fridge.

see how/where/what etc Can you just see who's at the door? | Let's see what happens if we add some oil.

seeing – saw – have seen

hear /hɪəʳ/ [v I/T] to be told about something: "Nina quit her job." "Yes, so I heard."

+ about He had heard about the accident from Helen.

+ (that) We heard there was a party at Bill's place, so we all went over there.

hear what/how/whether etc When will you hear whether you've got the job?

hearing – heard – have heard

> ⚠ You can say **I hear (that)** when you mean **I have heard (that)**: I hear you're moving to Toronto. (=someone told me that you are moving)

find /faɪnd/ [v T] to find out a fact or find out that something is true, especially by asking questions

+ that The survey found that more than 50% of teenagers had been offered drugs.

finding – found – have found

2 to try to find out about a crime, accident etc

investigate /ɪnˈvestɪɡeɪt/ [v I/T] to try to find out the truth about a crime, an accident, or a problem, especially by using careful and thorough methods: *Police are investigating an explosion at a city store.* | *We sent our reporter, Michael Gore, to investigate.*

⚠ Don't say 'investigate into the problem'. Say **investigate the problem**

look into sth /ˌlʊk 'ɪntuː (sth)/ [*phrasal verb* T] if someone in an official position **looks into** a problem or bad situation, they try to find out more about it so that the situation can be improved: *The manager promised to look into my complaint.* | *Police are looking into the possibility that the bomb warning was a hoax.*

solve /sɒlv‖sɑːlv, sɔːlv/ [*v* T] if someone **solves** a crime or a mystery, they get all the information they need so that they can explain exactly what happened: *Detectives are trying to solve the murder of a young girl.*

3 the process of finding out about a crime, accident etc

investigation /ɪnˌvestɪ̩'geɪʃən/ [*n* C] a process by which the police or other official organizations try to find out the truth about a crime or accident: *Following a major police investigation, two men have been arrested.*

+ **into** *The investigation into the cause of the air crash is continuing.*

carry out an investigation (=investigate) *Prison officials are carrying out a full investigation after two prisoners escaped from a prison vehicle.*

inquiry(also **enquiry**BRITISH) /ɪn'kwaɪəri‖ ɪn'kwaɪəri, 'ɪŋkwəri/ [*n* C] a series of official meetings at which people try to find out why something happened

+ **into** *Local people are calling for an inquiry into the accident.*

hold an inquiry (=have an inquiry) *An inquiry will be held to discover why the school's educational record is so bad.*

plural **inquiries**

inquest/'ɪŋkwest/ [*n* C] a legal process to find out why someone died: *The inquest heard that Mr Bovary was found hanging by a rope in his bedroom.*

+ **into** *an inquest into the death of a 54-year-old woman*

hold an inquest (=have an inquest) *An inquest will be held into the actor's death.*

FINISH

➡ look here for ...
• to finish doing something
• when you have used all of something
➡ see also **STOP, END, READY/NOT READY**

1 to finish doing something or making something

finish /'fɪnɪʃ/ [*v* I/T] to finish doing something or making something: *Have you finished your homework yet?* | *After we had finished our lunch, we went out for a walk.* | *The builders say they will have finished by Friday.*

finish doing sth *Give me a call when you've finished unpacking.*

finish with sth (=stop using something so someone else can use it) *Can I have a look at your newspaper when you've finished with it?*

have done/həv 'dʌn/ ESPECIALLY SPOKEN if you **have done** a piece of work, you have finished doing it: *Ask Jane if she's done that essay yet.* | *I've done all the dishes.*

complete/kəm'pliːt/ [*v* T] to finish making something, writing something, or doing something that takes a long time to finish: *The building is likely to be completed in two year's time.* | *Students who have completed the course usually find it fairly easy to find jobs.*

finalize (also **finalise** BRITISH) /'faɪnəlaɪz/ [*v* T] to finish making a plan, a business deal etc, by doing the last few things that need to be done: *Mr Samuels is flying to Detroit to finalize the details and sign the contract.* | *We still haven't finalized all the arrangements for the wedding.*

get it over with/get ɪt 'əʊvəʳ wɪð/ SPOKEN to do something that you have to do but do not want to do, so that you will not have to worry about it any more: *I hate going to the dentist, but I suppose I'd better go and get it over with.*

2 something that is finished

finished /'fɪnɪʃt/ [adj] something that is **finished** has all been done and dealt with in the way you wanted: *Can I read your assignment when it's finished?*

finished product/version (=finished and containing all its final details or features) *Looking at the finished product, you wouldn't know it was made from recycled paper.*

◯**be done** /bi: 'dʌn/ ESPECIALLY SPOKEN if something **is done**, you have finished doing it: *We'll send you a bill when the repairs are done.*

complete /kəm'pliːt/ [adj not before noun] use this about plans, arrangements, or activities with several different stages that are now all finished: *Building work should be complete in 20 weeks.* | *When your training is complete you will receive a special certificate.*

3 something that is not finished

not finished/unfinished /nɒt 'fɪnɪʃt, ˌʌn'fɪnɪʃt/ [adj] *On the desk was an unfinished letter to his mother.* | *The new swimming pool wasn't finished last time I drove past.*

incomplete /ˌɪnkəm'pliːt/ [adj] not finished, because not all of the work has been done on something, or because it does not have all the parts that it should have: *The excavation of the tunnel is still incomplete.* | *incomplete sentences*

⚠ **Incomplete** and **unfinished** are more formal than **not finished**

4 to finish a performance/ lesson/speech etc

finish/end /'fɪnɪʃ, end/ [v T] to finish a performance, lesson, speech etc that you are giving: *I finished my speech and sat down.* | *Our history teacher never ends her classes on time.*

finish/end sth with sth *He finished his lecture with a quotation from Shakespeare.*

finish/end sth by doing sth *I thought we'd end the evening by singing that old Irish favourite 'Danny Boy'.*

round off /ˌraʊnd 'ɒf‖-'ɔːf/ [phrasal verb T] to do something to end what you are doing in a special or suitable way

round off sth *To round off National Peace Week, a concert was organized in the park.*

round sth off with sth *They rounded the day off with a barbecue on the beach.*

5 to use all of something

finish /'fɪnɪʃ/ [v T] to eat or drink all of something, so that there is none left: *The kids have finished all the ice-cream.*

be finished (=when all of something has been used) *The butter's all finished. Can you buy some more?*

use up /ˌjuːz 'ʌp/ [phrasal verb T] to use all of something, especially when it is difficult or impossible to get more of it

use up sth *By 2100 we will probably have used up all our supplies of natural gas.*

use sth up *He'd used a whole week's money up by Monday evening.*

◯**be all gone** /bi: ˌɔːl 'gɒn‖-'gɔːn/ ESPE-CIALLY SPOKEN if something **is all gone**, there is none of it left: *"Are there any cookies left?" "No, they're all gone."*

run out /ˌrʌn 'aʊt/ [phrasal verb I] if something that you need **runs out**, there is none of it left because it has all been used; if you **run out of** something that you need, there is none of it left: *I was in a phone box and my money ran out before I'd finished.* | *We ran out of gas on the freeway last night.*

FIRE

HURT/INJURE
BURN   ACCIDENT
DESTROY ← see also → SAVE 2
KILL   HOT
EXPLODE   SMOKING

⚠ Don't say 'do you have fire?' if you want to light a cigarette. Say **do you have a light?**

1 a fire that damages a building, forest etc

fire

It took firefighters four hours to put out the blaze.

fire /faɪəʳ/ [n C/U] *30 people died in a fire in Chicago last night.* | *The fire quickly spread throughout the building.*
fire breaks out (=it starts suddenly) *A fire broke out in the hotel kitchen.*
start a fire *The fire was started by an electrical fault.*
forest fire *A huge forest fire is burning out of control in the south of France.*

blaze /bleɪz/ [n singular] a large and dangerous fire that burns very strongly: *Firefighters struggled to control the blaze at a huge chemical plant.* | *The church was completely destroyed in the blaze.*

⚠ **Blaze** is used especially in newspaper reports.

flames /fleɪmz/ [n plural] the bright parts of a fire that you see burning in the air: *I saw flames coming from the engine.*

2 when something is burning and being damaged by fire

be on fire /biː ɒn ˈfaɪəʳ/ if something **is on fire**, it is burning and being damaged by fire: *One of the plane's engines was on fire.* | *I can smell smoke. Something must be on fire.*

be in flames/be ablaze /biː ɪn ˈfleɪmz, biː əˈbleɪz/ if something **is in flames** or **is ablaze**, it is burning strongly and being very badly damaged by fire: *The ship was ablaze.* | *Within minutes the whole school was in flames.*

⚠ **Be in flames** and **be ablaze** are used especially in stories and newspaper reports.

3 a fire for making you warm, for cooking, or for burning unwanted things

fire /faɪəʳ/ [n C] *She sat down in front of the fire and read a book.*
log/coal fire *There's something very comforting about a real log fire.*
make a fire (=collect things you need for a fire) *The children collected some wood to make a fire.*
light a fire (=make a fire start burning) *Where are the matches? I need to light the fire.*

bonfire

bonfire /ˈbɒnfaɪəʳ‖ˈbɑːn-/ [n C] a large outdoor fire for burning dead leaves, wood, or things you do not need
build/make a bonfire *They piled up all the branches and made a big bonfire.*

4 to make something start burning

set fire to sth /set ˈfaɪəʳ tuː (sth)/ to make something start to burn, so that it gets damaged: *Vandals set fire to a disused warehouse near the docks last night.* | *Don't put up the barbecue there – you'll set fire to the trees.*

light /laɪt/ [v T] **light a cigarette/fire/candle etc** to make a cigarette, fire etc start to burn: *Ricky sat down and lit a cigarette.* | *We searched around for twigs and fallen branches, so we could light a fire.*
lighting – lit – have lit

arson /ˈɑːˑsən/ [n U] the crime of deliberately starting a fire in order to damage a building: *Police are treating the fire as a case of arson.*

5 to stop a fire

put out /ˌpʊt ˈaʊt/ [phrasal verb T] to make a fire stop burning
put out the fire/the blaze *It took firefighters four hours to put out the blaze.*
put sth out *She threw sand on the fire to put it out.*

extinguish /ɪkˈstɪŋgwɪʃ/ [v T] FORMAL to stop a fire burning: *He managed to extinguish the flames with his coat.*

blow out /ˌbləʊ ˈaʊt/ [phrasal verb T] to make a flame or fire stop burning by blowing on it
blow out a candle/a match/a fire *He blew out the candle and went to sleep.*
blow sth out *We tried to light a fire but the wind kept blowing it out.*

6 people whose job is to stop fires

firefighter /ˈfaɪəˑfaɪtəˑ/ [n C] someone whose job is to stop fires burning: *Firefighters rescued the children, who were trapped in an upstairs room.*

fireman /ˈfaɪəˑmən/ [n C] a man whose job is to stop fires burning
plural **firemen**

the fire brigade BRITISH **the fire department** AMERICAN /ðə ˈfaɪəˑ brɪˌgeɪd, ðə ˈfaɪəˑ dɪˌpɑːˑtmənt/ [n singular] the organization in a town or area that works to prevent fires and to stop fires burning: *The City Fire Department recommends that every home should have a smoke alarm.*

fire engine (also **fire truck** AMERICAN) /ˈfaɪər ˌendʒɪn, ˈfaɪəˑ trʌk/ [n C] a special vehicle that carries firefighters and their equipment, including the equipment used to shoot water at a fire

FIRST

➡ opposite **LAST**
➡ see also **BEGINNING, START**

1 before other things or people

first /fɜːˑst/ [adj] before everyone or everything else: *Laurie's name was first on the list.* | *I still remember my first day of school.* | *She had her first baby in 1984.* | *I only read the first chapter.* | *The first thing I noticed was that the front door had been smashed in.*
the first person to do sth *Yuri Gagarin was the first man to travel into space.*

first /fɜːˑst/ [adv] before you do any other things, or before anything else happens: *I always read the sports page of the newspaper first.* | *Shall we go out now, or do you want to eat first?* | *He's had a bad year. First he lost his job, then his girlfriend left him.*
first of all (=first, before a lot of other things) *First of all, fry the onions.*

be first/come first /biː ˈfɜːˑst, ˌkʌm ˈfɜːˑst/ to be the person who wins a race or a competition: *Joyner came first in the 200 metres.*

original /əˈrɪdʒɪnəl, -dʒənəl/ [adj only before noun] before all the others – use this about something that existed at the beginning, especially before a lot of things were changed: *The house still has its original stone floors.* | *Our original plan had been to go camping, but it was pouring with rain.*

initial /ɪˈnɪʃəl/ [adj only before noun] use this to talk about what happened at the beginning or how someone felt at the beginning, especially when this changes later
initial reaction/response/feeling *My initial reaction was one of complete disbelief.*
initial difficulties/problems/setbacks *Initial difficulties with the computer system were soon fixed.*

2 to do something for the first time

first /fɜːˑst/ [adv] for the first time – use this before a verb: *I first met Mari in 1975.* | *Howard first went to Egypt when he was a student.*

the first time /ðə ˌfɜːˑst ˈtaɪm/ use this to say what happened when you did something that you had never done before

F

+ (that) *The first time I went on a plane I was really nervous.* | *It was the first time that she had seen her mother cry.*

3 the first thing you want to say or ask

firstly/first/first of all /ˈfɜːʳstli, fɜːʳst, ˌfɜːʳst əv ˈɔːl/ [adv] what you say to introduce the first fact, reason, or question – use this when you are going to mention several more things: *First of all I'd like to thank you very much for all the lovely presents.* | *I wanted to change schools, firstly because I didn't like the teacher and secondly because it was too far away.*

FLAT/NOT FLAT

1 flat

flat

The countryside around Cambridge is very flat and you can see for miles.

flat /flæt/ [adj] a place that is **flat** has no hills or mountains; a surface that is **flat** is not sloping or has no raised parts: *The countryside around Cambridge is very flat and you can see for miles.* | *In those days the houses all had flat roofs.* | *The plant's broad, flat leaves are used for serving food.* | *We sat down on a big flat rock.*
flat – flatter – flattest

level /ˈlevəl/ [adj] a surface or area that is **level** does not slope in any direction, so every part of it is at the same height: *He looked for a strip of level ground where he could land the plane.* | *Make sure the shelves are level.*

smooth /smuːð/ [adj] a **smooth** surface feels completely flat and has no rough or raised parts, especially in a way that is

pleasant and attractive: *The marble table felt smooth and cold against her arm.* | *She had lovely smooth skin.*

horizontal /ˌhɒrɪˈzɒntl◄ǁˌhɑːrɪˈzɑːntl◄/ [adj] a **horizontal** line, position, or surface is straight, flat, and not sloping: *a T-shirt with red and blue horizontal stripes* | *horizontal layers of rock* | *The wine bottles should be kept in a horizontal position.*

2 to make something flat

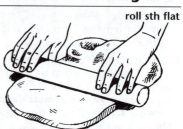

roll sth flat

Roll the pasty flat and cut out two 8-inch circles.

roll sth flat/press sth flat/ squash sth flat etc /ˌrəʊl (sth) ˈflæt, ˌpres (sth) ˈflæt, ˌskwɒʃ (sth) ˈflætǁ-ˌskwɔːʃ-/ to make something flat by rolling it, pressing it etc: *Roll the pastry flat and cut out two 8-inch circles.* | *A car ran over the ball and squashed it flat.*

flatten /ˈflætn/ [v T] to make something flat, especially something that is not usually flat: *The wind and rain had flattened the crops.* | *She flattened herself against the wall to avoid being seen.*

3 not flat

rough /rʌf/ [adj] not flat – use this about roads, walls, areas of land etc where the surface is not smooth because there are a lot of stones or small raised parts: *A rough dirt track led up to the farm.* | *rough mountain paths* | *the rough stone walls of the old castle*

bumpy /ˈbʌmpi/ [adj] a **bumpy** road, path, or area of land has a lot of holes and raised parts in it: *Neal drove the last mile down the bumpy road towards the highway.* | *The field was too bumpy to play football on.*
bumpy – bumpier – bumpiest

bump /bʌmp/ [n C] a small raised area that sticks up from the surface of something such as a road or piece of land: *The car rattled as we went over another bump in the road.*

uneven /ʌnˈiːvən/ [adj] an **uneven** surface has areas that are not flat or not all at the same level: *Be careful here – the sidewalk's very uneven.* | *His teeth were yellow and uneven.*

sloping /ˈsləʊpɪŋ/ [adj] something that is **sloping** is higher at one end than at the other: *The table's not straight – it's sloping.* | *A gently sloping bank led down to the stream.*

FOLD

to bend paper, cloth etc so that one part covers another

1 to fold something

fold

fold /fəʊld/ [v T] to bend a piece of paper or cloth, so that one part of it covers another: *She folded her clothes and put them on the chair.*
fold sth in two/in half (=across the middle) *I folded the letter in half and slipped it into an envelope.*
fold sth into a square/triangle (=so that it has the shape of a square or triangle) *The napkins were folded into neat triangles.*
    folded [adj] *She was carrying a pile of folded towels.*
fold up /fəʊld ˈʌp/ [phrasal verb T] to fold something, usually several times, in order to make it into a smaller or neater shape
fold up sth *The boy was having great trouble folding up his map.*
fold sth up *Don't just leave your clothes on the floor like that – fold them up.*

folding /ˈfəʊldɪŋ/ [adj only before noun] a **folding** bed, knife, bicycle etc is one that is specially designed so that it can be folded up and easily carried or stored: *I had to sleep on a folding bed in the living room.*

2 to open something that is folded

unfold /ʌnˈfəʊld/ [v T] *He unfolded the shawl and placed it around her shoulders.* | *We watched as she took out the letter and slowly unfolded it.*

FOLLOW

➡ if you mean 'happening after something else', go to **AFTER**

follow /ˈfɒləʊˈfɑː-/ [v I/T] to walk, drive, run etc behind someone else, going in the same direction as them: *Follow me and I'll show you where the library is.* | *You drive on ahead and I'll follow.* | *I had a horrible feeling that I was being followed.*
follow sb around (=follow someone wherever they go) *Journalists followed the couple around everywhere.*
followed by sb *The woman entered the room, followed by three little children.*
follow sb out/down/across etc *She didn't notice that Jack had followed her into the kitchen.*

run after sb/go after sb /ˌrʌn ˈɑːftər (sb), ˌgəʊ ˈɑːftər (sb)‖-ˈæf-/ [phrasal verb T] to run or walk quickly behind someone in order to catch them or talk to them, when they are going away from you: *A group of little boys ran after him to ask for his autograph.*

chase /tʃeɪs/ [v I/T] to run after someone in order to catch them, when they are trying to escape from you
chase sb across/up/down etc *The farmer chased the children across the field.*
+ after *Two men chased after the robbers but they managed to escape.*

When you see **EC**, go to the
ESSENTIAL COMMUNICATION section.

FOOD

RESTAURANTS/EATING AND DRINKING

MEAL · DRINK · EAT · see also · HUNGRY · COOK · FAT · TASTE · THIN

1 food

food /fuːd/ [n C/U] something that you eat: *They didn't even have enough money to buy food.* | *The doctor told him not to eat fatty foods.* | *What sort of food do you like best?* | *What's the food like at college?*

Qsomething to eat /ˌsʌmθɪŋ tu 'iːt/ ESPECIALLY SPOKEN food, especially a small meal that you eat quickly: *You should have something to eat before you go out.*

2 the kind of food someone usually eats

diet /'daɪət/ [n C] the particular combination of foods that a person or animal usually eats: *Changing your diet may help you sleep better.* | *A hedgehog's diet consists mainly of slugs, worms, and insects.*
+ of *a diet of raw fish* | *Kevin lived on a diet of peanut butter sandwiches.*
a low-fat/high-fibre etc diet (=when you only eat foods without much fat, with a lot of fibre etc)

3 food that is typical of a particular country or place

food /fuːd/ [n U] **French/Japanese/Italian etc food** the type of food that is typical of France, Japan etc: *I've never tried Korean food – what's it like?*

dish /dɪʃ/ [n C] several foods cooked together in a particular way, especially in a way that is typical of a country or place: *a delicious vegetable dish with a spicy nut sauce*
French/Moroccan/American etc dish *Paella is one of my favourite Spanish dishes.*
plural **dishes**

speciality BRITISH **specialty** AMERICAN /ˌspeʃi'æləti, 'speʃəlti/ [n C] a type of special food that a restaurant, country, or area is famous for: *The village is famous for its seafood specialties.*
local/regional speciality (=from a particular area) *Fish curry is a local speciality.*
plural **specialities/specialties**

4 to give someone food

serve /sɜːrv/ [v I/T] to give someone food by putting it in front of them, especially at a restaurant or a formal meal: *Dinner will be served at eight o'clock.* | *The chef serves important guests himself.* | *We're ready to serve.*
serve sb with sth *They served us with soup and bread.*
serve sth to sb *Andrew, will you serve coffee to the visitors?*

feed /fiːd/ [v T] to give food to a baby or animal: *My sister feeds the cats when we are away.* | *How often do you have to feed the baby?*
feed sb/sth on sth *Peggy feeds her dogs on raw meat and brown bread.*
feeding – fed – have fed

FORBID

to tell someone that they must not do something

➡ opposite **LET**

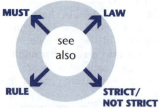

MUST · LAW · see also · RULE · STRICT/NOT STRICT

1 to forbid something

not let/not allow /nɒt 'let, nɒt ə'laʊ/ to say that someone must not do something, and to stop them doing it
not let sb do sth *My parents won't let me stay out after 11 o'clock.*
not allow sb to do sth *They do not allow anyone to enter the country without a visa.*

not allow sth *Joan and Bill don't allow smoking in their house.*

⚠ Not allow is more formal than **not let**.

tell sb not to do sth /ˌtel (sb) nɒt tə ˈduː (sth)/ to tell someone that they should not do something, especially because it is dangerous or harmful: *My mother always told us not to talk to strangers.* | *His doctor told him not to drink any alcohol for six weeks.*

forbid /fəˈbɪd/ [v T] FORMAL if a person or rule **forbids** something, they state clearly and firmly that it must not be done: *Their religion forbids the eating of pork.*
forbid sb to do sth *They ran away together after their parents forbade them to get married.*
forbidding – forbade – have forbidden

ban /bæn/ [v T] to officially forbid something – use this about activities that are forbidden by laws or agreements, especially because they are dangerous: *Many doctors now say that boxing should be banned.* | *a new international treaty banning all nuclear tests*
banning – banned – have banned

ban /bæn/ [n C] an official statement that forbids something, based on a law or a government decision
+ on *The city has imposed a ban on smoking in all restaurants.*
a total/complete ban *The government is considering a total ban on the sale of handguns.*
impose a ban (=ban something) *A ban has been imposed on the hunting and killing of whales.*
lift a ban (=stop having a ban) *President Clinton lifted the ban on homosexuals in the armed forces.*

2 **to forbid someone from taking part in an activity or sport**

suspend /səˈspend/ [v T] to remove someone from their job or their school for a limited period of time because they have done something wrong: *Martinez was suspended for a week because he attacked another student.*
suspend sb for doing sth *Three police*

officers have been suspended for accepting bribes.

ban /bæn/ [v T] to officially state that someone is not allowed to do something, especially as a punishment for something bad they have done
ban sb from doing sth *She was banned from driving for 6 months.* | *For many years, the Olympic Committee banned South Africans from taking part in the Games.*
banning – banned – have banned

disqualify /dɪsˈkwɒlɪfaɪ‖-ˈkwɑː-/ [v T often passive] to officially state that someone is no longer allowed to take part in a competition or activity, because they have broken a rule
disqualify sb from sth *Three athletes were disqualified from the championships after failing drugs tests.*
disqualify sb from doing sth *He was fined £500, and disqualified from holding any political office.*
disqualifying – disqualified – have disqualified

3 **when you are not allowed to do something**

not allowed /nɒt əˈlaʊd/ when a person or a rule says that you must not do something
sb is not allowed to do sth *We're not allowed to wear jewellery at school.* | *She wasn't allowed to go out with boys until she was 16.*
sth is not allowed *Smoking is not allowed anywhere in the building.*

be forbidden /biː fəˈbɪdn/ [adj] if something **is forbidden** or someone **is forbidden** to do something, there is a rule which says that they must not do it
sth is forbidden *The use of electronic calculators in the examination room is forbidden.*
sb is forbidden to do sth *Prisoners were forbidden to speak to each other while they were working.*
strictly forbidden *The use of mobile phones is strictly forbidden during take-off and landing.*

⚠ Be forbidden is more formal than **not allowed**

Q**can't** /kɑːnt‖kænt/ ESPECIALLY SPOKEN if you **can't** do something, you are not allowed to do it: *You can't park here.* | *My dad says I can't go out tonight.*

no smoking/no parking etc /nəʊ ˈsməʊkɪŋ, nəʊ ˈpɑːrkɪŋ (etc)/ used on signs and notices to say that you are not allowed to smoke, park your car etc: *There were 'no smoking' signs in every room.* | *Beside the lake was a large notice saying 'No Fishing'.*

be prohibited /biː prəˈhɪbɪ̩tɪ̩d‖-prəʊ-/ something that **is prohibited** is forbidden by a law or rule – used especially on official notices and warnings: *Cars are prohibited in the city centre.* | *Cameras are prohibited inside the cathedral.*

FORCE SB TO DO STH

to make someone do something that they do not want to do

➡ see also **MUST**

force /fɔːrs/ [v T] to make someone do something that they do not want to do: *You didn't have to come with us – nobody forced you.*
force sb to do sth *Government troops forced the rebels to surrender.*
force sb into doing sth *Her parents are trying to force her into marrying him.*

make /meɪk/ [v T] to force someone to do something: *I didn't want to go but my dad made me.*
make sb do sth *She made me promise never to mention the subject again.* | *We were made to work really hard.*
making – made – have made

⚠ **Make** is less formal than **force**.

put pressure on sb /ˌpʊt ˈpreʃər ɒn (sb)/ to keep trying to persuade someone to do something, for example by saying that it is their duty or that it will help other people
put pressure on sb to do sth *Our parents were putting pressure on us to get married.*

compel /kəmˈpel/ [v T] to make someone do something by using force or official power
compel sb to do sth *All the young men in the area were compelled to work in the quarries and coal-mines.*
compelling – compelled – have compelled

pressurize BRITISH **pressure** AMERICAN /ˈpreʃəraɪz, ˈpreʃər/ [v T] to make someone do something by persuading them very strongly and making them feel that they ought to do it
pressurize/pressure sb into doing sth *Many children are pressurized into studying subjects that they are not interested in.* | *Don't let them pressure you into buying something you don't need.*

⚠ **Pressurize** can also be spelled **pressurise** in British English.

FOREIGN

➡ see also **FROM, COUNTRY**

1 not from your own country

foreign /ˈfɒrɪ̩n‖ˈfɔː-, ˈfɑː-/ [adj] not from your own country or connected with your own country: *They are learning English as a Foreign Language.* | *Britain's car industry faces a lot of competition from foreign companies.* | *Mark collects foreign stamps.*

⚠ It is not polite to call people 'foreign'. It is better to say they are **from abroad** or to say which country they are from.

overseas /ˌəʊvərˈsiːz◀/ [adj only before noun] from or connected with a foreign country, especially one that is a long way away
overseas student/tourist/visitor *The university has a lot of overseas students.*
overseas trade/travel/trip/business *There has been an increase in overseas trade during the last year.*

from abroad /frəm əˈbrɔːd/ from another country or from other countries: *There is a shortage of medical staff, so a lot of the doctors here are from abroad.* |

They are not allowed to listen to radio broadcasts from abroad.

2 someone from a different country

foreigner /'fɒrɪnəʳ‖'fɔː-, 'faː-/ [n C] someone who comes from another country: *Any foreigner wishing to work in this country must have a work permit.* | *Saleem felt that people were suspicious of him because he was a foreigner.*

⚠ Many people think it is rude to call someone a **foreigner**, because this can sometimes mean they are strange or not welcome in your country.

immigrant /'ɪmɪgrənt/ [n C] someone who has left their own country and now lives permanently in another: *Many of the immigrants in France come from North Africa.*
illegal immigrant (=someone who does not have official permission to live and work in another country)

expatriate /eks'pætriət, -trieɪt‖eks'peɪ-/ [n C] someone who lives in a foreign country, for example because they have a job there or enjoy living there: *British expatriates living in Spain*

⚠ You can also use **expatriate** before a noun, like an adjective: *There are a lot of expatriate workers living in Dubai.*

3 in or to a different country

abroad /ə'brɔːd/ [adv] in or to a foreign country: *Katya will make her first trip abroad next month, to Japan.*
go/live/work etc abroad *Mike is planning on studying abroad for a year.*
be abroad *Mr Harris is abroad on business this week.*

⚠ Don't say 'he's gone to abroad'. Just say **he's gone abroad**.

overseas /ˌəʊvəʳ'siːz◄/ [adv] in or to a foreign country, especially one that is a long distance from your own: *The wood is shipped overseas from ports in the north west.*

go/work/travel etc overseas *Douglas travelled overseas a lot when he was in the army.*

⚠ Don't say 'to overseas'. Just say **overseas**.

emigrate /'emɪgreɪt/ [v I] to leave your own country in order to live permanently in another country
+ to *Jenny and Tim emigrated to Australia in 1958.*

FORGET

➡ opposite **REMEMBER**

1 to forget something

forget /fəʳ'get/ [v I/T] to no longer remember information, something that happened in the past, or something that you must do: *I'm sorry, I've forgotten your name.* | *It was an experience she would never forget.* | *It's his birthday tomorrow. I hope you haven't forgotten.*
forget what/where/how etc *She's forgotten where she parked the car.*
+ (that) *We forgot that it was Sunday and the banks would be closed.*
forget to do sth (=not do something because you forget) *I forgot to ask her for her phone number.*
+ about *Tom had forgotten about Tanya coming to stay.*
completely forget *I completely forgot about the meeting.*
I forget (=I have forgotten) *She had this boyfriend – I forget his name – who was an actor.*

forgetting – forgot – have forgotten

don't remember/can't remember

/ˌdəʊnt rɪ'membəʳ, ˌkɑːnt rɪ'membəʳ‖ˌkænt-/ [v I/T] to not be able to remember something that you want to remember: *"How did you get home after the party?" "I can't remember."* | *I was going to phone you, but I couldn't remember your number.*
not remember doing sth *Has she got an invitation? I don't remember inviting her.*
+ what/where/how etc *I don't remember exactly what happened.*

F

⟨ **it's on the tip of my tongue** /ɪts ɒn ðə ˌtɪp əv maɪ ˈtʌŋ/ SPOKEN use this to say that you know a name or word, but you are having difficulty remembering it at that moment: *That place we visited in Paris, what's it called? It's on the tip of my tongue...Oh yes, La Geode.*

your mind goes blank /jɔːʳ ˌmaɪnd gəʊz ˈblæŋk/ if **your mind goes blank**, you are suddenly unable to remember something at a time when you need to: *That's... Oh, my mind's gone blank – I can't remember her name. | When she saw the questions in the test her mind just went totally blank.*

2 to forget to bring something

forget /fəʳget/ [v T] to not bring something that you intended to bring, because you did not think of it: *Michael was at the airport before he realized he'd forgotten his passport. | How stupid of me! I forgot your photos – I must have left them on my desk.*

forgetting – forgot – have forgotten

leave /liːv/ [v T] to forget to take something with you when you leave: *I can't find my coat – I must have left it at work.*
leave sth behind *Oh hell! I think I left my credit card behind at the restaurant.*

3 to try to forget something

put sth out of your mind /ˌpʊt (sth) aʊt əv jɔːʳ ˈmaɪnd/ to make yourself stop thinking about something that makes you angry or sad: *She tried to put all thoughts of revenge out of her mind. | It's time to put her out of your mind and find a new girlfriend.*

take your mind off sth /ˌteɪk jɔːʳ ˈmaɪnd ɒf (sth)/ if an activity **takes your mind off** a worrying problem, it makes you forget about it for a short time: *Joe suggested a game of cards to take my mind off things. | I needed something to take my mind off the day's troubles.*

When you see **EC**, go to the **ESSENTIAL COMMUNICATION** section.

4 someone who often forgets things

have a bad memory /hæv ə ˌbæd ˈmeməri/ to not be good at remembering facts or information: *"We've met once before. At David's place." "Oh, I'm sorry – I have such a bad memory."*
+ for *I have a bad memory for names.*

forgetful /fəʳgetfəl/ [adj] someone who is, **forgetful** often forgets things, especially things that they have to do: *My grandfather's getting so forgetful – I have to remind him to take his medication. | Some forgetful person had left the door unlocked.*

absent-minded /ˌæbsənt ˈmaɪndɪd/ [adj] someone who is **absent-minded** often forgets things because they are thinking about other things: *He's a brilliant scientist but hopelessly absent-minded.*

have a memory like a sieve /hæv ə ˌmeməri laɪk ə ˈsɪv/ INFORMAL to not be able to remember facts or information, even for a short time: *You'd better remind him about the party – he has a memory like a sieve!*

FORGIVE

to stop being angry with someone for something bad they have done

➡ see also **SORRY**

1 to forgive someone

forgive /fəʳgɪv/ [v I/T] to stop being angry with someone for something bad they have done, especially when they have upset you or done something unkind: *Try to forgive him – he didn't mean to hurt you. | Hugh found his wife's behaviour hard to forgive.*
forgive sb for sth *He had lied to me, and I couldn't forgive him for that.*
forgive and forget (=forgive someone for something, and behave as if they had never done it) *He's the type of person who finds it hard to forgive and forget.*
forgiving – forgave – have forgiven

⚠ Don't say 'I am forgiving you'. Say **I forgive you**

excuse /ɪk'skjuːz/ [*v* T] to not be angry about something that someone has done, usually something that is not seriously wrong: *Please excuse my handwriting – I'm in a hurry.* | *He's always late, and I don't see why we should excuse it.*

> ⚠ You can politely ask someone to **excuse** something, when you want to welcome them and give them your attention: *Come in – and please excuse the mess.*

2 what you say to tell someone that you forgive them

that's all right/that's OK /ðæts ˌɔːl 'raɪt, ðæts ˌəʊ'keɪ/ SPOKEN say this when someone says they are sorry for something they did: *"Sorry I didn't phone you last week." "That's OK – I know how busy you've been."* | *"I must apologize for keeping you waiting so long." "That's all right."*

forget it /fəʳ'get ɪt/ SPOKEN INFORMAL say this to tell someone that you do not blame them for something, and you do not want them to mention it again: *"I feel so bad about upsetting your plans." "Oh, forget it, it really doesn't matter."*

> ⚠ **That's OK** and **forget it** are more informal than **that's all right**.

3 when something is too bad to be forgiven

unforgivable/unforgiveable /ˌʌnfəʳ'gɪvəbəl◂/ [*adj*] behaviour that is **unforgivable** is so bad that you cannot forgive it: *I think the way she spoke to her mother was unforgivable.*

4 to refuse to forgive someone

never forgive /ˌnevəʳ fəʳ'gɪv/ to refuse to forgive someone, because they have done something very bad

never forgive sb for sth *She never really forgave Roy for what he said.*

never forgive yourself *I'd never forgive myself if anything happened to the children while I was out.*

bear a grudge /ˌbeəʳ ə 'grʌdʒ/ to continue to feel angry with someone for a long time because they treated you badly in the past

+ against *Can you think of anyone who might bear a grudge against you?*

hold it against sb /ˌhəʊld ɪt ə'genst (sb)/ to dislike someone because of something they did in the past, even though it is no longer important: *Look, he made one mistake – you can't hold it against him for the rest of his life.*

FREE

1 something that costs no money

➡ look here for ...

- not costing any money
- able to do what you want
- not in prison

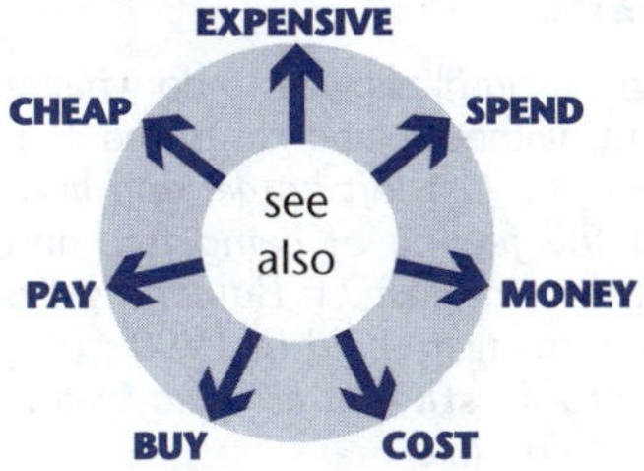

free /friː/ [*adj*] something that is **free** costs no money: *Parking is free after 6 p.m.* | *"How much is it to get into the concert?" "Oh, I think it's free."* | *I'm saving these tokens to get a free poster.*

cost nothing/not cost anything /ˌkɒst 'nʌθɪŋ, ˌnɒt kɒst 'eniθɪŋ‖ˌkɔːst-/ to be free, especially when this is unusual: *Luckily I was insured, so the treatment didn't cost anything.* | *It costs nothing to call the emergency number.*

2 when you can do something or get something without paying

free /friː/ [*adv*] when you can do something or get something without paying: *If you buy one pair of glasses we'll give you another pair completely free.* | *You can get into EuroDisney free with this special voucher.*

for nothing /fəʳ ˈnʌθɪŋ/ INFORMAL without having to pay for something that you would normally have to pay for: *He offered to fix the car for nothing.* | *My Dad owns the club, so we can get in for nothing.*

free of charge /ˌfriː əv ˈtʃɑːʳdʒ/ free – used especially in advertisements, official information etc, when someone wants you to take something that is free: *The leaflets are available free of charge at the tourist office.* | *When you've chosen your gift, we will wrap it for you free of charge.*

no charge /ˌnəʊ ˈtʃɑːʳdʒ/ if there is **no charge** for a service that someone provides, you do not have to pay for it: *You can leave your car at the hotel – there's no charge.*
+ for *There is no charge for cashing these traveller's cheques.*

3 allowed to do what you want

free /friː/ [adj] allowed to do whatever you want, without being controlled or restricted: *I had just left home, and was enjoying the feeling of being free and independent at last.* | *Bulgaria's first free elections were held in 1990.*
free to do sth *You are free to come and go as you like.*
free speech (=the right to say or write what you want without the police or government stopping you) *All Americans have the right to free speech.*
a free press (=when newspapers are not controlled by the government)

freedom /ˈfriːdəm/ [n U] the right to do what you want without being controlled or restricted: *There was a huge party at the Berlin Wall as East Germans celebrated their freedom.*
freedom to do sth *People here have the freedom to practise whatever religion they like.*

liberty /ˈlɪbəʳti/ [n U] FORMAL a person's legal right to do what they want, without being unfairly controlled by the government: *They were fighting for liberty and equality.* | *Many people think that compulsory ID cards interfere with personal liberty.*

freely /ˈfriːli/ [adv] if you can speak **freely**, travel **freely** etc, you can say what you like, go where you like etc, and no-one will try to prevent you: *For most of the year farmers allow the sheep to roam freely on the hillside.* | *At last Jim could talk freely and frankly about being gay.*

4 not in prison
➡ see also PRISON, ESCAPE

free /friː/ [adj not usually before noun] not in prison, or not being kept somewhere by force: *He was free again, after 10 long years in jail.* | *The hostages are now free after their five-day ordeal.*

out /aʊt/ [adj not before noun] no longer in prison, because the time of punishment is over: *Peters could be out in as little as 3 years.* | *Her husband gets out of jail next week.*

5 to let someone leave prison
➡ see also PRISON, ESCAPE

release /rɪˈliːs/ [v T] to let someone leave prison: *McKay moved to Newcastle after being released from prison.* | *They released ten political prisoners last year.*

let sb out /ˌlet (sb) ˈaʊt/ [phrasal verb T] to let someone leave a place where they are being kept, especially a prison: *Let me out! I'm innocent!*
+ of *She was let out of prison to attend her daughter's funeral.*

⚠ **Release** is more formal than **let sb out**

set sb free /ˌset (sb) ˈfriː/ to let someone leave a place where they are being kept by force: *The American hostages were set free last night.* | *Finally, in January 1987, they were set free.*

WORD BANK

FREE TIME
➡ see pages 302–305

FRIEND

➡ see also **FRIENDLY/UNFRIENDLY, GIRLFRIEND/BOYFRIEND, RELATIONSHIP**

1 a friend

friend /frend/ [n C] someone who you know well and enjoy spending time with, but who is not a member of your family: *Martha went to London with some friends.*

a friend of mine (=one of my friends) *I'm going out for a drink with a friend of mine.*

good/close friend (=someone you know very well and like very much) *Rob is one of my closest friends.*

best friend *Even my best friend didn't know my secret.*

old friend (=someone you have known well for a long time) *We spent the weekend with our old friends, Bill and Judy.*

mate BRITISH **buddy** AMERICAN /meɪt, 'bʌdi/ [n C] INFORMAL a friend: *I always go to the pub with my mates on Friday night.*

a mate/buddy of mine (=one of my friends) *Terry's an old buddy of mine.*
plural **buddies**

acquaintance /ə'kweɪntəns/ [n C] someone that you know and sometimes see, but who is not one of your close friends: *She's just an acquaintance – I sometimes see her at aerobics.*

2 a group of friends

circle of friends /ˌsɜːʳkəl əv 'frendz/ [n singular] all the people that you know well and often meet in social situations: *In New York, Marcia introduced him to her large circle of friends.*

⊂**the gang** /ðə 'gæŋ/ [n singular] SPOKEN a small group of close friends who often do things together – used especially by young people: *I usually go out with the gang on Saturday nights.*

⊂**the boys/the girls** /ðə 'bɔɪz, ðə 'gɜːʳlz/ [n plural] SPOKEN a group of male or female friends who often do things together: *Sally's having a night out with the girls from the office.*

3 to be someone's friend

be friends /biː 'frendz/ if two people **are friends**, they like each other and they enjoy doing things together: *Bill and I used to be good friends but we don't see each other much now.*

+ with *I've been friends with Andrea for about 10 years.*

get along (also **get on** BRITISH) /ˌget ə'lɒŋ, ˌget 'ɒn‖-ə'lɔːŋ, -'ɑːn/ [phrasal verb I] if two or more people **get along** or **get on**, they find it easy to talk and agree with each other, and so they feel relaxed when they spend time together

+ with *I used to argue a lot with my parents, but now we get along very well. | I like Julie, but I don't really get on with her brother. | He's a nice boy – very easy to get along with.*

be friendly with sb /biː 'frendli wɪð (sb)/ to have a good relationship with someone, even though you may not spend a lot of time together: *We're quite friendly with our neighbours, Mr and Mrs Webb. | I used to be very friendly with a girl from Boston.*

4 to become someone's friend

make friends /ˌmeɪk 'frendz/ to start to be someone's friend, especially when you make an effort to do this: *Caroline didn't find it easy to make friends.*

+ with *The children soon made friends with the kids next door.*

become friends /bɪˌkʌm 'frendz/ if two people **become friends**, they begin to be friends, often after knowing each other for a long time: *I'd known Nancy for years but we only became friends when we joined the same company.*

hit it off /ˌhɪt ɪt 'ɒf‖-'ɔːf/ INFORMAL if two people **hit it off**, they immediately become friends when they meet for the first time: *I knew you and Mark would hit it off!*

5 a friendly relationship with someone

friendship /'frendʃɪp/ [n C/U] *They first met when they were at college, and it was the start of a long friendship.*

FRIEND continues on page 306

FREE TIME

see also: DANCE, EXERCISE, SPORT, ART, THEATRE, TELEVISION AND RADIO, MUSIC, FILMS/MOVIES, PARTY, RESTAURANTS/EATING AND DRINKING

F

1 when you stay at home

stay in /ˌsteɪ ˈɪn/ [phrasal verb I] to stay at home and not go out: *Do you want to go and see a movie tonight, or shall we stay in? | I usually stay in when there's school next day.*

watch television/watch TV /ˌwɒtʃ ˈtelɪˌvɪʒən, ˌwɒtʃ tiː viː-ˌwɑːtʃ-/ *"Did you go out last night?" "No, we stayed in and watched TV."*

listen to music /ˌlɪsən tə ˈmjuːzɪk/ *Sometimes I like to just sit in my room and listen to music.*

play computer games /ˌpleɪ kəmˈpjuːtəʳ ˌgeɪmz/ *"Where's Fran?" "Up in her room playing computer games."*

read /riːd/ [v I/T] *I spend a lot of my free time reading. | She enjoys reading science fiction novels.*

get a video /ˌget ə ˈvɪdiəʊ/ to rent a film to watch on your own television: *Let's get a video. How about that new Bruce Willis movie?*

get a takeaway BRITISH **get takeout** AMERICAN /ˌget ə ˈteɪkəweɪ, ˌget ˈteɪkaʊt/ to buy food from a restaurant and take it home to eat: *I don't feel like cooking tonight. Let's get a takeaway.*

2 when you go to the cinema, a restaurant, a club etc

go out /ˌgəʊ ˈaʊt/ [phrasal verb I] to go out of your house and go to a restaurant, cinema, club etc: *"Did you go out last night?" "Yeah, We went to that new Mexican restaurant on 4th Avenue."*

go out to dinner/lunch /ˌgəʊ ˌaʊt tə ˈdɪnəʳ, ˈlʌntʃ/ (also **go out for a meal** /ˌgəʊ ˌaʊt fər ə ˈmiːl/ BRITISH) to go to a restaurant and have a meal: *It was Eleri's birthday, so we went out to dinner.*

go to the cinema BRITISH **go to the movies** AMERICAN /ˌgəʊ tʊ ðə ˈsɪnɪmə, ˌgəʊ tʊ ðə ˈmuːviːz/ to go and watch a film *Do you want to go to the movies tonight? | We haven't been to the cinema for ages.*

go to a concert /ˌgəʊ tʊ ə ˈkɒnsəʳt-ˈkɑːn-/ to go to listen to people playing music: *We went to a concert of Vivaldi's 'Four Seasons'. | I go to lots of pop concerts.*

go to a gig /ˌgəʊ tʊ ə ˈgɪg/ to go to listen to a band (=people who play popular music) *"I'm going to a gig tonight." "Who are you going to see?" "The Smashing Pumpkins."*

go clubbing/go to a club /ˌgəʊ ˈklʌbɪŋ; ˌgəʊ tʊ ə ˈklʌb/ to go to a place where you can dance and drink until late at night: *Michelle always goes clubbing on Friday night.*

go to a cafe/a bar/the pub /ˌgəʊ tʊ ə ˈkæfeɪ, ˈbɑːʳ, ðə ˈpʌb-kæˈfeɪ/ to go to a place where you can drink and talk to your friends: *On Friday we usually go to a bar after work.*

FREE TIME

F

go to the theatre BRITISH **go to the theater** /ˌgəʊ tə ðə ˈθɪətəʳ/ AMERICAN to go and watch a play being performed: *I haven't been to the theater in a long time.*

go shopping /ˌgəʊ ˈʃɒpɪŋ|-ˈʃɑːp-/ *We went shopping in Oxford Street.*

3 when you go outdoors

go to the beach /ˌgəʊ tə ðə ˈbiːtʃ/ *In the summer I go to the beach every day.*

have a picnic /ˌhæv ə ˈpɪknɪk/ to take a meal to a park or the countryside to eat it: *If the weather's nice we could have a picnic.*

go to the park /ˌgəʊ tə ðə ˈpɑːʳk/ *Jo and Tim are going to the park to play tennis.*

go for a walk /ˌgəʊ fər ə ˈwɔːk/ to walk in a nice place for fun: *Why don't we go for a walk? It's a beautiful day.*

go for a run /ˌgəʊ fər ə ˈrʌn/ to run somewhere, for fun or in order to get exercise:

FREE TIME continues on the next page

FREE TIME

I think I'll go for a run before it gets dark.

walk the dog/take the dog for a walk /ˌwɔːk ðə ˈdɒg, teɪk ðə ˈdɒg fər ə ˌwɔːk | -dɑːg-/ to walk somewhere with your dog, in order to exercise it: *I walk the dog every morning before school.* | *"Where's Nick?" "He's taking the dog for a walk."*

go sailing/climbing/skiing etc /ˌgəʊ seɪlɪŋ, klaɪmbɪŋ, skiː-ɪŋ (etc)/ *Did you go climbing while you were in Scotland?*

➡ if you want to talk about other sports, go to **SPORT**

4 when you spend time with your friends

have friends over /hæv ˈfrendz ˌəʊvəʳ/ (also **have friends round** /hæv ˈfrendz ˌraʊnd/ BRITISH) if you **have friends over** or **round**, they come to your house because you have invited them: *My parents don't like me having friends round during the week.*

have friends over/round for dinner *We had some friends over for dinner on Friday. Sam cooked lasagne.*

go over to sb's house /ˌgəʊ ˌəʊvəʳ tə (sb's) ˈhaʊs/ (also **go round to sb's house** /ˌgəʊ ˌraʊnd tə (sb's) ˈhaʊs/ BRITISH) *We're going over to Peter's house this evening – do you want to come?*

have a party /ˌhæv ə ˈpɑːti/ *Steve's having a party on Saturday.*

have a barbecue /ˌhæv ə ˈbɑːʳbɪkjuː/ to have a party where you cook food outside: *It was a warm evening, so we decided to have a barbecue.*

meet up with sb /ˌmiːt ˈʌp wɪð (sb)/ [*phrasal verb* T] to meet someone, at a time and place that you arranged before, so that you can do something together: *I met up with Jan and Peter outside McDonald's, and we all went shopping.*

go out with your boyfriend/girlfriend /ˌgəʊ ˌaʊt wɪð jɔːʳ ˈbɔɪfrend, ˈgɜːʳlfrend/ to spend time with someone that you have a romantic relationship with:

FREE TIME

"Is Sylvia coming tonight?" *"No, she's going out with her new boyfriend."*

hang out with sb /ˈhæŋ aʊt wɪð (sb)/ [*phrasal verb* T] SPOKEN to spend time somewhere with your friends, not doing very much: *"What did you do today?"* *"Oh, I just hung out with some friends."*

5 when you do something regularly in your free time

hobby /ˈhɒbi/ [*n* C] an activity that you do regularly in your free time: *My hobbies are wind-surfing and playing the guitar.* | *What are your hobbies?*
plural **hobbies**

take up sth /ˌteɪk ˈʌp (sth)/ [*phrasal verb* T] to become interested in an activity or subject and start doing it regularly: *I've just taken up pottery, and I'm really enjoying it.* | *He first took up boxing at school.*

collect /kəˈlekt/ [v T] to get and keep things of a similar kind, because you think they are attractive or interesting: *My sister collects old bottles.* | *I've started collecting foreign coins, and I have about fifty.*

collection /kəˈlekʃən/ [*n* C] a group of similar things that someone has kept because they are attractive or interesting: *Uncle Frank always wanted to show us his stamp collection.*
+ of *a valuable collection of Victorian postcards*

F

6 talking about your free time

What do you do in your free time? (=when you are not working or studying)

I like.../I enjoy... /aɪ ˈlaɪk, aɪ enˈdʒɔɪ/ *I like playing volleyball.* | *Most of all, I enjoy going to jazz concerts..*

I'm (really) into... /aɪm (ˈriːli) ˌɪntuː.../ SPOKEN INFORMAL (=I like or enjoy something very much) *I'm into all sports, especially tennis and basketball.* | *Simon's started learning Spanish, and he's really into it..*

In my free time/spare time... /ɪn maɪ ˌfriː taɪm, ˌspeər ˈtaɪm/ *In my free time, I'm learning Russian.* | *I like making jewellery in my spare time.*

At weekends... BRITISH **On weekends...** AMERICAN /ət ðə wiːkˈendz, ɒn ðə wiːkˈendz | -ˈwiːkendz/ *At weekends I usually see my friends.* | *Ben plays football on weekends.*

When I'm not studying/working... /wen aɪm ˌnɒt ˈstʌdiɪŋ, ˈwɜːrkɪŋ/ *When I'm not studying, I like going for long walks with my dog.*

Whenever I get the time... /wenˌevər aɪ get ðə ˈtaɪm/ *Whenever they get the time, they go climbing.* | *I go to the gym whenever I get the time.*

On Mondays/ Wednesdays... *On Thursdays I have dance class.* | *We usually go to the movies on Saturdays.*

In the evening... /ɪn ðiː ˈiːvnɪŋ/ *In the evening, Mario usually hangs out with his friends.*

FRIEND continued from page 301
+ **with** *I got to know Helen through her friendship with my sister.*

6 to stop being friends with someone

➡ see also **ARGUE**

fall out /ˌfɔːl ˈaʊt/ [phrasal verb I] to stop being friends because you have an argument: *It was the first time Bill and I had fallen out.*
+ **with** *It can be difficult if you fall out with someone you work with.*
+ **over** *Come on, there's no point in falling out over a silly game.*

FRIENDLY / UNFRIENDLY

DESCRIBING PEOPLE

NICE   **KIND**

POLITE   see also   **UNKIND**

RUDE   **RELATIONSHIP**

1 person

friendly /ˈfrendli/ [adj] behaving towards other people in a way that shows that you like them, you enjoy being with them, or you are pleased to see them: *The staff at the hotel are always polite and friendly.* | *She gave him a friendly smile.*
+ **to/towards** *The local people are generally friendly towards tourists.*
friendly – friendlier – friendliest

⚠ **Friendly** is an adjective, not an adverb, so don't say 'they treated me friendly'. Say **they treated me in a friendly way** or **they were friendly to me**

nice/pleasant /naɪs, ˈplezənt/ [adj] friendly and kind: *He's a really nice man.* | *I enjoyed my visit to Ireland – everyone I met there was so pleasant.* | *Ralph's new girlfriend seems nice.*

easy to get on with BRITISH **easy to get along with** AMERICAN /ˌiːzi tə get ˈɒn wɪð, ˌiːzi tə get əˈlɒŋ wɪð‖-əˈlɔːŋ-/ friendly, relaxed, and easy to work with or live with: *Fortunately my boss is fairly easy to get on with.* | *I have to admit, Tom isn't exactly easy to get along with.*

sociable /ˈsəʊʃəbəl/ [adj] someone who is **sociable** enjoys being with other people and talking to them: *Why don't you invite Chris for a drink? He seems a sociable kind of guy.*

hospitable /ˈhɒspɪtəbəl, hɒˈspɪ-‖hɑːˈspɪ-, ˈhɑːspɪ-/ [adj] someone who is **hospitable** is friendly and generous to you when you visit their home or their country: *Most of the people I met in Scotland were very hospitable and kind.*

hospitality /ˌhɒspɪˈtælɪti‖ˌhɑːs-/ [n U] someone's friendly, generous behaviour towards you when you visit their home or their country: *You must write to John and his family to thank them for their hospitality.*

2 situation/place/relationship

friendly /ˈfrendli/ [adj] a **friendly** situation, place, or relationship is one in which people behave in a friendly way: *You're lucky to work in such a friendly office.* | *The local bar had a really friendly atmosphere.*
friendly – friendlier – friendliest

welcoming /ˈwelkəmɪŋ/ [adj] a **welcoming** place or room makes you feel relaxed and happy to be there: *The fire burning in the grate made the room look bright and welcoming.*

amicable /ˈæmɪkəbəl/ [adj] FORMAL an **amicable** arrangement or solution is one when people who do not agree with each other are able to solve their problems in a friendly way: *The meeting between the two leaders was very amicable.*
amicable arrangement/divorce/solution *Both sides must try to find an amicable solution to the dispute.*

3 not friendly

unfriendly /ʌnˈfrendli/ [adj] not friendly: *It's very difficult to work with Lindsay – she's so unfriendly.* | *Big cities can be very unfriendly places.*

When you see **EC**, go to the **ESSENTIAL COMMUNICATION** section.

+ to/towards *The other girls weren't openly unfriendly towards her, but they never invited her along with them.*

cold /kəʊld/ [adj] behaving towards other people as if you do not like them or care about them: *His manner all evening was cold and unfriendly.* | *Next time she saw Harry he wasn't rude to her, just very cold and polite.*

> **coldly** [adv] *She coldly asked him to leave her house.*

anti-social /ˌænti ˈsəʊʃəl◂/ [adj] someone who is **anti-social** does not enjoy being with other people and tries to avoid meeting them or talking to them: *Not everyone who likes playing computer games is an anti-social loner.*

hostile /ˈhɒstaɪl‖ˈhɑːstl, ˈhɑːstaɪl/ [adj] very unfriendly, and ready to argue with someone or criticize them in a rude and angry way: *There was a crowd of hostile demonstrators waiting outside her door.*
+ to/towards *He's always had a very hostile attitude towards anyone in authority.*

FRIGHTENING/ FRIGHTENED

WORRYING/WORRIED
EXCITING/EXCITED
see also
SHAKE
MAGIC
STRANGE THINGS AND EVENTS

1 frightened of something or someone

frightened /ˈfraɪtnd/ [adj] feeling very nervous and afraid of someone or something, because you think something bad is going to happen to you because of them: *Don't be frightened. No-one's going to hurt you.* | *Two frightened children were hiding in a corner of the room.*
+ of *A lot of people are frightened of dentists.* | *Are you frightened of the dark?*

frightened of doing sth *He was frightened of making mistakes.*
+ that *I was frightened that my parents would get divorced.*

> ⚠ Don't confuse **frightened** (=feeling afraid) and **frightening** (=making you feel afraid). Don't say 'I am frightening' when you mean 'I am frightened'.

afraid /əˈfreɪd/ [adj not before noun] frightened
+ of *He had a terrible temper, and everyone was afraid of him.*
afraid of doing sth *I didn't tell anyone because I was afraid of being punished.* (=I thought I might be punished if I told anyone)
+ (that) *Kerry was afraid that he was going to hit her.*

> ⚠ **Afraid** means the same as **frightened**, but **afraid** is always followed by **of**, **that**, or the infinitive (to + verb), except in negative sentences like 'Don't be afraid' and 'I'm not afraid'.

scared /skeəʳd/ [adj not before noun] ESPECIALLY SPOKEN frightened: *The first time I went on a motorcycle I was really scared.*
+ of *She's always been scared of spiders.*
scared of doing sth *I think they were all scared of offending him.* (=they thought they might offend him)
+ that *I hate reading out my work in class – I'm scared that people are going to laugh at me.*
scared stiff/scared to death (=very scared) *When he came back he looked scared stiff, as if he'd seen a ghost.*

terrified /ˈterɪfaɪd/ [adj] extremely frightened: *At first, Anna was too terrified to speak.* | *the terrified faces of the refugees*
+ of *He's absolutely terrified of snakes.*
+ (that) *I was terrified that my father would find out I had lied to him.*
terrified of doing sth *She's never been outside the US – she's terrified of flying.*

> ⚠ Don't say 'very terrified'. Say **absolutely terrified**.

dread /dred/ [v T] to feel worried and frightened about something that you have to do, or about something that you know is going to happen: *I have to go to the dentist's tomorrow, and I'm dreading it.* **dread doing sth** *I dreaded having to tell Sam his dog had died.*

2 when you do not want to do something because you are frightened

be afraid/be frightened/be scared
/bɪ əˈfreɪd, biː ˈfraɪtnd, biː ˈskeəʳd/ to be unwilling to do something because you are frightened about what may happen if you do it

+ to do sth *Many old people are afraid to go out at night.*

+ of doing sth *She asked me to come with her because she was scared of going there on her own.* | *He's frightened of flying in case there's a bomb on the plane.*

⚠ **Be scared** is more informal than **be afraid** or **be frightened**.

3 suddenly frightened

get a fright /ˌget ə ˈfraɪt/ to be suddenly frightened by something that happens: *She got a terrible fright when the dog jumped out at her.*

get the fright of your life INFORMAL (=be suddenly very frightened) *I got the fright of my life when he suddenly spoke from out of the darkness.*

panic /ˈpænɪk/ [v I] if you **panic** in a dangerous situation, you start behaving in a way that is not sensible, because you are very frightened and you cannot think clearly: *Keep calm and don't panic.* | *As the fire raged through the ship, some passengers panicked and jumped into the sea.*

panicking – panicked – have panicked

4 something that makes you frightened

frightening /ˈfraɪtnɪŋ/ [adj] something that is **frightening** makes you feel frightened: *It was the most frightening experience of my life.* | *Driving in big cities can be pretty frightening for many people.*

terrifying /ˈterɪfaɪ-ɪŋ/ [adj] very frightening: *They stopped me, and they had a gun. It was terrifying.* | *There was a terrifying crash, and the house seemed to shake.*

⚠ Don't say 'very terrifying'. Just say **terrifying**.

scary /ˈskeəri/ [adj] ESPECIALLY SPOKEN frightening – use this especially about stories, films, or situations in which strange and frightening things happen: *She didn't like the film. It was too scary for her.* | *I had a really scary dream last night.* | *a big scary monster*

scary – scarier – scariest

spooky /ˈspuːki/ [adj] INFORMAL a place that is **spooky** is strange or frightening because it makes you think of ghosts: *The hotel was kind of spooky – big, dark, and empty.*

5 a film or story that is intended to make you frightened

horror /ˈhɒrəʳ‖ˈhɔː-, ˈhɑː-/ [adj only before noun] **horror film/movie/story/video** a film or story that is intended to make you feel frightened: *The movie is based on a horror story by Stephen King.*

thriller /ˈθrɪləʳ/ [n C] a film or book that is intended to be exciting and frightening because you do not know what will happen next: *'Psycho' is Hitchcock's greatest psychological thriller.*

6 to make someone feel frightened

frighten /ˈfraɪtn/ [v T] to make someone feel frightened: *Don't shout like that – you'll frighten the baby.* | *I don't care how tough he is – he doesn't frighten me.*

frighten sb into doing sth (=make someone do something by frightening them) *Their lawyers tried to frighten us into signing the contract.*

frighten sb off/frighten off sb (=frighten someone so that they go away or stop trying to do something) *The man pulled out a gun and managed to frighten off his attackers.*

scare /skeə^r/ [v T] ESPECIALLY SPOKEN to make someone feel frightened or very nervous: *There was a pale, white face at the window. It really scared me.*

scare the hell out of sb INFORMAL (=make someone feel very frightened) *The way he drives scares the hell out of me.*

⚠ **Scare** is more informal than **frighten** and you usually use it in spoken English.

terrify /ˈterɪfaɪ/ [v T] to make someone feel very frightened: *The idea of going down into the caves terrified her.*

terrifying – terrified – have terrified

startle /ˈstɑːrtl/ [v T] if someone or something **startles** you, they frighten you because you see them suddenly or hear them when you are not expecting them: *I'm sorry. I didn't mean to startle you.*

gives me the creeps /ˌgɪvz miː ðə ˈkriːps/ SPOKEN INFORMAL if a person or place **gives you the creeps**, they make you feel slightly frightened and nervous because they seem strange: *I hate this house. It gives me the creeps.*

7 the feeling of being frightened

fear /fɪə^r/ [n C/U] the feeling you have when you are very frightened, or the thought that something very unpleasant will happen: *Her hands were shaking with fear.* (=because she was frightened)
+ of *fear of flying | fears of another war in Europe*
+ that *There was always the fear that he might never return.*

terror /ˈterə^r/ [n U] a very strong feeling of fear when you think that something very bad is going to happen to you, especially that you will be killed
in terror (=because you are very frightened) *Shots were fired, and the children screamed in terror.*
sheer terror (=very great terror) *I'll never forget the look of sheer terror on her face.*

horror /ˈhɒrə^r/ [n U] a strong feeling of shock and fear, which you have when you see something terrible happen, or when you think of something terrible
in horror *The crowd watched in horror*

as the plane hit the ground and burst into flames.
to sb's horror (=making someone feel very frightened) *He suddenly realized to his horror that the brakes weren't working.*

panic /ˈpænɪk/ [n U] a sudden, strong feeling of fear when you are in a dangerous situation, which makes you do things that are not sensible because you cannot think clearly: *There was a sudden panic and everyone started rushing towards the door.*

FROM
to come from a place or to come from something else

➡ see also COUNTRY, TOWN, LIVE

1 when someone was born in a place or has lived there a long time

come from/be from /ˈkʌm frɒm, biː ˈfrɒm/ [phrasal verb T] if you **come from** or **are from** a particular place, that is where you were born or where you lived for a long time: *Where are you from? | She comes from Japan. | When we were on vacation we met a couple who came from the same town as us.*

2 when something has developed from something that existed before

come from sth /ˈkʌm frɒm (sth)/ [phrasal verb T] use this to say that something which exists now developed from something else that existed before: *The word 'origami' comes from the Japanese words 'ori', meaning 'folding', and 'kami', meaning 'paper'. | Many modern stories come from ancient Greek and Roman myths.*

be based on sth /biː ˈbeɪst ɒn (sth)/ if a film or story, or an idea or plan **is based on** something else, that is where its basic ideas or facts come from: *The movie 'The Far Pavilions' is based on a novel about India. | a new traffic policy, based on a six-month survey of road use*

origin/origins /ˈɒrɪdʒɪn(z)‖ˈɔː-, ˈɑː-/ [n C] the situation, ideas, events etc that something else developed from, especially when this helps to explain why something has developed
+ **of** *a TV programme about the origin of the universe* | *We had to write an essay on the origins of World War I.*

> ⚠ **Origin** and **origins** often mean the same, but use **origins** especially about something that has many different parts or stages: *the origins of the modern novel.* Use **origin** especially about something that developed from a single thing, cause, or situation: *Doctors are still not sure what the origin of the infection is.*

FULL

when nothing more can fit into a container, room, or space

➡ opposite **EMPTY**

1 full

full /fʊl/ [adj] if a container, room, or space is **full**, nothing more can go into it: *a full bottle of milk* | *I can't get anything more in this suitcase – it's full.* | *All the parking spaces were full.*

full

+ **of** *We found a box full of old letters.* | *The buses were full of people going to work.*

> ⚠ Don't say 'full with something'. Say **full of something.**

filled with sth /ˈfɪld wɪð (sth)/ full of something – use this about a container when a lot of things have been put into it: *an enormous vase filled with flowers* | *Pour the mixture into a tall glass filled with ice.* | *There were lots of tiny drawers filled with screws and nails.*

packed /pækt/ [adj] completely full of people – use this about a room, theatre, train, bus, etc: *"Were there many people on the train?" "Oh, it was packed!"* | *a packed theatre*

+ **with** *On the day of her funeral the church was packed with friends and relatives.*

crammed with sth /ˈkræmd wɪð (sth)/ completely full of things or people, so that they are all pressed together: *Security guards discovered a bag crammed with explosives.* | *small boats crammed with refugees* | *a shelf crammed with books*

overflowing /ˌəʊvəˈfləʊɪŋ◀/ [adj] a container that is **overflowing** is so full that the liquid or things inside it come out over the top: *The bath's overflowing! Who forgot to turn off the water?* | *The tables were covered with dirty coffee cups and overflowing ashtrays.*

overflowing

+ **with** *a trashcan overflowing with garbage*

overloaded /ˌəʊvəˈləʊdɪd/ if a vehicle or ship is **overloaded**, too many things have been put in it, so it is carrying too much: *The truck was completely overloaded, and things had started to fall out of the back.* | *an overloaded bus*

2 to become full

fill up /ˌfɪl ˈʌp/ [phrasal verb I] to gradually become full: *About half an hour before the performance, the theatre starts to fill up.* | *The drought has ended at last, and the reservoirs are filling up again.*

3 to make something full

fill /fɪl/ [v T] to put enough of something into a container to make it full: *Would you fill the watering can and water the flowers?*
fill sth with sth *We stood at the counter, filling our bowls with salad.* | *He had a notebook which he had filled with stories and poems.*

fill up /ˌfɪl ˈʌp/ [phrasal verb T] to fill a container that already has a small amount of something in it
fill up sth *Harold went around filling up everyone's glasses.*
fill sth up *If the oil tank is less than half full, tell them to fill it up.*
fill up sth with sth *I've filled up the freezer with fruit and vegetables.*

cram /kræm/ [v T] to push too many things into a container or space, so that they are all pressed together

cram sth into sth *I crammed all my clothes into the suitcase and then found I couldn't shut the lid.*

cramming – crammed – have crammed

stuff /stʌf/ [v T] to quickly fill something such as a bag or pocket by pushing things into it tightly

stuff sth into sth *She hurriedly stuffed some things into an overnight bag and left immediately.*

stuff sth with sth *The thieves had stuffed their pockets with $100 bills.*

refill /ˌriːˈfɪl/ [v T] to fill something again, after what was inside it has been used: *If you bring your empty bottles back to the store, we can refill them.* | *Can I refill anyone's glass?*

refill sth with sth *The tank was emptied, cleaned, and refilled with fresh water.*

FUNNY

JOKE   SMILE

see also

LAUGH   SERIOUS

1 when something or someone makes you laugh

funny /ˈfʌni/ [adj] something or someone that is **funny** makes you laugh: *It was the funniest story I'd ever heard.* | *He can be pretty funny when he's had a few drinks.*

very/really/so funny *You look really funny in that hat.*

it was funny *The goat was chasing Mark round and round the field – it was so funny.*

funny – funnier – funniest

make sb laugh /ˌmeɪk (sb) ˈlɑːf‖-ˈlæf/ to make someone laugh, for example by telling a joke or doing something funny: *I must tell Jerry what you said – it'll make*

him laugh. | *a great actor with a wonderful ability to make people laugh and cry*

amusing /əˈmjuːzɪŋ/ [adj] ESPECIALLY WRITTEN funny and entertaining enough to make you smile: *an amusing play about a shy young man* | *His speech was amusing at first, but then it got really boring.*

very/highly amusing *My mother was embarrassed, but I found the situation highly amusing.*

witty /ˈwɪti/ [adj] a person, speech, play, or remark that is **witty** uses words in a clever and amusing way: *Sam is intelligent, witty, and great fun to be with.* | *an entertaining speech full of witty comments*

witty – wittier – wittiest

humorous /ˈhjuːmərəs‖ˈhjuː-, ˈjuː-/ [adj] intended to be amusing – use this especially about stories, descriptions, letters, and other things that people write: *a book of humorous poems* | *a humorous account of a young man's travels in South America* | *humorous birthday cards*

hilarious /hɪˈleəriəs/ [adj] extremely funny – use this about situations, jokes, and stories, but not about people: *one of the hilarious scenes in a Marx Brothers film* | *The dancing was absolutely hilarious – we all kept tripping over each other.*

> ⚠ Don't say 'very hilarious'. Say **really hilarious** or **absolutely hilarious**.

2 something that is said or written to make people laugh

joke /dʒəʊk/ [n C] something that you say to make people laugh, especially a short funny story: *Have you heard the joke about the President's dog?* | *I always enjoy a good joke.*

make/tell a joke *It annoys me when people make jokes about women drivers.*

get/see the joke (=understand a joke) *Everyone laughed except Henry, who didn't see the joke.*

dirty joke (=a joke about sex)

comedy /ˈkɒmədi‖ˈkɑː-/ [n C] a film, play, TV programme etc that is intended to

entertain people and make them laugh: *a new romantic comedy starring Hugh Grant* | *a comedy show on Channel 4*
plural **comedies**

⚠ You can also use **comedy** before a noun, like an adjective: *the best comedy performance of the year* | *a TV comedy series called 'Cheers'*

3 someone whose job is to make people laugh

comedian/comic /kə'miːdiən, 'kɒmɪk‖ 'kɑː-/ [n C] someone whose job is to tell jokes and make people laugh

clown /klaʊn/ [n C] someone who entertains people by dressing in funny clothes and by doing silly things, especially in a circus

4 how you feel when you think something is funny

amused /ə'mjuːzd/ [adj] if you are **amused** by something, you think it is funny and it makes you smile: *When I told him what had happened, he sounded amused rather than annoyed.*
+ by/at *They seemed amused at his embarrassment.*
amused expression/smile/grin *She stood watching them with an amused expression on her face.*

amusement /ə'mjuːzmənt/ [n U] the feeling that you have when you think something is funny: *Larry's new haircut caused great amusement among his friends.*
watch/listen/notice etc with amusement *Everyone was watching the little dog with interest and amusement.*
(much) to sb's amusement (=making them feel very amused) *Suddenly, the teacher's chair collapsed, much to everyone's amusement.*

5 the ability to realize when something is funny

sense of humour BRITISH **sense of humor** AMERICAN /ˌsens əv 'hjuːməʳ‖-'hjuː-, -'juː-/ [n C usually singular] your ability to understand and enjoy jokes, funny situations etc: *I like Ann – she has such a*

good sense of humour. | *Maybe I'm losing my sense of humor but I didn't find that show at all funny.*

⟲**can take a joke** /kən ˌteɪk ə 'dʒəʊk/ ESPECIALLY SPOKEN to be able to laugh and not get angry when other people make jokes about you or do something that makes you look stupid: *I hope he can take a joke – have you seen what they've done to his car?*

FUTURE

➡ if you want to know how to form the future, go to the ESSENTIAL GRAMMAR section 5
➡ see also SOON, TIME, PAST

1 the time after now

future /'fjuːtʃəʳ/ [n singular] the time after now
the future *She's finishing college soon, and she doesn't really have any plans for the future*
of the future (=that will exist in the future) *The car of the future may run on solar-powered batteries.*
sb's future (=what will happen to someone in their job, their life etc) *I had a meeting with the boss to discuss my future.*
have a great future (=be likely to be very successful in the future) *She's a very talented musician, and we think she has a great future.*
a future leader/president/prime minister etc (=someone who will be a leader/president etc in the future) *He is regarded by many as a future president.*
a future date/time FORMAL *We agreed to consider the matter again at a future date.*

the outlook /ði 'aʊtlʊk/ [n singular] a general idea of what people expect to happen in the future, and whether they expect things to go well or badly: *The economic outlook is better than it has been for several years.*
+ for *With drought conditions continuing, the outlook for farmers is not very good.*

from now /frəm 'naʊ/ **an hour/10 years/ 2 weeks etc from now** an hour, 10 years etc from the time when you are speaking: *A couple of months from now, you'll probably have forgotten all about him.* | *There may be no rainforest left in 30 years from now.*

from now on /frəm ˌnaʊ 'ɒn/ use this to say that something will always happen in the future, starting from now: *From now on, I'm not letting anyone borrow my car.* | *From now on, you kids will have to make your own lunch.*

2 at some time in the future

in the future /ɪn ðə 'fjuːtʃər/ at some time in the future, but you do not know exactly when: *Global warming could become a major problem in the future.*

in the near future (=soon) *The new soft-ware will be available in the UK in the near future.*

some time /ˌsʌm 'taɪm/ at some time in the future, which has not been arranged yet: *Come over and see us some time.* | *Would you like to go out for a meal some time next week?*

one day/some day /ˌwʌn 'deɪ, ˌsʌm 'deɪ/ at some time in the future, especially a long time from now: *Perhaps one day we could all go to London together.* | *She always knew that some day he would leave her.*

then /ðen/ [adv] at a time in the future, which you have just mentioned: *Wait until I've finished my homework, then we'll take the dog for a walk.*

until then *School starts in September, and until then I'll be staying with friends.*

G

GAMBLING

when you try to win money by guessing the result of a race, competition etc

RISK   LOSE

see also

WIN   RESULT 3

1 to gamble

gambling /ˈgæmblɪŋ/ [n U] when you try to win money, for example by playing cards or guessing which horse will win a race: *Is gambling legal here?* | *The TV star admitted he was addicted to drugs and gambling.* | *We aim to give help and advice to people with gambling problems.*

gamble /ˈgæmbəl/ [v I/T] to try to win money, for example by playing cards or guessing which horse will win a race: *Eddie loved to gamble, and would spend most evenings at the roulette table.*

gamble away sth/gamble sth away (=waste a lot of money by gambling) *Roger gambled away all his money in a Las Vegas casino.* | *She inherited $50,000 but gambled it away.*

bet/have a bet /bet, ˌhæv ə ˈbet/ [v I] to try to win money by guessing who will win a race or game: *I don't bet very often.*

bet on sth/have a bet on sth (=gamble money on the result of a race or game) *We usually have a bet on the Grand Prix.*

bet £10/$100 etc on sth *He bet $1000 on a horse race last week.*

put £10/$20 etc on sth /pʊt (£10, etc) ɒn (sth)/ to gamble £10, $20 etc on the horse or team that you think will win a race or competition: *I put $20 on the Cowboys to win.*

put a bet on sth (=gamble on a horse, game etc) *I think I'll put a bet on the next race.*

2 someone who gambles

gambler /ˈgæmbləʳ/ [n C] someone who gambles, especially someone who gambles a lot and cannot stop: *Jack was a great drinker and gambler.*

3 ways of gambling

go to a casino /ˌgəʊ tʊ ə kəˈsiːnəʊ/ to go to a place where people try to win money by playing card games or games like roulette (=a game in which a ball falls into a hole with a number on it) *Did you go to the casino while you were in Monte Carlo?*

do the lottery BRITISH **play the lottery** AMERICAN /ˌduː ðə ˈlɒtəri, ˌpleɪ ðə ˈlɒtəri‖-ˈlɑː-/ to buy a ticket with numbers on it, so that you will win a lot of money if your numbers are chosen: *Thousands of people do the lottery every week.*

go to the races /ˌgəʊ tə ðə ˈreɪsɪz/ to go to watch horses racing, and often try to win money by guessing which one will win

play cards/poker/roulette /pleɪ ˈkɑːʳdz, ˈpəʊkəʳ, ruːˈlet/ to play a game in order to try to win money: *Miles and his friends used to sit up all night, drinking and playing poker.*

lose money on sth /luːz ˈmʌni ɒn (sth)/ to lose money by not guessing correctly the result of a game, race, or competition: *He claims that he lost all his money on a dice game.*

win money on sth /wɪn ˈmʌni ɒn (sth)/ to win money by correctly guessing the result of a game, race, or competition: *In the film, the star wins a lot of money on a gameshow.*

GAME

SPORT   GAMBLING

see also

WIN   LOSE

TAKE PART   COMPETITION

1 a game

game /geɪm/ [n C] an activity which you do for enjoyment which you play according to a set or rules: *Chess is such a difficult game.* | *Have you ever played Mah Jong? It's a Chinese game.*

computer game *Computer games are getting more and more violent these days.*

card game (=a game you play using a set of cards with numbers or pictures on them) *I'm not very good at card games. I always lose.*

board game (=a game played on a board with pieces of wood, plastic etc that you move around) *board games like Monopoly and Ludo*

⚠ You can also use **game** to mean a single occasion when you play a game: *We played three games of chess, and she beat me every time.*

2 to play a game

play /pleɪ/ [v I/T] to take part in a game: *Have you played backgammon before?* | *We're thinking of having a game of Monopoly. Does anyone else want to play?*

have a game /ˌhæv ə ˈgeɪm/ to play one game of something – use this especially when asking someone to play a game
+ of *Do you want to have a game of cards?*

3 someone who plays a game

player /ˈpleɪəʳ/ [n C] someone who plays a game: *Bridge is a game for 4 players.* | *The other players were much more experienced than I was.*

contestant /kənˈtestənt/ [n C] someone who takes part in a game on television or radio: *One lucky contestant will win tonight's star prize, a luxury car.*

4 the points that you get in a game

point /pɔɪnt/ [n C] a unit used for measuring how well you are doing in a game: *The first player to get a hundred points wins the game.*

score /skɔːʳ/ [n C] the number of points that one player or all the players have at the end of a game: *What's your highest ever score?* | *The final score was 4 all.* (=both players had 4 points)

GET

➡ see also **HAVE/NOT HAVE, OWN**

1 to get something

get /get/ [v T not in passive] to get something by buying it, asking for it, or working for it: *I got a really nice coat at Browns.* | *Where did he get the money for a new car?* | *I don't feel like cooking, let's go get a pizza.* | *I still haven't gotten a birthday present for Sherri.*

get sth from sb/sth *I wonder where they got those costumes from?*

get a job *Did you hear? Stuart got a new job.*

getting – got – have got BRITISH
have gotten AMERICAN

obtain /əbˈteɪn/ [v T] FORMAL to get something: *Maps and guides can be obtained at the tourist office.*

obtain sth from sb/sth *You have to obtain permission from the Principal if you want to leave early.*

get hold of /get ˈhəʊld ɒv/ to get something that is difficult to get, for example by finding it or borrowing it: *Do you know where I can get hold of Geraldine's address?* | *Somehow Scott had got hold of a gun.* | *That sort of information is very difficult to get hold of.*

gain /geɪn/ [v T] FORMAL to gradually get more of a useful skill or a good quality. Use **gain** with words like **experience, confidence, support, popularity, acceptance**: *It took her a long time to gain enough confidence to speak in public.* | *She stayed in the job for five years, gaining valuable experience.* | *His ideas are gaining a lot of support* (=more and more people are supporting them).

2 to be given something

get /get/ [v T not in passive] to be given something without having to ask for it or pay for it: *What did you get for your* *birthday?* | *You get a free CD with this magazine.*

get sth from sb *When she became sick, she didn't get any help from her family.*

getting – got – have got (BRITISH)
have gotten (AMERICAN)

receive /rɪˈsiːv/ [v T] to be given something, especially officially: *As from next month, single parents will receive reduced welfare payments.* | *We receive over 100 complaints a month about aircraft noise.*

receive sth from sb/sth *She received an honorary degree from Harvard in 1990.*

⚠ **Receive** is more formal than **get**.

be given sth /biː ˈɡɪvən (sth)/ to be given something, especially by someone in an important or powerful position: *He was given a 10 year jail sentence.* | *Why shouldn't disabled people be given the chance to compete in the Games?* | *New employees were given a complete medical check-up.*

be awarded sth /biː əˈwɔːrdɪd (sth)/ to be given a prize, especially by an important organization, for something that you have achieved: *The restaurant was awarded four stars in the 'Good Food Guide'.* | *Yasunari Kawabata was the first Japanese writer to be awarded the Nobel Prize.*

inherit /ɪnˈherɪt/ [v T] to be given someone's money or property after they die: *Who will inherit the house when he dies?*

inherit sth from sb *She inherited the money from her mother.*

3 to get a letter, telephone call, or message

get/receive /ɡet, rɪˈsiːv/ [v T] *I got a really strange phone call from Ann last night.* | *I'm sorry I didn't reply earlier, but I've only just received your letter.*

getting – got – have got BRITISH
have gotten AMERICAN

⚠ **Receive** is more formal than **get**.

4 to get a point or result in a game, test etc

get /ɡet/ [v T] to get a result in a test or examination: *I only got 35% in my history test.* | *Pam's really smart. She got straight A's at high school.*

getting – got – have got BRITISH
have gotten AMERICAN

score /skɔːr/ [v T] to get a number of points in a sports game, or in a test or examination: *The test was difficult, and no-one scored more than 45 points.*

score a goal/point/run *AC Milan scored a record number of goals this season.*

5 to get back something that you had before

get sth back /ˌɡet (sth) ˈbæk/ [phrasal verb T not in passive] to get back something that you had before, especially something that belongs to you: *Suzanna has my lecture notes – I won't be able to get them back until Monday.*

+ from *We never got our money back from the landlord.*

6 the person, place, company etc that you get something from

source /sɔːrs/ [n C] the person, place, or thing that you get something from: *They get their information from various sources.*

+ of *Beans and lentils are a very good source of protein.*

supplier /səˈplaɪər/ [n C] the person, company, or country that you regularly get a product from: *We can get the goods much more cheaply from foreign suppliers.*

+ of *In the past they have been one of the main suppliers of weapons to Iraq.*

GET RID OF

to remove a thing or person that you do not need or want any more

1 to get rid of an object, a piece of furniture or clothing etc
➡ see also **RUBBISH**

get rid of sth /ˌget ˈrɪd ɒv (sth)/ to remove something that you do not want or do not use any more, for example by giving it to someone else or throwing it away: *Let's get rid of some of these old books.* | *I hate these chairs. I wish we could get rid of them.*

throw away

throw   throw away

throw away /ˌθrəʊ əˈweɪ/ [phrasal verb T] to get rid of something by putting it in the bin (=container where you put unwanted things so they can be taken away)
throw away sth *Don't throw away those boxes – they might be useful.*
throw sth away *That bread is about two weeks old! You'd better throw it away.*

> ⚠ Don't confuse **throw** (=when you throw something through the air) and **throw away**.

throw out /ˌθrəʊ ˈaʊt/ [phrasal verb T] to get rid of something, especially when you are trying to make a place more tidy or to make space for new things
throw out sth *They were throwing out some old filing cabinets, so I asked if I could have one.*
throw sth out *You never wear these shoes – why don't you throw them out?*

dispose of sth /dɪsˈpəʊz ɒv (sth)/ [phrasal verb T] FORMAL to get rid of something that is difficult or unpleasant to get rid of: *a debate about the best way to dispose of nuclear waste* | *After killing her, Wells disposed of the body in a local lake.*

> ⚠ Don't say 'he disposed the body'. Say **he disposed of the body**

dump /dʌmp/ [v T] to throw away something unpleasant or dangerous by leaving it in a place where it should not be: *People dump all sorts of things in the woods.* | *Dangerous chemicals are being dumped in the ocean.*

disposable /dɪˈspəʊzəbəl/ [adj] something that is **disposable** is designed to be used once and then thrown away: *The nurses use disposable gloves.* | *Disposable plastic cups are bad for the environment.*

2 to get rid of a person
➡ see also **LEAVE 10**

get rid of sb /ˌget ˈrɪd ɒv (sb)/ INFORMAL to make someone leave because you do not want them or because they are causing problems: *The company has announced plans to get rid of 500 workers.* | *She stayed here talking for over three hours – I couldn't get rid of her!* | *He's not a very good teacher – I think they should get rid of him.*

3 to get rid of a system, law, plan etc

abolish /əˈbɒlɪʃ‖əˈbɑː-/ [v T] to officially end a law, legal right, or system, especially one that has existed for a long time: *an unpopular tax that was finally abolished in 1990* | *Wilberforce campaigned to abolish slavery.*
> **abolition** /ˌæbəˈlɪʃən/ [n U] when something is abolished: *a group that is fighting for the abolition of the death penalty*

scrap /skræp/ [v T] to end a system, law etc, or to decide not to use a plan that you were intending to use: *Plans to build a new airport have been scrapped because of lack of money.* | *Eventually, they hope to scrap border controls completely.*
scrapping – scrapped – have scrapped

> ⚠ **Scrap** is used especially in news reports.

4 to get rid of a problem or illness

get rid of sth /ˌget ˈrɪd ɒv (sth)/ to remove or deal with something that is causing you trouble, such as an illness or a problem: *I've had a cold for two weeks, and I just can't get rid of it.* | *a powerful fan that will get rid of unwanted tobacco smells*

GIRLFRIEND/ BOYFRIEND

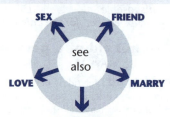

see also

SEX
FRIEND
LOVE
MARRY
RELATIONSHIP

1 a person that you have a romantic or sexual relationship with

girlfriend /'gɜːʳlfrend/ [n C] a girl or woman that you have a romantic relationship with, especially for a fairly long time: *I can't wait to meet my brother's new girlfriend.*

ex-girlfriend (=someone who used to be your girlfriend) *He keeps phoning his ex-girlfriend.*

boyfriend /'bɔɪfrend/ [n C] a boy or man that you have a romantic relationship with, especially for a fairly long time: *Josh was my first boyfriend.*

ex-boyfriend (=someone who used to be your boyfriend) *Oh, my God! I've just seen Alex, my ex-boyfriend.*

partner /'pɑːʳtnəʳ/ [n C] someone that you have a romantic and sexual relationship with, especially someone that you live with: *Partners are welcome at the office Christmas party.* | *We run a counselling service for anyone whose partner has died.*

⚠ Use **partner** about a man or woman who has had a relationship with someone else for a long time, especially when they live together, or when you do not know whether the person they are having a relationship with is male or female.

lover /'lʌvəʳ/ [n C] someone, especially a

man, that you have a sexual relationship with but do not live with: *The woman was attacked by a former lover.*

be lovers (=when two people have a sexual relationship) *Woody Allen and Mia Farrow were lovers for 12 years.*

mistress /'mɪstrɪ̩s/ [n C] a woman who has a sexual relationship with a man who is married to someone else: *She suspected her husband had a mistress, but could not prove it.*

plural **mistresses**

⚠ The word **mistress** is a little old-fashioned, but it is often used when talking about famous people, or about people in history or literature.

2 to have a girlfriend or boyfriend

go out with sb /ˌgəʊ 'aʊt wɪð (sb)/ [phrasal verb T] to have someone as your girlfriend or boyfriend: *She's going out with that guy who works at the gas station.*

be going out together *Mark and I have been going out together for four years.*

be seeing sb /biː 'siːɪŋ (sb)/ to have a romantic or sexual relationship with someone, especially a relationship that is not very serious and does not last very long: *Do you know if Tanya's seeing anyone at the moment?* | *A couple of years after they got married, he started seeing other women.*

3 a romantic or sexual relationship

relationship /rɪ'leɪʃənʃɪp/ [n C] when two people spend time together or live together because they are romantically or sexually attracted to each other: *After his marriage broke up, he had a series of disastrous relationships.*

+ with *I don't want to start a relationship with him because I'm going back to South Africa.*

affair /ə'feəʳ/ [n C] a secret sexual relationship between two people, when one or both of them is married to someone else: *The affair had been going on for years before her husband found out.*

have an affair with sb *I'd kill my husband if he had an affair with anyone!*

G

fling /flɪŋ/ [n C] INFORMAL a short and not very serious relationship: *Yes, I did go out with him, but it was just a fling.*
have a fling *They had a fling years ago.*

4 to end a relationship

split up/break up /ˌsplɪt ˈʌp, ˌbreɪk ˈʌp/ [phrasal verb I] if two people **split up** or **break up**, they stop having a relationship with each other: *Tim and I have split up.*
+ with *David has just broken up with his girlfriend. He's really upset.*

leave /liːv/ [v T] to end a serious relationship with someone you live with, especially your husband or wife: *His wife left him after 30 years of marriage.*
leaving – left – have left

finish with sb /ˈfɪnɪʃ wɪð (sb)/ [phrasal verb T] BRITISH to end your relationship with your boyfriend or girlfriend: *Frank? I finished with him years ago!*

GIVE

➡ see also GET, PROVIDE, TAKE/BRING
➡ if you mean 'give something to someone when they will give it back later', go to LEND

1 to give something to someone

give /gɪv/ [v T]
give sb sth *I gave him $10. | Why don't we give her some flowers for her birthday? | Let me give you some advice.*
give sth to sb *Would you give this letter to your uncle when you see him? | Russell was accused of giving secret information to the enemy.*
giving – gave – have given

> ⚠ Don't say 'give to her the book'. Say **give her the book** or **give the book to her.**
>
> ⚠ In the passive, you can say either 'I was given it' or 'it was given to me': *I was given this ring by my mother. | This ring was given to me by my mother.*

pass /pɑːs‖pæs/ [v T] to give something to someone by putting it in their hand or putting it near them, especially because

they cannot reach it themselves: *Could you pass the salt, please?*
pass sb sth *Would you pass me my sweater. It's on the back of your chair.*
pass sth to sb *Ellis quickly passed the note to the woman, looking around to check that no one had noticed.*

> ⚠ It is more polite to say **pass** than **give** when you are asking for something that you can see but cannot reach: *Could you pass me that book, please?*

hand /hænd/ [v T] to give something to someone by putting it into their hand
hand sb sth *The nurse handed me a glass of brown liquid and told me to drink it.*
hand sth to sb *Please hand your tickets to the man at the door.*

let sb have sth /ˌlet (sb) ˈhæv (sth)/ to give something to someone, especially something they have asked for or something they need: *If you could let me have your suggestions, it would be very helpful. | She lets her kids have anything they want.*

give away /ˌgɪv əˈweɪ/ [phrasal verb T] to give something that you own to someone else, especially because you do not want it or need it
give away sth *I gave away most of my old furniture because I didn't have room for it in my new apartment.*
give sth away *He decided to give all his money away and become a monk.*
give sth away to sb *I don't need all this stuff – I'll give it away to the first person who asks for it.*

provide /prəˈvaɪd/ [v T] to make sure that someone has what they need, by giving it to them or making it available to them: *The sports hall was built on land provided by the city authorities.*
provide sb with sth *Could you please provide us with full details of your previous experience?*
provide sth for sb *Jobs in restaurants provide a useful source of income for college students.*

present /prɪˈzent/ [v T] to give someone something at an official ceremony: *Who's going to present the prizes this year?*

> When you see EC, go to the
> **ESSENTIAL COMMUNICATION** section.

present sb with sth *The photo shows the Principal presenting me with my certificate.*

present sth to sb *A little girl presented a basket of flowers to the President.*

be presented with sth *She was presented with a gold medal for bravery.*

hand in/give in /ˌhænd ˈɪn, ˌgɪv ˈɪn/ [phrasal verb T] to give something to someone in authority, for example to the police or a teacher

hand/give in sth *When you leave the hotel please hand in your keys.* | *Luckily someone gave in her purse at the lost-and-found office.*

hand/give sth in *Have you given your English assignment in yet?*

2 to give something to everyone in a group

hand out/give out /ˌhænd ˈaʊt, ˌgɪv ˈaʊt/ [phrasal verb T] to give something to all the people in a group: *The princess plans to hand out gifts at a children's hospital tomorrow.* | *Don't start the test until I've finished giving out the question papers.*

hand/give out sth to sb *Outside the embassy, students were handing out leaflets to everyone who walked past.*

hand/give sth out *I need some volunteers to hand programs out tonight*

pass around (also **pass round** BRITISH) /ˌpɑːs (ə)ˈraʊnd‖ˌpæs-/ [phrasal verb T] if a group of people **passes** something **around**, one person takes it and gives it to the next person, who then gives it to the next person

pass around sth *They passed around a list and we each had to sign our name.*

pass sth around *Don't keep all the chocolates to yourself – pass them around!*

distribute /dɪˈstrɪbjuːt/ [v T] to give things out to a large number of people, especially in an organized way: *Anti-war protesters were distributing leaflets in the street.*

distribute sth to sb *The Red Cross has started distributing food and blankets to people in the flood area.*

distribute sth among *About $250,000 worth of medical supplies has been distributed among families affected by the epidemic.*

share out /ˌʃeər ˈaʊt/ [phrasal verb T] to divide something into equal parts and give a part to each person

share out sth *As long as they share out the profits fairly, everyone will be happy.*

share sth out *Bill shared the pizza out.*

share out sth among/between *More than £1.7 million has been shared out among victims of the disaster.*

serve /sɜːrv/ [v T] to give food and drinks to someone, for example in a restaurant or at a party: *Dinner will be served at 8.30.* | *Don't forget to serve the guests first.*

serve sth to sb *We don't serve alcohol to anyone under 21.*

serve sb with sth *As soon as they sat down they were served with steaming bowls of soup.*

3 to give money, food etc to help people who need it

give /gɪv/ [v I/T] to give money to an organization that will use it to help people who are poor, sick, in trouble etc: *We would be grateful for any donation that you are prepared to give.*

give sth to sb *Local people have given over $100,000 to our Help a Child appeal.*

give sb sth *The British give animal welfare organizations over £200 million per year.*

give generously (=give a lot of money) *Please give generously, these children need your help.*

giving – gave – have given

donate /dəʊˈneɪt‖ˈdəʊneɪt/ [v T] to give money, or something useful or valuable, in order to help people – use this especially about things that are given by companies or organizations: *The books were donated by a local publishing company.*

donate sth to sth *The concert organizers say they will donate all profits to charity.*

make a donation /ˌmeɪk ə dəʊˈneɪʃən/ to give an amount of money to an organization that will use it to help people: *We're collecting money to build a hostel for homeless people – would you like to make a donation?*

+ to *The company has made several large donations to charities.*

charity /ˈtʃærɪti/ [n C/U] an organization

that collects money or goods from people who give them, and uses them to help people who need help: *Elton John has campaigned for a number of AIDS charities.*

give sth to charity/go to charity (=when you give something or do something to help a charity) *All profits from the show will go to charity.*

do sth for charity *They aim to walk 30 miles for charity.*

plural **charities**

⚠ You can also use **charity** before a noun, like an adjective, to describe an event that makes money for charity: *Princess Diana was the guest of honour at the charity lunch.* | *a charity dance*

4 something you give someone on a special occasion, or in order to thank them

present /'prezənt/ [n C] something that you give to a friend or to someone in your family on a special occasion: *He got some nice presents for his birthday.*

+ from *The watch was a present from my mother.*

Christmas / birthday / anniversary etc present *We can't afford to spend much on Christmas presents this year.*

gift /gɪft/ [n C] something that you give to someone on a special occasion: *These candlesticks would be a lovely gift.*

+ from *In the hall was a magnificent vase, which was a gift from a Japanese businessman.*

⚠ You can also use **gift** before a noun, like an adjective: *a gift shop* | *gift wrap* (=paper used to wrap gifts in)

⚠ **Gift** and **present** usually mean the same, but in American English **gift** is more common than **present**, and in British English **present** is more common than **gift**. In British English, **gift** usually means something attractive rather than useful, and is used especially by people who make and sell such things.

reward /rɪ'wɔːrd/ [n C] something, especially money, that you give someone

because they have done something good or helpful

+ for *The police say there is a $50,000 reward for any information that helps them find the killer.*

5 to give something to someone, and receive something else from them

exchange /ɪks'tʃeɪndʒ/ [v T] to give something to someone and receive a similar thing from them at the same time: *We exchanged addresses and phone numbers.*

exchange sth for sth *Could I exchange this black jacket for a blue one?*

⚠ Use **exchange** especially in writing or in formal speech.

swap /swɒp‖swɑːp/ [v I/T] to exchange, especially with someone you know well, so that you each get something that you want: *My sister and I often swap clothes.* | *I'll read my book and you read yours, then we can swap.*

swap sth for sth *I'll swap this CD for two of your cassettes.*

trade /treɪd/ [v I/T] ESPECIALLY AMERICAN to exchange something that you have for something that someone else has: *She liked my T-shirt and I liked hers, so we traded.*

trade sth for sth *The report concluded that North had traded weapons for hostages.*

in exchange/in return /ɪn ɪks'tʃeɪndʒ, ɪn rɪ'tɜːrn/ if you give something or do something **in exchange** or **in return** for something else, you give it in order to get something else back: *They work at the hospital two hours a day and get free meals in return.*

+ for *He offered to take us out for dinner in exchange for helping him paint the apartment.*

6 to arrange for something to be given to someone after you die

leave /liːv/ [v T] to arrange for something to be given to someone after you die

leave sth to sb *He left £1000 to each of the nurses who had looked after him.*

leave sb sth *My aunt died last year and left me some of her furniture.*

leaving – left – have left

will /wɪl/ [n C] an official document that says who your money and possessions will be given to after you die: *Mrs Williams left her daughter $200,000 in her will.*

make a will (=write a will) *He made a will just hours before he died.*

be handed down /biː ˌhændᵻd ˈdaʊn/ if something **is handed down**, it is given to a younger person in the same family: *a ring that had been handed down from her grandmother*

be handed down from sb to sb *This recipe has been handed down from generation to generation for centuries.*

7 to give something to someone who had it before

give back /ˌgɪv ˈbæk/ [phrasal verb T] to give something to the person who gave it to you

give sth back *Don't forget to give my pen back when you've finished with it.*

give sth back to sb *He still hasn't given that book back to me.*

give sb sth back *I looked at the letter, then gave her it back.*

return /rɪˈtɜːʳn/ [v T] FORMAL to give something to the person or organization that owns it, especially after you have borrowed it from them: *You must return all your library books before the end of the year.*

return sth to sb *Your passport will be returned to you when you check out of the hotel.*

8 when several people give money in order to pay for something

contribute /kənˈtrɪbjuːt/ [v I/T] to give some of the money that is needed to pay for something

+ to *I'd like to thank all of you who contributed to the hospital appeal.*

contribute sth to/towards sth *My parents said they would contribute something towards the cost of my driving lessons.*

make a contribution /ˌmeɪk ə kɒntrᵻˈbjuːʃən‖-kɑːn-/ to give an amount of money which, when added to money given by other people, can be used to pay for something useful: *If we all make a contribution, we'll be able to get her something really nice.*

+ to/towards *Several local businesses have made contributions towards our new school bus.*

have a collection /ˌhæv ə kəˈlekʃən/ to collect money from each of the people in a group, especially in order to buy something for someone: *They had a collection at the bar and raised over $80.*

+ for *We're having a collection for Jane's birthday present.*

chip in /ˌtʃɪp ˈɪn/ [phrasal verb T] INFORMAL if everyone in a group **chips in** an amount of money, they each give an amount so that they can pay for something together: *We all chipped in to pay for the food and wine.*

chip in with $50/£10/$20 etc *Electronics firm Compol chipped in with over £20,000.*

9 to officially give someone the right to own something

hand over /ˌhænd ˈəʊvəʳ/ [phrasal verb T] to give property, goods, or power to someone else so that they officially own it or control it

hand over sth *Farmers were forced to hand over 60% of everything they produced.*

hand sth over to sb *The hijackers handed their weapons over to the army shortly after dawn.*

transfer /trænsˈfɜːʳ/ [v T] to make official arrangements so that money, property, or control of something is legally given to someone else

transfer sth to sb *In 1923 the ownership of the forest was transferred to a rich Dutch family.* | *a new constitution for Scotland, transferring power to a regional parliament*

transferring – transferred – have transferred

GO

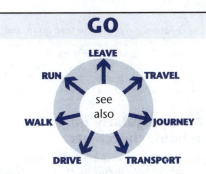

RUN   LEAVE   TRAVEL

WALK   see also   JOURNEY

DRIVE   TRANSPORT

1 to go somewhere

go /gəʊ/ [v I] to go away from where you are to another place: *We'd better go soon or we'll be late.* | *Where are you going?*
+ to/into/down/there etc *"Is Allie home?" "No, she's gone to a party."* | *Does this bus go past the university?*
go home *I called her at the office but she'd already gone home.*
go for a swim/drink/walk etc (=go somewhere to have a swim, a drink etc) *We all went for a walk after dinner.*
go and do sth/go do sth AMERICAN (=go somewhere in order to do something) *I'll just go and get my coat.*
going – went – have gone

⚠ British speakers say **go and do sth**. American speakers usually say **go do sth**: *Do you want to go see the baseball game?*

come /kʌm/ [v I] if someone or something **comes**, they go to the place where you are already, or to the place that you are going to: *Chris called to say he can't come.* | *Look – the bus is coming.*
+ to/from/here etc *Are you coming to lunch with us, Karen?* | *Come here at once!*
coming – came – have come

be off to /biː ˈɒf tuː‖-ˈɔːf-/ [phrasal verb T] ESPECIALLY SPOKEN if you **are off to** a place, you are about to go there, or you will go there very soon: *We're all off to Florida next week.* | *I'm just off to the shops. Is there anything you need?*

on your way/on the way /ˌɒn jɔːʳ ˈweɪ, ˌɒn ðə ˈweɪ/ if you are **on your way** somewhere, you have already left one place and you are travelling towards another

+ to/from/out etc *She was attacked on the way home from a nightclub.* | *I was already on my way to work when I realized I'd forgotten my briefcase.*

head /hed/ [v I] to travel towards a place, especially when the journey is long or difficult
+ towards/for *The ship was heading for Cuba.*
head north/west etc *Keep heading south until you reach the river.*

make your way /ˌmeɪk jɔːʳ ˈweɪ/ to go somewhere slowly, carefully, or with difficulty
+ to/through/there *It took us ages to make our way through the crowds.* | *After escaping from the prison camp, he made his way to the border.*

⚠ Use **make your way** especially in stories or descriptions of past events.

cross /krɒs‖krɔːs/ [v I/T] to go from one side of something to the other, for example across a river or road, or across a field or room: *How are we going to cross the river?* | *Before you cross, make sure there are no cars coming.* | *I crossed the hall and went towards the exit.*

2 to use a car, bus, train etc as a way of going somewhere

go by sth /ˈgəʊ baɪ (sth)/ [phrasal verb T]
go by car/bus/train/plane/boat to go to a place in a car, bus etc: *"Are you driving there?" "No we're going by bus."*

take /teɪk/ [v T] **take a taxi/bus/train** to pay to go somewhere in a taxi, bus, or train: *It was too far to walk, so we decided to take a taxi.*

taking – took – have taken

3 to go somewhere with someone

go with sb /ˈgəʊ wɪð (sb)/ [phrasal verb T] *One of his friends went with him to the hospital.* | *She wanted me to go back home with her, but I said no.*

come with sb /ˈkʌm wɪð (sb)/ [phrasal verb T] if you **come with** someone, you go with them to the same place that they are going: *We're going to the mall – do* you want to come with us? | Sorry I'm late – I came with Phil and his car broke down.

come along /ˌkʌm əˈlɒŋ‖-əˈlɔːŋ/ [phrasal verb I] to go with other people to a party, restaurant, film etc which they have already arranged to go to: We're going clubbing later – you're welcome to come along. | We went to the beach, and Jo came along too.

accompany /əˈkʌmpəni/ [v T often passive] FORMAL to go somewhere with someone, especially in order to give them protection or support: A bodyguard accompanies her wherever she goes.
be accompanied by Children under the age of 14 must be accompanied by an adult. | The President was accompanied by his wife, Hillary.

accompanying – accompanied – have accompanied

> ⚠ Don't say 'accompanied with someone'. Say **accompanied by someone**.

4 to go to a meeting, party, concert etc

go /gəʊ/ [v I] to go to a party, game, concert, meeting etc: She invited me to her party, but I didn't go.
+ to Did you go to the baseball game last weekend? | I have to go to a meeting this afternoon.
going – went – have gone

come /kʌm/ [v I] to go to a game, concert, meeting, party etc, either at the home of the person who invites you, or with someone who is also going there
+ to Can you come to my party? | You should have come to the concert, it was really good.
coming – came – have come

attend /əˈtend/ [v I/T] to go to an event such as a meeting or religious service: Several people were unable to attend because of the storm.
attend a meeting / service / interview / conference If you wish to attend the memorial service, please put your name on this list.

When you see **EC**, go to the **ESSENTIAL COMMUNICATION** section.

> ⚠ **Attend** is more formal than **go to**, and is used for talking about formal or official events: If you are unable to attend the interview, please let us know. Don't use **attend** for talking about things that you go to for pleasure, such as parties or concerts.

5 to regularly go to a school, church etc

go to /ˈgəʊ tuː/ [phrasal verb T] As a child I used to hate going to church. | He's been going to Spanish lessons for months and he still can't ask for directions.

attend /əˈtend/ [v T] WRITTEN to regularly go to a church, school, class etc: Both children attend Westwood Junior High.

be at /biː æt/ [phrasal verb T] if you **are at** a school, college, or university, you study there: I'm at Belton School. What about you?
be at school/college (=be a student) My husband and I met when we were both at college.

be in /biː ɪn/ [phrasal v T] AMERICAN if you **are in** a school or college, you study there: We can't afford to retire while Jessie and Joely are still in school. | We had the wildest parties when we were in school.

GOOD

➡ opposite **BAD**

1 something you like or enjoy very much

good /gʊd/ [adj] Did you have a good weekend? | It was the best party I've ever been to. | That smells good. What are you cooking?

very/really good *We enjoyed our trip to Canada. It was really good.*
good – better – best

nice /naɪs/ [adj] pleasant or enjoyable: *I hope you have a nice vacation.* | *Come over on Saturday. It would be good to see you.*
very/really nice *She made us a really nice dinner.*

⚠ **Nice** is rather an informal word. Use it in conversation and in letters to friends, but do not use it too much in your written work.

◯**great** /greɪt/ [adj] SPOKEN very good or very enjoyable: *It would be great if you could teach me to ski.* | *Thanks for a great day – we really enjoyed ourselves.*
really great *"What was the concert like?" "Great, really great."*

⚠ Don't say 'very great'. Say **really great**

excellent /ˈeksələnt/ [adj] extremely good: *There are excellent beaches close to the hotel.* | *an excellent opportunity to see wild animals in their natural surroundings*

⚠ Don't say 'very excellent'. Just say **excellent.**

marvellous/wonderful/fantastic /ˈmɑːrvələs, ˈwʌndərfəl, fænˈtæstɪk/ [adj] very good in a way that makes you feel happy or excited: *The kids had a marvellous time at the carnival.* | *You get a wonderful view of the mountains from here.*

⚠ Don't say 'very marvellous/wonderful/fantastic'. Say **absolutely marvellous/ wonderful/fantastic**

amazing/incredible /əˈmeɪzɪŋ, ɪnˈkred-ɪbəl/ [adj] very good in a surprising and exciting way: *Standing there on top of Mount Fuji was an amazing experience.* | *What a goal! That was incredible!*

⚠ Don't say 'very amazing/incredible'. Say **absolutely amazing/incredible.**

◯**brilliant** /ˈbrɪljənt/ [adj] BRITISH SPOKEN extremely good: *You should come to the new sports centre – it's brilliant.*

⚠ Don't say 'very brilliant'. Say **really brilliant** or **absolutely brilliant.**

◯**neat** /niːt/ [adj] AMERICAN SPOKEN very good or enjoyable: *That's such a neat car.*
really neat *The fireworks over Golden Gate Park were really neat.*

2 something that is of a high standard or good quality

good /gʊd/ [adj] *Yamaha make good pianos.* | *Lisa's work has been much better recently*
very good *Of course it's a very good car, but it is expensive.*
good – better – best

well /wel/ [adv] if something is done **well** or made **well**, it is done with a lot of care and skill, so it is of a high standard: *Jean's playing much better since you gave her some lessons.* | *This Lexus is one of the best designed cars on the market.*
very well *Both books are very well written and enjoyable to read.*
do well *Don't worry about the test – I'm sure you'll do well.*
well – better – best

excellent /ˈeksələnt/ [adj] extremely good: *The bank provides an excellent service for its customers.* | *They told me my English was excellent.*

⚠ Don't say 'very excellent'. Just say **excellent**

good quality/high quality /ˌgʊd ˈkwɒləti, ˌhaɪ ˈkwɒləti‖-ˈkwɑː-/ [adj only before noun] well made from good materials: *If you buy good quality shoes, they last longer.* | *We only use the highest quality ingredients for our pizzas.*
of good/high quality *handmade carpets of the highest quality*

impressive /ɪmˈpresɪv/ [adj] something that is **impressive** is of very good quality and you admire it: *The school's examination results were very impressive.* | *an impressive achievement*

impressed /ɪmˈprest/ [adj not before noun] if you are **impressed** by something, you think it is of very good quality, and so you admire it and feel pleased

C

about it: *When I saw the computer facilities at the college, I was really impressed.*
+ by/with *Everyone was very impressed by Kaori's English – she made almost no mistakes.*

outstanding /aʊt'stændɪŋ/ [adj] an **outstanding** performance or achievement is extremely good, much better than that of other people: *an outstanding performance by a talented young actor* | *Her work has been outstanding all year.*

3 in good condition

in good condition /ɪn ˌgʊd kən'dɪʃən/ something that is in **good condition** is not broken and has no marks or other things wrong with it: *The car hadn't been used much, and it was in very good condition.*

as good as new /əz ˌgʊd əz 'njuː‖-'nuː/ ESPECIALLY SPOKEN something that is **as good as new** is almost as good as when it was new – use this about things that have recently been cleaned or repaired: *I've just had the bike serviced, and it looks as good as new.*

4 a good idea, suggestion, plan etc

good /gʊd/ [adj] *A good way of dealing with the problem is to talk about it.* | *Have you got a better suggestion?*
good idea *"Why don't we hire a van?" "That's a good idea."*

good – better – best

excellent /'eksələnt/ [adj] extremely good: *We were given some excellent financial advice by Mr Samuel.* | *That sounds like an excellent idea to me.*

◯great /greɪt/ [adj] SPOKEN a **great** idea is one that you like very much
great idea *"Let's have a barbecue." "That's a great idea."*
great! *"You want to go the beach instead?" "Yeah, great, why not!"*

brilliant /'brɪljənt/ [adj] very clever and likely to succeed: *I think that's a brilliant suggestion – let's try it.* | *Hugh thought of a brilliant idea for a book.*

When you see **EC**, go to the
ESSENTIAL COMMUNICATION section.

5 someone who is good at doing something

good /gʊd/ [adj] able to do something well: *You should see him play tennis – he's pretty good.*
+ at *Ruth had always been good at languages.*
good at doing sth *You're much better at dealing with people than I am.*
good singer/teacher/actor etc *I like Robin Williams – he's a really good actor.* | *Lindy is probably the best dancer in the class.*
good with sth/sb (=good at dealing with them) *Mrs Hill is very good with children.* | *I've never been much good with money.*

good – better – best
  well [adv] *Dave plays the guitar very well.*

⚠ Don't say 'he's good in football'. Say **he's good at football**.

brilliant /'brɪljənt/ [adj] extremely good at doing something: *Paganini was a brilliant violinist.* | *Have you seen her dance? She's absolutely brilliant.*

skilful BRITISH **skillful** AMERICAN /'skɪlfəl/ [adj] someone who is **skilful** does something very well using their intelligence and their training: *Agassi is one of the most skilful players in professional tennis.* | *the artist's skillful use of color* | *Success in business depends on skilful management.*
  skilfully/skillfully [adv] *Ben steered the boat skilfully through the narrow channel.* | *a skillfully worded question*

skilled /skɪld/ [adj] someone who is **skilled** at a particular job has the training and experience to do it well
skilled worker/engineer/craftsman etc *There is a demand for carpenters, and other skilled craftsmen.*
skilled at doing sth *Our advisers are skilled at dealing with financial problems.*
highly skilled (=very skilled) *A highly skilled chef can earn a lot of money.*

outstanding/exceptional /aʊt'stændɪŋ, ɪk'sepʃənəl/ [adj] very good at doing something, so that people notice you are much better than others: *At Harvard Law School he was an outstanding student.* | *Sarah was quite a good artist, but not an exceptional one.*

talented /ˈtæləntɪd/ [adj] very good at doing something because you have a lot of natural ability

talented actor/musician/player etc *I remember Hugh being a talented actor when we were at school together.*

highly talented (=very talented) *The Brazilian team includes some highly talented young players.*

advanced /ədˈvɑːnst‖ədˈvænst/ [adj only before noun] someone who is **advanced** has reached a high level in a subject that they are studying: *This is an exercise for more advanced students.* | *The college has elementary, intermediate and advanced classes in French and Spanish.*

promising /ˈprɒmɪsɪŋ‖ˈprɑː-/ [adj] good at something, and likely to become very good in the future – use this about young people: *a promising young footballer* | *The most promising students were selected for special training.*

6 the ability to do something well

skill /skɪl/ [n C/U] the ability to do something well because you have learned it or practised it: *They teach you the skills you need to become a successful journalist.* | *The Australians played with great skill and determination.*

computer/management/language etc skills *You need good communication skills for this job.*

+ in *On the course you will develop skills in business management.*

ability /əˈbɪlɪti/ [n U] the ability to do something well: *a good player with a lot of natural ability*

ability to do sth *Paper 3 tests the student's ability to write in English.*

talent /ˈtælənt/ [n C/U] a natural ability to do something very well: *Her good looks and talent brought her immediate success in Hollywood.*

musical/theatrical/artistic etc talent *The boy's musical talents were first recognised by his teacher.*

+ for *She has a talent for languages.*

7 morally good people or behaviour

good /ɡʊd/ [adj] kind, honest, and helpful: *Jean's a very good person – she's always ready to help.* | *He had always tried to lead a good life.*

good – better – best

decent /ˈdiːsənt/ [adj] someone who is **decent** is good and honest according to the normal standards of society: *Decent citizens have nothing to fear from the police.* | *a decent, honest, hard-working woman*

ethical /ˈeθɪkəl/ [adj] morally correct according to the rules of behaviour in a particular job: *It would not be ethical for me, as a doctor, to talk to you about my patients.*

8 good enough, but not very good

good enough /ɡʊd ɪˈnʌf/ *If the weather's good enough we'll go camping.*

+ for *It's just a cheap wine but it's good enough for a picnic.*

good enough to do sth *Do you think she is good enough to be in the team?*

satisfactory /ˌsætɪsˈfæktəri/ [adj] something that is **satisfactory** reaches the expected standard, so it is good enough to be accepted: *You won't get paid unless your work is satisfactory.* | *Lynne got satisfactory grades and was offered a place at university.*

satisfactorily [adv] *The ship's disappearance has never been satisfactorily explained.*

> ⚠ **Satisfactory** is more formal than good enough.

not bad /nɒt ˈbæd/ SPOKEN use this to say that something is fairly good, and better than you expected: *"What was the food like?" "Oh, not bad – better than last time."* | *You know, that's not a bad idea.*

not too bad *"How was your test?" "Oh, not too bad. I think I passed."*

be all right/be okay /biː ɔːl ˈraɪt, biː əʊˈkeɪ/ SPOKEN to be good enough, although it is not especially good: *The children made the cakes. I hope they're* all right. | "What did you think of the movie?" "Oh, it was OK – nothing special."

+ for This book is okay for beginners but it's not really suitable for more advanced students.

Qwill do /wil 'duː/ SPOKEN you say that something **will do** when you think that it is good enough to use, although it is not exactly the right thing: *Don't worry if you haven't got any butter. Margarine will do.* | *This paint isn't quite the right colour but I suppose it'll do.*

WORD BANK
GOVERNMENT/ POLITICS

➡ if you mean 'organizations or companies owned or controlled by the government', go to **PUBLIC 1**

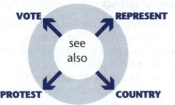

VOTE   REPRESENT

see also

PROTEST   COUNTRY

1 the people who govern a country

government /'gʌvəmənt, 'gʌvənmənt‖ 'gʌvərn-/ [n C] the people who govern a country, state, or local area, and who make all the important decisions about taxes, laws, relations with other countries etc: *The government promised to cut taxes.* | *Unemployment is a problem that faces most western governments.* | *the city government of Los Angeles*
the British/Japanese/German etc government *The French government has banned the sale of British beef.*

⚠ In British English, you can use **government** with a singular or plural verb: *The government has decided/have decided to introduce new laws against terrorism.* In American English, always use a singular verb.

⚠ You can also use **government** before a noun, like an adjective: *Government spending on education has risen by more than 10%.* | *fighting between government forces and rebels*

administration /ədˌmɪnɪ'streɪʃən/ [n C] use this especially to talk about the national government of the United States
the administration *The new administration is trying to improve standards in health care.*
the Kennedy/Reagan/Clinton etc administration (=the government when this person is president) *The Eisenhower administration refused to take military action in Vietnam.*

the authorities /ði ɔː'θɒrɪtiːz‖-ɔː'θɔːr-/ [n plural] the people or organizations that have the power to decide what people are allowed to do in a country or area: *The South African authorities arrested Mandela in August 1962.* | *The country was facing famine, and the authorities were doing nothing to prevent it.*

2 the people who make a country's laws

parliament /'pɑːrləmənt/ [n C] the group of people who are elected to make a country's laws: *Parliament will vote on the new divorce law today.* | *elections for the European parliament*

⚠ Most countries have their own name for their parliament. For example, in the UK it is called Parliament, in the US it is called Congress, and in Japan it is called the Diet.

⚠ In British English, you can use **parliament** with a singular or plural verb: *The Dutch parliament has introduced/have introduced new laws to control drug use.* In American English, always use a singular verb.

politician /ˌpɒlɪ'tɪʃən‖ˌpɑː-/ [n C] someone who works in politics, especially a member of a parliament: *Many right-wing politicians opposed the treaty.*

MP/member of parliament /ˌem 'piː, ˌmembər əv 'pɑːrləmənt/ [n C] someone who has been elected to a parliament, especially in Britain or in a country that has a similar system of government, such as India, Australia, or South Africa: *There are still very few women members of parliament.* | *Ken Livingstone, MP*

Labour/Conservative/Liberal MP *the Labour MP for Birmingham South*

plural **MPs/members of parliament**

congressman/congresswoman /ˈkɒŋɡrɪsmən, ˈkɒŋɡrɪsˌwʊmən‖ˈkɑːn-/ [n C] someone who is a member of the US Congress, especially of the House of Representatives: *Congressman Evan Kendrick*

plural **congressmen/congresswomen**

senator /ˈsenətəʳ/ [n C] a member of the US Senate or a similar institution: *Senator Kennedy* | *The President met with a group of senators and congressmen to discuss energy policy.*

3 a government that controls people's lives too much

dictatorship /dɪkˈteɪtəʳʃɪp/ [n C] a government in which one person or one small group has total power and uses it unfairly and cruelly: *Argentina's military dictatorship collapsed in 1983.*

police state /pəˈliːs ˌsteɪt/ [n singular] a country where the police have too much power and control people's lives too much: *They can't treat you like this – this is America, not a police state!*

totalitarian /təʊˌtælɪˈteəriən/ [adj usually before noun] a **totalitarian** country or system of government is one in which the government controls every part of people's lives and there is no freedom: *a writer who was imprisoned during Stalin's totalitarian rule*

oppressive /əˈpresɪv/ [adj] an **oppressive** government treats people in a cruel way, using military force to prevent any kind of opposition: *the oppressive rule of the Ceaucescus in Romania* | *The Nationalists passed more and more oppressive race laws.*

4 different systems of government

democracy /dɪˈmɒkrəsi‖dɪˈmɑː-/ [n U] a system of government in which everyone in the country can vote to choose the government: *In 1974 democracy returned to Greece after seven years of military rule.*

democracy [n C] a country in which everyone can vote to choose the government: *the democracies of Western Europe*

plural **democracies**

democratic /ˌdeməˈkrætɪk◄/ [adj] a **democratic** country, government, or political system is one in which the people vote to choose the government: *Pakistan's first ever democratic elections*

republic /rɪˈpʌblɪk/ [n C] a country whose leader is a president, not a king or queen: *the French Republic* | *Prime Minister Keating had plans to turn Australia into a republic.*

+ of *the People's Republic of China*

monarchy /ˈmɒnəʳki‖ˈmɑːn-/ [n C/U] a system of government in which a country is ruled by a king or queen: *questions about the future of the monarchy in Britain*

plural **monarchies**

5 one part of a government which deals with health, education, defence etc

department /dɪˈpɑːʳtmənt/ [n C] one of the separate parts of a government, which is responsible for a particular subject, such as health, education, or defence

the Department of Education/Health/Transport etc BRITISH *She is now head of the Department of Education.*

the Defense/Justice/Treasury Department AMERICAN *His brother Bobby was head of the Justice Department.*

ministry /ˈmɪnɪstri/ [n C] a government department in Britain and some other countries: *She works at the Ministry of Defence.*

plural **ministries**

minister /ˈmɪnɪstəʳ/ [n C] the politician who leads a government department in Britain and some other countries: *a meeting of European finance ministers in Bonn*

When you see **EC**, go to the **ESSENTIAL COMMUNICATION** section.

⚠ **Minister** is not the official job title of the leader of a government department in Britain, but it is often used. The official title is 'Secretary of State'. But this title has a different meaning in the US, where it means the person in charge of the US's relations with other countries.

6 the leader of a country

leader /'liːdəʳ/ [n C] someone, such as a president or prime minister, who is in charge of the government of a country: *World leaders are meeting in Geneva today to consider the peace plan.* | *former Soviet leader Mikhail Gorbachev*

⚠ **Leader** is not an official title.

president /'prezɪ̩dənt/ [n C] the official leader of a country that does not have a king or queen: *President Chirac*
+ **of** *the President of Egypt*

prime minister /ˌpraɪm 'mɪnɪ̩stəʳ/ [n C] the elected leader of the government in a country that has a parliament: *The British Prime Minister lives at 10 Downing Street.*
+ **of** *the Prime Minister of India*

ruler /'ruːləʳ/ [n C] someone, such as a king or queen or a military leader, who has the power to run the government of a country: *an unjust ruler* | *Nigeria's military rulers*
+ **of** *Ramses II, ruler of Egypt in 1300 BC*

king /kɪŋ/ [n C] a man who is the official leader of a country because he is a member of a royal family: *King George VI*
+ **of** *King Juan Carlos of Spain* | *the King of Morocco*

queen /kwiːn/ [n C] a woman who is the official leader of a country because she is a member of a royal family, or a woman who is the wife of a king: *Queen Elizabeth*
+ **of** *the Queen of Sweden*

7 to govern or rule a country

govern /'ɡʌvən‖-ərn/ [v I/T] if a political party or group **governs** a country, its members make all the important decisions

about laws, taxes, relations with other countries etc: *The Conservative Party has governed Britain for over 15 years now.*

run /rʌn/ [v T] to control a country – use this especially about a powerful person or group that controls a country but has not been elected: *Who's running this country, the government or the trade unions?* | *The revolutionary council ran the country until democratic elections were held.*
running – ran – have run

be in power /biː ɪn 'paʊəʳ/ if a political party or a leader **is in power** at a particular time, they are the government or leader of a country at that time: *Castro has been in power for more than 30 years.* | *Taxes were higher when the Social Democrats were in power.*

rule /ruːl/ [v T] if a king, queen, military leader, or a foreign government **rules** a country, they have official power over it: *At that time India was ruled by the British.* | *In 1860 Italy was a collection of small states ruled by princes and dukes.*
  rule [n U] when a country is ruled by a king or queen, a military leader or a foreign government: *For many years Algeria was under French rule (=was ruled by the French).*

8 activities and ideas that are connected with governing a country

political /pə'lɪtɪkəl/ [adj usually before noun] connected with the government of a country or local area: *There are two main political parties in the US.* | *the British political system* | *She began her political career as a city councillor.*

politics /'pɒlɪtɪks‖'pɑː-/ [n U] activities and ideas that are connected with governing a country or local area: *Gun control is one of the biggest issues in American politics at the moment.* | *Many young people aren't interested in politics.*
party politics (=when political parties are trying to get an advantage over each other)
local politics (=politics in a town or city) *She's always been deeply involved in local politics.*

go into politics (=start working in politics) *He didn't go into politics until he was over forty.*

GROUP

➡ if you mean 'a group of people who play music together', go to MUSIC
➡ see also CROWD, TYPE

1 a group of people together in one place

group /gruːp/ [n C] several people who are together in the same place
+ of *Outside the school, little groups of friends were talking to each other.* I *an old photograph of a group of soldiers sitting on the ground*
in groups (=forming separate groups) *Men stood in groups on street corners.*
get into a group (=make a group with other people so that you can do something together) *The teacher told us to get into groups of three.*

crowd /kraʊd/ [n C] a large number of people who are all together in the same place: *A big crowd gathered to see President Mandela.* I *a football crowd*
+ of *A crowd of reporters was waiting for her at the airport.*

⚠ In British English you can use **crowd** with a singular or plural verb: *The crowd was/were becoming impatient.* In American English, always use a singular verb: *The crowd was becoming impatient.*

⚠ You can say **crowds** of people when you mean a lot of people very close together: *Crowds of tourists were trying to get into the cathedral.*

2 a group of people who do things together

party /ˈpɑːʳti/ [n C] a group of people that someone has organized in order to go somewhere or do something
+ of *John was taking a party of tourists around the museum.* I *A party of Japanese businessmen will be visiting the factory next week.*

a search/rescue party (=a group of people trying to find and help someone who is in danger)
plural **parties**

bunch/crowd /bʌntʃ, kraʊd/ [n singular] INFORMAL ESPECIALLY SPOKEN a group of people who do things together or spend time together: *The people on my French course are a really friendly bunch.*
+ of *There was the usual crowd of students standing at the bar.*

gang /ɡæŋ/ [n C] a group of young people who spend time together, especially a group that causes trouble, fights with other groups etc
gang of youths/kids *There are always gangs of kids standing around the shopping mall.*
rival gang (=a gang that fights with another gang) *Fighting broke out between two rival gangs.*

3 a group of people who are similar in some way or have similar ideas

group /gruːp/ [n C] a number of people who are similar in some way, or who have the same ideas and aims: *Their policy was to keep people from different racial groups apart.*
+ of *The factory was burned down by a group of animal-rights activists.*
age group/income group etc (=all the people of about the same age, with about the same income etc) *Families in the lowest income group could not afford to educate their children.*

movement /ˈmuːvmənt/ [n C] a large group of people who share the same ideas and beliefs, and who work together to achieve something important: *She was active in a number of political movements, including the campaign to end slavery.*
the peace/environmental/independence etc movement *one of the leaders of the pro-democracy movement*

4 a group of people who work with each other

team /tiːm/ [n C] a group of people who work together to do a job: *There will be a meeting for all members of the team next Wednesday.*

G

+ of *The coins were discovered by a team of archaeologists.* | *Powell headed Mrs Thatcher's team of advisers.*

research/medical team *Dr Gaultier and his medical team worked in the refugee camps for over a year.*

⚠ In British English, you can use **team** with a singular or plural verb: *A team of police divers is/are searching the lake.* In American English, always use a singular verb: *A team of police divers is searching the lake.*

crew /kruː/ [n C] the people who work together on a ship or plane: *The captain and crew would like to welcome you on board Flight 381 to Geneva.*

committee /kə'mɪti/ [n C] a small group of people in an organization, company, or club who have been chosen to make decisions that affect everyone in the organization: *Bill Dean has been elected chairman of the committee.*

finance/health/housing committee *The finance committee has decided to raise membership fees for next season.*

be on a committee (=be a member of a committee) *She's been on the Church committee for 20 years.*

⚠ You can also use **committee** before a noun, like an adjective: *We have three new committee members this year.* | *a committee meeting*

⚠ In British English, you can use **committee** with a singular or plural verb: *The committee has decided/have decided to award you a scholarship.* In American English, always use a singular verb: *The committee has decided to award you a scholarship.*

5 a group of things together in one place or connected in some way

group /gruːp/ [n C] several things that are together in one place or connected in some way

+ of *The house was hidden behind a tall group of trees.* | *The letter 'F' is one of a group of consonants called 'fricatives'.* | *News International is a group of companies that produce newspapers and TV programmes.*

set /set/ [n C] a group of similar things that are used together, or a group of connected ideas, facts etc: *a chess set*

+ of *I gave an extra set of house keys to my neighbours.* | *a set of rules* | *We started the meeting by agreeing on a set of objectives.*

collection /kə'lekʃən/ [n C] a group of similar things that have been put together because they are interesting or attractive

+ of *The museum has a superb collection of Mexican pottery.*

art/stamp/postcard collection *Have you seen her record collection – it's enormous!*

bundle /'bʌndl/ [n C] several things of the same kind, such as papers, clothes, or sticks, that are fastened or tied together: *She keeps all his old letters, tied up in bundles.*

+ of *a bundle of firewood*

bunch /bʌntʃ/ [n C] a **bunch** of flowers is a collection of flowers tied together; a **bunch** of fruit is several pieces of fruit which grow together and which you buy as one piece: *a small girl carrying a huge bunch of roses* | *I bought a kilo of apples and a bunch of grapes.* | *a bunch of bananas*

plural **bunches**

6 a group of things on top of each other

pile /paɪl/ [n C] several things of the same kind placed one on top of the other

+ of *Greg carried the pile of ironed shirts upstairs.*

in piles *The books were arranged in neat piles on her desk.*

heap /hiːp/ [n C] a lot of things lying one on top of the other in an untidy way

+ of *There was a huge heap of blankets and pillows on the bed.*

in a heap *The children had left all their wet towels in a heap on the bathroom floor.*

7 to put things or people into groups

sort /sɔːrt/ [v T] to arrange a large number of things by putting them in different groups, so that you can deal with each group separately: *It takes a couple of hours to sort the mail in the morning.*

sort sth into sth *We sorted all the clothes into two piles.*

categorize (also **categorise** BRITISH) /ˈkætɪɡəraɪz/ [v T] to decide which group something should belong to, when there is a clear system of several groups
categorize sth according to sth *The hotels are categorized according to the standard of the rooms and services they offer.*
categorize sth as sth (=say which group it is in) *The store categorizes all records from Asia and Africa as 'World Music'.*

be grouped /biː ˈɡruːpt/ if people or things **are grouped**, they have been put together into separate groups according to a system
+ according to *The vehicles are grouped according to engine size.*
+ together *Non-fiction books are grouped together under different subjects.*
+ into *Most European languages can be grouped into two main families.*

GROW

➡ if you mean 'when a number or amount gets bigger', go to **INCREASE**
➡ see also **BIG**

1 when people, animals, or plants get bigger

grow

Sunflowers can grow to a height of ten feet.

grow /ɡrəʊ/ [v I] to become bigger or taller over a period of time: *Tom has really grown since I last saw him.*
+ to *Sunflowers can grow to a height of ten feet.*

grow one metre/two centimetres/six inches etc *Amy grew 9 inches last year.*
+ into *Within a few years, these saplings will grow into tall trees.*

growing – grew – have grown

develop /dɪˈveləp/ [v I] if a child, plant, or animal **develops**, it gradually changes into the form it will have as an adult: *The baby develops very quickly during the first few weeks of pregnancy.*
+ into *In less than 12 weeks the chicks will develop into adult birds.*

get taller/get bigger /ˌɡet ˈtɔːləʳ, ˌɡet ˈbɪɡəʳ/ to grow and become taller, especially in a short period of time: *Eleanor's getting bigger, isn't she? I hardly recognised her.* | *The grass got taller and taller over the summer.*

2 to make plants or vegetables grow

grow /ɡrəʊ/ [v T] to look after plants, vegetables, or crops so that they develop and grow: *Farmers in this area grow mainly wheat.* | *It's very satisfying growing your own vegetables.*

growing – grew – have grown

plant /plɑːnt‖plænt/ [v T] to put seeds or young flowers or plants into the soil so that they will grow: *Plant the seeds outside in late spring.* | *They planted an oak tree in the middle of the field.*

GUESS

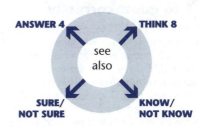

1 to guess something

guess /ɡes/ [v I/T] to give an answer or decide that something is probably true, when you do not know enough to be sure: *Are you sure Linda's pregnant, or are you just guessing?* | *We had to guess a* lot of the answers. | I didn't know all the answers, so I just had to guess some of them.

guess what/how/who etc Listen to the voices of these famous people and try to guess who they are.

+ (that) Detectives guessed that her attacker was someone she knew. | I guessed she was probably the new secretary.

have a guess BRITISH **take a guess** ESPECIALLY AMERICAN /ˌhæv ə ˈges, ˌteɪk ə ˈges/ to guess an answer, amount, or number: "How much rent do you pay for your apartment?" "Take a guess."

+ at Have a guess at the answer, then check it with your calculator.

estimate /ˈestɪmeɪt/ [v T] to say how much something will cost, or how many of something there are etc, partly by calculating and partly by guessing

+ that Police estimate that 10,000 people took part in the demonstration.

estimate sth at $350/£400 etc The mechanic estimated the cost of repairs at $350.

estimate what/where/how much etc Can you estimate how much fabric you will need for the curtains?

⚲**my guess is...** /maɪ ˈges ɪz/ SPOKEN say this when you are telling someone what you think has probably happened or will probably happen

+ (that) My guess is she'll move back to the States. | My guess is that they've been delayed in a traffic jam.

2 to guess correctly

guess /ges/ [v I/T] to guess correctly that something is true, or guess the right answer to something: "How old are you – about 27?" "Yes, how did you guess?"

guess what/who/where When I saw how upset she was, I guessed immediately what had happened.

+ (that) We'd already guessed that you were sisters – you look so alike!

guess the truth They had already guessed the truth about their son's disappearance.

3 to guess incorrectly

overestimate /ˌəʊvərˈestɪmeɪt/ [v T] to guess wrongly, by thinking that the amount, level, or cost of something is bigger, more expensive etc than it really is: People overestimated the risk of catching the disease.

underestimate /ˌʌndərˈestɪmeɪt/ [v T] to guess wrongly, by thinking that the amount, level, or cost of something is smaller, less expensive etc than it really is: They underestimated the amount of time it would take to finish the work.

4 an attempt to guess something

guess /ges/ [n C] an attempt to guess something: It'll probably take about 10 hours to get there, but that's just a guess.

make a guess (=try to guess something) I don't know why she left him, but I think I can make a guess.

⚲**good guess** ESPECIALLY SPOKEN "When was the house built – about 1600?" "Good guess – it was 1624."

rough guess (=one that is not intended to be exact) We think there are about 5 million users on the Internet, but this is only a rough guess.

guesswork /ˈgeswɜːrk/ [n U] when you try to understand something or find the answer to something by guessing, because you do not have all the information you need: The police investigation was largely based on guesswork.

speculation /ˌspekjʊˈleɪʃən/ [n U] when a lot of people, especially in newspapers and on television, try to guess what is happening or what will happen because they do not have much definite information

+ about There has been speculation about links between the Mayor and the Mafia.

+ that The latest defeat for the government led to increasing speculation that the Prime Minister would resign.

GUILTY / NOT GUILTY

responsible for a crime or for doing something bad

➡ look here for ...
- guilty of a crime or mistake
- feeling bad because you have done something wrong

➡ if you mean 'think or say that someone is responsible for a mistake or something bad', go to **BLAME**

ASHAMED   SORRY

see also

CRIME   COURT/TRIAL

1 guilty

guilty /ˈɡɪlti/ [adj] if someone is **guilty** of a crime, he or she is the person that did it
find sb guilty (=decide in a law court that someone is guilty) *The jury found Sewell guilty and he was sent to prison.*
guilty of murder/rape/a crime etc *A 23-year-old woman was found guilty of murder in the Central Court yesterday.*
plead guilty (=say in a law court that you are guilty of a crime) *Roberts pleaded guilty to driving without insurance.*

responsible /rɪˈspɒnsɪbəl‖rɪˈspɑːn-/ [adj] if someone is **responsible** for a crime, accident, or mistake, they did it or made it happen: *The other driver was responsible for the accident, and he should pay for the damage.*
+ for *Police believe a local gang is responsible for the recent burglaries.* | *Mrs Williams says that the hospital was responsible for her husband's death.*

⚠ Use **responsible** especially to talk about accidents and mistakes caused by carelessness, or when no-one knows for certain who did it.

2 not guilty

innocent /ˈɪnəsənt/ [adj] if someone is **innocent** of a crime they did not do it – use this especially about someone that other people think is guilty: *"I didn't kill anyone – I'm innocent!" Davies shouted.* | *Bates had allowed an innocent man to go to jail for his crime.*
+ of *Many people are kept in over-crowded prisons, even people who are innocent of any crime.*
   innocence /ˈɪnəsəns/ [n U] when you are not guilty of a crime: *Her parents were convinced of her innocence.*

not guilty /nɒt ˈɡɪlti/ if someone is **not guilty** of a crime, they did not do it – use this especially when a court has decided that someone did not do a crime
find sb not guilty (of sth) (=decide in a law court that someone is not guilty) *The two women were found not guilty of drug-trafficking.*

be acquitted /biː əˈkwɪtɪd/ if someone **is acquitted** by a law court, they are officially told that they are not guilty of a crime
+ of *McQuade has been acquitted of attempted murder.*

3 when you feel ashamed about doing something bad

feel guilty /ˌfiːl ˈɡɪlti/ to feel worried and unhappy because you have done something wrong or because you have upset someone: *I felt really guilty after spending all that money.* | *Are you feeling guilty because you didn't help her?*
+ about *Ed felt guilty about leaving work so early.*

be/feel ashamed /ˌbiː, ˌfiːl əˈʃeɪmd/ to feel very guilty and disappointed with yourself because you have done something wrong or behaved in an unpleasant or embarrassing way: *She felt thoroughly ashamed when she remembered how drunk she'd been.*
+ of *I feel ashamed of what I did.*
be/feel ashamed to do sth *I'm ashamed to admit it, but I wasn't really sorry when he died.*

G

be/feel ashamed of yourself (=feel very guilty about something that you have done) *You should be ashamed of yourself, being so rude to your grandmother.*

feel responsible /ˌfiːl rɪˈspɒnsᵻbəl‖ -ˈspɑːn-/ to feel that you made something bad happen, especially because you were careless or you could have prevented it from happening

+ for *For a long time afterwards I felt responsible for his death.*

feel bad /ˌfiːl ˈbæd/ ESPECIALLY SPOKEN to feel very sorry because you have upset someone or done something that you should not have done

+ that *I should have told Helen I was sorry. I feel really bad that I didn't.*

+ about *She feels bad about hitting the kids but she just can't stop.*

have a guilty conscience /hæv ə ˌgɪlti ˈkɒnʃəns‖-ˈkɑːn-/ to feel worried and unhappy for a long time because you know that you have done something wrong, especially something that other people do not know about: *"He's so nice – he's always buying flowers for his wife." "That's only because he has a guilty conscience about his mistress."*

guilt /gɪlt/ [n U] the feeling you have when you have done something that you know is wrong

feeling of guilt *People often have feelings of guilt after a divorce.*

G

H

HAIR

➡ see also **SHINE, DESCRIBING PEOPLE**

⚠ Don't say 'she has dark hairs'. Say **she has dark hair**. Never use 'hairs' to talk about all the hair on your head.

⚠ Don't say 'she has blonde long hair'. Say **she has long blonde hair**.

1 how long someone's hair is, or how much hair they have

short /ʃɔːʳt/ [adj] *She's a pretty girl with short black hair.*

long /lɒŋ‖lɔːŋ/ [adj] *That's my sister – the one with long blonde hair.* | *Jim's hair used to be quite long.*

shoulder-length /ˈʃəʊldəʳ leŋθ/ [adj] **shoulder-length** hair is long enough to reach your shoulders: *Do you know Melissa? She has shoulder-length brown hair.*

down to /ˈdaʊn tuː/ if someone's hair is **down to** their waist, shoulders etc, it is long enough to reach their waist, their shoulders etc: *When Gran was young, she had beautiful black hair down to her waist.* | *'I used to have hair down to here,' said Valerie indicating her shoulder.*

bald /bɔːld/ someone who is **bald** has little or no hair on their head: *a short bald man in a dark suit*
go bald (=lose your hair) *My father started going bald in his twenties.*

thick /θɪk/ [adj] if someone's hair is **thick** they have a lot of hair growing closely together: *Maria had beautiful thick dark hair.*

in a bob/bobbed /ɪn ə ˈbɒb, bɒbd‖-ˈbɑːb, bɑːbd/ if a woman's hair is **in a bob** or is **bobbed,** it is cut to the same length all around, except at the front, and it ends at about the level of her chin

ponytail /ˈpəʊniˌteɪl/ [n C] long hair tied together at the back of your head and hanging down like a tail: *Who's that guy over there with the ponytail?*
in a ponytail *Kathryn always wears her hair in a ponytail.*

2 how straight or curly someone's hair is

straight /streɪt/ [adj] **straight** hair does not have any curls: *Yuri's straight black hair was thick and shiny.*

wavy /ˈweɪvi/ [adj] **wavy** hair is not straight or curly, but has smooth curves in it: *Her wavy brown hair was tied back with a red ribbon.*
wavy – wavier – waviest

curly /ˈkɜːʳli/ [adj] **curly** hair has tight curls: *a chubby baby with blond curly hair*
curly – curlier – curliest

frizzy /ˈfrɪzi/ [adj] **frizzy** hair is full of stiff curls going in all directions, and looks as if it is difficult to control

3 what colour someone's hair is

dark /dɑːʳk/ [adj] **dark** hair is black or brown: *The attacker is described as 5ft 9ins tall, with short dark hair.* | *Her husband is tall and dark.* (=he has dark hair)

fair /feəʳ/ [adj] **fair** hair is light brown or yellow: *a little boy with fair hair and blue eyes*

blonde/blond /blɒnd‖blɑːnd/ [adj] **blonde** hair is very light brown or yellow – use **blonde** about women, and **blond** about men: *Janet's got beautiful long blonde hair.* | *Nicola has dark hair but her brother is blond.* (=he has blond hair)

red /red/ [adj] **red** hair is an orange-brown colour: *Ruth's the one with red hair.*

grey BRITISH **gray** AMERICAN /greɪ/ [adj] **grey** or **gray** hair is the colour between black and white, which most people's hair is when they are older: *a middle-aged businessman with grey hair and a grey suit*

highlights/streaks /ˈhaɪlaɪts, striːks/ [n plural] parts of your hair that have been made a lighter colour than the rest: *She has brown hair with blonde highlights.*

H

-haired /heəᵈd/ **dark-haired/fair-haired/red-haired** having dark hair, fair hair etc: *a tall, fair-haired guy* | *Two grey-haired ladies got on the bus.*

4 what shape someone's hair is

hairstyle /'heəʳstaɪl/ [n C] the shape of someone's hair and the way it has been cut: *I think it's time I changed my hairstyle.* | *You can get magazines that show you all the latest hairstyles.*

haircut /'heəʳkʌt/ [n C] the way someone's hair has been cut – use this either when someone's hair has just been cut, or to talk about a particular style of haircut: *I like your new haircut, Helen!* | *Her short, neat haircut and dark suit made her look rather serious.*

5 to have your hair cut or treated

have your hair cut /ˌhæv jɔːʳ 'heəʳ kʌt/ to pay someone to cut your hair: *Where do you have your hair cut?*
have your hair cut short *Lee had his hair cut really short.*

haircut /'heəʳkʌt/ [n C] when you have your hair cut: *I really need a haircut.*

hairdresser also **hairdresser's** BRITISH /'heəʳˌdresəʳ(z)/ [n C] the shop where you go to have your hair cut, washed, and put into particular styles: *I'm going to the hairdresser's – see you later.*
    hairdresser [n C] someone whose job is to cut and treat hair: *Teresa used to be a hairdresser.*

dye /daɪ/ [v T] to change the colour of someone's hair using chemicals: *Peter's hair is so black – I'm sure he dyes it.*
dye sb's hair blond/black etc *When she was fifteen she dyed her hair bright pink.*
    dyed [adj] *Do you think his hair is dyed?.*

perm /pɜːʳm/ [n C] when straight hair is made curly by using a chemical treatment
have a perm *Your hair would look thicker if you had a perm.*
    permed [adj] *permed hair*

When you see **EC**, go to the **ESSENTIAL COMMUNICATION** section.

6 to wash and brush your hair

wash /wɒʃ‖wɔːʃ, wɑːʃ/ [v T] to make your hair clean by using water and shampoo: *Do you wash your hair every day?*

shampoo /ʃæm'puː/ [n C/U] special liquid soap that you use to wash your hair
    shampoo [v T] to wash your hair

brush /brʌʃ/ [v T] to make your hair smooth and tidy using a brush: *She brushed her hair until it shone.*
    brush/hairbrush [n C] the thing you use to brush your hair: *"Where's my hairbrush?" "I think it's in the bathroom."*

comb /kəʊm/ [v T] to make your hair tidy by using a flat piece of plastic or metal with a row of thin teeth along one side: *Just give me a minute to comb my hair.*
    comb [n C] the thing you use to comb your hair: *Can I borrow your comb?*

blow-dry /'bləʊ draɪ/ [v T] to dry hair and shape it after washing it, using a hairdryer

HAPPEN

➡ see also START, FINISH

1 to happen

happen /'hæpən/ [v I] use this especially about things that have not been planned to happen or that people do not expect: *The accident happened at 2 pm yesterday.* | *What's happened? Why are you crying?* | *Before I knew what was happening, the man grabbed my bag and ran.* | *There's something happening in the street – come and look!*

take place /ˌteɪk 'pleɪs/ to happen – use this about events, performances, ceremonies and other things that have been planned to happen: *The wedding will take place on 23rd August.* | *Police are trying to prevent the demonstration taking place.*

⚠ **Take place** is more formal than **happen.**

there is /ðeər ɪz/ if **there is** an event, accident, change etc, it happens, especially when you do not expect it: *There* has been a serious accident on the Santa Monica Freeway. | You should see a doctor if there is any change in your condition. | There's a concert at the school next Saturday.

be going on /biː ˌgəʊɪŋ ˈɒn/ to be happening – use this especially about something that you think is bad or that you are unable to control: *The kids are being very quiet. I'd better see what's going on! | She says that women are discriminated against, and that this has been going on for years.*

occur /əˈkɜːr/ [v I] FORMAL to happen – use this especially about changes, chemical reactions, and other things that happen naturally: *Major earthquakes like this occur very rarely. | The metal becomes liquid if heated, and this occurs at temperatures of over 300°C. | Death occurred at approximately 12.30.*
occurring – occurred – have occurred

come true /ˌkʌm ˈtruː/ if a dream or wish **comes true**, it really happens after you have waited for it for a long time: *Patterson's dream came true when he won the Boston marathon on his first attempt.*

2 something that happens

event /ɪˈvent/ [n C] something that happens, especially something important or interesting, or something that has been organized and involves a lot of people: *The book discusses the events leading up to the outbreak of World War Two. | The Ryder Cup is the big golfing event this month. | 'The X Files' is a programme about strange and unexplained events.*
annual event (=an event held every year) *The beer festival is an annual event.*

incident /ˈɪnsɪdənt/ [n C] FORMAL something that happens, especially a crime or an accident: *A man has been charged with murder following an incident at a house in North London.*
without incident (=without any problems or trouble) *The fans were well behaved, and the game passed without incident.*

occasion /əˈkeɪʒən/ [n C] an important social event or celebration: *It's Mark's 21st birthday and we're having a party to*

celebrate the occasion. | *The President is only seen on important state occasions.*
special occasion *The hotel caters for weddings, birthdays, and other special occasions.*

affair /əˈfeər/ [n C] something that happens in politics or public life, especially something shocking or illegal, which is talked about in the newspapers and on television: *President Nixon was forced to resign after the Watergate affair. | Mr Major did nothing, hoping that the affair would soon be forgotten.*

3 when something happens to someone or something

happen to sb/sth /ˈhæpən tuː (sb/sth)/ [phrasal verb T] if something **happens to** someone or something, it happens and has an effect on them: *What's happened to Dave? He seems in a really bad mood. | A lot of people don't seem to care about what is happening to the environment.*

experience /ɪkˈspɪəriəns/ [v T] FORMAL if a person or organization **experiences** a problem, change etc, it happens to them: *Most of us will experience this kind of problem at some time in our lives. | Many local companies have recently experienced financial difficulties.*

⚠ **Experience** is more formal than **happen to.**

HAPPY

➡ opposite **SAD**

ENTHUSIASTIC/ UNENTHUSIASTIC

RELAX   **SMILE**

LAUGH   see also   **ENJOY**

EXCITING/ EXCITED   **SATISFIED/ DISSATISFIED**

COMFORTABLE/ UNCOMFORTABLE   **CONFIDENT/ NOT CONFIDENT**

1 feeling happy

happy /'hæpi/ [adj] someone who is **happy** seems relaxed and satisfied, and feels that their life is good, especially because they are in a situation, job, or relationship that they enjoy: *For the first five years of her marriage, they were extremely happy.* | *Liz seems a lot happier these days, doesn't she?* | *the children's happy faces*
happy doing sth *I was very happy working in that office – the people were all really friendly.*
a happy time/childhood/life/marriage (=a time when you are happy) *That year was the happiest time of my life.*
happy – happier – happiest

cheerful /'tʃɪəfəl/ [adj] someone who is **cheerful** seems to be always happy, for example by smiling, and friendly: *Ed's a very cheerful, friendly person.* | *'My name's Rosie,' she said with a cheerful smile.*

be in a good mood /biː ɪn ə ˌgʊd 'muːd/ to feel happy and behave in a happy, friendly way – use this about someone who is happy now, but is not always happy: *Their teacher was in an unusually good mood that morning.* | *Don't ask him now – wait till he's in a good mood.*

2 happy because something good has happened

happy /'hæpi/ [adj] feeling happy because something good has happened to you or is going to happen: *They returned home from their vacation feeling relaxed and happy.*
happy to do sth *I'm very happy to be back here again.*
+ about *Is she happy about being pregnant?*
+ (that) *He was very happy that Jane would be spending Christmas with them.*
happy – happier – happiest

pleased /pliːzd/ [adj not before noun] happy and satisfied with something that has happened, especially something that has happened to someone else or something good they have done: *"Did you know that Barbara had a baby girl?" "Oh, I am pleased."*

+ with *Amanda's teachers seem very pleased with her progress.*
be pleased to hear/see/say *You'll be pleased to hear that your application has been successful.*
+ (that) *I'm very pleased that so many people have agreed to help us.*

⚠ If someone tells you about something good that has happened, don't say 'I am happy'. Say **I am pleased** or **I am delighted**

glad /glæd/ [adj not before noun] pleased about a situation, especially because it has improved or because it is not as bad as it could have been: *We were all glad when it was time to go home.*
glad to be/hear/say/see *She was glad to hear he had arrived home safely.*
+ (that) *I'm really glad you like the present.* | *Maria looked around at the other guests – she was glad she had decided to wear her best clothes.*

delighted /dɪ'laɪtɪd/ [adj not before noun] extremely happy because something very good has happened: *She has been offered a job in Japan, and she's delighted of course.*
+ (that) *He was delighted that she had asked him to come.*
+ with/by/at *Wesley said he was delighted with the court's decision.*
delighted to be/hear/see etc *We're absolutely delighted to hear that you're getting engaged.*

⚠ Don't say 'very delighted'. Say **absolutely delighted**

satisfied /'sætɪsfaɪd/ [adj] pleased because something has happened in the way you want it to, or because something is as good as you expect it to be
+ with *I'm very satisfied with the results of our discussions.*
satisfied look/expression/smile *Blake leaned back with a satisfied smile.*

3 a happy feeling

happiness /'hæpinɪs/ [n U] the feeling you have when you are happy: *She married at the age of 56, and at last found true happiness.* | *I don't think he really cares about his wife's happiness.*

pleasure /ˈpleʒəʳ/ [n U] the feeling you have when you are doing something you enjoy or when something very nice has happened to you: *Most craftsmen get a lot of pleasure out of making things.*

give/bring pleasure to sb *His music has brought pleasure to people all over the world.*

for pleasure (=when you do something just for enjoyment, not because you have to) *reading for pleasure*

satisfaction /ˌsætɪsˈfækʃən/ [n U] the feeling of happiness you get when you have done a job well, or when you have worked hard to achieve something: *It was working with children that gave Diana the most satisfaction.*

great/deep satisfaction *Golding always said that writing was hard work but it gave him great satisfaction.*

get satisfaction from *She gets a lot of satisfaction from seeing her designs turned into actual products.*

job satisfaction (=the feeling you have when you enjoy your job)

joy /dʒɔɪ/ [n U] ESPECIALLY WRITTEN a feeling of very great happiness: *It's hard to describe the joy we felt, seeing each other again after so many years.*

4 happy because you are no longer worried about something

relieved /rɪˈliːvd/ [adj] happy because you are no longer worried about something, especially because something bad did not happen or something unpleasant has ended: *Kate looked relieved when she saw her husband walk through the door.*

relieved to see/know/hear etc *We were so relieved to hear that nobody was hurt in the accident.*

+ (that) *'I'm fine,' she replied, relieved that he was no longer angry with her.*

relief /rɪˈliːf/ [n singular/U] the feeling you have when you are no longer worried about something

it is a relief to do sth *It was a relief to get home after that terrible journey.*

with relief *Martha noticed with relief that the strange man was no longer looking at her.*

to sb's relief (=making someone feel relieved) *He ran back to the restaurant and, to his relief, found his wallet was still on the table.*

5 to make someone feel happy

make sb happy /ˌmeɪk (sb) ˈhæpi/ to make someone feel happy: *Would winning ten million dollars really make you happy?* | *Nothing I did ever seemed to make him happy.*

please /pliːz/ [v T] to make someone happy by doing what they want you to do: *I only got married to please my parents.* | *Tony will do anything to please the boss.*

satisfying /ˈsætɪsfaɪ-ɪŋ/ [adj] a **satisfying** job, activity, or experience is one that you enjoy, especially because you feel you are doing something good and useful: *Growing your own food can be very satisfying.*

cheer up /ˌtʃɪər ˈʌp/ [phrasal verb T] to make someone feel happy again after they have been unhappy

cheer up sb *Sending flowers is a great way to cheer up a friend who's depressed.*

cheer sb up *I'm taking Angie out to a restaurant to cheer her up.*

6 to feel happy again after feeling sad

cheer up /ˌtʃɪər ˈʌp/ [phrasal verb I] to feel happy again after you have been unhappy: *Matt soon cheered up when I offered to take him to the ball game.* | *Cheer up, Jenny! Things aren't so bad.*

HARD

➡ opposite **SOFT**
➡ if you mean 'hard to do or understand', go to **DIFFICULT**

1 something that does not bend or change its shape

hard /hɑːʳd/ [adj] something that is **hard** does not change its shape when you press on it: *The seats on the bus were hard and uncomfortable.* | *During the night* the ground had become frozen and hard. | Diamonds are the hardest known substance in the world.

solid /ˈsɒlɨd‖ˈsɑː-/ [adj] something that is **solid** is made of thick hard material, is not hollow, and is difficult to damage or break: That table looks pretty solid – why don't you put the computer there? | a solid concrete floor | a solid oak door

firm /fɜːrm/ [adj] not completely hard, but not changing shape much when you press it – use this about things that are sometimes soft, such as fruit, muscles, or the ground: exercises to make your stomach muscles nice and firm | I sat back and rested my head against a firm cushion.

stiff /stɪf/ [adj] not easy to bend – use this about things like paper or cloth: He stuck the photos onto a sheet of stiff black cardboard. | The collar of his shirt felt stiff and uncomfortable.

tough /tʌf/ [adj] meat that is **tough** is difficult to eat because it is not soft enough; materials that are **tough** are strong and difficult to break or damage: My steak's really tough – how's yours? | walking boots with tough rubber soles

2 to become hard or to make something hard

harden /ˈhɑːrdn/ [v I/T] to become hard or to make something hard: The glue needs about 24 hours to harden. | The steel is hardened by heating it to a very high temperature.

set /set/ [v I] if a liquid substance **sets**, it becomes harder – use this to talk about something that slowly becomes harder after it is mixed with water, for example, food or building materials: How long does it take for cement to set?
setting – set – have set

HATE

1 to hate someone or something
➡ see also LOVE, LIKE/NOT LIKE, ▣ OPINIONS

hate /heɪt/ [v T] to dislike someone or something very much: Dave hated his parents when he was a teenager. | Why do you hate school so much?
hate doing sth Like most people, Sally hated being unemployed, and she was very relieved when she found a new job.

can't stand/can't bear /ˌkɑːnt ˈstænd, ˌkɑːnt ˈbeəʳ‖ˌkænt-/ ESPECIALLY SPOKEN if you can't stand or can't bear a person or situation, they make you feel very uncomfortable, very angry or very unhappy, and you want to avoid them: They had loved each other once, but now they couldn't stand each other. | When I was pregnant, I couln't bear the smell of meat cooking.
can't stand/bear doing sth She couldn't bear seeing him in such pain.
can't stand/bear sb doing sth I can't stand people smoking while I'm eating.

detest/loathe /dɪˈtest, ləʊð/ [v T] to hate someone or something very much especially because they make you feel very angry: She always detested any form of cruelty. | Mrs Morel was married to a man whom she loathed.
detest/loathe doing sth Above all, Williams detested being shouted at by officers young enough to be his sons.

⚠ Use **detest** or **loathe** especially when you are writing stories or descriptions.

2 a feeling of hating someone or something

hatred /ˈheɪtrɨd/ [n U] an extremely strong feeling of hating someone or something: I could see the jealousy and hatred in Jeff's eyes.
+ of Tom had a hatred of any kind of authority.
+ for/towards use this about a feeling of hate for people, not things: Strangely, the murderer said he never felt hatred for any of his victims.

3 someone who hates you and wants to harm you
➡ opposite FRIEND

enemy /ˈenəmi/ [n C] Did your husband have any enemies?

make a lot of enemies (=make a lot of people hate you and want to harm you) *He made a lot of enemies while he was working as a police officer.*

plural **enemies**

HAVE/NOT HAVE

➡ see also **OWN, GET**

1 to have something such as a physical feature, a skill, or a quality

➡ see also **DESCRIBING PEOPLE**

have /hæv/ [v T] *He's a good teacher and he has a lot of patience.* | *The city has plenty of good hotels and restaurants.* | *My sweater has a hole in it.* | *Do you have any information about apartments to rent?*

having – had – have had

> ⚠ Don't say 'I am having', 'he is having' etc. Say **I have, he has** etc: *She has blue eyes.*

have got /həv ˈɡɒt‖-ˈɡɑːt/ [v T] ESPECIALLY BRITISH to have a feature, skill, or quality: *My sister's got blonde hair and blue eyes.* | *Our new car's got a sun roof and CD player.* | *She told us she'd got a lot of experience with computers.*

> ⚠ In spoken British English **have got** is more common than **have.**
>
> ⚠ **Have got** and **had got** are usually used in their short forms: **I've got, she's got, we'd got** etc.

with /wɪð, wɪθ/ [preposition] use this after a noun to describe the qualities, physical features etc that someone or something has: *Police are looking for a young man with a scar on his forehead.* | *The company needs more people with management experience.* | *a red shirt with a white collar*

there is/there are /ðeər ɪz, ðeər ɑːʳ/ use this to describe the things that a place has: *It's a big house – there are five bedrooms and two bathrooms.* | *Kyoto's a great place to visit. There are lots of fascinating old temples and gardens.*

possess /pəˈzes/ [v T] FORMAL to have a quality or skill, especially one that is very good or special: *All of Barbara's children possessed amazing musical ability.* | *Brown had always possessed great energy and ambition.*

> ⚠ **Possess** is more formal than **have** or **with**, and is used especially for describing parts of someone's character. Don't use **possess** for describing what people look like. Don't say 'He possesses dark hair and brown eyes'. Say 'He has dark hair and brown eyes'.

2 to own something such as a television, a car, or a house

have (also **have got** ESPECIALLY BRITISH) /hæv, həv ˈɡɒt‖-ˈɡɑːt/ [v T] to have something because you have bought it or someone has given it to you: *Over 25% of families in this country have two or more cars.* | *Jake's got a beautiful house.* | *Have you got a fax machine?* | *Do you have a fax machine?*

having – had – have had

> ⚠ Don't say 'I am having', 'she is having' etc. Say **I have, she has** etc: *She has a new car.*

with /wɪð, wɪθ/ [preposition] use this after a noun to say what someone owns: *a wealthy family with a big house in the country* | *Only people with a lot of money can afford to stay at this hotel.*

own /əʊn/ [v T] if you **own** something, especially something valuable such as a car, a house, or a company, it belongs to you legally: *Andy and his wife own a villa in Spain.* | *Who owns this car?* | *The company was previously owned by the French government.*

3 to have something with you or near you, so that you can use it

have (also **have got** ESPECIALLY BRITISH) /hæv, həv ˈɡɒt‖-ˈɡɑːt/ [v T] to have something with you or near you, for example in your pocket or bag or on your desk: *Do you have any change for the parking meter?* |

H

I have the tickets in my purse. | *Have you got a pen I could borrow?* | *Wait a minute. I think I've got a street map.*

having – had – have had

> ⚠ Don't say 'I am having', 'he is having' etc. Say **I have, he has** etc: *Don't worry, I have the passports.*

Qhave sth on you /ˌhæv (sth) ˈɒn juː/ ESPECIALLY SPOKEN to have something in your pocket, bag etc, so that you can use it or let someone else use it: *Do you have a calculator on you?* | *I realized I didn't have any money on me.*

have sth with you /ˌhæv (sth) ˈwɪð juː/ to have something useful in your pocket, bag etc when you are away from the place where you usually live or work: *You should have your identity card with you at all times.* | *Luckily I had my address book with me, so I called them to say I'd be late.*

4 to not have something

don't have /ˌdəʊnt ˈhæv/ *My parents don't have a TV.* | *Joe's family didn't really have much interest in his school work.*

haven't got /ˌhævənt ˈɡɒt‖-ˈɡɑːt/ ESPECIALLY BRITISH to not have something: *She hasn't got much artistic ability.* | *I'd love to come with you, but I haven't got the money at the moment.*

> ⚠ Be careful not to say 'I don't have got'. Say **I haven't got, she hasn't got** etc.

without /wɪðˈaʊt/ [preposition] use this after a noun to say that someone or something does not have or own something: *Billy came to class without his school books.* | *a house without a garden* | *There are so many people without jobs.*
be without sth (=not have basic things that you need) *Some families in the region are still without running water.*

be missing /biː ˈmɪsɪŋ/ if something **is missing**, you no longer have it, for example because you have lost it or it has been removed: *When I put my hand in my pocket, I realized my passport was missing.* | *Two of his front teeth were missing.*

lack /læk/ [v T] FORMAL to not have something important or something that you need: *Some schools lack even the basic equipment such as pens, pencils, and books.*
lack confidence/ability/experience *Tom has always lacked confidence.*

HEALTHY/ UNHEALTHY

1 not ill

healthy /ˈhelθi/ [adj] someone who is **healthy** is not often ill and has nothing physically wrong with them: *Karen has given birth to a healthy baby girl.* | *I feel much healthier since I stopped smoking.* | *Eating plenty of fresh fruit and vegetables will help you to stay healthy.*

healthy – healthier – healthiest

well /wel/ [adj not before noun] healthy – use this to say that someone feels or looks healthier than they usually do, or that they are healthy again after an illness: *Do you think he's well enough to travel?* | *Take plenty of rest and you'll soon be well again.*
look well *I saw Linda this morning. She looks really well after her vacation.*

Qfine /faɪn/ [adj not before noun] ESPECIALLY SPOKEN say this when someone has asked you how you feel and you are replying that you feel very well: *"How are you?" "I'm fine, thanks."* | *"Is Ted all right?" "Yes, he's fine."*

> ⚠ Don't say 'I'm very fine'. Just say **I'm fine**

better /ˈbetəʳ/ [adj not before noun] if someone is **better**, they are well again after being ill: *"How's your father now?"* *"Oh, he's much better, thanks."*

feel better *After a couple of days' rest, she felt a lot better.*

2 healthy and strong because you often do physical exercise

fit /fɪt/ [adj] ESPECIALLY BRITISH healthy and strong, especially because you play sport or do exercise regularly: *Sandy's very fit – he runs five miles every day.*

keep fit *Cycling is a good way to keep fit.*

 fitness [n U] *an exercise programme for people at all levels of fitness*

be in shape /biː ɪn ˈʃeɪp/ if you are **in shape** you are not fat and you can play sport or do exercise without getting tired

stay in shape/keep in shape *Walking to and from work helps me to stay in shape.*

in good shape *Both women played well and looked in good shape.*

3 how healthy/unhealthy someone is

health /helθ/ [n U] *It is now known that parents' smoking can affect their children's health.* | *a health and beauty magazine*

be in good/poor health (=be healthy/unhealthy) *Despite her age, your mother seems to be in good health.*

4 not healthy or fit

unhealthy /ʌnˈhelθi/ [adj] not healthy, and often ill: *James was a pale, unhealthy child.*

unfit /ʌnˈfɪt/ [adj] BRITISH someone who is **unfit** gets tired very easily when they do physical activities, for example because they eat or drink too much, or they do not get enough exercise: *I'm so unfit, I can't even run to the top of the stairs!* | *A lot of businessmen are overweight and unfit.*

out of shape/out of condition /ˌaʊt əv ˈʃeɪp, ˌaʊt əv kənˈdɪʃən/ if someone is **out of shape** or **out of condition**, they

get tired easily when they do sport or exercise, because they do it less often than they used to: *He used to play squash every day but now he's really out of condition.*

5 something that is good for your health

be good for you /biː ˈɡʊd fəʳ juː/ if a particular kind of food or activity **is good for you**, it helps you to stay healthy: *Citrus fruits such as oranges and lemons are very good for you.* | *She does yoga three times a week because she thinks it's good for her.*

healthy /ˈhelθi/ [adj usually before noun] **healthy** food or a **healthy** way of living helps you to stay healthy: *I'm trying to eat a healthier diet now, with less fat and sugar.*

healthy – healthier – healthiest

nutritious /njuːˈtrɪʃəs‖nuː-/ [adj] food that is **nutritious** contains the natural substances that your body needs in order to stay healthy or to grow: *Brown bread is more nutritious than white.* | *a light and nutritious lunch dish*

> ⚠ **Nutritious** is a slightly formal word, and is more common in written English.

6 something that is bad for your health

be bad for your health/be bad for you /biː ˌbæd fəʳ jɔːʳ ˈhelθ, biː ˌbæd fəʳ juː/ if a particular kind of food or activity is **bad for your health** or **bad for you**, it is likely to make you ill or less healthy: *Smoking is bad for your health.* | *Be careful when you're sunbathing – too much sun can be bad for you.*

unhealthy /ʌnˈhelθi/ [adj] **unhealthy** foods, places, situations etc are likely to make you ill or less healthy: *An unhealthy diet may make your headaches worse.* | *They work long hours in unhealthy and dangerous conditions.*

harmful /ˈhɑːʳmfəl/ [adj] if something is **harmful**, it has a bad effect on your health: *the harmful effects of radiation*

+ to *UV light can be harmful to the eyes.*

H

HEAR

➡ see also **LISTEN**
➡ see also **SOUND, LOUD, QUIET**

⚠ Don't confuse **hear** and **listen**. If you **hear** something, a sound comes into your ears: *I heard loud music coming from the next room.* If you **listen** to something, you want to hear it and you pay attention to what you hear: *I enjoy listening to music.*

1 to hear something or someone

hear /hɪəʳ/ [v I/T] *Did you hear that noise?* | *Suddenly we heard a knock at the door.* | *I pretended not to hear.*
hear sb/sth doing sth *We often hear our neighbours shouting at their children.* | *Do you hear that bird singing?*
hear sb/sth do sth *She ran outside and I heard the front door slam after her.* | *Did you hear them announce your name?*
hearing – heard – have heard

⚠ Don't say 'I am hearing', or are you hearing?' etc. You can say either **I hear, do you hear** etc, or (especially in British English) **I can hear, can you hear** etc, and it means the same: *I hear footsteps on the stairs* (=I can hear footsteps on the stairs). But don't use 'can hear' when you are talking about something that you hear often or regularly: *We often hear them arguing* (not 'we can often hear them arguing'). In the past tense, you can say **I could hear** and it usually means the same as **I heard**: *We could hear footsteps on the stairs* (=We heard footsteps on the stairs).

overhear /ˌəʊvəʳˈhɪəʳ/ [v T] to accidentally hear what someone is saying, when they do not realize that you can hear them: *I overheard a conversation between two of the doctors when I was in the waiting room.*
overhear sb saying/talking/arguing etc *We overheard Jenny and her friends talking about their boyfriends last night.*
overhearing – overheard – have overheard

2 the ability to hear

hearing /ˈhɪərɪŋ/ [n U] *Years of playing in a rock band resulted in a loss of hearing.* | *a hearing test* (=to find out how good or bad your hearing is)
my/her/his etc hearing *My hearing's not very good – can you speak a little louder please?*

3 when you cannot hear

can't hear /ˌkɑːnt ˈhɪəʳǁˌkænt-/ use this when you mean that you want to hear something but you are unable to hear it, for example because it is too quiet or there is too much other noise: *Can you turn the radio up – I can't hear the news.* | *The music was so loud that I couldn't hear what she was saying.*

didn't hear /ˌdɪdnt ˈhɪəʳ/ use this when you mean that you did not hear something at all, especially when you did not realize there was anything to hear: *I was outside in the yard, so I didn't hear the phone.* | *What time did you get back last night? I didn't hear you come in.* | *She didn't hear the car pulling up outside the house.*

didn't catch sth /ˌdɪdnt ˈkætʃ (sth)/ SPOKEN use this when you mean that you did not hear what someone said, because they were speaking too quietly or because you were not listening carefully: *I'm sorry, I didn't catch your name.* | *We were sitting at the back and didn't quite catch what he was saying.*

deaf /def/ [adj] someone who is **deaf** cannot hear well or cannot hear at all: *A lot of deaf children have additional problems in learning to speak.* | *She's partially deaf.*

hard of hearing /ˌhɑːrd əv ˈhɪərɪŋ/ someone who is **hard of hearing** cannot hear well: *My grandfather's a little hard of hearing, so he always has the TV turned up very loud.*

When you see **EC**, go to the **ESSENTIAL COMMUNICATION** section.

HEAVY

➡ opposite **LIGHT 5**

1 something that weighs a lot

heavy /'hevi/ [adj] something that is **heavy** weighs a lot or weighs more than you expect: *That table's too heavy for you to move on your own.* | *a truck carrying a heavy load* | *Boys are usually slightly heavier than girls at birth.*

heavy – heavier – heaviest

◯**weigh a ton** /ˌweɪ ə 'tʌn/ SPOKEN if something **weighs a ton**, it is very heavy and difficult to lift: *The box was full of books and weighed a ton.*

2 how heavy someone or something is

weigh /weɪ/ [v] to be a particular weight
weigh 50 kilos/30 tons etc *She weighs about 58 kg.* | *Each whale was about 40 feet long and weighed 45 tonnes.*
how much sb/sth weighs *How much does this parcel weigh?*
◯**what sb weighs** SPOKEN (say this to ask or talk about how much someone weighs) *What do you weigh now, Stephanie?*

weight /weɪt/ [n U] the amount that someone or something weighs: *Your weight is about right for someone of your height.*
+ of *The cost of postage depends on the weight of the package.*

how heavy /haʊ 'hevi/ use this to ask or say how much something weighs, especially something that is very heavy: *How heavy is the average small car?* | *You'd be surprised how heavy these sacks are.*

3 to find out how heavy someone or something is

weigh /weɪ/ [v T] to measure the weight of a person or thing: *Have you weighed yourself lately?* | *a special machine that weighs each truck and its cargo*

scales BRITISH **scale** AMERICAN /skeɪlz, skeɪl/ [n singular] a machine or piece of equipment for measuring the weight of people or things: *The scales showed I'd gained ten pounds in a week.*

HELP

➡ see also **ADVANTAGE/DISADVANTAGE, EXPLAIN**

1 to help someone

help /help/ [v I/T] to make it easier for someone to do something, by doing part of their work, showing them what to do, or giving them something they need: *Dad, I can't do my homework. Will you help me, please?* | *a charity which helps children in countries such as Bosnia and Romania* | *The new job was difficult at first but knowing foreign languages really helped.*
help sb to do sth *Steve helped her to clean up the mess.*
help sb do sth *If you write a list, it will help you remember what to buy.*
help (sb) with sth *Gavin helps with the housework.* | *Do you want me to help you with those bags?*
help sb across/down/along etc (=help someone to go somewhere) *The nurse helped him down the stairs.*
help sb out (=help someone who has problems and needs help) *Dad's helped us out on several occasions by sending us money.*

give sb a hand /ˌgɪv (sb) ə 'hænd/ SPOKEN to help someone to do something, especially by carrying or lifting things: *Dave wants to move some furniture and I promised I'd give him a hand.*
give sb a hand with sth *Could you give me a hand with the shopping?*

assist /ə'sɪst/ [v I/T] FORMAL to help someone by doing part of their work for them, especially the less important things
assist sb with/in sth *I was employed to assist the manager in his duties.*
+ with/in *Several of the guests assisted with the preparation of the food.*

⚠ Don't say 'I assist him to do his work'. Say **I assist him with his work**.

◯**do sb a favour** BRITISH **do sb a favor** AMERICAN /ˌduː (sb) ə 'feɪvər/ ESPECIALLY SPOKEN to do something to help someone, especially a close friend or someone you know well: *Could you do me a favour and post these letters on your way to school?*

H

do sb a big favour (=help someone a lot) *Simon did me a big favor by lending me his car.*

do sth for sb /'duː (sth) fɔːʳ (sb)/ [phrasal verb T] to help someone by doing something instead of them: *I'll do the shopping for you if you're feeling tired.* | *Judith's always doing her brother's homework for him.*

2 to make someone feel more confident and less worried

encourage /ɪnˈkʌrɪdʒ‖ɪnˈkɜːr-/ [v T] to say or do something that helps someone feel confident enough to do something: *She was always looking for ways to encourage her students.*

encourage sb to do sth *It was me who encouraged Rosie to give up her job and go to university.*

be supportive /biː səˈpɔːʳtɪv/ to make someone feel less worried and more confident, talking to them in a sympathetic way and giving them practical help: *Ever since I found out I was pregnant, my family has been very supportive.*

3 to help something to happen

help /help/ [v T] to make it more likely that something good will happen

help do sth *Going to Spain for a month should help improve her Spanish.*

help to do sth *A massage will help to relax your mind and your body.*

help sb (to) do sth *All this arguing isn't going to help us win the election.*

encourage /ɪnˈkʌrɪdʒ‖ɪnˈkɜːr-/ [v T] to make people more likely to want to do something, or make something more likely to happen: *Do you think that violence on TV encourages crime?*

encourage sb to do sth *If we had a better rail system, it would encourage people to leave their cars at home.*

promote /prəˈməʊt/ [v T] FORMAL to help something good to happen or develop and increase: *a meeting to promote trade between Korea and the UK* | *A balanced diet promotes good health and normal development.* | *The meetings*

are intended to promote good relations between the two communities.

4 when someone or something helps you

helpful /'helpfəl/ [adj] someone or something that is **helpful** gives you help or makes it easier for you to do something: *If you have problems with the computer, you may find the instruction manual helpful.* | *Thanks, Sam. You've been very helpful.*

it is helpful to do sth *It's helpful to prepare a list of questions before going to an interview.*

helpful advice/idea/suggestion *Does anyone have any helpful suggestions?* | *She gave us some helpful advice about renting apartments.*

> ⚠ Don't write 'helpfull'. The correct spelling is **helpful**.

be a help /biː ə 'help/ ESPECIALLY SPOKEN if someone or something **is a help**, they make it easier for you to do something that you are trying to do: *For the teachers, having more books and equipment would be a help.*

be a big/great/real help *Thanks for looking after the children. You've been a real help.*

5 someone who helps another person

assistant /əˈsɪstənt/ [n C] someone whose job is to help another person who has a more important job, by doing things for them: *Ryan got a job in a TV studio as a sound engineer's assistant.*

assistant to sb *Janet is the assistant to the Director of Finance.*

> ⚠ You can also use **assistant** before a noun, like an adjective: *the assistant manager* | *Peter is an assistant editor on a news programme.*

helper /'helpəʳ/ [n C] someone who helps other people, especially because they want to do it and not in order to earn money: *Ella works at the hospital once a week as a voluntary helper.*

accomplice /əˈkʌmplɪ̩s‖əˈkɑːm-, əˈkʌm-/ [n C] FORMAL someone who helps another person in a crime: *Evans could not have carried out the robbery without an accomplice.* | *The man held a knife to her throat while his accomplice snatched her keys.*

6 something that someone does in order to help

help /help/ [n U] something that someone does in order to help: *If I need any help I'll call you.* | *Please don't hesitate to ask for help if there's anything you don't understand.*
+ with *Do you need any help with those suitcases?*
help doing sth *I wouldn't mind some help moving that piano.*
with the help of *Ian pushed the car as far as the garage with the help of some friends.*

> ⚠ Don't say 'a help' in this meaning. Just say **help** or **some help, any help** etc.

assistance /əˈsɪstəns/ [n U] FORMAL help given to someone who needs it, often in the form of money, advice, or information: *The Association gives advice and practical assistance to motorists.*
financial assistance *Students here receive very little financial assistance from the government.*
be of assistance (=help someone) *Our tour guides will be pleased to be of assistance if you have any problems.*

aid /eɪd/ [n U] food, money, medicine, and other kinds of help that are given to countries or people who need them, because they are very poor or have serious problems: *Each year the US sends more than $1.8 billion worth of aid to sub-Saharan Africa.* | *Aid is not getting through to the refugees.*

> ⚠ Don't use **aid** in the plural. **Aid** is an uncountable noun.

> ⚠ You can also use **aid** before a noun, like an adjective: *aid agencies* | *the federal aid budget*

7 not giving any help

not helpful/unhelpful /nɒt ˈhelpfəl, ʌnˈhelpfəl/ not giving someone the help they need, especially when they have asked for help: *I found the sales assistants most unhelpful.* | *The authorities were not at all helpful when Rob reported that his passport had been stolen.*

useless /ˈjuːslɪ̩s/ [adj] ESPECIALLY SPOKEN not giving any help – use this when you are annoyed with someone or something because they should help you but they do not: *Those useless people in the tax office couldn't give me any advice.*
completely/absolutely useless *It's no good reading the instructions – they're completely useless.*

HERE   Ⓗ

➡ see also **PLACE**

1 here

here /hɪəʳ/ [adv] in, to, or from this place: *Were you born here?* | *I'll stay here and wait for the others.* | *I really love it here in Italy.*
be here *Check the names off the list to make sure everyone's here.*
come/get/arrive here (=come to this place) *What time did you get here?* | *We moved here about two years ago.*
around/near here (=near this place) *Do you live around here?*
right here (=in this exact place) *I put my keys right here in the drawer.*
from here (=from this place) *I know a really good Spanish restaurant not far from here.*
down/in/up here *'Hey, guys,' she called up to us, 'I'm down here in the basement.'*

> ⚠ Don't say 'come to here', 'arrive to here' etc. Say **come here, arrive here**: *We came here by bus.*

> ⚠ Don't say 'here the weather is nice'. Say **the weather is nice here**. Don't put 'here' at the beginning of a sentence.

be in /biː ˈɪn/ [phrasal verb I] to be in your home or at the place where you work: *Hello, Susan. Is Richard in?* | *She has to be in by 11 o'clock every night.*

be around /biː əˈraʊnd/ [phrasal verb I] SPOKEN if someone or something **is around**, they are here or somewhere near here, especially when you need them: *"Where's the iron?" "Oh, it must be around somewhere."* | *Are you going to be around at Christmas, or are you going away?*

be present /biː ˈprezənt/ FORMAL to be here – use this especially about people being at official meetings or ceremonies: *The President regrets he cannot be present at the meeting this afternoon.*

2 not here

not be here /nɒt biː ˈhɪəʳ/ *She wasn't here when the accident happened.* | *He hasn't been here long, but he's made a lot of changes already.*

not be around /nɒt biː əˈraʊnd/ INFORMAL if someone or something **is not around**, they are not here or near here, especially when you need them: *There's never a police officer around when you need one.* | *If Julie isn't around maybe Maria could help you.*

be out/not be in /biː ˈaʊt, nɒt biː ˈɪn/ [phrasal verb I] to not be in your home or at the place where you work, especially when someone wants to see you: *Mr Newton called while you were out – he'll call back later.* | *I'm sorry, I won't be in today – I have to go to the doctor's.*

be away /biː əˈweɪ/ [phrasal verb I] to not be at home or work for several days because you have travelled somewhere else, or not be at school or work because you are ill or on holiday: *She's going to be away for at least a week.*
be away on business *I'm sorry, Mr Hyam is away on business right now.*
be away from home/work/school *Because of her job, she is sometimes away from home for weeks at a time.*

be absent /biː ˈæbsənt/ if someone **is absent**, they are not at school or at the place where they work, especially because they are ill or on holiday

+ from *James was absent from school again today.*

> ⚠ **Be absent** is more formal than **be away**.

missing /ˈmɪsɪŋ/ [adj] someone or something that is **missing** is not in the place where you expect them to be, and it is difficult or impossible to find them: *The missing files were eventually found in Slater's apartment.*
+ from *Oh no! The last page is missing from this book!*

HIDE

➡ see also **SECRET, SHOW**

1 to hide things

hide /haɪd/ [v T] to make something difficult to see or find, for example by putting it somewhere secret, or by covering it: *The police had secretly hidden a tape recorder in Larry's apartment.* | *Hiding her face, she walked past the photographers towards her car.*
hide sth in/behind/under etc sth *He hid the money under his bed.*
hide sth from sb (=make sure someone cannot see or find something) *I shoved the cigarettes into my bag, to hide them from my Dad.*
hiding – hid – have hidden
hidden [adj] *a hidden microphone.*

conceal /kənˈsiːl/ [v T] to hide something, especially by covering it: *Several kilos of drugs were concealed in the back of the truck.*
concealed [adj] *a man carrying a concealed weapon*

> ⚠ **Conceal** is more formal than **hide**, and is often used when you are talking about things that are hidden for dishonest or criminal reasons.

cover /ˈkʌvəʳ/ [v T] if you **cover** something, you put something over it or on top of it so that it cannot be seen: *He reached for a towel to cover his naked body.*
cover sth with sth *Jane covered her face with her hands and started to cry.*

bury /'beri/ [v T] to put something in a hole in the ground and cover it with earth or sand in order to hide it: *Dogs like to bury bones.*

bury sth in/under etc sth *He murdered his wife and buried her body in a field.*

burying – buried – have buried

2 to hide yourself

hide /haɪd/ [v I] to go somewhere where people cannot easily see you or find you: *Dad's coming! Quick – hide!*

+ under/in/behind etc *I hid in a doorway until the man had gone.* | *I think there's someone hiding behind the door.*

+ from *Are you trying to hide from me?*

hiding – hid – have hidden

go into hiding /,gəʊ ɪntə 'haɪdɪŋ/ to go to a place where you can hide for a long time, because you are in danger or because the police are looking for you: *Many Jewish families went into hiding during World War Two.* | *Police believe the robbers have gone into hiding.*

3 to hide your feelings

hide /haɪd/ [v T] to deliberately not show your real feelings: *I couldn't hide my annoyance any longer.* | *'That's OK,' she said, trying to hide her disappointment.*

hiding – hid – have hidden

disguise /dɪs'gaɪz/ [v T] ESPECIALLY WRITTEN to not show your real feelings, by pretending to feel something else: *Kate gave a cheerful smile, somehow managing to disguise her embarrassment.* | *He didn't even attempt to disguise his amazement.*

4 to hide information

conceal /kən'siːl/ [v T] to hide information from people by not telling them all the facts, or by not telling them the truth about a situation: *He managed to conceal the fact that he had been in prison, and got a job as a security officer.*

conceal sth from sb *For years, Anna had concealed her true identity from everyone.*

cover-up /'kʌvər ʌp/ [n C] when an organization, for example the government or the police, tries to stop people from finding out the truth about something: *The Watergate cover-up finally led to Nixon's resignation.*

cover up /,kʌvər 'ʌp/ [phrasal verb T] to try to stop people from finding out about someone's mistakes or crimes

cover up sth *Lewis asked his wife to lie in an attempt to cover up the murder.*

cover sth up *He had made a big mistake, and I knew we wouldn't be able to cover it up for long.*

5 places to hide

hiding-place /'haɪdɪŋ pleɪs/ [n C] a place where someone can hide, or a place where you can hide something: *I've found a good hiding-place for the money.*

hideout /'haɪdaʊt/ [n C] a place where someone goes to hide from the police or from someone dangerous: *The kidnappers used an abandoned farmhouse as their hideout.*

HIGH

➡ opposite **LOW**
➡ look here for ...
   • a high mountain, building, tree etc
   • a high sound or voice
   • a high temperature, level etc

⚠ Don't use **high** to talk about people. Use **tall**.

1 a high building/mountain/tree

high

a high shelf   a tall tree

high /haɪ/ [adj] measuring a long distance from top to bottom – use this especially about mountains, walls, or buildings: *The castle was surrounded by high walls.* | *Mount Everest is the highest mountain in the world.* | *a high fence*

tall /tɔːl/ [adj] high and not wide or long – use this especially about trees and plants or about buildings and parts of buildings: *The main square was surrounded by tall grey buildings.* | *Two tall marble columns stood at either side of the entrance.* | *animals hiding in the tall grass*

> ⚠ Don't use **tall** about mountains or walls.

skyscraper /ˈskaɪˌskreɪpəʳ/ [n C] a very tall modern city building, especially one used for offices: *the skyscrapers of Manhattan*

high-rise /ˈhaɪ raɪz/ [adj only before noun] a **high-rise** building is a tall modern building, used either for apartments or for offices: *a high-rise apartment block*

2 a long distance above the ground

high /haɪ/ [adj/adv] *a large dining-room with a high ceiling* | *The shelf was too high for me to reach.*
+ in/into/above *The plane flew high above their heads.* | *Lava from the volcano was sent high into the air.*
+ up *The house was high up on a hill.*

3 how high something is

how high /ˌhaʊ ˈhaɪ/ use this to ask or say the height of something: *"How high is Mount Fuji?" "It's almost 4000 metres."* | *I'm not sure how high the ceiling is.*

30 m/100 ft etc high /(30 m etc) ˈhaɪ/ if a building or mountain is **30 m, 100 ft etc high**, the distance from top to bottom is 30 m, 100 ft etc: *Scotland's highest mountain is over 4000 ft high.* | *a 5 m high wall*

height /haɪt/ [n C/U] the distance between the top and the bottom of something, or the distance that something is above the ground
+ of *What's the height of that building?*
200 ft/30 m etc in height *Some of the pyramids are over 200 feet in height.*
a height of 25 m/100 ft etc *One of the climbers fell from a height of 25 m.*

level /ˈlevəl/ [n C] the height of something which you use as a basis for describing the height of something else: *Hold your arms out at the same level as your shoulders.*
+ of *We hung the painting just above the level of the window.*
sea level (=the height of the surface of the sea, used for measuring the height of mountains, hills etc) *The village is about 1500 metres above sea level.*

altitude /ˈæltɪˌtjuːd‖-tuːd/ [n C] the distance that something is above the ground – use this especially to talk about planes or about places in mountainous areas
at an altitude of 10,000 metres/30,000 feet etc *The plane is now flying at an altitude of 30,000 ft.*
at high altitudes *At high altitudes it is often difficult to breathe.*

> ⚠ **Altitude** is a more technical word than **height**.

4 a high sound/voice/ musical note
➡ see also SOUND

high /haɪ/ [adj] near the top of the range of sounds that humans can hear – use this about sounds, voices, or musical notes: *Most people can't sing such high notes.*

high-pitched /ˌhaɪ ˈpɪtʃt◂/ [adj] a **high-pitched** voice or sound is very high and is often unpleasant to listen to: *I could hear high-pitched laughter coming from the girls' room.*

piercing /ˈpɪəʳsɪŋ/ [adj usually before noun] very high and loud, in a way that is painful or unpleasant to listen to: *Sammy put his fingers in his mouth and gave a piercing whistle.*
piercing shriek/scream/cry (=the loud high noise someone makes when they are frightened or in pain) *Maggie let out a piercing scream as she saw the truck speeding towards her.*

5 a high temperature/ level/rate/cost

high /haɪ/ [adj] *In summer, temperatures can be as high as 40 °C.* | *The city has one of the highest crime rates in the world.* | *the high level of pollution in Britain's rivers*

HIT

ACCIDENTALLY
PUNISH   ACCIDENT
BREAK   see   KILL
         also
DRIVE   VIOLENT
ATTACK   HURT/INJURE
DELIBERATELY

1 to hit someone deliberately

hit /hɪt/ [v T] to deliberately hit someone with your hand, or with something that you are holding in your hand: *I was so mad I just wanted to hit her.*
hit sb with sth *Cathy turned around and hit the man with her umbrella.*
hit sb in the eye/on the nose/over the head *He hit a waiter over the head with a bottle during a drunken fight.*
hitting – hit – have hit

punch /pʌntʃ/ [v T] to hit someone hard with your closed hand, especially during a fight: *Steve swung around and punched Rick, knocking him to the ground.*
punch sb on the nose/in the eye/in the face *Sarah was arrested for punching a police officer in the eye.*

slap /slæp/ [v T] to hit someone quickly with the flat part of your hand making a loud sound: *Liz got really angry with her daughter and slapped her.*
slap sb across the face *He was so rude, I felt like slapping him across the face.*
slapping – slapped – have slapped

beat up /ˌbiːt ˈʌp/ [phrasal verb T] to hurt someone badly by hitting them again and again
beat sb up *Bob often used to get drunk and beat his wife up.*
beat up sb *The gang would beat up old women and steal their money.*

beat up on sb /ˌbiːt ˈʌp ɒn (sb)‖-ɑːn-/ [phrasal verb T] AMERICAN to hurt someone younger and weaker than yourself by hitting them again and again: *Wayne used to beat up on other kids in the class.*

When you see **EC**, go to the
ESSENTIAL COMMUNICATION section.

2 to hit someone or something by accident

hit /hɪt/ [v T] to hit someone or something without intending to: *Be careful with that ladder! You nearly hit me with it.* | *The bus hit a tree and the driver was badly injured.*
hit sb on the head/in the face etc *A flowerpot fell off the balcony, hitting a child on the head.*
hit your head/knee/elbow etc *He fell and hit his head on the side of the desk.*
hitting – hit – have hit

bump into sb/sth /ˈbʌmp ɪntuː (sb/sth)/ [phrasal verb T] to accidentally hit someone or something when you are walking or running, because you are not paying attention or you cannot see properly: *Mark ran around the corner and bumped into his teacher.* | *I kept bumping into things as I made my way across the dark yard.*

crash into sb/sth /ˈkræʃ ɪntuː (sb/sth)/ [phrasal verb T] to accidentally hit someone or something when you are moving very fast, causing a lot of damage and making a lot of noise: *The car crashed straight into a tree.* | *Eric came running down the corridor and crashed into me.*

bang /bæŋ/ [v T] to accidentally make part of your body, or something you are carrying, hit hard against something else, making a noise
bang sth on/against sth *They banged the piano against the wall as they carried it downstairs.*
bang your head/knee/elbow etc *Sean banged his knee getting up from the desk.*

collide /kəˈlaɪd/ [v I] if people or vehicles **collide**, they hit each other when they are moving in different directions: *Two planes collided in mid-air.*
+ with *He ran out of the door, and almost collided with Sally as she was coming in.*

3 to hit someone as a punishment

beat /biːt/ [v T] to hit someone many times with your hand or with a stick, gun etc in order to punish them: *The guards dragged Blair out of his cell and beat him.*

beat sb with sth *Two of the soldiers began beating her with rifles.*

beating – beat – have beaten

smack/spank/slap /smæk, spæŋk, slæp/ [v T] to hit a child who you think is behaving badly, using your hand: *Dad would sometimes shout at us, but he never smacked us.* | *Do you think that parents should be allowed to spank their children?*

slapping – slapped – have slapped

  smack/spank/slap [n singular] *Stop being so naughty or you'll get a smack!*

corporal punishment /ˌkɔːrpərəl ˈpʌnɪʃmənt/ [n U] when people, especially children in schools, are punished by being hit: *Corporal punishment was abolished in Britain in 1986.*

4 to hit a ball when playing a sport

hit /hɪt/ [v T] to hit a ball in a sport, usually with a bat, racket, or other piece of equipment: *You get three chances to hit the ball.* | *Torrance took a good look at the ball and hit it 80 yards up the fairway.*
hit sth hard *Hit the ball as hard as you can.*

hitting – hit – have hit

5 to hit a door, table, or window in order to get attention

knock /nɒk‖nɑːk/ [v I] to hit a door or window several times with your hand, because you want to go inside or talk to someone: *Please knock before you enter.* | *We kept knocking, but no-one opened the door.*
knock on/at the door *Was that someone knocking at the door?*
knock on/at the window *Ella knocked lightly on the car window to try and wake him up.*
  knock [n singular] *Dad gave a loud knock on the door.*

⚠ Don't say 'knock the door'. Say **knock on the door** or **knock at the door**.

bang /bæŋ/ [v I] to keep hitting a door, window, table etc, making a loud noise

bang on the door/window/table etc *Mum was banging on his bedroom door, screaming at him to turn the music down.* | *The students started banging on their desks.*

hammer /ˈhæməʳ/ [v I] to keep hitting a door or window loudly, especially because you are angry or impatient
hammer at/on the door *We were woken by the sound of the police hammering at the door.*
hammer at/on the window *Phil hammered on the window, hoping that someone would hear him.*

tap /tæp/ [v I/T] to hit a door, window, or table gently in order to make people notice you: *Mr Norton tapped his desk with a ruler until everyone was silent.*
tap on a door/window *She turned and saw a small boy tapping on the class-room window.*
tap at a door/window *I tapped three times at the door.*

tapping – tapped – have tapped

6 to make someone or something fall down by hitting them

knock out /ˌnɒk ˈaʊt‖ˌnɑːk-/ [phrasal verb T] to hit someone so hard that they fall down and become unconscious
knock sb out *He punched Colin hard on the head, knocking him out.*
knock out sb *Tyson knocked out his opponent in the second round.*

knock over/knock down /ˌnɒk ˈəʊvəʳ, ˌnɒk ˈdaʊn‖ˌnɑːk-/ [phrasal verb T] to accidentally hit someone or something that is standing, and make them fall: *A truck went out of control and knocked down a traffic light.* | *I bumped into Anna and almost knocked her over.*
get knocked down/over *As the crowd rushed towards the gate, several people got knocked over.*

run over /ˌrʌn ˈəʊvəʳ/ [phrasal verb T] to hit someone when you are driving a car, truck etc, and injure them or kill them
run sb over *A little boy stepped out in the street, and I almost ran him over.*
get run over *Get out of the road! You'll get run over!*

HOLD

➡ look here for ...
- hold something or someone
- drop something

➡ if you mean 'have something inside', go to **CONTAIN**

➡ see also **LIFT, CARRY, TAKE/BRING**

1 to have something in your hand

hold /həʊld/ [v T] to have something in your hand, with your fingers around it so that it does not fall: *The photo showed a young boy holding a flag.* | *Can you hold my coat while I try on this sweater?*
holding – held – have held

in your hand /ɪn jɔːʳ 'hænd/ if something is **in your hand**, you are holding it: *What's that in your hand?* | *He already had a glass in his hand when we arrived.*

handle /'hændl/ [v T] to touch or hold something – use this especially about things that you must be careful with such as weapons, food, or things that break easily: *It was the first time I had ever handled a gun.* | *Staff who handle food should have special training.* | *A sign on the box said 'Fragile. Handle with care'.*

2 to hold something tightly

grip /grɪp/ [v T] to hold something tightly: *I gripped the handrail and looked down at the people in the street below.* | *Gripping her arm tightly, Max pulled her away from the road.*
gripping – gripped – have gripped

clutch /klʌtʃ/ [v T] ESPECIALLY WRITTEN to hold something very tightly, especially because you are frightened or nervous or because you do not want to lose what you are holding: *I could feel his little hand clutching my arm.* | *Going out in the dark street, she clutched her bag tightly.*

hold on /ˌhəʊld 'ɒn‖-'ɑːn/ [phrasal verb I] to hold something tightly because you are afraid that you will fall or that you will lose what you are holding
+ to *I had to hold on to my hat to stop it blowing away.*

hold on tight *As the roller coaster turned upside down I shut my eyes and held on tight.*

3 to start to hold something

get hold of sth/take hold of sth /ˌget 'həʊld ɒv (sth), ˌteɪk 'həʊld ɒv (sth)/ to take something and hold it in your hand: *I took hold of the door handle and pulled as hard as I could.* | *When you get the fish out of the net, try to get hold of its tail.*

grab /græb/ [v T] to quickly and roughly take something and hold it: *She tried to grab the knife from him.* | *Suddenly, a police officer grabbed my arm.*
grab hold of sth *I grabbed hold of his leg and hung on.*
grabbing – grabbed – have grabbed

4 to hold someone

hold /həʊld/ [v T] to hold someone by putting your arms around their body, especially in order to make them feel less worried or upset: *I held him until he went to sleep.*
hold sb tight (=close to your body) *He held her tight and let her cry.*
holding – held – have held

hug /hʌg/ [v T] to hold someone for a short time, pressing their body with your arms in a friendly or loving way: *My father hugged me affectionately when I got home.*
hugging – hugged – have hugged
hug [n C] *Come and give me a hug.*

cuddle /'kʌdl/ [v I/T] to hold someone in your arms for a long time, especially a child, a small animal, or someone you love: *She had fallen asleep in her chair, cuddling a little teddy bear.*
kiss and cuddle (=when two people hold each other and kiss each other) *They were kissing and cuddling on the sofa.*
cuddle [n C] when you cuddle someone: *She was giving the baby a cuddle.*

put your arms around sb /ˌpʊt jɔːʳ 'ɑːʳmz əraʊnd (sb)/ ESPECIALLY WRITTEN to hold someone in a loving way, in order to kiss them or make them less upset: *I put my arms around her and kissed her.* | *She didn't speak, just put her arms around him and stroked his hair.*

H

⚠ **Put your arms around sb** is used especially in stories.

hold sb's hand /ˌhəʊld (sb's) 'hænd/ to hold someone's hand, as a sign of love or to make them feel safe: *Hold my hand, Billy. It's a dangerous road.*

hold hands (=when two people hold each other's hands) *two lovers walking along the beach, holding hands*

5 to stop holding something

let go /ˌlet 'gəʊ/ to stop holding something or someone: *Let go! You're hurting me.*
+ of *She wouldn't let go of the letter.*

drop /drɒp‖drɑːp/ [v T] to stop holding something suddenly, especially by accident, so that it falls to the ground: *Be careful not to drop any of those plates.* | *As soon as she saw him she dropped her suitcases and ran towards him.*

dropping – dropped – have dropped

HOLE

1 a hole that goes through something

hole /həʊl/ [n C] an empty space that goes right through something, so that water, air, light etc can pass from one side of it to the other: *I can't wear these socks – they're full of holes.*
+ in *We could see the sky through a hole in the roof.*
make a hole *Make a hole in the bottom of each plant pot to let the water drain out.*

leak /liːk/ [n C] a small hole or crack in a pipe, container etc, which should not be there and which lets liquid or gas flow out of it
+ in *There's a leak in the water tank.*

There's a leak in the bucket.

puncture

puncture BRITISH **flat tire** AMERICAN /'pʌŋktʃəʳ, ˌflæt 'taɪəʳ/ [n C] a hole made accidentally in a tyre, which allows air to get out and makes the tyre unsafe: *Do you know how to mend a puncture?*
get a puncture/flat tire *I got a flat tire and I was late for work.*

gap /gæp/ [n C] a space in the middle of something, for example in a wall or a fence, where a part of it is missing
+ in *The cows had escaped through a gap in the hedge.*

gap

The dog escaped through a gap in the fence.

2 a hole in the ground or in the surface of something

hole /həʊl/ [n C] an empty space in the ground or in the surface of something
+ in *There were huge holes in the road.*
make a hole *These holes in the tree trunk are made by tiny insects.*

hole

There were huge holes in the road.

dig /dɪg/ [v I/T] to make a hole in the ground, using a spade (=a tool for digging), a large machine, or your hands: *Some of the prisoners escaped through a tunnel they had dug under the wall.* | *a big black dog digging in the sand*

dig for sth (=in order to find something) *There were two fishermen on the beach digging for worms.*

dig a hole *The workmen began digging a hole in the middle of the road.*

digging – dug – have dug

HOLIDAY

FESTIVALS AND SPECIAL DAYS
VISIT   LAND AND SEA
STAY   see   COUNTRY
            also
JOURNEY   TRAVEL
BEAUTIFUL 6   TRANSPORT
       ORGANIZE/ARRANGE

1 time when you are allowed to be away from work or school

holiday /'hɒlɪdi‖'hɑːlɪdeɪ/ [n C/U] BRITISH a period of time when you do not have to work or go to school: *I have six weeks' holiday each year.* | *You look tired. What you need is a holiday.*
the holidays/summer holidays/school holidays (=the long periods when schools close) *July 20th is the first day of the summer holidays.*
Christmas/Easter holiday *Last year we spent most of the Christmas holiday at our grandma's.*

> ⚠ In American English, the period around Christmas is often called 'the holidays': *All the family will be together in St Louis over the holidays.*

vacation /vəˈkeɪʃən‖veɪ-/ [n C/U] AMERICAN a period of time when you do not have to work or go to school: *I'll see you next time I get a vacation.* | *The company allows us 25 vacation days a year.*
summer/Christmas vacation *I spent part of the summer vacation with friends in Seattle.*

break /breɪk/ [n C] a short holiday from your work or school: *The students get a few days' break in February.*
the Easter/autumn/fall break *Are you going home for the Easter break?*

2 a one-day holiday when shops, banks etc are closed

holiday /'hɒlɪdi‖'hɑːlɪdeɪ/ [n C] *We'd forgotten that July 14th was a holiday in France.*

national holiday (=a holiday for the whole country) *St Patrick's Day is a national holiday in Ireland.*
bank holiday/public holiday BRITISH (=an official holiday) *This shop is closed on Sundays and public holidays.* | *The roads are always busy on bank holidays.*

> ⚠ This meaning of **holiday** is the only one that is common in American English: *At the end of the summer we get a holiday for Labor Day.* For all the other meanings of **holiday**, Americans usually say **vacation**.

3 time when you travel to another place for enjoyment

holiday BRITISH **vacation** AMERICAN /'hɒlɪdi, vəˈkeɪʃən‖'hɑːlɪdeɪ, veɪ-/ [n C] a period of days or weeks that you spend in another place or country for enjoyment: *France is the ideal place for a family holiday.*
have a holiday/vacation *Have a nice holiday, and send us a postcard.*
take a holiday/vacation (=have a holiday) *We couldn't afford to take a vacation this year.*
be on holiday/vacation *We met when I was on vacation in Canada.*
go on holiday/vacation (=travel somewhere on holiday) *Maureen's going on holiday next week, to Turkey.*

> ⚠ You can also use **holiday** or **vacation** before a noun, like an adjective: *Have you made any holiday plans?* | *a vacation trip* | *a holiday resort*

honeymoon /'hʌnimuːn/ [n C] a holiday you take just after you get married: *We went to Barbados for our honeymoon.*
on honeymoon *Hawaii was full of couples on honeymoon.*

> ⚠ You can also use **honeymoon** before a noun, like an adjective: *a honeymoon couple* | *a honeymoon resort*

4 people on holiday

tourist /'tʊərɪst/ [n C] someone who travels around visiting places for interest and enjoyment: *Tourists are charged higher prices in the local shops.* | *The Tower of London is popular with tourists.*

H

holidaymaker BRITISH **vacationer**
AMERICAN /'hɒlɪˌdeɪkəʳ, vəˈkeɪʃənəʳ‖ˈhɑːlˌdeɪ-,
veɪ-/ [n C] someone who stays in a place
away from their home, when they are having a holiday: *The beach seems deserted
now that all the holidaymakers have
gone home.* | *He makes a lot of money
selling wooden carvings to vacationers.*

HOME

➡ if you mean that 'someone was
born in a place or has lived there a
long time', go to **FROM 1**

HOUSES/WHERE PEOPLE LIVE

1 where you live

home /həʊm/ [n C/U] the place where you
live: *John seems to have everything – a
wonderful family, a great job, and a
lovely home.* | *After three weeks in the
hospital, Ruth was glad to be back in her
own home.*
at home *Her daughter lives at college
during the week and at home on weekends.*

> ⚠ Don't say 'I'm going to home', 'he
> drove to home' etc. Say **I'm going home,
> he drove home** etc.

Helen's/my friend's/the Taylors'
etc ESPECIALLY SPOKEN the place where Helen,
my friend, the Taylor family etc live: *There's
a party at Helen's on Saturday night.* |
*I'm going to my friend's for a drink and a
chat.* | *Have you ever been to the Taylors'
– they have a beautiful apartment.*

place /pleɪs/ [n singular] ESPECIALLY
SPOKEN someone's house, apartment, or
room: *They've bought a beautiful place
out in the countryside near Oxford.*
my place/your place/our place etc *Let's
meet at my place at 8 o'clock.* | *Barbara
and Les have invited us over to their
place for a meal.*

address /əˈdres‖ˈædres/ [n C] the number
of the house or building, and the name of
the road and town where someone lives:
*He wrote his name and address on a
piece of paper and gave it to me.*
change of address *Please inform the
bank of any change of address.*

2 places for people to live

housing /'haʊzɪŋ/ [n U] houses or apartments in an area – use this to talk about
how many houses are available, what they
cost, and whether they are good or bad:
*There is a shortage of good, inexpensive
housing.*
poor housing (=housing that is in bad
condition) *health problems caused by
poor housing*

> ⚠ You can also use **housing** before a
> noun, like an adjective: *excellent housing
> conditions* | *an increase in housing costs*

**somewhere to live/a place to
live** /ˌsʌmweəʳ tə 'lɪv, ə ˌpleɪs tə 'lɪv/ a
house, apartment, or room – use this to
talk about the problems of getting a place
where you can live: *It's difficult to find
somewhere to live if you're poor and
unemployed.* | *I was starting college
and I needed somewhere to live.*

accommodation /əˌkɒməˈdeɪʃən‖ˌkɑː-/
[n U] ESPECIALLY BRITISH any place, such as a
house, apartment, or hotel, where people
can live or stay: *I spent a week looking
for accommodation before starting my
new job.*
rented accommodation (=a house, apartment, or room that you rent)

> ⚠ Don't say 'looking for an accom-
> modation' or 'looking for accommodations'.
> Say **looking for accommodation.**

> ⚠ Don't write 'accomodation' or
> 'acommodation'. The correct spelling is
> **accommodation** .

> ⚠ In American English, there is a plural
> noun **accommodations**, which means a
> place where you can stay for a short time,
> for example when you are on holiday: *We
> called the tourist office in Rome, but they said
> there were no accommodations available.*

3 things for using at home

domestic /dəˈmestɪk/ [adj only before noun]
domestic appliance/equipment/fuel etc
designed to be used at home, not in a factory or office: *The kitchen has all the latest domestic appliances – microwave, dishwasher etc.* | *Solar energy panels can provide domestic hot water.*

home /həʊm/ [adj only before noun] done at home or used at home
home computer/security system (=one for using at home, not in a factory or office)
home shopping/schooling/banking (use this about things you can do at home, which are usually done in other places)

4 to be in your home

be at home/be home /biː ət ˈhəʊm, biː ˈhəʊm/ to be in your home: *We kept trying to call her, but she was never home.* | *I hated being at home with the kids all day.*

Q**be in** /biː ˈɪn/ [phrasal verb I] ESPECIALLY SPOKEN if someone **is in**, they are at home, and you can talk to them or visit them: *Hi, Mrs Jones. Is Sally in?*

5 to not be in your home

Q**be out** /biː ˈaʊt/ [phrasal verb] ESPECIALLY SPOKEN to not be in your home for a short period: *"Can I speak to Frank?" "I'm sorry, he's out right now, but he'll be back soon."* | *While they were out, someone broke in and stole the TV.*

be away /biː əˈweɪ/ [phrasal verb I] to not be in your home for several days, weeks, or months: *Who's going to look after your cats while you're away?*
+ from *Jack worked as a pilot and was often away from home.*

6 to have no home

not have anywhere to live /nɒt hæv ˌeniweəʳ tə ˈlɪv/ to not have a house, apartment, or room: *Paul's staying with us at the moment because he doesn't have anywhere to live.*

homeless /ˈhəʊmləs/ [adj] someone who is **homeless** has no home to live in, especially because they are very poor or because their home has been destroyed:

There has been a big increase in the number of homeless people living on the streets | *The earthquake left thousands of people homeless.*
the homeless (=people who are homeless) *We distribute food and blankets to the homeless every evening.*

tramp BRITISH **vagrant** AMERICAN /træmp, ˈveɪgrənt/ [n C] someone, especially a man, who has no home or job and who begs for money on the streets: *As we walked over the bridge we saw an old tramp asleep by the river.*

HONEST

➡ opposite **DISHONEST**

1 someone who does not lie, steal, or cheat

honest /ˈɒnɪst‖ˈɑːn-/ [adj] someone who is **honest** does not lie, steal, or cheat: *As the job involves handling money, it's essential that our workers are honest.* | *I think he's one of the few honest politicians left in government.*

can trust /kən ˈtrʌst/ if you **can trust** someone, you are sure that they are honest and that you can depend on them: *Beth's an honest hardworking girl who I know I can trust.*
can trust sb to do sth *I knew I could trust Neil to look after the money.*

2 honest about telling people what you really think

honest /ˈɒnɪst‖ˈɑːn-/ [adj] if you are **honest**, you tell people what you really think, without hiding the truth
+ with *Sandra wanted to be honest with her children and tell them what was really happening.*

+ about *He's only interested in her money, but he's quite honest about it.*

your honest opinion (=what you really think) *If you want my honest opinion, I don't think she should marry him.*

honestly [adv] *I can honestly say that I've never been so bored in my life!*

○to be honest /tə biː 'ɒnʲst‖-'ɑːn-/ SPOKEN say this when you are telling someone what you really think, even though this may be surprising or shocking: *To be honest, I don't really like babies.*

to be perfectly honest *To be perfectly honest, I didn't enjoy the vacation at all.*

frank /fræŋk/ [adj] someone who is **frank** talks in an honest and direct way, especially about subjects that are difficult to talk about

+ with *The doctor was very frank with me and told me I didn't have long to live.*

○to be frank SPOKEN (=use this before saying what you really think or feel) *To be frank, George isn't very good at the job.*

○frankly [adv] SPOKEN say this before telling someone what you really think: *Quite frankly, I think it's your own fault.*

speak your mind /ˌspiːk jɔːʳ 'maɪnd/ to say exactly what you think, even if you offend people by doing this: *Liz wasn't afraid to speak her mind, even in front of the boss.*

sincere /sɪn'sɪəʳ/ [adj] someone who is **sincere** shows their true feelings and says what they really believe, and is not pretending: *She said she would love to come, but I wasn't sure if she was being sincere.*

3 an honest way of behaving

honesty /'ɒnʲsti‖'ɑːn-/ [n U] an honest way of talking or behaving, so you tell the truth, and do not try to cheat people or hide information from them: *Will talked about his experience of HIV with courage and honesty.* | *Honesty is important in any relationship.*

When you see **EC**, go to the **ESSENTIAL COMMUNICATION** section.

HOPE

➡ see also **WANT**

1 to hope that something will happen or that something is true

hope /həʊp/ [v I/T] to want something to happen or to be true, and think that this is possible: *See you soon, I hope!*

+ (that) *Let's hope no-one saw us leaving.* | *The President hopes that these talks will result in a permanent peace settlement.*

hope to do sth *Bob's hoping to travel to Africa next year.*

+ for *I'm hoping for a better salary in my next job.*

○I hope so SPOKEN (=when you hope that what was mentioned will actually happen) *"Is Laura coming to the party?" "I hope so."*

○I hope not SPOKEN *"Do you think Anna's lost?" "I hope not!"*

⚠ Don't say 'I hope him to come'. Say **I hope (that) he will come**.

⚠ Don't say 'I don't hope it rains'. Say **hope it doesn't rain**.

hopefully /'həʊpfəli/ [adv] use **hopefully** when you hope that what you are saying will happen or is true: *Hopefully, these problems can be solved quite quickly.* | *Karen might be feeling better by next week, hopefully.*

⚠ This use of **hopefully** is very common in both spoken and written english, but there are some people who think that **hopefully** should only be used to mean 'in a hopeful way', for example: *Waiting hopefully for a phone call.*

in the hope that (also **in hopes that** AMERICAN) /ɪn ðə 'həʊp ðət, ɪn 'həʊps ðət/ if you do something **in the hope that** it will have a good result, you do it because you hope it will make something good happen: *He showed me a photo of his wife, in the hope that I might have seen her.*

be hopeful /biː ˈhəʊpfəl/ if you **are hopeful** about a situation, you think it will probably have a good result in the end, even though it may be worrying at the moment
+ (that) *Police are still hopeful that the missing girl will contact her parents soon.*
+ about *After talking to the management, we felt a little more hopeful about the company's future.*

◯**keep your fingers crossed** /ˌkiːp jɔːr ˈfɪŋgərz ˌkrɒst‖-ˌkrɔːst/ SPOKEN to hope for good luck, so that something will happen in the way you want: *"Have you heard whether you got the job or not?" "No, but I'm keeping my fingers crossed."*

2 the feeling that things will happen in the way that you hope

hope /həʊp/ [n U] the feeling you have when you think that something good will probably happen: *This discovery will give new hope to cancer sufferers.*
be full of hope *We arrived in our new country full of hope.*
hope of doing sth *There is very little hope of finding any more survivors.*

optimistic /ˌɒptɪˈmɪstɪk◄‖-ˌɑːp-/ [adj] someone who is **optimistic** believes that everything will happen in the way that they want or that good things will happen in the future: *Most of the players were in an optimistic mood before the game.*
+ about *Senator Crosman, are you optimistic about the election results?*
　optimistically [adv] *They had promised – rather optimistically – to finish the job in three days.*

optimism /ˈɒptɪmɪzəm‖-ˈɑːp-/ [n U] the feeling that everything will happen in the way you want it to or that good things will happen in the future: *There is a mood of optimism among Socialist Party supporters tonight.* | *the optimism of the post-war period*

optimist /ˈɒptɪmɪst‖-ˈɑːp-/ [n C] someone who always thinks good things will happen in the future

3 something that you hope will happen

hope /həʊp/ [n C] something that you hope will happen: *My one hope was that I would see my family again one day.* | *The politicians didn't seem to understand the hopes and fears of ordinary people.*
have high hopes (=feel sure that good things will happen) *When we first got married we had such high hopes.*

4 something that makes you feel hopeful

encouraging /ɪnˈkʌrɪdʒɪŋ‖-ˈkɜːr-/ [adj]
encouraging signs, remarks, news etc make you feel more confident that things will improve or happen in the way you want: *The doctor's news was very encouraging – Ben was getting better every day.* | *There are encouraging signs that the economy is recovering.* | *encouraging comments*

promising /ˈprɒmɪsɪŋ‖ˈprɑː-/ [adj] something that is **promising** seems as if it is going to be good or successful in the future: *Beth gave up a promising business career to become an artist.* | *The team got off to a promising start, winning their first three games.*
get off to/make a promising start (=do very well at the beginning of something)

5 to stop hoping

give up hope/lose hope /ˌgɪv ʌp ˈhəʊp, ˌluːz ˈhəʊp/ to stop hoping that something good will happen or that things will get better: *Just when they had almost given up hope, Jenny became pregnant.*
give up/lose hope of doing sth *After the accident, he had given up hope of ever walking again.*
+ that *We never lost hope that one day we would see our son again.*

⚠ Don't say 'give up the hope' or 'lose the hope'. Say **give up hope** or **lose hope**.

despair /dɪˈspeər/ [n U] ESPECIALLY WRITTEN the feeling that things are so bad that there is nothing you can do to make the situation any better: *the years of loneliness and despair that followed her daughter's death*

H

in despair She turned to him in despair, with tears running down her cheeks.

HORRIBLE/ UNPLEASANT

BAD　　LIKE/NOT LIKE

HATE　　see also　　NICE

GOOD　　ENJOY

1 horrible person/ behaviour

horrible /ˈhɒrɪbəl‖ˈhɔː-, ˈhɑː-/ [adj] behaving in a very rude, unkind, or annoying way, especially towards people that you know well: *Her husband was a horrible man – violent, lazy, and always drunk.*
be horrible to sb *Why are you being so horrible to me? It's not my fault you lost your job.*

> ⚠ Don't say 'very horrible'. Say **really horrible** or just **horrible**.

nasty /ˈnɑːsti‖ˈnæsti/ [adj] deliberately very unkind – used especially by children or when you are talking to children: *The other boys played a nasty trick on him.*
be nasty to sb *Stop being so nasty to your sister!*

unpleasant /ʌnˈplezənt/ [adj] rude or unfriendly in the way you talk to people or answer their questions: *That man in the grocery store is always so unpleasant.*
be unpleasant to sb *You shouldn't have been so unpleasant to her – she was only trying to help.*

Ọnot very nice /nɒt veri ˈnaɪs/ SPOKEN unkind or unfriendly – use this especially about things people say to each other: *They just told us to shut up, which wasn't very nice.*
not very nice of sb *"He kept telling me how fat I was." "That wasn't very nice of him, was it?"*

mean /miːn/ [adj] AMERICAN INFORMAL someone who is **mean** behaves in a rude,

unfriendly, and sometimes cruel way: *Fratelli was a pretty mean character, and we were all scared of him.*

2 a horrible feeling/ experience/accident

horrible /ˈhɒrɪbəl‖ˈhɔː-, ˈhɑː-/ [adj] a **horrible** experience or feeling is one that makes you feel very worried and upset: *It was really horrible coming home and finding all our things had been stolen.* | *There was a horrible moment when she thought she had left all her files on the train.*

> ⚠ Don't say 'very horrible'. Say **really horrible**.

nasty /ˈnɑːsti‖ˈnæsti/ [adj] horrible – use this especially about events where there is violence, injury, or death: *There was a nasty accident on the freeway and seven people were killed.* | *a particularly nasty murder case* | *The news of his death came as a nasty shock.*

unpleasant /ʌnˈplezənt/ [adj] an **unpleasant** situation is one that makes you feel slightly worried, uncomfortable, or embarrassed: *I had an unpleasant feeling that someone was following me.* | *Phil and Jane just argued the whole time, so it was a pretty unpleasant evening.*

Ọnot very nice /nɒt veri ˈnaɪs/ SPOKEN unpleasant: *It's not very nice being stuck in an elevator for an hour.* | *Divorce is not a very nice business.*

> ⚠ People often use **not very nice** to describe something that is in fact extremely unpleasant.

nightmare /ˈnaɪtmeəʳ/ [n singular] a very unpleasant or frightening experience: *We were stuck in a traffic jam for about four hours – it was a nightmare.*
turn into a nightmare (=become very unpleasant) *The couple's honeymoon turned into a nightmare when Martin suddenly became very ill.*

> ⚠ You can also use **nightmare** before a noun, like an adjective: *a nightmare journey*

3 a horrible taste/smell/ sight etc

horrible/disgusting/revolting
/'hɒrɪbəl, dɪs'gʌstɪŋ, rɪ'vəʊltɪŋǁ'hɔː-, 'haː-/ [adj]
very bad – use this especially to talk about
things that taste or smell or look really
bad: *It was the most disgusting meal I've
ever eaten!* | *His teeth were a revolting
yellow color.* | *What a horrible smell!* |
*The villagers cooked a special stew,
which looked and smelled revolting.*

> ⚠ Don't say 'very horrible/disgusting/
> revolting'. Say **really horrible/disgusting/
> revolting.**

foul /faʊl/ [adj] a **foul** smell or taste is
extremely bad, and is caused especially by
things decaying: *There was a foul smell
coming up from the river.*

Q gross /grəʊs/ [adj] not before noun]
SPOKEN, ESPECIALLY AMERICAN very unpleasant
– use this to talk about food, smells, or
things people do that you dislike very
much: *Ooh, gross! I hate spinach!* | *Brad
threw up on the floor at the party. It was
really gross.*

HOT

➡ if you mean 'food that has a hot
taste', go to TASTE 7
➡ opposite COLD
➡ see also WEATHER

1 object/liquid/surface

hot /hɒtǁhaːt/ [adj] *Eat your dinner while
it's hot.* | *Each room has hot and cold
running water.* | *Be careful – that pan's
still very hot.*
red hot (=extremely hot) *By 10 o'clock,
the sand on the beach was red hot.*
hot – hotter – hottest

boiling/boiling hot /'bɔɪlɪŋ, ˌbɔɪlɪŋ
'hɒt◄ǁ-'haːt◄/ [adj] a liquid that is **boiling** or
boiling hot is extremely hot: *I'm not
getting into that bathtub yet. It's boil-
ing!* | *Boiling hot water poured out of
the radiator.*

scalding/scalding hot /'skɔːldɪŋ,
ˌskɔːldɪŋ 'hɒt◄ǁ-'haːt◄/ [adj] a liquid or drink

that is **scalding** or **scalding hot** is
extremely hot, so that it burns you if you
touch it or drink it: *She handed me a mug
of scalding hot coffee.*

2 room/place/weather

hot /hɒtǁhaːt/ [adj] *It was a hot summer's
day.* | *The Gobi Desert is one of the
hottest places on earth.*
it's hot (=when the weather is hot or a
room is hot) *It's hot in here – why don't
you turn the heater down?* | *It was too
hot to play volleyball.*
hot – hotter – hottest

heat /hiːt/ [n U] when something is hot,
especially the air in a room or outside:
*Several of her plants had died in the
heat.* | *The heat from the fire was
almost unbearable.* | *In the desert, the
heat of the day is soon lost when the sun
goes down.*

Q boiling/boiling hot /'bɔɪlɪŋ, ˌbɔɪlɪŋ
'hɒt◄-'haːt◄/ [adj] SPOKEN very hot: *a boiling hot day in August*
it's boiling/boiling hot *Open the door –
it's boiling in here.*

Q broiling /'brɔɪlɪŋ/ [adj] AMERICAN ESPE-
CIALLY SPOKEN weather that is **broiling** is
very hot and makes you feel uncomfortable: *The day of the pony race was
broiling hot.* | *the broiling heat of a
Mississippi summer*

sweltering /'sweltərɪŋ/ [adj] weather that
is **sweltering** is very hot and makes you
feel tired and uncomfortable: *Lucy came
to call one sweltering afternoon in
July.* | *the sweltering summer of 1995*

> ⚠ **Sweltering** is used especially in
> written descriptions.

heatwave /'hiːtweɪv/ [n C] a period of
time when the weather is much hotter
than usual: *The heatwave continued
throughout August and into September.*

3 warm, but not hot

warm /wɔːrm/ [adj] a little hot, but not very
hot, especially in a way that is pleasant: *I
didn't want to get out of my warm bed.* |
It's nice and warm in the kitchen. | *a
warm day* | *These plants only grow in
warm climates.*

H

warmth [n U] when an object, the weather, a place etc is warm: *The warmth of the sun was making them all sleepy.*

lukewarm /ˌluːk'wɔːᵊm◂/ [adj] food or drinks that are **lukewarm** are slightly warm, and not as hot or as cold as they should be: *The bartender handed me a mug of lukewarm beer.* | *The coffee was only lukewarm.*

4 when you feel hot

hot /hɒt‖hɑːt/ [adj not before noun] feeling hot, especially when this makes you uncomfortable: *I'm too hot – could you open the window?* | *The travellers were hot, tired, and thirsty.*

warm /wɔːᵊm/ [adj not usually before noun] feeling pleasantly warm, especially when you are in a cold place: *Are you warm enough?* | *We stamped our feet in order to keep warm.*
warm coat/boots/clothes etc (=which keep you warm when the weather is cold) *Put on some warm clothes if you're going out in the snow.*

boiling /'bɔɪlɪŋ/ [adj not before noun] SPOKEN feeling very hot: *I'd like a cold drink – I'm boiling!*

have a temperature /ˌhæv ə 'tempərətʃəᵊ/ if you **have a temperature**, your body is hotter than usual because you are ill: *The doctor said I had a temperature, and told me to stay in bed.*

5 when your body becomes wet because you are hot

sweat /swet/ [v I] if you **sweat**, small drops of liquid come from the surface of your skin because you are hot: *I was sweating after the long climb.*
sweat [n U] the liquid that forms on your skin when you are hot: *Ian came off the squash court covered in sweat.*

sweaty /'sweti/ [adj] covered with sweat: *Joe felt hot and sweaty, and decided to go for a swim.*

6 how hot something is

how hot /hau 'hɒt‖-'hɑːt/ *How hot is it outside?* | *She couldn't believe how hot it was in the car.*

temperature /'tempərətʃəᵊ/ [n C] a measurement of how hot or cold something is: *Test the temperature of the water to make sure it's not too hot.*
high/low temperature (=hot or cold) *Steel can only be produced at a very high temperature.* | *Expect low temperatures in the mountain regions tonight.*
a temperature of 30/70/100 etc degrees *Heat the oven to a temperature of 200 degrees.*

7 to become hot or warm

get hot/warm /ˌget 'hɒt, 'wɔːᵊm‖-'hɑːt-/ to become hot or warm: *You'd better switch the engine off – it's getting very hot.* | *As the weather gets warmer, birds begin to return from their winter nesting places.* | *The room got hotter and hotter as the afternoon went on.*

warm up /ˌwɔːᵊm 'ʌp/ [phrasal verb I] to gradually get warmer, especially so that a place reaches a more comfortable temperature: *It's pretty cold in here, but it'll soon warm up.* | *I'm not going horse-riding again until the weather warms up.*

overheat /ˌəʊvəᵊ'hiːt/ [v I] if an engine or machine **overheats**, it gets too hot so that it does not work properly: *There's a special cooling system that stops the engine from overheating.*

8 to make someone or something hot or warm

heat /hiːt/ [v T] to make something hot or warm using a fire, a heating system, or a cooker: *She heated the water in a pan.* | *How do you heat the house in the winter?*

heat up /ˌhiːt 'ʌp/ [phrasal verb T] to make food hot, especially food that has been cooked already and has gone cold
heat up sth *I usually just heat up some soup for my lunch.*
heat sth up *Heat the pitta bread up in the toaster.*

warm up /ˌwɔːᵊm 'ʌp/ [phrasal verb T] to make a place warmer or make yourself warmer, especially so that you feel more comfortable
warm sth/sb up *Here, have a glass of brandy. That'll warm you up.*
warm up sth *Dad lit the fire to warm up the living-room.*

turn up /ˌtɜːⁿ ˈʌp/ [phrasal verb T] to make something such as a heater or cooker produce more heat

turn up sth I'm freezing! Turn up the heater!

turn sth up After the cake has been baking for an hour, turn the heat up to 220°.

WORD BANK
HOUSES/ WHERE PEOPLE LIVE

➡ see pages 366–369

HUNGRY

MEAL TASTE COOK THIN EAT DRINK FOOD RESTAURANTS/ EATING AND DRINKING

see also

1 when you want to eat

hungry /ˈhʌngri/ [adj] if you are **hungry**, you feel that you need to eat something: Are you hungry? I can make you a sandwich. | Alan felt hungry after the game. | Have something before you go out, or you'll get hungry later.

⚠ Don't say 'I have hunger'. Say **I'm hungry**.

starving/ravenous /ˈstɑːⁿvɪŋ, ˈræv-ənəs/ [adj not before noun] SPOKEN very hungry: Can we stop for lunch now? I'm absolutely starving. | You haven't had dinner? You must be ravenous.

⚠ Don't say 'very starving' or 'very ravenous'. Say **absolutely starving/ravenous** or just say **starving** or **ravenous**.

peckish /ˈpekɪʃ/ [adj not before noun] BRITISH if you feel **peckish**, you feel a little hungry: I'm feeling a bit peckish. Is there anything in the fridge?

feel like something to eat /ˌfiːl laɪk sʌmθɪŋ tʊ ˈiːt/ SPOKEN if you **feel like something to eat**, you want to eat something: It's 12 o'clock – do you feel like something to eat?

2 not hungry

not hungry /nɒt ˈhʌngri/ if you are **not hungry**, you do not feel that you need to eat anything: "Would you like something to eat?" "No thanks, I'm not hungry."

lose your appetite /ˌluːz jɔːⁿ ˈæpɪtaɪt/ to not want to eat anything, for example because you are ill or worried: She isn't sleeping very well and she's lost her appetite.

not feel like anything /nɒt fiːl laɪk ˈeniθɪŋ/ SPOKEN INFORMAL say this to tell someone that you are not hungry: I had a really big lunch, so I don't feel like anything just now.

3 the feeling you have when you are hungry

appetite /ˈæpɪtaɪt/ [n C/U] the normal feeling of wanting to eat when you have not eaten for some time: The medicine might affect your appetite.

give sb an appetite (=make them feel hungry) All that exercise has given me an appetite.

have a good/big/healthy appetite (=want to eat a lot and enjoy eating) He certainly has a healthy appetite. He ate two plates of pasta in about 10 minutes.

hunger /ˈhʌngəⁿ/ [n U] the feeling you have when you have eaten very little food: By the end of the day, I was feeling weak with hunger.

4 when people are ill or dying because they do not have enough to eat

starving /ˈstɑːⁿvɪŋ/ [adj] someone who is **starving** has not had enough food for a long time and will die soon if they do not eat: TV pictures of starving children in Africa | People in western countries waste food while millions are starving.

HUNGRY continues on page 369

When you see **EC**, go to the **ESSENTIAL COMMUNICATION** section.

HOUSES/WHERE PEOPLE LIVE

Here are some words to help you describe the place where you live.

Is it a

HOUSE,

or an

APARTMENT

in a large building?

2 What type of apartment do you live in?

apartment /əˈpɑːrtmənt/ (also **flat** /flæt/ BRITISH) [n C] a set of rooms that are usually all on the same level and are part of a larger building

block of flats BRITISH **apartment building** /ˌblɒk əv ˈflæts, əˈpɑːrtmənt ˌblɒk‖ˌblɑːk-/ AMERICAN [n C] a building that consists of different levels and has several apartments on each level

condominium /ˌkɒndəˈmɪniəm‖ˌkɑːn-/ [n C] in the US, an apartment in a building that consists of several apartments, all of which are owned by the people who live in them

hall of residence (also **hall**) BRITISH **dormitory** (also **dorm**) AMERICAN /ˌhɔːl əv ˈrezɪdəns, hɔːl, ˈdɔːrmɪtəri, dɔːrm‖-tɔːri-/ [n C] a large building at a college or university that consists of separate rooms where students live

studio apartment AMERICAN **bedsit** BRITISH **studio flat** BRITISH /ˈstjuːdiəʊ əˌpɑːrtmənt, ˈbedsɪt, ˈstjuːdiəʊ ˌflæt‖ˈstuː-/ [n C] a small apartment with one main room, usually for only one person to live in

1 What type of house do you live in?

bungalow /ˈbʌŋgələʊ/ [n C] a small house in which all the rooms are on the same level

detached house /dɪˌtætʃt ˈhaʊs/ [n C] BRITISH a house that is not joined to another house

house /haʊs/ [n C] a building that people live in, especially a building on more than one level that is used by one family or group of people: *Are you coming to Sophie's house tonight?* | *There are some very old houses in this part of town.* | *He has an apartment in*

London as well as a country house. (=a house in the country)

ranch house /ˈrɑːntʃ ˌhaʊs‖ˈræntʃ-/ [n C] a house in the US in which all the rooms are on the same level, with a roof that does not slope much

semi-detached house /ˌsemi dɪˌtætʃt ˈhaʊs/ [n C] BRITISH a house that is joined to another house on one side

terraced house BRITISH **row house** /ˌterɪst ˈhaʊs, ˈrəʊ ˌhaʊs/ AMERICAN [n C] a house that is in a row of houses that are all joined together

HOUSES/WHERE PEOPLE LIVE

3 Which floor is your apartment on?

basement /'beɪsmənt/ [n C] the level of a building that is below the level of the ground: *Is anyone living in the basement?*
a basement flat/apartment *Carlo had a basement apartment in Grant St.*

floor /flɔːʳ/ [n C] **first/second/third etc floor** the first, second etc level in a building
on the first/second etc floor *Her apartment is on the third floor.*
a first-floor/second-floor etc apartment/flat *an eighth-floor apartment with a view of the ocean*

> ⚠ In American English, the **first floor** is on the same level as the ground, and the **second floor** is the next level above this. In British English, the part on the same level as the ground is called the **ground floor**, and the **first floor** is the next level above this.

ground floor /ˌgraʊnd 'flɔːʳ◄/ [n C] ESPE-CIALLY BRITISH the part of a building that is on the same level as the ground
on the ground floor *They live in a small flat on the ground floor.*
a ground-floor flat/apartment *The ground-floor apartment is empty at the moment.*

5 Is it owned by someone else?

landlord/landlady /'lændlɔːʳd, 'lænd-ˌleɪdi/ [n C] the man or woman that you rent a house or apartment from

rent /rent/ [v I/T] to pay money regularly to live in a house or apartment that someone else owns: *Hal's rented an apartment downtown.* | *We rented for a while before buying a place of our own.*
rent sth from sb *They rent the house from a retired businessman.*

rent /rent/ [n C/U] the money that you pay to live in a house or apartment that someone else owns: *The rent's pretty high – about $800 a month.*
pay the rent *We hardly earn enough money to pay the rent.*

rented /'rentɪd/ [adj usually before noun]
rented house/apartment/accommodation a house, apartment etc that you pay money to someone else to live in and do not own yourself

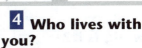

4 Who lives with you?
→ go to **LIVE**

6 What can you see from the window?

overlook /ˌəʊvəʳ'lʊk/ [v T] if a building or room **overlooks** a place that is on a lower level, you see that place from it when you look out of the window: *Our apartment overlooked a small courtyard.*
a house/apartment/room etc overlooking (=which overlooks) *an 8th-floor flat overlooking Hyde Park*

view /vjuː/ [n C] the whole area that you see when you look out of a window, especially when this area is very large or beautiful: *She stood on the balcony admiring the view.*
+ of *a spectacular view of San Francisco Bay*

HOUSES/WHERE PEOPLE LIVE continues on the next page

HOUSES/WHERE PEOPLE LIVE

7 What sort of area is it in?

area /'eəriə/ [n C] a particular part of a town or city: *My apartment's very small but I love the area.* | *a middle-class area* | *a residential area* (=where there are houses, but no offices or factories)

(housing) estate /('haʊzɪŋ) ɪ'steɪt/ [n C] BRITISH an area where there are a lot of houses or apartments which are very similar and were all built at the same time: *Conor was brought up on a big housing estate in Belfast.* | *There's a lot of crime on our estate.*

(housing) project /('haʊzɪŋ) ,prɒdʒekt‖ -prɑː-/ [n C] AMERICAN a group of houses or apartments for poor families, usually built with money from the government: *There are plans for a new housing project on the east side of town.* | *kids from the projects*

neighbourhood BRITISH **neighbor-**

hood AMERICAN /'neɪbərhʊd/ [n C] a small area of a town or city where people live: *a nice neighborhood of Boston*

in the neighbourhood *There's only one park in the whole neighbourhood.*

part of town /,pɑːrt əv 'taʊn/ [n C usually singular] an area of a town or city: *What part of town do you live in?*

suburb /'sʌbɜːrb/ [n C] an area outside the centre of a city, where many people live

the suburbs *I was brought up in the suburbs.*

+ of *a quiet suburb of Los Angeles*

Q**where sb lives** /weər (sb) 'lɪvz/ SPOKEN use this when you are describing the area where someone lives: *Where I live, there's nowhere for kids to play.* | *It's really nice where Sonia lives.*

➡ see also **TOWN**, **AREA**

8 Is it in the town or the country?
➡ go to **TOWN, COUNTRYSIDE**

9 How big is it?

one-bedroomed/two-bed-roomed etc /(one, etc) bedruːmd/ [adj only before noun] a **one-bedroomed, two-bedroomed etc** house or apartment has one bedroom, two bedrooms etc: *a one-bedroomed apartment* | *a three-bedroomed house*

overcrowded /,əʊvərˈkraʊdɪd◄/ [adj] an **overcrowded** house has too many people in it, and is unpleasant and uncomfortable to live in: *Many of these families are living in substandard or overcrowded housing.*

poky /'pəʊki/ [adj] a **poky** house or room is very small, and there is not enough room to move around in: *a poky little cottage*

spacious /'speɪʃəs/ [adj] a **spacious** house or room has plenty of space, so it is comfortable and pleasant to live in: *a spacious, comfortably furnished flat*

three-storey/four-storey etc BRITISH **three-story/four-story etc** AMERICAN /(three, etc) stɔːri/ [adj only before noun] a **three-storey, four-storey etc** house or building has three levels, four levels etc: *a five-story apartment block*

HUNGRY continued from page 365

starve /staɚv/ [v I] to have so little food to eat that you become ill or die: *I have a family to take care of – I can't let them starve.*

starve to death (=die because of lack of food) *Thousands of deer starve to death every winter.*

   starvation /staɚˈveɪʃən/ [n U] when you become ill or die because you do not have enough to eat: *The climbers were close to starvation when they were rescued.* | *Thousands of people could die of cold and starvation this winter.*

malnutrition /ˌmælnjʊˈtrɪʃən‖-nʊ-/ [n U] a serious health problem caused by not eating enough healthy food for a long time, which makes your body weak: *Many children from poor families were suffering from malnutrition.* | *Disease and malnutrition are widespread in the shanty towns.*

famine /ˈfæmɪ̯n/ [n C/U] when many people in a place are very hungry and some of them die, especially because the food they planted did not grow: *War and famine caused thousands of deaths in Africa last year.* | *During the Great Famine, millions of Irish people emigrated to the US.*

HURRY

➡ see also **FAST, SLOW, RUN**

1 to go somewhere or do something as quickly as you can

hurry /ˈhʌri‖ˈhɜːri/ [v I] to go somewhere or do something quickly, especially because you do not have much time: *The movie begins in ten minutes – we'll have to hurry.* | *There's no need to hurry – we still have an hour to spare.*

+ across/along/away/down etc *Dieter was hurrying along the platform to catch his train.* | *The children hurried away when they saw me coming.*

hurry to do sth *Anna was hurrying to finish her essay before lunchtime.*

hurrying – hurried – have hurried

---

10 How long have you lived there?

for /fər; *strong* fɔːr/ [preposition] use this to say how long you have lived somewhere: *My parents have lived in the same house for almost 30 years.*

since /sɪns/ [preposition/conjunction] if you have lived somewhere **since** a time or event, you started to live there at that time and you are still living there now: *They've lived here since they got married.*

since 1980/the summer etc *We've been living in the flat since last Christmas.*

I live in Hamburg in a rented apartment on the second floor of a large, old building that overlooks a busy street. The apartment is small and overcrowded, but the rent is cheap, and I like the area. It is a lively part of town full of bars, cafes, and restaurants.

in a hurry /ɪn ə ˈhʌri‖-ˈhɜːri/ if you do something **in a hurry**, you do it very quickly because you do not have much time, so you often make mistakes or forget things: *Bob left the house in a hurry, and forgot his keys.*

be in a hurry (=when you have to hurry) *Sorry, I can't stop – I'm in a hurry.*

be in a hurry to do sth *Why are you in such a hurry to get home?*

⚠ Don't say 'I am in hurry'. Say **I am in a hurry**.

rush/dash /rʌʃ, dæʃ/ [v I] to go somewhere or run somewhere very quickly, for example because you have to do something urgently or because someone is in danger

+ across/off/out/into etc *The neighbours came rushing out to see what had happened. | The last time I saw her she was dashing off to the airport.*

rush/dash to do sth *I dashed downstairs to answer the phone. | People were rushing into doorways to escape the bullets.*

hurriedly /ˈhʌrɪdli‖ˈhɜːr-/ [adv] WRITTEN if you do something **hurriedly**, you do it quickly because you do not have much time: *He hurriedly put on a pair of jeans and went to answer the door.*

⚠ Use **hurriedly** in stories and written descriptions.

2 what you say to tell someone to hurry

🔍 **hurry up/come on** /ˌhʌri ˈʌp, ˌkʌm ˈɒn‖ˌhɜːri-/ SPOKEN say this to tell someone to hurry, especially when you are impatient with them for being too slow: *Hurry up or we'll be late for school! | Come on – you should have finished packing by now!*

3 something that you do quickly because you are hurrying

quick /kwɪk/ [adj only before noun] a **quick** look, meal, visit, decision etc is done very quickly, because you do not have much time: *Mary went upstairs for a quick shower. | Could I just make a quick phone call?*

quick look/glance (=when you look at something or read something very quickly) *He had a quick glance at the newspaper before going to work.*

quick drink/lunch/coffee *Come on – let's have a quick drink in the bar.*

hasty /ˈheɪsti/ [adj only before noun] a **hasty** decision or action is done very quickly, without planning it or thinking carefully about the results: *Don't make any hasty decisions that you might regret. | Napoleon's army was forced to make a hasty retreat.*

hasty – hastier – hastiest

frantic /ˈfræntɪk/ [adj only before noun]
frantic activity/rush/search/effort when people are rushing around in a disorganized way, for example because they have to do something very urgently, or because someone is in danger: *The night before the wedding, the house was a scene of frantic activity. | a frantic search for the missing children*

frantically [adv] *The library was full of students, frantically trying to finish their final essays.*

rush /rʌʃ/ [n singular] a situation in which you have to hurry or work very fast in order to finish something

a rush to do sth *There was a rush to get everything arranged for the party.*

do sth in a rush *We had to pack our suitcases in a rush and leave the hotel.*

4 to make someone hurry

hurry sb up /ˌhʌri (sb) ˈʌp‖ˌhɜːri-/ [phrasal verb T] to make someone do something more quickly because they are taking too long: *Can you try and hurry the kids up? We're supposed to be leaving in ten minutes.*

rush/hurry /rʌʃ, ˈhʌri‖-ˈhɜːri/ [v T] to make someone do something more quickly, in an impatient way that makes them feel nervous or confused: *Don't rush me – I'm working as fast as I can. | It's an important decision, so don't let them hurry you.*

hurrying – hurried – have hurried

When you see **EC**, go to the **ESSENTIAL COMMUNICATION** section.

5 what you say to tell someone not to hurry

Q there's no hurry/there's no rush /ðeəʳz ˌnəʊ ˈhʌri, ðeəʳz ˌnəʊ ˈrʌʃ‖-ˈhɜːri/ SPOKEN say this to tell someone that they do not have to hurry or do something soon: *You can pay me for the ticket next week. There's no rush.*

Q take your time /ˌteɪk jɔːʳ ˈtaɪm/ SPOKEN say this to tell someone to do something slowly and carefully, because it is important to do it well: *Take your time and think carefully before you answer the question.*

Q what's the hurry?/what's the rush? /ˌwɒts ðə ˈhʌri, ˌwɒts ðə ˈrʌʃ‖-ˈhɜːri/ SPOKEN say this to someone who is hurrying or trying to make you hurry, to emphasize that there is plenty of time: *It'll only take us 20 minutes to get to the restaurant – what's the hurry?*

HURT/INJURE

MEDICAL TREATMENT
PAIN   DAMAGE
ACCIDENT   see also   THREATEN
FALL   CUT
BREAK   BETTER 4

1 hurt or injured in an accident, fight etc

be injured/be hurt /biː ˈɪndʒəʳd‖biː ˈhɜːʳt/ if someone **is hurt** or **is injured**, part of their body has been damaged, especially in an accident or fight: *"Did you hear about that fire in the school?" "Yes – thank God no one was hurt."* | *Four people have been injured in a road accident.*
badly/seriously injured *One man died, and another was seriously injured when a wall collapsed on a construction site.*
badly/seriously hurt *This man needs a doctor – he's badly hurt.*
slightly injured/hurt *A fireman was slightly injured, but all the people in the house were saved.*

get hurt *There's a huge crowd – someone could easily get hurt.*

⚠ Don't use the word 'damage' to talk about people. Cars, buildings, or equipment can get damaged, but people get **hurt** or **injured**.

be wounded /biː ˈwuːndɪd/ to be injured in a war, a fight etc, by a weapon such as a knife, gun, or bomb: *Two police officers were wounded in the attack.*
badly/seriously wounded *My father was badly wounded in 1945.*

2 to hurt a part of your body

hurt /hɜːʳt/ [v T] if you **hurt** a part of your body in an accident, a fight etc, you damage it so that it feels painful or you cannot move it easily: *He hurt his back, and the doctor said he would have to rest for a few weeks.* | *I can't go running this week – I've hurt my foot.*
hurt yourself *That's a sharp knife – be careful you don't hurt yourself!*
hurting – hurt – have hurt

injure /ˈɪndʒəʳ/ [v T] to hurt a part of your body, especially seriously and in a way that takes a long time to get better: *Tom injured his shoulder playing tennis.*

bruise /bruːz/ [v T] to hurt a part of your body when you fall or are hit, so that a dark, painful mark appears on your skin: *Shaun fell over and bruised his knee.*
   bruised [adj] *My arm was badly bruised, but not broken.*

sprain /spreɪn/ [v T] to injure your ankle, your knee, or another place where two bones are joined, by twisting or pulling it suddenly: *I sprained my ankle while I was playing basketball.*
   sprained [adj] *James can't play the piano because he has a sprained wrist.*

break /breɪk/ [v T] to break a bone in your body: *Nicola broke her leg when she went skiing.*
breaking – broke – have broken
   broken [adj] *I had three broken ribs and a broken arm.*

When you see **EC**, go to the **ESSENTIAL COMMUNICATION** section.

H

dislocate /'dɪsləkeɪt/ [v T] to injure your shoulder, knee, finger etc, so that one of the bones is moved out of its normal position: *He dislocated his shoulder in a riding accident.*

dislocated [adj] *The accident left her with bruises and a dislocated hip.*

3 to hurt someone

hurt /hɜːʳt/ [v T] to cause injury to someone's body and make them feel pain, especially by hitting them: *Let go of my arm! You're hurting me!* | *If he's hurt any of the children I'm going straight to the police.*

4 damage to part of your body

injury /'ɪndʒəri/ [n C/U] physical damage done to someone's body in an accident, a fight etc: *The glass roof collapsed onto the crowd, causing horrific injuries.*

serious injury *Wearing a helmet may protect you from serious injury.*

suffer an injury (=be injured) *He suffered serious injuries in a car crash, and died on the way to the hospital.*

plural **injuries**

wound /wuːnd/ [n C] an injury caused by a weapon such as a knife, gun, or bomb: *The wound was deep and needed 18 stitches.*

bullet/stab/gunshot wound *Barratt was taken to the hospital with stab wounds to his chest and neck.*

bruise /bruːz/ [n C] a dark, painful mark on your skin where you have fallen or been hit: *Her arms were covered in cuts and bruises.*

5 someone who is injured

injured /'ɪndʒəʳd/ [adj] hurt in an accident, fight etc: *Firefighters had to cut off the roof of the car, so that the injured man could be lifted out.*

the injured (=people who are injured) *The injured were rushed to St Thomas' Hospital.*

wounded /'wuːndɪd/ [adj] injured by a weapon such as a knife, gun, or bomb: *a wounded soldier* | *There are over 4000 refugees in the camp, many of them wounded.*

the wounded (=people who are wounded) *Helicopters have been sent in to rescue the wounded from the war zone.*

paralysed (also **paralyzed** AMERICAN) /'pærəlaɪzd/ [adj] unable to move part or all of your body because of a serious injury or illness: *The accident left him permanently paralysed.*

casualty /'kæʒuəlti/ [n C usually plural] someone who has been injured or killed in a war, attack, or accident: *The bomb caused serious damage to the building, but there were no casualties.* | *Indian troops have suffered more than 1200 casualties.*

6 not injured

unhurt /ʌn'hɜːʳt/ [adj not before noun] if you are **unhurt**, you are not hurt, even though you have been in an accident or have been attacked: *The driver of the car was unhurt, but his passenger was killed.*

unharmed /ʌn'hɑːʳmd/ [adj not before noun] if you are **unharmed**, you have not been harmed, even though you have been in a dangerous situation: *The boy was cold and hungry but otherwise unharmed.* | *All the hostages were released unharmed some time afterwards.*

I

IDEA

➡ see also **THINK, INVENT, IMAGINE**

1 a plan or suggestion that you think of

idea /aɪˈdɪə/ [n C] something that you think of and suggest to other people, for example a plan of what someone should do or a solution to a problem

good/great/fantastic etc idea *"We could go and see a movie." "Good idea!"*

have an idea *We're trying to think of a name for the product. Does anyone have any ideas?*

+ for *an idea for a new TV game show | Here are some new ideas for quick meals that taste great.*

it was sb's idea (=they thought of it: use this especially when you want to blame someone) *I didn't want to go to Spain – it was Sue's idea. | Whose idea was it to ask him to the party?*

get an idea from sb/sth *She got the idea from a picture in a magazine.*

thought /θɔːt/ [n C] an idea about what should happen or what someone should do, which you suggest although you are not sure if it is a good idea

have a thought *I've had a thought – do you think Nadia would like to come with us?*

sb's thoughts about sth *What are your thoughts about the holiday?*

⚲**(it was) just/only a thought** SPOKEN (say this when someone seems to disagree with an idea you suggested) *"We could paint the room yellow and blue." "Well, I'm not sure about that." "It's just a thought."*

2 an idea that explains something about life or the world

theory /ˈθɪəri/ [n C/U] a set of ideas that explains why something happens or why something is true, especially in science

+ about *There have been a lot of theories about the meaning of dreams.*

sb's theory of sth (used in the names of important scientific theories) *Darwin's theory of evolution | Einstein's theory of relativity*

+ that *There is a theory that Kennedy was killed by the CIA.*

plural **theories**

idea /aɪˈdɪə/ [n C] something that people think is true, for example their beliefs about why something happens

+ about *people's ideas about the origins of the universe*

+ that *What do you think of the idea that our lives are controlled by the stars?*

3 good at thinking of new ideas

creative /kriˈeɪtɪv/ [adj] someone who is **creative** is good at thinking of new ideas, designs, or ways of doing things, especially in art, music, literature etc: *Tarantino is one of Hollywood's most creative directors.*

full of ideas /ˌfʊl əv aɪˈdɪəz/ INFORMAL someone who is **full of ideas** has a lot of good new ideas and wants to tell other people about them: *Roy was full of ideas for the new show.*

imaginative /ɪˈmædʒɪnətɪv/ [adj] an **imaginative** plan, design, or way of doing something uses new and interesting ideas: *an imaginative solution to the city's crime problem | The film uses digital imaging techniques in an unusual and imaginative way.*

ILL/SICK

1 ill

⚠ **Ill** is more common than **sick** in British English. **Sick** is more common than **ill** in American English.

⚠ To **be sick** can also mean ‘to vomit’ (=bring up food from your stomach), especially in British English. And to **feel sick** can mean ‘to feel that you are going to vomit’. See Section 5.

ill /ɪl/ [adj not before noun] someone who is **ill** has an illness or does not feel well: *You look really ill. I'm going to call the doctor.* | *I was so ill I had to stay in bed for three months.*
feel ill *I felt ill for a week after I got back from Bolivia.*
seriously ill (=very ill) *His wife is seriously ill – they think it's cancer.*
critically ill (=so ill that you may die)
be taken ill (=suddenly become ill) *She was taken ill the day after her tenth birthday.*

⚠ Don't use **ill** about part of your body. Don't say ‘my head is ill’ or ‘my stomach is ill’. Say **I have a headache/a stomach ache**. See also PAIN.

⚠ Don't say ‘more ill’ or ‘iller’. Say **worse**: *The next morning she was even worse.*

sick /sɪk/ [adj] ill: *Where's Sheila? Is she sick?* | *She had spent months looking after her sick mother.*
get sick *If you take vitamin C every day, it helps to stop you from getting sick.*
be off sick (=not at work or school because of illness) *Lesley's off sick today.*
sick pay (=money you get from your employer when you cannot work because of illness)
the sick (=people who are sick) *At that time there were no state benefits for the old and the sick.*

⚠ Don't use **sick** about part of your body. Don't say ‘my leg is sick’ or ‘my head is sick’. See PAIN.

🔾**not very well** /ˌnɒt veri 'wel/ ESPECIALLY SPOKEN ill, but not seriously ill: *Sarah's not very well – she has a throat infection.*

🔾**under the weather** /ˌʌndəʳ ðə 'weðəʳ/ SPOKEN if you feel **under the weather**, you feel slightly ill: *Mike's feeling a little under the weather, so he couldn't come tonight.*

2 to become healthy again after being ill

get better /ˌget 'betəʳ/ if you **get better**, you become healthy again after an illness, operation, or injury; if a pain or an injury **gets better**, it stops hurting and you feel healthy again: *If you don't get better by tomorrow you'd better go to the doctor.* | *Did your headache get better after you took those pills?*

recover /rɪ'kʌvəʳ/ [v I] to become healthy again after a serious illness, operation, or injury: *Survivors of the fire are recovering in the city hospital.*
+ from *My father never really recovered from his first heart attack.*

⚠ **Recover** is more formal than **get better**, and is used especially about serious illnesses or injuries.

get well soon /ˌget wel 'suːn/ you say or write this to someone who is ill, to tell them that you hope they will soon get better: *Get well soon – we all miss you!*

3 someone who is ill

patient /'peɪʃənt/ [n C] someone who is looked after by a doctor or nurse because they are ill: *The hospital treats thousands of patients a year.* | *Dr Cobb is seeing a patient just now – could you wait ten minutes?*

invalid /'ɪnvəliːd, -lɪd‖-lɪd/ [n C] someone who is permanently ill and cannot look after themselves, especially someone who has to stay in bed: *Pregnant women do not want to be treated like invalids.*

unhealthy /ʌn'helθi/ [adj] someone who is **unhealthy** is often ill: *Tom was an unhealthy child, always catching colds and getting headaches.*

4 someone who often imagines they are ill

hypochondriac /ˌhaɪpə'kɒndriæk‖-'kɑːn-/ [n C] someone who worries a lot about their health, and often thinks they are ill when they are not: *He's such a hypochondriac. Every time he has a headache he thinks it's a brain tumour.*

5 when food comes up from your stomach and out of your mouth

vomit /ˈvɒmɪt‖ˈvɑː-/ [v I] if you **vomit**, food comes up from your stomach and out through your mouth, because you are ill or drunk: *The nurse gave her a bowl to vomit into.*

> **vomit** [n U] food that has come out of your mouth because you are ill or drunk

> ⚠ **Vomit** is more formal than **throw up** or **be sick** and is used especially by doctors and in formal written English.

○**throw up** /ˌθrəʊ ˈʌp/ [phrasal verb I] ESPECIALLY SPOKEN to vomit: *The baby threw up all over my shirt.*

> ⚠ **Throw up** is less formal than **vomit** and is the usual phrase to use in ordinary conversation.

be sick /biː ˈsɪk/ ESPECIALLY BRITISH to vomit: *Kelly ran into the bathroom and was violently sick.* | *I had to go out of the classroom because I thought I was going to be sick.*

> ⚠ **Be sick** is used in both written and spoken English.

feel sick /ˌfiːl ˈsɪk/ ESPECIALLY BRITISH to have the feeling that you are going to vomit: *Stop the car – I feel sick!* | *When I was pregnant the smell of coffee made me feel sick.*

nausea /ˈnɔːziə, -siə‖-ziə, -ʃə/ [n U] the feeling that you have when you think you are going to vomit: *The treatment sometimes causes headaches and nausea.*

ILLNESS/DISEASE

MEDICAL TREATMENT
ILL/SICK   DRUGS
BETTER 4   see also   WEAK
DOCTOR   SUFFER
PAIN   MENTALLY ILL
HEALTHY/UNHEALTHY

1 an illness

illness /ˈɪlnɪs/ [n C/U] a problem with your health that makes you feel ill, especially one that makes you stay in bed, or makes it difficult for you to work, have a normal life etc: *She died at the age of 82, after a long illness.* | *How many days off work have you had because of illness?*

mental illness (=an illness that affects your mind) *drugs that are used to treat mental illness*

serious illness (=one that could be dangerous) *In 1986 a serious illness ended her acting career.*

recover from an illness *Beth was still in the hospital, recovering from a serious illness.*

> ⚠ Don't use **illness** to talk about less serious problems such as headaches or colds.

disease /dɪˈziːz/ [n C/U] a particular kind of illness, especially one that spreads from one person to another or one that affects a particular part of your body: *Measles is a disease that is common among young children.* | *Mosquitoes spread diseases such as malaria.*

heart/lung/kidney disease *Smoking is a major cause of heart disease.*

suffer from a disease (=have a disease) *She suffers from a rare blood disease.*

infectious disease (=one that spreads from one person to another)

> ⚠ **Disease** can also be used to mean a lot of different diseases: *Thousands of refugees are dying of hunger and disease.*

infection /ɪnˈfekʃən/ [n C] a disease that spreads from one person to another and affects part of your body such as your eye, ear, or throat: *Dirty towels can spread infections.*

ear/eye/throat/chest infection *Richard's not at school because he has an ear infection.*

bug /bʌg/ [n C] INFORMAL a disease that is not serious, which spreads from one person to another, for example in the air or in food, and which a lot of people get: *There's a bug going around at school – everyone in my class has had it!*

stomach/tummy bug (=illness affecting the stomach) *Pete's been off work with a stomach bug.*

pick up a bug (=get a bug) *I think I picked up a bug while I was on vacation.*

problem /'prɒbləm‖'prɑː-/ [n C] when a part of your body has something wrong with it, for example when it is painful or it does not work properly

+ with *Simon's started to have problems with his back.*

back/chest/skin etc problems *A lot of people have skin problems when they are young.*

condition /kən'dɪʃən/ [n C] a serious problem that affects someone's health permanently: *High blood pressure is a condition that affects many elderly people.*

heart condition *Frank suffers from a rare heart condition.*

2 to have an illness

have (also **have got** BRITISH) /hæv, həv 'gɒt‖-'gɑːt/ [v T] to have an illness: *Beth has an awful cold. | I had all the usual child-hood illnesses. | Have you ever had pneumonia?*

suffer from sth /'sʌfər frɒm (sth)‖-frʌm-/ [phrasal verb T] to have a particular kind of illness or health problem, especially one that is serious or one that you have often: *Dewey had been in hospital for several weeks suffering from malaria. | She suffers from asthma attacks.*

there's something wrong with /ðeəʳz ˌsʌmθɪŋ 'rɒŋ wɪð‖-'rɔːŋ-/ INFORMAL use this to say that you have a medical prob-lem affecting part of your body, but you are not sure exactly what it is: *There's something wrong with my chest – it feels really tight. | We thought there might be something wrong with her hearing.*

with /wɪð, wɪθ/ [preposition] use this before the name of a disease, to say that someone has this disease: *"Where's Helen?" "She's in bed with flu." | The charity provides support for people with AIDS.*

When you see **EC**, go to the
ESSENTIAL COMMUNICATION section.

---

3 to start to have an illness

get /get/ [v T] to start to have an illness: *I feel all hot – I think I'm getting flu. | Smoking increases the risk of getting cancer.*

get sth from/off someone (=get an infec-tious disease from someone else) *He thinks he got the cold from someone in the office.*

catch /kætʃ/ [v T] to get a disease from someone else: *Luke has measles. I hope I don't catch it.*

catch sth from/off sb *I think I must have caught the flu from Sarah.*

catching – caught – have caught

go down with sth /ˌgəʊ 'daʊn wɪð (sth)/ [phrasal verb T] INFORMAL to start to have an illness, especially one that is not seri-ous: *I'm afraid we can't come this week-end – the baby's gone down with a sore throat.*

4 when a lot of people have an illness

outbreak /'aʊtbreɪk/ [n C] when a lot of people suddenly start to get an illness at the same time

+ of *Doctors are very concerned about an outbreak of tuberculosis in an East London school.*

epidemic /ˌepɪ'demɪk/ [n C] when very many people in an area or country get a disease, and it spreads very quickly

a flu/measles/cholera etc epidemic *Doctors warn that a flu epidemic may be on the way.*

5 when an illness is serious

serious /'sɪəriəs/ [adj] a **serious** illness or condition is very bad and may be danger-ous: *In February he suffered a serious heart attack. | Listeriosis is not usually a serious disease among healthy adults.*

something/anything/nothing serious *I hope it isn't anything serious, Doctor.*

seriously [adv] *Her mother is seriously ill with pneumonia.*

bad /bæd/ [adj] **bad cold/flu/fever/ cough/stomach ache etc** a cold etc that makes you feel very uncomfortable or that is very painful: *She has a bad cold.* | *a bad attack of bronchitis*

get worse *His cough seems to be getting worse.*

bad – worse – worst

terminal /'tɜːrmɪ̩nəl/ [adj] a **terminal** illness cannot be cured, so the person who has it will die from it, usually after quite a long period: *a patient suffering from terminal cancer* | *Should doctors tell patients that they have a terminal illness?*

fatal /'feɪtl/ [adj] a **fatal** illness makes the person who has it die: *The disease is almost always fatal.* | *The former president suffered a fatal heart attack this morning.*

6 when an illness is not serious

not serious /nɒt 'sɪəriəs/ [adj] *Don't worry, it's not serious. It's only a cold.*
nothing serious *My doctor told me it was nothing serious.*

slight /slaɪt/ [adj only before noun] **slight cold/cough/fever/headache etc** a cold etc that is not at all serious and does not make you feel very ill: *I have a slight cold.* | *The virus sometimes causes a slight fever.*

minor /'maɪnər/ [adj] a **minor** illness is not serious: *Most of these minor illnesses only last a few days or weeks.*

⚠ Don't use **minor** with the names of diseases.

IMAGINE

➡ look here for ...
• have a picture in your mind
• think that something is happening when it is not
➡ see also REAL 2, THINK, IDEA

1 to have a picture or idea of something in your mind

imagine /ɪ'mædʒɪ̩n/ [v T not in passive] to have a picture or idea in your mind about something that you have never seen or experienced: *The town was exactly how I had imagined it.*
+ (that) *Imagine that you won the lottery – what would you do with the money?*
+ what/how/where etc *I'm trying to imagine how the house will look when it's finished.*
imagine doing sth *It's hard to imagine living in a place like that.*
imagine sb doing sth *I can just imagine Sarah running her own business.*

⚠ Don't say 'imagine to do something'. Say **imagine doing something**: *Can you imagine having nowhere to live?*

picture /'pɪktʃər/ [v T not in passive] to form a clear picture in your mind of a person, place, or situation: *Can you picture it – you and me, lying on a beach in the sun.*
picture sb as *I had never met Graham, but I pictured him as tall and dark-haired.*
picture sb doing sth *I can't really picture him taking care of a baby.*

can see /kən 'siː/ ESPECIALLY SPOKEN to be able to imagine something, because you think it is likely to happen
can see sb doing sth *Jimmy's gone skiing. I can just see him arriving home with a broken leg.*
can see sb as sth *I can't really see her as a nurse.*

dream of /'driːm ɒv/ [phrasal verb T] to often think about something pleasant that you would like to do or that you wish would happen
dream of doing sth *When I was young, I used to dream of becoming a famous writer.*
dream of sth *They dreamed of a society where everyone was equal.*

2 to wrongly think that something is happening

imagine /ɪ'mædʒɪ̩n/ [v T] to wrongly think that something is happening when it is not really happening: *Had Luiz really spoken to her, or had she just imagined it?*
+ (that) *He was always imagining that people were talking about him behind his back.*

be seeing things/be hearing things /biː ˈsiːɪŋ θɪŋz, biː ˈhɪərɪŋ θɪŋz/ ESPECIALLY SPOKEN to think that you might have seen or heard something, although really you have not: *There's no one there – you must be seeing things.* | *Did someone call my name just then – or am I hearing things?*

3 something that you imagine

imaginary /ɪˈmædʒɪnəri‖-neri/ [adj] not real, but existing only as a picture or idea in your mind: *When Linda was a child, she had an imaginary friend called Booboo.* | *He held up an imaginary gun and pretended to shoot me.*

fantasy /ˈfæntəsi/ [n C] an exciting or enjoyable experience which you imagine happening to you, but which will probably never happen: *He's always talking about buying a beach house in Malibu, but it's just a fantasy.* | *sexual fantasies*
plural **fantasies**

4 your ability to imagine things

imagination /ɪˌmædʒɪˈneɪʃən/ [n C/U] *Reading is a good way to develop a child's imagination.* | *I don't have any pictures of the place, so you'll have to use your imagination.*
a vivid imagination (=when someone is very good at imagining unusual and exciting things) *Her stories show a particularly vivid imagination.*

⚠ Don't confuse **fantasy** and **imagination**. A **fantasy** is something that you imagine, but your **imagination** is your ability to imagine things.

IMMEDIATELY

➡ opposite LATER/AT A LATER TIME

1 immediately

immediately /ɪˈmiːdiətli/ [adv] quickly and without any delay: *If there's an accident in the school, you must report it immediately.* | *When I saw her face, I knew immediately that something was*

wrong. | *He turned over and immediately fell asleep.*
+ after/afterwards *We'll have to leave immediately after breakfast.* | *She was admitted to the hospital at 10 o'clock, and died almost immediately afterwards.*
immediate [adj usually before noun] happening or done immediately: *My immediate reaction was one of disappointment.* | *The baby had a fever, and needed immediate medical attention.*

at once/right away (also **straightaway** BRITISH) /ət ˈwʌns, ˌraɪt əˈweɪ, ˌstreɪtəˈweɪ/ if you do something **at once**, **right away**, or **straightaway**, you do it immediately, especially because it is urgent: *The principal wants to see you at once.* | *Moira phoned and I came straightaway.* | *If you offered me the job I could start right away.*

⚠ **Right away** is less formal than **at once** or **straightaway**, and is used especially in conversation.

this minute/right now /ˌðɪs ˈmɪnɪt, ˌraɪt ˈnaʊ/ SPOKEN say this when you are telling someone to do something immediately, especially in an angry way: *Tell him I want him in my office, right now!* | *You'd better go upstairs this minute and get in your bed.*

as soon as /əz ˈsuːn əz/ [conjunction] immediately after something has happened, or immediately after you have done something: *As soon as he felt well enough, he returned to Barcelona.*

⚠ When talking about the future, don't use the future tense after **as soon as**. Use the present tense: *I'll call you as soon as I get home* (not 'as soon as I will get home').

as soon as possible/as soon as you can /əz ˌsuːn əz ˈpɒsɪbəl, əz ˌsuːn əz juː ˈkæn‖-ˈpɑːrs-/ as soon as it is possible for you to do something: *Several other students need this book, so please return it as soon as possible.* | *We got back as soon as we could.*

instantly /ˈɪnstəntli/ [adv] immediately – use this when something happens at almost the same time as something else: *It* was a head-on crash, and both drivers died instantly. | I knew instantly that Kathy and I were going to be good friends.

at a glance /ət ə ˈglɑːns‖-ˈglæns/ **can see/know/tell sth at a glance** to know or realize something immediately, after only looking for a very short time: I could see at a glance how serious the situation was. | He can tell at a glance whether it's a real diamond or a fake.

IMPORTANT/ NOT IMPORTANT

➡ see also **DON'T CARE, FAMOUS, SERIOUS**

1 something that is important

important /ɪmˈpɔːrtənt/ [adj] something that is **important** has a big effect on people's lives and on the way things happen in the future, and a lot of things depend on it: Next Thursday's game is very important – if Italy lose they will be out of the World Cup. | I have an important announcement to make, so please listen carefully. | She didn't realize how important schoolwork was until it was too late.
   importance [n U] how important something is
+ of the importance of Einstein's discovery

significant /sɪgˈnɪfɪkənt/ [adj] **significant** events, changes etc are important enough to be noticed and considered or talked about: There has been a significant change in people's attitude to the environment. | Winning the award was a significant achievement. | a significant new discovery, which will improve our understanding of the AIDS virus

big /bɪg/ [adj only before noun] **big decision/event/occasion/day/moment** an important decision, event etc, especially one that will affect the rest of your life: This is a big decision – you'll have to give me time to think. | Graduation Day is one of those big occasions when everyone wants a souvenir photograph.

○**the big day** ESPECIALLY SPOKEN (=a very important day in someone's life) I hear you're getting married – when's the big day?

⚠ **Big** is more informal than **important**.

historic /hɪˈstɒrɪk‖-ˈstɔː-, -ˈstɑː-/ [adj only before noun] a **historic** event, moment etc is remembered as a part of history because it brings important changes that have a good effect for a long time: the historic moment when Nelson Mandela was released from prison | In his book, Churchill describes that historic first meeting with Roosevelt.

crucial /ˈkruːʃəl/ [adj] something that is **crucial** is extremely important because everything that happens afterwards depends on it: Evans scored two crucial points just before the end of the game.
+ to The result of these talks could be crucial to the future of the school.

⚠ Don't say 'very crucial'. Say **absolutely crucial**.

2 important and necessary

important /ɪmˈpɔːrtənt/ [adj] something that is **important** should be given special attention because it is very necessary: Young children should be given a healthy diet – that's very important.
it is important to do sth It is important to read the instructions carefully before you start.
it is important that It is important that everyone understands the risks involved in this plan.
   importance [n U] how important and necessary something is
+ of Most people realize the importance of getting enough sleep.

vital /ˈvaɪtl/ [adj] something that is **vital** is very important and necessary, and if it is not done correctly or dealt with there could be serious problems: nurses, police officers and other workers who provide vital services
+ to His evidence was vital to the defence case.
it is vital that It is vital that leaking gas pipes are fixed immediately.

3 more important than anything else

the most important /ðə ˌməʊst ɪmˈpɔːrtənt/ *the most important scientific discovery of the 20th century | For Muslims, this is the most important day of the year.*

the most important thing *If there is a fire, the most important thing is to get all the students out of the building immediately.*

main/chief/principal /meɪn, tʃiːf, ˈprɪn-sə̥pəl/ [adj only before noun] more important than anything else: *What was the main purpose of your visit? | Our chief concern is for the safety of the children. | Coffee is the country's principal export.*

> ⚠ **Main**, **chief**, and **principal** mean the same thing, but **main** is much more common than **chief** or **principal**. **Chief** and **principal** are used especially in written or formal spoken English.

biggest /ˈbɪɡə̥st/ [adj only before noun] the **biggest** decision, problem, event etc is the most important decision that you have to make, the most serious problem you have to deal with etc: *This music festival is the biggest thing that's ever happened in Knoxville. | Getting married was the biggest mistake of my life.*

> ⚠ **Biggest** is more informal than **most important**, **main** etc.

major /ˈmeɪdʒər/ [adj only before noun] one of the most important or serious things – use this especially when there is a small number of really important things, but a larger number of less important things: *Smoking is a major cause of heart disease. | All the world's major sporting events can be seen on HHS TV. | It's the Chief Executive who makes all the major decisions.*

basic /ˈbeɪsɪk/ [adj only before noun] use this about something that you need more than anything else, especially in order to do something or in order to live: *This book gives you the basic information about choosing a college course. | People's basic needs are food, housing, and health care.*

above all /əˌbʌv ˈɔːl/ use this to emphasize that what you are going to say is more important than the other things you have mentioned: *Keeping him in prison is pointless, expensive, and above all it's completely unfair. | Above all, she will be remembered for all the work she did in the community.*

> ⚠ Use **above all** in written or formal spoken English.

priority /praɪˈɒrə̥ti‖-ˈɔːr-/ [n C/U] the most important thing, which needs to be dealt with before anything else or given more attention than anything else: *First, let's decide what our priorities are.*

sb's priority is to do sth *My main priority is get through all my exams.*

first/top/number one priority *Safety has always been our number one priority.*

give priority to sth (=decide that something is very important, and deal with it urgently) *The President promised to give priority to reducing unemployment.*

plural **priorities**

4 someone or something that you care a lot about

important /ɪmˈpɔːrtənt/ [adj] if something is **important** to you, you care a lot about it, and it has an important influence on the way you think and behave: *Which is more important – your family or your career?*

be important to sb *While I was a student, my parents' support and encouragement were very important to me.*

the important thing (=the only important thing) *At least the children are safe – that's the important thing.*

> ⚠ Don't say 'money is important for me'. Say **money is important to me**.

Ⓠmean a lot to sb /ˌmiːn ə ˈlɒt tuː (sb)‖-ˈlɑːt-/ ESPECIALLY SPOKEN if someone or something **means a lot to** you, you care about them or worry about them a lot, and your happiness depends on them: *You mustn't discourage her – this job means a lot to her.*

mean everything to sb (=be more important than anything else) *Karen trained day and night – winning the gold medal meant everything to her.*

⚠ **Mean a lot to sb** is more informal than **important**.

5 an important person

important /ɪmˈpɔːˡtənt/ [adj] an **important** person has a lot of power or influence: *The school is having some very important visitors next week.* | *Several important politicians are calling for a change in the laws on gun control.*

leading /ˈliːdɪŋ/ [adj only before noun] a **leading** politician, scientist, doctor etc is well known or successful or has a lot of influence, often because they know more about a subject than anyone else: *a leading member of the government's environmental committee* | *a leading expert on heart disease*

play a leading part/role (=do something important to help something be successful) *The Norwegian prime minister played a leading part in the peace talks.*

VIP /ˌviː aɪ ˈpiː/ [n C] a very important, famous, or powerful person who is treated in a special way: *a special party for VIPs and celebrities*

⚠ You can also use **VIP** before a noun, like an adjective: *VIP guests* | *the VIP lounge at the airport*

6 not important

not important/unimportant /nɒt ɪmˈpɔːˡtənt, ˌʌnɪmˈpɔːˡtənt◄/ [adj] *"I forgot to get the milk." "Don't worry, it's not important."* | *I don't want to waste time arguing about unimportant details.*

⚠ **Unimportant** is more formal than **not important**.

minor /ˈmaɪnəˡ/ [adj usually before noun] **minor** problems, changes, injuries etc are only small, and therefore not important or worrying: *She suffered only minor injuries in the accident.* | *There have been some minor changes to the design.* | *Most of the problems we've had so far have been relatively minor.*

small /smɔːl/ [adj usually before noun] INFORMAL a **small** problem, detail, or thing to discuss is not important and will not take long to deal with: *Don't worry. It's only a small problem.* | *There were a couple of small things I wanted to talk to you about.*

it doesn't matter /ɪt ˌdʌzənt ˈmætəˡ/ SPOKEN say this to tell someone that something is not important and does not cause serious problems, even though it may seem bad: *"We've missed the train." "It doesn't matter, there's another one in 10 minutes."*

+ if/whether/when/what *It doesn't matter if you're late. We'll wait for you.* | *It doesn't matter what other people say. Do what you think is best.*

trivial /ˈtrɪviəl/ [adj] something that is **trivial** is so unimportant that you should not worry about it or waste time on it: *I'm sorry to bother you with such a trivial question.* | *My problems seem quite trivial compared with Suzie's.*

petty /ˈpeti/ [adj usually before noun] unimportant and annoying – use this about rules, arguments, or things people do that seem to be too concerned with unimportant things: *I'm sick of having petty arguments over money.* | *I liked the new school much better – it didn't have as many petty rules as the old one.*

IMPOSSIBLE

➡ opposite **POSSIBLE**
➡ see also **CAN/CAN'T**

impossible /ɪmˈpɒsᵻbəl‖ɪmˈpɑː-/ [adj] something that is **impossible** cannot be done: *an impossible task* | *We're supposed to do all this work by tomorrow, but it's impossible.*

it is impossible to do sth *The twins are so alike that it's impossible to tell them apart.*

it is impossible for sb to do sth *The street was narrow, and it was impossible for the two buses to pass.*

make it impossible *Her back injury made it impossible for her to play tennis anymore.*

find it impossible (=discover that you cannot do something) *When people leave prison, they often find it impossible to get a job.*

not possible /nɒt 'pɒsɪ̯bəl‖-'pɑː-/ [adj] impossible or very difficult to do – use this when the situation that you are in makes something extremely difficult to do: *We can't buy a new computer for every student – it's just not possible.*

it is not possible to do sth *It is not possible in a book this size to cover every aspect of the subject.*

it is not possible for sb to do sth *She's in a meeting, so I'm afraid it's not possible for you to see her now.*

◯**there's no way** /ðeəʳz ˌnəʊ 'weɪ/ SPO- KEN say this when you strongly believe that something is impossible: *There's no way we can get to the airport in less than an hour.*

out of the question /ˌaʊt əv ðə 'kwes- tʃən/ if an idea or suggestion is **out of the question**, it is completely impossible or it cannot be allowed: *I'd love to come with you, but with all the work I have to do it's out of the question.* | *The cost would be over $5000, which is quite out of the question.*

◯**can't possibly** /ˌkɑːnt 'pɒsɪ̯bli‖ˌkænt 'pɑː-/ ESPECIALLY SPOKEN say that you **can't possibly** do something in order to emphasize that you think it is impossible and that you are surprised someone thinks it is possible: *I can't possibly eat all that food.* | *We couldn't possibly afford the flight.*

IMPROVE

➡ see also **BETTER**

1 to get better

get better /get 'betəʳ/ to become better: *I hope the weather gets better soon.*

get a lot better *Yuri's English is getting a lot better.*

things are getting better (=a situation is getting better) *David has a new job, so things are getting better.*

get better and better (=continue to get better, in a way that makes you feel pleased) *Paloma's teacher says that her schoolwork is getting better and better.*

When you see **EC**, go to the **ESSENTIAL COMMUNICATION** section.

⚠ **Get better** is used in spoken English more than in written English.

improve /ɪm'pruːv/ [v I] to become better: *In the weeks that followed, his health continued to improve.*

improve dramatically (=improve a lot) *Conditions in prisons have improved dramatically in the last 20 years.*

⚠ **Improve** is more formal than **get better**. It is used mostly in written English or in formal spoken situations, but not usually in ordinary conversation.

◯**things are looking up** /ˌθɪŋz əʳ ˈlʊkɪŋ 'ʌp/ SPOKEN say this when good things have started to happen to you, and your life seems much better than it was: *Things are looking up – I've got a new job and a new boyfriend.*

2 to make something better

improve /ɪm'pruːv/ [v T] to make something better: *I wanted to improve my French, so I got a job in Paris.* | *Road and rail services have been improved.* | *Put some salt on it. It'll improve the taste.*

make sth better /ˌmeɪk (sth) 'betəʳ/ to improve a situation or improve someone's life: *Instead of making the traffic situation better, the new road has just made things worse.*

make things better *You won't make things any better by worrying about them.*

make life better for sb *Have computers really made life better for everyone?*

make improvements /ˌmeɪk ɪm'pruːv- mənts/ to make changes to something or add things to it in order to make it better, more useful, or more effective

+ to *Several improvements have been made to the original designs.* | *They made a lot of improvements to their house after they moved in (=for example by adding a new room or putting in a new heating system).*

◯**brush up sth/brush up on sth** /ˌbrʌʃ 'ʌp (sth), ˌbrʌʃ 'ʌp ɒn (sth)/ [phrasal verb T] ESPECIALLY SPOKEN to practise doing something that you have not done for a long time, in order to try to improve it – use this especially about speaking foreign languages: *I'd like to brush up my Italian before our trip.*

3 a change that makes something better

improvement /ɪmˈpruːvmənt/ [n C/U] a change that makes something become better

+ in *Have you noticed any improvement in his work?* | *Accidents have become less frequent, thanks to recent improvements in our safety checks.*

big / great / tremendous improvement *There's been a great improvement in the team's performance over the last three games.*

advance /ədˈvɑːns‖-ˈvæns/ [n C often plural] an important new idea or way of doing something, especially in science

+ in *Advances in medical science may make it possible for people to live for 150 years.*

big/enormous/major advance *The last 20 years have seen enormous advances in computer technology.*

IN CHARGE OF

to be the person who controls a person, organization, or activity

➡ see also **MANAGER, POWER, CONTROL**

be in charge /biː ɪn ˈtʃɑːrdʒ/ if you **are in charge** of an activity or a group of people, you are the person who has the power to control what happens, to tell other people what to do etc: *Who's in charge around here?*

+ of *the officer in charge of the investigation*

be in charge of doing sth *As senior supervisor, she is in charge of training new employees.*

put sb in charge *David Hughes has been put in charge of the school play this year.*

run /rʌn/ [v T] if you **run** a business or organization, you are the person who makes the important decisions about what will happen: *She runs a company called*

Sunshine Holidays. | *a drug counselling service that is run by ex-addicts*

running – ran – have run

be responsible for sth/sb /biː rɪˈspɒnsɪbəl fɔːr (sth/sb)‖-ˈspɑːn-/ if you **are responsible for** doing something, you have to make sure that everything is done correctly and that problems are dealt with; if you **are responsible for** someone, you have to make sure that they behave well and that they are safe: *You're responsible for the children while they are in your classroom.* | *the Minister responsible for foreign affairs*

be responsible for doing sth *Who is responsible for organizing the travel arrangements?*

responsibility /rɪˌspɒnsɪˈbɪlɪti‖rɪˌspɑːn-/ [n C/U] a duty that you have when you are in charge, for example making sure that problems are dealt with or that people are safe: *She's in charge of the whole hospital – it's a big responsibility.*

have responsibility for (doing) sth *In the past, it was usually the mother who had responsibility for child care.* | *The landlord is responsible for keeping the apartment in good condition.*

be sb's responsibility *Garbage collection is the responsibility of the city council.*

it is sb's responsibility to do sth *It's your responsibility to ensure that the passengers in your car are wearing seat-belts.*

plural **responsibilities**

lead /liːd/ [v T] to be in charge of a group of people, especially a political party, a group of soldiers, or a team of workers: *Margaret Thatcher led the British Conservative Party for fifteen years.* | *Lieutenant Capaldi is leading the murder investigation.* | *a research project led by Professor Johnson*

leading – led – have led

supervise /ˈsuːpərvaɪz, ˈsjuː-‖ˈsuː-/ [v T] if you **supervise** an activity or a group of people, your job is to watch what everyone is doing, in order to make sure that things are done correctly: *Who was supposed to be supervising the kids when the fire started?* | *The distribution of aid will be supervised by the International Red Cross.*

supervision /ˌsuːpərˈvɪʒən, ˌsjuː-‖ˌsuː-/ [n U] the activity of supervising people or activities: *The child needs constant supervision.*

under the supervision of sb (=while being supervised by someone) *You can try sailing or rock-climbing under the supervision of experienced instructors.*

leadership /ˈliːdərʃɪp/ [n U] the position of being in charge of a group or organization

+ of *Tony Blair took over the leadership of the party after John Smith died.*

INCLUDE/
NOT INCLUDE

➡ see also **HAVE/NOT HAVE, CONTAIN**

1 to include someone or something

include /ɪnˈkluːd/ [v T] if a group of people, things, ideas etc **includes** someone or something, it has them as one of its parts, but there are other parts as well: *Our tour party included several young families.* | *Today's programme will include a workshop on language learning games.* | *Symptoms of the disease include tiredness and loss of memory.*

⚠ Don't say 'it is including these things'. Say **it includes these things.**

including /ɪnˈkluːdɪŋ/ [preposition] use this to say that someone or something is part of the group that you have just mentioned: *Everyone in the class passed the test, including me.* | *You can play all kinds of games here, including tennis, basketball, and squash.*

consist of sth/be made up of sth /kənˈsɪst ɒv (sth), biː meɪd ˈʌp ɒv (sth)/ [phrasal verb T] use this when you are mentioning all of the parts that something includes: *The US government consists of the Congress, the Judiciary, and the President.* | *Up to 70% of your total body weight is made up of water.* | *For the first three or four months a baby's diet consists only of milk.*

⚠ Don't say 'it is consisted of these things'. Say **it consists of these things.**

⚠ Don't confuse **include** and **consist of.** Use **include** to mention only *some* of the things that something includes, but use **consist of** to mention *all* of the things that something includes: *The Romance family of languages includes French and Spanish.* | *The Romance family of languages consists of French, Spanish, Italian, and several other languages.*

contain /kənˈteɪn/ [v T] to include particular ideas, images, or information – use this about things like books, films, or reports: *The film contains some very unpleasant scenes of violence.* | *Her report contained some interesting suggestions.*

cover /ˈkʌvər/ [v T] to include information about every part of a subject or about a lot of different subjects – use this about a book, TV programme, class etc: *His book on European politics covers the period from 1914 to 1989.* | *Does your French class cover modern French literature?*

range from /ˈreɪndʒ frɒm‖-frʌm/ [phrasal verb T] if prices, ages, amounts etc **range from** one number or amount to another, they include both the lower and higher amounts and other amounts in between them: *My students' ages ranged from 20 to 55.* | *Prices for a week in one of our villas range from £75 to £335.*

2 when a number, total, or price includes something

include /ɪnˈkluːd/ [v T] *The price of the computer includes £500 worth of free software.* | *"It's $50 per night." "Does that include breakfast?"*

including /ɪnˈkluːdɪŋ/ [preposition] use this to say that something is included in a number, total, or price: *The final cost of the meal was $60, including a 10% service charge.* | *The phone costs £68, including batteries.*

come with sth /ˈkʌm wɪð (sth)/ [phrasal verb T] if something that you buy **comes with** something else, the second thing is included when you buy the first, and you do not have to pay any more for it: *All the dishes on this menu come with either*

French fries or salad. | *The carpets came with the house.*

with /wɪð, wɪθ/ [preposition] including a number or amount that is added to the total: *With tax, the hotel bill came to $400.*

3 to not include someone or something

leave out /ˌliːv ˈaʊt/ [phrasal verb T] to not include someone or something, either deliberately or accidentally

leave sb/sth out of sth *Fans were shocked that Giggs had been left out of the team.*

leave out sb/sth *You've left out a zero in this phone number.*

exclude /ɪkˈskluːd/ [v T] FORMAL to deliberately not include someone or something, especially in a way that seems wrong or unfair: *The new law protects most workers, but excludes those on part-time contracts.* | *She felt they were deliberately excluding her from their plans.*

omit /əʊˈmɪt, ə-/ [v T] FORMAL to not include something, especially a piece of information, either deliberately or because you forget: *How can you give a list of 'Great English Novelists' that omits Dickens?*

omit sth from sth *Sara's name had been omitted from the list of phone numbers.*

omitting – omitted – have omitted

miss out /ˌmɪs ˈaʊt/ [phrasal verb T] BRITISH to not include someone or something that should be included, often by mistake

miss out/miss sth out *You missed out several important facts.* | *Those are the people I'm inviting. Did I miss anyone out?*

4 when a number, total, or price does not include something

not include /ˌnɒt ɪnˈkluːd/ *The price does not include sales tax.*

not including *He used to earn about £300 a week, not including bonuses.* | *There were about 50 people on the plane, not including the crew.*

excluding /ɪkˈskluːdɪŋ/ [preposition] not including – use this especially when you are talking about prices or taxes: *The*

computer costs £1500, excluding VAT. | *Car rental charges are $50 a day, excluding the cost of gasoline.*

not counting /nɒt ˈkaʊntɪŋ/ ESPECIALLY SPOKEN use this to make it clear exactly which people or things you do not want to include in a total: *Jane's been away for a week now, not counting today.* | *I get 25 days' holiday a year, not counting public holidays.*

INCREASE

➡ look here for ...
- when a number or amount gets bigger
- when a feeling gets stronger
- when something happens more often

➡ see also **GROW, BIG, MORE**

1 when a number or amount gets bigger

increase /ɪnˈkriːs/ [v I] to become larger in number, amount, price, value etc: *Gradually the noise and traffic increased as they approached the city.*

increase by 10%/$100/2 million etc (=by a difference of 10% etc) *The price of cigarettes has increased by 30% in the last two years.*

increase to $1000/2 million etc (=to reach a total of $1000 etc) *The number of unemployed is expected to increase to four million by 2001.*

increase in number/value *an investment that is certain to increase in value*

increase considerably/greatly/enormously *The use of mobile phones has increased enormously over the past two years.*

increasing /ɪnˈkriːsɪŋ/ [adj only before noun] *An increasing range and variety of health foods are now available.*

an increasing number of/increasing numbers of *Increasing numbers of North American trees are being damaged by acid rain.*

> ⚠ Don't use **increase** about the level or standard of something. Use **go up** or **rise**: *The standard of living has risen* (not *'increased'*).

go up/rise /ˌgəʊ ˈʌp, raɪz/ [v I] to increase – use this about numbers, prices, or temperatures etc, but also about the level or standard of something: *My rent's gone up again. It's £100 a week now.* | *Spending on education has risen rapidly in recent years.* | *With more and more cars on the road, pollution levels are rising steadily.*

+ by 10%/$500 etc (=by a difference of 10% etc) *House prices went up by 20% last year.* | *Salaries have risen by 50% since 1987.*

+ to $1000/10 million etc *In summer, temperatures often rise to 40°.* | *The average price of a loaf of bread has gone up from 26p to 60p.*

rising – rose – have risen

⚠ **Go up** is more common in spoken English than **increase** or **rise**.

⚠ Don't confuse **raise** (=make something rise) with **rise** (=become more).

rising /ˈraɪzɪŋ/ [adj only before noun] increasing – use this about prices, numbers etc or about the level or standard of something: *Rising fuel costs have forced many airlines to put up the price of air tickets.* | *the country's rising standard of living*

rising unemployment/crime/inflation (=when problems increase and become more serious) *a period of economic difficulty and rising unemployment*

grow /grəʊ/ [v I] to increase gradually over a period of time – use this about numbers or amounts, or about the total amount of business activity or trade: *Sales of new cars have grown steadily since 1990.* | *China's economic output continues to grow at a remarkable annual rate.*

grow by 10%/5000 etc (=by a difference of 10% etc) *Last year, our profits grew by £50,000.*

growing – grew – have grown
  growing /ˈgrəʊɪŋ/ [adj only before noun] *Growing numbers of women are choosing to give birth at home.*

double /ˈdʌbəl/ [v I] to become twice as big: *The price of electricity has almost doubled in less than three years.*

shoot up /ˌʃuːt ˈʌp/ [phrasal verb I] to increase quickly and suddenly – use this especially about prices, costs, or amounts of money: *Water charges have shot up by 35% in only 12 months.*

+ from ... to ... *Profits shot up from $4000 to $34,000 last year.*

2 when a feeling gets stronger

growing /ˈgrəʊɪŋ/ [adj only before noun] **growing doubts/fears/interest/opposition etc** doubts, fears etc that are gradually becoming stronger: *women's growing interest in football* | *I listened to his story with growing disbelief.*

grow /grəʊ/ [v I] if a feeling **grows**, it gradually becomes stronger: *Her confidence grew, and soon she was able to go out driving on her own.* | *Fears are growing for the safety of the missing children.*

growing – grew – have grown

increase /ɪnˈkriːs/ [v I] to become stronger – use this especially about a feeling that a lot of people have: *The excitement is increasing inside the stadium as we wait for the teams to come out onto the field.* | *The President's popularity has increased enormously since the war.*

  increasing [adj only before noun] *There is increasing uncertainty about the company's future.*

build up /ˌbɪld ˈʌp/ [phrasal verb I] if a bad feeling such as anger **builds up**, it gradually increases, until it makes you decide to do something: *The pressure built up over the year, and eventually I had to leave my job.* | *I could feel the anger building up inside me.*

mounting /ˈmaʊntɪŋ/ [adj only before noun] **mounting anger/excitement/concern** anger, excitement etc that is quickly increasing and becoming very strong: *There is mounting concern about the use of guns by criminals.*

3 when something happens more often

increase /ɪnˈkriːs/ [v I] if an activity **increases**, it happens more often, and so it affects more and more people or situations: *Smoking is increasing among teenage girls.*

be on the increase /biː ˌɒn ðɪ ˈɪnkriːs/ if a problem in society **is on the increase**, it is happening more and more often: *Drug taking is on the increase.* | *Poverty and homelessness seem to be on the increase again.*

4 to make something increase

increase /ɪnˈkriːs/ [v T] to make something increase: *We must increase the amount of money that we spend on education.* | *Smoking increases the risk of getting lung cancer.* | *Mandela's imprisonment increased the opposition to white rule in South Africa.*
+ from ... to ... *The company is increasing its workforce from 350 to 500.*

put up /ˌpʊt ˈʌp/ [phrasal verb T] to increase the prices, taxes, or rents people have to pay
put up sth *If the landlord puts up the rent again, we may have to move out.*
put sth up *This used to be quite a cheap restaurant, but they've put their prices up recently.*

raise /reɪz/ [v T] to increase prices, taxes etc, or to make certain feelings stronger: *Before the election the President promised not to raise taxes.* | *Oil companies are planning to raise prices.*
raise hopes/expectations (=make people more hopeful)
raise doubts/fears/questions (=make people more uncertain or worried)

⚠ **Raise** is more formal than **put up**.

add to sth /ˈæd tuː (sth)/ [phrasal verb T] ESPECIALLY WRITTEN to increase an amount that is already large, or increase problems, worries etc that are already serious: *an insurance policy that adds significantly to the cost of the loan* | *The news of his exam results only added to his general feeling of gloom.*

double /ˈdʌbəl/ [v T] to increase a number or amount so that it is twice as big
+ from ... to ... *The landlord has doubled our rent.*

turn up /ˌtɜːrn ˈʌp/ [phrasal verb T] if you **turn up** a television, radio etc, you make it louder; if you **turn up** something used for heating or cooking, you make it produce more heat

turn up sth *He leaned forward and turned up the TV.*
turn sth up *I can't hear the news. Can you turn it up a little?* | *I wish they'd turn the heating up – it's so cold in here.*

5 an increase in an amount or number

increase /ˈɪŋkriːs/ [n C] when an amount or number increases
+ in *The company announced a 5% increase in profits.* | *There has been a big increase in the number of homeless people.*
pay/price/tax/rent increase *Large tax increases are expected if there is a change of government.*
a sharp/dramatic increase (=a big and sudden increase) *There has been a sharp increase in the number of people using the Internet.*

⚠ Don't say 'an increase of tax/profits' etc. Say **an increase in tax/profits** etc.

rise /raɪz/ [n singular] an increase in numbers, prices, taxes etc, or an increase in the level of something
+ in *The police have been unable to stop the rise in crime.* | *a sudden rise in temperature*
a sharp/dramatic rise (=a big and sudden increase) *The figures show a dramatic rise in sales of CDs.*

growth /ɡrəʊθ/ [n U] a gradual increase over a period of time, especially in the amount of business activity and trade
+ in *the steady growth in trade between the US and China*
+ of *The growth of the tourist industry has provided around 5000 jobs in the region.*
rapid growth (=very quick growth) *the rapid growth in the world's population is partly due to improved medical services.*

pay rise BRITISH **raise** AMERICAN /ˈpeɪ raɪz, reɪz/ [n C] an increase in the amount of money that you are paid: *It's time you had a pay rise.* | *The city simply can't afford to give all teachers a raise.*

build-up /ˈbɪld ʌp/ [n singular] a gradual increase in the level of something harmful, dangerous, or worrying

+ of *Industrialization has led to a build-up of gases such as carbon dioxide in the atmosphere* | *a build-up of troops on the Korean border*

INDEPENDENT

➡ look here for ...
- when a country is not ruled by another country
- when someone does not need help or money from other people

1 country

➡ see also **COUNTRY, GOVERNMENT/ POLITICS, FREE 3**

independent /ˌɪndɪˈpendənt◄/ [adj] an **independent** country is not ruled by another country and has its own government: *Many Scottish people want Scotland to be an independent country.*
become independent *India became independent in 1947.*

independence /ˌɪndɪˈpendəns/ [n U] when a country is not ruled by another country, but has its own government: *Mexico achieved independence from Spain in 1821.* | *the Irish people's fight for independence*

2 person

➡ see also **CONFIDENT/NOT CONFIDENT, DESCRIBING PEOPLE**

independent /ˌɪndɪˈpendənt◄/ [adj] an **independent** person can make their own decisions, organise their own life, and pay for the things they need, without help or advice from other people: *I've become much more independent since I started living on my own.* | *'Cosmopolitan' is a magazine for young independent professional women.*
financially independent (=when you don't need money from other people) *Carla had just started her first job, and she enjoyed being financially independent.*

◯ can take care of yourself (also **can look after yourself** BRITISH) /kən teɪk ˌkeər əv jɔːˈself, kən lʊk ˌɑːftər jɔːʳˈself/ ESPECIALLY SPOKEN if you **can take care of yourself** or **can look after**

yourself, you do not need other people to do things for you or tell you what to do: *Stop worrying about the kids – they can take care of themselves.*

stand on your own two feet /ˌstænd ɒn jɔːr ˌəʊn tuː ˈfiːt/ if you can **stand on your own two feet**, you can deal with difficulties and situations alone and you do not expect other people to do things for you: *I had to learn to stand on my own two feet when my husband left me.*

3 not independent

dependent /dɪˈpendənt/ [adj] unable to live or do things on your own, because you need the support or help of someone else: *My grandmother has become much more dependent since her illness.*
+ on *Over a million refugees in Zaire are dependent on foreign aid.*
financially dependent (=when you need money from someone in order to live) *Anne had never worked and was financially dependent on her husband.*
dependent on sb/sth for sth *Young children are dependent on their parents for love and emotional support.*

INFORMATION

DETAIL   COMPUTERS
FIND OUT   NEWS
see also
TELEVISION AND RADIO   TELL
ASK   NEWSPAPERS AND MAGAZINES

1 information

information /ˌɪnfəʳˈmeɪʃən/ [n U] facts or details that tell you about a situation, event, person, place etc
+ about/on *The book contains information on how to find a job abroad.*
give/provide information *The tourist office will be able to give you the information you need.* | *an organization that provides information about AIDS*
further information FORMAL (=more information) *For further information, please write to the following address.*

piece of information *a useful piece of information*

detailed information (=containing a lot of facts) *The guidebook has detailed information about the hotels in the area.*

⚠ Don't say 'informations'. Say **information**.

⚠ Don't say 'an information'. Say **a piece of information** or **some information**.

fact /fækt/ [n C usually plural] a piece of information that is known to be true: *I'm not interested in your opinions – I just want to know the facts.*
+ about *It's important that young people learn the facts about drugs.* | *a book full of interesting facts about plants*
+ that *It is a remarkable fact that no-one had ever been convicted under this law.*

details /'diːteɪlz‖dɪ'teɪlz/ [n plural] all the specific pieces of information that you need to know about something which you already know about in a general way: *There's a big jazz festival in May. I'll give you the details if you want.*
+ of *Please send us details of your bank account.*
further details FORMAL (=more details) *For further details, contact the conference organizer.*

data /'deɪtə, 'dɑːtə/ [n U] facts, numbers, and other information that has been collected and stored, especially on a computer: *All our data is stored on computer.*
+ on *Scientists have been collecting data on air pollution levels.*

2 a collection of information

file /faɪl/ [n C] a collection of information, about a person, subject etc which is kept by an organization such as a school, a company, or the police: *Only a few people are allowed to see these files.*
+ on *The FBI has files on all suspected terrorists.* | *Could you bring me the file on the West murder, please?*

record /'rekɔːd‖-ərd/ [n C usually plural] information that is collected gradually over a long period of time, so that it can be looked at when necessary: *I've checked*

the student records, and I can't find any mention of her name.* | *medical records*
+ of *the official records of births, marriages, and deaths*

keep a record (=write down details of things as they happen) *Keep a record of all your expenses during the trip.*

database /'deɪtəˌbeɪs/ [n C] a very large collection of information kept on a computer: *The bookstore now has a database which lists all the books in stock.*
+ of *a database of car-owners in the UK*

3 to write down information

record /rɪ'kɔːrd/ [v T] to write down information or store it on a computer, so that it can be looked at later, especially official information about numbers or amounts: *Only 13 cases of this disease have ever been recorded.* | *The meteorological office recorded the lowest rainfall in 10 years.*

INSTEAD

1 instead of another thing, place, or time

instead /ɪn'sted/ [adv] if you do one thing **instead** of another, you do the first thing after deciding not to do the other thing: *We didn't have enough money to go to a movie, so we went to the park instead.* | *I can't manage Thursday. Can we meet on Friday instead?*
+ of *Could I have soup instead of salad?*
instead of doing sth *You should talk to your teacher instead of just complaining to me about it.*

⚠ Don't say 'instead of it' or 'instead of that'. Just say **instead**: *We didn't go for a walk, but stayed at home instead.*

⚠ Don't say 'instead of to go' or 'instead to go'. Say **instead of going**.

rather than /'rɑːðər ðən‖'ræ-/ if you do one thing **rather than** another, you do the first thing because it seems better or more suitable: *A lot of young people are choosing to rent rather than buy their* own houses. | *Rather than waiting for the bus, Larry decided to take a taxi.*

in place of sth /ɪn ˈpleɪs ɒv (sth)/ if one thing is used **in place of** another, it is used instead of it or put in the place where the other thing used to be: *During this period, people were beginning to use coal as a fuel, in place of wood.*

in its place/in their place *The church was demolished, and an office block was built in its place.*

2 instead of another person

instead /ɪnˈsted/ [*adv*] *Chris couldn't go to the meeting, so I said I'd go instead.*
+ of *Gillespie will play in midfield instead of Cochrane.*

for /fər; *strong* fɔːr/ [*preposition*] if you do something **for** someone, you do it instead of them, especially in order to help them: *Let me carry that shopping for you.* | *Pat wasn't feeling well, so I said I would take care of the children for her.*

go in sb's place /ˌgəʊ ɪn (sb's) ˈpleɪs/ if you **go** somewhere **in someone's place** you go there instead of them: *Lauren was too busy to go to the concert, so Wendy went in her place.*

on behalf of sb /ɒn bɪˈhɑːf ɒv (sb)‖ -ˈhæf-/ if you do something **on behalf of** someone, such as giving a speech or making an official decision, you do it instead of them because they have asked you to be their representative: *On behalf of everyone here, I'd like to wish you a long and happy retirement.*
on sb's behalf *Richardson's lawyer agreed to speak to journalists on his behalf.*

3 to do something instead of someone or something else

take the place of/replace /ˌteɪk ðə ˈpleɪs ɒv, rɪˈpleɪs/ [*v* T] to do a job or do work that used to be done by someone or something else: *In most offices, computers have replaced the old typewriters.* | *One 'smart' card can now take the place of cash, cheques, and credit cards.* | *Schmidt will replace Thijssen as Minister of the Environment.*

take over /ˌteɪk ˈəʊvər/ [*phrasal verb* I/T] to start doing a job, especially an important job, that someone else used to do: *Perryman has agreed to take over until the club can find a new coach.*
take over sth *Kolchinsky took over the chairman's job in 1994.*
+ from *My father always expected me to take over from him and run the family business.*

stand in for sb /ˌstænd ˈɪn fɔːr (sb)/ [*phrasal verb* T] to do someone's job for them for a short time: *Can you stand in for Meg while she's on vacation?*

replacement /rɪˈpleɪsmənt/ [*n* C] a person, machine, system etc that does a job or does work instead of someone or something else: *When Steve announced he was leaving, the coach started looking around for a replacement.*
+ for *These fertilizers were developed as a replacement for the old nitrates.*

INSTRUCTIONS

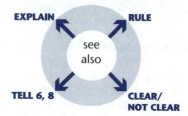

EXPLAIN   RULE

see also

TELL 6, 8   CLEAR/
                 NOT CLEAR

1 information about how to use something or what to do

instructions /ɪnˈstrʌkʃənz/ [*n* plural] written or spoken information telling someone what you want them to do or how something should be done: *Always wash clothes according to the instructions on the label.*
give sb instructions *Patricia was in the living room giving the babysitter her instructions.*
follow instructions (=do what the instructions tell you) *I've followed her instructions, but the computer still isn't working.*
+ about/on *Have you read the instructions about what to do if there's a fire?*

have instructions to do sth (=when someone has given you instructions) *The guards had strict instructions not to let anyone in.*

⚠ Remember to use **instructions** in the plural. Don't say 'You didn't follow my instruction'.

directions /dɪˈrekʃənz, daɪ-/ [n plural] instructions about how to go to a place
give sb directions *I've never been to his house before. Can you give me directions?*
follow sb's directions (=go where someone tells you to go) *She only got lost because she didn't follow my directions.*
+ to *Do you want me to give you directions to the restaurant?*

recipe /ˈresəpi/ [n C] instructions on how to make a particular kind of food: *This soup is really good – you must give me the recipe.*
+ for *I've found a recipe for barbecue sauce.*

2 a book or document with instructions

the instructions /ðiː ɪnˈstrʌkʃənz/ [n plural] a book or piece of paper that provides information about how to do something or how to use something: *I don't need to read the instructions – I've played this game before.* | *I can't get the computer to work and I've lost the instructions.*

manual /ˈmænjuəl/ [n C] a book that contains detailed instructions for using a complicated machine: *Before you try to use the camera, read the manual carefully.* | *a computer manual*

handbook /ˈhændbʊk/ [n C] a book containing useful information and advice for a group of people who need it, written by someone who knows a lot about the subject: *The students' handbook gives information on how to find accommodation.* | *a government handbook for teachers of deaf children*

cookbook (also **recipe book** BRITISH) /ˈkʊkbʊk, ˈresəpi bʊk/ [n C] a book that has instructions about how to cook different kinds of food

INTELLIGENT

➡ opposite **STUPID**
➡ if you mean 'behaving in a way that is reasonable and not stupid', go to **SENSIBLE**
➡ see also **GOOD 5**

1 good at learning, thinking, and understanding ideas

intelligent /ɪnˈtelɪdʒənt/ [adj] someone who is **intelligent** has a high level of mental ability and is good at learning, thinking, and understanding ideas: *Natalie was very charming and extremely intelligent.* | *He's probably the most intelligent student in the class.*
highly intelligent (=very intelligent) *a sensitive and highly intelligent young man*

clever ESPECIALLY BRITISH **smart** ESPECIALLY AMERICAN /ˈklevər, smɑːrt/ [adj] someone who is **clever** or **smart** is good at learning or understanding things quickly and at thinking of how to solve problems: *You're so clever! How did you think of that?* | *Laura's smart and she has plenty of ambition.* | *My sister's much smarter than I am.*

bright /braɪt/ [adj] children and young people who are **bright** are intelligent and likely to be successful at school or in their jobs: *She's one of the brightest kids in her class.* | *Tom was a model employee – bright and hard-working.*

brainy /ˈbreɪni/ [adj] INFORMAL someone who is **brainy** is very intelligent and good at studying: *At school, Karen was always one of the brainy ones.*
brainy – brainier – brainiest

2 extremely intelligent

genius /ˈdʒiːniəs/ [n C] someone with a very high level of intelligence, which only a few people have, especially someone who has original and important ideas: *Einstein was probably the greatest mathematical genius of all time.*

brilliant /ˈbrɪljənt/ [adj] a **brilliant** scientist, student, teacher etc is extremely intelligent and does very good or important work which people admire them for: *The brilliant physicist Paul Dirac first put forward this theory back in 1930.* | *a brilliant historian*

3 clever ideas, plans, or ways of doing things

clever /'klevə^r/ [adj] ESPECIALLY BRITISH a **clever** idea, plan, or way of doing something is good and works well: *Mark had lots of clever ideas for making money.*

> **cleverly** [adv] *The building has been cleverly designed to use as little energy as possible.*

ingenious /ɪn'dʒiːniəs/ [adj] an **ingenious** method, idea, or piece of equipment is cleverly designed to do a job or solve a problem in a very original way: *an ingenious method of sending secret information*

4 the ability to learn well

intelligence /ɪn'telɪdʒəns/ [n U] the ability to learn quickly, think clearly, and understand ideas well: *Most of the children at the school are of above average intelligence.*

brains /breɪnz/ [n plural] INFORMAL the ability to think quickly, study well, and remember a lot of facts: *With his brains, he'll easily get into university.*

5 an annoying person who thinks he or she is very clever

know-it-all (also **know-all** BRITISH) /'nəʊ ɪt ɔːl, 'nəʊ ɔːl/ [n C] INFORMAL someone who annoys you because they always think that they know more than other people: *All right then, know-it-all, you tell us what the answer is.*

6 good at getting advantages for yourself

clever ESPECIALLY BRITISH **smart** ESPECIALLY AMERICAN /'klevə^r, smɑːʳt/ [adj] someone who is **clever** or **smart** is good at getting advantages for themselves by using clever and sometimes dishonest methods: *Some smart lawyer got him out of prison.* | *a clever politician, who stayed in power by keeping his enemies divided*

> **cleverly** [adv] *He cleverly avoided saying what his real intentions were.*

cunning /'kʌnɪŋ/ [adj] someone who is **cunning** gets what they want by thinking carefully about it and making secret plans: *Hawkeye was very cunning – he always waited until his enemy was alone and unarmed before making his attack.*

> **cunningly** [adv] *A video camera had been cunningly hidden behind the mirror.*

streetwise /'striːtwaɪz/ [adj] someone who is **streetwise** has a lot of experience of life in big cities, so they know what to do in difficult or dangerous situations: *Kids nowadays are much more streetwise than we ever used to be.*

INTEND

1 to intend to do something

➡ see also ORGANIZE/ARRANGE, PREPARE

intend to do sth /ɪn,tend tə 'duː (sth)/ [v T] if you **intend to do** something, you have decided that you want to do it at some time in the future: *I intend to find out who is responsible for this.* | *Do you think Jones really intended to kill his wife?*

mean to do sth /,miːn tə 'duː (sth)/ ESPECIALLY SPOKEN to intend to do something – use this especially when you forgot to do something or did not have the chance to do it: *I've been meaning to phone Anne for ages.* | *I meant to tell you, but I forgot.*
meaning – meant – meant

be going to do sth /biː ,gəʊɪŋ tə 'duː (sth)/ if you **are going to do** something, you have arranged to do it at a particular time – use this to talk about definite arrangements: *Ruth and Al are going to open their own restaurant.* | *I'm going to go to the hospital tomorrow.*

plan to do sth /,plæn tə 'duː (sth)/ to intend to do something – use this especially when you have thought carefully about when and how you will do something: *Josie's planning to return to work after she's had the baby.* | *We're planning to go on vacation in October.*

set out to do sth /ˌset aʊt tə ˈduː (sth)/ to decide to do something and make plans for how you will achieve it, especially in a determined way: *He set out to make Newcastle the best football team in the country.* | *The film is about a New York gangster who is attacked and sets out to get revenge.*

2 to not intend to do something

➡ see also **ACCIDENTALLY/DELIBERATELY, MISTAKE**

not intend to do sth /nɒt ɪnˌtend tə ˈduː (sth)/ if you **do not intend to do** something, you have decided that you will not do it: *He doesn't intend to stay in this job all his life.* | *I was determined to go, and I did not intend to let them stop me.*

have no intention of doing sth /hæv ˌnəʊ ɪnˈtenʃən əv ˈduːɪŋ (sth)/ if you **have no intention of doing** something, you have firmly decided that you will definitely not do it: *She says she has no intention of going back to her husband.* | *Mr Birt announced that he had no intention of resigning.*

have no plans to do sth /hæv nəʊ ˌplænz tə ˈduː (sth)/ if you **have no plans to do** something, you have not made a decision to do it, although you may decide to do it at a later time: *At the moment, Hugh and his girlfriend have no plans to get married.*

◯**not mean to do sth** /nɒt ˌmiːn tə ˈduː (sth)/ ESPECIALLY SPOKEN use this to say that, although someone did something, they did not do it deliberately: *They hadn't meant to stay out so late.* | *"You really upset Frances last night." "I know – I didn't mean to, but I just got very annoyed."*

3 something that you intend to do

intention /ɪnˈtenʃən/ [n C] something that you intend to do: *I'm not sure what his intentions are.*
with the intention of doing sth *Kaori went to the US with the intention of getting a job at a university.*

intention to do sth *He has announced his intention to run for president at the next election.*

4 when something is intended to do something

be intended to /biː ɪnˈtendɪd tuː/ to be done or made for a particular purpose: *a speech that was clearly intended to reassure us* | *The restaurant was intended to be like a typical Moroccan restaurant.*

be meant to/ be supposed to /biː ˈment tuː, biː səˈpəʊzd tuː/ to be intended to have a particular result or effect – use this especially when the result or effect is not achieved: *This film was obviously meant to shock, but we just thought it was funny.* | *The new laws are supposed to prevent tax fraud.*

INTERESTING/ INTERESTED

➡ opposite **BORING/BORED**
➡ see also **EXCITING/EXCITED**

⚠ Don't confuse **interesting** (used about a subject, book, person etc that makes you want to pay attention) and **interested** (=how you feel when you want to find out more about something).

1 something that makes you feel interested

interesting /ˈɪntrɪstɪŋ/ [adj] if something is **interesting**, you give it your attention, because it is unusual or exciting or because it provides information that you want to know about: *an interesting film about African wildlife.* | *He's the most interesting person I've ever met.* | *We spent an interesting afternoon looking around the old part of the city.*
it is interesting to see/know/compare *It will be interesting to see which of these bands is still popular five years from now.* | *It would be interesting to know how much the painting costs.*
it is interesting that (use this about a fact that is interesting because it is unexpected or difficult to explain) *It is interesting that*

so few of the people here die from heart disease.

look/sound interesting *Susan's new job sounds really interesting.*

⚠️ Never say 'I am interesting in this'. Say **I am interested in this.**

interest /'ɪntrɪst/ [v T] if something **interests** you, it makes you feel interested: *There's a film about bears on the TV tonight. It might interest the children.*

⚠️ Don't say 'It is interesting me'. Say **it interests me.**

fascinating /'fæsɪneɪtɪŋ/ [adj] extremely interesting: *Istanbul is a fascinating city.* | *a fascinating story of mystery and adventure*

⚠️ Don't say 'very fascinating'. Say **absolutely fascinating.**

fascinate /'fæsɪneɪt/ [v T] if something **fascinates** you, it makes you feel extremely interested: *The idea of travelling to other planets fascinates me.*

intriguing /ɪn'triːgɪŋ/ [adj] if something is **intriguing**, you want to know more about it because it is strange or difficult to understand: *an intriguing question that continues to puzzle scientists* | *When I got home there was an intriguing message on my answerphone.*

stimulating /'stɪmjʊleɪtɪŋ/ [adj] something that is **stimulating** is interesting and enjoyable because it gives you new ideas to think about: *I would like to thank Professor Buchner for his stimulating lecture.* | *It was a stimulating experience, working among people from so many different countries.*

Q**I couldn't put it down** /aɪ ˌkʊdnt pʊt ɪt 'daʊn/ SPOKEN say this about a book which was so enjoyable that you did not want to stop reading it: *What an amazing book! I just couldn't put it down.*

2 feeling interested in something

interested /'ɪntrɪstɪd/ [adj not before noun] if you are **interested** in something, you give it your attention because you want to know more about it: *The children seemed very interested when I showed them my photographs.* | *I can't remember the name of the book, but if you're interested I can find out.*
+ in *I've never really been interested in politics.* | *Bob first got interested in motorcycles when he was about sixteen.*
interested to know/hear/see/learn *I'd be very interested to hear your opinion about this.*

find sth interesting /ˌfaɪnd (sth) 'ɪntrɪstɪŋ/ if you **find something interesting**, you feel very interested when you see it, read it, or hear about it, because it is the type of thing that you like to know about: *It's a book about travelling in India. I think you'll find it interesting.*

with interest /wɪð 'ɪntrɪst/ **watch/listen/read with interest** ESPECIALLY WRITTEN to be interested when you watch, listen, or read something: *Richard listened with interest to the conversation at the next table.*
with great interest *I read your letter with great interest.*

show interest/express interest /ˌʃəʊ 'ɪntrɪst, ɪkˌspres 'ɪntrɪst/ to say something to show that you are interested, especially in a suggestion or plan: *I suggested going camping, but none of my friends showed any interest.*
+ in *Several companies have already expressed interest in our research.*

Q**be into sth** /biː 'ɪntuː (sth)/ [phrasal verb T] INFORMAL, ESPECIALLY SPOKEN to be very interested in a subject or activity, and to spend a lot of time on it because you enjoy it: *I'm not very interested in science fiction, but my brother is really into it.*
be into doing sth *Lisa's into keeping fit – she goes to aerobics every day.*
get into sth (=become more interested in it) *I never used to like jazz, but I've been getting into it recently.*

3 to feel extremely interested in something

fascinated /'fæsˌneɪtˌd/ [adj not before noun] extremely interested in something that you are watching or listening to: *Julia watched the dancers for over an hour – she was fascinated.*
+ by *I was fascinated by her stories of her childhood in Africa.*

be absorbed in sth /biː əbˈsɔːrbd ɪn (sth)/ to be so interested in something that you give it all your attention: *She's totally absorbed in her work.* | *The children were so absorbed in their game that they didn't notice us.*

be obsessed with sth /biː əbˈsest wɪð (sth)/ to be too interested in something, so that you cannot stop thinking about it: *You're obsessed with sex – that's your problem.*
be obsessed with doing sth *As Forsyth grew older, he became obsessed with making money.*

obsession /əbˈseʃən/ [n C] when you cannot stop thinking about one particular thing: *Mario's interest in fast cars had become a dangerous obsession.*
+ with *the poet's unhealthy obsession with death*

4 when you are not interested in something
➡ see also **BORING/BORED**

not interested /nɒt ˈɪntrˌstˌd/ *I started telling them about my vacation, but they weren't very interested.*
+ in *He's not particularly interested in sport.*

not interest sb /nɒt ˈɪntrˌst (sb)/ if a subject or activity **does not interest** you, you do not want to know about it or learn about it: *To be honest, politics doesn't interest me at all.*

lose interest /ˌluːz ˈɪntrˌst/ to stop being interested in something that you were interested in before: *I used to go to photography classes every week, but then I just lost interest.*
+ in *Jenny seems to have lost all interest in her work.*

INTERFERE

to try to influence a situation that you should not be involved in

➡ see also **STOP 6**

1 to interfere

interfere /ˌɪntərˈfɪər/ [v I] to try to influence a situation that you should not be involved in, for example by telling someone what to do or giving them advice which they do not want: *For God's sake Dave, stop interfering!* | *I don't mean to interfere, but don't you think you should tell your parents about this?*
+ in *She has no right to interfere in her son's marriage like that.* | *The US was accused of interfering in China's internal affairs.*

    interference [n U] when someone interferes in a situation: *I think the Internet should be allowed to develop without any interference from the government.*
    interfering [adj only before noun] an **interfering** person annoys you because they keep interfering in things that they should not be involved in: *an interfering old woman*

meddle /'medl/ [v I] to interfere in a situation that you do not understand or know enough about, and which someone else is responsible for dealing with
+ in *In my opinion Church leaders shouldn't meddle in politics.*

poke your nose into sth /ˌpəʊk jɔːr ˈnəʊz ɪntuː (sth)/ INFORMAL, ESPECIALLY SPOKEN to ask questions about someone else's private life in a way that annoys them: *Just stop poking your nose into my private affairs.*

busybody /'bɪziˌbɒdi‖-ˌbɑːdi/ [n C] INFORMAL someone who always wants to know about or get involved in other people's private activities: *That woman's such a busybody – she knows everything about everyone!*
plural **busybodies**

> When you see **EC**, go to the **ESSENTIAL COMMUNICATION** section.

2 to not interfere

⌕mind your own business /ˌmaɪnd jɔːr əʊn ˈbɪznↄ̩s/ SPOKEN say this when you want someone to stop interfering or asking questions about something that is private: *Why don't you just mind your own business and leave us alone?* | *He asked me how much money I earned, and I told him to mind his own business.*

⌕stay out of it /ˌsteɪ ˈaʊt əv ɪt/ SPOKEN INFORMAL to not get involved in a fight or an argument between other people: *If I were you I'd stay out of it – Josh gets violent when he's drunk.*

INVENT

➡ if you mean 'think of an explanation, reason etc that is untrue', go to **TRUE/NOT TRUE 3**

⚠ Don't confuse **invent** (=think of something that did not exist before) and **discover** (=find something that people did not know about before).

1 to think of a new idea, design, or name for something

• see also **FIND 4, IDEA**

invent /ɪnˈvent/ [v T] to think of an idea for a new product, machine etc for the first time, and design it and make it: *Alexander Graham Bell invented the telephone.* | *Television was invented in the 1920s.*

　invention [n U] when someone has invented a new product: *a discovery that led to the invention of the nuclear bomb*

create /kriˈeɪt/ [v T] to make something new in art, literature, fashion etc: *Agatha Christie created the character Hercule Poirot.* | *Mary Quant created a whole new look for women's clothes in the 1960s.*

think up/come up with /ˌθɪŋk ˈʌp, ˌkʌm ˈʌp wɪð / [phrasal verb T] INFORMAL to produce a new idea, name, method etc by thinking carefully about it

think up sth/come up with sth *See if you can come up with a better name for it.* | *We need to think up some new ideas for the Christmas show.*

　think sth up *What a brilliant idea! I wonder who thought that up.*

devise /dɪˈvaɪz/ [v T] to invent a way of doing something, especially one that is clever and complicated: *The exercise program was devised by a leading health expert.* | *Scientists have devised a test that shows who is most likely to get the disease.*

2 someone who invents things

inventor /ɪnˈventəʳ/ [n C] someone who invents things
　+ of *Marconi, the inventor of radio*

creator /kriˈeɪtəʳ/ [n C] the writer, artist, or designer who first produced a well-known story, character, fashion etc
　+ of *Walt Disney, the creator of Mickey Mouse*

3 something that someone has invented

invention /ɪnˈvenʃən/ [n C] something that someone has invented: *The light bulb was Edison's most famous invention.*

INVITE

➡ see also **PARTY**

1 to invite someone

invite/ask /ɪnˈvaɪt, ɑːskǁæsk/ [v T] to ask someone to come to a party, wedding, meal etc: *It's going to be a big wedding – they've invited over a hundred people.* | *"Are you going to Emma's party?" "No, I haven't been asked."*

　invite/ask sb to a party/wedding etc *Are you going to invite Stephanie to the school disco?*

　invite/ask sb to do sth *Jane's parents have asked me to come and stay with them for a couple of weeks.*

　invite/ask sb for lunch/dinner *Madeline has invited us for dinner on Saturday.*

invite/ask sb in (=invite a visitor into your home) *He invited me in for a cup of coffee.*

> ⚠ Don't say 'she invited/asked me in her party'. Say **she invited/asked me to her party**.
>
> ⚠ You can use **invite** in written or spoken English. **Ask** is more informal, and is usually used in spoken English.

ask sb out /ɑːsk (sb) 'aʊt‖ˌæsk-/ [*phrasal verb* T] to ask someone to go to a restaurant, a film etc with you because you want to start a romantic relationship with them: *Why don't you ask her out? Or are you too shy?*

have sb over /ˌhæv (sb) 'əʊvəʳ/ [*phrasal verb* T] if you **have someone over**, they come to your home to have a meal or to spend time with you because you have invited them: *"What did you do last night?" "We had some friends over and we played cards."*

have sb over for drinks/dinner etc *We had Nick's parents over for dinner on Saturday.*

2 a message inviting someone

invitation /ˌɪnvˑɪ'teɪʃən/ [*n* C] a message inviting someone to a party, wedding etc: *Thanks for your invitation. I'd love to come.* | *a wedding invitation*
+ to *Did you get an invitation to the party?*

3 someone who you invite

guest /gest/ [*n* C] someone who is staying at your home, or who has come to your party, wedding etc because you invited them: *the wedding guests* | *We have guests staying with us this week.*

J

JEALOUS

1 because someone loves another person

➡ see also LOVE,
GIRLFRIEND/BOYFRIEND, RELATIONSHIP

jealous /'dʒeləs/ [adj] angry and unhappy because you think your husband, girlfriend etc loves someone else more than they love you

get jealous (=become jealous) *My girlfriend gets jealous if I even look at another woman.*

make sb jealous *I saw her talking and laughing with Bob. She was just trying to make me jealous.*

jealous husband/wife/lover *It's a story about a woman who is killed by her jealous lover.*

  jealously [adv] *He watched jealously as Rose danced with his brother.*

jealousy /'dʒeləsi/ [n U] the angry, unhappy feeling you have when you think your husband, girlfriend etc loves someone else more than they love you: *Morgan stabbed his girlfriend in a fit of jealousy.*

2 because you want something that someone else has

➡ see also WANT

jealous /'dʒeləs/ [adj] you feel **jealous** when someone has something that you want, and you are annoyed that they have it and you do not: *Wait till Andrea hears about my new job. She'll be really jealous.*

+ of *I felt jealous of Katie with her new baby.*

envious /'enviəs/ [adj] ESPECIALLY WRITTEN you feel **envious** when someone has something nice or special, and you wish that you had it too: *He cast an envious look at Simon's shiny red sportscar.*

+ of *I was always envious of the way Tracey looked good in whatever she wore.*

enviously [adv] *She glanced enviously at Emma's slim figure.*

envy /'envi/ [v T] to wish that you had the same abilities, possessions etc as someone else: *I wish I could play the piano like that – I really envy you!*

envy sb for sth *He always envied his brother for the way he made friends so easily.*

envying – envied – have envied

envy /'envi/ [n U] the feeling you have when you want something that someone else has: *It was difficult to hide her envy as Jim described his new job in Hawaii.*

green with envy (=very envious) *Tom will be green with envy when he sees your new computer.*

jealousy /'dʒeləsi/ [n U] the feeling of wanting something that someone else has, especially when this makes you angry or unhappy: *Ever since Clark won the lottery, he has had to cope with the jealousy and resentment of his former workmates.*

JOB

POSITION/RANK

WORK   COMPANY

see
also

MANAGER   PAY

EXPERIENCE   BUSINESS

1 a job

job /dʒɒb‖dʒɑːb/ [n C] the work that you do regularly in order to earn money, especially when you work for a company or a public organization: *My first job was in a record store.* | *Daniel starts his new job on Monday.* | *She has a well-paid job in the tax department.*

get/find a job *Her son still hasn't been able to find a job.* | *Ted got a job as a bartender.*

look for a job (=try to get one) *She's looking for a job in the music business.*

part-time job (=when you work less than the usual number of hours each week) *I* *had a part-time job while I was at college.*

job losses/job cuts (=when a lot of people lose their jobs)

⚠ Don't say 'What is your job?' or 'What is your work?' when you want to know what someone does to earn money. Say **What do you do?** or **What do you do for a living?**: *"What does your mother do?" "She's a doctor."*

work /wɜːʳk/ [n U] anything that you do to earn money: *My father started work when he was 14 years old.*

look for work (=try to find any job that you can) *Lena graduated from college six months ago and is still looking for work.*

find work *Mario was hoping to find work in a hotel or a restaurant.*

go back to work/return to work (=start working again) *A lot of women return to work when their children start school.*

to/at work (=to or at the place where you work) *He's marrying someone he met at work.* | *What time do you go to work?*

before/after work (=before you start/ after you finish your work each day) *Let's go for a drink after work tonight.*

⚠ Don't say 'a work'. **Work** is an uncountable noun.

profession /prəˈfeʃən/ [n C] an area of work such as law, medicine, or teaching, for which you need special training and education

the teaching/medical/legal profession *There are now a lot more women in the legal profession.*

go into/enter a profession *There was a big demand for accountants in the 1980s, and many graduates entered the profession at this time.*

occupation /ˌɒkjʊˈpeɪʃən‖ɑːk-/ [n C] the type of work that someone usually does: *Please state your age, address, and occupation in the space below.* | *Part-time workers often work in low-paid occupations.*

⚠ **Occupation** is a word used especially on official forms or for writing about the types of job that people do. Don't use **occupation** to talk about your own job.

post/position /pəʊst, pəˈzɪʃən/ [n C] FORMAL an important job in a company or organization

+ of *He was offered the post of ambassador to Mexico.*

hold a post/position (=have an important job in an organization) *She was the first woman ever to hold the position of Prime Minister.*

vacancy /ˈveɪkənsi/ [n C] a job that is available: *We'll contact you if we have any vacancies.*

+ for *Do you have any vacancies for sales staff?*

plural **vacancies**

professional /prəˈfeʃənəl/ [adj] a **professional** musician, sports player, photographer etc earns money by playing music, doing a sport etc, rather than doing it just for enjoyment: *Professional basketball players can earn a lot of money.*

turn professional (=become professional) *He had been a successful amateur boxer before he turned professional in 1988.*

  professional [n C] *It's a big golf tournament, with many of the world's top professionals taking part.*

2 to give someone a job

take on /ˌteɪk ˈɒn‖-ˈɑːn/ [phrasal verb T] if a company **takes** someone **on**, it gives them a job

take on sb *The store always takes on extra sales assistants for the Christmas period.*

take sb on *They've agreed to take me on for a year after I finish college.*

hire /haɪəʳ/ [v T] ESPECIALLY AMERICAN if a company **hires** someone, it gives them a job: *She was hired in April this year.* | *They're not hiring any new people at the moment.*

appoint /əˈpɔɪnt/ [v T] to choose someone for an important job: *The President has appointed a new Minister of Culture.*

appoint sb director/manager/principal etc *In 1989 he was appointed managing director.*

appoint sb to a job/position/post *This is the first time a woman has been appointed to such a senior position.*

recruit /rɪˈkruːt/ [v T] to find new people to work for a company, organization, or military force: *The police department is* *trying to recruit more black officers.* | *It's getting more and more difficult to recruit experienced staff.*

promote /prə'məʊt/ [v T often passive] to give someone who works in an organization a more important job than the one they had before
be promoted *Did you hear that David's been promoted?*
be promoted to *She was promoted to Assistant Principal.*

> **promotion** [n C/U] when someone is given a more important job in an organization: *What are my chances of promotion if I stay here?* (=am I likely to be promoted?) | *Darren has had two promotions since he joined the BBC in 1990.*

3 to take away someone's job

fire /faɪər/ [v T] to make someone leave their job, because they have done something wrong or because their work is not satisfactory: *She kept arriving late, and in the end they fired her.* | *You're fired!*
fire sb for (doing) sth *He was fired for being drunk at work.*

sack sb/give sb the sack /sæk (sb), ˌgɪv (sb) ðə 'sæk/ BRITISH to make someone leave their job, because they have done something wrong or because their work is not satisfactory: *They sacked the coach after the team lost 10 games in a row.*
+ for *She was given the sack for trying to organize a trade union.*

lose your job /ˌluːz jɔːr 'dʒɒb‖-'dʒɑːb/ if you **lose your job**, your job is taken away from you: *Things have been really difficult since Terry lost his job.* | *Thousands of workers lost their jobs when the car factory closed.*

get the sack /ˌget ðə 'sæk/ BRITISH if you **get the sack**, your job is taken away from you, especially because you have done something wrong or your work is not satisfactory: *He got the sack after he was caught stealing money.*

lay sb off/make sb redundant /ˌleɪ (sb) 'ɒf, ˌmeɪk (sb) rɪ'dʌndənt/ if a company **lays** someone **off** or **makes** them **redundant**, it makes them leave their job because it does not need them any more: *If sales*

keep falling, we'll have to lay off even more people. | *The two banks merged to form a single company, and hundreds of workers were made redundant.*

> ⚠ **Lay sb off** is used in both British and American English, and it can mean either that someone loses their job permanently, or that they lose it for a short period. **Make sb redundant** is used only in British English and means that someone loses their job permanently.

redundancy /rɪ'dʌndənsi/ [n C/U] BRITISH when a company takes away someone's job because it does not need them any more: *The decline in car sales led to many redundancies.*
redundancy pay/money (=money you receive from a company when you lose your job) *He used his redundancy money to buy a boat.*
plural **redundancies**

4 to ask for a job

apply /ə'plaɪ/ [v I] to formally ask to be considered for a job that has been advertised, especially by writing a letter or answering the questions on a form: *I applied in September, but I didn't hear from them till the following January.*
apply for a job/post/position *Dear Sir, I am writing to apply for the post of Training Officer.*
applying – applied – have applied

application /ˌæplɪ'keɪʃən/ [n C] a formal request to be considered for a job, often consisting of a form on which you have to answer questions about your education, your work experience etc
+ for *Ben's just sent off an application for a job in Dubai.*
application form (=a piece of paper on which you have to answer questions about yourself when you apply for a job) *You have to give details of your previous work experience on the application form.*
job application *She filled out hundreds of job applications before she got the job she wanted.*

applicant/candidate /'æplɪkənt, 'kændɪdət‖-deɪt, -dɪt/ [n C] someone who is being considered for a job: *We're interviewing applicants all week.*

+ for *How many candidates are there for the job?*

CV BRITISH **resumé** AMERICAN /,siː 'viː, 'rezʊ-meı‖'reı-, ,rezʊ'meı/ [n C] a written statement giving details of your education, the examinations you have passed, your previous jobs etc, which you send to an organization when you are trying to get a new job

5 when someone is asked questions to find out if they are suitable for a job

interview /'ıntə^rvjuː/ [n C] a formal meeting at which someone is asked questions in order to find out whether they are suitable for a job: *I'm always very nervous in interviews.*
+ for *She has an interview on Thursday for a job at MTV.*

interview /'ıntə^rvjuː/ [v T] to meet someone and ask them a lot of questions so that you can decide whether they are suitable for a job: *We're interviewing two candidates today and three more tomorrow.*

6 when someone does not have a job

unemployed /,ʌnım'plɔıd◂/ [adj] someone who is **unemployed** does not have a job: *a poor neighbourhood where 50 per cent of the men are unemployed*
the unemployed (=people who are unemployed) *What can the government do to help the unemployed?*

unemployment /,ʌnım'plɔımənt/ [n U] when people do not have jobs: *Unemployment increased by more than 30,000 last month.* | *The survey found that people's biggest worries were about crime and unemployment.*
high unemployment (=when a lot of people are unemployed) *The North-East is an area of high unemployment.*
unemployment benefit BRITISH (=money paid by the government to people who have no job)

be out of work (also **be on the dole** BRITISH) /biː ,aʊt əv 'wɜ^rk, biː ɒn ðə 'dəʊl/ to not have a job, especially for a long time: *My husband has been out of work for two years now.*

When you see **EC**, go to the **ESSENTIAL COMMUNICATION** section.

JOIN

➡ look here for ...
• join two things together
• when roads or rivers join together
• when people or countries join together
• join a club or organization
➡ if you mean 'join in', go to **TAKE PART**
➡ if you mean 'join two sides of a piece of clothing', go to **FASTEN/UNFASTEN**
➡ see also **CONNECTED/NOT CONNECTED, TOGETHER, SEPARATE**

1 to join things together by putting a wire, pipe, glue etc between them

join /dʒɔın/ [v T] to join two things together, for example by using glue or a piece of wood or metal: *Join the two pieces of wood using a strong glue.*
join sth together *Doctors had to use a metal rod to join the two pieces of bone together.* | *Join the sleeve and the shoulder parts together with strong thread.*

fix /fıks/ [v T] to join one thing firmly to another, using screws, nails, or glue, so that it stays there permanently
fix sth to sth *Now all I have to do is fix it to the ceiling.*
be fixed to sth *The chairs and tables were fixed to the floor.*

attach /ə'tætʃ/ [v T] to join one thing to another, so that it stays in position but can be removed later
attach sth to sth *It took a couple of minutes to attach the trailer to the back of the truck.* | *The doctor attached a tiny monitor to the baby's head.*
be attached to sth *Make sure your baggage tag is firmly attached to your suitcase.*

fasten /'fɑːsən‖'fæ-/ [v T] to fix one thing firmly to another, using string, wire, or tape, in a way that makes it easy to remove later
fasten sth to sth *Claire carefully fastened the brooch to her dress.*
be fastened to sth *Our bags were fastened to the roof of the car with thick ropes.*

connect /kəˈnekt/ [v T] to join two pieces of equipment together with a wire or a pipe, so that electricity, water, gas etc can pass from one to the other

connect sth to sth *Have you connected the speakers to the amplifier?* | *I don't know how to connect the Megadrive to the TV.*

be connected to sth *We're waiting for our house to be connected to the city water supply.*

link /lɪŋk/ [v T] to connect two computers, machines, or systems so that electronic signals can pass from one to the other: *The two TV stations are linked by satellite.*

link sth to sth *We'll link your computer to our system via your modem.*

2 when something forms a connection between two places, two machines etc

connect /kəˈnekt/ [v T] if a pipe, wire, bridge etc **connects** two things or places, it forms a connection between them

connect sth to/with sth *This wire connects the TV to the video recorder.* | *the umbilical cord connecting the baby to the placenta* | *The Golden Gate Bridge connects San Francisco with Marin County.*

be connected by sth *The two lakes are connected by a narrow canal.*

link /lɪŋk/ [v T] if a road, a railway, a plane service etc **links** two places, it connects them so that people can easily travel between them: *a new high-speed railway linking the two capitals*

link sth with sth *The Channel Tunnel has linked Britain with mainland Europe for the first time.*

link sth and sth *Interstate 5 links Los Angeles and San Diego.*

connection /kəˈnekʃən/ [n C] a wire or piece of metal that joins two parts of a machine or electrical system: *Carefully check all the electrical connections.*

loose connection (=one that is not joined properly) *There must be a loose connection somewhere – the phone isn't working.*

link /lɪŋk/ [n C] something that joins two places that are far apart, so that people can travel between them or communicate between them: *two TV stations joined by a satellite link*

+ between *Rebels bombed the Beira railroad, a vital link between the capital and the port.* | *a telephone link between the two presidents*

3 when roads, rivers etc come together and join

join /dʒɔɪn/ [v I/T] if two roads, rivers, pipes etc **join**, or if one **joins** another, they come together: *The two rivers join down in the valley.* | *Sometimes you get leaks where the pipes join.* | *The M1 motorway joins the M62 just outside Leeds.*

4 when people, countries etc join together

unite /juːˈnaɪt/ [v I] ESPECIALLY WRITTEN if people, organizations, or countries **unite**, they decide to work together or join together as a single unit, for example because they have the same aims as each other

unite to do sth *In 1960, British and Italian Somaliland united to form Somalia.* | *Various political and religious groups united to oppose the dictatorship.*

+ against *Police chiefs called on the local people to unite against the drug dealers.*

get together /ˌget təˈgeðər/ [phrasal verb I] if people or organizations **get together**, they work together in order to do something that would be difficult to do alone: *A group of parents got together and set up a youth club.*

get together to do sth *Several local stores got together to organize the festival.*

> ⚠ **Get together** is more informal than **unite**.

team up /ˌtiːm ˈʌp/ [phrasal verb I] if two or more people **team up**, they agree to work together, especially in business, music, theatre etc

+ with *I teamed up with a local journalist, and we worked on the story together.*

team up to do sth *It all started when Paul McCartney and John Lennon teamed up to form a band.*

merge /mɜːʳdʒ/ [v I] if two companies or organizations **merge**, they join to form a single company or organization: *The two banks are going to merge next year.*
+ with *The Liberal Party merged with the Social Democrats.*

alliance /əˈlaɪəns/ [n C] an agreement between two or more countries or groups of people to work together in order to achieve something: *the Anglo-Canadian alliance*
+ between *In the 1968 revolution there was an alliance between students and factory workers.*

5 to join a club, organization, or military force

➡ see also **MEMBER**

join /dʒɔɪn/ [v I/T] to join a club, company, organization, or military force: *Do you think we should join the union? | She joined the Conservative Party in 1952. | William joined IBM in 1979 as a programmer. | A lot of people want to join, so there's a big waiting list.*
join the army/navy/air force *Paul joined the army when he was 16.*

⚠ Don't say 'join in a club'. Say **join a club**.

⚠ Don't use **join** about going to a school or college. Say **she went to Harvard in 1990** (not 'she joined Harvard').

become a member /bɪˌkʌm ə ˈmembəʳ/ to join a club, organization, or political group, but not a company or a military force: *You have to be eighteen before you can become a member.*
+ of *I was hoping to become a member of the tennis club. | Several other countries had applied to become members of NATO.*

enlist/join up /ɪnˈlɪst, ˌdʒɔɪn ˈʌp/ [v I] to join the army, navy, or air force: *My grandfather went to join up on the day war broke out.*
enlist in the army/navy/airforce *Josie enlisted in the airforce and eventually became a pilot.*

When you see **EC**, go to the **ESSENTIAL COMMUNICATION** section.

JOKE

➡ see also **FUNNY, LAUGH, SERIOUS**

1 funny story

joke /dʒəʊk/ [n C] something you say or do to make people laugh, especially a funny story: *Do you know any good jokes?*
tell a joke *Tony told me a really funny joke last night, but I've forgotten it.*

⚠ Don't say 'say a joke'. Say **tell a joke**.

comedian/comic /kəˈmiːdiən, ˈkɒmɪk‖ ˈkɑː-/ [n C] someone whose job is to tell jokes and make people laugh: *Sandra Bernhard is an actor, singer, comedian, and a regular guest on the David Letterman show.*

2 when you pretend that something is true as a joke

be joking/be kidding /biː ˈdʒəʊkɪŋ, biː ˈkɪdɪŋ/ INFORMAL to say something that is not true, as a joke: *When he asked me to marry him, I thought he was joking! | Don't get mad – I was only kidding!*

pull sb's leg /ˌpʊl (sb's) ˈleg/ INFORMAL to try to make someone believe a story that is not true, as a joke: *He isn't really related to Madonna – he was only pulling your leg.*

3 to make someone seem stupid by making jokes about them

make fun of sb/sth /ˌmeɪk ˈfʌn ɒv (sb/sth)/ to try to make someone or something seem stupid by making jokes about them: *Stop making fun of me. | The other children at school are always making fun of Tom's clothes.*

⚠ Don't confuse **make fun of** and **have fun** (=enjoy yourself).

tease /tiːz/ [v I/T] to make jokes about someone, either in an unkind way, or in a friendly way that shows you like them: *The kids at school used to tease Sam because he was overweight. | Don't get upset, Stuart, she's only teasing.*
tease sb about sth *Kevin's always teasing me about my cooking.*

JOURNEY

LAND AND SEA — COUNTRY

TRAVEL — *see also* — HOLIDAY

STAY — VISIT

TRANSPORT — COUNTRYSIDE

journey /'dʒɜːᵗni/ [n C] the time during which you travel from one place to another, especially when you go a long way: *I've made us some sandwiches to eat on the journey.* | *We had an awful journey – there was heavy snow and the car broke down.*

bus/train/car journey *the long train journey to St Petersburg*

a two-hour/five-mile journey *They arrived in Nice after an eight-hour journey by car.*

make a journey *These birds make an incredible 10,000-kilometre journey to Africa every winter.*

plural **journeys**

⚠ Don't say 'do a journey'. Say **make a journey.**

⚠ Don't say 'Good journey' to someone who is about to make a journey. Say **Have a good journey** or **Have a safe journey.**

trip /trɪp/ [n C] a journey when you go to a place, stay there for a while, and then come back: *We had a lovely trip – the flight was fine and the hotel was fantastic.*

take a trip *They decided to take a trip to Paris.*

business/school/skiing trip *a school trip to the zoo*

on a trip (=taking a trip) *My husband's away on a business trip in China.*

a day trip (=when you go and come back on the same day) *a day trip to Oxford*

tour /tʊəᵗ/ [n C] an organized journey in which an entertainer, sports team, or politician visits several different places: *Did you see the Rolling Stones during their last tour?*

+ of *The President left Washington today for a tour of the Middle East.*

flight /flaɪt/ [n C] a journey in a plane: *All flights to Tokyo were delayed because of bad weather.*

a 30-minute/3-hour flight *From Athens it's a 30-minute flight to the island.*

drive /draɪv/ [n C] a journey in a car: *It was quite a pleasant drive along the coast to the cottage.*

a 12-hour/15-minute drive *It's about a 20-minute drive into the city from here.*

crossing /'krɒsɪŋ‖'krɔː-/ [n C] a short journey in a boat or ship from one side of a lake, river, or sea to the other: *The crossing from Dover to Calais is often very rough.*

voyage /'vɔɪ-ɪdʒ/ [n C] a long journey in a boat or ship: *In those days, the voyage to Australia was long and dangerous.*

⚠ Use **voyage** especially when you are writing stories.

JUMP

➡ see also **RUN, DANCE, FALL**

jump /dʒʌmp/ [v I] to push yourself off the ground using your legs: *How high can you jump?*

+ into/off/over *I bet you can't jump over that wall.* | *Boys were diving and jumping off the bridge.*

+ up/down *Jump down and I'll catch you.*

jump up and down (=jump several times, while staying in the same place) *Excited fans were jumping up and down and screaming.*

jump [n C] *Aziz won the event with a jump of 2.35 metres.*

leap /liːp/ [v I/T] to jump suddenly as far as you can

+ over/through/across *The barman leapt over the bar and tried to stop the fight.*

leaping – leapt – have leapt BRITISH

leaping – leaped – have leaped AMERICAN

When you see **EC**, go to the **ESSENTIAL COMMUNICATION** section.

K

KEEP

➡ see also **GET RID OF, INFORMATION**

1 to keep something in a place

keep /kiːp/ [v T] to keep something in a place, especially so that you can find it and use it when you need it: *Can you remember where she keeps her keys?*
keep sth in/on/under sth *Do you keep your car in a garage? | Nick always kept a bottle of whisky under the bed.*
keeping – kept – have kept

> ⚠ Don't say 'I am keeping', 'she is keeping' etc. Say **I keep, she keeps** etc.

store /stɔːʳ/ [v T] to keep something in a place or container where it will not be damaged or lost, especially if you intend to keep it for a long time: *The warehouse is being used to store food and clothes for the refugees. | Medicine should be stored in a cool dry place.*

2 to keep information

keep /kiːp/ [v T] to keep many different pieces of information together in one place, so that you can find them when you need them: *The police keep detailed information about everyone who has committed a crime. | Records of all births and deaths in the country are kept in London.*
keeping – kept – have kept

> ⚠ Don't say 'I am keeping', 'they are keeping' etc. Say **I keep, they keep** etc.

store /stɔːʳ/ [v T] to keep information in a computer: *Data regarding employees' salaries is stored on the computer at our main office.*

file /faɪl/ [v T] to keep written records and documents together using an organized system, so that everything is easy to find: *The students' records are filed alphabetically.*
file sth away (=put it in the correct file)

3 to keep something, and not sell it, give it away etc

keep /kiːp/ [v T] to keep something because you have decided not to sell it, give it away, or throw it away: *My mother kept all the love letters my father wrote. | I've decided to keep the car even though it's getting old. | Surely you don't want to keep all these old magazines!*
keeping – kept – have kept

4 to keep something for someone to use later

save /seɪv/ [v T] to keep something that you would normally use or throw away, so that someone else can use it later
save sth for sb *Let's save some of this pizza for Jill. | I save all Polly's old clothes for my sister's baby.*

reserve /rɪˈzɜːʳv/ [v T] to keep a table in a restaurant, a room in a hotel etc for someone to use: *I'm sorry Madam. All the tables have already been reserved.*
reserve sth for sb *I'll ask if they can reserve a room for us on December 22nd.*

keep /kiːp/ [v T] if a shop **keeps** something for someone, they do not sell it or give it to anyone else
keep sth for sb *If you want the necklace, we can keep it for you until Tuesday.*
keeping – kept – have kept

5 to keep things such as stamps, pictures, or coins because you are interested in them and you enjoy owning them

collect /kəˈlekt/ [v T] to keep things such as stamps, pictures, or coins because you are interested in them and you enjoy owning them: *My mother collects old china. | I used to collect shells when I was a kid.*
collector [n C] someone who collects things such as stamps, pictures, or coins

collection /kəˈlekʃən/ [n C] a set of stamps, pictures, coins etc that someone keeps because it is interesting or attractive: *Daniel has a fantastic stamp collection.*
+ of *a collection of fine china*

K

6 an amount that you are keeping to use later

supply /sə'plaɪ/ [n C] an amount of something that you keep so that there is always some available when you need it: *Food supplies were already running out.*
+ of *The hospital keeps a large supply of blood for use in emergencies.*
plural **supplies**

stock /stɒk‖stɑːk/ [n C] an amount of something that a shop keeps in order to sell: *Our stock of Italian wine is selling fast.* | *Buy now, while stocks last!*

KICK

to hit someone or something with your foot

➡ see also **HIT, ATTACK, HURT/INJURE**

kick /kɪk/ [v I/T] *The boy behind me kept kicking my chair.* | *He was dragged kicking and screaming to a waiting police car.*
kick sth along/over/around etc *Who kicked the ball over the fence?*
kick sb in the head/stomach etc *One of the gang kicked him in the stomach.*
kick [n C] a kicking action or movement: *A savage kick from his attacker just missed his knee.*

give sth a kick /ˌgɪv (sth) ə 'kɪk/ to kick something once: *If the door won't open, just give it a good hard kick.*

KILL

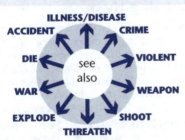

ILLNESS/DISEASE
ACCIDENT   CRIME
DIE   see   VIOLENT
         also
WAR   WEAPON
EXPLODE   SHOOT
THREATEN

1 to kill someone

kill /kɪl/ [v I/T] to make someone die, usually violently: *He claims that he didn't*
mean to kill his wife.* | *The explosion killed 32 people.* | *Many people do not realize that these drugs are dangerous and can kill.* | *The disease has already killed more than 2000 people in Latin America.*
be killed in a crash/accident etc *James Dean was killed in a car crash in 1955.*

murder /'mɜːʳdəʳ/ [v T] to deliberately kill someone, especially after planning to do it: *Wilson is accused of murdering his daughter and her boyfriend.* | *One of the country's top judges has been murdered by the Mafia.*

murder /'mɜːʳdəʳ/ [n C/U] the crime of deliberately killing someone: *He was convicted of murder and jailed for life.*
commit a murder (=murder someone) *The gun was found five miles from where the murder was committed.*

⚠ Don't confuse **murder** (=the crime of killing someone) and **murderer** (=the person who murders someone).

assassinate /ə'sæsɪneɪt‖-səneɪt/ [v T] to murder an important person, especially for political reasons: *President Lincoln was assassinated by John Wilkes Booth.* | *an attempt to assassinate the Pope*
assassination /əˌsæsɪ'neɪʃən‖-sən'eɪ-/ [n C/U]
+ of *The assassination of Indira Gandhi caused a crisis in India.*

massacre /'mæsəkəʳ/ [v T] to violently kill a large number of people who cannot defend themselves: *Hundreds of civilians were massacred during a peaceful protest.*
massacre [n C/U] *The whole world was shocked by the massacre in Rwanda.*

beat/kick/stab sb to death /biːt, kɪk, stæb (sb) tə 'deθ/ to kill someone by beating them, kicking them, or attacking them with a knife: *He beat his wife to death in a drunken argument.* | *A social worker was found stabbed to death in her office last night.*

2 to deliberately kill yourself

kill yourself /'kɪl jɔːʳˌself/ *He killed himself by taking an overdose of painkillers.* | *She had tried to kill herself several times before.*

suicide /'suːɪ̯saɪd, 'sjuː-‖'suː-/ [n C/U] when someone deliberately kills himself or herself: *Police think the man's death was suicide.* | *A record number of teenage suicides were reported last year.*
commit suicide (=kill yourself) *We were devastated when we heard the news that Kurt Cobain had committed suicide.*
suicide attempt (=when you try to commit suicide) *Stephen was rushed to the hospital after his suicide attempt.*
suicidal /ˌsuːɪ̯'saɪdl◂, ˌsjuː-‖ˌsuː-/ [adj] wanting to kill yourself because you are very unhappy or upset: *He became suicidal after his wife left him.*

3 someone who kills someone else

murderer /'mɜːʳdərəʳ/ [n C] someone who has deliberately killed another person: *A convicted murderer escaped from Dartmoor prison last night.*
sb's murderer (=the person who murdered someone) *She was determined to find her brother's murderer.*
mass murderer (=someone who murders a lot of people)

killer /'kɪləʳ/ [n C] someone who has deliberately killed another person – used especially in newspapers and news reports
+ of *The police are searching for the killer of a nine-year-old child.* | *The couple's killers have never been found.*
serial killer (=someone who has killed several people over a long period of time) *a serial killer who is targeting gay men in the area*

assassin /ə'sæsɪ̯n/ [n C] someone who has killed an important person, especially because they are paid for doing it: *Some people believe that the assassin was working for the government.*
sb's assassin (=the person who killed someone important) *Kennedy's assassin claims he was tricked by the FBI.*

4 when someone is killed as a punishment

be executed /biː 'eksɪ̯kjuːtɪ̯d/ to be legally killed by the government as punishment for a crime: *The leader of the rebels was caught and publicly executed.*

capital punishment /ˌkæpɪ̯tl 'pʌnɪʃmənt/ [n U] the system of killing criminals as a legal punishment: *I don't believe that bringing back capital punishment would reduce crime.* | *Most people that we questioned were in favour of capital punishment.*

> ⚠ Use **capital punishment** especially when you are talking about whether it is a good or a bad thing.

the death penalty /ðə 'deθ ˌpenlti/ [n singular] the legal punishment of being killed for a crime: *The death penalty does not exist in Britain.* | *In many countries, drug dealing carries the death penalty.* (=the punishment is death)

be on death row /biː ɒn ˌdeθ 'rəʊ/ if someone **is on death row**, they are in prison for a period of time before they are killed as punishment for a crime: *Some prisoners have spent more than ten years on death row.*

5 when someone is killed because they are very ill

euthanasia /ˌjuːθə'neɪziə‖-'neɪʒə/ [n U] when someone who is very ill is killed in order to stop their suffering: *Is it true that euthanasia is legal in the Netherlands?*

6 something that can kill you

fatal /'feɪtl/ [adj] a **fatal** accident, illness, or injury is one that causes death: *He suffered a fatal injury to the neck.*
+ to *A sudden shock could be fatal to anyone with a weak heart.*
fatally [adv] *The bank manager was fatally wounded during the robbery.*

lethal/deadly /'liːθəl, 'dedli/ [adj] likely or able to kill people – use this especially about weapons or poisons: *An ordinary kitchen knife can be a deadly weapon.* | *a lethal dose of drugs*

> ⚠ **Deadly** is sometimes also used about illnesses (but **lethal** is not): *a deadly form of skin cancer* | *the deadly AIDS virus*

7 to kill an animal

kill /kɪl/ [v T] *You shouldn't kill spiders just because you are scared of them.* | *I'm a vegetarian because I don't believe in killing animals.*

slaughter /'slɔːtəʳ/ [v T] to kill farm animals, either for their meat or skins, or because they are ill: *Farmers have been told to slaughter all flocks infected with the disease.* | *Hundreds of baby seals are slaughtered for their fur every year.*

have sth put down /ˌhæv (sth) pʊt 'daʊn/ to painlessly kill an animal, especially a pet, because it is very old, very ill, or badly injured: *Our cat was hit by a car, so we had to have her put down.*

KIND

➡ if you mean a kind of person or thing, go to **TYPE**

➡ opposite **UNKIND**

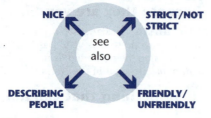

NICE
STRICT/NOT STRICT
see also
DESCRIBING PEOPLE
FRIENDLY/ UNFRIENDLY

1 kind

kind /kaɪnd/ [adj] someone who is **kind** tries to help people and make them happy or comfortable, and shows that they care about them: *The nurses were all very kind.* | *Luckily a kind man helped me with my bags.* | *It was a very kind thing to do.*
+ to *My host family in England were really kind to me.*
it is kind of sb (to do sth) *Wasn't it kind of Ross to lend us his car?*

> ⚠ Don't say 'they were kind with me' or 'they were kind for me'. Say **they were kind to me**.

kindness /'kaɪndnɪs/ [n U] kind behaviour: *I'd like to thank you for all your kindness.*

considerate /kən'sɪdərɪt/ [adj] someone who is **considerate** thinks about other people's feelings, and is careful not to make them unhappy or cause problems for them: *Louis was always considerate and sympathetic to others.*
it is considerate of sb (to do sth) *My boss gave me some time off when my mother died, which was very considerate of him.*

> ⚠ You often use **considerate** when complaining that someone is not considerate enough and should care more about other people's feelings: *I wish he would try and be a little more considerate.*

generous /'dʒenərəs/ [adj] someone who is **generous** often gives other people money or presents: *My sister's really generous. She's always buying things for the children.*
it is generous of sb (to do sth) *My dad offered to pay my plane fare, which was very generous of him.*

generosity /ˌdʒenə'rɒsɪti‖-'rɑː-/ [n U] generous behaviour: *The Prince was famous for his generosity to his friends.*

generously [adv] *These children need your help. Please give generously.*

it's nice of sb (to do sth) /ɪts 'naɪs əv (sb) (tə duː sth)/ SPOKEN say this when someone has helped you or pleased you by doing something kind: *It was nice of her to let you use her car.* | *"I've brought that book you wanted." "Oh, thanks – that's really nice of you."*

2 kind to people who have problems and difficulties

sympathetic /ˌsɪmpə'θetɪk◀/ [adj] if someone is **sympathetic** to you when you are having problems, they say kind things to you and show that they feel sad about your situation: *Everybody was very sympathetic when they heard I'd failed my test.* | *She gave him a sympathetic look.*

sympathetically [adv] *He listened sympathetically to her story.*

understanding /ˌʌndəʳ'stændɪŋ/ [adj] an **understanding** person is kind and patient when someone has a problem,

and does not get angry with them or criticize them: *I've missed a lot of work through illness – fortunately I have a very understanding boss.*
+ about *Thank you for being so understanding about all this.*

good /gʊd/ [adj not before noun] if someone is **good** to you, they help you and give you what you need, especially when you are having problems
+ to *My parents have been very good to me since I lost my job.*
it is good of sb (to do sth) *It was good of you to come and see me.*

3 to treat someone too kindly

spoil /spɔɪl/ [v T] to treat someone, especially a child, too kindly and give them everything they want whether they should have it or not: *Because he was their only son, his parents spoiled him.*

spoiling – spoiled (also **spoilt** BRITISH) – **have spoiled** (also **have spoilt** BRITISH)

KNOW/NOT KNOW

➡ look here for ...
• know a fact
• know a person

REALIZE   FIND OUT

see also

GUESS   SURE/ NOT SURE

1 to know a fact or piece of information

know /nəʊ/ [v I/T] to know a fact or piece of information: *This is a famous painting – do you know the name of the artist?* | *Jack's leaving. Didn't you know?*
+ (that) *I knew he was ill, but I didn't realize he had cancer.*
know how/what/where etc *Do you know where Andy is?*
+ about *We've known about the problem for some time.* •

know of sth (=know that something exists) *I know of one company where members of staff get their meals free.*
know a lot about sth *Keith knows a lot about computers.*

knowing – knew – have known

⚠ Don't say 'I am knowing', 'she was knowing' etc. Say **I know, she knew** etc.

realize (also **realise** BRITISH) /ˈrɪəlaɪz/ [v I/T] to know that a situation exists, and especially to know how important or serious it is: *None of us realized the danger we were in.* | *"The reason that she hasn't been in school is that she's pregnant." "Oh, really? I didn't realize."*
+ (that) *I realize that you are very busy, but could I talk to you for a few minutes?*
realize how/what/why *Do you think he realizes how much trouble he has caused?*

⚠ Don't say 'I am realizing', 'she was realizing' etc. Say **I realize, she realized** etc.

can tell /kən ˈtel/ ESPECIALLY SPOKEN to know that something is true because you can see signs that show this
+ (that) *His eyes were red, and I could tell he'd been crying.*
can tell whether/what/how etc *You can tell whether a coin is real by scratching its surface.*

be aware /biː əˈweəʳ/ FORMAL to know that a serious situation exists
+ of *We are aware of the problems faced by homeless people and are trying to deal with them.*
+ that *The question is, was the Chief of Police aware that so much corruption existed within the police department?*

2 someone who knows a lot about something

expert /ˈekspɜːʳt/ [n C] someone who knows a lot about a subject: *Our team of experts includes psychiatrists, psychologists and social workers.*
+ in/on *an expert in French history*
medical/legal/financial etc expert *Get advice from a financial expert first.*

⚠️ You can also use **expert** before a noun, like an adjective: *expert advice* (=advice from an expert) | *expert opinions*

specialist /'speʃəlˌɪst/ [n C] someone who has studied a very specific subject for a long time and knows much more about it than other people: *You really need a specialist for this job.*
+ in *Professor Williams teaches English Literature and is a specialist in the novels of George Orwell.*
computer/marketing/engine etc specialist *The Health Department is seeking the advice of a team of tropical disease specialists from London University.*

knowledgeable /'nɒlɪdʒəbəl‖'naː-/ [adj] someone who is **knowledgeable** knows a lot of different facts, especially about a particular subject or activity: *Talk to Mr Carew – he's knowledgeable and extremely helpful.*
+ about *He's very knowledgeable about garden plants.*

3 when most people know something

○**everyone knows** /ˌevriwʌn 'nəʊz/ ESPECIALLY SPOKEN say this when you think most people know something and you would be surprised if someone did not know it: *Haven't you heard Anja's pregnant? I thought everyone knew.*
+ (that) *Everyone knows Andy and Lynn are having an affair.*
everyone knows how/what/why etc *Surely everyone knows how to change a light bulb!*

well known /ˌwel 'nəʊn/ [adj] use this about facts and ideas that most people know about: *Mrs Thatcher's views on Europe were well known.*
it is well known that *It is well known that people who smoke are more likely to get lung diseases.*

⚠️ **Well known** is spelled with a hyphen when it comes before a noun: *It is a well-known fact that most crimes are committed by men.*

4 facts and information that you know

knowledge /'nɒlɪdʒ‖'naː-/ [n U, singular] facts and information that you know: *He doesn't have the skills or knowledge needed to do the job.*
+ of *Paula has a good knowledge of Japanese.*
scientific/medical/technical knowledge *theories based on scientific knowledge*

⚠️ Don't use **knowledge** in expressions like 'get more knowledge' or 'increase my knowledge'. It is better to use words like **learn** and **find out**: *I'd like to learn/find out more about using the Internet.*

5 to know a person

know /nəʊ/ [v T] if you **know** someone, you have met them before and you know things about them, such as where they live or what their job is: *Yes, I know Clive. I used to work with him.* | *Do you know anyone who could babysit tonight?*
know sb well *I know Paul very well – we were at college together.*
knowing – knew – have known

⚠️ Don't say 'I am knowing', 'she was knowing' etc. Say **I know, she knew** etc.

get to know /ˌget tə 'nəʊ/ to start to have a friendly relationship with someone by spending time with them and talking to them: *When you move to a new place, it can take a long time to get to know people.* | *I got to know Jenny when we worked together at IBM.*

acquaintance /ə'kweɪntəns/ [n C] someone you know, although you do not know them well, and they are not one of your friends: *Kim's just an acquaintance really – I've only met her a couple of times.*

6 to know a book, place, piece of music etc

know /nəʊ/ [v T] if you **know** a place, you have been there before and spent time there; if you **know** a book, song, film, etc you have read it or seen it or heard it before: *"Do you know Boston at all?" "Yes, I went to college there."* | *I didn't* know any of the songs they were singing. | Do you know that Hitchcock movie about a man who is being chased? What's it called?

know sth by heart (=know every word of a song, poem etc) I've heard that poem so often that I know it by heart.

know somewhere like the back of your hand INFORMAL (=know a place very well) Tony had spent a lot of time in Tokyo and knew the place like the back of his hand.

knowing – knew – have known

⚠ Don't say 'I am knowing', 'she was knowing' etc. Say **I know, she knew** etc.

be familiar with sth /biː fəˈmɪliəʳ wɪð (sth)/ FORMAL to know something well because you have seen it, read it, or used it before: Anyone applying for the job should be familiar with using a spreadsheet. | Are you familiar with the works of George Eliot?

7 when you have seen someone or something before

recognize (also **recognise** BRITISH) /ˈrekəgnaɪz, ˈrekən-/ [v T] to know who someone is or what something is, because you have seen them before: I didn't recognize him when he shaved his beard off. | Do you recognize this picture?

⚠ Don't say 'I am recognizing', 'she was recognizing' etc. Say **I recognize, she recognized** etc.

know /nəʊ/ [v T] to recognize someone or something, especially when you have not seen them for a long time: You'll know him when you see him. He hasn't changed at all. | The town has changed so much, I hardly know it any more.

know sb by sight (=be able to recognize someone, although you do not know their name) I've never spoken to her, but I know her by sight.

knowing – knew – have known

⚠ Don't say 'I am knowing', 'she was knowing' etc. Say **I know she knew** etc.

familiar /fəˈmɪliəʳ/ [adj] someone or something that is **familiar** is easy to recognize because you have heard or seen them many times before: a familiar tune | It was good to see all the old familiar faces again.

look/sound familiar The voice on the phone sounded familiar.

8 to not know something or someone

not know /nɒt ˈnəʊ/ to not know something or someone: "What time's the meeting?" "Sorry, I don't know." | I've met Tom a few times, but I don't know his sister.

not know how/what/why etc I don't know why they're so angry.

unfamiliar/not familiar /ˌʌnfəˈmɪliəʳ◂, nɒt fəˈmɪliəʳ/ ESPECIALLY WRITTEN [adj] if something is **unfamiliar** or **not familiar**, you have not seen it, heard it, or experienced it before: It took me a long time to get used to the unfamiliar surroundings.
+ to He was speaking a language that was not familiar to me.

be unaware/not be aware /biː ˌʌnəˈweəʳ, nɒt biː əˈweəʳ/ FORMAL to not know about a situation or about something that is happening, especially when you should know about it
+ of She was not aware of the man who had come quietly into the room. | The child was clearly unaware of the danger.
+ that His parents weren't aware that he smoked.

ignorant /ˈɪgnərənt/ [adj] someone who is **ignorant** does not know facts or information that they should know

ignorant of sth (=not knowing about a fact or situation) She remained ignorant of the real truth about her parents.

ignorant about sth (=not knowing about a subject) I'm very ignorant about politics.

ignorance /ˈɪgnərəns/ [n U] when someone does not know facts or information that they should know: a mistake that was the result of their ignorance
+ of He showed complete ignorance of the most basic historical facts.

9 what you say when you do not know the answer to a question

I don't know /aɪ ˌdəʊnt 'nəʊ/ SPOKEN say this when you do not know the answer to a question: *"What time is it?" "I don't know. I don't have a watch."*

I have no idea /aɪ hæv ˌnəʊ aɪ'dɪə/ SPOKEN say this when you do not know the answer to a question, and cannot even guess the answer: *"How long will it take to get there?" "I've no idea."*

who knows /ˌhuː 'nəʊz/ SPOKEN say this when you think it is impossible for anyone to know the answer to a question: *The world might end tomorrow. Who knows?*

who knows what/when etc *Who knows what could happen in the future?*

don't ask me/how should I know /ˌdəʊnt ɑːsk 'miː, ˌhaʊ ʃʊd 'aɪ nəʊ‖ -æsk-/ SPOKEN INFORMAL say this when it is impossible for you to know the answer to a question, and you are annoyed or surprised that someone has asked you: *"Why's Sharon in such a bad mood?" "How should I know, she never tells me anything."* | *"How do these modem things actually work?" "Don't ask me!"*

K

L

LAND AND SEA

➡ if you mean 'an area of land with its own government eg Japan, Germany', go to **COUNTRY**

➡ if you mean 'land where there are trees and fields and not many buildings', go to **COUNTRYSIDE**

ENVIRONMENT ← see also → BEAUTIFUL 6

TOWN ← → AREA

1 land that is owned by someone or is used for something

land /lænd/ [n U] land that is owned by someone or that can be used for farming or building houses: *They moved to the country and bought some land.* | *There was some empty land behind the office which had been turned into a parking lot.*
piece of land *Each family was given a small piece of land where they could grow food for themselves.*
farmland/building land (=land that can be used for farming, or for building houses, offices etc)
sb's land (=land owned by someone) *Get off my land.*

territory /'terɪtəri‖-tɔːri/ [n U] land that belongs to a country or that is controlled by a country during a war: *Miller had accidentally crossed into Iraqi territory and was arrested for spying.*
enemy territory (=land controlled by an enemy) *His plane was shot down over enemy territory.*

field /fiːld/ [n C] an area of land that is part of a farm, or that is used for playing sports: *cows grazing in the fields* | *a football field*
+ of *a field of wheat*

playing field BRITISH (=a field where sports are played) *We went out onto the school playing fields to watch a game of football.*

the grounds /ðə 'graʊndz/ [n plural] the gardens and land around a big building such as a castle, school, or hospital: *Have you ever been to Penryn Castle? The grounds are beautiful.*
the palace/school/hospital grounds *The nurse said I could go for a short walk around the hospital grounds.*

2 what you see in an area of land

landscape /'lændskeɪp/ [n C usually singular] the land that you see all around you, in the countryside or in the city, with its hills, fields, buildings etc: *the beauty of the New England landscape in the fall* | *Brad's apartment was in a poor part of town, and looked out on a desolate urban landscape of the industrial region.*

scenery /'siːnəri/ [n U] all the mountains, rivers, forests etc that you see around you, especially when these are beautiful: *a peaceful Alpine village surrounded by magnificent scenery*

3 the substance that forms the surface of the land

the ground /ðə 'graʊnd/ [n singular] the surface of the land: *The ground was covered in snow.* | *There was a big hole in the ground.*

⚠ Don't confuse **the ground** (=the surface of the land, outside a building) and **the floor** (=the surface you walk on inside a building): *The kitchen floor needs sweeping.* | *I sat down on the ground under a tree.*

earth /ɜːθ/ [n U] the substance that the ground is made of: *Thousands of tons of earth were moved to build the dam.* | *Outside, the sun beat down on the red baked earth of Provence.*

soil /sɔɪl/ [n U] the earth that plants grow in: *Roses grow best in a well-drained, slightly acid soil.*
fertile soil (=soil that plants grow well in) *The fertile soil of southern Italy is perfect for growing grapes and olives.*

L

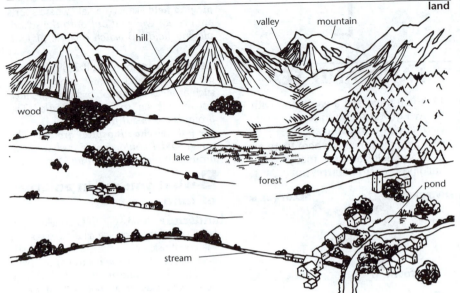

dirt /dɜːʳt/ [n U] AMERICAN loose dry earth: *The kids were playing in the yard, digging in the dirt.*

4 the land, compared with the sea or the air

land /lænd/ [n U] the land, not the sea: *After sailing across the ocean for 21 days we sighted land.*

on land *The sea turtle lays its eggs on land.*

the ground /ðə ˈɡraʊnd/ [n singular] the land, not the air – use this to talk about planes: *Our plane was flying only 100 feet above the ground.* | *Spectators watched in horror as the aircraft plunged to the ground.*

5 hills and mountains

mountain /ˈmaʊntɪn/ [n C] a very high piece of land with steep sides: *the Rocky Mountains* | *One day she wants to climb Mount Everest, the highest mountain in the world.*

hill /hɪl/ [n C] an area of land that is higher than the land around it, like a mountain but smaller: *A rough track led over the hill to the village.*

valley /ˈvæli/ [n C] an area of low land between two hills or mountains, often with a river flowing through it: *the Welsh*

valleys | *Carrie turned off the main road into a narrow valley.*

6 flat land

plain /pleɪn/ [n C] a large area of flat land: *the vast plains of central China*

7 land covered with trees

forest /ˈfɒrɪst‖ˈfɔː-, ˈfɑː-/ [n C/U] a large area of land that is covered with trees: *the thick forests of central Europe* | *Five hundred years ago, most of England was covered in forest.*

wood /wʊd/ [n C] an area of land with a lot of trees growing close together, like a forest but smaller: *There was a little wood at the bottom of the valley.*

⚠ You can also use **the woods** to mean an area covered with trees: *a walk through the woods* | *a story about two children who got lost in the woods*

rainforest/jungle /ˈreɪnˌfɒrɪst, ˈdʒʌŋɡəl‖ -ˌfɔː-, -ˌfɑː-/ [n C/U] a tropical forest with many large plants and tall trees growing close together, in an area where there is a lot of rain: *They had to cut a path through the thick leaves and branches of the jungle.* | *Environmental groups are campaigning against the destruction of the rainforest.*

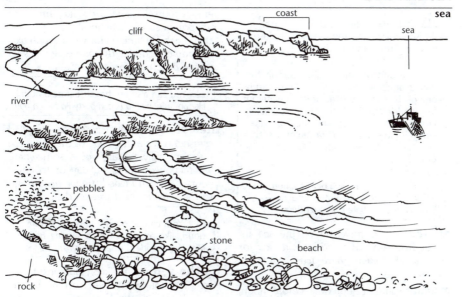

⚠ Use **rainforest** (not 'jungle') when you are talking about the environment.

8 dry land

desert /ˈdezəᵗt/ [n C/U] a large area of land in a hot place, where there is very little rain and very few plants or trees: *the Sahara Desert* | *Mauretania is a poor country and most of it is desert.*

9 rivers

river /ˈrɪvəᵗ/ [n C] a natural and continuous flow of water in a long line across land and into the sea: *the River Danube* | *Let's go for a swim in the river.*

stream /striːm/ [n C] a small river that is only one or two metres wide: *a mountain stream* | *We passed a couple of boys who were fishing in the stream.*

10 areas of water surrounded by land

lake /leɪk/ [n C] a large area of water surrounded by land: *There's a little island in the middle of the lake.* | *Lake Ontario*

pond /pɒnd‖pɑːnd/ [n C] a small area of water, especially one that has been made in a garden, park, or field: *A few village children were standing by the pond, feeding the ducks.*

pool /puːl/ [n C] a small area of water that is not moving, for example at the edge of the sea or forming part of a river: *The children hunted for crabs in the pools between the rocks.*

11 areas of land with water around them

island /ˈaɪlənd/ [n C] a piece of land completely surrounded by water: *a small island in the middle of the lake* | *the Hawaiian Islands* | *the island of Cyprus*
desert island (=a small tropical island far from other places with no-one living on it)

peninsula /pəˈnɪnsjʊ̈lə‖-sələ/ [n C] a long piece of land almost completely surrounded by water but joined to the rest of the land in one place: *a rocky peninsula that stretches out into the Atlantic Ocean* | *a city near the southern tip of the Malay Peninsula*

12 the sea

the sea ESPECIALLY BRITISH **the ocean** ESPECIALLY AMERICAN /ðə ˈsiː, ði ˈəʊʃən/ [n singular] the large area of salty water that covers most of the Earth's surface: *Do you like swimming in the sea?* | *She sat on the beach, gazing out at the ocean.* | *The sea was calm and there was a gentle breeze.*

⚠️ **The sea** is the word usually used in British English, and **the ocean** is the usual word in American English.

⚠️ **Sea** and **ocean** are also used in the names of large areas of water. An **ocean** is one of the five very large areas of water in the world: *the Pacific Ocean | the Indian Ocean*. A **sea** is a smaller area of water which is either part of an ocean or has land all around it: *the South China Sea | the Caspian Sea*.

⚠️ You can also use **sea** before a noun, like an adjective, in both British and American English: *the seashore | sea creatures*.

at sea /ət 'siː/ travelling on the sea far away from land: *We had been at sea for two weeks when there was a terrible storm.*

marine /mə'riːn/ [adj only before noun] **marine** plants and animals live in the sea: *She studies jellyfish and other marine life. | marine biology*

13 where the sea and land meet

the coast /ðə 'kəʊst/ [n singular] the part of a country that is close to the sea – use this when you are talking about a country or a large part of a country: *driving along the Californian coast, from San Francisco to LA*
on the coast (=on land that is close to the sea) *a little house on the coast of Brittany*
off the coast (=in the sea but close to the land) *They discovered oil off the northern coast of Scotland.*
+ of *The ship slowly made its way along the west coast of Africa.*

the shore /ðə ʃɔːr/ [n singular] the land along the edge of the sea or along the edge of a lake: *We could see a boat about a mile from the shore.*
the shore of/the shores of *a small town on the shores of Lake Ontario*

⚠️ You can say either **the shore of** or **the shores of**, and it means the same thing.

beach /biːtʃ/ [n C] an area of sand at the edge of the sea – use this especially to talk about a place where you go to relax and

enjoy yourself: *The area has miles of unspoiled sandy beaches.*
the beach *By nine o'clock the beach was already crowded with people. | Let's go to the beach tomorrow.*

⚠️ You can also use **beach** before a noun, like an adjective: *a beach party | a beach ball*

the seaside /ðə 'siːsaɪd/ [n singular] BRITISH a place at the edge of the sea – use this especially to talk about somewhere where you go for a holiday or to enjoy yourself: *When I was little we used to go to the seaside most weekends.*

⚠️ You can also use **seaside** before a noun, like an adjective: *a seaside holiday* (=at the seaside) *| a seaside town*

by the sea /baɪ ðə 'siː/ on land next to the sea: *We bought a small cottage by the sea. | walking by the sea in the early morning*

14 the study of countries, rivers, oceans etc

geography /dʒi'ɒgrəfiǁ-'ɑːg-/ [n U] the study of countries, rivers, oceans, towns etc: *She teaches geography in the high school. | I have to draw a map of India for my geography homework.*

LANGUAGE

➡ see also **WORD/PHRASE/SENTENCE**

1 the language used by a particular group of people

language /'læŋgwɪdʒ/ [n C] a system of words, phrases, and grammar that is used by the people who live in a particular country for speaking and writing to each other: *"What language do they speak in Brazil?" "Portuguese." | She can speak four different languages – French, German, English, and Dutch.*
foreign language *Children learn two foreign languages in school.*
official language (=the language used by the government) *English is the island's official language, but people also speak French and Creole.*

speak the language (=be able to speak the language of the country you are in) *It's difficult living in a country where you don't speak the language.*

> ⚠ Don't say 'I'm learning the Japanese language', 'Do you speak Italian language?' etc. Say **I'm learning Japanese, Do you speak Italian?** etc.
>
> ⚠ You can also use **language** before a noun, like an adjective: *language teaching | language classes*

dialect /'daɪəlekt/ [n C] a form of a language that is spoken by the people who live in one area of a country, which is different in some ways from the standard form of the language: *The people in this part of Germany speak a dialect called 'Plattdeutsch'. | In some northern English dialects, people say 'nowt' instead of 'nothing'.*

slang /slæŋ/ [n U] very informal words used by young people or by specific groups of people, for example soldiers or prisoners or people, who take drugs: *I was totally confused by the slang that the other kids spoke.*

jargon /'dʒɑːrgən‖-gən, -gɑɪn/ [n U] words used by people who do a particular job or who are interested in a particular subject, which are difficult for ordinary people to understand: *When you first learn about computers, there is a whole lot of jargon to understand.*
management/legal/medical/computer jargon *I hate all this management jargon about 'upskilling' and 'downsizing'.*

2 to change something from one language into another

translate /træns'leɪt, trænz-/ [v I/T] to change what someone has said or written from one language into another: *She has translated a number of his books. | Patrice doesn't speak English, so I'll have to translate.*
translate sth into Spanish/Japanese/ English *Can you translate this letter into French?*
translate from English into Japanese/ from Spanish into German etc *In the*

second exam we have to translate from Italian into English.

interpret /ɪn'tɜːrprɪt/ [v I] to translate what someone is saying immediately after they say it, so that people who speak different languages can talk to each other: *No-one in the tour group spoke Spanish, so we had to ask the guide to interpret.*
+ for *My boss doesn't speak any Japanese, but I interpret for her.*

translation /træns'leɪʃən, trænz-/ [n C/U] a piece of writing or speech that has been changed from one language into another: *I have only read the English translation of the book, not the Japanese original.*
do a translation (=translate something) *I have to do a translation for homework.*
in translation (=translated into a different language) *All of Brecht's plays are available in translation.*

3 someone who translates from one language into another

translator /træns'leɪtər, trænz-/ [n C] someone whose job is to translate what people say or write from one language into another: *She works as a translator in Geneva.*

interpreter /ɪn'tɜːrprɪtər/ [n C] someone whose job is to translate what has just been said, so that people who speak different languages can talk to each other: *Both Presidents were accompanied by their interpreters.*
through an interpreter (=using an interpreter) *Speaking through an interpreter, he said: 'I'm afraid to go back to my own country.'*

4 the language that you learn first

sb's first language /(sb's) ˌfɜːrst 'læŋgwɪdʒ/ the first language that you learn as a child – use this when you are comparing someone's first language with other languages that they learn at school or later: *My first language is Dutch.*

sb's mother tongue /(sb's) 'mʌðər ˌtʌŋ/ the first language that you learn as a child – use this especially to talk about someone who now lives in a country where a different language is spoken: *classes for students whose mother tongue is not English*

native speaker /ˌneɪtɪv ˈspiːkəʳ/ [n C] a **native speaker** of a language is someone who was born in the country where that language is spoken: *The book is aimed at learners of English, rather than native speakers.*

5 someone who can speak more than one language

bilingual /baɪˈlɪŋɡwəl/ [adj] someone who is **bilingual** can speak two languages perfectly: *Omar is bilingual – his parents speak Arabic, but he was brought up in France.*

sb's second language /(sb's) ˌsekənd ˈlæŋgwɪdʒ/ [n C] your **second language** is a language that you speak well and often use, but not the first language that you learned as a child: *Halima was born in Kenya. Her first language is Swahili, and her second language is English.*

6 the use of words to communicate

language /ˈlæŋgwɪdʒ/ [n U] the use of words, grammar etc to communicate with other people: *a fascinating study of the origins of language* | *Every child develops the natural ability to use language.*

linguistic /lɪŋˈgwɪstɪk/ [adj usually before noun] connected with people's use of language

linguistic ability/skills/studies/development *a child's linguistic development* | *She should be able to learn Russian fairly easily – she has plenty of linguistic ability.*

LAST

➡ opposite **FIRST**
➡ see also **END, FINISH**

1 coming at the end, after all the others

last /lɑːst‖læst/ [adj] happening or coming at the end, with no others after: *What time does the last train leave?* | *Could you repeat the last number for me*

please? | *That was the last time I ever saw her.* (=I never saw her again) | *the last game of the football season*

the last *That lecture was the last in a series.*

the last but one (=the person or thing before the last one) *Ours was the last car but one to leave the ferry.*

last [adv] *I expect they'll interview me last because my name begins with Y.*

come last/finish last/be last /ˌkʌm ˈlɑːst, ˌfɪnɪʃ ˈlɑːst, biː ˈlɑːst‖-ˈlæst/ to finish a race or competition in the last position: *Our team came last in the gymnastics competition.* | *I don't expect to win the race, but I don't want to be last.*

final /ˈfaɪnl/ [adj only before noun] last in a series of actions, events, or parts of a story: *the final chapter of the book* | *Could I mention just one final point?*

final days/years/moments *Klinsmann scored the winning goal in the final moments of the game.*

final stage (=the last part of a process or activity) *The final stages of the climb were particularly tiring.*

2 when something is the last thing you want to mention

finally /ˈfaɪnəl-i/ [adv] use this when something is the last thing you want to say, especially at the end of a long speech or piece of writing: *Finally, I'd like to thank all those people who helped make the conference such a success.*

lastly /ˈlɑːstli‖ˈlæst-/ [adv] use this to say that something is the last of a list of things, or when something is the last thing you want to say: *Firstly it's too big, secondly we can't afford it, and lastly we don't really need it.* | *Lastly, I want to ask all of you to keep this information secret.*

last but not least /ˌlɑːst bət nɒt ˈliːst‖ˌlæst-/ use this when you are mentioning the last person or thing in a list, to emphasize that they are just as important as all the others: *Last but not least, let me introduce Jane, our new accountant.*

3 most recent

last /lɑːst‖læst/ [determiner/adj only before noun] most recent: *We discussed this problem at the last meeting.*
last night/week/year/Monday etc (=the one that has just past) *Did you watch the game on TV last night?* | *We still haven't paid last month's rent.* | *Paul arrived back in England last Saturday.*
(the) last time (=the most recent occasion) *Last time I spoke to Bob he seemed happy and cheerful.* | *Do you remember the last time we came here?*
the last 10 minutes/20 years (=the period up to now) *Things have changed a lot in the last ten years.*
sb's last job/address/girlfriend etc (=the one they had just before this one) *Our last apartment was much smaller than this one.*
   last [adv usually before verb] most recently: *When I last saw her, she was going out with an Italian student called Giovanni.*

past /pɑːst‖pæst/ [adj only before noun] use this about the period of time up until now
the past year/few days/24 hours etc *During the past year there have been eleven accidents on this stretch of road.*

previous /ˈpriːviəs/ [adj only before noun] the **previous** time, event, or thing is the one before the one you have just mentioned: *Everyone knew what to do because we had planned all the arrangements the previous day.*
sb's previous job/address/visit etc (=the one they had or did before the one you have just mentioned) *She said she had left her previous job because she was unhappy.*

the day/week/year before /ðə (day, etc) bɪˈfɔːʳ/ the day, week, or year in the past before the one you have just mentioned: *Last week he was in Paris and the week before he was in Rome.*

When you see **EC**, go to the **ESSENTIAL COMMUNICATION** section.

LATE/NOT LATE

➡ look here for ...
• arriving or happening late
• late at night
➡ see also **EARLY**

1 arriving late

late /leɪt/ [adj/adv] arriving after the time that was arranged or after the time when you should arrive: *Cathy got there even later than I did.*
+ for *She often arrives late for work.*
be late *Sorry I'm late – my car broke down.*
5 minutes/2 days/3 weeks late *As usual, the bus was half an hour late.*
too late *By the time the doctor arrived, it was too late – the woman was already dead.*
late arrival/departure *We apologize for the late arrival of Flight AZ709.*

not on time /nɒt ɒn ˈtaɪm/ later than the time that was arranged: *Hurry up, or you won't get to school on time!* | *The train is never on time.*

miss /mɪs/ [v T] to arrive too late to see an event, film etc, or too late to get on a plane, train etc: *You'd better hurry or you'll miss the start of the show.*
miss the flight/train/bus/ferry *I missed the bus and had to wait half an hour for the next one.*

2 what you say when someone arrives late

Q**where have you been?** /ˌweəʳ həv juː ˈbiːn‖-ˈbɪn/ SPOKEN say this when someone arrives late and you want to know why, because you are worried or annoyed: *Where have you been? You said three o'clock!*

Q**what kept you?** /wɒt ˈkept juː/ SPOKEN say this when someone arrives late and you are annoyed: *It's nearly five already! What kept you?*

Q**about time too** /əˌbaʊt ˌtaɪm ˈtuː/ SPOKEN INFORMAL say this when someone or something arrives late, and you are annoyed because you have been waiting a long time: *"Look, the bus is coming." "And about time too!"*

L

3 to make someone arrive late

make sb late /ˌmeɪk (sb) 'leɪt/ to make someone arrive somewhere later than they should arrive
+ for *I don't want to make you late for work.* | *The car broke down again, which made her late for her meeting.*

be delayed /biː dɪ'leɪd/ if you **are delayed** by something, something unexpected happens and it makes you late
+ by *Our plane was delayed by fog.*
get delayed *There was an accident on the freeway and we got delayed.*

hold up /ˌhəʊld 'ʌp/ [phrasal verb T] to make someone stop or go more slowly when they are going somewhere
hold sb up *I won't hold you up – I can see you're in a hurry.*
be/get held up by sth *On her way to the hospital she got held up by heavy traffic.*

4 when something happens later than it should or later than usual

late /leɪt/ [adv/adj] when something happens later than usual, or someone does something later than they should: *The library stays open late on Fridays.*
be late *The harvest was late this year because of the bad weather.*
15 minutes/3 days/6 months late *Tony handed in his homework a day late.* | *Hurry up! We're already half an hour late.*
too late *He tried to warn them of the danger, but it was too late – they had already left.*
work late (=stay at work till later than usual) *I'm afraid I'll have to work late again tomorrow.*
get up late (=get out of bed late in the morning) *It's really nice to get up late on Saturday mornings.*
a late breakfast/lunch etc (=later than usual)

overdue /ˌəʊvəˈdjuː◄ǁ-'duː◄/ [adj] use this about payments that are late or library books that you give back later than you should: *I must take these books back to the library – they're overdue.*

three weeks/two months etc overdue
The rent's three weeks overdue.

be behind with sth /biː bɪ'haɪnd wɪð (sth)/ [phrasal verb T] if you **are behind**, with your work, you have done less of it than you should have done: *I have got to stay late tonight – I'm a little behind with my work.*

5 to make something happen later or more slowly

be delayed /biː dɪ'leɪd/ if an event or person **is delayed**, there is a problem that makes it happens later than it should, or take longer than it should: *President Chirac's visit had to be delayed because of security problems.*
be delayed for 5 hours/2 months etc *The opening of the new bridge may be delayed for several months.*
+ by *The start of the game was delayed by bad weather.*

hold up /ˌhəʊld 'ʌp/ [phrasal verb T] to make something happen late, or make it happen more slowly than it should
hold up sth *Protesters held up work on the new road.*
be held up by sth *The peace talks are being held up by continued fighting on the border.*
hold sb up *They should have finished that job on Friday – what's holding them up?*

6 something that makes you late

delay /dɪ'leɪ/ [n C] a situation in which you get delayed: *There were the usual delays at the border, but otherwise we had a good journey.*
long delay *The strike is causing long delays at airports.*
delay in doing sth *There have been a lot of complaints about delays in issuing passports.*

hold-up /'həʊld ʌp/ [n C] a delay that is unexpected but not very serious: *traffic hold-ups* | *There's been a hold-up with the builders, so the new office won't be ready until next month.*

7 **not late**

on time /ɒn ˈtaɪm/ at the time that was expected or planned: *The work must be completed on time.*

be on time (=arrive at the expected time) *Fortunately the train was on time.*

punctual /ˈpʌŋktʃuəl/ [adj] someone who is **punctual** is never late or not usually late: *I'm worried. Pat's not here yet, and she's usually so punctual.*

8 **late at night**

late /leɪt/ [adj/adv] late at night: *I must go home now, it's getting late.* | *I don't like coming home late to an empty house.*

stay up late (=not go to bed until late) *We usually let the children stay up late on Saturday evenings.*

have a late night (=when you go to bed very late) *I'm really tired today – I had a late night last night.*

in the middle of the night /ɪn ðə ˌmɪdl əv ðə ˈnaɪt/ late at night when most people are asleep: *I woke up in the middle of the night.*

LATER/ AT A LATER TIME

➡ if you mean 'see you later', go to
◧ **SAYING GOODBYE**
➡ see also **AFTER**

1 **at a later time**

later /ˈleɪtər/ [adv] not now, or not at the time you are talking about, but some time after this: *Sorry, I'm busy right now – I'll speak to you later.* | *We heard later that he had gone back to Japan.*

a month/two weeks/three years etc later *She became ill in 1993, and died two years later.*

much later (=a long time later) *I didn't find out the truth until much later.*

later that day/month/year etc *Later that afternoon, Anna called by to see me.*

later in the day/month/year etc *I spoke to him again later in the afternoon.*

later [adj only before noun] *The meat can be frozen and used at a later date.* | *In a later speech, Reagan admitted he had been wrong.*

later on /ˌleɪtər ˈɒn/ at a later time during the same period, day, week etc: *The weather was fine at first, but later on it started to rain.* | *Later on, I'll be interviewing the Vice-President, but first here is a summary of the news.*

in /ɪn/ [preposition] use this to say how far ahead in the future something will happen

in a minute/24 hours/a week etc *I'll be back in a couple of days.* | *The doctor would like to see you again in two weeks.*

in an hour's time/a few minutes' time etc *Just think, in a few hours' time we'll be in Seattle.*

from now /frəm ˈnaʊ/ **24 hours/a week/ 100 years etc from now** at a future time 24 hours from now, a week from now etc: *Three weeks from now the exams will be over.* | *A hundred years from now there may be no rainforest left.*

after /ˈɑːftər‖ˈæf-/ [preposition] use this to talk about something that happened in the past, and to say how much later than another event it happened

after two days/a week/a while etc *After a while, we got tired of waiting and went home.* | *She left the hospital in January, and the doctor saw her again after two weeks.*

2 **to decide to do something later**

postpone /pəʊsˈpəʊn/ [v T] to change the time when something was planned to happen, and arrange for it to happen later: *They decided to postpone the wedding until Pam's mother was out of the hospital.* | *Several of today's football games have been postponed because of heavy snow.*

put off /ˌpʊt ˈɒf‖-ˈɔːf/ [phrasal verb T] to decide to do something later than you planned to do it, for example because there is a problem or because you do not want to do it now

put sth off *I really should go to the dentist, but I keep putting it off.*

put off sth *The concert's been put off till next week.*

put off doing sth *The committee decided to put off making any decision until the new year.*

delay /dɪˈleɪ/ [v T] to arrange to do something later than you planned, because you are waiting for something else to happen first or you are waiting for a more suitable time: *He decided to delay his departure until after he'd seen the Director.*

delay doing sth *The police delayed making any announcement until the girl's relatives had been contacted.*

LAUGH

SMILE   HAPPY

FUNNY ← see also → ENJOY

JOKE   SERIOUS

1 to laugh because something is funny

laugh /lɑːf‖læf/ [v I] to laugh because something is funny or because you are enjoying yourself: *Jake made a funny face, and we all laughed.* | *I thought Dad would be angry, but he just laughed.*

+ about *I couldn't understand what they were all laughing about.*

+ at *No-one laughed at his jokes.*

burst out laughing (=suddenly laugh loudly) *We just looked at each other and burst out laughing.*

can't stop laughing (=laugh a lot because something is extremely funny) *Every time I thought about her hat, I couldn't stop laughing!*

　laugh [n C] *She gave a little nervous laugh and glanced towards Robyn.*

giggle /ˈgɪgəl/ [v I] to laugh quietly in the way that children laugh, because something is funny, or because you are nervous or embarrassed: *We never learned anything in history – we just sat at the back of the class giggling.* | *Mr Brogan asked her to dance, and she blushed and giggled.*

　giggle [n C] *I could hear giggles coming from my sister's bedroom.*

chuckle /ˈtʃʌkəl/ [v I] to laugh quietly, especially because you are thinking about something funny: *"Do you remember when Michelle fell in the river?" Morgan chuckled.* | *Simon sat reading a magazine, chuckling to himself.*

laughter /ˈlɑːftər‖ˈlæf-/ [n U] the sound you make when you laugh: *We could hear laughter coming from the next room.*

roar with laughter (=laugh very loudly) *The show was a great success, and the audience roared with laughter.*

2 to laugh in a cruel or nasty way

laugh at sb /ˈlɑːf æt (sb)‖ˈlæf-/ [phrasal verb T] to laugh at someone or make unkind jokes about them, because you think they are stupid or silly: *The other children laughed at Lisa because her clothes were old-fashioned.* | *Don't laugh at me – I told you I wasn't very good at Spanish.*

snigger BRITISH **snicker** AMERICAN /ˈsnɪgər, ˈsnɪkər/ [v I] to laugh quietly at something that is not supposed to be funny, for example when someone is hurt or embarrassed: *Ruth tripped and fell as she walked up the steps. The boys behind her sniggered.* | *As he walked across the stage, Billy could hear people snickering and whispering.*

make fun of sb/sth /ˌmeɪk ˈfʌn ɒv (sb/sth)/ to make someone or something seem stupid by laughing at them, or by saying things that make other people laugh at them: *Stop making fun of me!* | *The other girls used to make fun of the way she spoke.*

3 to make someone laugh

make sb laugh /ˌmeɪk (sb) ˈlɑːf‖-ˈlæf/ to make someone laugh by doing or saying something funny: *Rachel used to make us all laugh by imitating the teacher.* | *Thanks for your letter. It really made me laugh.*

When you see **EC**, go to the **ESSENTIAL COMMUNICATION** section.

LAW

STRICT/NOT STRICT

RULE   COURT/TRIAL

LET   see   POLICE
          also

FORBID   CRIME

LIMIT   PUNISH

1 an official rule that everyone must obey

law /lɔː/ [n C] an official rule that all the citizens of a country must obey

break the law (=disobey a law) *I didn't realize I was breaking the law.*

+ on *tough new laws on immigration*

+ against *There is a law against cruelty to animals.*

pass a law (=make a law) *Congress passed a law that allowed women to become pilots in the Air Force.*

⚠ If you talk about **the law**, this often means all the laws of a country and what they say you must and must not do: *It is the job of the police to make sure that people obey the law.*

legal /ˈliːgəl/ [adj only before noun] connected with laws and courts: *People on low salaries can get free legal advice.*

legal battle/dispute (=when two people or organizations disagree about something, and this is judged in a court of law) *Neither side wanted a long and expensive legal battle.*

act /ækt/ [n C] a law made by parliament or Congress – used in the official name of a law: *the 1991 Prevention of Terrorism Act* | *an Act of Congress*

legislation /ˌledʒɪˈsleɪʃən/ [n U] a set of laws, especially ones that are made to control a new problem: *Legislation is needed to stop the spread of computer pornography.*

+ on *new legislation on the sale of alcohol*

legal system /ˈliːgəl ˌsɪstm̩/ [n C] the laws and the way that they work in a particular country: *The Scottish legal system is different from that in England.*

2 when the law says you must do something or have the right to do it

legal /ˈliːgəl/ [adj only before noun] your **legal** rights, duties etc are the ones that the law says you must have: *the legal duties of parents*

legal right *Consumers have the legal right to demand their money back if a product is faulty.*

the legal owner (=the owner according to the law) *She now becomes the legal owner of the land.*

legally [adv] according to the law: *Legally, the house belongs to me.* | *If there is an accident, the owner of the vehicle will be legally responsible.*

by law /baɪ ˈlɔː/ if something must be done **by law**, the law says that you must do it: *By law, your employer has to make sure that your working environment is safe.*

it's the law /ɪts ðə ˈlɔː/ SPOKEN use this to tell someone that the law says that they must do something: *You have to wear a seatbelt – it's the law.*

3 allowed by law

legal /ˈliːgəl/ [adj] allowed by law: *This trade in foreign currency is perfectly legal.*

make sth legal *57% of people wanted abortion to be made legal.*

become legal *Divorce finally became legal in 1992.*

legally [adv] *Fuchs had entered the country legally on a tourist visa.*

legalize (also **legalise** BRITISH) /ˈliːgəlaɪz/ [T] to change the law so that something becomes legal: *a campaign to legalise cannabis*

4 not allowed by law

illegal /ɪˈliːgəl/ [adj] not allowed by law: *illegal drugs* | *In those days, abortion was illegal.*

it is illegal to do sth *It is illegal to sell tobacco to children under 16.*

be against the law /biː əˌgenst ðə ˈlɔː/ if something is **against the law**, it is not allowed by law: *Gambling is against the law in some countries.*

L

it is **against the law to do sth** *It is against the law to drive a car without insurance.*

it is **against the law for sb to do sth** *It is against the law for a teacher to hit a child.*

LAZY

when someone does not like working

1 lazy

lazy /ˈleɪzi/ [adj] someone who is **lazy** does not like work or physical activity, and tries to avoid it: *Marian didn't do well at school. She was intelligent, but very lazy.* | *Get up, you lazy thing! It's nearly lunchtime.*

a lazy day/week etc (=a time when you relax and do not work hard) *We spent a lazy afternoon at the beach.*

lazy – lazier – laziest

can't be bothered /ˌkɑːnt biː ˈbɒðəʳd‖ ˌkænt biː ˈbɑː-/ BRITISH SPOKEN if you **can't be bothered** to do something, you decide not to do it because you are feeling too lazy: *I was going to go shopping, but in the end I couldn't be bothered.*

can't be bothered to do sth *Let's go out for a meal – I can't be bothered to cook.*

2 to behave in a lazy way

sit around/laze around /ˌsɪt əˈraʊnd, ˌleɪz əˈraʊnd/ [phrasal verb I] INFORMAL to spend time sitting and relaxing and not doing any work: *We lazed around on the beach most of the day.* | *Why not finish your homework, instead of just sitting around doing nothing?*

not lift a finger /nɒt ˌlɪft ə ˈfɪŋgəʳ/ INFORMAL to give no help at all with work that must be done, such as cooking and cleaning: *Tim doesn't lift a finger when it comes to housework.*

not lift a finger to help *We spent the day moving furniture, but Sara didn't lift a finger to help.*

When you see **EC**, go to the **ESSENTIAL COMMUNICATION** section.

LEARN

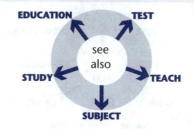

EDUCATION   TEST

see also

STUDY   TEACH

SUBJECT

1 to learn how to do something, or to learn about something

learn /lɜːʳn/ [v I/T] to learn how to do something, or to learn about a subject, especially by being taught or trained: *How long have you been learning German?* | *Young children learn much more easily than adults.*

learn to do sth *His daughter's learning to drive.* | *William learned to read when he was four.*

learn how to do sth (=learn a method or skill) *On this course, you will learn how to deal with communication problems.*

learning – learned (also **learnt** BRITISH) – **have learned** (also **have learnt** BRITISH)

study /ˈstʌdi/ [v I/T] to learn about a subject by reading books and going to classes at a school or university: *Less than 10% of girls choose to study science at school.* | *She's studying music at Berkeley College in Boston.*

study to be a doctor/lawyer/accountant etc *He's studying to be a lawyer.*

study for a test/diploma/an examination *"Is Ian coming with us?" "He can't – he's studying for his exams."*

studying – studied – have studied

train /treɪn/ [v I] to learn the skills and get the experience that you need in order to do a job

train to be a hairdresser/teacher/pilot/nurse *Julie is training to be a nurse.*

pick up /ˌpɪk ˈʌp/ [phrasal verb T] INFORMAL to learn something easily, without making much effort or having lessons

pick up sth *I picked up a few words of Turkish while I was in Istanbul.*

pick sth up *The rules of the game are really easy – you'll soon pick them up.*

get the hang of sth /ˌget ðə ˈhæŋ ɒv (sth)/ SPOKEN to learn how to do something that is fairly complicated: *Using the computer isn't difficult once you get the hang of it.*

2 to learn something so that you can remember it exactly

learn /lɜːʳn/ [v T] to learn facts, words, or numbers, especially at school, so that you can remember them exactly: *What songs have you learnt at school, then?*
learn sth by heart (=learn something so you can repeat it exactly without reading it) *We had to learn a lot of poetry by heart when we were children.*
learn your lines (=learn the words that you have to say in a play)
learning – learned (also **learnt** BRITISH) – **have learned** (also **have learnt** BRITISH)

memorize (also **memorise** BRITISH) /ˈmeməraɪz/ [v T] to learn numbers or words so that you can remember them exactly: *I'm not very good at memorizing phone numbers.* | *I memorised the message, then destroyed it.*

3 someone who is learning something

student /ˈstjuːdənt‖ˈstuː-/ [n C] someone who is studying at a school, college, or university: *a student at Harvard University* | *There's a special price for students.*
law/medical/engineering student *Law students always have a lot of work to do.*
student nurse/teacher (=someone who is studying to be a nurse or a teacher)

⚠ Don't say 'a student of Oxford' or 'a student in the high school'. Say **a student at Oxford, a student at the high school** etc.

trainee /ˌtreɪˈniː◄/ [n C] someone who is learning a skill while working in a company or organization: *I'm a trainee in a hairdressing salon.*
trainee accountant/reporter/salesman etc *I got a job as a trainee reporter on the 'Daily Star'.*

beginner /bɪˈgɪnəʳ/ [n C] someone who has recently started to learn something: *Japanese classes for beginners* | *The tennis club welcomes beginners as well as more advanced players.*

apprentice /əˈprentɪs/ [n C] someone who is learning all the skills that they need in order to do a job, especially a job that they do with their hands
apprentice electrician/bricklayer/hairdresser etc *I worked as an apprentice electrician for 18 months.*

4 to learn about things by experiencing them in your life

learn /lɜːʳn/ [v I/T] to learn how you should behave or how to deal with situations, because of experiences you have had in your life
+ (that) *I soon learned that it was best to keep quiet.*
learn to do sth *Gradually, I learned to trust her.*
learn from your mistakes (=remember mistakes you have made, and be careful not to make them again)
learn the hard way (=learn something by having an unpleasant experience) *Never lend money to your friends – that's something I learnt the hard way.*
learning – learned (also **learnt** BRITISH) – **have learned** (also **have learnt** BRITISH)

LEAST

the smallest number or amount

➡ opposite **MOST**
➡ see also **LESS**

the least /ðə ˈliːst/ [quantifier] the smallest amount of something: *Let's buy the one that costs the least.* | *the engine that uses the least fuel*
the least possible *We'll try to cause the least possible disturbance.*

⚠ Use **least** with uncountable nouns like 'money', 'food', or 'information'.

minimum /ˈmɪnɪ̯məm/ [adj/quantifier] the smallest number or amount that is possible or allowed

a minimum of 20/£100/95% etc You have to order a minimum of five CDs to get the discount.

the minimum age/level/wage (=the lowest age, level, or wage that is allowed) These workers are being paid less than the minimum wage.

keep sth to a minimum (=make sure that it is as small as possible) Costs must be kept to a minimum.

the absolute/bare minimum (=the lowest number or amount possible) He ate two cups of rice a day, the bare minimum needed for survival.

the lowest /ðə ˈləʊɪ̯st/ [adj] use this about numbers, prices, wages, temperatures, or levels: In the last election he was the candidate who got the lowest number of votes. | The lowest charge for a rented car is $20 a day.

the lowest for 6 months/15 years etc Interest rates are only 4%, the lowest for 25 years.

the fewest /ðə ˈfjuːɪ̯st/ [quantifier] the smallest number of people or things: Drivers aged under 25 have the most accidents, those over 50 have the fewest. | Our team scored the fewest goals in the competition.

⚠ Use **fewest** with countable nouns like 'pens', 'shops', or 'students'.

LEAVE

➡ see also **RETURN, START**

1 to go away from a room or building

leave /liːv/ [v I/T not in passive] to go away from a room or building: The phone rang just as I was leaving. | We left before the end of the show. | Before you leave the house, make sure all the windows are shut. | The police wanted to know what time Vicky left the office.

leaving – left – have left

When you see **EC**, go to the **ESSENTIAL COMMUNICATION** section.

⚠ Don't say 'I left from the house'. Say **I left the house**.

go /gəʊ/ [v I] ESPECIALLY SPOKEN to leave a place to go somewhere else: Let's go. | "Is Alan still here?" "No, he's just gone."

going – went – have gone

go out /ˌgəʊ ˈaʊt/ [phrasal verb I] to leave a room or building, especially when you will come back again soon: I'm sorry, I have to go out. I won't be long.

go out to do sth She's just gone out to buy some cigarettes.

+ of As he went out of the room, he slammed the door.

go away /ˌgəʊ əˈweɪ/ [phrasal verb I] to leave your home and go to another place for a few days or weeks: We're going away at the weekend, so could you feed the cat for us?

walk out /ˌwɔːk ˈaʊt/ [phrasal verb I] to leave angrily, for example after a quarrel: She threw her wine in his face and then walked out. | Several people walked out before the end of the movie.

slip out /ˌslɪp ˈaʊt/ [phrasal verb I] to leave quietly and without anyone noticing: No-one saw her slip out through the back door. | He just slipped out for a moment to speak with the principal.

sneak out/sneak off /ˌsniːk ˈaʊt, ˌsniːk ˈɒf‖-ˈɔːf/ [phrasal verb I] INFORMAL to leave secretly, taking care that no-one sees you, because you should not leave: I managed to sneak out while they were all busy talking. | The teacher caught Ron sneaking off early.

sneaking – sneaked (also **snuck** AMERICAN) **– have sneaked** (also **have snuck** AMERICAN)

2 to leave at the start of a journey

leave /liːv/ [v I/T not in passive] to leave a place when you are going on a journey: I'm leaving early in the morning to catch the train to Toronto. | When we got to Calais our boat had just left.

leave London/New York/Singapore etc Her plane leaves Hong Kong at 10:15.

leave for London/Paris/Chicago etc (=in order to go to London etc) Mr Mitchell's leaving for Paris tomorrow.

leaving – left – have left

⚠ Don't say 'I left from London'. Say **I left London**.

go /gəʊ/ [v I] ESPECIALLY SPOKEN to leave at the start of a journey: *What time does the next bus go?* | *We've packed all our bags and we're ready to go.*
going – went – have gone

set off /ˌset ˈɒf‖-ˈɔːf/ [phrasal verb I] to leave at the start of a journey, especially an important, exciting, or difficult journey: *As the sun came up, we set off up the mountain.*
set off for London/Paris/Chicago etc (=in order to go to London etc) *When he received the news that his sister was sick, he set off at once for London.*

⚠ **Set off** is used especially in the past tense, in stories or reports of past events.

take off /ˌteɪk ˈɒf‖-ˈɔːf/ [phrasal verb I] if a plane **takes off**, it leaves the ground at the beginning of a flight: *What time did your plane take off?*

3 to leave suddenly without telling anyone where you are going

disappear /ˌdɪsəˈpɪər/ [v I] to leave a place suddenly without telling anyone, so that no-one knows where you have gone: *After the concert I looked around and tried to find her, but she had disappeared.*

4 what you say when you are leaving
➡ see also ◪ SAYING GOODBYE

I have to go (also **I must go** BRITISH) /aɪ ˌhæv tə ˈgəʊ, aɪ ˌmʌst ˈgəʊ/ SPOKEN say this when you are leaving, because it is time to go or because you have to go somewhere else: *Sorry, I have to go or I'll miss my bus.* | *We must go – it's getting late.*

I'm off /aɪm ˈɒf/ SPOKEN INFORMAL say this when you are leaving: *I'm off, Peter. See you tomorrow.* | *We're off now – thanks for everything.*

5 ways of telling someone angrily to go away

⚠ These phrases are not polite. Only use them if you intend to be rude.

go away /ˌgəʊ əˈweɪ/ SPOKEN INFORMAL say this when you want someone to leave: *I wish you'd all just go away and leave me alone.* | *"Go away!" she shouted.*

get lost /ˌget ˈlɒst‖-ˈlɔːst/ SPOKEN INFORMAL say this when you want someone to leave because they are annoying you: *Get lost! I've told you already, I'm not interested.*

⚠ **Get lost** is ruder than **go away**.

get out /ˌget ˈaʊt/ SPOKEN say this to tell someone to leave your house, room etc, because you are very angry with them: *Get out! I never want to see you again!*
+ of *Give me back my money and get out of my house.*

6 to permanently leave the place where you live

leave /liːv/ [v I/T not in passive] to leave your home or the area where you live: *We've been so happy living here. I'll be really sorry to leave.* | *She was excited about leaving the village and going to live in London.*
leaving – left – have left

move /muːv/ [v I] to leave your house and go to live in another one: *When are you moving?* | *I've moved – here's my new address.*
+ to *We're looking forward to moving to Paris.*
move house BRITISH (=go to live in another house) *They moved house three times in five years.*

move out /ˌmuːv ˈaʊt/ [phrasal verb I] to permanently leave the house where you live, especially because there are problems that make it difficult for you to stay: *We'll have to move out if the landlord increases the rent again.* | *They quarrelled, and Anna moved out.*
+ of *Why do you want to move out of such a fantastic apartment?*

L

leave home /ˌliːv ˈhəʊm/ if a young person **leaves home**, he or she leaves their parents' house and goes to live somewhere else: *She left home when she was 18.* | *Now that the children have left home, I have more time for writing.*

run away /ˌrʌn əˈweɪ/ [phrasal verb I] if a young person **runs away**, he or she secretly leaves their parents' house or the place where they are living, because they are unhappy there: *When he was 15 he ran away and got a job on a ship.*

emigrate /ˈemɪ̩greɪt/ [v I] to leave your own country and go to live in another country: *His business failed, so he decided to emigrate.*
+ **to** *My parents emigrated to Australia in 1955.*

7 to make someone leave a place

throw sb out/kick sb out /ˌθrəʊ (sb) ˈaʊt, ˌkɪk (sb) ˈaʊt/ [phrasal verb T] INFORMAL to make someone leave the house or place where they live, especially because you are angry with them: *In the end her father threw her out.*
+ **of** *They can't just kick you out of the apartment for no reason.* | *Several foreign diplomats were kicked out of Russia for spying.*

evict /ɪˈvɪkt/ [v T] to legally force someone to leave the house where they live, either because they should not be there, or because they have not paid their rent: *If they evict us, we have nowhere else to go.*
be evicted from sth *The previous tenants were evicted from the house by the landlord.*

deport /dɪˈpɔːˑt/ [v T] if the government of a country **deports** a foreign person who is living there, they force them to leave the country: *Another five illegal immigrants were deported.*

8 to permanently leave a job or organization

leave /liːv/ [v I/T not in passive] to stop doing a job, or stop belonging to an organization: *Why did you leave your last job?* | *I had enjoyed teaching, and was sorry to leave.* | *Several leading*

Republicans are threatening to leave the party.
leaving – left – have left

resign /rɪˈzaɪn/ [v I] to officially leave your job, especially because you are unhappy with it or because you have done something wrong: *I wanted to resign, but my boss persuaded me to stay.*
+ **from** *Three more directors have just resigned from the board.*
> **resignation** /ˌrezɪgˈneɪʃən/ [n C/U] when someone officially leaves their job: *Hundreds of people wrote to the company, demanding the resignation of its chairman.*

retire /rɪˈtaɪəʳ/ [v I] to permanently leave your job, because you have reached the age when most people stop working: *In the UK, men usually retire at 65, and women at 60.*

quit /kwɪt/ [v I/T not in passive] INFORMAL to leave your job, school etc because you are not happy there: *I'd had enough of college and decided to quit.* | *He quit politics in '94 and went into banking.*
quitting – quit – have quit

9 to permanently leave your school or college

leave /liːv/ [v I/T not in passive] to permanently leave your school or college: *I hated school and was glad when I could leave.*
leave school/college/university *When he first left college, he worked in an office.*
leaving – left – have left

graduate /ˈgrædʒueɪt/ [v I] to successfully finish studying at a school or university: *What are you going to do after you graduate?* | *When I graduate I want to go to law school in New York.*
+ **from** *He graduated from Cambridge in 1979.*

> ⚠ In British English, you use **graduate** only to talk about leaving university. In American English, you can use **graduate** to talk about leaving high school or leaving university.

drop out /ˌdrɒp ˈaʊt‖ˌdrɑːp-/ [phrasal verb I] to leave school, college, or university before you have finished studying: *One-third of the students drop out at the end of the first year.*

+ of *When he was 15, he dropped out of school and joined a band.*

flunk out /ˌflʌŋk 'aʊt/ [phrasal verb I] AMERICAN INFORMAL to have to leave school or college because your work is not good enough

+ of *Bart messed around and flunked out of college.*

10 to make someone leave a job, school, or organization

fire /faɪəʳ/ [v T] ESPECIALLY AMERICAN to make someone leave their job, especially because they have done something wrong: *The boss fired him for being drunk.*

sack sb/give sb the sack /'sæk (sb), ˌgɪv (sb) ðə 'sæk/ [v T] BRITISH to make someone leave their job, especially because they have done something wrong: *The company has sacked three of its senior managers.* I *If I'd known what she was doing, I would have given her the sack long ago.*

kick sb out/throw sb out /ˌkɪk (sb) 'aʊt, ˌθrəʊ (sb) 'aʊt/ [phrasal verb T] INFORMAL to make someone leave a school, college, club etc, because they have done something wrong: *I said I'd kick them out if I caught them smoking again.*

+ of *Nick failed his exams and was thrown out of school.*

expel /ɪk'spel/ [v T] to make someone permanently leave a school or college, because they have behaved very badly: *The principal is expelling three boys who were caught taking drugs.*

get expelled (from/for) *She got expelled from her school for hitting one of the teachers.*

expelling – expelled – have expelled

suspend /sə'spend/ [v T] to make someone leave their school, job, or an organization for a period of time, because they have disobeyed rules or behaved badly: *Several police officers have been suspended for taking bribes.*

When you see **EC**, go to the **ESSENTIAL COMMUNICATION** section.

11 to be forced to leave your job

lose your job /ˌluːz ˌjɔːʳ 'dʒɒb‖-'dʒɑːb/ to be forced to leave your job: *Terry lost his job just before Christmas – it was terrible.* I *People don't complain – they're frightened of losing their jobs.*

be fired /biː 'faɪəʳd/ ESPECIALLY AMERICAN to be forced to leave your job, especially because you have done something wrong: *Did he resign or was he fired?*

be sacked/get the sack /biː 'sækt, ˌget ðə 'sæk/ BRITISH to be forced to leave your job, especially because you have done something wrong: *If you keep coming in late, you'll get the sack.*

be laid off (also **be made redundant** BRITISH) /biː ˌleɪd 'ɒf, biː ˌmeɪd rɪ'dʌndənt/ to lose your job, because your company does not need you any more: *Dad was laid off after 32 years in the steelworks.* I *250 people will be made redundant when the factory closes.*

redundancy /rɪ'dʌndənsi/ [n C/U] BRITISH when someone has to leave their job, because the company does not need them any more: *The men were offered shorter working hours as an alternative to redundancy.* I *more redundancies in the banking industry*

plural **redundancies**

LEND

to let someone use something that they will give back to you later

BORROW   BANKS

see also

OWE   MONEY

GIVE

⚠ Don't confuse **lend** and **borrow**. You **lend** something **to** someone (=you let them have it), but you **borrow** it **from** someone (=they let you have it).

Mark lent Julie £10. Julie borrowed £10 from Mark   Julie paid Mark back the following week.

1 to lend something to someone

lend (also **loan** AMERICAN) /lend, ləʊn/ [v T] to let someone have money which they will pay back later or let them use something that is yours, which they will give back to you later

lend/loan sb sth *Can you lend me $20?* | *I wish I'd never lent him my car.* | *I could loan you $100 if you need it.*

lend/loan sth to sb *Did you lend that book to Mike?* | *The camera had been loaned to him by his cousin.*

lending – lent – have lent

> ⚠ You **lend** or **loan** things that can be moved, but you **let someone use** a room, building etc.

let sb use sth /ˌlet (sb) ˈjuːz (sth)/ to let someone use something that belongs to you, for a short time, especially something such as a room, a house, or a piece of land: *Some friends are letting us use their house while they are on vacation.* | *Bob won't let me use his computer.*

on loan /ɒn ˈləʊn/ something that is **on loan**, especially a library book or a painting, has been lent to a person or organization: *I couldn't get that book from the library – all the copies are out on loan.*
+ from *The museum has an exhibition of paintings on loan from the Louvre.*

2 to lend houses, land, machines etc for money

rent out /ˌrent ˈaʊt/ [phrasal verb T] to allow someone to use a house, piece of land, or vehicle that belongs to you, in exchange for money

rent sth out *If you can't sell your house, why don't you rent it out?*
rent out sth *They rent out boats for pleasure cruises.*
rent sth out to sb *The field at the back of the house is rented out to a local farmer.*

lease /liːs/ [v T] to allow a company, organization etc to use buildings, land, or equipment for a fixed period of time, in exchange for money
lease sth to sb *The aircraft had been leased to a Nigerian airline.*

let BRITISH **rent** AMERICAN /let, rent/ [v T] to allow someone to use a room, house, or office in exchange for money
let/rent sth to sb *I've let my spare room to a Japanese student.* | *We usually rent our house to someone over the long vacation.*

To Let BRITISH **For Rent** AMERICAN (written on a sign to show that a room, house, or office is empty and can be rented)

letting – let – have let

3 money that is lent to someone

loan /ləʊn/ [n C] an amount of money that someone has borrowed: *The bank offered him a loan of £15,000 to set up a business.*

LESS

➡ opposite **MORE**
➡ see also **LEAST**
➡ if you want to know about using adjectives for comparing things, go to the **ESSENTIAL GRAMMAR**, section 14

1 a smaller amount or number

less /les/ [quantifier] a smaller amount of something: *You ought to eat less meat.* | *It'll cost about $50 – maybe less.*
+ than *Harry knows even less than I do about this business.*
+ of *I'd like to spend less of my time at work.*
less and less (=when an amount keeps getting smaller as time passes) *As the drought became worse, there was less and less food available.*

> ⚠ Use **less** with uncountable nouns like 'money', 'food', or 'information'. In formal writing it is incorrect to use **less** with countable nouns, like 'pens', 'shops', or 'students'. But in ordinary conversation, **less** is often used in this way.

fewer /'fjuːəʳ/ [quantifier] a smaller number of people or things: *There are fewer jobs available nowadays.*
+ than *Women are having fewer children than they used to.*
far fewer (=a lot fewer) *Far fewer people go to church these days.*

> ⚠ Use **fewer** with countable nouns like 'pens', 'shops' or 'students', and never with uncountable nouns.

not as much /ˌnɒt əz 'mʌtʃ/ less than an amount
+ as *The Chinese don't eat as much meat as the Americans.* | *Let's rent an apartment – it won't cost as much as a hotel.*

> ⚠ Use **not as much** with uncountable nouns, like 'time', 'money', or 'food', but never with countable nouns. Use **not as many** with countable nouns.

not as many /ˌnɒt əz 'meni/ fewer than a number of people or things
+ as *There weren't as many people there this year as last year.* | *I have quite a few CDs, but not as many as Becky has.*

> ⚠ Use **not as many** with countable nouns, like 'pens', 'shops', or 'students', but never with uncountable nouns.

lower /'ləʊəʳ/ [adj] less than another number or level – use this about prices, temperatures, marks for schoolwork, and other things that can be measured on a scale from high to low: *Foreign workers have fewer rights and get lower wages.* | *In the mountains the temperature is much lower.*
+ than *I got lower grades than the other students in my class.*

2 less than a particular number or amount

less than /'les ðən/ *Some of the miners were earning less than $2 an hour.* | *They've built another hotel less than a mile from here.*

under /'ʌndəʳ/ [preposition] less than a particular age, price, amount, or number: *It's illegal to sell cigarettes to children under 16.* | *Where can you get a meal for under $5?*
just under (=slightly less than) *The baby weighed just under three kilos.*

below /bɪ'ləʊ/ [preposition] less than a particular temperature, speed, limit, or level: *At night the temperature is often below freezing.*
fall below (=become less than) *The rate of inflation has fallen below 6%.*

3 less interesting, expensive, difficult, exciting etc

not as /'nɒt əz/ *Their first album sold over a million copies, but the second one wasn't as popular.*
not as...as *It's not as cold as it was yesterday.* | *Our house isn't as big as yours.* | *"How was the test?" "Not as bad as I expected."*

less /les/ [adv] *The dentist gave me an injection to make it less painful.*
less...than *I want something less formal than a traditional wedding dress.*

> ⚠ Don't use **less** with very short words. Don't say 'less good/bad/tall etc'. Say **not as good, not as bad, not as tall** etc. In spoken English, **not as** is more common than **less**.

4 when something happens less than before

less /les/ [adv]
+ than This type of problem still occurs, but less than it did in the past.
a lot less Since we got the car, we walk a lot less than we used to.
less and less (=when something keeps getting less as time passes) He seemed to care less and less about the band, and eventually decided to leave.

not as much /nɒt əz 'mʌtʃ/ She used to really hate her job, but she doesn't seem to complain as much now.
+ as "Do you still go swimming?" "Not as much as I used to."

⚠ **Less** and **not as much** mean the same, but they combine with different words. In spoken English, **not as much** is more common than **less**.

5 when prices, numbers etc become less

go down/come down /ˌgəʊ 'daʊn, ˌkʌm 'daʊn/ [phrasal verb I] to become less: The suicide rate has gone down in the last few years. | I'm hoping the price will come down if I wait a while.

fall/drop /fɔːl, drɒp‖drɑːp/ [v I] to become less, especially by a large amount: Airfares to Hong Kong have fallen dramatically because of increased competition.
+ to At night, the temperature drops to –20 °C.
fall/drop from sth to sth Profits fell from £98.5 million to £76 million.
falling – fell – have fallen
dropping – dropped – have dropped

⚠ **Fall** and **drop** are mostly used in written English. In spoken English, **go down** and **come down** are more common.

decrease /dɪ'kriːs/ [v I] to become less – used especially in writing about business or technical subjects: If a company improves its efficiency, its costs will decrease.
+ to The speed of rotation gradually decreases to zero.

decreasing [adj only before noun] decreasing levels of carbon dioxide in the air

6 to make something less

reduce /rɪ'djuːs‖rɪ'duːs/ [v T] to make something less in amount or level: Try to reduce the amount of fat in your diet. | I was hoping they would reduce the price a little. | Yoga and meditation can help to reduce stress.
reduce sth by half/10%/2 years etc The new road will reduce traffic through the town by 30%.
reduced [adj] Most airlines offer reduced rates for children.

lower /'ləʊər/ [v T] to reduce an amount, limit, or level – used especially in writing about business or technical subjects: After 20 minutes, lower the temperature to 200 degrees. | The Bundesbank is under pressure to lower interest rates.

turn down /ˌtɜːʳn 'daʊn/ [phrasal verb T] to reduce the level of sound, heat, or light, by turning a control
turn sth down Could you turn the TV down a little?
turn down sth The weather wasn't as cold, so we decided to turn down the central heating.

cut down /ˌkʌt 'daʊn/ [phrasal verb I] to reduce the amount of food that you eat, alcohol that you drink, or cigarettes that you smoke: If you can't give up smoking, at least try to cut down.
+ on I've cut down on the amount of meat I eat.

⚠ **Cut down** is more informal than **reduce.**

lessen /'lesən/ [v T] FORMAL to make a pain less severe, or make an unpleasant feeling less bad: Drugs can be used to lessen the pain. | We tried to be sympathetic, but nothing could lessen his disappointment.

7 a reduction in numbers, prices, levels etc

reduction /rɪ'dʌkʃən/ [n C] when a price, level etc is reduced – use this when something is reduced deliberately: We offer a reduction for groups of 10 or more.

+ in *Cleaner fuel has contributed to a reduction in air pollution.* | *a reduction in working hours*
reduction of £10/$5/25% etc (=a reduction by a particular amount) *There were reductions of up to 50% in some stores.*

decrease /ˈdiːkriːs/ [n C] when something happens less than it used to
+ in *There has been a 15% decrease in violent crime.* (=it has gone down by 15%)
a significant/marked decrease (=when something happens much less than it used to) *a significant decrease in the number of deaths from heart disease*

drop/fall /drɒp, fɔːl‖drɑːp/ [n singular] when a number or amount goes down suddenly or by a large amount
+ in *Charities have reported a 25% fall in donations during the past year.* (=donations have gone down by 25%) | *a sudden drop in the number of student nurses*
a sharp fall/drop (=when an amount goes down very suddenly) *a sharp fall in profits*

⚠ Don't say 'a drop of the birthrate' or 'a fall of the birthrate'. Say **a drop in the birthrate** or **a fall in the birthrate**.

cut /kʌt/ [n C] a reduction in the amount or size of something made by a government or large organization – use this especially for talking about politics or business
+ in *Cuts in the education budget have led to fewer teachers and larger classes.*
pay/job/tax cuts (=cuts in wages, number of jobs, or taxes) *Nurses are protesting about further pay cuts.* | *The new management has promised that there will be no job cuts.*

LET

➡ see also ▣ **PERMISSION**,
▣ **SUGGESTIONS, CAN/CAN'T**

1 to let someone do something

let /let/ [v T not in passive] *We wanted to go camping, but our parents wouldn't let us.*
let sb do sth *Sue never lets her children*

eat candy.* | *Thank you for letting me borrow your car.*
let sb in/out (=let someone go in or out of a place) *Let me in! It's cold out here!*
letting – let – have let

⚠ Don't say 'let me to borrow the car' or 'let me borrowing the car'. Say **let me borrow the car**.

allow /əˈlaʊ/ [v T] if someone such as a teacher, official, or parent **allows** someone to do something, they let them do it
allow sb to do sth *We do not allow people to smoke anywhere in the building.* | *What time was he allowed to go home?*
allow sb sth (=allow them to have it) *We allow passengers one item of hand luggage each.*
allow sb in/out etc (=allow someone to go into or go out of a place) *The manager doesn't allow children in the bar.*

⚠ **Allow** is more formal than **let**.

◯ say sb can do sth /ˌseɪ (sb) kən ˈduː (sth)/ ESPECIALLY SPOKEN to tell someone that you will allow them to do something: *Mum says I can go to the party.* | *I thought you said we could use this room.*

give permission /ˌgɪv pərˈmɪʃən/ if someone such as an official, teacher, or manager **gives permission**, they say that someone is officially allowed to do something
give sb permission to do sth *Who gave you permission to leave class early?* | *The pilot was given permission to land at Rome airport.*
+ for *The police have refused to give permission for a peace march through the centre of town.*

⚠ Don't say 'she gave us a permission' or 'she gave us the permission'. Just say **she gave us permission**.

agree to sth /əˈgriː tuː (sth)/ [phrasal verb T] to decide to allow someone to do something because you have been persuaded to allow it: *I'd like to go camping with my boyfriend but my parents would never agree to it.*

L

2 to be allowed to do something

can /kən; *strong* kæn/ [*modal verb*] to be allowed to do something: *Now that you're seventeen, you can learn to drive.* | *Can Jean stay at our house tonight?* | *You can't park there.*

> ⚠ Only use **can** in the present tense. The infinitive form of **can** is **to be able to**: *When you're 18, you'll be able to vote.* If you want to say that someone was allowed to do something on one occasion in the past, use **be allowed**: *After being questioned by the police, he was allowed to leave.*

> ⚠ Don't say 'you can to park here'. Say **you can park here**.

be allowed /biː əˈlaʊd/ to be allowed to do something, especially because a rule or law says you can do it
be allowed to do sth *Are we allowed to use calculators in the test?*
sth is allowed *Swimming is only allowed in the roped-off area of the lake.*
be allowed in/out/off/on etc (=be allowed to go in, out, off etc) *No-one was allowed off the plane at Harare.*

> ⚠ When talking about something that someone was allowed to do on one occasion in the past, use **was allowed to** not 'could'. Don't say 'he could leave at 10'. Say **he was allowed to leave at 10**.

be permitted /biː pərˈmɪtɪd/ FORMAL to be allowed to do something by an official order, rule, or law
be permitted to do sth *Orlov was arrested by the Soviet authorities, but his wife was permitted to leave.*
sth is permitted *Smoking is only permitted in the public lounge.*

may /meɪ/ [*modal verb*] FORMAL to be allowed to do something: *Thank you Mrs Prynn, you may go now.* | *Only authorized personnel may use this entrance.*

> ⚠ Only use **may** in the present tense. Do not use **may** to talk about permission which has already been given or refused. Use **could** or **was allowed**: *He said I could park in front of his house.* | *Only authorized personnel were allowed to use the entrance.*

> ⚠ Don't say 'you may to go'. Say **you may go**.

3 official permission to do something

permission /pərˈmɪʃən/ [*n U*] when someone officially allows you to do something
permission to do sth *I had to get official permission to visit the prison.*
with/without sb's permission *We're not allowed to camp here without the farmer's permission.* | *The changes to the book were all made with the author's permission.*

permit /ˈpɜːrmɪt/ [*n C*] an official document that gives you permission to do something, for example permission to work somewhere or visit somewhere: *You can't park here unless you have a permit.*
work permit (=a permit to work in a particular country)

licence BRITISH **license** AMERICAN /ˈlaɪsəns/ [*n C*] an official document that allows you to do something, for example to drive a car or to own a gun: *Do you have a licence for that gun?*
driving licence BRITISH **driver's license** AMERICAN *Do you have any ID? Like your driver's license?*

consent /kənˈsent/ [*n U*] formal permission from someone to do something important that will affect themselves, their family, or their property
with/without sb's consent *They had to get married without their parents' consent.*
give your consent (=say that you allow something to happen) *She refused to give her consent for the operation because of her religious beliefs.*

4 to let someone do something that is not usually allowed

bend the rules /ˌbend ðə ˈruːlz/ INFORMAL to let someone do something that is slightly different from what is usually allowed: *No-one is allowed in before six, but I suppose I could bend the rules a little.*

make an exception /ˌmeɪk ən ɪkˈsepʃən/ to allow someone to do something that is not usually allowed: *I'll make an exception* *this time, but next time you hand in an essay late I won't accept it.*

5 to let something happen by not stopping it

let /let/ [v T] to let something bad happen, especially by not trying to stop it
let sb/sth do sth *You shouldn't let your husband treat you like that.* | *I've been so busy, I've let the house get terribly untidy over the past few weeks.*
letting – let – have let

> ⚠ Don't say 'they let it to happen'. Say **they let it happen.**

allow /əˈlaʊ/ [v T] to let a situation continue or develop without doing anything to stop it or improve it
allow sb/sth to do sth *Allow the meat to defrost at room temperature.* | *The government has allowed the situation to get completely out of control.*

> ⚠ **Allow** is more formal than **let.**

LIE

➡ look here for ...
• lie on a bed or on the floor
• say something that is not true

1 to lie on a bed or on the floor

➡ see also **SIT, STAND**

lie /laɪ/ [v I] to lie flat on a bed or on the floor, or to get into this position: *In the next room, the old man lay dying.*
+ on *She switched off the light and lay on the bed.*
lie on your back *Jones was lying on his back smoking a cigarette.*
lying – lay – have lain

> ⚠ Don't confuse these three verbs: **lie** (past tense **lay**) =be flat on a bed; **lie** (past tense **lied**) =say something that is untrue; **lay** (past tense **laid**) =put something down.

lie down /laɪ ˈdaʊn/ [phrasal verb I] to put yourself into a flat position on a bed or the floor, in order to relax or go to sleep: *You*

look really tired. Why don't you go and lie down?
+ on *Hannah lay down on the grass and closed her eyes.*

stretch out /ˌstretʃ ˈaʊt/ [phrasal verb I] to lie or sit with your legs and body straight, in order to rest and relax
+ on *He likes to stretch out on the sofa and watch TV.*
stretched out (=lying with your legs and body straight) *Celia's dog lay stretched out on the rug.*

2 to say something that is not true

➡ see also **DISHONEST, CHEAT, TRICK/ DECEIVE, TRUE/NOT TRUE, TRUST/NOT TRUST**

lie /laɪ/ [v I] to deliberately tell someone something that is not true: *I looked at her face and I knew she was lying.*
+ about *Movie stars always lie about their age.*
+ to *Don't lie to me! I know you weren't working late last night.*
lying – lied – have lied

tell a lie /ˌtel ə ˈlaɪ/ to lie, especially on just one occasion: *I told a lie and said that I hadn't seen him.*
tell sb a lie *Of course it's true. I wouldn't tell you a lie.*

lie /laɪ/ [n C] something that you say which you know is not true: *Jim said he hadn't done it, but I knew it was a lie.* | *How can the newspapers print all these lies about her private life?*
a pack of lies (=so many lies that you feel shocked or angry) *I couldn't believe it! They just stood up in court and told a pack of lies!*

liar /ˈlaɪər/ [n C] someone who often tells lies: *How can you trust Graham? You know he's a liar.*

mislead /mɪsˈliːd/ [v T] to make someone believe something that is not true, by giving them information that is not complete or not completely true: *He deliberately misled the Senate.* | *The court decided that customers had been misled by the company's advertising.*
misleading – misled – have misled

> When you see **EC**, go to the **ESSENTIAL COMMUNICATION** section.

misleading [adj] a **misleading** statement, description etc does not give complete information or completely true information: *This tour brochure is attractive, but misleading.* | *a deliberately misleading answer*

3 to think of an untrue explanation or excuse

make up /ˌmeɪk ˈʌp/ [phrasal verb T] to think of an explanation, excuse etc that is untrue

make up sth *If you don't want to go out with Wanda, you'll have to make up some kind of excuse.*

make sth up *When I told them why I was late, they accused me of making it up!*

invent /ɪnˈvent/ [v T] to think of an explanation or excuse that is sometimes very complicated but completely untrue: *He used to invent stories about his rich lifestyle to impress the women he met.* | *I began to invent reasons for staying away from work.*

LIFE

ALIVE — DEAD
see also
EXIST — DIE

1 the time when someone is alive

life /laɪf/ [n C] the time when someone is alive: *The day our daughter was born was the happiest day of my life.* | *Sutcliffe was sent to jail for the rest of his life.*

spend your life *She had spent her life moving from one town to another.*

sb's early life (=when they were young) *He knew very little about his mother's early life in Africa.*

in later life (=when you are old) *Lack of calcium can lead to bone disease in later life.*

life expectancy (=how long people are expected to live) *Women have a longer life expectancy than men.*

plural **lives**

lifetime /ˈlaɪftaɪm/ [n singular] the time when someone is alive – use this when you are talking about how long someone lived and what happened in their life

in/during sb's lifetime *During her lifetime, my grandmother lived through two World Wars and saw the first steps on the Moon.* | *He suffered a lot of pain in his short lifetime.*

+ of *The king died in 1990, after a lifetime of service to the country.*

2 the kind of life that someone has

life /laɪf/ [n C] the kind of life that someone has: *Having a baby completely changes your life.*

a happy/hard/exciting life *Deborah has a very busy life as a doctor.*

lead a happy/quiet/exciting life *We've led a very quiet life since Ralph retired.*

a life of crime (=when you use crime to make money instead of having a normal job) *He left school at 15, and turned to a life of crime.*

plural **lives**

lifestyle /ˈlaɪfstaɪl/ [n C] the way someone lives and behaves, and the type of things they buy, eat etc: *Doctors are trying to persuade people to lead healthier lifestyles.* | *Her glamorous Hollywood lifestyle came to an end in 1987.*

way of life /ˌweɪ əv ˈlaɪf/ the way in which a person or group of people lives, and the type of things they usually do: *The modern way of life can be very stressful.* | *The tribe's traditional way of life is now under threat.*

the British/German/American etc way of life *Shopping is an important part of the American way of life.*

3 continuing for all of someone's life

all your life /ˌɔːl jɔːr ˈlaɪf/ for the whole of your life: *My father worked hard all his life.* | *I've known her all her life – we were neighbours when we were children.*

for life /fəʳ 'laɪf/ if something is **for life**, it will continue and not change for the rest of your life: *There's no such thing as a job for life these days.* | *As far as I'm concerned, when you're married, it's for life.*

lifelong /'laɪflɒŋǁ-lɔːŋ/ [adj only before noun] continuing for all of your life – use this about beliefs, feelings, or relationships that last for the whole of your life: *It was her lifelong ambition to write a best-selling novel.* | *a lifelong friendship that started when they were at school together* | *My father was a lifelong supporter of the Democrats.*

LIFT

to move something into a higher position

➡ see also **CARRY, HOLD, PUT**

1 to lift a person or thing

lift

I tried to lift the box onto the table
but it was too heavy.

lift /lɪft/ [v T] to take something in your hands, especially something heavy, and move it upwards to another position: *After the operation, I wasn't allowed to lift anything heavy.*
lift sth onto/over etc *We lifted the children over the wall.*
lift sb/sth up *I tried to lift the box onto the table but it was too heavy.*
lift up sb/sth *She lifted up the smallest boy so he could see the parade.*

pick up /ˌpɪk 'ʌp/ [phrasal verb T] to lift something up from the ground, from a table etc, especially something small or light
pick up sth *She picked up her bag and left the room.*

pick up

pick sth up *There are papers all over the floor – could you pick them up and put them away?*

raise

"Cheers, everyone!" said Larry, raising his glass.

raise /reɪz/ [v T] to move something to a higher position for a short time before lowering it again: *The bridge can be raised to allow ships to pass under it.* | *"Cheers, everyone!" said Larry, raising his glass.*

2 to lift a part of your body

raise /reɪz/ [v T] **raise your eyes/eyebrows/hand/arm** to move or turn your eyes, head etc upwards for a short time: *She was reading a book, but raised her eyes when Paul walked in.*

lift /lɪft/ [v T] **lift your arm/leg/head** to move your arm, leg etc upwards, especially when this is difficult to do: *I was feeling so weak that I could hardly lift my head from the pillow.*

put your hand up /ˌpʊt joʳ 'hænd ʌp/ to move your arm upwards and keep it in the air, for example because you want to speak in a class or meeting, or because you are being counted: *Put your hand up if you know the answer.* | *If you are not able to take part, please put your hand up.*

L

LIGHT

→ look here for ...
- not dark
- not heavy

1 light from the sun, a fire, an electric light etc

→ see also **DARK, BRIGHT/NOT BRIGHT, COLOUR/COLOR**

light /laɪt/ [n U] *Light was coming into the room through a crack in the door. | a gas lamp that gives as much light as a 100 watt bulb*

the light (=the amount of natural light in a place) *The light was fading and I was afraid we wouldn't be home before dark.*
good/strong/bright light *The light isn't good enough to take a photograph.*
blinding/dazzling light (=very strong light that hurts your eyes) *a sudden flash of blinding light*
by the light of the moon/the fire/a candle (=with only the moon etc to give light) *She sat reading by the light of the fire.*

it's light /ɪts ˈlaɪt/ use this to say that there is natural daylight: *Let's go now while it's still light. | It's not light enough to play outside.*

daylight /ˈdeɪlaɪt/ [n U] the natural light of day
in daylight *I'd like to look at the house again in daylight.*
daylight hours (=the time when it is light) *The park is open during daylight hours.*

sunlight /ˈsʌnlaɪt/ [n U] the light from the sun: *Her long blonde hair was shining in the sunlight. | Keep the plant out of direct sunlight.*
bright sunlight (=strong sunlight) *Maria stood blinking in the bright sunlight.*

moonlight /ˈmuːnlaɪt/ [n U] the light from the moon: *The trees looked strangely white in the moonlight.*

glare /gleəʳ/ [n singular] a very bright and unpleasant light that makes you want to close your eyes
+ of *the glare of the car's headlights*

glow /gləʊ/ [n singular] a soft pleasant light, especially from something that is burning: *Candles give a warm glow to the room.*
+ of *the orange glow of the sunset*

2 to make a place light

light up /ˌlaɪt ˈʌp/ [phrasal verb T] to shine lights on a place so that people can see it well, or so that it looks attractive
light up sth *The fireworks lit up the sky. | Their garden was lit up by dozens of coloured lamps.*

light /laɪt/ [v T] to put lights in a place so that people can see what is happening there: *What are you going to use to light the stage?*
be lit by/with *The room was lit by hundreds of candles.*
lighting – lit – have lit

switch/turn/put the light(s) on /ˌswɪtʃ, ˌtɜːn, ˌpʊt ðə ˈlaɪt(s) ɒn/ to turn or press a control to make an electric light produce light: *Can you put the light on? I can't see anything!*

3 something that provides light

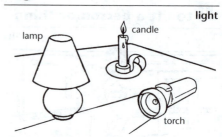

light

lamp   candle

torch

light /laɪt/ [n C] an electric light: *We could see the lights of Hong Kong across the bay.*
the light is on/off *There must be someone at home – the light's on in the kitchen.*
switch/turn/put the light on *It's getting dark. Can you turn the light on?*
switch/turn the light off *Don't forget to switch the lights off when you leave.*

lamp /læmp/ [n C] something that uses electricity, oil, or gas to produce light, especially a light that you can move from place to place: *There was a little oil lamp hanging from a hook in the ceiling. | a bedside lamp*

candle /ˈkændl/ [n C] a stick of wax that you burn to give light: *When there was a power cut, we had to use candles. | The cake had twelve candles on it.*

L

torch BRITISH *flashlight* AMERICAN /tɔːʳtʃ, ˈflæʃlaɪt/ [n C] a small electric lamp that you carry in your hand: *We shone our torches around the walls of the cave.*

4 colours/hair/skin
➡ see also **DARK, HAIR**

light /laɪt/ [adj] not dark in colour: *Her hair is a lighter colour than mine.*
light brown/blue/green etc *Mike has light brown hair. | The walls were a horrible shade of light green.*

> ⚠ Don't use **light** about the colour of people's skin. Use **fair** or **pale**.

pale /peɪl/ [adj] if someone is **pale**, their face is whiter than it usually is, especially because they are ill or frightened; a colour that is **pale** is very light: *You're very pale. Are you feeling sick?*
pale blue/green/pink etc *a pale pink dress | She has very pale blue eyes.*

> ⚠ Don't use **pale** about the colour of someone's hair. Say **fair hair** or **light brown hair.**

fair /feəʳ/ [adj] **fair** hair or skin is very light in colour: *People with fair skin should be careful when they go out in the sun. | Ulla has fair hair and blue eyes.*

5 not heavy
➡ opposite **HEAVY**

light /laɪt/ [adj] not heavy: *The equipment is light enough to carry around. | Modern tennis rackets are much lighter than the old-fashioned wooden ones.*

lightweight /ˈlaɪt-weɪt/ [adj] **light-weight** clothes, materials, or equipment are specially made so that they weigh very little: *a lightweight summer suit | a light-weight bicycle*

> When you see **EC**, go to the **ESSENTIAL COMMUNICATION** section.

LIKE/NOT LIKE

➡ look here for ...
  • think someone or something is nice
  • think someone or something is not nice
➡ if you mean 'similar to someone or something else', go to **same**

1 to like something

like /laɪk/ [v T] to think something is nice: *I like your dress – it's a beautiful colour. | Do you like spaghetti?*
like doing sth/like to do sth *He likes helping in the kitchen. | I like to see the children enjoying themselves.*
get to like sth (=start to like something) *At first she hated New York, but after a while she got to like it.*

> ⚠ Don't say 'I am liking it', 'she is liking it' etc. Say **I like it, she likes it** etc.

> ⚠ Don't say 'I like very much Paris'. Say **I like Paris very much**.

> ⚠ Usually it doesn't matter whether you use **like doing sth** or **like to do sth**, but when you mean someone likes the situation or place they are in, use **like doing sth**: *I like living in London* (not 'I like to live in London').

◯ love /lʌv/ [v T] ESPECIALLY SPOKEN to like something very much: *We had a great time at Disneyland. The kids loved it. | I love this song.*
love doing sth *Rachel loves driving.*

> ⚠ Only say 'love very much' about a person that you love. Don't use 'very much' with **love** when you are talking about a thing, place, or activity. Don't say 'I love Paris very much'. Just say **I love Paris**

be fond of sb/sth /biː ˈfɒnd ɒv (sb/sth)‖-ˈfɑːnd-/ to like something, especially something you have liked for a long time: *I know he's fond of Chinese food.* | *Gerry had always been fond of animals.*

be crazy about sth /biː ˈkreɪzi əbaʊt (sth)/ INFORMAL to be extremely interested in an activity and spend a lot of time doing it or watching it: *My kids are crazy about football.*

be into sth /biː ˈɪntuː (sth)/ [phrasal verb T] SPOKEN to like doing something, watching something, reading something etc: *My brother's really into rock-climbing.*

2 to like someone

like /laɪk/ [v T] to think someone is nice: *I've always liked Sally – she's such a friendly person.* | *He's an excellent teacher, and the students really like him.*

⚠ Don't say 'I am liking her', 'he is liking her' etc. Say **I like her, he likes her** etc.

be fond of sb /biː ˈfɒnd ɒv (sb)‖-ˈfɑːnd-/ to like someone very much, especially when you have known them for a long time: *You're very fond of Beryl, aren't you?* | *Miss Parker was very fond of the children in her class, although she was always strict with them.*

3 to like something or someone better than others

prefer /prɪˈfɜːr/ [v T] to like one thing more than another thing: *Do you prefer tea or coffee?*
prefer sth to sth *I prefer classical music to rock.*
prefer to do sth *Most of my friends take the bus to school, but I prefer to walk.*
preferring – preferred – have preferred

⚠ Don't say 'I prefer coffee than tea'. Say **I prefer coffee to tea.**

like sb/sth better /laɪk (sb/sth) ˈbetər/ ESPECIALLY SPOKEN to like one person or thing more than another: *Which do you like better, the red tie or the green one?*
+ than *I like this new teacher much better than the one we had before.*

⚠ **Like sb/sth better** is more informal than **prefer**.

⚠ Don't say 'I like better summer than winter'. Say **I like summer better than winter.**

like sth best /laɪk (sth) ˈbest/ ESPECIALLY SPOKEN to like something better than anything else – use this when you are asking someone to choose or when you are choosing: *Which of these dresses do you like best?* | *I think I like the red one best.*

4 the one you like better than any others

favourite BRITISH **favorite** AMERICAN /ˈfeɪvərɪt/ [adj only before noun] your **favourite** or **favorite** colour, food, teacher etc is the one that you like better than any other colour, food etc: *My favourite colour is purple.* | *Who is your favorite singer?* | *We're going to her favourite restaurant for a meal.*

⚠ Don't say 'most favourite'.

favourite BRITISH **favorite** AMERICAN /ˈfeɪvərɪt/ [n C] something that you like more than other things of the same kind
sb's favourite/favorite *I like all her books, but this one's my favourite.* | *Oh great! Chocolate ice-cream – my favourite!*

teacher's pet /ˌtiːtʃərz ˈpet/ [n singular] INFORMAL someone who is their teacher's favourite student, and who is not liked by the other students because of this

5 someone who likes something very much

fan /fæn/ [n C] someone who likes a particular sport, team, or famous entertainer very much: *Thousands of fans came to hear Oasis play.* | *a football fan*
+ of *Fans of Sylvester Stallone will enjoy this movie.*

lover /ˈlʌvər/ [n C] **music/jazz/art/animal lover** someone who likes music, art, or animals: *Every jazz lover dreams of visiting New Orleans.* | *a nation of animal lovers*

6 the kind of clothes, music etc that you like

taste /teɪst/ [n C/U] the kind of clothes, music, furniture, films etc that you like

+ in His taste in films and books is very different from mine.

have good/bad taste (=be good or bad at deciding which things are attractive) My grandmother's house was beautiful – she always had very good taste.

7 to not like someone or something

➡ see also **HATE**

not like /nɒt 'laɪk/ [v T] Why did you invite Claire? You know I don't like her. | I like the style of that dress, but I don't like the colour.

not like doing sth/not like to do sth I don't like walking home alone at night. | Jake didn't like to see her looking so sad.

not like sth/sb very much (use this when the feeling is not very strong) Mum didn't like Mark very much when she first met him.

dislike /ˌdɪs'laɪk/ [v T] to think someone or something is very unpleasant: He was a quiet person who disliked social occasions.

dislike doing sth Stephen dislikes having to get up early.

dislike sb/sth intensely (=dislike them very much) Muriel disliked Paul intensely.

> ⚠ **Dislike** is more formal than **not like**, and is not usually used in spoken English. If you **dislike** someone or something, you feel more strongly than if you **do not like** them.

◯hate /heɪt/ [v I] SPOKEN if you **hate** something, you do not like it at all because it is very unpleasant or very annoying: I hate those stupid talk shows on TV. | Don't you hate the way she interrupts you when you're talking?

hate it when I hate it when I'm in the shower and the phone rings.

◯don't think much of sth/sb /ˌdəʊnt θɪŋk 'mʌtʃ ɒv (sth/sb)/ SPOKEN to think that something is not very good or that someone is not very good at something:

The hotel was okay but I didn't think much of the food. | I don't think much of that new singer, do you?

not be very keen on sth /nɒt biː veri 'kiːn ɒn (sth)/ BRITISH INFORMAL to not like something, although you do not think it is very bad or very unpleasant: Actually, I'm not very keen on modern art. | I know you're not very keen on Japanese food, but try this!

◯not be sb's type /nɒt biː (sb's) 'taɪp/ ESPECIALLY SPOKEN if someone is **not your type**, they are not the kind of person you usually like: Vicky's friends are not my type. | Rob isn't her type at all.

◯go off sb/sth /ˌgəʊ 'ɒf (sb/sth)‖-'ɔːf-/ [phrasal verb T] BRITISH SPOKEN to stop liking someone or something that you used to like: I used to drink lots of coffee, but I've gone off it lately.

8 to stop someone from liking a person, thing, or activity

put sb off /ˌpʊt (sb) 'ɒf‖-'ɔːf/ [phrasal verb T] INFORMAL to stop someone from liking something or being interested in it: Don't let her put you off, it's a really good movie.

put sb off sth That weekend put me off camping for the rest of my life!

turn sb against sb /ˌtɜːrn (sb) ə'genst (sb)/ [phrasal verb T] to deliberately change someone's feelings, so that they stop liking someone that they used to like: My wife threw me out, and now she's trying to turn the children against me.

LIMIT

➡ see also **CONTROL, RULE, LAW**

1 the largest amount that is allowed or possible

limit /'lɪmɪt/ [n singular] the highest number, speed, temperature etc that is allowed by a law or rule

+ to There's a limit to the amount of French money you can take out of the country.

time/age/speed limit The Interstate speed limit is 65 m.p.h.

over/above the limit (=higher than the limit) *Pollution levels in the water were found to be over the official limit.*

set a limit on sth (=decide what the limit will be) *The Education Department has set a limit on the size of classes.*

maximum /ˈmæksɪməm/ [adj only before noun] the **maximum** number or amount is the largest number or amount that is possible, normal, or allowed: *After leaving Calais, the train soon reaches its maximum speed of 300 kph.* | *40 is the maximum number of passengers this bus is allowed to carry.*

maximum [n singular]
the maximum *You don't have to wait long for a new passport – 3 weeks is about the maximum.*

a maximum of £10/50%/30 degrees etc
The prisoners here can earn a maximum of £10 a week.

the most /ðə ˈməʊst/ [quantifier] the largest number or amount: *There are six people in the cab, and that's the most I'm allowed to take.* | *The most we can afford is $500 a month.*

2 the smallest amount that is allowed

the least /ðə ˈliːst/ [quantifier] the smallest number or amount: *The least you should offer her is $10 an hour.*

minimum /ˈmɪnɪməm/ [adj only before noun] the **minimum** number or amount is the smallest number or amount that is possible or allowed: *Is there a minimum wage in your country?* | *The minimum age for joining the army is 18.*

minimum [n singular]
the minimum *We need at least 8 students to make the course profitable – that's the minimum.*

a minimum of £10/50%/30 degrees etc
You have to stay for a minimum of 7 days.

3 when there are limits on what you can do

limits /ˈlɪmɪts/ [n plural] the rules or facts that control someone's freedom or their ability to do what they want

+ to/on *Are there any limits on the President's power?* | *There are practical limits to the number of cases we can deal with each day.*

within limits *Within certain legal limits, you can import anything you want.*

restrictions /rɪˈstrɪkʃənz/ [n plural] rules or laws that strictly control what you are allowed to do: *severe financial restrictions*

+ on/upon sth *Are there any restrictions on changing foreign currency?* | *Because of restrictions on reporting, the newspapers were not allowed to cover the story.*

impose restrictions (=officially order that something must be limited) *New restrictions have been imposed on immigration.*

limited /ˈlɪmɪtɪd/ [adj] if something is **limited**, only a fixed amount is allowed or available: *We only have a limited amount of time in which to finish the work.*

+ to *The class is limited to 20 students.*

be restricted to /biː rɪˈstrɪktɪd tuː/ if something **is restricted to** a particular amount, time, group etc, there are rules limiting it to that amount, time, group etc: *The sale of alcohol is restricted to people over 18.* | *Under the new rules working time is restricted to 45 hours a week.*

4 to put limits on something

limit /ˈlɪmɪt/ [v T] to stop a number or amount from becoming too large, or stop someone from doing whatever they want: *a new law limiting the number of foreign cars that can be imported* | *Men hold most of the top jobs, and this limits women's opportunities for promotion.*

limit sb/sth to sth *Try to limit your alcohol intake to 14 units per week.*

put/set/impose a limit /ˌpʊt, ˌset, ɪmˌpəʊz ə ˈlɪmɪt/ to officially control the size or amount of something by deciding what the limit will be

+ on *Governments should put strict limits on tobacco advertising.*

restrict /rɪˈstrɪkt/ [v T] to strictly control and limit the size, amount, or range of something: *The law restricts the sale of hand guns.*

restrict sth to sth *a population policy that restricted families to one child per couple*

5 when there is no limit

there is no limit /ðeər ɪz ˌnəʊ ˈlɪmɪt/ use this to say that someone can have or do as much of something as they want
+ to/on *If you buy one of these tickets there's no limit to the distance you can travel. | There's no limit on the number of applications you can make.*

unlimited /ʌnˈlɪmɪtɪd/ [adj] something that is **unlimited** has no fixed limit: *He has unlimited access to the firm's computer. | They seem to have unlimited amounts of money to spend on advertising.*

LINE

1 on paper, in a pattern, or on clothes

line /laɪn/ [n C] a long, thin, continuous mark on a surface: *The teacher had put a red line through my work. | If the ball goes over this line, it's out of play. | Don't park on the yellow lines.*

line

He drew a line on the paper.

straight line *Use your ruler to draw a straight line.*
lined [adj] paper that is **lined** has lines printed across it: *a letter written on pale blue lined paper*

stripe /straɪp/ [n C] a straight line of colour on cloth, paper etc, usually part of a pattern where the line is repeated many times: *He wore a grey suit with narrow blue stripes. | The car had green and white stripes painted along its side.*
striped [adj] clothing or material that is **striped** has stripes on it: *a yellow and white striped swimsuit*

crease

creases

crease /kriːs/ [n C] a line on a piece of clothing or material where it has been folded or crushed: *When I unpacked my suitcase, all my shirts had creases in them.*
creased [adj] clothes that are **creased** have a lot of creases in them: *When he unpacked his jacket, he found it was badly creased.*

2 on someone's skin

lines /laɪnz/ [n plural] lines that form on someone's skin: *The deep lines on his forehead showed that he was a worried man.*
lined [adj] if your skin or face is **lined**, it has lines on it: *His forehead was deeply lined with worry.*

wrinkles /ˈrɪŋkəlz/ [n plural] deep lines on someone's face or skin, caused by growing old: *His face was old and covered in wrinkles.*
wrinkled [adj] if your skin is **wrinkled**, it has deep lines on it: *her old wrinkled hands*

3 a line of writing or numbers

line /laɪn/ [n C] a line of writing that goes across a page: *Martin opened the letter and read the first few lines – it was bad news. | Start reading aloud at line 12.*
+ of *a few lines of poetry*

column /ˈkɒləm/ /ˈkɑː-/ [n C] a line of numbers, written under each other, that goes down a page: *Add up the numbers in the column on the right.*

column

4 a line of people or things

line /laɪn/ [n C] several people, trees, hills etc standing next to each other or one behind the other
in a line (=forming a line) *The photographer asked us to stand in a line.*
+ of *In front of the house there is a line of tall trees.*

When you see **EC**, go to the **ESSENTIAL COMMUNICATION** section.

row

The first two rows were empty.

row /rəʊ/ [n C] a line of people or things next to each other, especially one of several lines that are arranged one behind another
+ of *There were only three rows of chairs – everyone else had to stand.*
front/back row *Can you see me in the photo? I'm in the back row.*

procession /prə'seʃən/ [n C] a group of people or vehicles that move slowly along in a line, especially as part of a public ceremony: *We were held up by a long funeral procession. | The children were eager to take part in the carnival procession.*

5 a line of people waiting for something

queue

queue BRITISH **line** AMERICAN /kjuː, laɪn/ [n C] a number of people who are standing one behind another, waiting to do something: *There was a queue at the bus-stop.*
+ for *The line for the movie went right around the block.*
in a queue/line *We were stuck in a queue for half an hour.*

stand in line/wait in line /ˌstænd ɪn 'laɪn, ˌweɪt ɪn 'laɪn/ ESPECIALLY AMERICAN to stand in a line of people who are waiting to do something: *Jerry joined the crowd of people waiting in line outside the stadium.*

queue /kjuː/ [v I] BRITISH to stand in a line of people who are waiting to do something: *We had to queue for hours in the rain.*
queue for sth (=queue to get something) *I spent so long queuing for a ticket that I nearly missed the train.*
queue to do sth *There were hundreds of football fans queuing to get in.*
queue up (=form a queue) *Every night, people queue up outside Club 49.*
queuing – queued – have queued

6 the line that separates two areas or countries

border /'bɔːʳdəʳ/ [n C] the official line that separates two countries, or the area close to this line: *They escaped across the border into Thailand.*
+ with *Iraq had put thousands of troops along its border with Kuwait.*
+ between *The town lies on the border between Chile and Argentina.*
the German/Mexican/Swiss etc border *Strasbourg is very close to the German border.*

boundary /'baʊndəri/ [n C] the official line that marks the edge of an area of land, for example a farm or one of the parts of a country: *More and more people are moving outside the city boundaries.*
+ between *The Mississippi River forms the boundary between Tennessee and Arkansas.*
plural boundaries

LIQUID

➡ see also **MIX**

1 a liquid

liquid /'lɪkwɪd/ [n C/U] a substance, such as water or milk, that is not a solid and not a gas: *She screamed as the boiling liquid burned her skin. | Add most of the flour to the liquid and stir the mixture.*
liquid [adj usually before noun] use this about something which is a liquid, but which is usually a solid or a gas: *Treat your plants once a week with liquid fertiliser. | liquid soap | liquid oxygen*

fluid /ˈfluːɪd/ [n C/U] a liquid – a technical word used especially by doctors or scientists: *In extreme heat the body loses fluid and salt.* | *The fluids exchanged during sex can carry the HIV virus.*

2 an amount of liquid

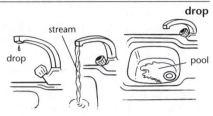

drop /drɒp‖drɑːp/ [n C] a very small amount of liquid that falls from somewhere in a round shape
+ of *Big drops of rain hit the window pane.* | *A drop of wax fell onto the carpet as she carried the candle across the room.*

stream /striːm/ [n C] a continuous line of moving liquid: *Water ran down the wall in a continuous stream.*
+ of *A thin stream of blood was pouring from his wound.*

pool /puːl/ [n C] an area of liquid lying on a surface
+ of *Trautman was lying in a pool of blood.* | *A pool of oil had collected under the car.*

3 liquid that flows easily

thin /θɪn/ [adj] a **thin** liquid flows very easily, especially because it is not quite thick enough: *This paint seems a little thin, it's dripping everywhere.* | *Don't make the mixture too thin or the pancakes will taste watery.*
thin – thinner – thinnest

runny /ˈrʌni/ [adj] INFORMAL food that is **runny** is liquid but should be thicker than it is: *a boiled egg with a runny yolk* | *runny custard*
runny – runnier – runniest

molten /ˈməʊltən/ [adj only before noun] molten rock, metal, glass etc has been made into a liquid by being heated to a very high temperature: *You can watch craftsmen make beautiful vases out of molten glass.* | *The town was buried under a river of molten lava.* | *molten wax*

4 liquid that flows slowly

thick /θɪk/ [adj] a **thick** liquid flows slowly because it is almost solid: *If you want to make the sauce thicker, add flour.* | *The soup was thick and creamy.*

lumpy /ˈlʌmpi/ [adj] a liquid that is **lumpy** contains small solid pieces, so it is not as smooth as it should be: *This gravy is lumpy.* | *I hate lumpy porridge.*

5 to become a liquid

melt /melt/ [v I/T] if something solid **melts** or if heat melts it, it becomes liquid: *The snow has all melted.* | *The chocolate had melted and was all over the inside of her pocket.* | *Melt the butter in a saucepan and stir in the sugar.*
melted [adj only before noun] *a pasta dish topped with melted cheese*

dissolve /dɪˈzɒlv‖dɪˈzɑːlv/ [v I/T] if something solid **dissolves** or if you **dissolve** it, it is added to a liquid and mixed with it, so that it becomes liquid itself: *The crystals dissolve in water to create a purple liquid.* | *Dissolve the salt in 125 ml of hot water.*

6 when liquid moves or comes out of somewhere

pour /pɔːr/ [v I] if a liquid **pours** out of something, down something etc, large amounts of it fall in that direction
+ out of/off/down *Water was pouring out of the crack in the ceiling.* | *Tears poured down her cheeks.*

flow /fləʊ/ [v I] if a liquid **flows**, it moves in a steady, continuous stream from one place to another: *The river flows more slowly here and it is safe to swim.*
+ into/out of/over *From here, factory waste flows straight into the sea.*

come out /ˌkʌm ˈaʊt/ [phrasal verb I] if liquid **comes out** of a pipe, container etc, it flows out slowly and in small quantities: *When I turned on the tap a brownish liquid came out.*
+ of *There's oil coming out of your engine.*

leak /liːk/ [v I] if liquid **leaks** from a container or pipe, or if a container or pipe **leaks**, the liquid comes out through a small hole or crack because the container or pipe is damaged: *I think the fuel tank is leaking.*

L

+ through/into/out of/from *Water was leaking from a pipe in the bathroom.* | *Yoghurt had leaked out of my lunchbox all over my bag.*

drip /drɪp/ [v I] if a liquid **drips**, it falls slowly and steadily, in drops

+ off/out/from/onto *The blood was still dripping from the cut on his lip.* | *We stood under a tree, with rain dripping onto our heads.*

dripping – dripped – have dripped

7 to make liquid come out of a container

pour /pɔːr/ [v T] to make liquid flow steadily from a container, by turning the container over or by making it lean to one side

pour

pour sth on/into/down sth *Pour the milk into a jug.* | *Nassim poured the whisky down the sink.*

spill /spɪl/ [v T] to accidentally make liquid come out of a container

spill sth onto/over/into sth *Someone had spilled red wine all over the carpet.* | *A tanker has spilled 6000 gallons of oil into the sea.*

spilling – spilled (also **spilt** BRITISH) – have spilled (also **have spilt** BRITISH)

spray /spreɪ/ [v T] to make liquid come very quickly out of a container as thousands of small drops, by forcing it through a small hole or many small holes

spray water/champagne/perfume etc over/onto sth *He shook up the bottle and sprayed champagne all over us.*

spray sth with sth *We regularly spray all our crops with pesticides.*

squirt /skwɜːrt/ [v T] to make liquid come out of a container in a short thin stream, especially by pressing the sides of the container

squirt sth into/onto/over sth *Mike squirted disinfectant onto the kitchen counter and began to wipe it down.* | *Squirt a little oil into the lock to loosen it.*

LIST

1 a list

list /lɪst/ [n C] a set of names of people, places, things that you have to do etc, which are written one below the other and kept as a record

+ of *a list of words that we had to learn*

be on a list *My name wasn't on the list of guests, so they didn't let me in.*

make a list *Make a list of all the people you want to send Christmas cards to.*

a waiting list (=a list of people who are waiting for something) *The English course is very popular so there might be a waiting list.*

a shopping list (=a list of things you need to buy)

cross sth off a list (=remove it from a list) *We have plenty of eggs, so you can cross them off the list.*

register /ˈredʒɪstər/ [n C] an official list containing the names of all the people, organizations, or things of a particular type

+ of *a register of qualified translators* | *a civil register of births, deaths, and marriages*

checklist /ˈtʃekˌlɪst/ [n C] a list of all the things that you need to do, to help you remember

+ of *When you go camping, it's a good idea to make a checklist of all the things you need to take with you.*

agenda /əˈdʒendə/ [n C] a list of all the things that will be discussed at a meeting: *Do you have an agenda for this morning's meeting?*

2 to provide a list

list /lɪst/ [v T] to give a written or spoken list of names, places etc: *a useful booklet, listing all the colleges that take part-time students*

be listed *The books are listed alphabetically, according to the name of the author.*

LISTEN

➡ see also **HEAR**

> ⚠ Don't confuse **listen** and **hear**. If you **listen** to something, you pay attention so that you can hear it well.

listen /'lɪsən/ [v I] to pay attention to what someone is saying or to a sound that you hear: *I didn't hear the answer because I wasn't listening when she read it out.*
+ to *Gordon was lying on his bed, listening to music.*
listen carefully *They all listened carefully while she was telling them the story.*
◯**Listen!** SPOKEN (say this when you want to get someone's attention) *Listen! I've just had a brilliant idea.*

> ⚠ Don't say 'I listen music'. Say **I listen to music**.

pay attention /ˌpeɪ ə'tenʃən/ to listen carefully to what someone is saying: *I have some important information about travel arrangements, so please pay attention.*
+ to *She went on talking, but I wasn't really paying attention to what she was saying.*

eavesdrop /'iːvzdrɒp‖-drɑːp/ [v I] to secretly listen to someone else's conversation by standing near them, hiding behind a door etc: *"How does Jake know that?" "He must have been eavesdropping."*
+ on *We talked very quietly so that no-one could eavesdrop on us.*

listen in /ˌlɪsən 'ɪn/ [phrasal verb I] to listen to someone else's telephone conversation when they do not know that you are listening
+ on *The police were listening in on their conversation.*

LITTLE/NOT MUCH

➡ if you mean 'not big', go to **SMALL**
➡ see also **FEW**

1 a small amount

a little /ə 'lɪtl/ [quantifier] a small amount of something
a little food/time/help etc *I think I'll have a little cream in my coffee.* | *They may need a little help.*
just a little (=only a small amount) *"Do you speak Japanese?" "Just a little."*
a little more/less *I wish he'd show a little more interest in his work.*

> ⚠ Don't say 'I speak a little of Spanish'. Say **I speak a little Spanish**.

a little bit (also **a bit** BRITISH) /ə ˌlɪtl 'bɪt, ə 'bɪt/ [quantifier] INFORMAL a small amount of something: *Don't buy a large pack – I only need a little bit.*
+ of *It's a good way of making a bit of extra money.*
a little bit more/less *Tell us a little bit more about your plans.*

not much /nɒt 'mʌtʃ/ [quantifier] only a small amount of something – use this especially when there is less than you need: *There's not much light in this room.* | *He doesn't have much experience of running a business.*
not very much *You haven't eaten very much.* | *We didn't have very much time, so we took a taxi.*

a drop /ə 'drɒp‖-'drɑːp/ [quantifier] INFORMAL a small amount of something that you drink: *"Do you take cream in your coffee?" "Yes, just a drop, please."*
+ of *Could I have a drop of milk in my tea?*

2 a very small amount

very little /ˌveri 'lɪtl/ [quantifier] a very small amount of something: *"How much do you know about computers?" "Very little, I'm afraid."* | *Fish contains very little fat.* | *Changing the law will make very little difference.*

hardly any /ˌhɑːʳdli 'eni/ [quantifier] such a small amount that there is almost none at all: *We need some more paper –*

there's hardly any left. | *Ian's learning to play the guitar, but he hardly gets any time to practise.*

scarce /skeə^rs/ [adj] if something that you need is **scarce**, it is available only in small amounts, so there is not enough of it: *After the war, food and clothing were scarce.* | *a waste of scarce natural resources*

3 a little tired/sad/older/bigger etc

a little /ə 'lɪtl/ [adv] *I'm feeling a little tired. I think I'll go upstairs and have a rest.* | *"Do you feel sad that you're leaving?" "Just a little."*

a little more *Business class costs a little more than economy class, but it's worth the extra money.*

a little bit (also **a bit** BRITISH) /ə ˌlɪtl 'bɪt, ə 'bɪt/ [adv] INFORMAL a little: *I'm feeling a little bit better today.* | *She looked a bit surprised when she saw me.*

slightly /'slaɪtli/ [adv] very little, but not enough to be important or easy to notice: *We're almost the same age. He's slightly older than me.* | *Sean's car is a slightly different colour.*

4 when something or someone moves or changes a little

a little /ə 'lɪtl/ *His work has improved a little since he came to the school.* | *I noticed that Mrs Ewing's hand was trembling a little.*

a little bit (also **a bit** BRITISH) /ə ˌlɪtl 'bɪt, ə 'bɪt/ INFORMAL a little: *Do you mind if I open the window a little bit.* | *The centre of the town has changed a bit, but everything else is just as I remember it.*

slightly /'slaɪtli/ [adv] a little, but not enough to be important or easy to notice: *The temperature had risen slightly, but it was still very cold.*

not much /nɒt 'mʌtʃ/ only a little and not as much as you might have expected: *Things haven't changed much over the past few years.*

When you see **EC**, go to the **ESSENTIAL COMMUNICATION** section.

LIVE

➡ opposite **DIE**
➡ if you mean 'not die', go to **ALIVE**
➡ see also **HOUSES/WHERE PEOPLE LIVE, HOME**

1 to live in a place

live /lɪv/ [v I] to have your home in a particular place: *Where do you live?*
+ in *Do you like living in Tokyo?* | *Do you live in an apartment or a house?* | *Judy lives in that nice house on the corner.*
+ at *In 1905 Russell was living at 4 Ralston Street.*

> ⚠ Use **in** before the name of a country or town: *John lives in Canada/in Toronto.* Use **at** before the exact address: *John lives at 78 Clancy Street.*
>
> ⚠ Don't confuse **live** (=live somewhere permanently) and **stay** (=live there for a short time): *We stayed at a small hotel close to the beach.*

grow up /ˌgrəʊ 'ʌp/ [phrasal verb I] to live in a place during the time when you are a child: *This is the place where I grew up.*
+ in *Margaret Hallworth was born in Manchester, but grew up in North Wales.*

settle /'setl/ [v I] to start to live permanently in a country or city, after you have lived in several different places
+ in *We lived in Thailand, then Singapore, and finally settled in Hong Kong.*

2 to live in the same house as someone else

live with sb /'lɪv wɪð (sb)/ [phrasal verb T] *I live with an old friend from college.* | *Do you still live with your parents?*

live together /'lɪv təˌgeðə^r/ [phrasal verb I] if two people **live together**, they live in the same house and have a sexual relationship: *These days, people often live together before getting married.*

share a house/apartment/room with sb /ʃeər ə 'haʊs, əˈpɑːtmənt, 'ruːm wɪð (sb)/ to live with someone who is not a member of your family and not your sexual partner: *My brother shares a house with four other students.* | *I used to share an apartment with a guy who played the drums.*

room with sb /ˈruːm wɪð (sb)/ [phrasal verb T] AMERICAN to live in the same room as someone at college: *Do you remember Diane? I roomed with her at college.*

flatmate BRITISH **roommate** AMERICAN /ˈflætmeɪt, ˈruːmˌmeɪt, ˈrʊm-/ [n C] someone that you share an apartment with, who is not a member of your family and not your sexual partner: *This is Rosalind, my flatmate.* | *You can't have a party without asking your roommate first.*

3 someone who lives in a place

⚠ If you want to say how many people live in a place, say 'a city/country with a population of 5 million' or 'a city/country with 5 million inhabitants'.

population /ˌpɒpjˈleɪʃən, ˌpɑːp-/ [n singular/U] all the people who live in a country or town or area, or the number of people who live in it: *In Ghana 46% of the population is under 16 years of age.*
+ of *The population of Singapore is almost 3 million.*
the adult/Muslim/black population (=all the people in a place who are adult, Muslim etc) *90% of the adult population is literate.*

resident /ˈrezˌdənt/ [n C] someone who lives in a particular area of a town, a particular street or apartment block etc: *Local residents are protesting about the new road.* | *Parking spaces are for residents only.*
+ of *Residents of Glacier Bay are complaining about the pollution caused by cruise ships.*

inhabitant /ɪnˈhæbˌtənt/ [n C usually plural] WRITTEN one of the people who live in a place, especially in a town or city or in an area of a country: *Copenhagen has about 1.4 million inhabitants.* | *This is a poor rural area, with only one doctor per 10,000 inhabitants.*
+ of *the inhabitants of the San Fernando Valley*

tenant /ˈtenənt/ [n C] someone who lives in a house, apartment, or room and regularly pays money to the person who owns it: *Tenants are not allowed to keep pets.* | *Have you found any tenants for your house yet?*

LONG

➡ look here for ...
- long hair, a long street etc
- a long book, list etc
- a long time

➡ opposite **SHORT**

➡ see also **MEASURE, TALL**

➡ if you mean 'after a long time', go to **END**

1 a long object/line/space etc

long /lɒŋ‖lɔŋ/ [adj] longer than usual from one end to the other: *The girl had long blonde hair.* | *There was a long line of people at the ticket office.* | *She led them down a long corridor, through countless swinging doors.* | *Rome has the longest shopping street in Europe.*

long

A cat was hiding in the long grass.

four inches/two metres/five miles etc long *The snake was more than three metres long.*

length /leŋθ/ [n C/U] how long something is: *These fish can grow to a length of four feet.* | *We need to measure the length and width of the room.*
four inches/two metres/five miles etc in length *The hotel pool is 15 metres in length.*

2 a long book/name/list/ speech etc

long /lɒŋ‖lɔŋ/ [adj] a **long** book, speech, name etc has a lot of pages, words, letters, details etc in it: *The place has a long Welsh name that I can't pronounce.* | *The principal gave a long, boring speech about discipline.* | *There was a long list of jobs that she needed to do that day.*

L

lengthy /'leŋθi/ [adj] FORMAL a **lengthy** book, speech, explanation, or document has a lot of words and details in it, and is often boring: *a lengthy, two-volume book on conditions in modern China* | *a lengthy financial report*

long-winded /,lɒŋ 'wɪndɪd◀,lɔːŋ-/ [adj] boring and much longer than it needs to be: *The book begins with a rather long-winded description of the historical background to the war.* | *I had to listen to his long-winded explanation as to why he was late.*

3 a long time

a long time /ə ,lɒŋ 'taɪm‖-,lɔːŋ-/

(for) a long time *He's lived here a long time.* | *The house has been empty for a long time.*

a long time ago *We met in August 1947, a long time ago.*

a very long time *We've been friends for a very long time.*

it's a long time since *It's a long time since I heard from Clive.*

a while /ə 'waɪl/ a fairly long time: *After a while people started to complain*

for a while *How's Lynn? I haven't seen her for a while.*

quite a while (=a long time) *He's been going out with her quite a while now, hasn't he?*

long /lɒŋ‖lɔːŋ/ [adv] for a long time: *Have you been waiting long?*

long before/after *Michelle was wearing platform shoes long before they came into fashion.*

⌕ages /'eɪdʒɪz/ [n plural] SPOKEN, ESPECIALLY BRITISH a very long time

for ages *I haven't been out for ages.*

wait/take/spend ages *I spent ages in town trying to find something to wear for the wedding.* | *We had to wait ages for a bus.*

it's ages since *It's ages since we played this game – I'd forgotten how good you are.*

ages ago (=a long time ago) *"When did you sell the car?" "Ages ago!"*

hours/months/years /aʊərs, mʌnθs, jɪərs/ [n plural] many hours, months, or years, and a lot longer than you expected: *It was years before we found out the truth.*

for hours/months/years *I'm worried – Robin's been out for hours.*

take (sb) hours/months/years *It took us months to paint the house.*

4 continuing for a long time

long /lɒŋ‖lɔːŋ/ [adj] continuing for a long time: *The play was good, but it was a little too long.* | *He died after a long illness.* | *It's a long flight – 15 hours.*

long-term /,lɒŋ 'tɜːrm◀‖,lɔːŋ-/ [adj only before noun] a **long-term** problem, situation, or effect is one that continues for a very long time: *Drugs such as Ecstasy may cause long-term damage to the brain.* | *long-term unemployment*

long-term relationship (=a sexual relationship that lasts for a long time) *I'm not ready for a long-term relationship right now.*

lasting /'lɑːstɪŋ‖'læs-/ [adj only before noun] strong enough or effective enough to continue for a long time

a lasting peace/friendship/agreement *The people of Northern Ireland are praying for a lasting peace.*

long-running /,lɒŋ 'rʌnɪŋ◀‖,lɔːŋ-/ [adj only before noun] **long-running dispute/row/debate/conflict** an argument, disagreement, or war that continues for a very long time: *The two countries have signed an agreement, ending a long-running dispute over fishing rights.*

interminable /ɪn'tɜːrmɪnəbəl/ [adj] FORMAL something that is **interminable** continues for much too long and makes you feel impatient or annoyed: *Tuesday was always a day of interminable meetings.* | *After an interminable delay, the bus finally left the station.*

5 something that you need a lot of time to do

take a long time /,teɪk ə ,lɒŋ 'taɪm‖-,lɔːŋ-/ if something **takes a long time**, you need a lot of time to do it: *I never go to work by train because it takes such a long time.* | *Your body takes a long time to recover after an operation.*

it takes (sb) a long time to do sth *It takes a long time to make friends when you move to a new town.* | *It took me a long time to learn how the system worked.*

take time /,teɪk ˈtaɪm/ if something **takes time** to do, it cannot be done quickly and you have to be patient: *Learning a new language always takes time.*
it takes time to do sth *It takes time to get to know people.*

time-consuming /ˈtaɪm kənˌsjuːmɪŋ‖-ˌsuː-/ [adj] an activity, process, or job that is **time-consuming** takes a very long time to do: *Checking all the calculations used to be a very time-consuming process.*

LOOK AFTER

➡ see also **CHILD, BABY**

1 to look after someone

look after sb /,lʊk ˈɑːftər (sb)‖-ˈæf-/ [phrasal verb T] to spend time with a child or with someone who is old or sick, and make sure they are safe and have the things they need: *Can you look after the kids for me while I'm out?* | *I took a week off work to look after my mother when she had her operation.*

take care of sb /,teɪk ˈkeər ɒv (sb)/ to look after someone, especially someone who is very young, very old, or very sick, and needs someone to help them all the time: *Taking care of young children is a full-time job.* | *My father became so ill that we couldn't take care of him at home any more.*
take good care of sb (=look after them well) *Don't worry, I'll take good care of him.*

care for sb /ˈkeər fɔːr (sb)/ [phrasal verb T] to look after someone who is very ill or very old by doing everything for them: *Elsie had to leave her job to care for her sick father.*

2 to look after children until they have grown up

bring up /,brɪŋ ˈʌp/ [phrasal verb T] to look after children until they have grown up: *His parents had a lot of problems, so he was brought up by his grandparents.*
bring up sb *I don't know how they managed to bring up six children with so little money.*
bring sb up *I brought my son up by myself.*

raise /reɪz/ [v T often passive] AMERICAN to look after children until they have grown up: *Raising a family is one of the toughest jobs in the world.*
be raised *My brother and I were raised on a small farm in Missouri.*

3 someone who is paid to look after children

babysitter (also **sitter** INFORMAL) /ˈbeɪbiˌsɪtər, ˈsɪtər/ [n C] someone who is paid to look after children while their parents go out for the evening

childminder /ˈtʃaɪldˌmaɪndər/ [n C] BRITISH someone who is paid to look after children while their parents are at work

nanny /ˈnæni/ [n C] a woman who is paid to look after someone else's children, and who lives in the house with the family
plural **nannies**

4 to look after something

look after sth /,lʊk ˈɑːftər (sth)‖-ˈæf-/ [phrasal verb T] to keep something in good condition and make sure that it does not get broken, damaged, or stolen: *You can have a new bike for Christmas if you promise to look after it.*
look after sth for sb *The neighbours are going to look after the house for us while we're away.*

take care of sth /,teɪk ˈkeər ɒv (sth)/ to look after something, especially something that is expensive or easily broken, or needs a lot of attention: *That car should run for another ten years if you take care of it.*
take good care of sth (=look after it well) *The boat was in good condition, and the previous owner had obviously taken very good care of it.*

keep an eye on sth /,kiːp ən ˈaɪ ɒn (sth)/ ESPECIALLY SPOKEN to look after something that belongs to someone else for a short time, by watching it to make sure that it does not get stolen or damaged: *Tom went into the library while I kept an eye on the bikes.* | *Can you keep an eye on my bags while I go to the toilet?*

maintain /meɪnˈteɪn, mən-/ [v T] to make sure that a car, machine, or building is in good condition by checking it and repairing it when necessary: *The car hadn't* been properly maintained, and it was very rusty.

maintenance /'meɪntənəns/ [n U] the job of maintaining a car, building, or machine: *A car is quite a big expense, especially when you consider maintenance costs.* | *The landlord is responsible for the maintenance of the building.*

LOOK AT

➡ see also SEE, WATCH

⚠ Don't confuse **see**, **watch**, and **look at**. When you **see** something, you notice it with your eyes, either deliberately or accidentally: *I saw an accident on my way to school today.* You **watch** things like films, sports games, or other situations where there is action and movement: *Dad was watching a basketball game on TV.* When you **look at** people, scenery, pictures, and other things that are not moving, you deliberately pay attention to them: *Look at this old picture of Sally!*

1 to look at someone or something

look /lʊk/ [v I] to turn your eyes towards something so that you can see it: *Look, there are swans on the river.*
+ at *"Come on, it's time to go," he said, looking at his watch.* | *Look at me when I'm talking to you.*
+ into/out of/through/down etc *Helen was looking out of the window, waiting for him to arrive.* | *Janie looked into her mail box, but there was nothing there.* | *The teacher stopped and looked around to see if there were any questions.*
look at sb/sth in amazement/disbelief/surprise etc (=in a way that shows you are surprised or shocked) *Sean looked at her in disbelief. "Are you sure?"*
look [n C] when you turn your eyes to look at someone or something: *Sarah needed only one look at her daughter's face to know that she was in trouble.* | *I was getting disapproving looks from the people around me.*

When you see **EC**, go to the ESSENTIAL COMMUNICATION section.

⚠ Don't say **look at** when you are talking about TV programmes, games, or things that are happening. Say **watch**: *I was watching a baseball game.* | *The kids are watching a video.*

have a look/take a look /ˌhæv ə 'lʊk, ˌteɪk ə 'lʊk/ ESPECIALLY SPOKEN to look at something, especially something interesting or unusual
+ at *We climbed to the top of the tower to have a look at the view.* | *"You'd better take a look at this," she said, passing me a letter.*

stare /steə^r/ [v I] to look directly at someone or something for a long time, without moving your eyes
+ at *Why are you staring at me like that?* | *She stared at the page for several minutes, trying to understand.*
+ into/out of etc *My cat spends all day staring out of the window.*
stare back (at sb) (=stare at someone who is looking at you)
stare in amazement/horror/disbelief (=in a way that shows you are surprised or shocked) *Donna stared in horror as the man fell to the floor.*
stare [n C] a long direct look: *Charles didn't reply. He just gave his daughter an angry stare.*

gaze /geɪz/ [v I] ESPECIALLY WRITTEN to look at someone or something for a long time, especially with a feeling of love or great pleasure
+ at *I lay back on the sand and gazed at the stars above.*
+ out/into/down etc *He was gazing into her eyes as he spoke.* | *Ruth gazed down at the sleeping child.*

⚠ **Gaze** is used especially in descriptions.

glare /gleə^r/ [v I] to look angrily at someone: *He sat there in silence, glaring angrily.*
+ at *Sarah glared at her father, "How dare you say that!"*

2 to look carefully

look carefully/closely /ˌlʌk 'keə^rfəli, 'kləʊsli/ to look carefully at something in order to see small details: *If you look carefully, you can see the artist's name in the corner of the picture.*

+ at *He looked closely at the pattern on the plate. "My Grandma used to have plates like this."*

🔍 **take a look at sth/have a look at sth** /teɪk ə 'lʊk æt (sth), hæv ə 'lʊk æt (sth)/ ESPECIALLY SPOKEN to look carefully at something in order to find out what is wrong with it or to find out something about it: *I've asked Ken to take a look at the car – the engine's making strange noises.* | *The doctor will be here soon to have a look at your ankle.*

take/have a good look at sth (=look very carefully and thoroughly) *The police asked me to take a good look at the photo, and tell them if I recognised anyone.*

examine /ɪgˈzæmɪ̞n/ [v T] to look at something carefully and thoroughly because you want to find out more about it: *When the police examined the gun, they discovered Wright's fingerprints on it.* | *A team of divers was sent down to examine the wreck.*

check/inspect /tʃek, ɪnˈspekt/ [v T] to look at something carefully and thoroughly to make sure that it is correct, safe, or working properly: *The factory is regularly inspected by a fire-safety officer.* | *Technicians would check the engines and replace any worn parts.*

check sth for damage/faults/cracks (=in order to find any damage) *After the explosion, they had to check the building for structural damage.*

go over sth/go through sth /ˌgəʊ ˈəʊvəʳ (sth), ˌgəʊ ˈθruː (sth)/ [phrasal verb T] to look carefully at every part of a document or plan in order to make sure that it is all correct: *I'd like to go over last month's accounts with you.* | *Marion's been through your report and she hasn't found any mistakes.*

examination /ɪgˌzæmɪ̞ˈneɪʃən/ [n C/U] when you look at something carefully in order to find out more about it: *National Transportation Safety Board investigators are continuing their examination of the crash.*

on closer examination (=when you look at something more carefully) *On closer examination the painting was found to be a clever copy.*

inspection /ɪnˈspekʃən/ [n C] an official visit to a school, factory, prison etc by someone whose job is to make sure that everything is being done correctly

+ of *There are regular inspections of the prison by government health officers.*

carry out an inspection (=make an inspection) *Admiral Naumenko personally carried out an inspection of the fleet.*

3 **to look quickly or secretly**

glance /glɑːns‖glæns/ [v I] to look quickly at something or someone, and then look away

+ at *Dr Morse kept glancing nervously at his watch.* | *I saw them glance at each other as if they shared a secret.*

+ into/down/through etc *Glancing into Neil's room, she noticed that his suitcase was packed.*

    glance [n C] a quick look: *A quick glance at the map showed that we were on the right road.*

take a quick look/have a quick look /teɪk ə ˌkwɪk 'lʊk, hæv ə ˌkwɪk 'lʊk/ to look at something quickly in order to check that everything is satisfactory

+ at/around/through etc *He took a quick look in the mirror, and went out of the house.* | *She had a quick look around the room before letting the guests in.*

peep /piːp/ [v I] ESPECIALLY BRITISH to look at something quickly and secretly, especially from a place where you cannot be seen

+ through/into/round *We peeped through a crack in the fence, and saw her talking to a strange-looking man.* | *Bobby peeped round the corner to see what was happening.*

peek/take a peek /piːk, ˌteɪk ə 'piːk/ [v I] AMERICAN to look at something quickly and secretly, especially from a place where you cannot be seen: *The children were peeking from behind the wall.* | *She quickly opened the door and took a peek inside.*

L

4 to look in a shop/market/place/place for tourists

look around/have a look around
/ˌlʊk əˈraʊnd, hæv ə ˌlʊk əˈraʊnd/ [phrasal verb I] to walk around a shop or market or a place where tourists go, looking at a lot of different things: *I think I'll just look around for a while – I'm not sure what I want.* | *You're welcome to have a look around. We have a wide range of sportswear.*

⚠ In British English, you can also say **look round** and **have a look round**.

browse /braʊz/ [v I] to spend time looking at things in a shop, especially books or records, without intending to buy anything: *Armando spent the afternoon browsing in Camden market.*
+ through *Joanne was standing in a bookstore browsing through some magazines.*

window-shopping /ˈwɪndəʊ ˌʃɒpɪŋ‖-ˌʃɑːp-/ [n U] the activity of looking at goods in shop windows without intending to buy anything: *We hadn't any money but we enjoyed window-shopping in Fifth Avenue.*

◯**I'm just looking** /aɪm ˌdʒʌst ˈlʊkɪŋ/ SPOKEN say this to tell someone who works in a shop that you are only looking at things, and you do not intend to buy anything just now: *"Can I help you?" "No thanks, I'm just looking."*

5 to stop looking at something

look away /ˌlʊk əˈweɪ/ [phrasal verb I] to turn your eyes away from something that you were looking at: *The accident was so horrible that I had to look away.*
+ from *She looked away from him, unable to tell him the truth.*

look up /ˌlʊk ˈʌp/ [phrasal verb I] to stop looking at something and turn your face upwards, in order to see someone or talk to them: *There was a loud bang outside the classroom and we all looked up.*
+ from *"Goodbye, then," she said, without even looking up from her newspaper.*

LOOK FOR
to try to find someone or something

1 to look for something you have lost or someone who is not where they should be
➡ see also **LOSE, LOST**

look for sb/sth /ˈlʊk fɔːr (sb/sth)/ [phrasal verb T] to try to find something that you have lost, or someone who is not in the place where you expected them to be: *I'm looking for Simon – have you seen him?* | *I've been looking everywhere for that key! Where did you find it?*

try to find sb/sth /ˌtraɪ tə ˈfaɪnd (sb/sth)/ to look for someone or something, especially when it is difficult to find them: *Jill was up in the attic trying to find her old school books.* | *I'm trying to find my daughter – she was here five minutes ago.*

◯**have a look** /ˌhæv ə ˈlʊk/ ESPECIALLY SPOKEN to look for someone or something, especially when you do it quickly or when you only look in one place: *"I can't find my green dress." "Have a look in my bedroom."*
+ for *I had a look for Clive but he wasn't in his office.*
have a quick look *I'll just have a quick look for that book before we go.*
have a good look (=look carefully and thoroughly) *We don't have time to find it now – we'll have a good look in the morning.*

search for sb/sth /ˈsɜːrtʃ fɔːr (sb/sth)/ [phrasal verb T] to look carefully and thoroughly for someone or something, especially when it is very important that you find them: *Detectives spent today searching for clues in the woods near the victim's home.* | *Friends and neighbours gathered to search for the missing boy.*

in search of sb/sth /ɪn ˈsɜːrtʃ ɒv (sb/sth)/ ESPECIALLY WRITTEN if you go **in search of** someone or something, you go somewhere in order to find them

go/set off in **search of** *She stayed and talked for a while, then went off in search of Flynn.*

2 to look for something or someone that you need

look for sth/sb /'lʊk fɔːʳ (sth/sb)/ [phrasal verb T] to try to find something or someone that you need: *Can you help me? I'm looking for a place to stay.* | *You should write to Data Corp – they're always looking for new staff.* | *I spent months looking for a job, with no luck.*

try to find sth/sb /ˌtraɪ tə 'faɪnd (sth/sb)/ to look for something or someone that you need, especially when it is difficult and takes a long time: *Doctors are still trying to find a cure for cancer.* | *I spent half an hour trying to find a parking space.*

in search of sth /ɪn 'sɜːʳtʃ ɒv (sth)/ ESPE-CIALLY WRITTEN if you go **in search of** something that you need, you go some-where to try to find it: *Menendez had travelled up from Mexico in search of a job.*

look up /ˌlʊk 'ʌp/ [phrasal verb T] to try to find information by looking in a book, on a list, in computer records etc
look up sth *I'll just look up her address – it's on the student database.*
look sth up *If you don't know what it means, look it up in the dictionary.*

be on the lookout for sth/sb /biː ɒn ðə 'lʊkaʊt fɔːʳ (sth/sb)/ to keep looking for something or someone that might be useful to you, always taking care that you do not miss any opportunity: *Maya was always on the lookout for a bargain.* | *The team is on the lookout for good, young players.*

3 when the police are looking for a criminal
➡ see also **POLICE, FOLLOW**

look for sb/search for sb /'lʊk fɔːʳ (sb), 'sɜːʳtʃ fɔːʳ (sb)/ [phrasal verb T] to look for someone who has been involved in a crime or who has escaped from prison: *Police are still looking for the prisoner who escaped yesterday.*

When you see **EC**, go to the
ESSENTIAL COMMUNICATION section.

be after sb /biː 'ɑːftəʳ (sb)‖-'æf-/ [phrasal verb T] INFORMAL to try to find and catch someone who has done something wrong: *She said she was frightened because the police were after her.* | *The man we're after is one of the biggest drug-dealers in Europe.*

hunt /hʌnt/ [v I/T] to search for a criminal or for someone who has disappeared – use this when a large number of police are making an organized search over a wide area
+ for *Police have been hunting for the missing woman for several days.*
hunt sb down (=search for a criminal until you find them) *The train-robbers were eventually hunted down in Australia.*

4 when the police are looking for drugs, guns etc
➡ see also **POLICE, DRUGS, WEAPON**

search /sɜːʳtʃ/ [v T] to look in every part of a place or to look in someone's clothes or bags in order to try to find drugs, guns, stolen goods etc: *All visitors to the prison are thoroughly searched.* | *A team of police officers had searched the whole area, but couldn't find the mur-der weapon.*

go through sth /'gəʊ θruː (sth)/ [phrasal verb T] to carefully search all of some-one's clothes, bags, or possessions to try to find guns or drugs: *Customs officials went through his baggage but found nothing.*

raid /reɪd/ [v T] if the police **raid** a place, they arrive there suddenly to look for crim-inals, drugs, or stolen goods: *The Casino nightclub has been closed since it was raided last month.* | *The army used to raid houses in the Catholic districts in search of guns.*

frisk /frɪsk/ [v T] if the police, airport officials etc **frisk** someone, they feel the person's clothes and body, looking for hidden weapons or drugs: *All the passen-gers were frisked before they got on the plane.*
frisk sb for sth *What a school! All the students are frisked for drugs before morning roll-call.*

5 an attempt to find something

search /sɜːrtʃ/ [n C] an attempt to find someone or something, especially when this is well organized and a lot of people are doing it

+ for a search for survivors of the plane crash | Their search for gold took them west to Washington State.

carry out a search (=search a place) FBI agents carried out a thorough search of all the nightclubs.

search party (=an organized group of people searching for someone who is lost) When the men did not return, the commanding officer sent out a search party.

house-to-house search (=when every house in an area is searched) House-to-house searches were carried out in the hope of finding the kidnapped baby.

hunt /hʌnt/ [n singular] an organized search by a lot of people, especially to find a criminal: Police have launched a nationwide hunt for the killer.

raid /reɪd/ [n C] a sudden visit by the police to a building in order to look for criminals, drugs, stolen goods etc: Two people were arrested today in a police raid on a house in South London.

LOOSE

not fitting tightly or not firmly fixed

➡ opposite **TIGHT**
➡ see also **FASTEN/UNFASTEN**

⚠ Don't confuse **loose** and **lose** (=to not be able to find something).

1 clothes

loose /luːs/ [adj] **loose** clothes do not fit your body tightly, so you feel comfortable when you wear them: She wore a long, loose linen jacket. | In hot weather, loose cotton clothes are more comfortable.

baggy /'bægi/ [adj] **baggy** clothes are designed to be big and loose and they hide the shape of your body: Bill was wearing

a polo shirt and baggy blue pants. | a comfortable baggy sweater

baggy – baggier – baggiest

stretch /stretʃ/ [v I] if clothes **stretch**, they become looser and do not fit you properly any more: Don't put that sweater in the washing machine – it'll stretch.

loosen /'luːsən/ [v T] to make a piece of clothing looser and more comfortable by unfastening it: Simon suddenly felt very hot, so he loosened his shirt and tie. | Loosen any tight clothing, and lay the patient on his side.

2 rope/knot/chain

loose /luːs/ [adj] a rope, knot, chain etc that is **loose** is not tied or stretched tightly, and is not as tight as it should be: The chain on my bicycle is loose – it keeps slipping.

come loose (=gradually become looser) The string around the package had come loose and some of the papers had fallen out.

loosely [adv] a scarf tied loosely around his neck

slack /slæk/ [adj] a rope or chain that is **slack** is not stretched as tightly as it should be: Our tent ropes were too slack, and the tent blew over in the night.

loosen /'luːsən/ [v T] to make something loose when it has been pulled or fastened tightly: She loosened the reins so that the horse could lower its head and drink. | Carl leaned back in his chair and loosened his belt.

3 something that is not fixed firmly enough

loose /luːs/ [adj] something that is **loose** is not firmly fixed in the place where it should be: Some of the floorboards are loose and they creak when you walk on them. | a loose tooth

come loose (=gradually become looser) This door handle's come loose.

a loose connection (=when wires or electrical parts are not firmly connected)

wobbly /'wɒbli||'wɑː-/ [adj] something that is **wobbly** shakes or moves from side to side because it is not fixed as firmly as it should be: Don't sit on that chair – one of the legs is wobbly. | a wobbly ladder

4 to make something loose that has been firmly or tightly fixed

loosen /'luːsən/ [v T] to make something loose in order to remove it, for example a screw or lid that has been tightly fixed: *I couldn't open the jar, so Paul loosened the top for me.* | *These screws are all rusty. Squirt some oil on to loosen them.*

LOSE

➡ look here for ...
  • when you can't find something
  • not win a game, fight, or war
    lose your home, job etc
➡ if you mean 'when you do not know where you are', go to **LOST**

⚠ Don't confuse **lose** and **loose** (=not fitting tightly).

1 when you can't find something or someone
➡ opposite **FIND**
➡ see also **LOOK FOR, DISAPPEAR**

lose /luːz/ [v T] to be unable to find something, especially because you cannot remember where you put it: *If you lose your credit card, phone this number immediately.* | *Sylvia lost her keys and couldn't get into the house.*
losing – lost – have lost

can't find /ˌkɑːnt 'faɪnd‖ˌkænt-/ to be unable to find something or someone, especially after you have spent a long time looking for them: *She searched through all her pockets, but she couldn't find the tickets.* | *I don't know what's happened to Eric – I can't find him anywhere.*

2 something or someone that you cannot find
➡ see also **LOOK FOR, DISAPPEAR**

missing /'mɪsɪŋ/ [adj] a **missing** object is lost and may have been stolen; a **missing** person cannot be found and may be in danger: *Police are still searching for the*

missing gold. | *She's been missing for three days now, and we're very worried.*
+ from *Suddenly I realized that my passport was missing from my handbag.*
go missing (from) BRITISH (=become lost or be stolen) *Every year, hundreds of books go missing from the library.*

lost /lɒst‖lɔːst/ [adj] if something is **lost**, no-one knows where it is: *Divers are searching for the plane's lost flight recorder.* | *Have you seen my calculator? I hope it isn't lost.*
get lost *I never received your parcel. It must have got lost in the mail.*

disappear /ˌdɪsə'pɪər/ [v I] if something or someone **disappears**, they cannot be found and you think they may have been stolen or may be in danger: *I left my purse here a moment ago, and now it's completely disappeared.* | *The girl was wearing a red coat when she disappeared.*

3 when you do not win in a game, argument, or war
➡ opposite **WIN**
➡ see also **SPORT, FIGHT, WAR**

lose /luːz/ [v I/T] to lose a game, competition, fight, or war: *I always lose when I play tennis with my sister.*
lose a game/fight/election etc *Everyone expected Truman to lose the election.*
lose to sb (=be beaten by a person, team etc) *England lost to Brazil in the final.*
lose by 1 goal/10 votes/20 points etc *In the end, we only lost by one point!*
losing – lost – have lost

be beaten /biː 'biːtn/ to lose a game, competition, or race: *The Yankees were beaten yesterday in an exciting game against the Red Sox.*
+ by *She reached the final, where she was beaten by Steffi Graf.*

be defeated /biː dɪ'fiːtɪd/ to lose an important or difficult battle, election, or game: *The king's army was defeated and he was taken prisoner.*
+ by *Last night England was defeated by a superior Brazilian team.*

be heavily defeated (=be very badly defeated) *Jimmy Carter was heavily defeated in the 1980 presidential election.*

⚠ Be **defeated** is more formal than **be beaten**.

defeat /dɪˈfiːt/ [n C/U] when a person, team, or army is defeated in a game, competition, election, battle etc
+ of *the defeat of Napoleon at Waterloo*
a crushing/humiliating defeat (=when you are very badly defeated) *This result represents a humiliating defeat for the President.*

surrender /səˈrendəʳ/ [v I] to officially announce that you want to stop fighting in a war because you know that you cannot win: *Finally, after months of fighting, the enemy surrendered.*
+ to *In May 1945, Germany surrendered to the Allied Forces.*

4 someone who loses in a game, competition etc

loser /ˈluːzəʳ/ [n C] the person or group that has lost a game, competition, or election: *The losers walked slowly off the field.* | *There was a silver cup for the winners, and medals for the losers.*

5 to no longer have something important

lose /luːz/ [v T] to no longer have something important or valuable, such as your job or your home, because it has been destroyed or taken away from you: *Thousands of people lost their homes in the earthquake.* | *I'll lose my job if the factory closes.* | *Another bank closed, and thousands of people lost their savings.*

losing – lost – have lost

cost /kɒst‖kɔːst/ [v T] if a mistake, accident etc **costs** you something important such as your job or your health, you lose that important thing because of it
cost sb sth *Another mistake like that could cost you your job.* | *All this delay has cost the company an important contract.*

costing – cost – have cost

When you see **EC**, go to the **ESSENTIAL COMMUNICATION** section.

LOST
when you do not know where you are

➡ see also **FIND**

1 to be lost

be lost /biː ˈlɒst‖-ˈlɔːst/ to not know where you are, or not know the way to the place that you want to go to: *Excuse me, I'm lost. Which way is the station?* | *Eventually the children realized they were lost.*

not know where you are /nɒt nəʊ ˌweəʳ juː ˈɑːʳ/ if you do **not know where you are**, you do not recognize the place that you are in: *I really don't know where we are – let's have a look at the map.* | *He was so drunk he didn't know where he was.*

2 to become lost

get lost /ˌget ˈlɒst‖-ˈlɔːst/ *I'll give you a map so that you don't get lost.* | *Sorry we're so late. We got lost.*

lose your way /ˌluːz jɔːʳ ˈweɪ/ if you **lose your way**, you go in the wrong direction or take the wrong road when you are trying to go somewhere: *The climbers had lost their way in the dark.* | *If you lose your way, just stop and ask someone.*

LOT

➡ see also **ENOUGH/NOT ENOUGH, FEW, LITTLE/NOT MUCH**

1 a large number of people or things

a lot of /ə ˈlɒt ɒv‖-ˈlɑːt-/ [quantifier] a large number of people or things: *There were a lot of words that I didn't understand.* | *A lot of students have weekend jobs.*

a lot more *She has a lot more problems than you have.*

quite a lot of (=a fairly large number) *There are quite a lot of computers in the school.*

a lot *I was surprised that so few people went to the concert – I thought there'd be a lot.*

lots of /ˈlɒts ɒv‖ˈlɑːts-/ [quantifier] INFORMAL a lot of people or things: *I've invited lots of people.* | *We went to lots of interesting places.*

many /ˈmeni/ [quantifier] a lot of people or things – use this especially in questions and negatives: *Did you get many Christmas cards this year?* | *There will be rain in many parts of the country overnight.*
not many *Not many people survived the crash.*
too many *There are too many cars on the road.*
for many years *She worked as a reporter on CBS news for many years.*
many of (=many among a larger number) *Many of the houses were over 100 years old.*

⚠ It is usually more natural to use **a lot of** rather than **many** in positive sentences, especially in spoken English. Don't say 'she has many friends'. Say **she has a lot of friends**. In written English, **many** is used especially in phrases such as **in many ways/places/cases**, and **for many years**.

plenty of /ˈplenti ɒv/ [quantifier] a lot of people or things that you want or need, especially when there are more than enough: *There are plenty of parking spaces further along the road.* | *The town has plenty of good bars and restaurants.* | *We have plenty of glasses, but not enough plates.*
plenty *"Are there any tickets left for tonight's show?" "Yes, plenty."*

a large number of/large numbers of /ə ˌlɑːʳdʒ ˈnʌmbəʳ ɒv, ˌlɑːʳdʒ ˈnʌmbəʳz ɒv/ [quantifier] a lot of a particular type of person or thing – used especially in newspapers and official reports: *Police seized a large number of weapons.* | *Large numbers of demonstrators were arrested during today's protest march.*
in large numbers *Japanese cars were first sold in large numbers in the 1960s* (=a lot of them were sold) .

be full of /biː ˈfʊl ɒv/ if something **is full of** people or things, there are a lot of

them in it: *In summer the town is full of tourists.* | *Her essay was full of mistakes.*

hundreds of/thousands of /ˈhʌn-drɪdz ɒv, ˈθaʊzəndz ɒv/ [quantifier] a lot of things or people – use this when you want to emphasize that you are talking about a very large number: *Driving conditions are very bad and there have been hundreds of accidents.* | *Thousands of people came to see the carnival.*

⚠ You can use **hundreds of** or **thousands of** in informal spoken English to talk about a large number which is actually less than a hundred: *Steve's had thousands of girlfriends.*

🔍 **quite a few** /ˌkwaɪt ə ˈfjuː/ [quantifier] SPOKEN a fairly large number of people or things: *I still have quite a few friends in Denver – I used to be in college there.*

2 **a large amount of something**

a lot of /ə ˈlɒt ɒv‖-ˈlɑːt-/ [quantifier] a large amount of something: *There was a lot of water on the floor.* | *a book that contains a lot of useful information* | *We spent a lot of time just lying on the beach.*
a lot *It's a big house – it must have cost a lot.*
quite a lot of (=a fairly large amount of something) *There's quite a lot of work involved, but the research is interesting.*
a lot to do/see/eat etc *There's still a lot to do before the wedding.*
a lot more/less *Ask Susan – she knows a lot more than I do.*

lots of /ˈlɒts ɒv‖ˈlɑːts-/ [quantifier] INFORMAL a large amount of something: *Don't worry – we still have lots of time.* | *It's a big apartment, so there's lots of room for all my things.*
lots to do/see/eat etc *We're never bored here – there's lots to see and do.*

much /mʌtʃ/ [quantifier] a lot of something – use this in questions and negatives: *Does he speak much English?*
not much *I don't know much about cars.* | *I didn't get much help from my family.*
too much *Don't make too much noise.*

L

much of sth FORMAL (=a large part of it) *Much of the city was destroyed in the attack.*

⚠ Don't say 'he earns much money'. Say **he earns a lot of money**. Use **a lot of** when you are talking about an amount in a positive sentence. Don't say 'too much people/cars etc'. Say **too many people/ cars etc**. Only use **much** with uncountable nouns: *too much work*

a great deal of /ə ˌgreɪt ˈdiːl ɒv/ [quantifier] a large amount of something such as time, money, work, trouble, or skill: *The job requires a great deal of patience and skill.* | *The storm caused a great deal of damage.*

⚠ **A great deal of** is more formal than **a lot of**.

⚠ Don't use **a great deal of** to talk about physical objects or substances.

plenty of /ˈplenti ɒv/ [quantifier] a large amount of something, that you want or need: *There's plenty of hot water if you want a bath.* | *Don't worry – I have got plenty of money.*
plenty *No thanks, I couldn't eat any more – I've had plenty.*

be covered in sth /biː ˈkʌvəʳd ɪn (sth)/ if a person **is covered in** something, they have a lot of it on their skin, their clothes, or their hair; if an object **is covered in** something, it has a lot of that thing on its surface: *My shoes are covered in mud.* | *At the end of the fight he was covered in blood.*

3 when there is a lot of something in many places

common /ˈkɒmən‖ˈkɑː-/ [adj] if an object, animal, idea etc is **common**, there is a very large number of objects, animals etc of this type in many different places: *Jones is a very common name in Britain.* | *Flatheads are a common type of fish and good to eat.*
common belief / attitude / problem / mistake (=one that a lot of people have or make) *My younger brother says politics is boring, which is a common attitude among teenagers.* | *You confused 'lie' and 'lay'. It's a common mistake.*

widespread /ˈwaɪdspred/ [adj usually before noun] a **widespread** feeling or attitude is one that a lot of people have in many different places; a **widespread** problem has a bad effect over a wide area
widespread opposition/support/interest etc *There was already widespread public support for women's rights.*
widespread damage/flooding/poverty etc *The bombing caused widespread damage.*

4 very much
➡ see also **VERY**

a lot /ə ˈlɒt‖-ˈlɑːt/ [adv not before verb] very much: *She's changed a lot since she's been here.* | *"How does your arm feel?" "It still hurts a lot."*
a lot better/worse/bigger/more etc *Your car's a lot bigger than ours.* | *It was a lot more interesting than I expected.*

⚠ **A lot** is more informal than **very much** and is used more in conversation.

much /mʌtʃ/ [adv] **much better/worse/ bigger/more etc** a lot better, worse, bigger etc: *You get a much better view if you stand on a chair.* | *a much more expensive car*
much too big/old/tall etc *I can't wear that coat. It's much too big!* | *The test was much too difficult for most of the students.*

⚠ You can also use **much** after a verb in questions and negatives: *Has he changed much?* | *"Did you enjoy the show?" "Not much."*

⚠ Don't confuse **much** and **very**. Don't say 'they are much different'. Say **they are very different**.

really /ˈrɪəli/ [adv only before verb] ESPECIALLY SPOKEN very much – use this especially to talk about your feelings: *I really like your dress.* | *What really annoys me is the way he never apologises when he's late.*

very much /ˌveri ˈmʌtʃ/ [adv] use this especially to talk about people's feelings: *"Do you like living in Rome?" "Yes, very much."*

like/admire/miss sb very much *Lara enjoyed being at college, but she missed her family very much.*

like/enjoy sth very much *It was a wonderful show – we enjoyed it very much.*

⚠ Don't say 'I like very much this colour'. Say **I like this colour very much.**

a good deal /ə ˌgʊd ˈdiːl/ [adv] FORMAL very much – use this especially to talk about changes, improvements, or differences: *Her work has improved a good deal over the past year.*

a good deal better/worse/bigger/more etc *The situation was a good deal worse than we had first thought.*

enormously /ɪˈnɔːʳməsli/ [adv] very much, especially in a good or positive way: *Diana enjoyed herself enormously at the party.* | *The breakup of the Soviet Union was an enormously important event.*

⚠ **Enormously** is more formal than the other words in this section.

LOUD

➡ opposite **QUIET**
➡ see also **SOUND**

1 loud sounds, music, machines etc

loud /laʊd/ [adj] something that is **loud** makes a lot of noise: *The music's too loud. Can you turn it down?* | *We heard a loud explosion.* | *loud laughter coming from the next room*

loudly [adv] *Bill had dozed off in his chair, and was snoring loudly.*

⚠ In informal English, you can also use **loud** as an adverb after 'as', 'so', and 'too': *I wish you wouldn't talk so loud.* | *You're playing that music too loud.* | *I shouted as loud as I could.*

noisy /ˈnɔɪzi/ [adj] use this about places where there is a lot of noise, or about people and machines that make a lot of noise, especially when this annoys you: *The nightclub was crowded and noisy.* | *Our new neighbours are really noisy.* | *The car has a noisy engine.*

noisy – noisier – noisiest

deafening /ˈdefənɪŋ/ [adj] a noise that is **deafening** is so loud that you cannot hear anything else: *Outside there was a deafening crash of thunder.* | *The cheers of the crowd were deafening.*

at full volume /ət ˌfʊl ˈvɒljuːm‖ -ˈvɑːljəm/ if you play music or have the radio or television on **at full volume**, it is as loud as it can be: *He annoyed everyone by playing heavy metal music at full volume.*

2 a noise

noise /nɔɪz/ [n C/U] a loud sound, especially an unpleasant one: *Traffic noise is a problem in inner-city areas.* | *The noise of the machines made it hard to talk.*

make (a) noise *Don't make too much noise – Dad's trying to work.*

racket /ˈrækɪt/ [n singular] INFORMAL a loud unpleasant noise: *It's impossible to work with that racket going on.*

make a racket *I wish those kids would stop making such a racket upstairs.*

3 to make music, a radio, or a television louder

turn up /ˌtɜːʳn ˈʌp/ [phrasal verb T] to make music, a radio etc louder by turning a control

turn sth up *Can you turn the television up? I can't hear the news.*

turn up sth *We turned up the music, and we all started dancing.*

4 how loud something is

volume /ˈvɒljuːm‖ˈvɑːljəm/ [n U] how loud a television, radio etc is: *This button here controls the volume.*

turn the volume up/down (=make it louder or quieter) *You can use the remote control to turn the volume up or down.*

When you see **EC**, go to the **ESSENTIAL COMMUNICATION** section.

LOVE

➡ opposite HATE

SEX — RELATIONSHIP
MARRY — see also — FAMILY
LIKE/NOT LIKE — GIRLFRIEND/ BOYFRIEND

1 to love someone in a sexual way

love /lʌv/ [v T] to have a strong feeling of liking someone, caring about them, and being sexually attracted to them: *My boyfriend finds it difficult to say "I love you."* | *He was the only man she had ever loved.*
love sb very much *We love each other very much and we're going to get married.*

be in love /biː ɪn ˈlʌv/ to love someone very much, so that you think about them all the time and want to be with them all the time: *"What's the matter with Lois?" "She's in love."*
+ with *How can you marry Adam when you're in love with someone else?*
be madly in love/very much in love (=very strongly in love) *We were both seventeen and madly in love.*

fall in love /ˌfɔːl ɪn ˈlʌv/ to begin to be in love with someone: *I suddenly realized that I'd fallen in love.*
+ with *I think Susie's falling in love with your brother.*

be crazy about sb /biː ˈkreɪzi əˌbaʊt (sb)/ INFORMAL to love someone very much, especially in a way that you cannot control: *He's obviously crazy about you. Why don't you ask him out?*

fancy /ˈfænsi/ [v T] BRITISH SPOKEN to be sexually attracted to someone, especially someone that you do not know very well: *All the girls fancied Bob.* | *My friend really fancies you.*
fancying – fancied – have fancied

When you see **EC**, go to the
ESSENTIAL COMMUNICATION section.

2 to love your parents, children, brothers and sisters etc

love /lʌv/ [v T] to love someone in your family, so that you care a lot about what happens to them, and you want them to be happy: *When my parents got divorced I thought they didn't love me any more.* | *He loved his stepdaughter as if she were his own child.*

adore /əˈdɔːr/ [v T] to love and admire someone very much and feel very proud of them: *Branwell Brontë adored his sister Anne.* | *She adores her grandchildren and is always buying them presents.*

close /biː ˈkləʊs/ [adj not usually before noun] if two people are **close**, they enjoy being together and they understand each other's feelings and thoughts: *My sister and I used to argue a lot but now we're very close.* | *We have always been a close family.*
+ to *He's never been close to his family.*

3 a feeling of love

love /lʌv/ [n U] a feeling of love, either for someone that you are sexually attracted to, or for a member of your family: *All children need love, attention, and encouragement.*
+ for *She wrote him a letter revealing her love for him.*
love at first sight (=when you love someone in a romantic way the first time you see them) *As soon as I met Tracy it was love at first sight.*

affection /əˈfekʃən/ [n U] a gentle feeling of love for a friend or member of your family, which makes you want to be kind to them and show them that you love them: *These orphans have never been shown any affection in their lives.*
+ for *Alison and I had been at school together, and I felt great affection for her.*

4 showing love or making you feel love

affectionate /əˈfekʃənɪt/ [adj] someone who is **affectionate** shows that they are very fond of another person by the way they behave towards them, for example by holding or kissing them: *She was an affectionate child, always wanting to hold my hand or sit on my knee.* | *He gave me an affectionate hug and jumped onto the train.*

romantic /rəʊˈmæntɪk, rə-/ [adj] something that is **romantic** gives you a feeling of love for your boyfriend, girlfriend, husband, wife etc – use this about situations, places, or things people do or say: *We went for a romantic walk by the lake.* | *He sent me a dozen red roses – it was very romantic.*

5 a relationship between two people who love each other

relationship /rɪˈleɪʃənʃɪp/ [n C] when two people spend a lot of time together or live together because they love each other in a romantic or sexual way: *In the past his relationships had never lasted for more than a few months.* | *The relationship ended badly and they never saw each other again.*
+ with *I don't want to start a relationship with him because I'm going back to South Africa.*

affair /əˈfeəʳ/ [n C] a secret sexual relationship between two people, when one of them is married to someone else, or they are both married to other people: *The affair had been going on for years before her husband found out.*
have an affair with sb *I would leave him if he had an affair with anyone.*

romance /rəʊˈmæns, rə-/ [n C] an exciting and usually short relationship between two people who are very much in love: *It was impossible for the couple to keep their romance a secret.*
holiday romance BRITISH **summer romance** AMERICAN (=while you are on holiday) *She knew it was just a holiday romance but she couldn't forget him.*

⚠ **Romance** is often used in newspaper stories.

6 stories, films etc about love

romance/love story /rəʊˈmæns, ˈlʌv ˌstɔːri/ [n C] a story about two people who are in love with each other: *'Romeo and Juliet' is one of the world's most famous love stories.* | *a well-known writer of popular romances*
plural **love stories**

romantic /rəʊˈmæntɪk, rə-/ [adj] a **romantic** story or film is about people who are in love: *a romantic comedy in which Meg Ryan plays a single mother looking for love*

LOW

➡ look here for ...
• a low wall, table etc
• a low sound
• a low temperature, level etc
➡ opposite **HIGH**
➡ see also **DEEP, TALL**

1 not high or not far off the ground

low

A low wall surrounded the garden.

low /ləʊ/ [adj] *A low wall surrounded the garden.* | *Some of the lowest branches were touching the ground.* | *In the middle of the room was a low table.*
low [adv] in, to, or towards a low position: *The plane flew low over the fields.* | *We had to bend down low to get through the little door.*

2 a low sound/voice/ musical note

low /ləʊ/ [adj] a **low** voice or musical note is not high on the scale of musical sound:

I can't sing the low notes. | *Her singing voice was lower than I expected.*

deep /diːp/ [adj] a **deep** voice is low, strong, and pleasant: *The men's deep voices echoed from the room below.*

3 a low temperature/level/rate/cost

low /ləʊ/ [adj] smaller than usual in level or number: *the lowest temperature ever recorded* | *Japan has a much lower crime rate than other countries.* | *the recent low level of unemployment*

LUCKY/UNLUCKY

1 a lucky person

lucky /'lʌki/ [adj] if you are **lucky**, good things happen to you and things go well for you, because you have good luck and not because of hard work, careful planning etc: *Isn't she lucky – she can eat what she wants and she never gets fat.* | *There are monkeys and zebra, and if you're lucky you might see a lion.*

lucky to do sth *The doctors say I'm lucky to be alive.*

+ (that) *Arthur left the front door unlocked – we're lucky that nothing was stolen.*

lucky – luckier – luckiest

fortunate /'fɔːrtʃənət/ [adj] lucky, especially when you are luckier than other people: *David managed to escape, but the others were not so fortunate.*

fortunate to do sth *I was very fortunate to have such supportive parents.*

⚠ **Fortunate** is more formal than **lucky**.

with luck/with any luck /wɪð 'lʌk, wɪð ˌeni 'lʌk/ use this to say that you will do something or will succeed in something if you are lucky and have no problems: *With any luck, we should reach the coast before dark.*

2 a lucky thing that happens

lucky /'lʌki/ [adj] a **lucky** event happens because of good luck, and not because of

hard work, careful planning etc: *"How did you know he'd be there?" "It was a lucky guess."* | *Italy got a lucky goal in the last five minutes of the game.*

it is lucky (that) *It was lucky that the weather was so nice.*

fortunate /'fɔːrtʃənət/ [adj] lucky – use this especially about something that happens which saves you from danger or serious trouble: *a fortunate escape*

it is fortunate (for sb/sth) that *It is extremely fortunate that there was no-one in the building when the bomb went off.* | *It was fortunate for Roy that we found him so quickly – he could have drowned!*

⚠ **Fortunate** is more formal than **lucky**.

luckily/fortunately /'lʌkɪli, 'fɔːrtʃənətli/ [adv] because of good luck – use this when something dangerous or unpleasant is avoided as a result of good luck: *I had forgotten my key, but luckily Ahmed was there and let me in.* | *Fortunately, there was no-one in the office when the fire started.*

+ for *Luckily for us it didn't rain till the evening.*

⌒**it's a good thing** /ɪts ə ˌɡʊd 'θɪŋ/ SPOKEN say this when something lucky happens that saves you from experiencing problems or danger

+ (that) *It was a good thing we brought some sandwiches, because there was no food available on the train.*

fluke /fluːk/ [n singular] INFORMAL something very surprising that only happens because of luck, not because of your skill or planning: *I'll have to win more than once, otherwise people will think it was a fluke.*

3 something that makes you have good luck

luck/good luck /lʌk, ˌɡʊd 'lʌk/ [n U] the way that good things happen to someone by chance, not because of hard work, careful planning etc: *They played pretty well, but they also had a lot of good luck.*

bring sb (good) luck (=make someone have good luck) *Some people think black cats bring good luck.*

pure/sheer luck (=only luck, and nothing else) *"How did you guess the right answer?" "It was pure luck!"*

for luck (=in order to bring luck)

lucky /'lʌki/ [adj] something that is **lucky** seems to help you to have good luck or be successful: *My lucky number is seven. | I have a feeling today's going to be my lucky day.*

lucky charm (=a small object, piece of jewellery etc that someone carries with them to bring them good luck)

4 to tell someone you hope they will be lucky and successful

Qgood luck/best of luck /ˌgʊd 'lʌk, ˌbest əv 'lʌk/ SPOKEN say this to tell someone that you hope they will be lucky and successful: *Good luck Archie! Enjoy your new job.*

+ with/in *Best of luck with your driving test.*

Qkeep your fingers crossed /ˌkiːp jɔːʳ 'fɪŋgəʳz ˈkrɒst‖-ˌkrɔːst/ SPOKEN say this when you are hoping for good luck for yourself or for other people: *We're hoping Bill will be well enough to play in the next game – we're keeping our fingers crossed, anyway.*

+ for *She's having her operation tomorrow, so keep your fingers crossed for her.*

wish sb luck /ˌwɪʃ (sb) 'lʌk/ to tell someone that you hope they will be lucky or successful, when they are about to do something difficult: *Wish me luck – I'll need it for this French exam.*

+ in/with *Brian asked me to wish you luck in your interview.*

5 an unlucky person

unlucky /ʌn'lʌki/ [adj] if you are **unlucky**, bad things happen to you and things go badly for you, because you have bad luck and not for any other reason: *Val's been so unlucky recently – on Monday her car was stolen and the day after she fell and broke her arm. | "Were you disappointed with the team's performance?" "No, not really, I think we were just unlucky."*

unlucky to do sth *Maya was unlucky not to pass her practical examination – she only failed by 2%.*

unfortunate /ʌn'fɔːʳtʃənɪt/ [adj] unlucky, especially when you are not as lucky as other people: *Some of the unfortunate victims were trapped inside the building for over 12 hours.*

be unfortunate (enough) to do sth *Two drivers were unfortunate enough to be crossing the bridge when it collapsed.*

⚠ **Unfortunate** is more formal than unlucky.

6 an unlucky thing that happens

unlucky /ʌn'lʌki/ [adj] an **unlucky** event happens simply because of bad luck, not because of bad planning, carelessness, stupidity etc: *The car in front braked suddenly and I went straight into it – it was just unlucky.*

it is unlucky (for sb) that *It was unlucky for Steve that the teacher walked in just at that moment.*

unfortunate /ʌn'fɔːʳtʃənət/ [adj] unlucky – use this especially about something that causes a lot of harm or problems: *Quarterback Brady Anderson was injured in an unfortunate collision with one of his team-mates. | an unfortunate coincidence*

it is unfortunate (for sb) that *It was very unfortunate that the ambulance was held up by heavy traffic.*

⚠ **Unfortunate** is more formal than unlucky.

unfortunately /ʌn'fɔːʳtʃənətli/ [adv] because of bad luck – use this when something annoying, unpleasant, or dangerous happens as a result of bad luck: *I would have been here an hour ago, but unfortunately I missed the train.*

unfortunately for sb *Several trees were blown down and, unfortunately for us, one of them fell on our car.*

Qjust my luck /ˌdʒʌst maɪ 'lʌk/ SPOKEN INFORMAL say this when something bad or annoying happens to you, to show that you are not surprised because you

L

always unlucky: *"I'm sorry, we sold the last tickets ten minutes ago." "Just my luck."*

7 something that makes you have bad luck

bad luck /ˌbæd ˈlʌk/ [n U] the way that bad things happen to someone by chance, not because of bad planning, carelessness, stupidity etc: *It wasn't her fault she missed the plane – it was just bad luck.* | *Tina was injured in the first five minutes of the game, which was very bad luck.*

unlucky /ʌnˈlʌki/ [adj] something that is **unlucky** makes you have bad luck: *Friday the 13th is supposed to be an unlucky day.*

it is unlucky to do sth *Some people think it's unlucky to walk under ladders.*

8 what you say when someone is unlucky

bad luck/hard luck /ˌbæd ˈlʌk, ˌhɑːʳd ˈlʌk/ SPOKEN say this to show that you are sorry when someone has been unlucky, for example when they do not succeed in doing something: *"No, I didn't get that job, I'm afraid." "Oh, hard luck."*

9 believing in luck

superstitious /ˌsuːpəʳˈstɪʃəs, ˌsjuː-‖ˌsuː-/ [adj] someone who is **superstitious** believes that some objects or actions are lucky and others are unlucky: *Tom's very superstitious – he won't go out without his lucky bracelet.* | *I don't mind having Room 13. I'm not superstitious.*

L

MACHINE

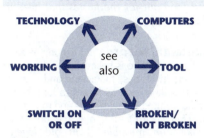

TECHNOLOGY   COMPUTERS

WORKING   ← see also → TOOL

SWITCH ON   BROKEN/
OR OFF   NOT BROKEN

1 a machine

machine /mə'ʃiːn/ [n C] a piece of equipment that does a particular type of work, either in your home or in a factory, office etc, using power from an engine or from electricity: *a machine that fills beer bottles* | *Nowadays machines do a lot of the jobs that people used to do.*
sewing/washing/fax machine (=a machine for sewing, washing clothes etc)
operate a machine (=make it work) *To operate the machine, select the drink you want and press the green button.*
by machine *The letters are sorted by machine.*

device /dɪ'vaɪs/ [n C] a piece of equipment that has been cleverly designed to do a particular job, for example one that makes measurements, records sounds or movements, or controls the operation of a machine: *An EEG is a device that records electrical activity in the brain.*
+ for *a thermostatic device for controlling temperature* | *The farmers there still use the 'Archimedes Screw', an ancient device for raising water from a lake or well.*
listening/measuring device *a listening device that enables you to hear when your baby is crying upstairs*

appliance /ə'plaɪəns/ [n C] FORMAL a piece of electrical equipment used in your home, such as a washing machine or TV: *The store sells a range of appliances and hi-fi equipment.*

domestic/household appliance *Their kitchen has all the latest domestic appliances – microwave, dishwasher etc.*

machinery /mə'ʃiːnəri/ [n U] machines in general, especially the large machines used in factories or on farms: *They are investing millions of dollars in new machinery for the factory.* | *a company that exports farm machinery*

robot /'rəʊbɒt‖-bɑːt, -bət/ [n C] a machine that is controlled by a computer and can do some of the complicated jobs that humans do, such as making things in a factory: *cars built by robots*

⚠ In stories and toys, robots are often made to look like humans (with arms, legs, heads, etc). But real industrial robots do not look like this.

2 a thing that produces power for a machine or vehicle

engine /'endʒɪn/ [n C] the part of a car, aircraft etc that produces the power that makes it move: *Every time I try to start the engine, there's a strange knocking sound.*
car/jet etc engine *The noise of the jet engines was deafening.*

motor /'məʊtər/ [n C] the part of a machine that makes it work or move, especially by using electrical power: *The lawnmower is powered by a small motor.*

3 connected with the way machines work

mechanical /mɪ'kænɪkəl/ [adj] using machines, or getting power from an engine: *They used a huge mechanical shovel to dig the foundations for the hotel.*
mechanical problem/fault/failure (=when a machine is not working properly) *Our ship had to return to port due to a mechanical problem.*
mechanically [adv] *Nowadays, the grape picking is all done mechanically.*

automatic /ˌɔːtə'mætɪk◄/ [adj] **automatic** machines, weapons etc are designed to operate by themselves, without much human control or attention: *A lot of* stores now have automatic doors. | We have an automatic time switch which makes the lights come on in the evening even when we're out.

automatically [adv] The doors open automatically when you go near them.

MAGIC

➡ see also **STRANGE THINGS AND EVENTS**

1 magic

magic /'mædʒɪk/ [n U] a secret power to make things happen or to do things that are normally impossible, by saying special words or doing special actions: In some villages, there were 'rainmakers', who used magic to bring rain. | people who believe in magic.

black magic (=using evil power) Several recent murders have been linked to a group practising black magic.

magic [adj only before noun] magic powers | The magic potion will make him fall in love with you.

witchcraft /'wɪtʃkrɑːft‖-kræft/ [n U] the use of magic to harm people and make bad things happen: At that time, hundreds of women were burned at the stake for witchcraft.

spell /spel/ [n C] special words, actions, plants, etc that are used in order to make something magic happen: a book of spells

put/cast a spell on sb (=make a spell that makes bad things happen to someone) The old man threatened to put a spell on the village and make the crops fail.

the occult /ði: 'ɒkʌlt‖-ə'kʌlt/ the study of spirits and magic, especially when this involves communicating with evil spirits: The major churches have always warned people against getting involved in the occult.

2 people with magic power

witch /wɪtʃ/ [n C] a woman who is believed to have magic power, which she uses especially to harm people or make bad things happen; in stories, witches are usually shown dressed in black with a tall,

pointed hat: In the story, Hansel and Gretel are captured by a wicked witch.

plural **witches**

fairy /'feəri/ [n C] an imaginary creature like a small person with wings, who has magic powers: When I was little I used to put food out for the fairies that lived in flowers.

plural **fairies**

magician/wizard /mə'dʒɪʃən, 'wɪzəᵈd/ [n C] a man who is believed to have magic power; in stories, magicians and wizards are usually shown as having a long beard and a pointed hat with stars and moons on it: The wizard's ring had the power to make him invisible. | an old legend about King Arthur and Merlin the magician

3 magic done as entertainment

magic /'mædʒɪk/ [n U] the skill of doing tricks that seem like magic, as a way of entertaining people: an evening of magic and comedy

trick /trɪk/ [n C] a skilful action that makes something happen which seems impossible, performed as entertainment

magic trick/conjuring trick She did a clever magic trick with a coin and a handkerchief.

card trick (=a trick done with playing cards)

magician/conjuror /mə'dʒɪʃən, 'kʌndʒərəᵈ‖'kɑːn-,'kʌn-/ [n C] someone who does magic tricks in order to entertain people: The children watched in amazement as the conjurer made the rings all disappear.

WORD BANK

MAIL, PHONE, AND FAX

➡ if you want to know what to say on the phone, go to **TALKING ON THE PHONE**

➡ see pages 470–473

When you see **EC**, go to the **ESSENTIAL COMMUNICATION** section.

MAKE

to produce something that was not there before

➡ see also **DO, INVENT, DESIGN**
➡ if you mean 'make someone do something', go to **FORCE SB TO DO STH**
➡ if you mean 'make a meal', go to **COOK**
➡ if you mean 'build a building', go to **BUILD**

1 to make something

make /meɪk/ [v T] to produce something which did not exist before: *Diana makes all her own clothes.* | *The furniture was made by a Swedish firm.* | *They've just finished making a movie about life during the Civil War.* | *My camera was made in Japan.*
made of (=made using a particular substance or material) *a bag made of leather*
made from (=made by putting together different materials, substances, and parts) *People were living in huts made from mud, stones, and straw.*
make sth from/out of sth (=use one thing to make something different) *a children's swing made out of an old tyre*
making – made – have made

produce /prə'djuːs‖-'duːs/ [v T] to make large quantities of food, equipment, or other goods by means of industrial processes, in order to sell them: *The dairy produces over 1500 tonnes of butter every year.* | *Japan produces and exports electronic goods all over the world.* | *a factory that produces high-quality steel*
production /prə'dʌkʃən/ [n U] when food, equipment, or other goods are made in large quantities, in order to be sold: *Crude oil is used in the production of plastics.* | *a big increase in grain production*

manufacture /ˌmænjʊˈfæktʃər/ [v T] to make machines, equipment, cars etc in factories: *The engines are manufactured in Portugal.* | *IBM manufactures and sells a wide range of computers.*

develop /dɪˈveləp/ [v T] to invent a new product, and gradually improve it so that it is ready to be produced and sold: *Scientists are developing new drugs to treat AIDS.* | *He helped to develop a well-known word-processing program.*

create /kriˈeɪt/ [v T] to invent something new and original in art, music, fashion etc: *Picasso created a completely new style of painting.* | *This dish was created by master chef Marco Pierre White.*

generate /ˈdʒenəreɪt/ [v T] to produce a lot of electricity, for example by burning gas, coal, oil etc in a special large building: *France generates a large part of its electricity from nuclear power.*

publish /ˈpʌblɪʃ/ [v T] to print a book, newspaper, or magazine and arrange for it to be sold: *The magazine is published four times a year.* | *He couldn't persuade anyone to publish his stories.* | *Darwin's famous book was first published in 1859.*

2 a company or country that makes something

producer /prəˈdjuːsər‖-ˈduː-/ [n C] a company or country that grows food or produces goods to be sold
oil/coffee/wine etc producer *Saudi Arabia is one of the world's biggest oil producers.*
+ of *She works for Toshiba, a leading producer of notebook computers.*

manufacturer /ˌmænjʊˈfæktʃərər/ [n C] a company that makes machines, equipment, cars etc in a factory: *Before you use the washing machine, read the manufacturer's instructions.*
car/aircraft/shoe etc manufacturer *a major weapons manufacturer*
+ of *Scantronic is a leading manufacturer of burglar alarms.*

publisher /ˈpʌblɪʃər/ [n C] a company that makes and prints books, newspapers, or magazines: *You can't make photocopies from this book unless you have permission from the publisher.*
+ of *a well-known publisher of educational books*

3 something that a company makes

product /ˈprɒdʌkt‖-ˈprɑː-/ [n C] something that a company makes in large quantities

MAKE continues on page 474

M

MAIL, PHONE, AND FAX

➡ see also **SEND, WRITE,** ◪ **TALKING ON THE PHONE**

1 communicate by mail, phone, or fax

get in touch with sb /ˌget ɪn 'tʌtʃ wɪð (sb)/ to write to someone or to speak to them on the telephone, especially someone you do not see very often or someone who is difficult to find: *I must get in touch with Lucy – I haven't spoken to her for ages.* | *They've been trying to get in touch with their daughter, but no-one knows where she is.*

contact /'kɒntækt‖'kɑːn-/ [v T] to write to, fax, e-mail, or telephone someone, in order to give or ask for important information: *If you need to contact me urgently, call me on my mobile phone.* | *Police are asking anyone who saw the accident to contact them.*

hear from sb /'hɪər frəm (sb)/ if you **hear from** someone, especially someone you know well, they write to you, or telephone you: *When was the last time you heard from Tina?* | *I haven't heard from her for a long time.*

> ⚠ **Hear from sb** is usually used in questions and negative sentences.
>
> ⚠ Don't use the word **communicate** when you are talking about writing, phoning, faxing etc a particular person. **Communicate** is usually used when you are talking generally about methods of exchanging information: *The Internet enables people to communicate with other computer users around the world.* | *How do birds communicate?*

2 mail

write /raɪt/ [v I/T] to write a letter to someone: *Write and let me know how you're getting on.*
write to sb *For further information write to Sam Carter at the BBC Helpdesk.*
write sb AMERICAN *I'll write you every day I'm away.*

write sb a letter *I wrote her several letters, but she never wrote back.*
write back (=reply to someone's letter)

send /send/ [v T] to arrange for a letter or package to be taken to another place by mail: *Have you sent all your Christmas cards yet?*
send sb a card/letter/present *My grandfather sent me a check for $100.*
send a card/letter to sb *He sent a postcard to Helen while he was in France.*

the mail ESPECIALLY AMERICAN **the post** BRITISH /ðə 'meɪl, ðə 'pəʊst/ the system for carrying letters and packages from one place to another: *There must be a problem with the mail. I sent her two letters last week and she didn't get either of them.*
be in the mail/post (=when something has already been sent by mail, but has not yet arrived) *Your photos are in the mail.*
by mail/post (=using the mail system) *You can apply for a new passport by post.*

mail ESPECIALLY AMERICAN **post** BRITISH /meɪl, pəʊst/ [v T] to send a letter or package using the mail system: *Did you remember to post that letter?*
mail/post sth to sb *George mailed his resumé to over 30 companies, but none of them wrote back.*
mail/post sb sth *I posted Margaret the cheque last Friday.*

address /ə'dres‖'ædres/ [n C] the number of the building and the name of the street and town where someone lives: *"What's their address?" "3317 Ellesmere Court, Walnut Creek 94598."*

post code BRITISH **zip code** AMERICAN /'pəʊst kəʊd, 'zɪp kəʊd/ [n C] the letters or numbers that show the exact area where a house is, so that letters can be delivered more quickly: *"What's your post code?" "N4 6XJ."*

3 e-mail

e-mail /'iː meɪl/ [n U] a system that lets you send a message directly from your computer to someone else's computer
be on e-mail (=have the necessary equipment to send and receive e-mail messages)

MAIL, PHONE, AND FAX

e-mail /'iː meɪl/ [n C] a message you send using e-mail: *"Does Glennis know about it?" "Yes, I sent her an e-mail."*

e-mail number/e-mail address /'iː meɪl ˌnʌmbəʳ, əˌdres‖-'ædres/ [n C] the letters and numbers that you type into the computer to send a message to a particular person using e-mail *What's Sylvia's e-mail number?*

e-mail /'iː meɪl/ [v T] to send someone a message by e-mail: *Will you e-mail me the date of the next meeting?*

message /'mesɪdʒ/ [n C] what you write and send to someone by e-mail: *When I got back from vacation there were 50 messages on my e-mail!*

4 fax

fax /fæks/ [n C] a letter, picture etc that is sent electronically down a telephone line using a fax machine and is then printed at the place that it has been sent to.
send a fax *He sent a fax to Mr McGee saying that he was resigning.*

fax /fæks/ [v T] to send someone a fax
fax sb sth *I'll fax you a map so you know how to get here.*
fax sth to sb *Can you fax these files to the Tokyo office?*

fax machine also **fax** /'fæks məˌʃiːn, fæks/ [n C] a machine that sends and receives faxes

fax number /'fæks ˌnʌmbəʳ/ [n C] the number that you use to fax someone
by fax *I'll send you the details by fax.*

5 phone

M

vocabulary

answering machine (also **answerphone** BRITISH) /'ɑːnsərɪŋ məˌʃiːn, 'ɑːnsəʳfəʊn‖'æn-/ [n C] a machine that answers your phone when you are out and lets people record messages so that you can listen to them later: *Chris wasn't in, so I left a message on his answering machine.* | *When I went out, I forgot to switch the answerphone on.*

answer the phone/telephone /ˌɑːnsəʳ ðə 'fəʊn, 'telɪfəʊn‖'æn-/ to pick up the receiver because the phone is ringing: *Could you answer the phone, Rob? I'm in the shower!*

busy AMERICAN **engaged** BRITISH /'bɪzi, ɪn'geɪdʒd/ [adj] if someone's phone is **busy** or **engaged**, you cannot speak to them because they are already having a phone conversation with someone else
it is busy/engaged *Every time I call Bob, it's always busy.* | *"Did you ring Melissa?" "I tried, but it was engaged."*

call /kɔːl/ [v I/T] to phone someone: *I'll call you tomorrow.*

call/phone call /kɔːl, 'fəʊn kɔːl/ [n C] when someone phones someone else: *Were there any calls for me while I was out?*
make a call/phone call *Can I use your phone – I need to make a quick call.*
give sb a call SPOKEN (=phone someone) *I'll give you a call at the weekend.*

MAIL, PHONE, AND FAX continues on the next page

MAIL, PHONE, AND FAX

❷ Jason **picks up the phone**......

I tried to call her this morning, but it was busy. Then I tried her mobile phone, but it wasn't switched on. I'll give her a call now. What's her phone number?

I don't know. Look in the phone book.

Ring! Ring!

I think I'll turn my cell phone off in case that's Jason trying to call me.

❸ Jason gets a **wrong number**.

Hi, Nina.

❹ The phone rings in Nina's house. Nina **answers** it.

Ring! Ring!

M

---

call back/phone back /ˌkɔːl ˈbæk, ˌfəʊn ˈbæk/ [*phrasal verb* I/T] to phone someone who has phoned you earlier, especially when you were out: *Has Bill phoned back yet?*
call sb back/phone sb back *Ian called while you were out. I said you'd phone him back.*

cellular phone (also **cell phone**) /ˈseljʊləʳ ˌfəʊn, ˈsel ˌfəʊn/ [*n* C] ESPECIALLY AMERICAN a phone that you can carry with you and use anywhere

hang up /ˌhæŋ ˈʌp/ [*phrasal verb* I] to finish a phone conversation by putting the receiver down: *'I'll call you again tomorrow,' she said, and hung up.*
hang up on sb (=put the receiver down before they have finished speaking)

leave the phone off the hook /ˌliːv ðə ˌfəʊn ɒf ðə ˈhʊk/ to not put the receiver on the phone, so

that people cannot phone you

message /ˈmesɪdʒ/ [*n* C] a piece of information that you ask someone to give to another person, when it is not possible to speak to that person directly
leave a message (=give a message to someone who answers the phone, or to an answering machine) *"Bill called when you were out." "Oh, did he leave a message?"*
⊙**can I take a message** SPOKEN (what you say when someone asks to speak to someone who is not available) *I'm afraid Martha's not home right now. Can I take a message?*

mobile phone (also **mobile** BRITISH) /ˌməʊbaɪl ˈfəʊn, ˈməʊbaɪl/ [*n* C] a phone that you can carry with you and use anywhere

phone /fəʊn/ [*v* I/T] to speak to someone using the

MAIL, PHONE, AND FAX

⑤ Nina **hangs up** on him.

Hi, Nina. It's Jason.

⑥ Jason **puts the phone down**. Nina **leaves the phone off the hook**.

She says she loves me.

M

telephone: *Has Anna phoned yet?* | *I'll phone you when I get to the airport.*

⚠ Don't say 'I phoned to Mary'. Say I **phoned Mary**.

phone book /'fəʊn bʊk/ [n C] a printed book containing the names, addresses, and phone numbers of the people who live in an area

phone number/telephone number /'fəʊn ˌnʌmbəʳ, 'telɪfəʊn ˌnʌmbəʳ/ [n C] the number that you use to phone a person or organization: *Do you know Rachel's phone number?*

pick up the phone /ˌpɪk ʌp ðə 'fəʊn/ to lift up your telephone receiver

put the phone down /ˌpʊt ðə 'fəʊn daʊn/ to put the receiver back onto the phone

receiver /rɪ'siːvəʳ/ [n C] the part of the phone that you pick up and speak into

ring /rɪŋ/ [v I] if the phone **rings**, it makes a sound to show that someone is phoning you

voice mail /'vɔɪs meɪl/ [n U] an electronic system on your phone that lets you leave messages for people who phone you when you are not available, and lets them leave messages for you

wrong number /ˌrɒŋ 'nʌmbəʳǁˌrɔːŋ-/ [n C] a number that is not the one you intended to call
  get a wrong number (=call someone that you did not intend to call, because you used an incorrect number)

MAKE continued from page 469

in order to sell it: *a new range of skin-care products* | *There was a ban on meat pies, gelatine, and other British beef products.*

4 made by a person, not a machine

homemade /ˌhəʊmˈmeɪd◄/ [adj] use this about food and drinks that are made at home, not in a factory: *Try one of these homemade cookies – they're delicious.* | *a bowl of homemade soup*

handmade /ˌhændˈmeɪd◄/ [adj] use this about furniture, clothes etc that are made by skilled workers, not by machines in a factory: *The shoes are expensive – they're handmade.* | *a beautiful handmade rug*

5 when a natural process makes something

form /fɔːʳm/ [v T] if a natural process or chemical reaction **forms** something, it makes it, especially when this happens over a period of time: *Hydrogen and oxygen combine to form water.* | *These rocks were formed millions of years ago.*

produce /prəˈdjuːs‖-ˈduːs/ [v T] if a natural process or a part of your body **produces** a substance, it makes it, usually for a particular purpose: *The stomach produces acids which help to digest food.* | *Carbon dioxide is produced during respiration.*

6 to be made of several different parts

consist of sth/be made up of sth /kənˈsɪst ɒv (sth), biː ˌmeɪd ˈʌp ɒv (sth)/ [phrasal verb T] if something **consists of** or is **made up of** different substances, parts, people etc, it has those things in it: *The spaghetti sauce consists of meat, onions, tomatoes, garlic, and herbs.* | *The image on a computer screen is made up of thousands of tiny dots.* | *a small committee, consisting of the Principal and four senior teachers*

When you see **EC**, go to the **ESSENTIAL COMMUNICATION** section.

MAN

➡ if you mean 'the man someone is married to', go to **MARRY**

1 a man

man /mæn/ [n C] an adult male person: *There were two men and a woman in the car.* | *Henry is a very rich man.* | *You wouldn't understand how she feels – you're a man!*
plural **men**

guy /gaɪ/ [n C] SPOKEN a man: *Dave's a really nice guy.* | *Is he the guy who used to live next door to you?*

bloke /bləʊk/ [n C] BRITISH SPOKEN a man: *Are you seeing this bloke again then?* | *He bought the car from a bloke at his office.*

gentleman /ˈdʒentlmən/ [n C] a man – use this as a polite way of talking about a man: *Can you serve that gentleman please, Sarah?* | *Mr Marks, an elderly gentleman, was travelling with his daughter.*
plural **gentlemen**

male /meɪl/ [adj] a **male** person is a man – use this especially when talking about jobs and work: *Most of the science teachers are male.*
male nurse/teacher/colleague etc *Salaries have increased for both male and female graduates.*

2 for men, or typical of men

male /meɪl/ [adj only before noun] for men or typical of men – use this about jobs or activities that men do, or about behaviour or attitudes that are typical of men: *More women are entering traditionally male jobs like engineering.* | *male aggression*

man's /mænz/ designed for men

a man's watch/suit/shirt etc *She was barefoot and wearing a man's shirt over her jeans.*

men's shoes/clothes/magazines etc *a shop selling handmade men's shoes*

manly /'mænli/ [adj] having the qualities that people admire in men, for example being strong and brave: *Her brother was tall and athletic, with a deep, manly voice.*

manly – manlier – manliest

macho /'mætʃəʊ‖'maː-/ [adj] a **macho** man behaves in a way that he thinks men are expected to behave, for example by doing dangerous things, by not showing his emotions, and by treating women as if they are not important: *He thinks he's too macho to put a sweater on, even when it's really cold.* | *Katie was getting tired of his macho attitudes.*

MANAGER

POSITION/RANK

BUSINESS   SHOP

see also

COMPANY   WORK

IN CHARGE OF   JOB

1 a manager

manager /'mænɪdʒəʳ/ [n C] someone whose job is to run one of the departments of a large organization, or to be in charge of a bank, shop, hotel etc: *I'd like to speak to the manager.*

bank/hotel/restaurant etc manager *He's a hotel manager. He has to work incredibly hard.*

marketing/sales/accounts etc manager *She's one of our regional sales managers.*

+ of *the advertising manager of a mail-order company*

> ⚠ Don't call someone 'manager' when you are talking or writing to them.

boss /bɒs‖bɔːs/ [n C] the person who is in charge of you at work: *Does your boss know you're looking for another job?* | *There's a new guy at work who's always trying to impress the boss.*

> ⚠ Boss is not an official name of a job and is not used in people's job titles.

foreman /'fɔːʳmən/ [n C] someone who is in charge of a group of factory workers or builders, whose job is to make sure that the workers do what the manager wants: *Anton hated the foreman, who was never satisfied with anyone's work.*

plural **foremen**

supervisor /'suːpəʳvaɪzəʳ, 'sjuː-‖'suː-/ [n C] someone who is in charge of a group of workers, such as cleaners or secretaries, in an office, factory, airport etc, whose job is to make sure that the workers do what the manager wants: *We still need to replace the office supervisor.*

deputy /'depjᵿti/ [n C] someone who does the manager's job when the manager is not there

deputy director/manager/principal etc *He became the deputy head of the FBI at the age of only 36.*

plural **deputies**

2 a top manager

director /dᵻ'rektəʳ, daɪ-/ [n C] one of the most important managers, especially the person who is in charge of one of the main departments: *The directors are meeting today to discuss the company's future.*

managing director BRITISH (=the person in charge of running an organization) *He's the managing director of a small printing firm.*

finance/sales/personnel etc director *Have you met the new finance director?*

+ of *Dr Jane Wilde, director of the Health Promotion Agency*

chief executive (also **chief executive officer/CEO** AMERICAN) /,tʃiːf ɪg'zekjᵿtɪv, ,tʃiːf ɪg'zekjᵿtɪv ,ɒfᵻsəʳ, ,siː iː 'əʊ‖-,ɑːf-, -,ɑːf-/ [n C] the top manager of a large company or organization, who is responsible for the whole business: *Universal Studios is looking for a new chief executive.*

+ of *the CEO of General Motors*

M

⚠️ The **chief executive** of a company makes the most important decisions, and does most of the planning. The **chairman** or **president** is responsible for the whole of the organization, and has the power to tell the **chief executive** what to do. Sometimes both jobs can be done by the same person: *He was the chairman and chief executive of a computer company.*

president /'prezɪdənt/ [n C] the most important person in a large company or organization, especially in the US: *Angry shareholders called for the resignation of the company president.*
+ of *the president of CBS news*

chairman /'tʃeəʳmən/ [n C] the most important person in a large company or organization, especially in Britain
+ of *Brian Cuthbertson was the chairman of the Associated Life Insurance Company.*
plural **chairmen**

⚠️ When the most important person in a company or organization is a woman, she can be called **chairman** or **chairwoman**.

head /hed/ [n C] the person in charge of an organization or department
+ of *the former head of MI5, the British Intelligence Service* | *She's the head of research and development.*

⚠️ **Head** is not usually used in official job titles.

the management /ðə 'mænɪdʒmənt/ [n singular] the people who are managers in an organization, not the ordinary workers: *Talks between the workers and the management broke down today.*

⚠️ In British English, you can use **the management** with a singular or plural verb: *The management has worked/have worked extremely hard to improve working conditions.* In American English, always use a singular verb.

the board /ðə 'bɔːʳd/ [n singular] the group of top managers in a company who meet regularly to make the most important decisions: *Carmichael was appointed to the board in July.*

the board of directors *There are only two women on the company's board of directors.*

⚠️ In British English, you can use **the board** with a singular or plural verb: *The board has appointed/have appointed a new Sales Director.* In American English, always use a singular verb.

3 the job of being a manager

management /'mænɪdʒmənt/ [n U] the job or skill of being a manager: *Val has finished college and is looking for a job in management.*
good/bad management *The failure of many small businesses is caused by bad management.*

⚠️ You can also use **management** before a noun, like an adjective: *a management training course*

managerial /ˌmænɪ'dʒɪəriəl◄/ [adj only before noun] connected with being a manager – use this about the jobs that managers do or the skills that they need
managerial job/skills/ability etc *This is her first managerial job.*

MARK

CLEAN — DIRTY

see also

WASH — DAMAGE

SPOIL

1 a mark on something that spoils its appearance

mark /maːʳk/ [n C] a spot or line on clothes, furniture, a wall, or floor etc, for example where it has been damaged,

mark

There was a mark on his new T-shirt

made dirty, or where someone has dropped liquid on it: *There are marks on the door where the cat has scratched it.*

dirty/greasy/sticky mark *How did you get that dirty mark on your T-shirt?*

stain /steɪn/ [n C] a large mark that is difficult to remove, made when a liquid such as coffee or wine falls onto something: *I can't get this stain out of the carpet.*

grass/coffee/wine/blood etc stain *Salt is the best remedy for a red wine stain.*

> **stained** [adj] with a stain on it: *She pushed the crumpled, stained sheets into the washing-machine.*
>
> **+ with** *His clothes were torn and stained with blood.*

spot /spɒt‖spɑːt/ [n C] a small round area on a surface, which is of a different colour from the rest of the surface and is made especially by drops of liquid: *There were grease spots on the front of his shirt.*

+ of *Detectives found a few spots of blood on the carpet.*

patch /pætʃ/ [n C] ESPECIALLY BRITISH an area where dirt, water, oil etc has made a mark on a floor, wall, or ceiling

greasy/dirty/damp patch *There's a damp patch under the window.*

patch of dirt/damp/grease *Patches of grease covered the kitchen walls.*

plural **patches**

smudge /smʌdʒ/ [n C] a dirty mark made when ink or paint is accidentally rubbed on a surface: *You can't hand your homework in with those smudges all over it.*

smudge

The ink was smudged.

+ of *Ella had a smudge of green paint on her cheek.*

2 to make a mark

stain /steɪn/ [v T] to make a large mark on something, which is difficult to remove: *The blackberry juice had stained their clothes and fingers.* | *Careful with your wine! If you spill it, it'll stain the carpet.*

mark /mɑːrk/ [v T] to damage the surface of something by making a mark on it: *Don't put that hot pan down – it'll mark the table.*

leave a mark/leave a stain /ˌliːv ə ˈmɑːrk, ˌliːv ə ˈsteɪn/ to make a mark or stain on something, often without realizing you have done this

+ on *The children walked through the kitchen in their boots, leaving muddy marks on the floor.* | *The chocolate sauce has left a stain on your shirt.*

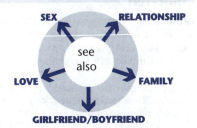

MARRY

SEX　　　　RELATIONSHIP

see also

LOVE　　　　FAMILY

GIRLFRIEND/BOYFRIEND

1 to get married

get married /ˌget ˈmærɪd/ to officially become husband and wife: *Jenny and Tom were very young when they got married.* | *My daughter's getting married in July.*

+ to *Is he getting married to Sophie at last?*

> ⚠ Don't say 'she got married with him'. Say **she got married to him**.

marry /ˈmæri/ [v T] to get married to someone: *Will you marry me?* | *She married an American guy that she met on vacation.*

marrying – married – have married

remarry /ˌriːˈmæri/ [v I] to get married again: *My mother died when I was very young and my father never remarried.*

remarrying – remarried – have remarried

2 the relationship of marriage

marriage /ˈmærɪdʒ/ [n C/U] the relationship between two people who are married: *She already has two children from a previous marriage.* | *Do you think marriage is still important to young people?*

M

+ to *Her marriage to Captain Phillips ended in divorce.*

a happy/unhappy marriage *Arnold's parents had had an unhappy marriage, which affected him deeply.*

a broken marriage (=a marriage that has ended) *It's the children who suffer in broken marriages.*

3 ceremonies, celebrations etc when people get married

wedding /'wedɪŋ/ [n C] an official ceremony at which two people get married, especially a religious ceremony: *I first met Jake at my cousin's wedding.*

> ⚠ You can also use **wedding** before a noun, like an adjective: *wedding photos* | *a lovely silk wedding dress* | *There were over 200 people at their wedding reception.* (=the party after the wedding)

honeymoon /'hʌnimuːn/ [n C] a holiday that two people go on when they have just got married: *We're thinking of going to Barbados for our honeymoon.*

bachelor party/stag party /'bætʃələr ˌpɑːrti, 'stæg ˌpɑːrti/ [n C] AMERICAN a party for a man and his male friends just before he gets married

stag night /'stæg ˌnaɪt/ [n C] BRITISH a party for a man and his male friends just before he gets married

bridal shower/wedding shower /'braɪdl ˌʃaʊər, 'wedɪŋ ˌʃaʊər/ [n C] AMERICAN a party for a woman and her female friends just before she gets married, when her friends give her gifts

hen night/hen party /'hen ˌnaɪt, 'hen ˌpɑːrti/ [n C] BRITISH a party for a woman and her female friends just before she gets married

4 people at a wedding

bride /braɪd/ [n C] the woman who is getting married: *Everyone turned to look at the bride as she came into the church.*

groom/bridegroom /gruːm, 'braɪdgruːm/ [n C] the man who is getting married: *a photo of the bride and groom together*

bridesmaid /'braɪdzmeɪd/ [n C] a woman or girl who helps the woman who is getting married on the day of her wedding: *The bridesmaids will be wearing long pink dresses.*

best man /ˌbest 'mæn/ [n singular] a male friend of the man who is getting married, who helps him on the day of his wedding: *Tony has asked me to be best man.*

5 to agree to get married

engaged /ɪn'geɪdʒd/ [adj not before noun] if two people are **engaged**, they have agreed to get married to each other at some time in the future

be engaged *Todd and Ellen have been engaged for about 3 months now.*

+ to *He's engaged to Paul's sister.*

get engaged (=become engaged) *We got engaged at Christmas.*

> ⚠ Don't say 'she got engaged with him'. Say **she got engaged to him**.

engagement /ɪn'geɪdʒmənt/ [n C] an agreement by two people to get married at some time in the future

announce your engagement (=tell everyone that you are going to get married) *Glennis and John announced their engagement yesterday.*

break off your engagement (=say that you do not want to be engaged any more) *Anita broke off her engagement when she found out that Paulo had been seeing another woman.*

engagement ring *Has he bought you an engagement ring yet?*

fiancé/fiancée /fi'ɒnseɪ‖ˌfiːɑːn'seɪ/ [n C] the man or woman that you are going to get married to: *I'd like you to meet Janice, my fiancée.* | *She didn't know Henry was Marie's fiancé.*

6 married

married /'mærɪd/ [adj] *Are you married or single?* | *Phil and I have been married for 15 years.*

+ to *She's married to a famous actor.*

married man/woman *a married man with three children*

> ⚠ Don't say 'married with someone'. Say **married to someone**.

wife /waɪf/ [n C] the woman that a man is married to: *Would you and your wife like to come over for dinner on Friday?* | *The men had gone out for the day, leaving their wives and children at home.*
plural **wives**

husband /'hʌzbənd/ [n C] the man that a woman is married to: *I don't like Francesca's husband very much.* | *Brian is her second husband.*

partner /'pɑːrtnər/ [n C] the person that someone lives with in a romantic relationship – use this whether they are married or not: *Can people bring their partners to the office party?*

couple /'kʌpəl/ [n C] two people who are married to each other, or who are having a romantic relationship: *The hotel is very popular both with families and with couples.* | *At one table there was an elderly couple who sat in total silence.*
married couple *They had come to live in England when they were a young married couple, in 1949.*

7 not married

not married /ˌnɒt 'mærɪd/ [adj] *He told her he wasn't married, but he was lying.* | *Jeff and Paula have two children, but they're not actually married.*

single /'sɪŋɡəl/ [adj] someone who is **single** is not married or is not in a romantic relationship with anyone: *a change in the tax laws for single people* | *I used to go out a lot more when I was single.*
single parent (=someone who has children, but who does not live with their partner) *It is extremely difficult being a single parent.*

unmarried /ˌʌn'mærɪd◄/ [adj] an **unmarried** person is someone who has never been married: *She has three unmarried sons.*

⚠ You may also see the words **bachelor** (=a man who has never been married) and **spinster** (=a woman who has never been married), but these words are rather old-fashioned.

8 not married any more

divorced /dɪ'vɔːrst/ [adj] someone who is **divorced** has officially ended their

marriage: *He's living with a divorced woman and her two children.*
be divorced *Yes, she used to be married, but she's been divorced since last year.*
get divorced (=officially end your marriage) *They got divorced only three years after they got married.*

divorce /dɪ'vɔːrs/ [n C/U] the legal process of ending a marriage: *She told me she wanted a divorce!* | *A third of all marriages in Britain end in divorce.*
get a divorce *It's much too easy to get a divorce nowadays.*

divorcee /dɪˌvɔːr'siː/ [n C] someone who is divorced, especially a woman

ex-husband/ex-wife /ˌeks 'hʌzbənd, ˌeks 'waɪf/ [n C] the man or woman that you used to be married to before getting divorced: *His ex-wife never lets him see the children.*

be separated /biː 'sepəreɪtɪd/ if a husband and wife **are separated**, they do not live with each other, because they are not happy together any more, but they are not divorced: *I didn't know Linda and Mike were separated.*

split up /ˌsplɪt 'ʌp/ [phrasal verb I] INFORMAL if two people **split up**, they end their marriage or they stop having a romantic relationship: *They're always arguing but I don't think they'll ever split up,*
+ with *Have you heard? Katie's splitting up with Andrew!*

widow /'wɪdəʊ/ [n C] a woman whose husband has died, and who has not got married again: *Mr Jarvis died suddenly, leaving a widow and four children.*

widower /'wɪdəʊər/ [n C] a man whose wife has died, and who has not got married again: *He's been a widower for eight years now.*

9 connected with people who are married

married life /ˌmærɪd 'laɪf/ [n U] your life as a married person: *After 30 years of married life, she couldn't imagine being on her own.*

marital /'mærɪtl/ [adj only before noun] FORMAL use this about problems that people have in their marriage
marital problems/violence/difficulties/breakdown *Their marital problems*

M

began when Martha lost her job. | Marital breakdown can have a devastating effect on the children.

marital status /ˌmærɪ̩tl ˈsteɪtəs‖-ˈsteɪtəs, -ˈstæ-/ [n singular] whether you are married, single, or divorced

> ⚠ **Marital status** is used especially on official forms: *Name: John Thorpe. Age: 26. Marital status: Single.*

marriage certificate /ˈmærɪdʒ səʳˌtɪfɪkət/ [n C] an official document that proves you are married

MATERIAL

any solid or liquid substance

1 material

substance /ˈsʌbstəns/ [n C] a type of solid or liquid, such as a chemical, a mineral, or something produced by a plant or tree: *Poisonous substances should be clearly labelled.* | *The animal's horns contain a substance called keratin.* | *Resin is a dark, sticky substance.* | *radioactive substances*

material /məˈtɪəriəl/ [n C/U] any solid substance that can be used for making things: *Steel is a stronger material than iron.* | *The company supplies building materials such as bricks and cement.* | *The wire is covered by an insulating material such as plastic.*

◯stuff /stʌf/ [n U] INFORMAL, ESPECIALLY SPOKEN a substance: *What's this sticky stuff on the floor?* | *Do you have any of that clear plastic stuff to cover food with?*

2 material for making clothes, curtains etc
➡ see **CLOTHES, DESIGN**

material /məˈtɪəriəl/ [n C/U] cloth used for making clothes or curtains, covering furniture etc: *She was wearing a long black dress of some silky material.*
dress/curtain material *Could I have six metres of that curtain material?*

fabric /ˈfæbrɪk/ [n C/U] cloth, especially cloth with different colours or patterns on

it: *I want to buy some fabric to make a skirt.* | *Man-made fabrics such as polyester are easy to wash and iron.*

cloth /klɒθ‖klɔːθ/ [n U] the substance that clothes are made from: *fine woollen cloth for making men's suits*

textiles /ˈtekstaɪlz/ [n plural] cloth for making clothes, curtains etc – use this for talking about the business of producing and selling cloth: *They make most of their money by exporting textiles.*

> ⚠ You can use **textile** before a noun, like an adjective: *textile workers* | *a large, up-to-date textile industry*

MAYBE

when you think something may happen or may be true, but you are not sure

➡ see also **SURE/NOT SURE, POSSIBLE, PROBABLY**

maybe/perhaps /ˈmeɪbi, pəʳˈhæps/ [adv] use this when you think that something may happen or may be true, but you are not sure: *"Are you going to the party?" "I don't know, maybe."* | *I wonder why she's late – maybe she missed the train.* | *The footprints belonged to a large cat, a tiger, perhaps.* | *Perhaps it would be better if you left now.*
maybe not/perhaps not *"It's not her fault that she can't get a job." "Well, maybe not, but she should make a little more effort."*

> ⚠ **Maybe** is more informal than **perhaps**. Use **maybe** in conversation or stories, but not in formal letters or reports.

may/might/could /meɪ, maɪt, kəd; *strong* kʊd/ [modal verb] use this with other verbs, to show that something is possible or likely, but you are not sure about it: *Take your umbrella – it might rain.* | *Hundreds of workers may lose their jobs if the strike continues.* | *We could be home before midnight if the traffic isn't too bad.*
may/might/could have done sth *"Bruce isn't here yet." "He may have decided not to come."*

> ⚠️ **Could** is more informal than **may** and **might**.

it is possible (that)/there is a chance (that) /ɪt ɪz 'pɒsɪbəl (ðæt), ðeəᵊz ə 'tʃɑːns (ðæt)‖-'pɑːs-, -'tʃæns/ use this when you think that something may happen or may be done, but that it is not very likely: *I might have to work on Saturday, so it's possible I won't be able to come to your party.*

it is just possible (that)/there is just a chance (that) (=when something is possible, but very unlikely) *There's just a chance that she left her keys in the office.* | *It's just possible we'll finish the job by tonight, but it'll probably be tomorrow.*

possibly /'pɒsɪbli‖'pɑː-/ [adv] use this when you think that something may be true, but you do not have enough information to be sure: *"Do you think she was murdered, inspector?" "Possibly."* | *He's playing in the US Open Golf Championships – possibly for the last time.* | *The cancer was possibly caused by exposure to asbestos.*

you never know /juː ˌnevər 'nəʊ/ SPOKEN say this when you are not sure whether something will happen, because no-one knows what will happen in the future: *"I don't think I'll ever get married." "Oh, you never know."* | *Let's buy a lottery ticket. You never know, we might win.*

MEAL
RESTAURANTS/EATING AND DRINKING

COOK · DRINK · see also · EAT · TASTE · FOOD · HUNGRY

1 a meal

meal /miːl/ [n C] the food that you eat in the morning, in the middle of the day, or in the evening, either at home or in a restaurant: *The hotel was nice, and the meals were really good.* | *Miriam was silent all through the meal.*

have a meal *We had an excellent meal in a Chinese restaurant.*

cook sb a meal *Jeff cooked us a delicious meal last night.*

go out for a meal (=go to a restaurant) *Would you like to go out for a meal sometime, Emma?*

take sb out for a meal (=take someone to a restaurant and pay for their meal) *It was Lisa's birthday so we took her out for a meal.*

main meal (=the biggest meal of the day) *We usually have our main meal in the middle of the day.*

something to eat /ˌsʌmθɪŋ tu 'iːt/ a meal, especially a small or quick meal: *Can I get you something to eat?*

have something to eat *We'll have something to eat, and then go out.*

snack /snæk/ [n C] something small such as an apple, some bread, or some chocolate that you eat between meals

have a snack *I'm not very hungry – I'll just have a snack.* | *The children have a snack at 11 o'clock – usually some fruit and a drink.*

takeaway BRITISH **takeout** AMERICAN /'teɪkəweɪ, 'teɪkaʊt/ [n C] a meal that you buy from a restaurant and then eat at home: *Dave just lives on beer and takeaways.* | *I don't feel like cooking tonight – let's get a takeout.* | *a takeout pizza*

M

2 a meal in the morning

breakfast /'brekfəst/ [n C/U] the meal you eat when you get up in the morning: *What do you want for breakfast – cereal or toast?* | *After breakfast we went for a walk on the beach.*

have breakfast *George was having his breakfast when the phone rang.*

> ⚠️ You can say 'eat breakfast' in American English, but in British English it is more usual to say **have breakfast**.

> When you see **EC**, go to the **ESSENTIAL COMMUNICATION** section.

3 a meal in the middle of the day

lunch /lʌntʃ/ [n C/U] the meal you eat in the middle of the day: *We had an early lunch and spent the afternoon shopping.* | *At work we are allowed one hour for lunch.* | *See you after lunch.*
have lunch *Shall we have lunch before we go out?*
plural **lunches**

> ⚠ You can say 'eat lunch' in American English, but in British English it is more usual to say **have lunch**.

4 a meal in the evening

dinner /ˈdɪnəʳ/ [n C/U] the meal you eat in the evening: *What shall we have for dinner?* | *Sarah cooked us a really nice dinner.*
go out for dinner (=go to a restaurant or to someone else's house) *We went out for dinner at the Ritz.*
have dinner *Why don't you come and have dinner with us?*

> ⚠ You can say 'eat dinner' in American English, but in British English it is more usual to say **have dinner**.

supper /ˈsʌpəʳ/ [n C/U] the meal you eat in the evening: *After supper we watched a video.* | *I had my supper and went to bed.*

> ⚠ You can say 'eat supper' in American English, but in British English it is more usual to say **have supper**.

> ⚠ In British English, **supper** is usually a less formal meal than **dinner**, and you have it at home, not in a restaurant.

tea /tiː/ [n C/U] BRITISH a meal you eat at home early in the evening: *What's for tea?*
have tea *The children came home from school, had their tea, and did their homework.*

> ⚠ Don't say 'eat tea'. Say **have tea**.

dinner party /ˈdɪnəʳ ˌpɑːʳti/ [n C] a formal meal in your home when you invite friends or guests

have a dinner party *We're having a dinner party on Tuesday, would you like to come?*
plural **dinner parties**

5 a meal outside

picnic /ˈpɪknɪk/ [n C] a meal that you take with you to eat outside: *We took a picnic down to the beach.*
have a picnic *It was a beautiful day – we had a picnic by the river.*

barbecue /ˈbɑːʳbɪkjuː/ [n C] a party when you cook and eat food outside: *I'll get some burgers and ribs for the barbecue.*
have a barbecue *If the weather's nice, we'll have a barbecue.*

6 part of a meal

course /kɔːʳs/ [n C] one of the parts of a meal, especially in a restaurant: *The waiter brought the first course, carrot soup.*
main course (=the biggest course in a meal) *For the main course we had roast turkey with vegetables.*
a three-course meal/a five-course meal *In La Porcetta you can get a really nice three-course meal for $20.*

starter BRITISH **appetizer** AMERICAN /ˈstɑːʳtəʳ, ˈæpɪˌtaɪzəʳ/ [n C] the first part of a meal in a restaurant: *What would you like for a starter – soup or garlic mushrooms?* | *a delightful appetizer of small clams*

dessert (also **pudding** BRITISH) /dɪˈzɜːʳt, ˈpʊdɪŋ/ [n C/U] the sweet part of a meal that you have at the end: *"Would you like a dessert, Madam?" "Yes please, I'll have the cheesecake."*
have sth for dessert/pudding *I had fruit salad for dessert.* | *What are we having for pudding?*

MEAN

➡ see also **WORD/PHRASE/SENTENCE, LANGUAGE**

1 to mean something

mean /miːn/ [v T] when a word, sign, or statement has a particular meaning: *What does 'abandon' mean?* | *It says 'not suitable for children', which means* *anyone under 16.* | *He said Sara was a very close friend, but I'm not sure what he meant.*

+ (that) *The flashing light means that we're running out of gas.* | *When it makes a 'bleep', that means it's switched on.*

meaning – meant – have meant

stand for sth /'stænd fɔːʳ (sth)/ [*phrasal verb* T] if a letter or group of letters **stands for** a word, name, or number, it is a short way of saying or writing it: *NATO stands for the North Atlantic Treaty Organization.* | *What does the F stand for in John F. Kennedy?*

in other words /ɪn ˌʌðəʳ 'wɜːʳdz/ use this to show that you are saying something again in a simpler way, in order to explain what it means: *If goods are faulty you are entitled to a full refund – you get your money back, in other words.* | *There are growing inequalities in the distribution of wealth – in other words, the rich are getting richer.*

2 meaning

meaning /'miːnɪŋ/ [*n* C/U] what a word, sign, or statement means: *The word 'spring' has several different meanings.*
+ of *There is a chart that explains the meaning of all the symbols on the map.* | *Semantics is the study of meaning.*

sense /sens/ [*n* C] one of the meanings of a word that has several meanings
+ of *In the dictionary the different senses of the word are marked by numbers.*
in the broadest/fullest sense (=in the most general meaning of the word) *I'm using the word 'education' in the broadest sense here.*

implication /ˌɪmplɪˈkeɪʃən/ [*n* C/U] a meaning which is not directly stated, but which seems to be intended: *He didn't actually accuse me of stealing, but that was the implication.*
+ that *Staff members were asked to work on Sundays, with the implication that they would lose their jobs if they refused.*
by implication (=the intended meaning is that) *The law bans organized protests and, by implication, any form of opposition.*

the gist /ðə 'dʒɪst/ [*n* singular] the main meaning of something such as a speech, report, or piece of writing, without considering all the specific details
+ of *The gist of the report seems to be that safety standards need to be improved.*
get the gist (of sth) (=understand the main meaning) *Read through the article quickly to get the gist of it.*

MEASURE

to find out the size, length, or amount of something

➡ see also **LONG, SHORT, AMOUNT/NUMBER**

1 to measure something

measure /'meʒəʳ/ [*v* T] to find out the size or amount of something, by using a special tool, machine, or system: *Can you measure the desk to see if it'll fit into that corner?* | *The GNP figure measures the rate of growth in the economy.* | *a device for measuring the speed of a tennis ball in flight*

measure

ruler

kitchen scales
BRITISH scale
AMERICAN

timer

½ cup

thermometer

cup

tape measure

stopwatch

measurement /ˈmeʒəʳmənt/ [n C] a number or amount that you get when you measure something: *What are the measurements of this room?*

take a measurement *I'll just take a few measurements, then I can tell you how much paint you will need.*

waist/chest/hip etc measurement (=how much you measure around your waist, chest etc)

weigh /weɪ/ [v T] to find out how heavy something is by measuring its weight with special equipment: *Weigh all the ingredients carefully before mixing them together.*

time /taɪm/ [v T] to measure how long it takes for someone to do something or for something to happen: *We timed how long it took us to get there.* | *The swimming teacher always times us over 100 metres.*

take /teɪk/ [v T] **take sb's pulse/temperature/blood pressure** to measure how hot someone is, how fast their heart is beating etc, as part of a medical examination: *The doctor will take your blood pressure and check your weight.*

taking – took – have taken

WORD BANK

MEDICAL TREATMENT

HEALTHY/UNHEALTHY
DOCTOR
DAMAGE
ILL/SICK
see also
DRUGS
PAIN
BREAK
HURT/INJURE
BETTER 4
MENTALLY ILL

M

1 the treatment of illness

medicine /ˈmedsən‖ˈmedᵻsən/ [n U] the science of understanding illness and injury, and the methods used for treating them: *Jane is studying medicine.* | *The discovery of penicillin revolutionized Western medicine.*

medical /ˈmedɪkəl/ [adj only before noun] connected with illness or injury and the methods used for treating them: *The*

insurance policy will pay all your medical expenses if you get sick.* | *Maria wants to go to medical school.* | *medical research*

medical attention (=treatment by doctors or nurses in a hospital) *After the accident, both drivers needed medical attention.*

the medical profession (=doctors and nurses)

treatment /ˈtriːtmənt/ [n C/U] a medical method of curing someone who is ill or injured, for example by means of drugs or an operation

+ for *He's receiving treatment for cancer.* | *Doctors are trying out a new treatment for depression.*

cure /kjʊəʳ/ [n C] a method of treating an illness, using drugs, operations etc, which makes the person with the illness completely better

+ for *the search for a cure for AIDS*

healthcare /ˈhelθkeəʳ/ [n U] the medical services that are available to people in a country: *The standard of healthcare in the area is excellent.* | *the rising cost of healthcare*

conventional medicine /kənˈvenʃənəl ˌmedsən‖-ˌmedᵻsən/ [n U] the usual form of medicine used in most European and North American countries, involving the use of drugs and operations

alternative medicine/complementary medicine /ɔːlˈtɜːnətɪv ˌmedsən, ˌkɒmplᵻˈmentəri ˌmedsən‖-ˌmedᵻsən/ [n U] medical treatments based on ideas that are completely different from the ideas of conventional medicine. Homeopathy, acupuncture, and herbal remedies are all types of **alternative medicine/complementary medicine**.

2 ordinary medical treatment

operation /ˌɒpəˈreɪʃən‖ˌɑːp-/ [n C] if you have an **operation**, a doctor cuts into your body to remove or repair a part that is damaged

have an operation *My mother's having an operation tomorrow – she's having her appendix removed.*

+ on *I had an operation on my knee last year.*

surgery /'sɜːʳdʒəri/ [n U] treatment by doctors in which they cut into someone's body to remove or repair a part that is damaged: *She needed emergency surgery after the accident.*

have/undergo surgery *Before undergoing surgery, patients can discuss their operation with a doctor.*

major/minor surgery (=serious/not very serious operations) *This is a dangerous condition, and she will require major surgery.*

⚠ **Surgery** is more technical than **operation**.

injection /ɪnˈdʒekʃən/ [n C] when a doctor or nurse gives someone a drug using a special needle: *I hate having injections.*

X-ray /ˈeks reɪ/ [n C] a medical examination that uses a beam of radiation to photograph the inside of someone's body: *The X-ray showed that William had broken his jaw.*

have an X-ray *The doctor said I had to have a chest X-ray.*

physiotherapy /ˌfɪziəʊˈθerəpi/ [n U] treatment for people who have injured their muscles, broken their legs etc, in which they have to do special exercises, have parts of their body rubbed and pressed etc

3 alternative medical treatment

homeopathic /ˌhəʊmiəˈpæθɪk◄/ [adj] **homeopathic** treatments or medicines are based on the idea of giving a person very small amounts of a substance which, in larger amounts, would give them an illness similar to the one they have

homeopathic remedy (=a homeopathic medicine) *a homeopathic cure for flu*

homeopathy /ˌhəʊmiˈɒpəθi‖-ˈɑːp-/ [n U] *Homeopathy is becoming more popular.*

reflexology /ˌriːflekˈsɒlədʒi‖-ˈsɑː-/ [n U] a treatment in which areas of a person's feet and hands are pressed in order to treat problems in another part of their body

aromatherapy /əˌrəʊməˈθerəpi/ [n U] a treatment using special oils which are used in a bath or rubbed into your skin

acupuncture /ˈækjʊˌpʌŋktʃəʳ/ [n U] a treatment in which many needles are put into your skin to stop pain or cure an illness

herbal remedy /ˌhɜːbəl ˈremɪdi‖ˌɜːr-, ˌhɜːr-/ [n C] a medicine that is made from special plants

4 medicines

medicine /ˈmedsən‖ˈmedɪsən/ [n C/U] a substance used for treating illnesses, especially a liquid that you drink: *Emergency supplies of food and medicine were sent to the earthquake area.* | *Chinese herbal medicines*

take medicine *Have you taken your medicine this morning?*

drug /drʌg/ [n C] a chemical substance used for treating illnesses: *a drug used in the treatment of stomach ulcers* | *The side effects of this drug may include fever and dizziness.* | *a big drug company*

medication /ˌmedɪˈkeɪʃən/ [n U] one or more drugs that your doctor has told you to take regularly: *Don't forget your medication*

be on medication *She's on medication for her heart.*

⚠ **Medication** is a word used especially by doctors.

dose /dəʊs/ [n C] a measured amount of a drug that you take at one time

+ of *a massive dose of insulin*

prescription /prɪˈskrɪpʃən/ [n C] a piece of paper from your doctor that says which medicine you need and allows you to get it

+ for *a prescription for sleeping tablets*

5 to give someone medical treatment

treat /triːt/ [v T] to try to make someone better when they are ill or injured, for example by giving them drugs or hospital care

treat sb for sth *Doctors are treating him for cancer.*

treat sth with sth *Many common infections can be treated with antibiotics.*

operate /ˈɒpəreɪt‖ˈɑː-/ [v I] if a doctor **operates**, he or she cuts someone open in order to remove or repair a part of their body that is damaged

M

+ on *It can be risky to operate on very old people.* | *They had to operate on my arm because it was broken in two places.*

examine /ɪgˈzæmˌn/ [v T] if a doctor **examines** someone who is ill, he or she looks carefully at them in order to find out what is wrong: *He was examined by three doctors, but none of them could find anything physically wrong.*

    examination /ɪgˌzæmˌˈneɪʃən/ [n U] when a doctor looks at someone who is ill in order to find out what is wrong with them

6 places where you can get medical treatment

◌the doctor's BRITISH **the doctor's office** AMERICAN /ðə ˈdɒktəʳz, ðə ˈdɒktəʳz ˌɒfˌs‖-ˈdɑːk-, -ˌɔːf-, -ˌɑːf/ ESPECIALLY SPOKEN the office where a doctor works, where people who are ill can go at certain times to be examined and treated: *You'd better go to the doctor's if your sore throat doesn't get any better.*

clinic /ˈklɪnɪk/ [n C] In the US, a place where several doctors have offices; in Britain, a place where people come for treatment or advice about a specific medical condition: *a family-planning clinic* | *a clinic for people with alcohol problems*

health centre BRITISH **health center** AMERICAN /ˈhelθ ˌsentəʳ/ [n C] in Britain, a building where several doctors have offices, and people can go to see them for treatment; in the US, a similar place in a college or university, where the students can go to see a doctor

surgery /ˈsɜːʳdʒəri/ [n C] BRITISH the office where a doctor works, where people can go to be examined and treated: *The waiting room at the surgery was full of people with colds and flu.*

    plural **surgeries**

hospital /ˈhɒspɪtl‖ˈhɑː-/ [n C] a large building where nurses and doctors work and where you stay while you are having medical treatment: *Dr Clark is a surgeon at a big hospital in Chicago.*

    in/to/from hospital BRITISH *My sister's in hospital having a baby.*

    in/to/from the hospital AMERICAN *After the accident, John was rushed to the hospital.*

casualty BRITISH **the emergency room** AMERICAN /ˈkæʒuəlti, ɪˈmɜːʳdʒənsi ruːm/ [n singular] the part of a hospital you go to for emergency treatment, for example if you have had an accident or if you suddenly become very ill: *We had to take Alistair to casualty after he fell downstairs.* | *I was waiting in the emergency room for three hours!*

MEET

➡ see also **VISIT, TALK**

1 when you have arranged to meet someone

meet /miːt/ [v I/T] to be in the same place as someone else because you have arranged to see them: *I'll meet you outside the theatre at 7 o'clock.* | *We agreed to meet again next Friday.* | *I used to meet her every week to discuss my work.*

    meet for lunch/coffee/a drink etc *Let's meet for lunch one day next week.*

    meet sb at the airport/station etc (=go to meet someone when they have just arrived somewhere) *My brother came to meet me at the airport.*

    meeting – met – have met

> ⚠ If you want to say that two people meet each other, it is better just to say **they meet**: *We met outside the theatre.*

meet with sb /ˈmiːt wɪð (sb)/ [phrasal verb T] ESPECIALLY AMERICAN to meet someone in order to discuss something: *She's flying to New York tomorrow to meet with her agent.*

meet up/get together /ˌmiːt ˈʌp, ˌget təˈgeðəʳ/ [phrasal verb I] INFORMAL if friends **meet up** or **get together**, they meet in order to do something together, for example to have a meal or a drink: *Let's meet up after work.*

    + with *I usually meet up with my friends on a Friday night and go for a drink.*

    + for lunch/coffee/a drink *We must get together for lunch some time.*

2 when you meet someone by chance

meet /miːt/ [v T not in passive] to see someone by chance and talk to them: *You'll never guess who I met yesterday!* | *I met Jill at the bus stop this morning.*
meeting – met – have met

bump into sb/run into sb /ˌbʌmp 'ɪntuː (sb), ˌrʌn 'ɪntuː (sb)/ [phrasal verb T] INFORMAL to meet someone that you know, by chance: *I'm glad I bumped into you. I wanted to ask you about tomorrow's history test.* | *She's always running into friends that she knows from school.*

chance meeting /ˌtʃɑːns 'miːtɪŋǁˌtʃæns-/ [n C usually singular] when you meet someone by chance: *It was a chance meeting that later led to a passionate love affair.*

3 when you meet someone for the first time

meet /miːt/ [v I/T not in passive] to meet someone you have not met before: *I was 15 years old when I met Andrew.* | *Have you ever met his wife?*
first meet *Where did you first meet Dr Steiner?* | *Janet and Pete first met when they were at university.*
meeting – met – have met

> ⚠ If you want to say that two people meet each other, it is better just to say they meet: *I remember the day we met.*

introduce /ˌɪntrə'djuːsǁ-'duːs/ [v T] if you **introduce** someone to a person they have never met before, you tell them each other's names: *Oh, Bob, let me introduce Rosie Webb, our new marketing manager.* | *Have you two been introduced?* (=to each other)
introduce sb to sb *Tom introduced me to his sister, Gloria.*

this is /'ðɪs ɪz/ [n C] SPOKEN say this when you are introducing someone to a person they have never met before: *"Sam, this is Julia – she's in college with me." "Hi Julia, nice to meet you!"*

> When you see **EC**, go to the **ESSENTIAL COMMUNICATION** section.

4 when a large group comes together in one place

gather /'gæðəʳ/ [v I] if a crowd or group of people **gathers**, they come together somewhere in order to do something or see something
+ in/at/on etc *The family gathered on the porch to say goodbye.* | *Eager fans are already gathering outside the stadium.*

assemble /ə'sembəl/ [v I] if a group of people **assembles**, they all come together in the same place, especially as part of an organized plan: *Prisoners must assemble in the courtyard every morning for exercise.* | *Foreign diplomats and their wives had assembled in the Great Hall to meet the President.*

5 a meeting

meeting /'miːtɪŋ/ [n C] an occasion when people meet in order to discuss something: *Sorry I can't come – I have to go to a meeting.* | *Peter's in London for a business meeting.*
have/hold a meeting *I think we'd better have a meeting to discuss these problems.*
attend a meeting FORMAL (=be at a meeting) *The President is attending a meeting in Prague today.*
call/arrange/organize a meeting *The principal has called a meeting for 4.00.*

conference /'kɒnfərənsǁ'kɑːn-/ [n C] an organized event, especially one that continues for several days, at which a lot of people meet to discuss a particular subject
+ of *a conference of women business leaders*
attend a conference FORMAL (=be at a conference) *She was in Boston attending a conference on the environment.*
hold a conference *The Institute of Accountants is holding its conference in Edinburgh this year.*

convention /kən'venʃən/ [n C] a large meeting of members of a political organization or professional group for a particular purpose: *the Democratic Party convention*
+ of *a convention of computer salespeople*

M

MEMBER

➡ see also **ORGANIZATION, JOIN**

1 a member of a club, political party etc

member /'membəʳ/ [n C] a person or organization that belongs to a club, a political party, or a similar organization: *Members can use the bar at any time.*
+ of *She's a member of the local drama society.* | *Is Switzerland a member of the European Union?*
a club/union/party member *Union members voted against the strike.*

2 to be a member of something

be a member of sth/belong to sth /biː ə 'membər ɒv (sth), bɪ'lɒŋ tuː (sth)‖ -'lɔːŋ-/ *My sister's a member of the Michael Jackson Fan Club.* | *Do you belong to any political party?*

join /dʒɔɪn/ [v T] to become a member of a club, a political party, a military force, or a company: *He joined the Marines at the age of 19, and fought in Vietnam.* | *I've joined the photographic club.* | *Williams joined Microsoft as a programmer in 1991.*

> ⚠ Don't use **join** to talk about going to a school or college. Say **she went to Oxford in 1995** (not 'she joined Oxford').

be in sth /biː ɪn (sth)/ [phrasal verb T] to be a member of an organization, especially a large, well-known one: *Nina's son is in the army.* | *I used to really enjoy camping when I was in the Boy Scouts.*

be on sth /biː ɒn (sth)/ [phrasal verb T] to be a member of a group or committee that meets to make official decisions
be on a committee/council/board/panel *Kathryn is on the school board for the district.*

3 being a member

membership /'membəʳʃɪp/ [n U] being a member: *What is the cost of membership?*

> When you see **EC**, go to the
> **ESSENTIAL COMMUNICATION** section.

+ of *Membership of political parties has been increasing.* | *Canada's membership of NATO*
+ in AMERICAN *Did you renew your membership in the sailing club?*

MENTALLY ILL

MEDICAL TREATMENT
CRAZY
DOCTOR
see also
MIND
DRUGS
ILL/SICK
BETTER 4

1 mentally ill

mentally ill /ˌmentəli 'ɪl/ someone who is **mentally ill** has an illness of the mind which affects the way that they behave: *Many of these homeless people have been mentally ill at some time.*
the mentally ill (=people who are mentally ill) *He works in a hostel for the mentally ill.*

mental illness /ˌmentl 'ɪlnɪs/ [n C/U] illness of the mind: *Depression is a mental illness and can be treated with drugs.* | *He had a history of mental illness and alcoholism.*

mental /'mentl/ [adj only before noun] connected with mental illness or people who are mentally ill
mental hospital/patient/institution *a hospital ward for non-violent mental patients*
mental problem/disorder/breakdown *We knew she had been having mental problems.*

insane /ɪn'seɪn/ [adj] permanently and seriously mentally ill, so that you cannot have a normal life: *Powell, who has attacked 13 women, was judged to be insane.*
go insane (=become seriously mentally ill) *Sometimes I thought I was going insane.*
insanity /ɪn'sænɪti/ [n U] permanent and serious mental illness: *Hobbs was found not guilty by reason of insanity.*

crazy (also **mad** ESPECIALLY BRITISH) /'kreɪzi, mæd/ [adj] mentally ill – use this in conversations or stories, but not in formal, medical, or legal English: *Some crazy guy walked into the store and started shooting people.* | *We soon realized that the old man was completely mad.*

go crazy/mad (=become crazy) *I wondered if I was going crazy. That guy was following me again.* | *After Hamlet rejects her, Ophelia goes mad and drowns herself.*

crazy – crazier -craziest

nervous breakdown /ˌnɜːrvəs ˈbreɪkdaʊn/ [n C] a medical condition in which you feel very tired, anxious, and upset, often because you have been working too hard or because of emotional problems: *After the divorce, Sonia had a nervous breakdown and had to stop work.*

2 not mentally ill

sane /seɪn/ [adj] not mentally ill, so that you are able to make sensible decisions and lead your life in a normal way: *Of course he isn't mad. He's as sane as you or I.* | *No sane person could believe such garbage.*

perfectly sane (=completely sane) *To his neighbours, Sutcliffe appeared perfectly sane.*

sanity /ˈsænəti/ [n U] when you are mentally healthy: *If you have your health and your sanity, money is not important.* | *I began to doubt Hamad's sanity as his story got stranger and stranger.*

MIDDLE

➡ see also **EDGE, SIDE**

1 the middle

the middle /ðə ˈmɪdl/ [n singular] the part of something, such as a space or area, a piece of writing, or a period of time, which is about half way between one side and the other, or halfway between the beginning and the end: *"Did you enjoy the movie?" "It was OK but I got a little bored towards the middle."*

+ of *Gary rowed out to the middle of the lake.* | *It was the middle of summer.* | *Going through the middle of Tokyo in the rush hour can be a nightmare.*

centre BRITISH **center** AMERICAN /ˈsentər/ [n C usually singular] the middle of a space, area, or object, especially the exact middle: *I love chocolates with soft centers.* | *The flower has white petals, and is deep pink at the centre.*

+ of *Draw a line through the centre of the circle.*

at the centre/in the centre (of) (=exactly in the middle of something) *One child stands at the centre of the circle, and the others dance around her.*

the heart of /ðə ˈhɑːrt ɒv/ the middle of an area, town, or city: *The hotel is located in the heart of Moscow.* | *a quiet village in the heart of the English countryside*

⚠ **The heart of** is used mainly in written descriptions of places, to make the place sound interesting, exciting, or very near to shops, theatres, trains etc.

2 in the middle

in the middle /ɪn ðə ˈmɪdl/ *a garden with a fish-pond in the middle*

+ of *Don't walk in the middle of the road!*

middle /ˈmɪdl/ [adj only before noun]
the middle drawer/shelf/finger etc (=the one in the middle) *You'll find the scissors in the middle drawer of my desk.* | *Jane was wearing a gold ring on her middle finger.* | *I am the middle child in a family of five.*

central /ˈsentrəl/ [adj] in the middle of an area, country, or town: *We are getting reports of bad weather in central Europe.* | *The houses face onto a central courtyard.* | *central London*

halfway /ˌhɑːfˈweɪ◂ ˌhæf-/ [adv] at the middle point between two places or of a period of time or event

+ across/between/down/up etc *Our car broke down halfway across the bridge.* | *We were halfway down the mountain when it started snowing.* | *Joe left the college halfway through the year.*

mid- /mɪd/ [prefix] in or near the middle of a period of time
mid-afternoon/mid-week/mid-December/mid-18th century/mid-1990s etc *The house was built in the mid-18th century.* | *That's how people used to wear their hair in the mid-80s.*

MIND

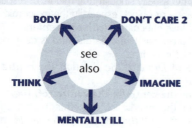

see also
BODY
DON'T CARE 2
THINK
IMAGINE
MENTALLY ILL

1 your mind

mind /maɪnd/ [n C] what you use to think and imagine things: *His mind was full of big ideas for developing the company.* | *I never know what's going on in her mind.* | *She had a picture of him in her mind – tall, blond, and handsome.* | *He had to push these worries out of his mind.* (=tried not to think about them)

brain /breɪn/ [n C] your ability to think and the way that you think: *My brain worked fast as I tried to decide what to do.* | *She has an excellent business brain.*

2 affecting your mind

mental /'mentl/ [adj usually before noun] affecting your mind or happening in your mind: *After months of overworking, Briggs was suffering from mental and physical exhaustion.* | *It takes a lot of mental effort to understand these ideas.*
mental picture/image (=a picture that you have in your mind)
mental illness/problem/breakdown (=an illness, problem etc of your mind, not your body)
  mentally [adv] *By the end of the day we were mentally and physically worn out.*

psychological /ˌsaɪkə'lɒdʒɪkəl◄ǁ-'lɑː-/ [adj] affecting the mind – use this especially about mental problems that influence the way someone behaves: *She works with children who have psychological problems.* | *The causes of a physical illness can often be psychological.*
  psychologically [adv] *psychologically disturbed children*

When you see **EC**, go to the **ESSENTIAL COMMUNICATION** section.

subconscious (also **unconscious**) /sʌb'kɒnʃəs, ʌn'kɒnʃəsǁ-'kɑːn-/ [adj] **subconscious** feelings, desires, worries etc are hidden in your mind and you do not realize you have them: *a subconscious fear of failure*
  subconsciously [adv] *Fathers are often subconsciously jealous of their sons.*

MISTAKE

see also
GUILTY/NOT GUILTY
WRONG
ADMIT
CARELESS
BLAME
ACCIDENTALLY
DELIBERATELY

1 a mistake

mistake /mɪ'steɪk/ [n C] something that is not correct, which you do, say, or write without intending to: *Your essay's full of mistakes.*
make a mistake *Sampras was playing badly, making a lot of mistakes.*
+ in *There's a mistake in the address.*
correct a mistake (=make it correct) *I hope you'll correct any mistakes I've made.*
spelling mistake (=when you spell a word wrongly) *Check your work carefully for any spelling mistakes.*

error /'erər/ [n C/U] a mistake – use this especially to talk about mistakes in calculating or in using a language, system, or machine: *the most common errors among students of English*
+ in *an error in the calculations*
human error (=when a mistake is caused by people, not by a machine) *The report decided that the accident was caused by human error.*
computer error (=a mistake caused by a computer) *Our enormous phone bill was due to a computer error.*

misprint /'mɪs-prɪnt/ [n C] a word that has been printed wrongly in a book or newspaper: *There were several misprints in the menu.*

2 a bad decision, idea etc that causes problems for you

mistake /mɪˈsteɪk/ [n C] something that you do or decide which is not at all sensible and which causes a lot of problems for you

make a mistake My first marriage was a terrible failure. I don't want to make the same mistake again.

it is a mistake to do sth It was a mistake to think that we could go on living on borrowed money.

big/serious mistake Buying the farm was the biggest mistake of her life.

3 to make a mistake

make a mistake /ˌmeɪk ə mɪˈsteɪk/ My spoken Spanish was okay, but I kept making mistakes in my written work. | Don't worry – everyone makes mistakes.

◯ get sth wrong /ˌget (stʃ) ˈrɒŋ‖-ˈrɔːŋ/ ESPECIALLY SPOKEN to make a mistake in something that you do, say, or write, especially when this has bad or annoying results: I've been there a year now, and my boss still gets my name wrong! | There was a report about it in the newspaper, but they got their facts wrong.

get it wrong This is a delicate operation. If we get it wrong the patient may die.

MIX

➡ see also **CONFUSED 4**

1 mix substances/liquids

mix /mɪks/ [v T] to mix different liquids or substances together so that they can no longer be separated

mix sth and sth You can make green by mixing blue and yellow paint.

mix sth with sth Shake the bottle well to mix the oil with the vinegar.

mix sth together Concrete is made by mixing gravel, sand, cement, and water together. | If these two chemicals are mixed together they will explode.

stir /stɜːʳ/ [v T] to mix things by moving them around in a container with a spoon or a stick: He sat on the front step stirring the paint to make it smooth.

stir in sth/stir sth in (=add something to a food mixture by stirring it) When the butter has melted, stir in the soy sauce and ginger. | Add the grated cheese to the sauce and stir it in.

stirring – stirred – have stirred

blend /blend/ [v T] to mix liquids or soft substances when you are preparing food, in order to make a single smooth substance

blend sth and sth Blend the sugar, eggs, and flour.

blend sth together The ingredients should be blended together until they are smooth.

dilute /daɪˈluːt/ [v T] to make a liquid weaker by mixing it with water: You should dilute the juice before you drink it.

2 when feelings, ideas, styles etc are mixed with each other

be a mixture of /biː ə ˈmɪkstʃər ɒv/ to contain different features or ideas, mixed together: The movie is a mixture of comedy and romance. | Her work is a mixture of classical and modern styles.

be a cross between /biː ə ˈkrɒs bɪtwiːn‖ -ˈkrɔːs-/ something that **is a cross between** one thing and another is a mixture of two different things: The expression on Paul's face was a cross between amusement and disbelief. | It's difficult to describe my job. I suppose I'm a cross between a secretary and a translator.

3 a mixture

mixture /ˈmɪkstʃəʳ/ [n C] several different things, ideas, feelings, or people mixed together

+ of The sauce is a mixture of flour, butter, milk, and cheese. | There was an interesting mixture of people at the party. | Sasha was looking at her with a mixture of admiration and curiosity.

combination /ˌkɒmbɪˈneɪʃən‖ˌkɑːm-/ [n C] a mixture of different people working together, or different ideas, problems etc happening together, which has a particular effect

+ of Our problems were due to a combination of bad management and lack of experience. | Their music is an odd combination of jazz and opera.

M

a good/bad/successful/disastrous etc combination They were a perfect combination – Anton as chef and Guy as restaurant manager.

4 not mixed with anything

pure /pjʊəʳ/ [adj] a material, substance etc that is **pure** has not been mixed with anything else: The jacket is pure silk. | a necklace made of pure gold

solid /ˈsɒlɪd‖ˈsɑː-/ [adj only before noun] not mixed with anything else – use this about wood or metals, especially expensive ones

solid gold/silver/pine/oak etc The necklace is solid gold. | We bought a solid pine chest for only £50.

neat/straight /niːt, streɪt/ [adj] not mixed with anything else – use this about strong alcoholic drinks that are usually made weaker by adding something else: Would you like your whisky neat or with water? | She was drinking straight vodka.

MODERN

➡ see also **NEW, FASHIONABLE/ UNFASHIONABLE**

1 modern machines/ buildings/methods

modern /ˈmɒdn‖ˈmɑːdərn/ [adj] using new methods, designs, or equipment: Seattle has a very modern public transportation system. | a bright, modern office building | the horrors of modern warfare

the latest /ðə ˈleɪtⱼst/ [adj only before noun] **the latest** machines, computers, and methods are the newest and best ones that are available: He was using one of the latest Japanese hand-held computers. | The latest model can print 15 pages every minute.

the very latest fast microprocessors that are produced using the very latest techniques

up-to-date /ˌʌp tə ˈdeɪt◄/ [adj] **up-to-date** equipment, machines, or methods are very modern, and much better than the ones that many other people or organizations are still using: This hospital has the

most up-to-date equipment in Europe. | up-to-date training methods

advanced /ədˈvɑːnst‖ədˈvænst/ [adj] **advanced** machines, weapons, and systems have been designed using the newest technical knowledge: We have the most advanced security system available. | advanced weapons technology

high-tech/hi-tech /ˌhaɪ ˈtek◄/ [adj] using very modern electronic equipment and machines, especially computers: a high-tech recording studio | the hi-tech industries of the 21st century

2 modern art/literature/ music/fashion

modern /ˈmɒdn‖ˈmɑːdərn/ [adj] **modern** art, literature, music etc uses styles that have been developed very recently – use this especially about styles which are deliberately different from traditional styles, and which some people dislike because of this: I like both modern dance and classical ballet. | Prince Charles has made several speeches criticizing modern architecture.

contemporary /kənˈtempərəri, -pəri‖ -pəreri/ [adj only before noun] **contemporary** art, music, literature etc was produced or written recently: Composers like Philip Glass have made contemporary music more popular.

contemporary artist/writer/composer etc a new exhibition of paintings by contemporary artists

the latest /ðə ˈleɪtⱼst/ [adj only before noun] **the latest fashion/style/design** is the one that is the most modern and the most fashionable: My sister says that black lipstick is the latest fashion.

the latest in sth (=the most fashionable type of) the latest in designer shoes

3 modern ideas/ways of thinking

progressive /prəˈgresɪv/ [adj] using new methods for dealing with social problems, education, crime etc, especially when these methods are less strict than traditional ones. You can use **progressive** with these words: **methods**, **ideas**, **views**, **education**, **school**, **government**, **policy**: The principal has very *progressive views on education.* | *progressive methods for dealing with young criminals*

4 to make something more modern

update /ʌpˈdeɪt/ [v I] to improve something, so that it includes the most modern equipment, methods, or information: *The school has just updated all its computer equipment.* | *Nursing staff were sent on training courses to update their skills.*

modernize (also **modernise** BRITISH) /ˈmɒdəˈnaɪz‖ˈmɑː-/ [v T] to make big changes to a place or organization, by putting in modern equipment or modern systems, and getting rid of old ones: *It was an old farmhouse that had been modernized by the previous owner.* | *attempts to modernize the Soviet economy*

MONEY

1 money

money /ˈmʌni/ [n U] what you use to buy things, what you earn by working etc: *We don't have enough money for a vacation this year.*

money to do sth (=money you can use to pay for something) *Dad, can I have some money to buy some new jeans?*

spend money *I spent far too much money on Christmas presents.*

save money (=not spend much money) *"Are you coming out with us on Saturday?" "No, I'm trying to save money."*

earn money *Accountants can earn a lot of money.*

make money (=earn money) *The restaurant makes a lot of money in the summer.*

lose money (=fail to make a profit in business, so that you spend more than you earn) *The state railway has been losing money for years.*

cash /kæʃ/ [n U] money, especially money that is available for you to spend: *I don't have much cash at the moment. Could I pay you next week?* | *She earns extra cash by working as a waitress.*

> ⚠ **Cash** is more informal than **money**.

a fortune /ə ˈfɔːrtʃən/ [n singular] INFORMAL a lot of money: *That dress must have cost a fortune – where does she get the money from?*

be worth a fortune *They bought their house really cheaply but it's worth a fortune now.*

sum /sʌm/ [n C] an amount of money – use this to say how large or small an amount is: *Stars like Chaplin earned $2000 a week, which was an enormous sum in those days.*

sum of money *My uncle left me a small sum of money when he died.*

2 money in the form of notes and coins

money /ˈmʌni/ [n U] notes and coins that you use for buying things: *He counted the money carefully before putting it in his pocket.* | *The Queen never carries any money.*

cash /kæʃ/ [n U] money – use this to emphasize that you mean coins and notes, and not cheques, bank cards etc: *Thieves escaped with cash and computer equipment worth over $100,000.*

in cash (=using cash) *I'll give you £50 in cash and a cheque for the rest.*

pay (in) cash *There's a 5% discount if you pay cash.*

currency /ˈkʌrənsi‖ˈkɜːr-/ [n C/U] the money used in a particular country

Italian/Malaysian/Japanese etc currency *I was carrying about £300 in Malaysian currency.*

foreign currency (=the currency of another country) *I'm taking £200 in traveller's cheques and £100 in foreign currency.*

plural **currencies**

change /tʃeɪndʒ/ [n U] money in the form of coins, or the money you get back when you pay for something with more money than it cost: *He emptied all the change out of his pockets.* | *The sales clerk handed me my change.*

in change (=in the form of coins) *I've got a £10 note and about £5 in change.*

change for $10/£5 etc (=coins in exchange for a note) *Do you have change for a $5 bill?*

3 money that you receive regularly

➡ see also **EARN, PAY**

income /ˈɪŋkʌm, ˈɪn-/ [n C/U] all the money that you receive regularly, for example from your job or from the government: *Their combined income is more than £250,000 a year.* | *Most of her income comes from savings and investments.*

an income of £800/$2000 etc *The whole family lives on an income of less than $400 a month.*

be on a low income (=earn very little money) *Families on low incomes get free medical care.*

pension /ˈpenʃən/ [n C] an amount of money that old people receive regularly after they have stopped working: *Many elderly people find it very difficult to live on their pensions.* | *Bill gets a big pension from General Motors – he worked there for 30 years.*

Social Security /ˌsəʊʃəl sɪˈkjʊərˌti/ [n U] money that people receive from the government in the US when they have finished working at 65: *Paying the rent uses all his Social Security money.*

> ⚠ In British English, **Social Security** is sometimes used to mean the same as **benefit**.

benefit /ˈbenˌfɪt/ [n C/U] money that the government gives to people who are very poor, who do not have jobs etc

unemployment/sickness/maternity benefit *You cannot receive unemployment benefit unless you are looking for a job.*

on benefit (=receiving benefit) *After I became too ill to work I was forced to live on state benefits.*

> ⚠ In American English, you usually say **benefits** rather than **benefit**, and it is a more formal word than in British English.

welfare /ˈwelfeər/ [n U] ESPECIALLY AMERICAN money that the government pays to people who are very poor, do not have jobs etc: *We don't get welfare because I have a part-time job.*

on welfare (=receiving this money from the government) *Over 50% of the families in this neighborhood are on welfare.*

> ⚠ You can also use **welfare** before a noun, like an adjective: *welfare payments* | *the welfare system*

allowance /əˈlaʊəns/ [n C] an amount of money that children get from their parents every week or every month: *My parents give me an allowance of $50 a month.*

pocket money /ˈpɒkˌt ˌmʌni‖ˈpɑː-/ [n U] BRITISH an amount of money that children get from their parents every week: *How much pocket money do you get?*

grant /grɑːnt‖grænt/ [n C] an amount of money that a government or other organization gives to someone to help pay for something good or useful, such as their education: *It's very difficult to get a grant to go to college.* | *You can get a grant from the council to repair your roof.*

scholarship /ˈskɒlərˌʃɪp‖ˈskɑː-/ [n C] money that a student receives from their school, college etc to pay for their education, especially because they have passed an examination

win a scholarship (=by passing an exam) *When she was 18, she won a scholarship to study at the Conservatoire in Paris.*

4 money that you make by doing business

profit /ˈprɒfˌt‖ˈprɑː-/ [n C/U] money that you make by doing business, for example when you sell something for more than it cost you to buy it or to produce it: *We aim to increase our profits by at least 5% every year.* | *For the first time, the company's annual profits were over $1 million.*

make a profit *They made a huge profit when they sold the business.*

M

profitable /ˈprɒfɪtəbəl‖ˈprɑː-/ [adj] a **profitable** business or activity makes a profit: *We don't sell children's clothes any more – it wasn't profitable enough.*

5 money that you pay to the government

tax /tæks/ [n C/U] money that you have to pay to the government, especially from the money you earn or as an additional payment when you buy something: *The Republicans promised to reduce taxes before the last election.*

tax on alcohol/cigarettes etc (=tax that is added to the price of alcohol, cigarettes etc)

income tax (=tax that you pay according to how much money you earn)

sales tax (=a tax added to the price of something you buy)

after tax (=after you have paid income tax) *I made over $600 a week, which was around $450 after tax.*

plural **taxes**

> ⚠ You can also use **tax** before a noun, like an adjective: *a tax inspector* | *filling in a tax form*

taxpayer /ˈtæksˌpeɪəʳ/ [n C] someone who pays tax

taxpayers' money (=money the government gets from taxes) *This defence project is simply a waste of taxpayers' money.*

the taxpayer (=all the people in a country who pay tax) *Bonus payments to top officials cost the taxpayer millions of pounds each year.*

6 additional money that you pay when you borrow money, or that you receive when you save money

interest /ˈɪntrɪst/ [n U] *If you had half a million dollars you could easily live off the interest.*

+ on *The interest on the loan is 16.5%.*

interest rate (=the amount of interest you pay or receive) *My bank charges really high interest rates.*

high/low interest *a high interest savings account*

7 money that you give to someone to make them do something dishonest

bribe /braɪb/ [n C] money that someone gives to a person in an official position, in order to persuade them to do something that they should not do

take/accept a bribe *The judge admitted that he had accepted bribes.*

pay (sb) a bribe (=give someone a bribe) *You won't get across the border unless you pay the guards a bribe of at least $500.*

> **bribery** [n U] when people give and accept bribes: *The inquiry showed that bribery was widespread.*

8 money for starting a business, paying for something important etc

finance /ˈfaɪnæns, fɪˈnæns‖fɪˈnæns, ˈfaɪnæns/ [n U] money that you borrow or receive in order to pay for something important and expensive, for example for starting a business: *We can't continue our research unless we get more finance.*

+ for *How will you get the finance for your university course?*

capital /ˈkæpɪtl/ [n U] a large amount of money that you can use to start a business or to pay for something that will eventually produce more money: *You can make a lot of money from renting property, but you need capital to get started.*

raise capital FORMAL (=get the money you need, for example by borrowing from a bank) *It took him just three months to raise the capital for making the movie.*

funding /ˈfʌndɪŋ/ [n U] money that a government or large organization provides to pay for education, theatre, music etc, not for business activities: *Nowadays, schools have to find funding from private industry as well as from the Education Department.* | *The daycare center couldn't survive without government funding.*

+ for *cuts in funding for the arts*

subsidy /ˈsʌbsɪdi/ [n C] money that the government provides to help a business or industry which might not be able to operate without this additional money:

M

Generous subsidies are available to farmers who produce wheat. | Without state subsidies, the railways couldn't survive.

plural **subsidies**

invest /ɪnˈvest/ [v I/T] to let a company, business, or bank use your money for a period of time, especially because you expect that you will eventually get back more money than you gave: *I want to invest the money my aunt left me.*
+ in *Investing in property is no longer as safe as it used to be.*
invest money in sth *I invested £5000 in my brother's printing business.*

> **investor** [n C] someone who invests money in a bank or business: *Most of the money came from foreign investors.*

put money into sth /ˌpʊt ˈmʌni ɪntuː (sth)/ to give money to a business to help it become successful, often in order to get back more money than you have given: *Unless they can find someone to put more money into it, the film studio will have to close.* | *The government ought to put more money into public transportation.*

9 connected with the way that money is used

financial /fɪˈnænʃəl, faɪ-/ [adj usually before noun] connected with money – use this about the way that people and organizations use and control their money: *Joan has a lot of financial problems at the moment.* | *Wall Street is the financial center of the US.* | *The accounts show that the school's financial position is very healthy.*

> **financially** [adv] *She wanted to go out to work and be financially independent.*

economic /ˌekəˈnɒmɪk◂, ˌiː-‖-ˈnɑː-/ [adj usually before noun] use this about the way that a country's money and wealth is produced, spent, and controlled: *The President's economic reforms have put a lot of people out of work.* | *a period of economic growth* | *the need for economic planning*

> **economically** [adv] *an economically advanced country*

economy /ɪˈkɒnəmi‖ɪˈkɑː-/ [n C] the economic system of a country, including its trade and industry: *the collapse of the German economy in the 1920s* | *one of the most successful economies in Asia*
the economy (=a country's economy) *This government has ruined the economy.*

plural **economies**

10 someone who wants a lot of money or always thinks about money

greedy /ˈgriːdi/ [adj] someone who is **greedy** wants a lot of money, even though they do not need it: *Britain has some of the greediest landlords in Europe.* | *corrupt and greedy politicians*
greedy – greedier – greediest

> **greed** [n U] when you keep wanting more money: *No-one needs to earn that much – it's just greed!*

materialistic /məˌtɪəriəˈlɪstɪk◂/ [adj] someone who is **materialistic** thinks that money and possessions are more important than anything else: *Bill has become so materialistic since he got that job – all he talks about is how much money he earns.*

11 having no money
➡ see also **POOR**

bankrupt /ˈbæŋkrʌpt/ [adj] a company or person that is **bankrupt** does not have enough money to pay their debts, and so they have to stop doing business: *Five years ago she was a successful actress, but now she is bankrupt.*
go bankrupt (=become bankrupt) *Many small businesses will go bankrupt unless interest rates fall.*

broke /brəʊk/ [adj not before noun] SPOKEN someone who is **broke** has no money or very little money: *"Can you lend me some money?" "Sorry, I'm broke."* | *When I was a student I was always broke.*

12 to have just enough money to live

get by /ˌget ˈbaɪ/ [phrasal verb I] to have just enough money to buy the things you need, but no more: *She does cleaning*

jobs in the evenings, and makes just enough to get by.
+ on *My grandmother gets by on just £50 a week.*

make ends meet /meɪk ˌendz ˈmiːt/ INFORMAL to have just enough money to buy what you need – use this when someone has so little money that life is very difficult for them: *Many families struggle to make ends meet, especially during the winter.* | *How am I supposed to make ends meet on $150 a month?*

live on sth /ˈlɪv ɒn (sth)/ [phrasal verb T] if you **live on** a particular amount of money, this is all the money that you have to buy everything you need: *You can't live on less than $25,000 a year in New York.* | *My salary doesn't really give me enough to live on.*

MORE

➡ opposite **LESS**
➡ if you want to know about using adjectives for comparing things, go to the **ESSENTIAL GRAMMAR**, section 14
➡ see also **MOST, ADD, INCREASE, ANOTHER**

1 more of the same thing, or another one of the same things

more /mɔːr/ [quantifier] more of something in addition to what is already there: *I gave him $200 last week and he's already asking for more.* | *We have enough tables but we need more chairs.*
+ of *I forced myself to swallow more of the medicine.* | *Do you have any more of those delicious cookies?*
three more/100 more etc *They walked for two more miles before they found a telephone.* | *Some of the students arrived today, and about 20 more of them are arriving tomorrow.*
some more/a few more/any more *Do you want any more tea?* | *You may need to buy some more books.*

another /əˈnʌðər/ [determiner/pronoun] one more thing, person, or amount that is the same as one you already had: *Look, your glass is cracked. I'll get you*

another. | *Would you like another drink?* | *Could you get another loaf of bread while you're out?*
another ten minutes/five miles/two gallons etc *Add the pasta and heat the soup for another ten minutes.*
another one *There were two cars in the driveway and another one in the garage.*
+ of *Is this another of your crazy ideas for making money?*

extra /ˈekstrə/ [adj/adv] more of something, in addition to the usual amount or number: *You'd better get some extra milk if Steve and Richard are staying the weekend.* | *Residents can use the hotel swimming pool at no extra cost.*
an extra ten minutes/three pounds/four litres etc *I asked for an extra day to finish my assignment.*
be/cost/earn extra (=extra money) *Dinner costs $15, but wine is extra.*

additional /əˈdɪʃənəl/ [adj only before noun] more than the amount that was agreed or expected at the beginning: *Our own car broke down, so we had the additional expense of renting a car.*
an additional £10/10 miles/10 minutes etc *They've extended his contract for an additional 12 months.*

further /ˈfɜːrðər/ [adj only before noun] FORMAL more, in addition to what there is already or what has happened already: *The doctors are keeping her in the hospital to do further tests.* | *For further information, contact the help line.*
a further £10/10 miles/10 minutes *Strike action will continue for a further 24 hours.*

2 more than a number or amount

more /mɔːr/ [quantifier] more than a number or amount: *Salaries are in the region of $200,000 a year, with top executives earning even more.*
+ than *I've been working here for more than ten years.* | *More than 50,000 people attended the open-air concert.*
much more/far more/a lot more *Diane earns much more than I do.*
10/100/$50 more (=more than another number) *It's a better hotel, but it costs about £50 more than the other one.*

or more *There must have been 200 people or more, all trying to crowd into the hall.*

over /'əʊvəʳ/ [preposition/adv] more than a number or amount: *I've been waiting over half an hour for you.* | *Jackson receives over 2000 fan letters a week.* | *The train was travelling at speeds of over 150 mph.*

just over (=slightly over) *She weighs just over 120 pounds.*

8/10/12 etc and over *The club is for children aged 10 and over.*

above /ə'bʌv/ [preposition/adv] more than a number or level on a scale that can be exactly measured: *The temperature was just 2 degrees above zero.* | *Anyone earning above $80,000 will pay more tax.*

3 years/6 metres/80% etc and above *Babies of 6 months and above need to be vaccinated.*

outnumber /aʊt'nʌmbəʳ/ [v T] if one type of person or thing **outnumbers** another, there are more of the first type than of the second: *Women teachers outnumber their male colleagues by two to one.*

greatly/far outnumber *a city where bicycles greatly outnumber cars*

3 more than before

more /mɔːʳ/ [quantifier/adv] more than before: *The new airport will just mean more traffic, more noise, and more pollution.* | *As mobile phones get cheaper, people are using them more.*

more quickly/slowly/easily etc *I wish she'd talk more slowly.*

more expensive/important/difficult etc *These days it's definitely more difficult to get into law school.*

+ than *People are travelling around more than they used to.* | *She seems more relaxed than she was last week.*

a lot more/much more/far more *There are a lot more game shows on TV than there used to be.* | *David earns far more now than he did in his old job.*

a little more/slightly more *Next time, try and be a little more patient.*

more and more /ˌmɔːr ənd 'mɔːʳ◄/ use this to say that something continues to happen more often than it did before or

continues to become more difficult, more expensive etc than it was before: *More and more students are using computers to do their schoolwork.* | *As the years passed, she depended more and more on her daughter.*

more and more expensive/tired/difficult etc *The concert was very long, and I began to feel more and more bored.*

more and more slowly/quickly/clearly etc *As the gas cools, the molecules move more and more slowly.*

increasingly /ɪn'kriːsɪŋli/ [adv] use this to say that something continues to happen more often than before, or continues to become more difficult, more expensive etc than it was before: *Increasingly, it is the female students who are getting the best grades.*

increasingly difficult/common/important/complex *It is looking increasingly likely that Tarrant will resign.* | *People have become increasingly interested in environmental issues.*

> ⚠ **Increasingly** and **more and more** mean the same, but there are some differences in the way they are used. **Increasingly** is used mainly in written English, and you can use it at the start of a sentence as a 'sentence adverb' (=one that describes the whole sentence): *Increasingly, criminals are carrying guns.* **More and more** is used in written and spoken English, and can be used directly before a plural noun: *More and more criminals are carrying guns.*

a growing number/an increasing number /ə ˌgrəʊɪŋ 'nʌmbəʳ, ən ɪnˌkriːsɪŋ 'nʌmbəʳ/ use this when the number of people that are doing something is not yet very large, but is increasing all the time

+ of *A growing number of refugees was entering the country.*

in growing/increasing numbers *Doctors are leaving the profession in increasing numbers.*

> ⚠ **Growing numbers** and **increasing numbers** mean the same as **a growing number** and **an increasing number**.

higher /'haɪəʳ/ [adj] use this about prices, speeds, or amounts that are bigger than they were before

higher price/proportion/level/rate *There is now a higher proportion of women in management jobs.*

+ than *The cost of student accommodation is higher than it was a year ago.*

greater /'greɪtəʳ/ [adj] FORMAL use this about a feeling or state that is stronger or more noticeable than it was before

greater interest/need/support/freedom *After the war, the country began to enjoy greater prosperity.*

+ than *The need for people with computing skills is greater than ever before.*

4 more than someone or something else

more /mɔːʳ/ [quantifier] more than another person, thing, or place: *My parents are both teachers, but my father earns more.* | *Ask Hilary. She knows more about it.*

+ than *It's not fair. He's got more than I have.* | *There is more oil in the Middle East than in any other part of the world.*

higher /'haɪəʳ/ [adj] use this about prices, speeds, or amounts that are bigger than someone else's

+ than *In the 1960s, Japan achieved a higher rate of economic growth than most other countries.* | *Car prices in Britain are higher than in many European countries.*

MOST

➡ opposite **LEAST**
➡ if you want to know about using adjectives for comparing things, go to the **ESSENTIAL GRAMMAR**, section 14
➡ see also **MORE**

1 most of an amount, number, total, group etc

most /məʊst/ [quantifier] the largest part of something, or the largest number of people, places, things etc

most people/things/days etc *What most people want is a peaceful life.* | *Most evenings we just stay in and watch TV.*

most of the students/my friends/her money etc (=most people or things in a group) *Most of the people I spoke to*

were very worried. | *Alex spends most of his allowance on books.* | *Most of what Hannah told me wasn't true.* | *This is a poor country, and most of it is desert.*

⚠ Don't say 'the most people drive to work'. Say **most people drive to work.**

⚠ Don't say 'almost Japanese people live in cities'. Say **most Japanese people live in cities.**

almost all/nearly all /ˌɔːlməʊst 'ɔːl, ˌnɪəʳli 'ɔːl/ not all, but almost all: *We got nearly all our food from the farm.*

+ of *I've read almost all of Jane Austen's novels.* | *Nearly all of my clothes are too small now.*

mostly/mainly /'məʊstli, 'meɪnli/ [adv] use this to say that most of the people or things in a group are of the same type: *A huge crowd of Oasis fans, mostly girls, waited outside the hotel.* | *Our customers are mainly young people interested in fashion.* | *She reads a lot of books, mostly science fiction stories.*

the majority /ðə mə'dʒɒrᵻti‖mə'dʒɔː-, mə'dʒɑː-/ [n singular] more than half of the people or things in a large group

+ of *In June the majority of our students will be taking examinations.*

the vast/great majority (=far more than half) *an education policy that will please the vast majority of parents* | *The great majority of accidents in the Alps occur while climbers are coming down.*

be in the majority (=be the largest part of a group) *Young people were in the majority at the meeting.*

⚠ Use a plural verb after **the majority (of):** *Some of the children go home for lunch, but the majority have their lunch in school.*

2 more than anyone or anything else

most /məʊst/ more than anything else – use this especially to talk about something that you like, want, need, or dislike more than anything else: *I want to study biology – that's what interests me most.* | *The part we enjoyed most was the trip to the Grand Canyon.*

most of all (=much more than anything else) *What the people here need most is food and clean water.*

the most /ðə 'məʊst/ a larger amount or number than anyone or anything else: *In a fair tax system those who earn the most should pay the most.*

the most things/points/votes etc *The player who scores the most points wins.*

the most money/fuel/information etc *Choose the program that gives you the most information.*

3 the largest possible amount

the most /ðə 'məʊst/ the largest amount that is possible: *I'm afraid £500 is the most I can offer you.* | *The most you can hope to achieve is a 10% increase in production.*

maximum /'mæksɪ̩məm/ [adj] the **maximum** amount of something is the largest amount that is possible or allowed

maximum amount/number/speed *Travelling at its maximum speed of 186 mph, the train reached Paris in less than two hours.* | *We want our message to reach the maximum number of people.*

the maximum (=the maximum number or amount) *Thirty students per class is the maximum.*

top /tɒp‖tɑːp/ [adj only before noun] **top speed/price/salary etc** the highest speed, price etc, or the most that is possible: *The 1.6 litre sports version has a top speed of 121 mph.* | *The top price paid was $1,200,000 for a print by Degas.*

⚠ **Top** is often used in newspapers, advertisements etc. **Maximum** is more formal or more technical than **top**.

4 most often

mostly/mainly /'məʊstli, 'meɪnli/ [adv] use this to say that someone does one thing more than they do anything else: *We eat mostly Italian food.* | *She has to travel abroad a lot, mostly to Spain and France.* | *a singer whose records are bought mainly by teenage girls*

in most cases /ɪn 'məʊst ˌkeɪsɪz/ use this to say that things happen in one way more often than in any other way, in the situation that you are talking about: *In most cases the new drug is very effective.* | *The seeds will start to grow within two weeks in most cases.*

most of the time /ˌməʊst əv ðə ˌtaɪm/ almost always: *Most of the time I just answer the phone and type letters.* | *This place is really busy most of the time.*

MOTHER

WOMAN   FATHER

see also

FAMILY   BABY

CHILD

1 mother

mother /'mʌðəʳ/ [n C] *Her mother is a teacher.* | *Like most mothers, I always felt anxious when my children came home late.* | *Terri Godwin, a mother of three, was attacked as she walked home yesterday.*

mum BRITISH **mom** AMERICAN /mʌm, mɒm‖mɑːm/ [n C] SPOKEN a name you use to talk to your mother or to talk about her: *My mum and dad are both doctors.* | *Mom, what's for dinner?*

mummy BRITISH **mommy** AMERICAN /'mʌmi, 'mɒmi‖'mɑːmi/ [n C] SPOKEN a name for your mother – used especially by young children or when you are talking to young children: *Ben, is your mommy coming to the Christmas concert?* | *"Goodnight, Mummy," said Sara.*

plural **mummies/mommies**

2 like a mother

maternal/motherly /məˈtɜːʳnl, ˈmʌðəʳli/ [adj] caring and kind like a mother – use this about women or their feelings: *Claire was very maternal towards the other children.* | *She kept a maternal eye on them all.* | *Mrs Woodrow, a good-natured motherly woman, took care of their children while they were at work.*

MOVE/NOT MOVE

➡ if you mean 'move house', go to
HOUSES/WHERE PEOPLE LIVE

see also: FAST, SLOW, SHAKE, GO, SLIDE, RUN, TRAVEL, WALK, STOP

1 to move from one place or position to another

move /muːv/ [v I] to go to a different place or to change the position of your body: *Every time I move I get a pain in my shoulder.* | *Will you move so that I can come past, please?* | *Don't get off the bus while it's moving.* | *Don't move, or I'll shoot!*
+ away/forward/toward etc *She moved away from the window.*
move around (=to different parts of an area) *I can hear someone moving around downstairs!*

movement /'muːvmənt/ [n C/U] when something or someone moves: *the dancer's graceful movements* | *Any movement will set off the alarm.*
+ of *Tourists come to see the mass movement of these animals across the plains of Africa.*

moving /'muːvɪŋ/ [adj only before noun] not staying still, but changing position or going from one place to another: *This photograph was taken from the window of a moving vehicle.* | *All the moving parts of the engine must be kept well oiled.*

2 to move something from one place or position to another

move /muːv/ [v T] to take something to a different place or change the position of something: *Will you move your car, please – it's blocking the road.* | *I think my hand is broken – I can't move my fingers.*

move sth to/into sth *We'll have to move the table into the hall.*

transfer /træns'fɜːr/ [v T] to move something and put it in a different place or container
transfer sth (from sth) to sth *Transfer the cookies to a wire rack to cool.* | *Information can be transferred from one computer to another.*

transferring – transferred – have transferred

⚠ Transfer is more formal than move.

3 to keep moving your body

fidget /'fɪdʒɪt/ [v I] to keep moving or playing with your fingers, hands, feet etc, because you are bored or nervous: *Stop fidgeting!*
+ with *Diana started fidgeting with her pencil.*

can't keep still /ˌkɑːnt kiːp 'stɪl/ ˌkænt-/ SPOKEN if you **can't keep still**, you keep moving your body because you are excited or nervous and you cannot relax: *I was so excited that I couldn't keep still all morning!*

twitch /twɪtʃ/ [v I] if part of your body **twitches**, it makes small movements that you cannot control: *My eyelid won't stop twitching.*

4 something that you can move from one place to another

portable /'pɔːrtəbəl/ [adj] a **portable** machine or piece of equipment is designed to be carried or moved easily: *We only have a little portable TV.* | *a portable computer*

5 unable to move or impossible to move

can't move /ˌkɑːnt 'muːv/ ˌkænt-/ ESPE-CIALLY SPOKEN if you **can't move**, you are unable to move, for example because you are injured: *I was so frightened that I couldn't move.*
can't move sth *I can't move my leg – I think it's broken.*

stuck /stʌk/ [adj not before noun] something that is **stuck** is fixed or trapped in a particular position or place and it cannot be moved: *I can't open the window – it's stuck.* | *The elevator's stuck again.*
+ in *Our bus was stuck in a traffic jam for three hours!*
get stuck (=become stuck) *They tried to drive through the snow, but the car got stuck.*

jammed /dʒæmd/ [adj not before noun] something that is **jammed** cannot be moved because it is trapped between two surfaces or trapped between parts of a machine: *This drawer's jammed – I can't get it open.*
+ in/under/between etc *The paper has got jammed in the printer again.*

stiff /stɪf/ [adj not usually before noun] if your fingers, back, neck, legs etc are **stiff**, it is difficult and usually painful for you to move them: *I slept on the hard ground, and woke up with a stiff neck.*

paralysed BRITISH **paralyzed** AMERICAN /ˈpærəlaɪzd/ [adj] someone who is **paralysed** or **paralyzed** cannot move, either because of an injury or because of fear, shock, etc: *A car crash in 1989 left him completely paralysed.*
+ by/with *His father had been partially paralyzed by the fall.* | *She stood at the side of the stage, paralysed with fear.*

6 not moving

still /stɪl/ [adj not before noun] not moving – use this especially about people who are not moving or about places where there is no wind: *There was no wind and the trees were completely still.* | *Anna looked out across the still water of the lake.*
keep/stand/sit still *Keep still while I tie your shoes.* | *I want you all to sit still and listen to the story.*

stationary /ˈsteɪʃənəri‖-neri/ [adj] **stationary car/vehicle/truck/traffic** a car, vehicle etc that is not moving: *The truck swerved and hit a stationary vehicle.* | *a four-mile queue of stationary traffic*

> ⚠ **Stationary** is more formal than 'not moving'.

at a standstill /ət ə ˈstændstɪl/ if traffic or a vehicle is **at a standstill**, it is not moving, especially when this is annoying: *Traffic was at a standstill on the motorway.* | *When I woke up, the train was at a standstill.*

WORD BANK

MUSIC

TELEVISION AND RADIO
DANCE   FREE TIME
SING   see   ART
         also
SOUND   FAMOUS
THEATRE   MODERN 2
FILMS/MOVIES

1 playing music

music /ˈmjuːzɪk/ [n U] the sounds made by people singing or playing musical instruments: *What sort of music do you like?* | *listening to music on the radio*
live music (=not recorded music) *The club has live music every Saturday night.*

> ⚠ **Music** can also mean the art and skill of writing or playing music: *studying music at school* | *music lessons* | *the Royal College of Music*

play /pleɪ/ [v I/T] to make music on a musical instrument: *Jane can play 'Yesterday' on the flute.* | *Do you play in an orchestra?*
play the piano/trumpet/drums etc *I didn't know you could play the violin.*

instrument/musical instrument /ˈɪnstrʊmənt, mjuːzɪkəl ˈɪnstrʊmənt/ [n C] an object such as a piano, a guitar, or a violin that you use to play music: *brass instruments*

perform /pərˈfɔːrm/ [v I/T] FORMAL to sing or play music in front of people who have come to listen: *She still gets very nervous about performing in public.* | *The orchestra will be at the Festival Hall tonight, performing a selection of works by Russian composers.*

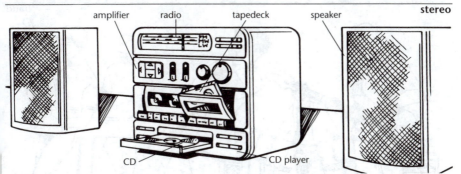

stereo

amplifier   radio   tapedeck   speaker

CD   CD player

2 listening to music

cassette/tape /kəˈset, teɪp/ [n C] a small flat plastic case containing a long thin piece of plastic material that is used for recording and playing sounds: *I bought him a cassette of folk music for Christmas.* | *a blank tape*

CD/compact disc /ˌsiː ˈdiː, ˌkɒmpækt ˈdɪsk‖ˌkɑːm-/ [n C] a shiny circular piece of hard plastic on which recorded music is stored

cassette player (also **tape recorder/ tape deck**) /kəˈset ˌpleɪəʳ, ˈteɪp rɪˌkɔːʳdəʳ, ˈteɪp dek/ [n C] a piece of electrical equipment used for playing cassettes

CD player /ˌsiː ˈdiː ˈpleɪəʳ/ [n C] a piece of electrical equipment used for playing compact discs

stereo /ˈsteriəʊ, ˈstɪə-/ [n C] a piece of electrical equipment used for playing cassettes and compact discs

Walkman /ˈwɔːkmən/ [n C] TRADEMARK a small cassette player or CD player that you can carry with you so that you can listen to music through headphones

headphones /ˈhedfəʊnz/ [n plural] a piece of equipment that you wear over your ears in order to listen to a radio, cassette, or compact disc: *a pair of headphones*

3 types of music

classical /ˈklæsɪkəl/ [adj] **classical** music is music which is regarded as serious and has been popular for a very long time, for example the music of Beethoven, Mozart, or Tchaikovsky: *a concert of classical music*

jazz /dʒæz/ [n U] music that was originally played by black Americans in the early 20th century, which has a strong beat and has parts in it that performers play alone: *My friend, Tony, plays trumpet in a jazz band.*

pop /pɒp‖pɑːp/ [n U] modern music that is popular with young people and usually has simple tunes and a strong beat: *one of Britain's most successful pop singers, George Michael* | *the 1970s pop group ABBA*

rock /rɒk‖rɑːk/ [n U] a type of popular modern music with electric guitars and a strong loud beat: *American rock bands such as Pearl Jam and Red Hot Chilli Peppers* | *veteran rock guitarist, Eric Clapton*

dance /dɑːns‖dæns/ [n U] a name for some types of modern music such as house, techno etc, that are made using electronic equipment and have a very fast, strong beat

> ⚠ Don't use **dance** to describe more traditional music that people dance to, such as music for the waltz or tango.

folk/folk music /fəʊk, ˈfəʊk ˌmjuːzɪk/ [n U] a type of traditional music in which people sing and play instruments without any electronic equipment: *a folk club*

world music /ˈwɜːʳld ˌmjuːzɪk/ [n U] music from places such as South America, Africa, the Middle East, and the Far East

4 people in music

musician /mjuːˈzɪʃən/ [n C] someone who play a musical instrument very well or someone who does this as their job: *one of our most talented young musicians*

M

conductor /kənˈdʌktəʳ/ [n C] someone who stands in front of a group of musicians or singers and directs their playing or singing

orchestra /ˈɔːrkəstrə/ [n C] a large group of people playing many different kinds of instruments and led by a conductor: *the Hallé Orchestra*

choir /kwaɪəʳ/ [n C] a large group of people who sing together, often in a church or school

band /bænd/ [n C] a small group of musicians who play popular music such as jazz, rock, or pop: *a jazz band*
be in a band *Lots of girls want to go out with Sonia's brother because he's in a band.*

singer /ˈsɪŋəʳ/ [n C] someone who sings, especially as their job: *Rosie's a singer in a rock band.* | *an opera singer*
lead singer (=the most important singer in a popular music group) *Jarvis Cocker is lead singer with Pulp.*

pop star /ˈpɒp ˌstɑːʳ‖ˈpɑːrp-/ [n C] someone who is famous and successful as a singer or musician in a pop group: *My sister has pictures of pop stars all over her bedroom wall.*

When you see **EC**, go to the
ESSENTIAL COMMUNICATION section.

5 going to see people play music

concert /ˈkɒnsəʳt‖ˈkɑːrn-/ [n C] a performance given by musicians: *a pop concert* | *the school concert*
+ of *a concert of orchestral music by Beethoven and Schubert*
go to a concert *On Friday we're going to a concert of modern African music.*

go to see /ˌgəʊ tə ˈsiː/ to go to see a particular singer or band perform – use this especially about going to see modern popular musicians: *We're going to see Oasis at Knebworth.*

performance /pəʳˈfɔːʳməns/ [n C] when a musician or group of musicians performs a piece of music
+ of *There are no tickets left for this evening's performance of Mozart's Requiem.*
give a performance *The band gave one of their best performances at the Woodstock Festival.*

gig /gɪg/ [n C] INFORMAL a performance by a musician or group of musicians playing modern popular music or jazz
do/play a gig (=perform at a concert) *They are doing about 30 gigs on their European tour.*
go to a gig *Let's go to a gig this weekend.*

festival /'festɪvəl/ [n C] an occasion when many different musical groups or singers perform, which happens at the same time and in the same place every year: *I first heard them play at the Pittsburgh Jazz Festival.* | *Are you going to the Glastonbury festival this year?*

concert hall /'kɒnsəˤt ˌhɔːl‖'kɑːn-/ [n C] a large building where concerts are performed

jazz club /'dʒæz ˌklʌb/ [n C] a place where you can listen to jazz bands and singers

venue /'venjuə/ [n C] a place where a concert, festival etc takes place: *The club is a popular venue for reggae bands.*

6 people who write music

composer /kəm'pəuzəˤ/ [n C] someone who writes music, especially classical music: *Henry Purcell was one of the greatest English composers.*

songwriter /'sɒŋˌraɪtəˤ‖'sɔːŋ-/ [n C] someone who writes songs: *Most of Elton John's early hits were written by songwriter Bernie Taupin.*

singer-songwriter (=someone who writes songs and sings them) *singer-songwriter Sheryl Crow*

7 writing music

compose /kəm'pəuz/ [v I/T] to write a piece of music, especially classical music: *a song composed by Schubert* | *The children will now play some pieces that they composed themselves.*

write /raɪt/ [v I/T] to write a song or a piece of music: *an opera written by Verdi*

MUST

FORCE SB TO DO STH

FORBID · LAW

see also

LET · SHOULD

RULE · STRICT/ NOT STRICT

1 when you have to do something

must /mʌst/ [modal verb] to have to do something, especially because you feel that you should do it or because there is a rule that says you have to do it

must do sth *All passengers must wear seatbelts.* | *I must go and do my homework.* | *Accidents must be reported to the safety officer.*

must sb do sth? FORMAL *Must you leave so soon?*

⚠ Only use **must** in the present tense. The past tense of **must** is **had to**: *At my old school, we had to wear a uniform.* The future tense of **must** is **will have to**: *If you fail the test, you will have to take it again.*

⚠ Don't say 'we must to go'. Say **we must go**.

⚠ You can say **I must** do something to mean that you feel you really should do it because it is important or urgent: *I must write to my mother.* | *I really must try to stop smoking.*

have to do sth /ˌhæv tuː 'duː (sth)/ if you **have to do something** you must do it, especially because the situation that you are in makes it necessary or because there is a rule that says you must do it: *I have to stay late today.* | *She had to leave early because she wasn't feeling well.* | *The doctor said I would have to have an operation.* | *Do we have to take our passports with us?*

have got to do sth BRITISH *I've got to return my library books today.*

need to do sth /ˌniːd tə 'duː (sth)/ to have to do something because you think it is necessary or someone else thinks it is necessary: *We need to buy some more potatoes.* | *She told me I needed to get my hair cut.* | *Do I really need to go to this meeting?*

be forced to do sth /biː ˌfɔːˤst tə 'duː (sth)/ to have to do something that you do not want to do because you are in a situation that makes it impossible to avoid: *She was forced to retire at the age of 50 because of health problems.* | *There was a train strike that day so we were forced to cancel the party.*

M

feel obliged to do sth /fiːl əˌblaɪdʒd tə 'duː (sth)/ to feel that you should do something because other people expect you to do it and will be disappointed or upset if you do not: *I felt obliged to invite them all.*

have no alternative /hæv ˌnəʊ ɔːl'tɜːrnətɪv/ to have to do something, even though you do not want to, because there is nothing else you can possibly do in the situation: *The police say they had no alternative: the man was armed and they had to shoot him.*

have no alternative but to do sth *He had no alternative but to resign.*

2 when you must not do something

➡ see also **FORBID**

must not/mustn't /'mʌst nɒt, 'mʌsənt/ use this to tell or order someone not to do something: *This book must not be removed from the library.*

must not/mustn't do sth *Remember, you mustn't tell Pat about this.*

> ⚠ Only use **must not/mustn't** in the present tense. When talking about the past, use **couldn't** or **wasn't/weren't allowed to**: *He couldn't stay in the US because he didn't have a green card.* | *The children were not allowed to watch horror movies.* When talking about the future use **will not be allowed to**: *Under the new rules, employees will not be allowed to smoke in the office.*
>
> ⚠ Don't say 'you mustn't to go'. Say **you mustn't go.**
>
> ⚠ Don't confuse **must not do something** (=when you are not allowed to to it) and **not have to do something** (=when you can do it, but you do not need to).

can't /kɑːnt‖kænt/ SPOKEN use this to say that someone is not allowed to do something: *"Ben wants to borrow the car." "Well tell him he can't."*

can't do sth *I'm sorry, you know I can't discuss my work – it's secret.*

> When you see **EC**, go to the **ESSENTIAL COMMUNICATION** section.

> ⚠ Only use **can't** in the present tense. When talking about the past, use **couldn't** or **wasn't/weren't allowed to**. When talking about the future, use **will not be allowed to**.
>
> ⚠ Don't say 'you can't to go'. Say **you can't go.**

not be allowed /nɒt biː ə'laʊd/ if something **is not allowed**, there is a rule that forbids it: *Smoking is not allowed on the train.*

sb is not allowed to do sth *You are not allowed to use a dictionary during the test.*

3 something that must be done

compulsory /kəm'pʌlsəri/ [adj] FORMAL something that is **compulsory** must be done because of a rule or law: *Compulsory education (=when all children have to go to school) was introduced in 1870.*

it is compulsory for sb to do sth *It's compulsory for all drivers to have insurance.*

necessary /'nesɪ̩səri‖-seri/ [adj] if something is **necessary**, there are very good reasons why it should be done, and it would not be sensible to avoid doing it: *If any changes are necessary, you can make them.*

it is necessary to do sth *Is it really necessary to keep all the doors locked?*

it is necessary for sb to do sth *The doctor says it may be necessary for me to have an operation.*

make it necessary to do sth *The heavy rain made it necessary to close several roads.*

essential/vital /ɪ'senʃəl, 'vaɪtl/ [adj] if something is **essential** or **vital**, it is very important to do it, and there could be serious problems if it is not done: *Choosing the right equipment is vital.* | *In cases of heart attack, immediate medical help is absolutely essential.*

it is essential/vital to do sth *It is vital to take precautions before handling toxic substances.*

it is essential/vital that *It is essential that you finish the job before Christmas.* | *It is vital that you keep accurate records of what you spend.*

4 when you do not have to do something

not have to do sth /nɒt hæv tə 'duː (sth)/ if you do **not have to do** something, you can do it if you want, but you are not forced to do it, either by a rule or by another person, or by the situation you are in: *Paola came from a wealthy family and didn't have to work.* | *You don't have to go if you don't want to.*

> ⚠ Don't confuse **not have to do something** (=when you are not forced to do it) and **must not do something** (=when you are not allowed to do it).

there is no need to do sth /ðeər ɪz ˌnəʊ 'niːd tə 'duː (sth)/ SPOKEN say this to tell someone that it is not necessary for them to do something: *There's no need to do the dishes – I'll do them in the morning.* | *There's no need to bring a towel – we have plenty.*

unnecessary/not necessary /ʌn-ˈnesəsəri, nɒt 'nesəsəri‖-seri/ [adj] if something is **unnecessary** or **not necessary**, is it not needed or there is no good reason for you to do it: *They want to build another shopping mall here, but we think it's completely unnecessary.*
+ to do sth *It's not necessary to oil your bike every day.*

not need to do sth (also **needn't do sth** BRITISH) /nɒt 'niːd tə 'duː (sth), 'niːdnt duː (sth)/ to not have to do something because it is not necessary and there will not be any problems if you do not do it: *You don't need to tell Sandy – she already knows.* | *You needn't come with me – I can find my own way to the station.* | *Marian had a rich husband and did not need to work.*

> ⚠ Don't say 'you needn't to pay now'. Say **you needn't pay now**.

> ⚠ Don't confuse **not need to do something** (=when something is not necessary) and **must not do something** (=when something is not allowed).

optional /'ɒpʃənəl‖'ɑːp-/ [adj] if something is **optional**, you do not have to do it or use it but you can if you want to: *We all had to study English, but Spanish was optional.*

voluntary /'vɒləntəri‖'vɑːlənteri/ [adj] a **voluntary** activity is one that you do because you want to do it, especially because you believe it is useful or will help other people, and not because you have to: *I do voluntary work at a young mothers' centre.* | *We get all our money from voluntary contributions.*

5 to say that someone must do something

insist /ɪn'sɪst/ [v I/T] to say firmly that someone must do something or that something must happen, and not let anyone refuse: *"You must stay," he insisted.*
insist (that) sb do sth *They insisted that we paid for the damage before we left.*
insist on doing sth (=say that you must be allowed to do something) *I insist on speaking to the manager.*

MYSELF/YOURSELF

➡ see also **ALONE**

1 when you do something yourself, instead of someone else doing it for you

yourself/myself etc [pronoun] if you do something **yourself**, no-one else does it for you: *I made these curtains myself.* | *Why can't your boyfriend cook lunch himself?* | *"Could you pass me that book?" "Get it yourself!"*

personally /'pɜːʳsənəli/ [adv] if an important person does something **personally**, they do it, although you would normally expect someone else to do it for them: *The President wrote to us personally to thank us for our hard work.*

in person /ɪn 'pɜːʳsən/ if you do something **in person**, you do it by going somewhere yourself, instead of writing, telephoning, or asking someone else to do it: *He delivered the document in person to*

Friedman's house. | *Do I have to come and get it in person?*

first-hand /ˌfɜːʳst ˈhænd◀/ [adj only before noun] **first-hand experience/knowledge/account etc** experience, knowledge etc that you get by doing or seeing something yourself, not by reading about it or hearing about it from someone else: *She has first-hand experience of the French education system, having taught there for five years.* | *a first-hand account of the robbery, by someone who witnessed it*

2 when someone only thinks about himself or herself

selfish /ˈselfɪʃ/ [adj] someone who is **selfish** only thinks about what they need or want, and never thinks about how other people feel: *Amy, don't be so selfish! Let the others have a turn.* | *a selfish old man* | *selfish motives*

selfishly [adv] *She selfishly refused to give us any of the food.*

selfishness [n U] when someone behaves in a selfish way: *a political philosophy based on selfishness and greed*

N

NAME

1 a person's name

name /neɪm/ [n C] *What's your name?* | *I'm not very good at remembering people's names.* | *His name is Raymond Ford.*
full name (=all your names) *Ayrton Senna's full name was Ayrton Senna da Silva.*

surname/last name /'sɜːrneɪm, 'lɑːst ,neɪm‖'læst-/ [n C] your last name, which is the same as your parents' name: *Smith is the most common English surname.*

> ⚠ Until recently, women always took their husband's **surname** or **last name** when they got married, but many women no longer do this.

first name /'fɜːrst ,neɪm/ [n C] the name that your parents choose for you when you are born, which in western countries comes at the beginning of your full name: *Her first name is Liz. I don't know her surname.*

maiden name /'meɪdn ,neɪm/ [n C] the surname that a woman had before she was married: *My mother kept her maiden name when she got married.* (=did not change her name to her husband's name)

initials /ɪ'nɪʃəlz/ [n plural] the first letters of your names: *There's no need to write out your full name. Just your initials will do.* | *a suitcase marked with the initials JR*

title /'taɪtl/ [n C] a word such as Mrs, Miss, Ms, Mr, Dr, or Professor that you put before your name: *The title 'Ms' became much more popular in the 1980s.*

2 your name when you write it on a cheque, at the end of a letter etc

signature /'sɪɡnətʃər/ [n C] your name as you usually write it, especially when you write it on an important document, a cheque, or a letter: *I can't read the signature on this letter.* | *We got more than 4000 signatures on our petition to save the park.*

autograph /'ɔːtəɡrɑːf‖-ɡræf/ [n C] a famous person's name that they write and give to someone who admires them: *Can I have your autograph?* | *I'd be too shy to ask for his autograph.*

3 a name that is not your real name

nickname /'nɪkneɪm/ [n C] a name given to someone by their friends or family, which is not their real name and is often chosen because of something about their appearance or behaviour: *At school, her nickname was Carrots because of her red hair.*

false name /ˌfɔːls 'neɪm/ [n C] a name that someone uses instead of their real name, so that people will not find out who they really are: *It is illegal to give a false name to your employer.* | *They used a false name to hire a car.*

stage name /'steɪdʒ ,neɪm/ [n C] the name used by an actor, singer etc instead of their real name: *Greta Garbo was the stage name of Greta Gustavson, born in Stockholm in 1905.*

4 the name of a place, object etc

name /neɪm/ [n C] *I've forgotten the name of the street where she lives.*
the Chinese/French etc name for sth *The Chinese name for this plant means 'cat's ears'.*

brand name /'brænd ,neɪm/ [n C] the name given to a product by the company that makes it, often including the name of the company itself: *Our customers prefer goods with brand names, such as Levi's or Adidas.*

5 to have a particular name

sb's name is /(sb's) 'neɪm ɪz/ *Hi! My name's Ted. I'm from Florida.* | *"Who's that man over there?" "His name is Lucio Mannonetti and he owns the company."*

be called /biː ˈkɔːld/ to have a particular name – use this about a person, thing, or place: *There's someone called Russell on the phone for you.* | *What's the new teacher called?* | *They are in favour of what is called 'sustainable development'.*

be named /biː ˈneɪmd/ ESPECIALLY AMERICAN someone who **is named** Paul, Jane etc has the name Paul, Jane etc: *Their new baby is named Caroline.* | *She went to the movies with some guy named Rudi.*

> ⚠ Don't say 'what's their son named?' Say **what's their son called?** Don't use **be named** in questions, use **be called**.

be known as /biː ˈnəʊn æz/ if someone or something **is known as** a particular name, that is the name that people call them, although it is not their real name: *He was known as Rambo to his friends.* | *This area is known as Little Odessa because there are a lot of Russians living here.*

6 to give a name to someone or something

call /kɔːl/ [v T] to give a name to someone or something
call sb Paul/Jane etc *My mother wanted to call me Yuri.* | *Guidebooks call Chicago 'The Windy City'.* | *This is what psychologists call 'body language'.*

name /neɪm/ [v T] ESPECIALLY AMERICAN to officially give someone or something a name: *Have they named the baby yet?*
name sb Paul/Jane etc *We named our daughter Sarah.*
name sb/sth after (also **name sb/sth for** AMERICAN) *Bill was named after his father.* | *The new college is going to be named for John F Kennedy.*

christen /ˈkrɪsən/ [v T] to give a baby its name at a Christian religious ceremony
christen sb Paul etc/be christened Paul etc *They christened him Patrick John.* | *She was christened Jessica, but everyone calls her Jess.*

rename /riːˈneɪm/ [v T] to change something's name: *New Amsterdam was renamed New York in the 17th century.*

> When you see **EC**, go to the **ESSENTIAL COMMUNICATION** section.

7 to publicly announce the name of someone

name /neɪm/ [v T] to publicly say who someone is, by telling people his or her name: *She refused to name the father of her child.*
name sb as sb *Police have named the dead woman as Annabel Tomms.*

identify /aɪˈdentɪfaɪ/ [v T] to officially recognize someone and say that you know who they are, for example in order to help the police: *The victim identified her attacker in court.* | *Greg had to identify the body of his wife.*
identifying – identified – have identified

8 what you call someone or something when you cannot remember their name

Q**what's his name/what's her name** /ˈwɒts hɪz neɪm, ˈwɒts həʳ neɪm/ SPOKEN INFORMAL say this when you cannot remember someone's name: *I saw Guy with what's her name in town yesterday.*

Q**what's its name/whatsit** (also **thingy** BRITISH) /ˈwɒts ɪts neɪm, ˈwɒtsɪt, ˈθɪŋiˈwɑːt-/ SPOKEN INFORMAL say this when you cannot remember the name of something: *"Can I have the whatsit for the TV?" "You mean the remote control?"*

NATURAL

not made by humans or changed by humans

➡ if you mean 'land where there are trees and fields and not many buildings', go to **COUNTRYSIDE**
➡ see also **LAND AND SEA, ENVIRONMENT**

1 plants/animals/places/substances

natural /ˈnætʃərəl/ [adj usually before noun] not made, caused, or changed by humans: *It was fascinating to see the elephants in their natural environment.* | *The river had worn away the rock to form a natural bridge.* | *a pipeline carrying natural gas from under the sea*

wild /waɪld/ [adj usually before noun] **wild flowers/plants/animals/birds** flowers, plants, and animals that are in their natural state and have not been changed or controlled by humans: *There were lots of wild flowers growing by the roadside.* | *Wildcats are usually much larger than domestic ones.*
grow wild *There were banana trees growing wild on the edge of the forest.*

2 food/drink

natural /ˈnætʃərəl/ [adj usually before noun] produced without using chemicals: *The manufacturers claim that only natural ingredients are used in their products.* | *These days, consumers prefer drinks that contain natural flavourings*

organic /ɔːˈɡænɪk/ [adj] **organic fruit/ vegetables/produce** fruit, vegetables etc that have been grown without using chemicals to help them grow: *Most supermarkets now sell organic produce.* | *Organic fruit is generally more expensive.*

pure /pjʊəʳ/ [adj only before noun] **pure** food or drink has not had anything added to it: *pure orange juice* | *The burgers are made of 100% pure beef.*

3 not natural

➡ opposite **REAL 1**
➡ see also **FALSE**

artificial /ˌɑːrtɪ̩ˈfɪʃəl◄/ [adj] not made of natural materials or substances: *The food contains no artificial colours or flavourings.* | *a type of artificial grass called Astroturf*

man-made /ˌmæn ˈmeɪd◄/ [adj] made by humans, but similar to something that is natural: *The Badesee is a man-made lake which is popular with swimmers.* | *a coat made of 80% wool and 20% man-made fibres*

> ⚠ **Artificial** and **man-made** are similar in meaning, but you can use **artificial** to give the idea that something is bad because it is not natural: *I don't like these artificial flowers, do you?*

synthetic /sɪnˈθetɪk/ [adj] **synthetic** materials, cloth, or substances are similar to natural ones but are made by a chemical process: *Her dress was made of some shiny synthetic material.* | *synthetic rubber*

processed /ˈprəʊsest‖ˈprɑː-/ [adj only before noun] **processed** food has been treated with chemicals in order to make it stay in good condition or to make it look good: *processed cheese* | *Processed food may lack the vitamins found in fresh food.*

NEAR

➡ opposite **FAR**
➡ if you want to know about words meaning 'next to', go to **POSITION & DIRECTION**

1 not far away

near / far

near /nɪəʳ/ [preposition/adv/adj] only a short distance from a person, place, or thing: *Bob was standing near enough to hear what they were saying.*
near sth/sb *We camped near a large lake.* | *Don't go near the fire.* | *Have you ever been to Versailles? It's near Paris.*
nearer to/nearest to *If we moved to Dallas we'd be nearer to my parents.*
near here *The accident happened somewhere near here.*

close /kləʊs/ [adj/adv] very near to something or someone, or almost touching them: *As we approached Abbeville, the gunfire sounded very close.*
+ to *Don't drive too close to the edge of the road.*
close together *The houses were built very close together.*
+ behind/beside *Suddenly we heard footsteps close behind us.* | *Nancy sat down close beside me.*
close by (=near where you are) *Is there a gas station close by?*

not far /nɒt ˈfɑːʳ/ not a very long distance away – use this about somewhere that is near enough to be easy to get to: *"How far's the station?" "Oh, not far – about ten minutes by car."*
+ from *Asti is not far from the French border.*
not far away *Our hotel was in the centre of town but the beach wasn't far away.*

nearby /ˌnɪəʳˈbaɪ◄/ [adv] near the place where you are or the place you are talking about: *Dave, who was sitting nearby, laughed when he heard this. | The house is nice, and a lot of my friends live nearby.*
nearby [adj only before noun] *Lucy was staying with her aunt in the nearby town of Hamilton.*

neighbouring BRITISH **neighboring** AMERICAN /ˈneɪbərɪŋ/ [adj only before noun] **neighbouring country/town/area etc** a country, town etc that is near the place where you are or the place you are talking about: *The fire quickly spread to the neighbouring areas.*

local /ˈləʊkəl/ [adj only before noun] **local store/hospital/school etc** a store, hospital etc that is in the area where you live and that you are most likely to use: *We spent the summer evenings on the beach or in the local park.*
sb's local school/cinema *You can find all these books in your local library.*
locally [adv] in the area near where you live or work: *We prefer to do all our shopping locally. | Do you live locally?*

within walking distance /wɪðɪn ˈwɔːkɪŋ ˌdɪstəns/ when a place is not far away, and you can walk there easily: *There are several good restaurants within walking distance.*
+ of *Dr Goldthorpe lived within walking distance of the University.*

2 the nearest house/ shop/station etc

the nearest /ðə ˈnɪərɪst/ **the nearest shop/station/bank etc** the shop, station etc that is closest to where you are: *Excuse me, where's the nearest subway station?*

the next /ðə ˈnekst/ **the next house/ street/room etc** the house, street etc that is closest to the one you are in or the one you are talking about: *The people in the next apartment were making a lot of noise.*

3 convenient because it is near

convenient for (also **handy for** BRITISH INFORMAL) /kənˈviːniənt fɔːʳ, ˈhændi fɔːʳ/ if your home, office etc is **convenient for** or **handy for** a particular place, that place is near it and easy to reach: *The place where we live now is very convenient for the school – it's only a couple of minutes on foot. | Our flat is on the High Street, so it's very handy for the shops.*

4 near enough to pick up or touch

handy /ˈhændi/ [adj] if something is **handy**, it is near enough for you to pick it up and use it quickly and easily
keep/have sth handy *Keep a pen and paper handy, because we'll be giving our phone number in a moment. | Make sure you have the manual handy when you install the new software.*
handy – handier – handiest

within reach /wɪðɪn ˈriːtʃ/ if something is **within reach**, it is near enough for you to take hold of it when you stretch out your hand: *As soon as she was within reach, he grabbed her wrist.*

5 to get nearer

get near/get close /ˌget ˈnɪəʳ, ˌget ˈkləʊs/ to go or come nearer to a person, place, or thing: *As Kay got near the house she began to feel nervous.*
+ to *Don't get too close to the microphone.*

approach /əˈprəʊtʃ/ [v I/T] to move gradually closer to a person, place, or thing: *The train slowed down as it started to approach the station. | We could hear footsteps approaching down the corridor.*

⚠ Don't say 'he approached to the place'. Say **he approached the place**.

catch up/be catching up /ˌkætʃ ˈʌp, biː ˌkætʃɪŋ ˈʌp/ to gradually get closer to a moving person or vehicle in front of you, by moving faster than they move:

Schumacher is still in front but the other Ferrari is catching up.
+ with Looking back, I could see that the other walkers were catching up with us.

NEED/NOT NEED

➡ see also **MUST, IMPORTANT/NOT IMPORTANT**

1 to need something

need /niːd/ [v T] if you **need** something, you must have it, because you cannot live, succeed, or do something without it: *It's cold outside – you'll need a coat.* | *I need time to think.* | *I think she might need a doctor.*
need sth for sth *He needs the information for an article he's writing.*
need to do sth (=when it is necessary for someone to do something) *That cat looks as if she needs to go to the vet.*
need sb to do sth *We need more volunteers to help clean up after the party.*
need cleaning/washing/mending etc (=need to be cleaned etc) *The plants need watering at least once a week.*
badly need sth (=need something very much) *The team badly needs some younger players.*

> ⚠ Don't say 'I am needing', 'he is needing', etc. Say **I need, he needs** etc.

require /rɪˈkwaɪər/ [v T] FORMAL to need something: *Is there anything further you require, sir?* | *Guests who require special diets should inform the catering manager.*
be required for sth *I regret that you do not have the qualifications required for this job.*

> ⚠ Don't say 'I am requiring', 'she is requiring' etc. Say **I require she requires** etc.

🔊**could do with sth/could use sth** /kʊd ˈduː wɪð (sth), kʊd ˈjuːz (sth)/ SPOKEN INFORMAL say that you **could do with** something or **could use** something when you feel that you need it and that it would improve things for you: *"Let's stop*

for a minute." "Sure, I could do with a rest." | *I could use some help around here.*

be desperate for sth /biː ˈdespərət fɔːʳ (sth)/ to urgently need something and want it very much: *I had to take the job – I was desperate for the money.* | *The heat was unbearable, and we were desperate for water and rest.*

2 when you cannot live without someone or something

can't do without /ˌkɑːnt duː wɪðˈaʊt‖ ˌkænt-/ to be unable to do the things that you have to do without someone who usually helps you or without something that you usually use: *He always says he couldn't do without his mobile phone.* | *My secretary's so efficient that I just can't do without her.*

depend on/be dependent on /dɪˈpend ɒn, biː dɪˈpendənt ɒn‖-ɑːn-/ [phrasal verb T] to be unable to live, exist, or continue normally without something or someone, because they provide you with what you need: *Since becoming blind she had been totally dependent on her husband.* | *Our research program depends entirely on gifts of money from private individuals.*
depend heavily/be heavily dependent on sth (=be very dependent on it) *Japan is heavily dependent on oil imports from the Middle East.*
dependent/be dependent on sth for sth *All young mammals depend on their parents for food and shelter.*

3 something you need

necessary /ˈnesəsəri‖-seri/ [adj] if something is **necessary**, you need to have it or do it: *Make sure you have all the necessary documents for your trip.*
if necessary (=if it is necessary) *If necessary, we will have to employ some extra people to finish the work.*
+ for *Fats in our diet are necessary for both heat and energy.*
it is necessary (for sb) to do sth FORMAL *It will be necessary to close the pool while the repairs take place.* | *The doctor says it may be necessary for me to have an operation.*

essential /ɪˈsenʃəl/ [adj] if something is **essential**, you need it because you cannot be successful, healthy, safe etc without it: *Computers form an essential part of any business nowadays.*

+ for *Calcium is essential for the development of healthy teeth and bones.*

it is essential to do sth *It is essential to read any document carefully before you sign it.*

it is essential that *It is essential that the oil is checked every 10,000 km.*

vital /ˈvaɪtl/ [adj] if something is **vital**, it is extremely important and you will have serious problems if you do not have it or do it: *One vital piece of evidence is missing – the murder weapon.* | *In this job, the ability to remain calm is vital.*

+ for *Efficient food production was vital for such a highly populated country.*

it is vital that *It is vital that you keep accurate records.*

sb's needs/the needs of sb /(sbˈs) ˈniːdz, ðə ˈniːdz ɒv (sb)/ the things that someone must have in order to live a normal, healthy, and comfortable life: *In designing new buildings we must consider the needs of disabled visitors.*

meet/satisfy sb's needs (=provide what someone needs) *Schools should try to meet the educational needs of every child.*

necessity /nɪˈsesɪti/ [n C] something that you need to have in order to live or to do your job: *Most Americans consider a phone a necessity rather than a luxury.*

an absolute necessity *A car is an absolute necessity for this job.*

the bare necessities (=the basic things that you must have, such as food and clothes) *Their wages are so low that they cannot even afford the bare necessities.*

⚠ Necessity is rather a formal word. In conversation it is more natural to say 'this is something we really need' (not 'this is a necessity').

plural **necessities**

4 the fact that something is needed

need /niːd/ [n singular] if there is a **need** for something, that thing is needed

+ for *the need for stricter safety regulations* | *Some politicians now believe there is a need for more discipline in schools.*

feel the need to do sth (=feel that you need to do something) *Don't you ever feel the need to take a vacation?*

5 to not need something

don't need /ˌdəʊnt ˈniːd/ to not need something or someone: *Do you want these text books? I don't need them any more.*

⚠ Don't say 'I am not needing', 'he is not needing' etc. Say **I don't need, he doesn't need** etc.

unnecessary/not necessary /ʌnˈnesəsəri, nɒt ˈnesəsəri‖-seri/ [adj] if something is **unnecessary** or **not necessary**, you do not need to have it or do it: *Don't fill your report with unnecessary information.* | *Dr Jacobs was furious when he discovered that the expense had been totally unnecessary.*

it is not necessary to do sth *It's not necessary to spend a lot of money on clothes to look good.*

unnecessarily [adv] *I think you're worrying unnecessarily. Just forget all about it.*

hardly necesssary /ˌhɑːrdli ˈnesəsəri‖ -seri/ not necessary at all – use this when you are surprised that someone thinks something is necessary: *They asked to see my passport, my driver's license, and my bank card, which was hardly necessary.*

spare /speər/ [adj usually before noun] use this about something which you do not need now, but which is available so that you can use it later or let someone else use it: *I always keep a spare can of oil in the garage.* | *We have two spare tickets for the game – do you want to come?* | *Do you have a spare pair of gloves I could borrow?*

can do without sb/sth /kən ˌduː wɪˈðaʊt (sb/sth)/ to not need someone or something, because you can live normally or do what you want to do without them: *The country now has a strong economy and can do without western aid.* | *He felt he could do without other people and was happy to live on his own.*

NEVER

➡ opposite **ALWAYS**
➡ see also **OFTEN, USUALLY, SOMETIMES**

1 never

never /ˈnevəʳ/ [adv] not once, or not at any time: *"Have you ever been to Paris?" "No, never."* | *The countryside was beautiful – I'll never forget it.* | *Ali had never seen snow before.* | *He never even says 'hello'.*

⚠ Don't use **never** with negative words like 'nobody', 'no one', and 'nothing'. Use **ever**: *Nobody will ever find me here.* You can use **never** with words like 'anybody', 'anything', and 'anywhere': *I'll never tell anyone.*

⚠ **Never** usually comes before the main verb: *He never told me.* If there is a modal or auxiliary verb (like **have, will, should** etc), **never** comes after this verb and before the main verb: *You must never speak to strangers.*

⚲never ever/never, never /ˌnevəʳ ˈevəʳ, ˌnevəʳ ˈnevəʳ/ SPOKEN say this when you want to emphasize strongly that something has never happened or will never happen: *You must never ever tell anyone what you heard tonight.* | *I'll never, never stop loving you.*

⚲not in a million years /ˌnɒt ɪn ə ˌmɪljən ˈjɪəʳz/ SPOKEN INFORMAL say this when you think it is completely impossible that something could ever happen: *You'll never get Kieran to give you that money – not in a million years!*

not once /nɒt ˈwʌns/ say this when you are surprised or annoyed because someone never did something, although they often had the opportunity to do it: *She's never said thank you – not once!* | *He hasn't once come here to see us.*

2 almost never

hardly ever /ˌhɑːʳdli ˈevəʳ/ almost never: *"How's Dorothy?" "I don't know. I hardly ever see her these days."* | *My grandmother hardly ever goes out of the house.*

When you see **EC**, go to the **ESSENTIAL COMMUNICATION** section.

⚠ **Hardly ever** is much more common in spoken English than **rarely** and **seldom**.

rarely/seldom /ˈreəʳli, ˈseldəm/ [adv] ESPECIALLY WRITTEN almost never: *Mr Gluck rarely went to bed before midnight, but tonight he felt very tired.* | *She seldom talked about her personal life.*

⚠ Don't say 'I go there seldom'. Say 'I **seldom** go there'. Use **seldom** before the main verb.

rare /reəʳ/ [adj] something that is **rare** does not happen often: *The disease is rare, but very dangerous.* | *On the rare occasions when I do go to the theatre, I really enjoy it.*

NEW

➡ opposite **OLD**
➡ see also **MODERN, SHINE 2**

1 recently made or produced

new /njuː‖nuː/ [adj] recently made, produced, or bought: *Do you like my new dress?* | *That's a nice bag – is it new?* | *the city's new hospital*

brand new (=completely new and almost unused) *Larry was very proud of his brand new BMW.*

buy sth new *I got a used video camera for $2000 – it would have cost twice that much if I'd bought it new.*

latest /ˈleɪtəst/ [adj only before noun] **the latest film/book/model/fashion** the film, book etc that has been produced or made most recently: *Have you seen Spielberg's latest movie?* | *the latest fashions from the Paris catwalks*

be just out /biː ˌdʒʌst ˈaʊt/ if a book, record, or film **is just out**, it has only recently arrived in the shops, cinemas etc: *REM's new album is just out.*

fresh /freʃ/ [adj] **fresh** food has been recently made, killed, or picked, and it still tastes good: *Make sure that the fish is fresh.*

fresh from the oven/sea/garden *The vegetables are picked fresh from the garden every day.*

freshly [adv] *These strawberries were freshly picked this morning.* | *freshly baked bread*

⚠ **Fresh** can also mean food that has not been frozen, dried, or put in cans: *fresh peas* | *fresh pasta*

2 instead of the one that you had before

new /njuː‖nuː/ [adj only before noun] your **new** job, home etc is the one you got most recently, and is different from the one you had before: *Are you enjoying your new job?* | *Have you met Keith's new girlfriend?* | *After the divorce, she went off to Canada to start a new life.*

another /əˈnʌðəʳ/ [determiner] if you want **another** job, **another** system etc, you want it instead of the one that you have now: *I decided to look for another job.* | *If you don't like one doctor, you can ask to see another.*

replace /rɪˈpleɪs/ [v T] if you **replace** something that is old or damaged, you put a new one in its place to be used instead of it: *The roof was in bad condition and needed to be completely replaced.*
replace sth with sth *They're replacing the old windows with modern ones.*

3 new ideas/methods/ information

new /njuː‖nuː/ [adj] **new** ideas, methods, or information did not exist before, or were not known about before: *important new scientific discoveries* | *Her lawyers have found new evidence that may prove her innocence.* | *the company's new non-smoking policy*

original /əˈrɪdʒɪnəl, -dʒənəl/ [adj] completely different from anything that has been thought of before
original idea/design/style *a jazz musician with a completely original style* | *My job is to think up creative and original advertising ideas.*

revolutionary /ˌrevəˈluːʃənəri‖-ʃəneri/ [adj] a **revolutionary** idea, method, or invention is completely different from anything that existed before, and is likely to bring important changes or improvements:

revolutionary technology for producing cheap, pollution-free energy | *a revolutionary new treatment for cancer*

4 a new government/ company

new /njuː‖nuː/ [adj] a **new** organization, government etc has only existed for a short time: *Within weeks of the election, the new government announced big tax cuts.* | *Thousands of new businesses are set up each year.* | *one of Europe's newest TV stations*

5 someone who has just started a new job, school etc

new /njuː‖nuː/ [adj] someone who is **new** has only recently arrived in a place, or has only recently started working in a job: *You're new here, aren't you?* | *All new employees are given training.*
+ to *Children who are new to the school may need extra help.*

newcomer /ˈnjuːkʌməʳ‖ˈnuː-/ [n C] someone who has only recently arrived in a place or has only recently started a job, sport, or other activity: *The villagers are very suspicious of newcomers.* | *The team includes some familiar faces as well as a few newcomers.*
+ to *Although she's a newcomer to the sport, she's already very successful.*

NEWS

➡ see also **INFORMATION, NEWSPAPERS AND MAGAZINES, TELEVISION AND RADIO**

1 news that people tell each other

news /njuːz‖nuːz/ [n U] information about something that happened recently
+ of *There hasn't been any news of him since he left home.*
+ that *He brought the news that their father was seriously ill.*
your/my/her news (=what you have been doing recently) *Sit down and tell me all your news.*
have good/bad news for sb *I'm afraid I have some bad news for you.*

hear news *Have you heard the news? Sara's going to have a baby.*
good/bad news *Good news! Ian passed his driving test!*

> ⚠ Don't say 'a news'. Say **a piece of news** or **some news**: *I heard an interesting piece of news yesterday.*

⚲the latest /ðə ˈleɪtɪst/ SPOKEN the most recent news: *Have you heard the latest? Phil's going out with Judy!*
+ on *What's the latest on the election?*

scandal /ˈskændl/ [n C/U] when shocking facts about someone's behaviour become publicly known: *a sex scandal involving senior politicians* | *the public's interest in scandal and gossip*

2 on television or in a newspaper

news /njuːz‖nuːz/ [n U] reports about recent events, printed in newspapers or given on television or radio: *I always read the sports news first.* | *It's a local paper, so most of the news is about local events.*
+ of *Later on, we'll bring you all the news of today's football games.*
the news (=a news programme on television or radio) *Do you want to watch the news?* | *the nine o'clock news*
on the news (=in a television or radio news programme) *It must be true – I heard it on the news this morning.*

> ⚠ You can also use **news** before a noun, like an adjective: *news broadcast* | *news item*

newsflash BRITISH **news bulletin** AMERICAN /ˈnjuːzflæʃ, ˈnjuːz ˌbʊlɪtɪn‖ˈnuːz-/ [n C] a piece of news that is so important that it is broadcast immediately, often in the middle of another programme: *We interrupt this programme to bring you a newsflash.*
plural **newsflashes**

the headlines /ðə ˈhedlaɪnz/ [n plural] the important points of the news, printed in big letters on the front page of a newspaper or read at the beginning of a news broadcast: *I stopped to read the front page headlines: 'KILLER ESCAPES FROM JAIL'.* | *This is the six o'clock news. First, the headlines ...*

⚡WORD BANK

NEWSPAPERS AND MAGAZINES

➡ if you mean 'information about something that has happened recently', go to **NEWS**
➡ see pages 518–521

NICE

HORRIBLE/UNPLEASANT
LIKE/NOT LIKE   BAD
ENJOY   see also   KIND
GOOD   POLITE
DESCRIBING PEOPLE   FRIENDLY/UNFRIENDLY

1 nice person

⚲nice /naɪs/ ESPECIALLY SPOKEN [adj] friendly and kind: *He's one of the nicest people I know.* | *Claire's really nice, isn't she?*
+ to *He's only nice to me when he wants something.*
it is nice of sb to do sth *It was nice of you to help me.*
nice – nicer – nicest

> ⚠ Be careful not to use **nice** too much in written English.

pleasant /ˈplezənt/ [adj] friendly, polite, and easy to talk to – use this especially about someone you do not know well: *I thought she was a quiet pleasant girl.* | *The Ambassador and his wife were surprisingly pleasant.*

likeable /ˈlaɪkəbəl/ [adj] nice, and easy to like: *The only likeable character in the whole movie is Judge White.*

lovely /ˈlʌvli/ [adj] INFORMAL, ESPECIALLY BRITISH very nice, kind, and friendly: *Old Dr Macintosh was a lovely man.*
lovely – lovelier – loveliest

NICE continues on page 522

WORD BANK NEWSPAPERS AND MAGAZINES

1 newspapers and magazines

newspaper/paper /ˈnjuːzˌpeɪpəʳ, ˈpeɪpəʳ‖ˈnuːz-/ [n C] a set of large folded sheets of paper containing news, articles, pictures etc, which is printed and sold every day or every week: *Can I have a look at your newspaper, please?* | *It says in the paper that they're getting divorced.*

> ⚠ Don't confuse **newspaper** and **journal**. A journal is a serious magazine on a particular subject, containing articles by university teachers, scientists, doctors etc: *the British Medical Journal* | *Their research was published in a scientific journal.*

Sunday paper /ˌsʌndi ˈpeɪpəʳ/ [n C] a paper that is sold every Sunday, and is usually bigger than papers sold on other days: *I like to sit in bed and read the Sunday papers.*

local paper /ˌləʊkəl ˈpeɪpəʳ/ [n C] a newspaper that gives news mainly about the town or area where it is printed: *Did you see Dave's picture in the local paper?*

magazine /ˌmægəˈziːn‖ˈmægəziːn/ [n C] a large, thin book with a paper cover, often printed on shiny paper, which contains stories, articles, photographs, and sometimes also news: *I bought some magazines for the journey – Cosmopolitan and Vanity Fair.* | *a photography magazine* | *a magazine for people interested in gardening.*
women's magazine (=a magazine intended especially for women)

the press /ðə ˈpres/ [n singular] newspapers and the people who write for them: *Do you think the press has too much influence on politics.* | *Princess Diana is followed by the press wherever she goes.*

the media /ðə ˈmiːdiə/ [n singular] all the organizations that are involved in providing information to the public, especially newspapers, television, and radio: *The letter must have been leaked to the media by a White House official.* | *The judge is worried that comments in the media might affect the result of the trial.*

tabloid /ˈtæblɔɪd/ [n C] a newspaper that does not contain much serious news, but has stories about famous people, sport, sex etc – use this especially about newspapers that you think are silly and not serious enough: *She claimed that she had had an affair with the President, and sold her story to one of the tabloids.*

the popular press /ðə ˌpɒpjə̣ləʳ ˈpres‖-ˌpɑː-/ [n singular] newspapers that are read by a lot of people and generally contain articles that are entertaining rather than serious, for example stories about people on television and in sport: *Smith strongly denies reports in the popular press that he is addicted to cocaine.*

comic (also **comic book** AMERICAN) /ˈkɒmɪk, ˈkɒmɪk ˌbʊk‖ˈkɑː-/ [n C] a magazine, especially for children, that consists of funny or exciting stories which are told using a series of pictures: *comic book characters such as Spiderman and Superman*

2 parts of a newspaper or magazine

headline /ˈhedlaɪn/ [n C] the words in big letters at the top of a newspaper report that tell you what the report is about: *The headline read: "SPACE ALIENS MEET WITH PRESIDENT'S CAT"*

letters page /ˈletəʳz ˌpeɪdʒ/ [n C] a page in a newspaper where letters from members of the public are printed

TV/sport/business/fashion page /ˈtiː viː, ˈspɔːʳt, ˈbɪznɪ̣s, ˈfæʃən ˌpeɪdʒ/ [n C] a page in a newspaper that tells you about television, sport, business, or fashion

listings /ˈlɪstɪŋz/ [n plural] lists of films, plays, and other events, with details of the times, dates, and places where they will happen

TV listings /ˈtiː viː ˌlɪstɪŋz/ [n plural] lists of programmes that are on the television and the times that they are on

3 what is written in newspapers and magazines

article /ˈɑːʳtɪkəl/ [n C] a piece of writing in a newspaper or magazine about a particular subject

NEWSPAPERS AND MAGAZINES

+ **on/about** Did you read that article about O J Simpson?

story /'stɔːri/ [n C] a report in a newspaper about a recent event: a front-page story in the New York Times

+ **about** Open any newspaper and you'll see many stories about shootings and muggings.

run a story (=report an event) The Post is running a story about one of the President's advisors being arrested for taking drugs.

feature /'fiːtʃər/ [n C] a special report in a newspaper or magazine about an interesting subject, place, or person: a special feature about the lives of homeless people

scoop /skuːp/ [n C] an important or exciting news story that is printed in one newspaper before any of the others know about it: Read our latest Royal Diary scoop!

editorial /ˌedɪˈtɔːriəl/ [n C] a piece of writing in a newspaper that gives the personal opinion of the editor about something that is in the news: Their editorials always criticize the government, whatever the government does.

exclusive /ɪkˈskluːsɪv/ [n C] a news story that is printed by one newspaper before any of the others know about it: a New York Times exclusive about a secret arms deal between a US company and Iraq

exclusive [adj] an exclusive interview with ex-President Bush

coverage /'kʌvərɪdʒ/ [n U] when something is reported in newspapers or magazines, or on television or radio, and the way in which it is reported: The release of Nelson Mandela was given massive coverage throughout the world

+ **of** The Daily Star's coverage of the election was very biased.

4 people who work for newspapers or magazines

reporter /rɪˈpɔːrtər/ [n C] someone whose job is to find out about news stories and write about them: She works as a junior reporter on a local paper. | A crowd of reporters were waiting outside the house all night.

journalist /'dʒɜːrnəlɪst/ [n C] someone who writes for a newspaper or magazine, or who appears on news programmes on television or radio: Cronkite's career as a journalist lasted over 30 years.

journalism /'dʒɜːrnəlɪzəm/ [n U] the work of being a journalist

correspondent /ˌkɒrɪˈspɒndənt‖ˌkɔːrɪˈspɑːn-, ˌkɑː-/ [n C] someone who writes about or talks about a particular subject, especially a serious one, for a newspaper or a news programme

political/foreign/education etc correspondent (=someone who reports news stories about politics, what is happening in other countries, education etc) 'Schools in Crisis', by our education correspondent Nick Bacon. | Martin Bell worked for many years as the BBC's war correspondent covering conflicts all over the world.

editor /'edɪtər/ [n C] the person in charge of a newspaper or magazine, whose job is to decide what should be written about: She's the editor of Cosmopolitan.

fashion/sports/political editor etc [n C] the person who is in charge of a particular part of a newspaper or magazine, and who decides what should be written about fashion, sport, politics etc: the chief political editor of The Times | Morrison is the paper's senior business editor.

hack /hæk/ [n C] INFORMAL a news reporter or journalist – use this about people you disapprove of or who you think produce bad quality writing: The editor sent one of his hacks to interview the murderer's girlfriend.

5 to write for a newspaper or magazine

write /raɪt/ [v I/T] to write news reports or other articles for a newspaper or magazine: She writes articles about health for a women's magazine.

+ **for** He's been writing for the Evening News ever since he left college.

NEWSPAPERS AND MAGAZINES continues on the next page

NEWSPAPERS AND MAGAZINES

report /rɪˈpɔːʳt/ [v I/T] to find out and write about news stories for a newspaper or news programme: *We try to report events as fairly as possible.*
+ on *She was sent to Bangladesh to report on the floods there.*
+ that *The newspaper wrongly reported that he had died.*

cover /ˈkʌvəʳ/ [v T] to report the details of an event or a series of events for a newspaper or news programme: *She was in New York to cover the St Patrick's Day celebrations.* | *Baxter had spent three weeks covering a big murder trial.*

6 people who read newspapers and magazines

reader /ˈriːdəʳ/ [n C] someone who reads a particular newspaper or magazine: *We'd like to wish all our readers a very happy Christmas!* | *2000 Cosmo readers took part in a survey about student life in the nineties.*

readership /ˈriːdəʳʃɪp/ [n U] the number of people or type of people who regularly read a particular newspaper or magazine: *The paper now has a readership of over 1.5 million.* | *The paper has a mainly middle-class readership.*

circulation /ˌsɜːʳkjəˈleɪʃən/ [n U] the number of copies of a newspaper or magazine that are sold in a day, a week, a month etc: *Circulation fell dramatically when the price of the magazine went up to $4.00.*

7 freedom of the press

Most people feel that **freedom of the press** is very important. It means that newspapers can report what they like, can criticize the government, and can carry out **investigative journalism** without worrying that they are breaking the law.

Where there is no freedom of the press, people are often not told the truth about what is really happening. Governments can use newspapers for their own **propaganda**, and can **censor** facts and opinions that they do not want people to read about.

vocabulary

biased /ˈbaɪəst/ [adj] a **biased** report or article is unfair, because it strongly supports or strongly opposes one particular group, opinion etc, and it does not give all the facts: *a biased newspaper article about the election campaign*
+ towards/in favour of *Much of the British press is biased in favour of the Conservative Party.*
+ against *They complained that the news report was biased against the police.*

censor /ˈsensəʳ/ [v T] to take out the parts of a written article, a television programme, a film etc that you do not want other people to read, see, or hear because you think the information is politically dangerous or immoral: *During the war, all newspapers and magazines were censored.*

censorship /ˈsensəʳʃɪp/ [n U] when a government or an official organization controls what people are allowed to read in newspapers, watch on television etc: *The government soon imposed strict censorship on the press.*

copy /ˈkɒpiˈkɑː-/ [n C] a single newspaper: *How many copies does the New York Times sell?*
+ of *There's a copy of yesterday's Guardian around somewhere.*

freedom of the press /ˌfriːdəm əv ðə ˈpres/ when newspapers are allowed to write about whatever they want, and to give whatever opinions they want, without there being any laws to stop them: *The new government has promised to allow complete freedom of the press.*

intrusive /ɪnˈtruːsɪv/ [adj] affecting or concerning people's personal lives in an annoying or upsetting way: *The family found many of the questions intrusive and sometimes offensive.*

NEWSPAPERS AND MAGAZINES

But in some cases, the newspapers themselves do not always tell the truth about what is happening. They sometimes try to influence people's political opinions, and newspaper reports can be **biased**. Many newspapers are more concerned with **sensationalism** than with serious news reporting, because this helps them to sell more **copies** of the paper.

In some countries, however, it can seem as if the press has too much freedom. Famous people sometimes feel that newspapers are **intrusive**, and print too much about their **private lives**. Many countries have laws that are designed to protect people's **privacy**.

If newspapers print something that is untrue about someone, they can be charged with **libel**, but this can still mean that people's lives, families, or jobs can be seriously damaged.

---

investigative journalism/reporting /ɪnˌvestɪ-gətɪv ˈdʒɜːrnəlɪzəm, rɪˈpɔːrtɪŋ‖-geɪtɪv-/ when journalists use their skill and determination to try to discover the truth about something serious that someone else is trying to keep secret: *President Nixon resigned after some excellent investigative reporting by two Washington Post journalists.*

libel /ˈlaɪbəl/ [n U] when a newspaper or magazine writes something untrue about someone: *He's suing the magazine for libel after they accused him of being a Nazi sympathizer.* (=he is taking the magazine to a law court to prove that they are guilty of libel)

privacy /ˈprɪvəsi, ˈpraɪ-‖ˈpraɪ-/ [n U] the idea that a person, especially an important or famous person, has the right to have a normal life with their family and friends, without newspapers telling people everything about them: *Though she's an interna-*tional superstar, she says her privacy is still very important to her.*

private life /ˌpraɪvɪt ˈlaɪf/ [n C] the way you live your life and what you do with your friends and family, rather than the things you do as part of your job or official position: *I think that what politicians do in their private lives is their own business.*

propaganda /ˌprɒpəˈgændə‖ˌprɑː-/ [n U] the use of newspapers, television, film etc to make people believe things that are not true, for example by giving only some of the facts or by giving false information about an opponent: *Early reports of the massacre were thought to be Communist propaganda.*

sensationalism /senˈseɪʃənəlɪzəm/ [n U] a way of reporting events or stories that makes them seem as strange, exciting, or shocking as possible: *The Daily Planet was accused of sensationalism in its reporting of the trial.*

NICE continued from page 517

sweet /swiːt/ [adj] INFORMAL someone who is **sweet** is kind and gentle, and tries to make other people happy: *He's a really sweet guy but I couldn't date him.*

it is sweet of sb to do sth *It was very sweet of you to buy me those flowers.*

2 something you like or enjoy

nice /naɪs/ [adj] ESPECIALLY SPOKEN *That's a nice jacket. Is it new?* | *Have a nice day!*

nice to do sth *It's really nice to see you again.*

+ for *It's much nicer for the kids when they have other kids to play with.*

look/taste/smell nice *You look really nice in that dress.*

nice big/quiet/long etc *I got a nice long letter from Andreas this morning.* | *a nice hot bath*

nice – nicer – nicest

> ⚠ Be careful not to use **nice** too much in written English.

lovely /ˈlʌvli/ [adj] INFORMAL, ESPECIALLY BRITISH very nice: *We had a lovely time at the beach.* | *Thank you for the lovely birthday present.*

it is lovely to do sth *It would be lovely to see you.*

look/taste/smell lovely *Anna's perfume smells lovely.*

lovely big/long etc *They've got a lovely big house.*

lovely – lovelier – loveliest

pleasant /ˈplezənt/ [adj] a **pleasant** place, occasion, or activity is one that you like, especially because it is peaceful, attractive, or relaxing: *We spent a very pleasant evening chatting.* | *Relax in the peaceful and pleasant surroundings of our hotel.* | *a pleasant little town*

pleasantly [adv] *It was pleasantly cool by the river.*

enjoyable /ɪnˈdʒɔɪəbəl/ [adj] an **enjoyable** experience or activity is one that you enjoy, because it is interesting, exciting etc: *We hope you will have an interesting and enjoyable trip.* | *I find aerobics more enjoyable than jogging.* | *an enjoyable day at the Carnival*

great/fantastic/wonderful /greɪt, fænˈtæstɪk, ˈwʌndərfəl/ [adj] extremely enjoyable – use this about holidays, parties, films, and other experiences that you enjoy very much: *I went to a fantastic party last night.* | *We had a wonderful month in Italy.* | *I think it's a great movie.*

> ⚠ **Great** and **fantastic** are more informal than **wonderful**, and should not be used in written English, except in personal letters.

> ⚠ Don't use 'very' with any of these words.

NONE/NOTHING

➡ see also **NEVER**

1 when there isn't any of something

none /nʌn/ [pronoun] not any of something, or no people or things: *I was going to offer you some cake, but there's none left.* | *"Coffee?" "None for me, thanks."*

+ of *None of her friends ever came to see her.* | *None of the equipment was actually working.*

none at all *"Do you have any objections to the plan, John?" "None at all."*

> ⚠ In spoken English, if **none of** is followed by a plural noun or pronoun, you can use it with a plural verb: *I invited some friends, but none of them were interested.* But in written English it is better to use a singular verb: *None of them was interested.*

not any /nɒt ˈeni/ [determiner/pronoun] none: *If you're looking for bread, you won't find any. I haven't been shopping yet.*

not any time/money/food etc *There won't be any time for questions after the lecture.*

not any shops/clothes/food/time etc *There aren't any good book stores in our town.* | *It was a big demonstration, but there wasn't any trouble.*

+ of *I haven't read any of Henry Miller's novels.*

no /nəʊ/ [determiner] not any or not one

no time/money/milk etc Do you mind having black coffee? There's no milk. | We've had no rain for three months.

no cars/houses/dogs etc There are no buses today. | a very plain room, with no pictures on the wall

no reason/reply/intention etc I knocked on the door, but there was no reply. | He just started hitting her for no reason.

no more There are no more classes until Monday.

nothing/not anything /ˈnʌθɪŋ, nɒt ˈeniθɪŋ/ [pronoun] There's nothing in this box. | These people don't know anything about computers. | I switched the TV on, but nothing happened. | "What are you doing?" "Nothing."

nothing new/serious/exciting etc Nothing exciting ever happens in this place!

nothing to eat/say/do etc There was nothing to do, so we just watched TV. | She hasn't had anything to eat all day.

nothing at all "Do you know anything about fixing cars?" "No, nothing at all."

2 **the number that means none**

zero /ˈzɪərəʊ‖ˈzɪːrəʊ/ [number] the number 0

⚠ In American English, **zero** is used more than in British English as a way of saying the number '0': I think her phone number is two zero five three zero. In British English, the usual way of saying '0' is **nought** or **o**, and **zero** is mostly used in scientific or technical language: The pressure increases from zero to maximum in 25 seconds.

nil /nɪl/ [number] none or nothing: The new machine has reduced our labour costs to almost nil. | The chances of finding them alive are virtually nil.

⚠ In British English, **nil** is also used when talking about sports results: United won the game three nil.

○ nought /nɔːt/ [number] BRITISH SPOKEN the number 0: The interest rate on this account is only nought point seven five per cent. (=0.75%)

When you see **EC**, go to the
ESSENTIAL COMMUNICATION section.

○ o /əʊ/ [number] SPOKEN, ESPECIALLY BRITISH the number 0: All Manchester numbers start with o-one-six-one. | You'll be in room two-o-four.

⚠ O is used especially when saying a telephone number, address, or room number, or a number after a decimal point.

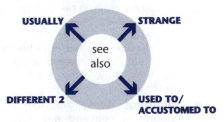

NORMAL/ ORDINARY

➡ opposite **UNUSUAL**

USUALLY **STRANGE**

see also

DIFFERENT 2 **USED TO/ ACCUSTOMED TO**

1 **ordinary, not special**

ordinary /ˈɔːrdənri‖-neri/ [adj] **ordinary** things are not special or unusual; **ordinary** people are not famous or powerful, and are not especially rich or clever: It's just an ordinary house in an ordinary street. | politicians who don't seem to care about ordinary people | Can you get connected to the Internet through an ordinary telephone line?

average /ˈævərɪdʒ/ [adj only before noun] an **average** person or thing is a typical example of a person or of a particular type of thing: The average family spends £50 a week on food. | In an average week I watch about 20 hours of TV. | Foreign affairs do not usually interest the average voter.

normal /ˈnɔːrməl/ [adj] something that is **normal** is just as you would expect it to be, because it is not special or different: The new Ford looks like any normal car, but it has a special advanced engine. | January 2nd is a public holiday in Scotland, but in England it is a normal working day.

normally [adv] Now the strike is over, and trains are running normally.

standard /'stændərd/ [adj usually before noun] normal – use this especially about products or methods that are the most usual type, without any special features
standard model / size / shape / pattern (=not special) *We make shoes in all standard sizes.* | *The standard model costs $4000 less than the luxury model.*
standard practice/procedure (=the way a job is usually done) *All hand-baggage was X-rayed – this is now standard practice at international airports.*
standard English/pronunciation/spelling (=normally accepted as correct)

routine /ˌruːˈtiːn◂/ [adj only before noun] use this about something that is done regularly as part of the normal system and not because of any special problem
routine check/inspection/examination etc *The fault was discovered during a routine check of the plane.* | *a routine visit to the dentist*

conventional /kən'venʃənəl/ [adj only before noun] a **conventional** method, piece of equipment, weapon etc is of the normal type that has been used for a long time – use this especially when you are comparing these things with something that is new or different: *A microwave cooks food much faster than a conventional oven.* | *conventional weapons* (=not nuclear weapons) | *The hospital provides both conventional and alternative medical treatments.*

day-to-day /'deɪ tə deɪ/ [adj only before noun] use this about the ordinary work, activities, and problems that happen every day: *As Director of Studies, I am responsible for the day-to-day management of the programme.*

2 normal behaviour or feelings

normal /'nɔːrməl/ [adj] if a person is **normal**, or if their behaviour or feelings are **normal**, there is nothing strange about them, and they are mentally and physically healthy: *Any normal boy of his age would be interested in football.* | *Her breathing was normal, but she had a very high temperature.*
it is normal (for sb) to do sth *It is quite normal for people to be afraid of the dark.*

perfectly normal (=completely normal) *Lisa seems a perfectly normal little girl.*
normally [adv] *Even a few hours before he committed suicide, he seemed to be behaving quite normally.*

natural /'nætʃərəl/ [adj] feelings that are **natural** are what you would normally expect in a particular situation, so there is no need to feel worried or embarrassed about them: *Anger is a natural reaction when you lose someone you love.*
it is natural (for sb) to do sth *I suppose it's natural for a mother to feel sad when her children leave home.* | *It isn't natural for a child to be so quiet.*
perfectly/quite natural (=completely natural) *It's perfectly natural to want to go home.*
it's only natural SPOKEN *Of course Jean misses her boyfriend – it's only natural.*

conventional /kən'venʃənəl/ [adj] **conventional** people, behaviour, and opinions are the kind that most people in society think are normal and socially acceptable, although some people think they are boring and old-fashioned: *My mother was very conventional – she didn't approve of my hippie lifestyle.* | *a young man with conventional tastes in clothes and music*
conventionally [adv] *She was dressed very conventionally in a rather dull grey suit.*

3 not ordinary/not normal

special /'speʃəl/ [adj] not ordinary, but more important, interesting, or impressive than usual: *Tomorrow is a very special day for us – it's our first wedding anniversary.* | *Students are not allowed to change to a different class unless there is a special reason.* | *She had a special talent for learning languages.*
something/anything/nothing special *"Are you doing anything this weekend?" "No, nothing special."*
special occasion (=an important social event or celebration) *I only wear this suit on special occasions, like weddings.*

abnormal /æb'nɔːrməl/ [adj] very different from what is normal, in a way that is strange, worrying, or dangerous: *abnormal behaviour that may be a sign of mental illness* | *an abnormal chest x-ray*

it is abnormal (for sb) to do sth *My parents thought it was abnormal for a boy to be interested in ballet.*

abnormally [adv] *abnormally low blood pressure | She seems abnormally fascinated by death.*

no ordinary /nəʊ ˈɔːʳdənri‖-neri/ **no ordinary dog/party/car etc** a dog, party, car etc that is not at all ordinary, but is very unusual, very impressive etc: *It was no ordinary birthday cake – it was over a metre high! | As soon as I got there, I realized that this was no ordinary family gathering.*

4 when something becomes normal again

get back to normal/return to normal /get ˌbæk tə ˈnɔːʳməl, rɪˌtɜːʳn tə ˈnɔːʳməl/ if a situation **gets back to normal** or **returns to normal**, it becomes normal again after a period when it was not normal: *After the war it took a long time for things to get back to normal. | The strike has caused serious problems, but we hope bus services will quickly return to normal.*

> ⚠ **Return to normal** is more formal than **get back to normal**.

NOT

➡ see also ⬛ **SAYING NO**

1 not

not /nɒt‖nɑːt/ [adv] *"Why don't you go to bed?" "I'm not tired." | They aren't here yet. | He told me not to worry. | He's not my boyfriend – he's just someone I work with.*

> ⚠ In spoken informal English, we usually use **n't** (the short form of **not**) *Don't worry, I won't hurt you.*

> ⚠ Don't use another negative word, for example 'nothing', 'nobody', or 'nowhere' in the same sentence as **not**. Use 'anything', 'anybody', 'anywhere' etc instead: *We didn't see anything. | They do not know anybody.*

neither /ˈnaɪðəʳ‖ˈniː-/ [adv] use this to say that a negative statement that has just been made about someone is also true about someone else

neither am I/neither does she/neither have we etc *"I've never been to Australia." "No, neither have I." | Tom didn't believe a word she said, and neither did the police.*

> ⚠ **Neither** can only be followed by these words: 'be', 'have', 'do', 'can', 'could', 'will', 'would', 'shall', 'should'.

not very/not particularly /nɒt ˈveri, nɒt pəʳˈtɪkjɣləʳli/ something that is **not very** big, **not very** pleasant etc is fairly small, fairly unpleasant etc: *Our apartment isn't very big. | I'm not particularly interested in soccer, but I did enjoy the World Cup.*

> ⚠ **Not very** and **not particularly** are often used as an indirect or polite way of expressing a strong idea: *She wasn't very pleased when she found out.* (=she was angry) *| The film wasn't particularly good.* (=it was bad)

not at all /ˌnɒt ət ˈɔːl/ use this to emphasize that something is definitely not true: *She's not at all happy about the situation. | No, no, that's wrong. That's not at all what I meant.*

not quite /nɒt ˈkwaɪt/ not completely, but almost: *We haven't quite finished yet. | The measurements are not quite accurate.*

by no means /baɪ ˈnəʊ miːnz/ **by no means certain/clear/complete/impossible/unusual etc** FORMAL not at all certain, clear etc – use this especially when other people think that something is certain, is clear etc, and you think they are wrong: *It is by no means certain that there was ever a real person called Robin Hood. | It's difficult, but by no means impossible.*

in no way /ɪn ˈnəʊ weɪ/ if something is **in no way** affected by something else, it is definitely not affected by it in any way: *This will in no way influence our original decision. | The damage is very slight and in no way reduces the value of the painting.*

N

2 not one thing and not the other

neither /ˈnaɪðəʳ‖ˈniː-/ [*determiner/pronoun*] use this to emphasize that you are talking about both of two people or things when you make a negative statement about them

+ of *Both the players have been warned, but neither of them seems to take it seriously.*

neither thing/person/place etc *Neither parent cares what happens to the child.*

neither ... nor /naɪðəʳ ... nɔːʳ/ use this to connect two peoople, actions, facts etc, when you want to make a negative statement about both of them: *He neither drinks nor smokes.* (=he does not drink, and he does not smoke) | *Neither Reagan nor his advisers knew anything about the plan.* | *She felt neither sad nor happy when she heard the news.*

> ⚠ Don't use 'or' after **neither**. Always use **nor**.
>
> ⚠ **Neither ... nor** is fairly formal. In informal English we express the same idea in a different way, for example *He doesn't drink or smoke* or *Reagan didn't know anything about the plan, and neither did his advisers.*

NOTICE

to see, hear, or feel something

➡ see also **REALIZE, SEE, SHOW 5**

➡ if you mean 'a sign that tells people something', go to **SIGN**

1 to notice someone or something

notice /ˈnəʊtɪ̈s/ [*v* I/T] to realize that something is there or that something is happening, when you see it, hear it, or feel it: *"Julie's home." "Yes, I noticed her bicycle outside."*

+ (that) *I was driving home, when I noticed that the engine was making a strange noise.* | *Dominic took a huge slice of cake, hoping no-one would notice.*

notice how/when/where etc *Did you notice what he was wearing?*

notice sb doing sth *I was about to leave when I noticed someone coming up the driveway.*

> ⚠ Don't use 'can' with **notice**. Don't say 'we can notice an improvement'. Say **we notice an improvement** or **we can see an improvement**.

can see/can tell /kən ˈsiː, kən ˈtel/ to know that something is true, because you notice signs that show you this

+ (that) *We could tell that she had been crying.* | *I can see you're not really enjoying this.*

I see (that) /aɪ ˈsiː ðət/ SPOKEN say this to mention something that you have noticed: *I see Pete's had his hair cut – it looks a lot better, doesn't it?* | *I see that new De Niro movie is on this weekend.*

spot /spɒt‖spɑːt/ [*v* T] to see something that is difficult to notice, or something that no-one else notices: *I'm glad you spotted that mistake before it was too late.* | *I dropped my keys in the grass, but luckily Jim spotted them.*

spotting – spotted – have spotted

become aware of sth /bɪˌkʌm əˈweər ɒv (sth)/ to gradually begin to notice something: *As he was reading, he became aware of someone watching him.* | *When did you first become aware of the problem?*

catch sb's eye /ˌkætʃ (sb's) ˈaɪ/ if something **catches your eye**, you notice it because it is unusual, interesting, or attractive: *I was walking through the market when this beautiful dress caught my eye – blue with silver flowers on it.* | *A newspaper headline caught her eye: 'Royal Divorce Shock'.*

2 to not notice something

not notice /nɒt ˈnəʊtɪ̈s/ *"Does Alex like your new hairstyle?" "He didn't even notice."* | *I saw Mike in town but he didn't notice me.*

not notice how/who/what etc *We were so busy we didn't notice how late it was.*

miss /mɪs/ [*v* T] to not notice something because it is difficult to see: *Jo spotted a mistake that everyone else had missed.* |

It's easy to miss the entrance – there's no sign outside.

overlook /ˌəʊvəˈlʊk/ [v T] to not notice something because you have not been careful enough: *They found some important evidence that the police had overlooked.*

3 good at noticing things

observant /əbˈzɜːʳvənt/ [adj] good at noticing things: *Men aren't usually very observant about things like hair and clothes.* | *An observant reader has pointed out a mistake on page 26.*

perceptive /pəʳˈseptɪv/ [adj] good at noticing things and understanding situations or people's feelings: *I like her novels – she's so perceptive about people's relationships.* | *A perceptive teacher noticed that Val was having problems.*

◯not miss much /nɒt ˈmɪs mʌtʃ/ SPOKEN if you do **not miss much**, you notice a lot about what is happening and what other people are doing or feeling: *"I think Alison and Peter are getting pretty friendly with each other." "You don't miss much, do you?"*

4 something that is easy to notice

obvious /ˈɒbviəs‖ˈɑːb-/ [adj] a fact that is **obvious** is easy to see or realize: *She tried to look grateful, but her disappointment was obvious.*
it is obvious (to sb) that *It's obvious that Paul is in love with Liz.* | *It was obvious to everyone that Gina was lying.*

noticeable /ˈnəʊtɪ̯səbəl/ [adj] easy to notice: *After two days there was a noticeable improvement in his health.* | *The new supermarket has had a noticeable effect on people's shopping habits.*
it is noticeable that *It was noticeable that no one at the party was under 40.*

conspicuous /kənˈspɪkjuəs/ [adj] FORMAL someone or something that is **conspicuous** is very easy to notice, because they look very different from everyone or everything around them: *It was a small country town, and Lauren looked very conspicuous in her fashionable New York clothes.*

eye-catching /ˈaɪ kætʃɪŋ/ **eye-catching** colours, designs, patterns etc are bright, attractive, and unusual, so everyone notices them: *The posters come in several eye-catching designs.* | *an eye-catching display of new children's clothes in a shop window*

stand out /ˌstænd ˈaʊt/ [phrasal verb I] if something **stands out**, it is easy to notice because it looks very different from everything around it: *A yellow background will make the black lettering stand out.*
+ against *The dark shapes of the trees stood out against the evening sky.*

◯you can't miss it /juː ˌkɑːnt ˈmɪs ɪt‖ -ˌkænt-/ SPOKEN say this when you are telling someone how to get to a place that is very easy to find or notice: *Their house has a pink door. You can't miss it.*

5 to make people notice you

get attention/attract attention /ˌget əˈtenʃən, əˌtrækt əˈtenʃən/ to try to make someone notice you, by doing something that they will notice: *Young children sometimes behave badly simply in order to get attention.*
get/attract sb's attention *Phil was trying to attract the waiter's attention.*

NOW

PAST   BEFORE 3, 4

FUTURE   see also   MODERN

TIME   NEW

1 now, at this moment or at this time

now /naʊ/ [adv] at this moment or at this time: *If we leave now, we'll be there before dark.* | *It's not raining now, but they said it might rain later.* | *Where do you go to school now?*

already /ɔːlˈredi/ [adv] if something is **already** happening or **already** true, it began to happen or be true before now:

He's only three and he's already reading. | "Should I tell Kay?" "She already knows." | The show has already started.

> ⚠️ **Already** usually comes before the main verb, or between an auxiliary or modal verb (like **be, have, can** etc) and a main verb: *She already knows about it.* | *Some cars can already run on this new petrol.* You can also use **already** at the end of a sentence to emphasize that something has happened sooner than you expected: *Is the taxi here already?*

currently /ˈkʌrəntli‖ˈkɜːr-/ [adv] now – use this when you are describing what the situation is at this time: *The firm currently employs 113 people.* | *Peterson is currently writing a book about his travels.*

> ⚠️ **Currently** is used especially in newspapers, official reports, and formal meetings. It is not usually used in ordinary conversations.

at present/at the moment (also **presently** AMERICAN) /ət ˈprezənt, ət ðə ˈməʊmənt, ˈprezəntli/ now – use this especially to say that something is happening now but you do not expect it to continue for a long time: *I'm working in a restaurant at the moment.* | *Miss Hellman is busy at present – can she contact you later?* | *She's presently working on her own talk show on TV.*

> ⚠️ **At present** is more formal than **at the moment** or **presently.**

◯right now /ˌraɪt ˈnaʊ/ SPOKEN at this moment or at this time

> ⚠️ In American English, **right now** means 'at this time', and is often used about a situation which you expect to change: *Right now, we're living with my mother.* | *I want to pay her back, but I don't have the money right now.* In British English, **right now** is usually used to emphasize that something is very urgent: *I want to see the manager, right now!*

◯just now /ˌdʒʌst ˈnaʊ/ BRITISH SPOKEN at this exact moment – use this especially to say that you cannot do something immediately: *Sorry, I'm busy just now – can I call you later?*

2 now, not in the past

now /naʊ/ [adv] use this when you are comparing the present situation with what happened in the past: *We used to be good friends, but I don't see her much now.* | *Julie has moved to a new school and she's much happier now.*

◯these days /ˈðiːz ˌdeɪz/ ESPECIALLY SPOKEN use this when you are describing how life is different now from the way it was in the past: *Children can't play in the street these days – the traffic's too bad.* | *I don't go to London much these days.*

nowadays /ˈnaʊədeɪz/ [adv] use this especially to talk about the way that society has changed: *It seems you're not allowed to smoke anywhere nowadays.* | *Nowadays divorce is more common.*

today /təˈdeɪ/ [adv] FORMAL at the present time, especially when compared with the past: *The car is the biggest cause of pollution in the world today.* | *Today, only a few of these beautiful animals survive.*

3 until now

so far /ˌsəʊ ˈfɑːr/ until now – use this when you are talking about a situation that will continue or develop after this time: *There haven't been any problems so far.* | *This is the hottest day we've had so far this summer.* | *"How many people say they will come to the party?" "About 20 so far."*

still /stɪl/ [adv] use this to say that a situation which started in the past continues to exist now, especially when this is surprising: *He's been studying French for five years, and still can't speak the language.* | *Are you still working at that restaurant?*

> ⚠️ **Still** comes after the main verb, or between an auxiliary or modal verb (like **be, have, can** etc) and a main verb: *He still loves her.* | *I can still remember it.* **Still** comes before a negative verb: *We still don't know.*

yet /jet/ [adv] use this in questions or negative statements, to talk or ask about things that you expected to happen before now: *Has the new washing machine arrived yet?* | *We are 30 minutes into the game, and neither team has scored yet.* | *"Have you finished your homework?" "Not yet."*

⚠ In British English, use the present perfect with **yet**: *Have you read that book yet?* In American English you can use the simple past or the present perfect: *Did you read that book yet?*

up to now/until now /ˌʌp tə ˈnaʊ, ənˌtɪl ˈnaʊ/ use this about a situation which has existed until now, but which has started to change or will change in the future: *I've been happy in that apartment up to now, but I'd really like to move to somewhere bigger.* | *Until now, there has been no effective treatment for this disease.*

4 things or situations that exist now
➡ see also **MODERN**

present /ˈprezənt/ [adj only before noun] the **present** situation is the one that exists now; your **present** job, address etc is the one that you have now: *Arnaud lived in Los Angeles before moving to his present home in New York.* | *He warned that the present situation in Northern Ireland could get much worse.*

current /ˈkʌrənt‖ˈkɜːr-/ [adj only before noun] use this about a situation or activity which is happening now, but which is not expected to continue for a long time: *in the current economic situation* | *Coca-Cola's current advertising campaign*
current level/rate/price *The aim is to reduce current pollution levels in the Black Sea.*

⚠ **Current** is used especially in newspapers, official reports, and formal meetings.

existing /ɪgˈzɪstɪŋ/ [adj only before noun] use this about things or situations that exist now, when you think they may be changed in the future: *The existing building is too small, and there are plans to replace it within the next five years.* | *Many people feel that the existing law discriminates against women.*

today's/of today /təˈdeɪz, əv təˈdeɪ/ [adj] use this about social, economic, or political conditions and attitudes that exist now, when you are comparing them with those that existed in the past: *The first computers were extremely slow by today's*

standards. | *The teenagers of today have a different attitude to sex.*

⚠ **Today's** and **of today** are used especially in news reports and articles.

5 happening now, but likely to change

for now/for the time being /fər ˈnaʊ, fər ðə ˌtaɪm ˈbiːɪŋ/ for a short time, but not permanently – use this about a temporary arrangement or way of dealing with a situation: *Leave the groceries there for now – I'll put them away later.* | *They will run the business from home for the time being, but they may need an office if things go well.*

for the moment /fər ðə ˈməʊmənt/ ESPECIALLY SPOKEN use this to say that something is true or happening now, but may change soon: *For the moment the city seems quiet, but the fighting could start again at any time.* | *"How's your apartment?" "It's fine for the moment, but I'd rather live nearer town."*

6 when something does not happen now, but used to happen

no longer/not any more /nəʊ ˈlɒŋgər, nɒt eni ˈmɔːr‖-ˈlɔːŋ-/ use this to say that a situation that existed until recently does not exist now: *Alice doesn't live here any more.* | *He no longer felt sure that he was right.*
no longer possible/necessary/available etc *The bridge had collapsed, and it was no longer possible to cross the river.*

⚠ **No longer** is more formal than **not any more**, and it always comes before the verb or adjective: *She no longer loved him.* | *She didn't love him any more.*

not now /nɒt ˈnaʊ/ use this to say that something happened in the past, but it does not happen now: *He's not in school now – he has a job.* | *People used to respect teachers, but they don't now.*

When you see **EC**, go to the **ESSENTIAL COMMUNICATION** section.

NUMBER

➡ see also **COUNT/CALCULATE, TOTAL**

1 a written number

number /'nʌmbə^r/ [n C] a word or sign that represents a quantity, which is used for example for counting or for showing the order in which things are arranged: *Six is my lucky number.* | *Football shirts usually have a number on the back.*

number 12/20/4 etc *She lives at number 853 Ocean Boulevard.*

even number (=2,4,6,8,10 etc) *Write down all the even numbers between 2 and 20.*

odd number (=1,3,5,7,9 etc) *All the doors on this side of the street have odd numbers.*

phone/passport/registration/licence number *What's your phone number?*

   numbered [adj] having a number: *The squares are numbered from one to ten.*

figure /'fɪgə^r‖'fɪgjər/ [n C] a number written as a sign, not as a word: *Write the amount in words and in figures.*

double figures (=more than 9 and less than 100) *Temperatures reached double figures yesterday, going as high as 14 degrees.*

single figures (=less than 10) *The inflation rate was still in single figures.* (=less than 10%)

five-figure/six-figure etc (=consisting of five, six numbers etc) *The chief executive earns a six-figure salary.* | *an eight-figure phone number*

2 a number used in calculating

number /'nʌmbə^r/ [n singular] a number of people, things etc, especially a number that has been calculated for official purposes: *There have been several cases of tubercolosis, and the number is rising.*

+ of *The number of cars on the roads increased by 22% last year.* | *The regulations limit the number of students in each class.*

a large/small etc number of *An enormous number of people wrote to complain about last night's show.*

figures /'fɪgəz‖'fɪgjərz/ [n plural] a set of numbers that are regularly calculated by a government, a company etc, especially in order to show how much something has increased or decreased: *Government figures show that unemployment is rising again.* | *Our sales figures have been steady this month.*

statistics /stə'tɪstɪks/ [n plural] information about financial matters, social changes etc, which is shown in the form of numbers: *Statistics show that the number of women managers has risen continuously for the last 25 years.* | *According to the latest government statistics, 2 million people retired last year.*

O

OBEY/DISOBEY

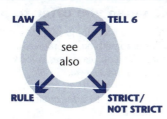

LAW   **TELL 6**

see also

RULE   **STRICT/ NOT STRICT**

1 to obey a person, rule, or law

obey /əʊˈbeɪ, ə-/ [v I/T] to do what someone tells you to do, or do what a law or rule says you must do: *Soldiers must always obey their commanding officer.* | *You can teach most dogs to obey simple commands.* | *I knew that if I didn't obey, I would be shot.*

⚠ Don't say 'he obeyed to the officer'. Say **he obeyed the officer.**

⚠ **Obey** is rather formal, and is used especially to talk about obeying the law or obeying military orders. **Do as you are told** is the usual expression for talking about children doing what their parents or teachers ask them to do.

do as you are told /ˌduː əz juː ɑːᵗ ˈtəʊld/ ESPECIALLY SPOKEN to obey without asking any questions – use this especially about children, when their parents or teachers tell them to do something: *"Oh Daddy, why?" "Don't ask why, just do as you're told."* | *If she doesn't do as she's told, send her to her room.*

comply with sth /kəmˈplaɪ wɪð (sth)/ [phrasal verb T] FORMAL if you **comply with** a law or a decision, you do what it says you must do: *Companies must comply with European employment laws.* | *Failure to comply with these conditions could result in prosecution.*

complying – complied – have complied

2 to not obey a person, rule, or law

disobey /ˌdɪsəˈbeɪ, ˌdɪsəʊ-/ [v I/T] to refuse to do what someone tells you to do, or what a rule or law says you must do: *No one dared to disobey the captain.* | *Black had disobeyed the judge's ruling, and he continued to harass his ex-wife.*

break a rule/break the law /ˌbreɪk ə ˈruːl, ˌbreɪk ðə ˈlɔː/ to not do what a rule or law says you must do: *Students who break the rules and smoke in school will have to leave.* | *If you don't buy a ticket before you get on the train, you are breaking the law.*

ignore /ɪgˈnɔːᵗ/ [v T] to pay no attention to a law or rule, or to what someone has told you to do, and behave as if it does not affect you: *Many cyclists ignore the law and ride around at night without lights.* | *I tell her to come home by 10 o'clock, but she just ignores me.*

not pay any attention (also **not take any notice** BRITISH) /ˌnɒt peɪ ˌeni əˈtenʃən, ˌnɒt teɪk ˌeni ˈnəʊtɪs/ ESPECIALLY SPOKEN to not do what someone has told you to do, in a way that annoys them: *We complained to the school about the state of the classroom, but no one paid any attention.* | *I keep telling him to do his homework, but he never takes any notice.*

rebel /rɪˈbel/ [v I] to deliberately behave in a way that is completely different from the way that your parents and people in general expect you to behave: *Her parents wanted her to go to university, but she rebelled and left school at 17.*
+ against *Teenagers tend to rebel against people in authority.*
rebelling – rebelled – have rebelled

3 always doing what you are told to do

obedient /əˈbiːdiənt, əʊ-/ [adj] someone who is **obedient** always does what their parents, teachers, or people in authority tell them to do – use this especially about children: *Bruno was a quiet and obedient little boy.* | *I wish my children were more obedient.*

obedience [n U] obedient behaviour: *The General demanded absolute obedience from his men.*

law-abiding /'lɔː əˌbaɪdɪŋ/ [adj] **law-abiding people/citizens etc** people who always obey the law and never break rules or do anything bad: *decent law-abiding people who go to church on Sundays and pay their taxes regularly*

4 refusing to obey

disobedient /ˌdɪsəˈbiːdiənt◄, ˌdɪsəʊ-/ [adj] someone who is **disobedient** refuses to do what their parents, teachers, or people in authority tell them to do – use this especially about children: *He's very disobedient, and he has a terrible temper.*

disobedience [n U] disobedient behaviour: *I've had enough of your disobedience.*

rebellious /rɪˈbeljəs/ [adj] someone who is **rebellious** deliberately behaves in a way that their parents or teachers disapprove of – use this about older children or young adults: *rebellious teenagers who run away from home*

OFFER

➡ see also ▣ OFFERS, REFUSE, ACCEPT

1 when you offer something to someone

offer /'ɒfəʳ‖'ɔː-, 'ɑː-/ [v T] to say that someone can have something if they want it
offer sb sth *She didn't even offer me a cup of tea.* | *I've been offered the job!*
offer sth to sb *Unfortunately, they offered the contract to someone else.*

○**would you like....?** /ˌwʊd juː ˈlaɪk/ SPOKEN say this as a polite way of offering something to someone: *We have some maps of the city – would you like one?*

○**can I get you.....?** /ˌkæn aɪ ˈget juː/ SPOKEN say this when you are offering someone a drink or food, for example at a party: *What can I get you? There's beer or wine.* | *Can I get you some coffee?*

○**help yourself** /ˌhelp jɔːʳˈself/ SPOKEN say this to tell someone they can take anything they want from the food and drink that is available: *There's plenty of food, so help yourselves.*

+ to *Help yourself to salad and bread.*

○**have** /hæv/ SPOKEN INFORMAL say this to persuade someone to take some food or drink that you are offering: *Have some of this salad – my Mum made it.* | *Go on, have another beer.*

2 when you offer to help

offer /'ɒfəʳ‖'ɔː-, 'ɑː-/ [v I/T] to say that you will do something in order to help someone: *"Do you want me to look after the children next week?" "No, but thanks for offering."* | *a teacher who was always ready to offer advice and encouragement*
offer to do sth *Charles offered to do some painting for us.*

⚠ Don't say 'I offered him to do it'. Say I offered to do it.

volunteer /ˌvɒlənˈtɪəʳ‖ˌvɑː-/ [v I] to offer to do something, especially something difficult or unpleasant: *Someone has to clean up all this mess. Who'll volunteer?*
volunteer to do sth *Jill volunteered to go with me to the hospital.*
+ for *No one volunteered for night duty.*

○**can I/would you like me to** (also **shall I** BRITISH) /'kæn aɪ, wʊd juː 'laɪk miː tuː, 'ʃæl aɪ/ SPOKEN say this when you are offering to do something for someone: *Can I take your bag – it looks heavy.* | *Would you like me to mail that letter for you?* | *Shall I make a copy for you?*

○**let me** /'let miː/ SPOKEN say this when you are offering to help someone, especially when you want to be kind or friendly to them: *Let me drive you to the station.* | *Why don't you let me cook dinner tonight?*

3 to offer money for something

offer /'ɒfəʳ‖'ɔː-, 'ɑː-/ [v T] to say that you will pay someone a particular amount of money in exchange for something
offer sb sth *My dad offered me $5 if I washed the car.* | *Chaldon was offered a huge salary to become team manager.*
offer sth for sth *Police are offering a reward for information about the robbery.* | *They said that they couldn't offer more than £2000 for the car.*

make an offer /ˌmeɪk ən ˈɒfəʳ‖-ˈɔː-/ to offer a particular amount of money in order to buy a house, car etc

+ for Has anyone made an offer for the house yet?

make sb an offer I'm prepared to make you a generous offer for the farm.

4 something that you offer

offer /ˈɒfəʳ‖ˈɔː-, ˈɑː-/ [n C] something that someone has offered to give you or do for you, such as money, help, or advice: I'll sell the car if I get an offer over $5000.

+ of They received several offers of help.

accept an offer (=say yes) Nasser decided to accept the offer of American aid.

refuse an offer (=say no) How could you refuse such a fantastic offer?

OFTEN

ALWAYS   SOMETIMES

see also

USUALLY   NEVER

1 when something happens many times

often /ˈɒfən, ˈɒftən‖ˈɔːf-/ [adv] when something happens many times: Rosi often works till 7 or 8 o'clock in the evening. | I often see her walking past with the children. | You should come and visit us more often.

very often I have a mobile phone, but I don't use it very often.

how often "How often do you see your parents?" "Only two or three times a year."

⚠ **Often** usually comes before a verb: He often plays tennis in the evening. When there is a modal or auxiliary verb (like 'have', 'can', or 'must'), **often** comes between this and the main verb: You can often buy cheap tickets. **Often** comes after the verb 'be': In summer the beach is often so crowded that you cannot find space to sit down.

○**a lot** /ə ˈlɒt‖-ˈlɑːt/ [adv] SPOKEN if you do something **a lot**, you often do it: It's nice to meet you. Wendy's talked about you a lot.

quite a lot BRITISH She goes abroad on business quite a lot.

tend to do sth /ˌtend tə ˈduː (sth)/ if something **tends to** happen, it often happens and it is likely to happen: Recent studies show that girls tend to be better at languages than boys.

frequently /ˈfriːkwəntli/ [adv] often: Passengers complain that trains are frequently cancelled. | Heat the sauce gently, stirring frequently.

⚠ **Frequently** is more formal than **often**.

frequent /ˈfriːkwənt/ [adj] happening often: His job involved making frequent trips to Saudi Arabia. | The treatment was effective, and her headaches became less frequent.

regularly /ˈregjʊ̈ləʳli/ [adv] often and at regular times, for example every day, every week, or every month: I used to go to church regularly. | Dave likes to keep fit, and he plays squash regularly.

regular /ˈregjʊ̈ləʳ/ [adj usually before noun] happening often, for example every hour, every day, or every week, with the same amount of time between each event: It is very important to take regular exercise. | There is a regular bus service from the airport to the town.

repeatedly /rɪˈpiːtɪ̈dli/ [adv] use this to emphasize that someone did something many times: Graham's doctor had repeatedly warned him not to work so hard. | Max was punched and kicked repeatedly as he lay on the ground.

again and again /əˌgen ənd əˈgen/ many times, much more often than you would expect: She kept asking the same question again and again. | Again and again, the little boat was almost smashed against the rocks.

2 very often, in a way that makes you annoyed

○**keep doing sth** /ˌkiːp ˈduːɪŋ (sth)/ ESPECIALLY SPOKEN to do something many times, in a way that is annoying: Dad,

Bobby keeps hitting me. | How can I explain if you keep interrupting me? | I keep forgetting to mail this letter.

always/all the time /'ɔːlweɪz, -wɪz, ɔːl ðə 'taɪm/ [adv] very often, in a way that is annoying: *She just complains all the time and never tries to help*

be always doing sth *I'm sick of Harold – he's always telling me what to do.*

> ⚠ **Always** comes before the main verb, but after the verb 'be': *He always forgets to bring his pen.* | *They are always complaining.*

time and time again /,taɪm ənd taɪm ə'gen/ use this to say that something has been done many times, but without any effect: *I've told you time and time again not to play with matches – it's dangerous.*

continually/constantly /kən'tɪnjuəli, 'kɒnstəntli‖'kɑːn-/ [adv] use this when you are very annoyed because something seems to keep happening over a long period of time: *They seemed to be continually arguing.* | *I wish you'd clean up your room without having to be constantly reminded.*

> **continual/constant** [adj only before noun] *It's impossible to work with these constant interruptions.* | *We've had continual problems with the computer system ever since it was installed.*

OLD

➡ look here for ...
• someone or something that is old
• something that has been used before

➡ if you want to talk about exactly how old someone or something is, go to **AGE**

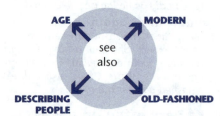

AGE   MODERN

see also

DESCRIBING   OLD-FASHIONED
PEOPLE

1 things
➡ opposite **NEW**

old /əʊld/ [adj] *They live in a big old*

house. | *She was wearing jeans and an old blue jacket.* | *The Luna Baglioni is one of the oldest hotels in Venice.* | *How old is your car?* | *That's a really old joke – I've heard it lots of times.*

ancient /'eɪnʃənt/ [adj] very old – use this about buildings, cities, countries, languages, or customs that existed many hundreds of years ago: *Rome is famous for its ancient monuments.* | *the Pyramids of ancient Egypt* | *an ancient Greek vase*

the ancient Egyptians/Chinese/Greeks etc (=the people who lived in Egypt etc many hundreds of years ago)

antique /æn'tiːk◄/ [adj only before noun] **antique** furniture, jewellery, clocks etc are old and valuable, and often beautiful to look at: *a lovely antique desk*

antique /æn'tiːk/ [n C often plural] something such as a piece of furniture or a beautiful object that is old and valuable: *The house is full of valuable antiques.*

antique shop/dealer/market (=one that sells antiques)

2 people
➡ opposite **YOUNG**

old /əʊld/ [adj] *The old lady was rather deaf.* | *You shouldn't marry him – he's much too old for you.* | *How old is the oldest person in the world?*

get old (=become old) *She's getting old now, and she needs someone to take care of her.*

the old (=old people) *The old and the sick have been allowed to leave.*

> ⚠ Be careful about using **old** to talk about people. It is more polite to use **elderly**.

elderly /'eldəˡli/ [adj] old – use this as a polite way of talking about old people: *a group of elderly ladies drinking coffee*

the elderly (=old people) *a retirement home for the elderly*

elder /'eldəˡ/ [adj only before noun] **elder brother/sister** someone's older brother or sister: *My elder brother's an actor.*

> ⚠ Don't say 'elder people', 'elder students' etc. Only use **elder** to talk about members of the same family.

eldest /ˈeldɪst/ [adj] **eldest brother/sister/son/daughter** someone's oldest brother, sister, son, or daughter: *Her eldest son is in college.* | *I shared the bedroom with my eldest sister.*
the eldest (=the oldest) *Rosie was the eldest of four daughters.*

senior citizen (also **senior** AMERICAN) /ˌsiːniəʳ ˈsɪtᵻzən, ˈsiːniəʳ/ [n C] someone who is above the age of 60 – use this to talk about older people as a group, and their particular interests, rights etc: *They have special prices for senior citizens.* | *Many seniors have very active lives.*

pensioner/old age pensioner /ˈpenʃənəʳ, ˌəʊld eɪdʒ ˈpenʃənəʳ/ [n C] BRITISH an old person who has stopped working and receives money from the government: *Many pensioners cannot afford to heat their homes in winter.* | *Old age pensioners can travel free on the buses.*

3 food

stale /steɪl/ [adj] **stale** bread or cake is hard, dry, and unpleasant to eat because it is no longer fresh: *I found some stale cake at the back of the cupboard.*
go stale (=become stale) *The bread's gone stale – you'd better throw it away.*

mouldy BRITISH **moldy** AMERICAN /ˈməʊldi/ [adj] **mouldy** cheese, bread etc has a soft green or black substance growing on it because it has been kept too long: *There was nothing in the fridge except a piece of mouldy cheese.*
go mouldy (=become mouldy) *Someone left coffee in my mug, and it's gone mouldy.*
mouldy – mouldier – mouldiest

rotten /ˈrɒtn‖ˈrɑːtn/ [adj] **rotten** food, especially eggs or fruit, has been kept too long and it smells bad: *At the back of the cupboard was a bag of rotten apples.* | *Some of the tomatoes were rotten.*

4 the time when someone is old

old age /ˌəʊld ˈeɪdʒ/ [n U] the time in someone's life when they are old: *the problems of old age*

When you see **EC**, go to the **ESSENTIAL COMMUNICATION** section.

in his/her old age (=when he/she is old) *Her grandfather's getting a bit forgetful in his old age.*

5 when something has been used before

old /əʊld/ [adj only before noun] **old** clothes, books, chairs etc have already been worn or used a lot by someone else: *I was the youngest in the family, so I had to wear all my brothers' old clothes.* | *Do you have any old magazines the kids can cut up?* | *My dad just bought a new TV, and he's giving me the old one.*

second-hand /ˌsekənd ˈhænd◄/ [adj] **second-hand** books, clothes, cars etc have already been owned by someone else and are then sold: *Max spent a whole afternoon looking around a second-hand book store.* | *Do you know where I can buy a second-hand bicycle?*
buy/get sth second-hand *"Is that table new?" "No, we got it second-hand."*

used /juːzd/ [adj only before noun] a **used** car is one that someone else has already owned, which is then sold: *He made his money buying and selling used cars.*

OLD-FASHIONED
not modern, or not suitable for the present time

1 clothes/styles/words

old-fashioned /ˌəʊld ˈfæʃənd◄/ [adj] **old-fashioned** clothes, styles, words etc are no longer considered modern or fashionable, although some people still wear them or still use them: *I don't wear that skirt now – it looks so old-fashioned.* | *'Wireless' is an old-fashioned word for radio.*

dated /'deɪtɪd/ [adj not usually before noun] use this about clothes or styles that used to be fashionable, especially until recently, but now seem old-fashioned: *Just look at the hairstyles in this photo – they're so dated.* | *The song was a big hit last year, but it's already starting to sound dated.*

2 opinions/methods/systems/people

old-fashioned /ˌəʊld 'fæʃənd◄/ [adj] **old-fashioned** opinions and ways of living were common in the past, but are not the way most people think and behave now: *In those days, people believed that divorce was morally wrong, but this now seems very old-fashioned.* | *He has some very old-fashioned ideas about women.*

> ⚠ You can also use this about people who have old-fashioned opinions: *Her parents were very old-fashioned and wouldn't let her go out with boys.*

outdated /ˌaʊt'deɪtɪd◄/ [adj] **outdated** opinions, methods, or systems are not suitable for modern times and need to be changed and made more modern: *The British legal system is hopelessly outdated.* | *The school's approach to teaching English is totally outdated.*

traditional /trə'dɪʃənəl/ [adj] **traditional** opinions, methods, or customs have existed for a long time, and have not been changed or affected by modern ideas: *The local people still use traditional farming methods which have been used for hundreds of years.* | *the traditional idea that a woman's place is in the home* | *Tom went to a very traditional all-boys school.* (=a school using traditional methods)

> ⚠ **Outdated** is always used in a negative way, but **old-fashioned** and **traditional** are sometimes used in a positive way, to talk about ideas or methods: *old-fashioned family values* | *They want to bring back traditional teaching methods.*

> When you see **EC**, go to the **ESSENTIAL COMMUNICATION** section.

3 machines/equipment

old-fashioned /ˌəʊld 'fæʃənd◄/ [adj] **old-fashioned** machines and equipment have a design that is no longer modern: *He rides one of those old-fashioned bikes with high handlebars.* | *A lot of the machines at the factory are very old-fashioned.*

outdated /ˌaʊt'deɪtɪd◄/ [adj] use this about machines or equipment that use old-fashioned designs, and should be replaced with more modern ones: *It is hard to run a business with outdated equipment.* | *a rebel army, equipped only with outdated Russian weapons*

obsolete /'ɒbsəliːt‖ˌɑːbsə'liːt/ [adj] use this about machines and equipment that are no longer being produced, and that seem old-fashioned because newer machines have been invented which can do the same job much better: *The old 5¼ inch floppy disks are now obsolete.*
make sth obsolete *a new type of 'Network Computer', which could make existing PCs obsolete within five years*

4 books/information

out of date /ˌaʊt əv 'deɪt/ [adj] use this about books, maps etc that do not contain the most recent information, or about information that is no longer right because the facts have changed: *The map we had with us was completely out of date.*

> ⚠ **Out of date** is written with hyphens when it comes before a noun, but without hyphens when it comes after a noun: *out-of-date medical records* | *Your medical records are out of date.*

5 old-fashioned in a pleasant way

old-fashioned /ˌəʊld 'fæʃənd◄/ [adj] old-fashioned in a way that reminds you of nice things in the past: *good old-fashioned home cooking* | *The town has a lovely old-fashioned charm about it.*

quaint /kweɪnt/ [adj] old-fashioned and unusual, but attractive and interesting – use this about small buildings or places, or about customs and beliefs: *We stayed in a quaint little fishing village in Cornwall.* | *quaint country cottages*

ONE

➡ see also **ALONE**

1 one person or thing

one /wʌn/ [number] *I have four sisters and one brother.* | *Turn to page one.* | *There were two signs saying 'Welcome to Wales', one on each side of the road.*
+ of *one of your friends*
one-legged/one-eyed/one-armed   etc (=having only one leg, one eye etc) *a one-eyed cat*

> ⚠ Don't say **one** when you should say **a** or **an**. Say 'he offered me a cigarette' (not 'one cigarette'). Use **one** to emphasize that you really mean only one, and not a larger number. Compare: *In the middle of the room there was a big table.* | *There were five small tables and one big table.*

> ⚠ With measurements (like month, mile, metre etc), it is more usual to say **a** than **one**: *I saw her a week ago.* | *It's about a mile from here.* | *a hundred litres of water*

single /'sɪŋgəl/ [adj only before noun] only one – use this especially when it is surprising that there is only one: *a vase with a single red rose in it* | *They won the game by a single point.* | *These dealers can earn $10,000 in a single day.*
not a single (=not even one) *It was 3 a.m. and there wasn't a single car on the road.*

solo /'səʊləʊ/ [adj only before noun] use this about something that one person does alone, but which is usually done by several people together: *a solo attempt to climb Mount Everest* | *Ridgeway's solo voyage across the Atlantic* | *This is his first solo album.* (=he made the record on his own, not with a band)
solo [adv] *When did you first fly solo?*

2 one time

once /wʌns/ [adv] one time or on one occasion: *I've only met her once.* | *He rang the bell once, then waited.*
once a day/week/month (=once every day, week etc) *We feed the dog once a day.* | *a desert region, where it only rains once or twice a year*
once more (=one more time) *Breathe in slowly once more.*

ONLY

➡ if you mean 'the largest or smallest amount that is allowed', go to **LIMIT**
➡ see also **FEW**

1 only one, or only a small number

only /'əʊnli/ [adj/adv] only one person or thing, or only a small number of people or things, and not anyone or anything else: *There was only one dress that she really liked.* | *Only rich people were able to travel abroad in those days.* | *You can only take one piece of hand baggage onto the plane.* | *You get only two chances – if you fail the exam twice you can't take it again.*
the only person/thing/place etc *She's the only woman I've ever loved.*
be only for sb (=only one person or group can use something) *These seats are only for first class passengers.*

just /dʒʌst/ [adv] ESPECIALLY SPOKEN only one person, thing, type, or group, especially when this is surprising: *"Were there a lot of people there?" "No, just me and David."* | *He started his own small shop – at first selling just newspapers, then books and magazines.* | *"Does everyone have to wear uniform?" "No, just the first-year students."*

the one /ðə 'wʌn/ **the one thing/person/time/problem etc** the only person, thing etc and no others – use this to emphasize that there really is only one person or thing of this type: *She was the one friend that I could trust.* | *The one thing I don't like about my car is the colour.* | *The one disadvantage of the new software is that it uses up a lot more space on your disk.*

all /ɔːl/ [pronoun] the only thing or things, especially when this is disappointing, annoying, or surprising: *All Kevin ever talks about is football.* | *We were so hungry, but all we could find was some stale bread.* | *All I wanted was a bit of sympathy.*

nothing but /'nʌθɪŋ bʌt/ only – use this especially when you feel disappointed, annoyed, or surprised that this is the only thing there is or the only thing someone does: *They did nothing but argue for the whole journey.* | *She answered the door wearing nothing but a towel.*

2 a surprisingly small price/number/amount etc

only /'əʊnli/ [*adv*] use this to say that a number, amount, price, size etc is surprisingly small: *Four chairs for only $99.* | *We only have a very small garden.* | *"Is it far?" "No, it's only a mile away."* | *She was only 17 when she got married.*

just /dʒʌst/ [*adv*] only a small amount, number, period of time etc, especially when this is surprising and good: *There is a beautiful park just 300 metres from the busiest shopping street.* | *It took the firefighters just three minutes to arrive.* | *His car hit a wall, but he escaped with just cuts and bruises.*

just a little (also **just a bit** BRITISH) SPOKEN (=only a small amount, number etc) *"Do you take milk?" "Just a little, please."*

is that all? /ɪz ðæt 'ɔːl/ SPOKEN say this when you are surprised because you expected a number, price etc to be higher: *"The tickets are $10." "Is that all?"*

3 for only one reason, and no others

only /'əʊnli/ [*adv*] for only one reason or purpose, and not for any others – use this especially when explaining why someone does something: *She only married him for his money.* | *Ms Walker said she only started stealing because her children were hungry.*

just /dʒʌst/ [*adv*] ESPECIALLY SPOKEN only – use this when explaining why someone does something: *I think she just wanted someone to talk to.* | *I didn't mean to interfere – I was just trying to help.*
just because *People think they know me just because they've seen me on TV.*

merely /'mɪəˈli/ [*adv*] FORMAL use this to emphasize that you are doing something only for the reason you say, and not for any other reason, especially when someone seems annoyed or upset: *The committee does not blame any individual; we are merely trying to find out how the accident happened.*

4 someone or something that is not important, special, or interesting

only/just /'əʊnli, dʒʌst/ [*adv*] use this to emphasize that someone or something is not particularly important, special, or interesting: *Don't ask me – I'm only the cleaner.* | *"What's for dinner?" "Just pasta – nothing exciting."*
only another/just another *It's just another one of those daytime talk shows.*

⚠ **Just** is used especially in spoken English.

merely /'mɪəˈli/ [*adv*] FORMAL use this to emphasize that someone or something is not really important or special, although they may seem to be: *The President's position is merely ceremonial; it is the Chancellor who holds real power.*

OPEN

➡ opposite **SHUT/CLOSE**
➡ see also **FASTEN/UNFASTEN, TIE/UNTIE**

1 to open a door, window, drawer etc

open /'əʊpən/ [*v* T] to open a door, window, drawer etc: *It's very hot in here. Do you mind if I open the window?* | *The drawer was stuck, but Tom eventually managed to open it.*

unlock /ʌn'lɒk‖-'lɑːk/ [*v* T] to turn the lock on a door, drawer, cupboard etc so that you can open it: *Unlock the door! We can't get out!* | *Which of these keys unlocks the cupboard?*

force open /ˌfɔːˈs 'əʊpən/ to open a drawer, window, cupboard etc by using force, often with a tool
force sth open *The door's stuck – we'll have to force it open.*
force open sth *The burglars had forced open the window with an iron bar.*

break the door down /ˌbreɪk ðə 'dɔːˈ daʊn/ to hit or push a locked door very hard so that the lock breaks and the door opens or falls down: *Firefighters had to break the door down.* | *This is the* *police! Open the door or we'll break it down.*

wind down the window BRITISH **roll down the window** AMERICAN /,waɪnd daʊn ðə 'wɪndəʊ, ,rəʊl daʊn ðə 'wɪndəʊ/ to open a car window, especially by turning a handle: *The driver wound down his window and asked us the way to the stadium.* | *Mom, will you roll down your window a little?*

2 when a door or window opens

open /'əʊpən/ [v I] if a door or window **opens**, it moves so that it is no longer shut: *The door opened and Dr Neil came in.* | *I can't get this window to open.*

burst open/fly open /,bɜːʳst 'əʊpən, ,flaɪ 'əʊpən/ to open very suddenly: *Suddenly the door flew open with a bang.* | *The door burst open and Flora came running in.*

⚠ Use **burst open** or **fly open** especially in stories or descriptions.

3 an open door or window

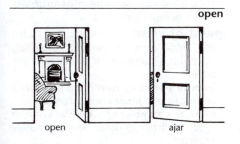

open

open   ajar

open /'əʊpən/ [adj] *Carrie stood in front of the open window.* | *The office door was open, and I could hear everything they said.*

wide open (=open as much as possible) *He always leaves the door wide open when he's getting changed.*

ajar /ə'dʒɑːʳ/ [adj not before noun] WRITTEN a door that is **ajar** is slightly open: *She had left her bedroom door ajar and could hear her parents talking downstairs.*

When you see **EC**, go to the **ESSENTIAL COMMUNICATION** section.

⚠ Use **ajar** especially in stories and written descriptions.

4 to open a container

open /'əʊpən/ [v T] to open a bottle, box, or other container by removing or lifting its top or lid: *Ask the waiter to open another bottle of champagne.* | *Jonah opened his tool box and pulled out a hammer.* | *It's a little gadget that helps you to open jars.*

unscrew /ʌn'skruː/ [v T] to remove the top or lid of a bottle or container by turning it: *Charlie unscrewed the top and held out the bottle, offering me a drink.*

5 to open a packet or something that is folded

open /'əʊpən/ [v T] to remove or partly remove the outside covering of something so that you can reach what is inside it: *Aren't you going to open your letter?* | *Judy opened another pack of cigarettes.*

unwrap /ʌn'ræp/ [v T] to open a package by removing the paper that is wrapped around it: *I just love unwrapping Christmas presents!* | *Sarah sat down and unwrapped her sandwiches.*

unwrapping – unwrapped – have unwrapped

unfold /ʌn'fəʊld/ [v T] to open something that was folded, such as a piece of paper or cloth: *They unfolded the tablecloth and set out the picnic.* | *The wind was so strong that it was impossible to unfold the map.*

6 to open your eyes or mouth

open your eyes/open your mouth /,əʊpən jɔːr 'aɪz, ,əʊpən jɔːʳ 'maʊθ/ *She opened her eyes and sat up in bed.* | *The dentist told me to open my mouth a little wider.*

open /'əʊpən/ [adj not usually before noun] when your mouth or eyes are open: *I was so tired I could hardly keep my eyes open.*

wide open (=open as much as possible) *Ben was staring at her with his mouth wide open.*

O

7 when a shop, bank, restaurant etc opens

open /ˈəupən/ [v I] if a shop, bank, restaurant etc **opens** at a particular time in the day, people can use it from that time: *"What time do the banks open?" "They normally open at 9.30."* | *On Saturdays, the restaurant opens at 7 p.m.*

⚠ You can also use **open** to say that a new shop, bank, restaurant etc starts to be available for people to use: *A new McDonalds has opened in St Petersburg.* | *The store first opened in 1976.* You can also say that someone **opens** a new shop, bank, restaurant etc, meaning that they make it available for people to use: *They plan to open a new superstore just outside of town.*

open /ˈəupən/ [adj not before noun] if a shop, bank, restaurant etc is **open**, it is available for people to use: *The World Café is open from 10 a.m. till 11 p.m.*
stay open *In some places, the bars stay open all night.*

OPINION

🖭 OPINIONS   LIKE/NOT LIKE

AGREE   see also   DISAGREE

AGAINST   SUPPORT

🖭 DISAGREEING   🖭 AGREEING

1 what you think about something

opinion /əˈpɪnjən/ [n C] what you think about a subject or situation
my/your/her etc opinion *Do you want my opinion? I don't think the colour really suits you.*
in my/your/her etc opinion *In my opinion, most lawyers are overpaid.* | *This is, in the opinion of the critics, their best record for years.*
+ about/on *Can I ask your opinion about something, Michael?*

give your opinion (=say what you think) *Do you think it's a good essay? Give me your honest opinion.*

⊙ what you think of/about sth

/ˌwɒt juː ˈθɪŋk ɒv, əbaut (sth)/ ESPECIALLY SPOKEN your opinion about something, especially whether you think it is good or bad: *What do you think of the new Oasis record?* | *You still haven't said what you think about my idea.*

view /vjuː/ [n C] your opinion about something, especially about a serious or important subject: *It is quite natural for children to have different views from their parents.*
+ that *I don't agree with the view that longer prison sentences stop people from committing crime.*
in my/his/John's view *In Freud's view, people's dreams often reveal their unconscious fears.*
+ on *She has strong views on environmental issues.*

attitude /ˈætɪtjuːd‖-tuːd/ [n C] what you think and feel about something or someone, especially when this is shown in the way you behave: *I don't understand your attitude. Why don't you trust her?*
+ to/towards *Since the 1960s, there has been a big change in people's attitudes to sex before marriage.*

point of view /ˌpɔɪnt əv ˈvjuː/ [n C] what you think about something, especially when this is influenced by the situation you are in
from sb's point of view *From a farmer's point of view, foxes are a nuisance.*
listen to sb's point of view *She's always ready to listen to other people's points of view.*
plural **points of view**

public opinion /ˌpʌblɪk əˈpɪnjən/ [n U] what most people in a country think about a particular subject, idea, or problem: *The government responded to public opinion and introduced new controls on guns.* | *Public opinion is strongly in favour of the death penalty.*

position /pəˈzɪʃən/ [n singular] the official opinion of a government, political party, or organization
+ on *What is the party's position on abortion?*

2 what other people think about you

reputation /ˌrepjʊˈteɪʃən/ [n C] someone's **reputation** is the general opinion that other people have about them, for example whether they are good or bad

excellent/good/bad reputation *No parent wants to send their child to a school with a bad reputation.*

+ as *She had a reputation as a very efficient organizer.*

+ for *a car with a reputation for reliability*
damage sb's reputation *Nixon's reputation was damaged so badly that he had to resign.*

image /ˈɪmɪdʒ/ [n singular] the idea that people have about a well-known person, company, or product – use this especially about an idea that is deliberately created through newspaper stories, advertising etc: *Pepsi's image is as a drink for fashionable young people.*

be bad/good for sb's image *The President's advisers said it would be bad for his image to be photographed with union leaders.*

OPPOSITE

➡ look here for ...
- when two things are completely different
- in the opposite direction
- when two people or things are facing each other

➡ see also **DIFFERENT, SAME**

1 when two things or people are completely different

opposite /ˈɒpəzɪt‖-ɑːp-/ [adj] as different as possible from something else: *The medicine was supposed to make him sleep, but it had the opposite effect.* | *During the summer there wasn't enough rain, but now we have the opposite problem!* | *John and I have opposite opinions on almost everything.*

When you see **EC**, go to the **ESSENTIAL COMMUNICATION** section.

the opposite /ði ˈɒpəzɪt‖-ɑːp-/ [n singular] a person or thing that is as different as possible from someone or something else, or a word whose meaning is as different as possible from the meaning of another word: *They asked for our advice, and then did the opposite!*

+ of *'Hard' is the opposite of 'soft'.*

just the opposite (=exactly the opposite) *Larry is friendly and outgoing, but his brother is just the opposite.*

◯**the other way around** /ði ˌʌðəʳ weɪ əˈraʊnd/ SPOKEN if a situation is **the other way around**, it is the opposite of what you thought or of what someone has just said: *No, the street was named after the college, not the other way around.* (=the college was not named after the street) | *I thought he was the boss and she was his secretary, but in fact it was the other way around.*

2 in the opposite direction

the other way /ði ˌʌðəʳ ˈweɪ/ **go/come/look/face the other way** to go, look etc in the opposite direction: *She didn't see me – she was looking the other way.* | *Their car hit a truck which was coming the other way.*

⚠ The other way is more informal than in the opposite direction.

in the opposite direction/in the other direction /ɪn ði ˈɒpəzɪt dɪˈrekʃən, ɪn ði ˌʌðəʳ dɪˈrekʃən‖-ɑːp-/ in the direction that is opposite to the one in which someone is going: *I saw him and hurried away in the opposite direction.* | *The road is very narrow, so slow down if you meet another car coming in the other direction.*

in opposite directions *Two trains travelling in opposite directions had collided.*

3 **when two people or things directly face each other**

opposite

They sat opposite each other.

opposite /'ɒpəzᵻt‖'ɑːp-/ [adj/adv/preposition] something that is **opposite** something else is facing it, for example on the other side of the street or on the other side of a table: *When you get off the bus, you'll see a grocery store on the opposite side of the street.* | *She recognized the man who was sitting opposite.*
be opposite sb/sth *The bathroom is opposite the bedroom.*
directly opposite (=exactly opposite) *The entrance to the park is directly opposite our house.*

> ⚠ Don't say 'the cinema is opposite of the station'. Say **the cinema is opposite the station.**

across /ə'krɒs‖ə'krɔːs/ [preposition] **across the street/river/table** opposite where you are, and on the other side of the street, river etc: *She lives across the road.* | *From the hotel you can see the pretty villages across the bay.*
across the street/table from sth *Across the street from where we were standing was a little park.*

on the other side /ʌn ði ˌʌðəʳ 'saɪd/ on the opposite side of a road, river etc: *If you look across the lake, you can see Ruskin's house on the other side.*
+ of *You have to park on the other side of the road.*

face /feɪs/ [v T] if one person, building, seat etc **faces** another, they are opposite each other, and each of them has their front towards the other: *Rita's apartment faces the harbour.* | *The seat facing mine was empty.* | *They stood facing each other for a few minutes.*

face to face /ˌfeɪs tə 'feɪs/ if two people are **face to face**, they are sitting or standing opposite each other, and they are very close: *The two men stood face to face, glaring at each other.* | *We sat face to face across the table.*

ORDER

the order in which things are arranged, or the order in which things happen

➡ if you mean 'order someone to do something', go to **TELL**

1 **order**

order /'ɔːʳdəʳ/ [n U] the way that events happen or that information is arranged, showing which is first, which is second, and so on
in this/that/what/any order *Safety checks must be carried out in the following order: One – make sure all electrical equipment is switched off, two – ...* | *It doesn't matter which order you answer the questions in.*
+ of *We were given a printed sheet showing the order of events for the day.*
in order of importance/difficulty/size etc (=when the most important thing is first, then the next most important etc) *Their main exports, in order of importance, are copper, coal, and maize.* | *The subjects that students enjoyed most were, in order of popularity, music, history, and art.*
in alphabetical order (=with 'a' first, then 'b', then 'c' etc)

sequence /'siːkwəns/ [n C] the specific order in which a number of events, actions, or pieces of information follow one another

+ of *Police are not sure of the exact sequence of events that led to the riot.* | *The dance is basically a sequence of steps that you repeat over and over again.* | *Basic computer code consists of sequences of ones and zeros.*

pattern /ˈpætən‖ˈpætərn/ [n C] the order in which things usually happen or someone usually does something, which you notice because it seems to be regular: *It's a common pattern: failure at school, unemployment, leading to a life of crime.*
+ of *a familiar pattern of events*
follow a pattern (=happen in the same way) *Police say that each of the murders follows the same pattern.*

2 in the correct order

in the right order /ɪn ðə ˌraɪt ˈɔːrdər/ if a set of things, actions, or events is **in the right order**, it is correctly arranged or it happens in the correct order: *Have you put all the pages in the right order?* | *It is important to add each ingredient in the right order.*

3 in the wrong order

in the wrong order /ɪn ðə ˌrɒŋ ˈɔːrdər‖ -ˌrɔːŋ-/ if a set of things, actions, or events is **in the wrong order**, it is not correctly arranged: *All the files were in the wrong order, so it took me hours to find her letter.* | *If you give commands in the wrong order, the computer will not respond.*

mixed up /ˌmɪkst ˈʌp◂/ [adj not before noun] in the wrong order, especially when this has been done deliberately: *It's an exercise in which the sentences are all mixed up and you have to put them in the right order.*

backwards /ˈbækwədz/ [adv] starting at the end and finishing at the beginning: *Can you say the alphabet backwards?*

When you see EC, go to the ESSENTIAL COMMUNICATION section.

ORGANIZATION

a group of people who do something together, or who work for a particular purpose

0

➡ see also **MEMBER, COMPANY, JOIN**

organization (also **organisation** BRITISH) /ˌɔːrgənaɪˈzeɪʃən‖-gənə-/ [n C] a large organized group of people who work together in business, politics, education, sport etc: *Greenpeace is an international organization that works to protect the environment.* | *Most big organizations employ their own legal experts.* | *the World Health Organization*

institution /ˌɪnstɪˈtjuːʃən‖-ˈtuː-/ [n C] an organization that does educational, scientific, or financial work, especially a large and important organization that has existed for a long time: *librarians working in educational institutions* | *banks, insurance companies, and other financial institutions* | *A major study of women and heart disease is being carried out by the Johns Hopkins Medical Institution.*

party /ˈpɑːrti/ [n C] an organization of people who all have the same political ideas, which you can vote for in elections: *The Republican Party now has a majority in Congress.* | *the new right-wing political parties in Russia*
join a party *He joined the Communist Party when he was a student.*
plural **parties**

⚠ You can also use **party** before a noun, like an adjective: *Party leaders met today to discuss the crisis.* | *This is not party policy.* | *party members*

⚠ In British English, you can use **party** with a singular or plural verb: *The Labour Party is likely/are likely to oppose any change in the law.* In American English, always use a singular verb.

club /klʌb/ [n C] a group of people who meet regularly in their free time to do something that they are all interested in, especially a sport
tennis/photography etc club *a member of the local tennis club*
join a club *How much does it cost to join the golf club?*

belong to a club (=be a member of a club) *She belongs to the college chess club.*

society /sə'saɪ₃ti/ [n C] an organization for people who have the same interest or aim, especially a large official organization: *the Royal Society for the Protection of Birds | the university film society | the president of the American Historical Society*
plural **societies**

> ⚠ **Clubs** are usually for sport and other activities that people do in their free time, such as photography or gardening. **Societies** are interested in subjects like art, literature, and science, or in working to help people or animals that have problems.

association /ə,səusi'eɪʃən, ə,səuʃi-/ [n C] an important organization for people in a particular sport, profession, activity etc, which officially represents its members and has the power to make rules: *The new health care proposals have been criticized by the British Medical Association. | The National Basketball Association negotiates TV rights for important games.*

> ⚠ The word **association** is almost always used in the name of an organization.

union /'juːnjən/ [n C] an organization formed by workers to protect their rights and improve their pay and working conditions: *The largest teachers' union supports the education reforms. | the National Union of Mineworkers*
trade union BRITISH **labor union** AMERICAN (=union) *The President could not rely on the support of the labor unions.*
join a union *Some workers refused to join the union.*

> ⚠ You can also use **union** before a noun, like an adjective: *Union members have voted against a strike. | a union official*

> ⚠ In British English, you can use **union** with a singular or plural verb: *The union has rejected/have rejected the latest pay offer.* In American English, always use a singular verb.

When you see **EC**, go to the
ESSENTIAL COMMUNICATION section.

ORGANIZE/ ARRANGE

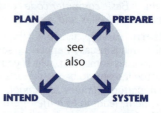

1 to make preparations for something to happen

arrange /ə'reɪndʒ/ [v I/T] to make preparations for a meeting, party, journey etc, for example by choosing a suitable time and place and telling people about it: *Ann's arranging a surprise party for Russell's birthday. | We're going on Friday – it's all arranged.*
arrange to do sth *They arranged to meet the following day.*
arrange for sb to do sth *He arranged for her to leave on the next flight home.*
it is arranged that *It was arranged that our visitors should stay at a nearby hotel.*

organize (also **organise** BRITISH) /'ɔːrgənaɪz/ [v T] to make preparations for an event, especially a big public event that needs a lot of preparation and planning: *I've been asked to organize this year's Summer Carnival. | an exhibition organised by the local camera club*
> **organizer** (also **organiser** BRITISH) [n C] someone who organizes a large public event: *the organizers of the Dartmouth Music Festival | conference organizer*

make arrangements /,meɪk ə'reɪndʒ-mənts/ to arrange all the details of an event, such as dates, times, and places after you have decided what you are going to do
+ for *Rita and Howard are busy making arrangements for their wedding.*

set up /,set 'ʌp/ [phrasal verb T] to make all the arrangements that are necessary so that a meeting can happen or a system can start working
set up sth *I'll get my secretary to set up a meeting for all of the sales executives. |*

We need to set up emergency procedures to deal with this sort of problem.

set sth up *There will be an inquiry into the accident, and Judge Mather has been asked to set it up.*

fix up /ˌfɪks ˈʌp/ [phrasal verb I/T] BRITISH INFORMAL to arrange a meeting, a visit, a journey etc

fix up sth *We should fix up a meeting. Are you free on Thursday?*

fix up to do sth *I've fixed up to go to the airport with Bill.*

fix up for sb to do sth *He fixed up for her to go and see Dr Graham.*

2 plans and preparations for an event

arrangements /əˈreɪndʒmənts/ [n plural] all the preparations that must be made for something to happen and be successful

+ for *Who is in charge of the arrangements for the President's visit?*

make arrangements *Her nephew has made all the funeral arrangements.*

travel/seating/sleeping arrangements *Lena wasn't very happy about the travel arrangements.*

plans /plænz/ [n plural] things that you have planned to do and arranged to do: *I'd bought everything for a picnic, but the weather spoiled our plans.*

+ for *What are your plans for tonight?*

appointment /əˈpɔɪntmənt/ [n C] an arrangement to meet someone such as a doctor, a lawyer, or a business person at a particular time and place: *What time is your appointment at the hospital?*

have an appointment with sb *I have an appointment with the dentist on Monday afternoon.*

make an appointment *If you want to see the manager, you'll have to make an appointment.*

3 something that is well organized

well-organized (also **well-organised** BRITISH) /ˌwel ˈɔːʳgənaɪzd◄/ [adj] organized in a careful and thorough way, and therefore likely to be successful: *The exhibition was very well-organized. | a clear, well-organized report | a well-organized political campaign*

efficient /ɪˈfɪʃənt/ [adj] use this about an organization, method, or system in which all the parts work well together and good results are achieved without any money or time being wasted: *The passport office is very efficient – I got a new passport in just 48 hours. | We need more efficient methods of transporting goods.*

well-run /ˌwel ˈrʌn◄/ [adj] use this about an organization or business that is successful because the people in charge organize it well: *The Klausner is a comfortable, well-run hotel.*

4 someone who organizes things well and gets good results

well organized (also **well organised** BRITISH) /ˌwel ˈɔːʳgənaɪzd◄/ [adj] someone who is **well organized** plans things well so that they achieve what they want to achieve: *If you work as a personal assistant, you need to be well-organized. | Well-organized rebel forces have succeeded in recapturing the town.*

efficient /ɪˈfɪʃənt/ [adj] someone who is **efficient** works well and does what needs to be done without wasting time: *Friendly and efficient staff are essential.*

businesslike /ˈbɪznɪˌslaɪk/ [adj] someone who is **businesslike** deals with people effectively and does not waste time on things that are not important: *At work, she becomes efficient and businesslike. | Gates gave a brief, businesslike explanation of his plans for the company.*

5 something that is badly organized

badly organized (also **badly organised** BRITISH) /ˌbædli ˈɔːʳgənaɪzd◄/ [adj] use this about events or activities that are not successful, because they have not been planned well: *The show was very badly organized, and nobody seemed to know what they were doing.*

disorganized (also **disorganised** BRITISH) /dɪsˈɔːʳgənaɪzd/ [adj] use this about people who are bad at organizing things, and who do not know where anything is or what they should be doing: *Graham's far too disorganized to be a good teacher.*

0

chaos /'keɪ-ɒs‖-ɑːs/ [n U] a very confused situation in which nothing seems to be organized, especially when something bad has happened unexpectedly: *The floods have caused widespread chaos.*

in chaos *The country was in chaos following the death of the President.*

   chaotic /keɪ'ɒtɪk‖-'ɑːt-/ [adj] use this about situations in which everything seems confused and nothing seems organized: *Traffic in the cities is chaotic.*

confusion /kən'fjuːʒən/ [n U] a situation in which no one is sure what is happening and there is a lot of noise and activity: *the noise and confusion of the marketplace* | *The bombers escaped in the confusion that followed the explosion.*

be a mess/be a shambles /biː ə 'mes, biː ə 'ʃæmbəlz/ INFORMAL if a situation or event **is a mess** or **a shambles**, no one seems to be in control and nothing good or useful is being achieved: *The country's economy is a shambles.* | *My life seems to be a mess at the moment.*

6 to put things or people in a particular order

arrange /ə'reɪndʒ/ [v T] to put a group of things or people into a particular order or position, according to a plan or design: *Nina arranged the roses in a tall vase.* | *A photographer was arranging the children for the school photograph.*

arrange sth in a circle/in rows etc *The chairs had been arranged in a circle around the piano.*

organize (also **organise** BRITISH) /'ɔːʳgənaɪz/ to arrange in order information, ideas etc according to a system, so that they will be more effective or easier to use: *Organize your notes very carefully before giving a speech.*

organize sth into piles/groups etc *The book is organized into three sections.*

set out /ˌset 'aʊt/ [phrasal verb T] to arrange a group of things on the floor, on a table, on a shelf etc for people to use, take, or look at

set out sth *Let's set out the chairs so they'll be ready for tonight's meeting.*

set sth out *A waiter brought drinks and sandwiches, and set them out on a low table beside the pool.*

rearrange /ˌriːə'reɪndʒ/ [v T] to arrange things in a different order or position from the way they were arranged before: *Who's been rearranging the furniture?* | *With a word processor you can easily rearrange the paragraphs when you've finished writing.*

7 to put things into the correct order

put sth in order /ˌpʊt (sth) ɪn 'ɔːʳdəʳ/ to arrange things so that they are in the correct order: *Collect all the pages together, put them in order, and file them.*

put sth in alphabetical/numerical order *We need to put all the names in alphabetical order.*

sort out /ˌsɔːʳt 'aʊt/ [phrasal verb T] to organize something that is untidy or unclear, so that it is tidier and easier to use

sort out sth *I spent most of the morning sorting out my desk.*

sort sth out *Sort the files out, and throw away any we don't need.*

8 the way that things are arranged

arrangement /ə'reɪndʒmənt/ [n C] a group of things that are arranged according to a pattern or in order to look attractive

+ of *a simple design consisting of a geometrical arrangement of circles and rectangles*

flower arrangement (=flowers that have been cut and arranged attractively)

layout /'leɪaʊt/ [n C] the way that a building, town, garden, book etc is arranged according to a plan, so that it looks attractive or works well: *a computer program to help you design page layout*

+ of *the architects who had planned the layout of our hospital*

When you see **EC**, go to the
ESSENTIAL COMMUNICATION section.

OWE

LEND　　　BANKS

see also

BORROW　　　PAY

MONEY

1 to owe money to someone

owe /əʊ/ [v T] if you **owe** someone money, you have to pay them, either because you borrowed money from them or because you got something from them and have not yet paid for it

owe sb sth/owe sth to sb *I owe him £5.* | *We owe a lot of money to the bank.*

owe money/$50 etc *The business collapsed, owing $50 million.*

owe sb sth for sth *They still owe us money for the car.*

be in debt /biː ɪn 'det/ if you **are in debt**, you owe a lot of money and you have difficulty paying it: *The helpline offers financial advice to people who are in debt.*

get into debt (=start being in debt) *We got into debt when my wife lost her job.*

be £1000/$2000 etc in debt (=owe that amount) *The report showed that most students were over £1000 in debt.*

be heavily in debt (=owe a very large amount of money) *Several companies were heavily in debt by the end of the 1980s.*

be overdrawn /biː ˌəʊvəˈdrɔːn/ to owe money to your bank because you have spent more than you had in your bank account: *I was overdrawn at the end of last month.*

be $100/£200 etc overdrawn *The bank wrote to tell us we were $500 overdrawn.*

be in the red /biː ɪn ðə 'red/ INFORMAL if you **are in the red**, you owe more money than you have: *I'm always in the red by the middle of the month.*

be £100/$500 etc in the red (=owe that amount) *At the end of the war, Britain was about $50 million in the red.*

2 money that you owe

debt /det/ [n C/U] money that you owe, especially a large amount: *Debt is one of the main social problems of our time.*

+ of *The government now has debts of $2.5 billion.*

pay off a debt (=pay all the money that you owe) *It took us three years to pay off all our debts.*

overdraft /ˈəʊvəˈdrɑːft‖-dræft/ [n C] an amount of money that you owe to your bank when you have spent more money than you had in your bank account: *I've already got an enormous overdraft.*

a £100/$1500 etc overdraft *When he left college, he had a $3000 overdraft.*

3 to not owe any money

be in credit /biː ɪn 'kredɪt/ if your bank account **is in credit**, there is money in it, and you do not owe the bank anything: *We offer free banking for customers whose accounts remain in credit.*

OWN

➡ if you mean 'on your own', go to **ALONE**

➡ see also **HAVE/NOT HAVE, GET**

1 to own something

own /əʊn/ [v T] if you **own** something, especially something big like a house, a car, or a company, it is your property and you have the legal right to have it: *We don't own the apartment, we're just renting it.* | *Clark owns about 40 companies in northern Europe.* | *The horse is owned by an Italian businessman.*

⚠ Don't say 'I am owning this house'. Say **I own this house**.

have (also **have got** ESPECIALLY BRITISH) /hæv, həv ˈɡɒt‖-ˈɡɑːt/ [v T] to own something, especially something that ordinary people are likely to own: *What kind of car has she got?* | *We don't have a TV.* | *How many of your students have a computer?*

having – had – have had

⚠ Don't say 'he is having a car'. Say **he has a car.**

be mine/yours/John's etc /biː (mine, etc)/ if something **is mine**, **yours**, **John's** etc, it belongs to me, you, John etc: *Sorry! I didn't know it was yours.* | *"Whose bike is that?" "It's Martin's."*

possess /pəˈzes/ [v T] FORMAL to own something – use this especially in negative sentences to say that someone does not own something that most people own: *Very few families in this area possess a telephone.* | *He never wore a suit – I don't think he possessed one.* | *They lost everything they possessed in the earthquake.*

⚠ Don't say 'everything that they are possessing'. Say **everything that they possess.**

belong to sb /bɪˈlɒŋ tuː (sb)‖-ˈlɔːŋ-/ [phrasal verb T] if something **belongs to** someone, they own it: *This watch belonged to my grandfather.* | *Who does that Walkman belong to?*

⚠ Don't say 'the bag is belonging to her'. Say **the bag belongs to her.**

my own/your own etc /maɪ ˈəʊn, jɔːr ˈəʊn (etc)/ if something is **your own**, it belongs to you and not anyone else: *You can rent skis or you can bring your own.* | *Joe left the company to set up his own business.*

a room/car/house etc of your own *When we move to the new house, I'm going to have a room of my own.*

2 the person who owns something

owner /ˈəʊnər/ [n C] the person who owns something: *The previous owner painted the outside of the house yellow.*

+ of *The owners of the company live abroad.*

home/car/dog etc owner *Car owners are facing a 10% rise in the price of gasoline.*

landlord/landlady /ˈlændlɔːrd, ˈlændleɪdi/ [n C] someone who owns a building and is paid money by the people who live in it or use it: *Our landlord has promised to fix the heating by Tuesday.*

plural **landladies**

3 the things that someone owns

property /ˈprɒpərti‖ˈprɑː-/ [n U] things that someone owns, especially large, expensive things such as buildings, land, or cars: *The boys have been charged with damaging school property.* | *Some of the stolen property was discovered in an empty warehouse.*

⚠ Don't say 'properties' when you mean the things that someone owns.

possessions /pəˈzeʃənz/ [n plural] all the things that a person owns, which they keep in their home or carry with them: *They lost all their possessions in the floods.* | *This book is one of my most treasured possessions.*

things /θɪŋz/ [n plural] SPOKEN things such as clothes, records, and books that you own: *She always leaves her things all over the floor.*

stuff /stʌf/ [n U] SPOKEN INFORMAL your clothes, furniture, plates, pans etc: *I don't know how I'm going to fit all my stuff into the new apartment.*

belongings /bɪˈlɒŋɪŋz‖bɪˈlɔːŋ-/ [n plural] things you own such as clothes, equipment, bags etc, especially things you take with you when you are travelling somewhere: *Please keep your belongings with you at all times.* | *They packed all their belongings into the car and left the city that night.*

valuables /ˈvæljuəbəlz, -jʊbəlz‖ˈvæljʊbəlz/ [n plural] small valuable things, such as jewellery or cameras, which may get stolen if you do not look after them: *The hotel management advises guests not to leave any valuables in their rooms.*

When you see **EC**, go to the **ESSENTIAL COMMUNICATION** section.

P

PAIN

HURT/INJURE   DOCTOR

ILL/SICK   *see also*   BETTER 4

BREAK   SUFFER

ILLNESS/DISEASE   MEDICAL TREATMENT

1 when part of your body hurts

hurt /hɜːʳt/ [v I] if a part of your body **hurts**, you feel pain in it, for example because you have hit it or cut it, or because you are ill: *My neck felt stiff and my shoulder hurt.* | *I fell and banged my knee, and it really hurts.*

it hurts SPOKEN (say this when part of your body hurts) *It hurts when I move my arm.*

hurting – hurt – have hurt

painful /ˈpeɪnfəl/ [adj] a **painful** injury or a **painful** part of your body makes you feel pain: *Jim's knee was still painful where he had fallen on it.* | *a painful back injury*

> ⚠ Don't say 'she is painful'. Say she is in pain. Don't say 'I am painful'. Say my leg/back etc hurts.

ache /eɪk/ [v I] if a part of your body **aches**, you feel a pain in it that is continuous but not very strong – use this about pains in your arms, legs, or back, or in your head or stomach: *My arms ached from carrying all the groceries.* | *She felt hot and her head was beginning to ache.* | *I went to dance class last week, and I've been aching ever since.*

sore /sɔːʳ/ [adj] if a part of your body is **sore**, it hurts when you touch it or use it – use this about painful areas of your skin, for example where you have cut yourself: *Her hands were still sore from scrubbing*

the floors. | *I cut my finger last week, and it's still sore.*

sore throat (=when the inside of your throat is sore, especially because you have a cold) *Honey is very good for a sore throat.*

sting /stɪŋ/ [v I] to feel a sudden sharp pain for a short time – use this about your eyes or your skin: *The smoke made our eyes sting.*

stinging – stung – have stung

stiff /stɪf/ [adj] if a part of your body is **stiff**, it is difficult to move and the muscles around it hurt: *"How do you feel?" "My legs are a little stiff, but otherwise I'm fine."*

stiff neck/leg/back etc *Long car journeys always give me a stiff neck.*

2 when something or someone hurts you

hurt /hɜːʳt/ [v I/T] if something or someone **hurts** you, they make you feel pain: *The dentist's drill really hurt.* | *Stop it – you're hurting me.*

hurting – hurt – have hurt

sting /stɪŋ/ [v I/T] to cause a sudden sharp pain on your skin or in your eyes for a short time: *The antiseptic might sting a little.* | *The smoke stung my eyes.* | *She felt a stinging pain as the bullet grazed her arm.*

stinging – stung – have stung

3 the feeling you have when part of your body hurts

pain /peɪn/ [n C/U] the feeling you have when part of your body hurts: *The pain is getting worse.* | *You won't feel any pain during the operation.* | *He told the doctor he was suffering from chest pains.*

a pain in your chest/leg/back etc *I have a terrible pain in my left arm.*

be in pain (=be feeling pain) *The old man looked white and was obviously in pain.*

be in great pain/be in a lot of pain *She's in a lot of pain with her back.*

severe pain (=very bad pain) *A slipped disc can cause severe back pain.*

ease the pain (=make a pain hurt less) *These pills should help to ease the pain.*

ache /eɪk/ [n C] a pain that continues for a long time but is not very sharp: *The ache in my leg muscles had almost disappeared.*

dull ache (=a continuous annoying ache) *Lisa felt a dull ache spreading up her arm.*

be in agony /biː ɪn ˈægəni/ to have a lot of severe pain: *Yves lay in agony on the slope. He was sure that he had broken his leg.*

headache/toothache/backache/ stomach ache /ˈhedeɪk, ˈtuːθeɪk, ˈbækeɪk, ˈstʌmək eɪk/ [n C/U] a continuous pain in a part of your body: *Is your backache any better?*

have/get a headache *I always get a headache when I've been using the computer.*

have toothache/backache/stomach ache BRITISH *I'm not surprised you have stomach ache – you eat too fast.*

have a toothache/a backache/a stomach ache AMERICAN *My daughter has a really bad toothache.*

a splitting headache (=a very bad headache)

> ⚠ Don't say 'I have headache' or 'it gives me headache'. Say **I have a headache** or **it gives me a headache.**

4 when something does not hurt

not hurt /nɒt ˈhɜːrt/ if something **does not hurt**, it is not painful: *This won't hurt at all. Just sit still while I remove the bandage.*

painless /ˈpeɪnləs/ [adj] something that is **painless** does not hurt, especially when you are worried that it might hurt: *The operation is simple and painless.*

not feel a thing /nɒt ˌfiːl ə ˈθɪŋ/ SPOKEN to not feel any pain at all: *Don't worry about the injection – you won't feel a thing.*

> When you see **EC**, go to the
> **ESSENTIAL COMMUNICATION** section.

PAINT

BRIGHT/NOT BRIGHT

ART

DRAW

see also

DECORATE

PICTURE

PATTERN

COLOUR/COLOR

1 to paint pictures

paint /peɪnt/ [v T] to make a picture of something or someone, by putting paint onto a surface with a brush: *Geraint was sitting on the beach, painting the seagulls and the fishing boats.*

paint a picture (of sth/sb) *I'm going to paint a picture of the church.* | *a picture painted by Monet*

painting [n U] the activity of painting pictures: *I'm not very good at painting.* | *a painting class*

painter /ˈpeɪntər/ [n C] someone who paints pictures: *This is by the great Spanish painter, Goya.*

portrait painter (=someone who paints pictures of people)

landscape painter (=someone who paints pictures of places, the countryside etc)

artist /ˈɑːrtᵻst/ [n C] someone who produces works of art, especially paintings or drawings: *an exhibition of works by Italian artists* | *We asked a young local artist to come and show her work to the students.*

2 to paint walls/doors/ rooms

paint /peɪnt/ [v I/T] to put paint on walls, doors, pieces of furniture etc: *I'm going to paint the bathroom tomorrow.*

paint sth blue/red/white etc *She painted the walls yellow.* | *What colour did you paint the doors?*

decorate /ˈdekəreɪt/ [v I/T] ESPECIALLY BRITISH to paint the inside of a house or put paper on the walls: *They've just finished decorating the kitchen.* | *We spent all weekend decorating.*

have sth decorated (=pay someone to decorate it) *Mum had the whole house decorated before she moved in.*

painter /ˈpeɪntər/ [n C] someone who paints houses, walls etc as their job

---

PART

➡ see also **PIECE**

1 part of an object/area

part /pɑːrt/ [n C] *When you have filled in the form, keep the top part and send the other part to the bank.*
+ of *The front part of the car was badly damaged.* | *Malaria is still common in many parts of Africa.*

bit /bɪt/ [n C] BRITISH SPOKEN a small part of an object or area: *The bit you've painted looks really nice.*
+ of *that bit of the garden where the fruit trees are*

piece /piːs/ [n C] one of several different parts that must be joined together to make something: *a 1000-piece jigsaw puzzle*
in pieces (=as separate pieces) *The huge structure had to be taken apart and transported in pieces.*

section /ˈsekʃən/ [n C] one of several parts that a place, shop, container etc is divided into: *You'll find her books in the 'English Classics' section.*
+ of *The spoons go in the front section of the drawer.* | *the non-smoking section of the plane*

2 part of a story/book/film/play etc

part /pɑːrt/ [n C] *Jane Austen's 'Pride and Prejudice', adapted for radio in six parts*
+ of *The first part of the story takes place in Crete.*
Part One/Part Two etc (=one of the main parts that a book, TV story etc is divided into) *Part One ends with the death of the hero's father.*

bit /bɪt/ [n C] BRITISH SPOKEN a small part of a story or film: *My favourite bit was when they try to escape from the prison.*
+ of *Some bits of the film were really boring.*

chapter /ˈtʃæptər/ [n C] one of the parts that a book is divided into: *Read the first two chapters before next week's class.*
Chapter One/Chapter Two etc *I've only read as far as Chapter 6.*

scene /siːn/ [n C] one of the parts that a play or film is divided into: *The ghost appears in the first scene.* | *a love scene*

3 part of an organization

branch /brɑːntʃ‖bræntʃ/ [n C] a shop, office, or bank in a particular area that is part of a larger organization: *Our store has branches all over the country.*
+ of *The North-East Branch of the charity is based in Newcastle.*

> ⚠ You can also use **branch** before a noun, like an adjective: *He was appointed Branch Manager.* | *a branch office*

department /dɪˈpɑːrtmənt/ [n C] a **department** of a large organization, such as a company, a school, or a hospital, is a part of it that is responsible for a particular kind of work: *Our department deals mainly with exports.*
Sales/Accounts/Planning etc Department (=in a company or large organization) *Melissa is in charge of the Marketing Department.*
Art/History/Science etc Department (=in a school or university)

4 part of an activity/job/period of time

part /pɑːrt/ [n C] *Organizing the party was easy – the hardest part was getting my parents to agree to it.*
+ of *Which part of your job do you enjoy most?* | *She spent the early part of her life in Barcelona.* | *Part of the research program involved interviewing teenagers in inner-city areas.*

bit /bɪt/ [n C] BRITISH SPOKEN a part of an activity, plan, or job: *Filling in the application form is the easy bit – it's the interview I find stressful.*
+ of *The last bit of the climb was really difficult because it started to snow.*

stage /steɪdʒ/ [n C] one of several parts of a long process, which happen one after another

+ **of** *Many women feel a little depressed during the early stages of pregnancy.*

+ **in** *Safety checks are carried out at every stage in the production process.*

at this stage *At this stage of the election campaign, it is impossible to say who will win.*

phase /feɪz/ [n C] a separate part in the development or growth of something

+ **in** *There are three phases in the life of a butterfly.*

initial/final phase (=the first or last part) *The initial phase of the project should take about three months.*

⚠ **Phase** is a more technical word than **stage**.

5 part of a situation/subject/someone's character

aspect /ˈæspekt/ [n C] one of the many parts of a situation or subject, which can each be considered separately: *The book describes the postwar period in all its aspects – social, political, and economic.*

+ **of** *Drug addiction can affect all aspects of a person's life.* | *There are aspects of the problem that we haven't discussed.*

side /saɪd/ [n C] one part of a situation or of someone's character – use this especially when you are comparing one part with another: *Weiskopf was a talented and successful man, but he did have a cruel side.* | *I'm in charge of production, and Martha takes care of the marketing side.*

+ **of** *Many people seem to forget the religious side of Christmas.* | *Try to see the funny side of the situation.*

6 of an amount/number

➡ see also **AMOUNT/NUMBER**

proportion /prəˈpɔːʳʃən/ [n C] a part of an amount or number – use this when you are comparing the part with the whole amount or number

+ **of** *What proportion of your income do you spend on food?*

high/large proportion *A high proportion of married women also have part-time jobs.*

small proportion *We get a small proportion of our funding from the government.*

fraction /ˈfrækʃən/ [n C] a small part of an amount or number, especially a very small part

+ **of** *Employees' salaries are only a fraction of the total cost of the project.*

a small fraction *a problem that affects only a small fraction of the total population*

percentage /pəʳˈsentɪdʒ/ [n C] a part of an amount or number that is expressed as part of a whole which is 100

+ **of** *What percentage of our students passed the exam?* | *a percentage of the profits that is less than 50%*

high/large percentage *A high percentage of the coffee they produce goes to the US.*

small percentage *Only a small percentage of the population has private medical insurance.*

PARTLY

➡ for words meaning the opposite, go to **COMPLETELY**

partly /ˈpɑːʳtli/ [adv] *The road was partly blocked by a fallen tree.* | *What he told us was only partly true.*

partly because *The accident happened partly because we were having an argument in the car.*

partially /ˈpɑːʳʃəli/ [adv] if something is **partially** done, it has not been completely done or finished: *The house was partially destroyed by the explosion.* | *The ice had partially melted and there was a pool of water on the table.*

partially successful *The advertising campaign was only partially successful.*

⚠ **Partially** is more formal than **partly**.

half /hɑːf‖hæf/ [adv] **half-eaten/half-dressed/half-finished etc** partly eaten, partly dressed etc: *I found him sitting on his bed, half-dressed.* | *a half-smoked cigarette in the ashtray* | *The houses were half-submerged by flood water.*

to some extent /tə ˈsʌm ɪkˌstent/ use this when you want to say that something is partly true but not completely true: *Doing well in examinations is to some extent a matter of luck.* | *To some extent it was our own fault that we lost the contract.*

PARTY

FESTIVALS AND SPECIAL DAYS
INVITE   **FOOD**
ENJOY   see also   **DRINK**
FREE TIME   **DRUNK**
MUSIC   **DANCE**

1 a party

party /ˈpɑːti/ [n C] a social event, especially in someone's house, when people talk, drink, eat, and dance: *Are you going to Susie's birthday party?* | *I really enjoyed your party last night.*

have a party *We're having a party next Saturday. Would you like to come?*

throw a party (=have a big party, with lots of food and drink etc) *Sheikh Mahmood would regularly throw lavish parties at the Sheraton Hotel.*

invite sb to a party *I've been invited to a party at Dave's tonight.*

dinner party (=a party at someone's house in the evening, when people have a meal)

fancy-dress party BRITISH **costume-party** AMERICAN (=a party where people wear strange, funny, or historical clothes)

plural **parties**

> ⚠ You can also use **party** before a noun, like an adjective: *party games* | *a party invitation*

celebration /ˌseləˈbreɪʃən/ [n C] a party or other enjoyable event that is organized because something good has happened or because it is a special day: *We had a big family celebration for my father's 60th birthday.* | *New Year celebrations in Scotland go on for three days.* | *celebrations to mark the 50th anniversary of the country's independence*

> ⚠ The plural form, **celebrations**, is used especially to talk about big public events that take place to celebrate important occasions, such as New Year. The singular form, **celebration**, is used especially to talk about a party to celebrate a personal or family event such as a birthday.

celebrate /ˈseləbreɪt/ [v I/T] to show that a happy event or occasion is important by doing something enjoyable, for example by having a party or going to a restaurant: *Congratulations on your new job – we must go out and celebrate.* | *We went to a club to celebrate the end of the school year.* | *My mother bought some champagne to celebrate my 21st birthday.*

celebrate by doing sth *We celebrated by going out for a drink.*

celebrate sth with sth *She celebrated her election victory with a party at the Hilton Hotel.*

2 people at a party

host /həʊst/ [n C] the person who invites people to a party and provides them with food and drink: *The host brought in some more wine.*

> ⚠ **Host**, **hostess**, and **guest** are all rather formal words, used for talking about formal parties.

hostess /ˈhəʊstəs/ [n C] a woman who invites people to a party and provides them with food and drink: *Pam was a wonderful hostess – everyone enjoyed her parties.*

guest /gest/ [n C] someone who goes to a party: *There were 100 guests at the garden party.*

PASS

➡ look here for ...
- be successful in an examination
- go past a person or place
- when time passes

1 to be successful in a test or examination

➡ see also **TEST, DRIVE, EDUCATION**

pass /pɑːs‖pæs/ [v I/T] to reach a high enough standard to succeed in an examination or test: *"I'm taking my driving test today." "Do you think you'll pass?"* | *You'll never pass the exam if you don't work!*

⚠ Don't say 'pass in an exam'. Say **pass an exam**.

qualify /ˈkwɒlɪ̥faɪ‖ˈkwɑː-/ [v I] to pass all the examinations that you need in order to become a doctor, lawyer, engineer etc: *After qualifying, she joined the NatWest Bank as a corporate advisor.*
+ as *I decided to return to college and qualify as a teacher.*
qualifying – qualified – have qualified

graduate /ˈgrædʒueɪt/ [v I] to pass all your final examinations at university or college, and get a degree
graduate from Oxford/Stanford etc *Mitch graduated from Stanford in 1993 with a degree in Law.*
graduate in history/French/medicine etc *She graduated in modern languages and now works as an interpreter.*

⚠ In American English, **graduate** also means to successfully complete your high school education: *Jerry will be graduating from high school this year.*

scrape through /ˌskreɪp ˈθruː/ [phrasal verb I/T] INFORMAL to only just pass an examination, by getting only a few marks more than are necessary: *I might scrape through if I'm lucky.* | *Daniel only just scraped through the entrance exam.*

2 to go past a place or person
➡ see also **DRIVE, WALK, RUN**

past /pɑːst‖pæst/ [adv/preposition]
walk/drive/rush/run past *An ambulance rushed past on its way to the accident.* | *Will you be going past the library on your way home?* | *The children were frightened of walking past the old ruined house.*

by /baɪ/ [adv] going past, especially not very quickly
go/pass/walk/sail by *I lay on the grass and watched the clouds floating by.*

pass /pɑːs‖pæs/ [v I/T] to go past a place or person: *I'll get you some aspirin – I pass the drugstore on the way to work.* | *They kept quiet until the soldiers had passed.* | *A big Cadillac passed us as we walked up the hill.*
passing [adj only before noun] going past: *noise and fumes from the passing traffic*

overtake /ˌəʊvəˈteɪk/ [v I/T] ESPECIALLY BRITISH to pass a moving vehicle in order to go in front of it: *Before you start to overtake, make sure the road ahead is clear.* | *Hill overtook Schumacher just before the last bend.*
overtaking – overtook – have overtaken

3 when time passes

go by/pass /ˌgəʊ ˈbaɪ, pɑːs‖pæs/ [v I] *Several years passed before she learned the truth.* | *The days passed slowly.* | *As you get older, time seems to go by more quickly.*

go quickly /ˌgəʊ ˈkwɪkli/ if time **goes quickly**, it seems to pass quickly: *The last few days of the holiday went far too quickly.*

○**time flies** /ˌtaɪm ˈflaɪz/ SPOKEN say this when you are surprised at how quickly the time has passed: *Is Martin eight already? How time flies!* | *Time flies when you're having fun!*

go slowly /ˌgəʊ ˈsləʊli/ if time **goes slowly**, it seems to pass slowly: *Time always goes slowly when you're bored.*

PAST

➡ if you want to know how to form the past, go to the **ESSENTIAL GRAMMAR**, section 4

1 the past

the past /ðə ˈpɑːst‖-ˈpæst/ [n singular] the time that existed before the present time: *My grandfather enjoys talking about the past.* | *The Queen's horse-drawn carriage is a nostalgic reminder of the past.*
in the past (=during the time before now) *I decided to ask Anna, as she had always been very helpful in the past.* | *In the past, US foreign policy was mainly based on its opposition to communism.*

past /pɑːst‖pæst/ [adj only before noun] **past** events, experiences etc happened before now: *He's learned a lot from past experiences.* | *Judging by her past performance, I'd say Rowena will do very well.*
the past 10 years/2 weeks etc (=the 10 years, 2 weeks etc before now) *The past few months had been very difficult for Mary.* | *For the past two weeks, I have been doing my boss's job while she's away on business.* | *The enormous changes of the past 30 years.*

history /ˈhɪstəri/ [n singular] all the things that have happened in the past, especially to a country, a town, or an organization
the history of sth *a book about the history of the United Nations* | *India has been invaded several times in its history.*

sb's past /(sb's) ˈpɑːst‖-ˈpæst/ all the things that have happened to someone in the past: *The newspapers have been investigating the President's past, hoping to find some scandal.*

2 when something happened in the past, but does not happen now

used to /ˈjuːst tuː/ [modal verb] if you **used to** do something, you did it for a period of time in the past, or you did it regularly in the past, but you do not do it now: *"Do you smoke?" "No, but I used to."*
used to do sth *We used to live in Glasgow when I was young.*
there used to be *There used to be a market in the town.*
didn't used to *I was surprised to see her driving – she didn't used to.*

once/at one time /wʌns, ət ˌwʌn ˈtaɪm/ [adv] during a period of time in the past, but not now – use this when it is not important to say exactly when this period was: *a sports car once owned by Paul McCartney* | *He once worked for the FBI.* | *It is a big city now, but at one time the population was only 50,000.*

then/at that time /ðen, ət ðæt ˈtaɪm/ [adv] during a particular period of time in the past – use this when you are comparing that period with the present: *I was a student in the 1950s, and things were very different then.* | *We were married before the war, and at that time most married women stayed at home.*

in the past /ɪn ðə ˈpɑːst‖-ˈpæst/ use this to talk about a situation that existed in history but does not exist now: *In the past, most children didn't go to school at all.* | *Women were not allowed to own property in the past.*

in those days /ɪn ˈðəʊz deɪz/ use this to talk about a time long ago in your life, or in your parents' or grandparents' lives, when things were different: *He was paid £5 a week, which was a lot of money in those days.* | *In those days there was no bridge over the river, and we crossed it by boat.*

formerly /ˈfɔːrməˈli/ [adv] WRITTEN in the past, before the present situation existed: *The school was formerly a hospital.* | *Peru was formerly ruled by the Spanish.*

3 on one occasion in the past

once /wʌns/ [adv] *She once called me a liar – I've never forgiven her.* | *Once, when I was a little boy, I found a gold watch.*

one time /ˈwʌn ˌtaɪm/ INFORMAL on one occasion in the past: *One time we went out fishing on the lake at night.*

one day/one morning/one afternoon /wʌn ˈdeɪ, wʌn ˈmɔːrnɪŋ, wʌn ˌɑːftərˈnuːn‖-æf-/ on a day, morning, or afternoon in the past – use this when you are telling a story and it is not important to say exactly which day you mean: *One day he went away and never came back.* | *I was having my breakfast one morning when the telephone rang.*

PATTERN

a regular arrangement of shapes, colours, or lines

DESIGN ART
CLOTHES PAINT
see also
MATERIAL 2 DRAW
DECORATE COLOUR/COLOR

pattern /ˈpætən||ˈpætərn/ [n C] a regular arrangement of shapes, colours, or lines on a surface, especially one that is used to decorate paper, cloth, plates etc: *Do you have any wallpaper with the same pattern but a different colour?*
+ of *patterns of sunlight and shadow on the ground*

design /dɪˈzaɪn/ [n C] a pattern which is used to decorate a surface such as cloth or paper: *This design is very common on Turkish carpets.* | *You can get curtains and bedcovers for children, decorated with 'Lion King' designs.*

markings /ˈmɑːrkɪŋz/ [n plural] the natural patterns on the skin, fur, or feathers of animals or birds: *a bird that you can recognize by its unusual red and yellow markings*

patterned /ˈpætənd||ˈpætərnd/ [adj] **patterned** clothes, materials etc have patterns on them: *Patterned leggings were very fashionable last year.* | *a horrible green patterned carpet*

PAY

MONEY
EARN COST
BUY FREE
see also
SPEND CHEAP
SHOP OWE
EXPENSIVE

1 to pay for something

pay /peɪ/ [v I/T] to give money in exchange for goods or services: *Several fans tried to get in without paying.* | *Please pay at the desk.*
+ for *Have you paid for the tickets?*
pay £20/$40 etc for sth *She paid $5,000 for three nights in a classy hotel.*
pay a bill/the rent *He hardly earns enough to pay the rent.* | *I thought you already paid the phone bill.*
paying – paid – have paid

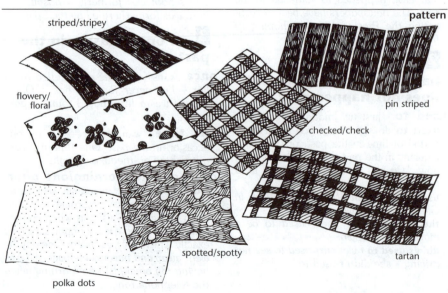

pattern

striped/stripey

flowery/floral

pin striped

checked/check

spotted/spotty

tartan

polka dots

payment /'peɪmənt/ [n C] an amount of money that you pay for something, especially when it is only one part of the total amount you have to pay: *Your first payment is due on 16th July.* | *mortgage payments*

make a payment *He makes monthly payments into his ex-wife's bank account.*

on credit /ɒn 'kredɪt/ **buy/get sth on credit** to buy something and pay for it later, usually by small regular payments: *In 1991, 56% of new cars were bought on credit.*

2 to pay for someone else's food, drink, ticket etc

pay /peɪ/ [v I] to pay for someone else, for example for their meal, drink, or ticket: *When they go out for a meal, his girlfriend always expects him to pay.*

+ for *Let's go to the zoo. I'll pay for you and the children.* | *Did your parents pay for your driving lessons?*

paying – paid – have paid

treat /triːt/ [v T] to buy something such as a meal or theatre ticket for someone, because you like them or you want to celebrate: *As it's your birthday, I thought I'd treat you.*

treat sb to sth *We treated Sally to lunch at the Savoy.*

3 to be able to pay for something

can afford /kən ə'fɔːrd/ if you **can afford** something, you have enough money to pay for it: *I'd love to visit Australia, but I just can't afford it.*

can afford to do sth *How can you afford to eat in restaurants all the time?*

4 to pay someone to do something

pay /peɪ/ [v T] to pay someone for work

pay sb for (doing) sth *They still haven't paid her for the work she did last year.* | *Did she pay you for taking care of her kids?*

be/get paid *We get paid at the end of every month.*

pay sb £100/$200 etc *Ziedler was ready to pay her $2000 a week.* | *How much do they pay you?*

well/highly paid (=paid a lot) *He has a very well-paid job in finance.* | *a highly paid executive*

badly paid (=not paid much) *Most badly paid jobs are done by women.*

paying – paid – have paid

bribe /braɪb/ [v T] money that someone gives to a person in an official position, in order to persuade them to do something that they should not do: *I had to bribe the customs official.*

bribe sb to do sth *He bribed a guard to smuggle a note out of the prison.*

bribe [n C] money that you give to someone to bribe them: *The judge was accused of accepting bribes.*

bribery [n U] when people are being bribed

bribery and corruption (=bribery and dishonest behaviour) *There was widespread bribery and corruption in the police department.*

5 to provide money to help someone do something

subsidize (also **subsidise** BRITISH) /'sʌbsɪdaɪz/ [v T] if a government or other organization **subsidizes** something, it pays part of the cost of it: *Many companies subsidize meals for their workers.* | *a government-subsidized health service* | *The city council subsidizes the local orchestra.*

sponsor /'spɒnsər‖'spɑːn-/ [v T] if a company **sponsors** something such as a sports event, a theatre, or an art show, it provides some of the money that is needed, often as a form of advertising: *The new league will be sponsored by Pepsi Cola.* | *The bank is sponsoring an art exhibition.*

6 to give money back to someone

pay back /ˌpeɪ 'bæk/ [phrasal verb T] to give someone back money that you have borrowed from them

pay sb back *I'll pay you back tomorrow.*

pay back sth/pay sth back *How are you going to pay back all that money?*

repay /rɪ'peɪ/ [v T] to pay a large amount of money that you owe, especially to a bank: *The loan has to be repaid within two years.*

repaying – repaid – have repaid

P

pay off /ˌpeɪ ˈɒf‖-ˈɔːf/ [phrasal verb T] to finish paying back an amount of money that you have borrowed

pay off a debt/loan/mortgage *Twenty years later they still hadn't paid off their mortgage.*

pay a debt/loan/mortgage off *They hope to pay all their debts off by 2002.*

give sb their money back/give sb a refund /ˌgɪv (sb) ðeəʳ ˈmʌni ˌbæk, ˌgɪv (sb) ə ˈriːfʌnd/ to give back to someone the money that they paid for something, especially because they are not satisfied with what they bought: *We'll give you a refund if you're not entirely satisfied. | It's the wrong size. Do you think they'll give me my money back?*

refund [n C] the money you get when someone gives you a refund: *You can't have a refund unless you bring us the receipt.*

7 a piece of paper that shows how much you must pay

bill /bɪl/ [n C] a piece of paper that tells you how much you must pay for services you have received or for work that has been done for you: *We've just had a huge telephone bill.*

pay a bill *They left the hotel without paying the bill.*

a bill for £50/$100 etc *The garage sent me a bill for $400.*

⚠ In British English, you can also use **bill** when you are talking about paying in a restaurant: *Ask the waiter for the bill.*

check /tʃek/ [n C] AMERICAN a piece of paper that tells you how much you must pay in a restaurant: *A waiter came over and handed me the check.*

pay the check *Let me pay the check.*

invoice /ˈɪnvɔɪs/ [n C] a piece of paper that a company sends you to tell you how much money you owe them for goods or for work they have done: *The repairs are all finished. We'll send you an invoice by the end of the month.*

When you see **EC**, go to the **ESSENTIAL COMMUNICATION** section.

8 paid/not paid for doing a job, activity, or sport

professional /prəˈfeʃənəl/ [adj only before noun] a **professional** sports player, musician, actor etc gets paid for playing, acting etc, and they do it as their job: *Professional basketball players can earn millions of dollars.*

professional [n C] someone who gets paid for doing a job, sport, or activity that most people do for enjoyment: *I learned to play golf by watching the professionals on TV.*

amateur /ˈæmətəʳ, -tʃuəʳ, -tʃəʳ, ˌæməˈtɜːʳ/ [adj only before noun] an **amateur** sports player, musician, actor etc does not get paid for playing, acting etc, but they do it for enjoyment: *A group of amateur actors performed 'Romeo and Juliet'. | an amateur photographer*

amateur [n C] someone who does an activity or sport just for enjoyment, and does not get paid for doing it: *The orchestra is made up entirely of amateurs.*

voluntary /ˈvɒləntəri‖ˈvɑːlanteri/ [adj usually before noun] **voluntary** work is done by people who do it because they want to do it and they believe it is useful, and who do not expect to be paid for their work: *When she retired, she did a lot of voluntary work for the Red Cross.*

PEACE

when there is no war

➡ opposite **WAR**

1 when there is no war

peace /piːs/ [n U] when there is no war: *There has been peace in the region for six years now. | a dangerous situation that threatens world peace*

peace talks/negotiations (=when enemies meet and talk, to try and achieve peace) *The warring groups will meet for peace talks in Sarajevo.*

the peace process (=a continuing attempt, over a long period, to achieve peace between enemies)

⚠ Don't say 'a peace'. **Peace** is uncountable.

peacetime /'piːstaɪm/ [n U] a period when a country is not fighting a war – use this when comparing this period with a time when there is war: *A country's army may be quite small during peacetime.* | *In peacetime the Hercules aircraft has been used for distributing food to famine areas.*

peaceful /'piːsfəl/ [adj] use this about changes or events that happen without war or fighting: *a peaceful solution to the troubles in former Yugoslavia* | *a peaceful transfer of power from the military government to the new democracy*

peacefully [adv] *Can they achieve their independence peacefully?*

2 when two countries agree to stop fighting

make peace /ˌmeɪk 'piːs/ if two countries **make peace**, they stop fighting and agree to end the war: *France and Spain made peace in 1659 after a war lasting 25 years.*
+ **with** *The two armies made peace with each other in 1918.*

ceasefire /'siːsfaɪəʳ/ [n C] an agreement to stop fighting for a limited period, especially in order to talk about making peace: *The ceasefire won't last unless both sides are prepared to compromise.*
ceasefire agreement *Both leaders signed the ceasefire agreement.*

peace treaty /'piːs ˌtriːti/ [n C] a written agreement between enemies saying that they agree to end the war: *Both countries agreed to work towards a peace treaty.* | *The peace treaty was finally signed in 1919.*
plural **peace treaties**

3 someone who is against war

pacifist /'pæsɪfɪst/ [n C] someone who believes that all war and violence is wrong: *Bergson was imprisoned as a pacifist during World War I.*

anti-war /ˌænti 'wɔːʳ◄/ [adj only before noun] strongly against war, especially a war that your country is fighting at the present time
anti-war protest/demonstration/campaigner *During the Gulf War, there were several big anti-war demonstrations.* | *Anti-war feeling was very strong in the US during the Vietnam conflict.*

PERFECT

➡ see also **BEST, SUITABLE/UNSUITABLE, GOOD**

1 very good, with nothing wrong

perfect /'pɜːʳfɪkt/ [adj] someone or something that is **perfect** is good in every way and could not be any better: *We had a wonderful vacation – the weather was perfect.* | *It's an old car, but it's in perfect condition.*
absolutely perfect *The meal was absolutely perfect.*
the perfect husband/secretary/couple etc *Beth and Martin always seemed to be the perfect couple.*
perfectly [adv] *It's a beautiful dress, and it fits perfectly.*

flawless/faultless /'flɔːləs, 'fɔːltləs/ [adj] FORMAL completely perfect, with no mistakes or faults at all: *Hiroshi's English was flawless.* | *She gave a faultless performance as the Sleeping Beauty.*

model /'mɒdl‖'mɑːdl/ [adj only before noun] **a model husband/wife/student etc** someone who has all the qualities that a husband, wife, student etc should have: *Karen was a model student; hardworking, intelligent, and enthusiastic.*

2 the best and most suitable person or thing

ideal /aɪ'dɪəl◄/ [adj] an **ideal** person or thing is very suitable and is exactly what you want: *The house was not ideal – it was too small – but it was in a nice part of town.*
+ **for** *This place is ideal for families with young children.*
my ideal man/woman/job/house etc (=one that has all the qualities you like best) *My ideal man would be someone like Mel Gibson.*

perfect /ˈpɜːʳfɪkt/ [*adj*] completely suitable for a person or situation: *A dry white wine is perfect with any fish dish.*

+ for *This dress will be perfect for the summer party.* | *perfect weather for a picnic*

the perfect place/time/job etc *That sounds like the perfect job for you.*

just right /ˌdʒʌst ˈraɪt/ SPOKEN suitable in every way: *"Do the curtains look OK?" "Yes, they're just right."*

+ for *I'm glad they're getting married – they're just right for each other.*

PERSON/PEOPLE

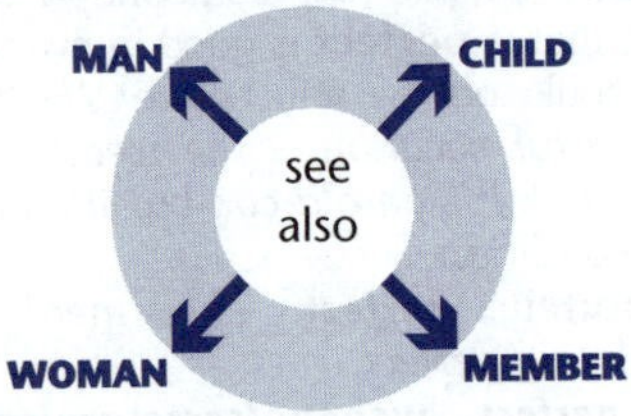
MAN
CHILD
see also
WOMAN
MEMBER

1 a person

person /ˈpɜːʳsən/ [*n C*] *I think she's a really nice person.* | *He's the only person I know who can speak Chinese.* | *There were over 200 people at the meeting.* | *I like the people I work with.*

plural **people**

someone/somebody /ˈsʌmwʌn, ˈsʌmbɒdi, -bədi‖-ˈbɑːdi, -bədi/ [*pronoun*] a person – use this when you do not know who the person is, or when it is not important to say who it is: *Someone phoned you, but I didn't get their name.* | *What would you do if somebody tried to rob you in the street?*

someone else/somebody else (=another person) *Can't you get someone else to clean the kitchen?*

human being/human /ˌhjuːmən ˈbiːɪŋ, ˈhjuːmən/ [*n C*] a person – use this when you are comparing people with animals or machines: *Chimpanzees are very closely related to human beings.* | *Computers have replaced humans in many factories.*

2 people in general

people /ˈpiːpəl/ [*n plural*] people in general: *People are getting very worried about rising crime.* | *I don't want people to feel sorry for me.*

most people *Most people hate writing essays, but my brother enjoys it!*

> ⚠ Don't say 'peoples'. **People** is a plural noun.

everyone/everybody /ˈevriwʌn, ˈevriˌbɒdi‖-ˌbɑːdi/ [*pronoun*] ESPECIALLY SPOKEN all people – use this to make general statements about how people behave, what people like etc: *Don't you like ice-cream? I thought everyone liked it!* | *Everybody has the right to a good education.* | *Everyone knows that smoking is bad for you.*

> ⚠ Use a singular verb with **everyone** and **everybody**.

the human race /ðə ˌhjuːmən ˈreɪs/ all the people in the world, considered as one group: *Pollution is threatening the future of the human race.* | *the origins of the human race*

society /səˈsaɪəti/ [*n U*] people in general – use this to talk about people as an organized group with a system of laws and accepted behaviour: *We want our students to become useful and responsible members of society.* | *the position of women in Islamic society* | *The judge described Smith as 'a danger to society'.*

social /ˈsəʊʃəl/ [*adj only before noun*] use this about conditions, problems, and changes that affect all the people in society: *Rising unemployment led to even more social problems.* | *social changes that have brought women greater freedom*

the public /ðə ˈpʌblɪk/ [*n singular*] ordinary people who do not belong to the government, the police etc, and do not have any special rights: *The castle is open to the public during the summer.* | *The public ought to know how the money from taxes is being spent.*

members of the public *Some of these politicians never meet ordinary members of the public.*

public [*adj only before noun*] use this about the actions or feelings of ordinary people: *Public attitudes towards homosexuality are gradually changing.* | *The* *plan cannot succeed without public support.*

> ⚠ In British English, you can use **the public** with a singular or plural verb: *The public is always/are always interested in stories about the Royal Family.* In American English, always use a singular verb: *The public isn't interested in foreign affairs.*

3 all the people in a group, town, or country

community /kə'mjuːnɨti/ [n C] a group of people who live in the same area, especially when they all belong to the same religious group or race: *The local community was shocked by the murder.*
the Jewish/Muslim/Greek etc community *New York's Jewish community*

plural **communities**

⟲**everyone/everybody** /'evriwʌn, 'evrɨˌbɒdi‖-ˌbɑːdi/ [pronoun] ESPECIALLY SPOKEN all the people in a group or in a place: *There's plenty of food for everybody.* | *It's the sort of place where everyone knows everyone else.*

> ⚠ Use a singular verb with **everyone** and **everybody**.

population /ˌpɒpjʊ'leɪʃən‖ˌpɑː-/ [n singular] all the people who live in a town or country – use this when saying how many people live there, or giving some facts about them
the population of Tokyo/Greece etc *In 1966 the population of Lima was about two million.*
a population of five million/twenty million etc *New Jersey has a population of around 7.6 million.*
the black/Catholic/male population (=all the black people, Catholic people etc in a place) *30% of the male population suffers from heart disease.*

the people /ðə 'piːpəl/ [n plural] all the people who live in a particular place
the people of Paris/China etc *the awful sufferings of the people of Sarajevo*
the British/Korean/Nigerian etc people *Reagan's views were shared by a majority of the American people.*

> When you see **EC**, go to the **ESSENTIAL COMMUNICATION** section.

4 about people, not animals or machines

human /'hjuːmən/ [adj usually before noun] use this about people's abilities, character, or behaviour, when you are comparing people with animals or machines: *the effects of pollution on the human and animal population* | *Bacteria cannot be seen with the human eye.*

5 for each person

per person /pəʳ 'pɜːʳsən/ **$500/two pieces etc per person** (=$500, two pieces etc for each person) *There were only two pieces of bread per person.* | *The annual income per person is less than $250.*

a head /ə 'hed/ use this to say how much something costs for each person
$10/£5 etc a head *We paid £5 a head for our Christmas dinner.*

6 no people

no-one/no one/nobody /'nəʊ wʌn, 'nəʊbədi/ [pronoun] no person or people: *No-one was home, so I left a note.* | *He explained what had happened but nobody believed him.*

PERSUADE

➡ see also **ADVERTISING**

1 to persuade someone to do something

persuade /pəʳ'sweɪd/ [v T] to make someone agree to do something, by giving them reasons why they should do it: *Neil didn't want to come at first, but we persuaded him.*
persuade sb to do sth *I persuaded Tom to lend me his car.*

get sb to do sth /ˌget (sb) tə 'duː (sth)/ INFORMAL to make someone do what you want them to do, by persuading them over a long time: *I finally got them to agree, by offering them more money.* | *My girlfriend's always trying to get me to stop smoking.*

influence /ˈɪnfluəns/ [v T] to affect what someone decides to do, but without directly persuading them: *It's your choice; don't let anyone else influence you.* | *I hope you weren't influenced by anything that your brother said.*

⚠ Don't say 'TV influences on children'. Say **TV influences children**.

encourage /ɪnˈkʌrɪdʒ‖ɪnˈkɜːr-/ [v T] to try to persuade someone to do something, because you think it will be good for them
encourage sb to do sth *Patricia encouraged me to apply for the job.* | *We want to encourage more children to use the library.*

talk sb into sth /ˌtɔːk (sb) ˈɪntuː (sth)/ [phrasal verb T] INFORMAL to persuade someone to do something that they do not want to do
talk sb into doing sth *I managed to talk them into giving me more money.*
talk sb into it *I didn't really want to go to the party, but Dave talked me into it.*

2 to persuade someone not to do something

persuade sb not to do sth /pəˈrsweɪd (sb) nɒt tə ˈduː (sth)/ to make someone decide not to do something, by giving them reasons why they should not do it: *Catherine persuaded him not to resign.*

talk sb out of sth /ˌtɔːk (sb) ˈaʊt ɒv (sth)‖-ɑːv/ [phrasal verb T] INFORMAL to persuade someone not to do something that they were planning to do
talk sb out of doing sth *Everyone tried to talk me out of buying the car.*
talk sb out of it *I nearly cancelled the wedding, but my best friend talked me out of it.*

discourage /dɪsˈkʌrɪdʒ‖-ˈkɜːr-/ [v T] to stop someone wanting to do something, by making them think that it will be difficult or unpleasant: *We need to discourage the use of cars.*
discourage sb from doing sth *Girls are sometimes discouraged from studying subjects like engineering and physics.*

deterrent /dɪˈterənt‖-ˈtɜːr-/ [n C] something that is intended to stop people from wanting to do something: *Prison is supposed to be a deterrent.*

+ to *Window locks are a cheap and effective deterrent to burglars.*

3 to persuade someone that something is true or right

convince /kənˈvɪns/ [v T] to make someone believe that something is true, especially when they doubted it before: *You still don't believe me, do you? What do I have to do to convince you?*
convince sb that *It took him a long time to convince the police that he was telling the truth.*

persuade /pəˈrsweɪd/ [v T] to make someone believe that something is true or right, by telling them things that seem to prove it
persuade sb that *She won't lend me the car unless I can persuade her that I'm a safe driver.*

4 something that persuades you

persuasion /pəˈrsweɪʒən/ [n U] things that you say in order to persuade someone to do something: *It took a lot of persuasion to get Dad to agree to the idea.* | *They got what they wanted with a mixture of persuasion and threats.*

convincing /kənˈvɪnsɪŋ/ [adj] a **convincing** reason, explanation, or excuse makes you believe that something is true or right: *That's not a very convincing excuse for being late!* | *There is convincing evidence that smoking causes heart disease.*

persuasive /pəˈrsweɪsɪv/ [adj] good at persuading people: *Ben can be very persuasive if he wants something.* | *The salesman had a smooth persuasive manner.*

PICTURE

COLOUR/COLOR

ART   PATTERN

see
also

PAINT   DESIGN

DRAW   DECORATE

1 a picture that you paint or draw

picture /'pɪktʃəʳ/ [n C] a painting or drawing: *Van Gogh's 'Sunflowers' is one of the most famous pictures in the world.*
+ of *There was a picture of a windmill on the bedroom wall.*
sb's picture (=a painting or drawing of someone) *The house belonged to the Duke of Wellington, and his picture hangs in the hall.*
draw/paint a picture *She drew some beautiful pictures of the church.*
do a picture INFORMAL (=draw or paint a picture) *Jamie loves doing pictures of cats.*

painting /'peɪntɪŋ/ [n C] a picture that someone has painted: *an exhibition of Cezanne's paintings*
+ of *a painting of the Grand Canal in Venice by Canaletto*
do a painting *She enjoys doing paintings of wildflowers.*

drawing /'drɔːɪŋ/ [n C] a picture that someone has drawn using a pen or pencil: *Sylvia's teacher was very impressed by her drawings.*
+ of *On the wall was a drawing of a woman's head.*
do a drawing *Monet did a series of drawings of waterlilies.*

sketch /sketʃ/ [n C] a picture consisting of a few lines drawn quickly with a pen or pencil
+ of *I thought your sketches of the garden were very attractive.*
do a sketch *The architect did a sketch of how the building will look when it's finished.*
quick/rough sketch (=a sketch done very quickly) *Gabriella did a quick sketch of her baby daughter.*
plural **sketches**

illustration /ˌɪləˈstreɪʃən/ [n C] a picture in a book, which shows people or events that have been mentioned in the book: *Who did the illustrations for the Winnie-the-Pooh books? | The new encyclopedia is full of colour illustrations and photographs.*

cartoon /kɑːʳˈtuːn/ [n C] a funny drawing in a newspaper or magazine, often with a joke written under it: *a cartoon showing the President's wife dressed as a witch in a black cloak*

poster /'pəʊstəʳ/ [n C] a very large picture or photograph printed on paper, which you put on a wall for decoration
+ of *Anna's bedroom wall was covered in posters of James Dean and Marilyn Monroe.*

portrait /'pɔːʳtrɪt/ [n C] a painting, drawing, or photograph of a person
+ of *A portrait of the Queen hung on the wall.*
paint a portrait *He has painted the portraits of a lot of famous people.*

landscape /'lændskeɪp/ [n C] a painting showing an area of countryside

2 a photograph

photograph /'fəʊtəɡrɑːf‖-ɡræf/ [n C] a picture made using a camera: *an exhibition of war photographs*
+ of *a book full of photographs of Kenya*
take a photograph *Visitors are not allowed to take photographs inside the museum.*
sb's photograph (=a photograph of someone) *The police have her photograph and are hoping to find her soon.*
wedding/passport/school photograph *The guests stood still and posed for the wedding photographs.*
photograph album (=a book that you put photographs in)

⚠ **Photograph** is more formal than **photo** or **picture**.

photo/picture /'fəʊtəʊ, 'pɪktʃəʳ/ [n C] a photograph – use this especially to talk about photographs of you, your friends or family, or places you have visited: *Who's that woman in the picture? She looks familiar.*
+ of *That's an awful photo of me – it makes me look really stupid!*
take a photo/picture *We always take lots of photos of the children.*
sb's photo/picture (=a photo of someone) *Let me take your picture by the swimming pool. | We saw her photo in the local paper.*
wedding/passport/school photo *I must remember to get some passport photos.*

⚠ You can also use **photo** before a noun, like an adjective: *a photo album* | *a silver photo frame*

snap ESPECIALLY BRITISH **snapshot** ESPECIALLY AMERICAN /snæp, 'snæpʃɒt‖-ʃɑːt/ [n C] INFORMAL a photograph which you take yourself, for example of your family or on holiday, not one that is taken by a professional photographer: *Patrick was showing his holiday snaps to everyone in the office.*
take a snap/snapshot *Did you take any snaps in Greece?*
+ of *She showed me a snapshot of her three children.*

photography /fə'tɒgrəfi‖-'tɑː-/ [n U] the art or profession of taking photographs: *Chris is studying photography at night school.*

3 what you see in a mirror, on a screen, or on water

image /'ɪmɪdʒ/ [n C] a picture on the screen of a television, cinema, or computer: *The images on a computer screen are made up of thousands of tiny dots.* | *the flickering images of an old silent movie*

reflection /rɪ'flekʃən/ [n C] what you see when you look in a mirror or at the surface of water: *Anna stood looking at her reflection in the mirror.* | *the reflection of the moon on the surface of the lake*

4 the front or back of a picture

foreground /'fɔːˈgraʊnd/ [n C usually singular] the nearest part of a scene in a picture or photograph
in the foreground *There was a group of people sunbathing in the foreground of th photo.*

background /'bækgraʊnd/ [n C usually singular] the area behind something or someone in a picture or photograph
in the background *It was a photo of everyone in my class, with the school building in the background.*

When you see **EC**, go to the **ESSENTIAL COMMUNICATION** section.

PIECE

➡ see also **PART, CUT**

1 part of something that has been separated from the rest

piece /piːs/ [n C] an amount of something that has been broken, cut, or separated from something larger: *Tim cut the cake into eight pieces.* | *a pack of chicken pieces*
+ of *There were pieces of broken glass all over the road.* | *a simple boat made from a few pieces of wood*
in pieces (=broken into many pieces) *The vase lay in pieces on the floor.*

bit /bɪt/ [n C] ESPECIALLY BRITISH a small piece of something: *"Do you want some of this Christmas pudding?" "Yes, I'll try a bit."*
+ of *Use a bit of soft cloth to apply the lotion.*
little/small/tiny bits *There were little bits of food all over the carpet.*

scrap /skræp/ [n C] a small piece of paper, material, or food that is left after you have used the main part
+ of *I wrote down her address on a scrap of paper.* | *We made some pretty bags out of scraps of curtain material.*

slice /slaɪs/ [n C] a thin flat piece of food that you cut from a larger piece
+ of *Have a slice of bread and butter.*
cut sth into slices *Cut the pork into thin slices and fry it for five minutes.*

2 a piece that has a regular shape

block /blɒk‖blɑːk/ [n C] a large solid piece of wood, stone, or ice that has straight sides: *a building made out of concrete blocks*
+ of *The fish were lying on huge blocks of ice to keep them cold.*

cube /kjuːb/ [n C] a solid object with six equal square sides: *Cut the cheese into small cubes.*
ice/sugar cube *Charlie kept putting ice cubes down my back.*
+ of *a cube of sugar*

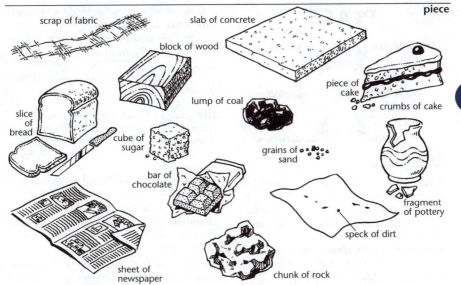

scrap of fabric | slab of concrete | block of wood | piece of cake | crumbs of cake | slice of bread | lump of coal | cube of sugar | grains of sand | bar of chocolate | fragment of pottery | speck of dirt | sheet of newspaper | chunk of rock

P

slab /slæb/ [n C] a heavy piece of stone or rock, which is long and wide but not very thick

stone/concrete/marble slab *The floor was made out of stone slabs.*

+ of *His grave is covered by a huge slab of marble.*

sheet /ʃiːt/ [n C] **sheet of glass/paper/ steel/metal** a flat thin piece of glass, paper etc: *She took a sheet of paper and began to write.* | *The roof is made of sheets of corrugated iron.*

bar /bɑːʳ/ [n C] a piece of metal, soap, or chocolate that has a long or square shape with straight sides: *The gold bars were transported in a security vehicle.*

+ of *a bar of chocolate*

3 a piece that does not have a regular shape

chunk /tʃʌŋk/ [n C] a piece of something solid that does not have a regular shape: *Cut the potatoes into chunks and boil them for 15 minutes.*

+ of *A large chunk of plaster had fallen from the ceiling.* | *The lions were eating a huge chunk of red meat.*

lump /lʌmp/ [n C] a small piece of something solid that does not have a regular shape

+ of *He threw some more lumps of coal onto the fire.* | *I was almost hit by a lump of rock that fell from the cliff.*

> ⚠ Don't use **lump** to talk about pieces of food, unless you want to say that something was unpleasant: *The sauce was horrible; it was full of lumps.*

4 a very small piece

grain /ɡreɪn/ [n C] a single small piece of sand, salt, or rice

+ of *I could feel grains of sand between my toes.*

speck /spek/ [n C] **a speck of dust/dirt** a piece of dust or dirt that is so small you can hardly see it: *The apartment was very clean – not a speck of dust anywhere.*

crumbs /krʌmz/ [n plural] very small pieces of food such as bread or cake: *The tablecloth was covered in crumbs.* | *brushing crumbs off her skirt*

fragment /ˈfræɡmənt/ [n C] ESPECIALLY WRITTEN a very small piece that has been broken or torn from something bigger

+ of *A fragment of cloth, caught on a nail, showed that someone had been that way.* | *The doctor removed some fragments of bone from the wound.*

PLACE

LAND AND SEA   COUNTRY

AREA   see also   UGLY

TOWN   BEAUTIFUL 6

1 a place

place /pleɪs/ [n C] *Have you put your passport in a safe place? | This is the place where the accident happened. | the coldest place on earth | She lives in a place called Tientsin.*
a place to live/eat/park etc *I was looking for a place to park the car.*
+ for *a great place for a party*
the right/wrong place *I thought I'd gone to the wrong place – I didn't recognize anyone there.*

⚠ In spoken English, you often just use **where**, **somewhere**, or **anywhere** instead of saying 'the place', 'a place' etc: *I'll show you where I was born. | I need somewhere to put my books. | I couldn't find anywhere to park the car.*

position /pəˈzɪʃən/ [n C] the exact place where something or someone is, especially in relation to other things or people: *Jessica moved to a position where she could see him better. | We need to know the enemy's positions before we can plan our attack. | Make sure the decimal point is in the right position.*
+ of *From the position of the sun, I guessed that it was about two o'clock.*

spot /spɒt‖spɑːt/ [n C] INFORMAL a place where something happened, or a pleasant place where people go to relax: *People had left flowers at the spot where the police officer was killed. | We camped in a pleasant, shady spot beside the river.*
+ for *a favourite spot for picnics*
beauty spot (=a place that is famous for being beautiful) *We spent the afternoon at a local beauty spot.*

location /ləʊˈkeɪʃən/ [n C] FORMAL the place where an office, shop, hotel, or house is built: *a hotel in an extremely attractive location*
+ for *This is the ideal location for the company's new head office.*

⚠ **Location** is used especially in advertisements or in business English.

site /saɪt/ [n C] an area of ground where something is going to be built, or where something important or interesting happened or existed in the past: *an archaeological site*
+ of *the site of the Battle of Waterloo | A home for the elderly will be built on the site of the old hospital.*
building site BRITISH **construction site** AMERICAN (=place where a new building is being built)

point /pɔɪnt/ [n C] an exact place or position: *At this point the river is half a mile wide. | We reached a point where the road divided. | the distance between two points on the map*

surroundings /səˈraʊndɪŋz/ [n plural] ESPECIALLY WRITTEN everything in the general area that a place or person is in, such as the buildings or the countryside – use this to say whether a place is pleasant, unpleasant etc: *The hotel is in beautiful surroundings on the edge of a lake. | We had the chance to watch great football in comfortable surroundings. | Sara felt nervous in the unfamiliar surroundings of her new school.*

2 to be in a place

be /bi; strong biː/ [v I] *Where are my keys?*
+ in/on/near/there etc *Egypt is in North Africa. | There's a bank on the corner.*
being – was – have been

stand /stænd/ [v I] use this about buildings, furniture, trees, or tall objects: *There is a parking lot now where the old school once stood.*
+ in/near/on there etc *The house stood next to a church. | A single tall candle was standing in the middle of the table.*
standing – stood – have stood

⚠ Use **stand** especially when you are writing descriptions and stories.

lie /laɪ/ [v I] use this about paper, clothes, books, or other things that have been placed flat on a surface

+ in/on/near etc *His letter was lying on the table.* | *The children's clothes lay on the bed, ready to be put on.*

lying – lay – have lain

be situated/be located /biː ˈsɪtʃu-eɪtɪd, biː ləʊˈkeɪtɪd‖-ˈləʊkeɪtɪd/ FORMAL use this about towns, buildings, offices etc

+ in/on/near *Soweto is an African township situated to the south west of Johannesburg.* | *The company's offices are located in downtown Manhattan.*

conveniently/pleasantly/ideally situated *a new hotel, conveniently situated close to the airport*

be based /biː ˈbeɪst/ if a company or organization **is based** in a place, its main offices are there

+ in/at *The United Nations is based in New York.*

London-based/Tokyo-based etc *a London-based insurance company*

3 when something is usually kept in a place

go/belong /gəʊ, bɪˈlɒŋ‖-ˈlɔːŋ/ [v I] ESPE-CIALLY SPOKEN if something **goes** or **belongs** in a place, it should always be put there when it is not being used: *Put those books back where they belong.*

+ in/on/under etc *"Where do these plates go?" "They go in the cupboard above the sink."*

4 not in any place

nowhere/not anywhere /ˈnəʊweəʳ, nɒt ˈeniweəʳ/ [adv] not in any place or to any place: *Where's Nick? I can't find him anywhere.* | *I'm not going anywhere.* | *a path that seems to lead nowhere*

nowhere else/not anywhere else (=no other place) *They're staying here because there's nowhere else they can go.*

nowhere to live/sit/stay *The hall was already full, and there was nowhere to sit.*

When you see **EC**, go to the **ESSENTIAL COMMUNICATION** section.

PLAN

DESIGN   PREPARE

see also

INTEND   ORGANIZE/ ARRANGE

1 a plan to do something

plan /plæn/ [n C] something that you have decided to do, and the methods you will use to do it: *Her plan is to finish her degree and then go and teach in Japan.* | *You can't start a new company if you don't have a good business plan.*

+ for *NASA has announced plans for a new space mission to Mars.*

plan to do sth *The school has plans to build a computer centre.*

go according to plan (=when things happen exactly as you intended) *Everything went according to plan, and we all crossed the river safely.*

strategy /ˈstrætɪdʒi/ [n C usually singular] a carefully designed plan for achieving something that is difficult and may take a long time: *the President's long-term economic strategy*

+ for *We need a new strategy for increasing our sales in Europe.* | *Murdoch bought several TV stations, as part of his strategy for building a media empire.*

plural **strategies**

programme BRITISH **program** AMERICAN /ˈprəʊgræm/ [n C] a series of activities, organized by a government or other large organization, that is designed to achieve something important and will continue for a long time

+ of *The irrigation project is part of a programme of aid to West Africa.*

training/research/space etc programme *a major research program, aimed at developing cheaper fuels*

2 a plan to do something bad

plot /plɒt‖plɑːt/ [n C] a secret plan to do something bad, especially to the members of a government

P

plot to do sth *a plot to assassinate the President*

conspiracy /kən'spɪrəsi/ [n C/U] a secret and usually complicated plan made by two or more people to do something bad or illegal together

conspiracy to do sth *a conspiracy to defraud the company of millions of dollars*
+ **against** *Members of the Secret Service were involved in a conspiracy against the elected government.*

plural **conspiracies**

3 a plan of the times when things will happen

timetable BRITISH **schedule** AMERICAN /'taɪm,teɪbəl, 'ʃedjuːl‖'skedʒʊl, -dʒəl/ [n C] a written list that shows the exact times when something will happen, for example when planes or buses leave, or when classes at school take place: *The timetable said there was another train at 6.15.*
+ **of** *I want a schedule of flights from Boston to New York.*

schedule /'ʃedjuəl‖'skedʒʊl, -dʒəl/ [n C] a detailed plan of what someone is going to do and when they will do it, especially someone important: *The President's schedule includes a two-day visit to St Petersburg.*

busy/tight schedule (=when you plan to do a lot of things in a short time) *She has a pretty tight schedule, but she may be able to meet you for lunch.*

programme BRITISH **program** AMERICAN /'prəʊgræm/ [n C] a plan that shows the order of activities at a ceremony, sports meeting, public event etc: *The next race on today's program is the women's 1000 metres.* | *Who is organizing the conference programme?*

4 to make plans
➡ see also **ARRANGE**

plan /plæn/ [v I/T] to think carefully about something you are going to do, and decide how you will do it: *Sue spent months planning her trip.* | *The burglary had obviously been very carefully planned.*

plan ahead (=make plans for the future) *Now that you're pregnant, you'll have to plan ahead.*

planning – planned – have planned

planning [n U] the activity of deciding how you will do something that you intend to do: *financial planning* | *After weeks of planning, the big day finally arrived.*

make plans /ˌmeɪk 'plænz/ to think about and talk about something that you intend to do, especially something that needs to be carefully planned: *We sat around the table, talking, laughing, and making plans.*
+ **for** *I've already started to make plans for the wedding – there's so much to do.*

⚠ If you **make plans** for something, you think about it in a general way. If you organize times, travel etc in detail you **make arrangements.**

plot /plɒt‖plɑːt/ [v I/T] to make secret plans to harm a person or organization: *The girls were in the kitchen, plotting their revenge.*

plot to do sth *The woman was accused of plotting to murder her boss.*
+ **against** *Plotting against the government was punishable by death.*

plotting – plotted – have plotted

5 not planned

unplanned /ˌʌn'plænd◄/ [adj] *On the way to Denver, we made an unplanned visit to my mother's.* | *More than 4 out of every 10 pregnancies are unplanned.*

spontaneous /spɒn'teɪniəs‖spɑːn-/ [adj] something that is **spontaneous** is done because you suddenly feel you want to do it, not because you have arranged to do it or been asked to do it: *The crowd gave a spontaneous cheer when the news was announced.* | *an act of spontaneous generosity*

spontaneously [adv] *Quite spontaneously, members of the audience started leaving the theatre.*

WORD BANK

POLICE

➡ see pages 569–571

When you see **EC**, go to the **ESSENTIAL COMMUNICATION** section.

POLICE

CRIME
DRUGS   CATCH
KILL   see   PRISON
         also
STEAL   LAW
ATTACK   COURT/TRIAL

1 the police

the police /ðə pə'liːs/ [n plural] the organization and the people whose job is to catch
criminals and make sure that people obey the
law: *He was stopped by the police and
arrested for dangerous driving.* | *Any
attack should be reported to the police.*
call the police *I heard a gunshot and called
the police.*
the riot police /ðə 'raɪət pə'liːs/ a group of
police officers with special equipment and
special training whose job it is to control
large crowds of people who have become
violent: *The riot police killed a student
protester who was taking part in an anti-
government demonstration.*

> ⚠ You can also use **police** before nouns,
> like an adjective: *a police car* | *a police
> helicopter* | *Police divers found a body at the
> bottom of the lake.*

the police force /ðə pə'liːs fɔːʳs/ the police
organization in a country or large area: *Jason
joined the police force when he was 19.*

police department [n C] AMERICAN /ðə
pə'liːs dɪˌpɑːʳtmənt/ the police organization in
a particular city: *the Los Angeles Police
Department*

P

2 people in the police

police officer (also **officer**) /pə'liːs ˌɒfˌɪsəʳ,
ˈɒfˌsəʳ‖-ˈɔːr-/ [n C] a man or woman whose job
is to catch criminals and to make sure people
obey the law

policeman/woman /pə'liːsmən, pə'liːs-
ˌwʊmən/ [n C] a male or female police officer

detective /dɪ'tektɪv/ [n C] a police officer
whose job is to discover information that will
result in criminals being caught

cop /kɒp‖kɑːp/ [n C] INFORMAL, ESPECIALLY AMERI-
CAN a police officer

plainclothes /ˈpleɪnkləʊðz, -kləʊz/ [adj only
before noun] **plainclothes** police wear
ordinary clothes, instead of a special uniform,
so that people do not know they are police
officers: *There were two plainclothes detectives waiting outside in an unmarked car.*

uniformed/in uniform /ˈjuːnɪˌfɔːʳmd, ɪn
ˈjuːnɪˌfɔːʳm/ wearing the special clothes worn
by the police: *Uniformed officers went to an
incident in Victor Road on Friday evening.*

---

vocabulary

arrest /ə'rest/ [v T] if the police **arrest** someone,
they take them to a police station because they
believe that person has done something illegal
be/get arrested *Gallagher was arrested yesterday
on suspicion of possessing cocaine.*

bail /beɪl/ [n U] money left with the court, so that
someone who is waiting for their trial is allowed to
stay out of prison until the trial. If the person does not
come back for their trial, the court keeps the money.
refuse sb bail (=not let someone stay out of prison
until their trial)
on bail (=released from prison because bail has
been paid)
release sb on bail (=let someone out of prison until
their trial, because bail has been paid) *He was
released on bail of £10,000.* (=he had to leave
£10,000 with the court)

catch /kætʃ/ [v T] to find a criminal and arrest him or her

charge /tʃɑːʳdʒ/ [v T] if the police **charge** someone,
they officially tell that person that they believe he or
she is guilty of a crime

charge sb with murder/theft/assault etc *William
Loeb was arrested and charged with rape.*
be charged with doing sth *A 13-year-old boy was
charged with shooting and killing a woman.*

commit /kə'mɪt/ [v T] if someone **commits** a crime,
they do something illegal

> ⚠ Never say 'do a crime'. Say **commit a
> crime.**

criminal /ˈkrɪmˌnəl/ [n C] someone who has done
something illegal: *Four dangerous criminals
escaped from prison last night.*
petty criminal (=one who commits crimes that are
not very serious) *Johnson was a petty criminal,
involved in shoplifting and car theft.*

crime /kraɪm/ [n C/U] an action that is illegal, such as
stealing something or killing someone

evidence /ˈevˌdəns/ [n U] information that helps to
prove whether someone is guilty of a crime

POLICE continues on the next page

POLICE

3 the work of the police

1 When a **crime** is **committed**...

2 ... someone **reports** it to the police. The police carry out an **investigation,** and try to **catch** the **criminal** involved.

3 They **interview** the **victim,**...

4 ...and they **interview** any **witnesses.**

I saw a man coming out of the house carrying a television.

5 They collect **evidence, search** buildings...

fingerprint

+ that *There is no evidence that Williams was in the park on the night that the murder took place.*
collect/gather evidence (=look for and get evidence) *The police are still gathering evidence in the case involving a boy who was kidnapped and assaulted.*
evidence against sb *Blood was found on his clothing -- a key piece of evidence against him.*
in custody /ɪn ˈkʌstədi/ if someone is **in custody,** they are being kept in a police station or in prison because the police think they have done something illegal
hold sb in custody (=keep them in a police station or in prison) *A man is being held in custody in connection with the robbery.*
interview /ˈɪntəʳvjuː/ [v T] ESPECIALLY BRITISH to ask someone questions about a crime: *Police would like to interview two men who were seen at the scene of the crime.*
interview room BRITISH **interrogation room** AMERICAN /ˈɪntəʳvjuː ˌruːm, ɪnˌterəˈɡeɪʃən ˌruːm/ [n U] a room in a police station where people are asked questions about a crime

investigation /ɪnˌvestɪˈɡeɪʃən/ [n C] when the police try to find out who committed a crime, for example by asking questions and looking for evidence
+ into *Los Angeles county police are continuing their investigation into a series of armed robberies in a shopping mall.*
carry out an investigation (=try to find out about a serious crime, especially using a lot of police officers) *The FBI is carrying out an investigation into the shootings.*

⚠ Don't say 'do an investigation'. Say **carry out an investigation.**

on remand /ɒn rɪˈmɑːnd‖-ˈmænd/ BRITISH if someone is **on remand,** they are being kept in prison while they are waiting for their trial: *He was beaten up by other prisoners while on remand in Parkhurst Prison.*
police station /pəˈliːs ˌsteɪʃən/ [n C] the building where the police work, where you go if you want to report a crime, and where people are taken when

POLICE

6 and interview any **suspects**.

7 When they have enough evidence, they **arrest** someone, and **take them in for questioning**.

handcuffs

8 The police hold them **in custody** and **question** them. If the police think that the **suspect** is guilty, they **charge** them with the crime.

9 Then the **suspect** is either kept **on remand**,...

10 ....or released on **bail** until the **trial**.

POLICE · DEPARTMENT

➡ for the second part of this story, go to **COURT/TRIAL**

---

they are arrested

question /ˈkwestʃən/ [v T] to ask someone questions to find out what they know about a crime, especially someone that the police think may be guilty
question sb about sth *The police questioned him about the missing $10,000.*

report /rɪˈpɔːʳt/ [v T] if you **report** a crime, you tell the police that it has happened
report sth to the police *We saw a gang of men fighting outside a bar, and reported it to the police.*

search /sɜːʳtʃ/ [v T] if the police **search** a building or place, they look in it for stolen goods, weapons, drugs, or evidence

suspect /ˈsʌspekt/ [n C] someone that the police think may have committed a crime: *Police regard the murder victim's ex-wife as their main suspect.* | *More than 20 suspects have been questioned.*

take sb in for questioning BRITISH **bring sb in for questioning** AMERICAN /ˌteɪk, ˌbrɪŋ (sb) ɪn fəʳ ˈkwestʃənɪŋ/ to take someone to the police station, because the police think that they have done something illegal and want to get information from them

trial /ˈtraɪəl/ [n C] a process in a law court in which it is officially decided whether or not someone is guilty of a crime

victim /ˈvɪktɪm/ [n C] someone who has been attacked, robbed, murdered, or harmed in some way in a crime: *The police believe that the victim knew her attacker.*
murder/rape etc victim *Many rape victims do not report the crime.*
+ of *He had been the victim of a serious assault three months previously.*

witness /ˈwɪtnəs/ [n C] someone who tells the police or a law court what they know about a crime or the person involved in it: *Police are appealing for witnesses* (=they want anyone who knows anything about the crime to talk to them) *after the death of 4-year-old boy last night.*
key witness (=someone whose evidence is extremely important) *The former basketball star is regarded as a key witness in the trial.*

POLITE

behaving in a way that is socially correct and shows respect for other people

➡ opposite **RUDE**
➡ see also **NICE, FRIENDLY/UNFRIENDLY, KIND**

polite /pəˈlaɪt/ [adj] someone who is **polite** follows the rules of social behaviour and shows respect for other people and their feelings: *He seemed a very polite young man.* | *a polite request*
it is polite to do sth *I didn't really care what she thought about the book, but I thought it would be polite to ask her.*
politely [adv] *'I hope your mother is well?' he asked politely.*
politeness [n U] when people are polite: *During my stay in Japan, I was treated with great politeness by everyone I met.*

good manners /ˌɡʊd ˈmænəʳz/ [n plural] someone who has **good manners** knows how to behave politely in social situations, for example, when to say 'please' and 'thank you': *My mother was impressed with Tony's good manners.* | *At least she had the good manners to let us know she would be late.*

well-behaved /ˌwel bɪˈheɪvd◄/ [adj] a **well-behaved** child is polite and does not cause trouble or make noise: *His older brother was quieter and far better-behaved.*
well-behaved – better-behaved – best-behaved

tactful /ˈtæktfəl/ [adj] careful not to mention something that might embarrass or upset someone: *I wish you'd be more tactful – didn't you know she was divorced?*
it is tactful of sb to do sth *It wasn't very tactful of you to ask whether she'd put on weight.*
tactfully [adv] *Claire tactfully changed the subject when someone mentioned the war.*
tact [n U] when people are tactful: *This job requires tact and patience.*

When you see **EC**, go to the **ESSENTIAL COMMUNICATION** section.

POOR

➡ opposite **RICH**

EARN   BORROW

MONEY   see also   SUFFER

OWE   EXPENSIVE 3

1 having very little money

poor /pʊəʳ/ [adj] having very little money: *They were so poor they couldn't afford to buy shoes for their children.* | *Ethiopia is one of the poorest countries in the world.*
the poor (=poor people) *the growing gap between the rich and the poor*

be broke/be hard up /biː ˈbrəʊk, biː ˌhɑːʳd ˈʌp/ ESPECIALLY SPOKEN to have very little money, either permanently or just at the present time: *Most students are too hard up to spend much money on clothes.* | *We're always broke at the end of the month.* | *I'm a little hard up just now – can I pay you back next week?*

poverty /ˈpɒvəʳtiǁˈpɑː-/ [n U] when people have very little money: *Charles was shocked by the poverty he saw in India.* | *Poverty and unemployment are two of the biggest causes of crime.*
live in poverty *Old people should not have to live in poverty.*

2 an area where poor people live

slum /slʌm/ [n C] a house in bad condition in a poor area of a city: *Maria lives with her eight children in a slum outside Montevideo.*
the slums (=an area where there are a lot of slums) *I grew up in the East London slums.*

⚠ You can also use **slum** before a noun, like an adjective: *a slum area* | *slum dwellers*

inner city /ˌɪnəʳ ˈsɪti/ [n C] the part near the middle of a city where the buildings are in bad condition and where a lot of poor people live: *the problems of Britain's inner cities*

plural **inner cities**

  inner-city [adj] *inner-city schools*

ghetto /'getəʊ/ [n C] a poor and crowded part of a city, where people live separately from the rest of the population, especially people of one race or from one country: *a novel about life in the ghettos of New York*

plural **ghettos** or **ghettoes**

POPULAR/ UNPOPULAR

LIKE/NOT LIKE   LOVE

WANT   SELL 5

see also

ENJOY   OPINIONS

HORRIBLE/ UNPLEASANT   ENTHUSIASTIC/ UNENTHUSIASTIC

1 people/places/activities that a lot of people like

popular /'pɒpjʊlər‖'pɑː-/ [adj] if things or people are **popular**, a lot of people like them: *Lisa's one of the most popular girls in class.* | *a popular holiday resort* | *Is baseball America's most popular sport?*
+ with *The nightclub is very popular with tourists.*

2 a popular book/film/song

bestseller /ˌbest 'selər/ [n C] a book that a lot of people buy: *Jackie Collins' latest book is certain to be a bestseller.*

blockbuster /'blɒkˌbʌstər‖'blɑːk-/ [n C] a film that a lot of people watch and that makes a lot of money, especially a film with a lot of exciting action: *Bruce Willis's new blockbuster took $10.6 million in its first weekend.*

hit /hɪt/ [n C] a record, song, or play that a lot of people buy, listen to, or watch: *When I first heard the song I knew it would be a hit.*

hit song/single/musical *a new hit single from Janet Jackson* | *the hit musical 'Cats'*

big hit *The album was a big hit in the States.*

3 when something becomes popular again

revival /rɪ'vaɪvəl/ [n C] when something or someone becomes popular and fashionable again, for example, a kind of music, a style of clothes, a writer, or a singer: *Sixties pop music enjoyed a big revival in the mid-90s.* | *There's been something of a Raymond Chandler revival recently.*

4 not popular

unpopular /ʌn'pɒpjʊlər‖-'pɑː-/ [adj] if things or people are **unpopular**, a lot of people do not like them: *The government is more unpopular now than it has been for years.* | *Mr Venables must be the most unpopular teacher in the school.*
+ with *The new uniforms were extremely unpopular with the students.*

POSITION/RANK

your position in an organization, company etc, which shows how important you are

➡ see also **CLASS IN SOCIETY**

1 your position or rank

position /pə'zɪʃən/ [n C] your job in an organization, company, or profession – use this to talk about how important someone is and how much responsibility they have: *Because of her position in the company, she is responsible for the major financial decisions.* | *He eventually became Lord Chancellor, the most powerful position in the British legal system.*
hold a position (=have a position) *Thorn holds one of the most senior positions in the Federal Bank.*

level /'levəl/ [n C] all the jobs in an organization that are similar in importance and that pay the same amount of money: *We* provide training for staff at all levels in the company. | There are not many part-time workers in the middle and higher levels of management.

rank /ræŋk/ [n C] someone's position in an organization such as the army or police force: *He joined the Los Angeles police department and was quickly promoted to the rank of lieutenant.*

⚠ Don't use **rank** about someone who works in a company, a school etc.

2 someone who has a high position

senior /'siːniəʳ/ [adj only before noun] a **senior** manager, official etc is one who has an important position in an organization or company: *He's a senior executive at Volkswagen.* | *a job in senior management* | *one of the country's most senior judges*

top /tɒp‖tɑːp/ [adj only before noun] **top manager/lawyer/executive etc** someone who has one of the most powerful jobs in business, or one of the most important jobs in a profession: *The President met with top Korean businessmen.* | *There are still not many women in top jobs.* | *a top fashion designer*

high-ranking /ˌhaɪ ˈræŋkɪŋ◀/ [adj only before noun] **high-ranking officer/official/member etc** someone who has a high position in an organization like the police or army, or in a government department, but not in business: *A high-ranking State Department official was accused of selling secret information.* | *a high-ranking officer in the air force*

3 someone who has a lower position than someone else

junior /'dʒuːniəʳ/ [adj only before noun] a **junior** doctor, officer etc does not have as much power or responsibility as other doctors, officers etc, especially because he or she has not been in the job for very long: *She started work as a junior reporter on a local newspaper.* | *The most junior officers wore a red stripe on their sleeves.*

assistant /ə'sɪstənt/ [adj only before noun] **assistant manager/editor/director etc** someone whose job is just below the position of a manager etc: *My mother is assistant principal at a school in Washington.*

POSSIBLE

➡ opposite **IMPOSSIBLE**

1 when something can be done

possible /'pɒsɪbəl‖'pɑː-/ [adj] if something is **possible**, it can be done: *Travel to other planets may soon be possible.* | *The only possible way of getting your money back is to go to the police.* | *Detectives can now check every criminal's records, which wouldn't be possible without computers.*

it is possible to do sth *Is it possible to find a room in a good hotel for less than $100?*

if possible (=if it is possible to do it) *I want to get back by 5 o'clock if possible.*

as soon/quickly as possible *Please let me know your answer as soon as possible.* (=as soon as you can) | *We must get her to the hospital as quickly as possible.*

everything possible (=everything that can possibly be done) *The doctors did everything possible to save her life.*

can be done /kən biː 'dʌn/ if something **can be done**, it is possible to do it: *The job can be done by Friday if we all make an effort.* | *I'm sure that more could be done to help the homeless.* | *Val got her MA while she was working full-time, so it can be done, you see.*

possibility /ˌpɒsɪ'bɪlɪti‖ˌpɑː-/ [n C] one of the things that you could try to do: *One possibility is that we could offer him more money.* | *Beth decided that she wanted to start her own business, and began to explore the possibilities.*

consider/discuss the possibility of doing sth (=consider whether you could do it) *We are considering the possibility of providing a new class for advanced students.*

2 when something can happen

possible /ˈpɒsᵻbəl‖ˈpɑː-/ [adj] if something is **possible**, there is a chance that it may happen or it may be true: *Accidents are always possible in heavy industries like mining.* | *"I think I saw Jack in the street yesterday." "That's not possible! He's in Kenya at the moment."* | *technological changes and their possible effects on our lives*
it is possible for *It is possible for more than one person to win the competition.*
it is possible that *It is possible that the children are still alive.*
> **possibly** [adv] *He could possibly be released from prison within three years.*

possibility /ˌpɒsᵻˈbɪlᵻti‖ˌpɑː-/ [n C] something that can happen or may happen: *A Republican victory in next month's elections now seems to be a real possibility.*
+ of *We could not ignore the possibility of an enemy attack.*
a distinct possibility (=something that is likely to happen) *There's a distinct possibility that there will be another earthquake.*

can /kən; *strong* kæn/ [modal verb] if something **can** happen, it is possible for it to happen at some time: *Anyone can make a mistake.* | *A lot can happen in two years.*

> ⚠ Don't say 'it can to happen'. Say **it can happen.**

potential /pəˈtenʃəl/ [adj only before noun] a **potential** problem, advantage, effect etc is not a problem, advantage etc now, but it may become one in the future: *Why was the chemical factory built so close to the town? Didn't people realize the potential risks?*
potential customer/buyer/student etc (=someone who may become a customer, buyer etc in the future) *one way of making the college more attractive to potential students*

there is a chance/there is a possibility /ˌðeər ɪz ə ˈtʃɑːns, ˌðeər ɪz ə ˌpɒsᵻˈbɪlᵻti‖-ˈtʃæns, -ˌpɑː-/ use this to say that it is possible that something will happen

+ of *On the northern hills there is always the possibility of a snow shower, even in June.*
+ that *Is there any chance that he will recover from his injury in time for the race?*

3 to make something possible

make sth possible /ˌmeɪk (sth) ˈpɒsᵻbəl‖-ˈpɑː-/
make sth possible *We are grateful to Mr Johnson, who made this event possible by letting us use his land.*
make it possible for sb to do sth *Satellite broadcasting made it possible for people all over the world to watch the 1960 Olympic Games.*

allow/enable /əˈlaʊ, ɪˈneɪbəl/ [v T] ESPECIALLY WRITTEN to make it possible for someone to do something that they want to do
allow/enable sb to do sth *The Internet allows people to send messages all over the world.* | *The money from her aunt enabled Maxine to buy a small restaurant.*

POWER

1 the ability to control people and events

power /ˈpaʊəʳ/ [n U] the ability or the right to control other people and make decisions that affect them: *Do you think the police have too much power?* | *Stalin's desire for power*
great/enormous power *the enormous economic power of the United States*
+ over *The big Hollywood studios have a lot of power over what kind of films get made.*
have the power to do sth *Only Parliament has the power to make new laws.*

⚠ Don't say 'he wanted the power'. Say he wanted power.

influence /ˈɪnfluəns/ [n U] if someone has **influence**, they can use their important social position or their wealth to persuade other people to do things: *The Catholic Church has always had a lot of influence in Polish politics.*
+ over *The banks had too much influence over government policy.*

authority /ɔːˈθɒrɪti, ə-‖əˈθɑːr, əˈθɔːr-/ [n U] the right to make decisions and control people, which a person has because of their job or official position: *No one dared to question the principal's authority.*
+ over *In the British system, the mayor has no authority over the local police.*
the authority to do sth *Every manager has the authority to dismiss employees.*

⚠ Use **authority** to talk about the rights and power that people have, but not to talk about the power that countries have.

2 someone who has a lot of power

powerful /ˈpaʊərfəl/ [adj] a **powerful** person, organization, or country has a lot of power, and can control people and influence events: *Parliament had become more powerful than the King.* | *one of the most powerful men in US politics* | *Berlusconi was the owner of a powerful media empire.*

influential /ˌɪnfluˈenʃəl◄/ [adj] someone who is **influential** can influence events, because they are rich, important, or greatly respected, and therefore people pay attention to what they say: *Her uncle is a rich and influential businessman.* | *She is probably the most influential member of the finance committee.* | *an influential film critic*
highly influential (=very influential) *Galbraith was a highly influential writer on economic affairs.*

strong /strɒŋ‖strɔːŋ/ [adj] powerful – use this about a political group that is supported by a lot of people: *The Communists were strong in all the big industrial cities.* | *There has been a strong anti-nuclear movement in Japan for many years.*

dominant /ˈdɒmɪnənt‖ˈdɑː-/ [adj] more powerful than other people, groups, countries etc: *Gradually, Microsoft became the dominant company in the software business.* | *At that time Portugal was the dominant naval power in the Mediterranean.*

3 to have official power

in power /ɪn ˈpaʊər/ a person or political group that is **in power** has political control of a country or government: *The Socialists have been in power since the 1965 revolution.* | *Gorbachev could not remain in power without the support of the Red Army.*

in authority /ɪn ɔːˈθɒrɪti‖-əˈθɑː-, -əˈθɔː-/ someone who is **in authority** has a job or position that gives them the right to tell other people what to do: *My mother demanded to speak to someone in authority.* | *Problems arise when people in authority can't keep discipline.*

rule /ruːl/ [v I/T] to have the power to control what happens in a country – use this especially about a person or group that has not been elected: *In 1860, Italy was a collection of small states ruled by princes and dukes.*
+ over *The Romans ruled over a large empire.*
rule [n U] when a person or group rules a country: *British rule in India came to an end in 1947.*
ruling [adj only before noun]
the ruling party/class/group the political party, social class, or group of people that has most power in a country: *Australia's ruling Labor Party* | *the struggle between the workers and the ruling class*

come to power /ˌkʌm tə ˈpaʊər/ to take political control of a country, especially by being elected: *De Gaulle came to power in 1958.*

4 someone who has no power

powerless /ˈpaʊərləs/ [adj not before noun] someone who is **powerless** has no power to control or influence what happens: *Blocked by the Republicans in Congress, Clinton seemed powerless.*

+ against *The people of Hungary were powerless against the tanks of the Red Army.*

powerless to do sth *The UN was powerless to prevent the war spreading.*

weak /wiːk/ [adj] someone who is **weak** does not have much power because they cannot make other people respect them or obey them: *These policies failed because the government was weak and ineffective.* | *a weak, indecisive principal*

weakness [n U] *The king's mercy towards the rebels was regarded as a sign of weakness.*

PRACTISE/ PRACTICE

to do something a lot in order to improve your skill at it

➡ see also **IMPROVE, BETTER, GOOD 5, 6**

1 to practise for a competition, test, or performance

practise BRITISH **practice** AMERICAN /'præktɪs/ [v I/T] to do an activity a lot in order to improve your skill: *I'm learning to play the piano, and I practise every day.* | *We're going to Paris for a few days, so that Bill can practice his French.*

practise doing sth *Try to practise speaking slowly and clearly.*

⚠ Don't use **practise** about sports. For example, don't say '*I practise tennis/golf every weekend*'. Say **I play tennis/golf every weekend**. But you can use **practise** about doing a particular movement in a sport in order to improve it. For example, you can say *I need to practise my backhand*.

train /treɪn/ [v I] to prepare for a race or game by exercising and practising: *If you're really going to run in the marathon, you need to start training now.*

+ for *Tyson is training for the big fight next week.*

rehearse /rɪ'hɜːrs/ [v I/T] to practise a speech, play, or concert so that you will be ready to perform it: *The producer made us rehearse the last scene again.* | *His band has been rehearsing at the TV studio all day.*

2 activities people do in order to practise

practice /'præktɪs/ [n U] things you do regularly in order to improve your skill at something: *She's playing pretty well now – she just needs a little more practice.*

piano/football/choir etc practice (=time that you spend practising the piano etc) *I scored two goals at hockey practice tonight.* | *Anna never misses her violin practice.*

training /'treɪnɪŋ/ [n U] time that you spend practising and doing exercise in order to improve your skill at a sport: *The team captain got a knee injury during training.*

a training course/session/programme *I have to go to the weekly training session at the gym.*

⚠ Don't say '*a training*' or '*trainings*'. **Training** is an uncountable noun.

rehearsal /rɪ'hɜːrsəl/ [n C] an occasion when all the people in a play, concert etc practise it before performing it in public

+ of *We're having our first rehearsal of 'Hamlet' tonight.*

3 when you have not practised something for a long time

be out of practice /biː ˌaʊt əv 'præktɪs/ if you are **out of practice**, you cannot do something as well as you could in the past, because you have not done it for a long time: *Sam said he's a little out of practice, but he'll play if we need him.*

rusty /'rʌsti/ [adj] if your skill at something is **rusty**, it is not as good as it used to be because you have not used it for a long time: *My Spanish is very rusty these days.*

rusty – rustier – rustiest

When you see **EC**, go to the **ESSENTIAL COMMUNICATION** section.

PRAISE

to say that you admire or approve of someone or something

➡ opposite **CRITICIZE**

ADMIRE   BEST
GOOD ⟵ see also ⟶ BEAUTIFUL
BETTER   LIKE/NOT LIKE

1 to praise someone or something

praise /preɪz/ [v T] to say that you admire someone or approve of something good that they have done: *Fire chiefs praised a 10-year-old girl who saved her brother's life yesterday.* | *The play was widely praised when it first appeared on Broadway.*
praise sb for sth *Local people were praised for their calm response to the crisis.*

congratulate /kənˈɡrætʃʊleɪt/ [v T] to tell someone that you are pleased because they have achieved something special or because something good has happened to them: *She got the job? I must go and congratulate her.*
congratulate sb on doing sth *The President congratulated him on winning the title.*

> ⚠ Don't say 'congratulate someone for something'. Say **congratulate someone on something**.

compliment /ˈkɒmplɪment‖ˈkɑːm-/ [v T] to tell someone that you like the way they look or that you are pleased with something that they have done
compliment sb on sth *He complimented her on the perfume she was wearing.* | *Everyone complimented me on my new hairstyle.*

flatter /ˈflætəʳ/ [v T] to say nice things that you do not mean about someone, especially in order to get something from them: *Flatter her a little – tell her she's beautiful.*

2 what you say when you praise someone

⟲**well done** BRITISH **good job** AMERICAN /ˌwel ˈdʌn, ˌɡʊd ˈdʒɒb‖-ˈdʒɑːb/ SPOKEN say this to someone when they have done something well or succeeded in doing something difficult: *Well done! You got all the answers right.* | *Good job, John! That was a great shot.*

congratulations /kənˌɡrætʃʊˈleɪʃənz/ say or write this: *Congratulations! Is it a girl or a boy?*
+ on *Congratulations on your new job, Jenny.*
congratulations on doing sth *Congratulations on passing your driving test.*

> ⚠ Don't say 'congratulation'. **Congratulations** is always plural.

⟲**way to go** /ˌweɪ tə ˈɡəʊ/ AMERICAN SPOKEN INFORMAL use this to praise someone who has just done something very good or impressive: *"I got accepted at Stanford." "Way to go!"* | *Way to go, Sam! Good hit!*

3 remarks that praise someone

praise /preɪz/ [n U] things you say to someone to show that you admire them or approve of what they have done
+ for *The police deserve a lot of praise for the way they handled the situation.*
be full of praise for sb/sth (=praise someone a lot) *Most parents are full of praise for the school.*
win/earn praise FORMAL (=be praised for something) *The charity has earned widespread praise for its work.*

compliment /ˈkɒmplɪmənt‖ˈkɑːm-/ [n C] what you say when you tell someone they look nice or they have done something well: *He said my English was almost as good as his – it was quite a compliment!*
pay sb a compliment (=give someone a compliment) *He's always paying her compliments and buying her flowers.*

flattery /ˈflætəri/ [n U] nice things that you say about someone, which may not be true, in order to get something that you want from them: *She used a mixture of persuasion and flattery to get what she wanted.*

PREPARE

➡ if you mean 'make food', go to **COOK**
➡ if you mean 'ready to do something' or 'ready to be used', go to **READY/NOT READY**

➡ if you mean 'organize a meeting, party etc', go to **ORGANIZE/ARRANGE**

1 to make something ready to be used

prepare /prɪˈpeəʳ/ [v T] to make something ready: *Before you start painting, prepare the walls by cleaning them and filling any cracks.*
prepare sth for sth *His job was to prepare dead bodies for burial.*
prepare a talk/presentation/speech/lesson *Teachers spend a long time preparing lessons.*

get sth ready /ˌget (sth) ˈredi/ to make sure a room, building, or piece of equipment is ready to be used
+ for *I spent the afternoon getting everything ready for the party.* | *Blake was down at the marina, getting his boat ready for the trip.*

set up /ˌset ˈʌp/ [phrasal verb T] to make a piece of equipment ready to work, by putting all the pieces of it together and putting it in the right place
set up sth *Ask Keith to set up your computer for you.*
set sth up *It'll take me a few minutes to set the camera up.*

2 to prepare for something that will happen soon

prepare /prɪˈpeəʳ/ [v I] to do things so that you will be ready for something that is going to happen soon: *I'm worried about tomorrow's interview – I haven't had enough time to prepare.*
+ for *Captain Harper told the flight crew to prepare for take-off.*
prepare to do sth *Jane was busy preparing to go abroad.*

get ready /ˌget ˈredi/ to do the things you need to do so that you will be ready to go somewhere, such as getting washed and changing your clothes: *You'd better go and get ready – it's nearly 7 o'clock.*

+ for *John took ages getting ready for the party.*
get ready to do sth *I was just getting ready to go out when Tim arrived.*

make preparations /meɪk ˌprepəˈreɪʃənz/ to do all the things you need to do so that you will be ready for an important event
+ for *We started to make preparations for the wedding about a year ago.*

train /treɪn/ [v I] to prepare for a race or game by exercising and practising: *The team is training at a secret location in Hampshire.*
+ for *She's training for next month's marathon.*

be prepared /biː prɪˈpeəʳd/ if you **are prepared** for something unpleasant or difficult that might happen, you expect it and you have made yourself ready for it
+ for *The children were sea-sick last time, so this time we'll be prepared for it.*
be well prepared *When the hurricane came, we made sure we were well prepared.*

3 things you do to prepare for something

preparation /ˌprepəˈreɪʃən/ [n U] the time and work that is needed to prepare for something: *Months of preparation have gone into organizing the festival.*
in preparation for sth (=as part of the preparation for something) *The hospital was being repainted in preparation for the Queen's visit.*

preparations /ˌprepəˈreɪʃənz/ [n plural] all the things you have to do so that you will be ready for an important event
+ for *She's busy with preparations for the school concert.*
make preparations *Belgium is making preparations for next year's centenary celebrations.*

PRESS

➡ see also **PUSH, PULL**

1 to push something firmly, especially with your fingers

press /pres/ [v T] to push something firmly

with your fingers or with your feet: *The doctor gently pressed her stomach.* | *I pressed the brake pedal, but nothing happened.*

press sth down *Press the lid down hard to seal the tin.*

press a button/bell/key (=in order to make a machine work, a bell ring etc) *Which key do I press to delete it?* | *To get coffee, put your money in the machine and press the green button.*

squeeze /skwiːz/ [v T] to push something firmly inwards with your hands or fingers: *I squeezed the toothpaste tube, but nothing came out.* | *squeezing a damp cloth to get the water out*

squeeze sb's arm/hand (=as a sign of love or friendship) *Alice squeezed my arm affectionately, and said goodbye.*

pinch /pɪntʃ/ [v T] to press someone's skin tightly between your fingers and thumb, so that it hurts: *Dad! Katy just pinched me!*

touch /tʌtʃ/ [v T] ESPECIALLY AMERICAN to press a button, for example on a telephone or a computer screen, in order to make a choice, get information, or make something work – used especially in instructions: *For room service, touch button 9.*

2 to press something so hard that it breaks or becomes flat

squash /skwɒʃ‖skwɑːʃ, skwɔːʃ/ [v T] to damage something, especially something soft, by pressing it and making it flat: *Someone sat on my hat and squashed it.* | *Careful you don't squash those peaches.*

    squashed [adj] *a squashed tomato*

crush /krʌʃ/ [v T] to press something so hard that it gets damaged or broken into pieces: *His leg was crushed in the accident.* | *a machine for crushing rocks*

    crushed [adj] *The path was made of crushed shells.*

mash /mæʃ/ [v T] to press fruit or cooked vegetables with a fork or similar tool, until they are soft and smooth: *Mash the bananas and add them to the mixture.*

    mashed [adj] *pie and mashed potatoes*

grind /graɪnd/ [v T] to break something such as corn or coffee beans into powder,

using a machine or special tool: *Grind some black pepper over the salad.*

grinding – ground – have ground

    ground [adj] *freshly ground coffee*

PRETEND

➡ if you mean 'pretend to have a feeling or opinion', go to **FALSE 3**

1 to pretend that something is true

pretend /prɪˈtend/ [v I/T] to behave as though something is true when you know that it is not: *We thought he had really hurt himself, but he was just pretending.*

+ (that) *The kids were pretending that they were in a space rocket.*

pretend to do sth *She pretended to listen, but I could tell she was thinking about something else.*

put it on/be putting it on /ˌpʊt ɪt ˈɒn, biː ˌpʊtɪŋ ɪt ˈɒn‖-ˈɑːn/ SPOKEN to pretend to be ill, upset, injured etc, because you want to avoid doing something or you want people to feel sorry for you: *Kelly's not really ill – she's just putting it on because she doesn't want to go to school.*

2 to pretend to be someone else

pretend /prɪˈtend/ [v T] to behave as if you are someone else and try to make other people believe this

pretend to be sb *We pretended to be students and went along to the party too!*

+ (that) *They got into the house by pretending they worked for the electricity company.*

impersonate /ɪmˈpɜːrsəneɪt/ [v T] to behave as though you are someone with official power or someone famous, either for dishonest reasons or in order to entertain people: *I got home to find him impersonating Elvis Presley in front of the mirror.* | *It's illegal to impersonate a police officer.*

do an impersonation/do an impression /duː ən ɪmˌpɜːʳsəˈneɪʃən, duː ən ɪmˈpreʃən/ to speak, walk, or behave like someone else, in order to make people laugh

+ of *Stuart did a brilliant impersonation of the boss.* | *a comedian who used to do impressions of famous politicians*

role-play /ˈrəʊl ˌpleɪ/ [n C/U] when you pretend to be someone else and behave as they would behave, especially as a way of learning about a situation or developing a skill: *Role-play is often used as a teaching method in language classes.*

3 to pretend not to notice someone or something

pretend not to see/hear/notice /prɪˌtend nɒt tə ˈsiː, ˈhɪəʳ, ˈnəʊtɪs/ *She winked at me, but I pretended not to notice.* | *She pretended not to see the look of surprise on Karen's face.*

pretend (that) you have not noticed/ seen/heard *I called out his name, but he pretended that he hadn't heard me.*

ignore /ɪgˈnɔːʳ/ [v T] if you **ignore** someone, you rudely pretend you have not seen them or heard them; if you **ignore** something, you pretend you have not noticed it, especially because it does not seem important: *John totally ignored her and went on talking to his new girlfriend.* | *Someone made a rude noise, which the teacher decided to ignore.*

○ not take any notice BRITISH **not pay any attention** AMERICAN /nɒt ˌteɪk eni ˈnəʊtɪs, nɒt ˌpeɪ eni əˈtenʃən/ ESPECIALLY SPOKEN to not let someone's words or behaviour affect what you do or affect the way you feel: *I keep telling them to turn the music down, but they don't take any notice.* | *We complained to the school about it, but no one pays attention.*

not take any notice of/not pay any attention to *Don't take any notice of him – he's just jealous.*

When you see **EC**, go to the **ESSENTIAL COMMUNICATION** section.

4 pretending to have feelings you do not have

insincere /ˌɪnsɪnˈsɪəʳ◄/ [adj] someone who is **insincere** says things that they do not really mean, for example when they praise you or say something friendly: *'It's so good to see you again,' she said, with an insincere smile.* | *an insincere compliment* | *He always praised everyone, so it was difficult to tell if he was being insincere or not.*

hypocritical /ˌhɪpəˈkrɪtɪkəl◄/ [adj] pretending to be morally good or to have beliefs that you do not really have: *I think it's a little hypocritical to get married in a church when you don't believe in God.* | *Politicians are so hypocritical – they preach about 'family values' while they all seem to be having affairs.*

hypocrite [n C] someone who pretends to have strong opinions about how people should behave, but who does not behave like this themselves: *My dad is such a hypocrite – he says I shouldn't smoke, but he smokes 20 a day.*

false /fɔːls/ [adj] emotions or feelings that are **false** are not real, and you are only pretending to feel them: *'Merry Christmas,' she said, with false cheerfulness.* | *The politician greeted them with a false smile.*

PRISON

FREE 3, 4   **LAW**

CRIME   see also   **PUNISH**

POLICE   **ESCAPE**

COURT/TRIAL   **CATCH**

1 a place where people are kept as a punishment

prison /ˈprɪzən/ [n C/U] a building where people are kept as a punishment for a crime: *Conditions in the prison were appalling.* | *a maximum security prison*

in prison *She's been in prison for eight years.*

be sent to prison *Davis was sent to prison for selling illegal drugs.*

be released from prison (=be allowed to leave) *Forbes will be released from prison next week.*

⚠ You can also use **prison** before a noun, like an adjective: *a long prison sentence | prison officers*

⚠ **Prison** and **jail** mean the same, and both words can be used in most situations. But **prison** is the usual word in more formal or official contexts, or when someone is sent there for a very long time.

⚠ Don't use 'a' or 'the' with **prison** if you are talking about prisons in general: *He spent half his life in prison* (not 'in the prison'). | *She was sent to prison.*

jail /dʒeɪl/ [n C/U] a prison – use this especially about a situation in which someone is sent to prison for a fairly short time: *This is the jail that Butch Cassidy escaped from in 1887.*

in jail *She was released after just three days in jail.*

⚠ You can also use **jail** before a noun, like an adjective: *a jail sentence*

cell /sel/ [n C] a small room in a prison or police station, where someone is kept as a punishment: *The prisoners spend most of the day locked in their cells.*

2 someone who is kept in prison

prisoner /ˈprɪzənəʳ/ [n C] someone who is kept in prison as a punishment: *The prisoners are allowed an hour's exercise every day.*

convict /ˈkɒnvɪkt‖ˈkɑːn-/ [n C] someone who has been proved guilty of a crime and has been sent to prison: *There was a report on the news about an escaped convict.* | *Stubbs was an ex-convict who got a job as a security guard.*

⚠ **Convict** is used especially in news reports.

hostage /ˈhɒstɪdʒ‖ˈhɑːs-/ [n C] someone who is kept as a prisoner by an enemy or a group of criminals, and is threatened

with death or injury if their government, their family etc does not do what the enemy or criminals want: *They say they will kill the hostages if we don't agree to their demands.*

3 to put someone in prison

put sb in prison/send sb to prison /ˌpʊt (sb) ɪn ˈprɪzən, ˌsend (sb) tə ˈprɪzən/ to officially order someone to be taken to a prison and kept there: *Eventually, her attacker was caught and put in prison.* | *The judge sent him to prison for seven years.*

lock up /ˌlɒk ˈʌp‖ˌlɑːk-/ [phrasal verb T] ESPECIALLY SPOKEN to put someone in prison
lock sb up/lock up sb *Rapists deserve to be locked up for the rest of their lives.* | *a new law allowing the courts to lock up very young criminals*

⚠ Use **lock up** especially when you mean that someone deserves to be in prison because they are very bad or dangerous.

imprison /ɪmˈprɪzən/ [v T] FORMAL to put someone in prison, especially when you think this is wrong or unfair: *The government has arrested and imprisoned all opposition leaders.* | *Mandela and Sobukwe were imprisoned on Robben Island.*

imprisonment [n U] when someone is put in prison, or the time that someone spends in prison: *The maximum penalty is three years' imprisonment.* | *His confession led to the arrest and imprisonment of several gang members.*

4 to force someone to stay in a place as a prisoner

keep /kiːp/ [v T] to force someone to stay in a place, as if they were a prisoner
keep sb in sth *West had abducted a young girl and kept her in his basement for 10 days.*
keep sb prisoner *The rebels kidnapped her and kept her prisoner for three months.*

take sb hostage /ˌteɪk (sb) ˈhɒstɪdʒ‖-ˈhɑːs-/ if an enemy or group of criminals **takes** someone **hostage**, they keep that person as a prisoner, and threaten to kill or injure them unless they get what they want: *The Ambassador and his wife have been taken hostage by terrorists.*

> ⚠ Don't say 'take someone as a hostage'. Say **take someone hostage**.

hold /həʊld/ [v T] to keep someone in a place and not allow them to leave – used especially in news reports: *Police are holding two men in connection with the robbery.*

hold sb prisoner/hostage/captive *Several tourists were being held captive by rebels in Kashmir.*

holding – held – have held

be imprisoned /biː ɪmˈprɪzənd/ to be kept somewhere and prevented from leaving: *the castle where Mary Queen of Scots was once imprisoned* | *Many old people are too frightened to go out, and feel as if they are imprisoned in their own homes.*

PRIVATE

➡ look here for ...
- not for other people to use
- not for other people to know about
- not controlled by the government

➡ opposite **PUBLIC**

➡ see also **MEDICAL TREATMENT, EDUCATION**

1 not for other people to use

private /ˈpraɪvɪt/ [adj] a **private** room, piece of land etc can only be used by one person or group, and is not for everyone: *All the rooms have private bathrooms.* | *The hotel has its own private beach.* | *Private property. No entry!*

2 not for other people to know about

private /ˈpraɪvɪt/ [adj] someone's **private** feelings, discussions, letters etc concern themselves or their family and friends, and are not for other people to know about: *You shouldn't be listening to a private conversation!* | *The book contains extracts from his diary and private letters.*

sb's private life (=things they do that are not connected with their work) *The newspapers are full of stories about the private lives of famous people.*

personal /ˈpɜːrsənəl/ [adj] someone's **personal** problems, relationships, letters etc are connected with their private life, not with their work: *There is a letter marked 'personal' for you.* | *I'd like to talk to you about a personal matter.* | *Are we allowed to make personal calls on the office phone?*

secret /ˈsiːkrɪt/ [adj only before noun] someone's **secret** thoughts and feelings are ones that they never tell anyone else about: *The diaries reveal all his secret hopes and fears.* | *a secret ambition*

secretly [adv] *He told her not to worry, but secretly he still blamed her for the accident.*

◯ be none of sb's business /biː ˌnʌn əv (sbs) ˈbɪznəs/ ESPECIALLY SPOKEN use this when you think someone has no right to ask about something, because it is private: *What I do at the weekend is none of your business!* | *Why should I tell Dan who I'm seeing? It's none of his business.*

3 not controlled by the government

private /ˈpraɪvɪt/ [adj usually before noun] **private school/hospital/education/pension etc** a school, hospital etc that is not owned by the government and that you must pay money to use: *Do you think the teaching in private schools is better than in state schools?*

privately [adv] *privately educated* (=at a private school) | *Journalists flew in on a privately chartered plane.*

commercial /kəˈmɜːrʃəl/ [adj only before noun] **commercial TV/radio/channel** a television or radio company that is not paid for by the government, but gets its money from advertising: *the most popular commercial radio station in London*

> When you see **EC**, go to the **ESSENTIAL COMMUNICATION** section.

PROBABLY

when it is likely that something will happen, or that something is true, but it is not definite

➡ see also **MAYBE, SURE/NOT SURE, POSSIBLE**

1 probably

probably /ˈprɒbəbli‖ˈprɑː-/ [adv] when something will probably happen or is probably true: *"Are you going to Lucy's party?" "Yes, probably."* | *We're probably going to move to New York next year.* | *Archaeologists think the temple was probably built in the 3rd century AD.* | *He wrote dozens of books, but this is probably his best-known novel.*

> ⚠ Be careful about the position of **probably**. It comes before an ordinary verb: *She probably left the car at home.* But it comes after an auxiliary or modal verb (like **have, will, can** etc): *It was probably an accident.* | *We will probably be late.*

likely /ˈlaɪkli/ [adj] something that is **likely** will probably happen or is probably true: *A peace settlement now seems likely.* | *The likeliest result is a win for the Democrats.*
likely to do sth *Men are more likely to die from heart attacks than women.* | *The price of books is likely to rise again this year.*
it is likely that *It is likely that the murdered girl knew her killer.*
very likely (=almost certain) *There will be a lot of cloud tomorrow, and rain is very likely.*

likely – likelier – likeliest

probable /ˈprɒbəbl‖ˈprɑː-/ [adj] FORMAL likely to be true or likely to happen: *This seems the most probable explanation.* | *Could you please inform us of the probable cost of the repairs?*
it is probable that *It is probable that they would have won the war if they had continued fighting.*
probable cause *The report states that the probable cause of death was a heart attack.*
highly probable (=when something will almost certainly happen) *A victory for the*

Communist Party now seems highly probable.

> ⚠ **Probable** is more formal than **likely**.

I suppose (also **I should think** BRITISH **I guess** AMERICAN) /aɪ səˈpəʊz, aɪ ʃʊd ˈθɪŋk, aɪ ˈges/ SPOKEN say this when you think something is likely to be true or likely to happen: *She's a year or two older than you, I should think.*
+ (that) *There was no reply when I phoned – I suppose she's still at school.* | *I should think you must be tired after your journey.* | *I guess Kathy will want to bring her boyfriend.*
I suppose so/I should think so/I guess so (=use this to say 'yes' to a question) *"Is Bill coming too?" "Yes, I suppose so."*

it looks as if/it looks like /ɪt ˈlʊks əz ɪf, ɪt ˈlʊks laɪk/ SPOKEN say this when you think that something is very likely to happen, based on what you know about a situation: *It's almost 11, so it looks as if Fred isn't coming tonight.* | *I can't see any buses – it looks like we'll have to take a taxi.*

I wouldn't be surprised if /aɪ ˌwʊdnt biː səˈpraɪzd ɪf/ SPOKEN say this when you think that something which seems unlikely is in fact quite likely to happen: *You know, I wouldn't be surprised if they decided to get married.*

2 how likely it is that something will happen

likelihood /ˈlaɪklihʊd/ [n U] how likely it is that something will happen
+ of *What's the likelihood of the war ending this year?* | *As you get older, the likelihood of illness increases.*
+ that *There is little likelihood that the number of college places will go up this year.*

chances /ˈtʃɑːnsɪz‖ˈtʃæn-/ [n plural] how likely it is that something you hope for will actually happen
chances of sth/of doing sth *The new treatment will increase her chances of survival.* | *For these men the chances of getting another job are not very high.*

probability /ˌprɒbəˈbɪləti‖ˌprɑː-/ [n U] how likely it is that something will happen – use this especially about situations where you can calculate fairly exactly how likely something is

+ of *The probability of catching the disease from your partner is extremely low.*

+ that *There is a 90% probability that the hurricane will hit the coast of Florida later today.*

probably not /ˌprɒbəbli ˈnɒtǁˌprɑː-/ *Her parents probably won't let her go.* | *I'll come and see you again, but probably not before Christmas.* | *"Do you think they'll offer you the job?" "Probably not."*

3 when something will probably not happen

unlikely /ʌnˈlaɪkli/ [adj] something that is **unlikely** will probably not happen or is probably not true: *She might let you borrow the car, but it's very unlikely.*

unlikely to do sth *A small amount of the drug is unlikely to have any harmful effects.*

it is unlikely (that) *It is unlikely that anyone saw the attack.*

doubtful /ˈdaʊtfəl/ [adj] very unlikely

it is doubtful whether/that *It seems doubtful whether the terrorists will ever be found.*

PROBLEM

➡ see also **DEAL WITH**

1 something that causes difficulties and must be dealt with

problem /ˈprɒbləmǁˈprɑː-/ [n C] a bad situation that must be dealt with, because it is causing harm or inconvenience, or it is stopping you from doing what you want to do

big/serious problem *Our biggest problem is lack of money.* | *Teenage crime is a serious problem.*

have a problem *If you have any problems, give me a call.*

+ with *Sue's had a lot of problems with her neighbours recently.*

cause/create problems *The new traffic system is causing problems for everyone.*

solve a problem (=find a way to deal with it) *Scientists still have not solved the problem of what to do with nuclear waste.*

the drug problem/crime problem etc *a new way of dealing with the drug problem*

the problem of sth *the problem of industrial pollution*

> ⚠ Don't say 'an important problem'. Say **a serious problem** or **a big problem**.

trouble /ˈtrʌbəl/ [n U] problems that someone or something is causing you, especially when this makes you worried or annoyed

have trouble with sth *We've had a lot of trouble with our bank.*

cause trouble *She seems to cause trouble wherever she goes.*

have trouble doing sth (=when something is difficult and causes problems) *We had a lot of trouble borrowing the money we needed.*

> ⚠ Don't say 'troubles' or 'a trouble'. **Trouble** is uncountable in this meaning.

difficulty/difficulties /ˈdɪfɪkəlti, ˈdɪfɪkəltiz/ [n U/plural] problems that make it difficult to do what you want to do

face/experience difficulty (=have difficult problems that you must deal with) *Without more rain, the farmers will face serious difficulties.* | *Some parents experienced difficulty when they tried to move their children to other schools.*

run into difficulty/difficulties (=start to have difficulties, especially about money) *The magazine ran into difficulties after only a few months.*

be in difficulty/difficulties (=experiencing problems) *Manchester United won easily, and they never seemed to be in any difficulty.*

setback /ˈsetbæk/ [n C] something that happens which stops you making progress or which makes things worse than they were before

have/suffer a setback *The peace talks have suffered a series of setbacks.*

+ for *This latest scandal is a major setback for the President's election campaign.*

snag /snæg/ [n C] a problem which seems small or not very serious, but which spoils your plans or causes you a lot of inconvenience: *It's a great place for a vacation – the only snag is that it's full of mosquitoes.*

hassle /'hæsəl/ [n C/U] INFORMAL an annoying problem that causes a lot of work or inconvenience for you when you are trying to do something: *the hassles of getting a visa*
it's too much hassle (=there are too many things to do) *I don't want to organize a big party – it's too much hassle.*

2 something wrong with a machine, system, plan etc

problem /'prɒbləm‖'prɑː-/ [n C] something that stops a machine or system from working normally
have problems *Please call 5326 if you have any computer problems.*
+ with *There seems to be some kind of problem with the cooling system.*

trouble /'trʌbəl/ [n U] something wrong with a machine, car etc, especially when you do not know exactly what is causing it: *engine trouble*
+ with *We've had trouble with the air-conditioning.*
the trouble (=the specific thing causing the problem) *I think we've found out what the trouble is.*

fault /fɔːlt/ [n C] something wrong with one of the parts of a machine that prevents it from working
+ in *I think there's a fault in one of the loudspeakers.*
electrical/mechanical/technical fault *The rocket launch was delayed because of a technical fault.*

defect /'diːfekt, dɪ'fekt/ [n C] something wrong with a product or machine, caused by a mistake in the way it was made or designed: *All the computers are checked for defects before they leave the factory.*
+ in *Investigators found a defect in the design of the ship.*

flaw/weakness /flɔː, 'wiːknᵻs/ [n C] something wrong with a plan or set of ideas, which may make the whole plan or set of ideas useless or ineffective

When you see **EC**, go to the **ESSENTIAL COMMUNICATION** section.

+ in *There are several obvious flaws in his argument.* | *One major weakness in the study is that it is based on a very small sample.*

3 something that makes you feel worried and unhappy

problem /'prɒbləm‖'prɑː-/ [n C often plural] something that happens in your life that makes you feel worried and unhappy
have a problem *Bill isn't sleeping well – I think he's having problems at school.*
personal/emotional problems *She's had a lot of personal problems – her mother died when she was eight.*

troubles /'trʌbəlz/ [n plural] things that make you feel worried and unhappy, especially problems that have continued for a long time: *It's nice to talk to someone about your troubles.* | *family troubles*

4 to have a lot of problems

be in trouble /biː ɪn 'trʌbəl/ to be in a difficult situation and have a lot of problems
be in deep/serious/big trouble *Their marriage was in serious trouble.*
get into trouble (=start to have problems) *A lot of people get into trouble when they borrow money.*

be in a mess /biː ɪn ə 'mes/ INFORMAL if something is **in a mess**, there are so many problems that there is not much hope that things will get better: *The economy is in a complete mess.*
get into a mess *How did you manage to get into this mess in the first place?*
sb's life is a mess (=they have a lot of problems and seem unable to deal with them) *Her boyfriend left her and she lost her job – her life is just a mess at the moment.*

5 what you say when you are explaining about a problem

the trouble is/the problem is /ðə 'trʌbəl ɪz, ðə 'prɒbləm ɪz‖-'prɑː-/ SPOKEN say this when you are explaining why something is difficult or what is causing problems: *The trouble is, there's no-one here who really understands computers.*

+ **that** *The problem is that we can't really afford the plane fare.*

the trouble/problem with sth is *The trouble with using credit cards is that it's so easy to get into debt.*

○**the thing is** /ðə ˈθɪŋ ɪz/ SPOKEN INFORMAL say this when you are explaining to a friend why you cannot do what they want: *The thing is, I have an important exam next week.*

6 what you say to ask someone about a problem

○**what's wrong?/what's the matter?** /ˌwɒts ˈrɒŋ, ˌwɒts ðə ˈmætər‖ -ˈrɔːŋ-/ SPOKEN say this when you are asking someone what is causing a problem, for example why they are upset, or why a machine will not work: *What's the matter? You look as if you've been crying.*
+ **with** *What's wrong with the TV?*

○**what's up?** /ˌwɒts ˈʌp/ SPOKEN INFORMAL say this when you are asking someone if there is a problem that they want to talk about: *"Karen, can I talk to you for a minute?" "What's up?"*
what's up with sb? (=say this when someone seems to have a problem) *What's up with Larry today?*

○**what's the problem?** /ˌwɒts ðə ˈprɒbləm‖-ˈprɑː-/ SPOKEN say this when you are asking why someone cannot do something or why something will not work: *"I can't finish the last question." "Why? What's the problem?"*
+ **with** *What's the problem with the coffee machine this time?*

○**do you have a problem with that?** /ˌduː juː hæv ə ˈprɒbləm wɪð ðæt‖ -ˈprɑː-/ SPOKEN, ESPECIALLY AMERICAN say this to ask someone if they are unhappy about something you just said or suggested, because they think it may cause problems for them: *"So you think we should let Karen borrow the car?" "Yeah, do you have a problem with that?"*

7 someone who causes a lot of problems

troublemaker /ˈtrʌbəlˌmeɪkər/ [n C] someone who deliberately causes problems, especially by complaining a lot or trying to make people fight or argue: *The*

violence was started by a small group of troublemakers.

difficult/awkward /ˈdɪfɪkəlt, ˈɔːkwərd/ [adj] someone who is **difficult** or **awkward** causes a lot of problems, because they behave in an unreasonable or unhelpful way: *Darren's always been such a difficult child.*
+ **about** *She's being really awkward about the divorce.*

PROMISE

to tell someone that you will definitely do something or that something will definitely happen

➡ see also **AGREE 4**

1 to promise something

promise /ˈprɒmɪs‖ˈprɑː-/ [v I/T] to tell someone that you will definitely do something that they want you to do or expect you to do: *"I can't take you to the beach today." "But you promised!"*
+ **(that)** *Hurry up, we promised we wouldn't be late. | He promised that he wouldn't tell anyone about our secret.*
promise to do sth *The government has promised to investigate why the accident happened.*
promise sb (that) *Harper promised her he would get the money somehow.*

assure /əˈʃʊər/ [v T] to tell someone that something will definitely happen or is definitely true, so that they are less worried
assure sb (that) *The doctor assured me that I wouldn't feel any pain. | The airline has assured travellers there will be no further delays.*

give sb your word /ˌgɪv (sb) jɔːr ˈwɜːrd/ to promise someone very seriously and sincerely that you will do something: *I have to go and meet her. I've given her my word.*
+ **(that)** *Phil gave me his word that he wouldn't ever take drugs again.*

guarantee /ˌgærənˈtiː/ [v T] to say that something will definitely happen, or will definitely be provided, especially when you feel very certain about this
+ **(that)** *Can you guarantee that there won't be any job losses when the*

company is taken over? | It's a great movie – I guarantee you'll enjoy it.

guarantee sth *The authorities could not guarantee the safety of UN observers.* | *Companies can no longer guarantee 'jobs for life'.*

guarantee sb sth *Have you been guaranteed a place in the team?*

swear /sweə^r/ [v T] make a very serious promise, especially publicly or in a law court

+ (that) *During the ceremony you swear that you will serve the country loyally.*

swear to sb (that) *Swear to me that you will never mention it again.*

swear to do sth *Do you swear to tell the truth?*

swearing – swore – have sworn

2 a promise

promise /'prɒmɨs‖'prɑː-/ [n C] a statement telling someone that you will definitely do something that they want you to do

+ of *The refugees are relying on promises of food and aid from the West.*

make a promise *I made a promise to help her, and that's what I'm going to do.*

promise to do sth *She seemed to have forgotten her promise to drive us to the airport.*

+ that *He left with a promise that he would be back before six.*

keep a promise (=do what you have promised) *I said I would take her out, so I have to keep my promise.*

break a promise (=not do what you have promised) *She never forgave her father for breaking his promise.*

3 what you say when you promise something

Ǫ**I promise** /aɪ 'prɒmɨs‖-'prɑː-/ SPOKEN *"Promise me you'll write to me." "I promise."*

+ (that) *I promise I won't forget.*

Ǫ**I give you my word** /aɪ ˌgɪv juː maɪ 'wɜː^rd/ SPOKEN FORMAL say this when you want to make a very serious and sincere promise: *You won't regret this – I give you my word.*

+ (that) *I give you my word that I'll do everything I can.*

When you see **EC**, go to the **ESSENTIAL COMMUNICATION** section.

4 when a company makes a promise about its products

guarantee /ˌgærən'tiː/ [n C] a formal written promise by a company to repair or replace a product free if it has a fault within a fixed period: *The VCR comes with a two-year guarantee.*

be under guarantee (=be protected by guarantee) *Your watch will be repaired free if it is still under guarantee.*

be guaranteed /biː ˌgærən'tiːd/ if a product **is guaranteed**, the company that made it has formally promised to repair or replace it free if it has a fault within a fixed period of time: *All our computers are fully guaranteed for two years.*

PROTECT

to prevent someone or something from being harmed or damaged

➡ see also **DEFEND, LOOK AFTER**

1 to protect someone or something

protect /prə'tekt/ [v T] to keep someone or something safe from harm, injury, damage, or illness: *new laws that are intended to protect the environment* | *The painting is protected by thick glass.* | *He came towards me with a knife, and I put my arm up to protect myself.*

protect sb/sth from sth *Try to protect your skin from the sun.*

protect sb/sth against sth *Garlic was once thought to protect people against evil spirits.*

guard /gɑː^rd/ [v T] to stay close to a person, a valuable object etc and watch them carefully, in order to make sure that they do not escape, get stolen, or get attacked: *They took turns to guard the prisoner during the night.*

guard sb/sth against sth *Soldiers have been called in to guard the embassy against further attacks.*

shelter /'ʃeltə^r/ [v T] to provide a place where someone or something is protected, especially from danger or bad weather:

I tried to shelter the baby with my umbrella.

shelter sb/sth from sth *A low hill sheltered us from enemy gunfire.* | *Plant roses next to a wall to shelter them from the wind.*

sheltered [adj] protected from wind, rain etc: *We found a sheltered beach where we could sunbathe.*

2 someone who protects a person or place

guard /gɑːʳd/ [n C] someone whose job is to watch a place, person, or valuable object, in order to protect them or stop them escaping: *There were guards on all the gates of the castle.*

security guard (=someone whose job is to guard a building) *Two men overpowered the security guard and stole $20,000.*

armed guard (=with guns) *The captain put armed guards all around the camp.*

bodyguard /ˈbɒdigɑːʳd‖ˈbɑː-/ [n C/U] a person, or a group of people, whose job is to protect someone important: *The President arrived, surrounded by bodyguards.* | *a member of the Emperor's bodyguard*

3 something that protects a person, animal etc

protection /prəˈtekʃən/ [n U] something that protects you against harm or damage
+ against *Their light summer clothes were no protection against the bitter cold.*
give/provide protection (=protect someone) *Vitamin C provides some protection against minor illnesses.*
+ from *At the moment, the law gives women very little protection from violent husbands.*

shelter /ˈʃeltəʳ/ [n U] a place where you will be protected from danger or from bad weather: *It began to rain and we all ran for shelter.*
the shelter of sth *William hurried towards the shelter of the old cowshed.*
take shelter (=find a safe place) *When the bombing started, we took shelter in the basement.*

protective /prəˈtektɪv/ [adj only before noun] **protective** clothes, covers, substances etc protect someone or something

from being hurt or damaged: *a tortoise's protective shell* | *Remove the hard disk from its protective packaging.*

protective clothing *Always wear protective clothing when you are working in the laboratory.*

4 someone who wants to protect people

protective /prəˈtektɪv/ [adj] someone who is **protective** wants to protect someone else from harm: *Philip noticed Maggie's protective attitude to the girl.*
+ towards *It is normal for parents to feel protective towards their children.*

overprotective /ˌəʊvəʳprəˈtektɪv◄/ [adj] someone who is **overprotective** tries too hard to protect someone else, in a way that restricts their freedom: *Maria's father was an overprotective man, who wouldn't let her meet any boys at all.*

PROTEST

when people show publicly that they do not agree with something

1 to protest about something

protest /prəˈtest/ [v I/T] if people **protest** about something, they show that they think it is wrong or unfair, for example by holding public meetings or writing letters to politicians: *When the army took power, huge crowds gathered in the capital to protest.*
+ about/against *Prisoners had climbed onto the roof to protest about conditions in the jail.*
protest sth AMERICAN *a huge crowd of students protesting the Vietnam War*

demonstrate /ˈdemənstreɪt/ [v I] to protest about something in an organized

way, by having a large outdoor meeting or by marching through the streets: *Police arrested 120 people who were demonstrating outside an army base.*
+ against *a large crowd demonstrating against US arms exports*

march /mɑːrtʃ/ [v I] to walk with a large group of people from one place to another, in order to show that you do not agree with something
+ through/to *Over three hundred farmers marched through Brussels to protest against the new tax.*

boycott /ˈbɔɪkɒt‖-kɑːt/ [v T] to not buy something, not go somewhere, or not take part in an event, in order to protest about the actions of a country or company: *We are asking people to boycott stores that sell furniture made from rainforest wood.* | *Several countries have said they may boycott next year's Olympic Games.*

2 things that people do in order to protest

protest /ˈprəʊtest/ [n C/U] anything that you do to protest about something: *The hospital was closed down, despite the protests of local people.*
as a protest/in protest *The Cuban delegates walked out of the meeting in protest.*
+ against *The refugees are refusing to eat, as a protest against their arrest.*

> ⚠ You can also use **protest** before a noun, like an adjective: *a big protest meeting*

demonstration (also **demo** BRITISH INFORMAL) /ˌdemənˈstreɪʃən, ˈdeməʊ/ [n C] when a large number of people come together to protest about something, by having an outdoor meeting or marching through the streets: *The police had to break up yesterday's animal rights demonstration.*
+ against *a huge demonstration against the French nuclear tests*

march /mɑːrtʃ/ [n C] when a large group of people walk in an organized way from one place to another in order to protest about something: *The march ended in front of the White House.*

protest march *I went on a lot of protest marches when I was a student.*

boycott /ˈbɔɪkɒt‖-kɑːt/ [n C] when people protest against the actions of a country or company, for example by not buying its products, not attending its events etc
+ of *The international boycott of South African products led to the release of Nelson Mandela.* | *a boycott of the peace talks*

3 people who protest

protester /prəˈtestər/ [n C usually plural] someone who comes together with other people to protest about something: *Some of the protesters climbed onto the roof of the police station and refused to leave.*

demonstrator /ˈdemənstreɪtər/ [n C usually plural] someone who takes part in an organized event, such as a march or an outdoor meeting, to protest about something: *Thirteen demonstrators were killed when soldiers started shooting.*

marcher /ˈmɑːrtʃər/ [n C] someone who takes part in an organized walk though an area in order to protest against something: *The Rev. Jesse Jackson led 1000 marchers through downtown Detroit to protest state welfare cuts.*

PROUD

pleased with your achievements, abilities etc

EMBARRASSED   SHY

see also

ASHAMED   DESCRIBING PEOPLE

CONFIDENT/NOT CONFIDENT

1 to feel proud

proud /praʊd/ [adj] someone who is **proud** of their achievements, their school, their family etc is very pleased with them and feels that they are very good or special: *I felt so proud when my son went up to collect his medal.* | *the proud parents with their new baby*

+ of *Jane's very proud of her new car.* | *My students have worked hard, and I'm proud of them.*

proud to be/do sth *Morris was proud to be part of such a brilliant team.*

+ that *He's very proud that his work has finally been published.*

> **proudly** [*adv*] *She turned to the crowd, proudly holding up the silver cup.*

pride /praɪd/ [*n U*] the feeling of being proud because of something special you have achieved, someone special you are connected with etc: *a sense of national pride*

do sth with pride *He talked with great pride about his father's work.*

bursting with pride (=feeling extremely proud) *Bursting with pride, she stood up to receive her prize.*

take pride in sth /ˌteɪk ˈpraɪd ɪn (sth)/ to feel proud of your work, your appearance etc, and always try to keep them at a high standard: *The people of the Basque country take great pride in their local cuisine.*

take pride in doing sth *The owners of the hotel take pride in offering an excellent service.*

2 too proud

conceited/big-headed /kənˈsiːtɪd, ˌbɪgˈhedɪd◂/ [*adj*] someone who is **conceited** or **big-headed** is too proud of their own achievements or abilities, in a way that annoys other people: *You're the most conceited, selfish person I've ever met!* | *I know this sounds big-headed, but I think these photos of mine are really good.*

> ⚠ **Big-headed** is more informal than **conceited**.

arrogant /ˈærəgənt/ [*adj*] someone who is **arrogant** behaves as if their opinions are more important than other people's, and thinks that they are always right: *a rude and arrogant young man* | *his arrogant disregard for other people's opinions*

> **arrogantly** [*adv*] *They arrogantly assumed that their form of democracy was better than anyone else's.*
>
> **arrogance** [*n U*] when someone behaves as if their opinions are more important than other people's and thinks that they

are always right: *the arrogance of people who have been in government for too long and think they can never be wrong*

vain /veɪn/ [*adj*] someone who is **vain** thinks they are very good-looking, special, or intelligent: *He's always admiring himself in the mirror – he's so vain!*

be pleased with yourself /biː ˈpliːzd wɪð jɔːˌself/ to feel very satisfied because of something you have achieved – use this especially about someone who seems too satisfied: *Ed walked out of the examination room looking very pleased with himself.* | *He's a nice young man, I suppose, but perhaps a little too pleased with himself.*

3 someone who thinks they are better than other people

snob /snɒb‖snɑːb/ [*n C*] someone who thinks that they are better than people from a lower social class: *My mother was a real snob – she wouldn't let me play with the local children.*

> **snobbish** [*adj*] like a snob: *Don't be so snobbish!* | *snobbish attitudes*

stuck-up /ˌstʌk ˈʌp◂/ [*adj*] INFORMAL someone who is **stuck-up** thinks that they are better than people from a lower social class, and behaves in a proud, unfriendly way: *The children who go to that school are so stuck-up.*

pompous /ˈpɒmpəs‖ˈpɑːm-/ [*adj*] someone who is **pompous** tries to sound important, especially by using very long or formal words: *The headteacher gave a pompous speech about 'the values of learning'.*

look down on sb /ˌlʊk ˈdaʊn ɒn (sb)‖ -ɑːn-/ [*phrasal verb T*] if you **look down on** other people, you think you are better or more important than them: *He looks down on anyone who hasn't had a college education.*

4 to talk too proudly about yourself

boast /bəʊst/ [*v I/T*] to talk too proudly about your achievements or possessions, because you want people to admire you:

'I can do better than any of them,' she boasted.

+ about *He's always boasting about how many girlfriends he's had.*

+ that *She liked to boast that she could speak six languages fluently.*

show off /ˌʃəʊ 'ɒf‖-'ɔːf/ [phrasal verb I] to keep doing things and saying things to show people how clever you are, how brave or strong you are etc, and make them admire you: *Ben was at the pool, showing off to the girls.* | *"I can say it in French, Spanish, Japanese, and Greek." "Oh, stop showing off!"*

> **show-off** /'ʃəʊ ɒf‖-ɔːf/ [n C] someone who is always doing or saying things to make people admire them: *Don't be such a show-off!*

5 a feeling of respect for yourself

self-respect /ˌself rɪ'spekt/ [n U] a feeling of respect and confidence in yourself and in your abilities: *It is difficult to keep your self-respect when you have been unemployed for a long time.* | *Serious illness often results in a loss of confidence and self-respect.*

dignity /'dɪgnɪ̩ti/ [n U] the ability to behave in a calm way that shows that you respect yourself, even in difficult situations
do sth with dignity *Very sick people should be allowed to die with dignity.*
lose your dignity *She lost her home and all her money, but she never lost her dignity.*

pride /praɪd/ [n U] the feeling that you deserve to be respected by other people – use this especially when someone finds it difficult to admit they need help or that they are wrong: *He has too much pride to say he's sorry.* | *Her pride would not allow her to ask for help.*
hurt sb's pride *Don't offer her money – you'll hurt her pride.*

dignified /'dɪgnɪ̩faɪd/ [adj] behaving in a calm way, even in a difficult situation, that makes other people respect and admire you: *She was a quiet, dignified old lady.* | *Jo listened to their criticisms in dignified silence.*

> When you see **EC**, go to the
> **ESSENTIAL COMMUNICATION** section.

6 when someone does not talk proudly about themselves

modest /'mɒdɪst‖'maː-/ [adj] someone who is **modest** never talks proudly about their abilities and achievements: *Fame didn't affect him – he remained a charming and modest man.* | *She was too modest to tell you that she got top marks in the test.*

> **modestly** [adv] *"It was really brave of you." "Oh, it was nothing," he replied modestly.*

modesty /'mɒdɪsti‖'maː-/ [n U] a modest way of talking or behaving: *'I couldn't have done it without the rest of the team,' he said, with typical modesty.*

PROVE

to show that something is true or correct

➡ see also **COURT/TRIAL, TRUE/NOT TRUE**

1 to prove something

prove /pruːv/ [v T] to show that something is definitely true, by providing facts or information

+ (that) *Can you prove that you were at home at the time of the attack?* | *He wanted to prove that he was just as clever as his sister.*

prove sb wrong/innocent/guilty *I would love to prove him wrong.*

prove sth to sb *I'm telling the truth, and I can prove it to you.*

proving – proved – have proved (also **have proven** ESPECIALLY AMERICAN)

show /ʃəʊ/ [v T] if facts or actions **show** that something is true, they prove that it is true: *The Prime Minister's comments show his ignorance of people's feelings.*

+ (that) *Her record shows that Graf is one of the best players of all time.*

show how/what *These figures show how serious the company's problems are.*

showing – showed – have shown

> ⚠ People or things can **prove** something, but only things can **show** something.

demonstrate /'demənstreɪt/ [v T] to do something or provide information which makes it very clear to people that something is true: *The studies demonstrate a clear link between smoking and heart disease.*
+ that *The President is anxious to demonstrate that he has a strong foreign policy.*

⚠ Demonstrate is more formal than show.

confirm /kən'fɜːᵣm/ [v T] if a piece of new information **confirms** an idea or belief that people already have, it shows that it is definitely true: *Police have found new evidence that confirms his story.*
+ that *The discovery seems to confirm that people lived here over 10,000 years ago.*

2 to prove that something is not true

disprove /dɪs'pruːv/ [v T] to prove that something is wrong or not true: *She was able to produce figures that disproved Smith's argument.*
disproving – disproved – have disproved (also **have disproven** ESPECIALLY AMERICAN)

3 the information that proves something

proof /pruːf/ [n U] information or facts that prove that something is true: *He was the only person in the room when the money disappeared – what more proof do you want? | The police knew she was guilty, but they had no proof.*
+ of *You can't drink in bars without some proof of your age.*
+ that *There is no proof that he did it.*

⚠ Don't say 'proofs' or 'a proof'. Just say proof.

evidence /'evɪdəns/ [n U] information that helps to prove whether something is true or not: *The police did not have enough evidence to charge anybody with the murder.*
+ that *There is some evidence that a small amount of alcohol is good for you.*
+ of/for *evidence of life on other planets*

medical/scientific evidence *There is no scientific evidence to support this theory.*

⚠ Don't say 'an evidence'. Say **a piece of evidence**.

PROVIDE

to make something available for someone who needs it or wants it

➡ see also **GIVE, MONEY 8**

provide /prə'vaɪd/ [v T] if a person or organization **provides** something, they make it available for someone who needs it or wants it: *They deal with general inquiries, and also provide free legal advice.*
provide sth for sb *Free parking is provided for hotel guests. | The university should provide more facilities for disabled students.*
provide sb with sth *The money will be used to provide the school with new computer equipment.*

supply /sə'plaɪ/ [v T] to provide things for people, especially regularly and over a long period of time
supply sth to sb *The company supplies beauty products to several major stores.*
supply sb with sth *The US government supplied the rebels with weapons.*
supplying – supplied – have supplied

supplier /sə'plaɪəᵣ/ [n C] a company or country that supplies things to people
+ of *one of the world's biggest suppliers of defense equipment*

PUBLIC

➡ opposite **PRIVATE**
➡ look here for ...
• for everyone to use
• controlled by the government
• when a lot of people can see you
➡ if you mean 'people in general', go to **PERSON/PEOPLE 2**
➡ see also **GOVERNMENT/POLITICS**

1 for everyone to use

public /'pʌblɪk/ [adj only before noun] a **public** place or **public** service is one that anyone can use, not one that is only for a particular person or group: *a public telephone* | *proposals to ban smoking in public places* | *Is this a public beach?* | *public toilets*

public transport BRITISH **public transportation** AMERICAN (=buses, trains etc, not cars) *If more people used public transport, there would be less pollution.*

2 owned or controlled by the government

public /ˈpʌblɪk/ [adj only before noun] **public** schools, libraries, hospitals etc are provided and paid for by the government, not by private companies: *a public library* | *garbage collection and other public services* | *We need to raise taxes to pay for better public healthcare.*

public spending/expenditure (=money spent by the government to provide public services) *a big increase in public spending*

publicly owned [adj] owned by the government, not by private companies: *Thatcher privatized publicly owned industries like electricity and telecommunications.*

state /steɪt/ [adj only before noun] owned, controlled, or paid for by the government: *the state education system* | *State aid has been promised for the victims of the flood.* | *China's state radio station*

> ⚠ When you are talking about the US, Canada, or Australia, **state** has a different meaning. A **state** is one of the separate parts of the country which has its own government. So in these countries, a 'state university', for example, is one that is run and paid for by one of the states.

nationalized (also **nationalised** BRITISH) /ˈnæʃənəlaɪzd/ [adj only before noun] **nationalized industry/company etc** an industry or company that used to be private but is now owned and run by the government: *The government is trying to sell off as many nationalized industries as it can.*

3 when a lot of people can see you or know about what is happening

in public /ɪn ˈpʌblɪk/ if you do something **in public**, you do it in a place where a lot of people can see or hear you: *Most people feel nervous about speaking in public.* | *Her husband was always very nice to her in public, but not at home.*

appear in public (use this to say that a famous person is seen in public by ordinary people) *The Prince has not appeared in public since the announcement.*

publicly /ˈpʌblɪkli/ [adv] if you do or say something **publicly**, you do or say it so that everyone knows about it, and you do not try to keep it secret: *He was put in prison after publicly criticizing the military government.* | *They plan to announce their engagement publicly in the New Year.*

public /ˈpʌblɪk/ [adj only before noun] **public** statements, meetings, or events happen in places where everyone can see them or know about them: *In a public statement, Jackson and his wife announced their intention to get divorced.* | *a country where they still hold public executions*

openly /ˈəʊpənli/ [adv] if you do something **openly**, you do it in a public place and without being embarrassed or trying to hide what you are doing: *He was the first person to talk openly on TV about having AIDS.* | *Drugs are sold openly on the city streets.*

PULL

➡ see also **PUSH, PRESS**

1 to pull something with your hands

pull

pull /pʊl/ [v I/T] to hold something and make it move towards you by moving your arms: *You need to pull this lever to start the machine.*

pull sth up/towards/away etc *He pulled her towards him and kissed her.* | *Pull the chair nearer to the fire.*

pull hard (=pull using a lot of effort) *Take hold of the rope and pull hard.*

tug /tʌg/ [v I/T] to pull something using short quick movements: *Mandy was tugging my sleeve.*

+ at *I tugged at the dog's collar but he wouldn't move.*

tugging – tugged – have tugged

yank /jæŋk/ [v T] INFORMAL to pull something with a sudden, strong movement

yank sth off/out/from etc *I picked up the box and yanked the lid off.*

yank sth open *Bruno rushed to the door and yanked it open.*

2 to pull something heavy

pull /pʊl/ [v T] to make a vehicle or piece of machinery move aong behind – use this especially about animals or heavy vehicles pulling things: *a tractor pulling a plough* | *The Queen's carriage was pulled by two white horses.*

drag /dræg/ [v T] to pull something along the ground, especially because it is too heavy to carry

drag sth along/over/away etc *They dragged the boat out of the water and up the beach.* | *Pick up your chair. Don't drag it along the floor.*

dragging – dragged – have dragged

haul /hɔːl/ [v T] to pull something heavy, with a strong continuous movement, often using a rope

haul sth along/out/away etc *Andrew helped them haul the cart from the ditch.*

haul in a net/rope (=pull it towards you) *We watched the fishermen hauling in their nets.*

tow

tow /təʊ/ [v T] if a vehicle or boat **tows** something, it pulls it behind it: *What's the speed limit for cars towing trailers?*

tow sth to/from/away etc *The damaged ship was towed to the nearest port.* | *The police had towed his car away because it was blocking the road.*

heave /hiːv/ [v I/T] to pull something very heavy with one great effort: *Everyone pull together now. Are you ready? Heave!*

heave sth onto/into/over etc *He heaved the sack onto his shoulder.*

PUNISH

to do something unpleasant to someone because they have done something wrong

see also

COURT/TRIAL   CRIME

LAW ←   → BAD 8, 9

PRISON   STRICT/ NOT STRICT

1 to punish someone

punish /ˈpʌnɪʃ/ [v T] to do something unpleasant to someone because they have done something wrong, for example by putting them in prison, or making them do something that they do not want to do: *The teacher punished us by making us do extra homework.*

punish sb for sth *Campbell was never punished for the murder.*

punish sb for doing sth *He wanted to punish her for deceiving him.*

fine /faɪn/ [v T] to make someone pay money as a punishment: *Inspectors have the power to fine any passenger travelling without a ticket.*

be fined £10/$100 etc *She was fined $50 for careless driving.*

sentence /ˈsentəns/ [v T] to announce officially in a court what punishment someone will be given for a crime

sentence sb to 20 years/life imprisonment etc *The judge sentenced her to a year in jail.* | *Lund was sentenced to eight years' imprisonment for the murder.*

sentence sb to death (=say officially that someone will be killed as a punishment) *60 prisoners have been sentenced to death.*

2 a way of punishing someone

punishment /'pʌnɪʃmənt/ [n C/U] something that is done to someone in order to punish them: *In cases of sheep-stealing, the usual punishment was hanging.*
+ for *Billy was sent to bed early as a punishment for his bad behaviour.*
capital punishment (=the system of punishing people by killing them) *Some people are demanding the return of capital punishment for murder.*
corporal punishment (=punishing people, especially children, by hitting them) *Do you agree with corporal punishment?*

> ⚠ Don't say a punishment is 'big', 'heavy', or 'strict'. Use **harsh** or **severe**: *Losing a day's pay seems quite a severe punishment for being 10 minutes late!*

penalty /'penlti/ [n C] an official punishment for someone who breaks a law, rule, or legal agreement
+ for *The penalty for treason was always death.*
the death penalty (=being officially killed as a punishment) *Drug smugglers face the death penalty if they are caught.*
a heavy/severe/stiff penalty *The contract includes stiff financial penalties for failure to complete the work on time.*
plural **penalties**

fine /faɪn/ [n C] an amount of money that you are ordered to pay as a punishment
get a fine (=be told to pay a fine) *I got a £40 fine for speeding.*
a heavy fine (=a large fine) *There are heavy fines for drink-driving.*

sentence /'sentəns/ [n C] a punishment given by a judge in a court
a prison sentence *He got a 10-year prison sentence.*
the death sentence (=when someone is punished by being killed) *The victim's family are demanding the death sentence for his attacker.*
a life sentence (=a very long time in prison)

a heavy/light sentence (=a long/short time in prison) *Evans was given a light sentence because he had given information to the police.*

3 to be punished for something bad you have done

be punished /biː 'pʌnɪʃt/ to be punished for something bad that you have done: *If you commit a crime you must expect to be punished.*
+ for *Ellen was punished for being rude to her teacher.*
be severely punished *Anyone who disobeyed his orders was severely punished.*

get/be given /get, biː 'gɪvən/ to be officially given a punishment: *He deserves to get at least 10 years in prison.* | *You'll probably just get a fine.* | *McLean was given a life sentence for his part in the bombing.*

be in trouble /biː ɪn 'trʌbəl/ ESPECIALLY SPOKEN if you **are in trouble**, you are likely to be punished because you have done something bad: *You'll be in trouble if they catch you cheating!*
be in trouble with the police/the authorities *My sister's in trouble with the police again.*
get into trouble *I'll get into trouble if my parents see me smoking.*

4 to punish someone because they harmed you

get revenge/take revenge /get rɪ'vendʒ, teɪk rɪ'vendʒ/ to do something to punish someone who has harmed you, your family, or your friends
+ on *She took revenge on her husband by cutting up all his best clothes.*
+ for *Flavio was determined to get revenge for the murder of his sister.*

get your own back/get back at sb /get jɔːr 'əʊn bæk, get 'bæk æt (sb)/ INFORMAL to do something which causes problems for someone, because they have done something that causes problems for you: *Okay, she made me look stupid, but I'll get my own back!* | *He wanted to get back at his supervisor for criticizing him in public.*

+ on *He kept looking for a chance to get his own back on Freddie.*

5 when someone is not punished

escape punishment/avoid punishment /ɪˌskeɪp ˈpʌnɪʃmənt, əˌvɔɪd ˈpʌnɪʃmənt/ to avoid being punished for something wrong that you have done: *He managed to escape punishment by saying that he was mentally ill.*

get away with sth /get əˈweɪ wɪð (sth)/ [phrasal verb T] to not be punished for something bad you have done
get away with doing sth *How does he manage to get away with being so cheeky to the teacher?*
get away with it *You're not supposed to park here, but you'll probably get away with it.*

> ⚠ **Get away with sth** is more informal than **escape punishment** or **avoid punishment**.

let sb off /ˌlet (sb)ˈɒf‖-ˈɔːf/ [phrasal verb T] to not punish someone, or give them a less severe punishment than they deserve: *I'll let you off this time, but don't do it again!*
let sb off with a warning/a fine etc (=only give them a warning etc, although they deserve a worse punishment) *The police let him off with a warning.*

PURE

not mixed with anything else

pure /pjʊəʳ/ [adj only before noun] a **pure** substance or material contains only one substance and is not mixed with anything else: *pure cotton | Our burgers are made from pure beef. | When it first comes out of the ground, the oil is not very pure.*

> ⚠ Water or air that is **pure** is very clean and does not contain any harmful substances or chemicals *The water in the stream was pure enough to drink.*

solid /ˈsɒlɪd‖ˈsɑː-/ [adj only before noun]
solid gold/silver/pine etc gold, silver

etc that has not been mixed with any other metal or wood: *My parents gave me a solid gold necklace for my 18th birthday. | a table made of solid oak*

100% /ˌhʌndrəd pəʳˈsent◂/ if food or material is **100%** beef, **100%** cotton etc, it is made only from beef or cotton, and has no other food or material added to it: *The label said '100% wool'.*

neat/straight /niːt, streɪt/ [adj] if you have a strong alcoholic drink **neat** or **straight**, you do not mix it with another drink or with water: *He always drinks his whisky neat. | I'll have a straight vodka please.*

PURPOSE

what an event or action is supposed to achieve

➡ if you mean 'on purpose', go to **DELIBERATELY**
➡ see also **REASON**

purpose /ˈpɜːʳpəs/ [n C] the thing that you want to achieve, when you do something or make a plan
+ of *The purpose of the study is to find out people's attitudes towards drugs.*
the main purpose (=the most important purpose) *The main purpose of the meeting is to discuss who will be in the team.*
sb's purpose in doing sth *My purpose in writing this book was to draw attention to the problem of global warming.*
for this/that purpose *Clifford intended to buy a restaurant, and he had borrowed the money for this purpose.*

> ⚠ **Purpose** is a fairly formal word, so in ordinary conversation it is better to say something like 'why did you do it?' (not 'what was your purpose?') or 'I did it because ...' (not 'my purpose was ...').

aim /eɪm/ [n C] the thing that someone hopes to achieve: *Their aims may be difficult to achieve.*
+ of *The aim of the bombers was to destroy public property and get maximum publicity.*
sb's/sth's aim *The organization's aims are to provide food for homeless people and help them find somewhere to live.*

with the aim of doing sth *He started going to the gym, with the aim of improving his fitness.*

⚠ Don't say 'with the aim to do it'. Say **with the aim of doing it**.

the point /ðə ˈpɔɪnt/ [n singular] the purpose of something that you are doing or planning – use this especially when someone does not understand what the purpose is

+ of *The point of the experiment is to show how this chemical reacts with water.*

the whole point (=exactly the purpose of doing something) *Of course it'll annoy Dad – that's the whole point!*

see the point of sth (=understand why someone does something) *I can't see the point of travelling all that way and then only staying for one day.*

the idea /ðə aɪˈdɪə/ [n singular] the effect or result that you hope to achieve by doing something – use this especially when you are doubtful whether that effect or result can be achieved: *We make toys that are both fun and educational – at least that's the idea.*

the idea is to do sth *The idea of the centre was to provide a place where old people could go during the day.*

objective /əbˈdʒektɪv/ [n C] FORMAL the thing that someone is trying to achieve in business or politics: *The President believes that all military objectives have been achieved.*

PUSH

to make someone or something move away from you by pressing against them

➡ see also **PRESS, PULL**

1 to push someone or something

push /pʊʃ/ [v I/T] to make something or someone move away from you, by putting your hands or your shoulder against them and pressing them hard: *We kept pushing but we couldn't get the door open.* | *Stop pushing me!*

push sb into/away/back etc *I was pushed into the car with my hands tied behind my back.* | *She tried to kiss him but he pushed her away.* | *We pushed the chairs back against the wall and rolled up the carpet.*

pushing and shoving (=when people in a crowd keep pushing each other) *There was a lot of pushing and shoving as they all tried to get nearer the stage.*

give sth/sb a push /ˌgɪv (sth/sb) ə ˈpʊʃ/ to push something or someone, with a single firm movement: *Suddenly, someone gave him a push from behind.* | *If the door is stuck, just give it a push.*

nudge /nʌdʒ/ [v T] to gently push someone with your elbow to get their attention, especially when you do not want anyone else to notice: *Toby nudged my arm. 'That's the guy I told you about,' he whispered.*

poke /pəʊk/ [v T] to push someone or something with your finger or with something sharp: *I poked the fish with my finger to see if it was still alive.*

poke sb in the eye/side/ribs *Careful with that stick! You nearly poked me in the eye with it.*

shove /ʃʌv/ [v T] to push someone or something roughly, without caring if you hurt them

shove sb into/aside/against etc *He was shoved into a van, which then drove off at high speed.* | *The police were shoving people aside to make way for he President's car.*

2 to push something so that it keeps moving

We ran out of petrol and had to push the van.

push /pʊʃ/ [v T] **push a cart/trolley/ car/pram etc** to push something that has wheels on it so that it moves along: *Bert*

*was pushing a wheelbarrow loaded with
sand.*
push sth along/around/into/up etc
*Three men helped her push the car into
a side-street.*

roll /rəʊl/ [v T] to push a round object so
that it keeps turning and moves forward
roll sth along/across/down/up etc *He
rolled the barrel gently up the slope. |
The kids were rolling an enormous
snowball along the ground.*

3 to push something into a small space or into something soft

stick /stɪk/ [v T] to push a sharp object into
something soft, or push something into a
small space
stick sth into/up/inside etc sth *They
stuck pins into a map to show where the
enemy camps were. | The doctor had to
stick a tube down my throat in order to
examine my stomach.*
sticking – stuck – have stuck

force /fɔːrs/ [v T] to push something into a
small space using a lot of strength
force sth into/through/down sth *She
tried to force her feet into the shoes but
they were too small. | The burglar must
have forced his hand through the window bars and reached the lock inside.*

stuff/shove /stʌf, ʃʌv/ [v T] INFORMAL to
push something quickly and carelessly into
a pocket, or bag, or a small space
stuff/shove sth into/up/down sth *She
shoved two more sweaters into her
bag. | Just before the police arrived,
Jamie stuffed the package down the side
of the sofa.*

4 to push something to operate a machine

push/press /pʊʃ, pres/ [v T] **push/press
a button** to push something that makes a
machine operate: *To send a fax, put the
paper in here, then push the red but-
ton. | It's a very easy camera to use –
just point it in the right direction and
press the shutter.*

When you see **EC**, go to the
ESSENTIAL COMMUNICATION section.

PUT

➡ see also **LIFT, MOVE 2, SPREAD 5**

1 to put something somewhere

put /pʊt/ [v T] to move something to a
place or position and leave it there
put sth in/on/there etc *Just put the bags
on the table. | I can't remember where
I put my keys.*
put sth back (=put it in the place where it
was before or where it should be) *Can you
remember to put everything back when
you've finished. | I put the letter back in
the envelope.*
put sth away (=put it where it is usually
kept) *Could you put your books away
now, please?*
put sth down/put down sth (=put something that you were holding onto a surface) *I'll have to put them down for a
minute – I'm exhausted!*
put sth up/put up sth (=fasten something
to a wall, ceiling, or in a high position) *I'm
not allowed to put up any posters in my
bedroom.*
putting – put – have put

Ostick /stɪk/ [v T] SPOKEN to put something somewhere, especially quickly or
carelessly
stick sth on/in/over sth *"Where shall I
put these groceries?" "Oh just stick them
on the table."*

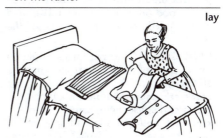
lay

lay /leɪ/ [v T] to put something on a surface
so that it is flat
lay sth on/across sth *She unfolded the
map and laid it on the table.*
lay sth out/lay out sth (=arrange something carefully on a surface) *Before you
start packing, lay out all the clothes on
the bed.*
laying – laid – have laid

P

lean /liːn/ [v T] to put something in a sloping position against something such as a wall, fence, or tree

lean sth against sth *She leaned the ladder against the wall and climbed up.*

leaning – leaned (also **leant** BRITISH) – **have leaned** (also **have leant** BRITISH)

lean

He leaned the ladder up against the wall.

hang /hæŋ/ [v T] if you **hang** clothes somewhere you put them up on a hook, door etc; if you **hang** a picture you put it on a hook or nail on the wall

hang sth on/over/in sth *The room would look better if you hung a few pictures on the walls.* | *Hang your coat over the back of the chair.*

hang

He hung his jacket up as soon as he got home.

hang sth up/hang up sth *Take off your wet clothes and hang them up to dry.*

hanging – hung – have hung

2 to put several things on top of each other

pile /paɪl/ [v T] to put a lot of things on top of each other, especially in an untidy way

pile sth on/onto/there etc *Don't pile so much food onto your plate!* | *We piled all the furniture into the middle of the room.*

stack /stæk/ [v T] to put things neatly on top of each other: *I'll start stacking the chairs.*

stack sth against/in/on sth *Unload the boxes and stack them in that corner.*

stack sth up (=put a lot of things on top of each other in a tall pile) *Dirty plates were stacked up in the sink.*

3 to put one thing onto another, so that they are joined

attach /əˈtætʃ/ [v T] to put one thing onto another and join them using pins, glue, thread etc

attach sth to sth *Attach a recent photograph to your application form.*

fix /fɪks/ [v T] to join one thing to another so that it will stay there permanently

fix sth to sth *It took me hours to fix the shelf to the wall.*

fix sth on (=join one thing onto another) *I managed to fix the top on with some glue.*

fasten /ˈfɑːsən‖ˈfæ-/ [v T] to join one thing to another, using a pin, string, rope etc, in a way that lets you remove it easily when you need to

fasten sth to sth *She fastened the badge to her dress.* | *You have to fasten the rope to a tree.*

4 to put things into a bag, box, car etc before taking them somewhere

pack

pack /pæk/ [v I/T] to put things into cases, bags, boxes etc so that you can take them somewhere: *We're going to Greece tomorrow, and I haven't started packing yet!* | *Did you remember to pack the suntan lotion?*

pack a bag/suitcase (=put things into a bag etc) *She packed her suitcase and set off for the airport.*

pack sth into sth *We packed all our books into boxes.*

load

load /ləʊd/ [v T] to put goods, furniture, or other large objects into a large vehicle so that they can be taken somewhere load sth into/onto sth *I started loading the boxes into the truck.*

5 to put equipment in a place and make it ready to be used

put in /ˌpʊt 'ɪn/ [phrasal verb T] to put a new piece of machinery or equipment into a room or building

put in sth *The landlord has promised to put in a new heating system.*

put sth in *The workmen are coming to put the new windows in today.*

putting – put – have put

install /ɪn'stɔːl/ [v T] to put a new piece of machinery or equipment into a room or building, and connect it to the electricity supply, water supply etc: *Crime has dropped since the video cameras were installed in the shopping mall.* | *The company is installing a new computer system.*

⚠ **Install** is more formal than **put in**.

fit /fɪt/ [v T] to put a new part or piece of equipment into or onto something such as a machine or car: *I had to fit new locks after the burglary.*

fit sth with sth *All the new cars are fitted with alarms.*

fit sth to sth *We decided to fit bars to the ground floor windows.*

fitting – fitted or fit – have fitted

6 to put seeds or plants in the ground

plant /plɑːnt‖plænt/ [v T] to put plants or seeds in the ground so that they can grow: *We've planted some new rose bushes in the yard this year.*

sow /səʊ/ [v I/T] to put seeds in the ground so that they can grow: *The seeds should be sown in spring.*

sowing – sowed – have sown

7 to put something under the ground

bury /'beri/ [v T often passive] if you **bury** something, you put it in a hole in the ground and put soil over it: *The bodies were buried in a nearby field.* | *Police found guns and ammunition buried in the yard.*

burying – buried – have buried

When you see **EC**, go to the **ESSENTIAL COMMUNICATION** section.

Q

QUIET

→ opposite **LOUD**
→ if you mean 'someone who does not talk much', go to **TALK 8**
→ see also **SOUND**

⚠️ Don't spell this as 'quite'. The correct spelling is **quiet**.

1 when a place is quiet

quiet /'kwaɪət/ [adj] if a place is **quiet**, there is not much noise there: *Inside the church it was quiet and peaceful.* | *David and I found a quiet corner where we could talk.*

quiet [n U] when there is little or no noise: *There was a moment of quiet before the shouting started again.*

silent /'saɪlənt/ [adj] WRITTEN if a place is **silent**, there is no noise at all: *The streets of the city were silent in the moonlight.* | *Apart from the humming of the bees, all was silent and still.*

⚠️ Don't say 'very silent'. Say **completely silent**.

⚠️ Use **silent** especially in stories or descriptions of events.

peaceful /'piːsfəl/ [adj] if a place is **peaceful**, it makes you feel calm and relaxed because there is no unpleasant noise or activity: *It was so peaceful in the garden that Philip almost forgot about his problems.* | *a quiet peaceful valley*

silence /'saɪləns/ [n C/U] when there are no sounds at all: *Nothing disturbed the silence of the night.* | *There was a long silence before anyone answered.*

peace /piːs/ [n U] when there is no unpleasant noise or activity, so you can feel calm and relaxed: *The square was a little oasis of peace, only minutes from the heart of the city.*

peace and quiet *I'm going to my room for a bit of peace and quiet.*

2 when music, sounds, or voices are quiet

quiet /'kwaɪət/ [adj] **quiet** sounds, voices, or music are not loud: *He spoke in a quiet yet confident voice.* | *There was a quiet knock at the door.*

quietly [adv] *We were talking quietly so as not to wake the baby.*

low /ləʊ/ [adj] a **low** voice or sound is quiet and deep: *A low humming noise was coming from the refrigerator.*

in a low voice (=speaking quietly) *'Take care,' he said in a low voice.*

soft /sɒft‖sɔːft/ [adj] **soft** sounds, voices, or music are quiet, gentle, and pleasant: *He spoke with a soft Irish accent.* | *a whisper so soft that I could scarcely hear it*

softly [adv] *Music was playing softly in the background.*

3 when people or machines are quiet

quiet /'kwaɪət/ [adj] if someone or something is **quiet**, they make little or no noise: *I want you all to be very quiet and listen carefully.* | *Our new washing machine is much quieter than the old one.*

quietly [adv] *The children were reading quietly at their desks.*

silent /'saɪlənt/ [adj] WRITTEN not making any sound at all: *The engine is almost silent.* | *The children remained silent and watchful as the police questioned their parents.*

fall silent (=stop talking) *The crowd fell silent as he stood up to speak.*

silently [adv] *Silently, the mist crept closer.*

⚠️ Use **silent** especially in stories or descriptions of events.

in silence /ɪn 'saɪləns/ ESPECIALLY WRITTEN if you do something **in silence**, you do it without speaking: *Thousands of protesters stood in silence outside the prison gates.* | *We drank our coffee in silence.*

in total/complete silence *The two of them walked all the way to Matilda's house in complete silence.*

⚠ Use **in silence** especially in stories or descriptions of events.

not make a sound /nɒt ˌmeɪk ə ˈsaʊnd/ to not make any noise at all: *Sit still and don't make a sound.*

without making a sound *She managed to get into the house without making a sound.*

4 to become quieter

go quiet /gəʊ ˈkwaɪət/ to stop speaking or making any noise at all, for example because you are shocked or embarrassed: *Laurie went very quiet after Jo told him how she felt.*

fade away /ˌfeɪd əˈweɪ/ [phrasal verb I] if a sound **fades away**, it gradually becomes quieter until you cannot hear it any more: *The sound of a police siren was slowly fading away into the distance.*

lower your voice /ˌləʊə^r jɔː^r ˈvɔɪs/ to speak more quietly because you do not want other people to hear what you are saying: *Kath lowered her voice so that Mike wouldn't hear.*

5 to make someone or something quieter

quieten sb down BRITISH **quiet sb down** AMERICAN /ˌkwaɪətn (sb) ˈdaʊn, ˌkwaɪət (sb) ˈdaʊn/ [phrasal verb T] to make someone quieter and calmer, when they are making a lot of noise because they are angry or upset: *I spent half the lesson trying to quieten them down.* | *Sue managed to quiet us both down and stop us arguing.*

silence /ˈsaɪləns/ [v T] FORMAL to make someone suddenly stop speaking: *Mrs Talbot silenced me with an angry look.*

⚠ Use **silence** when you are writing stories.

shut sb up /ˌʃʌt (sb) ˈʌp/ [phrasal verb T] INFORMAL to make someone stop talking, especially by speaking to them rudely or angrily: *Can't you shut those kids up?* | *The only way to shut her up is to give her something to eat.*

6 what you say to someone to tell them to be quiet

⌕ssh /ʃ/ SPOKEN say **ssh** when you want someone to speak more quietly or make less noise: *Ssh, keep the noise down, Timmy's asleep.*

⌕shut up /ˌʃʌt ˈʌp/ SPOKEN INFORMAL a rude way of telling someone to stop talking: *Just shut up, will you?*

⚠ Only use **shut up** with people you know very well. It is not polite.

⌕be quiet /biː ˈkwaɪət/ SPOKEN say **be quiet** to tell someone to stop talking or to make less noise, especially when you are annoyed with them: *'Be quiet, James!' she snapped.*

R

RACE

one of the main groups of people in the world, who have the same colour of skin and physical appearance

➡ if you mean 'a sports race', go to **SPORT 2**

1 race

race /reɪs/ [n C/U] one of the main groups of people in the world, who have the same colour of skin and physical appearance as each other: *People should be treated equally, regardless of their race, age, or sex.* | *people of all races and religions*
race relations (=the relationship between people of different races) *The group is working to improve race relations in our cities.*

> ⚠ Use **race** to talk about people of the same colour and physical type. To talk about people who have the same history, language, customs etc use **nation**.

ethnic /'eθnɪk/ [adj only before noun]
ethnic group/community/minority a group from one race or country living in a place where many of the people are different from them: *The city's population includes a wide range of different ethnic groups.*
ethnic origin/background (=the ethnic group that someone belongs to) *fighting in Bosnia between people from different ethnic backgrounds*

2 when people are treated badly because of their race

racism /'reɪsɪzəm/ [n U] unfair treatment of people because of their race: *The company has been accused of racism after firing three Algerian workers.* | *the struggle against racism in our society.*

racial /'reɪʃəl/ [adj only before noun]
racial discrimination/prejudice/violence/attack when people are treated unfairly or attacked because of their race: *Some people complained of racial discrimination in the way housing was allocated.* | *Racial attacks are relatively uncommon.*

racist /'reɪsɪst/ [adj] **racist** statements, jokes, behaviour, or opinions are based on a dislike of people from other races and a feeling that your race is better than others: *racist attitudes* | *a comedian well known for his racist and sexist jokes*
racist [n C] someone who has racist opinions: *Kamal had been attacked by a gang of white racists.*

3 including people from several races

multiracial/multicultural /ˌmʌlti-'reɪʃəl, ˌmʌlti 'kʌltʃərəl/ [adj only before noun] **multiracial society/school/community** a society, school etc where people from several different races live together or work together, especially in a friendly way: *a school providing a multi-cultural environment* | *a multiracial neighbourhood*

REACH

1 when something is long or high enough to reach something

reach /riːtʃ/ [v I/T] to be long enough, high enough, or deep enough to get to a particular place or point: *The snow was very deep and it almost reached my knees.* | *You see, the paint doesn't quite reach the edge of the paper.* | *a long ladder reaching as far as the third floor*

stretch /stretʃ/ [v I] if a river, road, or area of land **stretches** to a place that is far away, it continues as far as that place
+ into/to *The highway stretched into the distance.*
+ as far as *There were poppy fields stretching as far as the eye could see.*

> ⚠ **Stretch** is used especially in stories and descriptions.

2 when a number reaches a particular level

reach /riːtʃ/ [v T] if a number or amount **reaches** a particular level, it increases or decreases until it gets to that level: *Gold prices have reached their lowest level for 15 years.* | *Inflation continued to rise, reaching a peak of 28%.*

reach $500/100 kph etc *a car which can reach 140 mph*

hit /hɪt/ [v T] to reach a very high or very low level: *The temperature hit 40°C in parts of the country yesterday.* | *As oil production increased, prices hit an all-time low.*

hitting – hit – have hit

⚠️ **Hit** is used especially in newspaper and television reports.

3 when someone can reach something

reach /riːtʃ/ [v I/T] to be able to touch something or take hold of it, by stretching your arm or moving your body: *Can you get that cup down for me? I can't reach.* | *She can reach the top shelf if she stands on a chair.*

reach

4 to reach a place that you are travelling to

➡ see also **ARRIVE, TRAVEL, JOURNEY**

reach /riːtʃ/ [v T] to arrive at a place, especially after a long or difficult journey: *We didn't reach the hotel until midnight.* | *In winter, some parts of Northern Canada can only be reached by plane.*

⚠️ Don't say 'we reached at the hotel' or 'we reached to Paris'. Say **we reached the hotel** or **we reached Paris**.

Ϙ **get** /get/ [v I] ESPECIALLY SPOKEN if you **get** to a place, you reach it

+ to *By the time we got to York, it was pouring with rain.*

+ home/here/there *What time did you get home?*

+ as far as *We only got as far as the end of the road, then the car broke down.*

getting – got – have got (BRITISH) **– have gotten** (AMERICAN)

Ϙ **make it** /'meɪk ɪt/ ESPECIALLY SPOKEN to arrive at a place, especially when you were not sure that you would be able to get there: *The weather looked so bad that I wasn't sure we would make it.* | *If we run, we should be able to make it before the bus leaves.*

+ to/across/home etc *He couldn't swim, but somehow he managed to make it to the side of the pool.*

READ

➡ see also **BOOKS/LITERATURE, NEWSPAPERS AND MAGAZINES**

1 to read something

read /riːd/ [v I/T] *Read the instructions carefully before you start.* | *Have you read 'A Tale of Two Cities'?* | *Don't believe everything you read in the newspapers.*

+ about *Did you read about that terrible car crash?*

read to sb/read sb a story (=read something aloud, so that people can listen) *Our mother used to read to us every evening.*

+ that *Steve was amazed when he read that his sister had won a prize*

reading – read – have read

  reading [n U] the skill or activity of reading: *Children are taught reading and writing in their first years at school.* | *I like to do a lot of reading when I'm on vacation.*

  reader [n C] someone who reads something: *The newspaper is trying to attract more women readers.*

read out /ˌriːd 'aʊt/ [phrasal verb T] to read something and say the words so that people can hear it, especially the words or numbers that are written in a message, list etc

read out sth *He opened the envelope and read out the name of the winner.*

read sth out *Read the numbers out and I'll write them down.*

read sth out to sb *Sarah left a message – I'll read it out to you.*

browse through sth /ˈbraʊz θruː (sth)/ [*phrasal verb* T] to turn the pages of a magazine or book, stopping to read parts that interest you: *I was browsing through the magazines at the station bookstall when I noticed Susan.*

read through/read over /ˈriːd θruː, ˈriːd əʊvəʳ/ [*phrasal verb* T] to read something carefully from beginning to end, in order to check details or find mistakes
read through/over sth *Always read through what you have written before you leave the exam room.*
read sth through/over *Before you sign the contract, read it through carefully.*

2 to be able to read

can read /kən ˈriːd/ *Tom is only four and he can read already.* | *Two hundred years ago, few ordinary people could read or write.*

literate /ˈlɪtərɪt/ [*adj*] someone who is **literate** can read and write – use this about adults or older children: *People have become healthier, more literate, and better educated.* | *Every student should be literate by the time he or she leaves primary school.*
   literacy /ˈlɪtərəsi/ [*n* U] the ability to read and write: *a program to improve standards of literacy*

3 to not be able to read

can't read /ˌkɑːnt ˈriːd‖ˌkænt-/ *We run courses to help adults who can't read.* | *Of course she can't read – she's only 3!*

illiterate /ɪˈlɪtərɪt/ [*adj*] someone who is **illiterate** cannot read or write – use this about adults or older children: *His father was an illiterate farm worker.* | *If 70% of the population is illiterate, how do people know who they are voting for?*

4 writing that is easy to read

legible /ˈledʒɪbəl/ [*adj*] written clearly enough for you to read: *Is the date on the coin still legible?* | *Her writing was so tiny that it was barely legible.*

5 writing that is impossible to read

can't read sth /ˌkɑːnt ˈriːd (sth)‖ˌkænt-/ *I can't read your handwriting – it's so messy.*

illegible /ɪˈledʒɪbəl/ [*adj*] writing that is **illegible** is impossible to read because it is not clear: *I don't know what this note says – Dad's handwriting is totally illegible!* | *The label had got wet and was now illegible.*

READY/NOT READY

➡ see also **PREPARE, HURRY**

1 when you are ready to do something

ready /ˈredi/ [*adj* not before noun] if you are **ready** for something, you have done everything that needs to be done in order to prepare for it: *Are you ready? The taxi's here.* | *When everyone is ready, I will give the signal to start.*
ready to do sth *Everything is packed and we're ready to leave.*
+ for *I don't want to take the test until I'm ready for it.*
get ready (=prepare yourself to do something) *We have to leave in 10 minutes, so you'd better go and get ready.* | *We've spent the last few days getting ready for Christmas.* | *Get ready to start the engine when I tell you.*

⚠ We often use **get ready** to mean 'get washed and dressed in the right clothes': *I got ready for bed.* | *She's getting ready to go out.*

prepared /prɪˈpeəʳd/ [*adj* not before noun] ready to deal with a situation, because you were expecting it or because you have made careful preparations
+ for *The police were prepared for trouble.* | *I was not prepared for all those questions.*
well prepared *When the storm came, we were well prepared.*

2 ready to be used or eaten

ready /'redi/ [adj not before noun] if something is **ready**, you can use it or eat it immediately: *I'll let you know when lunch is ready.* | *When the pasta is ready, add the sauce.* | *Your suit will be ready on Wednesday, sir.* | *I'm sorry, your car isn't ready yet.*

ready to eat/drink/wear etc *In a year's time the wine will be ready to drink.*
+ for *Is everything ready for the party?*
get sth ready (=prepare it) *They were getting the boat ready for a long voyage.*

ripe /raɪp/ [adj] ready to eat – use this about fruit that has been on the plant for long enough: *The apples were ripe and juicy.* | *Is this melon ripe enough to eat?*

REAL

➡ see also FALSE, NATURAL, IMAGINE

1 not false or artificial

real /rɪəl/ [adj] not false or artificial: *That's a nice watch – is it real gold?* | *Are those flowers real or artificial?* | *Sinbad's not his real name.*

genuine /'dʒenjuɪn/ [adj] real, not just seeming to be real or pretending to be real: *For years people thought the picture was a genuine Van Gogh, but in fact it's a fake.* | *a system for dealing with genuine refugees*

authentic /ɔː'θentɪk/ [adj] **authentic** food, music, clothes etc are correct for the place or the period in history that they are supposed to be from: *a friendly restaurant offering authentic Greek food* | *They play music on authentic medieval instruments.*

2 not imagined or invented

real /rɪəl/ [adj only before noun] actually existing, and not just imagined or invented: *There are some real advantages to the system.* | *Children often think that fairies are real.*

in real life (=not in a story, film, or your imagination) *Many great comic actors are anxious and depressed in real life.*

actual /'æktʃuəl/ [adj] real – use this especially to compare how something really is with what you expected it to be or intended it to be: *How does the actual cost compare with the original estimate?* | *The actual number of people without jobs is much higher than the government claims.*

actually [adv] *He looks quite young, but he's actually about 50.*

3 when someone really feels something

really /'rɪəli/ [adv] when you **really** feel something, **really** want something etc, and you are not just pretending to feel it: *Do you think she's really sorry?* | *Do you really want to come with us? It'll be very boring for you.* | *He talks about wanting equality, but I don't think he really believes it himself.*

sincere /sɪn'sɪər/ [adj] if you are **sincere**, or have **sincere** feelings, you really care about something, want something, or feel sorry about something: *a sincere wish for peace*
+ in *They seemed to be sincere in their concern for the children's welfare.*
sincere thanks/apologies FORMAL *I would like to express my sincere thanks to all those who helped us.*

sincerely [adv] *I believe they sincerely want to find a peaceful solution to the dispute.*

genuine /'dʒenjuɪn/ [adj] **genuine** feelings are real and not pretended – use this especially when you are surprised that someone has these feelings: *I'm not sure if her sympathy was really genuine.* | *a genuine attempt to improve relations between the two countries*

genuinely [adv] *He seemed genuinely interested in our work.*

4 pictures/books that make things seem real

realistic /rɪə'lɪstɪk/ [adj] use this about books, pictures, and films that show or describe things as they really are: *I loved the drawings, they were so realistic.* | *The documentary gave a very realistic account of the war.*

lifelike /ˈlaɪflaɪk/ [adj] use this about pictures and models that look very like the real person or thing: *On the shelf was a very lifelike plastic bird.*

REALIZE

to notice or understand something that you did not notice or understand before

R

➡ see also **UNDERSTAND/NOT UNDERSTAND, NOTICE, KNOW/NOT KNOW**

realize (also **realise** BRITISH) /ˈrɪəlaɪz/ [v I/T] to notice or understand something that you did not notice or understand before: *Tim only realized his mistake the next day.* | *Without realising it, we had gone the wrong way.* | *Oh, is that your chair? Sorry, I didn't realize.*
+ (that) *She woke up and realised that there was someone moving around downstairs* | *I never realized you were from Rome!*
realize how/what/why etc *I'm sorry, I didn't realize how upset you were about all this.*

occur to sb /əˈkɜːr tuː (sb)/ [phrasal verb T] if something **occurs to you**, you suddenly realize that it may be true
it occurs to sb that *It suddenly occurred to me that maybe she was lying.* | *Didn't it ever occur to you that they would probably like to be alone together?*
occurring – occurred – have occurred

become aware /bɪˌkʌm əˈweər/ ESPECIALLY WRITTEN to gradually begin to realize that something is happening or is true
+ of *I was slowly becoming aware of how much Melissa was suffering.*
+ that *He became aware that the man sitting opposite was staring at him intently.*

sink in /ˌsɪŋk ˈɪn/ [phrasal verb I] if a new piece of information **sinks in**, you gradually understand it and realize how important, serious, or good it is: *The news of the President's assassination had only just begun to sink in.* | *"How do you feel about winning this award?" "It hasn't really sunk in yet."*

dawn on sb /ˈdɔːn ɒn (sb)‖-ɑːn-/ [phrasal verb T] if a fact **dawns on you**, you slowly begin to realize it, especially something that you should have realized before: *The awful truth only dawned on me later.*
it dawns on sb that *It slowly dawned on her that they were all making fun of her.*

REASON

➡ see also **CAUSE, PURPOSE**

1 why something happens or why someone does something

reason /ˈriːzən/ [n C] what makes something happen, or what makes someone do something: *"Why didn't Mike come to the party?" "I don't know, but there must be a reason."*
+ for *The reason for the price rise was the increase in the cost of materials.*
reason for doing sth *What was your reason for leaving your last job?*
reason why *There's no reason why Johnnie can't come with us.*
+ (that) *The only reason she didn't win was that she had injured her knee.*
for personal/health/business etc reasons *For security reasons, there were video cameras at the school entrance.*
for some reason ESPECIALLY SPOKEN (=for a reason that you do not know or understand) *No, he isn't here – he had to go back to Poland for some reason.*

⚠ Don't say 'the reason of something'. Say **the reason for something**: *What was the reason for her strange behaviour?*

explanation /ˌekspləˈneɪʃən/ [n C] a fact, statement, or idea that helps you to understand why something has happened: *I don't know where your bike is. The only explanation I can think of is that someone borrowed it.*
+ for *What is the explanation for these changes in climate?*

motive /ˈməʊtɪv/ [n C] the reason that makes someone decide to do something, especially something bad or dishonest
+ for *Police believe the motive for the murder was jealousy.*

motive for doing sth *What was her real motive for phoning me?*

2 why something is right or should be done

reason /ˈriːzən/ [n C/U] a fact that makes it right or fair for someone to do something

reason why *The reason why we need these laws is to protect children from violent adults.*

reason to do sth *I can think of lots of reasons to get married.*

with good reason (=when it is right or fair that someone does something) *The school is proud of its record, and with good reason.*

that's no reason to do sth *I know I'm late but that's no reason to shout at me.*

argument /ˈɑːᵊgjᵿmənt/ [n C] one of the reasons that someone uses to try to persuade someone to agree with them

+ that *the argument that violence on TV makes people behave violently*

+ for/against (=a reason why something should or should not be done) *What are the arguments for the legalization of cannabis?*

argument for/against doing sth *The main argument against smoking is that it's bad for your health.*

justification /ˌdʒʌstɪ̯fɪ̯ˈkeɪʃən/ [n C/U] a reason that someone gives for doing something that seems wrong to most people: *She had her residence permit taken away, without any justification.*

+ for *There's no justification for cruelty.*

justification for doing sth *What justification can there be for paying women lower wages?*

3 a reason explaining why you did something wrong

excuse /ɪkˈskjuːs/ [n C] something that you say to try to explain why you did something bad, so that people will forgive you: *Oh shut up Bill, I'm tired of listening to your excuses.*

excuse for doing sth *"What's your excuse for being late?" "My alarm clock didn't go off, so I overslept."*

explanation /ˌekspləˈneɪʃən/ [n C] something that you say which gives good reasons

for something wrong which you have done: *This work should have been finished a week ago. What's your explanation?*

+ for *He offered no explanation for his absence at the previous day's meeting.*

4 to tell someone the reason for something

say why/tell sb why /ˌseɪ ˈwaɪ, ˌtel (sb) ˈwaɪ/ to tell someone why something happened: *I knew she was annoyed, but she wouldn't say why.* | *Can anyone tell us why there are no buses today?*

explain /ɪkˈspleɪn/ [v I/T] to tell someone the reason for something, so that they understand the situation better: *She just doesn't like me. How else can you explain her behaviour?* | *I don't have time to explain now – just come with me quickly!*

explain why/how/what etc *Doctors are unable to explain why the disease spread so quickly.*

+ that *Sarah explained that she hadn't been feeling well recently.*

+ to *It was difficult explaining to the children why their father was leaving home.*

⚠ Don't say 'he explained me it', 'he explained me why he left' etc. Say **he explained it to me, he explained why he left** etc.

give a reason /ˌgɪv ə ˈriːzən/ to tell someone why you are doing something, especially something surprising: *"He says he's not coming." "Oh, did he give a reason?"*

give sb a reason *The landlord told us we had to go, but we were never given any reason.*

5 to be the reason why something happened

be the reason /biː ðə ˈriːzən/ to be the reason why something happened or why someone did something

+ for *Nick's teachers think that problems at home are the reason for his poor schoolwork.*

be the reason why/(that) *He borrowed too much money, and that's the main reason why his business failed.*

R

explain /ɪkˈspleɪn/ [v T] if a fact or situation **explains** something, it helps you to understand why it happened: *We were all puzzled: what could explain his sudden change of mind?*

explain why/what/how *Mark couldn't sleep last night, which explains why he was in such a bad mood this morning.*

account for sth /əˈkaʊnt fɔːʳ (sth)/ [phrasal verb T] FORMAL to be the reason that explains why something strange or surprising happened: *If it's true that he was taking drugs, that would account for his strange mood swings.*

RECENTLY

➡ see also **GRAMMAR 6**

1 a short time ago

recently /ˈriːsəntli/ [adv] if something happened **recently**, it happened a short time before now, especially a few days or weeks ago: *The President has recently returned from a five-day tour of South America.*

only recently *I only recently started eating meat again.*

until recently *He lived in Boston until quite recently.*

very recently *"When did she go back to Italy?" "Oh, very recently – just a couple of days ago."*

recently discovered/completed/built etc *a recently published textbook*

just /dʒʌst/ [adv] very recently, for example only a few minutes, hours, or days ago: *I've just heard that Julie's getting married.*

only just *You haven't missed much of the show – it's only just started.*

just this minute (=a moment ago) *"Where's Karen?" "I saw her leaving the building just this minute."*

> ⚠ In British English, use the present perfect tense with **just**: *They have just arrived.* Notice that **just** comes between 'have' and the main verb. In American English, use the simple past tense with **just**: *They just arrived.*

not long ago /nɒt ˈlɒŋ əˈɡəʊ‖-ˈlɔːŋ-/ use this especially about something that seems quite recent, although it actually happened quite a long time ago: *Now the French are saying they oppose nuclear testing, but not long ago they were carrying out tests themselves.*

not so long ago/not very long ago *Not so long ago, India and Pakistan were one country.*

a minute ago/a moment ago /ə ˈmɪnɪt əˈɡəʊ, ə ˈməʊmənt əˈɡəʊ/ a few minutes ago: *Michael was looking for you a moment ago.* | *What did I do with my glasses? I had them in my hand a minute ago.*

2 when something has been happening during the recent period

recently /ˈriːsəntli/ [adv] use this to say that something has been happening for a few weeks or months, and it is still happening now: *Her schoolwork has been much better recently.*

just recently *Just recently I've been thinking about changing my job.*

lately /ˈleɪtli/ [adv] recently – used especially in questions and negative sentences: *Have you done any painting lately?*

just lately BRITISH *Gerry hasn't been feeling very well just lately.*

> ⚠ **Lately** is more informal than **recently**.

in the last few days/weeks/months/ years /ɪn ðə ˈlɑːst fjuː (days etc)‖-læst-/ during the days, weeks, months, or years closest to now: *We've had very little rain in the last few months.* | *Crimes against elderly people have risen sharply in the last few years.*

3 something that happened recently

recent /ˈriːsənt/ [adj] use this about something that happened recently, especially a few days or weeks ago: *He hadn't completely recovered from his recent illness.* | *A recent report said that small amounts of alcohol were good for the health.*

in recent weeks/months/years *She's had a lot of problems at school, but in recent weeks things have improved.*

latest /'leɪt̬st/ [adj only before noun] someone's latest book, record, film etc is the one produced most recently; the latest news reports etc include all the newest information: *In her latest movie she plays an LA cop.*
the latest news *What's the latest news from home?*

REFUSE

➡ look here for ...
• refuse to do something
• say no when someone offers you something
• not accept someone for a job or course

➡ see also ☞ **SAYING NO**

1 to say that you will not do something
➡ opposite **AGREE**

refuse /rɪ'fjuːz/ [v I/T] to tell someone firmly that you will not do what they asked you to do: *I'm sure if you ask her to help you, she won't refuse.*
refuse to do sth *If they refuse to leave, call the police.*
flatly refuse (=refuse very firmly) *Mother flatly refused to see the doctor.*
refuse sb sth (=refuse to give them something) *The US authorities refused him a visa.*

refusal /rɪ'fjuːzəl/ [n C/U] when someone refuses to do something that they have been asked to do: *He was upset by her refusal.* | *a polite refusal*
refusal to do sth *his refusal to admit that he was wrong* | *Refusal to do military service was a criminal offence.*

⚠ Don't say 'refusal of doing something'.

Q**say no** /ˌseɪ 'nəʊ/ ESPECIALLY SPOKEN to tell someone that you will not do what they asked you to do: *I asked Dad to lend me some money, but he said no.*
+ to *They asked me so nicely, I couldn't really say no to them.*

Q**will not/won't** /ˌwɪl 'nɒt, wəʊnt/ ESPE-CIALLY SPOKEN if someone **will not** or **won't** do something that they have been asked to do or told to do, they are deter-mined not to do it: *He's so naughty – he won't do what I tell him.* | *I simply will not sign the contract unless they offer me more money.*

⚠ **Will not** is stronger and more definite than **won't**.

Q**I'm not prepared to do sth** /aɪm ˌnɒt prɪˌpeə'd tə 'duː (sth)/ SPOKEN say this to emphasize that you refuse to do some-thing, and that you think it is wrong or unfair that anyone expects you to do it: *I'm not prepared to help her if she just criticizes me all the time.* | *The landlord says that he is not prepared to pay for the repairs.*

2 to say no when someone makes an offer or suggestion
➡ opposite **ACCEPT**

refuse /rɪ'fjuːz/ [v T] to say you do not want something that you have been offered: *Their offer is too good to refuse.* | *He never refuses a drink, does he?*

not accept sth /nɒt ək'sept (sth)/ to say no to an offer or invitation, because you think it would not be right to accept it: *She's given us all this stuff and she won't accept any money for it.* | *I decided not to accept their invitation.*

Q**say no** /ˌseɪ 'nəʊ/ ESPECIALLY SPOKEN to say no when someone makes an offer or suggestion: *I asked him if he wanted a drink, but he said no.* | *I'll offer to buy it from her, but I expect she'll say no.*
+ to *John's so unhelpful – he just says no to everything I suggest.*

reject /rɪ'dʒekt/ [v T] to say no very firmly to an offer or suggestion, especially in a way that seems rude or unhelpful: *Sarah rejected her parents' offer of financial help.* | *The government has rejected the latest ceasefire proposals from the rebels.*

⚠ **Reject** is more formal than **not accept** and **say no**.

R

turn down /ˌtɜːʳn ˈdaʊn/ [phrasal verb T] to say no to an offer – use this especially when someone refuses a good offer or opportunity, and this is surprising

turn sth/sb down *They offered her a really good job, but she turned it down.*

turn down sth/sb *If you turn down the opportunity to go to college, you'll always regret it.*

3 to refuse to give someone a job, a chance to study etc

reject/turn down /rɪˈdʒekt, ˌtɜːʳn ˈdaʊn/ [v T] to officially tell someone that you will not offer them the job or the chance to study at college which they asked for: *Ian was rejected by the army because of his bad eyesight.*

turn sb down *I applied to six different colleges but they all turned me down.*

turn down sb *We turn down any candidate who makes a spelling mistake on their application.*

⚠ Reject is more formal than turn down.

rejection /rɪˈdʒekʃən/ [n C/U] when a company, college etc tells someone they cannot have the job or the chance to study which they asked for: *You'll have to expect a lot of rejections if you want to work in TV.*

REGULAR

➡ see also USUALLY, SOMETIMES, OFTEN

1 when you do something regularly, or something happens regularly

regularly /ˈregjʊləʳli/ [adv] if you do something **regularly**, you do it on many different occasions, usually with the same amount of time in between: *Bryan and Martha regularly play golf together, about twice a month.* | *Don't forget to take your medicine regularly.*

regular /ˈregjʊləʳ/ [adj usually before noun] a **regular** event or activity happens every hour, every week, every month etc, usually with the same amount of time in

between: *It's important to visit your dentist for regular check-ups.* | *The Parent-Teacher Association has regular meetings – usually one every month.* | *She needs regular injections of insulin.*

on a regular basis (=regularly) *We give our students tests on a regular basis.*

at regular intervals (=with equal amounts of time between) *The prison is inspected at regular intervals by government health officers.*

every day/every week/every year etc /evri (day, etc)/ *Marilyn cycles to work every day.* | *Every Sunday we go to my mother's for lunch.* | *They bring out a new record about every six months.*

⚠ Don't spell this as 'everyday'. The correct spelling is as two separate words: **every day**: *I phoned her every day.*

hourly/daily/weekly/monthly etc [adj only before noun] happening every hour, every day etc: *There are daily flights to Frankfurt.* | *a weekly current affairs TV show* | *a monthly magazine*

hourly/daily etc [adv] *The news is broadcast hourly on Network Five.* | *Do you get paid monthly or weekly?*

every 5 miles/every 3 kilometres etc /evri (5 miles, etc)/ happening regularly after a particular distance: *You should change the oil every 7000 kilometres.* | *After every 100 yards, Grandpa had to stop and sit down.*

2 not regularly

every now and then/every so often /ˌevri ˌnaʊ ənd ˈðen, ˌevri səʊ ˈɒfən‖-ˈɔːfən/ sometimes, but not very often and not regularly: *Chris goes to visit his mother in Paris every now and then.* | *Every so often the silence was broken by the sound of gunfire.*

on and off /ˌɒn ənd ˈɒf‖ˌɑːn ənd ˈɔːf/ ESPECIALLY SPOKEN if you do something **on and off** during a long period, you do it for short periods but not regularly: *I've been trying to learn Spanish on and off for the past five years.*

When you see **EC**, go to the **ESSENTIAL COMMUNICATION** section.

RELATIONSHIP

the way that people or groups
behave and feel towards each other

FRIEND　　MARRY

see
also

FAMILY　　SEX

GIRLFRIEND/BOYFRIEND

1 the relationship between two people or groups

relationship /rɪ'leɪʃənʃɪp/ [n C] the way that two people or groups feel about each other and behave towards each other
+ with His relationship with his parents had never been very good.
+ between the relationship between doctor and patient
a close relationship (=when you know someone very well and like them a lot) They'd known each other for years and had a very close relationship.

⚠ Don't say 'relationship to someone'. Say **relationship with someone**.

relations /rɪ'leɪʃənz/ [n plural] the public relationship between groups, organizations, or countries, especially when this affects how well they work together
+ between Relations between management and workers have improved.
+ with Will this dispute damage our relations with the United States?
race relations (=between people of different races)
diplomatic relations (=between the governments of two countries) New Zealand broke off diplomatic relations with France because of the nuclear tests.
industrial relations BRITISH **labor relations** AMERICAN (=between workers and managers)

⚠ Use **relationship** especially to talk about the personal relationship between two people. Use **relations** especially to talk about the public, working relationship between large groups, countries etc.

2 when you have a good relationship

have a good relationship /hæv ə ˌgʊd rɪ'leɪʃənʃɪp/ when two people or groups are friendly towards each other and work well together: My boss and I have a very good relationship.
+ with It's important that the school has a good relationship with the students' parents.

get along (also **get on** BRITISH) /get ə'lɒŋ, get 'ɒn‖-ə'lɔːŋ, -'ɑːn/ [phrasal verb I] if people **get along** or **get on**, they have a friendly relationship with each other: We all get on really well, so we're going to share a flat next year.
+ with He's very easy to get along with.

⚠ **Get along** and **get on** are more informal than **have a good relationship**.

be on good terms /biː ɒn gʊd 'tɜːmz/ if people are **on good terms**, they have a polite relationship and they can work well together, but they are not close friends: The members of the band were on good terms, but they never spent much time together socially.
+ with We're on good terms with all our neighbours.

close /kləʊs/ [adj] if two or more people are **close**, they like each other very much, and can talk to each other about their feelings, their problems etc: Dad and I have always been very close. | close friends from my schooldays
+ to She was never very close to her stepmother.

3 when you have a bad relationship

not get along (also **not get on** BRITISH) /nɒt get ə'lɒŋ, nɒt get 'ɒn‖-ə'lɔːŋ, -'ɑːn/ if people do **not get along** or do **not get on**, they have a bad relationship and they often argue and disagree with each other: Barney and I just don't get along.
+ with He's not getting on very well with his new boss.

fall out /ˌfɔːl 'aʊt/ [phrasal verb I] BRITISH if friends or relatives **fall out**, they have an argument and stop being friendly with

R

each other: *They fell out last year, and they won't even speak to each other now.*
+ with *He's fallen out with his girlfriend again.*

4 when a relationship ends

split up /ˌsplɪt ˈʌp/ [*phrasal verb* I] INFORMAL if people who are married or having a romantic relationship **split up**, they end their relationship: *Steve's parents split up when he was four.*
+ with *Have you heard? Tim's split up with his girlfriend.*

separate /ˈsepəreɪt/ [*v* I] if people who are married **separate**, they stop living together: *It's the children who suffer when their parents separate.*
    separation /ˌsepəˈreɪʃən/ [*n* C/U] when a husband and wife agree to live apart: *So many marriages end in separation or divorce.*

get divorced /ˌget dɪˈvɔːrst/ if people who are married **get divorced**, they officially end their marriage by means of a legal process: *They got divorced only two years after they were married.*
    divorce [*n* C/U] the legal process of ending a marriage: *About a third of marriages in Britain end in divorce.*

breakup /ˈbreɪkʌp/ [*n* C/U] when a marriage or romantic relationship ends: *the effects of marital breakup on children*

RELAX

➡ see also **REST, WORRYING/WORRIED**

1 to make yourself feel calmer and more comfortable

relax /rɪˈlæks/ [*v* I] to make yourself feel calmer, more comfortable, and less worried, by resting or doing something enjoyable: *Just wait! In two weeks time I'll be relaxing on a beach in Greece.* | *Trained staff will look after your children, so that you can relax and enjoy yourself.* | *Relax! It'll be okay.*

When you see **EC**, go to the **ESSENTIAL COMMUNICATION** section.

⚠ Don't say 'relax yourself'. Just say **relax**.

unwind /ʌnˈwaɪnd/ [*v* I] to gradually relax after you have been working hard or worrying a lot: *A hot bath is a pleasant way to unwind.* | *I need a drink to help me unwind.*
unwinding – unwound – have unwound

2 feeling calm and comfortable

relaxed /rɪˈlækst/ [*adj*] feeling calm, comfortable, and not worried or annoyed: *How can you be so relaxed when you have an interview tomorrow?* | *Gail was lying in the sun looking very relaxed.*

laid-back /ˌleɪd ˈbæk◄/ [*adj*] INFORMAL someone who is **laid-back** always seems relaxed, and does not easily get worried or annoyed: *My parents are pretty laid-back and don't mind me staying out late.* | *She seems to have a fairly laid-back attitude to life.*

3 making you feel calm and comfortable

relaxing /rɪˈlæksɪŋ/ [*adj*] making you feel calm, comfortable, and not worried: *We had a lovely holiday – it was very relaxing.* | *a relaxing massage*

WORD BANK

RELIGION

1 a religion or a religious group

religion /rɪˈlɪdʒən/ [*n* C] a set of beliefs that a group of people has about a god, and the ceremonies, customs, and rules that go with these beliefs: *a book about the religion of ancient Egypt* | *"What religion are you?" "I'm a Christian."* | *one of the great world religions*

faith /feɪθ/ [*n* C] a religion, especially one of the large important world religions: *People of all faiths are welcome to come to our church.*
the Jewish / Christian / Islamic / Hindu faith *Most of the island's population belong to the Islamic faith.*

sect /sekt/ [n C] a religious group that is part of a larger religious group, and has its own beliefs and ceremonies: *Islam has two main sects: the Sunnis and the Shias.* | *The Quakers are a Christian religious sect who strongly oppose violence and war.*

church /tʃɜːrtʃ/ [n C] a religious group that is part of the Christian religion: *Which church do you belong to?* | *a meeting of church leaders* | *The Pope is the head of the Catholic Church.*

cult /kʌlt/ [n C] a small religious group which is not part of one of the main world religions, especially a group that has very unusual ideas which they believe very strongly: *Several members of the cult were found dead in a forest in France.*

2 religions in general

religion /rɪˈlɪdʒən/ [n U] religions and religious beliefs and activities in general, for example as a subject that people talk about or study: *They spent hours discussing politics and religion.* | *Discrimination on the grounds of religion is strictly forbidden by law.*

⚠ When you are talking about religions in general, don't say 'the religion'. Just say **religion**.

3 things that you believe because of your religion

beliefs /bɪˈliːfs/ [n plural] all the ideas that someone believes because of their religion: *They were persecuted because of their religious beliefs.* | *people with very traditional Christian beliefs*

faith /feɪθ/ [n U] a strong belief in a particular god or religion: *When her husband died, she found great comfort in her faith.*
+ in *Nothing could shake his faith in God.*

4 connected with religion

religious /rɪˈlɪdʒəs/ [adj only before noun] connected with religion: *Kusbu doesn't eat meat for religious reasons.* | *Religious education is compulsory in British schools.* | *a religious ceremony*

holy /ˈhəʊli/ [adj usually before noun] a **holy** place, person, or object is one that people think is special because it is connected with God and religion: *Jerusalem is a holy city for Jews, Christians, and Muslims.* | *holy water* | *Criminals could not be buried in holy ground.*
holy – holier – holiest

spiritual /ˈspɪrɪtʃuəl/ [adj] your **spiritual** feelings and ideas are your most private feelings about religion, the meaning of life, and other things that are not connected with the ordinary experiences of daily life: *He seems to have no interest in spiritual matters.* | *The materialism of the 1980s failed to satisfy people's spiritual needs.*

5 someone who believes in a religion

religious /rɪˈlɪdʒəs/ [adj] someone who is **religious** believes strongly in a particular religion: *He was raised as a Muslim but he isn't very religious.*
deeply religious (=very religious) *Her father was a deeply religious man, who spent hours praying each day.*

practising BRITISH **practicing** AMERICAN /ˈpræktɪsɪŋ/ [adj only before noun] a **practising** Catholic, Muslim etc does not just say they are a Catholic, Muslim etc, but regularly goes to religious ceremonies and lives according to the rules of their religion

devout /dɪˈvaʊt/ [adj] a **devout** Catholic, Muslim etc is someone who has strong and sincere religious beliefs, and who carefully obeys all the rules of their religion: *Devout Muslims pray to Allah five times a day.*

fundamentalist /ˌfʌndəˈmentəl-ɪst/ [n C] someone who has a strong belief that the laws of their religion must be followed very strictly: *Fundamentalists believed that women should not be educated.* | *Christian fundamentalists who believe that every word in the Bible is true*

6 things that people do as part of their religion

pray /preɪ/ [v I] to speak to God, silently or aloud, especially in order to ask for help or to thank him for something: *He got down on his knees and began to pray.*

+ to *Abdullah prayed to God to help him.*

pray for sb (=ask God to help someone) *The minister asked us to pray for the dead girl's family.*

pray for sth (=ask God to make something happen) *Let us pray for peace.*

prayer /preə^r/ [n C] words that you say when you are praying: *a prayer for the dead*

say a prayer (=say a fixed set of words) *An old lady was kneeling in front of the statue, saying a prayer.*

say your prayers (=say prayers as a duty you regularly have to do) *Make sure the children say their prayers before they go to bed.*

worship /'wɜːʃɪp/ [v I/T] FORMAL to pray, sing, or take part in a religious ceremony, in order to show your love of God: *Muslims come to worship and study at the mosque.* | *The Ancient Egyptians worshipped many gods.*

worshipping – worshipped –
have worshipped also worshiping –
worshiped – have worshiped AMERICAN

worship [n U] when you worship: *The building has been used for worship for centuries.*

hymn /hɪm/ [n C] a song praising God sung in a church or at a religious ceremony: *a well-known Christian hymn*

sing hymns *They gather on Sundays to pray and sing hymns.*

fast /faːst‖fæst/ [v I] to eat no food for a period of time, for religious reasons: *Muslims fast during Ramadan.*

meditate /'medɪteɪt/ [v I] to sit quietly and think deeply, to make your mind completely empty, as a form of religious training: *The monks spend hours every day meditating.*

meditation /ˌmedɪ'teɪʃən/ [n U] when you sit quietly and calmly, and try to make your mind completely empty

7 someone who does not believe in God

atheist /'eɪθi-ɪst/ [n C] someone who believes that there are no gods: *Dr Conan has been an atheist all her adult life.*

agnostic /æg'nɒstɪk, əg-‖-'nɑː-/ [n C] someone who thinks it is impossible to know whether God exists or not: *Though brought up in the Jewish faith, he became an agnostic in later life.*

8 not connected with religion

secular /'sekjʊlə^r/ [adj] not connected with any religious belief or organization – use this especially when comparing religious and non-religious institutions, ideas etc: *The choir sang a mixture of secular and religious music.* | *They want to change the country from a secular state to an Islamic republic.*

9 buildings for religion

church /tʃɜːrtʃ/ a holy building where Christians go to pray and to have their religious ceremonies

chapel /'tʃæpəl/ a small church, or a church where particular Christian groups go to pray and to have their religious ceremonies: *the Austin Baptist Chapel*

temple /'tempəl/ a holy building where people pray and religious ceremonies take place, in religions such as Buddhism, Hinduism, Sikhism, and Shinto: *the Buddhist Temple in Ladakh*

mosque /mɒsk‖mɑːsk/ a holy building where Muslims go to pray and to have their religious ceremonies: *the Great Mosque of Damascus*

synagogue /'sɪnəgɒg‖-gɑːg/ a holy building where Jews go to pray and to have their religious ceremonies

REMAIN

to still exist after everything else has gone

➡ if you mean 'continue to be the same', go to CONTINUE 3

1 to remain

left /left/ [adj not before noun] something or someone that is **left** is still there after everything else has gone or has been used: *Is there any milk left?* | *By 5 o'clock there was no one left in the office.* | *If Tracey leaves, I'll be the only girl left in the class.*

have sth left *How much time do we have left to finish this?*

be left over /biː left ˈəʊvəʳ/ something that **is left over**, especially money or food, is still there after you have used everything that you need: *I pay all the bills and save any money that is left over.*

+ from *Was there any food left over from the party?*

remain /rɪˈmeɪn/ [v I] FORMAL if something **remains**, it still exists or is still available after everything else has gone, or been used, or been dealt with: *Not much of the house remained after the fire. | We have dealt with most things, but a few small problems remain. | Some elements of the old class system still remain.*

remain to be done *A few problems remain to be discussed.*

2 someone or something that remains

the rest /ðə ˈrest/ [n singular or plural] what is left after everything or everyone else has gone, or been used, or been dealt with: *You carry these two bags and I'll bring the rest. | Four of the attackers were killed, the rest escaped.*

+ of *What will you do with the rest of the money? | He'll be in a wheelchair for the rest of his life.*

the remains /ðə rɪˈmeɪnz/ [n plural] **the remains** of something are the small parts of it that are left after most of it has been destroyed or has disappeared

+ of *Archaeologists have discovered the remains of an ancient Roman village.*

remaining /rɪˈmeɪnɪŋ/ [adj only before noun] ESPECIALLY WRITTEN the **remaining** people or things are the ones that are left when all the others have gone, or been used, or been dealt with: *The few remaining guests were in the kitchen finishing off the wine. | The only remaining question is whether we can borrow the money. | the Navy's one remaining aircraft-carrier*

what is left of sth /wɒt ɪz ˈleft ɒv (sth)/ the small amount that remains after everything else has gone or been used: *As the noise of the explosion died away, he looked up at what was left of his roof. | At last she went, and I settled down to enjoy what was left of the afternoon.*

leftovers /ˈleftəʊvəʳz/ [n plural] INFORMAL food that has not been eaten at the end of a meal: *We used the leftovers to make soup the next day.*

REMEMBER

➡ opposite **FORGET**

1 to remember something from the past

remember /rɪˈmembəʳ/ [v I/T] if you **remember** something that happened, something you did, or something you used to know, the thought of it comes back into your mind: *Do you remember your first day at school? | I couldn't remember her name. | Where are my keys? Oh, I remember, I left them in the kitchen.*

remember who/what/where/how *I can't remember where I put my bag.*

+ (that) *Suddenly I remembered that I'd left the iron on!*

remember doing sth *He remembered meeting her at a party once.*

remember sth well/vividly *That was a wonderful Christmas – I remember it well.*

> ⚠ Don't say 'I am remembering that day'. Say **I remember that day** or **I can remember that day**.

> ⚠ Don't say 'I remember to have seen him'. Say **I remember seeing him**.

I will never forget /aɪ wɪl ˌnevəʳ fəʳˈget/ ESPECIALLY SPOKEN use this to say that you will remember something for a long time because it was very shocking, very enjoyable, very frightening etc: *I'll never forget the sight of him lying there in the hospital. | I can promise you an experience you will never forget!*

think back/look back /ˌθɪŋk ˈbæk, ˌlʊk ˈbæk/ [phrasal verb I] to think about something that happened in the past because you want to remember it: *She tried to think back and remember exactly what Jim had said.*

+ to *Thinking back to when I was first married, I realize now that I made a lot of mistakes.*

look back on *When I look back on those days, it always makes me sad.*

memory /ˈmeməri/ [n C often plural] something that you remember from the past about a person, place, or experience
+ of *I have lots of happy memories of my time in Japan.*

bring back memories (=when something makes you think of a happy time in the past) *Those old songs bring back memories!*

plural **memories**

nostalgia /nɒˈstældʒə‖nɑː-/ [n U] the slightly sad feeling you have when you remember happy things from the past: *There's a mood of nostalgia throughout the whole book.*
+ for *nostalgia for the 'good old days' of steam trains*

> **nostalgic** [adj] making you remember happy times in the past: *a nostalgic visit to my home town*

2 to remember something that you must do

remember /rɪˈmembər/ [v I/T] to think of something that you must do, get, or bring, and not forget about it: *I hope he remembered the wine.* | *Just remember, I want you to be home before midnight.*
remember to do sth *Remember to close the windows before you go out.*

not forget /ˌnɒt fərˈget/ to remember something you must do – use this especially when it seems likely that you will not remember something: *Don't worry, I won't forget.*
not forget to do sth *I hope he doesn't forget to water the plants.*
+ (that) *I might be home a little late, but I haven't forgotten that we're going out.*

3 to learn something so that you can remember it

memorize (also **memorise** BRITISH) /ˈmeməraɪz/ [v T] to learn facts, numbers, lines from a play or poem etc, so that you can remember them later: *I memorised huge lists of names and dates before the exam.* | *You have to memorize this number – don't write it down!*

4 to make someone remember something they must do

remind /rɪˈmaɪnd/ [v T] to make someone remember something they must do or something they need to know: *I must pay the gas bill – I'll put it here to remind myself.*

remind sb about sth *Pauline phoned to remind you about the party.*

remind sb to do sth *Remind me to buy some batteries for my Walkman.*

remind sb (that) *I just want to remind you that your assignments must be completed by Friday.*

remind sb how/what/when *a few notes to remind yourself what you want to say*

reminder /rɪˈmaɪndər/ [n C] a spoken or written message to help you remember something that you might forget: *When your next check-up is due, the dentist will send you a reminder.* | *Finally, a reminder that the school concert will be on 17 December.*

don't forget /ˌdəʊnt fərˈget/ SPOKEN say this to tell someone to remember something that you think they might forget: *Don't forget your keys.*

don't forget to do sth *Don't forget to mail that letter, will you?*

+ (that) *Don't forget that we're going out on Friday evening.*

5 when something makes you remember something from the past

remind /rɪˈmaɪnd/ [v T] if something **reminds** you of a person, thing, or time from the past, it makes you remember them

remind sb of sb/sth *The perfume always reminded him of his mother.* | *It's horrid! It reminds me of the lumpy custard we had at school!*

> ⚠ Don't say 'it reminds me her'. Say **it reminds me of her**.

> ⚠ Don't use **remind** (=make you remember) when you mean **remember**.

make sb think of sth /ˌmeɪk (sb) 'θɪŋk ɒv (sth)/ to remind you of something that you experienced in the past: *I hate that smell – it makes me think of hospitals.*

6 something that is easy to remember

memorable /'memərəbəl/ [adj] a **memorable** event or occasion is so good, so enjoyable, or so unusual that you remember it for a long time: *the memorable day when our team won 5-0* | *She gave a memorable performance as Lady Macbeth.*

unforgettable /ˌʌnfəˈgetəbəl/ [adj] an **unforgettable** experience, sight, etc affects you so strongly that you will never forget it: *A visit to India is a truly unforgettable experience.* | *those awful unforgettable images of starving children*

7 the ability to remember things

memory /'meməri/ [n singular] your ability to remember things: *I had a good memory, and usually did well in tests.* | *You know what your memory's like – you're sure to forget!*

have a good/bad memory for sth (=be good/bad at remembering something) *I have a terrible memory for names.*

REMOVE

to take something away from the place where it is

➡ if you mean 'take off your clothes', go to **CLOTHES**

1 to remove something from inside something

take out /ˌteɪk 'aʊt/ [phrasal verb T] to take something from inside a container, space, room etc

take out sth *She opened her briefcase and took out a letter.* | *We'll have to take out the engine to fix the gearbox.*

take sth out *Roland reached inside his jacket and took his passport out.*

take sth out of sth *Take that bicycle out of the house!*

remove /rɪ'muːv/ [v T] to take something from inside something: *Cut the fruit in half and remove the stones.*

remove sth from sth *Someone had removed an important document from the file.*

> ⚠ **Remove** is more formal than **take out** and is used especially in writing.

get sth out /ˌget (sth) 'aʊt/ [phrasal verb T] to remove something that is deep inside something else, especially when this is difficult to do: *My keys fell down a drain, but I got them out with a piece of wire.*
+ of *Did you manage to get all the glass out of the wound?*

pull out /ˌpʊl 'aʊt/ [phrasal verb T] to suddenly take something out from a place where it cannot be seen, for example from a pocket, bag etc
pull out sth *The man pulled out a gun and fired three shots.*
pull sth out *She pulled out a chequebook and started writing a cheque for £500.*

2 to remove something from a surface

➡ see also **CLEAN**

take off /ˌteɪk 'ɒf‖-'ɔːf/ [phrasal verb T] to remove something that is on a surface, or that covers a surface
take off sth *You will be able to take off the bandages in about a week.*
take sth off sth *Take the sheets off your bed and I'll wash them.* | *Could you take all those things off the table?*

remove /rɪ'muːv/ [v T] to take something off the surface of something else, especially dirt, marks, or something that should not be there: *You can use lemon juice to remove the grease.* | *A waiter came and removed the empty bottles.*
remove sth from sth *Remove any dirt from the negative before printing the photograph.*

wipe off /ˌwaɪp 'ɒf‖-'ɔːf/ [phrasal verb T] to remove something such as dirt, paint, or liquid from a surface by moving a cloth over it

R

wipe off sth *Make sure you wipe off all those marks.*

wipe sth off *Angela wiped her lipstick off and washed her face.*

wipe sth off sth *Werner sat down, wiping the sweat off his forehead with a handkerchief.*

rub off /ˌrʌb ˈɒf‖-ˈɔːf/ [phrasal verb T] to remove dirt, marks etc from a surface by rubbing it hard with a cloth or brush

rub sth off sth *I tried to rub the dirt off my shoes with a tissue.*

rub off sth *I managed to rub off most of the mud, but my coat was still filthy.*

scrape off /ˌskreɪp ˈɒf‖-ˈɔːf/ [phrasal verb T] to remove something from a surface, using a knife or sharp tool

scrape off sth *We started by scraping off the old wallpaper.*

scrape sth off sth *Kevin was scraping some burnt food off the bottom of a pan.*

3 to remove something that is fixed or joined to something else

take off /ˌteɪk ˈɒf‖-ˈɔːf/ [phrasal verb T] to remove something that is fixed to something else

take sth off *I took the lid off and tasted the soup.*

take off sth *We had to take off the handles to get it through the door.*

remove /rɪˈmuːv/ [v T] to take off something that forms a piece or part of something else or that covers something else: *Remove all the fat, then cut the meat into cubes.*

remove sth from sth *She was in the hospital, having a lump removed from her breast.* | *Turn off the power, then remove the cover from the computer.*

⚠️ **Remove** is more formal than **take off** and is used especially in writing.

break off /ˌbreɪk ˈɒf‖-ˈɔːf/ [phrasal verb T] to remove a part of something by breaking it

break off sth *She broke off a piece of chocolate and gave it to me.*

break sth off sth *George broke a branch off the tree and threw it on the fire.*

cut off /ˌkʌt ˈɒf‖-ˈɔːf/ [phrasal verb T] to remove a part of something by cutting it with a knife or with scissors

cut off sth *At the end of the play, he cuts off Macbeth's head.*

cut sth off *Do you want me to cut the label off?*

tear off /ˈteər ˈɒf‖-ˈɔːf/ [phrasal verb T] to remove part of a piece of paper or cloth, by pulling it so that it tears

tear off sth *Tear off the coupon and send it to this address.*

tear sth off sth *I tore the corner off my newspaper and wrote her phone number on it.*

4 to remove writing, film, or music from paper, a tape, a computer etc

delete /dɪˈliːt/ [v T] to remove part or all of a document in a computer, so that it no longer exists: *I think you should delete the second paragraph.* | *The computer automatically deletes any files that you have not saved.*

rub out BRITISH **erase** AMERICAN /ˌrʌb ˈaʊt, ɪˈreɪz‖ɪˈreɪs/ [v T] to remove writing or pictures from paper by rubbing with a piece of rubber, or to remove writing or pictures from a board by rubbing with a cloth: *Use a pencil so you can erase your mistakes.*

rub sth out/rub out sth *I had to rub the whole thing out and start again.*

cross out /ˌkrɒs ˈaʊt‖ˌkrɔːs-/ [phrasal verb T] to draw a line through a word to show that it was a mistake or that you want to change what you have written

cross out sth *Someone had crossed out my name.*

cross sth out *That's not right. Cross it out and start again.*

erase /ɪˈreɪz‖ɪˈreɪs/ [v T] to remove writing, film, or music that has been recorded on a machine: *You can erase what you have recorded by pressing this button.* | *I accidentally erased the movie I had recorded before I had a chance to watch it.*

5 the process of removing something

removal /rɪˈmuːvəl/ [n U]

+ of *Police arranged for the removal of*

the wreckage. | the removal of Russian troops from the area | an operation for the removal of her appendix

---

REPAIR

➡ see also **BROKEN, DAMAGE**

1 to repair something that is broken or damaged

repair /rɪˈpeəʳ/ [v T] if you **repair** something that is broken or not working properly, you work on it so that it is in good condition again: *The builders are coming to repair the roof today.* | *The plane was too badly damaged to be repaired.*
get/have sth repaired (=pay someone else to repair it) *How much will it cost to have the TV repaired?*

> ⚠ **Repair**, **fix**, and **mend** mean the same, and you can use any of them in most situations: *We had to pay someone to repair/fix/mend the roof.* **Fix** is more informal than the other two, and is used especially about repairing machines, cars etc. **Mend** is used especially about repairing things that have holes in them, such as clothes and shoes, roofs, roads, or fences.

fix /fɪks/ [v T] to repair something that is broken or not working properly, especially a machine: *The radio isn't working – can you fix it?*
get/have sth fixed (=pay someone else to fix it) *I must get my camera fixed before we go to France.*

mend /mend/ [v T] to repair something that is broken or not working, or something that has a hole in it: *When are you going to mend the fence?* | *a gang of workers mending the road*

service /ˈsɜːʳvɪs/ [v T] to look at a vehicle or machine in order to make sure that it is working properly, and repair it if necessary: *Has the heating system been serviced recently?*
have/get sth serviced (=pay someone else to service it) *I'm having the car serviced next week.*

> When you see **EC**, go to the **ESSENTIAL COMMUNICATION** section.

2 work done to repair something

repairs /rɪˈpeəʳz/ [n plural] work done to repair something: *The roof repairs cost £650.*
carry out repairs/do repairs *We will send workmen to carry out emergency repairs.*
+ to *$8000 for repairs to the church roof*

maintenance /ˈmeɪntənəns/ [n U] regular work done to check and repair something so that it stays in good condition: *Smoke detectors require routine maintenance.*
+ of *The department is responsible for the maintenance of roads and bridges.*

> ⚠ You can also use **maintenance** before a noun, like an adjective: *maintenance work* | *maintenance costs*

REPRESENT

to speak and do things for someone else because they have asked you to, for example in a meeting, competition, or a law court

➡ see also **COURT/TRIAL, GOVERNMENT/ POLITICS**

1 to represent a person or group

represent /ˌreprɪˈzent/ [v T] if you **represent** a person or organization at a meeting or in a law court or parliament, you give their opinions and take action for them; if you **represent** a country, school etc in a competition, you have been chosen to compete for that country or school: *Who will be representing the UK in the next round of peace talks?* | *Students will elect two people to represent them on the School Council.* | *the athletes representing China in this year's Olympic Games*
be represented by sb *Wilson was represented in court by a top criminal lawyer.*

on behalf of /ɒn bɪˈhɑːf ɒv‖-ˈhæf-/ if you do something **on behalf of** someone, you do it because they want you to or have asked you to: *On behalf of everyone*

R

here, I'd like to wish Ted a long and happy retirement. | The woman who bought the painting said she was acting on behalf of a New York art gallery.

on sb's behalf The letter had been signed on the manager's behalf by his assistant.

speak for sb/act for sb /'spiːk fɔːʳ (sb), ˌækt fɔːʳ (sb)/ to represent someone by speaking for them in an official discussion or court, or by making legal decisions for them: David Blunkett, speaking for the Labour Party, said more money should be spent on higher education. | The family has instructed me to act for them in this case.

2 someone who represents a group

representative /ˌreprɪ'zentətɪv/ [n C] someone who has been chosen to represent an organization or country: Japan, Britain, and the US are all sending representatives to the talks in Geneva. | John Kohorn is the company's representative in Prague.

REST

➡ if you mean 'spend time in a place', go to **STAY**

RELAX   SLEEP

see also

TIRED   HOLIDAY

1 to rest

rest /rest/ [v I] to stop working or stop being active, and sit down or lie down so that you become less tired: If you're tired, we'll stop and rest for a while. | The doctor told me to take some time off work and try to rest.

have a rest/take a rest /ˌhæv ə 'rest, ˌteɪk ə 'rest/ to stop doing something for a short time because you are tired and need to rest: Halfway up the mountain we stopped to have a rest.

have a break/take a break /ˌhæv ə 'breɪk, ˌteɪk ə 'breɪk/ to stop what you are doing for a short time, so that you can rest: Let's take a break and have some coffee. | Is it alright if we have a break at about 10:30?

relax /rɪ'læks/ [v I] to do something that makes you feel calm and comfortable and helps you to forget about your work and problems: relaxing on the beach after a hard week's work | Try to relax at lunchtime, perhaps with a drink.

> ⚠ Don't say 'relax yourself'. Just say **relax**.

2 a period when you rest

rest /rest/ [n C/U] a period of time when you do not have to do anything tiring or active, and you can relax or sleep: We painted the walls and then stopped for a rest. | She needs plenty of rest.

a good rest (=one that makes you feel completely relaxed) Make sure you have a good rest at the weekend.

break /breɪk/ [n C] a short time when you stop what you are doing so that you can rest or eat: OK, let's run through it again straight after the break.

without a break (=not stopping to rest or eat) Harry had worked for eight hours without a break.

coffee/tea/lunch break I'll phone you during my lunch break.

recess AMERICAN **break** BRITISH /rɪ'ses, breɪk‖ 'riːses/ [n U] a time between classes when the children in a school can go outside and play: The children played kickball during recess. | Come and see me at break, Tom.

RESTAURANTS/ EATING AND DRINKING

WORD BANK

➡ see pages 623–625

RESTAURANTS/EATING AND DRINKING

1 places to eat

restaurant /'restərɒnt|-rənt, -rɑːnt/ [n C] a place where you buy and eat a meal, which is usually brought to your table, especially a place that you go to with other people as a social event: *Have you ever been to 'La Porchetta'? It's a really nice restaurant.*
a Chinese/Italian/Mexican/etc restaurant *A new Japanese restaurant just opened on Upper Street.*

café/cafe /'kæfeɪ|kæ'feɪ, kə-/ [n C] a place where you can drink coffee or tea and sometimes alcoholic drinks, and eat cakes or small meals: *We found a small café just off the main street.*

canteen BRITISH **cafeteria** AMERICAN /kæn'tiːn, ˌkæfə'tɪərɪə/ [n C] a place in a school, factory, or company building where the students or workers can buy and eat meals

fast food restaurant /'faɪst fuːd ˌrestərɒnt|'fæst-, -rɑnt/ [n C] a place where you can buy and eat small meals such as hamburgers that are ready to eat so that you do not have to wait for them: *Fast food restaurants such as McDonald's and Burger King can be found in almost every country in the world.*

diner /'daɪnər/ [n C] AMERICAN a small restaurant where you can buy cheap meals: *They stopped for breakfast at a roadside diner.*

deli /'deli/ [n C] a shop that sells cheese, salads, cooked meats etc, and where you can also buy small meals and sandwiches

sandwich bar /'sænwɪdʒ ˌbɑːr|'sændwɪtʃ-/ [n C] a place where you can buy sandwiches and drinks that you can take away to eat or drink somewhere else

takeaway /'teɪkəweɪ/ [n C] BRITISH a place that sells complete meals that you take away to eat at home, or one of the meals it sells: *a Chinese takeaway | Shall we get a takeaway tonight?*

2 places to drink

bar /bɑːr/ [n C] a place where you can buy and drink alcoholic drinks: *I met her in a bar in Manhattan.*

pub /pʌb/ [n C] a place, especially in Britain or Ireland, where people meet their friends and drink alcoholic drinks

wine bar /'waɪn ˌbɑːr/ [n C] a fashionable, fairly expensive place that serves many different types of wine and small meals

coffee shop /'kɒfi ʃɒp|'kɔːfi ʃɑːp/ [n C] a small café where you drink coffee, tea, and other non-alcoholic drinks, and which also sells cakes, sandwiches etc

microbrewery /'maɪkrəʊˌbruːəri/ [n C] a place in the US where you can buy meals and drink beer that is made by the bar's owners: *The number of microbreweries has increased dramatically in recent years.*

3 when you go somewhere to eat or drink

eat out /iːt 'aʊt/ [phrasal verb I] to have a meal in a restaurant, not at home: *I don't feel like cooking tonight – let's eat out.*

go out to dinner/lunch /gəʊ aʊt tə'dɪnər, lʌntʃ/ (also **go out for a meal** /gəʊ aʊt fər ə 'miːl/ BRITISH) to go to a restaurant and have a meal: *We went out to lunch as a celebration. | When was the last time we went out for a meal?*

go out for a drink /gəʊ ˌaʊt fər ə 'drɪŋk/ to go to a bar, pub etc in order to meet your friends and drink alcoholic drinks: *"What did you do at the weekend?" "Oh nothing much – just went out for a drink on Friday."*

RESTAURANTS/EATING AND DRINKING
continues on the next page

RESTAURANTS/EATING AND DRINKING

4 in a restaurant

① I don't feel like cooking tonight. Let's **eat out**.

Yeah, why not? We haven't been out for a meal for a long time. There's a new Italian restaurant that's just opened in town – let's go there.

② Do we need to **book a table**?

No. It's not usually busy during the week.

③ waitress

waiter

Good evening.

Good evening, **a table for two** please.

④ Can I get you anything to drink?

Can we see the **wine list**?

A mineral water for me, please.

⑤ Shall we have the **set menu**?

I think I'd rather have pizza.

vocabulary

bill BRITISH **check** AMERICAN /bɪl, tʃek/ [n C] a piece of paper with a list of what you have had and how much you must pay

book a table /ˌbʊk ə ˈteɪbəl/ ESPECIALLY BRITISH (also **make a reservation** /ˌmeɪk ə resəˈveɪʃən/ AMERICAN) [v I/T] to tell the restaurant that you want to eat there, so they do not give your table to someone else

dessert /dɪˈzɜːʳt/ [n C/U] the sweet part of your meal that you have after the main course

eat out /iːt ˈaʊt/ [phrasal verb I] to have a meal in a restaurant, not at home

house wine/house red/house white /haʊs ˈwaɪn, haʊs ˈred, haʊs ˈwaɪt/ [n U] ordinary, inexpensive wine that you can buy in a restaurant to eat with your meal

Ⓠ**I'll have...** /aɪl hæv/ SPOKEN say this to tell the waiter or waitress what you want to eat

main course /meɪn kɔːʳs/ [n C] the biggest separate part of a meal

menu /ˈmenjuː/ [n C] a list of all the meals that a restaurant serves

order /ˈɔːʳdəʳ/ [v I/T] to tell the waiter or waitress what you want to eat or drink

RESTAURANTS/EATING AND DRINKING

set menu /ˌset ˈmenjuː/ [n C] BRITISH a complete meal that you pay a fixed price for, instead of ordering and paying for the different parts separately

starter BRITISH **appetizer** AMERICAN /ˈstaːrtər, ˈæpəˌtaɪzər/ [n C] the part of a meal that you have before the main course

table for two/three etc /ˈteɪbəl fɔːr (two, etc)/ say this to the waiter or waitress when you arrive, so that they know how many people are with you: *We'd like a table for four, please.*

tip /tɪp/ [n C] money that you give to the waiter or waitress, as a way of showing your thanks, in addition to the money you pay for your meal
   leave a tip (=put a tip on the table when you leave)

waiter /ˈweɪtər/ [n C] a man who serves food and drink at the tables in a restaurant

waitress /ˈweɪtrɪs/ [n C] a woman who serves food and drink at the tables in a restaurant

⚠ In American English, **waitperson** is sometimes used instead of **waiter** or **waitress**

wine list /ˈwaɪn lɪst/ [n C] a list of all the alcoholic drinks that a restaurant serves

RESULT

1 something that happens or exists because of something else

➡ see also CAUSE, REASON

result /rɪ'zʌlt/ [n C] something that happens because of someone's actions or because of something else that happened before
+ of *Her constant cough was the result of many years of smoking.*
with the result that *More and more people are using cars, with the result that the roads are much more polluted.*
as a result *Jobs are hard to get and, as a result, more young people want to continue their education.*
a direct result of sth (=caused by only one thing even if people think there may be other causes) *Her parents believe that her death was a direct result of medical errors.*

effect /ɪ'fekt/ [n C] the way that a person or situation is changed by something that happens or something that someone does:
+ of *the harmful effects of radiation*
have an effect *All my efforts to persuade them were beginning to have an effect.*
+ on *The death of a parent can have very serious and long-lasting effects on a child.*
have a bad/good effect (on) *Any increase in fuel costs could have a bad effect on business.*
side effects (=unwanted effects of a drug or medicine) *The side effects of Seproxan can include headaches and tiredness.*

⚠ Don't confuse **effect** and **affect**. **Effect** is a noun and **affect** is a verb.

outcome /'aʊtkʌm/ [n C] the situation that exists at the end of a meeting, activity, or series of events, especially when no one knows what this will be until it actually happens: *Whatever the outcome, I hope we remain friends.* | *The talks had a better outcome than we originally hoped.*
+ of *the final outcome of the dispute*

consequence /'kɒnsɪkwəns‖'kɑːnsɪkwens/ [n C usually plural] the **consequences** of an action, decision etc are the things that happen as a result of it, which are usually bad: *Safety procedures had been ignored, with tragic consequences.*
+ of *The environmental consequences of the oil leak were horrific.*

⚠ **Consequence** is more formal than **effect**.

2 when one thing happens because of another

➡ see also CAUSE, REASON

because of /bɪ'kɒz əv‖bɪ'kɔːz-/ if something happens **because of** an earlier problem, event etc, it happens as a result of the problem, event etc: *Sampras is likely to miss the US Open because of a back injury.* | *Because of problems with the fuel system, the launch has been put back a week.* | *She was chosen for the Peace Prize because of her courageous fight for democracy.*

be the result of sth /biː ðə rɪ'zʌlt ɒv (sth)/ to happen because of something else that happened or was done: *Our success is the result of a great deal of hard work.* | *The big population increase in the US was partly the result of immigration.*

as a result of sth /əz ə rɪ'zʌlt ɒv (sth)/ happening because of something else: *He died as a result of cold and exhaustion.* | *Over 60 drugs have been removed from sale as a result of recent tests.*

resulting /rɪ'zʌltɪŋ/ [adj only before noun] ESPECIALLY WRITTEN happening or existing because of something else that happened before: *During the storm the dam collapsed. The resulting floods caused several deaths.*

3 the result of a game, competition, or election

➡ see also SPORT, VOTE, TEST

result /rɪ'zʌlt/ [n C usually plural] the final number of points, votes etc at the end of a competition, election etc: *These are excellent results for the Christian Democratic Party.*

When you see **EC**, go to the **ESSENTIAL COMMUNICATION** section.

+ of *And now, the results of last week's competition.*

⚠️ In British English, you can also use **result** to talk about sport: *Turn to BBC1 for the latest football results.* In American English, use **score**.

score /skɔːʳ/ [n C] the number of points that each team or person has at the end of a game: *What was the score?* | *The final score was 2-1 to Juventus.* | *listening to the baseball scores on the radio*

4 to decide how well a student has done in a test etc

➡ see also **TEST**

mark (also **grade** AMERICAN) /mɑːʳk, greɪd/ [v T] to look at students' work or examination papers and give them numbers or letters to show how good they are: *Mrs Parry, have you marked our tests yet?* | *I have 48 English papers to grade this evening.*

RETURN

to go back to the place where you were before

➡ see also **GO**

go back /ˌgəʊ 'bæk/ [phrasal verb I] to go back to the place you started from, or to a place you have been to before: *I've had my treatment, but I have to go back next week for a check-up.*
+ to *When will you be going back to Japan?*
+ there/inside/downstairs etc *It's cold out here, let's go back indoors.*
go back for sth (=go back in order to get something) *Richard forgot his wallet and had to go back for it.*

⚠️ If someone goes back to visit a place where they were before and then comes back here, you can say they **have been back**: *He left Germany in 1950 and he's only been back there once.*

come back /ˌkʌm 'bæk/ [phrasal verb I] if someone **comes back**, they return to the place where you are: *Rachel's left me,*

and I don't think she'll ever come back.
+ to/from *When will you be coming back to London?* | *He's just come back from a vacation in Miami.*

return /rɪ'tɜːʳn/ [v I] to go back or come back to the place where you were before, especially to your home or your country: *I left early, but promised to return the next day.*
+ to/from *He had to return to India to look after his mother.* | *Alastair returned from the office late that night.*

⚠️ **Return** is more formal than **go back** and **come back**.

⚠️ Don't say 'return back'. Just say **return**.

return /rɪ'tɜːʳn/ [n singular] FORMAL the time when someone returns to a place: *We eagerly await your return.*
on sb's return (=after they return) *On her return to Washington, she immediately went to the French Embassy.*

go home /ˌgəʊ 'həʊm/ to return to your home or to the country where you were born: *It's late, I should be going home.* | *John used to go home once a month when he was at college.*
+ to *Isabelle is going home to France on Saturday.*

⚠️ Don't say 'go to home'. Just say **go home**.

be back /biː 'bæk/ ESPECIALLY SPOKEN [phrasal verb I] to be in the place where you were before you went away: *Don't worry, I'll be back soon.* | *Jane, what a surprise! How long have you been back?*

RICH

➡ opposite **POOR**
➡ see also **MONEY, EXPENSIVE, EARN**

1 rich people

rich /rɪtʃ/ [adj] someone who is **rich** has a lot of money: *He's marrying the daughter of a rich lawyer.* | *If I was rich I'd buy a Ferrari.* | *Bill Gates is one of the richest men in the world.*

wealthy /ˈwelθi/ [adj] rich – use this especially about someone whose family has owned a lot of land or property for a long time: *a wealthy landowner* | *She came from one of Boston's wealthiest families.*

wealthy – wealthier – wealthiest

wealth /welθ/ [n U] FORMAL the large amount of money and property that makes someone rich: *His Hollywood films brought him wealth and fame.*

well off /ˌwel ˈɒf◀-ˈɔːf◀/ [adj not before noun] not very rich, but with enough money to have a comfortable life and do the things that you want to do: *a relatively well off family* (=richer than most people) | *They were sufficiently well off to buy their own apartment.*

better off (=having more money than before or more than someone else) *Most families will be better off when the tax changes are introduced.*

millionaire /ˌmɪljəˈneəʳ/ [n C] someone who is extremely rich and has at least a million pounds or a million dollars: *He had his own company at 25 and was a millionaire by 30.* | *You'd have to be a millionaire to afford a place like that.*

the rich /ðə ˈrɪtʃ/ [n plural] people who are rich, especially when you are comparing them to people who are poor: *the wide gap between the rich and the poor*

2 rich countries

rich /rɪtʃ/ [adj] a **rich** country has a lot of money, so most of the people living there have comfortable lives: *Many of the former Soviet republics have received aid from their richer neighbours.*

developed /dɪˈveləpt/ [adj only before noun] a **developed** country is rich and has modern industrial, health, and education systems: *Typhoid and cholera are not now serious problems in developed countries.*

3 to become rich

Ω**get rich** /ˌget ˈrɪtʃ/ ESPECIALLY SPOKEN to become rich, especially to make a lot of money quickly: *Roger got rich selling second-hand cars.*

make a fortune /ˌmeɪk ə ˈfɔːʳtʃən/ INFORMAL to become rich by earning or winning a lot of money: *A good salesman can make a fortune if he works hard.*

make a fortune doing sth *He had made a fortune gambling in Las Vegas.*

RIGHT

➡ look here for ...
• correct and without any mistakes
• when someone's behaviour is reasonable
• morally right
• legal rights and rights in society
➡ opposite **WRONG**
➡ see also **SUITABLE/UNSUITABLE, GOOD**

1 correct and with no mistakes

right /raɪt/ [adj] something that is **right** is true, or has no mistakes in it, or is the way that it should be: *Yes, that's the right answer.* | *Is that the right time?* | *Make sure you use the right amounts of flour and sugar.* | *Put the words in the right order to make a sentence.*

sb is right (=what they say is right) *I think you're right – there's not going to be enough food for everyone.*

Ω**that's right** SPOKEN (use this to emphasize that what someone has said is true) *"Your mother's a teacher isn't she?" "Yes, that's right."*

be right about sb/sth (=have the right opinion about someone or something) *You're right about Tara. You can't trust her.*

get sth right (=be right in what you say or write) *Make sure you get people's names right when you're sending out the invitations.*

correct /kəˈrekt/ [adj] **correct** answers, facts, methods etc are right, for example because they contain no mistakes or they break no rules: *The first ten correct answers will win a prize.* | *This information is no longer correct.* | *Did the police use the correct procedure when they interrogated him?*

⚠ **Correct** is more formal than **right**.

⚠ Don't use **correct** about people. Use **right**: *You're right, Maria.*

accurate /ˈækjʊ̈rət/ [adj] information, measurements, descriptions etc that are **accurate** are completely correct and all the details are true: *She gave the police an accurate description of her attacker.* | *It is vital that measurements are accurate.*

2 in the right way

○**right** /raɪt/ [adv] ESPECIALLY SPOKEN if you do something **right**, you do it without making any mistakes: *Have I spelled your name right?* | *Most people can't do it right the first time.*

correctly /kəˈrektli/ [adv] if you do something **correctly**, you do it in the way that it should be done and without making any mistakes: *The drug is quite safe if used correctly.* | *You're not holding the racket correctly.*

> ⚠ **Correctly** is more formal than **right**.

properly /ˈprɒpəˈli‖ˈprɑː-/ [adv] ESPECIALLY BRITISH if you do something **properly**, you do it in a satisfactory way or in the way that it should be done: *Make sure you put the lid on properly.* | *He accused me of not doing my job properly.*

3 to make something correct

correct /kəˈrekt/ [v T] to change something wrong that someone has said or written, and make it right: *We read through the first version, correcting the errors.* | *It's a program that lets you say a sentence, then corrects you if it's wrong.*

correction /kəˈrekʃən/ [n C] a mark or note that corrects something in a piece of writing: *My homework was covered with corrections.*
make a correction *I still have a few last-minute corrections to make.*

4 when you think it is right to do something

right /raɪt/ [adj] use this to talk about what someone has done, to say that you agree with what they did because it was fair or reasonable
be right to do sth *You were right to complain – the waiter was rude and the food was awful.*

the right thing to do *Believe me, it's the right thing to do. You can't let him treat you like this.*

justified /ˈdʒʌst̬ɪfaɪd/ [adj] if you say that someone is **justified** or that something they do is **justified**, you believe they have good reasons for what they do, because of what you know about the situation: *I don't think Colin's criticisms were really justified.*
be/feel justified in doing sth *The government feels justified in using military force to protect its own citizens.* | *Do you think the principal was justified in expelling those students?*

reasonable /ˈriːzənəbəl/ [adj] if someone does something **reasonable**, you think they are behaving in a fair and sensible way: *The police say they only used 'reasonable force' to break up the demonstration.*
it is reasonable to assume/expect/suppose *It is reasonable to assume that about half of the students will pass.*

○**I don't blame you/her etc** /aɪ ˌdəʊnt ˈbleɪm (you, etc)/ SPOKEN INFORMAL say this when you can understand why someone has behaved in a particular way, and you think they were right: *"Sheila's left her husband." "Well, I don't blame her!"*
+ for (doing) sth *I don't blame you for losing your temper with Ann – she was being so annoying.*

justify /ˈdʒʌst̬ɪfaɪ/ [v T] to show that there are good reasons for doing something that seems wrong to most people: *How can you justify a 200% pay rise!* | *a desperate attempt to justify his decision*
justify doing sth *I don't think anyone can justify spending so much money on weapons.*
justifying – justified – have justified

rightly /ˈraɪtli/ [adv] FORMAL if someone says or does something **rightly**, you believe that they are right to say it or do it: *His opponents point out, quite rightly, that government money is really taxpayers' money.*

5 your beliefs about what is right and wrong

conscience /ˈkɒnʃəns‖ˈkɑːn-/ [n C/U] the part of your mind that tells you what is right or wrong, and makes you feel guilty if you do something wrong: *My conscience told me that I shouldn't accept the money.*

guilty conscience (=a guilty feeling because you know you have done something wrong) *Paul couldn't sleep: 'A sign of a guilty conscience,' he thought.*

with a clear conscience (=when you feel sure you have not done anything wrong) *Ben had treated her so badly, she felt she could leave him with a clear conscience.*

R

principles /ˈprɪnsɪpəlz/ [n plural] your beliefs about what is morally right or wrong, which help you to decide what you should or should not do: *Some politicians are only interested in power, and don't seem to have any principles at all!*

against sb's principles (=not morally acceptable to them) *I never borrow money – it's against my principles.*

6 to think that something is right

right /raɪt/ [adj] if you think something is **right**, you believe that there are good reasons for doing it, or that it is not morally wrong: *I don't think they should test drugs on animals. It's not right.*

it is right to do sth *Do you think it is ever right to lie to someone?*

approve /əˈpruːv/ [v I] if you **approve** of what someone does, you think it is morally good or not morally wrong; if you **approve** of someone, you like them because you think they are sensible, honest etc; *Martha wants to get a motorcycle but her parents don't approve.*

+ of *Most people approve of the changes in the gun laws.* | *Tom's mother doesn't approve of his new girlfriend.*

approve of sb doing sth *Would you approve of your teenage son smoking?*

⚠ Don't say 'I approve it'. Say **I approve of it.**

agree with sth /əˈgriː wɪð (sth)/ [phrasal verb T] to think that an action, decision, or type of behaviour is the right thing to do – used especially in questions or negative sentences: *I do not agree with the use of violence.* | *Do you agree with the administration's immigration policy?*

⚠ Don't say 'I agree this decision'. Say **I agree with this decision.**

⚠ Don't confuse **agree with sth** (=think that something is right) and **agree to do sth** (=say that you will do it): *He agreed to meet me after work.*

believe in sth /bɪˈliːv ɪn (sth)/ [phrasal verb T] to think that a type of behaviour is morally right or is a sensible thing to do: *Hilary doesn't believe in sex before marriage.* | *I don't believe in all these silly diets.*

believe in doing sth *We've always believed in letting the children have plenty of freedom.*

be in favour of sth BRITISH **be in favor of sth** AMERICAN /biː ɪn ˈfeɪvər ɒv (sth)/ if you are **in favour of** something, especially something that affects a lot of people, such as a government plan or policy, you strongly support it because you think it is the right thing to do: *Are you in favour of the death penalty?*

be in favour of doing sth *80% of those interviewed were in favour of banning nuclear weapons.*

approval /əˈpruːvəl/ [n U] the feeling that something is good, right, or sensible: *When the awards were announced there was general public approval.* | *shouts of approval from the crowd*

7 the legal right to do something

right /raɪt/ [n singular] something that you are legally or officially allowed to do

the right to do sth *Women fought very hard for the right to vote.*

have the right to sth *Everyone should have the right to a decent education.*

give sb the right to do sth *Having a European passport gives you the right to travel and work anywhere in the European Union.*

⚠ Don't say 'the right of something' or 'the right of doing something'. Say **the right to something** or **the right to do something.**

rights /raɪts/ [n plural] the political and social freedom that everyone in a country should have: *laws that have gradually taken away workers' rights*

human rights (=the basic rights that all people should have, including the right to be treated fairly and without cruelty by their government) *The country has a bad record on human rights.*

equal rights (=the right of everyone to be treated fairly and equally) *equal rights for women*

be entitled to sth /biː ɪnˈtaɪtld tuː (sth)/ FORMAL to be legally allowed to have something or do something: *You may be entitled to compensation for loss of earnings.*

be entitled to do sth *If she marries him, will she be entitled to live in this country?*

RISK

the possibility that something bad might happen

➡ see also DANGEROUS, GAMBLING

1 a risk

risk /rɪsk/ [n C/U] the possibility that something harmful or unpleasant might happen: *There are a lot of risks involved when you start your own business.*

+ of *People continue to smoke, despite all the risks of heart disease, cancer etc.*

reduce/increase the risk of *Clean the wound thoroughly to reduce the risk of infection.*

risk of doing sth *Drivers often break the speed limit, and there's little risk of getting caught.*

+ that *There is always the risk that someone may press the wrong button and cause an accident.*

danger /ˈdeɪndʒəʳ/ [n singular/U] the possibility that something dangerous or very unpleasant might happen

+ of *Is there any danger of Grant being sent to prison?* | *Cover your head and drink plenty of fluids, to reduce the danger of sunstroke.*

+ that *There's a real danger that Britain's forests may disappear completely within the next 50 years.*

threat /θret/ [n singular] a strong possibility that something very bad will happen, especially something that affects many people

+ of *Once again the people of Sudan face the threat of famine.*

2 actions or situations that are full of risk

risky /ˈrɪski/ [adj] a **risky** action or situation is one that involves the risk that something harmful or unpleasant might happen: *It's always risky leaving your car out in the street all night.* | *a risky investment*

risky – riskier – riskiest

3 to do something even though there is a risk

take a risk /ˌteɪk ə ˈrɪsk/ to decide to do something, even though you know that something bad might happen: *I knew we were taking a risk when we lent him the money.* | *Sometimes it's worth taking a few risks to get what you want.*

take a chance /ˌteɪk ə ˈtʃɑːns‖-ˈtʃæns/ INFORMAL to decide to do something even though there is a risk, because you think that you will succeed: *I was offered a job in Hong Kong and decided to take a chance.*

take chances *You can trust them if you like, but I'm not taking any chances!*

risk /rɪsk/ [v T] if you **risk** doing something, you do it even though you know it is risky

risk doing sth *He couldn't risk phoning her at home – her husband might have been there.*

risk it (=risk doing something in spite of possible problems or danger) *They said the snow was too deep for cars to travel, but we decided to risk it.*

> ⚠ Don't say 'risk to do something'. Say **risk doing something.**

4 to be in a situation where there are risks

risk /rɪsk/ [v T] to get into a situation where something very unpleasant might happen to you

R

risk death/punishment/defeat etc (=do something that might result in you being killed, punished etc) *risking death or imprisonment to escape from Vietnam*
risk doing sth *I don't want to risk offending your parents.*
risk your life (=risk dying) *She risked her life trying to rescue a cat from a blazing building.*

be in danger /biː ɪn ˈdeɪndʒəʳ/ to be in a situation in which something very dangerous might happen: *It was a terrible storm, and the little ship was in danger.* | *With the rise of the fascist movement, democracy itself was in danger.*
+ of *Thousands of refugees are now in danger of starvation.*
be in danger of doing sth *The island's traditional culture is in danger of being destroyed.*

threaten /ˈθretn/ [v T] if actions or events **threaten** something, they cause danger for it and make it likely to be harmed or destroyed: *Severe droughts often threaten the rice crop.* | *According to some scientists, global warming threatens the survival of the whole human race.*

put sb/sth at risk /ˌpʊt (sb/sth) ət ˈrɪsk/ to do something that makes it more likely that someone or something will be harmed: *The pilot has been accused of putting his passengers' lives at risk.* | *Your stupid behaviour could put your whole future at risk.*

ROAD/PATH

➡ see also **DRIVE, WALK**

1 in a town

road /rəʊd/ [n C] a long area of ground with a hard, flat surface, for cars, buses, bicycles etc to travel on: *They're building a new road around the city centre.*
along/down/up the road *The boys go to the school down the road.* | *The park is just along the road from our house.*
across/over the road (=on the other side of the road) *Who lives in that house across the road?*
main road (=a large road with a lot of traffic) *It's very noisy living on a main road.*

cross the road (=walk to the other side) *Stop, look, and listen before you cross the road.*
busy road (=a road with a lot of traffic) *It's a busy road, so be careful when you cross.*

street /striːt/ [n C] a road close to the centre of a town, with houses, shops, or offices and a path down each side for people to walk on: *There were stores on both sides of the street.*
side street (=a small quiet street) *You can park in one of the side streets.*
in a street BRITISH **on a street** AMERICAN *Meg lived in the same London street all her life.* | *We used to have an apartment on 23rd Street.*
a one-way street (=where you can only drive in one direction) *You can't turn here, it's a one-way street.*

high street BRITISH **main street** AMERICAN /ˈhaɪ striːt, ˈmeɪn striːt/ [n C] the main street in the middle of a town where most of the shops, hotels, and offices are: *Our bank used to have a branch in every high street.* | *The small town of Whitehorse, Alaska consists of a half-mile long main street and a few scattered houses.*

alley /ˈæli/ [n C] a very narrow street or path between buildings in a town, especially one that is dirty, dark, or unpleasant: *homeless people sleeping in alleys*
plural **alleys**

2 outside a town

road /rəʊd/ [n C] a road that connects towns or cities: *Route 66 used to be one of the main roads across the States.* | *I like driving on the French roads – they're so straight, and there isn't much traffic.*
+ to *As you leave the city, turn right and take the road to Madrid.*

lane /leɪn/ [n C] a narrow road in the countryside, connecting villages or farms: *We rode our bicycles along pretty country lanes.*

track /træk/ [n C] a narrow road, usually without a hard surface, leading to a farm or field: *The track was only wide enough for one car.* | *A dirt track led up to the cottage.*

3 a road for travelling quickly

motorway BRITISH **freeway** AMERICAN /'məʊtəˈweɪ, 'friːweɪ/ [n C] a wide road connecting cities and towns, on which cars can travel fast for long distances: *The speed limit on motorways is 70 mph.* | *We headed east on the Pasadena freeway.*

⚠ When talking about motorways, people say 'the M1', 'the M62' etc: *Take the M4 to Swindon.* | *heavy traffic on the M6*

highway /'haɪweɪ/ [n C] AMERICAN a wide fast road that connects cities and towns: *I got onto the highway and drove as fast as I could.*
Highway 61/70 etc *There's a rest stop somewhere on Highway 61.*

freeway/expressway /'friːweɪ, ɪk-'spresweɪ/ [n C] AMERICAN a wide fast road that takes traffic into and out of a big city: *They took the expressway to the airport.*

bypass /'baɪpɑːs‖-pæs/ [n C] BRITISH a road that goes around a town, so that people can avoid driving through the town

4 an area for people to walk on

path /pɑːθ‖pæθ/ [n C] a long, narrow piece of ground for people to walk along: *A narrow path took us down to the river.* | *a path though the woods*

pavement BRITISH **sidewalk** AMERICAN /'peɪvmənt, 'saɪdwɔːk/ [n C] a path built along the side of a street for people to walk on

footpath /'fʊtpɑːθ‖-pæθ/ [n C] BRITISH a public path for people to walk on in the countryside: *They followed the coastal footpath into the village.*

trail /treɪl/ [n C] AMERICAN a path in the mountains or in the forest: *hiking trails* | *The trail follows the river most of the way to Avalanche Lake.*

5 a place where roads or paths join

junction /'dʒʌŋkʃən/ [n C] ESPECIALLY BRITISH a place where two or more roads cross or join: *Kerry slowed down as she approached the junction.*

+ of *Turn left at the junction of Abbots Road and Church Street.*

intersection /'ɪntərˌsekʃən/ [n C] ESPECIALLY AMERICAN a place, especially in a city, where two or more roads cross each other: *The accident happened at a busy intersection downtown.*

crossroads /'krɒsrəʊdz‖'krɔːs-/ [n C] a place where two small roads or streets cross each other: *Go straight on at the crossroads.*
plural **crossroads**

R

RUBBISH

things that you throw away because you do not want them

➡ see also GET RID OF

rubbish /'rʌbɪʃ/ [n U] BRITISH all the paper, empty bottles, cans, pieces of food etc that you throw away: *The dustmen collect the rubbish on Wednesdays.*
a rubbish bin (=a container for rubbish)
a rubbish dump (=a large open area where people's rubbish is taken after it is collected)

garbage/trash /'gɑːrbɪdʒ, træʃ/ [n U] AMERICAN all the paper, empty bottles, cans, pieces of food etc that you throw away: *There were piles of trash in the backyard.* | *Empty the wastebaskets and take out the garbage.*
a garbage/trash can (=a container for garbage)

litter /'lɪtər/ [n U] empty bottles, packets, and pieces of paper that people have dropped on the street or in a park: *You can be fined £100 for dropping litter.*
litter bin BRITISH **litter basket** AMERICAN (=a container for people to put litter in)

refuse /'refjuːs/ [n U] FORMAL all the things that are regularly thrown away from the houses, shops, factories etc in an area: *the weekly refuse collection*

waste /weɪst/ [n U] useless materials which are left over, especially after an industrial process, and which must be thrown away: *Too much waste has been dumped into the North Sea.* | *We've been trying to recycle our household waste.*

industrial/toxic/nuclear waste *Industrial waste had leaked into the water supply.*

RUDE

➡ opposite **POLITE**
➡ see also **FRIENDLY/UNFRIENDLY, DESCRIBING PEOPLE**

1 not polite, and likely to upset people or make them angry

rude /ruːd/ [adj] someone who is **rude** upsets or offends people by not following the rules of good social behaviour: *He's so rude! I was talking to him and he just walked away! | I heard her making rude remarks about your furniture.*
be rude to sb *My mother doesn't like my boyfriend because he was rude to her once.*
be rude about sth *My French friends are always rude about English food.*
it is rude to do sth *It's rude to interrupt people when they are speaking.*
it is rude of sb to do sth *I thought it was very rude of her not to answer my letter.*
  rudely [adv] *Blair rudely pushed his way to the front of the line.*

impolite/not polite /ˌɪmpəˈlaɪt, ˌnɒt pəˈlaɪt/ [adj] not following the rules of good social behaviour, especially when someone does this without realizing it: *I was tired, but I thought it might not be polite to leave so early. | In Senegal it is considered impolite if you do not share your food.*

> ⚠ **Impolite** and **not polite** are used mostly about things that people do or say, not about people themselves.

offensive /əˈfensɪv/ [adj] **offensive** words, jokes, or actions make people angry, because they show no respect for people's moral or religious beliefs: *His racist jokes are really offensive.*
find sth offensive (=think it is offensive) *Some viewers may find the language in this film offensive.*

insulting /ɪnˈsʌltɪŋ/ [adj] something that you say or do that is **insulting** criticizes someone, or shows in a very rude way that you think they are stupid or unimportant: *He kept making insulting remarks about women drivers. | She talks to me as if I'm stupid. It's so insulting.*

tactless /ˈtæktləs/ [adj] someone who is **tactless** upsets or embarrasses someone else, without intending to, by mentioning something that it would be better not to talk about: *I wanted to know about her divorce, but I thought it would be tactless to ask. | It's so tactless of him to keep complaining about his job when Sam is unemployed. | tactless remarks*

cheeky /ˈtʃiːki/ [adj] BRITISH use this about a child who says something rude to a parent or teacher: *I don't like teaching that class – the children are all so cheeky.*
cheeky – cheekier – cheekiest

bad manners /ˌbæd ˈmænərz/ [n plural] someone who has **bad manners** does not behave politely in social situations, for example by not saying 'please' and 'thank you': *Marilyn apologized for her husband's bad manners.*
it is bad manners to do sth *It's bad manners to talk with your mouth full.*

2 to say or do something rude

insult /ɪnˈsʌlt/ [v T] to be very rude and unpleasant to someone, either by saying rude things to them or by making them feel stupid or unimportant: *Jarvis was fired for insulting a customer. | They offered me $20 for a whole day's work – I felt really insulted.*

offend /əˈfend/ [v T] to make someone angry or upset by doing something that they think is socially or morally unacceptable: *I think I offended Kevin by not inviting him to the party. | Many people are offended by sex scenes on television.*

swear /sweər/ [v I] to deliberately use words that shock people because they are considered to be very rude, especially words about sex or religion: *Don't swear in front of the children.*
+ at *The other driver got out of his car and started swearing and shouting at me!*
swearing – swore – have sworn

3 rude things that people say

insult /'ɪnsʌlt/ [n C] something that some-one says to someone else, which is very rude because it criticizes their intelligence, character, or appearance: *Outside the bar, a drunk was shouting insults at everyone who came past.*

bad language /ˌbæd 'læŋgwɪdʒ/ [n U] words that are considered to be very rude, especially words about sex or religion: *My mother is coming to stay, so no smoking, no drinking, and no bad language. | There were hundreds of complaints about the bad language in the film.*

RULE

rule /ruːl/ [n C often plural] an instruction that says what people are allowed to do or not allowed to do, for example in a game, or in a school or organization: *Do you want me to explain the rules of the game? | It says in the rules that every child has to wear school uniform.*

break a rule (=not obey it) *Anyone breaking the rules will be punished. | If you put a plural verb with a singular noun, you're breaking a basic rule of grammar.*

rules and regulations (use this when you think there are too many official rules) *Businessmen are tired of all these rules and regulations.*

be against the rules (=not be allowed by the rules) *You can't smoke in here – it's against the rules.*

regulation /ˌregjʊ'leɪʃən/ [n C usually plural] an official rule made by a government or organization, which is part of a set of rules: *recent changes in health and safety regulations | The new regulations are very strict about what you can and cannot bring into the country.*

bureaucracy /bjʊə'rɒkrəsi‖-'rɑː-/ [n U] a complicated official system which is annoying because it takes a long time to do anything and it has a lot of unnecessary rules: *It takes ages to get a visa these days – there's so much bureaucracy.*

RUN

➡ if you mean 'be in charge of an organization', go to **IN CHARGE OF**

1 to run

He had to run to catch the bus.

run /rʌn/ [v I] *You'll have to run or you'll miss the bus. | He kept on running until he was out in the open country.*

+ across/through/along/out etc *A dog ran straight out in front of my car. | She ran upstairs and slammed her bedroom door.*

run for the bus/train (=in order to catch it) *Just running for the bus leaves me out of breath.*

run away/off (=run fast in order to leave a place) *They grabbed her purse and then ran off towards the subway.*

run after sb/sth (=chase someone) *Her dog was running after a rabbit and did not hear her calling.*

running – ran – have run

dash /dæʃ/ [v I] to run very quickly for a short distance, because you have to do something urgently

R

+ around/into/across etc *He dashed forward and pulled the child away from the road.*

dash for sth/make a dash for sth (=run quickly towards something) *She got up and made a dash for the door.*

sprint /sprɪnt/ [v I] to run as fast as you can over a short distance: *A man sprinted past, then five seconds later two policemen came running after him.*

trot /trɒt‖trɑːt/ [v I] to run fairly slowly, taking short steps

trot along/back/off *Paul walked quickly, with his little dog trotting along behind.*

trotting – trotted – have trotted

2 to run as a sport or for exercise

run /rʌn/ [v I/T] to run in a race or for exercise: *Omar's running the marathon this year.*

go running/go for a run (=go out and run for exercise) *I usually go running on Saturday afternoons.*

run 2 miles/400 metres etc *She runs a couple of miles twice a week.*

running – ran – have run

runner [n C] someone who runs, especially in a race: *a long-distance runner*

jog

I started jogging to lose a little weight.

jog /dʒɒg‖dʒɑːg/ [v I] to run fairly slowly for a long distance, for exercise, and to keep healthy: *I started jogging to lose a little weight.*

jog along/down/past etc *When I lived in Washington I jogged along the river every morning.*

go jogging/go for a jog (=go out and jog) *Sharon goes for a jog every evening after work.*

jogging – jogged – have jogged

When you see **EC**, go to the
ESSENTIAL COMMUNICATION section.

S

SAD

➡ opposite **HAPPY**
➡ see also **CRY, SATISFIED/DISSATISFIED**

1 feeling sad or unhappy about something

sad /sæd/ [adj not usually before noun] not happy, especially because a happy time has ended, or because you feel sorry about someone else's unhappiness: *She felt sad as she waved goodbye.* | *Why is Sandra looking so sad?*

sad to see/hear/learn/leave/go etc *We were very sad to hear about your father's death.*

+ about *I was glad to be going home, but sad about leaving all my friends.*

sad look/expression/voice/face *There was such a sad look in her eyes.*

sad – sadder – saddest

> **sadly** [adv] *She shook her head sadly and sighed.*

unhappy /ʌnˈhæpi/ [adj] not happy, because you are in a situation, job, or relationship that you do not enjoy at all, and it seems likely to continue for a long time: *He was very unhappy at school.* | *Her parents' divorce left her feeling confused and unhappy.*

desperately/deeply unhappy (=very unhappy) *I was desperately unhappy after Sean left me.*

unhappy – unhappier – unhappiest

> **unhappily** [adv] *"What a fool I've been," said James, unhappily.*

upset /ʌpˈset/ [adj not before noun] unhappy because something very unpleasant or disappointing has happened, so that you feel shocked or you want to cry: *Miss Hurley is too upset to speak to anyone at the moment.* | *The children were very upset when we told them that we wouldn't be going to Disneyland.*

+ about *She's still upset about her uncle's death.*

depressed /dɪˈprest/ [adj not before noun] very unhappy for a long time, and feeling that your life will never get any better: *Her husband's been very depressed since he lost his job last year.*

+ about *Gretta gets depressed about her weight.*

> ⚠ **Depressed** can also be used about someone who is suffering from a serious medical condition in which they feel so unhappy that they cannot lead a normal life.

feeling sorry for yourself /ˈfiːlɪŋ ˈsɒri fər jɔːˈself‖-ˈsɑːri-/ ESPECIALLY SPOKEN spending all your time thinking about how unlucky you are or how unfairly you have been treated, and not doing anything to improve the situation: *You've got to stop feeling sorry for yourself and try to find a job.*

homesick /ˈhəʊmˌsɪk/ [adj] unhappy because you are a long way from your home, your family, and your friends, and you wish you were back there: *My sister was very homesick when she first went to college.*

2 unhappy because someone has been unkind to you

upset /ʌpˈset/ [adj not before noun] unhappy because someone has been unkind to you, so that you want to cry: *She's upset because Dan didn't invite her to his party.*

get upset (about) *It was an awful thing for him to say, but there's no point in getting upset about it.*

+ that *She was very upset that Matthew hadn't told her he was leaving.*

hurt /hɜːrt/ [adj not before noun] upset and shocked because someone has been unkind to you, especially someone that you trusted and thought was a friend: *Bill felt very hurt when he realized she had lied to him.*

deeply hurt (=extremely hurt) *Jackson was said to be 'deeply hurt' by the newspaper reports about him.*

offended /əˈfendɪd/ [adj not before noun] upset and angry because you think someone has treated you rudely or without respect: *She'll be offended if you don't thank her for her help.*

get offended *He gets very offended if you criticize his work.*

3 something that makes you feel sad

sad /sæd/ [adj usually before noun] use this about a story, piece of music, period of time etc that makes you feel sad

sad time/day/moment/occasion etc *The day her son left home was one of the saddest days of her life.*

sad news/story/song/film etc *Fairuz sang a sad song that made us all homesick.* | *I don't like movies with sad endings.*

it is sad that *It's very sad that she died before her children grew up.*

sad – sadder – saddest

unhappy /ʌnˈhæpi/ [adj] **unhappy childhood/marriage/year etc** a time when you are unhappy because you are in a difficult or unpleasant situation that you do not enjoy at all: *Phil was married for three unhappy years.* | *Looking at that photo always brings back unhappy memories.* | *an unhappy love affair*

unhappy – unhappier – unhappiest

depressing /dɪˈpresɪŋ/ [adj] a **depressing** experience, story, place, piece of news etc makes you feel that there is nothing to be happy about and not much hope for the future: *What a depressing novel!* | *It's such a depressing town – there's nothing to do here!* | *the depressing news that violent crime has increased again*

> ⚠ Don't say **depressive** when you mean **depressing**. A **depressive** is a person who gets depressed very easily.

upsetting /ʌpˈsetɪŋ/ [adj] an **upsetting** experience or event has a strong emotional effect on you, and makes you want to cry: *She can't talk about her son's death – she finds it too upsetting.* | *Being burgled can be a very upsetting experience.*

4 to make someone sad

make sb sad/make sb unhappy /ˌmeɪk (sb) ˈsæd, ˌmeɪk (sb) ʌnˈhæpi/ to make someone feel sad, or make them feel unhappy: *Something at school was making her unhappy, but she didn't want to talk about it.* | *It made me sad to see her looking so old and ill.*

upset /ʌpˈset/ [v T] if something **upsets** you, it makes you feel as if you want to cry, especially because someone has been unkind to you or because you have had a very unpleasant experience: *I'm sorry if I upset you – I didn't mean to.*

it upsets sb to see/hear/think sth *Her parents got divorced when she was 10, and it still upsets her to think about it.*

upsetting – upset – have upset

hurt /hɜːʳt/ [v T] to make someone feel upset by being unkind to them or not thinking enough about their feelings, especially someone who trusts you and thinks you are their friend: *I would never do anything to hurt her.*

hurt sb's feelings *I didn't really like her boyfriend, but I couldn't tell her that – I didn't want to hurt her feelings.*

it hurts sb to see/hear/learn etc *It hurt me to think that Jane had lied to me.*

hurting – hurt – have hurt

get sb down /ˌget (sb) ˈdaʊn/ [phrasal verb T] INFORMAL if something **gets you down**, it makes you feel unhappy and tired because it has continued for too long: *I know it's a boring job, but don't let it get you down.* | *The endless rain was beginning to get him down.*

5 a sad feeling

sadness /ˈsædnɪs/ [n U] a sad feeling, caused especially when a happy time is ending, or when you feel sorry about someone else's unhappiness: *Her eyes were full of sadness.*

with (great) sadness *I remembered with great sadness all the friends I had left behind.*

unhappiness /ʌnˈhæpinɪs/ [n U] the unhappy feeling you have when you are in a very difficult or unpleasant situation: *After years of unhappiness, she finally decided to leave him.*

grief /griːf/ [n U] ESPECIALLY WRITTEN great sadness that you feel when someone that you love has died: *He was overcome with grief when his wife died.*

depression /dɪˈpreʃən/ [n U] a mental illness that makes someone feel so unhappy that they have no energy or hope for the future, and they cannot live a normal life

severe depression *My father had suffered from severe depression for many years.*

6 to make someone feel less sad

cheer sb up /ˌtʃɪəʳ (sb) ˈʌp/ [phrasal verb T] to make someone feel happier when they are disappointed or sad about something: *She failed her test, so I'm taking her out to cheer her up.*

comfort /ˈkʌmfəʳt/ [v T] to make someone feel less upset by being kind to them and telling them not to worry: *Bill stroked her hair gently, trying to comfort her.* | *We did our best to comfort him, but he was obviously very upset.*

cheer up /ˌtʃɪːr ˈʌp/ SPOKEN say this to tell someone to stop feeling disappointed or sad and try to be more cheerful: *Cheer up, Phil! It's only a game, and you can't win every time.*

it's all right/it's OK /ɪts ˈɔːl raɪt, ɪts ˈəʊkeɪ/ SPOKEN say this to make someone feel calmer or make them stop crying, when they are very upset and worried about something: *It's all right, honey, I'm here now.*

SAFE

➡ opposite **DANGEROUS**
➡ see also **RISK**

1 when you are not in danger

safe /seɪf/ [adj not before noun] not in danger of being harmed or attacked: *Will she be safe in the house on her own?* | *I feel safer in London than I do in New York.*
+ from *The ants live in underground nests where they are safe from birds and lizards.*
safe and sound (=safe and unharmed after being in danger) *We're praying that she will come back safe and sound.*

safely /ˈseɪfli/ [adv] without being harmed: *Did you get home safely last night?* | *The pilot managed to land the plane safely.*

safety /ˈseɪfti/ [n U] when you are safe from danger, harm, or accidents: *I worry*

about the children's safety if they are late home from school.
in safety (=without any danger) *From behind a glass screen, we could watch the experiment in complete safety.*
for your own safety (=in order to make sure you are safe) *For your own safety, please do not smoke until you get off the plane.*

⚠ **Safety** is a noun, not an adjective. Use **safe** (not 'safety') in sentences like this: *She's a very safe driver.* | *We always feel safe here.*

be out of danger /biː ˌaʊt əv ˈdeɪndʒəʳ/ to be safe, after being in danger of dying or of being harmed or attacked: *The patient is out of danger, but he's still very weak.* | *We're not out of danger yet – they're still following us.*

2 something that will not cause harm

safe /seɪf/ [adj] not likely to cause any injury or harm: *That bridge doesn't look very safe.* | *a safe driver* (=someone who drives carefully and does not cause accidents)
it is safe to do sth *Is it safe to swim in the water here?*
+ for *We want the streets to be safe for our children.*
safely [adv] *The nuclear waste is safely buried in the deepest part of the ocean.*

harmless /ˈhɑːʳmləs/ [adj] an animal or chemical that is **harmless** will not harm or injure anyone, even though it may seem dangerous: *Our dog makes a lot of noise, but he's perfectly harmless.* | *Barnes claims that cannabis is a relatively harmless drug.*

3 when something will not get lost, stolen, or damaged

safe /seɪf/ [adj] *Your money will be safer in the bank.*
in a safe place *Keep your keys in a safe place.*
it is safe to do sth *Would it be safer to park my car in the driveway?*
keep sth safe *Leave your necklace with me – I'll keep it safe.*

4 a place where someone or something is safe

safety /'seɪfti/ [n U] a place where you are safe from danger: *By the time the men reached safety, they were exhausted and half starved.*
in/to/from the safety of sth *She rushed back to the safety of her own house.*
carry/lead/take sb to safety *The firefighters carried the children to safety.*

refuge /'refjuːdʒ/ [n C/U] a place that you go in order to escape from a dangerous or unpleasant situation
+ from *The basement provided us with a refuge from the fighting.*
take refuge (=go somewhere that is safe) *During the flooding, people took refuge in the hills.*
seek refuge from sth (=try to find a safe place, to escape from a dangerous situation) *Thousands of families came here seeking refuge from the civil war.*

out of harm's way /aʊt əv ˌhaːᵊmz 'weɪ/ if someone or something is **out of harm's way**, they are in a place where they cannot be hurt or damaged: *Keep all medicines out of harm's way, where children cannot reach them.* | *She put the glass vases on the top shelf, out of harm's way.*

5 things done to make people and places safer

security /sɪ'kjʊərᵻti/ [n U] things that are done to make sure that someone does not get attacked or robbed: *They need to improve security here – anyone could just walk in.*
tight security (=very careful security) *There is tight security at the airport and all baggage is being searched.*

⚠ You can also use **security** before a noun, like an adjective: *Strict security measures were in force during the President's visit.* | *a security guard* (=someone whose job is to protect a person or building).

safety /'seɪfti/ [n U] ways of preventing dangerous accidents: *the importance of safety in the workplace*
road safety (=rules and methods for using roads safely) *All children should be taught road safety from an early age.*

⚠ You can also use **safety** before a noun, like an adjective: *Unless safety standards are improved, there could be a major accident.* | *Read the safety instructions first.*

SAME

➡ if you mean 'have the same score as another team', go to **SPORT 10**
➡ look here for ...
- the same thing or person
- similar to another thing or person
➡ see also **DIFFERENT, ANOTHER, CONTINUE 3**

⚠ **The same** can be used in two different ways. Compare these sentences: *She's so rich, she never wears the same dress twice* (=when you are talking about one dress). | *I saw someone wearing the same dress as me* (=when you are talking about two dresses that look the same).

1 the same one

the same /ðə 'seɪm/ the same place, person, or thing, not a different one: *My friend and I went to the same school.* | *They work in different offices, but they have the same boss.*
the same ... as *She was born on the same day as me.* | *I was staying in the same hotel as Bill Clinton. Can you believe it!*

⚠ Don't use 'same' on its own. Always say **the same**.

⚠ Don't say 'the same with' or 'the same like'. Say **the same as**.

2 exactly like another one

the same /ðə 'seɪm/ [adj only before noun] the same as another thing, place, situation etc: *They were both wearing the same shoes.*
look/sound/taste etc the same *The houses on the street all look the same.*
just the same/exactly the same (=not different in any way) *I tried three different types of wine, but they all tasted just the same to me.*

the same ... as *They were doing the same jobs as the men, but being paid less.*

do the same *We've opened up stores in the UK and we hope to do the same in the rest of Europe.*

◯**it's the same** SPOKEN (=say this when you mean that two or more situations are the same) *"We always get up late on Saturdays." "It's the same in our house."*

⚠ Don't use 'same' on its own. Always say **the same**.

⚠ Don't say 'the same like' or 'the same with'. Say **the same as**.

just like/exactly like /ˌdʒʌst ˈlaɪk, ɪgˌzæktli ˈlaɪk/ if someone or something is **just like** or **exactly like** someone or something else, there is very little difference between them: *Clare looks just like her mother.* | *This song sounds exactly like that one by The Beatles.*

identical /aɪˈdentɪkəl/ [adj] two or more things that are **identical** are exactly the same in every way: *To me the two patterns looked identical.*
+ to *The picture is identical to the one in the Museum of Modern Art in New York.*

◯**can't tell the difference** /ˌkɑːnt tel ðə ˈdɪfərəns‖ˌkænt-/ ESPECIALLY SPOKEN if you **can't tell the difference** between two things or people, they seem exactly the same to you: *The twins were so alike that I really couldn't tell the difference.*
+ between *People who are colour-blind can't tell the difference between red and green.*

be no different from sth /biː nəʊ ˈdɪfərənt frɒm (stʰ)/ use this especially when you expect something or someone to be different from another thing or person, but in fact they are the same: *People often think that movie stars are special in some way, but really they're no different from anybody else.* | *Life on the island is no different from life on the mainland.*

When you see **EC** , go to the **ESSENTIAL COMMUNICATION** section.

3 the same height/age/ amount etc

the same /ðə ˈseɪm/ [adj only before noun] *Both stores are charging the same price for CD players.*
the same height/age etc as *Her sister is the same age as me.*
exactly the same *We're both exactly the same height.*

⚠ Don't use 'same' on its own. Always say **the same**.

⚠ Don't say 'the same with' or 'the same like'. Say **the same as**.

be as old/long/strong etc as /biː əz (old, etc) əz/ to be the same age, length etc as someone or something else: *At 14, Richard was already as tall as his father.*

equal /ˈiːkwəl/ [adj] two or more amounts, totals, levels etc that are **equal** are the same as each other: *You should spend an equal amount of time on each question in the test.*
+ to *A pint is equal to about half a litre.*

equally /ˈiːkwəli/ [adv]
equally good/bad/difficult etc (=as good, bad etc as something else) *Both schools seem equally good.*
divide/share sth equally (=so that everyone has the same amount) *The money was divided equally between their three children.*

4 the same as before

the same /ðə ˈseɪm/ *I hadn't seen John for ages, but he was still just the same.*
the same as ever *School's the same as ever – too much work and not enough time to do what I really want!*
just the same/exactly the same (not changed in any way) *We went to the office Christmas party, but it was just the same as last year's.*

◯**hasn't changed** /ˌhæzənt ˈtʃeɪndʒd/ ESPECIALLY SPOKEN if someone or something **hasn't changed**, they are the same as they were before, even though you have not seen them for a long time: *I went back to my old school and it hadn't changed.*

hasn't changed at all (also **hasn't changed a bit** BRITISH) *He hasn't changed at all – he's still crazy about football.*

5 always the same

stay the same /ˌsteɪ ðə ˈseɪm/ to continue to be the same and not change: *The word 'sheep' doesn't add 's' in the plural – the ending stays the same.* | *Tamara lived in a government apartment, and the rent stayed the same for five years.*

constant /ˈkɒnstənt‖ˈkɑːn-/ [adj] an amount, temperature, speed etc that is **constant**, stays the same and does not change: *The number of deaths from road accidents has remained constant over the last five years.* | *It is important to store wine at a constant temperature.*

> ⚠ **Constant** is a more technical way of saying that something stays the same.

6 similar to someone or something else

like /laɪk/ [preposition] similar to or almost the same as something or someone else: *It has teeth like sharp knives.*
be like *The houses here are like the ones in Northern France.* | *I can't describe the taste – it was like vanilla but not quite.*
look/sound/feel etc like *It looks like meat and tastes like meat, but it's actually made from vegetable protein.* | *What lovely material – it feels like velvet.*

similar /ˈsɪmələʳ, ˈsɪmɪləʳ/ [adj] if one thing is **similar** to another, or if two or more things are **similar**, they are like each other but not exactly the same: *We have similar tastes in music.*
+ to *The plane is similar to the one that crashed in Nepal.*
similar in size/appearance/style etc *The two dresses were similar in style.*

alike /əˈlaɪk/ [adv] if two people are **alike**, they look like each other or they have a similar character: *My mother and I are very alike.*
look alike *A lot of couples look alike.*

> When you see **EC**, go to the
> **ESSENTIAL COMMUNICATION** section.

remind you of sb/sth /rɪˈmaɪnd juː ɒv (sb/sth)‖-ɑːv-/ [phrasal verb T] to be similar to another person, thing, or event, and make you think of them: *My brother really reminds me of my father sometimes.* | *The restaurant reminded her of the ones she used to go to in Paris.*

take after sb /ˈteɪk ɑːftəʳ (sb)‖-æf-/ [phrasal verb T] to be like your mother, father, grandmother etc, because you look like them or you have a similar character, similar abilities etc: *Neil takes after his father.* | *Jennie's good at languages. She takes after her grandmother in that way.*

have a lot in common /hæv ə ˌlɒt ɪn ˈkɒmən‖-ˌlɑːt ɪn ˈkɑːmən/ if two or more people **have a lot in common,** they have the same interests, opinions, experiences etc, so they are likely to have a good relationship: *You'll like Paul. I think the two of you have a lot in common.*
+ with *I had nothing in common with her, and didn't know what to talk about.*

7 ways in which people or things are similar

similarity /ˌsɪmɪˈlærɪti/ [n C/U] a way in which people, things, or events are similar
+ between *Detectives said there were similarities between the two murders.*
+ with/to *The English language has certain similarities with German.*
striking similarity (=one that is very easy to notice) *There are some striking similarities between the two stories.*
plural **similarities**

resemblance /rɪˈzembləns/ [n C/U] if there is a **resemblance** between two people or things, they look like each other
+ between *The resemblance between him and Andy was remarkable.*
bear a strong/striking/close resemblance to FORMAL (=look very like someone or something else) *The two paintings bore a striking resemblance to each other.*

SATISFIED/ DISSATISFIED

HAPPY   COMPLAINING

ENJOY   see also   COMPLAIN

LIKE/NOT LIKE   COMFORTABLE/ UNCOMFORTABLE

1 when you think that something is good enough

satisfied /'sætɪsfaɪd/ [adj] how you feel when you think that something is as good as it should be, for example someone's work or something you buy: *I did the whole essay again, but she still wasn't satisfied.*
+ with *His boss seems satisfied with his work.* | *95% of passengers say they are satisfied with the bus service.*

> ⚠ Don't say 'I'm satisfied of it'. Say **I'm satisfied with it.**

be happy with sth /biː 'hæpi wɪð (sth)/ to be satisfied with a situation, decision, or arrangement: *The doctor said he was happy with the way the operation had gone.*
be perfectly happy with sth *Until now she seemed perfectly happy with the arrangement.*

> ⚠ **Be happy with sth** is less formal than **satisfied** and is used especially in spoken English.

satisfactory /ˌsætɪs'fæktəri◄/ [adj] something that is **satisfactory** is good enough because it is of a high enough standard or it gives you what you need: *You can only take the advanced class if your work is of a satisfactory standard.* | *I wrote and complained, but I still haven't had a satisfactory answer.*

pleased /pliːzd/ [adj] how you feel when you think something is very good and you feel very satisfied with it: *Were you pleased when you saw the results?*

+ with *Tom's teacher was pleased with his progress, and gave him an 'A' on his report card.* | *"How's your new car?" "It's great – I'm really pleased with it."*

2 when you have what you want in your life, your job etc

satisfied/happy /'sætɪsfaɪd, 'hæpi/ [adj not before noun] happy because you have what you want and you do not want anything more or anything different
+ with *I'd be quite happy with a part-time job, so long as the money's OK.* | *I don't really want a bigger house – I'm satisfied with what I have.*
keep sb satisfied/happy *They have to make bigger and bigger profits to keep the bosses happy.*

> ⚠ **Happy** is more common in spoken English than **satisfied**.

content /kən'tent/ [adj not before noun] happy and satisfied with everything in your life, so that you do not want to change anything
+ with *Although Lawrence was poor, he was basically content with life.*
content to do sth *At present he seems content to just sit at home and watch TV.*

3 the feeling you have when you are satisfied

satisfaction /ˌsætɪs'fækʃən/ [n U] the feeling of being satisfied, especially because you have achieved something good or useful: *She finished her essay, and read it through with satisfaction.*
get satisfaction from sth *He enjoys coaching the hockey team, and gets a lot of satisfaction from it.*
express satisfaction FORMAL (=say you are satisfied) *Most users have expressed satisfaction with the new system.*

4 not satisfied

not satisfied/dissatisfied /nɒt 'sætɪsfaɪd, dɪ'sætɪsfaɪd/ how you feel when something is not as good as you want it to be or expect it to be: *Eliott won the race, but said that he wasn't entirely satisfied – "I was hoping to beat the world record."*

+ with *The teacher told James that she wasn't satisfied with his work.* | *Paul had become increasingly dissatisfied with his job and his marriage.*

⚠️ **Dissatisfied** is more formal than **not satisfied**.

not be happy with sth /nɒt biː ˈhæpi wɪð (sth)/ to feel dissatisfied or disappointed because something has not been done well enough, or because you have not achieved what you wanted: *The director wasn't happy with her performance, and they had to shoot the scene again.*

5 **the feeling you have when you are not satisfied**

dissatisfaction /dɪˌsætɪsˈfækʃən/ the feeling you have when you are not satisfied: *Teaching standards are low and there is widespread dissatisfaction among the students.*
+ with *Opinion polls show increasing dissatisfaction with the way the country is being governed.*

SAVE

➡ look here for ...
• to save money
• to save someone from a dangerous situation
• to keep something so that you can use it later
➡ see also **SPEND, MONEY, BANKS**

1 **to save money**

save /seɪv/ [v I/T] to gradually collect money by not spending all the money you have, especially when you regularly put some of it in a bank: *I find it really difficult to save – I just spend everything I get.*
save money/£500/$400 etc *He's managed to save $800 so far.* | *I try to save a little money each month.*
+ for *She starts saving for Christmas in the middle of July!*

save up /ˌseɪv ˈʌp/ [phrasal verb I/T] to save money in order to buy something or do something special: *I'm trying to save up enough money to buy a computer.*

save up to do sth *We're saving up to go to the Caribbean next year.*
+ for *If you want a new bike, you'll have to save up for it.*

savings /ˈseɪvɪŋz/ [n plural] the money that you have saved: *I'm paying for my Spanish classes out of my savings.*
life savings (=all the money you have saved in your life) *My parents spent their life savings on a retirement home in Florida.*

2 **to save someone from danger or from an unpleasant situation**
➡ see also **FIRE, ACCIDENT**

save /seɪv/ [v T] if you **save** someone, you stop them from being killed or badly hurt: *He almost fell off the cliff, but she put out her arm and saved him.*
save sb from sth *His cycling helmet saved him from serious injury.*
save sb from doing sth *A lifeguard dived into the pool and saved her from drowning.*
save sb's life *Wearing a seat belt can save your life.*

rescue /ˈreskjuː/ [v T] if you **rescue** someone, you take them away from a dangerous situation, so that they do not get killed or badly hurt: *Paramedics and firefighters worked for two hours to rescue people who were trapped in the bus.*
rescue sb from sth *The couple were rescued from the burning building by neighbours.*

rescue/come to the rescue /ˈreskjuː, ˌkʌm tə ðə ˈreskjuː/ if you **rescue** someone or **come to the rescue**, you help them when they are in a difficult or unpleasant situation: *Luckily, Sally came to the rescue and lent us her car.* | *I was stuck talking to Mrs Roberts until Mum rescued me.*
come to sb's rescue *I couldn't remember the man's name. Fortunately Maria came to my rescue.*

3 **to save something to use later**

save/keep /seɪv, kiːp/ [v T] to keep something and not use it now, so that you can use it later: *Save some of the cheese to sprinkle on top of the dish.*

save/keep sth for sth *He got out the bottle of champagne that he'd been saving for this occasion.*

save/keep sth for later *We can keep the rest of the food for later.*

keeping – kept – have kept

SAY

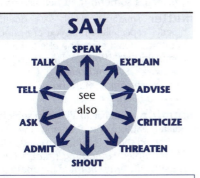

SPEAK
TALK　EXPLAIN
TELL　see also　ADVISE
ASK　CRITICIZE
ADMIT　THREATEN
SHOUT

⚠ Don't confuse **say**, **tell**, **talk**, and **speak**. You **say** words to someone. You **tell** someone facts or information about something. You **talk** to someone about a subject. You **speak** (=you say words) or you **speak** a language.

1 to say something

say /seɪ/ [v I/T] to say something using spoken or written words: *"I must be going," she said.* | *"Where's Pam going?" "I don't know. She didn't say."*

+ (that) *James wrote to the bank and said we needed a loan.* | *It says in today's paper that gas prices are going up again.*

say what/where/why etc *The doctor didn't say how long the operation would take.*

say hello/sorry/yes etc (to sb) *Lauren came over to say goodbye to us.* | *I asked Dad if he'd lend me some money, but he said no.*

say sth to sb *What did you say to her?*

saying – said – have said

⚠ Don't say 'say someone that ...'. Say **say that** ... or **tell someone that** ...: *She said that she was going home.* | *She told me that she was going home.*

⚠ Use **say** (not 'tell') when you are reporting someone's actual words: *"I'm going home," she said.*

---

tell /tel/ [v T] to give someone information, using spoken or written words

tell sb (that) *Rosie told me that she might be late.*

tell sb sth *He refused to tell me his name.*

tell sb who/what/where etc *There are signs telling you where the exits are.*

tell sb about sth *Sit down and tell me all about it.*

telling – told – have told

point out /ˌpɔɪnt 'aʊt/ [phrasal verb T] to tell someone something that they had not noticed or had not thought about: *As Sharon pointed out, the story was rather hard to believe.*

point out sth *an article pointing out the similarities between the Watergate scandal and the problems that Clinton has now*

+ that *It's worth pointing out that very few people ever die of this disease.*

mention /'menʃən/ [v T] to talk about someone or something, but without giving details or saying very much about them: *He mentioned something about a party, but he didn't say when it was.* | *When I mentioned her name, he looked embarrassed.*

+ (that) *I forgot to mention that I won't be in tomorrow.*

⚠ Don't say 'mention about something'. Say **mention something**.

---

add /æd/ [v T] to say something more, after what has already been said or written: *Is there anything you'd like to add, Peter?* | *"Finally," she added, "I would like to thank my family for their support."*

+ that *I should add that I do not agree with Dr Mitchell.*

put it /'pʊt ɪt/ to express an idea in a particular way, choosing your words carefully to explain what you mean simply and clearly: *If you don't understand, I'll try and put it another way.*

⚲**put it this way** SPOKEN (use this when you are trying to say something in the clearest possible way) *Put it this way: if we don't make a profit, we're out of a job.*

express /ɪk'spres/ [v T] to let someone know your feelings, by putting them into words

express concern/satisfaction/annoyance/ sympathy etc (=say that you are worried, satisfied etc) *Ollie found it hard to express his feelings about the war.* | *Parents have expressed concern about the amount of violence in some children's shows.*

express yourself (=make people understand what you are thinking or feeling) *Young children often find it difficult to express themselves in words.*

2 publicly or officially

say /seɪ/ [v T] to say something publicly or officially, using spoken or written words

+ (that) *The President said he had no intention of resigning.* | *The sports club rules say that sports shoes must be worn in the gym at all times.*

say what/how/who/when etc *Did they say who will take over as Chairman?*

saying – said – have said

announce /əˈnaʊns/ [v T] to officially tell people what has happened or what will happen, in a written or spoken public statement: *The company announced profits of $400 million.*

+ (that) *The Prime Minister has just announced there is to be a General Election next month.*

state /steɪt/ [v T] FORMAL to say something publicly or officially in clear, definite language

+ that *The law states that you are innocent until proved guilty.* | *Justice Cohen stated clearly that no further action would be taken.*

confirm /kənˈfɜːrm/ [v T] if you **confirm** something that other people have already said is true, you say publicly that it is definitely true: *Mr Eastwood refused to confirm or deny the rumour.*

+ that *Police have confirmed that they are questioning a woman about the disappearance of baby Kelly Truman.*

make a statement /ˌmeɪk ə ˈsteɪtmənt/ say or write something publicly in order to tell people what you intend to do, what your opinion is etc – use this about politicians, business leaders, and other important people: *The President is expected to make a statement on the crisis later this afternoon.*

3 quietly or unclearly

whisper /ˈwɪspər/ [v T] to say something very quietly, using your breath rather than your voice: *"Don't wake the baby," whispered Cecilia.* | *Fran leant over and whispered something in her sister's ear.*

mutter /ˈmʌtər/ [v T] to say something quietly, especially when you are annoyed but do not want someone else to hear you complaining: *"Why do I have to do all the work?" she muttered.* | *Grant went out, muttering something about having to see a client.*

mumble /ˈmʌmbəl/ [v T] to say something quietly without pronouncing the words clearly, so that it is difficult to understand: *He mumbled something I didn't hear.* | *Kaye could only mumble an apology.*

4 in an indirect way

imply /ɪmˈplaɪ/ [v T] to say one thing which seems to show that another thing is true, but without saying the other thing directly

+ (that) *Michael did imply that I could have the job if I wanted it.* | *The article implied that unemployed people are lazy and do not want to work.*

implying – implied – have implied

suggest /səˈdʒest‖səg-/ [v T] to say something in an indirect way, especially something bad that you prefer not to say directly: *What are you suggesting? Do you think I'm a thief?*

+ (that) *His letter seemed to suggest that he wasn't satisfied with my work.*

hint /hɪnt/ [v I/T] to say something in a very indirect way, but so that other people can guess what you really mean

+ (that) *Harry hinted that his friendship with Mona might have contributed to his marriage break-up.*

+ at *The President hinted at the possibility of military action.*

hint [n C] something that you say in a very indirect way, but so that other people can guess what you really mean

drop a hint (=say something very indirectly) *He kept dropping hints about what he wanted for Christmas.*

When you see **EC**, go to the
ESSENTIAL COMMUNICATION section.

5 to say that something is definitely true or not true

claim /kleɪm/ [v T] to say that something is true, even though it has not been proved and people may not believe it
+ (that) *Martin claimed that he was with friends at the time of his wife's murder.*
claim to be/do sth *Doctors claim to have discovered a cure for the disease.*

swear /sweə^r/ [v T] to promise very seriously that something is definitely true
swear (that) *Vic swears he saw a ghost standing at the end of his bed.* | *Una swore that she hadn't stolen the money.*
swearing – swore – have sworn

deny /dɪˈnaɪ/ [v T] to say that you have not done something bad that people say you have done: *Bowlam denies all charges of selling drugs to children.*
+ (that) *Gallagher denies that he copied the tune from an old Beatles song.*
deny doing sth *Joanna denied ever having lied to me.*
flatly/categorically deny (=deny very strongly) *Leeman categorically denied any involvement in the robbery.*
denying – denied – have denied

⚠ Don't confuse **deny** (=say you have not done something) and **refuse** (=say you will not do something): *He denied that he had given her the gun.* | *He refused to give her the gun.*

insist /ɪnˈsɪst/ [v T] to keep saying that something is true, especially when a lot of people say it is not true
+ (that) *Barker insisted that he was the legal owner of the car.* | *Miller insisted he had never had an affair with the actress.*

6 to say that someone has done something bad or illegal

accuse /əˈkjuːz/ [v T] to say or write that someone is guilty of a crime or of doing something bad
accuse sb of doing sth *Are you accusing me of cheating?*
accuse sb of sth *The article accused the company of sex discrimination.*

accusation /ˌækjʊˈzeɪʃən/ [n C] a statement saying that someone is guilty of a crime or of doing something bad
make an accusation *You can't go around making accusations without proof.*
+ of *There have been accusations of racism in the Los Angeles police department.*
+ against *The accusations against Dr Jones were found to be false.*

allege /əˈledʒ/ [v T] to say publicly that someone has done something bad or illegal, even though this has not been proved
+ (that) *Mrs Taylor alleges that she lost her job because she was pregnant.*
be alleged to have done sth *He was alleged to have planted a bomb in the parliament building.*
the alleged murderer/rapist/attacker etc (=the person someone alleges is a murderer etc) *The alleged terrorists are in the custody of the German police.*

⚠ **Allege** is used especially in newspapers and news reports.

allegation /ˌælɪˈgeɪʃən/ [n C usually plural] a public statement saying that someone has done something bad or illegal, but giving no proof
make an allegation *He has made some serious allegations concerning the company's financial dealings.*
+ of *There were allegations of corruption in the police department.*
+ about *allegations about the senator's private life*
+ that *The newspaper printed allegations that politicians had been accepting bribes.*
deny an allegation (=say it is false) *Weimar denied allegations of financial mismanagement.*

say /seɪ/ [v T] ESPECIALLY SPOKEN to say or write that someone has done something bad or illegal
+ (that) *Are you saying I'm a liar?* | *His ex-wife says that he used to beat her.*
saying – said – have said

7 to say something again

repeat /rɪˈpiːt/ [v T] to say something again, for example because someone did not hear you or understand you: *Could you please repeat the question?*

+ that *She repeated that anyone who really needed help would get it.*

repeat yourself (=say something again, without realizing it) *Have I told you this before? Please stop me if I'm repeating myself.*

◯**say sth again** /ˌseɪ (sth) əˈgen/ ESPE-CIALLY SPOKEN to say something again, either because someone did not hear you or because you want to emphasize it: *Sorry, would you say that again?* | *I've said it before and I'll say it again: I never trusted that man.*

8 how you ask someone to say something again

◯**sorry?/pardon?** (also **excuse me** AMERICAN) /ˈsɒri, ˈpɑːʳdn, ɪkˈskjuːz miː‖ˈsɑːri, ˈsɔːri/ SPOKEN say this when you want to ask someone politely to repeat what they just said because you did not hear it: *"It's hot today, isn't it?" "Pardon?"*

◯**what?/what did you say?** /wɒt, ˌwɒt dɪd juː ˈseɪ/ SPOKEN INFORMAL say this when you did not hear what someone said, or when you are surprised by what they said: *"Are you going to the bar?" "What? Oh, yes, I suppose so."* | *"Oh shut up!" "What did you say?"*

⚠ Some people think it is rude to say **what?** or **what did you say?**

9 to say something that someone else has said

quote /kwəʊt/ [v I/T] to repeat exactly something that someone else has said or written, especially someone famous: *He was always quoting clever sayings from Oscar Wilde's plays.*

+ from *Let me quote from the report: "6000 children die each day from curable diseases."* | *Phil can quote from any Shakespeare play you mention.*

quotation /kwəʊˈteɪʃən/ [n C] a sentence or phrase from a book, poem etc, which you repeat because it is interesting or funny, or because it supports what you are saying

+ from *Spencer began his speech with a quotation from Karl Marx.*

10 to say what will happen in the future

predict /prɪˈdɪkt/ [v T] to say what you think will happen in the future: *Most of the papers are predicting an easy victory for the Dallas Cowboys.* | *a major earthquake that no-one had predicted*

+ that *Some experts predict that the Earth's temperatures will rise by as much as 5° over the next 20 years.*

prediction /prɪˈdɪkʃən/ [n C] a statement saying what you think will happen in the future: *Despite their confident predictions, sales of the new car have not been very good.*

make a prediction *It's too early to make any predictions about the election results.*

forecast /ˈfɔːʳkɑːst‖-kæst/ [v T] to publicly say what will happen in the future with the weather or with the economic or political situation, especially when you have special or technical knowledge: *UK politicians are forecasting a big improvement in employment opportunities.*

forecast rain/fine weather/snow etc *Rain is forecast for all parts of southern England tomorrow.*

+ that *Hardly anyone had forecast that the drought would last so long.*

forecasting – forecast or **forecasted – have forecast** or **have forecasted**

forecast /ˈfɔːʳkɑːst‖-kæst/ [n C] a public statement saying what is likely to happen with the weather or with the economic or political situation, based on special or technical knowledge

the weather forecast (=a statement in a newspaper, or on the TV or radio, saying what the weather will be like during the next few days) *According to the weather forecast, it's going to stay hot for the rest of the week.*

give/make a forecast *It is impossible to give an accurate forecast of company sales 10 years from now.*

11 something that someone says

remark /rɪˈmɑːʳk/ [n C] something that you say, for example an opinion or something you have noticed: *I ignored his rude remarks about my clothes.*

make a remark (=say something) *Mr Hill sat down and made a few remarks about the weather.*

comment /'kɒment‖'kɑː-/ [n C/U] something that you say or write, especially to give an opinion or explanation: *OK, that's what we are suggesting – does anyone have any comments?*
+ on/about *She had written some useful comments on my essay.*
make a comment *We were discussing her new movie, and Jill made some interesting comments about it.*
Ǫno comment SPOKEN (=used by politicians, business leaders etc when they do not want to publicly answer a question) *"What is your view of the affair, Prime Minister?" "No comment."*

Ǫthing to say /θɪŋ tə 'seɪ/ ESPECIALLY SPOKEN **a strange/stupid/horrible etc thing to say** a remark that is strange, stupid etc: *What an awful thing to say about your mother! | I said I was crazy about her. I know it was a silly thing to say.*

point /pɔɪnt/ [n C] something that you say, which people had not thought about or discussed until you mentioned it: *That's a good point, and we should take it into consideration.*
make a point (=say something in a discussion, which people had not thought of before) *In his speech, Marks made the point that far more people died from smoking tobacco than from taking drugs.*

announcement /ə'naʊnsmənt/ [n C] a public or official statement telling people what has happened or what will happen: *The announcement was heard by millions of radio listeners this morning.*
+ of/about *I read the announcement of her death in today's newspaper.*
make an announcement *Silence, please. Mr Bennett is about to make an announcement.*

statement /'steɪtmənt/ [n C] something that someone says or writes publicly in order to tell people what they intend to do, what their opinion is etc: *In a statement, the BBC admitted that it had given incorrect information.*
make a statement (=say something publicly) *The President will make a statement to the press this afternoon.*

12   what people say about something

according to /ə'kɔːdɪŋ tuː/ use this to tell someone what someone else has said or written
according to John/my sister/the newspaper etc *According to the paper, 20 people died in the fire. | Rob's got a new girlfriend, according to Janine.*

Ǫthey say/people say /ðeɪ 'seɪ, ˌpiːpəl 'seɪ/ SPOKEN use this to say what a lot of people believe and are talking about
+ (that) *They say her husband's in prison.*
so they say (=when you are not sure whether something is true) *The test isn't difficult, or so they say.*

Ǫapparently /ə'pærəntli/ [adv] SPOKEN use this to say what you have read or been told, although you do not know about it yourself: *It's going to be hot this weekend, apparently. | Apparently, Jim's a really good tennis player.*

rumour BRITISH **rumor** AMERICAN /'ruːmər/ [n C/U] a story that is passed from one person to another among a lot of people, and which may or may not be true
+ about *Have you heard the rumor about him and his secretary?*
+ that *There are rumors that the band may be splitting up.*
spread a rumour (=tell other people a rumour) *Someone's been spreading nasty rumours about me.*

gossip /'gɒsɪp‖'gɑː-/ [n U] things people tell each other about other people's private lives, which may or may not be true: *I got back from my vacation eager to hear all the latest gossip.*

> ⚠ Don't say 'gossips'. Just say **gossip**.

13   not saying anything
➡ see also **QUIET**

silent /'saɪlənt/ [adj] ESPECIALLY WRITTEN not speaking: *She was silent for a moment as she tried to think.*
fall silent (=become silent) *The crowd fell silent as the President stood up to speak.*

☺I didn't know what to say /aɪ ˌdɪdnt nəʊ wɒt tə 'seɪ/ SPOKEN say this when you are suddenly surprised or embarrassed about something, and you cannot think of anything suitable to say: *I didn't know what to say. It was such a wonderful present.*

speechless /'spiːtʃləs/ [adj not before noun] unable to say anything because you are very angry, surprised, or upset: *Anna was speechless. She had never seen such luxury before.*
speechless with anger/rage/horror etc *Laura stared at him, absolutely speechless with rage.*

SECRET

when only a few people know about something, and they do not tell anyone else

➡ see also PRIVATE, TELL, HIDE

1 information/plans/places/meetings

secret /'siːkrɪt/ [adj] if something is **secret**, not many people know about it, and they agree not to tell anyone else about it: *The tunnel had a secret entrance, which only the children knew about.* | *The decision was made at a secret meeting yesterday.*
top secret (=when an official document is very secret) *I was allowed to see top secret plans for a new fighter plane.*
  secretly [adv] without anyone else knowing: *They were secretly married last week.*

secret /'siːkrɪt/ [n C] something that you do not want other people to know about: *Her exact age remained a secret.*
  ☺be a secret ESPECIALLY SPOKEN *Don't tell anyone. It's a secret.* | *The recipe is a family secret.*
  tell sb a secret *I'll tell you a secret if you promise not to tell anyone else.*
  state secret (=information that a government keeps secret from other countries) *Burgess was accused of giving away state secrets to the Russians.*

When you see **EC**, go to the
ESSENTIAL COMMUNICATION section.

confidential /ˌkɒnfɪˈdenʃəl◄ˌkɑːn-/ [adj] **confidential** information is known only by a few official people, and must not be told to anyone else, for example because it contains military secrets or private details about people: *We can't give out confidential information about our patients.* | *confidential records on each employee*
highly confidential (=very confidential) *This is a highly confidential matter – can she be trusted?*
  confidentially [adv] *Wyatt had been told confidentially that the President planned to invade Grenada.*

in secret /ɪn 'siːkrɪt/ if you do something **in secret**, you do it secretly, especially because other people do not want you to do it: *They planned the attack in secret.* | *Church services were held in secret, because they were not officially allowed.*

in private /ɪn 'praɪvɪt/ if you talk to someone or discuss something **in private**, you do it where other people cannot see you or hear you: *I'd like to talk to you in private.* | *The judge heard the case in private.*

undercover /ˌʌndərˈkʌvər◄/ [adj only before noun] working secretly – use this about the activities of the police, the army etc
undercover agent/detective/police officer *The bomb was found by an undercover detective.*
undercover operation/investigation *Six members of a drug-smuggling gang were arrested after an 18-month undercover police operation.*

2 thoughts/feelings

secret /'siːkrɪt/ [adj] **secret** thoughts and feelings are ones that you do not tell anyone else about: *Her secret ambition was to be a dancer.* | *He kept a secret diary for fifteen years.*
  secretly [adv] *He was secretly ashamed of his family.*

private /'praɪvɪt/ [adj] **private** thoughts and feelings are about you, your family, and your friends, and you do not think other people should know about them: *She used to write down all her most private thoughts in a book that she kept under the bed.* | *I don't want to discuss it with you – it's private.*

3 to not tell other people about a secret

not tell sb /nɒt 'tel (sb)/ to not tell someone about something: *I didn't tell my parents in case they got worried.*
+ about *Vinny didn't tell the police about his visit to Mahoney's apartment.*
+ (that) *She didn't tell anyone she was leaving.*

keep sth secret /ˌkiːp (sth) 'siːkrɨt/ to not tell other people something, because you want it to remain a secret: *They wanted to keep their relationship secret for as long as possible.*
+ from *Many of Stalin's actions were kept secret from the world until after his death.*

keep sth from sb /'kiːp (sth) frɒm (sb)/ [phrasal verb T] to deliberately not tell someone about something, especially because you think they would be upset if they knew the truth: *Edward never told anyone about his illness. He even tried to keep it from his wife.*

keep quiet /ˌkiːp 'kwaɪət/ INFORMAL to deliberately not talk about something in public, especially something you are ashamed or embarrassed about
+ about *He paid his secretary to keep quiet about their affair.*
keep sth quiet (=keep something secret) *Let's try to keep it quiet until we've talked to Steve.*

SEE

➡ if you mean 'see someone doing something wrong', go to **CATCH 4**
➡ see also **WATCH, LOOK AT, NOTICE**

⚠ Don't confuse **see**, **watch**, and **look at**. When you **see** something, you notice it with your eyes, either deliberately or accidentally: *I saw an accident on my way to school today.* You **watch** things like films, sports games, or other situations where there is action and movement: *Dad was watching a basketball game on TV.* When you **look at** people, scenery, pictures, and other things that are not moving, you deliberately pay attention to them: *Look at this old picture of Sally!*

1 to see someone or something

see /siː/ [v T] *I saw your brother in town this morning.* | *Have you seen my pen anywhere?* | *If you see either of these men, inform the police immediately.*
see sb doing sth *I saw Matt coming out of the cinema with Jane.*
see sb do sth *Did you see Jim leave?*
see who/what/where *It was too dark for her to see who the woman was.*
can see sb/sth *Shh! I can see someone moving in the bushes.*
seeing – saw – have seen

⚠ In the present tense, it is more usual to say **I can see, she can see** etc, than to say 'I see', 'she sees' etc, or 'I am seeing', 'she is seeing' etc.

see

She was blindfolded so she couldn't see.

She enjoyed looking at her friend's photographs.

He was watching television.

catch sight of/catch a glimpse of /ˌkætʃ 'saɪt ɒv, ˌkætʃ ə 'glɪmps ɒv/ ESPECIALLY WRITTEN to see someone or something for only a second, and not very clearly: *Rick caught sight of the driver's face as the car raced past.* | *Lynn caught a brief glimpse of herself in the mirror.*

spot /spɒt‖spɑːt/ [v T] to suddenly see someone or something that you have been looking for, or something interesting or unusual: *Yates was spotted by police as he drove through the centre of Manchester.* | *I was just browsing through the job adverts when I spotted it.*

spotting – spotted – have spotted

witness /'wɪtnᵻs/ [v T] to see something happen, especially an accident, a crime, or an important event: *Police are appealing for information from anyone who witnessed the attack.* | *The crash was witnessed by millions of viewers who were watching the race on TV.*

⚠ **Witness** is a more formal or official word than **see**, and is not usually used in normal conversation.

make out /ˌmeɪk 'aʊt/ [phrasal verb T] to see someone or something, but only with difficulty
make out sth *It was dark, and Patrick could just make out the shape of a woman in front of him.*
make out what/where/who *It was difficult to make out where the rocks ended and the sea began.*

⚠ **Make out** is used especially in stories or descriptions of events.

2 something that you see

sight /saɪt/ [n C] something that you see: *Sunrise over the Himalayas is a magnificent sight.*
the sight of sth (=when you see something) *I can't stand the sight of blood.*
a familiar sight (=something that you often see) *Homeless kids are now a familiar sight on London's streets.*
the sights (=the interesting things for tourists to see in a place) *Klaus took me around Munich and showed me the sights.*

view /vjuː/ [n C] the whole area that you see from somewhere, for example when you look out of a window or down from a hill and see a beautiful place
get/have a view (=be able to see all of it) *She had a great view from her window across the park.*
+ of *a view of the surrounding countryside*

scene /siːn/ [n C often plural] what you see in a place, especially when you are describing a place where something unusual or shocking is happening: *Reporters described the horrific scenes which followed the bombing.*
scenes of confusion/suffering/violence etc *There are scenes of confusion here as refugees pour out of the city.*

3 when something can be seen

visible /'vɪzᵻbəl/ [adj] if something is **visible**, it can be seen: *I examined the animal, but there were no visible signs of injury.*
clearly visible *The bullet-marks are still clearly visible in the walls.*

in sight /ɪn 'saɪt/ if someone or something is **in sight**, you can see them from where you are: *The only building in sight was a small wooden cabin.* | *Meredith looked around – there was no-one in sight.*

show /ʃəʊ/ [v I] if something **shows**, people can see it, especially when you do not want them to: *Don't worry about that mark – it won't show.* | *The baby's head was just showing from under the blanket.*

showing – showed – have shown

appear /ə'pɪəʳ/ [v I] if someone or something **appears**, you begin to see them or you suddenly see them
+ at/in/on etc *At that moment, Kenny appeared in the doorway.*
+ from behind/under *A man suddenly appeared from behind the bushes.*

in front of sb /ɪn 'frʌnt ɒv (sb)/ if something happens **in front of** someone, it happens where they can see it, especially when it is something shocking or unpleasant: *The man was shot in front of his wife and three children.*

right in front of sb (use this to emphasize how shocking something is) *He lit up a cigarette right in front of the head teacher!*

come into view /ˌkʌm ɪntə 'vjuː/ WRITTEN if someone or something **comes into view**, you start to see them as you get nearer to them or as they come closer: *As we turned the corner, the house came into view.*

> ⚠ **Come into view** is used especially in stories and written descriptions.

4 when something cannot be seen

invisible /ɪnˈvɪzəbəl/ [adj] if something is **invisible**, it cannot be seen: *The gas is invisible but highly dangerous.*

out of sight /ˌaʊt əv 'saɪt/ if someone or something is **out of sight**, you cannot see them because they are too far away, or because they are behind something else: *Jim waited until his parents' car was out of sight and then left the house.*

5 someone who cannot see

blind /blaɪnd/ [adj] someone who is **blind** cannot see at all: *Blake is now over 90, and almost blind.*

go blind (=become blind) *Helena went blind at the age of 30.*

the blind (=people who are blind) *a radio programme specially for the blind*

> ⚠ Don't say 'become blind'. Say **go blind**.

blind [v T often passive] to make someone unable to see, either for a short time or permanently: *As I came out of the tunnel, I was blinded by the sun.* | *A riding accident left her blinded in one eye.* (=she can still see with the other one)

⌕can't see /ˌkɑːnt 'siː‖ˌkænt-/ ESPECIALLY SPOKEN if you **can't see**, you are unable to see things, either because there is something wrong with your eyesight, or because something is preventing you seeing clearly: *My mother can't see very well.* | *When I woke up, I found I couldn't see.*

6 the ability to see

sight /saɪt/ [n U] the ability to see: *There are five senses: sight, smell, hearing, taste, and touch.*

lose your sight (=become unable to see) *He lost his sight in an accident.*

eyesight /ˈaɪsaɪt/ [n U] the ability to see – use this to talk about how well or badly someone can see: *My eyesight's got a lot worse over the last few years.* | *William has perfect eyesight.*

can see /kən 'siː/ if you **can see**, you are able to see things, especially after you have been unable to: *Thanks to a new operation, Ann can see for the first time in her life.* | *Turn the light on so we can see!*

7 something that you can see through

clear /klɪər/ [adj] if water, air, or glass is **clear**, you can easily see through it: *The lake was so clear that you could see the plants on the bottom.* | *On a clear day, you can see Mount Fuji from Tokyo.*

transparent /trænˈspærənt/ [adj] use this about objects or materials that you can see through, especially things made of plastic: *The box has a transparent plastic lid so you can see what's inside.*

see-through /ˈsiː θruː/ [adj usually before noun] **see-through** clothes are made of thin material that you can see through: *a see-through blouse*

8 things that help you to see

glasses /ˈɡlɑːsɪz‖ˈɡlæ-/ (also **spectacles** FORMAL) [n plural] something that you wear in front of your eyes in order to see more clearly, consisting of two pieces of glass in a frame

spectacles /ˈspektəkəlz/ [n plural] FORMAL glasses

sunglasses /ˈsʌnˌɡlɑːsɪz‖-ˌɡlæ-/ [n plural] dark glasses that you wear to protect your eyes when the sun is very bright

contact lenses /ˈkɒntækt ˌlenzɪz‖ˈkɑːn-/ [n plural] two small round pieces of plastic that you wear on the surface of your eyes in order to see more clearly

telescope /'telɪskəʊp/ [n C] a piece of equipment like a tube that you look through in order to see things that are very far away

microscope /'maɪkrəskəʊp/ [n C] a piece of scientific equipment that you look through in order to see extremely small things

SEEM

➡ see also **SHOW 5**

1 to seem

seem /siːm/ [v] if someone or something **seems** to be happy, dishonest, true etc, that is what you think they are, even though you are not completely certain
seem nice/worried/honest/unfair etc *She seemed happy at her new school.*
sth seems strange/unfair/important etc (to sb) *The whole situation seems very strange to me.*
seem to be/do sth *Lack of money seems to be the main problem.* | *At first the crowd didn't seem to notice him.*
it seems (that)/it seems to sb (that) (use this to say what you think about a situation) *It seems that someone forgot to lock the door.* | *It seemed to Jim that Amy was worried about something.*
seem like sth ESPECIALLY SPOKEN (=seem to be) *Kevin seems like a nice guy.*
there seems to be *There seems to be something wrong with the TV.*
it seems as if *There were so many delays – it seemed as if we would never get home.*
it seems likely/possible/probable (that) *It seems likely that they will release the hostages soon.*

⚠ Don't say 'she is seeming', or 'it was seeming' etc. Say **she seems, it seemed** etc.

appear /ə'pɪər/ [v] FORMAL to seem
appear to be/appear to do sth *The company appears to be making a profit at last.* | *My father appeared to be in good health.*
appear calm/rude/angry etc *It's difficult to ask someone their age without appearing rude.*

it appears that *It appeared that no-one was at home.*

look /lʊk/ [v] if someone or something **looks** good, bad, tired etc, that is how they seem to you when you look at them
look good/happy/tired etc *That book looks interesting.* | *Warren looked tired after his long drive.*
look like sth *The burglar was holding what looked like a shotgun.*
look as if *You look as if you haven't slept all night.*
it looks as if (use this to say how a situation seems to you) *It looks as if we are going to need more help.*

⚠ Don't say 'she looked like excited'. Say **she looked excited.**

sound /saʊnd/ [v] if someone or something **sounds** good, bad, strange, angry etc, that is how they seem to you when you hear about them or read about them
sound good/bad/awful/angry etc *Istanbul sounds really exciting.* | *He sounds a pretty strange person.*
sound like sth *Serge's idea for a party sounded like fun.*
it sounds (to me) as if (use this to say how a situation seems to you when you hear about it) *It sounds to me as if he needs to see a doctor.*

strike sb as sth /'straɪk (sb) əz (sth)/ [phrasal verb T] if a person or situation **strikes** you **as** strange, interesting, unusual etc, this is your opinion of how they seem: *What strikes me as odd is the fact that she didn't report the burglary to the police.* | *Clare didn't strike me as the type who would want to be a teacher.*
strike sb as being/having *He never struck me as being very interested in politics.*

2 when a feeling or situation seems to be real

apparent /ə'pærənt/ [adj only before noun] **apparent** abilities, feelings, or attitudes seem to be real, but you cannot be sure if they are real: *She was upset by her father-in-law's apparent dislike of her.* | *What shocked me was the parents' apparent lack of interest in their child.*

apparently /ə'pærəntli/ [adv] He walked away from the crash, apparently unhurt.

on the surface /ɒn ðə 'sɜːrfɪs/ if a person, place, or situation is pleasant, normal, calm etc **on the surface**, they seem that way until you know them better: On the surface, life seemed normal in Beirut at that time. | Mike was very pleasant on the surface, but he had a nasty temper.

3 the way something seems

appearance /ə'pɪərəns/ [n C/U] if someone or something has the **appearance** of being a particular kind of person or thing, they seem to be like that, but in fact they may not be

give the appearance of (=seem like) Karen gives the appearance of being confident, but she isn't really.

to all appearances (=it seems to everyone) To all appearances, Ken and Gina were a happily married couple.

impression /ɪm'preʃən/ [n C] your **impression** of someone or something is the way they seem to you

+ of What's your impression of Frank as a boss?

get the impression (that) (=think something is a fact, because it seems true) We got the impression that Sally wasn't very pleased to see us. | For some reason she got the impression that you didn't like her.

give sb the impression that (=make people believe something, by making it appear to be true) In her book, she gives the impression that she was a close friend of the Prince, but in fact she only met him twice..

first impression (=how someone or something seems to you the first time you see them) My first impression of England was of a grey and rainy place.

⚠ Don't say 'what's your impression about him?' Say what's your impression of him?

When you see **EC**, go to the **ESSENTIAL COMMUNICATION** section.

SELL

BUY   EXPENSIVE
SHOP   see   COST
        also
BUSINESS   MONEY
CHEAP   ADVERTISING

1 to sell something

sell /sel/ [v T] to give something to someone in exchange for money: Tom's thinking of selling his motorcycle and buying a new one. | Postcards and souvenirs were being sold outside the cathedral.

sell sb sth The woman who sold us the apartment went to live in Florida.

sell sth to sb It is illegal to sell tobacco to anyone under the age of 18. | The picture was sold to an art gallery in Philadelphia.

sell sth for £250/$50 etc I managed to sell my old car for £2000.

selling – sold – have sold

export /ɪk'spɔːrt/ [v T] if a country or company **exports** its products, it sends them to another country in order to sell them: Japanese companies export televisions and hi-fi systems all over the world.

export sth to sb In 1986 they exported 210,000 cases of wine to the UK.

exporter [n C] Saudi Arabia is one of the world's leading exporters of oil.

deal in sth /'diːl ɪn (sth)/ [phrasal verb T] to buy and sell products for business purposes, but usually not in a shop – use this especially about valuable things like paintings or gold, about farm products, or about stolen or illegal goods: a wholesale commodity firm dealing in cotton and corn | Slater had made a good living by dealing in stolen car radios.

bring out sth /ˌbrɪŋ 'aʊt (sth)/ [phrasal verb T] if a company **brings out** a new product, they produce it and make it available for people to buy: Microsoft has just brought out a new edition of its multimedia encyclopedia. | We're bringing out a new sports car early next year.

the sale of sth /ðə 'seɪl ɒv (sth)/ the business of selling something: *The sale of marijuana is illegal in Britain.* | *They make most of their profits from the sale of farm machinery.*

2 available for people to buy

for sale /fəʳ 'seɪl/ if something is **for sale**, the person who owns it wants to sell it: *There are several houses for sale in our street.* | *There was a notice in the window. "For Sale: Black and White Kittens".*

on sale /ɒn 'seɪl/ if a product is **on sale**, you can buy it in the shops: *These cameras are on sale in most electrical stores.*
go on sale (=begin to be available) *The new model Toyota goes on sale next month.*

on the market /ɒn ðə 'mɑːʳkɪt/ goods that are **on the market** are available for people to buy – use this especially when comparing products of the same general type: *It's one of the cheapest computers on the market.* | *There are so many different shampoos on the market that it's hard to know which one to buy.*

⚠ Don't say 'in the market'. Say **on the market**.

3 someone who sells something

sales assistant (also **shop assistant** BRITISH **sales clerk** AMERICAN) /'seɪlz ə,sɪstənt, 'ʃɒp ə,sɪstənt, 'seɪlz ˌklɑːk‖ 'ʃɑːp-, -ˌklɜːrk/ [n C] someone who deals with customers in a shop and sells them things: *Rowan worked as a sales assistant in a Beverly Hills shopping mall.* | *a shop assistant in the shoe department*

salesman/saleswoman /'seɪlzmən, 'seɪlz,wʊmən/ [n C] someone whose job is to persuade people, shops, and companies to buy their company's products: *I worked for a while as a salesman for a big computer corporation.* | *Gail has been the firm's top saleswoman for the last two years.*
plural **salesmen, saleswomen**

seller /'seləʳ/ [n C] the person who sells something to someone – use this either to talk about the buyer and seller in a business deal, or about someone who sells things to people in the street: *It was a good time for both buyers and sellers of houses.*
a fruit/flower/ice-cream/soft-drink etc seller *Outside the theatre, there was a row of flower sellers.*

dealer/pusher /'diːləʳ, 'pʊʃəʳ/ [n C] someone who buys and sells illegal drugs: *Dealers were selling heroin to teenagers outside the stadium.*
drug dealer/pusher *Drug pushers have been warned to stay away from the club.*

4 something that is sold

goods /gʊdz/ [n plural] things that are produced in order to be sold: *The store sells a wide range of goods.*
electrical/household/luxury goods *We import a lot of electrical goods from Japan.*

product /'prɒdʌkt‖'prɑː-/ [n C] anything that is made, grown, or designed in order to be sold: *There is less demand now for products like coal and steel.* | *I'm allergic to dairy products, like milk and cheese.*

⚠ **Products** can be things made in factories or grown on farms, but they can also be services like insurance or holidays: *We sell pensions, life insurance, and a range of financial products.*

exports /'ekspɔːʳts/ [n plural] goods that are sent to another country to be sold: *The value of China's exports to the US rose by over 50% last year.*

5 when a lot of something gets sold

sales /seɪlz/ [n plural] the number of products that a business sells, or the value of the products it sells: *A big price increase led to a fall in sales.*
+ of *Sales of computer games have risen dramatically over the past five years.*

⚠ You can also use **sales** before a noun, like an adjective: *sales figures* | *The department failed to achieve its sales target.*

sell /sel/ [v I] to be sold in large numbers: *Tickets for the concert just aren't selling.*
sell well *Rolls-Royces sell very well in the Far East.*

selling – sold – have sold

sell out /ˌsel ˈaʊt/ [phrasal verb I] if a shop, ticket office etc **sells out** of goods or tickets, all of them are sold so there are no more available: *I went to the store to get some bread but they had sold out.*
+ of *They opened at 8 o'clock, and by 8.30 they had sold out of tickets for the big game.*
be sold out (=when all the tickets for a performance or sports event have been sold) *We couldn't get tickets anywhere – the show was completely sold out.*

best-selling /ˌbest ˈselɪŋ◄/ [adj only before noun] a **best-selling** product is sold in large numbers, especially more than other products of the same kind: *Coca-Cola is the world's best-selling soft drink.* | *Stephen King has written several best-selling novels.*

SEND

GET　GIVE

see also

COMPUTERS　MAIL, PHONE, AND FAX

1 thing/letter/message

send /send/ [v T] to send a letter, package, message, or object to another person or place: *How many Christmas cards did you send?* | *Send a cheque for £50 with your order.*
send sb sth *Could you send me a copy of the report?* | *Mary's boyfriend sent her a dozen red roses on her birthday.*
send sth to sb *Diego sent a fax to the managing director telling him about his decision.*

sending – sent – have sent

> ⚠ Don't say 'I sent to him a letter'. Say I **sent him a letter**.

post BRITISH **mail** AMERICAN /pəʊst, meɪl/ [v T] to send a letter, package etc by putting it in a letter box or taking it to the post office: *I must remember to post Joey's birthday card.* | *Her letter had been mailed from Paris.*
post/mail sth to sb *Could you mail those photographs to me?*

send off /ˌsend ˈɒf‖-ˈɔːf/ [phrasal verb T] to send something somewhere so that it can be dealt with
send sth off *I must send this film off to be processed.*
send off sth *Did you send off your application form?*

send back /ˌsend ˈbæk/ [phrasal verb T] to return something by sending it to the place it came from
send sth back *She sent all Patrick's letters back without opening them.*
send back sth *Complete all the details, then send back the form.*

fax /fæks/ [v T] to send someone a message using a fax machine: *Shall I fax the report or mail it?*
fax sth to sb *The order will be faxed directly to the manufacturer.*
fax sb sth *They've agreed to fax us their proposals tomorrow.*

e-mail /ˈiː meɪl/ [v T] to send a message directly from one computer to another computer in a different place: *You can e-mail Richard in Sydney.*

2 person

send /send/ [v T] to make someone go somewhere, especially so that they can do something for you
send sb to/into/there etc *I've sent Michael to the supermarket to get some wine.* | *French troops were later sent into the war zone.*

sending – sent – have sent

SENSIBLE

not behaving in a stupid or unreasonable way

➡ opposite **STUPID, CRAZY**

1 person

sensible /'sensɪbəl/ [adj] someone who is **sensible** is unlikely to do anything stupid, because they judge situations well and make good decisions: *Laura is a very sensible girl – she wouldn't talk to strangers.* | *I wish you'd be more sensible – you can't go out without a coat on in this weather!*
+ about *People are far more sensible about what they drink now.*

> ⚠ Don't confuse **sensible** (=likely to make good decisions and not do stupid things) and **sensitive** (=good at realizing how other people feel).

reasonable /'riːzənəbəl/ [adj] someone who is **reasonable** makes sensible decisions that are fair to everyone: *He's a reasonable man; I'm sure he'll lend you the money when you explain the problem.* | *Let's try and discuss this in a calm and reasonable way.*
◯**be reasonable!** SPOKEN *Be reasonable! – you can't expect her to do all the work on her own!*

responsible /rɪ'spɒnsɪbəl‖rɪ'spɑːn-/ [adj] someone who is **responsible** can be trusted to do what they ought to do and to think about the results of their actions: *If Mary was a little more responsible, I wouldn't mind lending her the car.* | *We aim to educate our children to become responsible citizens.*

mature /mə'tʃʊər/ [adj] a child or young person who is **mature** behaves in a sensible way, as you would expect an older person to behave: *She's very mature for her age.* | *After two years of college, the students have a much more mature attitude.*

rational /'ræʃənəl/ [adj] if someone is **rational**, their actions are based on a clear understanding of the facts of a situation, and are not influenced by their feelings or imagination: *He says he wants to quit college because his girlfriend left him – he's not being rational.*
rationally [adv] *Do people behave completely rationally when they vote in elections?*

◯**talk sense** /ˌtɔːk 'sens/ ESPECIALLY SPOKEN if someone **talks sense**, they express sensible ideas or opinions that you agree

with: *I know he's rather bigheaded, but he does talk a lot of sense.*

2 decision/plan/idea/ action

sensible /'sensɪbəl/ [adj] a **sensible** decision, plan etc is likely to have good results because it is based on good, practical reasons and judgements: *I think that's a very sensible suggestion.* | *a sensible solution to a difficult problem*
it is sensible to do sth *It would have been more sensible to save the money than to spend it all on clothes.*
◯**the sensible thing to do** SPOKEN *The sensible thing to do would be to rest until you feel better.*
sensibly /'sensɪbli/ [adv] *She had sensibly decided to leave the car at home.*

reasonable /'riːzənəbəl/ [adj] a **reasonable** idea, request, action etc seems sensible and fair, and you can understand the reasons for it: *I thought her request for more information was reasonable, but it was refused.* | *You don't have to go. You have a perfectly reasonable excuse.*
it is reasonable to assume/believe/suppose *It's reasonable to assume that prices will rise again soon.*

◯**make sense** /ˌmeɪk 'sens/ ESPECIALLY SPOKEN if something **makes sense**, it seems a very sensible thing to do: *You don't live here but you're still paying rent? It doesn't make sense!*
it makes sense (for sb) to do sth *It made sense for Sam to live nearer the college.*

wise /waɪz/ [adj] a **wise** decision or action is based on good judgement and on your experience of life: *So Raymond's going to retire? I think he's made a wise decision.*
it is wise (for sb) to do sth *He thought it might be wise not to tell her what had happened.* | *Do you think it's wise for him to travel alone?*

logical /'lɒdʒɪkəl‖'lɑː-/ [adj] a **logical** action or decision seems to be clearly the right thing to do, because it is based on thinking intelligently about all the facts of a situation, and not based on feelings or emotions: *As I wanted to travel to other countries, studying languages was the logical choice.* | *This is the logical place to build a new airport.*

it is/it seems logical to do sth *It seemed logical to start by visiting the scene of the crime.*

rational /ˈræʃənəl/ [adj] **rational argument/behaviour/decision/explanation etc** a decision, way of behaving etc that is based on real facts or scientific knowledge, and not influenced by feelings or imagination: *It can't just have disappeared! I'm sure there's a perfectly rational explanation.* | *The doctor should give you the facts so that you can make a rational decision.*

realistic /rɪəˈlɪstɪk◂/ [adj] based on a good understanding of what is or is not possible and practical: *Starting my own business is not a realistic idea at the moment.*
it is realistic to do sth *It's not realistic to expect my parents to lend us any more money.*

○**be a good idea** /biː ə ˌɡʊd aɪˈdɪə/ ESPECIALLY SPOKEN if a plan, decision, or action **is a good idea**, it seems sensible and seems to be the right thing to do: *Yes, I think a short meeting this afternoon would be a good idea.*
it's a good idea to do sth *It's a good idea to tell a friend if you are going on a date with someone you don't know well.*

3 the ability to make sensible decisions

common sense /ˌkɒmən ˈsens◂ˌkɑː-/ [n U] the ability to make sensible, practical decisions, based on experience: *She has a lot of common sense.* | *Common sense should tell you that this is not a good idea.*
use your common sense! *It's not difficult to work out the answer – you just have to use your common sense!*

sense /sens/ [n U] the ability to behave in an intelligent and sensible way, and to avoid doing anything stupid
have the sense to do sth (=be sensible enough to do what is needed in order to avoid problems, danger etc) *Luckily, Sheena had the sense to call the police before Baxter left the building.*
have enough/little/not much sense *I'm sure she has too much sense to give him her address.*

SEPARATE

ALONE   JOIN

see also

TOGETHER   RELATIONSHIP

1 not together

separate /ˈsepərɪt/ [adj] not together: *They sleep in separate beds.* | *a university with three separate campuses*
+ from *Their house was separate from the rest of the village.*
keep sth separate *He likes to keep his work and his family life separate.* | *Keep your bank card and your PIN number separate.*

apart /əˈpɑːrt/ [adv] if people or things are **apart**, they are in different places and there is a distance between them: *Jo and Sam decided to try living apart for a while.* | *Since the universe began, the galaxies have gradually moved further apart.*
+ from *Helen noticed one little boy standing apart from the rest of the group.*
keep sb apart *The two sets of rival fans had to be kept apart by the police.*

separately /ˈsepərɪtli/ [adv] not together, but at separate times or in separate places: *The couple arrived separately at London Airport yesterday.* | *Each problem should be considered separately.*

2 to separate two things, people, or groups

separate /ˈsepəreɪt/ [v T] to put people or things that were together into different places or groups: *If you two don't stop talking during class, I'll have to separate you.*
separate sth from sth *Farmers separate calves from their mothers when they are only a few days old.* | *Break an egg and separate the white from the yolk.*
separate sth into groups/piles/parts etc *Sheila had separated the clothes into two piles.*

divide /dɪˈvaɪd/ [v T] to separate something into a number of smaller parts

divide sth into two/three etc (=into two, three etc parts or pieces) *We divided the pizza into three and had a slice each.* | *The country is divided into seven provinces.*

divide sth between/among (sb) *They divided the money equally between them.*

be divided into *Most of these big old houses have been divided into apartments.*

split /splɪt/ [v T] to separate something that used to be a single thing or a single group into two or more completely different parts: *Rutherford first split the atom on 3rd January 1919.*

split sth in half/in two (=so that it makes two equal parts) *Why don't you just split the money in half?*

split sth into two/three etc (=into two, three etc parts or pieces) *For this exercise, I'm going to split the class into three groups.*

splitting – split – have split

segregate /ˈsegrɪgeɪt/ [v T often passive] to separate one group of people from others, especially because of their race, sex, religion etc: *The school system should not segregate children with disabilities.*

be segregated from *Male prisoners were strictly segregated from the females.*

segregated [adj]
segregated school/hotel/cinema/housing etc (=for only one group or race, and not for others) *At that time, the beaches in South Africa were segregated.*

3 when something becomes separated into different parts

divide /dɪˈvaɪd/ [v I] to become separated into two or more parts

a road/path/river divides *They came to a point where the river divided.*

+ into *The single cell divides into two identical cells.*

split /splɪt/ [v I] if a group of people **splits**, it becomes separated into two or more smaller groups

split into two/three etc *The class split into two. Half of us went to the museum*

and half to the cathedral. | *a political party that split into three separate groups*

splitting – split – have split

SERIOUS

➡ look here for ...
• a serious problem, accident, illness, crime
• not joking
➡ see also **JOKE**

1 a serious problem/accident/illness/crime

serious /ˈsɪəriəs/ [adj] very bad – use this about problems, accidents, illnesses, or crimes: *There was a serious accident on the freeway.* | *serious head injuries* | *Unemployment is a serious problem in many countries.* | *Drug smuggling is a serious crime.*

seriously [adv]
seriously ill/injured/affected *Her father is seriously ill in the hospital.*

bad /bæd/ [adj] serious enough to cause problems or make you feel worried – use this especially about accidents or illnesses: *I stayed home yesterday with a bad cold.* | *a bad car crash*

badly [adv]
badly injured/damaged/affected *Several people were killed or badly injured in the attack.* | *The furniture was badly damaged by fire.*

> ⚠ Don't say 'her hands were burned badly'. Say **her hands were badly burned**. **Badly** comes before a past participle.

desperate /ˈdespərɪt/ [adj] use this about a very serious or dangerous situation, especially when people will die if it does not improve: *The situation is getting desperate – we've had no rain for months.* | *a desperate shortage of food and medical supplies*

nasty /ˈnɑːsti‖ˈnæsti/ [adj] ESPECIALLY SPOKEN use this about small accidents or illnesses that are worse than you would normally expect them to be: *That cough sounds nasty – you ought to see a doctor.* | *He had a nasty cut on his head.*

nasty – nastier – nastiest

2 when you really mean what you say

be serious /biː ˈsɪəriəs/ to really mean what you say, or really intend to do something: *Listen! I'm serious! I'm not lending you any money.* | *Barratt had threatened them, but no-one was sure if he was serious.*

be serious about doing sth *I hope Jeff's serious about giving up smoking.*

be perfectly/absolutely serious (=be serious, even though this seems very unlikely) *"Look!" he said, "I am perfectly serious. I'm willing to give you $10,000 for your land."*

not joking /nɒt ˈdʒəʊkɪŋ/ SPOKEN if you are **not joking**, you really mean what you say, even though it seems surprising or unlikely: *There must have been about 10 of them in that car – I'm not joking.* | *She told him she'd call the police if he bothered her again, and she wasn't joking.*

seriously /ˈsɪəriəsli/ [adv] SPOKEN say this to emphasize that something surprising is really true, or to ask whether something surprising is really true: *Seriously, I think you're making a big mistake.* | *"She's quit her job." "Seriously?"*

mean /miːn/ [v T] if someone **means** what they say, they are being serious when they say it, and they are not pretending or lying

mean it ESPECIALLY SPOKEN *I mean it – I'll scream if you don't let me go.* | *She told me she loved me, but I wasn't sure if she meant it.*

mean what you say *I meant what I said – I never want to see you again.*

meaning – meant – have meant

mean business /ˌmiːn ˈbɪznɪs/ INFORMAL if someone **means business**, it is very clear that they will definitely do what they say or what they are threatening to do: *The man had a gun. It was obvious he meant business.*

3 someone who does not tell jokes or laugh

serious /ˈsɪəriəs/ someone who is **serious** is quiet and sensible, and does not seem to enjoy laughing and joking: *Friends described him as a serious and thoughtful man.*

+ about *Laura was always very serious about her work.*

SEX

LOVE   RELATIONSHIP

see also

MARRY   BABY

GIRLFRIEND/BOYFRIEND

1 male or female

sex /seks/ [n C/U] someone's **sex** is whether they are male or female: *Put your name, age, and sex on the form.* | *Teachers of both sexes are employed by the school.*

the opposite sex (=the sex which is not your own) *He has never shown much interest in members of the opposite sex.*

plural **sexes**

2 sexual activities

sex /seks/ [n U] the activity of having sex with someone: *She had no interest in sex after the baby was born.*

have sex *Many people first have sex when they are at college.* | *The average couple have sex three times a week.*

safe sex (=methods of protecting yourself against sexual diseases while you are having sex)

sexual /ˈsekʃuəl/ [adj] **sexual activity/behaviour/relationship/problems/feelings etc** activity, behaviour etc involving sex: *Dr Ruth offers advice on sexual problems.*

sexual intercourse FORMAL (=sex) *It is illegal to have sexual intercourse with a girl under 16 years of age.*

sexual abuse (=when someone forces a child to have sex or touches them in a sexual way) *Sexual abuse and violence against children are increasing every year.*

sexual harassment (=when someone at work, at college etc talks to you or touches you in a sexual way when you do not want them to) *Victims of sexual harassment at* work are often afraid of losing their jobs if they complain about it.

sleep with sb/sleep together /ˈsliːp wɪð (sb), ˈsliːp təˌɡeðəʳ/ [phrasal verb] to have sex with someone that you are not married to, especially regularly and over a period of time: *She's been sleeping with this guy Mark since the summer.* | *When did you first find out that Betty and your husband were sleeping together?*

make love /ˌmeɪk ˈlʌv/ if two people **make love**, they have sex because they like or love each other: *All day they made love on the unmade bed.*
+ with *When I first made love with him, we were both a little shy and nervous.*

⚠ **Make love** is used especially in stories or descriptions of past events.

rape /reɪp/ [v T] to force someone to have sex when they do not want to: *The woman was raped and then murdered by her kidnapper.* | *He was accused of raping his ex-girlfriend.*
rape [n C/U] the crime of raping someone: *Rape victims receive special counselling and are treated very sensitively.*

seduce /sɪˈdjuːs‖-ˈduːs/ [v T] to persuade someone to have sex with you, especially someone who is younger than you or has less sexual experience than you: *He knew that Antonia was engaged but decided, quite shamelessly, to seduce her.*

fancy /ˈfænsi/ [v T] BRITISH INFORMAL to be sexually attracted to someone, especially someone that you do not know very well: *All the girls fancied Bob.* | *My friend really fancies you.*
fancying – fancied – have fancied

mate /meɪt/ [v I] if birds and animals **mate**, they have sex in order to produce babies: *The birds mate in April and the eggs are hatched by June.*

3 sexually attractive

attractive /əˈtræktɪv/ [adj] someone who is **attractive** has a personality or appearance that makes other people sexually attracted to them
+ to *I don't know what makes Jamie so attractive to women.*

find sb attractive (=think they are attractive) *She's very nice but I don't really find her attractive.*

sexually attractive *Young, rich, intelligent, and sexually attractive – she had it all!*

sexy /ˈseksi/ **sexy** people or clothes make you feel sexually excited: *sexy lace underwear* | *He's the sexiest man I've ever met.*
sexy – sexier – sexiest

4 books/movies/jokes/ conversations etc about sex

pornography /pɔːʳˈnɒɡrəfi‖-ˈnɑːr-/ [n U] films, magazines, or pictures that show sexual acts and are intended to make people feel sexually excited: *Is there a link between pornography and sex crimes?*
hard-core pornography (=very pornographic materials, which may be illegal) *Two trucks full of illegal hard-core pornography were seized by customs officials today.*

porn /pɔːʳn/ [n U] INFORMAL films, magazines, or pictures that show sexual acts in order to make people feel sexually excited: *Teachers and parents are worried about porn on the Internet.*
hard porn (=very pornographic material) *a back-street movie theater showing hard-porn movies*
soft porn (=not very pornographic) *81 per cent of our readers said they regularly watched soft-porn movies.*

pornographic /ˌpɔːʳnəˈɡræfɪk◄/ [adj] a **pornographic** film, magazine, or picture shows or describes sexual acts in order to make people sexually excited: *He admitted possessing nude photographs, but denied they were pornographic.* | *She was offered $50,000 to pose for a pornographic magazine.*

erotic /ɪˈrɒtɪk‖ɪˈrɑː-/ [adj] an **erotic** book, film, painting etc shows or describes sexual acts in a way that is deliberately sexually exciting but is also artistic: *He writes both poetry and erotic literature.* | *A number of scenes in the film were very erotic.*

obscene /əbˈsiːn/ [adj] **obscene** words or pictures are about sex and are very offensive: *'Lady Chatterley's Lover' was banned as an obscene book.* | *He was*

charged with smuggling obscene materials into the UK.

> ⚠ **Obscene** is used especially about something that is illegal.

dirty /'dɜːʳti/ [adj only before noun] INFORMAL **dirty** books, jokes, films etc are about sex – use this especially to show that you think these things are unpleasant: *They just sit around telling dirty jokes – it's very boring.* | *He used to keep a collection of dirty books hidden under his bed.*

dirty – dirtier – dirtiest

5 someone who is sexually attracted to their own sex

gay /geɪ/ [adj] sexually attracted to people of your own sex: *When did you first tell your parents you were gay?* | *I'm sure Tony isn't having an affair with your wife. He's gay.*
gay bar/club/newspaper (=for gay people) *Wednesday night is gay night at the Pink Flamingo Club.*
the gay community (=people who are gay, considered as a group) *The decision to show the film has outraged the gay community.*
   gay [n C] a gay man or woman: *San Francisco has the highest population of gays in the United States.*

homosexual /ˌhəʊməˈsekʃʊəl◄, ˌhɒ-‖ˌhəʊ-/ [adj] sexually attracted to people of your own sex: *Homosexual men and women are fighting for the right to join the army.* | *Do you think homosexual couples should be allowed to get married?*
   homosexual [n C] a gay man: *Steve was 18 when he told his parents he was a homosexual.*

> ⚠ **Homosexual** is more formal than **gay**.

lesbian /'lezbiən/ [n C] a woman who is sexually attracted to other women: *a telephone chatline for lesbians*
   lesbian [adj only before noun] *lesbian writers*

> When you see **EC**, go to the **ESSENTIAL COMMUNICATION** section.

6 sexually attracted to people of the opposite sex

heterosexual/straight /ˌhetərəˈsekʃʊəl◄, streɪt/ [adj] someone who is **heterosexual** or **straight** is sexually attracted to people of the opposite sex: *I haven't told my straight friends that I'm gay.* | *a heterosexual relationship*

> ⚠ **Straight** is mostly spoken and is more informal than **heterosexual**.

7 when someone has sex with a person who is not their husband, girlfriend etc

unfaithful /ʌnˈfeɪθfəl/ [adj] if someone is **unfaithful**, they have sex with someone who is not their husband, girlfriend etc: *Why do women stay with unfaithful partners?* | *Jeff promised he'd never be unfaithful again.*
+ to *He accused me of being unfaithful to him.*

affair /əˈfeəʳ/ [n C] a secret sexual relationship between two people when at least one of them is married to someone else: *Their affair lasted for six years.*
have an affair (with) *My wife thinks I'm having an affair with someone at work.*

adultery /əˈdʌltəri/ [n U] when someone who is married has sex with someone who is not their husband or wife: *In some countries, adultery is a crime.*
commit adultery FORMAL (=have sex with someone who is not your husband or wife) *60% of men admit to committing adultery at some time during their marriages.*

cheat on sb /ˈtʃiːt ɒn (sb)‖-ɑːn-/ [phrasal verb T] INFORMAL if someone **cheats on** their husband, girlfriend etc, they secretly have sex with someone else: *He'd been cheating on her with a teacher at the high school.*

8 when someone only has sex with their husband, girlfriend etc

faithful /'feɪθfəl/ [adj] someone who is **faithful** only has sex with their husband, girlfriend etc: *I've always been faithful. I've never cheated on you, not once!*

+ to *This is the longest time she's ever been faithful to anyone.*

9 someone who has never had sex

virgin /'vɜːᵗdʒ₃n/ [n C] someone who has never had sex: *I was still a virgin when I got married.*

SHAKE

1 when things shake

shake /ʃeɪk/ [v I] if something **shakes**, it makes small quick movements from side to side or up and down: *The branches of the trees were shaking in the wind.* | *Suddenly the ground began to shake beneath my feet.* | *The floor shook as they danced faster and faster.*

shaking – shook – have shaken

rattle /'rætl/ [v I] if something **rattles**, it makes a noise because it keeps shaking and hitting something else: *The windows were rattling in the storm.* | *Mike knocked against the table and made the coffee cups rattle.*

wobble /'wɒbəl‖'wɑː-/ [v I] if something **wobbles**, it moves from side to side because it is not steady or not well balanced: *The pile of books wobbled and almost fell.* | *I wish this desk would stop wobbling!*

vibrate /vaɪ'breɪt‖'vaɪbreɪt/ [v I] if something **vibrates**, it shakes continuously with very small, very fast movements: *When you switch on the engine, you can feel the whole car vibrate.*

2 when someone's body, hand etc shakes

shake /ʃeɪk/ [v I] if you **shake**, you make small quick uncontrolled movements with your body, for example because you are frightened, nervous, or angry: *My hands were shaking so much I could hardly write my name on the exam paper.*

shake with **fear/anger/laughter** (=shake because you are frightened, angry etc) *The others were all shaking with laughter.*

shaking – shook – have shaken

tremble /'trembəl/ [v I] to shake very slightly because you are frightened or upset: *Jane's lip began to tremble and I thought she was going to cry.* | *The dog sat trembling in a corner.*

shiver /'ʃɪvəᵗ/ [v I] to shake because you are cold: *Julia shivered and pulled her coat more tightly around her.* | *You're shivering! Do you want to go indoors?*

3 to make something shake

shake /ʃeɪk/ [v T] to make something move up and down or from side to side with small quick movements: *Shake the bottle before you open it.* | *She shook the blanket to get rid of all the dust.* | *a huge explosion that shook houses up to five miles away*

shaking – shook – have shaken

make sth shake /,meɪk (sth) 'ʃeɪk/ to make a place or object shake – use this especially about loud noises or strong movements or explosions: *The music was so loud that it made the floor shake.* | *The distant earthquake made all the furniture shake.*

give sth a shake /,gɪv (sth) ə 'ʃeɪk/ ESPECIALLY BRITISH to hold something and shake it a few times: *I gave the box a shake to see if there was anything inside.* | *She gave the cloth a shake and put it back on the table.*

4 to shake hands as a greeting

shake hands /,ʃeɪk 'hændz/ *The two leaders shook hands and walked into the White House.*

+ with *The picture shows him shaking hands with Saddam Hussein.*

SHAPE

1 the shape of something

shape /ʃeɪp/ [n C/U] the shape that something is, for example a square, a circle etc: *You can get pasta in lots of different shapes.* | *What shape is the swimming pool?*

2 to have a particular shape

be round/square/rectangular etc
use this to say what shape something is:
The windows were round, like the windows on a ship. | *"What shape is the table?" "It's long and rectangular."*
be round/square etc in shape WRITTEN *The dining-room was square in shape, and simply furnished.*

> ⚠ When you want to describe the shape of something, don't say 'it has a square/circular etc shape' or 'its shape is square/circular etc'. Say **it is square/circular** etc.

shaped /ʃeɪpt/ [adj] **star-shaped/heart-shaped/L-shaped etc** when something has the shape of a star, a heart, the letter L etc: *The lounge was L-shaped.* | *He gave me some heart-shaped chocolates.*
shaped like sth *Her birthday cake was shaped like a train.*

in the shape of sth /ɪn ðə ˈʃeɪp ɒv (sth)/
when something has the same shape as something, for example of a bird or animal: *a beautiful blue bowl in the shape of a flower*

SHARE

1 to use something with another person

share /ʃeər/ [v I/T] if two or more people **share** something, they all use it together: *We don't have enough books, so some of you will have to share.* | *I have my own room but we share the kitchen and bathroom.*
share sth with sb *I shared a room with Tom while I was at college.*

2 to do something with another person

share /ʃeər/ [v T] if two people **share** a job or activity, they each do part of it: *Judy and I shared the driving, so it wasn't too tiring.*
share sth with sb *She shares the job with another woman who also has a young child.*

take turns/take it in turns /ˌteɪk ˈtɜːrnz, ˌteɪk ɪt ɪn ˈtɜːrnz/ if two or more people **take turns** or **take it in turns** to do something, they do it one after the other, and each person does it several times: *If the housework is too much for one person, why don't you take it in turns?*

shape

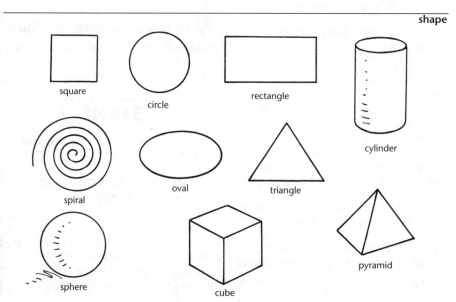

square | circle | rectangle | cylinder | spiral | oval | triangle | sphere | cube | pyramid take turns/take it in turns to do sth *The parent birds take turns to guard the nest.*

3 when several people each have part of something

share/share out /ʃeəʳ, ʃeər aʊt/ [v T] to divide something so that several people have a part of it: *We agreed that we would share the prize money if we won.*
share sth (out) among/between sb *She shared the cake between the children.* | *Profits from the sale of tickets were shared out among the members of the band.*

split /splɪt/ [v T] if a small number of people **split** something, especially money, they divide it into equal parts and take a part each: *They planned to rob a bank, split the money, and leave the country.*
split sth among/between sb *He said that the land should be split between his four sons.*
splitting – split – have split

divide/divide up /dɪˌvaɪd, dɪˌvaɪd ˈʌp/ [v T] to separate something into two or more parts
divide sth (up) between sb *Hitler and Stalin agreed to divide Poland between them.*
divide (up) sth between sb *We divided up the rest of the pie between us.*

4 to share the cost of something

share/split /ʃeəʳ, splɪt/ [v T] to share the cost of something so that each person pays part of it: *The two families shared the cost of the wedding.* | *We usually share all the bills.*
splitting – split – have split

go halves /gəʊ ˈhɑːvz‖-ˈhævz/ SPOKEN INFORMAL if two people **go halves**, they each pay half of the cost of something that they buy together
go halves with sb (on sth) *I'll go halves with you on the tickets if you like.*

5 the part of something that someone gets or owns

share /ʃeəʳ/ [n C] the part of something

that one person gets or owns when something is shared between several people
+ of *When Grandpa died we each got a share of his money.* | *Wilson's share of the business is worth $500,000.*

SHARP/NOT SHARP

➡ see also **CUT**

1 sharp

sharp /ʃɑːʳp/ [adj] something that is **sharp** can easily cut things or make holes in them, because it has a very narrow edge or point:

Be careful. That knife's very sharp. | *You'll need some sharp scissors.*
razor-sharp (=extremely sharp) *Sharks have razor-sharp teeth.*

pointed /ˈpɔɪntɪ̩d/ [adj] long, thin, and ending in a point: *a plant with long pointed leaves* | *He picked up a pointed stick and began drawing in the sand.*

2 not sharp

blunt /blʌnt/ [adj] not sharp: *This knife's blunt – it's no good for anything.* | *a blunt pencil* | *Police say the man was killed with a blunt instrument, possibly a hammer.*

3 to make something sharp

sharpen /ˈʃɑːʳpən/ [v T] to make something sharper: *I'll just sharpen my pencil.* | *a special stone for sharpening knives*

SHINE

➡ see also **BRIGHT/NOT BRIGHT, NEW, CLEAN**

1 when light comes from the sun, a lamp etc

shine /ʃaɪn/ [v I] if the sun, a lamp etc **shines**, it sends out bright light: *The sun was shining, so we decided to go to the beach.* | *She could see the lights of Hong Kong shining in the distance.*
shining – shone – have shone

glow /gləʊ/ [v I] to make a warm soft light that is not very bright: *The evening sun glowed in the sky.* | *A few lumps of coal still glowed in the fire.*
　　glow [n singular] *the soft glow of the candles*

⚠ Use **glow** when you are writing stories or descriptions.

flash /flæʃ/ [v I] to make a bright light for a very short time: *Lightning flashed across the sky.* | *The light on top of the police car was flashing.*
　　flash [n C] *There was a blinding flash of light as the bomb exploded.*

flicker /ˈflɪkəʳ/ [v I] use this about a weak flame or light which keeps becoming almost dark, so that it seems to be about to stop shining: *The candle suddenly started to flicker.* | *The flashlight is flickering. I guess it needs a new battery.*

2 when something has a bright surface

shiny /ˈʃaɪni/ [adj] something that is **shiny** has a smooth bright surface: *The little girl's shoes were made of shiny black leather.* | *Use this shampoo for thicker, shinier hair.* | *a big shiny limousine*

shiny – shinier – shiniest

glossy /ˈglɒsi‖ˈglɑːsi, ˈglɔːsi/ [adj] **glossy** hair or fur looks shiny and healthy; **glossy** magazines and books use expensive shiny paper: *She stroked the horse's glossy neck.* | *There was a stack of glossy magazines on the table.* | *glossy travel brochures*

glossy – glossier – glossiest

gleaming /ˈgliːmɪŋ/ [adj usually before noun] **gleaming** objects or vehicles are shiny because they are very new or clean: *A gleaming Porsche was parked in front of the house.* | *a gleaming white kitchen*

shine /ʃaɪn/ [v I] if something with a smooth surface **shines**, it is very bright and sends back any light that falls on it: *He polished the silver plates until they shone.*

sparkle /ˈspɑːkəl/ [v I] something that **sparkles**, such as jewellery or water, looks attractive because there are many small bright points of light on its surface: *Her diamond ring sparkled in the sunlight.* | *a sparkling mountain stream* | *The children's eyes sparkled with excitement.*

SHOOT

1 to shoot someone

shoot /ʃuːt/ [v T] to kill or injure someone by firing bullets from a gun: *Ruth Ellis shot her lover in a pub in London.* | *It's the President! He's been shot!*
　　shoot sb in the back/chest/leg etc *He had been shot in the chest but managed to crawl to safety.*
　　shoot sb dead (=shoot someone and kill them) *A tourist was shot dead by muggers in New Orleans last night.*

shooting – shot – have shot

be hit /biː ˈhɪt/ to be injured or damaged by bullets: *I didn't realize he'd been hit until he fell to the ground.* | *One of our planes was hit.*

2 to shoot a gun or other weapon

shoot /ʃuːt/ [v I] to point a gun towards someone, and make bullets come out of it: *Don't shoot! We surrender!* | *Make sure you hold the gun steady and shoot straight.*
　　+ at *We used to shoot at empty bottles for practice.*

shooting – shot – have shot

fire /faɪəʳ/ [v I/T] to make bullets come out of a gun, or shoot a bomb or explosive object into the air: *The police fired into the air to make the crowd break up.*
　　+ at *As soon as we crossed the border, enemy troops started firing at us.*
　　fire a shot/bullet *Kendrick fired three shots at the President's car.*

fire a missile/ rocket US warships began firing cruise missiles into Iraq.

3 the sound of shooting

shot /ʃɒt‖ʃɑːt/ [n C] the noise made by a gun when it is fired: *One witness claimed she had heard eight shots.*

a shot rings out WRITTEN (=when you hear a loud shot) *Suddenly, a shot rang out.*

gunfire /ˈgʌnfaɪəʳ/ [n U] the sound made by several guns being fired, especially in a war: *Enemy gunfire could be heard from several kilometres away.*

SHOP

➡ if you mean 'go shopping', go to **BUY**

SELL · ADVERTISING · CHEAP
COST · see also · BUSINESS
SPEND · MONEY
FREE · FREE TIME
EXPENSIVE

1 a shop

shop ESPECIALLY BRITISH **store** ESPECIALLY AMERICAN /ʃɒp, stɔːʳ‖ʃɑːp/ [n C] a building or place where things are sold: *There's a store across the street that sells ice cream.*

clothes/record/furniture etc shop/store *Have you been to that new clothes shop on Park Road yet? | She works in a video store on Tenth Avenue.*

go to the shops BRITISH **go to the store** AMERICAN *Helen's gone down to the shops to get a few things.*

⚠ **Shop** is the usual word to use in British English, and **store** is the usual word to use in American English. In British English, **store** is often used in newspapers and in business reports, especially when talking about big shops: *All the big stores are open from 8am till 8pm. | High street stores are getting ready for Christmas.*

⚠ **Go to the shops** or **go to the store** means to go to your local shops to buy food and other small things you need. **Go shopping** means to go to look at things in

shops and buy things that you do not buy regularly, such as clothes or records.

chain store /ˈtʃeɪn stɔːʳ/ [n C] one of a group of shops that have the same name and are owned by the same company: *The big chain stores have made it very difficult for smaller shops to do business.*

2 different types of shop

⚠ If you want to talk about a shop that sells a particular kind of thing, you usually say a **clothes shop, record shop, furniture shop** etc in British English, and a **clothes store, record store, furniture store** etc in American English. **Bookshop** (BRITISH) and **bookstore** (AMERICAN) are usually written as one word.

supermarket (also **grocery store** AMERICAN) /ˈsuːpəʳˌmɑːrkɪt, ˈgrəʊsəri ˌstɔːʳ/ [n C] a large shop that sells a wide range of things, especially food, cleaning materials, and other things that people buy regularly

convenience store /kənˈviːniəns ˌstɔːʳ/ [n C] AMERICAN a shop in your local area that sells food, alcohol, magazines etc and is often open 24 hours a day

corner shop /ˈkɔːʳnəʳ ʃɒp‖-ʃɑːp/ BRITISH a small local shop, usually on the corner of a street, that sells food, alcohol, magazines etc

bakery (also **baker's** BRITISH) /ˈbeɪkəri, ˈbeɪkəʳz/ [n C] a shop that sells bread and cakes, especially one that also makes the bread and cakes

plural **bakeries** or **bakers**

butcher's /ˈbʊtʃəʳz/ [n C] a shop that sells meat

plural **butchers**

delicatessen (also **deli** INFORMAL) /ˌdelɪkəˈtesən, ˈdeli/ [n C] a shop that sells high quality food such as cheeses and cold meats, often from different countries

off licence BRITISH **liquor store** AMERICAN /ˈɒf ˌlaɪsəns, ˈlɪkəʳ ˌstɔːʳ/ [n C] a shop that sells beer, wine, and other alcoholic drinks which you drink at home

chemist's BRITISH **drugstore** AMERICAN /ˈkemɪsts, ˈdrʌgstɔːʳ/ [n C] a shop that sells medicines, beauty and baby products etc

plural **chemists**

⚠ In the US, the part of a **drugstore** where medicines are prepared and sold is called the **pharmacy**.

pharmacy /ˈfɑːrməsi/ [n C] ESPECIALLY AMERICAN a shop or part of a shop where medicines are made and sold

plural **pharmacies**

hardware store (also **hardware shop** BRITISH) /ˈhɑːrdweər ˌstɔːr, ˈhɑːrdweər ˌʃɒp‖-ˌʃɑːp/ [n C] a shop that sells equipment and tools that you can use in your home or garden

newsagent's/newsagent /ˈnjuːzˌeɪdʒənt(s)‖ˈnuːz-/ [n C] BRITISH a shop that sells newspapers and magazines, cigarettes, chocolates etc

plural **newsagents**

newstand /ˈnjuːzstænd‖ˈnuːz-/ [n C] a small movable structure on a street, which sells newspapers and magazines

kiosk /ˈkiːɒsk‖-ɑːsk/ [n C] a very small shop on a street, which has an open window where you can buy newspapers, cigarettes, chocolate etc

3 a very large shop

department store /dɪˈpɑːrtmənt ˌstɔːr/ [n C] a very large shop which is divided into several big parts, each of which sells one type of thing, such as clothes, furniture, or kitchen equipment

superstore /ˈsuːpərstɔːr, ˈsjuː-‖ˈsuː-/ [n C] a very large modern shop, especially one that is built outside the centre of a city

DIY store BRITISH **home center** AMERICAN /ˌdiː aɪ ˈwaɪ ˌstɔːr, ˈhəʊm ˌsentər/ [n C] a very large shop that sells equipment and tools for repairing and decorating your home

garden centre BRITISH **nursery** AMERICAN /ˈgɑːrdn ˌsentər, ˈnɜːrsəri/ [n C] a place that sells a wide range of plants, seeds, and things for your garden

4 a lot of shops together in one place

shopping centre BRITISH **shopping center** AMERICAN /ˈʃɒpɪŋ ˌsentər‖ˈʃɑːp-/ [n C] an area in a town where there are a lot of shops that have all been built together in the same space

mall/shopping mall /mɔːl, ˈʃɒpɪŋ mɔːl‖ˈʃɑːp-/ [n C] ESPECIALLY AMERICAN a very large building with a lot of shops inside it, and often also cinemas, restaurants etc

market /ˈmɑːrkət/ [n C] an area outside where people buy and sell many different types of things

market stall (=one of the tables that things are sold from in a market)

5 people who work in a shop

sales assistant (also **shop assistant** BRITISH **sales clerk** AMERICAN /ˈseɪlz əˌsɪstənt, ˈʃɒp əˌsɪstənt, ˈseɪlz ˌklɑːrk‖ˈʃɑːp-, -ˌklɜːrk/) [n C] someone whose job is to serve customers and sell things in a shop, especially in a big shop such as a department store

⚠ **Sales assistant** is more formal than **shop assistant** or **sales clerk**.

manager /ˈmænɪdʒər/ [n C] someone who is in charge of a shop

shopkeeper BRITISH **storekeeper** AMERICAN /ˈʃɒpˌkiːpər, ˈstɔːrˌkiːpər‖ˈʃɑːp-/ [n C] someone who owns or manages a small shop

store detective /ˈstɔːr dɪˌtektɪv/ [n C] someone whose job is to watch the customers in a large shop, to stop them from stealing things

SHORT

➡ look here for ...
- a short distance or length
- a short person
- a short time

1 short in length or distance
➡ opposite LONG

short /ʃɔːrt/ [adj] if something is **short**, there is only a small length or distance from one end of it to the other: *a girl with short blond hair* | *The curtains are much too short.* | *The hotel is just a short distance from the station.* | *There was a short path leading up to the house.*

short walk/drive/ride (=a short distance to walk, drive etc) *It's only a short walk to the bus stop.*

2 someone who is short in height

➡ opposite **TALL**
➡ see also **SMALL**

short /ʃɔːᵗt/ [adj] not as tall as most people: *She was short and fat. | a short, heavy-looking man with powerful shoulders | Mr Haddad was several inches shorter than his wife.*

not very tall /nɒt veri 'tɔːl/ fairly short: *She's not very tall – about 1.4 metres, I'd say.*

small /smɔːl/ [adj] not as big or as tall as most people: *a small man in a dark suit* **small for his/her age** (=smaller than other children of the same age) *Bobby's small for his age, but he's perfectly healthy.*

> ⚠ **Short** means 'not tall'. **Small** means 'not tall, and also 'not fat'. People are often described as 'short and fat', but not 'small and fat'.

3 a short time

a short time /ə ˌʃɔːᵗt 'taɪm/ [n singular] *Unfortunately, we could only spend a short time together. | How did you manage to do all this in such a short time? | Your friends left a short time ago.*

a while /ə 'waɪl/ [n singular] a period of time that is neither very short nor very long: *After a while, he came back.* **for a while** *We lived in Seattle for a while after we got married. | Can you stay for a while, or do you have to leave right now?* **a little/short while** (=a short period of time) *Bob's only been working here a short while.*

a minute/a moment /ə 'mɪnɪt, ə 'məʊmənt/ [n singular] a very short time, no more than a few minutes: *Where's Charles gone? He was here a moment ago. | Wait a minute, I'm nearly ready.* **a minute or two** *It took me a minute or two to realize what she meant.*

a second/an instant /ə 'sekənd, ən 'ɪnstənt/ [n singular] an extremely short time, no more than a few seconds: *In an instant her mood had changed from sadness to anger.* **for a second/an instant** *Liz hesitated, but only for a second. | Just for an instant I thought he was going to hit me.*

> ⚠ A **second** and an **instant** mean the same thing, but use an **instant** especially when you are writing stories or descriptions of events.

a bit /ə 'bɪt/ [n singular] BRITISH SPOKEN INFORMAL a short time, usually just a few minutes: *Oh, wait a bit, can't you?* **for a bit** *I think I'll lie down for a bit.*

4 continuing for only a short time

short /ʃɔːᵗt/ [adj] continuing for only a short time: *The meeting was shorter than I'd expected. | the shortest day of the year*

quick /kwɪk/ [adj only before noun] a **quick** action takes only a very short time, because you are in a hurry **quick look/drink/shower** *I took a quick look at the map. | Do I have time for a quick shower before we go out?*

brief /briːf/ [adj] a **brief** pause, visit etc is short, especially because there is not much time available: *It was impossible to see everything during one brief visit to Paris. | After a brief intermission the performance continued. | a brief period of calm*

> ⚠ **Brief** is more formal than **short**, and is used mostly in written English rather than in conversation.

not take long /nɒt teɪk 'lɒŋ‖-'lɔːŋ/ if something does **not take long**, you do it and finish it in a short time: *Let me show you how to use the computer – it won't take long.* **it does not take long to do sth** *It didn't take long to solve the problem.*

temporary /'tempərəri, -pəri‖-pəreri/ [adj] something that is **temporary** is expected to continue for only a short time and will not be permanent: *Ben's found a* *temporary job, till November.* | *They're living in temporary accommodation at the moment.*

temporary workers/staff (=doing temporary jobs)

temporarily [adv] for a limited period of time: *The library is temporarily closed for repairs.*

short-lived /ˌʃɔːʳt ˈlɪvd◄‖-ˈlaɪvd◄/ [adj] WRITTEN something that is **short-lived** ends sooner than you want it to – use this especially about a feeling, or a relationship: *We were glad to be home, but our happiness was short-lived.* | *The President's popularity may be short-lived.*

5 a short piece of writing

short /ʃɔːʳt/ [adj] a **short** piece of writing does not have many pages or words: *a book of short stories* | *a short letter from my employer* | *Your essay is too short.*

brief /briːf/ [adj] **brief note/description/ comments/outline/account** a note, description etc that has been written using very few words, to give only the most important information without a lot of details: *I sent them a brief note saying what the problem was.* | *The book begins with a brief outline of the history of modern China.*

> ⚠ **Brief** is more formal than **short**. Don't use **brief** about a whole book or story.

6 a shorter way of saying or writing something

abbreviation /əˌbriːviˈeɪʃən/ [n C] a shorter way of writing or saying a word or phrase: *the Central Intelligence Agency, usually known by the abbreviation CIA*
+ for/of *'Dr' is the written abbreviation of 'Doctor'.*

be short for sth /biː ˈʃɔːʳt fɔːʳ (sth)/ if a word, a name, or a set of letters **is short for** something, it is a shorter way of saying or writing it: *They call me Beth – it's short for Elizabeth.* | *What's 'etc' short for?*

for short /fəʳ ˈʃɔːʳt/ if you call someone or something a name **for short**, you use a

shorter form of their real name: *His name's Moses – Mo for short.* | *They are chlorofluorocarbon gases, or CFCs for short.*

7 a short statement giving the main ideas and facts

summary /ˈsʌməri/ [n C] a short statement that gives only the main ideas and facts of something that has been written or said
+ of *Write a two-page summary of the results of your research.* | *I've made a summary of the main points in the Secretary General's speech.*
news summary (=a short programme reporting the main events in the news)
plural **summaries**

outline /ˈaʊtlaɪn/ [n C] an **outline** of a plan or of a series of historical events is a short statement that gives only the main points and facts
+ of *an official statement giving a general outline of the Middle East peace plan* | *The book begins with an outline of the events that led to the First World War.*

8 to give the main ideas or facts of something

summarize (also **summarise** BRITISH) /ˈsʌməraɪz/ [v T] to make a short statement giving only the main information, but not the details, of a report, plan, event etc: *Your final paragraph should summarize the main points of your essay.*

sum up /ˌsʌm ˈʌp/ [phrasal verb I/T] to make a very short statement, especially at the end of a speech, report, or discussion, giving the main ideas or facts: *The chairman's job is to introduce the speakers and then sum up at the end of the discussion.*
sum up sth *In these few words Churchill summed up the feelings of the whole nation.*
summing – summed – have summed

in short /ɪn ˈʃɔːʳt/ FORMAL use this when you have been writing or talking about something, and you want to say in a few words what the most important fact or idea is: *In short, I believe that we need to change our whole attitude towards cars.*

⚠ Only use **in short** in formal written or formal spoken English.

9 to make something shorter

shorten /ˈʃɔːʳtn/ [v T] to make something shorter: *Could you shorten the sleeves for me?*

shorten sth to sth *The three-year course has been shortened to two years.* | *Diana's name is often shortened to Di.*

cut /kʌt/ [v T] to make a film or piece of writing shorter by removing parts from it: *Even after it had been cut, the film was still over three hours long.*

cut sth down *This last paragraph is too long – you'll have to cut it down.*

cutting – cut – have cut

⚠ Use **cut something down** only about pieces of writing.

SHOULD

➡ see also **MUST, DESERVE**

1 when you should do something because it is right and it is your duty

should /ʃʊd/ [modal verb] if you **should** do something, it is your duty to do it, or it is the best thing to do because it is right, fair, or honest: *I don't want to go to the meeting but I suppose I should.*

should do sth *I think you should tell her the truth.* | *He should visit his parents more often.* | *All accidents should be reported to the Health and Safety Officer.* | *Should we contact Joe's parents and tell them what's happened?*

should not/shouldn't do sth *You shouldn't leave young children at home alone.*

should have done sth (=it was the right thing to do, but someone did not do it) *They should have given you your money back.*

shouldn't have done sth (=it was the wrong thing to do, but someone did it) *I'm sorry, I shouldn't have shouted at you.*

⚠ Don't say 'you should to go'. Say **you should go**. **Should** is followed by an infinitive without 'to'.

⚠ **Should** is often used in instructions: *Students should register for courses before September 30th.*

ought to do sth /ɔːt tə ˈduː (sth)/ use this to say that someone should do something because it is right or it is the best thing to do in a situation: *I think you were very rude and you ought to apologize.* | *Do you think we ought to get permission before we do this?* | *The Government ought to spend more on education.*

ought not/oughtn't to do sth *I think that animals have rights, and we ought not to use them for experiments.*

ought to have done sth (=it was the right thing to do, but someone did not do it) *It was a serious matter. They ought to have called the police.*

⚠ **Ought to** is less common than **should** in written and spoken English.

had better do sth /həd ˌbetəʳ ˈduː (sth)/ ESPECIALLY SPOKEN use this to say that you think someone should do something because it would be the correct, polite, or fair thing to do: *You had better phone Alan and tell him you're going to be late.* | *If anyone wants to borrow the car, they'd better ask Dad first.*

had better not do sth *We'd better not tell anyone about this just yet.*

⚠ Don't say 'we better go' or 'we'd better to go'. Say **we'd better go.**

be supposed to do sth /biː səˌpəʊzd tə ˈduː (sth)/ use this to say that someone should do something because there is a rule that says they should, because they have been told to do it, or because it is part of their job: *You're supposed to knock before you come in.* | *Put that cigarette out! You're not supposed to smoke in here.* | *I was totally confused, and had no idea what I was supposed to do next.*

it is sb's job to do sth /ɪt ɪz (sb's) ˌdʒɒb tə ˈduː (sth)‖-ˌdʒɑːb-/ use this to say that someone is responsible for doing something, because it is officially part of their job, or because they have agreed to do it: *It's my job to check that the equipment is in good working order.* | *I thought we'd agreed it was Mike's job to send out all the invitations.*

◯ it's up to sb to do sth /ɪts ˌʌp tə (sb) tə ˈduː (sth)/ SPOKEN say this to emphasize that a particular person is responsible for doing something: *It's up to parents to teach their children the difference between right and wrong.*

it is sb's duty to do sth /ɪt ɪz (sb's) ˌdjuːti tə ˈduː (sth)‖-ˌduːti-/ FORMAL use this to say that someone should do something because it is their legal or moral duty: *It is the judge's duty to give a fair summary of both sides of the case.*

2 when you should do something because it is sensible or it is good for you

should /ʃʊd/ [modal verb] if you **should** do something, it is the best thing to do because it is good for you or it will help you: *Everyone keeps telling me I should give up smoking.* | *You should go to bed early if you're feeling tired.*
should not/shouldn't do sth *They shouldn't worry so much. Everything will be all right.*
should have done sth (=it was the best thing to do, but someone did not do it) *Yes, I know. I should have spent more time studying.*
shouldn't have done sth (=it was not a sensible thing to do but someone did it) *We shouldn't have bought such a big car.*

> ⚠ Don't say 'you should to go'. Say **you should go**. **Should** is followed by an infinitive without 'to'.

ought to do sth /ˌɔːt tə ˈduː (sth)/ use this to say that you think someone should do something because it is good for them or will help them: *The doctor told Dan he ought to exercise more.* | *You ought to ask Eric. I'm sure he'd be happy to help.*
ought not to do sth/oughtn't to do sth *She oughtn't to drive if she's been drinking.*

> ⚠ **Ought to** is less common than **should** in written and spoken English.

◯ had better do sth /həd ˌbetəʳ ˈduː (sth)/ ESPECIALLY SPOKEN use this to say that you think someone should do something because it is sensible or it will help them avoid problems: *You'd better ask your teacher for advice.* | *It was starting to snow and we thought we had better go home.*

> ⚠ Don't say 'you better go home' or 'you'd better to go home'. Say **you'd better go home**.

◯ it's/that's a good idea /ɪts, ðæts ə ˌgʊd aɪˈdɪə/ SPOKEN say this to emphasize that you think an idea or suggestion will help someone or prevent problems: *"I'll check the oil before we set off." "Yes, that's a good idea."*
it's a good idea to do sth *It's a good idea to write down the serial number of your computer in case it gets stolen.*

SHOUT
to say something very loudly

shout /ʃaʊt/ [v I/T] to say something very loudly, because you want to make sure that someone hears you, or because you are angry or excited: *"Get out!" she shouted angrily.* | *There was so much noise from the engine that we had to shout to hear each other.* | *The protesters marched through the streets, shouting slogans.*
+ at *I wish you'd stop shouting at the children.*
  shout [n C] *As we got near the stadium, we could hear the shouts of the crowd.*

scream /skriːm/ [v I/T] to make a loud, high noise, or say something in a high, loud voice, because you are excited, frightened, angry, or in pain: *The man took out a gun and everyone started screaming.* | *"Help me!" she screamed.*
+ at *Maria felt like screaming at her husband.*
scream with pain/delight/terror etc *She woke up screaming with terror.*
  scream [n C] *We could hear screams coming from the burning building.*

yell /jel/ [v I/T] INFORMAL to shout very loudly, either because you are excited, angry, or in pain, or because you want to make sure that someone can hear you: *The audience was yelling and clapping.* | *"Don't touch me!" she yelled.*

+ at *Children were yelling at each other across the street.*

yell [n C]

give/let out a yell (=yell once) *Thomas gave a sudden yell of excitement.*

cheer /tʃɪəʳ/ [v I/T] to shout in order to show that you like or approve of a person, team, performance etc: *The crowd cheered as the President's car drove past.* | *The speaker was cheered loudly when he called for a total ban on nuclear weapons.*

cheer [n C] *There was a big cheer as the band came onto the stage.*

call out /ˌkɔːl ˈaʊt/ [phrasal verb I/T] to shout something in order to get someone's attention, for example to warn them or ask them for help: *She opened her mouth to call out, but no sound came.*

call out sth *A voice from the back of the room called out "Never!"*

call sth out *When I call your name out, put up your hand.*

raise your voice /ˌreɪz jɔːʳ ˈvɔɪs/ to speak more loudly than usual, because you are angry: *I never heard my father raise his voice.*

raised voices (=the sound of people talking loudly because they are angry) *I heard raised voices coming from the next room.*

SHOW

➡ if you mean 'show that something is true/not true or correct', go to **PROVE**

➡ if you mean 'show someone how to do something', go to **EXPLAIN**

➡ if you mean 'show off', go to **PROUD 4**

1 to let someone see something

show /ʃəʊ/ [v T] to let someone see something, especially by holding it out in front of them: *Everyone has to show their identity cards at the entrance to the building.*

show sb sth *Stephanie showed us her engagement ring.* | *Has he shown you his pictures from his vacation yet? They're really good.*

show sth to sb *Show your ticket to the inspector, Charlie.*

showing – showed – have shown

let sb see sth /ˌlet (sb) ˈsiː (sth)/ ESPECIALLY SPOKEN to show something to someone, especially because they have asked to see it: *She won't let anyone see the painting until it is finished.* | *Could you let me see the menu?*

show off /ˌʃəʊ ˈɒf‖-ˈɔːf/ [phrasal verb T] to show something that you are proud of to other people, because you want them to admire it

show off sth *He couldn't wait to show off his new car.*

show sth off to sb *Rosa showed her new baby off to all her friends.*

2 to show someone where something is

show /ʃəʊ/ [v T] to show someone where something is

show sb where *The secretary showed her where to put her coat.*

show sb sth *Uncle Joe showed me the best place to go fishing.*

show sb the way (=go somewhere with someone when they do not know how to get there) *I'll show you the way to the station – it's not far.*

show sb around (=show someone all the interesting or important parts of a place) *Jan has offered to show me around Oxford tomorrow.*

showing – showed – have shown

point /pɔɪnt/ [v I] to show someone where something is, by pointing towards it with your finger

+ to *"That's your desk," he said, pointing to a table piled with files and books.*

point out sth/point sth out (=show something to someone, when there are many of the same things together) *We drove along Market Street, and she pointed out the house where she was born.*

3 when a machine or sign shows information or measurements

show /ʃəʊ/ [v T] to show information about something: *There was a thermometer showing the temperature of the water in the pool.*
+ (that) *This light shows that the machine is switched on.*
showing – showed – have shown

say /seɪ/ [v T] SPOKEN to show a particular distance, time, or speed: *The clock said three o'clock when we left.* | *I was surprised that the fuel gauge still said half full.*
saying – said – have said

display /dɪˈspleɪ/ [v T] if a computer or sign **displays** information, it shows the information in a way that makes it easy to see or notice: *The computer displays the date in the top right corner of the screen.* | *The parking restrictions are displayed on a small yellow sign.*

4 paintings/art

be shown/be on show /biː ˈʃəʊn, biː ɒn ˈʃəʊ/ if a work of art **is shown** or **is on show**, it is put in a public place so that people can look at it: *Some of the artist's paintings are on show at the National Gallery.* | *This is the first time the jewels have been shown outside Russia.*

exhibition /ˌeksɪˈbɪʃən/ (also **show** /ʃəʊ/ ESPECIALLY AMERICAN) [n C] an event at which paintings, photographs etc are shown to the public for a period of time: *We went to see the Picasso exhibition at the Museum of Modern Art.*

5 when actions, behaviour, or events show that something is true

show /ʃəʊ/ [v T] to show that something is true
+ (that) *The election results showed that people weren't satisfied with the government.* | *The case shows that women still face discrimination at work.*
show how/why/what etc *I'm glad he sent me flowers – it shows how much he still cares about me.*
showing – showed – have shown

demonstrate /ˈdemənstreɪt/ [v T] FORMAL to show very clearly that something is true: *The Chernobyl disaster demonstrated the dangers of nuclear power.*
+ that *The results of the experiment demonstrate that there is no difference between girls' and boys' abilities at this age.*

⚠ **Demonstrate** is more formal than **show**. It is often used in official or technical contexts, but not usually in conversation.

be a sign /biː ə ˈsaɪn/ if an event or action **is a sign** of something else, it is one of the things that shows that something is probably true
+ that *When a dog shakes his tail it's a sign that he's happy.*
+ of *He kept fiddling with the pen, which I thought was a sign of nervousness.*

suggest /səˈdʒest‖səɡˈdʒest/ [v T] to show that something is probably true, even though there is no definite proof
+ (that) *There was nothing in his letter that suggested he might be unhappy.*
strongly suggest (=show that something is very likely) *The door had not been forced open, which strongly suggests that the victim knew the killer.*

mean /miːn/ [v T] if an event or action **means** something, you can guess from it that something is true
+ (that) *The lights are on in the window – that means he must still be there.* | *Just because I asked her out for a meal, it doesn't mean I'm madly in love with her.*
meaning – meant – have meant

indicate /ˈɪndɪkeɪt/ [v T] if scientific facts, tests, official figures etc **indicate** something, they show that it is likely to be true
+ that *Research indicates that the drug can be harmful to pregnant women.* | *A recent survey has indicated that viewers want a wider choice of programmes on TV.*

6 to show your feelings, abilities, or attitudes

show /ʃəʊ/ [v T] to behave in a way that shows people how you feel or what your character is like
show interest/surprise/enthusiasm/anger etc (=show that you are interested,

surprised etc) *Paul didn't show much interest in the idea.*

show how angry/upset/unhappy etc you are *I was determined not to show how upset I felt.*

show courage/determination/skill/confidence etc (=show that you are brave, determined etc) *The hostages showed great courage in a very frightening situation.*

showing – showed – have shown

express /ɪkˈspres/ [v T] to tell people what you are feeling or thinking: *He finds it very hard to express his feelings.*

express anger/doubts/surprise/concern etc FORMAL (=say you are angry, uncertain etc) *Relatives of the murdered man expressed anger that the police had done so little.*

can't hide /ˌkɑːnt ˈhaɪd‖ˌkænt-/ if you **can't hide** a strong feeling, you cannot stop yourself from showing it: *Kris couldn't hide his delight.* | *She didn't know if she could hide her feelings for much longer.*

SHUT/CLOSE

➡ opposite **OPEN**

1 door/window/box etc

shut /ʃʌt/ [v T] to move a door, window, gate etc so that it is no longer open: *Come in and shut the door behind you.* | *Someone had shut the gate to stop the sheep from getting out onto the road.* | *She heard Charlotte downstairs shutting the windows and locking up for the night.*

shutting – shut – have shut

close /kləʊz/ [v T] to shut something: *Do you mind if I close the window?* | *She took the necklace out of the box and closed the lid.*

⚠ In most situations, **shut** and **close** mean exactly the same: *She shut the door = She closed the door.* But if you want to say that someone shuts a door slowly and quietly, you usually say **close**: *She closed the door carefully behind her so as not to wake the children.*

be shut/be closed /biː ˈʃʌt, biː ˈkləʊzd/ [adj not before noun] not open: *Make sure all the windows are shut before you go out.* | *The gates were closed, and there was no other way in.* | *Keep your eyes closed.*

slam /slæm/ [v T] to shut a door quickly so that it makes a loud noise, especially because you are angry: *Jane marched out of the room, slamming the door behind her.* | *He slammed the door so hard that the glass cracked.*

slamming – slammed – have slammed

lock /lɒk‖lɑːk/ [v T] if you **lock** something, you turn a key so that people cannot open it or go into it: *Don't forget to lock the back door.* | *I can't remember if I locked the car.*

locked [adj] *I need to get my coat out of your car – is it locked?* | *Karl kept his gun in a locked drawer in his bedroom.*

draw the curtains/close the curtains /ˌdrɔː ðə ˈkɜːtnz, ˌkləʊz ðə ˈkɜːtnz/ to close curtains by pulling them across a window: *Let's draw the curtains. We don't want people looking in.*

2 eyes/mouth

close/shut /kləʊz, ʃʌt/ [v T] to close your eyes or mouth: *I lay down and closed my eyes.* | *He shut his eyes and listened to the music.*

shutting – shut – have shut

closed/shut [adj not before noun] *The girl was lying on the bed with her eyes closed.* | *He kept his mouth tightly shut.*

3 to become shut

close/shut /kləʊz, ʃʌt/ [v I] to become shut: *He walked out and the door closed behind him.* | *There was a bang as the gate shut.* | *Her eyes closed, and she fell into a deep sleep.*

shutting – shut – have shut

slam (also **slam shut**) /slæm, ˌslæm ˈʃʌt/ [v I] if a door **slams** or **slams shut**, it shuts quickly and makes a loud noise: *Outside in the street, car doors slammed and people were shouting.* | *She heard a door slam shut and the sound of footsteps on the path.*

slamming – slammed – have slammed

4 shop/office

shut/close /ʃʌt, kləʊz/ [v I] if a shop or office **shuts** or **closes**, it stops being open for business: *"What time does the bank shut?" "Four o'clock."* | *Most of the stores close at 6:30.*
shutting – shut – have shut

be shut/be closed /biː ˈʃʌt, biː ˈkləʊzd/ if a shop or office **is shut** or **is closed**, it is not open for business: *The ticket office was closed.* | *It was nine o'clock and all the stores were shut.*

SHY

➡ opposite **CONFIDENT/NOT CONFIDENT**

shy /ʃaɪ/ [adj] nervous and embarrassed about talking to other people, especially people you do not know: *David was always rather quiet and shy at school.* | *Carrie gave him a shy smile.* | *I was too shy to ask her out on a date.*
  shyly [adv] *"Would you like to go for a drink?" he asked shyly.*
shy – shyer – shyest
  shyness [n U] shy feelings or behaviour: *Alan forgot his shyness and began asking them questions.*

timid /ˈtɪmɪd/ [adj] frightened to talk to people or to give your opinion, because you have very little confidence: *Ralph's wife was a small, timid woman who hardly ever spoke.*
  timidly [adv] *"Can I go home now?" Sue asked, timidly.*

reserved /rɪˈzɜːrvd/ [adj] someone who is **reserved** tries not to show their feelings to other people and does not talk a lot: *English people have a reputation for being very reserved.*

SIDE

➡ see also **MIDDLE, EDGE**

1 the part of an area that is furthest from the middle

side /saɪd/ [n C] one of the parts of an area that is furthest from the middle and closest to the edge

+ of *We walked along the side of the road.*

on the side of sth *There were high walls on all four sides of the prison yard.*

side

I left the book on the side of the desk.

edge /edʒ/ [n C] the part around an object or area that is furthest from its centre, or the part along its side where its surface ends
+ of *The edges of the carpet were torn.* | *Keep away from the edge of the cliff – you might fall.*

on the edge of sth *Just leave it on the edge of your plate.*

at the edge of sth (=next to the edge) *The house stood right at the edge of the lake.*

edge

The edges of the paper were ragged.

end /end/ [n C] one of the two parts of a long object or area that are furthest from each other
+ of *He cut a thick slice from the end of the loaf.*

at one end of sth *Mrs Deacon sat at one end of the long table and I sat at the other.*

at both ends/at each end *There are scoreboards at both ends of the stadium.* | *A dumbbell is an iron bar with a heavy weight at each end.*

border /ˈbɔːrdər/ [n C] a line or band around the edge of something such as a picture or a piece of cloth: *a tablecloth with a brightly patterned border*
+ around *The card had a blue border around it.*

margin /ˈmɑːrdʒɪn/ [n C] the empty space on the left or right side of a page: *Someone had written a note in the left-hand margin.*

margin

margin

When you see **EC**, go to the **ESSENTIAL COMMUNICATION** section.

2 one of the two areas on either side of a line, wall, river etc

side /saɪd/ [n C]
+ of *This side of the fence is private property.* | *From the other side of the wall came the sounds of children playing.* | *We crossed the bridge to the north side of the river.*

bank /bæŋk/ [n C] the land along the side of a river

on the bank of/banks of sth *a new theatre on the south bank of the Thames* | *the vineyards along the banks of the Rhone*

⚠ Don't confuse **bank** (of a river or stream), **shore** (of a sea or large lake), and **coast** (the part of a country that is close to the sea).

3 not the back or front

side /saɪd/ [n C] one of the two surfaces of a building, vehicle, or boat that is not the back, front, top, or bottom
+ of *A truck ran into the side of the car, killing the driver and two passengers.*
at the side of sth *There was another entrance at the side of the building.*

⚠ **Side** is also used to mean one of the two surfaces of something flat, such as a sheet of paper, a coin etc: *Write on both sides of the paper.*

4 the left or right half of an object, area, or road

side /saɪd/ [n C]
+ of *The left side of the brain controls the right side of the body.* | *The dancers came on from both sides of the stage.*
on the left-hand/right-hand/other side *In Japan they drive on the left-hand side of the road.*

5 towards the side

sideways /'saɪdweɪz/ [adv] moving, looking, or facing to the left or right instead of straight ahead: *The car skidded sideways off the road.*

to one side/to the side /tə ˌwʌn 'saɪd, tə ðə 'saɪd/ if someone or something moves **to one side** or **to the side**, they move from where they are to the left or to the right: *She pushed her plate to one side and leaned forward.* | *Could you move a little to the side so we can get past?*

from side to side /frəm ˌsaɪd tə 'saɪd/ moving continuously, first to one side then to the other: *The tractor swayed from side to side, almost throwing me out of my seat.*

SIGN

➡ if you mean 'write your name', go to **WRITE 2**

1 a written sign that gives instructions or information

sign

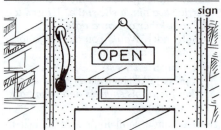

sign /saɪn/ [n C] something with words or shapes on it, which is put in a public place to show the name of a building, town etc, or to give a warning or information: *The sign said 'No smoking'.* | *There was a big sign above the entrance.* | *Didn't you see the speed limit signs?*

traffic/road sign (=a sign that gives information to drivers)

the signs for (=the signs on a road that show how to go to a place) *Follow the signs for Atlanta.*

notice

notice /ˈnəʊtɪs/ [n C] a piece of paper giving instructions or information, which is put in a place where people can see it: *The details of the trip are on that notice over there.*
put up a notice (=attach it to a wall) *I'll put up a notice about the meeting.*
take down a notice (=remove it from a wall)

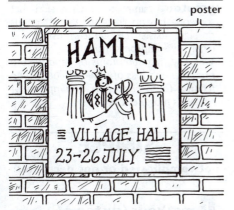
poster

poster /ˈpəʊstəʳ/ [n C] a large printed piece of paper which is put on a wall in a public place, and which gives information about something that is going to happen, for example a film or concert
+ for *There are posters for the Van Gogh exhibition everywhere.*
election poster (=a poster that tells you to vote for a party or person in an election)

2 a picture or shape that has a special meaning

sign /saɪn/ [n C] a picture or a shape which has a particular meaning, and which is well known and often used: *You've forgotten to put the dollar sign before the total amount.* | *Where's the percentage sign on this keyboard?*

symbol /ˈsɪmbəl/ [n C] a picture, shape, or design that has a special meaning or represents an idea: *The walls were covered with magical symbols.* | *The singer Prince now uses a symbol instead of his name.*
+ of *The dove is a symbol of peace.*
+ for *What is the mathematical symbol for 'infinity'?*

logo /ˈləʊgəʊ/ [n C] a sign that has been designed to represent an organization or product: *The baseball team has a new logo.* | *bags with our company logo on them*

emblem /ˈembləm/ [n C] a picture of an object, flower, animal etc that is used to represent a country or organization: *England's national emblem is the rose.*
+ of *The hammer and sickle is the emblem of the Communist Party.*

3 a movement or sound that you make to tell someone something

sign /saɪn/ [n C] a movement that you make in order to tell someone something: *He raised his hand in a sign of greeting.*
sign for sb to do sth *When the teacher puts her finger to her lips, it's a sign for us to be quiet.*

signal /ˈsɪgnəl/ [n C] a sound or movement that you make in order to tell someone to do something
give a signal *Don't start yet – wait until I give the signal.*
signal to do sth *The soldiers were waiting for the signal to start firing.*
signal for sb to do sth *When I blow my whistle, that's the signal for you to start filming.*

gesture /ˈdʒestʃəʳ/ [n C] a movement of your hands, arms, or head that shows how you feel, especially when you are very worried or angry
+ of *Jim raised his hands in a gesture of despair.*
make a gesture *Someone in another building started making gestures and pointing towards our kitchen.*
make a rude gesture *The fight started when one of the drivers made a rude gesture at someone.*

4 to make a movement or sound to tell someone something

make a sign /ˌmeɪk ə ˈsaɪn/ to make a movement, especially with your hand, in order to tell someone something: *I'll make a sign when I'm ready.*
make a sign to show/tell etc *The President made a sign to indicate that he wanted to leave.*

S

signal /'sɪgnəl/ [v I/T] to make a movement or sound in order to give instructions or information: *A sailor began signalling with two flags.*
+ to *Capone finished his drink and signalled to the waiter.*
+ that *An official signalled that it was time for the race to begin.*

signalling – signalled – have signalled
BRITISH

signaling – signaled – have signaled
AMERICAN

wave /weɪv/ [v I/T] to move your hand or arm from one side to the other, for example in order to get someone's attention or to tell them something
+ at *Who's that waving at you?*
wave goodbye (=wave to someone who is leaving) *Her parents stood in the doorway and waved goodbye.*
wave sb through/on (=wave to show someone that they can go through or continue their journey) *At the border the customs officer just waved us through.*

    wave [n C]
    give sb a wave (=wave at someone in order to say hello or goodbye) *I gave him a friendly wave.*

wink /wɪŋk/ [v I] to quickly close and open one eye, in order to show that you are joking or that you share a secret with someone
+ at *Ben grinned and winked at his father.*

    wink [n C] when you close and open one eye quickly: *"Don't worry," he said with a wink. "I won't tell anyone about this."*

5 something that shows what is true or what is happening

sign /saɪn/ [n C] an event or fact that shows that something is true or that something is happening
+ of *the first signs of the disease*
+ (that) *A score of 80 or more is a sign that you are doing very well.*
be a sure sign of/(that) (=show that something is definitely true) *When Emma offers to help you it's a sure sign that she wants something from you!*
a good/hopeful/encouraging sign (=a sign that things are improving) *He ate all his food, which is a good sign.*

evidence /'evɪdəns/ [n U] facts, objects etc that show that something exists or is true
+ of *People have been looking for evidence of life on other planets for years.*
+ that *There is no evidence that he ever worked for the company.*

> ⚠ Don't say 'a lot of evidences'. Say **a lot of evidence.**

symptom /'sɪmptəm/ [n C] a sign that someone has an illness or that a serious problem exists: *Dr Duncan asked me what my symptoms were.*
+ of *The first symptoms of hepatitis are tiredness and loss of weight.* | *The Bishop regards these crimes as a symptom of society's moral decline.*

SIMPLE
not complicated or not decorated

1 methods/systems/ explanations/words
➡ opposite **DIFFICULT**

simple /'sɪmpəl/ [adj] not complicated, and therefore easy to understand: *All you have to do is to follow a few simple instructions.* | *There must be a perfectly simple explanation for what has happened.* | *Speak slowly and use simple words so that everyone can understand.*

    simply [adv] *Try to express your ideas more simply.* (=using simple language)
    simplicity /sɪm'plɪsɪti/ [n U] when something is easy to use or understand: *The simplicity of the system is its great advantage.*

straightforward /streɪt'fɔːʳwəʳd/ [adj] simple – use this especially about explanations, instructions, and methods which contain nothing difficult or unexpected: *The new accounting system is fairly straightforward – there shouldn't be any problems.* | *The rules of the game are very straightforward.*

plain English /ˌpleɪn 'ɪŋglɪʃ/ English that ordinary people can understand, without any difficult or confusing words: *I wish they'd write in plain English, instead of all this business jargon.*

2 food/clothes/rooms designs

simple /'sɪmpəl/ [adj] **simple** food, clothes, or designs do not have a lot of decoration or unnecessary things added, but they are usually attractive or enjoyable: *a simple black dress* | *The meal was simple, but delicious.*

plain /pleɪn/ [adj] **plain** food, clothes, or designs do not have anything added or any decoration, and may be a little boring: *English food tends to seem rather plain compared to French food.* | *She always wore plain, ordinary-looking clothes.* | *The chapel was a small, plain, white-washed building.*

basic /'beɪsɪk/ [adj] **basic** food, rooms, or designs only have the necessary features, and do not include things that make them more comfortable, more attractive etc: *Some of the hotels in the mountains are pretty basic.* | *The basic model of this car is £7000 including insurance and car tax.*

3 machines/tools

simple /'sɪmpəl/ [adj] a **simple** machine or tool has only a few parts and is not made in a complicated way: *The tribes of Central New Guinea use very simple tools such as hammers and axes.*

basic /'beɪsɪk/ [adj] **basic** machines, equipment, or tools only have the most necessary features and you cannot use them to do unusual, difficult, or complicated things: *The hospital lacked even the most basic medical equipment.* | *The basic tool-kit is good enough for most everyday repairs.*

4 to make something simpler

simplify /'sɪmpləfaɪ/ [v T] to make something simpler and easier to use or understand: *The government is planning to simplify the tax laws.*

simplifying – simplified – have simplified

simplified [adj] something that is **simplified** has been made easier to understand: *a simplified version of Jonathan Swift's novel, 'Gulliver's Travels'*

SING

➡ see also **MUSIC, DANCE**

1 to sing

sing /sɪŋ/ [v I/T] to make musical sounds with your voice, especially the words of a song: *Sophie sings in the church choir.* | *I could hear someone singing downstairs.*

sing a song/tune/hymn *They sat together and sang songs.* | *All the family sang 'Happy Birthday' as Dad came in.*

sing sb a song/tune *Come on, David, sing us a song!*

sing to sb *She sat in a corner, singing softly to her baby.*

sing along (=sing with someone who is already singing) *Sing along if you know the words.*

singing – sang – have sung

hum /hʌm/ [v I/T] to make musical sounds with your voice, but with your mouth closed: *Carole hummed to herself as she worked.* | *He walked along, humming a tune.*

humming – hummed – have hummed

whistle /'wɪsəl/ [v I/T] to make musical sounds by blowing air out between your lips: *Sam was painting the door, whistling softly as he worked.*

whistle a song/tune *You've been whistling that tune all day.*

2 someone who sings

singer /'sɪŋər/ [n C] someone who sings, especially as their job: *He's a really good singer.*

opera/jazz/blues/rock singer *Jodie dreamed of being a rock singer.*

lead singer (=the main singer in a pop group) *Mick Jagger, the lead singer with the Rolling Stones*

choir /kwaɪər/ [n C] a large group of singers who regularly sing in a church or school or with an orchestra (=large group of musicians): *I used to be in the school choir.*

3 something that you sing

song /sɒŋ‖sɔːŋ/ [n C] a short piece of music with words for singing: *It's one of Bob Dylan's most famous songs.* | *an old*

Beatles song | The song was originally written by Schubert.

hymn /hɪm/ [n C] a religious song that people sing in church

SIT

➡ see also **STAND, LIE**

1 to be sitting in a chair, on the floor etc

sit /sɪt/ [v I] to be in a chair, on the floor etc, with the weight of your body resting on your bottom, not on your feet: *It was a lovely day, and we sat outside in the sun.* | *Billy was sitting on the edge of the desk, swinging his legs.*
sit at a desk/table/bar/counter *I used to spend all day sitting at a desk.*
sit back (=sit and lean back against something) *Just sit back and relax.*
sit up (=sit with your back straight) *It's better for your back if you sit up straight.*
sit still (=sit quietly without moving) *I wish you children would sit still for 10 minutes.*
sitting – sat – have sat

> ⚠ Sit: which preposition? You **sit on** something with a flat surface, such as the floor, a bed or table, a sofa or bench, or a plain chair or stool. You **sit in** a comfortable chair or armchair. You **sit at** a desk, table, or bar (meaning that you sit facing it, for example to work or to eat a meal). And you **sit in front of** a television, computer, or fire.

sit up /ˌsɪt ˈʌp/ [phrasal verb I] to move your body so that you are sitting, after you have been lying down: *The day after the operation, he was allowed to sit up in bed.* | *Anna sat up at once, looking startled.*

2 to sit after you have been standing

sit down /ˌsɪt ˈdaʊn/ [phrasal verb I] to sit on a chair, bed, floor etc, after you have been standing: *Come in and sit down.*
+ in/on/next to/beside etc *Fay sat down on the edge of the bed.*

sit /sɪt/ [v I] to sit down after you have been standing
+ in/on/next to/beside etc *Come and sit next to me.* | *Let's go and sit by the window.*
sitting – sat – have sat

3 a place where you can sit

seat /siːt/ [n C] something you can sit on, especially in a bus, train, plane, theatre etc: *Our seats were right at the front of the bus.* | *He leaned back in his seat and lit a cigarette.*
back/front seat (=in a car)

place /pleɪs/ [n C] a seat – use this especially to talk about whether seats are available: *There are still some places at the back of the hall.* | *Are there any places left on tonight's flight to Rio?*

chair /tʃeəʳ/ [n C] a piece of furniture for one person to sit on: *He sat down in his favourite chair by the fireplace.*

> ⚠ You say sit **on** a chair if it is a plain piece of furniture with a hard seat. You say sit **in** a chair if it is a comfortable piece of furniture with a soft seat.

sofa/couch /ˈsəʊfə, kaʊtʃ/ [n C] a comfortable piece of furniture which is big enough for two or three people to sit on: *Roy was lying on the sofa.* | *Come and sit with me on the couch.*

armchair /ˈɑːʳmtʃeəʳ, ɑːʳmˈtʃeəʳ/ [n C] a large comfortable chair with parts at the sides where you can rest your arms: *Dad was dozing in the armchair.*

bench /bentʃ/ [n C] a long hard seat made of wood or metal that several people can sit on, which does not have a back or arms

stool /stuːl/ [n C] a seat for one person, which has three or four legs and has no back or arms: *a bar stool*

4 what you say to tell someone to sit

◯**sit down** /ˌsɪt ˈdaʊn/ SPOKEN *Sit down, I have something to tell you.* | *Will you sit down and finish your breakfast!*

◯**have a seat/take a seat** /ˌhæv ə ˈsiːt, ˌteɪk ə ˈsiːt/ SPOKEN say this when telling someone politely to sit down: *Have a seat – the dentist won't be long.*

SITUATION

what is happening in a particular place or at a particular time

➡ see also **PLACE**

situation /ˌsɪtʃuˈeɪʃən/ [n C usually singular] the combination of all the things that are happening in a particular place and at a particular time, especially when this is causing problems: *With no rain for six months, the situation was becoming desperate.* | *I tried to explain the situation to my boss.*
economic/political situation *The economic situation in the US is getting better.*
a difficult/awkward/tricky situation *It's a rather difficult situation – I need to borrow some money, but I don't want my parents to know.*
be in a situation *It's good to be able to talk to other people who are in the same situation as yourself.*

circumstances /ˈsɜːʳkəmstænsɪz/ [n plural] the situation at a particular time, which influences what you do, what you decide, and what can happen: *TV cameras are sometimes allowed in the courts, but it depends on the circumstances.*
in some/certain circumstances *In some circumstances you may have to work on Saturdays.*
under normal circumstances *Under normal circumstances she would never have left the children with a stranger.*
in the circumstances/under the circumstances (=use this to say that you think something should happen because of the situation now) *In the circumstances, it might be better if you took a few days off work.*

⚠ Don't say 'a circumstance' or 'the circumstance'. Say **the circumstances**.

Q things /θɪŋz/ [n plural] INFORMAL, ESPECIALLY SPOKEN the general situation that exists, especially the way it affects your life: *Don't worry! Things can't get any worse.* | *Things haven't changed much since I wrote to you last.*

position /pəˈzɪʃən/ [n C usually singular] the way things are at the present time, in a situation that is likely to change: *The position now is that the peace talks are continuing.*
in a good/bad/strong/difficult position *The latest economic news puts the President in a strong position.*

conditions /kənˈdɪʃənz/ [n plural] the things that make your life or your work comfortable or uncomfortable, for example whether you have enough food or money, whether the place where you are living or working is warm enough, safe enough etc: *Conditions in the city are getting worse every day.* | *How can people bring up a family in such dreadful conditions?*

⚠ Don't say 'a condition' or 'the condition'. Always say **conditions** in this meaning.

environment /ɪnˈvaɪərənmənt/ [n C] all the things that influence the way you live, work, and develop, such as the physical conditions you live in and the people around you: *Do girls learn better in an all-female environment?*
working/home environment *We have comfortable offices and an enthusiastic young team – it's a pleasant working environment.*

SIZE

how big or small something is

➡ see also **BIG, SMALL, MEASURE**

size /saɪz/ [n C/U] how big or small something is: *Your desk is exactly the same size as mine.* | *The price of a carpet will depend on its size and quality.*
be twice the size/be half the size (=be twice as big or half as big) *Their apartment is half the size of ours.*
of different sizes/of various sizes *There were several pieces of wood of different sizes.*
vary in size (=be of different sizes) *The American states vary enormously in size, from very large to very small.*
... the size of sth (=when something is the same size as something else) *an area of forest the size of Luxembourg*

... this/that size (=as big as this one or that one) *In a class this size, there will always be a few problems.*

⚠ When you are asking about someone's clothes size, you can say **what size are you?** or **what size do you take?** (BRITISH) or **what size do you wear?** (AMERICAN). When you are talking about your clothes size, you say **I'm a 6/12/42 etc** or **I take a size 6/12 etc** (BRITISH), or **I wear a size 6/12 etc** (AMERICAN).

how big /haʊ ˈbɪɡ/ use this to ask or talk about the size of something: *How big is the table?* | *We need to know how big the hall is.*

area /ˈeəriə/ [n C/U] the size of a flat surface such as a floor or a field
+ of *Calculate the area of the walls and ceiling before you buy the paint.* | *Forest fires caused damage over an area of about 5000 square miles.* | *a room with a floor area of 20 square metres*

be 5 metres high/2 miles long/6 centimetres wide etc use this to say how high, how long etc something is: *The River Nile is over 6000 kilometres long.* | *In some places the path is only a couple of feet wide.*

be 10 metres by 15 metres/be 5 cm by 20 cm etc use this to say what the size of an area, object, or room is, for example, **10 metres by 5 metres** means 10 metres long and 5 metres wide: *The kitchen is 4 metres by 2 metres.*
measure 10 m by 15 m/5 cm by 20 cm etc *The photographs should measure 3 cm by 2 cm.*

SLEEP

➡ see also **TIRED, REST, WAKE UP/GET UP**

1 to sleep

sleep /sliːp/ [v I] *The baby was sleeping peacefully.* | *I had to sleep on the floor.*
sleep well *"Did you sleep well?" "Yes, thanks."*
sleep like a log INFORMAL (=sleep very well)
sleep badly/not sleep well *I haven't been sleeping well recently.*

sleep in (=deliberately sleep until a later time than usual, and get up late) *We usually sleep in on Sundays.*
sleep rough BRITISH (=sleep outside or in an empty building, because you have no home) *Hundreds of homeless people sleep rough every night in London.*
sleeping – slept – have slept

⚠ Don't confuse **sleep** and **go to bed**. Use **go to bed** to talk about getting into your bed at the end of the day: *I went to bed at midnight, and slept for eight hours.* Don't say 'I slept at midnight'.

sleep /sliːp/ [n singular/U] time when you are sleeping: *Lack of sleep can make you bad-tempered.*
in your sleep (=while you are sleeping) *Katie sometimes talks in her sleep.*
get some sleep (=spend time sleeping, especially when you are very tired and need to sleep) *I didn't get much sleep last night.*
a good night's sleep (=a long sleep at night, which makes you feel relaxed and comfortable) *What you need is a good night's sleep.*
have a sleep BRITISH (=sleep for a short time, especially in the daytime) *The baby usually has a sleep after lunch.*

be asleep /biː əˈsliːp/ to be sleeping: *Nicky was still asleep.* | *We found Mom asleep on the sofa.*
be fast asleep (=be sleeping very well) *The kids were all fast asleep in the back of the car.*

oversleep /ˌəʊvəˈsliːp/ [v I] to sleep for too long, so that you are late for something: *I'm sorry I'm late – I overslept.*
oversleeping – overslept – have overslept

have a nap/take a nap /ˌhæv ə ˈnæp, ˌteɪk ə ˈnæp/ to sleep for a short time during the day: *The children have a nap every morning at about 11 o'clock.*

doze /dəʊz/ [v I] to sleep for a short time while sitting in a chair, often waking up and going back to sleep again: *Grandpa was dozing by the fire.*

2 to start sleeping

go to sleep /ˌɡəʊ tə ˈsliːp/ to start sleeping: *Shut up and go to sleep!* | *I didn't* go to sleep until after midnight. | "I'll stay with her till she goes to sleep," said Theo.

fall asleep /ˌfɔːl əˈsliːp/ to start sleeping, especially when you do not intend to: *The movie was so boring that I fell asleep halfway through it.* | *As usual, he had fallen asleep in front of the TV.*

doze off /ˌdəʊz ˈɒf‖-ˈɔːf/ [phrasal verb I] INFORMAL to start sleeping when you do not intend to, and sleep for just a short time: *I must have dozed off for a few minutes.*

3 to get into your bed at the end of the day

go to bed /ˌgəʊ tə ˈbed/ *I usually go to bed at about eleven-thirty.* | *"Can I speak to Andrea?" "Sorry, she's already gone to bed."*

> ⚠ Don't confuse **go to bed** (=start sleeping) and **sleep** (=be asleep).

4 what you say to someone when they are going to bed

⚲goodnight (also **night** INFORMAL) /ɡʊdˈnaɪt, naɪt/ SPOKEN say this when you are going to bed, or to someone else who is going to bed: *Goodnight, everyone.* | *"Night Dad." "Night Steve."*

say goodnight *I said goodnight to my parents and went up to bed.*

⚲sleep well /ˌsliːp ˈwel/ SPOKEN say this to someone who is going to bed, especially someone in your family or a close friend: *Goodnight, Paula. Sleep well!*

5 not asleep

awake /əˈweɪk/ [adj not before noun] not sleeping: *"Are you awake?" he whispered.*

wide awake (=not asleep and not tired) *It was 3 o'clock in the morning, but Peter was still wide awake.*

lie awake (=lie in bed, but not be able to sleep) *I lay awake all night worrying about it.*

keep sb awake (=prevent someone from sleeping) *The noise of the party kept us awake for most of the night.*

stay awake (=deliberately not go to sleep) *One of us should stay awake and keep watch.*

can't get to sleep /ˌkɑːnt get tə ˈsliːp‖ˌkænt-/ use this when you cannot sleep although you want to: *Mum, I can't get to sleep.* | *There was so much noise that I couldn't get to sleep till four o'clock in the morning.*

conscious /ˈkɒnʃəs‖ˈkɑːn-/ [adj not before noun] awake and able to understand what is happening around you – use this about someone who is ill or has had an accident: *The driver was still conscious but in great pain.*

fully conscious (=completely conscious)

insomnia /ɪnˈsɒmniə‖ɪnˈsɑːm-/ [n U] someone who has **insomnia** cannot sleep – use this about people who have a medical problem that often prevents them from being able to sleep: *Strong coffee can cause insomnia.*

6 when someone cannot feel anything and seems to be asleep

unconscious /ʌnˈkɒnʃəs‖-ˈkɑːn-/ [adj] if you are **unconscious**, you cannot see, hear, or feel anything, for example because you have had an accident or been given a drug: *She was lying unconscious on the floor.*

be knocked unconscious (=become unconscious because you have been hit on the head) *There was a fight, and Mark was knocked unconscious.*

faint /feɪnt/ [v I] to become unconscious and fall down, for example because you are feeling very hot or hungry: *I need to go outside. I think I'm going to faint.* | *Several of the fans fainted and had to be carried out of the concert.*

in a coma /ɪn ə ˈkəʊmə/ unconscious for a long time because of a serious accident or illness: *Her father has been in a coma for six months.*

go into a coma (=start to be in a coma) *Ellen went into a coma and died soon afterwards.*

> When you see **EC**, go to the **ESSENTIAL COMMUNICATION** section.

SLIDE

1 to slide

slide /slaɪd/ [v I] to move smoothly across a surface

+ along/around/down etc *The children were having fun sliding around on the ice.* | *Several glasses slid off the tray and crashed to the floor.*

sliding – slid – have slid

slip /slɪp/ [v I] to accidentally slide a short distance, especially when you then fall down: *He slipped and fell – I think he's broken his arm.* | *The floor's wet – careful you don't slip!*

+ on *I slipped on some ice and landed on my back.*

slipping – slipped – have slipped

skid /skɪd/ [v I] if a vehicle **skids**, it suddenly slides to the side and it is difficult for the driver to control it: *The car rounded the bend, skidded, and crashed into a tree.*

+ across/on/off etc *Nineteen people were injured today when a bus skidded off the road into a ditch.*

skidding – skidded – have skidded

2 a surface that makes you slip

slippery /'slɪpəri/ [adj] a **slippery** surface is so smooth or wet that it is difficult to stand or move safely on it: *Be careful – the floor is very slippery.* | *Black ice is making the roads slippery today.*

SLOW

➡ opposite **FAST**

1 moving slowly or doing something slowly

slow /sləʊ/ [adj] not moving quickly or not doing something quickly: *The train was slow, noisy, and uncomfortable.* | *a slow graceful dance* | *a race in which the slowest runners were soon left behind* | *My computer's really slow compared to the ones at school.*

be slow to do sth (=not do it quickly enough) *The police car was very slow to arrive, and the thieves had already gone.*

slowly /'sləʊli/ [adv] *He got up slowly out of his chair and came towards me.* | *Can you speak more slowly? I can't understand what you're saying.* | *A big white cloud drifted slowly across the sky.*

2 happening slowly or changing slowly

slow /sləʊ/ [adj] taking a long time: *She's making a slow recovery after her illness.* | *For the first few months my progress was extremely slow.* | *Rebuilding the country's economy is likely to be a long, slow process.*

slowly /'sləʊli/ [adv] *The situation is slowly improving.* | *Slowly, prices began to fall.*

gradually/little by little /'grædʒuəli, ,lɪtl baɪ 'lɪtl/ [adv] happening slowly by a series of small amounts or changes, over a long period of time: *Our climate is gradually becoming warmer and drier.* | *Little by little, Guy's health improved.* | *I was gradually beginning to realize the seriousness of the situation.*

> ⚠ **Little by little** is used especially in stories or descriptions of past events.

gradual /'grædʒuəl/ [adj] happening or changing slowly over a long period of time – use this about a process or change, or an increase or reduction: *I had noticed a gradual improvement in her written work.* | *a gradual fall in the number of unemployed people*

take too long /,teɪk tuː 'lɒŋ‖-'lɔːŋ/ if something **takes too long**, it happens too slowly, or you need too much time to do it: *I won't read out the whole statement – that would take too long.*

take too long to do sth *I've changed my mind – it would take too long to explain why.*

3 to become slower or make something slower

slow down /,sləʊ 'daʊn/ [phrasal verb I/T] *You're driving too fast – slow down!*

slow sth/sb down *The bad weather slowed us down a lot.*

slow down sth *Clinton was able to slow down the rate of US inflation.*

SMALL

➡ if you mean 'to become smaller in amount, or to make sth smaller in amount', go to **LESS**

➡ opposite **BIG**

1 small in size

⚠ Small and little mean the same, but always use **small** (not **little**) when you are simply talking about the size of something or giving information about its size. Use **little** when you want to show your feelings or opinion about a small thing or person.

small /smɔːl/ [adj] *His office was a small room at the top of the building.* | *These shoes are too small for me.* | *a small insect that can give you a nasty bite* | *Arthur was 16, but he was small for his age.* | *Her father owns a small printing business.* | *a small town in Missouri* | *Which is the smallest state in the US?*

little /'lɪtl/ [adj only before noun] small – use this especially to show how you feel about someone or something, for example to show that you like them, dislike them, or feel sorry for them: *It's just a little souvenir I brought back from Italy.*

⌕**nice little/lovely little** ESPECIALLY SPOKEN *What a lovely little dog!* | *They've bought a nice little house in the country.*

⌕**poor little** SPOKEN (=when you feel sorry for someone) *a poor little bird with a broken wing*

⌕**silly little/horrible little etc** SPOKEN *silly little coffee cups that only hold one mouthful of coffee* | *What a horrible little boy!*

⚠ Don't use 'very', 'more', or 'most' with **little**.

tiny /'taɪni/ [adj] very small: *the baby's tiny fingers* | *The apartment has two bedrooms and a tiny kitchen.*

⌕**tiny little** ESPECIALLY SPOKEN *The box was full of tiny little blue beads.*

tiny – tinier – tiniest

minute /maɪ'njuːt‖-'nuːt/ [adj] extremely small and difficult to see: *minute pieces of broken glass* | *Her handwriting is minute.* | *The problem was caused by minute particles of dust getting into the disk drive.*

⚠ Minute is more formal or more technical than **tiny**.

cramped /kræmpt/ [adj] a room, space, or vehicle that is **cramped** is uncomfortable because there is not enough space inside it for people to move around: *I hated working in that cramped little office.* | *Conditions on board the ship were extremely cramped.*

2 small numbers/amounts

small /smɔːl/ [adj] *Our drinking water contains small quantities of fluoride and calcium.* | *The car industry is dominated by a small number of very powerful companies.*

⚠ Don't use **little** to talk about numbers or amounts – use **small**.

⚠ Don't use **small** about prices and wages – use **low**.

low /ləʊ/ [adj] **low** prices, wages, levels etc are less than usual or less than they should be: *It's a good time to buy a computer, because prices are low.* | *Farm workers are complaining about long hours and low wages.* | *low interest rates*

⚠ Don't say 'a low amount'. Say **a small amount**.

tiny /'taɪni/ [adj usually before noun] a **tiny** amount or number is very small: *Only a tiny fraction of our profit comes from book sales.*

a tiny minority (=a very small number of a much larger group) *Millions of people buy lottery tickets, but only a tiny minority ever win anything.*

tiny – tinier – tiniest

3 small changes/ differences/problems

small /smɔːl/ [adj] *a small increase in unemployment* | *I want to make a few small changes to the design.* | *There is still one small problem that we haven't dealt with.*

slight /slaɪt/ [adj usually before noun] small and not very important or noticeable: *There has been a slight change of plan.* | *The doctor says there has been a slight improvement in her condition.*

the slightest change/difference (=one that is extremely small and difficult to measure) *a thermometer that can record the slightest change in temperature*

⚠ Don't say 'slighter'.

minor /'maɪnər/ [adj only before noun] use this about small changes or problems that are not important enough or serious enough to worry about

minor change/difference/problem/injury/ detail *Except for one or two minor changes, the course is the same as last year.* | *She fell off her horse, but suffered only minor injuries.*

4 to become smaller

➡ see also LESS

get smaller /ˌget 'smɔːlər/ *The dot got smaller and smaller, and vanished from the screen.* | *Am I getting fatter or is this dress getting smaller?*

shrink /ʃrɪŋk/ [v I] if clothes **shrink**, they get smaller when they are washed: *Don't wash that sweater in hot water – it'll shrink.*

shrinking – shrank – have shrunk

When you see **EC**, go to the **ESSENTIAL COMMUNICATION** section.

SMELL

➡ see also TASTE

1 a smell

smell /smel/ [n C] something that you notice by using your nose: *What's that smell? Is something burning?* | *the smells from the factory* | *cooking smells*
+ of *There was a lovely smell of freshly baked bread.*

⚠ When **smell** is used without an adjective, it usually means an unpleasant smell: *Can we open the window and get rid of the smell?*

stink /stɪŋk/ [n singular] a strong and very unpleasant smell: *The stink from the drains is almost unbearable in summer.*
+ of *There was a stink of dead fish coming from the garbage can.*

odour BRITISH **odor** AMERICAN /'əʊdər/ [n C] a strong smell that is easy to recognize, especially an unpleasant smell: *Get rid of unpleasant household odours with new Fleur!*
+ of *A strong odour of sweat filled the air.*

⚠ In British English, **odour** is more formal than **smell** and is mostly used in writing. But in American English, **odor** is often used as another way of saying 'smell'.

aroma /ə'rəʊmə/ [n C] a pleasant smell, especially from food or coffee: *Each of these herbs has its own flavour and aroma.*
+ of *The aroma of fresh coffee made Paul stop in front of a small café.*

scent/fragrance /sent, 'freɪgrəns/ [n C] a pleasant smell, especially from flowers, plants, or fruit: *The rose has a delicate fragrance.*
+ of *the scent of jasmine*

2 to have a particular kind of smell

have a nice/horrible/strange etc smell /hæv ə (nice etc) 'smel/ *The house was empty, and the rooms had a stale, damp smell.* | *The drink has an unusual smell, but it tastes very nice.*

smell /smel/ [v] to have a particular smell
smell nice/good/awful/sweet etc *The air smelled clean and fresh after the storm.*
+ of *The house still smells of paint.* | *She smelled of alcohol and was unsteady on her feet.*
smell like sth *It smells like a hospital in here.*
smelling – smelled (also **smelt** BRITISH) – **have smelled** (also **have smelt** BRITISH)

> ⚠ When **smell** is used without an adjective, it always means that something has an unpleasant smell: *Those socks really smell.*

3 to have a bad smell

smell /smel/ [v I] to have an unpleasant smell: *Does my breath smell?* | *It's time you cleaned the bird cage out – it's starting to smell.*
smell awful/terrible/disgusting *What's in this bag? It smells absolutely awful.*
smelling – smelled (also **smelt** BRITISH) – **have smelled** (also **have smelt** BRITISH)

stink /stɪŋk/ [v I] to have a strong and unpleasant smell: *How can you eat that cheese – it stinks!*
+ of *The house stank of cigarette smoke.*
stinking – stank – have stunk

smelly /ˈsmeli/ [adj] something that is **smelly** has a bad smell: *smelly socks* | *The water in the pond had turned brown and smelly.*
smelly – smellier – smelliest

reek of sth /ˈriːk ɒv (sth)/ [phrasal verb T] to have a very strong smell of something unpleasant: *The whole place reeked of garlic.* | *After days of travelling in the tropical heat, their bodies reeked of sweat.*

4 to smell something

smell /smel/ [v T not in passive] to notice the smell of something, especially by putting your nose near it: *Smell these roses – aren't they lovely?* | *Have you been drinking? Let me smell your breath.* | *If you smell gas, call this number immediately.*

can smell (=notice a smell) *I'm sure I can smell something burning.*
smelling – smelled (also **smelt** BRITISH) – **have smelled** (also **have smelt** BRITISH)

> ⚠ Don't say 'I am smelling gas'. Say **I can smell gas.**

sniff /snɪf/ [v I/T not in passive] to take quick breaths through your nose in order to smell something: *He opened the milk and sniffed it.* | *She stopped to sniff the evening air.*
+ at *The dog was rushing around excitedly, sniffing at the ground.*

sense of smell /ˌsens əv ˈsmel/ [n singular] the ability to notice smells: *These dogs have a very good sense of smell.*

5 something that you put on your body to make it smell nice

perfume /ˈpɜːrfjuːm/ [n C/U] a liquid that a woman puts on her neck or body to make it smell nice: *The pillow smelled of cheap perfume.*

fragrance /ˈfreɪɡrəns/ [n C] a perfume for women or for men – used especially in advertisements: *Calvin Klein's exciting new fragrance for men – available now!*

cologne /kəˈləʊn/ [n C] a liquid that you put on your face or body to make it smell nice, similar to perfume but with a less strong smell

aftershave /ˈɑːftərʃeɪv‖ˈæf-/ [n C/U] a liquid that a man puts on his face and neck to make it smell nice, especially after shaving (=cutting hair from his face)

deodorant /diˈəʊdərənt/ [n C/U] something that you put on your skin to prevent or hide unpleasant smells

SMILE

LAUGH   FUNNY

see
also

HAPPY   JOKE

FRIENDLY/UNFRIENDLY

1 to smile

smile /smaɪl/ [v I] to make your mouth curve upwards, as a sign that you are happy or amused or that you want to be friendly: *She smiled and said "Good morning". | Rosie's such a cheerful girl – always smiling.*
+ at *The twins turned and smiled at each other, sharing a private joke.*

⚠ Don't say 'he smiled to me'. Say **he smiled at me.**

grin /grɪn/ [v I] to give a big happy smile: *Hank was grinning with pleasure. | Grinning shyly, he offered her a drink.*
+ at *She kept grinning at me as if we were old friends.*
grinning – grinned – have grinned

beam /biːm/ [v I] to smile for a long time, because you are very pleased about something or proud of something you have achieved: *Her parents stood there beaming as she went up to receive the prize.*
+ at *The bride and groom walked out of the church, beaming at everyone they passed.*

smirk /smɜːʳk/ [v I] to smile in an unpleasant way, for example because you are pleased about someone else's bad luck or because you know something that they do not know: *She sits there smirking as if she's the only one who knows the answer.*
+ at *What are you smirking at?*

sb's face lights up /(sb's) ˌfeɪs laɪts ˈʌp/ if **someone's face lights up**, they suddenly look very happy: *The children's faces lit up when we told them we were going to Disney World.*

+ with joy/pleasure *Chantal's face lit up with joy as Max came towards her.*

⚠ Use this especially in stories and descriptions of past events.

2 a smile

smile /smaɪl/ [n C] the look on your face when you make your mouth curve upwards to show that you are happy, friendly, amused etc: *Helga has a lovely smile.*
give sb a smile (=smile at them) *Barry gave the old lady a warm smile.*
a big smile *"See you later," she said, giving us all a big smile.*
with a smile on your face *He fell asleep with a contented smile on his face.*

grin /grɪn/ [n C] a big happy smile: *That's Larry on the left of the picture, the one with the big grin on his face.*
give sb a grin (=grin at them) *William gave her a friendly grin as he walked past.*

smirk /smɜːʳk/ [n C] an unpleasant, satisfied smile, for example when you are pleased about someone else's bad luck or when you think you know something that they do not know: *"You didn't pass, then?" Richard asked with a smirk.*

SMOKING

➡ see also **BURN, FIRE**

1 to smoke a cigarette, pipe etc

smoke /sməʊk/ [v I/T] *How old were you when you started smoking? | Do you mind if I smoke? | My father smokes a pipe. | He sat behind his desk, smoking a fat cigar.*
smoke 20/30 a day (=smoke 20, 30 cigarettes every day) *Anyone who smokes 40 a day can expect to have a lot of health problems.*
chain-smoke (=smoke cigarettes continuously) *While he was directing a movie, he would chain-smoke and drink black coffee.*

smoking /'sməʊkɪŋ/ [n U] the habit of smoking: *Smoking is bad for your health.*

passive smoking (=when you breathe in the smoke from other people's cigarettes)

puff on sth /'pʌf ɒn (sth)‖-ɑːn-/ [phrasal verb T] to take small amounts of smoke into your mouth from a cigarette, cigar, or pipe: *Barry was puffing on his pipe and looking thoughtful.*

smoker /'sməʊkəʳ/ [n C] someone who smokes regularly: *The survey shows that most smokers would like to stop smoking.* | *The average smoker spends about £18 a week on cigarettes.*

heavy smoker (=someone who smokes a lot) *I knew she was a heavy smoker when I saw the yellow stains on her fingers.*

2 to not smoke

don't smoke /,dəʊnt 'sməʊk/ [v T] if you **don't smoke**, you never smoke cigarettes or other tobacco products: *"Would you like a cigarette?" "No, thanks, I don't smoke."*

give up smoking ESPECIALLY BRITISH **quit smoking** ESPECIALLY AMERICAN /,gɪv ʌp 'sməʊkɪŋ, ,kwɪt 'sməʊkɪŋ/ to stop smoking, especially when you make a firm decision that you will not smoke again: *I'm trying to give up smoking, but it isn't easy.*

> ⚠ In American English, you can also just say **quit**, and it means the same: *"Do you still smoke?" "No, I quit two years ago."*

non-smoker /nɒn 'sməʊkəʳ‖-nɑːm-/ [n C] someone who never smokes: *This part of the restaurant is reserved for non-smokers.* | *Non-smokers get cheaper health insurance.*

no-smoking /,nəʊ 'sməʊkɪŋ/ [adj only before noun] use this about rules or signs that say you must not smoke

a no-smoking sign/policy/ban *There were big no-smoking signs on all the walls.* | *The company has a no-smoking policy in all its offices.*

> When you see **EC**, go to the **ESSENTIAL COMMUNICATION** section.

non-smoking /nɒn 'sməʊkɪŋ‖-nɑːm-/ [adj] use this about places or buildings where you are not allowed to smoke: *I asked for a seat in the non-smoking section of the plane.*

3 to light a cigarette, pipe etc

light /laɪt/ [v T] to make a cigarette, cigar, or pipe start burning: *The old man struck a match and lit his pipe.* | *I leaned forward to light her cigarette.*

lighting – lit (also **lighted**) **– have lit** (also **have lighted**)

have you got a light? BRITISH **do you have a light?** AMERICAN /,hæv juː gɒt ə 'laɪt, ,duː juː hæv ə 'laɪt‖-gɑːt-/ SPOKEN say this to ask someone for a match or a lighter to light your cigarette: *Excuse me, do you have a light?*

> ⚠ Don't say 'have you got fire?' or 'do you have fire?'

4 to make a cigarette, pipe etc stop burning

put out /,pʊt 'aʊt/ [phrasal verb T] to make a cigarette, cigar, or pipe stop burning
put out sth/put sth out *Bill put out his pipe and stood up to leave.*

extinguish /ɪk'stɪŋgwɪʃ/ [v T] FORMAL to put out a cigarette, cigar, or pipe – used especially in official notices or announcements: *Passengers are requested to extinguish all cigarettes when the red light goes on.*

stub out /,stʌb 'aʊt/ [phrasal verb T] to put out a cigarette by pressing the end of it against something
stub out sth/stub sth out *She nervously stubbed out her cigarette, and immediately lit another one.*

SOFT

➡ opposite **HARD**

soft /sɒft‖sɔːft/ [adj] not hard, and easy to press or crush, or pleasant to touch: *I need a softer pillow.* | *shoes made of very soft leather* | *The ground was soft after all the rain.*

softness [n U] when something is not hard, and is easy to press or crush: *She loved the softness of the cat's fur.*

tender /'tendər/ [adj] use this about meat and vegetables that are soft and easy to cut because they have been cooked well: *Fry the chicken for a further 15 minutes, until it is tender.*

smooth /smuːð/ [adj] use this about skin or fur that is soft and pleasant to touch: *Her skin was as smooth as silk.*

SOME

➡ look here for ...
- some but not many
- some but not much
- some but not all

NUMBER — LOT
see also
FEW — AMOUNT/NUMBER
LITTLE/NOT MUCH

1 some, but not a large number

some /səm; *strong* sʌm/ [determiner/pronoun] a number of people or things, but not a large number – use this when you are not saying exactly what the number is: *There were some children playing in the street.* | *"Do you have any tools?" "Yes, there should be some in the back of the car."*
some more/some other *I've got some more pictures of her upstairs.* | *There are some other reasons besides those I have mentioned.*

⚠ Don't use **some** in negative sentences. Use **any**. Don't say 'I don't have some cigarettes'. Say **I don't have any cigarettes**.

⚠ In questions, you can use either **some** or **any**: *Do you want any chips?* | *Do you want some chips?* But use **some** especially when you think that the other person will answer 'yes'.

a few /ə 'fjuː/ [quantifier] a small number of people, things, facts etc: *"Are there any chocolates left?" "Only a few."* | *They went to China a few years ago.* | *We know a few people who work in advertising.* | *There are a few problems I'd like to discuss with you.*

⚠ Don't confuse **a few** (=a small number) and **few** (=almost none): *She has few friends* (=almost no friends). | *She has a few friends* (=some friends).

⚠ Don't confuse **a few** (=a small number) and **a little** (=a small amount). **A few** is only used with plural nouns.

several /'sevərəl/ [quantifier] more than a few people or things, but not a large number: *The President visited several states on his tour.* | *Several people complained about the noise from the party.* | *I've been to Japan several times.*

a number of /ə 'nʌmbər ɒv/ FORMAL several: *A number of people said they had seen the gunman earlier in the day.* | *We have received a number of complaints about last night's television programme.*

a series of /ə 'sɪəriːz ɒv/ several things of the same kind that happen one after the other: *There has been a series of robberies in the area recently.* | *We are planning a series of concerts to raise money for charity.*

2 some, but not a large amount

some /səm; *strong* sʌm/ [determiner/pronoun] an amount of something, but not a large amount – use this when you are not saying exactly what the amount is: *Can I borrow some money, Dad?* | *I need some time to think about what you've said.* | *"We've run out of milk." "Do you want me to go and get some?"*
some more *Would you like some more meat?*

⚠ Don't use **some** in negative sentences. Use **any**. Don't say 'I don't have some money'. Say **I don't have any money**.

⚠ In questions, you can use either **some** or **any**: *Do you want some wine?* | *Do you want any wine?* But use **some** especially when you think that the other person will answer 'yes'.

a certain amount of /ə ˌsɜːᵗtn əˈmaʊnt ɒv/ a fairly large amount – use this to talk about people's feelings, abilities etc, not to talk about things: *a job that required a certain amount of intelligence and skill* | *A certain amount of stress is unavoidable in daily life.*

3 some, but not all

some/some of /sʌm, ˈsʌm ɒv/ [quantifier] some but not all of a number or amount: *Some students only come here because they want to have fun.* | *"Have you met Jack's friends?" "Some of them."* | *I've already spent some of the money.* | *Some trees lose their leaves in the autumn; others remain green all through the winter.*

a few of /ə ˈfjuː ɒv/ [quantifier] a few but not all of a number of people or things: *I'm going to the club with a few of my friends.*

several of /ˈsevərəl ɒv/ [quantifier] several but not all of a number of people or things: *Several of us are going on a trip to France.* | *Several of the islands have beautiful beaches.*

SOMETIMES

When you see **EC**, go to the **ESSENTIAL COMMUNICATION** section.

sometimes /ˈsʌmtaɪmz/ [adv] on some occasions, but not always: *Sometimes I drive to work and sometimes I walk.* | *Traffic noise is sometimes a problem.* | *The journey takes about an hour, sometimes even longer.*

⚠ Don't forget the 's' at the end of **sometimes**.

occasionally /əˈkeɪʒənəli/ [adv] use this to talk about something that only happens a few times, and does not happen often: *Occasionally we go out to restaurants, but mostly we eat at home.*

very occasionally (=not at all often) *He lives in Australia now, so we only see him very occasionally.*

occasional [adj only before noun] happening a few times, but not at all often: *Prisoners are allowed occasional visits from their relatives.*

⚠ You can also say **the occasional ...** when you mean **an occasional ...**: *Apart from the occasional Christmas card, we never heard from her again.*

now and then/every now and then /ˌnaʊ ənd ˈðen, ˌevri naʊ ənd ˈðen/ sometimes, but not regularly: *Now and then she would look up from her work and smile at him.* | *You see stories like this in the newspapers every now and then.*

from time to time /frəm ˌtaɪm tə ˈtaɪm/ sometimes, but not regularly and not often: *This is the kind of problem that we all have from time to time.* | *Tax rates may vary from time to time.*

the odd /ðiː ˈɒd‖-ˈɑːd/ [adj only before noun] **the odd drink/game/occasion/weekend etc** ESPECIALLY SPOKEN a few drinks, games etc at various times, but not often and not regularly: *Jim and I have the odd drink together.* | *We get the odd complaint from customers, but mostly they're very satisfied.*

off and on/on and off /ˌɒf ənd ˈɒn, ˌɒn ənd ˈɒf/ ESPECIALLY SPOKEN for short periods, but not continuously or regularly, over a long period of time: *We've been going out together for five years, off and on.* | *I worked in bars on and off for two years before I decided to go back to college.*

can be /ˈkæn biː/ sometimes – use this to talk about what may happen in a particular situation: *These dogs can be quite aggressive if they are not well trained.* | *She can be really stubborn once she has made up her mind about something.*

SOON

> ⚠ Don't confuse **soon** (=in a short time) and **early** (=before the usual time).

➡ see also **EARLY, LATER/AT A LATER TIME**

1 soon

soon /suːn/ [adv] in a short time from now, or a short time after something else happens: It'll soon be Christmas. | Driving in the city was hard at first, but she soon got used to it. | She arrived home sooner than we expected.

as soon as possible Please reply as soon as possible.

as soon as you can I came as soon as I could.

the sooner the better (=when it is important that something is done very soon) The sooner we get him to the hospital the better.

soon after/afterwards They set off soon after breakfast.

before long /bɪˌfɔːʳ ˈlɒŋ‖-ˈlɔːŋ/ if something happens **before long**, it happens after a fairly short time: The bus will be here before long. | He joined the business as Sales Director, but before long he was running the whole company.

shortly /ˈʃɔːʳtli/ [adv] soon – use this especially about something that you know will happen soon: We apologize for the delay – the train will be leaving shortly. | The President will shortly be on his way to Italy for a trade conference.

shortly after/before Her last novel was published shortly after her death.

> ⚠ **Shortly** is more formal than **soon**.

in the near future /ɪn ðə ˌnɪəʳ ˈfjuːtʃəʳ/ use this to talk about something that will happen in the next few weeks or months, although you do not know exactly when: She doesn't have a driver's license, but is hoping to pass her test in the near future. | Successful candidates will be contacted in the near future.

> When you see **EC**, go to the **ESSENTIAL COMMUNICATION** section.

2 very soon

in no time /ɪn ˈnəʊ taɪm/ use this to talk about something good that will happen very soon or that happened a very short time after something else: Take this medicine and you'll be feeling better in no time.

in no time at all In no time at all they were back together again.

○**in a minute** /ɪn ə ˈmɪnɪt/ ESPECIALLY SPOKEN use this to talk about something that will happen within a few minutes, especially something you are waiting for or hoping for: "I'm bored. Can we go now?" "OK – in a minute!" | Coffee will be ready in a minute. | Dale climbed into the plane beside her, and in a minute they were on their way.

○**any minute now** /ˌeni mɪnɪt ˈnaʊ/ SPOKEN use this to talk about something that will happen or start very soon, especially something exciting or important: We will be bringing you the first live pictures from Jupiter any minute now.

quickly /ˈkwɪkli/ [adv] if you do something **quickly**, you do it very soon after something else happens: We quickly realised that something was wrong when we saw her expression. | Alex was knocked to the ground, but he quickly recovered.

3 something that will happen soon

imminent /ˈɪmɪnənt/ [adj] ESPECIALLY WRITTEN an important or worrying event that is **imminent** will happen very soon: By then, war was imminent. | With a general election imminent, Churchill returned to London.

in imminent danger of sth (=when something bad is likely to happen very soon) Whole sections of the ruined abbey are in imminent danger of collapse.

○**be coming up** /bɪ ˌkʌmɪŋ ˈʌp/ ESPECIALLY SPOKEN if something **is coming up**, it is going to happen soon: Katie's working much harder now that her final exams are coming up.

have sth coming up You have a birthday coming up, haven't you?

SORRY

➡ look here for ...
- feel sorry because you have done something bad or stupid
- feel sad for someone because they are in a bad situation

🔡 APOLOGIZING   EMBARRASSED

see
also

ASHAMED   GUILTY/
                                       NOT GUILTY

1 to tell someone you are sorry you did something

say you are sorry /ˌseɪ juː əʳ ˈsɒri‖-ˈsɑːri/ to tell someone you are sorry because you have upset them or done something that causes problems for them: *Sometimes it's not easy to say you are sorry.*
+ (that) *She finally arrived, and said she was sorry we had been kept waiting.*

🔍**say sorry** /ˈseɪ sɒri‖-ˈsɔːri/ ESPECIALLY SPOKEN to tell someone, especially a member of your family or close friend, that you are sorry because you have upset them or done something bad: *She says she won't see him again unless he says sorry.*
+ to *Go and say sorry to your mother, Andrew.*

apologize (also **apologise** BRITISH) /əˈpɒlədʒaɪz‖əˈpɑː-/ [v I] to tell someone you are sorry, especially in a formal or official situation: *The hotel manager apologized and agreed to give us our money back.*
+ for *British Airways apologizes for the late arrival of flight BA297.*
+ to *The US has apologized to Britain for an accident in which two British soldiers were killed.*
apologize for doing sth *She apologized for causing us so much inconvenience.*

⚠ Don't say 'I apologized her'. Say **I apologized to her.**

apology /əˈpɒlədʒi‖əˈpɑː-/ [n C] something that you say or write to tell someone that you are sorry: *The story was full of lies, and the paper had to print an apology.*

accept sb's apology/apologies *I hope you will accept our sincere apologies.*
demand an apology *Blake was wrongfully arrested and is now demanding an apology from the police.*
plural **apologies**

2 what you say to tell someone you are sorry

🔍**sorry/I'm sorry** /ˈsɒri, aɪm ˈsɒri‖ -ˈsɑːri/ SPOKEN say this to tell someone you are sorry that you upset them or caused problems for them; you can also say this as a polite way of excusing yourself for a small mistake: *I'm sorry, I didn't mean to be rude.* | *Sorry, did I step on your foot?*
I'm very/really/terribly sorry *I'm really sorry, Joanna. I've broken one of your glasses.*
+ (that) *I'm sorry that I shouted at you.* | *Sorry we're late, Shelley.*
+ about *Sorry about all the noise.*
sorry to do sth *I'm sorry to bother you, but I need to discuss my essay.*

⚠ **Sorry** is more informal than **I'm sorry.**

🔍**excuse me** /ɪkˈskjuːz miː/ SPOKEN, ESPECIALLY AMERICAN say this to tell someone you are sorry because you accidentally touched them or made a small or embarrassing mistake: *Oh, excuse me, is that your bag I just stood on?* | *Excuse me – I didn't realize there was anyone in here.*

🔍**I beg your pardon** /aɪ ˌbeg jɔːʳ ˈpɑːʳdn/ SPOKEN FORMAL say this when you make a small mistake and you want to say sorry politely: *"That's my pen." "Oh, I beg your pardon – I thought it was mine."*

3 to feel sorry about something you have done

be sorry/feel sorry /biː ˈsɒri, ˌfiːl ˈsɒri‖ -ˈsɑːri/ to feel sad, embarrassed, or annoyed about something bad or stupid that you have done, and wish you had not done it
+ (that) *Now she felt sorry that she had never written to her parents.* | *I didn't enjoy myself and I was sorry I ever agreed to go with them.*
be/feel sorry for sth (=sorry for something bad you have done) *I hope you're sorry for the trouble you have caused.*

be/feel sorry about sth (=sorry about something that has happened) *He's lost his job, but he doesn't seem very sorry about it.*

regret /rɪˈgret/ [v T] to wish that you had not done something, especially because it has bad results that affect you for a long time: *I decided to leave my job – a decision which I later regretted.* | *It was a stupid thing to say, and I immediately regretted it.*

regret doing sth *I've always regretted giving up my piano lessons.*

+ (that) *I think she regrets now that she never went to college.*

regretting – regretted – have regretted

> ⚠ **Regret** is more formal than **be/feel sorry.**
>
> ⚠ Don't say 'I regret to do it' or 'I regret to have done it'. Say **I regret doing it** or **I regret that I did it.**

regret /rɪˈgret/ [n C/U] a feeling of sadness because you wish you had not done something, or you wish the situation was different: *Burgess left with a feeling of regret, knowing that he would never return.*

with great/deep regret *We have accepted her resignation with deep regret.*

have no regrets (=not regret anything) *I moved to the US ten years ago, and I have no regrets.*

wish you had/wish you hadn't /ˈwɪʃ juː hæd, ˈwɪʃ juː hædnt/ to feel that you have done the wrong thing, and wish that you had behaved differently: *I wish I had told him the truth.* | *She wished now that she had not agreed to marry him.*

4 to feel sorry because someone else is in a bad situation

be sorry /biː ˈsɒri‖-ˈsɑːri/ to feel sad about something bad that has happened to someone else

+ (that) *I'm sorry she didn't get the job – I think she really deserved it.*

be sorry to hear/see/read *We were all sorry to hear about your accident.*

feel sorry for sb /ˌfiːl ˈsɒri fɔːʳ (sb)‖ -ˈsɑːri-/ to feel sad for someone because they have had very bad luck or they are in

a bad situation: *He felt sorry for Tina – she seemed so lonely.* | *It's his wife I feel sorry for.*

sympathize (also **sympathise** BRITISH) /ˈsɪmpəθaɪz/ [v I] to feel sad for someone who is having problems, because you understand how they feel: *I know what it's like to be alone in a strange country, and I do sympathise.*

+ with *They say they sympathize with people who are unemployed, but how do they know what it's like?*

sympathy /ˈsɪmpəθi/ [n U] the feeling you have when you feel sorry for someone who is having problems, and you understand how they feel: *Relatives of the air-crash victims were treated with great sympathy.*

have sympathy for sb *I have a lot of sympathy for her – divorce is a very upsetting experience.*

pity /ˈpɪti/ [v T] to feel very sorry for someone who is in a much worse situation than you: *I pity anyone who has to feed a family on such a low income.*

pitying – pitied – have pitied

> ⚠ You can also use **pity** to talk in a joking way about someone whose problems are not very serious: *He spends all his time cleaning and polishing the car – I pity his poor wife!*

5 what you say when you feel sorry for someone

I'm sorry /aɪm ˈsɒri‖-ˈsɑːri/ SPOKEN say this to tell someone you are sad that something bad has happened to them: *I heard about your father's death; I'm very sorry.* | *I really am sorry. I hope Jim finds another job soon.*

bad luck /ˌbæd ˈlʌk/ SPOKEN say this to show your sympathy for someone who has tried to do something and failed: *Bad luck, Paul. I'm sure you'll pass next time.*

poor /pʊəʳ/ [adj only before noun] ESPECIALLY SPOKEN use this when talking about someone that you feel sorry for: *The poor girl gets blamed for everything that goes wrong.*

poor old INFORMAL (used about someone you know well) *I hear poor old Steve broke his ankle.*

SOUND

➡ see also **LOUD, QUIET, MUSIC**

1 a sound

sound /saʊnd/ [n C/U] something that you hear: *The only sound in the house was the ticking of the clock.* | *The TV's broken – you can see the pictures, but there's no sound.*
+ of *We could hear the sound of laughter in the next room.*
a clicking/tapping/buzzing etc sound *There's a funny rattling sound coming from the back of the car.*

noise /nɔɪz/ [n C/U] a sound, especially a loud or unpleasant one: *The children are making a lot of noise.* | *street noises*
+ of *The noise of the traffic kept me awake.*
a banging/scratching etc noise *What's that banging noise?* | *We heard a creaking noise, and saw the door begin to open.*

⚠ Don't say 'a big noise'. Say **a loud noise**.

echo /'ekəʊ/ [n C] a sound which repeats the last part of a loud sound made, for example, in a large empty room or near a high wall
+ of *the faint echo of thunder in the distance*
plural **echoes**

2 to make a sound

make a sound/make a noise /ˌmeɪk ə 'saʊnd, ˌmeɪk ə 'nɔɪz/ *I knew that if I made any noise, they would find me.* | *The lamb was making a sound like a baby crying.*

◯**go** /gəʊ/ [v] **go bang/beep/pop etc** ESPECIALLY SPOKEN to make a short loud sound: *I was using the hairdryer and suddenly it went bang.*
going – went – have gone

echo /'ekəʊ/ [v I] if a sound **echoes**, you hear the last part of it again because it was made in a large empty room, near a high wall etc: *I heard footsteps echoing down the corridor.*
echoing – echoed – have echoed

with /wɪð/ [preposition] **with a bang/crash/thud etc** making a loud sound: *The picture fell to the floor with a loud crash.* | *Fighter planes flew low over the village, with a great 'whoosh'.*

go off /ˌgəʊ 'ɒf‖-'ɔːf/ [phrasal verb I] if something **goes off**, it starts to make a noise – use this about bells that warn you about danger, clocks that tell you it is time to get up etc: *My neighbour's car alarm went off three times last night.* | *Our alarm clock goes off at 7:15 every morning.*

3 to make a sound because you are in pain, are disappointed etc

groan /grəʊn/ [v I] to make a long sound in a deep voice, because you are in great pain or you are very disappointed: *Alex groaned as the pain got worse.* | *Everyone groaned when Tim walked into the room.*
groan [n C] the sound you make when you groan: *There was a loud groan from the crowd as Shearer's shot missed the goal.*

sigh /saɪ/ [v I] to breathe in and out deeply and loudly because you feel disappointed, bored, or impatient: *Pamela sighed and looked at her watch.*
sigh [n C] the sound you make when you sigh: *John gave a sigh and sat down.*

4 when a sound stops

fade away/die away /ˌfeɪd ə'weɪ, ˌdaɪ ə'weɪ/ [phrasal verb I] if a sound **fades away** or **dies away**, it gradually becomes quieter and quieter until you cannot hear it any more: *The noise of the bombing died away and the town was quiet once more.*

SPACE

➡ see also **HOLE**

1 space that is available to use

space /speɪs/ [n C/U] an empty area of any size, which can be used or filled by things or people: *I wish we had more* space in our office. | There's a space on the form where you write the name of your school. | parking spaces

+ for We don't have enough space for all our furniture.

space to do sth Could you find me a space to store these boxes in?

make/clear a space (=make a space by moving things) She cleared a space on the desk for her computer.

room /ruːm, rʊm/ [n U] enough space for something to fit into: I can't sit there, there isn't enough room.

+ for Is there room for my camera in your bag?

room to do sth I had to back the car out of the driveway – there wasn't enough room to turn around.

make room for sb/sth (=move people or things closer together so there is room for another person or thing) Can you move and make room for Jerry, please?

2 a space between things

space /speɪs/ [n C] an empty area between two things: There was an empty space on the shelf where the book had been.

+ between The children hid in the space between the wall and the sofa.

gap /gæp/ [n C] a space where there should not be one, for example because something has been removed or something is missing

+ in We'll have to fix this gap in the fence.

+ between The dentist says the gaps between her teeth may cause problems later.

opening /ˈəʊpənɪŋ/ [n C] a small hole or space that you can pass through or see through

+ in The guards passed food to the prisoners through an opening in the wall. | The children were peeping through an opening in the curtains.

When you see **EC** , go to the **ESSENTIAL COMMUNICATION** section.

SPEAK

SAY — TALK

see also

TELL — LANGUAGE

⚠ Don't confuse **say**, **tell**, **talk**, and **speak**. You **say** words to someone. You **tell** someone facts or information about something. You **talk** to someone about a subject. You **speak** (=by producing words) or you **speak** a language.

1 to speak

speak /spiːk/ [v I] to produce words with your voice: She had a sore throat and couldn't speak. | How old are babies when they learn to speak?

speak up (=speak louder) Can you speak up? – I can't hear you.

speaking – spoke – have spoken

talk /tɔːk/ [v I] to produce words with your voice in order to have a conversation, tell people what you think etc: Please don't all talk at the same time. | You're not supposed to talk in the library.

stammer/stutter /ˈstæməʳ, ˈstʌtəʳ/ [v I/T] to speak with difficulty because you cannot stop yourself repeating the first sound in some words: She always used to stutter when she was nervous. | "I d-d-don't know," he stammered.

whisper /ˈwɪspəʳ/ [v I] to speak very quietly, using your breath rather than your voice: We had to whisper because Jill's mother was in the next room. | What are you two whispering about?

mumble /ˈmʌmbəl/ [v I] to speak quietly and not at all clearly, so that it is difficult for people to understand you: Don't mumble – I can't hear what you're saying.

speech /spiːtʃ/ [n U] the ability to speak: Only humans are capable of speech. | The left side of the brain controls speech.

2 to speak a language

speak /spiːk/ [v T] to be able to speak a language: *Nadia speaks six languages.*
speak French/Japanese/Russian etc *Is there anyone here who can speak Arabic?*

speaking – spoke – have spoken

⚠ Don't say 'he can speak in English'. Say **he can speak English**.

⚠ Don't say 'he talks English', 'I talk Japanese' etc. Say **he speaks English, I speak Japanese** etc.

⚠ Don't confuse **she is speaking English** (=she is speaking it now) and **she speaks English** (=she can speak it).

fluent /'fluːənt/ [adj] very good at speaking a language, so that you can speak it quickly without stopping and you understand it very well
fluent in English/German etc *Danielle is fluent in Cantonese.*
fluent French/Arabic/Japanese etc *Ann speaks fluent Italian.*
fluently [adv] *Douglas speaks Hindi fluently.*

⚠ Use **fluent** and **fluently** about languages you have learned, not about your own first language.

bilingual /baɪ'lɪŋgwəl/ [adj] able to speak two languages very well: *Their children are completely bilingual.*

speaker /'spiːkəʳ/ [n C] someone who can speak a particular language
speaker of English/Russian/Arabic etc *Speakers of Cantonese often cannot understand speakers of Mandarin.*
English/Spanish/Urdu etc speaker *The hotel has two English speakers on its staff.*
native speaker (=someone who was born in the country where a language is spoken, so that is the language they usually use) *All our English teachers are native speakers.*

3 the way someone speaks

pronunciation /prəˌnʌnsi'eɪʃən/ [n singular] the way someone says the words and sounds of a language: *Gianni has problems with his grammar but his pronunciation is very good.*

⚠ Don't write 'pronounciation'. The correct spelling is **pronunciation**.

accent /'æksənt‖'æksent/ [n C] the way someone speaks a language, which shows which country or which part of a country they come from, and which sometimes shows which social class they come from: *She speaks Spanish with a Mexican accent.* | *I knew from his accent that he was Scottish.*
a strong/broad accent (=an accent that is easy to notice) *Her companion had a strong French accent.*
an upper-class accent (=typical of people from a high social class)

speech /spiːtʃ/ [n U] the way someone speaks, especially when this is affected by illness, drugs etc: *He was drunk, and his speech slow and unclear.*
speech impediment (=a permanent speech problem, which makes it difficult to pronounce certain sounds) *She was born with a slight speech impediment.*

4 spoken, not written

spoken /'spəʊkən/ [adj usually before noun] **spoken** language is produced with the voice, not written down: *This book will help you with both spoken and written English.*

oral /'ɔːrəl/ [adj usually before noun] using spoken language rather than written language – use this especially about tests and exams
oral test/exam *We had a 15-minute oral exam in German.*

5 unable to speak

can't speak /ˌkɑːnt 'spiːk‖ˌkænt-/ to be unable to speak because you are too ill, weak, frightened, or shocked: *I was so terrified, I couldn't speak*

lose your voice /ˌluːz jɔːʳ 'vɔɪs/ to become unable to speak because of illness, or because you have been using your voice too much: *All that shouting has made her lose her voice.*

dumb /dʌm/ [adj] permanently unable to speak: *Martin was born deaf and dumb.*

> ⚠ **Dumb** is not used by doctors, and is often considered offensive.

SPECIAL

➡ see also **UNUSUAL, DIFFERENT, FESTIVALS AND SPECIAL DAYS**

1 special

special /'speʃəl/ [adj] something that is **special** is different from other things, for example because it is better, more important, or intended for a particular purpose: *They have special meals for children.* | *United Airlines is offering a special $299 return fare to London.* | *I made a special effort to be nice to him.*
+ for *Today is a very special day for her.*
special occasion (=a wedding, birthday, or other time when people celebrate something) *He has a dark suit, which he only wears on special occasions.*
something special about sb/sth (=something good about a person, place etc which makes you like them very much) *There's something special about the countryside in this part of France.*

specially /'speʃəli/ [adv] **specially designed/made/built/chosen/trained/prepared etc** designed, made, built etc for a special purpose: *a new range of beauty products specially designed for teenagers* | *Customs officers use specially trained dogs to search for drugs.*

particular /pəˈtɪkjʊlər/ [adj only before noun] use this to say that something is clearly different or separate from other things of the same kind, or that something is more important than other things: *Each flower has its own particular smell.* | *Is there any particular reason why you want to go back to Japan?* | *Each class will focus on one particular aspect of American culture.*
be of particular interest/importance (=be especially interesting or important to a particular person or group) *This discovery is of particular interest to scientists studying the origins of the universe.*

unique /juːˈniːk/ [adj] so special and unusual that it is the only one of its kind – use this especially about things or people that you think are extremely good: *It was a unique achievement – no-one has ever won the championship five times before.* | *The exhibition provides a unique opportunity to see all of the artist's work.*

> ⚠ Don't say 'very unique'. Just say **unique**.

SPEND
to spend money or time

➡ look here for ...
• spend money
• spend time

1 to use money to buy things

spend /spend/ [v T] to use money to buy things
spend £5/$10 etc *I bought two skirts and a T-shirt and I only spent $50.*
spend £5/$10 etc on sth *We spend about £85 a week on food.* | *The government should spend more on education.* | *She spends far too much money on clothes.*
spend money on doing sth *Carrie spends most of her money on travelling to school.*

spending – spent – have spent

> ⚠ Don't say 'I spent $50 for this jacket'. Say **I spent $50 on this jacket**.

pay £5/$10 etc for sth /peɪ (£5/$10 etc) fər (sth)/ [phrasal verb T] to spend £5, $10 etc in order to buy something: *They paid over $100 each for tickets.* | *The set meal costs £15 but you have to pay extra for wine.*

⚠ Use **pay for** to talk about what you must pay for something because that is what it costs. Compare: *We pay more for food than people in America* (=because food is more expensive here). | *French people spend more on food than British people* (=they choose to spend more of their money on food).

Q**blow** /bləʊ/ [v T] SPOKEN to spend a lot of money on something expensive and enjoyable, especially something that you do not really need
blow £50/$100 etc on sth *We blew $3000 on a trip to Barbados.*
blow the lot BRITISH **blow it all** AMERICAN (=spend everything) *He won £500,000 in the National Lottery, but he's blown the lot.*

blowing – blew – have blown

2 to spend less money

cut down /ˌkʌt ˈdaʊn/ [phrasal verb I/T] to reduce the amount of money that you regularly spend: *He's spending much more than he can afford – he'll have to cut down.*
+ on *She's already cut down on going out and buying clothes, but she still doesn't have enough money.*

economize (also **economise** BRITISH) /ɪˈkɒnəmaɪz‖ɪˈkɑː-/ [v I] to spend less money by buying only what you really need, or by buying cheaper things: *Sorry, I can't come out tonight – I'm trying to economize.*
economize on sth (=spend less money on something) *Families on low incomes had to economize on food and heating costs.*

3 the amount of money you spend

spending /ˈspendɪŋ/ [n U] the amount of money that is spent, especially by a government
public/government spending *increases in government spending*
health/education/defence spending *In recent years the government has reduced defence spending.*

⚠ You can also use **spending** before a noun, like an adjective: *a survey of people's spending habits* | *big spending cuts*

costs /kɒsts‖kɔːsts/ [n plural] the money that a person or organization has to spend regularly on heating, rent, electricity etc: *What are your annual fuel costs?*
cut costs (=reduce costs) *Falling sales have forced companies to cut costs.*
running costs (=the costs of owning and using a car or machine) *I'm looking for a car with low running costs.*

expenses /ɪkˈspensɪz/ [n plural] the money that you need to spend in order to buy the things you need: *John and Rachel have a new baby, so they have a lot of expenses right now.*
travel / living / medical / legal expenses *Living expenses are much higher in London.* | *The company doesn't pay my travel expenses.*

4 someone who hates spending money

stingy /ˈstɪndʒi/ [adj] not generous with your money, even though you are not poor: *It's no use asking him – he's too stingy to give money to charity.*
stingy – stingier – stingiest

mean /miːn/ [adj] BRITISH someone who is **mean** does not like spending money or sharing what they have with other people: *He's so mean, he never even buys his wife a birthday present.*
+ with *Marsha has always been mean with her money.*

Q**cheap** /tʃiːp/ [adj] AMERICAN, ESPECIALLY SPOKEN someone who is **cheap** does not like spending money, and always tries to avoid spending it: *Uncle Matt was really cheap – he used to stay with us for weeks, and he never paid for anything.*

miser /ˈmaɪzər/ [n C] someone who hates spending money, and tries to spend as little as possible, especially someone who stores their money in a secret place: *Everyone said Mr Henny was a miser who had thousands of pounds hidden under his bed.*

When you see **EC** , go to the **ESSENTIAL COMMUNICATION** section.

5 someone who likes spending money

extravagant /ɪk'strævəgənt/ [adj] spending a lot of money on things that you do not really need: *$200 on a dress? You're so extravagant!*

throw your money around /ˌθrəʊ jɔːʳ 'mʌni ə,raʊnd/ INFORMAL someone who **throws their money around** has a lot of money and enjoys spending it: *a luxury skiing resort, full of rich people throwing their money around*

6 to spend time

➡ see also **STAY**

spend /spend/ [v T] to spend time somewhere, with someone, or doing something: *I never seem to have any time to spend with the children.* | *Dani spends hours on the phone.*
spend time doing sth *Fay spent a year in Italy teaching English.*
spending – spent – have spent

pass the time /ˌpɑːs ðə 'taɪm‖ˌpæs-/ to spend time doing something unimportant, because you have nothing else to do: *I started doing a crossword to pass the time.*
pass your time *The security guards used to pass their time playing cards.*

waste /weɪst/ [v T] to use your time badly, by doing nothing or by doing something that is not useful: *Stop wasting time. We have to finish this by five o'clock.* | *I must have wasted two whole hours trying to fix this machine.*

kill /kɪl/ [v T] **kill time/a couple of hours etc** INFORMAL to make the time pass more quickly while you are waiting for something by doing something that you do not need to do: *I was early, so I sat in a café, killing time.* | *The train doesn't leave till two, so we have a couple of hours to kill.*

When you see **EC**, go to the **ESSENTIAL COMMUNICATION** section.

SPOIL

to make something less attractive, less enjoyable, or less effective

DAMAGE   BREAK
see also
MARK   DESTROY

spoil /spɔɪl/ [v T] *That new supermarket has really spoiled the view from the house.* | *Yes, it rained a lot, but we didn't let that spoil our vacation.*
spoil sth for sb (=make it less enjoyable or exciting for them) *Don't tell me the ending of the movie – you'll spoil it for me.*
spoil everything/spoil things (=completely spoil someone's plans) *If you don't come it'll spoil everything.*
spoiling – spoiled (also **spoilt** BRITISH) – **have spoiled** (also **have spoilt** BRITISH)

mess up /ˌmes 'ʌp/ [phrasal verb T] SPOKEN to spoil something important or something that has been carefully planned
mess up sth *The travel agents messed up the arrangements and there was no room for us at the hotel.* | *He's messed up my whole life.*
mess sth up *We secretly organized a party for her, but then Bill messed everything up by telling her about it.*

ruin /'ruːɪn/ [v T] to spoil something completely: *John and Sandy argued all the time, which completely ruined the evening for the rest of us.* | *My new white dress was totally ruined!* | *If the newspapers find out about this, it could ruin his career.*

wreck /rek/ [v T] to completely spoil something important so that it can never exist again or be like it was before: *The bombing was a deliberate attempt to wreck the peace talks.* | *a dreadful car crash that wrecked their lives*

SPORT

COMPETITION   THROW 2

EXERCISE   see   CATCH
                also
FREE TIME   GAME

TAKE PART   ORGANIZATION

1 sport

sport /spɔːʳt/ [n C/U] a physical activity in which people or teams play against each other and try to win: *My favourite sports are basketball and motor-racing.*
do sport ESPECIALLY BRITISH **play sport** ESPECIALLY AMERICAN *Do you play any sports? | I haven't been doing much sport lately.*
  sports [adj only before noun] used for sport or connected with sport: *My son belongs to a local sports club. | sports equipment*

⚠ **Sport** can also be an uncountable noun, especially in British English, meaning 'sports in general'. So you can say either **good at sport** (ESPECIALLY BRITISH) or **good at sports** (ESPECIALLY AMERICAN).

⚠ Don't say 'make sport'. Say **play sport** or **do sport**.

game /geɪm/ [n C] a sport that you play against another player or team, according to a set of rules: *At school, we played team games like football and hockey. | Tennis is a popular game in the summer.*

⚠ Don't confuse **sport** and **game**. **Sport** includes all sorts of physical activities, games, races, and things like climbing and fishing. **Games** are usually played either between two people or between two teams. Sports that involve racing, such as swimming, athletics, and horse-racing, are not **games**.

2 an occasion when people compete against each other in a sport

game /geɪm/ [n C] an occasion when two people or two teams compete against each other in a sport: *Barcelona beat Real Madrid 3–2 in a thrilling game. | Who won the game? | I got two tickets for the Bulls' game.*
game of tennis/squash etc *How about a game of tennis this evening?*
basketball/football etc game *I'm going to watch a volleyball game this Saturday.*

match /mætʃ/ [n C] ESPECIALLY BRITISH an occasion when two people or two teams compete against each other in a sport: *Are you going to the match tomorrow?*
a football/cricket/boxing match *A cricket match was in progress on the school sports field.*

⚠ Don't say 'a match of tennis/football/chess etc'.

⚠ Americans never use **match** to mean a game played between two teams. They only use it for games where one person competes with another or fights with another: *a wrestling match*

race /reɪs/ [n C] a competition in which several people try to run, drive, ride, swim etc faster than each other: *Hill won the race, and Schumacher finished second.*
horse race *Her husband spent all their money gambling on horse races.*

3 to play a sport

play /pleɪ/ [v I/T] to take part in a sport – use this especially about games in which you try to win against another person or team: *I'm playing in a basketball game this Sunday.*
play football/tennis/golf/baseball etc *It's a long time since I played hockey.*
+ against *The Rams played against the Giants twice in three weeks.*

playing – played – have played

do /duː/ [v T] ESPECIALLY SPOKEN use this especially with the names of sports that are not team sports: *I do aerobics twice a week.* | *He used to do karate, but he gave it up.*

doing – did – have done

go /gəʊ/ [v T] use this about sports whose names end in '-ing'

go climbing / swimming / running / riding etc *John goes running every morning.*

going – went – have gone

4 someone who does a sport

player /ˈpleɪəʳ/ [n C] someone who belongs to a sports team or who regularly does a sport: *One of the players had been injured.*

baseball/basketball etc player *one of the best tennis players in the country*

sportsman/sportswoman /ˈspɔːʳts-mən, ˈspɔːʳtsˌwʊmən/ [n C] someone who is very good at sport, especially someone who does it as their job: *A special Olympic village has been built for the sportsmen and sportswomen to live in.*

plural sportsmen/sportswomen

athlete /ˈæθliːt/ [n C] someone who is good at sport, especially someone who does athletics (=sports such as running, throwing things, or jumping over high bars): *All athletes now have to be regularly tested for drugs.*

5 a group of people who play against another group

team /tiːm/ [n C] a group of people who play together against another group in a sport: *Which team do you support?*

be in a team BRITISH be on a team AMERICAN *We haven't decided who is going to be on the team yet.*

⚠ In British English, you can use team with a singular or plural verb: *Our team is wearing red/are wearing red.* In American English, only use a singular verb.

side /saɪd/ [n C] BRITISH one of two teams who are playing against each other: *Both sides played really well.* | *Our side only needs one more goal to win.*

captain /ˈkæptₐn/ [n C] the main player in a team, who tells the other players what to do

+ of *the captain of the England football team*

6 a place where you do a sport

field /fiːld/ [n C] a large area of ground, usually covered in grass, where team sports are played: *The crowd cheered as the players ran onto the field.*

baseball/football/sports etc field (=a field where baseball, football etc is played): *The football field was too muddy to play on, so the game was cancelled.*

pitch /pɪtʃ/ [n C] BRITISH a sports field: *The fans rushed onto the pitch at the end of the match.*

cricket/football etc pitch (=a pitch where cricket or football is played)

court /kɔːʳt/ [n C] an area with lines painted on the ground, where two people or teams play a game such as tennis, badminton, basketball, or netball

tennis/basketball/squash etc court (=a court where tennis etc is played)

leisure centre /ˈleʒəʳ ˌsentəʳ‖ˈliː-/ [n C] BRITISH a building where you can do various different sports: *There's a really nice swimming pool at the leisure centre.*

gym /dʒɪm/ [n C] a large room where there are machines that you can use to do exercises and make your body stronger: *Are you going to the gym today?*

pool/swimming pool /puːl, ˈswɪmɪŋ puːl/ [n C] a place where you can swim, consisting of a large hole in the ground that has been built and filled with water, either outdoors or inside a building

stadium /ˈsteɪdiəm/ [n C] a large sports field with seats all around it, where people go to watch team sports: *a baseball stadium*

7 someone who watches a sport

spectator /spekˈteɪtəʳ‖ˈspekteɪtəʳ/ [n C] someone who goes to a game and watches people playing a sport

fan /fæn/ [n C] someone who likes a particular team or player and often goes to watch them play: *Thousands of fans queued to buy tickets.*

supporter /sə'pɔːʳtəʳ/ [n C] BRITISH someone who likes a particular team, especially a football team, and often goes to watch it play: *Several supporters were arrested outside the stadium.*
Milan/Liverpool etc supporter (=a supporter of Milan/Liverpool etc)

support /sə'pɔːʳt/ [v T] BRITISH to like a particular team, and want it to win: *"Which team do you support?" "Oh, United, of course!"*

⚠ Don't say 'I am supporting Juventus'. Say **I support Juventus**.

8 the person who makes sure that players obey the rules

referee/umpire /ˌrefə'riː, 'ʌmpaɪəʳ/ [n C] the person in charge of a game, who makes sure that the players obey the rules and decides who has won

⚠ Use **referee** about football, basketball, hockey, and boxing.

⚠ Use **umpire** about baseball, cricket, and tennis.

judges /'dʒʌdʒɨz/ [n plural] the people who decide which person is the best in a competition

⚠ Use **judges** about sports in which people do not compete in teams, such as skating, horse-riding, and gymnastics.

9 the points you get when you are playing a sport

point /pɔɪnt/ [n C] a unit used for measuring how well you are doing in a sport or game: *Steve Jones is 15 points ahead. | Damon Hill leads the Formula 1 Championship, with 58 points from 6 races.*
get/score a point *We lost the game when the Giants scored 14 points in the last quarter.*

goal /gəʊl/ [n C] the point you get when you make the ball go into the net in sports such as football or hockey
score a goal (=get a goal)

score /skɔːʳ/ [n C] the number of points that the two teams or players have in a

game: *What's the score? | The score at half time was 12–18.*
final score (=the score at the end of the game)

10 when two teams or players have the same score

draw ESPECIALLY BRITISH **tie** ESPECIALLY AMERICAN /drɔː, taɪ/ [n C] when both players or teams have the same number of points at the end of a game: *"What was the result of the Barcelona v Real Madrid game?" "It was a draw."*
end in a draw/tie *The game ended in a tie.*

○ **be two all/be four all etc** /biː (two etc) 'ɔːl/ SPOKEN say this when both players or teams have two points, four points etc in a game: *It's two all at the moment, but United seems the better team. | "What was the final score?" "One all."*

SPREAD

to cover a larger area or affect a larger group of people

1 when fire/liquid etc spreads

spread /spred/ [v I] if fire, liquid, smoke etc **spreads**, it moves outwards in all directions to cover a larger area: *The fire spread quickly through the building.*
+ through/across/to etc *By now the flood water had spread across 80 square miles of farmland. | She knocked over her glass, and a dark pool of wine spread over the tablecloth.*
spreading – spread – have spread

2 when information/ ideas/feelings etc spread

spread /spred/ [v I/T] if information, an idea, or a feeling **spreads**, or if you **spread** it, more and more people begin to know about it or be affected by it: *News of the President's death spread quickly.*
+ to/into/through etc *a feeling of panic that spread through the whole army*

spread lies/rumours/gossip (=deliberately tell untrue information to a lot of people) *Someone's been spreading lies about Nancy again.*

spreading – spread – have spread

spread [n singular]
the spread of sth (=when ideas, feelings etc are spread) *the spread of liberal ideas in the 19th century*

get around /ˌget əˈraʊnd/ [phrasal verb I] INFORMAL if news or information **gets around**, people tell other people, so that soon many people know about it: *News soon got around that Nick was back in town.* | *It's a small place, so news and gossip get around pretty quickly.*

3 when diseases spread

spread /spred/ [v I/T] if a disease **spreads**, or if it **is spread**, it is passed from one person to another, and it affects more and more people: *Some diseases are spread by insects.*
+ through/to/across *Cholera is spreading through the refugee camps at an alarming rate.*

spreading – spread – have spread

spread [n singular]
the spread of sth (=when a disease spreads) *the spread of AIDS*

infectious /ɪnˈfekʃəs/ [adj] an **infectious** disease is spread by being passed from one person to another: *infectious diseases such as typhoid*
highly infectious (=very infectious) *Measles is a highly infectious illness that can be extremely serious.*

4 when people go in many directions

spread out /ˌspred ˈaʊt/ [phrasal verb I] if a group of people **spreads out**, they move apart from each other so that they cover a larger area: *"Spread out!" shouted the sergeant. "We have to search the whole forest."* | *Small groups of survivors spread out across the plain.*

scatter /ˈskætəʳ/ [v I] if a group of people **scatter**, they all suddenly move in different directions, especially to avoid something dangerous: *A gun went off and the crowd scattered.* | *The rioters scattered when police vans arrived.*

5 to put butter, glue etc on a surface

spread /spred/ [v T] to put a thin layer of a soft substance, such as butter or glue, on a surface, so that it covers it
spread sth on sth *Spread the glue evenly on both surfaces.* | *He spread plaster on the walls.*
spread sth with sth *two slices of toast spread with peanut butter*

spreading – spread – have spread

6 to open something out and arrange it on a surface

spread/spread out /spred, ˌspred ˈaʊt/ [v T] to open something such as a sheet, a map, or a newspaper, and arrange it so that it lies flat on a table, the floor, or another surface
spread out sth *Jim spread out a blanket for her to sit on.*
spread sth out/over/on *He took the map and spread it out on the table.* | *I spread the towels over the radiator to dry.*

7 when things are spread over a wide area

scattered /ˈskætəʳd/ [adj] things that are **scattered** are spread over a large area in an irregular or untidy way
+ about/over/among etc *Tiny cottages were scattered all over the hillside.*

spread out /ˌspred ˈaʊt/ [adj not before noun] things that are **spread out** are spread over a large area with a lot of space between them
+ on/among/across etc *Diane had her papers spread out all over the floor.*

STAND

➡ if you mean 'can't stand something', go to **BAD 6**
➡ see also **SIT, LIE**

1 to be in a standing position

stand /stænd/ [v I] to be in a standing position: *I was standing next to the entrance.* | *There were no seats, so we* had to stand. | *Who's that girl standing over there?*

stand doing sth (=stand while you are doing something) *She stood watching him as he turned to go.*

stand up straight (=with your back and legs straight) *The ceilings were so low that Mark couldn't stand up straight.*

stand still (=stand without moving) *Stand still a moment while I brush your hair.*

standing – stood – have stood

be on your feet /biː ɒn jɔːʳ ˈfiːt/ to be standing, especially for a long time, with the result that you feel tired – use this especially about people who have to stand and walk a lot in their jobs: *I've been on my feet all day and I need to rest.*

on tiptoe/on tiptoes /ɒn ˈtɪptəʊ (z)/ standing on your toes, especially when you stretch your body in order to see something or reach something: *She stood on tiptoe and tried to see over the fence.*

lean /liːn/ [v I] to stand while resting part of your body against a wall, a table etc
+ against/on *Kay was leaning against the school wall, smoking a cigarette.* | *Joe leaned on the gate and watched them drive away.*

leaning – leaned (also **leant** BRITISH) – **have leaned** (also **have leant** BRITISH)

2 to stand after sitting or lying down

get up /ˌget ˈʌp/ [phrasal verb I] to stand after you have been sitting, bending, or lying down: *She got up and turned off the TV.*
get up from a chair/seat/sofa etc *Max got up from his chair and shook her hand.*
get up off the floor/ground/grass etc *One of her friends helped her to get up off the floor.*
get up to do sth *I was left with Maria when the others got up to dance.*

stand up /ˌstænd ˈʌp/ [phrasal verb I] to stand after you have been sitting: *"I must go now," she said, standing up.* | *Everyone stood up as the bride and her father entered the church.*

get to your feet /ˌget tə jɔːʳ ˈfiːt/ to stand up, especially slowly or when it is difficult for you: *He got to his feet, looking pale and anxious.* | *Somehow Jenny*

managed to get to her feet and stumble out of the room.

3 to put your foot down on something

stand on sth/step on sth (also **tread on sth** BRITISH) /ˈstænd ɒn (sth), ˈstep ɒn (sth), ˈtred ɒn (sth)‖-ɑːn-/ [phrasal verb T] to put your foot down on something while you are standing or walking, especially accidentally: *I think I must have stood on some glass.* | *Be careful! You nearly trod on my foot.*

stamp on sth /ˈstæmp ɒn (sth)‖-ɑːn-/ [phrasal verb T] to deliberately put your foot down very hard on something: *There was a big cockroach in the kitchen and Barbara stamped on it.*

START

➡ opposite **STOP**
➡ see also **BEGINNING, FINISH, END**

1 to start doing something

start /stɑːʳt/ [v I/T] *We can't start until Carol gets here.* | *I'm starting a new job next week.* | *Have you started that book yet?* (=started reading it)
start doing sth *I've just started learning German.* | *If the baby starts crying, give her some milk.*
start to do sth *Has Gemma started to write that report yet?*
start by doing sth (=do something as the first part of an activity) *Start by melting the butter in the frying-pan.*
start with sth (=do something or deal with something as the first part of a long activity) *Tina wanted to paint the whole apartment, and she decided to start with the kitchen.*
get started (=start a journey, activity etc, especially one that will take a long time) *It was a fine morning, and the boys were eager to get started.*

begin /bɪˈgɪn/ [v I/T] ESPECIALLY WRITTEN to start doing something: *When the children were quiet, Martha began.* | *They began their journey in Venice.*

begin to do sth *Ann began slowly to climb the steps to the castle.* | *I began to realize that she no longer loved me.*

begin doing sth *The audience suddenly began shouting and cheering.*

begin by doing sth (=do something as the first part of an activity) *They began by asking me questions about my previous job.*

+ with *The speaker began with a short introduction about the history of the town.*

> ⚠ **Begin** means the same as **start**, but **begin** is more formal. It is not usually used in conversation, but it is often used when you are describing past events or telling a story.

beginning – began – have begun

get down to sth /get 'daʊn tuː (sth)/ [phrasal verb T] INFORMAL to finally start doing something, after you have been avoiding doing it or after something has prevented you from doing it: *Come on Bill – it's time you got down to some homework.*

get down to doing sth *Once the summer's here we must get down to painting the outside of the house.*

◯ get cracking /get 'krækɪŋ/ SPOKEN INFORMAL to start doing something immediately, because you are in a hurry or there is a lot to do: *Come on! – get cracking. I want this whole house clean when I get back.* | *You'd better get cracking if you want to get to the airport by ten.*

> ⚠ Only use **get cracking** in the infinitive or in commands. Don't say 'we got cracking' etc.

2 to start doing something regularly

start/begin /staːʳt, bɪˈgɪn/ [v T] to start doing something which you then do regularly

start/begin doing sth *I started doing aerobics two years ago.* | *She was only 16 when she began seeing Alan, who was already married.*

start/begin to do sth *His parents got divorced last year – that's when he started to take drugs.*

beginning – began – have begun

> ⚠ **Begin** is more formal than **start**, and is not usually used in conversation.

take up sth /ˌteɪk 'ʌp (sth)/ [phrasal verb T] to become interested in a sport or activity, and start to spend time doing it: *When did Bryan take up golf?*

turn to sth /ˈtɜːʳn tuː (sth)/ [phrasal verb T] **turn to crime/drugs/alcohol etc** to start doing something dangerous or illegal: *Hal turned to drinking after his wife and kids were killed in a car crash.* | *Research shows that young people without jobs are most likely to turn to crime.*

3 when something starts happening

start/begin /staːʳt, bɪˈgɪn/ [v I] *Do you know what time the class starts?* | *My day starts at 5 or 6 o'clock, when the baby wakes up.* | *The movie was just beginning when Richard and James arrived.* | *Work on the new bridge will begin next year.*

beginning – began – have begun

> ⚠ **Begin** is more formal than **start**, and is not usually used in conversation.

break out /ˌbreɪk 'aʊt/ [phrasal verb I] to start happening – use this about unpleasant things like fires, wars, or diseases: *A fire broke out on the top floor of the building.* | *Fighting broke out between gangs of rival football fans.*

outbreak /ˈaʊtbreɪk/ [n C] when something unpleasant starts happening, such as a fire, war, or disease

+ of *There's been an outbreak of food poisoning at the hotel.*

4 to make something start happening

start /staːʳt/ [v T] to make something start happening: *The referee couldn't start the game because there were fans on the field.* | *Don't drop your cigarette here – you could start a fire.* | *Jim parked in someone else's space, and that's what started the fight.*

launch /lɔːntʃ/ [v T] **launch an attack/ appeal/inquiry/campaign** to start a public or military activity, when there is a clear aim that you want to achieve: *The local hospital has launched a campaign to raise money for new X-ray equipment.* | *Police are launching a major murder inquiry.* | *Rebel forces launched an attack on Kabul.*

introduce/bring in /ˌɪntrəˈdjuːs, ˌbrɪŋ ˈɪn‖ -ˈduːs/ [v T] to officially start a new system, method, or rule for the first time: *The company is thinking of introducing medical tests for all employees.* | *New safety measures will be introduced next month.* | *They have promised to bring in a minimum wage if they win the election.*

5 to start a new business or organization

start/start up /staːrt, ˌstaːrt ˈʌp/ [v T] to start a new business or organization: *Luigi's family came here in 1966 and started up a chain of restaurants.* | *John decided to start his own textile business shortly after the war.*

open /ˈəʊpən/ [v T] to start a business that provides services to the public, such as a shop, a restaurant, or a hotel: *They just opened a new supermarket on Van Nuys Boulevard.*

set up /ˌset ˈʌp/ [phrasal verb I/T] to start a new business by making all the necessary arrangements, buying equipment etc
set up sth *Bruno and his partner are setting up their own printing business.*
set up in business (=start to run your own business) *People attend the college to learn how to set up in business on their own.*
set up as *Sean got a bank loan to set up as an architect in his own studio.*

found /faʊnd/ [v T] to start an organization, school, hospital etc, especially by providing the money for it – use this especially about something that was started a long time ago: *Pierpont was one of the group who founded Yale College in 1701.*
be founded *The bank was founded 60 years ago in Munich.*

6 to start doing something again

start again /ˌstaːrt əˈgen/ [phrasal verb I/T] to start doing something again, or to start happening again: *The Middle East peace talks have started again.*
start sth again *After her vacation, Trish really didn't feel like starting work again.* | *She failed her degree, so she had to start her course again.*

start over /ˌstaːrt ˈəʊvər/ [phrasal verb I] ESPECIALLY AMERICAN to start doing something again from the beginning, especially because you want to do it better: *If you make a mistake, just press 'delete' and start over.*

bring back sth /ˌbrɪŋ ˈbæk (sth)/ [phrasal verb T] to start using a custom, system, law etc again, which was used in the past but then stopped: *Do you think they should bring back the death penalty?* | *They're talking about bringing back formal grammar teaching.*

go back to sth /ˌgəʊ ˈbæk tuː (sth)/ [phrasal verb T] to start doing something again, after a period when you did something else: *Some mothers go back to full-time work only a few weeks after their baby is born.*
go back to doing sth *This time, Ben was determined not to go back to using drugs again.*

STAY

➡ look here for ...
• stay in a place and not leave it
• spend time in a place
• stay in someone's house or a hotel
➡ if you mean 'continue to be the same', go to **CONTINUE 3**

1 to stay in the same place, job, school etc and not leave it

➡ opposite **LEAVE**

stay /steɪ/ [v I] to continue to be in the same place, job, school etc and not leave it: *Stay there – I want to take a photograph of you.*
+ with *He stayed with the baby until she fell asleep.*
stay at home *My husband wants me to stay at home and look after the children.*

stay at school BRITISH **stay in school** AMERICAN (=continue to go to school) *Most students stay at school until they are 16 or 17.*

stay in a job *Alice has never stayed in the same job for more than a year.*

stay behind (=stay somewhere after other people have left) *After the party a few of us stayed behind to help clean up.*

stay in /ˌsteɪ 'ɪn/ [phrasal verb I] to stay in your house and not go out, especially in the evening: *The others went out to a club, but I stayed in and watched television.*

stay on /ˌsteɪ 'ɒn‖-'ɑːn/ [phrasal verb I] to stay in a place, job, school etc for a longer time than you had planned, or after other people have left: *We've had such a great time that we're thinking of staying on here for another week.*

stay on at school/university *He stayed on at college for an extra year to do a Master's degree.*

remain /rɪ'meɪn/ [v I] to stay in the same place, job, or school: *Picasso remained in Paris throughout the rest of the war.*

remain at home/at school/at work *In those days, unmarried daughters usually remained at home.*

⚠ **Remain** is more formal than **stay**. It is used especially in written English.

2 to spend some time in a place

stay /steɪ/ [v I] to spend a period of time in a place that is not your permanent home: *I'm planning to stay in Paris for a couple of months. | How long are you staying in New York?*

⚠ Don't confuse **stay** (=be somewhere temporarily, for a few days, weeks, or months) and **live** (=be somewhere permanently, or for several years, in your own home).

be there /biː 'ðeəʳ/ to be staying somewhere – use this to talk about a place that has just been mentioned: *"Have you ever been to Prague?" "Yes, I was there in 1978." | While you're there you should go and see the Louvre.*

3 to stay at a hotel or at someone's house

➡ see also **HOLIDAY, VISIT**

stay /steɪ/ [v I] to spend a few days, weeks etc at someone else's house or at a hotel, but not live there permanently

stay at a hotel/at sb's house *I'm staying at my brother's house for a couple of weeks. | Which hotel are you staying at?*

stay with sb (=stay at their house) *You could stay with John and Anne while you're in London.*

stay the night BRITISH **stay over** AMERICAN (=sleep at someone else's house) *Is it all right if I stay the night?*

come to stay *One of Sarah's friends is coming to stay with us this summer.*

visit /'vɪzɪt/ [v I/T] to go to the house of a friend or relative and stay there for some time, because you want to see them: *Aunt Jane usually visits us for two or three weeks in the spring.*

guest /gest/ [n C] someone who is staying with friends or relatives or at a hotel: *The hotel bar is for guests only. | I'm really busy – I'm expecting guests this weekend.*

⚠ **Guest** is rather a formal word. In spoken English you often say **someone staying** or **someone coming to stay** instead of **guest**: *I have someone staying with me at the moment.*

4 a place where you can stay for a short time, such as a hotel

○**a place to stay/somewhere to stay** /ə ˌpleɪs tə 'steɪ, ˌsʌmweəʳ tə 'steɪ/ ESPECIALLY SPOKEN a place where you can stay, for example a hotel or a room in someone's house: *She needs somewhere to stay while she's at college. | We're going to Tokyo – do you know any good places to stay?*

accommodation (also **accommodations** AMERICAN) /əˌkɒmə'deɪʃən(z)‖əˌkɑː-/ [n U/plural] a place where you pay money to stay, for example a hotel or a room that you rent: *The cost of rented accommodation keeps going up. | The travel agency will help you find accommodations.*

⚠ **Accommodation** is more formal than **a place to stay**, and is often used when talking in a general way about places where people can pay to stay: *a shortage of accommodation for students*

⚠ Don't say 'an accommodation'.

5 to let someone stay in your home

◎**put sb up** /ˌpʊt (sb) ˈʌp/ [*phrasal verb* T] ESPECIALLY SPOKEN to let a friend stay in your home for a short time, and provide them with a bed to sleep in: *"Where are you staying?" "Carole's putting us up for a couple of days."*

6 the time when you stay somewhere

stay /steɪ/ [*n* singular] the time when you stay in a place, for example when you go somewhere on holiday or for business: *I met her during my stay in Venice.* | *Did you enjoy your stay?*

visit /ˈvɪzɪ̯t/ [*n* C] the time when you go to stay somewhere, especially in order to see people or see a place: *It was my first visit to my wife's parents' house.*

STEAL

LAW   POLICE

see also

CRIME   PUNISH

⚠ Don't confuse **steal** and **rob**. A thief **steals** money or property, but a robber **robs** a shop, a bank, or another person (=steals money etc from them).

1 to steal something

steal /stiːl/ [*v* I/T] to take something that does not belong to you: *Thousands of cars get stolen every year.* | *In the end he had to steal in order to survive.*
+ **from** *drug addicts who steal from their friends and families*

steal sth from sb/sth *Thieves stole paintings worth $5 million from a Paris art gallery.*

stealing – stole – have stolen

⚠ Don't say 'steal someone'. Say **steal money, clothes etc from someone.**

stolen /ˈstəʊlən/ [*adj*] *The three men escaped in a stolen car.*

take /teɪk/ [*v* T] to steal something, especially money or things that can be carried away: *Someone has been taking money from the cash box.* | *The burglars took our TV and stereo, but they didn't find the jewellery.*

taking – took – have taken

◎**nick/pinch** /nɪk, pɪntʃ/ [*v* T] BRITISH SPOKEN to steal something: *I wonder where she got that coat – do you think she nicked it?*

nick/pinch sth from sb/sth *Jimmy was caught pinching money from his mum's purse.*

◎**rip off** /ˌrɪp ˈɒf‖-ˈɔːf/ [*phrasal verb* T] SPOKEN, ESPECIALLY AMERICAN to steal something

rip off sth *The store was very crowded, and someone ripped off my purse.*

2 to steal from a house, shop, bank etc

rob /rɒb‖rɑːb/ [*v* T] if someone **robs** a bank, shop etc, they take money or property from it, especially by using threats or violence: *He got five years in jail for robbing a gas station.* | *Two men robbed the Central Bank yesterday, escaping with over $1 million.*

robbing – robbed – have robbed

burgle BRITISH **burglarize** AMERICAN /ˈbɜːrɡəl, ˈbɜːrɡləraɪz/ [*v* T] to illegally enter a house or office and steal things: *He was caught burgling the house of a police officer.* | *Our apartment has been burglarized twice since we moved here.*

⚠ You can say 'we've been burgled', or 'we were burglarized', when you mean 'our house has been burgled'.

shoplift /ˈʃɒpˌlɪft‖ˈʃɑːp-/ [*v* I only in -ing form] to take things from shops without paying for them, especially by hiding them in your clothes or in a bag: *I started shop-lifting when my parents got divorced.*

hold up sth /ˈhəʊld ʌp (sth)/ [*phrasal verb* T] to go into a bank, shop etc with a gun and demand money: *The men who held up the store were wearing Halloween masks.*

3 to steal from someone in the street

rob /rɒb‖rɑːb/ [*v* T] if someone **robs** you, they take money or property from you, especially in a public place such as a street: *Two men tried to rob him as he left the restaurant.*
robbing – robbed – have robbed

mug /mʌg/ [*v* T usually in passive] to violently attack someone in the street and rob them: *Since she was mugged she's been scared to go out on her own.*
mugging – mugged – have mugged

4 someone who steals

thief /θiːf/ [*n* C] someone who steals things, usually secretly and without violence: *The thieves had been careful not to leave any fingerprints.*
car thief/jewel thief etc (=someone who steals cars, jewels etc)
plural **thieves**

robber /ˈrɒbəʳ‖ˈrɑː-/ [*n* C] someone who steals from banks, offices, houses etc, especially by using threats or violence: *The robbers forced bank staff to give them £4000 in cash.*
bank robber (=someone who robs a bank)
armed robber (=a robber with a gun)

burglar /ˈbɜːʳgləʳ/ [*n* C] someone who illegally gets into a house, office etc and steals things: *No-one saw the burglar, but I think he got in through the kitchen window.*

pickpocket /ˈpɪkˌpɒkɪt‖-ˌpɑːk-/ [*n* C] someone who steals from people in a public place, by taking things from their pockets or bags without them noticing: *There are a lot of pickpockets in crowded tourist areas, so look after your belongings.*

shoplifter /ˈʃɒpˌlɪftəʳ‖ˈʃɑːp-/ [*n* C] someone who takes things from shops without paying for them, especially by hiding them in their clothes or in a bag: *The store has*

installed hidden cameras to catch shoplifters.

mugger /ˈmʌgəʳ/ [*n* C] a thief who violently attacks someone in the street and robs them: *Harry suffered serious head injuries when he was attacked by a gang of muggers.*

5 the crime of stealing

robbery /ˈrɒbəri‖ˈrɑː-/ [*n* C/U] the crime of stealing money or other things from a bank, shop etc, especially by using threats or violence: *He took part in his first robbery when he was 17.*
armed robbery (=using guns) *Spencer was jailed for eight years for armed robbery.*
bank robbery *Police are investigating a series of bank robberies.*
plural **robberies**

burglary /ˈbɜːʳgləri/ [*n* C/U] the crime of illegally entering a house, office etc and stealing things: *Call the police – there's been a burglary.* | *Most burglaries occur when a house or apartment is empty.*
plural **burglaries**

theft /θeft/ [*n* C/U] FORMAL when something is stolen
+ of *the theft of £150 from the office*
car/bicycle theft (=when a car or bicycle is stolen) *Bicycle theft is a major problem in the city.*

break-in /ˈbreɪk ɪn/ [*n* C] when someone breaks a door or window in order to enter a place and steal things: *There was a break-in at the college last night – they took all the computers.*
plural **break-ins**

hold-up /ˈhəʊld ʌp/ [*n* C] when someone goes into a bank or shop with a gun and demands money: *A man was shot dead in a hold-up at a downtown bank.*
plural **hold-ups**

mugging /ˈmʌgɪŋ/ [*n* C] a violent attack on someone in the street in order to rob them: *The number of muggings in the area has doubled in the last year.*

shoplifting /ˈʃɒpˌlɪftɪŋ‖ˈʃɑːp-/ [*n* U] the crime of taking things from shops without paying for them: *Shoplifting cost the major stores millions of dollars last year.*

STICK

to join one thing to another thing, especially using glue

➡ see also JOIN

1 to stick something

stick /stɪk/ [v T] to join one thing to another thing, especially by using glue or tape with glue on it

stick sth on/in sth *It took hours to stick all the stamps on these letters.* | *Stick a label on each box to say what's inside it.*

stick sth together *We gathered up the pieces and stuck the vase back together again.* | *Some of the pages were stuck together.*

sticking – stuck – have stuck

glue /gluː/ [v T] to use glue to join things together, when you are making something or repairing something

glue sth to/onto sth *I tried to glue the handle back onto the cup.*

glue sth together *You make the model by cutting out these shapes and gluing them together.*

2 when one thing sticks to another

stick /stɪk/ [v I] if something **sticks** to something else, it becomes joined to it when it touches it, because it has glue or a sticky substance on it: *She pressed down the flap of the envelope, but it didn't stick.*

+ to *Peter was very hot, and his shirt was sticking to his back.*

sticking – stuck – have stuck

sticky /'stɪki/ [adj] something that is **sticky** sticks to other things, and sticks to your fingers when you touch it: *There was a horrible sticky mess on the table.* | *Add flour to the mixture to prevent it from becoming sticky.*

sticky – stickier – stickiest

3 a substance that you use to stick things

glue /gluː/ [n C/U] a liquid or soft substance that you use to join things together: *Wait for the glue to dry before you paint the model.*

Sellotape BRITISH **Scotch tape** AMERICAN /'seləteɪp, ˌskɒtʃ 'teɪp‖ˌskɑːtʃ-/ [n U] TRADEMARK transparent tape with glue on it that you use to join things together: *He was wearing glasses that were held together with Sellotape.*

STOP

➡ look here for ...
• stop doing something
• stop something from happening
• stop moving
➡ opposite START
➡ see also FINISH, END, REST

1 to stop doing something

stop /stɒp‖stɑːp/ [v I/T] to no longer do something that you have been doing or that you used to do: *That baby is always crying – doesn't he ever stop?*

stop doing sth *Everyone stopped talking as soon as she entered the room.* | *They stopped making the 3-litre Austin-Healey sportscar in 1967.*

◯**stop it/that** SPOKEN (=say this to tell someone to stop doing something) *Stop it! You're hurting me.*

stop work *At five o'clock we stopped work and went home.*

⚠ Don't say 'she stopped to cry'. Say **she stopped crying**.

stopping – stopped – have stopped

quit /kwɪt/ [v I/T] ESPECIALLY AMERICAN to stop doing something, especially something that is difficult or unpleasant, or something that annoys other people: *"Have you found it?" "No, and if I don't find it soon I'm going to quit."*

quit doing sth *I wish he'd quit bothering me.* | *She's trying to quit smoking.*

◯**quit it/that** SPOKEN (say this to tell someone to stop doing something annoying) *Quit it, Robby, or I'll tell Mom.*

quitting – quit – have quit

give up /ˌgɪv 'ʌp/ [phrasal verb T] to stop doing something, especially something that you used to do regularly

give up sth *I had to give up tennis when I injured my knee.*

give up smoking/drinking/fatty food etc
(=stop smoking, drinking etc because you
want to be healthy) *Michelle gave up
smoking three years ago.*
give up doing sth *After about 10 minutes, I gave up trying to explain it to her.*
give it up *I used to play a lot of football,
but I had to give it up because of an
injury.*

abandon /ə'bændən/ [v T] **abandon a
plan/attempt/search/policy etc** to
stop something before you finish it, especially because it is too difficult to continue
or there are too many problems: *They
had to abandon the search because of
the bad weather.* | *We abandoned the
climb after Collins fell and broke his leg.*

2 to stop doing something for a short time

stop /stɒp‖stɑːp/ [v I] to stop doing something for a short time, before continuing
again: *Can we stop for a moment – I
want to look at the map.*
stop for coffee/lunch/a break etc (=stop
what you are doing, so you can have
coffee, lunch etc) *We'll stop for lunch at
12:30.*
stop to look/listen/watch/talk/rest etc
(=stop in order to look at something etc)
*We stopped to listen to a couple of boys
who were playing guitars in the street.* |
I stopped to rest for a few minutes.
stopping – stopped – have stopped

pause /pɔːz/ [v I] WRITTEN to stop speaking
or stop doing something for a very short
time, before starting again: *Lawrence
paused and turned to me: "Look, if you
don't think it's a good idea ..."*
pause for breath (=because you need to
rest for a moment) *She talked for about
twenty minutes without even pausing
for breath.*
pause to do sth (=in order to do something) *We waited while Graham paused
to light a cigarette.*

⚠ Use **pause** especially in written stories
or descriptions of events.

hesitate /'hezɪteɪt/ [v I] to stop for a
moment and wait before doing something,
because you feel unsure or nervous about
it: *She hesitated for a moment before*
replying. | *Barry stood at the door
hesitating. Should he walk straight in or
knock?*
hesitation /ˌhezɪ'teɪʃən/ [n U] when
someone hesitates: *After some hesitation, one of them began to speak.*

◯**take a break** /teɪk ə 'breɪk/ ESPECIALLY
SPOKEN to stop working for a short time in
order to rest, eat etc: *We're all getting
tired. Let's take a break for ten minutes.*

3 a period of time when you stop doing something

break /breɪk/ [n C] a long or short period
when you stop your work or normal activities, before continuing them again later:
*She returned to her career after a six-
month break.*
+ from *Murray felt he needed a break
from studying.*
lunch/coffee/tea break (=when you stop
work to have lunch, coffee etc)

pause /pɔːz/ [n C] WRITTEN a short period of
time when you stop speaking or stop
doing something before starting again:
*After a long pause, Barney said: "Yes, I
suppose you're right."*
+ in *There was a pause in the conversation
as everyone turned to say hello to Paul.*

4 to stop happening

stop /stɒp‖stɑːp/ [v I] to stop happening:
Let's wait until the rain stops. | *The
noise stopped as suddenly as it had
begun.*
stopping – stopped – have stopped

end /end/ [v I] if an event, activity, or story
ends, it finally stops when it reaches its
end: *When the war ended, there were
over a million refugees.* | *Our journey
ends on the banks of the River Ganges.*

finish /'fɪnɪʃ/ [v I] to end – use this about an
organized event such as a meeting, party,
or lesson, especially to say what time it
ends: *The meeting finished at
lunchtime.* | *What time does your
Spanish class finish?*

come to an end /ˌkʌm tu ən 'end/ to
finally end – use this about things that
have continued for a long time: *Their
marriage came to an end after twenty-
two years.* | *The war in Vietnam finally
came to an end in 1975.*

fade away /ˌfeɪd əˈweɪ/ [phrasal verb I] if a sound **fades away**, it gradually gets quieter and finally stops: *He waited until the sound of the engines had faded away.* | *As the music faded away the audience broke into applause.*

5 to make something stop happening

stop /stɒp‖stɑːp/ [v T] to make someone stop doing something, or make something stop happening: *The referee stopped the fight when one of the boxers was badly injured.* | *A power failure stopped the concert half-way through.*
stop sb doing sth *I gave him some chocolate to stop him crying.*
stopping – stopped – have stopped

put an end to sth /ˌpʊt ən ˈend tuː (sth)/ to permanently stop something, so that it can never start again: *A broken ankle put an end to her career as a dancer.* | *The war put an end to their romance.*

put a stop to sth /ˌpʊt ə ˈstɒp tuː (sth)‖ -ˈstɑːp-/ to stop something unpleasant or harmful that has been happening for a long time: *The UN commander was determined to put a stop to the fighting.*

stamp out /ˌstæmp ˈaʊt/ [phrasal verb T] to completely stop a bad or illegal activity, by making rules about it and making sure that people obey them
stamp out sth *The police are determined to stamp out street robberies.*

6 to make it impossible for someone to do what they want to do

prevent /prɪˈvent/ [v T] to make it impossible for someone to do something that they want to do
prevent sb from doing sth *A leg injury may prevent Shearer from playing in tomorrow's game.* | *There were reports that some people had been prevented from voting in the election.*

stop /stɒp‖stɑːp/ [v T] to stop someone from doing something that they want to do, especially by controlling them in an unreasonable way: *I've made up my mind to leave home, and you can't stop me.*
stop sb (from) doing sth *My parents tried to stop me seeing Anna.* | *The*

BBC was stopped from broadcasting a programme about the Secret Service.

> ⚠ Don't say 'stop someone to do something'. Say **stop someone doing something** or **stop someone from doing something**.

stopping – stopped – have stopped

get in the way of sth /ˌget ɪn ðə ˈweɪ ɒv (sth)/ if something **gets in the way of** something you want to do or something you must do, it makes you too busy to do it: *Don't let your social life get in the way of your education.*

7 to stop someone from going somewhere

stop /stɒp‖stɑːp/ [v T] to prevent someone or something from going somewhere: *We were stopped and searched when we tried to enter the building.* | *The police are stopping drivers to ask questions about the accident.*
stopping – stopped – have stopped

be in the way /biː ɪn ðə ˈweɪ/ if someone or something **is in the way**, they are in a position that stops you from going where you want to go: *There's a car in the way and I can't get out of the garage.*
be in sb's way *Could you move please, Sonia. You're in my way.*

block /blɒk‖blɑːk/ [v T] if objects or people **block** a road, entrance etc, they lie or stand right across it, so that no-one can pass through: *A big truck had turned over on its side, and it was blocking the road.* | *Hundreds of protesters blocked the entrance to the President's palace.*

8 to make sure that something does not happen

prevent /prɪˈvent/ [v T] to make sure that something will not happen or cannot happen, especially something bad: *The rules are intended to prevent accidents.* | *Managers and union leaders are hoping to prevent the strike.*
prevent sth from doing sth *The chemical is stored in sealed tanks to prevent poisonous gases from escaping.*
prevention [n U] when something is prevented: *the prevention of crime*

stop /stɒp‖stɑːp/ [v T] to make sure that something bad that is happening cannot continue and become worse: *If it can help to stop the spread of AIDS, it's worth trying.*
stop sth from doing sth *They had to stop the fire from reaching the oil storage tanks.*
stopping – stopped – have stopped

cancel /'kænsəl/ [v T] to change a previous arrangement, so that a meeting, concert, game etc which was planned will not happen: *We've cancelled the meeting because Wayne can't come. | I forgot to cancel my doctor's appointment.*
cancelling – cancelled – have cancelled
BRITISH
canceling – canceled – have canceled
AMERICAN

call off /ˌkɔːl 'ɒf‖-'ɔːf/ [phrasal verb T] to stop a meeting or event that you have organized, just before it is going to start
call off sth *If it goes on raining, we'll have to call off the game. | Damian called off the wedding at the last moment.*
call sth off *"Will there be a train strike tomorrow?" "No, the union called it off."*

9 to stop someone from working, paying attention etc

interrupt /ˌɪntəˈrʌpt/ [v I/T] to stop someone when they are working, talking, or having a meeting, especially because you want to ask a question or tell them something: *Don't interrupt – I haven't finished yet. | I'm sorry to interrupt your meeting, but I have an important announcement.*
interruption [n C] when someone interrupts you: *It's hard to study with so many interruptions.*

disturb /dɪˈstɜːrb/ [v T] to stop someone who is busy doing something, for example by asking them a question or making a noise: *Sorry to disturb you, but could I ask you a quick question? | Try not to disturb your Dad – he's working.*

distract /dɪˈstrækt/ [v T] to stop someone who is trying to work, study, or read, by making them look at or listen to something else: *The couple behind us kept distracting everyone by talking during the movie.*
be distracted by sth *I was distracted by the sound of a car alarm in the street.*

put sb off /ˌpʊt (sb) ɒf/ [phrasal verb T] BRITISH to make it difficult for someone to do something, by preventing them from paying attention and thinking clearly about what they are doing: *Seles couldn't concentrate on the game – the photographers were putting her off.*

10 to stop moving

stop /stɒp‖stɑːp/ [v I] to stop moving: *I stopped and picked up the coin. | What's happened? Why have all the cars stopped?*
stop to do sth (=stop in order to do something) *He stopped to buy a newspaper on the way home.*
stop dead (=stop very suddenly) *My horse stopped dead, and I was thrown forward.*
stopping – stopped – have stopped

come to a halt/come to a stop /ˌkʌm tʊ ə 'hɔːlt, ˌkʌm tʊ ə 'stɒp‖-'stɑːp/ ESPECIALLY WRITTEN to gradually slow down and then stop – use this about trains, cars etc: *As the train came to a stop he jumped off and ran away. | The bus finally came to a halt half-way up a very steep hill.*

brake /breɪk/ [v I] to make a car, train, bicycle etc stop or go more slowly by using the brake (=the control that reduces the speed): *I had to brake suddenly to avoid a dog that ran into the road.*

pull in/pull over /ˌpʊl 'ɪn, ˌpʊl 'əʊvəʳ/ [phrasal verb I] to make your car stop at the side of the road: *If you start to feel tired on long journeys, pull in and have a rest.*

11 when a train, bus, or plane stops somewhere

stop /stɒp‖stɑːp/ [v I] to stop somewhere to let passengers get on or off – use this about trains or buses
+ at/near/outside etc *Does this train stop at York? | The bus stops just outside my house.*
stopping – stopped – have stopped

stop /stɒp‖stɑːp/ [n C] a place where a bus or train regularly stops to let passengers get on or off: *Get off at the third stop.*
bus stop *We live miles from the nearest bus stop.*

call at /ˈkɔːl æt/ [phrasal verb T] if a train or ship **calls at** a place, it stops there while it is on the way to somewhere else: *This is the 10:30 to Bristol, calling at Reading and Bath.* | *The ship calls at Madeira to collect cargo.*

direct /dɪˈrekt, daɪ-/ [adj/adv] if a journey is **direct**, or if you travel **direct**, you go straight from one place to another without stopping to change planes, trains etc: *With this ticket you can travel direct from Paris to Berlin overnight.*
direct flight/bus/train *There are no direct flights from Rochester to Cincinnati.*

non-stop /ˌnɒn ˈstɒp◂‖ˌnɑːn ˈstɑːp◂/ [adj only before noun] a **non-stop** flight, plane, train etc goes from one place to another without stopping anywhere: *There are three non-stop flights to Hong Kong every day.*
non-stop [adv] *You can travel from Paris to London non-stop on the Eurostar.*

STORY

a description of a series of events that is told to entertain people

➡ see also **BOOKS/LITERATURE, FILMS/MOVIES**

1 a story

story /ˈstɔːri/ [n C] a description of real or imaginary events, which is told or written to entertain people: *a book of short stories*
tell/read sb a story *Our teacher used to read us a story every afternoon.*
+ about *Grandpa's always telling us stories about when he was a boy*
the story of (=a well-known story about someone) *the story of Cinderella*
fairy/ghost/love story (=a story about magic/ghosts/love) *We sat around the fire telling ghost stories.*

true story (=about events that really happened) *Have you seen 'Schindler's List'? Apparently it's based on a true story.*
plural **stories**

tale /teɪl/ [n C] an exciting story of imaginary events: *'Treasure Island' – a tale of pirates and adventure*
fairy tale (=a story for children with magic in it) *Hans Christian Andersen's fairy tales*

myth /mɪθ/ [n C/U] a very old story, about gods and magical creatures: *The myth tells of how the gods sent fire to the earth in flashes of lightning.* | *a ballet based on a Greek myth*

legend /ˈledʒənd/ [n C/U] an old story, usually about strange events or people with magic powers: *According to legend, the whole castle was washed into the sea.*
+ of *the legend of Robin Hood*

anecdote /ˈænɪkdəʊt/ [n C] a short funny story about something that really happened: *The book is full of amusing anecdotes about his time in the police force.*

2 a person in a story

character /ˈkærɪktəʳ/ [n C] one of the people in a story: *The two main characters in the book are a young boy and his teacher.*

hero /ˈhɪərəʊ/ [n C] the man or boy who is the main character in a story, especially when he is very good, very brave etc: *At the end of the story, the hero rescues the princess and they get married.*
+ of *James Bond is the hero of the film.*
plural **heroes**

heroine /ˈherəʊɪn/ [n C] the woman or girl who is the main character in a story, especially when she is very good, very brave etc
+ of *Tess is the tragic heroine of the novel.*

3 the way the events in a story are arranged

plot /plɒt‖plɑːt/ [n C] the series of events that happen in a book, play, film etc, and the way they are all connected: *The plot of 'Twin Peaks' was so complicated that I couldn't follow it.*

storyline /'stɔːrɪlaɪn/ [n C] the main story of a book, play, film etc: *The play has a strong storyline which will appeal to children as well as adults.* | *Anna's marriage problems form the main storyline in Episode One.*

STRAIGHT

➡ see also **BEND**

1 when lines or objects are straight

straight

a straight road across the desert

straight /streɪt/ [adj] **straight** lines, roads, edges etc have no bends or curves: *First, draw two straight lines.* | *Her hair is blonde and very straight.* | *a long straight avenue*
dead straight ESPECIALLY BRITISH (=completely straight) *The road ran dead straight for 50 miles across the desert.*

2 travelling or moving in a straight line

straight /streɪt/ [adv] *Terry was so drunk he couldn't walk straight.*
straight ahead/down/towards etc *If you look straight ahead, you'll see the church in the distance.* | *The truck was heading straight towards us.*

Ⓠ**go straight on** BRITISH **go straight** AMERICAN /ˌgəʊ streɪt 'ɒn, ˌgəʊ 'streɪt/ SPOKEN to continue travelling ahead in the same direction as before, without turning left or right – use this when you are telling people which way to go: *When you get to the intersection, go straight.* | *Keep going straight on through the town and when you come to the school, turn left.*

in a straight line /ɪn ə ˌstreɪt 'laɪn/ if something moves **in a straight line**, it does not turn to the left or to the right: *Light always travels in a straight line.* | *It's difficult to walk in a straight line with your eyes closed.*

direct /dɪ'rekt, daɪ-/ [adj] going straight from one place to another without changing direction
direct route/line/path/way *Which is the most direct route to London from here?*

3 sitting or standing straight

upright /'ʌpraɪt/ [adv] sitting or standing with your back and neck straight, not bent: *We couldn't stand upright in the cave.*
bolt upright (=sitting with your back very straight) *There was a sudden noise outside, and she sat bolt upright in bed.*

4 to make something straight

straighten /'streɪtn/ [v T] *He was standing outside the manager's office, straightening his tie.*
straighten your legs/arms/back *Gradually straighten your legs until you are standing upright.*

STRANGE

unusual, in a way that makes you feel surprised, frightened, worried etc

UNUSUAL   CRAZY

see also

NORMAL/   STRANGE
ORDINARY   THINGS AND
            EVENTS

1 strange object/ situation/experience

strange /streɪndʒ/ [adj] very different from what you expect or from what usually happens, in a way that makes you feel a little frightened or surprised: *A strange noise woke her up.* | *I had a strange feeling that I'd been there before.*

it is strange that *It's strange that you've never met him – he lives in your street.*

funny/odd /ˈfʌni, ɒdǁɑːd/ [adj] ESPECIALLY BRITISH something **funny** or **odd** is a little strange and it makes you feel slightly worried, because you cannot explain it or you do not know what it is: *There's a funny smell coming from the fridge.*

it is odd/funny that *It seems odd that no-one noticed him coming in.*

◖**that's funny/that's odd** SPOKEN (say this when something seems odd) *"Your keys aren't here." "That's odd – I'm sure I left them on the table."*

peculiar /pɪˈkjuːliəʳ/ [adj] strange and slightly unpleasant: *This meat tastes peculiar.* | *The walls were painted a very peculiar shade of green.*

mysterious /mɪˈstɪəriəs/ [adj] use this about something that people know very little about and that is difficult to explain or understand: *His father died of a mysterious illness.* | *I kept getting mysterious phone calls where the caller would hang up as soon as I answered.* | *his mysterious disappearance*

mysteriously [adv] *Mysteriously, no-one had noticed anyone leave or enter the room.*

weird /wɪəʳd/ [adj] a **weird** experience, feeling, sight, or sound is strange and very different from what you are used to: *She always wears really weird clothes.* | *a weird dream* | *It's a weird feeling to go back to a place that you lived in a long time ago.*

ironic /aɪˈrɒnɪkǁaɪˈrɑː-/ [adj] an **ironic** situation seems strange and amusing, because something happens that you would not expect at all: *Her car was stolen from outside the police station, which is pretty ironic.*

it is ironic that *It's ironic that athletes are often such unhealthy people.*

2 strange person/ behaviour

strange /streɪndʒ/ [adj] someone who is **strange** behaves differently from most people, and seems unusual or a little

frightening: *Pearl was a strange girl who never played with the other children.* | *He's very strange – you never really know what he's thinking.*

strangely [adv] *Conor was acting very strangely last night – do you think he's all right?*

> ⚠ Don't confuse a **strange** person (=someone who behaves in a strange way) and a **stranger** (=someone you have never met before).

funny/odd /ˈfʌni, ɒdǁɑːd/ [adj] ESPECIALLY BRITISH someone who is **funny** or **odd** behaves strangely and is difficult to understand: *Did Anna warn you that her aunt is rather ... well, rather odd?* | *He's a bit funny – sometimes he's very friendly, other times he just ignores you.*

mysterious /mɪˈstɪəriəs/ [adj] a **mysterious** person is someone that people know very little about, and who therefore seems strange or interesting: *The package had been left outside the door by a mysterious visitor.*

eccentric /ɪkˈsentrɪk/ [adj] an **eccentric** person has strange and slightly crazy habits or ideas, which people find amusing: *Our neighbour is an eccentric old lady who has about 25 cats.*

weird /wɪəʳd/ [adj] INFORMAL a **weird** person is very strange and makes you feel frightened or uncomfortable: *She's living with this really weird guy who's into witchcraft and black magic.*

WORD BANK

STRANGE THINGS AND EVENTS

MAGIC   STRANGE

see also

SURPRISING/   FRIGHTENING/
SURPRISED   FRIGHTENED

When you see **EC**, go to the **ESSENTIAL COMMUNICATION** section.

1 things that happen which cannot be explained by science

the paranormal /ðə ˌpærəˈnɔːˈməl/ [n singular] strange things that happen or exist but cannot be explained by science: *She has written two books about the paranormal – one on UFOs, and the other on poltergeists.* | *There seems to be a growing interest in the paranormal.*
  paranormal [adj] *paranormal experiences*

supernatural /ˌsuːpəˈrˈnætʃərəl◄, ˌsjuː-‖ ˌsuː-/ [adj] **supernatural** powers, creatures, or events cannot be explained by science, and are therefore believed to be connected with magic or gods: *a horror movie about a little girl with supernatural powers* | *supernatural beings*
  the supernatural [n singular] *His stories mingle realism with the supernatural.*

mystery /ˈmɪstəri/ [n C] something strange that no-one can understand or explain: *Her disappearance would remain forever a mystery.*
  + of *the mystery of the lost city of Atlantis*

mysterious /mɪˈstɪəriəs/ [adj] if something is **mysterious**, no-one can understand it or explain it: *the mysterious deaths of three nuclear scientists in separate incidents*
  mysteriously [adv] *Mysteriously, the food on the plates was still warm, but the ship was deserted.*

2 creatures from other parts of the universe

alien /ˈeɪliən/ [n C] a creature that is from another part of the universe: *Thousands of Americans claim to have been kidnapped by aliens and taken to their spaceships.*

alien

  alien [adj] *The photograph seems to show a UFO above the city. Is this evidence of an alien visit?* | *creatures from an alien planet*

UFO

UFO /ˈjuːfəʊ, juː ef ˈəʊ/ [n C] a strange object in the sky that people believe is a space vehicle from another planet: *There have been several UFO sightings in this area.*

3 spirits and ghosts

ghost /gəʊst/ [n C] a dead person who appears again after they have died, either as an image that you see or as something that you feel is really there: *Do you believe in ghosts?* | *There was a ghost at the end of my bed – a woman in a long, white dress.*
  the ghost of sb *The church is haunted by the ghost of a young man who was killed there on his wedding day.*

ghost

spirit /ˈspɪrɪt/ [n C] the part of a person that, according to some people's beliefs, continues to live after they have died: *In Japan, people believe that the spirits of the dead return to earth every summer, during the Obon festival.*
  evil spirits (=spirits that want to harm people) *They wear these charms to protect themselves against evil spirits.*

poltergeist /ˈpɒltəˈrgaɪst‖ˈpəʊl-/ [n C] a type of ghost you cannot see, which moves furniture and throws things around: *The poltergeist threw books around the room and smashed plates.*

haunt /hɔːnt/ [v T] if a ghost **haunts** a place, it appears there often: *The ghost of* the murdered prince still haunts the castle.

be haunted by sth *The wood is a spooky, secret place, said to be haunted by a headless man on a horse.*

haunted /'hɔːntɪd/ [adj] a place that is **haunted** has ghosts in it: *a haunted house* | *The people refused to go into the forest alone because they thought it was haunted.*

ghostly /'gəʊstli/ [adj] looking like a ghost, or making you think of ghosts

ghostly figure (=a ghost, or something that could be a ghost) *A ghostly figure hovered at the top of the stairs.*

ghostly voice/hand/footsteps *She felt the touch of a ghostly hand on her shoulder.*

spooky /'spuːki/ [adj] INFORMAL a place that is **spooky** feels strange and makes you feel that there might be ghosts there: *Let's get out of here. This place is really spooky.* | *What a spooky castle! It would be a great place to make a film.*

4 when someone has mental powers that seem impossible

psychic

psychic /'saɪkɪk/ [adj] someone who is **psychic** or has **psychic** powers has the ability to know, see, or do things that most people believe are impossible, for example to know what is happening in another place without being told: *She uses her psychic abilities to help the police find people who are missing.* | *psychic healing*

psychic phenomena (=things such as communicating with dead people, or knowing things without using your usual senses)

psychic /'saɪkɪk/ [n C] someone who has psychic powers: *As a psychic, she could*

sense when evil things had happened in a place.

telepathic /ˌtelɪ'pæθɪk◂/ [adj] someone who is **telepathic** has the ability to know what someone else is thinking or feeling without being told, even if the other person is a long way away: *The twins are telepathic, and each one always knows what the other is feeling.*

telepathy /tɪ'lepəθɪ/ [n U] the ability to know what someone else is thinking without them telling you: *It was like some kind of telepathy, the way they finished each other's sentences.*

5 when someone knows what will happen in the future

clairvoyant /kleə'vɔɪənt/ [n C] someone who has the ability to know what will happen in the future: *A clairvoyant predicted that something terrible would happen to the President.*

clairvoyance /kleə'vɔɪəns/ [n U] the ability to know what will happen in the future

fortune teller

fortune teller /'fɔːtʃən ˌtelər/ [n C] someone who tells people what will happen to them in the future and is paid for doing this: *I went to see a fortune teller, and she told me that I would have three children.*

see into the future /ˌsiː ɪntə ðə 'fjuːtʃər/ someone who can **see into the future** has the ability to know what will happen before it happens: *If I could only see into the future and know how this would all end.*

predict /prɪ'dɪkt/ [v T] to correctly say what will happen in the future: *Nostradamus predicted many of the key events of the 20th century.*

prediction [n C] something that you say will happen in the future

premonition /ˌpreməˈnɪʃən, ˌpriː-/ [n C] a strange feeling that you know about something that is going to happen in the future, especially something bad: *The night before we sailed, I had a terrible premonition of danger ahead.*

6 when someone tries to talk to the spirits of dead people

medium /ˈmiːdiəm/ [n C] someone who claims that they can hear messages from the spirits of dead people

seance /ˈseɪɑːns, -ɒns‖-ɑːns/ [n C] a meeting where someone tries to help people to talk to the spirits of dead people: *Helen was a medium, and once a month she held a seance in her house.*

STRICT/NOT STRICT

RULE   PUNISH

see also

LAW   LIMIT

OBEY/DISOBEY

1 strict person

strict /strɪkt/ [adj] someone who is **strict** makes clear rules and expects people always to obey them: *a strict teacher*
+ with *I think Jill's parents are too strict with her.*
+ about *The manager is very strict about people getting to work on time.*
   strictly [adv] *They brought their children up very strictly.*

firm /fɜːrm/ [adj] if you are **firm** with someone, you tell them that they must accept your decision because you are not going to change it: *The principal was polite but firm – her answer was 'no'.*
+ with *You'll just have to be firm with him and tell him he can't have any more money.*
   firmly [adv] *"No," she said firmly, "you can't go." | Bill was firmly opposed to any change in the plans.*

tough /tʌf/ [adj] very strict, and determined that your orders will be obeyed – use this especially when you think that someone is right to be strict
+ on *Ray was a baseball coach, and known for being tough on his players.*
get tough with sb (=start being very strict with them) *The police have been told to get tough with drunken teenagers in the town centre.*

> ⚠ **Tough** is more informal than **strict** or **firm**.

2 strict rule/law

strict /strɪkt/ [adj usually before noun] a **strict** rule or law is very clear and must always be obeyed: *There are strict rules about the use of dangerous chemicals. | He had strict instructions to return the key to me.*
   strictly [adv] *Smoking is strictly forbidden in this area.*

harsh /hɑːrʃ/ [adj] a **harsh** law or system of government has severe punishments – use this especially about something that you think is unfair and too strict: *The laws concerning alcohol are very harsh. | a harsh military regime*
   harshly [adv] *Young offenders were treated very harshly.*

tough /tʌf/ [adj] **tough** laws or rules are very strict and do not allow much freedom: *The federal government is introducing tough new rules to control immigration. | The athletes had to undergo a tough training programme.*

> ⚠ **Tough** is more informal than **strict** or **harsh**.

3 not strict

lenient /ˈliːniənt/ [adj] not strict in the way that you punish people or control their behaviour: *The younger teachers generally had a more lenient attitude towards the students' behaviour.*
+ with *The judge was criticized for being too lenient with young offenders.*
   leniently [adv] *He asked the police to deal leniently with the boys.*
   leniency [n U] when someone is not strict: *This report shows that wealthy*

people are treated with more leniency when they break the law.

easy-going /ˌiːzi ˈgəʊɪŋ◀/ [adj] someone who is **easy-going** does not care about being strict, and is usually calm and relaxed: *Our parents are pretty easy-going, and they don't mind if we stay out late.*

STRONG

➡ look here for ...
- a strong person or thing
- a strong government or leader
- a strong feeling or belief
- a strong taste or smell

➡ opposite **WEAK**

➡ see also **BRAVE/NOT BRAVE**

1 strong person

➡ see also **EXERCISE, SPORT**

strong /strɒŋ‖strɔːŋ/ [adj] someone who is **strong** has big muscles and can lift heavy things, do a lot of physical work etc: *It took four strong men to lift the piano.* | *strong hands*

strength /streŋθ, strenθ/ [n U] the ability to lift or carry heavy things, to do a lot of physical work etc: *Bill was doing a lot of exercise to build up his strength.*
the strength to do sth *I didn't have the strength to climb any further.*
with all your strength (=as hard as you can) *Diana pulled on the rope with all her strength.*

energetic /ˌenərˈdʒetɪk◀/ [adj] someone who is **energetic** likes to be active or busy, and has the ability to work hard for a long time: *With a new and energetic director, the company was soon doing well again.* | *For more energetic visitors, there are many sports and activities.*

energy /ˈenərdʒi/ [n U] the feeling of physical and mental strength that helps you to do a lot of things without getting tired easily: *Vitamin pills can give you extra energy.* | *I don't have the time or the energy to go out much during the week.*

powerful /ˈpaʊərfəl/ [adj] very strong – use this about someone's body, arms,

muscles etc: *a tall man with a powerful physique* | *The birds have very powerful wing muscles.* | *the crocodile's powerful jaws*

muscular /ˈmʌskjʊlər/ [adj] someone who is **muscular** looks strong because you can see that they have big muscles: *She liked men who were tall and muscular.* | *He had broad shoulders and muscular arms.*

athletic /æθˈletɪk‖əθ-/ [adj] someone who is **athletic** has a strong but fairly thin body, and looks as if they are good at sports: *She was tall, athletic, and very attractive.* | *long athletic legs*

stamina /ˈstæmɪnə/ [n U] the ability to work hard, run, play sports etc for a long time without getting tired: *You need stamina to be a long-distance runner.* | *exercises to increase your strength and stamina*

2 strong government/ leader/organization

➡ see also **POWER, GOVERNMENT/ POLITICS**

strong /strɒŋ‖strɔːŋ/ [adj] a **strong** government, leader, manager etc has clear ideas about what should be done, and takes firm control of what happens: *This country needs a strong government to solve the economic crisis.* | *The school's main problem is that it lacks strong leadership.*

powerful /ˈpaʊərfəl/ [adj] a **powerful** person, group, or organization has a lot of influence over events, for example because they are very rich or they hold an important position: *The Senator has powerful allies in America's business community.* | *Murdoch controls dozens of newspapers and TV stations, and is an immensely powerful man.*

3 strong thing/material

strong /strɒŋ‖strɔːŋ/ [adj] something that is **strong** cannot be broken or destroyed easily: *The bags are made of strong black plastic.* | *You'll need a strong piece of rope for towing the car.*
strength [n U] how strong something is: *testing the strength of the steel beams*

solid /'sɒlɟd‖'saɪ-/ [adj] a building or piece of furniture that is **solid** is strong and well made: *The table seemed solid enough, so I climbed up onto it.* | *rows of solid little houses built of local stone*

tough /tʌf/ [adj] not easily broken, cut, or damaged – use this about cloth, leather, plastic, or natural substances: *jackets made from tough waterproof cotton* | *a pair of tough leather boots* | *Before cooking the artichoke, cut off the tough outer leaves.*

4 strong feeling/belief

strong /strɒŋ‖strɔŋ/ [adj] if you have **strong** feelings, beliefs, or opinions about something, your feelings affect you a lot and you are very serious about them: *The subject of abortion always arouses strong emotions.* | *These plans faced strong opposition from local people.* | *a strong sense of family loyalty*

   strongly [adv] *If you feel very strongly about this, write to your Congressman and complain.*

   strength [n U] how strong someone's feelings are: *The President could not ignore the strength of public opinion.*

intense /ɪn'tens/ [adj] a feeling that is **intense** is so strong that you can hardly control it: *We were waiting for the winner to be announced, and the excitement was intense.* | *intense pleasure* | *Every car was stopped and searched, which caused intense annoyance to the drivers.*

   intensely [adv] *From the moment I first met him I disliked him intensely.*

deep /diːp/ [adj usually before noun] very strong – use this especially about a feeling of love, sympathy, sadness, or disappointment: *The news came as a deep disappointment to us all.* | *the deep sorrow that we all felt when Arthur died*

   deeply [adv] *I was deeply offended by their remarks.*

extreme /ɪk'striːm/ [adj] **extreme** opinions or beliefs about politics, religion etc are too strong and most people regard them as unreasonable: *extreme nationalist views* | *an extreme left-wing party*

> When you see **EC**, go to the **ESSENTIAL COMMUNICATION** section.

5 strong taste/smell

strong /strɒŋ‖strɔŋ/ [adj] a **strong** smell or taste is one that you notice easily: *This cheese has a very strong taste.* | *There's a strong smell of gas.*

   strongly [adv] *His breath smelled strongly of garlic.*

6 to make something stronger

make sth stronger /ˌmeɪk (sth) 'strɒŋgəʳ‖ -'strɔŋ-/ to make something physically stronger: *I've put in some extra posts to make the fence stronger.*

strengthen /'streŋθən, 'strenθən/ [v T] to make something stronger, physically or emotionally: *The ship's decks will have to be strengthened to carry the extra weight.* | *Her parents' opposition only strengthened her determination to succeed.* | *This trade agreement will strengthen the links between our countries.*

STUDY

TEST   TEACH

see also

LEARN   SUBJECT

EDUCATION

1 to study something at school, university etc

study /'stʌdi/ [v I/T] to learn about a subject by reading books, going to classes, and doing work that your teacher asks you to do: *It's difficult to study when the weather's so hot.* | *I've been studying English for six years now.*

study to be a doctor/engineer etc *She's at business school, studying to be an accountant.*

studying – studied – have studied

take /teɪk/ [v T] to study a subject – use this to talk about subjects that you choose to

study at a school or university: *In my final year, I decided to take English, French, and Economics.*
taking – took – have taken

do /duː/ [v T] BRITISH INFORMAL to study a subject at school or university: *I can't decide whether to do German or Spanish next year.* | *Did you do computing at school?*
do a course *Why not do a language course at your local college?*
doing – did – have done

major in sth /ˈmeɪdʒər ɪn (sth)/ [phrasal verb T not in passive] AMERICAN to study something as your main subject at university: *Diane majored in psychology at Berkeley.* | *What are you majoring in?*

take lessons/have lessons /ˌteɪk ˈlesənz, ˌhæv ˈlesənz/ to pay for lessons from a teacher in order to study a subject or skill in your free time: *My mother wants me to take violin lessons.* | *I'm having Spanish lessons after work.*

⚠ Don't say 'do lessons'.

revise /rɪˈvaɪz/ [v I/T] BRITISH to read books, notes etc in order to prepare for an examination that you are about to take: *Ahmed's upstairs, revising.*
revise for a test/examination *The library was full of students revising for the final exams.*

2 to study something in order to discover new facts

study /ˈstʌdi/ [v T] to examine something carefully, do tests on it etc, in order to find out more about it and discover new facts: *Scientists are studying the development of the disease in children.* | *She spent several years studying the behaviour of gorillas in Africa.*
studying – studied – have studied

analyse (also **analyze** AMERICAN) /ˈænəlaɪz/ [v T] to carefully examine information, reports, the results of tests etc, in order to understand something better: *The detective's main job is to analyze all the evidence relating to a crime.* | *We use a special computer program to analyse all the sales figures.*

do research /ˌduː rɪˈsɜːʳtʃ/ to study a subject in a careful, detailed way, in order

to discover new information or produce new ideas about it: *She got a degree in biology and then went to work for a drug company, doing research.*
+ into/on *a team of scientists doing research into the causes of heart disease*

3 the work that you do when you study

studies /ˈstʌdiz/ [n plural] all the work that you do when you are a student at school or university
his/her/your etc studies *My uncle asked me if I was enjoying my studies.* | *He graduated in history at Stanford, then went to continue his studies at Harvard.*

homework /ˈhəʊmwɜːʳk/ [n U] work that a school pupil is given to do during free time, not during lessons: *Mrs Burgess isn't very popular – the children say she gives them too much homework.*
do your homework *I'm going to the library to do my French homework.*

⚠ Don't say 'homeworks'. Say **homework**.

⚠ Don't say 'I made my homework'. Say **I did my homework**.

coursework /ˈkɔːʳswɜːʳk/ [n U] all the work that a student has to do as part of a course of study, apart from what they do in examinations: *Half of the marks are for the exam, and half are for coursework.*

research /rɪˈsɜːʳtʃ, ˈriːsɜːʳtʃ/ [n U] careful, detailed work that you do in order to discover new information or produce new ideas about a particular subject: *Recent research has shown that human language is much older than we previously thought.*
+ into/on *More research is needed into the ways in which this virus is spread.*
medical/historical etc research *the latest scientific research*
do research *She's doing research into the connection between crime and poverty.*

⚠ Don't say 'a research' or 'researches'. Just say **research**.

⚠️ Don't say 'make research'. Say **do research**.

revision /rɪ'vɪʒən/ [n U] BRITISH when you read books, notes etc in order to prepare for an examination that you are going to do: *How is your history revision going?*
do revision *I can't come out tonight – I have a lot of revision to do.*

STUPID

➡ see also **SENSIBLE, INTELLIGENT, CRAZY**

1 people who behave in a stupid way

stupid /'stjuːpɪd‖'stuː-/ [adj] someone who is **stupid** behaves in a way that shows very bad judgement and that is likely to cause problems for themselves or for other people: *You stupid boy! I've told you never to play with matches.* | *He told me a lot of lies, and I was stupid enough to believe him.* | *If your stupid brother hadn't left the door open, we wouldn't have been robbed.*
it is stupid of sb to do sth *I should have called the police – it was stupid of me not to.*
stupidly [adv] *I stupidly agreed to lend him some money.*

⚠️ You can use **stupid** about yourself, but it is rude to say someone else is **stupid**. People usually say this only when they are very annoyed with someone.

dumb /dʌm/ [adj] INFORMAL, ESPECIALLY AMERICAN stupid: *She told him Jeff was just a friend, and he was dumb enough to believe her.*

silly /'sɪli/ [adj] someone who is **silly** behaves in a way which is not at all sensible or serious, and which they may be embarrassed about later: *The children were running around and shouting and being very silly.* | *I think you're silly to worry so much about your hair.*
silly – sillier – silliest

When you see **EC**, go to the **ESSENTIAL COMMUNICATION** section.

crazy /'kreɪzi/ [adj] someone who is **crazy** behaves in a way that does not seem normal, for example because they do something very strange or very dangerous: *You're crazy to think of hitch-hiking on your own.* | *I said I enjoyed doing exams, and she looked at me as if I was crazy!*

⚠️ Don't say 'very crazy'. Say **completely/totally/absolutely crazy**: *Put that gun down! Are you completely crazy?*

crazy – crazier – craziest

idiot/fool /'ɪdiət, fuːl/ [n C] someone who does something very stupid or embarrassing: *You lost the tickets? How could you be such a fool?* | *Some idiot in a fast car was trying to overtake me.*
be a fool/idiot to do sth *I realized later that I was a fool to believe all his lies.*
make a fool of yourself (=do something that makes you seem very stupid) *Sorry I made such a fool of myself yesterday. I had far too much to drink.*

childish /'tʃaɪldɪʃ/ [adj] someone who is **childish** annoys you by being unreasonable and unhelpful, or by complaining and being rude, as if they were a small child: *He said he wouldn't go out with us if Jerry was going too – he's so childish!* | *It would be very childish to walk past without saying hello.*

immature /ˌɪmə'tʃʊər◄‖-'tʊər◄/ [adj] someone who is **immature** behaves as if they were younger than they really are, so they are not as sensible or responsible as you expect them to be: *Teenage boys are often more immature than girls.* | *I was 19 when I went to college, but still very immature.*

2 stupid things that people do or say

stupid /'stjuːpɪd‖'stuː-/ [adj] **stupid** questions, ideas, actions, or situations annoy you because they show a lack of sensible thinking or good judgement: *It's a stupid idea and it'll never work.*
a stupid question/remark/comment *Of course you have to pay! What a stupid question!*
a stupid thing to do/say *You followed her home? That was a really stupid thing to do.*

it is stupid to do sth *I think it's stupid not to keep copies of your work on disk.*

dumb /dʌm/ [*adj*] INFORMAL, ESPECIALLY AMERICAN stupid: *She's always asking such dumb questions.* | *Don't do anything dumb, or they might shoot you!*

silly /ˈsɪli/ [*adj*] **silly** behaviour, jokes, mistakes etc show that someone is not very sensible or serious or does not think carefully about what they do: *I'm tired of Paul and his silly jokes.* | *Her work is rather careless, and she keeps making the same silly mistakes.*

a silly thing to do/say *I had locked myself out, which was a silly thing to do.*

silly – sillier – silliest

crazy /ˈkreɪzi/ [*adj*] **crazy** ideas, plans, or situations make you feel annoyed or very surprised, because they are not at all sensible or reasonable: *Ian's got a crazy plan to drive all the way across Africa.* | *I don't know why I thought we'd be happy together. It was a crazy idea.* | *The farmers can make more money by not planting crops – it's crazy, isn't it?*

> ⚠ Don't say 'very crazy'. Say **completely/totally/absolutely crazy**: *"There's only one computer for a class of 35 students." "That's absolutely crazy."*

crazy – crazier – craziest

ridiculous/absurd /rɪˈdɪkjᵊləs, əbˈsɜːʳd/ [*adj*] use this about plans, suggestions, situations etc which are so stupid that you cannot believe anyone would think of them or allow them to happen: *They're asking a ridiculous rent for that apartment.* | *What an absurd suggestion!*

it is ridiculous/absurd that *It's ridiculous that you have to wait six weeks to get the books you ordered.*

irrational /ɪˈræʃənəl/ [*adj*] irrational actions, feelings, or beliefs are not based on clear thinking or sensible reasons: *an irrational fear of flying in airplanes* | *irrational behaviour*

daft /dɑːft‖dæft/ [*adj*] BRITISH stupid, but often also amusing: *Is this another one of your daft ideas?* | *What a daft thing to say!*

3 not intelligent

not very bright/not very intelligent /nɒt veri ˈbraɪt, nɒt veri ɪnˈtelɪ̈dʒᵊnt/ [*adj*] someone who is **not very bright** or **not very intelligent** is unable to learn and understand things quickly and easily: *Sometimes I think that woman just isn't very bright.* | *Franco works hard but he isn't really very intelligent.*

stupid /ˈstjuːpɪ̈d‖ˈstuː-/ [*adj*] not at all intelligent: *She talks to us as if we're completely stupid.* | *Poor Larry's too stupid to realize when you're making fun of him.*

> ⚠ It is rude to say someone is **stupid**, so usually we say that they are **not very bright** or **not very intelligent**.

dumb /dʌm/ [*adj*] INFORMAL, ESPECIALLY AMERICAN not at all intelligent: *The athletic guys were seen as 'cute but dumb'.* | *You're so dumb, Clarissa!*

thick /θɪk/ [*adj*] BRITISH INFORMAL not at all intelligent: *He's a nice boy, but he's a bit thick, isn't he?*

SUBJECT

what you talk about, write about, or study

1 something that you talk about, write about etc

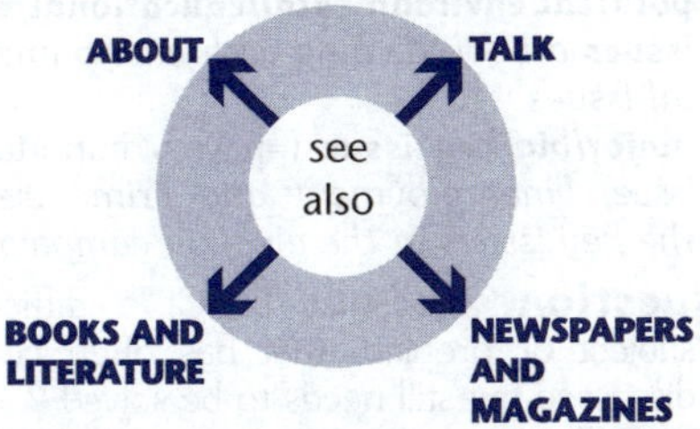

subject /ˈsʌbdʒɪkt/ [*n C*] something that is talked about or written about, for example at a meeting, in an essay or newspaper article, or in a conversation: *I read a lot of books about astronomy. It's a very interesting subject.* | *We talked about all sorts of subjects.*

the subject of crime/racism/animal rights etc (=crime etc as a subject that people write about or talk about) *Until about 20 years ago, the subject of the environment was hardly ever discussed.*

change the subject (=start talking about something different) *I could see John was embarrassed, so I changed the subject.*

thing /θɪŋ/ [n C] SPOKEN something that people talk about or think about: *The first thing we have to discuss is the price.* | *I had a lot of things to think about.*

topic /'tɒpɪk‖'tɑː-/ [n C] a subject that people often discuss or write about, in books, newspapers, at school etc: *The rise of Islam is a popular topic these days.* | *Our teacher gave us a list of topics to choose from.*

topic of conversation (=something you talk about with other people) *Their main topic of conversation seems to be football.*

theme /θiːm/ [n C] an important idea that appears several times in a book, film etc, and slowly influences the way it develops: *One of the themes of the book is the relationship between humans and nature.* | *The idea of duty is a favourite theme in the President's speeches.*

main/central theme (=the most important theme) *The play's central theme is greed and its corrupting effects.*

issue /'ɪʃuː, 'ɪsjuː‖'ɪʃuː/ [n C] an important subject that people discuss and argue about: *The control of nuclear weapons is an important issue.*

+ of *the issue of drugs in sports*

political/environmental/educational etc issues *a book dealing with environmental issues*

major/big/key issue (=a very important issue) *Unemployment and crime were the key issues in the election campaign.*

question /'kwestʃən/ [n C] a difficult subject or problem that has often been discussed but still needs to be solved

+ of *The question of where to hold the conference has still not been settled.*

the Irish/Bosnian etc question (=the political problems of Ireland, Bosnia etc)

raise a question (=make people consider a problem) *These operations can save lives, but they raise difficult questions about animal rights.*

the point /ðə 'pɔɪnt/ [n singular] the main subject of a meeting, discussion, speech etc

stick to the point (=keep talking about the main subject, not about other less important things) *Just stick to the point, John – what we want to know is how much the plan will cost.*

come/get to the point (=start talking about the main subject, not about unimportant details) *Mr Bailey came straight to the point and asked me why I wanted the job.*

miss the point (=not realize what the main subject is)

2 a subject that you study at school or university

➡ see also EDUCATION, TEST, LEARN, STUDY, TEACH

subject /'sʌbdʒɪkt/ [n C] one of the things that you study at school or university, such as English, history, or mathematics: *English was my favourite subject at school.*

course (also **class** AMERICAN) /kɔːrs, klɑːs‖klæs/ [n C] a series of lessons in one subject, often with an exam at the end: *Are you enjoying the course?*

language/computing/history etc course/class *The college is offering three basic computer courses this year.*

+ in/on *a course in journalism*

take a course/class (also **do a course** BRITISH INFORMAL) *She's taking a class in art history.*

> ⚠ Don't say 'a course/class of business studies'. Say **a course/class in business studies.**
>
> ⚠ Don't say 'make a course/class' or 'attend a course/class'. Say **take a course/class.**

major /'meɪdʒər/ [n C] AMERICAN the main subject that you study at university: *"What was your major?" "Political Science."*

> When you see **EC**, go to the **ESSENTIAL COMMUNICATION** section.

SUCCEED

➡ opposite **FAIL**
➡ see also **WIN, IMPROVE**

1 to succeed in doing what you hoped to do or tried to do

succeed /sək'siːd/ [v I] to do something that you hoped to do, tried to do, or wanted to do: *She wanted to be the first woman to climb Mount Everest and she almost succeeded.*
succeed in doing sth *In one year we've succeeded in increasing profits by 40%.* | *If they succeed in getting across the border, the police will never catch them.*

⚠ Don't say 'he succeeded to do it'. Say **he succeeded in doing it**.

⚠ **Succeed** is fairly formal, and is not often used in conversation. Don't say 'I succeeded in my course/studies/exam'. It is better to say **I did well**.

◯**do well** /duː 'wel/ ESPECIALLY SPOKEN to achieve good results at school, in your job, in a sport etc: *She's working for a record company in London – I think she's doing very well.* | *Bill and Jim always did well in the swimming races.*

successfully /sək'sesfəli/ [adv] if you do something **successfully**, you try to do it and you succeed: *Mr Malik has successfully completed the advanced course in Business Management.* | *The film successfully combines a good storyline with a serious political message.*

manage /'mænɪdʒ/ [v I/T] to succeed in doing something difficult after trying very hard, especially when you almost do not succeed: *She has to do all that work before Friday – do you think she'll manage?*
manage to do sth *He finally managed to find an apartment near his office.* | *I couldn't manage to get it downstairs – it was so big.*
◯**manage it/that** ESPECIALLY SPOKEN *You got him to change his mind? How did you manage that?* | *I said we'd be there by seven, but I doubt if we'll manage it.*

achieve /ə'tʃiːv/ [v T] to succeed in doing something important, especially something that other people will admire you for: *She's achieved a lot in the short time she's been with the company.* | *He hopes to achieve his dream of playing for the Red Sox.* | *When you get your MA, you really feel that you've achieved something.*

make progress /ˌmeɪk 'prəʊgres‖-'prɑː-/ to gradually start to achieve something that you want to achieve, by working hard: *I'm not very good at Japanese yet, but I feel I am making progress.*
+ with *At last I began to make some progress with my research.*

2 when something has the result that you want it to have

succeed /sək'siːd/ [v I] if something that you plan to do or try to do **succeeds**, you get the result that you hoped for: *If the terrorists' plan had succeeded, the bomb would have killed hundreds of people.* | *The new government's efforts to control inflation are unlikely to succeed.*

successful /sək'sesfəl/ [adj] if something that you plan to do or try to do is **successful** you get the result that you hoped for: *If the treatment is successful, she could be back at school next month.* | *successful peace negotiations*
highly successful (=very successful) *a highly successful election campaign*

work /wɜːrk/ [v I] if a plan or method **works**, it produces the result that you want: *"I can't open the jar." "Try putting it in hot water. That sometimes works."* | *The recipe works just as well if you cook the fish in a microwave.*

go well /ˌgəʊ 'wel/ if something **goes well**, such as a meeting, party, or performance, everything happens in the way you wanted and there are no problems: *Did the party go well?* | *If everything goes well, we'll be on the plane to the US by this time next week.*

effective /ɪ'fektɪv/ [adj] a method or action that is **effective** is very good because it does exactly what it is intended to do: *the most effective way of cleaning glass* | *The ad was simple but very effective.*

effective **in (doing) sth** *Penicillin is effective in the treatment of many common diseases.* | *New laws have been effective in reducing radiation levels.*

highly effective (=very effective) *a method of teaching foreign languages that has proved highly effective*

⚠️ Don't say 'this drug is effective to treat cancer'. Say **it is effective in treating cancer**.

3 a successful book/film/product etc

successful /sək'sesfəl/ [adj] *a* **successful** book, film, product etc is one that a lot of people buy or enjoy: *This is his most successful movie since 'Robocop'.*

highly successful (=very successful) *Harper Lee's highly successful novel – over 11 million copies were sold*

do well /ˌduː 'wel/ if a product **does well**, it is successful because a lot of people buy it, especially over a long period of time: *The magazine has continued to do well despite new rivals.* | *Our perfumes and cosmetics are doing very well in Japan.*

be a success /biː ə sək'ses/ if a product, show etc **is a success**, it is very popular and it makes a lot of money: *The new sports car was launched six months ago, and looks like being a real success.*

be a great success *The musical was a great success on Broadway, though it didn't do so well in London.*

hit /hɪt/ [n C] INFORMAL *a record, film, play etc that is very popular and successful:* *It's more than 30 years since 'Love Me Do', the Beatles' first hit.* | *another big hit for Spielberg* | *the hit musical 'Cats'*

4 a successful person or business

successful /sek'sesfəl/ [adj] *a* **successful** person achieves good results in their job, in a sport etc, and people admire them for this; *a* **successful** business makes a lot of money: *He has trained many of Britain's most successful athletes.* | *She retired in 1992, after a successful career in journalism.* | *a successful electronics company*

promising /'prɒmɪsɪŋ||'praː-/ [adj] *a* **promising** young player, student, manager etc is doing well and seems likely to be very successful in the future: *one of the most promising young players in the Italian league* | *Promising employees are quickly promoted.*

top /tɒp||taːp/ [adj only before noun] **top player/model/designer etc** one of the best and most successful players, designers etc: *All the world's top tennis players will be taking part in the tournament.* | *a conference attended by some of Europe's top scientists*

5 something successful that you do

success /sək'ses/ [n C/U] *when someone or something is successful:* *Steffi says success hasn't changed her at all.* | *After her recent successes in Tokyo and New York, Bjork has returned to perform in England.*

+ of *Auster was surprised at the success of his latest novel.*

success in doing sth *Did you have any success in persuading Adam to come?*

+ in *Success in business depends on hard work, determination, and good ideas.*

plural **successes**

achievement /ə'tʃiːvmənt/ [n C] *something important that you succeed in doing by your own efforts and that other people admire:* *Winning three gold medals is a remarkable achievement.*

progress /'prəʊgres||'praː-/ [n U] *when you gradually get closer to the result you want to achieve:* *We are very pleased with your son's progress at school.*

+ in *Progress in technology has changed people's lives dramatically.*

+ towards *progress towards equal status for men and women*

breakthrough /'breɪkθruː/ [n C] *an important discovery or achievement, especially one which happens suddenly after people have been trying for a long time*

+ in *Scientists are claiming a major breakthrough in the treatment of AIDS.*

make a breakthrough *Police say they have made a breakthrough in their search for the killer of Diane Sutton.*

SUDDENLY

➡ opposite **SLOW 2**
➡ see also **SURPRISING/SURPRISED**

1 suddenly

suddenly /'sʌdnli/ [adv] if something happens **suddenly**, it happens quickly when you are not expecting it: *Robert died very suddenly last week.* | *Suddenly there was a loud bang and all the lights went out.* | *I suddenly realized that there was someone following me.*

all of a sudden /ˌɔːl əv ə 'sʌdn/ suddenly – use this especially in stories or descriptions of past events: *We waited and waited, then all of a sudden we saw a sail on the horizon.*

out of the blue /ˌaut əv ðə 'bluː/ INFORMAL if something happens **out of the blue**, you are not expecting it at all, and you are very surprised by it: *Do you remember Jane? Well, she phoned me yesterday, completely out of the blue.*

without warning /wɪðˌaut 'wɔːʳnɪŋ/ if something bad or dangerous happens **without warning**, it happens suddenly and there were no signs that it was going to happen: *The earthquake in California came without warning.* | *Without warning, the car swerved across the road and hit a tree.*

on the spur of the moment /ɒn ðə ˌspɜːʳ əv ðə 'məumənt/ if you do something **on the spur of the moment**, you suddenly decide to do something that you had not planned to do: *I bought the car on the spur of the moment.* | *On the spur of the moment, Ian leaned across and kissed her.*

> **spur-of-the-moment** [adj only before noun] *a spur-of-the-moment decision*

2 something that happens suddenly

sudden /'sʌdn/ [adj] happening suddenly: *a sudden sharp pain in my stomach* | *Rebecca's decision to leave was very sudden.* | *There was a sudden increase in the price of oil.*

dramatic /drə'mætɪk/ [adj] a **dramatic change/improvement/increase/fall/**

rise etc a sudden very noticeable change, which makes things either much better or much worse: *a dramatic change in temperature* | *There has been a dramatic increase in homelessness over the last few years.*

> **dramatically** [adv] *The sales figures improved dramatically last year.*

SUFFER

when something very painful or unpleasant happens to you

1 to suffer

suffer /'sʌfəʳ/ [v I/T] to experience physical or emotional pain when something bad happens to you: *Children always suffer when their parents get divorced.* | *Anne still suffers a lot of pain in her leg.*
+ from *My sister has suffered from nightmares since the accident.*

endure /ɪn'djuəʳ‖ɪn'duəʳ/ [v T] ESPECIALLY WRITTEN to experience pain or have difficult and unpleasant experiences over a long period – use this especially about people who are brave and patient: *She has endured ten years of painful back operations.* | *They were lost in the mountains for ten days, enduring hunger, thirst, and intense cold.*

go through sth /'gəu θruː (sth)/ [phrasal verb T] to experience a lot of problems in your life over a long period of time: *Peter had lost his job, and the family was going through a very difficult time.*

2 something painful or unpleasant that you suffer

suffering /'sʌfərɪŋ/ [n U] very unpleasant, painful, or upsetting conditions – use this especially about a situation that affects a lot of people: *The earthquake has caused* massive damage and a great deal of human suffering. | *Reporters described the suffering they had seen in Somalia.*

hardship /'hɑːʳdʃɪp/ [n C/U] when your life is difficult and uncomfortable, especially because you are very poor: *the hardships of life for the early settlers in the US*

great hardship (=serious difficulties) *Rising food prices caused great hardship for most of the population.*

financial/economic hardship *Many students suffer financial hardship.*

3 someone who suffers

victim /'vɪktᵻm/ [n C] someone who suffers because of an illness, accident, crime etc: *Our aim is to help victims of crime.* | *Heart attack victims stand a better chance if they are treated immediately.*

SUGGEST

➡ see also 🞂 **SUGGESTIONS, WARN**

⚠ Compare **suggest** and **advise**. If you **suggest** something to someone, you give them your ideas about what they could do, or about what you and they could do together: *I suggested a walk in the park.* If you **advise** someone to do something, you tell them that you think they should do it, because it is the most sensible thing to do: *I advised her to put locks on all the windows.*

⚠ After **suggest that**, **propose that**, and **recommend that**, you can either use **should** or you can leave out **should**: *I suggested that we should meet for a drink.* | *I suggested that we meet for a drink.* In American English, **should** is usually left out.

1 to suggest something

suggest /sə'dʒest‖seg'dʒest/ [v T] to tell someone your ideas about what they should do, where they should go etc, or about what you and they should do together: *"Why don't you come with us?" Alan suggested.* | *It was a sunny afternoon, and Jim suggested a trip to the beach.*
+ (that) *My Dad suggested that I should apply for the job.* | *I suggest we take a break and finish this later.*

suggest doing sth *It was raining heavily, and she suggested calling a taxi.*

⚠ Don't say 'he suggested me to go'. Say **he suggested that I go** or **he suggested that I should go**.

make a suggestion /ˌmeɪk ə sə'dʒest-ʃən‖-səg-/ to suggest something that you think will help someone or will solve a problem: *Can I just make a suggestion? I think there's an easier way to do this.*

recommend /ˌrekə'mend/ [v T] to suggest something to someone because you know that it is good and you are sure that they will like it: *Can you recommend a comfortable hotel near here?*
recommend sth to sb *Oh, that book? Karen recommended it to me.*

⚠ Don't say 'I recommend to read this book'. Say **I recommend this book**.

2 to make a formal suggestion in a meeting, report etc

propose /prə'pəʊz/ [v T] to formally suggest that something should be done, especially at a meeting: *The Russians proposed a treaty banning all nuclear tests.*
+ that *I propose that we continue the meeting tomorrow.*

⚠ In this meaning, don't say 'I propose to ban cars from the city centre'. Say **I propose that we ban cars from the city centre** or **I propose that cars be banned from the city centre**.

recommend /ˌrekə'mend/ [v T] to officially suggest that something should be done, after you have considered the situation carefully: *The report recommends a number of changes in the existing law.*
+ that *The committee recommended that the money should be given to charity.* | *It is recommended that the number of cars on the roads be reduced by 10%.*

⚠ Don't say 'I recommend to increase the price'. Say **I recommend that we increase the price** or **I recommend that the price be increased**.

put forward /ˌpʊt ˈfɔːʳwəʳd/ [phrasal verb T] to suggest new plans or ideas for people to discuss and make decisions about
put forward sth *The UN has put forward a peace plan.* | *ideas put forward by environmental advisers*

nominate /ˈnɒmɪneɪt‖ˈnɑː-/ [v T] to formally suggest someone for an important job or prize, especially when people will vote to make a decision
nominate sb for sth *Jane Campion was one of the people nominated for the 'Best Director' award.*
nominate sb as sth *Gorbachev unexpectedly nominated Yanayev as Vice-President.*
nomination /ˌnɒmɪˈneɪʃən‖ˌnɑː-/ [n C/U] when someone is suggested for an important job or prize: *His nomination to the Supreme Court was blocked by political opponents.*

3 something that someone suggests

suggestion /səˈdʒestʃən‖səg-/ [n C] something that someone suggests: *That's an excellent suggestion.*
make a suggestion *She made some useful suggestions about places we could visit.*
+ that *Barry ignored my suggestion that he should try phoning her again.*
have a suggestion (=want to make a suggestion) *Does anyone have any other suggestions?*

proposal /prəˈpəʊzəl/ [n C] a formal or official suggestion that something should be done: *They will consider our proposal at their next meeting.*
proposal to do sth *Their proposal to build a new airport has finally been rejected.*
+ for *American proposals for a Middle East peace settlement*

4 what you say to suggest something

➡ see also ▣ **SUGGESTIONS**

◯**I suggest** /aɪ səˈdʒest‖-səg-/ SPOKEN say this especially to suggest something that you think is a sensible or helpful thing to do

I suggest (that) sb do sth *I suggest we take a half-hour break and start again at 3.* | *If you don't know the answer, I suggest you try the encyclopedia.*

⚠ **I suggest** is more formal than all the other expressions here.

◯**let's** /lets/ **let's go/do/have/meet etc** SPOKEN say this to suggest to someone what you and they should do together: *Let's have a meal after the concert.*
let's not *Let's not argue – it's my birthday!*

◯**why don't you?/why not?** /ˈwaɪ dəʊnt juː, ˈwaɪ nɒt/ SPOKEN say this to suggest something to someone, especially to help them decide what to do: *Why not get Andreas a book for his birthday?* | *Why don't you just phone and tell them you can't come?*

◯**shall we?/shall I?** /ˈʃæl wiː, ˈʃæl aɪ/ SPOKEN, ESPECIALLY BRITISH say this to suggest what you might do, and to ask someone if they agree: *Shall I get the theatre tickets?* | *Shall we go shopping this afternoon, then?*

◯**do you want to?** /duː juː ˈwɒnt tuː‖-ˈwɑːnt-/ SPOKEN say this to suggest something that you and someone else could do together, and to ask the other person if they agree: *Do you want to go out for a meal?*

◯**how about?/what about?** /ˈhaʊ əbaʊt, ˈwɒt əbaʊt/ SPOKEN INFORMAL say this to suggest something which you think is a good idea: *We need a break – how about a weekend in London?* | *Well, if the car's too small, what about renting a bigger one?*

◯**could always** SPOKEN /kʊd ˈɔːlwɪz‖-weɪz/ say this to suggest something that may solve a problem: *You could always stay with me if you miss the train.* | *I suppose I could always get Rosie some perfume for Christmas.*

When you see ▣ , go to the
ESSENTIAL COMMUNICATION section.

SUITABLE/ UNSUITABLE

➡ see also **CONVENIENT/NOT CONVENIENT, BEST, PERFECT**

1 suitable

suitable /'suːtəbəl, 'sjuː-‖'suː-/ [adj] something or someone that is **suitable** is the right kind of thing or person for a purpose, job, or situation: *I still haven't found a suitable job.* | *You must wear something suitable – preferably black.*
+ **for** *The house would be suitable for a large family.* | *choosing a suitable bride for the prince*
  suitably [adv] *suitably dressed for a wedding*

> ⚠ Don't say 'suitable to something' or 'suitable to do something'. Say **suitable for something**.

right /raɪt/ [adj] the **right** thing or person is exactly suitable: *I've found some curtains that are just the right colour.* | *I don't know the right word to describe it.*
+ **for** *It's a good school, but it wasn't really right for Melissa.* | *We all agree that Carey is the right person for the job.*
just right (=completely suitable) *I moved into a small apartment close to the college – it was just right.*

proper /'prɒpər‖'prɑː-/ [adj only before noun] **the proper equipment/clothes/ methods/training etc** ESPECIALLY BRITISH the equipment, clothes etc that are generally considered to be right for a purpose: *You can't climb a mountain without the proper equipment.* | *I must have the proper tools for the job.*
  properly [adv] *The machine operators had not been properly trained.*

appropriate /ə'prəʊpri-ət/ [adj] suitable for a situation or purpose – use this especially about something that has been carefully chosen for a particular situation: *Considering the warnings he's had, I think the punishment was appropriate.* | *You will be given your orders at the appropriate time.*

+ **for** *Each member is given a special exercise routine that is appropriate for his or her needs.*
  appropriately [adv] *a delightful place that was appropriately named Mount Pleasant*

> ⚠ **Appropriate** is more formal than **right** or **proper**.

Qgood /ɡʊd/ [adj only before noun] ESPECIALLY SPOKEN very suitable for a purpose or job – use this especially when there are several suitable people or things to choose from: *Bates would be a good person to have on the team.*
+ **for** *The big jars are good for storing rice or pasta.*

good – better – best

ideal /aɪ'dɪəl/ [adj] the **ideal** thing or person is the most suitable one you can possibly choose, when there are many to choose from: *If you're setting up your own company, our Business Starter Loan would be ideal.*
+ **for** *With its tough suspension and 4-wheel drive, it's ideal for driving in the desert.*

suit /suːt, sjuːt‖suːt/ [v T not in passive] something that **suits** a person, purpose, or situation is suitable for them: *Make sure you choose a computer that suits your needs.* | *a job that would suit a young science graduate* | *They found us a house close to the campus, which suited us very well.*

> ⚠ Don't say 'it suits to me' or 'it suits with me'. Say **it suits me**.

2 not suitable

unsuitable/not suitable /ʌn'suːtəbəl, nɒt 'suːtəbəl, -'sjuː-‖-'suː-/ [adj] *We never planted vines there because the climate was not suitable.*
+ **for** *violent movies that are totally unsuitable for children* | *The road is not suitable for heavy vehicles.*

wrong /rɒŋ‖rɔːŋ/ [adj] not the right one for a particular job or purpose: *You're using the wrong spoon – this is the soup spoon.* | *This is a very important job, so we don't want to choose the wrong* person. | *I think you picked the wrong time to call her.*

inappropriate/not appropriate
/ˌɪnəˈprəʊpri-ɪ̩t, nɒt əˈprəʊpri-ɪ̩t/ [*adj*] FORMAL not suitable for a situation or purpose – use this especially about something that has been done or chosen without enough care or thought: *I thought his remarks were quite inappropriate on such a serious occasion.* | *This is not an appropriate use of taxpayers' money.*

+ for *It was a very powerful computer, completely inappropriate for someone like me.*

out of place /ˌaʊt əv ˈpleɪs/ if something or someone looks or feels **out of place**, they do not seem suitable for the place or situation that they are in, especially because they look very different: *I felt completely out of place among all those rich fashionable people.* | *a large concrete building that looked out of place in such a pretty mountain village*

not cut out for sth /nɒt kʌt ˈaʊt fɔːr (sth)/ INFORMAL if you are **not cut out for** a type of work or way of life, you do not have the right qualities to enjoy it or to be successful in it: *Obviously, Paul was not cut out for army life.* | *I've decided I'm not cut out for teaching.*

SUPPORT

➡ look here for ...
- agree with someone or something
- help someone
- stop something from falling down

➡ see also **DEFEND**

1 to support an idea, person, or political party
➡ opposite **AGAINST**
➡ see also **PROTEST, AGREE, DISAGREE**

support /səˈpɔːrt/ [*v* T] to say that you agree with an idea, plan, political party etc, and want it to succeed: *I've always supported the Democrats.* | *a newspaper article that supports the idea of a minimum wage for workers*

strongly support *Plans for a new school were strongly supported by local residents.*

⚠ Don't say 'I am supporting them'. Say **I support them**.

be in favour of sth BRITISH **be in favor of sth** AMERICAN /biː ɪn ˈfeɪvər ɒv (sth)/ to support a plan or suggestion because you think it is a good idea: *Most UN delegates are in favor of the peace plan.*

be in favour of doing sth *Some teachers were in favour of retaining the existing system.*

be all in favour of sth ESPECIALLY SPOKEN (=completely agree with it) *I'm all in favour of people having smaller cars.*

⚠ Don't say 'I'm in favour with it' or 'I'm in favour to do it'. Say **I'm in favour of it**.

pro- /prəʊ/ [*prefix*] **pro-democracy/pro-government/pro-independence etc** supporting democracy, the government etc: *The pro-independence group has been attacked and suppressed.* | *pro-western forces* | *The 'pro-choice' group believes in the right to abortion.*

⚠ **Pro-** is usually used in newspapers, on TV etc.

be on sb's side /biː ɒn (sb's) ˈsaɪd/ to support one person or group against another in an argument, war etc: *Why did you keep agreeing with my parents? I thought you were on my side.* | *With most of the newspapers on their side, they have a good chance of winning.* | *Whose side are you on?*

2 someone who supports a person, political party, idea etc

supporter /səˈpɔːrtər/ [*n* C] someone who supports a person, political party, or idea: *a Labour Party supporter*

+ of *Supporters of women's rights are protesting against the court's decision.*

follower /ˈfɒləʊər‖ˈfɑː-/ [*n* C] someone who supports the ideas of a political or religious leader: *Marx and his followers were convinced that capitalism would not survive.*

+ of *the followers of Mahatma Gandhi*

sympathizer (also **sympathiser** BRITISH) /ˈsɪmpəθaɪzəʳ/ [n C] someone who supports the ideas of a political organization but does not belong to it, especially an organization that is illegal: *His opponents accused him of being a Nazi sympathiser.* | *Money for the group's terrorist activities has been provided by sympathisers in the US.*

following /ˈfɒləʊɪŋ‖ˈfɑː-/ [n singular] all the people who support a person or organization: *The civil rights movement attracted a large following in the northern cities.*

3 to support someone with money or with help

support /səˈpɔːʳt/ [v T] to give help, encouragement, money etc to someone because you want them to succeed: *The rebels were supported by the former South African government, which provided arms and money.* | *Employers support the training program by offering places for young people.*

in support of /ɪn səˈpɔːʳt ɒv/ if you do something **in support of** someone or something, you do it to show that you support them: *The miners were striking in support of the nurses.* | *a big demonstration in support of democratic reforms*

back /bæk/ [v T] to support a person or plan by providing money or practical help – used especially in newspapers to talk about governments or other powerful groups that support something: *Several major insurance companies have agreed to back the healthcare reforms.* | *The plans for a new shopping mall are backed by the city council.*

4 the money or help that you give when you support someone

support /səˈpɔːʳt/ [n U] the help and encouragement that you give to someone when you want them to succeed: *I couldn't have finished my degree without the support of my family.*
+ for *the growing support for Greenpeace in Australia and New Zealand*

financial support (=money given to support something) *political parties that receive financial support from foreign businessmen*

backing /ˈbækɪŋ/ [n U] money or practical help given to support a person or plan, especially by a government or other powerful group: *Does this policy have government backing?*
+ of *a magazine that originally started with the backing of the TV companies*

5 to support an object so that it does not fall down

support/hold up /səˈpɔːʳt, ˌhəʊld ˈʌp/ [v T] to hold something or someone up and stop them from falling down
support sth *The ceiling was supported by huge stone columns.*
hold sth up *The only thing holding it up was a frail-looking section of scaffolding.*
hold up sth *The poles hold up the outer part of the tent.*

> ⚠ Hold up is more informal than support.

prop up /ˌprɒp ˈʌp‖ˌprɑːp-/ [phrasal verb T] to stop something from falling by putting something else against it or under it
prop up sth *The builders have propped up the walls with steel beams.*
prop sth up *I sat down and propped my feet up on the edge of the desk.*

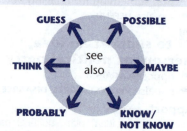

SURE/NOT SURE

GUESS   POSSIBLE

THINK ← see also → MAYBE

PROBABLY   KNOW/ NOT KNOW

1 when you feel sure about something

sure /ʃʊəʳ/ [adj not before noun] if you are sure about something, you feel that it is almost certainly true or correct

+ (that) *You've worked so hard, I'm sure you'll do well in your exams.* | *Are you quite sure that he understood your instructions?*
+ about/of *I think children are influenced by these films, but it's impossible to be sure about this.*
feel sure *I'm surprised she isn't here – I felt sure she would come.*

> ⚠ Don't say 'it is sure'. Say **I'm sure**: *I'm sure that the food will be nice.*

certain /ˈsɜːʳtn/ [adj not before noun] completely sure that something is true
+ (that) *Are you absolutely certain you didn't leave your keys at home?*
+ about/of *She won't let you borrow the car – I'm certain of that.*

> ⚠ Don't say 'very certain'. Say **quite certain** or **absolutely certain**: *We're quite certain that Hayes is guilty.*

convinced /kənˈvɪnst/ [adj not before noun] sure that something is true, even if you have no information to support this belief
+ (that) *We've had no news of him, but we're convinced he's still alive.* | *She became convinced that her boyfriend was seeing someone else.*
+ of *Brown's wife was convinced of his innocence.*

> ⚠ Don't say 'very convinced'. Say **completely/absolutely convinced**: *She seems absolutely convinced that she's going to fail.*

Q positive /ˈpɒzɪ̩tɪv‖ˈpɑː-/ [adj not before noun] ESPECIALLY SPOKEN completely sure that something is true – use this especially when other people are saying it might not be true: *"Are you sure you locked the door?" "Yes, I'm positive."*
+ (that) *She said she was positive the exam was next Tuesday.*

confident /ˈkɒnfɪ̩dənt‖ˈkɑːn-/ [adj not before noun] sure that something good will happen, or that you will be able to achieve what you want: *They asked Cantona about tomorrow's game, and he seems very confident.*
+ (that) *Doctors are confident that he'll make a full recovery.*

Q I bet /aɪ ˈbet/ SPOKEN INFORMAL say this when you feel sure that something is true:
+ (that) *I bet you're tired after such a long journey.* | *I bet she hasn't told her parents about this.*

Q must /mʌst/ [modal verb] ESPECIALLY SPOKEN if you say that something **must** be true or **must** have happened, you are sure about it, because of information you have or things you have noticed which make it seem very likely: *They must be having a party next door, judging by all the cars parked outside.*
must have *Kim didn't answer when I called – she must have gone to bed.* | *The lights aren't working – there must have been a power cut.*

> ⚠ The opposite of **must** in this meaning is **can't**. Use **can't** to say you are sure that something is not true or has not happened: *She can't have gone to bed yet – it's only 8 o'clock* (=I am sure that she has not gone to bed).

2 when something is definitely true and there are no doubts at all

certainly/definitely /ˈsɜːʳtnli, ˈdefɪ̩nətli, ˈdefn̩tli/ [adv] use this to emphasize that something is definitely true, especially when other people think that it might not be: *I'm sorry if I upset you. I certainly didn't mean to.* | *We don't know exactly when the house was built, but it's certainly over 100 years old.* | *I definitely posted the cheque last week, so it should have arrived by now.*
certainly not/definitely not *"Would you accept less than a thousand for it?" "No, definitely not."*

Q surely /ˈʃʊəʳli/ [adv] ESPECIALLY SPOKEN use this to emphasize that you think something must be true, and you are asking someone else to agree with you: *Surely, he must have realized that the money was stolen.* | *Surely your car is worth more than £1000, isn't it?*

there is no doubt /ðeər ɪz nəʊ ˈdaʊt/ use this to say that, in your opinion, something is definitely true
+ (that) *There is no doubt that smoking contributed to Margaret's heart attack.*

Q**there is no doubt about it/that** ESPE-CIALLY SPOKEN *Paul's under a lot of stress. There's no doubt about that.*

3 when something will definitely happen

certainly/definitely /'sɜːˈtnli, 'defɪnˌtli, 'defənˌtli/ [adv] use this to say that you are completely sure that something will happen or that someone will do something: *Brad and Andy are certainly coming to the party, but I don't know about Bob. | We'll definitely be back by 7 o'clock. | Gascoigne is injured and will definitely miss the game on Saturday.*

certain /'sɜːˈtn/ [adj not usually before noun] if something is **certain**, you believe it will definitely happen: *Computer prices will continue to fall – that's certain.*

it is certain (that) *It's now almost certain that the President will resign.*

certain death/failure/disaster etc (=when something very bad is definitely going to happen) *He was alone on the mountain, his leg broken, facing almost certain death.*

definite /'defɪnˌt, 'defənˌt/ [adj] something that is **definite** has been agreed or decided, and it is certain that it will happen: *I think I have a good chance of getting the job, but it's not definite yet.*

> ⚠ **Definite** is used especially in questions or negative sentences.

be sure to do sth/be certain to do sth /biː ʃuəˈ tə duː (sth), biː 'sɜːˈtn tə duː (sth)/ use this to say that you strongly believe that something will happen, because of what you know about the situation: *Drivers heading for the coast are certain to face long delays this weekend. | There's sure to be someone that you know at the party.*

be bound to do sth /biː 'baʊnd tə duː (sth)/ if you say something **is bound to** happen, you think it certainly will happen, because that is what normally happens: *Chris is bound to arrive late – he always does. | His new record isn't very good, but it's bound to be a hit.*

be sure of doing sth /biː ʃuər əv 'duːɪŋ (sth)/ if you **are sure of doing** something, you will definitely get what you want

or achieve what you want: *If they win tonight's game, they are sure of winning the championship. | To be sure of arriving on time, I took an earlier train.*

inevitable /ɪn'evɪˌtəbəl/ [adj] something unpleasant that is **inevitable** will certainly happen and is impossible to prevent: *War now seems inevitable.*

inevitable result/consequence *Bread prices were doubled, with the inevitable result – food riots.*

it is inevitable (that) *It is inevitable that some people won't like the new arrangements.*

> **inevitably** [adv] *Inevitably, some people will lose their jobs when the two companies merge.*

4 not sure about something

not sure /nɒt 'ʃuəˈ/ *"What time does the film start?" "I think it's 8.30, but I'm not sure."*

not sure how/whether/when etc *I'm not sure where she lives.*

+ about/of *If you're not sure about the meaning of a word, look it up in a dictionary. | Use the 'Filesearch' function if you are not sure of the name of a file.*

Q**can't be sure** SPOKEN (when you think something is true, but you are not completely sure) *I can't be sure, but I think I saw Maggie coming out of the hospital this morning.*

not know /nɒt 'nəʊ/ to not be at all sure what you should decide, whether something is true etc: *"How old is she?" "Oh, I don't know – fifty, fifty-five?"*

not know if/whether/how etc *He didn't know whether he should accept their offer or not. | I don't know if I really agree with that.*

Q**not know for sure** ESPECIALLY SPOKEN *It could be this week but it might be much later. We don't know for sure.*

doubt /daʊt/ [n C/U] a feeling of not being sure whether something is true or right

+ about/as to *There are still some doubts about her suitability for the job.*

have (your) doubts (=not be sure that something is really the right thing to do) *My parents thought I should go to business school, but I had my doubts.*

5 **something that you cannot be sure about**

uncertain /ʌnˈsɜːʳtn/ [*adj*] if a situation is **uncertain**, you cannot be sure what will happen, because nothing is definite: *Our holiday plans are still uncertain.* | *The company faces an uncertain future.*
it is uncertain whether *It is still uncertain whether the conference will actually take place.*

not clear /nɒt ˈklɪəʳ/ if something is **not clear**, people do not know enough or understand enough to be sure about it: *The causes of the dispute are not entirely clear.*
it is not clear how/why/whether etc *It isn't clear how the fire started.*

be doubtful/be in doubt /biː ˈdaʊtfəl, biː ɪn ˈdaʊt/ if the success or future of something **is doubtful** or **is in doubt**, you cannot be sure what will happen, but you think it is likely to be something bad: *With more and more cuts in government spending, the school's future now looks doubtful.* | *After yet another injury, his football career is in doubt.*

6 **to do something in order to be sure that something else will happen**

make sure /ˌmeɪk ˈʃʊəʳ/ to do something in order to be sure that something else will happen: *I think Harry knows the way, but I'll go with him just to make sure.*
+ (that) *Make sure that you lock your car.*

ensure BRITISH **insure** AMERICAN /ɪnˈʃʊəʳ/ [*v* T] to do something in order to be sure that something else will happen
+ (that) *It is the company's responsibility to ensure that everyone knows the safety rules.*

⚠ Ensure and insure are more formal than make sure.

◯**see that/see to it that** /ˈsiː ðət, ˈsiː tʊ ɪt ðət/ ESPECIALLY SPOKEN if you **see that** or **see to it that** something happens, you make sure that it happens, often by getting someone else to do this for you: *Don't worry. I'll see that he gets the*

message. | *We see to it that all our guests receive a very high standard of service.*

SURPRISING/ SURPRISED

➡ see also **SUDDENLY, EXPECT 6**

1 **feeling surprised**

surprised /səʳˈpraɪzd/ [*adj*] if you are **surprised** by something that happens, you do not expect it, so it seems strange or unusual: *I was really surprised when I passed my driving test first time.* | *Carrie looked surprised. "I didn't expect to see you here!"*
surprised to see/hear/learn etc *We were surprised to see Drew's picture in the newspaper.*
+ (that) *I'm really surprised that he remembered my birthday.*
+ at/by *He was surprised at how late it was.* | *Julia seemed a little surprised by my question.*

⚠ Don't say 'surprised for'. Say **surprised at** or **surprised by**.

amazed/astonished /əˈmeɪzd, əˈstɒnɪʃt‖ əˈstɑː-/ [*adj*] extremely surprised by something that happens, because it seems so unlikely: *Liz was amazed when she found out how much the meal had cost.*
+ that *I'm amazed that the bank keeps lending him money.*
+ at *Everyone was astonished at how calm and relaxed she was before her big speech.*
amazed to see/learn/find out etc *We were amazed to see John looking so well, so soon after his operation.*
astonished to see/hear/discover/find etc *Sarah was astonished to see Neil and Beth kissing.*

startled /ˈstɑːʳtld/ [*adj*] ESPECIALLY WRITTEN surprised and a little frightened or worried because of something that has suddenly happened or something that someone said: *"Have we met somewhere before?" The man looked startled for a moment.*
+ by *They were startled by a sudden flash in the sky.*

to my/her/their surprise /tuː (my etc) səʳpraɪz/ use this when you are telling a story or describing past events, to say that someone was surprised by something: *He asked her to go out with him and, to his surprise, she agreed immediately.*

⚠ Don't use **to my/her/their surprise** at the end of a sentence.

can't believe /ˌkɑːnt bɪˈliːv‖ˌkænt-/ ESPECIALLY SPOKEN if you **can't believe** something, you are very surprised by it because it does not seem possible
can't believe it *I can't believe it! Jane and Richard are getting married!*
+ (that) *She was a brilliant pianist – we couldn't believe that she was only fifteen.*

taken aback /ˌteɪkən əˈbæk/ so surprised or shocked by what someone has done or said to you that for a moment you do not know what to say
be/look/seem taken aback *When I asked her to marry me, she looked rather taken aback.*
+ by *Bill was taken aback by her rude and aggressive behaviour.*

speechless /ˈspiːtʃləs/ [adj] so surprised, by something very good or very bad, that you do not know what to say: *When I told her I was pregnant, she was totally speechless.*

2 surprised and upset because something very bad has happened

shocked /ʃɒkt‖ʃɑːkt/ [adj] surprised and upset by something very bad that has happened: *When they heard that Janet was in hospital they were really shocked.*
+ by *The whole town was shocked by the news.*
shocked to hear/learn/find *We were shocked to hear of Brian's death – he was so young.*

horrified /ˈhɒrɪfaɪd‖ˈhɔː-, ˈhɑː-/ [adj] extremely shocked by something very unpleasant or frightening that has happened: *Horrified passengers saw the man fall under the train.*
+ by *Sam's parents were horrified by his injuries.*

horrified to see/hear/find *They looked out of the window, and were horrified to see two men attacking each other with knives.*

stunned /stʌnd/ [adj] so shocked that you are unable to speak or do anything: *When I heard about the accident I was stunned.*
+ by *Staff were stunned by the news that 200 people were to lose their jobs.*

3 to make someone surprised

surprise /səʳpraɪz/ [v T] if something **surprises** you, it makes you feel surprised: *Diana's reaction surprised him – he hadn't realized that she was so upset.* | *The exam was actually quite easy, which surprised me.*
it surprises sb that *It surprised me that he could still walk.*

amaze /əˈmeɪz/ [v T] to make someone feel extremely surprised: *Dave amazed his friends by leaving a well-paid job to travel around the world.*
it amazes sb that *It amazes me that no-one thought of the idea sooner.*

come as a surprise /ˌkʌm əz ə səʳpraɪz/ if something **comes as a surprise**, it surprises you because you were not expecting it at all
+ to *Richard's marriage came as a surprise to everyone.*
come as a complete surprise *I didn't think I'd get the job, so it came as a complete surprise when they offered it to me.*

take sb by surprise /ˌteɪk (sb) baɪ səʳpraɪz/ if something **takes you by surprise**, it happens suddenly at a time when you are not expecting it: *The President's resignation took everyone by surprise.*

shock /ʃɒk‖ʃɑːk/ [v T] if something very bad or unpleasant **shocks** you, it makes you feel very surprised and upset: *What really shocked me was that no-one seemed to care about all the beggars.*
it shocks sb to see/realize/hear etc *It shocked us to see how ill she looked.*

come as a shock /ˌkʌm əz ə ˈʃɒk‖-ˈʃɑːk/ if something unpleasant **comes as a shock**, it makes you feel surprised and upset because you were not expecting it to happen: *We knew he had been ill, but Robert's death still came as a shock.*

come as a complete/terrible shock (to sb) *It came as a terrible shock to Richard when his wife told him she was seeing another man.*

○**make sb jump** /ˌmeɪk (sb) ˈdʒʌmp/ ESPECIALLY SPOKEN to make someone feel surprised and nervous by making a sudden noise or movement, especially when they did not know you were there: *I'm sorry, I didn't mean to make you jump.*

4 when something makes you surprised

surprising /səˈpraɪzɪŋ/ [adj] something that is **surprising** makes you feel surprised: *A surprising number of 16-year-olds leave school without being able to read and write.* | *a surprising choice*
it is surprising (that) *It is surprising that so few people came to the party.*
it is surprising how/what *It was surprising how quickly we got used to the new house.*
　surprisingly [adv] *The restaurant was surprisingly cheap.* | *Surprisingly, very few people complained about the show.*

amazing /əˈmeɪzɪŋ/ [adj] very surprising – use this especially about something very good or impressive: *an amazing achievement* | *Hong Kong is an amazing city, with all those tall modern buildings.*
it is amazing how/what *It's amazing how fast these Grand Prix cars can go.*
it is amazing that *It's amazing that the inscriptions are still clear enough to read after 2000 years.*
　amazingly [adv] *Chris was amazingly lucky to pass the exam.* | *Five cars crashed into each other, but amazingly no-one was hurt.*

unexpected /ˌʌnɪkˈspektɪd◂/ [adj] something **unexpected** is surprising, because you did not think that it would happen: *the unexpected success of her first novel* | *His decision to leave was completely unexpected.*
　unexpectedly [adv] *Phil arrived unexpectedly while we were having lunch.*

startling /ˈstɑːrtlɪŋ/ [adj] a **startling** fact is one that you would never have expected to be true: *There had been a startling*

increase in the numbers of homeless people.* | *startling new discoveries about the way the universe began*

unbelievable/incredible /ˌʌnbɪˈliːvəbəl, ɪnˈkredɪbəl/ [adj] extremely surprising and difficult to believe: *He's so rude. It's unbelievable!* | *Over the next two weeks, we saw an incredible change in her character.*
it is unbelievable/incredible that *They were driving much too fast. It's incredible that no-one was hurt.*
　unbelievably/incredibly [adv] *Throughout the crisis, Bill remained incredibly calm.* | *It was a fantastic hotel, and unbelievably cheap.*

staggering /ˈstægərɪŋ/ [adj] a **staggering** number or amount is very surprising because it is so large: *There has been a staggering rise in the number of attacks and murders in our cities.* | *We spend a staggering £2.4 billion a year on food for our pets.*

5 something surprising that happens

surprise /səˈpraɪz/ [n C] something that you did not expect, especially something nice
it is a surprise/it was a surprise *It was a real surprise when Tony walked in. We thought he was still in America.* | *We've got Katie a bike for her birthday, but don't tell her – it's a surprise.*
a complete surprise (=one that you did not expect at all) *Anita didn't expect to get the job – it was a complete surprise.*
○**what a surprise!** SPOKEN *Flowers? For me? What a lovely surprise!*

shock /ʃɒk‖ʃɑːk/ [n C] something very bad or unpleasant that happens to you and that you did not expect: *"The bill came to almost £500." "That must have been a shock."*
get a shock *She got a shock when she opened the letter and saw who it was from.*
give sb a shock *It gave me a shock to realize that I had nearly been killed.*

6 when something does not make you surprised

not surprising/hardly surprising /ˌnɒt səˈpraɪzɪŋ, ˌhɑːrdli səˈpraɪzɪŋ/ if something is **not surprising** or **hardly surprising**, you are not surprised by it because the situation makes it very likely to happen: *Now she's frightened to go out at night, which is hardly surprising after what happened to her.*

it is not surprising/hardly surprising (that) *It's not surprising you're tired – you've been out every night this week.*

> **not surprisingly** [adv] *Not surprisingly, she's very annoyed* (=it is not surprising that she is annoyed).

I'm not surprised /aɪm ˌnɒt səˈpraɪzd/ SPOKEN say this when you can clearly see why something has happened: *"I'm starving." "I'm not surprised. You haven't eaten all day."*

+ (that) *I'm not surprised she's fed up with him.*

no wonder /nəʊ ˈwʌndər/ SPOKEN say this when you realize the reason why something happened, so that it is not surprising any more: *No wonder my camera wasn't working – there's no battery in it!*

come as no surprise /ˌkʌm əz nəʊ səˈpraɪz/ if something **comes as no surprise**, you are not surprised when it happens, because you expected it to happen

it comes as no surprise when *It came as no surprise when President Santos announced his resignation.*

SWITCH ON OR OFF

to make a light, machine, radio etc start or stop working by pressing or turning something

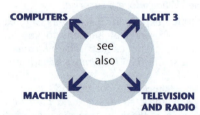

COMPUTERS   LIGHT 3

see also

MACHINE   TELEVISION AND RADIO

1 to switch something on

switch on /ˌswɪtʃ ˈɒn‖-ˈɑːn/ [phrasal verb I/T] to make something start working, for example by pressing a button – use this about things that use electricity, for example, lights, televisions, or computers

switch on sth *Can you switch on the television? | I switched on the radio to listen to the news.*

switch sth on *Do you mind if I switch the light on?*

turn on /ˌtɜːrn ˈɒn‖-ˈɑːn/ [phrasal verb T] to make something start working, for example by turning a tap or pressing a button – use this about things that use electricity, gas, or water

turn on sth *He went into the bathroom and turned on the shower.*

turn sth on *Do you want me to turn the lights on?*

put sth on /ˌpʊt (sth) ˈɒn‖-ˈɑːn/ [phrasal verb T] **put the light/radio/TV/kettle etc on** to make a light, radio etc start working: *Eva put the kettle on to make a cup of coffee. | Put the light on, then we can see what we're doing.*

start /stɑːrt/ [v T] **start a car/engine/motor** to make a car, engine, or motor start working: *She started the car and backed slowly out of the garage.*

2 to switch something off

switch off /ˌswɪtʃ ˈɒf‖-ˈɔːf/ [phrasal verb I/T] to make something stop working, for example by pressing a button – use this about things that use electricity, for example, lights, televisions, or computers

switch off sth *Always switch off your computer when you've finished.*

switch sth off *It's OK – I switched it off before I went out.*

turn off /ˌtɜːrn ˈɒf‖-ˈɔːf/ [phrasal verb T] to make something stop working, for example by pressing a button or turning a tap – use this about things that use electricity, gas, or water

turn off sth *She got up and turned off the TV. | Could you turn off the heater before you go to bed?*

turn sth off *Who forgot to turn the tap off?*

stop /stɒp‖stɑːp/ [v T] to make an engine or machine stop working: *George stopped the engine and got out of the car. | We had to stop the pump and unblock it.*

When you see **EC**, go to the **ESSENTIAL COMMUNICATION** section.

3 when something is switched on

on /ɒn‖ɑːn, ɔːn/ [adj/adv not before noun] if something is **on**, it is working – use this about lights, machines, and other things that use electricity, gas, or water: *Is the heating on? I'm freezing.*

leave sth on *Did you leave the kitchen light on?*

keep sth on *In the winter, I keep the gas fire on all day.*

come/go on (=start working) *The heating comes on automatically.*

be switched on /biː ˌswɪtʃt 'ɒn‖-'ɑːn/ use this about things that use electricity, for example, machines, computers, or heating equipment: *A green light shows that the computer is switched on.* | *Have you checked that the power is switched on?*

be turned on /biː ˌtɜːʳnd 'ɒn‖-'ɑːn/ use this about machines or about the electricity, gas, or water supply: *If the boiler fails to light first check that the gas is turned on.*

be running /biː 'rʌnɪŋ/ if an engine or a machine **is running**, it is working and its parts are moving: *Do not touch the machine while it is running.*

leave sth running *Nick left the engine running while he ran into the house.*

4 when something is switched off

off /ɒf‖ɔːf/ [adj/adv not before noun] if something is **off**, someone has switched it off to make it stop working – use this about lights, machines, and other things that use electricity, gas, or water: *Is the cooker off? I can smell gas.* | *I don't think anyone's at home. All the lights are off.*

go off (=stop working) *The heating goes off at 10:30.*

be switched off /biː ˌswɪtʃt 'ɒf‖-'ɔːf/ use this about things that use electricity, for

example, machines, computers, or heating equipment: *Do you mean the alarm was switched off all night?*

be turned off /biː ˌtɜːʳnd 'ɒf‖-'ɔːf/ use this about lights, machines, or about the electricity, gas, or water supply: *Make sure everything's turned off before you leave the house.*

go out /ˌgəʊ 'aʊt/ [phrasal verb I] if a light **goes out**, it stops shining because it has been switched off, or because there is no electricity: *I watched the house until all the lights had gone out.*

SYSTEM

the way in which something is organized

➡ see also **ORGANIZE/ARRANGE, ORDER**

system /'sɪstɪm/ [n C] the way that something is organized, following fixed rules and methods, in order to provide a service or achieve an aim: *a system for dealing with enquiries from our customers*

+ of *What we need is a cheap and reliable system of public transportation.* | *a democratic system of government*

education/transport/banking system *Most teachers are opposed to recent changes in the education system.* | *the French legal system*

set-up /'set ʌp/ [n singular] INFORMAL the way in which things are organized or done within a company, school etc: *My last school was quite traditional, but it's a different set-up at the new one.* | *It's a very strange set-up – everyone here earns exactly the same salary.*

network /'netwɜːʳk/ [n C] a system of lines, tubes, wires, roads etc that are connected to each other: *A 24-hour strike brought the railway network to a standstill.*

+ of *A network of veins and arteries carries the blood around the body.*

T

TAKE/BRING

➡ if you mean 'take something out', go to REMOVE
➡ see also STEAL, CARRY

1 to take someone or something from one place to another

take /teɪk/ [v T] to have someone or something with you when you go to another place: *Don't forget to take your keys.*
take sth to/out/into *"Where's Dan?" "He's taken the car to the garage."* | *Let's take the kids to the beach.*
take sb sth *I took Alice a cup of tea.*
take sth/sb with you *Did they take the tent with them on their holiday?*
taking – took – have taken

bring /brɪŋ/ [v T] if someone **brings** a person or thing to the place where you are, they have that person or thing with them when they come: *I brought my camera so that I could take pictures of all of you.* | *We've brought someone to see you.*
bring sth to/into/out *Will you bring your CD player to the party?*
bring sb sth *Robert asked the waiter to bring him the check.*
bring sth/sb with you *I hope he hasn't brought his brother with him.*
bringing – brought – have brought

drive /draɪv/ [v T] to take someone from one place to another in a car
drive sb to/from/away *Bill offered to drive me to the airport.* | *The man was driven away in a police van.*
driving – drove – have driven

fly /flaɪ/ [v T] to move people or goods from one place to another in a plane
fly sb to/from *His company is flying him to New York for the meeting.*
fly sth into/to/out *The Red Cross is flying emergency supplies into the earthquake zone.*
flying – flew – have flown

deliver /dɪˈlɪvəʳ/ [v T] to take letters, newspapers, goods etc to someone's home or office: *The store will deliver your new washing-machine tomorrow morning.*
deliver sth to *Unfortunately the package was delivered to the wrong address.*
delivery [n C/U] when letters, newspapers, goods etc are taken to someone's house or office: *We offer free home delivery for every purchase over $150.*

transport /trænˈspɔːʳt/ [v T] to move large quantities of goods or large numbers of people from one place to another, especially over a large distance: *It is much cheaper to transport goods by ship.* | *a large plane that is used for transporting military personnel*
transport sth to/from/across *Meat is transported across Europe in refrigerated containers.*

2 to go to a place and take someone or something from there

get /get/ [v T] to go to the place where someone or something is, and bring them back, or tell them to come back: *I'll get my coat and then we can go.* | *Dinner's ready. Can you get Jo?*
get sb sth (=get something for someone) *Could you get me my keys from the kitchen?*
go and get sb/sth *Go and get your father. He's in the garden.*
getting – got – have got (BRITISH) **– have gotten** (AMERICAN)

pick up /ˌpɪk ˈʌp/ [phrasal verb T] to go to a place where someone or something is waiting for you or ready for you, and take them with you
pick up sb/sth *I'll pick up the airline tickets on my way home from work.*
pick sb/sth up *Omar and Nadia are waiting for you to pick them up at the airport.*

collect /kəˈlekt/ [v T] BRITISH to go to a place where someone or something is waiting for you, and bring them back: *I'm at the station. Can you come and collect me?*
collect sb/sth from *I have to go and collect a parcel from the post-office.*

fetch /fetʃ/ [v T] ESPECIALLY BRITISH to go to get someone or something that you need and bring them back: *Quick! Fetch a ladder.* | *Jim went off to fetch a policeman.*

fetch sb/sth from *Martha fetched a towel from the bathroom.*
fetch sb sth (=fetch something for someone) *Could you fetch me a screwdriver?*

3 to take someone or something back to the place where they came from

take back /ˌteɪk ˈbæk/ [phrasal verb T]
take sb/sth back to *Paul asked the taxi driver to take him back to his hotel.*
take sb/sth back *The dress was too big for me so I took it back.* | *I'll take you back after the party.*
take back sth *Did you remember to take back all your library books?*

bring back /ˌbrɪŋ ˈbæk/ [phrasal verb T]
to bring someone or something back to the place where you are now or to your home
bring sb/sth back *Mrs Ali will bring you back from school today.*
bring back sth *I've brought back the book you lent me.* | *They brought back some lovely cheese from France.*

return /rɪˈtɜːrn/ [v T] to bring or take something back to the place where you got it from: *Penny has still not returned the office keys.*
return sth to *If there is a problem with the computer you can return it to the store.*

> ⚠ **Return** is more formal than **take back** or **bring back**.

4 to take something from someone

take /teɪk/ [v T] to take something out of someone's hands: *Let me take your bags – you look exhausted.*
take sth from sb *He walked across the room and took the gun from her.*
taking – took – have taken

grab/snatch /græb, snætʃ/ [v T] to take something from someone with a sudden violent movement, for example because you are angry or you want to steal something: *A thief snatched her purse while she was walking down the street.*
snatch/grab sth from sb *Larry tried to grab the letter from me.*
grabbing – grabbed – have grabbed

take away /ˌteɪk əˈweɪ/ [phrasal verb T]
to take something important from someone, such as a posession or a right, either as a punishment or in a way that is wrong or unfair
take away sth *a new law that would take away the rights of workers to go on strike*
take sth away from sb *Johnson failed a drugs test, and his gold medal was taken away from him.*

confiscate /ˈkɒnfɪskeɪt‖ˈkɑːn-/ [v T] to officially take something away from someone, either as a punishment or because they are not allowed to have it: *The teacher confiscated my Walkman.* | *Police will confiscate nets and rods from anyone found fishing illegally.*

5 to take something from the place where it is

take /teɪk/ [v T] to take something from the place where it is: *Have you taken my keys? I can't find them.*
take sth from/off/down etc *He took a dictionary down from the shelf.*
take sth away (=take something permanently from a place) *They haven't taken the garbage away for two weeks.*
taking – took – have taken

take out /ˌteɪk ˈaʊt/ [phrasal verb T] to take something from a place where it could not be seen, for example from a pocket, drawer, or container
take out sth *He reached into his pocket and took out a handkerchief.*
take sth out *Sally opened a pack of cigarettes, took one out and lit it.*
take sth out of sth *Take that chewing gum out of your mouth!*

pull out /ˌpʊl ˈaʊt/ [phrasal verb T] to quickly take something from a place where it was hidden or could not be seen
pull out sth *He pulled out a gun and fired three shots.*
pull sth out *I saw her pull a bag out from under the seat.*

remove /rɪˈmuːv/ [v T] to take something away from the place where it is, especially something that you do not want or something that should not be there: *Please do not remove this notice.* | *She was in the hospital, having her appendix removed.*

remove sth from sth *Remove all the packaging from the pizza and place it in a preheated oven.*

> ⚠ **Remove** is more formal than **take off**, **take out** etc.

6 to take someone away using force

take sb away /ˌteɪk (sb) əˈweɪ/ [phrasal verb T] if soldiers, the police etc **take** someone **away**, they force that person to go with them: *The soldiers took my son away and I never saw him again.* | *Our neighbour was taken away in a police car.*

kidnap /ˈkɪdnæp/ [v T] to take someone away by force and keep them as your prisoner, in order to make their family or their government give you money or other things you want: *Terrorists have kidnapped a French officer and are demanding $400,000 from the French government.*
kidnapping – kidnapped – have kidnapped
    kidnapping [n C] when someone is kidnapped: *Most diplomats now travel with bodyguards, following a series of kidnappings.*

abduct /əbˈdʌkt, æb-/ [v T] to take someone away by force, especially a child or young person, often in order to kill them or sexually attack them – used especially in news reports: *Several young women had been abducted from their villages and forced to work as prostitutes.*

take sb hostage /ˌteɪk (sb) ˈhɒstɪdʒ‖ -ˈhɑː-/ to take someone and keep them as a prisoner, especially for political reasons, and threaten to kill them if their government does not do what you demand: *Rebel forces have taken five UN peacekeepers hostage.*

> When you see **EC**, go to the
> **ESSENTIAL COMMUNICATION** section.

TAKE PART
to do something together with other people

➡ see also **SPORT, COMPETITION, GAME**

1 to take part in an event, activity, discussion etc

take part /ˌteɪk ˈpɑːʳt/ to do something together with other people, by joining them in an activity, discussion, event etc: *There is an information session about illegal drugs, and local police officers will be taking part.*
+ in *She was invited to take part in a TV debate on drugs.* | *Police have arrested a number of people who took part in the riot.*

be involved /bɪː ɪnˈvɒlvd‖-ˈvɑːlvd/ to take part in an activity with a small number of other people, often something bad or illegal: *Choosing a school is an important decision, and both parents ought to be involved.*
+ in *Mason says he wasn't involved in the kidnapping.* | *At least three politicians are involved in the scandal.*

participate /pɑːʳˈtɪsɪ̩peɪt/ [v I] FORMAL to take part in an activity, especially an organized activity: *There are regular class discussions, but some of the students never participate.*
+ in *Over 300 local firms participated in the survey.* | *Members can participate in any of the trips organized by the club.*
    participation /pɑːʳˌtɪsɪ̩ˈpeɪʃən/ [n U] when people participate: *Our partners demand full participation in decision-making at management level.*

2 to start taking part

join in /ˌdʒɔɪn ˈɪn/ [phrasal verb I/T] to start taking part in something that other people are already doing, especially something enjoyable such as a game, or a song: *When we get to the chorus I want everybody to join in!* | *We all wanted to join in the fun.*
+ with *She was a shy girl, and wouldn't join in with the other children's games.*

get involved in sth /ˌget ɪnˈvɒlvd ɪn (sth)‖-ˈvɑːlvd-/ to start to take part in something, especially something that will cause you problems or take a lot of your time: *I don't want to get involved in their family arguments.* | *When did you first get involved in local politics?* | *The US are unwilling to get involved in another war.*

get caught up in sth /get ˌkɔːt ˈʌp ɪn (sth)/ to become involved in something dangerous, unpleasant, or illegal, without wanting to or intending to do this: *It is easy for young people to get caught up in crime when there are so few jobs.*

3 to take part in a competition

compete/take part /kəmˈpiːt, ˌteɪk ˈpɑːrt/ [v I] to take part in a competition or race: *Only cars over 50 years old are allowed to compete.* | *The competition was a great success. Nearly two hundred people took part.*
+ in *How many runners will be competing in the marathon?* | *Please contact Debbie if you would like to take part in the charity swim.*

enter sth/go in for sth /ˈentər (sth), ˌgəʊ ˈɪn fɔːr (sth)/ [v T] to say that you will take part in a competition or race, for example by putting your name on a list: *You have to be under 18 to enter the painting competition.* | *Dad says he's going in for the talent contest.*

⚠ **Enter** is more formal than **go in for**, and **go in for** is only used in British English.

4 someone who takes part

competitor /kəmˈpetɪ̹tər/ [n C] someone who takes part in a race, game, or competition: *Two of the competitors failed to turn up for the race.*

participant /pɑːrˈtɪsɪ̹pənt/ [n C] FORMAL someone who takes part in an organized event or activity: *At the end of the conference, all the participants were given a questionnaire.*
+ in *an active participant in the protest movement*

5 to not take part

not take part /nɒt teɪk ˈpɑːrt/ *The President was invited to appear on the program but decided not to take part.*
+ in *I noticed that Darren was not taking part in the discussion.*

pull out/drop out /ˌpʊl ˈaʊt, ˌdrɒp ˈaʊt‖ ˌdrɑːp-/ [phrasal verb I] INFORMAL to suddenly decide not to take part in something, that has already started or is about to start, especially when this causes problems: *The show was cancelled when the star guest pulled out.*
+ of *Dave wants to drop out of the team.* | *It's too late to pull out of the agreement now.*

have nothing to do with sth /hæv ˌnʌθɪŋ tə ˈduː wɪð (sth)/ to not be involved in any way in something bad or illegal – use this especially when other people think that you were involved: *Tell the police that you had nothing to do with the robbery.* | *She had nothing to do with the break-up of my marriage.*

take no part in sth /ˌteɪk ˌnəʊ ˈpɑːrt ɪn (sth)/ FORMAL to deliberately not take part in something, because you disagree with it or think it is wrong: *They were pacifists and would take no part in the war.*

withdraw /wɪðˈdrɔː, wɪθ-/ [v I] to decide not to take part in a competition, race, discussion etc, which you previously agreed to take part in
+ from *Clare had to withdraw from the race after injuring her knee.*
withdrawing – **withdrew** – **have withdrawn**

6 to not let someone take part

leave sb out /ˌliːv (sb) ˈaʊt/ [phrasal verb T] to not include someone in an activity or in a group: *They considered twenty candidates, but Melissa was left out.*
leave sb out of sth *It would be very unfair to leave him out of the team.*

exclude /ɪkˈskluːd/ [v T] to prevent someone from taking part in an activity, or from joining a group
exclude sb from sth *The black majority in South Africa was excluded from politics under apartheid.* | *The Church had*

previously excluded women from the priesthood.

drop /drɒp‖drɑːp/ [v T often passive] to decide that someone can no longer be in a team

+ from *She was dropped from the badminton team because she missed practice too often.*

dropping – dropped – have dropped

TALK

SAY   SPEAK

see also

TELL   SUBJECT

LISTEN

⚠ Don't confuse **say**, **tell**, **talk**, and **speak**. You **say** words to someone. You **tell** someone facts or information about something. You **talk** to someone about a subject. You **speak** (=you say words) or you **speak** a language.

1 to have a conversation

talk /tɔːk/ [v I] if two or more people **talk**, they have a conversation: *We sat around talking for hours.* | *two friends talking on the phone*

+ about *They talked about their favourite pop stars.*

+ to *Danny was talking to a girl he'd just met at the bar.* | *It's been nice talking to you.*

talk with sb AMERICAN *I left Mario talking with my mother.*

get talking (=start having a conversation with someone that you do not know) *Kay got talking to a taxi-driver.*

speak to sb /'spiːk tuː (sb)/ [phrasal verb T] to say something to someone or have a conversation with them: *Natalie's on the phone. She wants to speak to you.* | *He hasn't spoken to me since we quarrelled.*

speaking – spoken – have spoken

chat/have a chat /tʃæt, ˌhæv ə 'tʃæt/ [v I] to talk in a friendly and informal way, especially about things that are not very important: *The girls were sitting on the steps, chatting.* | *Just call me if you feel like having a chat.*

+ about *We drank our coffee and chatted about our experiences.*

+ with/to *Harry chatted to a couple of Australian tourists as we waited for the show to begin.*

chatting – chatted – have chatted

visit /'vɪzət/ [v I] AMERICAN to talk in a relaxed way to someone you know well: *Mom and Aunt Jo were sitting drinking coffee and visiting.*

+ with *I don't see him that often, but I like to go and visit with him when I can.*

gossip /'gɒsəp‖'gɑː-/ [v I] if people **gossip**, they exchange information about other people's private lives, often in an unkind way because they enjoy talking about other people's problems: *They sat in the kitchen, drinking coffee and gossiping.* | *Don't tell Anne about this. You know how she gossips.*

+ about *People often gossip about each other in a small town.*

gossip [n singular/U] conversation about other people's private lives: *There has been a lot of gossip about her divorce.* | *I stopped by at Marsha's house for a gossip.*

conversation /ˌkɒnvər'seɪʃən‖ˌkɑːn-/ [n C/U] when people talk to each other, especially in an informal situation: *a telephone conversation* | *The noise of the traffic made conversation almost impossible.* | *They didn't realize their conversation was being recorded.*

have a conversation (with) *Vicky was having a long conversation with the bartender.*

get into conversation (with sb) (=start talking to someone you do not know) *While I was on the train to Cambridge, I got into conversation with an American.*

2 to talk to someone about a problem, plan, or serious subject

talk /tɔːk/ [v I] *I think we need to talk.*

+ about *If you have a problem at school, let's sit down and talk about it.*

+ to *Gerry wants to talk to his girlfriend before he makes a decision.*

talk with sb AMERICAN *If you need more money you should talk with Richard.*

speak to sb (also **speak with sb** AMERICAN) /ˈspiːk tuː (sb), ˈspiːk wɪð (sb)/ [*phrasal verb* T] to talk to someone about something that you are worried about or annoyed about: *The King's envoy travelled to Rome to speak to the Pope.*

+ about *I intend to speak to the manager about the way I've been treated.* | *Have you spoken with Michael about your problem?*

have a word with sb /ˌhæv ə ˈwɜːrd wɪð (sb)/ to talk to someone alone for a short time, for example because you need their advice or because you want to tell them something privately or criticize them for something they have done wrong: *The boss wants to have a word with me.*

+ about *Could I have a word with you about my homework assignment?*

discuss /dɪˈskʌs/ [*v* T] if people **discuss** a subject or situation, they exchange ideas and opinions about it, so that it is easier to make a decision or make plans: *The two families got together to discuss the wedding arrangements.*

discuss sth with sb *Don't make any plans yet – I want to discuss this with Jamie first.*

discuss what/how/where etc *We need to discuss what kind of food we want at the party.*

talk over /ˌtɔːk ˈəʊvər/ [*phrasal verb* T] to talk to someone about all the details of a serious problem or difficult situation, in order to understand it better

talk sth over/talk over sth *If you're worried about your work, come and see me and we'll talk it over.*

talk sth over with sb *It's often useful to talk things over with a trained counsellor.*

negotiate /nɪˈgəʊʃieɪt/ [*v* I/T] to discuss a political problem or business arrangement in order to try to reach an agreement – use this about political or business leaders

+ with *The government refuses to negotiate with terrorists.*

negotiate an agreement/deal/price etc *Colombia and Venezuela are currently negotiating a trade agreement.*

3 **a meeting where people talk seriously about something**

discussion /dɪˈskʌʃən/ [*n* C/U] when people exchange ideas and opinions about something, especially in order to make a decision

+ about *a discussion about cars and pollution*

+ with *After a long discussion with her father, she decided not to take the job.*

have a discussion *I need to have a discussion with my boss before I can give you an answer.*

under discussion FORMAL (=being discussed) *A new road-building project is now under discussion.*

negotiations /nɪˌgəʊʃiˈeɪʃənz/ [*n* plural] when people who represent governments, companies etc meet to discuss a problem or business arrangement and try to reach an agreement: *The trade negotiations between the US and Japan are going very well.*

+ with *Negotiations with the Turkish government are due to begin tomorrow.*

talks /tɔːks/ [*n* plural] a series of discussions between political or business leaders, which may continue for several days or weeks and are intended to solve a difficult problem: *the Strategic Arms Limitation Talks, known as 'SALT'*

hold talks *The peace talks are being held in Geneva.*

+ with *The company's managers have begun talks with union leaders.*

+ between *trade talks between France and Korea*

debate /dɪˈbeɪt/ [*n* C] a formal public discussion, for example in parliament or on television, in which two or more groups of people make speeches giving different opinions about a subject, and people vote on it afterwards: *The law was passed, after a long and sometimes angry debate.*

+ on/about *a televised debate on abortion*

4 **when someone makes a speech**

speech /spiːtʃ/ [*n* C] a formal talk to a group of people, for example in a parliament or at an official meeting or

T

ceremony: *She left early to write her speech for the next day.* | *an election speech*

make/give a speech *After the concert the mayor made a speech, congratulating the school.*

+ about/on *a speech on the economy*

plural **speeches**

talk /tɔːk/ [n C] a planned, but not very formal talk about a particular subject, for example at a meeting or on the radio: *a series of radio talks by well-known writers*

give a talk on/about sth *Mr. Munroe gave an interesting talk on his recent visit to Peru.*

give a talk to sb *Alice Walker has been invited to give a talk to the literary group this evening.*

> ⚠ Compare **speech** and **talk**: **Speeches** are often about politics. **Talks** are about things like literature, science, art, or history, but not usually about politics.

speak /spiːk/ [v I] to make a speech, for example in parliament or at an official meeting or ceremony: *I've been invited to speak at the party's annual conference.*

+ to *The President will speak to the nation tonight on television.*

talk /tɔːk/ [v I] to speak publicly to a group of people about a particular subject

+ about *This evening Professor Welch will be talking about Shakespeare's historical plays.*

speaker /'spiːkəʳ/ [n C] someone who makes a speech in public: *the first speaker in tonight's debate*

public speaker *Kennedy was known as a brilliant public speaker.*

guest speaker (=someone who has been invited to come and give a speech or talk)

5 to mention someone or something when you are talking

mention /'menʃən/ [v T] to say something about a person, plan, event etc during a conversation, but without giving any details or saying very much: *When you were talking to Barbara, did she mention her mother?* | *One of the students*

mentioned something about a party on Thursday.

mention sth to sb *I mentioned the idea to Joan, and she seemed to like it.*

+ (that) *He mentioned that he was having problems, but he didn't say what they were.*

refer to sth/sb /rɪ'fɜːʳ tuː (sth/sb)/ [phrasal verb T] to talk about a person, plan, event etc in a conversation, speech, or piece of writing: *She didn't mention any names, but everyone knew who she was referring to.* | *In his speech the President referred to the achievements of the Olympic team.*

> ⚠ **Refer to** is more formal than **mention**.

bring up /ˌbrɪŋ 'ʌp/ [phrasal verb T] to start to talk about a subject during a conversation or meeting

bring up sth *She wished she'd never brought up the subject of money.*

bring sth up *If you think safety is a problem, I suggest you bring it up at the next meeting.*

6 to talk when someone else is already speaking

interrupt /ˌɪntə'rʌpt/ [v I/T] to start speaking when someone else is already speaking: *I wish you wouldn't interrupt all the time.* | *She's always interrupting people before they've finished talking.*

butt in /ˌbʌt 'ɪn/ [phrasal verb I] INFORMAL to interrupt someone rudely: *Will you please stop butting in!*

7 someone who talks a lot

talkative /'tɔːkətɪv/ [adj] someone who is **talkative** talks a lot: *The wine was making her more relaxed and talkative.*

chatterbox /'tʃætəʳbɒks‖-bɑːks/ [n C] INFORMAL someone, especially a child, who talks a lot in a friendly way

plural **chatterboxes**

go on /ˌgəʊ 'ɒn‖-'ɑːn/ [phrasal verb I] ESPECIALLY SPOKEN to keep talking or complaining about something, in a way that is annoying or boring: *Doesn't she go on? She's always complaining.*

+ about *I wish you'd stop going on about how expensive everything is.*

go on and on (=keep talking for a long time) *He went on and on until we were all practically falling asleep.*

8 someone who does not talk much

➡ see also QUIET

quiet /ˈkwaɪət/ [adj] someone who is **quiet** does not talk much: *The new girl's quiet, but nice enough.* | *Steven's a very quiet boy who loves reading.*

silent /ˈsaɪlənt/ [adj not usually before noun] WRITTEN if someone is **silent**, they do not say anything
remain silent *Alice was laughing and joking, but her sister remained silent.*
fall silent (=suddenly stop talking) *When the priest entered the room, everyone fell silent.*

9 what you say to tell someone to stop talking

➡ see also QUIET

◯**be quiet** /biː ˈkwaɪət/ SPOKEN say this when you want someone to stop talking: *Please be quiet for a moment.*

⚠ Only say **be quiet** to children or to someone that you know well.

◯**shut up** /ˌʃʌt ˈʌp/ SPOKEN INFORMAL a rude way of telling someone to stop talking: *Oh, shut up! I don't want to hear your excuses.*
+ about *We know you won, but just shut up about it, okay?*

⚠ Only say **shut up** to people you know very well, because it is not polite.

TALL

HIGH   LOW

see also

SHORT   DEEP

DESCRIBING PEOPLE

1 tall

tall /tɔːl/ [adj] a **tall** person, building, tree etc has a greater height than average: *You'll recognize him – he's very tall and thin.* | *a tall building like the Sears Tower* | *The photographer asked the tallest people to stand at the back of the group.*

⚠ Use **tall** about people, and about things that are high but not wide or long, such as trees or some buildings. Use **high** about things that are wide or long as well as being high, such as mountains or walls, or about things that are far above the ground, such as ceilings or shelves.

⚠ **Short** is the opposite of **tall** when you are talking about a person: *He's short and fat with grey hair.*

2 how tall someone is

how tall /ˌhaʊ ˈtɔːl/ use this to ask or talk about someone's height: *"How tall are you?" "I'm about 1 metre 65."* | *I hadn't seen her for five years and I was amazed at how tall she was.*

6ft tall/2m tall etc /(6ft etc) ˈtɔːl/ use this to say exactly how tall someone is: *John is 1.78 metres tall and weighs 95 kilos.*

⚠ Don't say 'I am tall 180 cm'. Say **I am 180 cm tall.**

height /haɪt/ [n U] how tall someone or something is: *They need to know your age, weight, and height.*
+ of *What's the height of the Eiffel Tower?*
be the same height (as) *My daughter is only 14 but she is nearly the same height as me.*
of medium height (=someone who is not tall and not short) *a man of medium height*

When you see **EC**, go to the **ESSENTIAL COMMUNICATION** section.

TASTE

FOOD   EAT
DRINK   see   TRY 4
also
COOK   SMELL
MEAL   RESTAURANTS/
EATING AND
DRINKING

1 the taste of food or drink

taste /teɪst/ [n singular] the feeling that something produces in your mouth when you eat it or drink it: *I never drink beer, I just don't like the taste.*
+ of *Have some water to take away the taste of the medicine.*

⚠ Don't say 'this cake is good taste'. Say **this cake tastes good**.

flavour BRITISH **flavor** AMERICAN /'fleɪvəʳ/ [n C/U] the interesting, pleasant, or strong taste that a type of food or drink has, which makes it different from any other food or drink: *This sauce has a really unusual flavour.* | *We have three flavors of ice-cream – strawberry, chocolate, and vanilla.* | *The wine wasn't bad, but it didn't have much flavour.*

2 when food has a particular taste

taste /teɪst/ [v I] use this to say that food has a particular taste
taste good/awful/strange/sweet etc *This milk tastes strange – do you think it's OK to drink?*
taste of sth (=have the taste of something) *I ordered chocolate ice-cream but it tasted of coffee.*
taste like sth *It's a vegetarian pie, but it tastes just like meat!*

⚠ Don't say 'it is tasting good/awful etc'. Say **it tastes good/awful etc.**

have a strong/sweet/unpleasant etc taste /hæv ə (strong etc) 'teɪst/ use

this when you want to describe exactly what something tastes like: *The soup had a very strong, spicy taste.*

flavoured BRITISH **flavored** AMERICAN /'fleɪvəʳd/ [adj] **lemon-flavoured/choco-late-flavoured etc** with the taste of lemon, chocolate etc added: *an orange-flavoured drink*

3 food that tastes good

delicious /dɪ'lɪʃəs/ [adj] something that is **delicious** tastes very good, and you enjoy eating it or drinking it: *Thank you, that was a delicious meal.* | *"What do you think of the wine?" "Mmm, delicious!"*

⚠ Don't say 'very delicious'. Say **absolutely delicious** or **really delicious**: *The tomato soup was absolutely delicious.*

◯**good** (also **nice** ESPECIALLY BRITISH) /gʊd, naɪs/ [adj] ESPECIALLY SPOKEN pleasant to eat or drink: *This is a really good pizza. I think I'll have another slice.* | *You can get very nice bread at Walker's Bakery.*
taste good/nice *This sauce tastes nice. How did you make it?*
good – better – best

tasty /'teɪsti/ [adj] food that is **tasty** has a strong taste that you like: *These sausages are very tasty – where did you buy them?* | *tasty apple pie*

⚠ Don't confuse **tasty** (which is used about food) and **tasteful** (which is used about things such as furniture and clothes that look attractive).

mouth-watering /'maʊθ ˌwɔːtərɪŋ/ [adj usually before noun] **mouth-watering** food makes you feel hungry because it looks or smells very good: *There was a mouth-watering selection of cakes to choose from.* | *the mouth-watering aroma of freshly made fish soup*

4 food that tastes bad

disgusting/revolting /dɪs'gʌstɪŋ, dɪz-, rɪ'vəʊltɪŋ/ [adj] food or drink that is **disgusting** or **revolting** has an extremely unpleasant taste: *This hamburger tastes disgusting – I wonder what they put in it.* | *It wasn't a bad meal, but the coffee was absolutely revolting.*

⚠ Don't say 'very disgusting' or 'very revolting'. Say **absolutely disgusting** or **absolutely revolting**

5 food that tastes sweet

sweet /swiːt/ [adj] food or drink that is **sweet** has a taste like sugar: *Italian oranges are much sweeter than the ones we buy in Britain.* | *a cup of hot sweet tea*

sugary /ˈʃʊgəri/ [adj] very sweet or too sweet because a lot of sugar has been added: *Eat fruit between meals, and try to avoid sugary snacks.*

6 food that does not taste sweet

bitter /ˈbɪtər/ [adj] food or drink that is **bitter** has a taste like the taste of strong coffee without milk or sugar, or the taste of very dark chocolate: *The medicine tasted bitter and Jessie spat it out.*

sour /saʊər/ [adj] something that is **sour**, especially fruit, has a sharp taste like a lemon: *The strawberries are a little sour – you may need to put sugar on them.*

savoury /ˈseɪvəri/ [adj] BRITISH **savoury** foods are not sweet but have the taste of meat, cheese, fish etc: *You can use this herb to flavour almost any savoury dish.* | *As a child I didn't like sweet things, but I loved potato chips, nuts, and anything savoury.*

dry /draɪ/ [adj] a **dry** wine is not sweet at all: *We drank dry white wine with our fish.* | *dry sherry*

dry – drier – driest

7 food that has a hot taste

hot /hɒt‖hɑːt/ [adj] food that has a **hot** taste seems to burn your mouth, and makes you want to drink a lot of water: *Bring me the hottest curry on the menu.* | *The sauce had a hot peppery taste.*

hot – hotter – hottest

spicy /ˈspaɪsi/ [adj] **spicy** food has various strong hot pleasant tastes in it: *Remember, my mother doesn't like spicy food, so don't put too much ginger in it.* | *The meat is served with a spicy peanut sauce.*

spicy – spicier – spiciest

8 food that has no taste

have no taste/not taste of anything /ˌhæv nəʊ ˈteɪst, nɒt ˈteɪst əv ˌeniθɪŋ/ *What's this soup supposed to be? It doesn't taste of anything to me.* | *Watermelon is refreshing on a hot day but it doesn't have much taste.*

bland/tasteless /blænd, ˈteɪstləs/ [adj] use this about food or drink that has no strong noticeable taste, and is not interesting or enjoyable: *Food tastes very bland if you stop using salt.* | *a plate of tasteless, overcooked vegetables*

TEACH

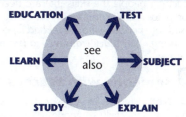

see also

EDUCATION · TEST · LEARN · SUBJECT · STUDY · EXPLAIN

1 to teach

teach /tiːtʃ/ [v I/T] to help someone to learn a subject or skill, by giving them lessons or instructions, especially when this is your job: *She teaches at the local high school.*

teach sth *I got a job teaching French and Spanish.* | *He was working at the technology school, teaching classes in computer programming.*

teach sb *I didn't enjoy teaching teenagers.*

teach sb sth *You remember Mr Hughes – he used to teach us history.*

teach sb to do sth/how to do sth *Who taught you to drive?* | *It was my mother that taught me how to cook.*

teaching – taught – have taught

train /treɪn/ [v T] to teach someone the practical skills and knowledge that they need to do a job: *She works at the flying school, training pilots.*

train sb to do sth *All our staff will be trained to use the new computer system.* | *They had trained the dog to detect illegal drugs.*

train sb in sth *We train people in skills such as typing and business administration.*

trained [adj] *a shortage of trained medical staff*

teaching /'tiːtʃɪŋ/ [n U] the work that a teacher does, or the job of being a teacher: *Andrea took some time off from teaching when her children were small.*

go into teaching (=become a teacher) *What made you decide to go into teaching?*

⚠️ **Teaching** can also be used before a noun, like an adjective: *Do you have any teaching experience?* | *a teaching job*

training /'treɪnɪŋ/ [n U] the process of teaching people the skills that are needed for a job: *The equipment can only be used by people who have had special training.* | *military training* | *a training course*

2 someone who teaches

teacher /'tiːtʃər/ [n C] someone who teaches, especially someone whose job is to teach children in a school: *She's a teacher in the high school.*

English/science/chemistry etc teacher *The school doesn't have enough French teachers.*

+ of *a conference for high-school teachers of Spanish*

a good/bad teacher *I gave her some driving lessons, but I'm afraid I'm not a very good teacher.*

tutor /'tjuːtər‖'tuː-/ [n C] someone who gives lessons to just one student or a small group of students: *When she was ill she studied at home with a private tutor.* | *They hired a tutor to help Carlos with his English.*

instructor /ɪn'strʌktər/ [n C] someone who teaches a sport or a practical skill

a swimming/driving/riding etc instructor *Do you know any good driving instructors?* | *a ski instructor*

coach /kəʊtʃ/ [n C] someone who trains a person or a team in a sport, and helps them to improve their skill

a basketball/football/tennis coach *a successful football coach*

professor /prə'fesər/ [n C] a university teacher – used in Britain to mean a teacher of the highest rank, and in the US to mean any university teacher who has a higher degree such as a PhD: *a linguistics professor*

+ of *She's a professor of history at Oxford.*

⚠️ You can also use **professor** as a title: *Our guest speaker today is Professor Julius Weissman from the University of Chicago.*

⚠️ Never use **professor** to mean a school teacher.

lecturer /'lektʃərər/ [n C] BRITISH someone who teaches at a university or college: *a chemistry lecturer*

+ in *a lecturer in economics*

3 books, games etc that teach something

educational /ˌedjʊ'keɪʃənəl◄‖ˌedʒə-/ [adj] **educational** books, games, television programmes etc are designed to help you to learn something: *educational toys for 7 to 11 year-olds* | *a leading publisher of educational books and software*

WORD BANK

TECHNOLOGY

➡ see pages 756–759

WORD BANK

TELEVISION AND RADIO

NEWSPAPERS AND MAGAZINES

ACTOR/ACTRESS   ▣ OPINIONS

FREE TIME   see also   MUSIC

NEWS   ADVERTISING

SWITCH ON OR OFF   FILMS/MOVIES

When you see ▣, go to the **ESSENTIAL COMMUNICATION** section.

1 television

television/TV /'telɪˌvɪʒən, ˌtelɪ'vɪʒən, ˌtiː 'viː/ [n U] the system of broadcasting pictures and sound, or the programmes that are broadcast in this way: *Television brings events like the Olympic Games into millions of homes.* | *the educational uses of television*

watch television/TV *She just sits there all day watching television.*

on television/TV (=shown on television) *products that you see advertised on TV*

television/TV (also **television set** FORMAL) [n C] the box-shaped thing with a glass screen on which you watch programmes: *a wide-screen TV* | *He was sitting on the floor in front of the television.*

> ⚠ You can also use **television** or **TV** before a noun, like an adjective: *a television company* | *the television studios* | *a TV program*

> ⚠ You can say someone works **in television** (not 'in TV') when they have a job in the business of making or selling television programmes. Don't confuse **on television** (you watch a programme **on television**) and **in television** (=in the television business).

> ⚠ Don't say 'see television'. Say **watch television**. But you can use **see** to talk about a particular programme in the past: *Did you see 'Star Trek' last night?*

telly /'teli/ [n C/U] BRITISH SPOKEN INFORMAL the programmes that are broadcast on television or the box-shaped thing with a screen on which you watch programmes: *We've just bought a new telly.*

watch telly *You can watch telly after you've done your homework.*

on telly (=shown on television) *Is there anything good on telly tonight?*

2 radio

radio /'reɪdiəʊ/ [n U] the system of broadcasting sound, or the programmes that are broadcast in this way: *The story was specially written for radio.*

listen to the radio *In the evening I usually watch TV or listen to the radio.*

on the radio (=broadcast on the radio) *I've often heard that song on the radio, but I can't think what it's called.*

radio [n C] the piece of electronic equipment that you listen to: *Do you have a radio in your car?*

> ⚠ You can also use **radio** before a noun, like an adjective: *a radio play* | *radio programmes* | *a radio station* (=a company that broadcasts radio programmes).

> ⚠ Don't say 'hear the radio'. Say **listen to the radio**. But you can use **hear** when you are talking about a particular programme in the past: *Did you hear the local news today?*

3 when a programme is broadcast on television or radio

be on /biː 'ɒn‖-'ɑːn/ [phrasal verb I/T] if a programme **is on**, you can watch it on television or listen to it on the radio, especially at a particular time: *The Breakfast Show's on between 8 and 10 in the morning.* | *You shouldn't call him while the football's on.*

be on television/TV/the radio *There's a good concert on the radio this evening.* | *What's on TV tonight?*

show /ʃəʊ/ [v T] if a television company **shows** a particular programme, it makes the programme available for people to watch: *Highlights of the game will be shown on Channel 5.* | *They're showing 'Dangerous Liaisons' on Saturday night.*

showing – showed – have shown

broadcast /'brɔːdkɑːst‖-kæst/ [v T usually passive] if a television or radio company **broadcasts** a programme, they send it out so that people can watch it on television or listen to it on the radio: *The funeral was broadcast to the whole nation.*

be broadcast live (=when an event is shown at the same time that it is happening) *The whole race will be broadcast live from Monza.*

broadcasting – broadcast – have broadcast

> ⚠ **Broadcast** is more formal than **show**.

TELEVISION AND RADIO continues on page 760

TECHNOLOGY

➡ see also **COMPUTERS**

Technology affects nearly every area of our lives...

1 communication

We can talk to other people in almost any part of the world by phone, **satellite**, or computer.

People can also take part in **teleconferencing, online** discussions, or do some **home shopping**.
But this can also mean that people may spend less time actually with their families and friends, and may spend much more time in their houses. This could have a very bad effect on local **communities**.
Many areas of the world do not yet have the technology to take part in **global** communication.

vocabulary

advance /ədˈvɑːns‖-ˈvæns/ [n C] an **advance** in science or technology is when a new process is invented or something new is discovered, which makes it possible for people to do things they could not do before
+ in *Advances in medical technology have dramatically reduced the amount of time that patients spend in hospital.*

automated /ˈɔːtəmeɪtɪd/ [adj] using machines to do a job or industrial process: *a fully automated dialling and answering system*

balance of nature /ˌbæləns əv ˈneɪtʃər/ [n singular] the natural situation in which many different living things can exist at the same time, without one type of plant, animal etc completely destroying or being destroyed by another: *Though some insects are harmful to crops, getting rid of them with pesticides may seriously upset the balance of nature.*

bank account /ˈbæŋk əˌkaʊnt/ [n C] an arrangement with a bank that lets you keep your money with that bank and take it out when you need it: *My salary is paid directly into my bank account.*

biological weapon /ˌbaɪəlɒdʒɪkəl ˈwepən‖-lɑː-/ [n C] the use of bacteria or viruses in weapons that can make people suffer from diseases which could seriously injure or kill them: *a biological weapon that can infect people with a deadly genetically engineered virus*

breed /briːd/ [v T] to make animals or plants produce young in a controlled way, in order to develop new and better types: *Horses are deliberately bred so that each generation can run faster, but this means their legs are thinner and lighter, and break much more easily.*

cancer /ˈkænsər/ [n C] a very serious disease in which the cells in a part of the body start to grow quickly in a way that is not normal, often causing death: *Her uncle died of lung cancer.* | *skin cancer*

card crime /ˈkɑːd ˌkraɪm/ [n U] when criminals use the information from other people's credit cards or bank cards to steal money or to pay for goods

cashless society /ˌkæʃləs səˈsaɪəti/ [n singular] when no-one needs to use money in the form of coins or notes, because they can pay for everything using plastic cards

cell /sel/ [n C] the smallest part of a plant, animal, or human that can exist independently. All living things are made up of cells: *red blood cells* | *The cell divides to become two identical separate cells.*

TECHNOLOGY

2 work

A lot of boring or complicated jobs can now be done by computers, machines, or **robots** instead of people.
Some **manufacturing** processes and services are now fully **automated**.
This can lead to high **unemployment** as more jobs are done by machines or computers…

…and many people would rather deal with a person than with a machine.

3 cards, money and information

Smart cards can carry a lot of information on a **magnetic strip**, and you can sometimes use them to work electronic machines. Soon we may no longer need to use coins or banknotes, as **credit cards** and **smart cards** can be used to pay for things.

community /kəˈmjuːnᵻti/ [n C] all the people who live in the same area: *plans for a new recreation centre that will benefit the whole community*

computer fraud /kəmˈpjuːtəʳ ˌfrɔːd/ [n U] the use of computers for dishonest or criminal activities, for example using a computer illegally to change financial records

confidential /ˌkɒnfᵻˈdenʃəl◀ˌkɑːn-/ [adj] information that is **confidential** is intended to be kept secret, for example because it includes personal details about someone: *confidential documents containing information about members of staff*
  highly confidential (=very confidential) *She was fired for giving highly confidential information to a newspaper.*

credit card /ˈkredᵻt ˌkɑːʳd/ [n C] a plastic card given to you by a financial organization such as Visa® or MasterCard®, which you can use to buy things, and then pay the money back later: *We accept all major credit cards.* | *Can I pay by credit card?* (=using a credit card)

ethical /ˈeθᵻkəl/ [adj] **ethical** problems or questions concern difficult moral decisions, about whether or not it is right to do something that has become possible because of science: *the ethical implications of using aborted foetuses for research*

fertility treatment /fəˈtɪlᵻti ˌtriːtmənt/ [n C/U] a type of medical treatment in which a woman is helped to become pregnant when she cannot do this naturally: *There are several different types of fertility treatments available.*

gene /dʒiːn/ [n C] an extremely small part of the material in a cell of a living thing, which controls the way a person, plant, or animal grows and develops. Genes are passed on from parents to children: *Scientists say they have discovered a gene that causes people to be overweight as adults.* | *Your genes determine the colour of your eyes and skin, and whether you will be tall or short.*

genetic /dʒᵻˈnetɪk/ [adj] related to or caused by genes: *a genetic illness* (=caused by your genes or those of your parents)

gene therapy /dʒiːn ˌθerəpi/ [n U] a type of medical treatment that changes someone's genes to help them get rid of a disease or cure a medical condition

genetic engineering /dʒəˌnetɪk endʒᵻˈnɪərɪŋ/ [n U] when scientists change the genes of a person, plant or animal in order to make it stronger, healthier, bigger, more attractive etc: *As a result of genetic engineering, all the apples from this farm are*

TECHNOLOGY continues on the next page

TECHNOLOGY

This could lead to a **cashless society**. But some people are worried that **confidential** information stored on cards, such as their **medical records** or **bank account** details might be seen or used by other people.
Most people have no way of checking what personal information about themselves is stored on a smart card.
There has also been a big increase in **card crime** and **computer fraud**.

4 medicine

Advances in **medical science** mean that many more diseases can be cured or treated than ever before. New techniques include the use of **lasers** in operations, and new equipment makes it possible for doctors to see what is happening inside a patient's body on a **monitor**.

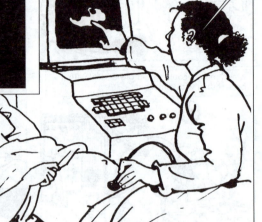

...And there's the baby's head, Mrs Brown...

exactly the same size and colour. | *There are fears that genetic engineering could lead to the creation of harmful viruses that cannot be controlled.*
genetically engineered [adj] *a genetically engineered cow that can produce low fat milk*

global /'gləʊbəl/ [adj] including or affecting the whole world: *Modern technology has made global communication fast and inexpensive.* | *a global ban on the dumping of nuclear waste*

home shopping /həʊm 'ʃɒpɪŋ‖-'ʃɑːp/ [n U] a service that lets you buy things without leaving your home, using a credit card and a computer, a phone, or a television: *Call in at this web site for the very latest in home shopping and online services.*

laser /'leɪzəʳ/ [n C] a piece of equipment that produces a powerful narrow beam of light that can be used in medical operations, to cut things, and to play CDs: *The hospital has just spent over £1m on new laser equipment.* | *Later on, there was a laser and firework show.*

magnetic strip /mæg,netɪk 'strɪp/ [n C] a dark area on a plastic card that contains information stored electronically. You cannot see this information with your eyes, but it can be read by a machine: *Using the magnetic strip on the driver's license, police can instantly call up people's driving records.*

manufacturing /,mænjɜ'fæktʃərɪŋ/ [n U] the process or business of producing things in factories: *the decline of manufacturing in the UK* | *The car industry has lost thousands of manufacturing jobs in the past few years.*

medical records /,medɪkəl 'rekɔːdz‖-kərdz/ [n plural] information about someone's health and physical condition, for example what illnesses they have had, how many children they have, whether they smoke etc: *The report was based on the medical records of babies born to drug addicts.*

medical science /,medɪkəl 'saɪəns/ [n U] the use of science and technology to understand and treat diseases: *Medical science still cannot explain what causes cancer.*

microsurgery /maɪkrəʊ,sɜːʳdʒəri/ [n U] a way of doing medical operations, in which doctors can repair or remove parts of the body that are so small they can only be seen with a microscope: *His hand was attached again using the latest microsurgery techniques.*

monitor /'mɒnɪtəʳ‖'mɑː-/ [n C] a screen connected to a computer system or video camera

multiple birth /,mʌltɪpəl 'bɜːθ/ [n C] when a woman has three or more babies at the same time

TECHNOLOGY

Organ **transplants, microsurgery,** and **fertility treatments** are now all very common. But new treatments can also mean new moral or **ethical** problems, for example whether people should be kept alive by machines when naturally they would have died. Some people think that fertility treatment should not be used when it might result in **multiple births** or if the woman receiving it is too old to have children naturally.
Other people believe that all new medical techniques should be available to anyone who wants or needs them.

5 genetic engineering

Scientists can use **genetic engineering** to grow crops and **breed** animals that cannot be harmed by common diseases, and which provide more food for people to eat.
Genetic engineering or **gene therapy** can also be used to treat some diseases in humans, for example the **cells** that cause **cancer** can be changed. It is also possible for doctors to stop people with genetic diseases from passing them on to their children.

However, **genetically engineered** plants and animals are unnatural and may affect the **balance of nature**. Many people believe it is cruel to breed genetically engineered animals. **Biological weapons** can be made that can change **viruses** which are normally harmless into **viruses** that can kill people. There may be harmful effects of **genetic engineering** that we do not yet know about.

---

online /ˌɒn laɪn‖ˈɑːn/ [adj] **online** services, discussions, games etc take place or exist on the Internet (=the system of connections that allows computers all over the world to communicate with each other): *You can get online help for all your computer problems.* | *They provide an online library and reference service.*

radiation /ˌreɪdiˈeɪʃən/ [n U] a form of energy that comes especially from nuclear reactions (=when the central part of an atom is split) which is very harmful to people, animals, and plants if it is present in large amounts

robot /ˈrəʊbɒt‖-bɑːt, -bət/ [n C] a machine that can move and do jobs, for example in a factory or in space: *The use of robots in industry is greater in Japan than anywhere else.* | *a robot that does your housework for you*

satellite /ˈsætₗlaɪt/ [n C] a machine that has been sent into space and goes around the Earth, which is used for sending radio and television signals, and for other types of electronic communication

smart card /ˈsmɑːᵗt kɑːᵗd/ [n C] a plastic card with an electronic part that records and stores information, which can also be used to pay for things, make electronic machines work etc

technology /tekˈnɒlədʒi‖-ˈnɑː-/ [n U] the use of scientific knowledge and scientific discoveries to develop new machines and systems: *rapid advances in computer technology* | *nuclear technology*

new technology (=computers, electronic equipment etc) *At first, many businesses were slow to adapt to new technology.*

technological /ˌteknəˈlɒdʒɪkəl‖-ˈlɑː-/ [adj] *The steam engine was one of the most important technological developments of the 18th century.*

teleconferencing /ˌtelₐˈkɒnfrənsɪŋ‖-ˈkɑːn-/ [n U] a way of having a meeting between people who are in different places, using video cameras and computer systems that are connected to each other

transplant /ˈtrænsplɑːnt‖-plænt/ [n C] a medical operation in which an unhealthy organ is replaced with an organ from someone else's body: *a heart transplant* | *He's in hospital waiting for a kidney transplant.*

unemployment /ˌʌnɪmˈplɔɪmənt/ [n U] when people who want to work cannot get jobs: *Unemployment rose steadily throughout the 1980s.* | *government attempts to tackle unemployment*

high unemployment (=when a lot of people do not have a job)

virus /ˈvaɪərəs/ [n C] an extremely small living thing that can cause infectious illnesses in people: *HIV, the virus that causes AIDS* | *a normally harmless virus that can be dangerous to very young children*

TELEVISION AND RADIO continued from page 755

4 a television or radio programme

programme BRITISH **program** AMERICAN /ˈprəʊgræm/ [n C] a play, show, discussion etc that you can watch on television or listen to on the radio: *a news program* | *See today's paper for a list of TV programmes in your area.*

+ on/about *Programmes on gardening are very popular.*

broadcast /ˈbrɔːdkɑːst‖-kæst/ [n C] something that is broadcast on the radio or on television, especially a speech, discussion, or news programme: *The government banned all broadcasts by opposition parties.* | *In a nationwide TV broadcast, President Nixon explained why he was resigning.*

channel /ˈtʃænl/ [n C] a particular set of programmes that is broadcast by one television company; there are usually several different channels, and you can choose which one you want to watch: *the sports channel on satellite TV* | *This is boring. Do you mind if I switch over to another channel?* | *The final episode will be shown on Channel 4 tonight.*

5 programmes to entertain people

show /ʃəʊ/ [n C] a programme on television or the radio, that is intended to be entertaining or funny: *the Chris Tarrant Show* | *Good evening and welcome to the show.* | *After the show we received over 200 calls complaining about bad language.*

chat show

chat show BRITISH **talk show** AMERICAN /ˈtʃæt ʃəʊ, ˈtɔːk ʃəʊ/ [n C] a programme, especially on television, in which famous people talk about themselves and answer questions about their lives, opinions etc

quiz show /ˈkwɪz ʃəʊ/ [n C] ESPECIALLY BRITISH a programme in which people or teams compete against each other by answering questions

game show

game show /ˈgeɪm ʃəʊ/ [n C] a programme on television in which people play games and answer questions in order to win prizes

> ⚠ In American English, **quiz show** means the same as **game show**.

cartoon

cartoon /kɑːˈtuːn/ [n C] a film, especially a story for children, that is made by photographing a series of drawings of people, animals etc, so that they seem to move: *a Mickey Mouse cartoon*

sitcom /'sɪtkɒm‖-kɑːm/ [n C] an amusing programme in which there is a different story each week about the same group of people: *popular American sitcoms, like 'Cheers' and 'Roseanne'*

breakfast show BRITISH **morning show** AMERICAN /'brekfəst ʃəʊ, 'mɔːrnɪŋ ʃəʊ/ [n C] a programme that is broadcast early in the morning, which includes news and regularly tells you what time it is; there are also usually songs and jokes and conversations with famous people

drama

drama /'drɑːmə‖'drɑːmə, 'dræmə/ [n C] an exciting but serious play on radio or television

radio/television/TV drama *a new TV drama series about drug-trafficking*

a police/political/hospital drama *an exciting police drama starring Helen Mirren*

soap opera/soap /'səʊp ˌɒpərə, səʊp‖ -ˌɑːp-/ [n C] a television or radio story about a group of people and their lives, which is broadcast regularly for many years

6 serious programmes to inform and educate people

the news /ðə 'njuːz‖-'nuːz/ [n singular] a programme that is broadcast several times each day, which tells you about all the important events that are happening in the world

phone-in (also **call-in** AMERICAN) /'fəʊn ɪn, 'kɔːl ɪn/ [n C] a programme, especially on the radio, in which people telephone the programme in order to give their opinions or ask a famous person questions

the weather forecast

the weather/the weather forecast /ðə 'weðər, ðə 'weðər ˌfɔːrkɑːst‖-kæst/ [n singular] a short programme that tells you what the weather will be like

wildlife programme

wildlife programme BRITISH **nature programme** AMERICAN /'waɪldlaɪf ˌprəʊgræm, 'neɪtʃər ˌprəʊgræm/ [n C] a television programme about wild animals or plants

documentary /ˌdɒkjʊ'mentəri‖ˌdɑːk-/ [n C] a programme that gives you facts and information about a serious subject, such as history, science, or social problems plural **documentaries**

7 a number of programmes about the same subject, the same people etc

series /'sɪəriːz/ [n C] a set of separate programmes, each of which tells the next part of a story, or deals with the same subject: *a police drama series | a series about the Russian Revolution*

serial /ˈsɪəriəl/ [n C] ESPECIALLY BRITISH a story that is broadcast in several separate parts

episode /ˈepɪ̩səʊd/ [n C] one of the parts of a story that is being broadcast in several separate parts

8 the people on television or radio

➡ see also **ACTOR**

presenter BRITISH **announcer** AMERICAN /prɪˈzentəʳ, əˈnaʊnsəʳ/ [n C] someone on a TV or radio programme who tells you what the programme will be about, and introduces the other people in it

host /həʊst/ [n C] someone who introduces the people on a TV or radio show, especially a game show or quiz show

newsreader BRITISH **anchor** AMERICAN /ˈnjuːzˌriːdəʳ, ˈæŋkəʳ‖ˈnuːz-/ [n C] someone who reads the news on TV or radio, and introduces news reports

commentator /ˈkɒmənteɪtəʳ‖ˈkɑːm-/ [n C] someone on television or radio who describes an event as it is happening, especially a sports game

DJ /ˈdiː dʒeɪ/ [n C] someone who plays records and talks to people on a music programme on the radio

contestant /kənˈtestənt/ [n C] a person who takes part in a competition on TV or the radio

guest /gest/ [n C] a famous person who is invited to appear on a show for just one programme

9 someone who watches television or listens to the radio

viewer /ˈvjuːəʳ/ [n C] someone who watches television – used especially by people in the television business: *a programme that appeals to younger viewers*

listener /ˈlɪsənəʳ/ [n C] someone who listens to the radio – used especially by people in the radio business

When you see **EC**, go to the **ESSENTIAL COMMUNICATION** section.

10 equipment for recording television programmes

video BRITISH **VCR** ESPECIALLY AMERICAN /ˈvɪdiəʊ, ˌviː siː ˈɑːʳ/ [n C] a machine used for recording television programmes or for showing recorded programmes or films

video /ˈvɪdiəʊ/ [n C] a copy of a film or television recording on video tape, which can be shown using a video machine

tape (also **video** BRITISH) /teɪp, ˈvɪdiəʊ/ [v T] to record a television programme using a video machine: *Could you video 'The Elvis Presley Story' for me at 8.00? | Did you tape the Super Bowl?*

TELL

➡ look here for ...
- tell someone about something
- order someone to do something

⚠ Don't confuse **say, tell, talk,** and **speak.** You **say** words to someone. You **tell** someone facts or information about something. You **talk** to someone about a subject. You **speak** (=you say words) or you **speak** a language.

1 to give someone information

tell /tel/ [v T] to give someone spoken or written information

tell sb (that) *Jane told me you have a new job. | She wrote to tell us that she was getting married.*

tell sb sth *Let's have a cup of coffee and you can tell me all the details.*

tell sb who/what/where etc *Just tell me what happened. | This leaflet tells you how to apply for a driving licence.*

tell sb about sth *Have you told anyone about this?*

telling – told – have told

⚠️ You must always say who you are telling. Don't say 'he told that he was going'. Say **he told me that he was going**. Don't say 'he told about it'. Say **he told me about it**.

⌕**let sb know** /ˌlet (sb) 'nəʊ/ ESPECIALLY SPOKEN to tell someone something important that they need to know or want to know: *If you ever need any help, just let me know.*

+ about *I said we'd let her know about the job by the end of the week.*

let sb know sth *I'll let you know our new address as soon as I have it.*

+ (that) *When you get there, will you phone and let me know you arrived safely?*

let sb know what/where/how etc *Could you let us know what time you'll be home?*

inform /ɪnˈfɔːʳm/ [v T] to officially or formally give someone information about something: *Do you think we ought to inform the police?*

inform sb of sth *You should inform your bank of any change of address.*

inform sb (that) *I am sorry to inform you that your application has been unsuccessful.*

keep sb informed /ˌkiːp (sb) ɪnˈfɔːʳmd/ to give someone regular information about decisions, events etc so that they know what is happening: *I've very concerned about this, so please keep me informed.*

+ of/about *Some parents felt the school had not been keeping them informed about their children's progress.*

give /ɡɪv/ [v T] to provide information about something, especially written information

give information/details/instructions etc *Please give details of all your previous jobs.* | *The handbook gave full instructions on how to change the oil.*

give an account/description/report *The article gave a vivid account of life after the earthquake.*

give sb information/details etc *Could you give me some information on how to apply for a loan?*

giving – gave – have given

break the news /ˌbreɪk ðə ˈnjuːz‖-ˈnuːz/ to tell someone some bad news or something that might upset them

+ to *After Jack's body was found, a policewoman had to break the news to his mother.*

communication /kəˌmjuːnɪ̩ˈkeɪʃən/ [n U] when people exchange information and tell each other about their decisions and ideas: *Good communication is essential in a large organization.*

+ between *There seems to have been a breakdown in communication between the police and the army.*

⚠️ You can also use **communication** before a noun, like an adjective: *You need good communication skills to be a teacher.* | *communication problems between managers and employees*

2 to publicly tell a lot of people about something

announce /əˈnaʊns/ [v T] to make a public statement in order to tell people about a decision or about something important that has happened or will happen: *The winner of the award will be announced at a dinner at the Sheraton Hotel.*

+ (that) *Lord McGowan has announced that he will retire at the end of the year.*

⚠️ Don't say 'she announced us that ...'. Just say **she announced that ....**

report /rɪˈpɔːʳt/ [v I/T] to give people news about what is happening, in newspapers, on television, or on the radio: *The local newspaper has reported several cases of meningitis in the area.*

+ (that) *Our correspondent in Rwanda reports that conditions in the refugee camps are filthy and overcrowded.*

+ on *She was sent to Chechnya to report on the independence struggle.*

publicize (also **publicise** BRITISH) /ˈpʌb-lɪ̩saɪz/ [v T] to use the newspapers, television etc to provide information about something such as a new product or a special event, because you want everyone to know about it: *She did a series of radio interviews to publicize her new book.*

well publicized (=mentioned often in newspapers or on television or radio) *The parade was well publicized and thousands came to see it.*

publicity /pʌˈblɪsɪ̪ti/ [n U] when newspapers and television or radio reports attract people's attention to particular information or events: *The judge was forced to resign because of the publicity surrounding his divorce.*
get/receive/attract publicity *Princess Diana's tour of Angola received a lot of publicity.*

3 to tell someone about your feelings

confide in sb /kənˈfaɪd ɪn (sb)/ [phrasal verb T] to tell someone you trust about personal matters which you are worried about and which you do not want anyone else to know: *Maria felt she had no-one she could confide in.*

communicate /kəˈmjuːnɪ̪keɪt/ [v I] to make your feelings or thoughts clear to other people by talking to them: *Counselling may help married couples to start to communicate again.*
+ with *She's not very good at communicating with young people.*

4 to tell something that was a secret

tell /tel/ [v T] to tell someone something that should be kept secret: *What did she say? Tell me!*
tell sb where/what/who etc *He didn't tell me where he got this information.*
tell sb about sth *Don't tell anyone about this just yet.*
tell sb a secret *I'll tell you a secret – Beth has a new boyfriend!*

reveal /rɪˈviːl/ [v T] ESPECIALLY WRITTEN to let people know about something that was previously kept secret, especially something embarrassing: *What actually happened to the gold has never been revealed.*
+ (that) *Markov revealed that he had once worked for the CIA.*

leak /liːk/ [v T] to deliberately give secret government information to a newspaper or television company: *The Congressman was furious that the report had been leaked.*

leak sth to sb *The contents of the fax were leaked to the press.*
leak [n C] *The scandal began with a leak to 'The Times'.*

5 to tell the police about a crime or criminal
➡ see also **CRIME, POLICE**

report /rɪˈpɔːʳt/ [v T] to tell the police or someone in authority about a crime, an accident etc: *I'd like to report a theft.*
report sth to sb *Sally was too scared to report the attack to the police.*

inform on sb /ɪnˈfɔːʳm ɒn (sb)‖-ɑːn-/ [phrasal verb T] to secretly tell the police that someone you know is responsible for a crime: *He informed on his brother, who was later arrested for drug-dealing.*

talk /tɔːk/ [v I] to give the police information about a crime when they ask you questions about it: *The suspect was questioned for six hours but refused to talk.*

tip off /ˌtɪp ˈɒf‖-ˈɔːf/ [phrasal verb T] to secretly tell someone such as the police about a crime that is planned, so that they can prevent it
tip off sb *Someone must have tipped off the police. They were already waiting at the house.*
tip sb off *I wonder who tipped them off.*
tip-off [n C] a piece of information, secretly given to someone such as the police, about a crime that is planned: *Acting on a tip-off, customs officers searched the vehicle for drugs.*

informer /ɪnˈfɔːʳməʳ/ [n C] someone who is part of a criminal group but who secretly tells the police about its activities: *An informer had warned the police about the bombing.*

6 to tell someone that they must do something

tell /tel/ [v T] to tell someone that they must do something: *"Wait here!" he told the children.*
tell sb to do sth *Tell her to come and see me as soon as possible!*
tell sb not to do sth *She told him not to phone her again.*
tell sb what to do *I'm sick of being told what to do by my parents.*

tell sb (that) *Ian's teachers keep telling him that he must work harder.* | *The doctor told me I should give up smoking.*

Qdo as you're told! SPOKEN (used to tell children to obey) *Do as you're told and go and wash your hands!*

> ⚠ Don't say 'he told to me to stop'. Say **he told me to stop**.

order /ˈɔːʳdəʳ/ [v T] to tell someone to do something, either officially or in an angry, threatening way: *'Don't move,' he ordered.*

order sb to do sth *The judge ordered Timms to pay £20,000 in legal costs.* | *Army units have been ordered to advance towards the river.*

order sb into/out of/back etc (=order them to go somewhere) *She pointed her gun at him, ordering him out of the room.*

order sth (=give an order that something must happen) *After the plane crash, the Government ordered a full public inquiry.*

ask sb to do sth /ˌɑːsk (sb) tə ˈduː (sth)‖ˌæsk-/ to tell someone politely but firmly to do something or to stop doing something: *Mr Evans, I must ask you to come with me to the police station.*

ask sb not to do sth *Would you ask visitors not to park their cars in front of the entrance.*

give orders/give instructions /ˌgɪv ˈɔːʳdəʳz, ˌgɪv ɪnˈstrʌkʃənz/ if someone such as a leader or officer **gives orders** or **gives instructions**, they tell other people exactly what they must do

give sb orders/instructions to do sth *The General has given them orders to bomb the city.*

+ that *We were given strict instructions that nobody should enter the building without a security card.*

on sb's orders/on sb's instructions /ɒn (sb's) ˈɔːʳdəʳz, ɒn (sb's) ɪnˈstrʌkʃənz/ if you do something **on** someone's **orders**, or **on** someone's **instructions**, you do it because they have officially told you to do it: *On the instructions of the new military government, soldiers burned books and other documents.*

acting on sb's orders/instructions (=doing what someone has told you to do) *Sergeant Dean claims that he was acting on the orders of the police chief.*

7 to give orders in a rude, unpleasant way

order sb around (also **order sb about** BRITISH) /ˈɔːʳdəʳ (sb) əˈraʊnd, ˈɔːʳdəʳ (sb) əˈbaʊt/ [phrasal verb T] if someone **orders you around** or **orders you about**, they keep telling you what to do in an annoying or unfair way, and they seem to enjoy it: *I hate the way she's always ordering us around.* | *You have no right to order the children around like that.*

push sb around /ˌpʊʃ (sb) əˈraʊnd/ [phrasal verb T] to tell someone what to do in a rude or threatening way: *Tom was a bully who enjoyed pushing the younger kids around.* | *Don't let Mary push you around – she's not your boss!*

bossy /ˈbɒsi‖ˈbɔːsi/ [adj] someone who is **bossy** enjoys telling other people what to do, although they may not have the right to do it: *Let Simon do things his way, and stop being so bossy!*

8 a statement telling someone to do something

order /ˈɔːʳdəʳ/ [n C] an official statement ordering you to do something, given by someone with the power to do this, especially a military officer: *The commander's orders must be obeyed at all times.* | *We are still waiting for orders from HQ.*

order to do sth *We received an order to attack.*

give (sb) an order *The captain gave the order to fire.*

my/your/their orders (=the orders you have been given) *My orders are to give this letter to the Commissioner.*

instructions /ɪnˈstrʌkʃənz/ [n plural] a statement telling someone what they should do and how they should do it: *The coach kept shouting instructions at his team.*

follow/obey instructions *If you had followed my instructions none of this would have happened.*

instructions to do sth *Scott has just received instructions to return to Washington.*

T

+ on *We were given strict instructions on what to do in an emergency.*

TEST

➡ look here for ...
- a test or examination
- a test done in order to find out about something

➡ if you mean 'something that you get when you finish a course successfully', go to **EDUCATION 12**

EDUCATION   DRIVE
RESULT   see   STUDY
also
TRY   SUBJECT
PASS   LEARN

1 a test of your knowledge or skill

test /test/ [n C] a set of spoken or written questions or practical activities, which are intended to find out how much someone knows about a subject or skill

spelling/reading/biology etc test *Don't forget there's a chemistry test tomorrow.*

driving test *Did Lauren pass her driving test?*

+ on *Listen carefully, because there will be a test on this next week.*

exam /ɪgˈzæm/ [n C] an important test that you do at the end of a course of study or at the end of the school year: *How did you do in your exams?*

history/French/biology etc exam *We have a biology exam tomorrow, and I haven't done any work for it yet.*

entrance exam (=an exam you must pass to enter a school or university)

> ⚠ You can also use **exam** before a noun, like an adjective: *an exam paper* (=the piece of paper that has the exam questions on it) | *When do you get your exam results?*

examination /ɪgˌzæmɪˈneɪʃən/ [n C] FORMAL an exam: *Students are not allowed to talk during the examination.*

quiz /kwɪz/ [n C] AMERICAN a quick short test that a teacher gives to a class: *Oh no, I think we're having a history quiz today.* plural **quizzes**

oral exam (also **oral** BRITISH) /ˈɔːrəl ɪgˌzæm, ˈɔːrəl/ [n C] an exam in which you answer questions by speaking, instead of writing, for example to test how good you are at speaking a foreign language: *I failed the oral exam because my pronunciation was so bad.* | *Nicky got an A in her Spanish oral.*

practical /ˈpræktɪkəl/ [n C] BRITISH an exam that tests your ability to do or make things, rather than your ability to write about them, for example in subjects such as chemistry or cooking: *We've got our chemistry practical tomorrow morning.*

finals /ˈfaɪnlz/ [n plural] the last exams that you take at the end of a university course: *During my finals, I was revising till 3 o'clock in the morning most days.*

> ⚠ In American English, a **final** (singular) is an important exam that you take at the end of a set of classes: *I have a final in chemistry tomorrow.*

2 to do a test or exam

take /teɪk/ [v T] to do a test or exam: *Anna will be taking her music exam in the summer.* | *I took my driving test when I was 18.*

taking – took – have taken

> ⚠ Don't confuse '**take** an exam' (=do it) and '**pass** an exam' (=be successful in it) *Only 25% of the students who took the exam passed it.*

have (also **have got** ESPECIALLY BRITISH) /hæv, həv ˈgɒt‖-ˈgɑːt/ [v T] if you **have** an exam tomorrow, next week etc, you are going to do it then: *I have a written test in the morning, and an interview in the afternoon.* | *Lucy's got her driving test next week.*

having – had – have had

3 to be successful in a test or exam

pass /pɑːs‖pæs/ [v I/T] to achieve a good enough standard to be successful in a test or exam: *Congratulations! I hear you passed all your exams.* | *"Did you pass?" "Yeah, I got a B."*

scrape through /ˌskreɪp ˈθruː/ [phrasal verb I/T] to only just pass a test or exam: *I didn't do very well in Biology – I just scraped through.*
scrape through sth *Jim scraped through his history paper.*

graduate /ˈgrædʒueɪt/ [v I] to get a first degree from a university or college, or to successfully finish your studies in an American high school: *After he graduated, he got a job with a law firm.*
graduate from Harvard/high school/ Manchester University etc *He graduated from Harvard with a degree in Economics in 1982.*
graduate in Law/English/History etc *She graduated in Modern Languages and got a job as an interpreter.*

qualified /ˈkwɒlɪfaɪd‖ˈkwɑː-/ [adj] ESPE-CIALLY BRITISH a **qualified** doctor, teacher, lawyer etc has passed all the exams need-ed to become a doctor, teacher, lawyer etc: *My sister's a qualified nurse.*
get qualified *How long does it take to get qualified?*
fully qualified (=when you have passed all the necessary exams) *She's training to be an accountant, but she's not fully qualified yet.*

4 the result of an examination or school test

grade /greɪd/ [n C] the letter that is put on a student's work to show how good or bad it is: *How were your grades last semes-ter?*
good/bad grade *If Dan gets good enough grades he'll get a scholarship to Michigan State.*

mark /mɑːrk/ [n C] BRITISH the number or letter that is put on a student's work to show how good or bad it is: *"What mark did you get?" "B".*
good/high mark *The highest mark in the class was 75%.*
bad/low mark *You have to do the course again if you get low marks.*
get full marks (=get the highest possible marks) *I got full marks in the history test.*

results /rɪˈzʌlts/ [n plural] BRITISH all the marks that a student gets in a set of tests or examinations, which show whether he or she has been successful or not: *His exam results weren't very good, so he's not sure what he's going to do.*
get good results *Ceri got better results than she expected.*

score /skɔːr/ [n C] AMERICAN the number that shows how well or badly a student has done in an exam, especially an important exam: *Test scores are falling, which means fewer kids get to college.*
high/low score *He's worked so hard he's sure to get a really high score.*

5 to fail a test or exam

fail /feɪl/ [v I/T] to not pass a test or exam: *I failed my Spanish exam three times.* | *"How did Chris do in his driving test?" "He failed."*

flunk /flʌŋk/ [v T] AMERICAN INFORMAL to fail an exam: *I thought I was going to flunk Math, but I got a C.*

6 to give students a test

give sb a test /ˌgɪv (sb) ə ˈtest/ to make someone do a test: *I hope you've been listening carefully, because tomorrow morning I'm going to give you a test.*
+ on *The French teacher gave us a test on irregular verbs, and I got 100%.*

test /test/ [v T] to ask someone written or spoken questions to find out what they know about a subject
test sb on sth *Tomorrow you'll be tested on the main events of the Civil War.*

7 to study in order to prepare for an exam

revise BRITISH **study** AMERICAN /rɪˈvaɪz, ˈstʌdi/ [v I] to spend time reading things again, making notes etc, in order to pre-pare for an exam: *I'm not surprised you failed – you didn't study at all!*
+ for *I was up all night revising for my German literature exam.*
revision /rɪˈvɪʒən/ [n U] BRITISH work you do to prepare for an exam: *She tries to do four hours' revision a day.*

When you see **EC**, go to the **ESSENTIAL COMMUNICATION** section.

8 a test on something to check it or find out about it

test /test/ [n C] a process that is used for finding out important information about something, for example whether a machine is working properly, whether a substance is safe, or whether someone has an illness: *a simple test to show whether the alarm system is working*
carry out a test/do a test *Car designers do tests using wind tunnels.*
+ on *We carry out safety tests on all our products.*
a test for sth (=to find out if something exists) *There is a simple test for diabetes.*
eye/blood/skin etc test (=when your eyes, blood etc are tested) *All our pilots have regular eye tests.*

⚠ Don't say 'make a test'. Say **do a test** or **carry out a test**.

experiment /ɪkˈsperɪmənt/ [n C] a scientific test to find out how something is affected when you do something to it
do/carry out/perform an experiment *They are doing experiments to learn more about the effects of alcohol on the brain.*
experiment on sth (=an experiment using something) *experiments on animals*

trial /ˈtraɪəl/ [n C] a test in which a new product, such as a drug, a weapon, or an aircraft, is used by a small number of people in order to find out if it is safe and effective
+ of *Trials of a new anti-cancer drug have begun in the US.*

9 to do a test on something in order to check it or find out about it

do a test/experiment /ˌduː ə ˈtest, ɪkˈsperɪmənt/ *Today we did an experiment with magnesium.*
+ on *Doctors are doing tests on Greg's heart.*

test /test/ [v T] to do a test on something to find out whether it works or to get more information about it: *Test your brakes to check they are working correctly.* | *testing nuclear weapons*

test sth on sb/sth *These products have not been tested on animals.*
test sth for sth (=to find out whether it has a substance in it) *The water is being tested for signs of chemical pollution.*

experiment on sth /ɪkˈsperɪment ɒn (sth)‖-ɑːn-/ [phrasal verb T] to use something in scientific tests in order to find out how it is affected when you do something to it: *I think it's cruel to experiment on animals.*

THANK YOU

➡ see also **EC THANKING**

1 to say thank you to someone

thank /θæŋk/ [v T] to tell someone that you are pleased and grateful for something they have given you or done for you: *I spent three hours helping her and she didn't even thank me.*
thank sb for sth *We must write and thank Cathy for the present.*
thank sb for doing sth *The Governor publicly thanked the people of Arizona for supporting him during his campaign.*

thanks /θæŋks/ [n plural] what you say, write, or do to thank someone
letter/message of thanks *He wrote me a short letter of thanks.*
without a word of thanks (=without saying thank you) *She got up and left without a word of thanks.*

thank-you letter/thank-you note etc /ˈθæŋk juː (letter etc)/ [n C] a letter etc that you send to someone to thank them, for example when they have given you a present or when you have stayed at their house: *We spent three days after the wedding writing thank-you letters for all the presents we'd had.*

○**say thank you** /seɪ ˈθæŋk juː/ SPOKEN to thank someone for what they have done: *This little gift is our way of saying thank you to everyone who worked so hard.*

When you see **EC**, go to the
ESSENTIAL COMMUNICATION section.

2 when you feel that you want to thank someone

grateful /ˈɡreɪtfəl/ [adj] feeling that you want to thank someone, especially because they have done something for you and helped you a lot: *Dr. Shah has received hundreds of letters from grateful patients.*
grateful to sb for sth *I'm really grateful to you for all your help.*
   gratefully [adv] *We gratefully accepted her offer.*

> ⚠ Don't confuse **thankful** (=happy because something good has happened or something bad has been prevented) and **grateful** (=wanting to thank someone).

gratitude /ˈɡrætˌtjuːd‖-tuːd/ [n U] when you feel grateful: *I'd just like to express my gratitude for all the help I've received.*

3 when someone does not thank you

ungrateful /ʌnˈɡreɪtfəl/ [adj] someone who is **ungrateful** does not thank you when you do something for them, and this makes you annoyed or upset: *Our children are so ungrateful! They don't realize how much we do for them.*

WORD BANK THEATRE

NEWSPAPERS AND MAGAZINES
FREE TIME **FILMS/MOVIES**
MUSIC **ART**
see also
DANCE **ACTOR/ACTRESS**
OPINIONS **BOOKS/LITERATURE**
TELEVISION AND RADIO

1 a place where you go to watch plays

theatre ESPECIALLY BRITISH **theater** AMERICAN /ˈθɪətəʳ/ [n C] a place where people go to watch plays being performed: *They're building a new theatre in the town centre.*
   go to the theatre/theater (=go to a theatre to see a play) *When was the last time you went to the theatre?*

2 the plays that are performed in the theatre

play /pleɪ [n C] a story that is written to be performed by actors in a theatre, or on the television or radio: *his new play 'Fat Men in Skirts'*

theatre

see a play *There's a new play on at the Leeds Playhouse that I'd like to see.*

a Shakespeare play/a Brecht play etc (=a play written by Shakespeare, Brecht etc)

drama /ˈdrɑːmə‖ˈdrɑːmə, ˈdræmə/ [n U] plays in general, especially when they are considered as a form of literature: *the influence of Greek drama on modern playwrights* | *a course in 20th century American drama*

the theatre BRITISH **the theater** AMERICAN /ðə ˈθɪətəʳ/ [n singular] theatres in general – use this to talk about the work of acting in plays, writing plays etc: *a Hollywood actor, who began his career in the theatre* | *a play on the TV which was originally written for the theatre*

production /prəˈdʌkʃən/ [n C] a play, opera, or show performed in a theatre: *a new production of 'Private Lives' at the Curren Theater*

performance /pəʳˈfɔːʳməns/ [n C] when a play is performed: *There are two performances every day, one in the afternoon and one in the evening.*

3 types of play

comedy /ˈkɒmədi‖ˈkɑː-/ [n C/U] a play that is intended to make you laugh: *a comedy starring Julie Walters and Bob Hoskins*

tragedy /ˈtrædʒədi/ [n C/U] a serious play that deals with the bad, violent, or harmful side of human nature, and usually ends with the death of the main character

musical /ˈmjuːzɪkəl/ [n C] a play in which the characters speak, sing, and dance to tell a story: *Andrew Lloyd Webber's musical 'Cats'*

opera /ˈɒpərə‖ˈɑːp-/ [n C] a play in which all the words are sung: *Verdi's last and best opera 'Falstaff'*

opera singer *Luciano Pavarotti, the Italian opera singer, will be appearing tonight in Berlin.*

4 people in the theatre

actor /ˈæktəʳ/ [n C] someone who acts in a play

actress /ˈæktrɪs/ [n C] a woman who acts in a play

⚠ You can use **actor** about a man or woman. Some women prefer to be called **actors** and do not use the word **actress**.

cast /kɑːst‖kæst/ [n singular] all the actors who act in a play: *After the play, there was a big party for the cast.*

a strong cast (=when all the actors in a play are very good)

director /dɪˈrektəʳ, daɪ-/ [n C] the person who is in charge of a play, and who tells the actors what to do

playwright/dramatist /ˈpleɪraɪt, ˈdræmətɪst/ [n C] someone who writes plays: *Ben Jonson was a 17th-century playwright.*

5 to perform in a play

act /ækt/ [v I/T] to perform in a play, especially as a job: *Secretly, she had always wanted to act.*

well/badly acted *I thought the whole play was very well acted.*

play /pleɪ/ [v T] to say the words and do the actions of a particular character in a play: *She is currently playing Ophelia in a new production of 'Hamlet'.*

play the part of *I once played the part of Stella in 'A Streetcar Named Desire'.*

be in/appear in /biː ɪn, əˈpɪər ɪn/ if someone **is in** a play or **appears in** a play, they act as one of the characters in it: *Sir Alec Guinness will be appearing in a new play this autumn.*

rehearse /rɪˈhɜːʳs/ [v I/T] if actors **rehearse**, or **rehearse** a play, they practise their words and actions so they will be ready to perform: *The cast has been rehearsing all summer.*

rehearsal [n C] when actors practise what they must say and do in a play

direct /dɪˈrekt, daɪ-/ [v I/T] to be in charge of a play and tell the actors what to do: *a famous production of 'A Midsummer Night's Dream', directed by Peter Hall*

performance /pəʳˈfɔːʳməns/ [n C] the way in which an actor plays his or her part in a play – use this especially to say how good or bad the acting is

give a powerful/stunning/magnificent performance *She gives a powerful performance as Amelia, the daughter.*

acting /'æktɪŋ/ [n U] the work or skill of performing in plays: *She has done some acting, but is best known as a model.* | *The best thing about this production is the quality of the acting.* | *the acting profession*

6 the person that an actor pretends to be in a play

character /'kærɪktər/ [n C] a person in the story of a play: *Many of the characters in O'Neill's plays are based on his own family.*
main character *The main character is Jerome, a penniless writer living in Brooklyn.*

part /pɑːrt/ [n C] the words and actions of one of the characters in a play: *'Hamlet' is the part that every young actor dreams of.*
play the part of *He played the part of Thomas More in 'A Man for All Seasons'.*

role /rəʊl/ [n C] a character played by an actor in a play
the lead role (=the most important part) *Derek Jacobi is currently playing the lead role in 'Becket'.*

7 what happens in a play

plot /plɒt‖plɑːt/ [n C] the events that happen in a play, and the way in which these events are connected: *a complicated plot*

act /ækt/ [n C] one of the parts that a long play is divided into
first act/second act etc *The main character doesn't appear until the second act.*
Act 1/Act 4 etc *In Act 1, Macbeth decides to kill the king.*

⚠ An **act** is usually divided into several **scenes**.

scene /siːn [n C] a part of a play in which there is no change in time or place: *During the first few scenes of the play, Porter is shown as a vicious bully.*
scene 1/scene 6 etc *The queen dies in Act 5, Scene 6.*
opening scene/closing scene (=the first/last scene) *In the opening scene, we see Leon lying on a bench.*

ending /'endɪŋ/ [n C] what happens at the end of a play: *a happy ending*

8 objects, clothes etc that are used in the theatre

scenery /'siːnəri/ [n C] the wooden or cloth surfaces at the back and sides of the stage, which are painted to look like a house, garden, castle etc

costume /'kɒstjuːm‖'kɑːstuːm/ [n C] the clothes worn by an actor in a play

prop /prɒp‖prɑːp/ [n C] an object or piece of furniture that is used by an actor in a play

lighting /'laɪtɪŋ/ [n U] the way that lights are used to light the stage in a theatre

set /set/ [n C] the whole appearance of the stage, including the scenery, the lighting, and the way things are arranged on the stage

9 the words and noises of a play

script /skrɪpt/ [n C] the words that the actors say in a play

sound effects /'saʊnd ɪˌfekts/ [n plural] noises made in order to create a particular effect during a play, for example the noise of a storm, a gun, or something breaking

10 describing a play

be about /biː əˈbaʊt/ [phrasal verb T] if a play **is about** a person, idea, or set of events, that is the main subject of the play: *It's a play about a group of kids living in Harlem.*

be set in /biː ˈset ɪn/ if a play **is set in** a place or period of time, the story happens in that place or during that time: *The play is set in South Carolina right after the Civil War.*

theme /θiːm/ [n C] one of the main ideas in a play, which the writer develops though the words and actions of the actors: *The main theme of 'Hamlet' is revenge.*

When you see **EC**, go to the **ESSENTIAL COMMUNICATION** section.

THICK

➡ opposite **THIN**
➡ see also **WIDE/NARROW, FAT, LIQUID**

1 thick

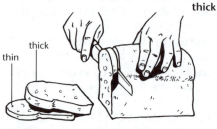
thick
thick
thin

thick /θɪk/ [adj] if something such as a wall, a book, or a piece of glass is **thick**, there is a large distance between its two flat surfaces: *It's an old house with very thick stone walls.* | *The ground was covered in a thick layer of snow.* | *a thick slice of bread* | *shoes with thick rubber soles*

fat /fæt/ [adj only before noun] **fat book/envelope/wallet/briefcase/cigar** a book, envelope etc that is thick because there is a lot in it – use this especially as a humorous way of describing something that looks very thick: *He pulled out a fat wallet stuffed with banknotes.* | *a man smoking a fat cigar* | *a big fat book*

2 how thick something is

how thick /haʊ 'θɪk/ *The price of the glass will depend on how thick it is.* | *How thick is the ice on the lake?*

2 cm thick/1 m thick etc /(2 cm etc) θɪk/ use this to say exactly how thick something is: *Cut the carrots into slices about half an inch thick.* | *In some places, the walls are over two metres thick.*

thickness /'θɪknɪs/ [n C/U] the distance between the opposite surfaces of a solid object or material: *It's about the same thickness as a £1 coin.* | *steel plate in a range of different thicknesses*
+ of *Just look at the thickness of those old walls.*

When you see **EC**, go to the **ESSENTIAL COMMUNICATION** section.

THIN

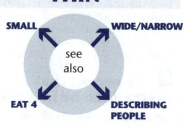
SMALL   WIDE/NARROW
see also
EAT 4   DESCRIBING PEOPLE

1 thin person
➡ opposite **FAT**

thin /θɪn/ [adj] someone who is **thin** has very little fat on their body: *She looked pale, thin, and unhealthy.* | *I wish my legs were thinner.*
thin – thinner – thinnest

slim /slɪm/ [adj] thin in a way that is attractive: *She was tall, slim, and good-looking.* | *You're looking very slim – have you lost weight?*
slim – slimmer – slimmest

skinny /'skɪni/ [adj] very thin, especially in a way that is unattractive: *I was really skinny when I was a teenager.* | *When he wore a T-shirt, you could see how skinny his arms were.*
skinny – skinnier – skinniest

emaciated /ɪ'meɪʃieɪtɪd‖-sieɪtɪd/ [adj] extremely thin as a result of illness or serious lack of food: *News came of the famine, and there were pictures of emaciated children on the TV.* | *I was shocked when I saw her in the hospital – she looked so emaciated.*

2 thin object, layer etc
➡ opposite **THICK**

thin /θɪn/ [adj] if something is **thin**, there is a very small distance between its two flat surfaces: *The lake was covered with a thin layer of ice.* | *a box made of thin plastic* | *a knife with a long, thin blade* | *Despite the cold weather, she was wearing a thin summer dress.*
thin – thinner – thinnest

⚠ Don't use **thin** about roads, rivers, paths etc. Use **narrow**: *a narrow street leading down to the bay*

fine /faɪn/ [adj] very thin – use this about lines, thread, wire etc: *fine lines at the corners of her eyes* | *A fine wire had been stretched across the path.* | *The pencil was sharpened to a fine point.*

3 when someone becomes thinner

lose weight /ˌluːz ˈweɪt/ to become thinner and weigh less: *The best way to lose weight is to do lots of exercise.* | *I'm really worried about my grandmother – she's lost a lot of weight recently.*

lose 5 kilos/7 pounds etc *"How's your diet going?" "Pretty well. I've lost 3 pounds this week."*

go on a diet /ˌɡəʊ ɒn ə ˈdaɪət/ to eat less food than usual, or eat special combinations of food because you want to become thinner and weigh less: *We're both going on a diet after Christmas.*

be on a diet *"Would you like some chocolate?" "No thanks, I'm on a diet."*

THING

→ see also TOOL, EQUIPMENT

1 a thing

thing /θɪŋ/ [n C] use this instead of the name of something when you do not need to say its name or when you do not know what it is called. You can use **thing** when you mean a physical object, or something such as an event, an idea, or something that someone says: *What's that thing on the kitchen table?* | *There were several things that I wanted to discuss.* | *A strange thing happened to me yesterday.* | *The first thing I noticed about him was that he seemed very nervous.*

something /ˈsʌmθɪŋ/ [pronoun] a thing – use this especially when you do not know what the thing is, or you have not decided yet what it will be: *I need to get something for Greg – it's his birthday tomorrow.* | *There was something floating in my coffee.*

something new/different/strange etc *She told me something really funny.* | *He wanted to get her something special, something expensive.*

something else (=another thing) *I've just remembered something else I wanted to tell you.*

something to eat/wear/read etc *I must have something to eat before I go out.*

or something (=or something similar) *There's a stone or a nail or something stuck in my shoe.*

⚠ Don't spell this as 'some thing'. The correct spelling is **something**.

object /ˈɒbdʒɪkt‖ˈɑːb-/ [n C] a solid thing, especially one that you can touch or hold in your hand: *His foot struck a hard object, and he fell.* | *There were many beautiful objects in the room, but the clock was really special.*

⚠ Use **object** especially in writing.

item /ˈaɪtəm/ [n C] one of several things in a list or group of objects, things for sale, or things to be discussed: *The most expensive item we bought was the washing machine.* | *the next item on the agenda for today's meeting*

an item of clothing/furniture/jewellery (=one piece of clothing, furniture, or jewellery) *Thieves broke into the store and stole several items of clothing.*

⚠ **Item** is fairly formal, and is used mostly in business or official contexts.

2 several things of different types

things /θɪŋz/ [n plural] use this when you are talking about two or more things of different types and you do not need to say what they are: *I just threw a few things into a bag and rushed to catch the train.*

🔊**my/your/their things** SPOKEN (=the things that you own or that you are carrying with you) *Don't forget your things.*

all sorts of things (=a lot of different types of things) *They sell furniture, toys, cards – all sorts of things.*

🔊**stuff** /stʌf/ [n U] SPOKEN INFORMAL objects or possessions of different types: *I don't know how we're going to get all this stuff into the car.*

my/your/their stuff *Someone broke in and took most of her stuff.*

junk /dʒʌŋk/ [n U] SPOKEN things that are not useful and should be thrown away, for example because they are old or broken: *I must clean out this cupboard – it's absolutely full of junk.*

odds and ends /,ɒdz ənd 'endz‖,ɑːdz-/ [n plural] several different things, especially small things that are not of much value: *In the drawer she found a photograph, an old hairbrush, and various other odds and ends.*

THINK

➡ look here for ...
- use your mind
- have an opinion

SURE/NOT SURE 🔟 OPINIONS

IDEA see also IMAGINE

REMEMBER BELIEVE/ NOT BELIEVE

1 to think about something

think /θɪŋk/ [v I] to use your mind in order to solve a problem, remember something, make a decision etc: *"Are you going to accept their offer?" "I'm not sure, I need more time to think."*

+ about *She thought about Harry and how kind he'd been.*

think carefully *Think carefully before you answer her letter.*

think hard (=think a lot about something important) *We need to think hard about what we're going to do in the future.*

thinking – thought – have thought

consider /kən'sɪdər/ [v T] to think about something carefully before deciding what to do: *Before buying a car you should consider the cost of insuring it.*

consider doing sth *Have you considered working as a journalist?*

> ⚠ Don't say 'they're considering to sell their house'. Say they're considering selling their house.

think over /,θɪŋk 'əʊvər/ [phrasal verb T] to think carefully about an idea, suggestion, or offer before deciding what to do

think sth over *I just need a few days to think it over before I reply.*

think over sth *I've been thinking over what you said and you're absolutely right.*

2 to think carefully about what you are doing

pay attention /,peɪ ə'tenʃən/ to think carefully about what you are doing, so that you do not make any mistakes

+ to *If you had been paying more attention to your driving, the accident would never have happened. | The teacher said I needed to pay attention to spelling.*

concentrate /'kɒnsəntreɪt‖'kɑn-/ [v I] to think very carefully about something that you are doing, and not allow yourself to be interrupted or to think about anything else: *Turn that music down, please – I'm trying to concentrate.*

+ on *Katie was too upset to concentrate on her book.*

concentration /,kɒnsən'treɪʃən‖,kɑn-/ [n U] the ability to think about something carefully for a long time: *The job requires a lot of concentration, and it's best to be in a room on your own.*

lose concentration *It's easy to lose concentration when driving for long distances.*

keep your mind on sth /,kiːp jɔːr 'maɪnd ɒn (sth)/ to keep thinking about what you are doing, even though you want to think about something else: *Ken was worried about his daughter and found it hard to keep his mind on his work.*

3 to have a particular opinion

think /θɪŋk/ [v T]

+ (that) *I didn't think that the concert was very good. | She thinks I'm crazy to leave this job. | We all thought that the new teacher was very nice.*

what do you think of sb/sth? (=what is your opinion about them?) *What do you think of my new hairstyle?*

thinking – thought – have thought

⚠ Don't say 'I am thinking', 'he is thinking' etc. Say **I think, he thinks** etc: *I think it's a very good movie.*

believe /bɪ'liːv/ [v T] to have an opinion that you are sure is right, especially about something important such as life, religion, or politics
+ (that) *Some people believe that abortion is wrong.* | *We believe the rich should pay higher taxes.*

⚠ Don't say 'I am believing', 'we are believing' etc. Say **I believe, we believe** etc.

feel /fiːl/ [v T] to have a strong opinion, but one which is based on your feelings rather than on facts
+ (that) *Liz's parents feel she isn't old enough to leave home.* | *I just feel that I should have helped him more.*
feeling – felt – have felt

⚠ Don't say 'I am feeling', 'they are feeling' etc. Say **I feel, they feel** etc.

consider /kən'sɪdə^r/ [v T] FORMAL to have an opinion about something, especially after thinking about it carefully
+ (that) *My client considers that she was unfairly dismissed from her job.*
consider sth important/necessary, unsuitable etc *The doctors considered it too dangerous to operate on him.*

regard/see /rɪ'gɑːrd, siː/ [v T] to think that someone or something is a particular kind of person or thing
be regarded/seen as sth *Forty years ago television was regarded as a luxury.* | *America was seen as the land of opportunity.*
regard/see sb as sth *She seemed to regard me as an enemy.* | *She sees herself more as an entertainer than a singer.*
seeing – saw – have seen

figure /'fɪgər‖'fɪgjər/ [v T] AMERICAN INFORMAL to form an opinion about something, after thinking about the situation for a while
+ (that) *I figured he was too drunk to drive.* | *Costello figured that he'd better leave before the police arrived.* | *We figure that they must have got in through the back window.*

⚲ **reckon** /'rekən/ [v T] SPOKEN to have an opinion about something and say what it is: *I think it's quite a good idea – what do you reckon, Peter?*
+ (that) *They reckon the French team's better than ours.*

4 to think something is true, but not be sure

think /θɪŋk/ [v T]
+ (that) *I think I must have left my wallet at work.* | *Jim says he thinks there's something wrong with the engine.*
thinking – thought – have thought

⚠ Don't say 'I am thinking', 'he is thinking' etc. Say **I think, he thinks** etc.

believe /bɪ'liːv/ [v T] to feel almost sure that something is true, because you have information which makes it seem very likely
+ (that) *Scientists now believe that these are the ruins of an ancient temple.* | *Darwin had believed that humans had evolved from apes and similar animals.*

⚠ Don't say 'I am believing', 'he is believing' etc. Say **I believe, he believes** etc.

⚠ **Believe** is more formal than **think**.

suspect /sə'spekt/ [v T] to think that something is probably true, especially something bad, although you cannot prove it
+ (that) *I suspect she was lying.* | *She suspected that he had never really loved her.*

⚠ Don't say 'I am suspecting', 'he is suspecting' etc. Say **I suspect, he suspects** etc.

have a feeling (that) /,hæv ə 'fiːlɪŋ (ðət)/ to think that something is true, although you do not have a definite reason to think this: *He had a feeling he'd been there before.* | *I had a feeling that Ruby didn't really want to talk to me.*

get the impression (that) /,get ðiː ɪm'preʃən (ðət)/ to start to think that something is true because of what you have noticed about a situation: *I get the impression that it's a very good company to work for.* | *We got the impression that most of the people at the party were students.*

5 what you say when you think something is true but you are not sure

Q I think/I believe /aɪ ˈθɪŋk, aɪ bɪˈliːv/ SPOKEN *Carol lives in Toronto now, I think.*
+ (that) *I think that Daniel changed jobs in January. | I believe she's back in Japan now.*
I think so/I believe so (say this to answer 'yes' to a question when you are fairly sure that something is true) *"Has James gone home?" "Yes, I think so."*

⚠ **I believe** is more formal than **I think**.

Q I suppose /aɪ səˈpəʊz/ SPOKEN, ESPE-CIALLY BRITISH say this when you think that something is probably true but are not really sure: *Having a burglar alarm makes you feel safer, I suppose.*
+ (that) *I suppose we can pay by credit card but we'd better check first.*
I suppose so (say this to answer a question) *"Will the children be disappointed?" "Yes, I suppose so."*

Q I guess /aɪ ˈges/ SPOKEN, ESPECIALLY AMER-ICAN say this when you think that something is probably true or has probably happened: *I never married – I just didn't find the right girl, I guess.*
I guess so/not (say this to agree with something that someone has said) *"Looks like Danny will be leaving home soon." "I guess so." | "Ella wasn't happy." "I guess not."*

Q as far as I know /əz ˌfɑːr əz aɪ ˈnəʊ/ SPOKEN say this when you think that something is true, although you realize that you may not know all the facts: *As far as I know, the research program is going well.*

Q I imagine /aɪ ɪˈmædʒɪn/ SPOKEN say this when you think that something is likely to be true, although this is only based on your own opinion about the situation: *You'll want to leave as soon as possible, I imagine.*
+ (that) *I imagine that she feels very lonely now the kids have left home.*

⚠ **I imagine** is more formal than the other expressions here.

6 to wrongly think that something is true when it is not true

think /θɪŋk/ [v T]
+ (that) *I thought you were at work. What's wrong? Are you sick? | She wore a lot of make-up to make them think that she was older.*
thinking – thought – have thought

be under the impression (that) /biː ˌʌndər ði ɪmˈpreʃən (ðət)/ to wrongly believe that something is true, because of something you have heard or seen: *Your mother seems to be under the impression that you want to marry Sophie. | I had always been under the impression that all Americans were rich.*

⚠ **Be under the impression (that)** is more formal than **think**.

imagine /ɪˈmædʒɪn/ [v T] to have an idea in your mind about something, which is in fact the wrong idea
+ (that) *Many people imagine that writers have glamorous and exciting lives.*
you're/he's imagining it *"I think she doesn't like me." "No – you're imagining it."*

7 to think something is probably not true

don't think /ˌdəʊnt ˈθɪŋk/
+ (that) *I don't think there'll be many people at the party.*
Q I don't think so SPOKEN (say this to answer 'no' to a question) *"Is there any coffee left?" "No, I don't think so."*

doubt /daʊt/ [v T] to think that something is probably not true or will probably not happen
doubt if/whether *He doubted whether anyone would believe his story.*
+ (that) *I doubt we'll be going on vacation this year.*
Q I doubt it SPOKEN *"Do you think Bill will have time to help us?" "I doubt it."*

⚠ Don't say 'I'm doubting it'. Say **I doubt it**.

Q I'd be surprised if /aɪd biː səˈpraɪzd ɪf/ SPOKEN say this when you think that something is very unlikely to happen or to be true: *I'd be surprised if Ronnie gets the job – he just doesn't have the right experience.*

8 to decide that something is true, although you have no proof

the idea of sth /ðiː aɪˈdɪə əv (sth)/ what you think about something that might happen to you, for example whether it would be good or bad: *I've never liked the idea of being a father.* | *The idea of working from home is very attractive to many people.*

assume /əˈsjuːm‖əˈsuːm/ [v T] to think that something is true although you have no proof
+ (that) *I just assumed that the woman standing next to Jack was his wife.* | *I assume you all know what you're supposed to be doing today.*

take it for granted (that) /ˌteɪk ɪt fəʳ ˈɡrɑːntɪd (ðət)‖-ˈɡræn-/ to believe that something is true without ever thinking that it might not be – use this especially when in fact you are wrong: *I'm sorry. I just took it for granted that the tickets were free.* | *Nowadays you take it for granted that everyone has a phone.*

presumably /prɪˈzjuːməbli‖-ˈzuː-/ [adv] use this to say that it is likely that something is true, based on what you know about it: *The film was presumably intended for an American audience.* | *"Where's the money for all these wonderful reforms coming from?" "The tax-payers, presumably."*

9 to have an idea or thought in your mind

think /θɪŋk/ [v I/T] to have an idea or thought in your mind, especially one that appears suddenly: *I kept thinking, "What if someone saw me come in?"*
+ of *I've just thought of a really good idea.* | *Has she thought of any names for the baby?* | *We're trying to think of a good place for a picnic.*
think (that) *I thought that I might go to see 'Braveheart' tonight.*
thinking – thought – have thought

have an idea /ˌhæv ən aɪˈdɪə/ to think of an idea about something: *I've had an idea. Why don't we buy her a book about gardening?* | *Let me know if you have any good ideas.*

thought /θɔːt/ [n C] something that you think of: *She told him all her most secret thoughts.*
have a thought *I've just had a thought – why don't we ask Judith?*
+ about *Have you had any thoughts about what you are going to do after university?*
the thought of doing sth *The thought of spending a weekend with Emma made him feel very excited.*
the thought (that) *He couldn't bear the thought that his wife was lying.*
sb's first thought (=the first thing that someone thinks) *My first thought was that he had been taken away by the police.*

cross sb's mind /ˌkrɒs (sb's) ˈmaɪnd‖ˌkrɔːs-/ if a thought **crosses your mind**, you think about it, but only for a short time because you do not want to believe it or think about it: *Leave him? Well actually that thought had crossed my mind.*
it crossed sb's mind (that) *It crossed her mind that maybe Jo was right.*
it never crossed my mind *"Did you think he was lying?" "No, it never crossed my mind."*

10 to think about something too much

be obsessed /biː əbˈsest/ to keep thinking about something all the time, so that you find it difficult to think about anything else
+ with/by *writers who seem obsessed with sex*

obsession /əbˈseʃən/ [n C] a very strong, continuous interest in a particular thing or person, which stops you thinking about anything else: *All they ever talk about is food – it's becoming an obsession.*
+ with *the British obsession with class*

can't get sb/sth out of your mind /ˌkɑːnt get (sb/sth) aʊt əv jɔːʳ ˈmaɪnd‖ˌkænt-/ INFORMAL to be unable to stop thinking about someone or something, even when you do not want to think about them: *He'd only seen the girl once but he couldn't get her out of his mind.*

T

THREATEN
to say you will harm someone if they do not do what you want

CRIME · HURT/INJURE
SHOOT · VIOLENT · see also
KILL · CRUEL

1 to threaten someone

threaten /ˈθretn/ [v T] to tell someone that you will hurt them or cause serious problems for them if they do not do what you want

threaten to do sth *When they found out he was an American, the soldiers threatened to kill him.* | *Every time we have a quarrel, she threatens to leave me.*

threaten sb with a knife/a gun etc *After threatening the manager with a knife, he stole £300 and ran off.*

threaten sb with violence/jail/legal action etc (=say you will hurt someone, put them in prison etc) *I was threatened with jail if I published the story.*

threaten sb *Then he started threatening me, and saying that my family might get hurt.*

blackmail /ˈblækmeɪl/ [v T] to force someone to give you money or do what you want, by threatening to tell embarrassing secrets about them: *Gina tried to blackmail him by threatening to tell his wife about their affair.*

blackmail sb into doing sth *The FBI blackmailed her into informing on the other members of the gang.*

intimidate /ɪnˈtɪmɪdeɪt/ [v T] to try to make someone do what you want by behaving in a way that makes them feel afraid: *He's being kept in jail until the trial so that he can't intimidate any of the witnesses.*

intimidate sb into doing sth *Some voters say they were intimidated into supporting the government.*

When you see **EC**, go to the
ESSENTIAL COMMUNICATION section.

2 words or actions that threaten someone

threat /θret/ [n C] when you tell someone that you will hurt them or cause serious problems for them if they do not do what you want

make threats against sb *Threats have been made against the judge who is investigating the case.*

death threat (=when someone threatens to kill you) *She's decided to leave Hollywood because of the death threats.*

carry out a threat (=do what you threatened to do)

receive a threat *Black families in the area have received threats from right-wing extremist groups.*

threatening /ˈθretnɪŋ/ [adj] **threatening** words or actions are intended to make someone feel afraid, so that they do what you want: *'You listen to me!' His voice was threatening.*

threatening letter/phone call *Before the attack I'd received several threatening phone calls.*

intimidation /ɪnˌtɪmɪˈdeɪʃən/ [n U] when you try to make someone do what you want by making them feel afraid: *Grugel used intimidation and violence to get money from local restaurant owners.*

blackmail /ˈblækmeɪl/ [n U] when you force someone to give you money or do what you want, by threatening to tell embarrassing secrets about them: *They demanded $10,000 for the photos – I knew it was blackmail, but what could I do?* | *Bates got a 5-year jail sentence for blackmail.*

THROW

➡ if you mean 'throw something away because you do not need it', go to **GET RID OF**

1 to throw something

throw /θrəʊ/ [v T] to make something fly through the air by moving your arm quickly and letting it go

throw sth on/onto/across/down etc *Wallace stood on the beach, throwing stones into the waves.*

throw sth at sb (=when you want to hit them) *She was so angry that she threw the pan straight at my head.*

throw sb sth (=when you want someone to catch something) *'Got a light?' Carrie threw him a box of matches.*

throwing – threw – have thrown

toss /tɒs‖tɔːs/ to throw something, especially in a careless, relaxed way

toss sth on/into/at etc *Debbie tossed her purse onto the counter.*

toss sb sth *Could you toss me that pack of cigarettes?*

chuck /tʃʌk/ [v T] INFORMAL to throw something, especially in a careless way

chuck sth on/into/at etc *Tom took off his jacket and chucked it on the bed.*

chuck sb sth (=throw something to someone) *Could you chuck me that book?*

hurl /hɜːrl/ [v T] to throw a heavy object in a violent way, especially because you are angry

hurl

hurl sth at sb (=when you want to hit them) *Some demonstrators began hurling bricks at the police.*

hurl sth into/out of/across etc *He picked up his chair and hurled it across the room.*

flip a coin (also **toss a coin** BRITISH) /ˌflɪp ə ˈkɔɪn, ˌtɒs ə ˈkɔɪn‖ˌtɔːs-/ to throw a coin up into the air and watch which side it falls on, so that you can make a decision about something: *We couldn't decide which movie to go to, so in the end we just flipped a coin.*

flip

2 to throw the ball in a game

➡ see also **SPORT**

pass

pass /pɑːs‖pæs/ [v I/T] to throw the ball to another player in your team, in a game in which the ball is moved by hand

+ to *Johnson passes to White, White passes to Eliot, and Eliot scores!*

pass the ball to sb *The quarterback passed the ball to Olson, who ran in for a touchdown.*

pitch

pitch /pɪtʃ/ [v I/T] to throw the ball when you are playing baseball so that someone from the other team can try to hit it with the bat: *It was Corgan's turn to pitch.*

+ to *He pitched to 8 batters before leaving the game.*

bowl /bəʊl/ [v I/T] to throw the ball when you are playing cricket so that someone from the other team can try to hit it with the bat

bowl

+ to *Cork is bowling to Waugh.*

throw /θrəʊ/ [v T] to throw a ball when you are playing a sport or game: *He threw the ball as hard as he could.*

throw the ball to sb (=so that they can catch it) *Cromartie catches the ball and throws it back to the pitcher.*

throwing – threw – have thrown

TIDY

neatly arranged, with everything in the right place

➡ opposite **UNTIDY**
➡ see also **CLEAN**

1 tidy place/room

tidy /ˈtaɪdi/ [adj] a **tidy** place, room, desk etc looks nice because everything is neatly arranged and in the right place: *Andrew's* *apartment is always so tidy.* | *Try and keep your bedroom a bit tidier.*

clean and tidy *We spent the morning getting the whole house clean and tidy.*

tidy – tidier – tidiest

   tidily [*adv*] *She put her things away tidily in the closet.*

neat /niːt/ [*adj*] carefully arranged or carefully shaped in a way that is nice to look at, with straight lines and clear edges: *He put his clothes in a neat pile on the bed.* | *Mrs Woodie cut the sandwiches in neat squares.* | *rows of white houses with neat little lawns*

neat and tidy *Be sure to leave everything neat and tidy.*

   neatly [*adv*] *All the books were neatly arranged on the shelves.*

immaculate /ɪˈmækjʊlɪt/ [*adj*] extremely clean and tidy: *She keeps the house immaculate – everything's beautifully clean and tidy.*

2 to make a place tidy

tidy /ˈtaɪdi/ [*v* T] to make a room, desk, or drawer tidy: *Tidy your bedroom and then you can go out.* | *I must tidy my desk before I leave.*

tidying – tidied – have tidied

tidy up /ˌtaɪdi ˈʌp/ [*phrasal verb* I/T] BRITISH to make a place tidy, by putting everything back in its right place and removing things that you no longer need: *I haven't had time to tidy up yet.*

tidy up sth *We have to tidy up the house before my parents come to visit.*

tidy sth up *The garden looked much better after we'd tidied it up.*

straighten/straighten up /ˈstreɪtn, ˌstreɪtn ˈʌp/ [*v* T] ESPECIALLY AMERICAN to make a place tidy by putting things in the right place or arranging them neatly: *I spent half an hour straightening the living room.* | *Hogan straightened the pile of papers on his desk.*

clean up /ˌkliːn ˈʌp/ [*phrasal verb* I/T] ESPECIALLY AMERICAN to make a place tidy and clean, by putting things away and removing dust or dirt

clean sth up/clean up sth *Sloan said he had to clean up the house before his in-laws arrived.*

clear up /ˌklɪər ˈʌp/ [*phrasal verb* I/T] BRITISH to get rid of all the things that are making a place dirty or untidy: *Who's going to clear up after the party?*

clear up sth/clear sth up *Clear up the mess you left in the kitchen!* | *It'll take ages to clear this up.*

clear up after sb (=tidy a place after someone else has made it untidy) *I spend my life clearing up after the children.*

3 tidy person

tidy /ˈtaɪdi/ [*adj*] ESPECIALLY BRITISH someone who is **tidy** always likes to keep things neat and in their right place: *Neither she nor Nick were particularly tidy at home.* | *a tidy man who hated messy people*

tidy – tidier – tidiest

neat /niːt/ [*adj*] AMERICAN someone who is **neat** always likes to keep things in their right place: *I've never been very neat but my husband is just the opposite.*

immaculate /ɪˈmækjʊlɪt/ [*adj*] looking perfectly neat and clean, because you take a lot of care about your clothes, your hair etc: *Emma always looks immaculate.* | *James was wearing an immaculate white shirt.*

4 tidy work/writing

neat /niːt/ [*adj*] work or writing that is **neat** has been done very carefully: *Gina has very small neat handwriting.*

TIE/UNTIE

➡ see also **FASTEN**

1 to fasten things together, using rope, string etc

tie /taɪ/ [*v* T] to join one thing to another using rope, string, wire etc

tie sth to/around/onto sth *Don't forget to tie this label onto your suitcase.* | *The washing line was tied to a tree.* | *Saul tied one end of the rope around a large rock and lowered himself over the cliff.*

tie a package/parcel (=keep it closed by putting string or rope around it)

tying – tied – have tied

2 to prevent someone escaping by tying rope around them

tie up /ˌtaɪ ˈʌp/ [phrasal verb T] to tie someone's arms and legs with rope so that they cannot move
tie sb up *The soldiers tied them up and beat them.*
be tied up *Mrs Bennett had been tied up and left in the back of a van.*

tie /taɪ/ [v T] to prevent someone from escaping by tying them with rope etc
tie sb to sth *The terrorists tied the hostages to their chairs.* | *Her horse was tied to a tree.*
tie sb's hands/feet together *The kidnappers had tied his hands together and blindfolded him.*
tying – tied – have tied

⚠ Don't say 'they tied him'. Say **they tied him up, they tied him to the chair** etc.

3 to remove string or rope from something

undo /ʌnˈduː/ [v T] to remove the string or rope from something so that it is no longer held together: *I can't undo the string!* | *She undid the ribbon and let her hair fall over her shoulders.*
undoing – undid – have undone

untie /ʌnˈtaɪ/ [v T] to remove or unfasten the string or rope that joins one thing to another: *Someone had untied the boat and it floated away.* | *It was several hours before anyone found me and untied me.*
untying – untied – have untied

TIGHT

➡ opposite **LOOSE**

1 tight clothes

tight /taɪt/ [adj] **tight** clothes or shoes are only just big enough for you to wear, and they are often uncomfortable: *This skirt is far too tight.* | *tight shoes*

skintight /ˌskɪnˈtaɪt◀/ [adj] **skintight** clothes are very tight and fit exactly to the shape of your body, especially in a way that looks sexually attractive: *skintight jeans*

2 pulled or stretched tight

tight /taɪt/ [adj] rope, wire, cloth etc that is **tight** has been pulled or stretched as far as possible so that it is straight or it cannot move: *If the straps aren't tight enough, the saddle might slip.* | *Drive forward slowly until the towing rope is tight.*

taut /tɔːt/ [adj] WRITTEN stretched very tight – use this with these words: **rope/string/skin/muscles**: *The skin of her face felt dry and taut.* | *Rambo crouched, his muscles taut and ready for action.*

3 fastened tight

tight /taɪt/ [adj] a screw, lid, cover etc that is **tight** has been firmly fixed and is difficult to move: *Check that the screws are tight.* | *The lid's really tight. I can't open it.*

firmly /ˈfɜːrmli/ [adv] if something is **firmly** closed or fixed, it has been closed or fixed so that it cannot move: *Make sure that you put the cork back firmly in the bottle.* | *The posts must be fixed firmly in the ground.*

securely /sɪˈkjʊərli/ [adv] if something is **securely** fastened or fixed, it has been carefully fastened or fixed so that it will not move or open, in order to prevent accidents: *We made sure that our bags were severely fastened to the roof of the car.*

4 to make something tight

tighten /ˈtaɪtn/ [v T] to make something tight, either by fastening it firmly so that it cannot move, or by pulling it until it is tight
tighten a screw/bolt (=by turning it) *Tighten the screws gradually until the wheel is firmly in place.*
tighten a rope/belt/string etc *You can tighten your seat belt by pulling it at this end.*

pull sth tight /ˌpʊl (sth) ˈtaɪt/ to pull a string, rope etc hard, so that it becomes tight: *Brian wrapped some string around the package and pulled it tight.* | *Pull the laces tight and tie them firmly.*

stretch /stretʃ/ [v T] to pull a piece of rope, cloth, rubber etc so that it becomes tight, making it slightly longer than it normally is: *Stretching the cord to its fullest extent, she carried the phone to the other end of the room.*
stretch sth over/between etc *First, stretch the canvas over the frame.*

TIME

➡ if you mean 'spend time', go to
SPEND 6

1 time that can be measured in hours, days etc

time /taɪm/ [n U] what we measure in hours, days, years etc: *How much time do we have for the test?*
spend time (=use your time doing something) *I'd like to spend more time with my family.*
time goes by/passes *The time passed very slowly when I was in prison.* | *As time went by, things started to improve.*

2 a time when something happens

time /taɪm/ [n C] a specific time when something happens or someone does something: *It's my favourite film – I've seen it five times.*
+ (that) *It was the only time I saw her lose her temper.*
time when *Do you remember the time when Dad lost the car keys?*
every/each time *Every time I meet her she asks me about the children.*
next/last/this time *Give us a call next time you're in town.* | *Last time I saw him he was driving a Porsche.* | *We'll do the test again, and this time you can use a calculator.*
the first/second/third time *Is this the first time you've played pool?*

occasion /əˈkeɪʒən/ [n C] FORMAL a time when something happens

on an occasion *Hamilton visited Paris twice that year, and on both occasions he stayed at the Ritz.* | *She had met Zahid on a previous occasion.*

moment/point /ˈməʊmənt, pɔɪnt/ [n C] an exact time when something happens, during a longer process or series of events: *The play went well, apart from one embarrassing moment when I dropped my cup.* | *At several points during the meeting, Adler threatened to walk out.*
at this point/at that moment etc *At that moment there was a knock on the door.* | *At this point the surgeon realized that things were going wrong.*

3 what hour of the day something happens

time /taɪm/ [n C/U] the particular minute or hour of the day when something happens or someone does something
+ of *a notice giving the dates and times of the final examinations*
what time *What time did you get up this morning?*
lunchtime/dinnertime (=the time when you have a meal)

4 asking what time it is

ask sb the time/ask sb what time it is /ˌɑːsk (sb) ðə ˈtaɪm, ˌɑːsk (sb) wɒt ˈtaɪm ɪt ɪz‖ˌæsk-/ to ask someone to tell you the time: *I'd forgotten my watch, so I had to ask someone the time.* | *Go and ask Dad what time it is*

what time is it? (also **what's the time?** BRITISH) /wɒt ˈtaɪm ɪz ɪt, ˌwɒts ðə ˈtaɪm/ SPOKEN say this to ask someone you are with to tell you the time

have you got the time? BRITISH **do you have the time?** AMERICAN /ˌhæv juː gɒt ðə ˈtaɪm, ˌduː juː hæv ðə ˈtaɪm‖ -ˈgɑːt-/ SPOKEN say this to ask someone the time, when you do not know whether they have a watch: *Excuse me, do you have the time?*

When you see **EC**, go to the
ESSENTIAL COMMUNICATION section.

5 telling someone the time

it's five o'clock /ɪts
ˌfaɪv əˈklɒk‖-ˈklɑːk/

it's just after five
/ɪts ˌdʒʌst ɑːftəʳ ˈfaɪv‖-æf-/

it's nearly five /ɪts
ˌnɪəʳli ˈfaɪv/

**it's four forty-five/
it's a quarter to
five** (also **it's a
quarter of five**
AMERICAN) /ɪts ˌfɔːʳ fɔːʳti
ˈfaɪv, ɪts ə ˌkwɔːʳtər tə
ˈfaɪv, ɪts ə ˌkwɔːʳtər əv
ˈfaɪv/

it's ten past five
BRITISH **it's ten after
five** AMERICAN /ɪts ˌten
pɑːst ˈfaɪv, ɪts ten ɑːftəʳ
ˈfaɪv‖-pæst-, -æf-/

it's five thirty (also
it's half past five
BRITISH) /ɪts ˌfaɪv ˈθɜːʳti, ɪts
ˌhɑːf pɑːst ˈfaɪv‖-ˌhæf
pæst-/

6 how to say when something happened or will happen

at /ət; *strong* æt/ [*preposition*] use this with hours and minutes of the day, special holidays, or the beginning or end of a period of time

**at six o'clock/half-past four/midnight/
lunchtime** He starts work at 10, and finishes at 6:30.

at Christmas/Easter/New Year We get a week's holiday at Easter.

at the end/the beginning Frank joined the navy at the beginning of the war.

on /ɒn‖ɑːn, ɔːn/ [*preposition*] use this with particular days: We have a test on the first day of each month.

on Monday/Tuesday/Friday evening etc We're going out to dinner on Friday.

on August 12th/March 2nd etc She was born on May 12th, 1913.

on my birthday/their wedding day It rained on our wedding day.

in /ɪn/ [*preposition*] use this with parts of the day, particular years or particular months, and seasons of the year

in the morning/afternoon/evening I'm usually too tired to cook a meal in the evening. | I went to bed at 3 o'clock in the morning.

in 1892/1997 etc In 1996 the Olympic Games were held in Atlanta.

in January/February/the autumn etc I came to England in the summer of 1995.

> ⚠ Don't use **at, on** or **in** before these words when talking about time: **next, last, that, this.** Say **I'm leaving next Wednesday/this afternoon** etc (not 'on next Wednesday' etc), or **she left last January/that morning** etc (not 'in last January' etc).

> ⚠ In American English, you can say **Mondays, nights, evenings, weekends** etc, without a preposition, when you mean 'every Monday', 'every night' etc: Weekends, I stay with my parents.

ago /əˈɡəʊ/ [*adv*] use this to say how far back in the past something happened

5 minutes/an hour/100 years ago Michael left the office 20 minutes ago.

a long/short time ago *I met your father once, a long time ago.*

a minute/a moment ago *I had my keys a minute ago, and now I can't find them.*

in /ɪn/ [preposition] use this to say how much time will pass before something happens

in an hour/in three days etc *Closed for lunch. Back in one hour.* | *In three days we'll be going off to Italy.*

in an hour's time/100 years' time etc (=in the future, an hour from now, a hundred years from now etc) *You'll be feeling much better in a month's time.*

7 within a period of time

during /'djʊərɪŋ‖'dʊə-/ [preposition] at one point in a period of time, or through the whole of a period of time: *Henry died during the night.* | *She has seen many changes during her life.* | *This place was used as an air-raid shelter during the war.* | *Foxes remain hidden during the day.*

> ⚠ Don't confuse **during** and **for**. Don't say 'I studied French during 5 years'. Say **I studied French for 5 years**. Use **for** to say how long something continues.

in /ɪn/ [preposition] between the beginning and end of a period of time: *They painted the whole house in a single day.*

in the last few months/in the next ten minutes etc *You should get a reply in the next few weeks.*

within /wɪð'ɪn‖wɪð'ɪn, wɪθ'ɪn/ [preposition] during a period or before the end of a period – use this to emphasize that it is a short or limited period of time: *There have been five serious accidents within the last few days.* | *If we do not hear from you within 14 days, we will contact our solicitors.*

by /baɪ/ [preposition] if something happens **by** a particular time, it happens at some time before that time: *If she's not back by 10 o'clock, I'm calling the police.* | *By Christmas, our money problems had become much worse.*

> When you see **EC**, go to the
> **ESSENTIAL COMMUNICATION** section.

8 all through a period of time

through /θruː/ [preposition] during the whole of a period of time, continuing until the end: *The party continued through the night until dawn.*

all through/throughout /ɔːl 'θruː, θruː'aʊt/ [preposition] through – use this to emphasize that something continues from the beginning to the end of a long period: *It closes down all through the winter, and opens again in April.* | *Throughout her career she has worked hard and maintained high standards.*

all day/all morning/all week etc /ɔːl (day etc)/ through all of the day, the morning, the week etc – use this especially when the day, morning etc has not finished yet: *We've been travelling around all week.* | *I haven't seen Sara all day – where is she?*

all the time/the whole time /ɔːl ðə 'taɪm, ðə ˌhəʊl 'taɪm/ through the whole of a period of time – use this especially to talk about something unpleasant or annoying that happens

+ (that) *I was miserable all the time you were away.* | *The whole time we were there he never said thank you, not once!*

9 between two times

between /bɪ'twiːn/ [preposition] in the time between two times or events: *This house was built sometime between 1930 and 1935.* | *We usually go and see Jan's parents between Christmas and the New Year.*

meanwhile/in the meantime /'miːnwaɪl, ɪn ðə 'miːntaɪm/ [adv] during the time between now and a future event, or between two events in the past: *The doctor will be here soon. In the meantime, try to relax.* | *The plane will be ready soon. Meanwhile, please wait in the departure lounge.*

10 how long something continues, someone waits etc

how long /haʊ 'lɒŋ‖-'lɔːŋ/ use this to ask about or talk about how many minutes, hours, days, or years something continues for: *How long have you lived here?* | *I didn't know how long the operation would take.*

for /fər; *strong* fɔːr/ [preposition] use this to say how long something continues
for an hour/two days/a long time etc *It rained continuously for three days.* | *We talked for a while.* | *Eggs should stay fresh for a week or two.*

> ⚠ You can leave out **for** after the verbs 'stay', 'wait', and 'last': *I waited a long time.* | *He stayed nearly three months.*

until (also **till** ESPECIALLY SPOKEN) /ʌnˈtɪl, ən-, tɪl/ [preposition/conjunction] if something happens **until** or **till** a time or event, it continues and then stops at that time or event: *David worked as a teacher until 1989.* | *I'll be at home until 5:30 if you want to phone me.* | *She polished the car until it shone.* | *I didn't learn to drive until I was 31.* | *The library's only open till five on Saturdays.* | *Just wait till I've finished my coffee.*

from ... until ... /frəm ... ʌnˈtɪl .../ use this to say that something starts happening at one time or event and continues until another time or event: *We worked from nine in the morning until late at night.* | *Max edited the paper from 1950 until he retired in 1989.*

from ... to ... /frəm ... tuː .../ use this to say that something starts at a particular time and stops at a later time
from May to September/from 9am to 5pm etc *The hotel is open from March to October.* | *Eisenhower was President from 1952 to 1956.*

through /θruː/ [preposition] **May through September/Monday through Friday etc** AMERICAN starting in May and continuing until September, starting on Monday and continuing until and including Friday, etc: *The store is open Monday through Saturday.*

Monday–Friday/6:00–8:00 WRITTEN starting on Monday and continuing until and including Friday, starting at 6 o'clock and continuing until 8 o'clock etc – used on signs and notices: *Visit the exhibition of modern art, open every day, 9:30-6:00.* | *A special fishing licence is required for the season (May-September).*

11 how long something has been happening

> ⚠ Don't confuse **for** and **since**. Use **for** with periods of time: *I've been waiting here for 25 minutes.* | *We've lived here for six years.* Use **since** with the date, time, year etc when something started: *I've been waiting here since 7 o'clock.* | *I've lived here since 1991/since my husband died.*

for /fər; *strong* fɔːr/ [preposition] during the whole of a period of time until now: *Omar's been learning English for two years now.* | *I haven't phoned my mother for over a week.*

since /sɪns/ [preposition/conjunction/adverb] all the time from a time or event in the past until now: *I've had this car since 1992.* | *Graham's become a lot more confident since he finished his training.* | *I saw her this morning, but I haven't seen her since.*
since then *He arrived in Hollywood back in 1952. Since then he's appeared in over 100 movies.*
ever since (=since a time or event a long time ago) *I read that poem when I was at school, and I've remembered it ever since.* | *She's been interested in animals ever since she was a little girl.*

> ⚠ Don't say 'I lived here since 1985' or 'I live here since 1985'. Say **I've lived here since 1985**. Always use a verb in the perfect tense with **since**.

12 to happen over a period of time

last /lɑːst‖læst/ [v I] to continue happening for a period of time: *No-one knows how long the war will last.*
+ for/until *The hot weather lasted for almost six weeks.*
last 2 hours/all day/a long time etc *Each lesson lasts an hour.* | *a storm that lasted all night*
not last long *Tanya's bad mood didn't last long.*

take /teɪk/ [v T] if something **takes** two minutes, six months etc, that is the time needed to do it

take 2 hours/6 months etc *The drive takes three hours.*

it takes (sb) 2 hours/6 months etc to do sth *It often takes several months to get a visa.* | *It only took us half an hour to get here.* | *How long did it take to get here?*

taking – took – have taken

13 a period of time

period /ˈpɪəriəd/ [n C] ESPECIALLY WRITTEN a particular length of time with a beginning and an end: *You shouldn't sit in front of a computer screen for long periods without a break.*
period of time *The work had to be completed within a limited period of time.*
a ten-day/three-year etc period *The money can be paid back over a five-year period.*
a period of 3 weeks/2 years etc *The project will last for a period of 2 years.*

time /taɪm/ [n singular] a period of time – use this especially to talk about a period in the past, or when you are not saying whether the period was long or short: *Bill had lost his job, and it was a difficult time for him.* | *I really enjoyed my time at university.*
during that/this time *He played for Barcelona for four years, and during that time they won two major competitions.*
for a time *He chatted to us for a time, then left.*
after a time *After a time, I began to feel more relaxed.*

a while /ə ˈwaɪl/ a period of time – use this when you do not want to say definitely how long the period is: *You'll have to wait a while. We're very busy.* | *He lived in Japan for a while.*
a little while *I spoke to Ken a little while ago and he seemed fine then.*
a long while *For a long while, she sat and stared out of the window.*

some time /ˌsʌm ˈtaɪm/ a period of time, especially a fairly long period: *Roach died yesterday. He had been suffering from cancer for some time.* | *Some time later, we all met again.* | *Of course, all this happened some time ago.*

14 a long time

a long time /ə ˌlɒŋ ˈtaɪm‖-ˌlɔːŋ-/ *They've been married for 30 years – that's a long time.* | *The house has been empty for a long time.* | *The accident happened such a long time ago that I can't remember much about it.*
a very long time *It's very well built and should last for a very long time.*

ages /ˈeɪdʒɪz/ [n plural] SPOKEN, ESPECIALLY BRITISH a very long time: *I've been standing here for ages.* | *It's ages since we saw Mark.* | *It takes ages to get to Glasgow by bus.*

hours/weeks/years many hours, weeks, or years and much longer than you think it should be: *My wife had to wait for hours at the hospital.* | *It'll take them years to repair all the damage.*

15 a short time

a minute/a moment /ə ˈmɪnɪt, ə ˈməʊmənt/ [n singular] a very short time: *Helen was here a minute ago. You've just missed her.* | *Can I show you something? It'll only take a minute.* | *Luke thought for a moment and then said: 'Would you like to come too?'*

a second (also **a sec** INFORMAL) /ə ˈsekənd, ə ˈsek/ SPOKEN a very short time – use this especially when asking someone to wait for a short time: *Just a second – I think it's on the desk upstairs.*

not long /nɒt ˈlɒŋ‖-ˈlɔːŋ/ a short time: *"How long will it take?" "Oh, not long – just a couple of hours."* | *His book was published not long after he died.*

a bit /ə ˈbɪt/ [n singular] BRITISH SPOKEN a short time: *Wait a bit, I've nearly finished.* | *Do you mind looking after the kids for a bit while I go out?*

16 at the same time as something else

at the same time /ət ðə ˌseɪm ˈtaɪm/ *Charlie and I arrived at the same time.*
+ as *I arrived at the same time as Charlie.* | *You must have been at Harvard at the same time as I was.*

at once /ət ˈwʌns/ if two or more things happen **at once**, they happen at the same time, and this is annoying or it causes problems: *I can't understand what you're saying when you both talk at once.* | *The problem with my job is that I have to do several things at once.*

as /əz; *strong* æz/ [*conjunction*] ESPECIALLY WRITTEN if something happens **as** something else is happening, it happens at the same time: *As I walked towards the desk, he closed his book and stood up.*
just as (=at exactly the same time) *Just as I was getting into the shower, the phone rang.*

simultaneously /ˌsɪməlˈteɪniəsliǁˌsaɪ-/ [*adv*] if two or more things happen **simultaneously**, they happen at exactly the same time: *The two men aimed their pistols at each other and fired simultaneously.* | *The system can simultaneously search up to 16 databases.*
    simultaneous [*adj*] happening at exactly the same time: *Police carried out simultaneous drug raids on several houses in the area.*

> ⚠ **Simultaneously** is more formal than **at the same time**.

🔢 17 while something else is happening

while /waɪl/ [*conjunction*] during the same period of time that something is happening: *I bought a magazine while I was waiting for the train.* | *I'll just make a phone call while you finish the dishes.*

meanwhile /ˈmiːnwaɪl/ [*adv*] while something else is happening: *Bill was upstairs, talking on the phone. Meanwhile, a burglar had broken in downstairs.*

🔢 18 not too late

on time /ɒn ˈtaɪm/ if you do something **on time**, you do it at the arranged time, not too late: *I'm never going to finish this work on time!*
be on time *The meeting starts at 10 a.m – try to be on time.*
right on time (=exactly at the correct time) *The train arrived right on time.*

in time /ɪn ˈtaɪm/ before it is too late: *If I get home in time, I'll take you swimming.*

just in time (=almost not in time) *You're just in time, Jill. We were about to leave without you.*
+ for *You've arrived just in time for the start of the game.*
in time to do sth *Luckily, we still got to the airport in time to catch the plane.*

punctual /ˈpʌŋktʃuəl/ [*adj*] someone who is **punctual** arrives at the time that was arranged, and does not come late: *It's very important to be punctual for appointments.*
    punctually [*adv*] *The guests arrived punctually at 8 o'clock.*

🔢 19 the right or wrong time to do something

the right time /ðə ˌraɪt ˈtaɪm/ the best time to do something, when you are most likely to get the result that you want
the right time to do sth *It seemed like the right time to start planning something new.* | *I don't think it's the right time to tell Jeff .*
come at the right time (=happen at a time when you need it) *I lost my job last month, so this offer has come at just the right time.*

the wrong time /ðə ˌrɒŋ ˈtaɪm‖-ˌrɔːŋ-/ a time when you should not do something, because you will probably not be successful
the wrong time to do sth *I think this is probably the wrong time to ask for a pay increase.*
come at the wrong time (=happen at a time that is likely to cause problems) *These economic problems have come at the wrong time for the Republican Party.*

a good time /ə ˌɡʊd ˈtaɪm/ a suitable or convenient time: *I'd like to come on Saturday – would that be a good time?*
a good time to do sth *Now is a good time to start applying for jobs.* | *When would be a good time to have a meeting?*

a bad time /ə ˌbæd ˈtaɪm/ an unsuitable or inconvenient time when there are a lot of other problems: *She called at a really bad time – I had just started my homework.*
a bad time to do sth *It's a bad time to be trying to sell your house.*

T

20 the time when something is planned to happen

time /taɪm/ [n C] the time when something is planned to happen

the time of sth *The letter doesn't give the time of the meeting.* | *This leaflet lists the dates and times of all the concerts.*

opening/closing/arrival time *The plane's estimated arrival time is 19:45.*

date /deɪt/ [n C] the day when something is planned to happen: *We need to arrange a date for the next meeting.* | *What date is the wedding?*

+ **of** *June 9th is the date of the European elections.*

timetable BRITISH **schedule** AMERICAN /'taɪm,teɪbəl, 'ʃedjuːl‖'skedʒuːl -dʒəl/ [n C] a list that shows the times when something will happen, for example when planes or buses leave, or when classes at school take place: *Teachers will be giving out copies of the new timetable in the first class today.* | *The schedule's on the bulletin board.*

+ **of** *I want a schedule of flights from Boston to New York.*

schedule /'ʃedjuːl‖'skedʒʊl, -dʒəl/ [n C] a detailed plan of activities that have been organized, showing for example the times when someone will do something, or the times when activities will start and finish: *The President's schedule includes a two-day visit to St Petersburg.*

+ **for** *Do you have a schedule for the tour?*

ahead of/behind schedule (=earlier or later than was planned) *The work is already behind schedule.*

timetable /'taɪm,teɪbəl/ [n C] a plan that shows when parts of an important and long process, especially a political one, will happen

+ **for** *The minister announced a timetable for the discussions.*

> When you see **EC**, go to the
> **ESSENTIAL COMMUNICATION** section.

21 when you have enough time

have time /ˌhæv 'taɪm/ to have enough time to do something: *Could you go and see Jean if you have time?*

have time to do sth *We're so busy at work that I hardly have time to eat.*

+ **for** *Do you have time for a drink?*

there is time /ˌðeər ɪz 'taɪm/ use this to say that there is enough time available to do something or to go somewhere: *I thought we could go to the museum, and maybe an art gallery too if there's time.*

there is time for sth/time to do sth *If we leave now, there should be time for a little shopping.*

find time/make time /ˌfaɪnd 'taɪm, ˌmeɪk 'taɪm/ to arrange your plans so that you have enough time to do something, because you think it is important

+ **for** *I'm really busy but I try to make time for my family.*

find/make time to do sth *a nurse who always finds time to talk to her patients*

22 when you do not have enough time

not have time/have no time /nɒt hæv 'taɪm, hæv ˌnəʊ 'taɪm/ to not have enough time to do something: *I can't talk now – I don't have time.*

+ **to do sth** *She had to leave immediately – she had no time to explain why.*

+ **for** *She doesn't have much time for reading.*

there is no time /ˌðeər ɪz ˌnəʊ 'taɪm/ use this to say that there is not enough time available to do something: *We can't stop to fix it now – there's no time.*

there is no time to do sth *There was no time to say goodbye to everyone.*

run out of time /ˌrʌn aʊt əv 'taɪm/ if you **run out of time**, the time that is available ends before you have finished doing something: *I didn't finish all the questions in the test. I ran out of time.*

TIRED

➡ see also **SLEEP, BORING/BORED, WAKE UP/GET UP**

⚠ Don't confuse **tired** (=when you feel that you must rest) and **tiring** (=when something makes you feel tired) *I'm really tired.* | *What a tiring day!*

1 tired after exercise or work

tired /taɪəʳd/ [adj] if you are **tired**, you feel that you want to rest because you have done a lot of work, walked or travelled a long way etc: *I usually feel too tired to cook dinner after a day at the office.* | *the tired faces of the children in the back of the car*
get tired (=start to feel tired) *Can we stop soon? I'm getting really tired.*
tired out (=very tired) *We were tired out after a long day's skiing.*

exhausted /ɪgˈzɔːstɪd/ [adj] very tired, especially because you have been doing a sport or other hard physical activity, and you have used all your energy: *By the end of the race the runners all looked exhausted.*
completely/absolutely exhausted *We had been walking for over 20 miles, and we were completely exhausted.*

worn out /ˌwɔːʳn ˈaʊt/ [adj not before noun] so tired that you cannot do anything more, especially because you have been working hard: *Come in and sit down. You look worn out.* | *She had spent the whole morning cleaning, washing, and ironing, and now she was completely worn out.*

⚠ Don't say 'very worn out'. Say **completely worn out**.

🔍**knackered** BRITISH **beat** AMERICAN /ˈnækəʳd, biːt/ [adj not before noun] SPOKEN INFORMAL very tired: *I've been up since four o'clock this morning – I'm absolutely knackered!* | *You look beat – what have you been doing?*

⚠ **Knackered** is very informal. Only use it when you are talking to friends, especially young people.

2 wanting to sleep

tired /taɪəʳd/ [adj] if you are **tired**, you feel that you want to sleep: *The kids were really tired, so we sent them to bed.* | *I was going to watch the late-night movie, but I was just too tired.*

sleepy /ˈsliːpi/ [adj] if you are **sleepy**, you want to sleep immediately and your eyes are starting to close: *It was 11.30, and I was starting to feel sleepy.* | *We arrived at the hotel late at night, and were too sleepy to notice how beautiful it was.*
sleepily [adv] *"What time is it?" she said sleepily.*

drowsy /ˈdraʊzi/ [adj] starting to sleep because you are in a warm place or because you have drunk alcohol or taken medicine: *Lisa leaned back in her chair. The wine had made her drowsy.* | *You shouldn't drive after taking these pills – they can make you drowsy.*

yawn /jɔːn/ [v I] to open your mouth very wide and breathe in very deeply through your mouth because you are tired: *I couldn't stop yawning, I was so tired.* | *Vanessa yawned. "I'm going to bed. Night!"*
yawn [n C] the movement and sound you make when you yawn: *There was a big yawn from someone in the back row.*

3 making you feel tired

tiring /ˈtaɪərɪŋ/ [adj] something that is **tiring** makes you feel tired: *The journey was really tiring.*
a tiring day/week *I've had such a tiring day. I just want to take a bath and go to bed.*

exhausting /ɪgˈzɔːstɪŋ/ [adj] something that is **exhausting** makes you feel very weak and very tired: *I had to drive for nine hours without a break. It was exhausting.* | *The band has just finished an exhausting world tour.*

hard /hɑːʳd/ [adj] a **hard** day, journey etc is one that makes you feel very tired because you have to work very hard, travel a long distance, or deal with a lot of problems: *I've had a really hard day at the office – I think I'll go straight to bed.* | *It was a long hard walk back to the nearest town.* | *Looking after babies is hard work.*

strenuous /'strenjuəs/ [adj] **strenuous** activity, work, or exercise needs a lot of physical effort: *My doctor says I mustn't do any strenuous exercise until I'm fully recovered.*

4 the feeling of being tired

exhaustion /ɪgˈzɔːstʃən/ [n U] the feeling of being extremely tired and weak because you have used all your energy: *After two days marching the troops were close to exhaustion.*
from/with exhaustion (=because of exhaustion) *One of the players collapsed with exhaustion, and had to be carried off the field.*

tiredness /'taɪərdnɪs/ [n U] the feeling of being tired: *Tiredness and headaches are common signs of stress.*

drowsiness /'draʊzɪnɪs/ [n U] the feeling of wanting to sleep that you sometimes get when you are in a warm place or when you have drunk alcohol or taken medicine: *The drug can cause drowsiness.*

TOGETHER

TWO   MIX

see also

JOIN   SEPARATE

CONNECTED/NOT CONNECTED

1 together in the same place

together /tə'geðər/ [adv] *The whole family spent Christmas together.* | *Nicola and I were at school together.* | *I keep all my school books together in my desk.*

⚠ Don't say 'I live together with my parents'. Say **I live with my parents** or **my parents and I live together**.

live side by side /lɪv ˌsaɪd baɪ 'saɪd/ if two different groups of people **live side by side**, they live together peacefully and do not fight with each other: *German and Polish peasants had lived side by side there for generations.*

2 doing things together

together /tə'geðər/ [adv] when two or more people do something with each other: *"Did you build that wall yourself?" "My brother and I did it together."* | *We're thinking of going on vacation together.* | *The police and the army worked together to track down the terrorists.*

⚠ Don't say 'I play golf together with Marie'. Say **Marie and I play golf together**.

side by side /ˌsaɪd baɪ 'saɪd/ if two different groups of people fight or work **side by side**, they fight or work together to achieve something, even though there may be big differences between them: *Communists and Nationalists fought side by side.* | *Feminists and religious groups found themselves working side by side to oppose pornography.*

in partnership with /ɪn 'pɑːrtnərʃɪp wɪð/ if people, organizations, or countries work **in partnership with** each other, they work together to do something important or useful: *The city council is working in partnership with local businesses to build new sports facilities in the area.*

3 things done by people working together

joint /dʒɔɪnt/ [adj only before noun] a **joint** decision, statement, effort, report etc is made by people or groups working together, not by just one of them: *We both wanted to move to Canada – it was a joint decision.* | *a joint declaration by Israeli and Palestinian leaders*

combined /kəm'baɪnd/ [adj only before noun] **combined** actions are done by people or groups who try to do something together which they could not do alone: *It took the combined efforts of four police officers and two paramedics to lift the driver from the wreckage.* | *a combined operation involving troops from the US and Europe*

collective /kəˈlektɪv/ [adj only before noun] a **collective** decision, action, or agreement is made by everyone in a group or organization, not by just one or two of its members: *The US wanted the United Nations to take collective action against Iraq.*
collective responsibility (=when everyone in a group shares responsibility for its decisions)

4 when two things are used together, or added together

together /təˈgeðəʳ/ [adv] *Mix the butter and the sugar together.* | *That skirt and jacket look really good together.* | *Together, these two paintings are worth more than £10,000.*

combined /kəmˈbaɪnd/ [adj only before noun] a **combined** amount includes two or more amounts added together; the **combined** effect of two or more things is the effect that they have together: *The combined value of the investments is $5 billion.* | *Her two latest records have sold a*

combined total of 14 million copies. | *He was suffering from the combined effects of heat and exhaustion.*

TOOL
a piece of equipment you use for repairing, cutting, or making things

REPAIR   CUT

see also

EQUIPMENT   MACHINE

tool /tuːl/ [n C] a thing that you hold in your hand and use to repair, cut, or make something: *He couldn't finish repairing the engine because he didn't have the right tools.* | *I keep all my tools in the garage.* | *gardening tools*
+ for *a tool for cutting metal*
tool kit (=a set of tools that are kept together)
tool box (=a strong box that tools are kept in)

instrument /ˈɪnstrʊmənt/ [n C] a small tool used especially by doctors and scientists, for doing careful or delicate work: *I*

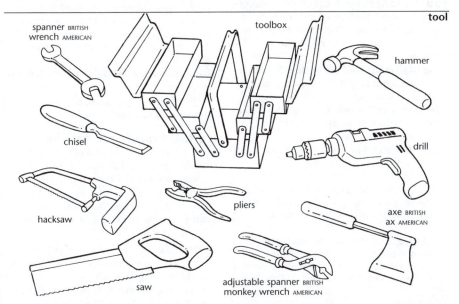

tool

spanner BRITISH
wrench AMERICAN

toolbox

hammer

chisel

drill

hacksaw

pliers

axe BRITISH
ax AMERICAN

saw

adjustable spanner BRITISH
monkey wrench AMERICAN

sat in the dentist's chair and looked at the row of instruments beside me.

gadget /ˈgædʒɪt/ [n C] a small tool that has been cleverly designed to help you do something more easily: *a clever little gadget that lets you chop vegetables into attractive shapes* | *electronic gadgets, such as a watch that you can use as a phone*

device /dɪˈvaɪs/ [n C] a piece of equipment that has been cleverly designed to do a particular job, for example one that makes measurements, records sounds or movements, or controls the operation of a machine: *An EEG is a device that records electrical activity in the brain.*

+ for *a thermostatic device for controlling temperature* | *The farmers there still use the 'Archimedes Screw', an ancient device for raising water from a lake or well.*

TOO/TOO MUCH

⚠️ Don't confuse **too** (=more than enough, more than is right, or more than is necessary) and **very**. Don't say 'it's too interesting'. Say **it's very interesting** or **it's really interesting**.

1 too

too /tuː/ [adv] more than is right or necessary, or more than you want: *They didn't give him the job. They said he was too old.* | *You mustn't work too hard.* | *It's too hot in here.*

too big/small/tired etc to do sth *The car was too wide to get through the gate.* | *She's still too upset to talk about it.*

far too small/much too big etc *$200! That's far too expensive.* | *He was driving much too fast.*

too old/quick/big etc for *My room's too narrow for a king-size bed.*

⚠️ Don't say 'it's a too big house'. Say **the house is too big**. Don't use **too big**, **too fast**, **too difficult** etc before a noun.

⚠️ Don't say 'he was too much old'. Say **he was too old** or **he was much too old**. Don't use **too much** before an adjective that is not followed by a noun. Just use **too**.

2 too much or too many

⚠️ Use **too much** before uncountable nouns, and **too many** before countable nouns. Don't say 'there are too much cars'. Say **there are too many cars**.

too much /tuː ˈmʌtʃ◄/ [quantifier] use this about amounts or costs: *Jim drinks too much.* | *That kid talks too much.* | *You spend too much time worrying about things.*

far too much *$200 for a room? That's far too much.* | *I'm afraid I put far too much salt in the soup.*

+ for *There was too much baggage for one person to carry.*

too many /tuː ˈmeni◄/ [quantifier] use this about numbers of people or things: *I've brought some more chairs – I hope I didn't bring too many.* | *She can't come – she says she has too many things to do.*

far too many *Far too many people are unemployed.*

+ for *There were too many bags for one person to carry.*

⚠️ **Too many** is used with countable nouns. **Too much** is used with uncountable nouns.

excessive /ɪkˈsesɪv/ [adj] use this about an amount, cost, or level which is much too high, especially when you think it is wrong or unfair that it is so high: *the excessive use of chemicals in farming* | *$15 for two cups of coffee seems excessive.*

3 to do something too much

⚠️ Don't say 'she works too much'. Say **she works too hard**.

try/think/push etc too hard /(try etc) tuː ˈhɑːˮd/ to do something with too much effort, so that you do not get the result you want: *Don't try too hard to impress people. Just be yourself.* | *You're hitting the ball too hard.* | *I think you've been working too hard – you need a rest.*

overdo it /ˌəʊvəˮˈduː ɪt/ ESPECIALLY SPOKEN to do something too much, especially to do too much work or exercise: *You need to take more exercise, but don't* *overdo it.* | *I've been overdoing it lately – it's time I had a vacation.*

overdoing – overdid – have overdone

overreact /ˌəʊvəriˈækt/ [v I] to get too angry or too worried when something happens which is not in fact very serious: *Don't you think you're overreacting a little? I'm only ten minutes late.*
+ to *People have overreacted to the advertisement – we didn't intend to offend anyone.*

4 to say something is much bigger, worse etc than it really is

exaggerate /ɪgˈzædʒəreɪt/ [v I/T] to say that something is much bigger, better, worse, more important etc than it really is: *"He said you walked 30 miles." "Oh, no! He's exaggerating."* | *Newspapers tend to exaggerate their influence on the way people vote.*

exaggeration /ɪgˌzædʒəˈreɪʃən/ [n C/U] when someone says that something is bigger, better, worse, more important etc than it really is: *The report says that 500 people were killed in the blast, but I think that's an exaggeration.*
it is an exaggeration to say/suggest etc sth *It would be an exaggeration to say that we never disagreed, but we certainly worked well together.*

5 not too much

not too much /nɒt tuː ˈmʌtʃ/ *Not too much pizza for me please, I'm on a diet.*
not eat/drink/talk etc too much *Don't talk too much now – you need to rest.*

moderate /ˈmɒdərɪt‖ˈmɑː-/ [adj] not too much – use this about eating, drinking, and other things that could be unhealthy if you did them too much: *Moderate exercise, such as walking and swimming, can help to prevent heart disease.* | *Some doctors believe that moderate drinking is good for you.*

in moderation /ɪn ˌmɒdəˈreɪʃən‖-ˌmɑː-/ if you eat or drink something **in moderation**, you do not eat or drink too much of it: *In moderation, fatty foods are not bad for you.* | *He only drinks in moderation.*

TOTAL
the number or amount that there is when everything has been counted

➡ see also **COUNT/CALCULATE, NUMBER**

1 a total

total /ˈtəʊtl/ [n C] the number or amount that there is, when everything has been counted or added together: *If you add 30 and 45, the total is 75.*
a total of *The three defendants were jailed for a total of 30 years.* | *A total of $950 million was spent on the new transportation system.*

total /ˈtəʊtl/ [adj only before noun] the **total** number or amount is the number that there is when everything has been counted. You can use **total** with these words: **number, amount, cost, value, income, earnings, population, workforce**: *The total cost was far higher than we had expected.* | *People of Chinese origin made up about 10% of the total population.*

altogether/in all /ˌɔːltəˈgeðəʳ◀, ɪn ˈɔːl/ [adv] use this when saying or asking what the total amount is, including everything that could be included: *If you include the crew, there were 40 of us in all.* | *How much do I owe you altogether?*

2 when several numbers produce another number as a total

come to sth /ˈkʌm tuː (sth)/ [phrasal verb T] if the price of something **comes to** £50, $100 etc, this is the total amount when everything is counted: *Including wine, the bill came to $70.* | *How much does it all come to?*

reach /riːtʃ/ [v T] if a total **reaches** 10, 50, 100 etc, it keeps increasing until it is equal to that number: *The famine appeal has reached £45,000.* | *The city's population is expected to reach 12 million by the year 2010.*

make /meɪk/ [v T not in passive] if numbers added together **make** 10, 50, 100 etc, that is the answer or the total: *Two* *plus two makes four.* | *If Jane comes, that makes six of us.* | *There are also eight submarines, making a total fleet of 34 ships.*

making – made – have made

add up to sth /ˌæd ˈʌp tuː (sth)/ [*phrasal verb* T] if a set of several numbers **adds up to** 10, 50 etc, that is the total when you add them all together: *The numbers in each line add up to nine.* | *With the hotel, the flights, and the food, it all added up to much more than I had expected.*

TOUCH

1 to put your hand on someone or something

touch /tʌtʃ/ [*v* T] to put your fingers or hand onto someone or something: *Don't touch the plates – they're hot!* | *I cut my knee last week, and it still hurts if I touch it.* | *Someone's hand touched her arm. She turned around and saw it was Maria.*

feel /fiːl/ [*v* T] to touch something in order to find out how hard, soft, hot, cold etc it is: *Just feel this material – it's so soft!* | *The nurse felt his forehead to see if he had a fever.*

feeling – felt – have felt

run your hand over/along/across/through etc /ˌrʌn jɔːʳ ˈhænd (over etc)/ to move your hand gently across the surface of something, for example to feel what it is like: *She ran her hand over the glossy cover of the magazine.* | *Mr Roberts ran his hand across his bald head and smiled nervously.*

rub /rʌb/ [*v* T] to move your hands or fingers quickly backwards and forwards over part of your body, while pressing down, especially in order to make a pain less severe: *Colin yawned and rubbed his eyes.* | *Bill had fallen on the path, and was rubbing his knee.*

rubbing – rubbed – have rubbed

scratch /skrætʃ/ [*v* I/T] to rub your finger nails hard on part of your skin, for example because it feels painful or uncomfortable: *Don't scratch. It'll make the*

itching worse. | *She was scratching her arm where the mosquito had bitten her.* | *He sat scratching his head, trying to think of the answer.*

fiddle with sth/play with sth /ˈfɪdl wɪð (sth), pleɪ wɪð (sth)/ [*phrasal verb* T] to hold something small in your hands and keep moving it around, especially because you are nervous or bored: *She fiddled nervously with her watch strap.*

2 to touch someone in a gentle or loving way

stroke /strəʊk/ [*v* T] to move your hand or fingers over part of someone's body in a gentle, loving way: *Tim sat beside her and began stroking her arm.* | *Every time you try to stroke the cat it bites your hand.*

pat /pæt/ [*v* T] to touch someone lightly several times with the flat part of your hand, in order to comfort them or to show them that you are pleased: *"Don't worry,"* he said, patting her hand gently.

pat sb on the shoulder/arm/head *She bent down and patted the dog on the head.*

patting – patted – have patted

tickle /ˈtɪkəl/ [*v* T] to move your fingers quickly and gently over a sensitive part of someone's body in order to make them laugh: *Stop tickling my feet!*

caress /kəˈres/ [*v* T] WRITTEN to move your hand or fingers gently over part of someone's body in a loving, or sexual way: *Barbara lovingly caressed the baby's cheek.* | *He put his arms around her and began caressing her.*

3 when one thing touches another

touch /tʌtʃ/ [*v* I/T] if one thing **touches** another thing, it hits the other thing gently; if two things **are touching**, there is no space between them: *It's possible that part of the crane touched the electricity cable.* | *My head almost touched the ceiling.*

be touching *Max and Kate sat side by side, their shoulders touching.*

lean against sth /ˈliːn əgenst (sth)/ [*phrasal verb* T] if something **leans**

against a wall, a fence etc, it touches the wall, fence etc and is supported by it: *There was an old bicycle leaning against the side of the shed.*

4 what something feels like when you touch it

feel /fiːl/ [v] if something **feels** cold, hot, smooth, rough etc, this is the feeling it gives you when you touch it: *When I touched his hands they felt really cold.*
feel like sth *The material feels like cotton but it's actually synthetic.*
feeling – felt – have felt

texture /'tekstʃər/ [n C/U] the way a surface, material, or substance feels when you touch it, especially how rough or smooth it feels: *The wood had a lovely smooth texture.*
in texture (=in the way something feels) *The skin of the fruit is rather coarse in texture.*

⟲**feel** /fiːl/ [n singular] ESPECIALLY SPOKEN the way something feels when you touch it, especially something that feels pleasant
+ of *I like the feel of soft wool against my skin.*

⎡WORD
BANK⎤ ## TOURISM

➡ see pages 796–798

TOWN

➡ see also **COUNTRYSIDE, AREA, HOUSES/WHERE PEOPLE LIVE**

1 a place with houses, streets, and shops

town /taʊn/ [n C] a place with houses, streets, shops etc, which is bigger than a village and smaller than a city: *a small town in the Midwest* | *I live in a town near Paris called St Germaine-en-Laye.*

city /'sɪti/ [n C] a big and important town: *You should visit San Francisco. It's a beautiful city.* | *More and more people moved to the cities, which became increasingly overcrowded.*
the city of Belfast/Jerusalem/Boston etc WRITTEN *The city of Barcelona is famous for its wonderful architecture.* | *the ancient city of Petra*
plural **cities**

⚠ You can also use **city** before a noun, like an adjective: *I don't much like city life.* | *city traffic* | *the old city walls*

village /'vɪlɪdʒ/ [n C] a place with a few houses, shops etc, which is in the countryside and is much smaller than a town: *There are some nice pubs in the villages around here.* | *Benjamas left her village in the north of Thailand and went to live in Bangkok.*

⚠ American people do not usually use the word **village** to talk about places in the US. They usually say **small town**.

capital /'kæpɪtl/ [n C] the city where the government of a country or state is: *Rome is one of the world's most beautiful capitals.*
the capital of France/Korea etc *"What's the capital of Kenya?" "Nairobi."*
state capital (=of one of the states in a large country) *Sacramento is the state capital of California.*
capital city (=the capital) *Dublin, the capital city of Ireland*

urban /'ɜːrbən/ [adj only before noun] in or connected with a city or cities – use this about places or people in cities, or about things that happen in cities or affect cities: *The problem of air pollution is especially serious in urban areas.* | *China's growing urban population* | *urban planning*
urban poverty/unemployment etc *Urban unemployment continues to rise.*

2 the centre of a town or city

centre BRITISH **center** AMERICAN /'sentər/ [n C] the part of a town or city where most of the shops, banks, theatres etc are
+ of *I work in the centre of London, so I can easily go shopping after work.*
city centre/city center *A bomb went off in the city center and 19 people were killed.*
town centre BRITISH *She's gone into the town centre to do some shopping.*

TOWN continues on page 799

TOURISM

see also

HOLIDAY → TRAVEL

VISIT ← → JOURNEY

STAY → TRANSPORT

❶

*Are you going on **vacation**?*

*Yes I went to the **travel agent's** and got these **brochures**, but I can't decide where to go.*

❷ Last year I went to Florida Keys. I like **watersports** so I went **windsurfing, waterskiing**, and **scuba diving**.

❸ I want to **relax** and **laze around** by the pool but my girlfriend's really interested in **culture**. She likes to go to **museums** and **galleries** and places like that.

T

vocabulary

accommodation ESPECIALLY BRITISH **accommodations** AMERICAN /əˌkɒməˈdeɪʃ(ə)n(z)‖əˌkɑː-/ [n U/plural] a room or other place to stay when you are away from home, for example a hotel: *The Tourist Office can help you find accommodations.* | *The accommodation was great, but the food was awful.*

⚠ Accommodations is never used in British English.

B&B/bed and breakfast /biː ənd ˈbiː, ˌbed ənd ˈbrekfəst/ [n C] *We stayed in a little B & B in the Coltswolds.*

book ESPECIALLY BRITISH **make a reservation** ESPECIALLY AMERICAN /bʊk, ˌmeɪk ə rezəˈveɪʃən/ [n T] if you **book** a flight, a room etc, you arrange to travel on a plane, stay in a hotel etc at a particular time in the future: *Have you booked your flight yet?* | *I've made a reservation at the Holiday Inn.*

⚠ In American English, **book** is mostly used about flights rather than hotels

brochure /ˈbrəʊʃər, -ʃʊərˈ‖brəʊˈʃʊər/ [n C] a book advertising the holidays that a company sells, usually printed on shiny paper and full of photographs

camping /ˈkæmpɪŋ/ [n U] when you visit an area and stay in a tent: *The children love camping.*
go camping *We went camping last summer.*

campsite BRITISH **campground** AMERICAN /ˈkæmpsaɪt, ˈkæmpɡraʊnd/ [n C] a place where you can stay in a tent for a holiday, usually with a water supply and toilets, and often with other services such as a swimming pool and a shop: *It was late Friday when we arrived at the campground.*

condominium (also **condo**) AMERICAN **apartment** BRITISH /ˌkɒndəˈmɪniəm, ˈkɒndəʊ, əˈpɑːˈtmənt/ [n U] a set of rooms, including a kitchen and a bathroom, that you can

TOURISM

4 Last year I went **camping**. The **campsite** was good but the weather was terrible. So this year I'm going to stay in a **hotel** or a **B&B**, or maybe I'll rent a **condominium**.

5 You can get some really good **package deals**, you know - especially **off-season**. It's much cheaper than booking your **flight** and **accommodations** separately. And they organize **excursions** so you can see the **sights**.

6 I want to go to a lively **resort** where the **nightlife** is good.

---

rent and stay in when you are on holiday: *We've rented a condo in Texas.* | *a holiday apartment in Spain*

culture /ˈkʌltʃər/ [n U] the art, music, literature, and history of a country or area

excursion /ɪkˈskɜːrʃən‖-ʒən/ [n C] a short journey arranged so that tourists can visit an interesting place, especially while they are already on holiday: *We went on an excursion to the Pyramids.*

flight /flaɪt/ [n C] a journey on a plane: *Did you have a good flight?* | *I booked my flight to Moscow today.*

hotel /həʊˈtel/ [n C] a building when you pay to stay and eat meals.

⚠ Hotels are given 'stars' to show their quality. Five-star hotels are the very best hotels: *a four-star hotel with two restaurants and a swimming pool*

laze around /ˌleɪz əˈraʊnd/ [phrasal verb I] to relax and enjoy yourself by sitting or lying down and not doing anything active like walking or swimming

nightlife /ˈnaɪtlaɪf/ [n U] entertainment in the evening and night, such as bars and nightclubs: *The only nightlife in the town is based on a few discos and cheap bars.*

off season /ˌɒf ˈsiːzən◀‖ˌɔːf-/ [adj/adv] during the time of year when not many people go on holiday

package deal (also **package tour** AMERICAN **package holiday** BRITISH /ˈpækɪdʒ ˌdiːl, ˈpækɪdʒ tʊər, ˈpækɪdʒ ˈhɒlɪdi/) [n C] a holiday arranged by a company that includes travel, a place to stay, and sometimes meals, all for a fixed price

relax /rɪˈlæks/ [v I] to make yourself feel calmer, less tired and less worried, by resting or doing something enjoyable: *He works hard all year and like to relax when he's on vacation.*

resort /rɪˈzɔːrt/ [n C] a town where a lot of people often go for holidays

TOURISM continues on the next page

TOURISM

But I don't want to go any where that's too **touristy**. There are too many **tourists** in some resorts.

THEN

8 Some places have been ruined by **mass tourism**.

NOW

---

a seaside/beach/mountain/ski resort *We spent two days in Bangkok, and four days in the seaside resort of Pattaya.*

scuba diving /'skuːbə ˌdaɪvɪŋ/ [n U] the sport of swimming under water using special breathing equipment

sights /saɪts/ [n plural] the famous and interesting places that tourists often visit

see the sights (=spend time visiting the sights) *We spent the afternoon walking around Rome, seeing all the sights.*

sightseeing /'saɪtˌsiːɪŋ/ when you visit famous or interesting places as a tourist: *By this time, I was sick of sightseeing.*
go sightseeing *After lunch, we went sightseeing.*

tourism /'tʊərɪzəm/ [n U] the business selling holidays and providing things for people to do, places for them to stay etc while they are on holiday: *The country depends on tourism for most of its income.*

mass tourism (= when there are very many tourists in an area and this changes its character.)

tourist /'tʊərɪst/ [n C] someone who travels or visits a place for pleasure

touristy /'tʊərɪsti/ INFORMAL a place that is **touristy** has a lot of tourists visiting it, often with the result that it becomes less attractive or interesting: *Vancouver's Chinatown is less touristy than San Francisco's.*

travel agent's/travel agency /'trævəl ˌeɪdʒənts, 'trævəl ˌeɪdʒənsi/ [n C] a business that arranges travel and holidays

vacation AMERICAN **holiday** BRITISH /vəˈkeɪʃən, ˈhɒlɪdeɪ||veɪ-, ˈhɑːlɪdeɪ/ [n C] a time when you leave your home and stay in another place to rest and enjoy yourself
go on vacation/go on holiday *She went on vacation to the Bahamas for two weeks.*

water skiing /'wɔːtər ˌskiːɪŋ/ [n U] a sport where you wear skis and are pulled across the surface of the sea by a boat
go water skiing *I went water skiing – it was great fun.*

watersports /'wɔːtərˌspɔːrts/ [n plural] sports played on or in water

windsurfing /'wɪnd ˌsɜːrfɪŋ/ [n U] the sport of sailing across water by standing on a board and holding on to a large sail

TOWN continued from page 795

downtown /ˈdaʊntaʊn/ [adv] AMERICAN in or to the part of a city where most of the shops, banks, theatres etc are: *She lives in a really beautiful apartment downtown.*
go downtown *I have to go downtown later.*
> **downtown** [adj only before noun] *a downtown hotel* | *Rick got into his car and headed in the direction of downtown San Francisco.*

Q in town /ɪn ˈtaʊn/ BRITISH SPOKEN in the part of a town or city where most of the shops, theatres etc are: *I suggest we meet somewhere in town and have lunch together.*
go into town *I'm going into town. Do you want anything?*

inner city/inner-city /ˌɪnəʳ ˈsɪti/ [adj only before noun] **inner city** areas are areas close to the centre of a big city, where many poor people live and there are often social problems: *Crime is a big problem in inner-city areas.* | *children from inner city schools* (=schools in inner city areas)

3 the areas at the edge of a town or city

suburb /ˈsʌbɜːʳb/ [n C] an area outside the centre of a city, where many people live because it is quieter and there is more space than in the centre
the suburbs *More and more people are moving to the suburbs every year.*
a suburb of Tokyo/New York etc *They have just bought a house in Pacific Palisades, a wealthy suburb of Los Angeles.*
> **suburban** /səˈbɜːʳbən/ [adj] in the suburbs: *a typical suburban house*

> ⚠ Don't say 'I live in the suburb' or 'I live in suburbs'. Say **I live in the suburbs.**

the outskirts /ðiː ˈaʊtskɜːʳts/ [n plural] the areas around the edge of a city or just outside it
the outskirts of Tokyo/London etc *By 9 o'clock we reached the outskirts of Berlin.*
on the outskirts *There are plans to build a giant shopping centre on the outskirts of Glasgow.*

> ⚠ Don't say 'in the outskirts'. Say **on the outskirts.** *We live on the outskirts of town.*

out-of-town /ˈaʊt əv taʊn/ [adj only before noun] **out-of-town** shops are built outside a town, so that people from the town have to drive to them: *an out-of-town shopping centre*

4 the town where you are from

home town /ˈhəʊm taʊn/ [n C] the town where you were born or where you lived as a child, or where you live now: *Johnson lived in Seattle for ten years before returning to his home town of Cody, Wyoming.* | *Sarajevo is my home town and I did not want to leave.*

> ⚠ In spoken English use **I'm from** when you want to say where you were born or lived as a child: *I'm from Tokyo. Where are you from?*

home /həʊm/ [n C] the place where you were born or the place where you usually live, especially if this is where you feel happy and want to live: *I've lived in Paris for many years, and it feels like home to me now.* | *Her home, she said, was in Hong Kong, but she hadn't been there since she was a child.*

TRADITION
a belief or custom that has existed among a group of people for a very long time

➡ see also **FESTIVALS AND SPECIAL DAYS, MARRY**

1 a tradition

tradition /trəˈdɪʃən/ [n C] a belief, custom, or a way of doing something that has existed for a very long time in a particular country or among a particular group of people: *A lot of the old traditions are dying out.* | *We always go for a long walk on Christmas morning – it's a family traditon.* | *The story of Dracula is based on various Eastern European traditions.*

+ of *The region has a tradition of wine-making which goes back to Roman times.*

+ that *the tradition that the eldest son inherits all the money*

traditional /trə'dɪʃənəl/ [adj] belonging to the traditions of a country or group of people – use this about music, food, clothes, customs etc: *They play traditional Irish music.* | *dancers wearing traditional African costume* | *the traditional British breakfast of eggs, bacon, and sausages*

it is traditional to do sth *In the US it is traditional to hang candy canes on the Christmas tree.*

traditionally [adv] *a special dish that is traditionally eaten at New Year*

custom /'kʌstəm/ [n C] a way of behaving that has existed for a long time among a group of people, and is considered normal or polite – use this especially to talk about other countries or other times: *an old Chinese custom*

it is the custom (for sb) to do sth *It is the custom in Japan to take your shoes off when you go into someone's house.* | *In those days it was the custom for farmers to give part of their crop to the lord of the manor.*

the custom of doing sth *The custom of sending birthday cards began in the 19th century.*

2 all the customs and beliefs of a country or group

tradition /trə'dɪʃən/ [n U] all the beliefs and ways of behaving that have existed for a very long time in a particular country or among a particular group of people: *Many Americans originated from Ireland, so there is a great respect for Irish tradition in the US.*

by tradition (=according to a tradition) *By tradition, it is the bride's parents who pay for the wedding.*

folklore /'fəʊklɔːʳ/ [n U] old stories which the people in a country or area have told each other for a very long time, and which often contain historical or religious ideas: *According to folklore, Arthur will one day return to become King of Britain.* | *In folklore the snake is often a symbol of evil.*

3 a special event that is part of a tradition

ceremony /'serɪməni‖-məʊni/ [n C] a special formal event which is part of the religious or social tradition of a place, and in which there is a fixed set of words and actions: *After the ceremony we went to a reception at the bride's parents' house.*

hold a ceremony (=have a ceremony) *A ceremony is held every year to remember those who died in the war.*

plural **ceremonies**

ceremonial /ˌserɪ'məʊniəl◄/ [adj] use this about something that is part of a ceremony or that is used in a ceremony: *a ceremonial sword*

ritual /'rɪtʃuəl/ [n C/U] a set of words and actions that are always done in the same way as part of a religious ceremony: *As part of this ancient ritual, the people paint their faces blue to symbolize the ghosts of childhood.*

perform a ritual *The ritual is performed in order to thank the Sun Goddess for the rice harvest.*

WORD BANK **TRANSPORT**

➡ see pages 802–805

TRAVEL

TRANSPORT HOLIDAY

GO — see also → DRIVE

JOURNEY TOURISM

1 to travel to a place

go /gəʊ/ [v I] to go to a place that is far from where you live, especially for a holiday or for business

go to/across etc *We're going to Malta this summer.* | *Mexico? I've never been there.* | *She often goes to Tokyo on business.*

go abroad (=go to a different country) *My grandparents have never been abroad.*
going – went – have gone/have been

> ⚠ **Have gone** and **have been** are used in different ways. Compare these sentences: *She's gone to Moscow* (=she is there now and has not come back yet). | *I've been to Moscow* (=I have visited it at some time in the past, but I'm not there now).

travel /'trævəl/ [v I] to make a journey from one place to another – use this either to talk about going to a place that is far away, or about a journey that you make regularly, for example to work or school
travel to/through/there etc *Jack spent the summer travelling around Europe.*
travel 50 km/100 miles etc *Some of these people had travelled 50 miles to find food.*
+ to *I usually travel to work by car.*
travelling – travelled – have travelled
BRITISH

traveling – traveled – have traveled
AMERICAN

> ⚠ Use **go** to talk about where you go to. Use **travel** to talk about the journey itself.

2 the activity of travelling

travel /'trævəl/ [n U] the activity of travelling: *The job involves a lot of travel.*
air/space/road/rail/travel *New technology has made air travel much safer.*

> ⚠ You can also use **travel** before a noun, like an adjective: *a travel writer* (=someone who writes about travelling) | *travel expenses* (=money that your employer pays you for travelling somewhere)

> ⚠ Don't say 'the travel' when you mean 'the journey' or 'the trip': *The journey to Scotland took over 5 hours* (not 'the travel').

3 different ways of travelling

drive /draiv/ [v I] to travel in a car: *Jenny drove down to the coast for the weekend.*
driving – drove – have driven

fly /flai/ [v I] to travel by plane: *My mother never liked flying.* | *Russell flew to New York with United.*
flying – flew – have flown

sail /seil/ [v I] to travel by any kind of boat or ship: *We sailed from Southampton on May 6th.*

by car/boat/plane/train /bai 'kɑːr, 'bəʊt, 'plein, 'trein/ travelling in a car, boat, plane, or train: *"Did you come by car?" "No, I took the train."* | *Some of the beaches can only be reached by boat.*

> ⚠ Don't say 'with the train', 'with my car' etc. Say **by train, by car** etc.

on foot /ɒn 'fʊt/ if you go somewhere **on foot**, you walk there: *They are trying to cross the Antarctic on foot.*

> ⚠ Don't say 'by foot'. Say **on foot**.

take /teik/ [v T] if you **take** a train, bus, or plane, you travel in it: *We can take the train or drive – it doesn't matter.*
taking – took – have taken

by air/by sea/by land /bai 'eər, bai 'siː, bai 'lænd/ if you travel **by air**, **by sea**, or **by land**, you travel by plane, in a boat, or on land: *It's much quicker if you go by air, but it's also more expensive.*

4 someone who is travelling

traveller BRITISH **traveler** AMERICAN /'trævələr/ [n C] someone who is on a journey: *The First Class section is mostly used by business travellers.* | *an interesting book about European travellers in Africa in the 19th century*
air/rail travellers *80,000 air travellers pass through the terminal every day.*

passenger /'pæsindʒər, -sən-/ [n C] someone who is travelling in a car, boat, plane, or train, but is not the driver or pilot: *The driver and his three passengers were all killed in the crash.* | *The airport is full of angry passengers held up by the strike.*

tourist /'tʊərɪst/ [n C] someone who travels around and visits places for pleasure, while they are on holiday: *Oxford is full of tourists in the summer.*

TRAVEL continues on page 806

> When you see **EC**, go to the **ESSENTIAL COMMUNICATION** section.

TRANSPORT

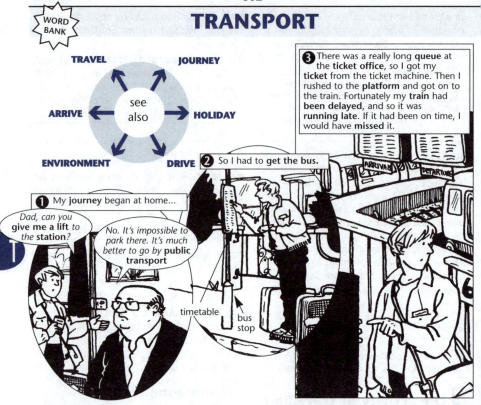

WORD BANK

TRAVEL   JOURNEY

see also

ARRIVE ← → HOLIDAY

ENVIRONMENT   DRIVE

❸ There was a really long **queue** at the **ticket office**, so I got my **ticket** from the ticket machine. Then I rushed to the **platform** and got on to the train. Fortunately my **train** had **been delayed**, and so it was **running late**. If it had been on time, I would have **missed** it.

❷ So I had to **get the bus**.

❶ My **journey** began at home...

Dad, can you **give me a lift** *to the* **station***?*

No. It's impossible to park there. It's much better to go by **public transport**

timetable

bus stop

vocabulary

airport /ˈeəpɔːrt/ [n C] the building where you go at the beginning and end of a journey by plane

arrivals /əˈraɪvəlz/ [n U] the area in an airport where you go after you get off the plane

arrivals board /əˈraɪvəlz ˌbɔːrd/ [n C] a large piece of equipment at an airport or station which shows information about which planes or trains are arriving and at what time

board /ˌbɔːrd/ [v I/T] to get on a plane, ship, train or bus

boarding card /ˈbɔːrdɪŋ ˌkɑːrd/ [n C] a piece of card with your name and seat number printed on it, you show before you get on a plane or ship

bus stop /ˈbʌs stɒp‖-ˌstɑːp/ [n C] the place at the side of the road where buses stop for passengers

by bus/taxi/train/ferry/car etc /ˌbaɪ (bus, etc)/ using a bus, a taxi etc: *"Did you come by car?" "No, by train."*

cabin /ˈkæbɪn/ [n C] a small room inside a ship where you can sleep

change /tʃeɪndʒ/ [v I/T] to get out of one train, bus, or plane and get into another in order to continue your journey
+ at *"Is it a direct flight?" "No, we have to change at Bangkok."*

check in /ˌtʃek ˈɪn/ [phrasal verb I] to go to the desk at an airport to show your ticket, give them your bags and get a boarding card

check-in desk BRITISH **check-in counter** AMERICAN /ˈtʃek ɪn ˌdesk, ˈtʃek ɪn ˌkaʊntərr/ [n C] the place at an airport where you check in

customs /ˈkʌstəmz/ [n U] the place where your bags are checked for goods that you should not bring into a country
go through customs (=walk through the part of the airport or port where your bags are checked)

deck /dek/ [n C] a flat area that you can walk on on the outside or upper surface of a ship

be delayed /ˌbiː dɪˈleɪd/ if a train, plane etc **is delayed**, it will arrive or leave later than the time expected
be delayed by 15 minutes/2 hours etc *Our flight was delayed by 2 hours.*

departures /dɪˈpɑːrtʃərz/ [n plural] the place in an airport where you go before you get on the plane

departures board /dɪˈpɑːrtʃərz ˌbɔːrd/ [n C] a large piece of equipment at an airport or station which shows information about which planes or trains are leaving and at what time

departure lounge /dɪˈpɑːrtʃərz ˌlaʊndʒ/ [n C] the place in an airport where you sit and wait just before you get on your plane

destination /ˌdestɪˈneɪʃən/ [n C] the place that you are travelling to

dining car also **buffet car** BRITISH /ˈdaɪnɪŋ ˌkɑːr, ˌbʊfeɪ ˌkɑːr‖-bəˈfeɪ/ [n C] the part of a train where

TRANSPORT

④ The train journey wasn't too bad, and I managed to get some sandwiches and some coffee from the **dining car**.

⑥ The train was **packed**.

⑤ My train arrived in London. Then I had to get **the underground** to the airport.

*OK, so I go three **stops** along this **line**, and then **change**.*

T

---

you can buy food or drink

duty-free /ˌdjuːti ˈfriː◂ˌduː-/ [*adj*] **duty-free** goods are things such as cigarettes, alcohol, and perfume you can buy at airports or on ships without paying the full price because there is no tax on them

ferry /ˈferi/ [*n C*] a boat that carries people, and sometimes also cars, across a river or across narrow parts of a sea

by ferry *We went to Manhattan by ferry.*

flight /flaɪt/ [*n C*] a journey on a plane: *Did you have a good flight?* | *I booked my flight to Cairo today.*

fly /flaɪ/ [*I*] to travel by plane: *You can fly direct from London to Tokyo.*

gate /geɪt/ [*n C*] the place where you leave the airport building to get on a plane: *Would passengers for flight BA423 please proceed to gate 34.*

get a bus/train/taxi BRITISH **take a bus/train/taxi** AMERICAN /ˈget ə (bus, etc), ˈteɪk ə (bus, etc)/ to use a bus, train or taxi in order to travel somewhere

get on /ˌget ˈɒn‖-ˈɑːn/ [*phrasal verb I/T*] to go into a bus, train etc at the beginning of a journey: *Vince got on the plane and found his seat.*

get off /ˌget ˈɒf‖-ˈɔːf/ [*phrasal verb I/T*] to leave a bus, train etc at the end of a journey: *The train stopped and I got off, but then I realized I'd left my bag behind.*

⚠️ You **get on** a bus, train, plane, or ship, but you **get in** or **get into** a car or taxi: *She kissed him, and then got into her car and drove away.*
You **get off** a bus, train, plane, or ship, but you **get out of** a car or taxi: *Both drivers got out of their cars and started shouting at each other.*

get to /ˌget tuː/ [*phrasal verb T*] to arrive at the place you are travelling to

give sb a lift BRITISH **give sb a ride** AMERICAN /ˌgɪv (sb) ə ˈlɪft, ˌgɪv (sb) ə ˈraɪd/ to take someone somewhere in your car

go by bus/taxi/train/ferry/car etc /ˈgəʊ baɪ (bus, etc)/ to travel by bus, taxi etc: *It'll be much quicker if we go by taxi.*

journey/trip /ˈdʒɜːni, trɪp/ [*n C*] when you travel from one place to another: *Did you have a good trip?*

train/car/bus etc journey an eight hour car journey

train/car/bus etc trip *The bus trip back to Fort Lewis took two hours.*

TRANSPORT continues on the next page

TRANSPORT

7 I arrived at the **airport**, found the right **terminal**, and got a **trolley**. Then I went to **check in**.

check-in desk

Here's your **boarding card**. Go to **gate** 17.

ARRIVALS→
←DEPARTURES

8 I went through **security**, where my bag was **scanned**.

Did you **pack** this bag yourself?

9 I went to the **duty-free** shop, and then waited in the **departure lounge**. I waited there a long time - my **flight** was **delayed** by 4 hours.

DUTY FREE

T

⚠ In American English, **trip** is the usual word for any journey.
In British English, **trip** is the usual word when you travel somewhere, stay for a short time, and then travel back again.
Journey is used especially when you travel a long way or for a long time.

land /lænd/ [v I] if a plane lands, it moves down onto the ground at the end of a journey

line /laɪn/ [n C] the track that a train travels along regularly, stopping at the same stops every time

luggage /ˈlʌɡɪdʒ/ [n U] the bags and cases that you take with you when you are travelling

miss /mɪs/ [T] to be too late for your train, flight etc so that it leaves before you can catch it: *Guy overslept and almost missed his flight.*

on time /ɒn ˈtaɪm/ arriving at the correct time and not late: *These buses are never on time.*

pack /pæk/ [I/T] to put things into a bag or case to take with you on a journey: *Have you packed yet?*

packed /pækt/ [adj] INFORMAL extremely crowded, so that you cannot move easily, and it is difficult to find anywhere to sit or stand

passenger /ˈpæsɪndʒəʳ, -sən-/ [n C] someone who pays to travel on a boat, bus, train, or plane etc

passport control /ˈpɑːspɔːʳt kənˌtrəʊl‖ˈpæs-/ [n U] the place where your passport is checked when you leave or enter a country
go through passport control (=walk through the part of an airport or port where your passport is checked)

platform /ˈplætfɔːʳm/ [n C] the place beside a railway track where you get on and off a train in a station

port /pɔːʳt/ [n C] a place where ships start and finish their journeys

public transport BRITISH **public transportation** AMERICAN /ˌpʌblɪk ˈtrænspɔːʳt, ˌpʌblɪk trænspɔːʳˈteɪʃən -trænspər-/ [n U] buses, trains etc that are provided for anyone to pay and use: *If more people used public transport instead of cars, there would be less pollution.*

queue BRITISH **line** AMERICAN /kjuː, laɪn/ a line of people waiting to enter a building, buy something etc

running late /ˌrʌnɪŋ ˈleɪt/ arriving and leaving later than the planned or expected time
be running late *There has been an accident and all the trains are running late.*

scan /skæn/ [T] if a machine **scans** a bag, it produces a picture of what is inside the bag on a screen, so that officials can check that the bag doesn't contain anything dangerous or illegal

seasick /ˈsiːsɪk/ [adj] feeling as if you want to vomit because of the movement of a boat that you are travelling on

seat /siːt/ [n C] a place on a bus, train etc where you

TRANSPORT

10 Eventually we **boarded** and then **took off**. There was a lot of **turbulence** during the flight, and some of the other **passengers** got very nervous.

11 We **landed** in Athens, and I went through **passport control** and **customs**. You can **fly** to Crete, but it's cheaper to go by **ferry**, so I got a taxi to the **port**. I couldn't afford a **cabin** on the **ferry**, so I just got a **seat**.

12 The **ferry** took 12 hours and I was **seasick**. Eventually I arrived at my **destination**, and **got off** the boat.

---

can sit

security /sɪˈkjʊərᵻti/ [n U] the part of an airport where people's bags are checked for weapons, bombs, or other illegal articles
go through security (=walk through the part of the airport where security checks are made)

station (also **train station** ESPECIALLY AMERICAN) /ˈsteɪʃən, ˈtreɪn ˌsteɪʃən/ [n C] a place where trains stop so that people can get on or off: *The city's central station is right next to the river.*

stop /stɒp‖stɑːp/ [n C] a place where a bus or train regularly stops for people to get on or off: *I must get off - this is my stop.*

take 10 minutes/three hours etc /teɪk (10 minutes, etc)/ if a journey **takes 10 minutes/three hours etc,** you need 10 minutes/three hours, etc to make the journey

take off /teɪk ˈɒf‖-ˈɔːf/ [I] if a plane **takes off**, it goes up into the air at the beginning of a flight

terminal /ˈtɜːrmᵻnəl/ [n C] a large building at an airport or port where people begin and end their journeys

ticket /ˈtɪkᵻt/ [n C] a small printed piece of paper that shows you have paid to travel on a train, bus, plane etc

ticket machine /ˈtɪkᵻt məˌʃiːn/ [n C] a machine that you put money in to get a ticket

ticket office /ˈtɪkᵻt ˌɒfᵻs‖-ˌɔːf-/ [n C] a place where

you can buy tickets

timetable BRITISH **schedule** AMERICAN /ˈtaɪmteɪbəl, ˈʃedjuːl‖-ˈskedʒʊl/ [n C] a list of the times when buses or trains arrive and leave

track /træk/ [n C] the two metal lines that trains travel along

transport BRITISH **transportation** AMERICAN /ˈtræn-spɔːrt, ˌtrænspɔːˈteɪʃən‖-ˌtrænspər-/ [n U] a system for carrying people and goods from one place to another

trolley BRITISH **baggage cart** AMERICAN /ˈtrɒli, ˈbægɪdʒ ˌkɑːrt‖ˈtrɑː-/ [n C] a metal basket or frame on wheels that you put your bags on to move them around in an airport or station

turbulence /ˈtɜːrbjᵿləns/ [n U] irregular movements of a plane caused by strong movements of air which can make your journey uncomfortable

the underground /ðiː ˈʌndəˈɡraʊnd/ [n singular] in London, the system of trains that run under the ground

> ⚠ In London the underground train system is called **the underground** or **tube**, in Paris it is called **the metro**, and in New York and other American cities it is called **the subway**.

TRAVEL continued from page 801

5 buying a ticket

reserve (also **book** BRITISH) /rɪ'zɜːˤv, bʊk/ [v T] to arrange for a seat on a plane, bus, or train to be kept for you to use: *I'd like to reserve a seat on the six o'clock flight to Miami.* | *We booked our tickets months in advance.*

reservation /ˌrezəˤ'veɪʃən/ [n C] an arrangement for a seat on a plane, bus, or train to be kept for you to use: *Do you have a reservation?*

make a reservation *I managed to make a reservation on the last flight to Houston that night.*

ticket /'tɪkᵻt/ [n C] a piece of paper or card which shows that you have paid to travel on a bus, train, plane etc

one-way ticket (also **single ticket** BRITISH) (=a ticket to go to a place, but not to come back)

round-trip ticket (also **return ticket** BRITISH) (=a ticket to go to a place and come back)

season ticket (=a ticket that you can use every day for a period of time)

> ⚠ In British English you can also say a **single** (=a single ticket) or a **return** (=a return ticket) *A single to Cambridge, please.*

fare /feəˤ/ [n C] the amount of money you pay to travel on a bus, train, plane etc: *Last year fares went up by 20%.*

air/rail/train/bus/taxi fare *cheap air fares to New York*

TRICK/DEVEIVE

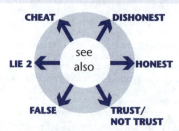

see also

CHEAT
DISHONEST
LIE 2
HONEST
FALSE
TRUST/ NOT TRUST

1 to deliberately make someone believe something that is not true

trick /trɪk/ [v T] to make someone believe

something that is not true, in order to get something from them or make them do something: *I realized then that I had been tricked, but it was too late.*

trick sb into doing sth *The old man's sons had tricked him into signing the papers.*

trick sb out of sth (=take something from someone by tricking them) *They tricked her out of all her money.*

deceive /dɪ'siːv/ [v T] ESPECIALLY WRITTEN to make someone who trusts you believe something that is not true because it is useful for you if they believe it: *He had been deceiving his wife for years – she thought he was working late but all the time he was with Paula.* | *This was a deliberate attempt to deceive the public.*

fool /fuːl/ [v T] to make someone believe something that is not true by using a clever but simple trick: *His false moustache didn't fool anyone.*

fool sb into doing sth *They managed to fool the police into thinking they had left the country.*

☊you can't fool me SPOKEN *You can't fool me – I know he's already given you the money.*

mislead /mɪs'liːd/ [v T] to make people believe something that is not true, by deliberately not giving them all the facts or by saying something that is only partly true: *McFarlane admitted he had misled Congress.* | *They were accused of misleading customers about the nutritional value of their product.*

mislead – misled – have misled

misleading [adj] **misleading** information or statements make people believe something that is not true, especially by not giving them all the facts: *The article was misleading, and the newspaper has now apologized.*

2 something you do in order to trick someone

trick /trɪk/ [n C] a clever plan designed to make someone believe something that you want them to believe, or do something that you want them to do: *The phone call from the hospital was a trick to get him out of the office.*

a trick question (=a question that is cleverly designed to make someone give a wrong answer)

trap /træp/ [n C] a clever plan designed to harm someone, for example by making them go somewhere where they will be caught or attacked, or making them say something they did not intend to say: *Suspecting a trap, I didn't take the money with me.*
fall into a trap (=be deceived because you did not realize someone was trying to trick you) *King asked her a question about taxes, and she fell into his trap.*

TRUE/NOT TRUE

see also

RIGHT   DISHONEST
LIE 2   HONEST
CHEAT   FALSE
TRUST/NOT TRUST   TRICK/DECEIVE

1 true

true /truː/ [adj] something that is **true** is based on real facts and was not invented or imagined: *Everything I have told you is true.* | *The film is based on a true story.*
it is true (that) *Is it true that Tom and Lesley are getting married?*

the truth /ðə ˈtruːθ/ [n singular] the true facts about a situation: *It took the police a long time to find out the truth.*
+ about *We may never know the truth about what really happened to Marilyn Monroe.*
◯**be the truth** SPOKEN (=be true – use this especially to persuade someone that you are not lying) *I've never seen this man before, and that's the truth.*
◯**the truth is (that)** SPOKEN (use this when you are explaining the true facts about something, especially when they are different from what people think) *The truth is she's worried about losing her job.*

tell the truth /ˌtel ðə ˈtruːθ/ to say what really happened or what the true situation is: *Why won't you believe me? I'm telling the truth!*

tell sb the truth *You should have told him the truth.*

> ⚠ Don't say 'she's saying the truth'. Say **she's telling the truth.**

accurate /ˈækjʊrət/ [adj] **accurate** information, figures, descriptions etc are based on facts that are exactly right, and do not contain mistakes: *It is important that people suffering from the disease get accurate information about it.* | *He gave an accurate account of what had happened.*

it is a fact /ɪt ɪz ə ˈfækt/ use this to emphasize that something is definitely true, especially when it is surprising or difficult to believe
+ that *It is a fact that more young people die in road accidents than from any other cause.*

> ⚠ Use **it is a fact** especially in reports and discussions.

2 not true

not true/untrue /nɒt ˈtruː, ʌnˈtruː/ [adj not before noun] *"No-one ever helps me." "That's not true!"* | *There were various rumours about her private life, but they were all untrue.*
it is untrue/not true that *It is not true that all women want to go out to work.*
completely/totally untrue *The papers said he had beat up his wife, which was completely untrue.*

> ⚠ In spoken English, **not true** is much more common than **untrue.**

false /fɔːls/ [adj] not true or not correct – use this about statements or beliefs that are based on untrue information: *He gave a false name and address to the police.* | *This article gives a totally false impression of life in Russia today.* | *Decide whether these statements are true or false.*

not be the case /nɒt biː ðə ˈkeɪs/ to not be true – use this to say that something is not true even though many people believe that it is: *Recent reports suggest that violent crime is increasing, but this is simply not the case.*

> ⚠️ **Not be the case** is fairly formal, and is used especially when writing or talking about politics or other serious subjects.

there is no truth in sth /ðeər ɪz nəʊ ˈtruːθ ɪn (sth)/ if you say that **there is no truth in** something, you mean that it is completely untrue and that people are wrong to suggest that it is true: *There is no truth in the rumour that Collins and his wife are about to divorce.* | *Someone told me the company was losing money, but Bill says there's no truth in this.*

misleading /mɪsˈliːdɪŋ/ [adj] **misleading** information or statements make people believe something that is not true, especially by not giving them all the facts: *The holiday brochure is deliberately misleading, because the hotels it shows are not the ones you actually stay in.* | *These statistics give a misleading impression of what is happening to the economy.*

3 to think of a reason, explanation etc, especially one that is untrue

make up /ˌmeɪk ˈʌp/ [phrasal verb T] to think of a reason, explanation, excuse etc that is untrue
make up sth *If you don't want to go out with Wanda, you'll have to make up some kind of excuse.*
make sth up *When I told them why I was late, they accused me of making it up!*

invent /ɪnˈvent/ [v T] to think of a reason, explanation, or excuse that is sometimes very complicated but completely untrue: *He used to invent strories about his rich lifestyle to impress the women he met.* | *I began to invent reasons for staying away from work.*

> ⚠️ **Invent** is more formal than **make up**, and is used especially in written English.

> When you see **EC**, go to the **ESSENTIAL COMMUNICATION** section.

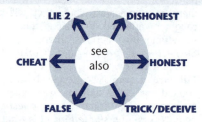

TRUST/NOT TRUST

see also: LIE 2, DISHONEST, CHEAT, HONEST, FALSE, TRICK/DECEIVE

1 when you think someone is honest

trust /trʌst/ [v T] to believe that someone is honest and will not tell lies, cheat you, or do anything that would harm you
can trust sb (=you feel sure that someone is honest) *David's one of my oldest friends – I trust him completely.* | *We found he had been stealing cash from the store, so how can we trust him now?* | *She needs someone to take care of the jewels for her – someone she can trust.*

> ⚠️ Don't say 'I am trusting him'. Say **I trust him**.

trustworthy /ˈtrʌstˌwɜːʳði/ [adj] ESPECIALLY WRITTEN if someone is **trustworthy**, you can trust them because they are completely honest: *Her school report described her as 'an intelligent and trustworthy girl'.* | *We got the information from a trustworthy source.*

2 when you can be sure that someone will do what you want

can depend on sb/can rely on sb /kən dɪˈpend ɒn (sb), kən rɪˈlaɪ ɒn (sb)/ if you **can depend on** or **can rely on** someone, you can be sure that they will do what you want them to do or what you have asked them to do: *"You won't tell anyone about this, will you?" "You can depend on me."*
can depend/rely on sb to do sth *We knew we could rely on Tom to bring some good records.*

reliable /rɪˈlaɪəbəl/ [adj] someone who is **reliable** can be trusted to do what they say they will do and not make any mistakes: *It's strange Ben isn't here: he's usually so reliable.* | *Reliable and hard-working cleaner needed for 3 hours each week.*

responsible /rɪ'spɒnsˌbəl‖rɪ'spɑː-/ [adj] someone who is **responsible** can be trusted to behave in a sensible way, so you do not need to worry that they will do something stupid: *I'm not sure if she's responsible enough to go on vacation without her parents.*

loyal /'lɔɪəl/ [adj] ESPECIALLY WRITTEN someone who is **loyal** can be trusted to always give help or support to their friends, their country, their political party etc: *a loyal supporter of the Green Party* | *She was described as a loyal friend of the Princess.* | *The company fired him, after 30 years of loyal service!*
+ **to** *Most MPs remained loyal to their party leader.*
> **loyalty** [n C/U] loyal behaviour: *The attempted coup failed, thanks to the loyalty of the army.*

3 something that you can trust

reliable /rɪ'laɪəbəl/ [adj] a **reliable** machine, system etc always works well; **reliable** information, books etc do not contain mistakes and are likely to be correct: *I wish we had a more reliable computer system.* | *Do you have a reliable map of the area?*

can rely on sth/can depend on sth /kən rɪ'laɪ ɒn (sth), kən dɪ'pend ɒn (sth)/ if you **can depend on** or **can rely on** something, you can be sure that it will always work well: *You can rely on the postal service here. It's very good.* | *What I need is a car I can really depend on.*

4 not trust

not trust /nɒt 'trʌst/ to not trust someone: *I don't trust these politicians, do you?*
not trust sb with sth (=when you will not let someone have something, because you think they will damage it or steal it) *I wouldn't trust him with my money.*

can't rely on/can't trust (sb/sth) /ˌkænt rɪ'laɪ ɒn, ˌkænt 'trʌst (sb/sth)‖ˌkænt-/ to be unable to trust someone to do what

they say they will do, or to be unable to trust a machine, system etc to work well: *You can't rely on the buses. They're often late.*
can't rely on sb/sth to do sth *That boy's hopeless – I can't rely on him to do anything.*

unreliable /ˌʌnrɪ'laɪəbəl/ [adj] if someone is **unreliable**, you cannot be sure that they will do what they say they will do; if a machine, car etc is **unreliable**, it often stops working and you cannot be sure it will work well: *We could ask our neighbours to feed the cat, but they're a little unreliable.* | *My old car was becoming very unreliable.*

be suspicious of sb/sth /biː sə'spɪʃəs ɒv (sb/sth)/ to have a feeling that you should not trust someone or something, although you are not sure why: *I'm always suspicious of people who offer me money.*
deeply suspicious (=very suspicious) *Parents and teachers are deeply suspicious of the government's plans for education.*

TRY

➡ look here for ...
• try to do something
• try something to see if it is good
➡ see also **TEST**

1 to try to do something

try /traɪ/ [v I/T]
try to do sth *Tim tried to get another job, but he had no luck.* | *I can't come out tonight – I'm trying to finish all my homework before the weekend.*
try not to do sth *Try not to worry – I'm sure she'll be home soon.*
try sth (=try to do something) *If you finish section one, try the exercises on page 25.*
try *"Can Larry fix the car?" "He said he'd try, but I'll probably have to take it to a garage."*
try and do sth *"What time does the game start?" "I don't know. I'll try and find out."*
trying – tried – have tried

⚠️ **Try and do something** means the same as **try to do something**, but is less formal and is not used in past tenses or in the progressive.

attempt /əˈtempt/ [v T] to try to do something, especially something difficult, dangerous, or bad

attempt to do sth *He was attempting to climb Mount Everest without oxygen.* | *They were charged with attempting to overthrow the government.*

attempt sth *Bad weather conditions prevented us from attempting the jump.*

⚠️ **Attempt** is more formal than **try**.

🔾**see if you can do sth** /ˌsiː ɪf juː kən ˈduː (sth)/ SPOKEN to try to do something – use this either to offer to do something for someone, or to ask someone to do something for you

I'll see if I can do sth *If you want to come to the show, I'll see if I can get you a ticket.*

see if you can do sth *See if you can get him to change his mind.*

🔾**have a try** (also **have a go** BRITISH) /ˌhæv ə ˈtraɪ, ˌhæv ə ˈɡəʊ/ SPOKEN to try to do something, even though you think you may not succeed: *"I can't get the lid off this jar." "Here, let me have a try."* | *I've never been windsurfing before, but I'll have a go.*

2 to try hard to do something

try hard /ˌtraɪ ˈhɑːʳd/ to make a lot of effort, because you really want to do something: *You must try harder to get all your homework done on time.* | *No matter how hard I tried, I couldn't get the window to open.*

do your best/try your best /ˌduː jɔːʳ ˈbest, ˌtraɪ jɔːʳ ˈbest/ to try as hard as you can, even when the situation is difficult and you are not sure if you will succeed: *"Can you get it finished by Friday?" "We'll do our best, but we're very busy at the moment."*

do/try your best to do sth *Harry did his best to sound calm, but it was obvious that he was really annoyed.*

make an effort to do sth /ˌmeɪk ən ˈefəʳt tə duː (sth)/ to try hard to do something, especially something which you do not want to do but which you think you should do: *I made an effort to sound interested in what he was saying.* | *I wish you'd make an effort to be friendly to her.*

work at sth /ˈwɜːʳk æt (sth)/ [phrasal verb T] to try hard to improve the way you do something, by practising a lot: *You'll have to really work at it if you want to become a professional dancer.*

3 when you try to do something

attempt /əˈtempt/ [n C] when you try to do something, especially something difficult, dangerous, or bad: *After four attempts, Mike finally passed his driving test.*

attempt to do sth *another attempt to find a solution to the problem* | *It was a deliberate attempt to mislead the voters.*

make an attempt to do sth *The climbers will make another attempt to reach the summit today.*

in an attempt to do sth *The government built hundreds of cheap houses in an attempt to solve the homelessness crisis.*

effort /ˈefəʳt/ [n C/U] the work you do and the energy you use when you try to do something

sb's efforts to do sth *All our efforts to convince her failed.*

put a lot of effort into sth (=work very hard to do it) *Margaret had put a lot of effort into making the party a success.*

4 to eat, use, or do something to find out if it is good, if it works etc

➡️ see also **TASTE**

try /traɪ/ [v T] to eat, use, or do something in order to find out if you like it or if it is successful: *Have you ever tried that chewing gum that's supposed to help you stop smoking?* | *I tried aerobics once, but I didn't really enjoy it.*

try doing sth (=do something to see if it has a successful result) *If the sauce is too thin, try adding some cream.*

trying – tried – have tried

try out /ˌtraɪ ˈaʊt/ [phrasal verb T] to use a new method, product etc, in order to find out how good it is

try out sth I want to try out some of the recipes that I've seen on TV.

try sth out She had just bought a new computer, and couldn't wait to try it out.

taste /teɪst/ [v T] to eat or drink a small amount of something to find out what it tastes like: Come here and taste the soup. Do you think it needs more salt?

experiment with sth /ɪkˈsperɪment wɪð (sth)/ [phrasal verb T] to try different things or methods to find out what effect they have – use this especially about drugs or about styles in art and music: Some children start experimenting with drugs when they are 14 or 15. | The band has been experimenting with different styles and different instruments.

TURN

➡ see also **BEND, AROUND**

1 to turn your head or body

turn /tɜːʳn/ [v I] to turn your head or body so that you are looking in a different direction: Campbell turned and walked out of the room.

turn to sb (=turn to look at someone so that you can say something to them) 'What do you think we should do?' she said, turning to her husband.

turn to do sth She turned to face him and saw that he had been crying.

turn away (=turn in order to avoid seeing something) Julie turned away while the doctor put the needle in her arm.

turn around (also **turn round** BRITISH) /ˌtɜːʳn (ə)ˈraʊnd/ [phrasal verb I] to turn your body so that you are looking in the opposite direction: I turned round quickly to see if anyone was following me. | "Is my skirt too short?" "Turn around and let me see the back."

turn over /ˌtɜːʳn ˈəʊvəʳ/ [phrasal verb I] to change the position of your body while you are lying down, so that you are facing in a different direction: The bed squeaks every time I turn over. | If you find it uncomfortable to sleep on your back, try turning over onto your side.

2 to make something turn

turn /tɜːʳn/ [v T] to make something turn by moving it with your hand: Tim turned the handle slowly and pushed open the door. | We dragged the box into the hall, and turned it on its side.

turn sth around (=so that it is facing the opposite direction) If we turn the table around we can fit more chairs in the room.

turn sth over (=so that its top is facing down and its bottom is facing up) When the pancakes are cooked on the bottom, turn them over and cook the other side.

twist /twɪst/ [v T] to turn something with a quick firm circular movement: "I can't get the top off." "Try twisting it the other way." | She pushed the knife into his stomach and twisted it hard.

3 when something such as a wheel goes around

turn /tɜːʳn/ [v I] if something **turns**, it moves around a fixed central point: Slowly, the wheels of the train began to turn. | We watched in terror as the handle turned and the door creaked open.

go around (also **go round** BRITISH) /ˌgəʊ (ə)ˈraʊnd/ to move in a continuous circular movement: When the fan goes around it moves the air and cools the room.

go around and around (=go around many times) The big wheel went around and around.

spin /spɪn/ [v I] to turn around many times very quickly: The wheels were spinning in the mud, but the car wouldn't move.
+ around The hard disk spins around several times every second.

spinning – spun – have spun

4 to change your direction when you are walking or driving

turn /tɜːʳn/ [v I] to change your direction when you are walking or driving: He saw a police car up ahead, so he turned and went down a side street.

When you see **EC**, go to the **ESSENTIAL COMMUNICATION** section.

turn left/right *Turn left at the next intersection.*

turn back (=turn and go back towards the place that you came from) *After sailing north for an hour, we had to turn back because of fog.*

turn off (=leave a street in order to go down another street) *Turn off Delaney Road just after the church.*

turn onto/into (=start going along another street after changing direction) *Turn onto South Street, then go straight for three blocks.*

change direction /ˌtʃeɪndʒ dɪˈrekʃən/ to turn while you are moving so that you start going in a different direction: *Changing direction on skis isn't difficult once you've learned the technique.*

swerve /swɜːʳv/ [v I] if a vehicle or its driver **swerves**, they change direction very suddenly, especially in order to avoid hitting something: *The driver swerved to avoid a child, and crashed into a signpost.*

5 when a road or river changes direction

bend /bend/ [n C] a place where a road or river curves: *The taxi went around the bend at an alarming speed.*
+ in *a bend in the river*

curve /kɜːʳv/ [n C] a place where a road curves: *He lost control of the car on a sharp curve.*

⚠ In American English, **curve** is more common than **bend** in this meaning.

turn (also **turning** BRITISH) /tɜːʳn, ˈtɜːʳnɪŋ/ [n C] a place in a road where you can turn and go onto another road: *We wanted to go west toward Newark, but I think we missed the turn.* | *Take the first turning after the traffic lights.*

6 when a vehicle turns over in an accident

turn upside down /tɜːʳn ˌʌpsaɪd ˈdaʊn/ if a car, plane, boat etc **turns upside down**, it turns over so that its top is facing down and its bottom is facing up: *The plane had turned upside down and was out of control.*

turn over /ˌtɜːʳn ˈəʊvəʳ/ [phrasal verb I] if a car, train etc **turns over**, it turns upside down or falls on its side as a result of an accident: *The car turned over and burst into flames.*

capsize /kæpˈsaɪz‖ˈkæpsaɪz/ [v I] if a boat or ship **capsizes**, it turns upside down, or falls on its side, and usually sinks: *193 passengers died when their ferry capsized in the English Channel.*

TWO

1 two

two /tuː/ [quantifier] 2: *We have two dogs and three cats.* | *There used to be five churches in the town. Now there are only two.* | *It takes two hours to get there.*
+ of *Two of the boys in the hockey team were sick.*

pair /peəʳ/ [n C] two things of the same type that are used together
a pair of shoes/socks/gloves/earrings etc *I need a new pair of shoes.*

a couple /ə ˈkʌpəl/ [quantifier] BRITISH INFORMAL two: *I haven't got any stamps – could you lend me a couple?*
+ of *I've got a couple of tickets for the game on Saturday.* | *She lived in Japan for a couple of years.*

⚠ In American English, **a couple** usually means 'a small number', but in British English it usually just means 'two'.

2 two people together

couple /ˈkʌpəl/ [n C] two people who are together, especially because they are married or have a sexual relationship: *The couple who live next door are always arguing.* | *a young couple walking hand in hand along the beach*
a married couple (=a couple who are married)

⚠ In British English, you can use **couple** with a singular or plural verb: *An old couple was sitting/were sitting at the next table.* In American English, always use a singular verb.

pair /peə^r/ [n C] two people who are doing something together, or who are similar or connected in some way

+ of a pair of dancers | Annie and Jane were all dressed up, and looked like a pair of movie stars.

in pairs (=working in groups of two) Do the next exercise in pairs.

a strange/funny/friendly etc pair Bill and his brother were a rather odd-looking pair.

3 each one of two people or things

both /bəʊθ/ [predeterminer/quantifier] use this to talk about two people or things together: Paul and I are both scared of spiders. | I can't decide which dress to buy. I like them both. | Both drivers were injured, but not seriously.

both the/these/my etc Both the robbers were wearing masks. | Both her parents are doctors.

both of them/us/the dogs etc Both of us felt sick after eating the fish. | Both of the windows had been broken.

> ⚠ Don't say 'both my children goes to the same school'. Say **both my children go to the same school**. **Both** is followed by a plural verb.

> ⚠ Don't say 'I don't like both of them'. Say **I don't like either of them**. Use **either** in negative statements, not **both**.

> ⚠ When you use **both** with a noun, you can use any of these patterns, and they all have the same meaning: The cats are both black = Both the cats are black = Both cats are black. When you use **both** with a pronoun, you can say either **we both/they both etc** or **both of us/both of them etc** and the meaning is the same: We both like Kung Fu movies = Both of us like Kung Fu movies.

each /iːtʃ/ [determiner/pronoun] use this to talk about two people or things when you think of them as separate: My wife and I each have our own bank account.

each of them/us/the teams etc Each of the teams can use three substitutes.

> When you see **EC**, go to the **ESSENTIAL COMMUNICATION** section.

> ⚠ **Each** is followed by a singular verb, except when it comes after a plural noun or pronoun, so we say: Each girl has her own room. | Each of the girls has her own room. But They/The girls each have their own room.

> ⚠ Don't say 'each boys' or 'each of boys'. Say **each boy** or **each of the boys**.

either /ˈaɪðə^r‖ˈiː-/ [determiner/pronoun] use this to talk about one of two people, places, or things, especially when it does not matter which one: "Would you like tea or coffee?" "Either – I don't mind." | You can operate the controls with either hand.

either of them/you/the men etc If you see either of these men, contact the police immediately. | She says she never met either of them before.

either sth or sth I usually drink either coke or beer.

neither /ˈnaɪðə^r‖ˈniː-/ [determiner/pronoun] not one of two people, places, or things, and not the other: "Do you want milk or lemon in your tea?" "Neither thanks." | The game wasn't very exciting, and neither team played well.

neither of them/you/the girls etc Luckily, neither of the passengers was hurt in the crash.

neither sth nor sth Neither her mother nor her father knew about her boyfriend.

> ⚠ Don't say 'I don't like neither of them'. Say **I don't like either of them**.

> ⚠ You can say **neither team was playing well** or **neither of the teams was playing well**. They both mean the same, and in both cases you use a singular verb.

each other/one another /iːtʃ ˈʌðə^r, wʌn əˈnʌðə^r/ [pronoun] use this to say that each of two people does the same thing to the other, or has the same feeling about the other: The twins looked at one another and giggled. | My boyfriend and I don't talk to each other very much.

each other's/one another's Ron and Joe didn't like each other's girlfriends. (=Ron didn't like Joe's girlfriend and Joe didn't like Ron's)

4 two children born on the same day to the same mother

twin /twɪn/ [n C] one of two children who were born on the same day to the same mother: *She dressed the twins in the same clothes.* | *Joey's my twin.*

twin brother/sister *Bill and his twin sister got married on the same day.*

identical twins (=twins who look exactly the same)

5 intended for two people

for two /fəʳ ˈtuː/ **dinner/a holiday/a table etc for two** dinner, a holiday etc intended for only two people: *We'd like a table for two please.* | *a romantic weekend in Paris for two*

double /ˈdʌbəl/ [adj only before noun] **double room/bed/mattress** a room, bed etc intended for two people: *The room was so small, there was hardly enough space for a double bed.* | *Double rooms cost $80, single rooms are $50.*

6 when something happens two times

twice /twaɪs/ [adv] *The weather was great – it only rained twice in three weeks.* | *She's been married twice before.*

twice a day/month/year etc (=when something happens regularly two times every day, month etc) *I play golf twice a week.* | *Staff meetings are held twice a month.*

7 when a number or amount is twice as big as another

twice /twaɪs/ [predeterminer/adv] **twice as big/fast/much/many etc** bigger, faster etc by 100%: *This sweater would have cost twice as much if I'd bought it in England.*

twice the size/my salary/his age etc *He married a woman who was twice his age.* | *It's about twice the length of a football field.*

double /ˈdʌbəl/ [predeterminer] **double the amount/number/weight/size/**

cost etc twice the amount, number etc: *Over 30% of marriages end in divorce, which is double the number 20 years ago.* | *The house was now worth double the amount they paid for it.*

TYPE

1 a type of person or thing

type/kind/sort /taɪp, kaɪnd, sɔːʳt/ [n C] a group of people or things that are similar to each other in some way, or a thing or person that belongs to such a group: *I'll get you some ice-cream. What kind would you like?*

+ of *The floor was made of three different types of wood.* | *What sort of fish is this?* | *She's the kind of person you can always rely on.* | *There are two sorts of politician – the ones who really want to help people, and the ones who just want power.*

of this/that type etc *Accidents of this type are extremely common.* | *It's a club for writers and actors and people of that sort.*

of various/many/different types etc *They export farm machines and tools of various kinds.*

> ⚠ Type, kind, and sort mean the same, and they can all be used in most situations. Kind and sort are more common than type in conversation. Type is the usual word to use when you are talking about technical subjects or when you are describing something in an exact way: *To do this, you need a special type of screwdriver called a Phillips screwdriver.*

> ⚠ You can use type, kind, and sort in the singular or plural, followed by a singular or uncountable noun: *a type of flower* | *several kinds of bread* | *I like all kinds of music.* Don't use them with plural nouns: don't say 'this type of computers'. Say **this type of computer**. Don't use them in the singular after words like 'all', 'many', or 'these': don't say 'many kind of car/food etc'. Say **many kinds of car/food etc.**

species /ˈspiːʃiːz/ [n C] a group of animals or plants that are all similar and can breed

together to produce young animals or plants of the same type
+ of *There are over forty species of bird living on the island.* | *They discovered a new species of Eucalyptus tree.*
endangered species (=one that might not exist for much longer) *The giant panda is an endangered species. There are fewer than a thousand living in the wild.*
plural **species**

⚠ **Species** is a technical word for a specific type of animal or plant that can be described exactly.

○**like this/like that** /laɪk 'ðɪs, laɪk 'ðæt/ ESPECIALLY SPOKEN of the type that you have just been talking about: *The children need new pens and pencils and things like that.* | *People like that really annoy me.* | *I'm not sure what to do. I've never been in a situation like this before.*

category /'kætɪgəri‖-gɔːri/ [n C] a group that people or things of the same type are divided into for a particular purpose – use this when there are several groups and there is a clear system for deciding which group something belongs to: *Emma Thompson won an Oscar in the 'Best Actress' category.*
+ of *Insurance companies identify six main categories of driver.* | *The novels are divided up into three categories: historical, romantic, and crime.*
plural **categories**

style /staɪl/ [n C] a particular type of building, art, literature, music etc: *The new library is a blend of various architectural styles.*
+ of *a completely new style of painting*
western-style/Japanese-style etc *The room was simply furnished, Japanese-style.*

2 **a type of product**

brand /brænd/ [n C] a type of product made by a particular company – use this about products that you use every day such as food or drink or cleaning materials
+ of *Coke and Pepsi are the most popular brands of cola.* | *my favourite brand of toothpaste* | *They sell all the usual kinds of coffee, but also some less well-known brands.*

make /meɪk/ [n C] a type of product made by a particular company – use this about things such as machines, equipment, and cars, not about food or drink: *What make is your washing machine?*
+ of *"What make of car was she driving?" "A Mercedes."*

model /'mɒdl‖'mɑːdl/ [n C] one particular type of car or machine from among the various types that a company produces: *"What make is the car?" "It's a Ford." "And what model?" "An Escort 1.8L."* | *We produce a range of different computers, but this is our most popular model.*

TYPICAL
when something or someone is a good example of the type that they belong to

➡ see also **USUALLY**

1 **a typical thing or person**

typical /'tɪpɪkəl/ [adj] use this to say that someone or something is a normal example of a particular type of person or thing, and has all the features that you would expect: *With his bright shirt and camera around his neck, he looked like a typical American tourist.* | *a typical middle class family* | *We had some warm weather, and quite a lot of rain – it was a typical English summer.*
+ of *This painting is typical of the work that Matisse did in the 1920s.*

⚠ Don't say 'it's a typical restaurant' or 'this house is very typical' etc. You must also say what something is typical of, for example: *It's a typical Japanese/Spanish restaurant.* | *This house is typical of the style of this region.*

be a good example /biː ə ˌgʊd ɪg'zɑːmpəl‖-'zæm-/ something that **is a good example** of a type of thing is very typical of it: *There are many beautiful Norman churches in this part of England. Iffley church is a good example.*

+ of *The fox is a good example of a wild animal that has adapted to living in towns.*

representative /ˌreprɪˈzentətɪv/ [adj] FORMAL someone or something that is **representative** is very typical of the group that they belong to and shows what everyone or everything else in the group is like **+ of** *Are his views representative of the other teachers at the school?*

a representative group/sample/selection/cross-section (=a small group, chosen because it is typical of a larger group) *We asked a representative group of teenage girls what they thought about marriage.*

classic /ˈklæsɪk/ [adj usually before noun] **a classic case/example etc** a very typical and very good example of something: *Tiredness, headaches and bad temper are the classic signs of stress.* | *The invention of the X-ray was a classic case of an accidental discovery.*

stereotype /ˈsteriətaɪp/ [n C] a fixed idea which most people have in their minds about what people of a particular type or from a particular country are like, but which is not actually true: *The film is full of stereotypes: a stupid blonde, a fat American tourist, and a gay man with huge muscles.*

racial stereotypes (=fixed ideas about people of certain races)

+ of *the stereotype of Asian girls as quiet and hard-working*

2 when someone's behaviour or character is exactly what you would expect

typical /ˈtɪpɪkəl/ [adj] behaviour that is **typical** of a person is exactly what you would expect them to do – use this especially when what they do is annoying: *"Kate put the wrong address on the letter." "That's just typical!"* | *He said he was too tired to wash the dishes. Typical man!*

+ of *It's typical of Ramon to waste time when we're already late.*

it's just like/that's just like /ɪts ˌdʒʌst ˈlaɪk, ðæts ˌdʒʌst ˈlaɪk/ SPOKEN say this when someone has behaved in exactly the way that you would expect them to behave: *It's just like Uncle Roy to invite us all to lunch and then forget to tell Aunt Sarah.* | *Helen stayed to help us clean up, which is just like her.*

U

UGLY

not nice to look at

➡ opposite BEAUTIFUL

1 people

⚠ In conversation, we usually avoid saying someone is **ugly** or **unattractive** because it sounds very rude. Instead, you can say that someone is **not very good looking** or **not very attractive**.

unattractive/not attractive /ˌʌnə-ˈtræktɪv◄, nɒt əˈtræktɪv/ [adj] not nice to look at and not sexually attractive: *Like many teenage girls, she was worried that she was unattractive.* | *He wasn't a particularly attractive man, but there was something about him that women liked.*
find sb unattractive (=think that someone is unattractive) *She was crazy about Carl, and couldn't understand why we found him unattractive.*

not very good-looking /nɒt veri gʊd ˈlʊkɪŋ/ not nice to look at – use this as a less direct way of saying someone is unattractive: *He's a nice guy, but not very good-looking.*

ugly /ˈʌgli/ [adj] extremely unattractive, with a face that is not at all nice to look at: *We hated our uncle. He was ugly and fat and treated us cruelly.* | *An ugly little man came over and offered to buy me a drink.*

ugly – uglier – ugliest

plain /pleɪn/ [adj] someone who is **plain**, especially a woman, is not ugly but is not at all good-looking: *Catherine, who had been rather plain as a child, was now an attractive young woman.*

homely /ˈhəʊmli/ [adj] AMERICAN someone who is **homely** is not at all good-looking: *The waitress was a homely girl from Kansas.* | *Brad was a serious boy, very ordinary-looking but not downright homely.*

2 objects/buildings etc

ugly /ˈʌgli/ [adj] very unpleasant to look at: *The room was bare except for a few pieces of ugly furniture.* | *The new shopping centre is one of the ugliest buildings in the city.*

ugly – uglier- ugliest

an eyesore /ən ˈaɪsɔːr/ [n singular] a large and very ugly building that you cannot avoid seeing: *They built a huge office block right next to the old cathedral – what an eyesore!*

hideous /ˈhɪdiəs/ [adj] extremely ugly: *One of our wedding presents was a hideous clock.* | *Emma was wearing an absolutely hideous purple and orange dress.*

UNDERSTAND/ NOT UNDERSTAND

➡ see also REALIZE

1 to understand something

understand /ˌʌndərˈstænd/ [v I/T] to know the meaning of what someone says, or to know why something happens or how something happens: *She spoke slowly and clearly so that everyone could understand.* | *I don't understand the second question.*
understand how/what/why etc *Scientists are beginning to understand how the universe was formed.* | *I've never really understood why she married him.*
fully understand (=understand completely) *Doctors still do not fully understand the process by which the disease is transmitted.*
easy/difficult to understand *The instructions on the packet are easy to understand*

understanding – understood – have understood

⚠ Don't say 'I am understanding', 'are you understanding?' etc. Say **I understand, do you understand?** etc.

⚠ You can also say 'I **can** understand' or 'I **can't** understand', and it means the same as 'I understand' or 'I don't understand'.

understanding – understood – have understood

Q**see** /siː/ [v I/T] ESPECIALLY SPOKEN to understand the truth about a situation, or understand the reasons for something: *Don't you see? She never wanted to marry him in the first place.*
see what sb means *Yes, I see what you mean – it would be better if we didn't tell her.*
see why/how/what etc *I can see why people don't like him.*
+ that *After a time, Clara saw that she had been wrong to blame Jim.*
see a reason *Can you see any reason why it shouldn't work?*

seeing – saw – have seen

Q**I see** /aɪ ˈsiː/ SPOKEN say this to tell someone that you understand what they have told you: *"The door's a little stiff – just give it a push here." "Oh yes, I see."*

Q**I get it** /aɪ ˈget ɪt/ SPOKEN say this to tell someone that you understand what they have told you, especially when they have explained it more than once: *Oh right, I get it. So you only get paid if you sell at least 10 copies.*

follow /ˈfɒləʊ‖ˈfɑː-/ [v T] to understand a story, explanation, or talk that continues for a long time: *I had difficulty following the story – there are so many different characters.*
difficult/hard/easy to follow *The lecture was very hard to follow.*

figure out/work out /ˌfɪgər ˈaʊt, ˌwɜːrk ˈaʊt‖ˌfɪgjər-/ [phrasal verb T] to think about something until you understand it, especially something complicated
+ how/why/what etc *Detectives are still trying to work out what happened.*
figure/work sth out *In case you haven't figured it out yet, we've been tricked.*

2 to understand how someone feels

understand /ˌʌndərˈstænd/ [v I/T] to understand how someone feels, and feel sympathy for them, especially when they are upset or have problems: *Try telling your teacher about your problem. I'm sure she'll understand. | My wife doesn't understand me.*
understand how/what/why etc *I understand how you feel, but I still think you should apologize to her.*

understanding – understood – have understood

⚠ Don't say 'I am understanding'. Say **I understand**.

appreciate /əˈpriːʃieɪt/ [v T] FORMAL to understand clearly how someone feels or what problems they have: *The Senator failed to appreciate the amount of anger that people felt about this issue.*
+ (that) *I appreciate that it's not easy for you, but you must try to get here on time.*

see /siː/ [v T] to understand how someone feels and why they feel that way, especially because the reasons are very clear
see why/how/what *You can see why Clare was so annoyed, can't you?*
+ (that) *Martha saw that Bob was getting upset, so she changed the subject.*

seeing – saw – have seen

know how sb feels /ˌnəʊ haʊ (sb) ˈfiːlz/ to understand how someone feels, because you have had the same feelings or experiences yourself: *"My children are driving me crazy." "I know how you feel – they're very difficult at that age."*

3 when you cannot understand something

don't understand/can't understand /ˌdəʊnt ˌʌndərˈstænd, ˌkɑːnt ʌndərˈstænd‖kænt-/ *They didn't understand a single word she said. | Tell me if you don't understand.*
+ how/why/what etc *I really can't understand why so many people like her music.*

Q**don't/can't see** /ˌdəʊnt, ˌkɑːnt ˈsiː‖ˌkænt-/ SPOKEN to not understand the reason for something
+ why/how/what/where *I didn't see how they could sell it so cheaply. | All my friends liked that book, but I just can't see why.*

○**not get it** /nɒt 'get ɪt/ SPOKEN to feel confused, and be unable to understand why something has happened or what someone has told you: *I don't get it – why would he take the money if he knew they would find out?* | *I keep telling her that Steve isn't interested in her, but she just doesn't get it.*

puzzling /'pʌzəlɪŋ/ [adj] a **puzzling** situation makes you feel confused, because you have tried to understand it or explain it, but you cannot: *I don't know why she left – it's all very puzzling.*

○**it's a mystery to me/it beats me** /ɪts ə 'mɪstəri tə miː, ɪt ˌbiːts 'miː/ SPOKEN say this when you cannot understand why something happens or how someone does something, and you find it very surprising: *"Why does she stay with her husband then?" "It beats me."*

+ how/what/why etc *It's a mystery to me how he can get so much work done in such a short time.*

4 to not understand something correctly

misunderstand /ˌmɪsʌndəˈstænd/ [v I/T] to think that someone means one thing when in fact they mean something else: *I think she misunderstood the question.* | *I'm sorry, I must have misunderstood you.*

misunderstanding – misunderstood – have misunderstood

miss the point /ˌmɪs ðə 'pɔɪnt/ if you **miss the point**, you think you understand what someone says or what is important about a situation, but in fact you are wrong: *I soon realised that he had completely missed the point.*

misunderstanding /ˌmɪsʌndəˈstændɪŋ/ [n C/U] a problem caused when someone does not understand something correctly: *There seems to have been a misunderstanding. I didn't order steak.* | *Cultural differences between people from different countries can sometimes lead to misunderstandings.*

UNFORTUNATELY
when you wish that something had not happened or was not true

➡ see also **SORRY, LUCKY/UNLUCKY**

unfortunately /ʌnˈfɔːrtʃənˌtli/ [adv] use this to show that you wish something had not happened, or you wish something was not true: *There's nothing I can do about it, unfortunately.* | *Unfortunately, Dr Cole cannot spend as long with each patient as she would like.* | *We took some fantastic photos, but unfortunately the film got damaged.*

sadly /'sædli/ [adv] unfortunately – use this to talk about events or situations that are very sad: *Alice was rushed to the hospital, but sadly she died two hours later.* | *Sadly, this fine old theatre was destroyed by fire in 1993.*

⚠ **Sadly** is more formal than **unfortunately**, and used about serious situations.

○**it's a pity/it's a shame** /ɪts ə 'pɪti, ɪts ə 'ʃeɪm/ SPOKEN say this to show that you feel disappointed, sad, or annoyed about something that has happened: *They've cut down all those beautiful trees. It's a shame.*

+ (that) *It's a shame you can't come with us.* | *I don't mind you going out – it's just a pity you didn't ask me first.*

+ about *It's a shame about the weather.*

what a pity/what a shame! (say this to show that you feel sad or sympathetic about something) *"Janet didn't get that job." "Oh, what a pity!"*

it's sad /ɪts 'sæd/ use this to show that you feel upset about something sad that has happened, and you wish the situation was different

it's sad (that) *It's so sad that your father can't be here to see this.*

it's sad when *It's sad when a marriage breaks up, especially after all those years.*

When you see **EC** , go to the **ESSENTIAL COMMUNICATION** section.

UNKIND

➡ opposite **KIND**
➡ see also **CRUEL**

1 treating someone unkindly

unkind /ˌʌnˈkaɪnd◄/ [adj] if you are **unkind** to someone, you speak to them or treat them in a way that makes them unhappy: *It is all right to correct your students' mistakes, but try not to be unkind.* | *It was a really unkind thing to say.*
+ to *I'm sorry – I didn't mean to be so unkind to you yesterday.*
it is unkind (of sb) to do sth *It was very unkind of them to keep making jokes about her cooking.*
  unkindly [adv] *She described him, rather unkindly, as a boring little man.*

cruel /ˈkruːəl/ [adj] someone who is **cruel** is very unkind, and does not seem to care about other people's feelings: *He's not ugly! How can you be so cruel?* | *a cruel laugh*
+ to *The other kids were cruel to him because he was so fat.*
  cruelly [adv] *She wanted to leave him but, as he cruelly reminded her, she had nowhere else to go.*

nasty /ˈnɑːstiǁˈnæsti/ [adj] someone who is **nasty** is deliberately unkind, and seems to enjoy making people unhappy: *What a nasty thing to do!* | *He has a really nasty side to his character.*
+ to *Don't be so nasty to your sister!*
nasty – nastier – nastiest

spiteful /ˈspaɪtfəl/ [adj] deliberately unkind to someone because you are jealous of them or angry with them: *Failure had made him bitter and spiteful.*
  spitefully [adv] *"I never liked her anyway," Rob said spitefully.*

bitchy /ˈbɪtʃi/ [adj] INFORMAL someone who is **bitchy** says unkind things about another person, especially about the way they look or behave
bitchy comments/remarks *She's always making bitchy comments about other people's clothes.*
+ about *She was being really bitchy about Martha.*

⚠ **Bitchy** is used especially by women when talking about other women.

2 unkind, but not deliberately unkind

thoughtless/inconsiderate /ˈθɔːtləs, ˌɪnkənˈsɪdərɪt◄/ [adj] someone who is **thoughtless** or **inconsiderate** only thinks about their own situation, their own enjoyment etc, and does not think about the effects that their actions will have on other people: *A few thoughtless people spoiled the trip for everyone.* | *A lot of drivers these days are really rude and inconsiderate.*

insensitive /ɪnˈsensɪtɪv/ [adj] someone who is **insensitive** does not notice when other people are upset or when something that they do might upset other people: *I thought it was very insensitive, the way she kept talking about her new baby – she knows that Pam can't have children.* | *insensitive treatment of rape victims*

UNTIDY

➡ opposite **TIDY**
➡ see also **DIRTY**

1 place/room

untidy /ʌnˈtaɪdi/ [adj] if a place is **untidy**, things have been left carelessly in different parts of it instead of being neatly arranged: *Dad is always complaining that my bedroom's untidy.* | *an untidy desk* | *I'm afraid the garden's very untidy.*
untidy – untidier – untidiest

be a mess/be in a mess /biː ə ˈmes, biː ɪn ə ˈmes/ INFORMAL if a place **is a mess** or **is in a mess**, it is very untidy and dirty: *Please sit down. Sorry everything's such a mess.* | *The whole house was in a mess, but I didn't have time to clean it up.*

messy /ˈmesi/ [adj] INFORMAL very untidy and dirty: *I can't find anything in your bedroom – it's so messy!* | *a messy sinkful of dishes*
messy – messier – messiest

cluttered /ˈklʌtəˈd/ [*adj*] untidy because there are too many things in a small space: *a cluttered little office*
+ with *The room was tiny, its walls cluttered with paintings and old photographs.*

◯ **a dump** /ə ˈdʌmp/ [*n* singular] SPOKEN INFORMAL a dirty and untidy room, building, or place: *Do something about your room – it's a dump.*

2 person/clothes/hair etc

untidy /ʌnˈtaɪdi/ [*adj*] someone who is **untidy** does not keep their house, clothes, hair etc neatly arranged: *The children are so untidy – they leave their things all over the floor.* | *Her hair was untidy and her lipstick was smudged.*

look a mess /ˌlʊk ə ˈmes/ INFORMAL to look very untidy: *When the police called, I had just got up, and my hair looked a mess.*

scruffy /ˈskrʌfi/ [*adj*] someone who is **scruffy** is wearing old, untidy clothes: *My parents think I look scruffy in these jeans.*
scruffy clothes/jeans/sweater etc *She's wearing that scruffy old sweater again.*
scruffy – scruffier – scruffiest

3 when things are spread around in an untidy way

mess /mes/ [*n* singular] when things are spread around everywhere in a dirty, untidy way: *We spent the morning tidying up the mess after the party.* | *There were cups and ashtrays everywhere – what a mess!*
make a mess (=make a place dirty and untidy) *You can do some baking if you promise not to make a mess in the kitchen.*

chaos /ˈkeɪ-ɒs‖-ɑːs/ [*n* U] when everything is very untidy, nothing is organized, and there is no order or system: *We've just moved into the new office and I've no idea where anything is – it's chaos!*
in chaos (=in a state of chaos) *I arrived home to find the house in chaos.*

When you see **EC**, go to the **ESSENTIAL COMMUNICATION** section.

UNUSUAL

➡ opposite **NORMAL/ORDINARY**

⚠ Don't confuse **unusual** (=different from what usually happens) and **strange** (=unusual, and also a little frightening, surprising, or difficult to understand).

1 not what usually happens

unusual /ʌnˈjuːʒuəl, -ʒəl/ [*adj*] different from what usually happens, or different from the ordinary kind: *We had snow in April, which is very unusual.* | *She had an unusual last name – Peachtree or Plumtree or something like that.*
it is unusual for sb to do sth *We were beginning to worry. It was unusual for Dave to be so late.*
unusually [*adv*] *The office was unusually quiet that morning.*

special /ˈspeʃəl/ [*adj* usually before noun] a **special** occasion, situation, method etc is one that is different from what normally happens, and usually better: *There were special security arrangements for the President's visit.* | *Prince William is the school's most famous student, but he doesn't get special treatment or special privileges.*
special event/occasion *a special event to celebrate the 200th anniversary of the revolution*
in special circumstances *Prisoners are only allowed to visit their families in special circumstances.*

exceptional /ɪkˈsepʃənəl/ [*adj*] an **exceptional** situation is very unusual and happens very rarely; an **exceptional** person or quality is so good that there are very few like them: *A few of the top executives are women, but this is still exceptional.* | *a man of exceptional intelligence*

in exceptional circumstances/cases *Exit visas are only given in exceptional circumstances.*

exceptionally [*adv*] *an exceptionally talented athlete*

uncommon/not common /ʌnˈkɒmən, ˌnɒt ˈkɒmən‖-ˈkɑːmən/ [*adj*] something that is **uncommon** or **not common** is unusual because it does not happen very often: *The disease mostly affects older people, and is not common among younger people.*

it is uncommon/not common (for sb) to do sth *It is uncommon for small babies to sleep more than four hours without waking.*

⚠ **Uncommon/not common** is more formal than **unusual**.

⚲**it's not like sb** /ɪts nɒt ˈlaɪk (sb)/ SPOKEN say this when you mean that someone is behaving in a way that they do not usually behave, so you think they may be ill or have some kind of problem: *Don't you want any more to eat? That's not like you.*

it's not like sb to do sth *It's not like Sally to get so upset – I think she's been working too hard.*

2 different from the way most people think or behave

unconventional /ˌʌnkənˈvenʃənəl◂/ [*adj*] someone who is **unconventional** lives, behaves, or does things in ways that are very different from the way that most ordinary people live or behave: *She comes from an unconventional family.* | *unconventional teaching methods*

UP

➡ if you mean 'a price, number etc goes up', go to **INCREASE**
➡ opposite **DOWN**
➡ see also **CLIMB**

1 moving up to a higher place or level

up /ʌp/ [*prep/adv*]
go/climb/walk etc up *There's a great view from the top – you should go up and have a look.*

up a hill/tree/wall etc *Tim had climbed up a tree to get a better view.*

+ onto/into/at etc *Don't let the cat jump up onto the table.* | *You mustn't go up there – it's dangerous.*

upwards/upward /ˈʌpwə^rd(z)/ [*adv*] towards a higher position, especially towards the sky: *Most plants grow upwards, towards the light.*

+ into/above/over etc *With a loud bang, the rocket shot upward into the sky.*

upward [*adj* only before noun] *She massaged my back with a light upward movement.*

⚠ Don't say 'they walked upwards the hill'. Say **they walked up the hill**.

uphill /ˌʌpˈhɪl◂/ [*adv*] going up a hill: *When I'm driving uphill the engine makes a terrible noise.* | *The bus crawled uphill for another mile.*

uphill [*adj* only before noun] *a long uphill climb through the snow*

upstairs /ˌʌpˈsteə^rz/ [*adv*] **go/walk/run etc upstairs** to go towards a higher level in a building by going up the stairs: *Guy ran upstairs quickly.* | *Don't go upstairs yet – I think Sara's wrapping your present.*

rise /raɪz/ [*v* I] WRITTEN to move straight up into the air or sky: *The balloon rose slowly into the air.* | *We got up, just as the sun was rising.*

rising – rose – have risen

climb /klaɪm/ [*v* I/T] WRITTEN to move up a slope, or to move up into the sky in a sloping direction: *The bus began to climb the steep hill out of the valley.* | *The plane climbed higher and higher until it was out of sight.*

2 facing up, looking up, or pointing up

up /ʌp/ [*adv*]
look/point/stare up (=look, point etc upwards) *Caroline looked up and laughed.*

+ at/into/towards etc *The dog just sat and stared up at me.*

straight up (=directly up) *He was pointing his rifle straight up in the air.*

upwards (also **upward** AMERICAN) /ˈʌp-wəʳd(z)/ [adv] facing or pointing up, especially towards the sky: *She stretched out her hands with the palms upwards.* | *Their faces were turned upward, fixed on the man on the ledge.*

vertical /ˈvɜːʳtɪkəl/ [adj] lines, walls, surfaces etc that are **vertical** go straight up: *The wallpaper had vertical pink and white stripes.* | *First, the surgeon makes a three-inch vertical cut in the abdomen.*

> **vertically** [adv] *The cliffs rose vertically out of the sea.*

upright /ˈʌp-raɪt/ [adj/adv] standing straight up: *The ceiling was so low that we couldn't stand upright.*

hold/keep sth upright *Keep the bottle upright, in case it leaks.*

3 in a higher position

upstairs /ˌʌpˈsteəʳz◂/ [adv] on a higher floor of a building, especially just above where you are: *"Where's John?" "He's upstairs, doing his homework."* | *We got a note from the woman who lives upstairs.*

> **upstairs** [adj only before noun] *The burglars got in through an upstairs window.*

> ⚠ Don't say 'she lives in upstairs'. Just say **she lives upstairs.**

up in/up on/up there etc /ˈʌp ɪn, ˈʌp ɒn, ʌp ˈðeəʳ (etc)/ in a higher position than where you are: *I think your old bike's still up in the attic somewhere.* | *Put the bottles up on the shelf where the baby can't reach them.* | *Is it safe up there?*

4 to move a part of your body up

raise /reɪz/ [v T] ESPECIALLY WRITTEN to move part of your body up: *She raised her head and looked at him.* | *raising his hands to protect his face*

put up /ˌpʊt ˈʌp/ [phrasal verb T] to move your hand or arm above your head

put up your hand/arm *Put up your hand if you know the answer.*

put your hand/arm up *I put my hand up to shield my eyes from the sun.*

5 when a road or path goes towards a higher level

up /ʌp/ [adv/prep] *A track continues up the hillside towards the church.*

+ into/towards/over etc *paths leading up into the mountains*

go up/go uphill /ˌgəʊ ˈʌp, ˌgəʊ ʌpˈhɪl/ [phrasal verb I] to go towards a higher level: *After the next village, the road goes up steeply.* | *The path went uphill for another two miles.*

6 when the level of water goes up

rise /raɪz/ [v I] *The level of water in the lake was rising fast.* | *In 1956 the river rose by more than 6 metres.*

> **rising – rose – have risen**

USE

➡ see also **WASTE**

1 to use something

use /juːz/ [v T] to use something for a purpose: *Do you mind if I use your phone?* | *Are we allowed to use a dictionary in the test?* | *I use the library a lot.*

use sth to do sth *Use a calculator to check your answers.* | *some techniques you can use to help yourself relax*

use sth for doing sth *We use the shed for storing our firewood.*

use sth as sth *We decided to use the second bedroom as a junk room.*

with /wɪð, wɪθ/ [preposition] if you do something **with** a spoon, a hammer etc, you use a spoon, hammer etc to do it: *Beat the egg with a fork.* | *Do you have anything I can open the bottle with?*

make use of sth /ˌmeɪk ˈjuːs ɒv (sth)/ to use something that is available, especially something that can help you or give you an advantage: *Not enough people are making use of the company's fitness centre.*

make good/full use of sth *While she was at college, she made good use of all the computing facilities.*

2 to use an amount of fuel, water, food etc

use /juːz/ [v T] to use an amount of something: *It's a big car, and it uses a lot of gas.* | *You'll need to use at least two cans of paint.*

consume /kənˈsjuːm‖-ˈsuːm/ [v T] FORMAL to use fuel, energy, water, and other natural products – use this especially to talk about the amount of fuel, energy etc used by people in general: *The US imports 45% of the oil that it consumes.* | *industrialized countries which consume natural resources in huge quantities*

> **consumption** /kənˈsʌmpʃən/ [n U] the amount of fuel, energy etc that people use: *The government is urging people to reduce their water consumption.*

3 to use something again

recycle /ˌriːˈsaɪkəl/ [v T] to put bottles, newspapers, cans etc through a process so that they can be used for making new bottles, newspapers etc: *new techniques for recycling plastics*

> **recycled** [adj] *All our envelopes are made from recycled paper.*

re-use /ˌriːˈjuːz/ [v T] to use something again after you have used it before: *The supermarket encourages shoppers to re-use plastic bags.*

4 when a seat, room, machine etc is being used

be in use /biː ɪn ˈjuːs/ if a room or machine **is in use**, it is being used by someone at the present time, so no-one else can use it: *The meeting room is in use at the moment, so we'll have to go somewhere else.* | *All the photocopiers are in use. Could you come back later?*

be taken /biː ˈteɪkən/ ESPECIALLY SPOKEN use this about a seat on a train, in a theatre etc that someone else has already bought or arranged to use, even if they are not there at the moment: *Is this seat taken?* | *I'm sorry, you can't sit there. It's taken.*

> When you see **EC**, go to the
> **ESSENTIAL COMMUNICATION** section.

5 not being used

unused /ˌʌnˈjuːzd◄/ [adj] not being used at the present time: *After Grandad died, his car sat unused in the garage.* | *Farmers were paid special subsidies for unused fields.*

disused /ˌdɪsˈjuːzd◄/ [adj only before noun] ESPECIALLY BRITISH a **disused** factory, mine, railway etc is old and is not used any more: *The drugs were found in a disused warehouse.*

6 when something is not being used, so you can use it

available /əˈveɪləbəl/ [adj] something useful that is **available** is ready to be used and you can use it if you want to: *They built the shelter using old wood and plastic – just whatever was available.* | *We had filled all the available space, so there was nowhere to store the books.*

free /friː/ [adj] use this about a chair, room, table etc that you can use because no-one else is using it: *The office next door is free if you need somewhere to work.* | *There's just one free table, over there in the corner.*

spare /speər/ [adj only before noun] a **spare tyre/pen/key etc** a tyre, key etc which you are not using at the moment, but which you keep in case the one you are using breaks, gets lost etc: *We keep a spare key in the garage.* | *Do you have a spare pen I could borrow?*

empty/vacant /ˈempti, ˈveɪkənt/ [adj] use this about buildings that no-one is using: *Fire broke out in a vacant office block early this morning.* | *The house has been empty for over a year.*

> ⚠ **Vacant** is more formal than **empty**.

7 officially allowed to be used

valid /ˈvælɪd/ [adj] if a ticket, passport etc is **valid**, you can legally use it and it will be officially accepted: *My passport is valid for 10 years.* | *Do you have a valid driver's license?*

8 what something can be used for

use /juːs/ [n C often plural] one of the ways in which something can be used: *The land has been developed for tourism and other recreational uses.* | *the industrial uses of hydrogen*

be for /biː ˈfɔːʳ/ [phrasal verb T] to be used for doing a particular job: *This cream is for removing make-up.* | *What's that switch for?*

function /ˈfʌŋkʃən/ [n C] the purpose for which something is intended to be used
+ of *The main function of the bars is to protect the driver's legs.*

> ⚠ **Function** is used especially in technical or scientific writing.

9 to use something in the wrong way

misuse /mɪsˈjuːz/ [v T] to use something in the wrong way or for the wrong purpose: *The word 'schizophrenia' is frequently misused.* | *Politicians misused public money on entertaining their business friends.*

> **misuse** /mɪsˈjuːs/ [n C/U] when something is used in the wrong way or for the wrong purpose: *Opponents of genetic engineering see it as a misuse of scientific knowledge.*

abuse /əˈbjuːz/ [v T] to use something for a bad purpose, especially in a way that is unfair or that harms other people: *Local politicians abused their privileges to make themselves rich.* | *people who abuse the welfare system*

> **abuse** /əˈbjuːs/ [n C/U] when something is used for a bad purpose: *There was widespread abuse of power.* | *drug abuse*

USED TO/ ACCUSTOMED TO

when something seems normal to you because you have often done it or experienced it before

➡ if you mean 'did something regularly in the past', go to **PAST 2**

1 used to something

be used to sth /biː ˈjuːst tuː (sth)/ if you are **used to** something, you have often done it or experienced it before, so it does not seem strange, new, or difficult to you
be used to doing sth *She's used to getting up early because she lives on a farm.*
be used to sth *At first Omar hated the rain in England but he's used to it now.*
get used to (doing) sth *Mary never really got used to living on her own after her husband died.* | *It's quite a simple system – you'll soon get used to it.*

> ⚠ Don't confuse **I used to do it** (=I regularly did it in the past, but I don't do it now) and **I am used to doing it** (=I often do it, so it doesn't seem unusual to me): *When I worked on a farm, I used to get up early every day.* | *I work on a farm, so I'm used to getting up early.*
>
> ⚠ Don't say 'I am used to do this'. Say **I am used to doing this**: *I'm used to making all my own food.*

be accustomed to sth /biː əˈkʌstəmd tuː (sth)/ FORMAL to be used to something, especially because it is a normal part of your life: *Zara was accustomed to a life of luxury.*
be accustomed to doing sth *Larry remained completely relaxed – he was accustomed to dealing with difficult customers.*
become/grow accustomed to sth *After a time, she became accustomed to all the media attention.*

adjust to sth /əˈdʒʌst tuː (sth)/ [phrasal verb T] to gradually get used to a new situation, by changing your attitudes or the way you do things: *It took us a while to adjust to the tropical climate.* | *Some of*

the staff found it hard to adjust to all the changes in technology and working methods.

settle in /ˌsetl 'ın/ [phrasal verb I] to gradually get used to a new place or a new way of life, so that you feel relaxed and confident: *Paul never really settled in at his last school.*

settle into sth *It didn't take Charlie long to settle into his new job.*

familiar /fə'mɪliəʳ/ [adj] a **familiar** place, idea, situation etc is one that you are used to and that you know well: *It was good to be back in familiar surroundings.* | *the familiar sounds of home*
+ to *This kind of problem will be familiar to many married couples.*

2 not used to something

not be used to sth /nɒt biː 'juːst tuː (sth)/ *I'm still not used to the new computer system.*
not be used to doing sth *Jane wasn't used to having so much money, and she didn't know what to do with it.*

be unaccustomed to sth /biː ˌʌnə-'kʌstəmd tuː (sth)/ FORMAL to not be used to something, especially when this makes you annoyed or worried: *Curtis was a country boy, unaccustomed to city life.*
be unaccustomed to doing sth *Teachers may be unaccustomed to having their teaching methods criticised.*

unfamiliar /ˌʌnfə'mɪliəʳ◄/ [adj] an **unfamiliar** place, idea, situation etc is one that you are not used to or do not know much about: *the unfamiliar experience of driving on the left-hand side of the road* | *a new place, with all its unfamiliar sounds and smells*
+ to *Some of these expressions may be unfamiliar to your students.*

strange /streɪndʒ/ [adj only before noun] a **strange** country, food, custom etc is one that you are not used to because you have never been there before, experienced it before etc, and this may make you feel anxious: *The strange food made her ill.* | *She was all alone in a strange city.*

USEFUL/ NOT USEFUL

➡ see also **CONVENIENT/NOT CONVENIENT 2**

1 useful

useful /'juːsfəl/ [adj] something that is **useful** makes it easier for you to do something or to get something: *See page 35 for a list of useful addresses.* | *The bank gave us a lot of useful advice about starting our own business.* | *a useful skill*
useful for doing sth *Scotch tape is very useful for making quick repairs.*
+ to *information that may be useful to the enemy*
Q**come in useful** SPOKEN (=be useful in a particular situation) *Keep the rest of the paper – it might come in useful later.*

handy /'hændi/ [adj] INFORMAL useful and easy to use: *a handy chart for converting pounds into kilos* | *This handy booklet tells you everything you need to know about getting connected to the Internet.*
handy for doing sth *There's a special brush, which is handy for cleaning the stairs.*
Q**come in handy** SPOKEN (=be useful in a particular situation) *Bring a sleeping bag – it might come in handy.*

practical /'præktɪkəl/ [adj] designed to be useful rather than attractive – use this especially about clothes and things you use in your house: *a type of floor covering that is simple, practical, and cheap*

Q**be good for sth** /biː 'gʊd fɔːʳ (sth)/ ESPECIALLY SPOKEN to be suitable and useful for a particular job or purpose: *The old table does take up a lot of space, but it's good for parties.*
be good for doing sth *The big jars are good for storing pasta.*

invaluable /ın'væljuəbəl, -jəbəl‖ın'væljʊ̈bəl/ [adj] FORMAL extremely useful – use this about something that you are very pleased to have because it will help you a lot, for example someone's advice or help: *Thank you, your advice has been invaluable.* | *My six months at IBM gave me invaluable experience of the computer business.*

versatile /'vɜːsətaɪl‖'vɜːrsətl/ [adj] something that is **versatile** can be used in a lot of different ways: *Eggs are good value for money and so versatile.* | *a versatile blue cotton jacket*

2 not useful

useless /'juːsləs/ [adj] not at all useful: *useless information* | *Without the proper electric cable, it's useless.*
completely/totally/absolutely useless *I'm going to throw this old vacuum cleaner away – it's absolutely useless.*
+ for *It's only a simple claculator, so it's useless for doing anything complicated.*

pointless /'pɔɪntləs/ [adj] if someone does something that is **pointless**, it does not seem to have any useful purpose and will not help anyone: *The argument was completely pointless.* | *pointless drug testing on animals*
it is pointless doing sth *It's pointless trying to speak to the manager – she's always too busy.*

◯**there's no point/what's the point?** /ðeəʳz ˌnəʊ 'pɔɪnt, ˌwɒts ðə 'pɔɪnt/ ESPECIALLY SPOKEN say this when you think that it is useless to do something because it will not achieve any useful purpose: *"Why don't you try and sort out your argument with Mike?" "There's no point – he never listens."*
there's no point (in) doing sth *There's no point in waiting any longer – she obviously isn't coming.*
◯**what's the point of doing sth?** SPOKEN *What's the point of taking the exam if you know you're going to fail?*

◯**be a waste of time** /biː ə ˌweɪst əv 'taɪm/ ESPECIALLY SPOKEN if you say that doing something **is a waste of time**, you mean that it is very unlikely to achieve any useful result and so no-one should spend their time doing it
be a complete waste of time *These meetings are a complete waste of time. Nothing ever gets decided.*
it is a waste of time doing sth *So many people wanted that job, that I thought it was a waste of time even applying for it.*

When you see **EC**, go to the
ESSENTIAL COMMUNICATION section.

USUALLY

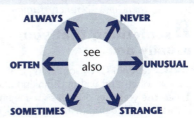

1 usually

usually/normally/generally /'juːʒuəli, 'nɔːrməli, 'dʒenərəli/ [adv] on most occasions or in most situations: *I usually get up at about 7 o'clock.* | *The journey normally takes me about 45 minutes.* | *Usually, I do all the housework and Peter does the garden.* | *Women are generally paid less than men.*

⚠ Put **usually, normally,** and **generally** before the main verb in a sentence, except when the main verb is the verb 'to be': *They usually make a lot of noise.* | *They are usually very noisy.*

as usual /əz 'juːʒuəl/ in the same way as things usually happen: *Tickets cost $20, and as usual there is a special price for students.*

⚠ Don't say 'as usually'. Say **as usual**: *As usual, the bus was full.*

⚠ In spoken English, **as usual** is often used to say that something annoying has happened, when you mean that this happens very often: *I tried to find Larry, but as usual he was outside having a cigarette.*

◯**nine times out of ten** /ˌnaɪn taɪmz aʊt əv 'ten/ SPOKEN if something happens **nine times out of ten**, it nearly always happens or is nearly always true: *Nine times out of ten, he works late and I have to look after the kids.*

2 usual

usual/normal /'juːʒuəl, 'nɔːrməl/ [adj usually before noun] use this to describe the situation that usually happens, the thing that someone usually uses etc: *She was sitting in her usual chair by the fire.* | *They're selling CDs at half the normal price.*

colder/better/later etc than usual *The journey took much longer than usual, because there was so much traffic.*

3 something that you usually do

habit /ˈhæbɪt/ [n C/U] something that you do very often and without thinking about it, because you have done it so many times before: *smoking and drinking and all his other bad habits*
have a habit of doing sth *She has an annoying habit of leaving her books all over the floor.*

get into the habit of doing sth (=start doing something regularly) *You ought to get into the habit of planning your work each morning.*

routine /ˌruːˈtiːn◄/ [n C/U] all the things that you usually do in the same order every day: *Try to make exercise a part of your daily routine. | Most babies soon develop a routine of sleeping and eating.*
routine [adj] a **routine** action or process is done as a normal part of a job or system: *The drugs were found during a routine check by customs officers.*

V

VERY

➡ see also **LOT 4, COMPLETELY, LITTLE/NOT MUCH**

1 very

very /'veri/ [adv] We had a very good time. | The test was very difficult. | She described the scene very well. | Try again, but move your arms very slowly.

◯**really** /'rɪəli/ [adv] ESPECIALLY SPOKEN very – use this especially to talk about your feelings or what you think about something: It's really cold out there. | I feel really hungry. | Bob played really well.

highly /'haɪli/ [adv] FORMAL very – you can use **highly** with these words: **successful**, **intelligent**, **profitable**, **effective**, **efficient**, **educated**, **skilled**: He runs a highly successful company. | a team of highly skilled engineers

◯**real** /rɪəl/ [adv] AMERICAN SPOKEN INFORMAL very: I think he's a real smart guy. | You can take the car but be real careful. | driving real fast

2 even more than very

extremely /ɪk'striːmli/ [adv] ESPECIALLY WRITTEN use this when you want to use a stronger word than 'very': It is extremely difficult to work in these conditions. | The article contains some extremely important information. | The conference was extremely badly organized.

absolutely /'æbsəluːtli, ˌæbsə'luːtli/ [adv] as much as it is possible to imagine – use this to emphasize adjectives that already have a strong meaning

absolutely marvellous/wonderful/delicious etc We had an absolutely marvellous day. | The cake tastes absolutely delicious – did you make it?

absolutely filthy/disgusting/awful etc When they came in from the yard, they were absolutely filthy.

absolutely terrified/exhausted/delighted/furious etc She stood in the middle of the stage looking absolutely terrified.

completely /kəm'pliːtli/ [adv] in every possible way: What's he doing? Has he gone completely crazy? | By Friday I'm always completely exhausted. | a place where you can feel completely relaxed

◯**very, very** /ˌveri 'veri/ SPOKEN say this when you want to emphasize 'very': a very, very important decision | She's intelligent, and she's very, very efficient.

incredibly /ɪn'kredɪbli/ [adv] use this when something is so good, so bad, so fast etc that you are surprised by it or you find it hard to believe: They all work incredibly hard. | Their house is incredibly cold – I don't think they heat it at all. | I've been incredibly lucky in my career.

3 less than very, but more than a little

fairly /'feəli/ [adv] if something is **fairly** heavy, **fairly** easy etc it is more than a little heavy or easy, but it is not very heavy or very easy: The house has a fairly big living room. | She was fairly certain that she had been there before. | Maria sings fairly well, but she needs more lessons.

quite /kwaɪt/ [adv, predeterminer] ESPECIALLY BRITISH if something is **quite** heavy, **quite** easy etc, it is more than a little heavy or easy, but it is not very heavy or very easy: The hotel was quite expensive. | The door opened quite easily. | I quite like it here, but I'd rather live in Manchester.

quite a long way/nice day/a good book etc It's quite a long way to the church from here. | I thought it was quite an interesting movie.

⚠ In American English, 'quite good', 'quite funny' etc means 'very good', 'very funny' etc.

pretty /'prɪti/ [adv] INFORMAL fairly: It's pretty cold today. | I was pretty embarrassed when I realized that she'd been listening. | "Hi Beth, how are you?" "Pretty good."

⚠ In British English, **pretty** is used mostly in conversation. But in American English, **pretty** is much more common, and it is the most usual way of saying **fairly**.

rather /'rɑːðəʳ‖'ræ–/ [adv, predeterminer] ESPECIALLY BRITISH fairly – use this especially about things that are bad or unsuitable: *Gail seems rather unhappy today.* | *a rather annoying delay*

rather a long way/short dress etc *That's rather a large whisky; I don't think I can drink it all.*

rather a lot *She was wearing rather a lot of make-up at the party.*

> ⚠ **Rather** is more formal than the other words in this section.

VIOLENT

likely to attack or hurt people

ATTACK   CRUEL
SHOOT   CRIME
see also
HIT   THREATEN
KILL   FILMS/MOVIES

1 violent person/animal/ behaviour

violent /'vaɪələnt/ [adj] someone who is **violent** often attacks people, and sometimes causes injury or death, especially because this is part of their character: *My father was a violent man who couldn't control his temper.* | *There was a violent protest outside the court, and a police officer was injured.*

violent crime *Everyone is worried about the increase in violent crime.*

> **violently** [adv] *He was violently attacked by a gang of youths.*

aggressive /ə'gresɪv/ [adj] someone who is **aggressive** behaves in an angry way, and always seems to want to fight or argue: *Some of the crowd were very aggressive, shouting and banging on windows.* | *Kids who play video games show much more aggressive behaviour than those who don't.*

> **aggressively** [adv] *Why do you always drive so aggressively?*

brutal /'bruːtl/ [adj] violent and cruel: *The prison guards were brutal and corrupt.* | *a brutal dictator who killed all his opponents*

brutal murder/attack/killing *Carter was jailed for the brutal murder of a young mother.*

> **brutally** [adv] *Opponents of the regime were brutally tortured.*

vicious /'vɪʃəs/ [adj] a **vicious** person or animal is likely to attack and injure people suddenly and for no reason: *Police shot dead a vicious Rottweiler dog.*

vicious attack/assault *Stephanie was the victim of a vicious sex attack.*

fierce /fɪəʳs/ [adj] a **fierce** animal looks very frightening and is ready to attack people: *A fierce dog was standing at the gate, guarding the house.*

2 violent film/story

violent /'vaɪələnt/ [adj] **violent** films, stories, or television programmes contain a lot of fighting and killing: *I think Tarantino's films are too violent.*

gory /'gɔːri/ [adj] **gory** films, descriptions etc clearly show or describe violent injuries, blood, death etc: *a gory horror movie*

3 violent actions

violence /'vaɪələns/ [n U] fighting, killing, and other violent behaviour: *complaints about sex and violence on TV* | *In some parts of the city, teachers have to deal with violence in the classroom.*

+ against *male violence against women*

force /fɔːʳs/ [n U] violent action or the threat of violent action, used in order to make someone do something: *We want to end the demonstration without force.*

use force *The police do not use force when arresting people unless it's absolutely necessary.*

by force (=using force) *Her husband tried to get the children back by force.*

aggression /ə'greʃən/ [n U] angry behaviour that often causes fights: *Drugs can be used to control aggression.* | *Some people think aggression in children may be caused by the food they eat.*

VISIT

to go and spend time in a place or with a person

STAY • FREE TIME • TRAVEL • HOLIDAY — see also

1 to visit a person

visit /'vɪzɪt/ [v I/T] to go and spend time with someone, especially in their home: *We're going to visit Vicky this weekend.* | *Paul visited her every day when she was in the hospital.*

> ⚠ Visit is a fairly formal word. In informal English, **go to see** is more common.

go to see /ˌgəʊ tə 'siː/ to go and spend time with someone, either for enjoyment or in order to get advice or help from them: *We went to see Kim last weekend.* | *He goes to see his mother every evening.* | *You should go to see the doctor about that cough.*

> ⚠ In spoken English, you can also say **go and see**: *Why don't you go and see your mother?* In American spoken English you can also say **go see**: *You really should go see the bank manager.*

> ⚠ In the past tense, always say **went to see** (not 'went see'): *I went to see an accountant about my tax problems.*

stop in/stop by /ˌstɒp 'ɪn, ˌstɒp 'baɪ‖ˌstɑːp-/ [phrasal verb I] to visit someone for a short time while you are on your way to somewhere else: *Bruce and Betty stopped by on their way to the mall.*

Q drop in/drop by /ˌdrɒp 'ɪn, ˌdrɒp 'baɪ‖ˌdrɑːp-/ [phrasal verb I] ESPECIALLY SPOKEN to visit someone for a short time, especially when they are not expecting you: *Guess who dropped in earlier – Aunt Leone!* | *Lizzie said she'd drop by later and let us know the arrangements for tonight.*

Q come by /ˌkʌm 'baɪ/ [phrasal verb I] AMERICAN, ESPECIALLY SPOKEN to visit someone in their home, especially for a short time: *Can you come by on Tuesday to pick up the keys?*

Q call in/call round /ˌkɔːl 'ɪn, ˌkɔːl 'raʊnd/ [phrasal verb I] BRITISH, ESPECIALLY SPOKEN to visit someone in their home while you are on your way to somewhere else: *Fred calls round sometimes on his way to the sports centre.* | *I'll call in tomorrow, Mum.*

see /siː/ [v T] to visit a doctor, lawyer etc at their place of work, in order to get professional help or advice: *You should see a doctor if your back doesn't get any better.* | *I've come to see the Planning Officer.*

seeing – saw – have seen

2 to visit a place

go to /'gəʊ tuː/ [phrasal verb T] to visit a place: *We're going to Hawaii for our vacation.* | *I've been to Germany several times.* | *Have you ever been to the National Gallery in London?*

go to see /ˌgəʊ tə 'siː/ to visit a well-known place or building while you are in a city or country: *If you're in Paris, you must go to see the Pompidou Centre.*

> ⚠ In spoken English, you can also say **go and see**: *Let's go and see the cathedral.* In American spoken English you can also say **go see**: *Why don't we go see the Statue of Liberty?*

> ⚠ In the past tense, always say **went to see** (not 'went see').

visit /'vɪzɪt/ [v T] to go somewhere, especially as part of your official duties: *The Ambassador visited Hong Kong in 1982.* | *The photo shows Mr Clinton visiting an automobile factory.*

> ⚠ Don't say 'we visited the cinema/ Disneyland etc'. Say **we went to the cinema/Disneyland** etc. Use **visit** to talk about important people when they officially go to a city, a country, a factory etc.

> ⚠ Don't say 'he visited to the town'. Say **he visited the town**.

stop off /ˌstɒp ˈɒf‖ˌstɑːp ˈɔːf/ [*phrasal verb* I] to make a short visit to a place while you are on your way to somewhere else
+ at/in *We stopped off in Boston on our way to New York.* | *I'll stop off at the library on the way home.*

sightseeing /ˈsaɪtˌsiːɪŋ/ [*n* U] when you travel around a place to look at the famous and interesting places there: *We did a lot of walking and sightseeing while we were in London.*
go sightseeing *Let's go sightseeing tomorrow. I'd like to see the Empire State Building and Central Park.*

⚠ Don't say 'a sightseeing'. Say **some sightseeing** or **a lot of sightseeing**.

3 someone who visits

visitor /ˈvɪzɪtər/ [*n* C] someone who visits a person or place: *The museum had over a million visitors last year.* | *We have visitors staying with us at the moment.* | *Prisoners are allowed only two visitors a week.*

guest /gest/ [*n* C] someone that you have invited to visit you or stay with you at your house: *They were guests of an Arab banker at his apartment in the south of France.*

⚠ **Guest** is a rather formal word. In spoken English, it is more usual to say 'someone visiting' or 'someone staying': *We have some friends visiting us this weekend.*

tourist /ˈtʊərɪst/ [*n* C] someone who is visiting a place while they are on holiday: *Cambridge is full of tourists in the summer.*

4 a time when you visit

visit /ˈvɪzɪt/ [*n* C] a time when you visit a person or a place: *Jenni was getting quite excited at the thought of her mother's visit.*
+ to *It's the President's first visit to Moscow.*

pay sb a visit (=visit someone) FORMAL *Melissa decided to pay a visit to her old teacher.*

a flying visit (=a very short visit when you do not have much time) *Do you have time to stay for a meal, or is this just a flying visit?*

VOTE

➡ see also **GOVERNMENT/POLITICS, REPRESENT, PROTEST**

1 to vote

vote /vəʊt/ [*v* I/T] to show which person you want to choose, or to show whether you agree with a plan, by putting your hand up or making a mark on a piece of paper
vote for sb/sth (=vote to support them) *I haven't decided who I'm going to vote for.* | *70% of the population voted for independence.*
vote against sth (=vote to say that you do not agree with a plan or suggestion) *Only two people voted against the proposal.*
vote to do sth *Congress voted to increase spending on foreign aid.*
vote on sth (=vote in order to make a decision about something) *Teachers will be voting on a proposal to accept the 5% pay offer.*
vote *In tomorrow's election, many young people will be voting for the first time.*
vote Republican/Labour etc (=vote for a political party) *I've voted Democrat all my life.*
   the vote [*n* singular] the right to vote: *It wasn't until 1918 that women were given the vote.*

have a vote/take a vote /ˌhæv ə ˈvəʊt, ˌteɪk ə ˈvəʊt/ if a group of people **have a vote** or **take a vote**, they decide something by putting their hands up to show which idea they agree with: *We may need to take a vote if we can't decide.*
+ on *Let's take a vote on it* (=decide it by voting) .

elect /ɪˈlekt/ [*v* T] to choose a government, leader, or representative by voting: *At tonight's meeting, we will elect a new chairperson.* | *The present mayor was elected two years ago.*
elect sb leader/chairman/president etc (=choose someone to be leader etc by voting) *When was Mr Yeltsin elected president?*

veto /ˈviːtəʊ/ [*v* T] if someone **vetoes** a decision that other people have agreed on, they use their official power to refuse to allow it: *The bill was vetoed by the President because it contained too many tax increases.*

vetoing – vetoed – have vetoed

2 an occasion when people vote

election /ɪˈlekʃən/ [n C] when people vote to choose a government or leader: *Since the last election, unemployment has increased.*

hold an election *South Africa held its first multi-racial elections in 1994.*

presidential election (=an election to choose a president)

general election BRITISH (=an election to choose a government)

referendum /ˌrefəˈrendəm/ [n C] when everyone in a country votes to say what they think about an important political question

hold a referendum *A referendum held in the Ukraine showed strong support for independence.*

+ on *The Irish people voted 'no' in a referendum on divorce in 1986.*

ballot /ˈbælət/ [n C] when members of an organization decide something by marking what they want on a piece of paper, especially in order to make sure that it is secret: *The result of the ballot showed that nurses were not in favour of a strike.* | *a secret ballot*

vote /vəʊt/ [n singular] when a group of people, especially a committee or parliament, vote to decide something: *Winterton announced that he would not be supporting the plan in Monday's vote.*

3 someone who votes

voter /ˈvəʊtəʳ/ [n C] someone who votes in a political election: *Italian voters have shown what they think of the corrupt old party system.*

Republican/Labour etc voters (=people who vote for the Republican Party etc)

W

WAIT

➡ see also EXPECT, STAY

1 to wait

wait /weɪt/ [v I] to spend time not doing very much, while you are expecting something to happen or expecting someone to arrive: *Wait here until I get back.* | *Hurry up, everyone's waiting.*

wait for sb/sth (=wait until someone arrives, is ready etc) *I'll stay here and wait for Suzie.*

wait (for) a minute/two hours/a long time etc *Where have you been? I've been waiting for ages.* | *You'll have to wait a few minutes – I'm not ready yet.*

wait to do sth *Are you waiting to use the phone?*

wait for sb/sth to do sth *She waited for him to reply.*

keep sb waiting (=make someone wait, for example by arriving late) *I'm so sorry I kept you waiting.*

wait and see (=be patient until you find out) *I've sent the letter – now I'll just have to wait and see what happens.*

⚠ Don't say 'I'll wait you', 'they waited the bus' etc. Say **I'll wait for you, they waited for the bus** etc.

⚠ You can say **I waited an hour** or **I waited for an hour**. Both are correct.

hold on /ˌhəʊld ˈɒn‖-ˈɑːn/ [phrasal verb I] SPOKEN to wait a little longer: *I can hold on for a few minutes if you like.*

hang around /ˌhæŋ əˈraʊnd/ [phrasal verb I] INFORMAL to wait in one place without doing anything, so that you are wasting time: *Sally hung around for over an hour but no-one came.*

keep sb hanging around *You knew I was in a hurry. Why did you keep me hanging around?*

When you see **EC**, go to the **ESSENTIAL COMMUNICATION** section.

2 what you say to tell someone to wait

wait /weɪt/ SPOKEN *Wait – I must phone Les before we go.*

wait a minute/second/moment *Wait a minute, I'll get my coat.*

just a minute/just a second /ˌdʒʌst ə ˈmɪnɪt, ˌdʒʌst ə ˈsekənd/ SPOKEN say this when you want someone to wait a short time before going somewhere or doing something: *Just a minute – I have to check I locked the back door.*

hold on/hang on /ˌhəʊld ˈɒn, ˌhæŋ ˈɒn‖-ˈɑːn/ SPOKEN INFORMAL say this to tell someone to wait for a short time: *Hold on – I haven't finished yet.*

+ a minute/moment/second etc *Hang on a minute while I find her phone number.*

wait up /ˌweɪt ˈʌp/ AMERICAN SPOKEN say this to tell someone to stop, because you want to talk to them or go with them: *Wait up, you guys! I can't walk so fast.*

hold the line /ˌhəʊld ðə ˈlaɪn/ SPOKEN say this in a business telephone conversation to ask someone to wait for a moment, until the person they want to speak to is ready to answer: *Hold the line, please, I'll see if he's available.*

bear with me /ˈbeəʳ wɪð miː/ SPOKEN FORMAL say this to ask someone to wait patiently, while you explain something or while you finish what you are doing: *If you just bear with me, I'll explain.*

3 to stand in a line of people waiting

queue/queue up /kjuː, ˌkjuː ˈʌp/ [v I] BRITISH to stand in a line of people who are all waiting for the same thing: *Students were queuing up at the bus-stop.*

queue (up) to do sth *It's worth queuing up to get the best tickets.*

queue (up) for sth (=in order to get something) *The refugees had to queue for food and water.*

stand in line/wait in line /ˌstænd ɪn ˈlaɪn, ˌweɪt ɪn ˈlaɪn/ AMERICAN to stand in a line of people who are all waiting for the same thing: *people waiting in line outside a nightclub*

stand/wait in line to do sth *We stood in line for two hours to get into the stadium.*

line up /ˌlaɪn ˈʌp/ [phrasal verb I] if people **line up**, they go and stand in a line and wait to do something or be given something: *The prisoners were told to line up at the gate.*

line up to do sth *They lined up to receive their prizes.*

queue BRITISH **line** AMERICAN /kjuː, laɪn/ [n C] a line of people who are all waiting for the same thing: *The queue went right round the block.* | *After waiting an hour, we got to the front of the line.*

join a queue/line (=start waiting in it) *I joined the queue for a taxi.*

4 able to wait quietly and calmly

patient /ˈpeɪʃənt/ [adj] able to wait calmly without becoming annoyed or bored: *I'm sure she'll write soon. Just try to be patient.*

patiently [adv] *The audience waited patiently for the show to begin.*

patience [n U] when you can wait calmly without becoming annoyed or bored: *It's easy to grow your own plants – all you need is a little time and patience.*

5 unable to wait quietly and calmly

impatient /ɪmˈpeɪʃənt/ [adj] becoming annoyed because you have been waiting for a long time: *Don't be so impatient. I'm doing it as fast as I can.*

get/become/grow impatient *I could see that Max was getting impatient.*

impatiently [adv] *The customs officer waved them on impatiently.*

impatience [n U] annoyance caused by waiting for a long time: *People were beginning to show signs of impatience.*

WAKE UP/GET UP

➡ see also **TIRED, SLEEP**

1 to stop sleeping

wake up/wake /ˌweɪk ˈʌp, weɪk/ [phrasal verb I] to stop sleeping: *I woke up at five o'clock and couldn't get back*

to sleep again. | *Babies often wake because they are hungry.*

waking – woke – have woken

> ⚠ Wake is more formal than wake up.

be awake /biː əˈweɪk/ to not be asleep: *"Are you awake, Lucy?" she whispered.* | *I'm usually awake before anyone else.*

be wide awake (=be completely awake) *It was past midnight, but Jill was still wide awake.*

come round BRITISH **come around** AMERICAN /ˌkʌm (ə)ˈraʊnd/ [phrasal verb I] to gradually become conscious again after being given a drug or being hit on the head: *She was coming round after her operation, but she still felt dizzy and very sleepy.*

2 to make someone stop sleeping

wake/wake up /weɪk, ˌweɪk ˈʌp/ [v T] *Be quiet, or you'll wake my parents.* | *We were woken by a loud banging on the door.*

wake sb up *The alarm clock woke me up at 8 o'clock.*

wake up sb *They were making enough noise to wake up the whole street!*

waking – woke – have woken

disturb /dɪˈstɜːrb/ [v T] to accidentally wake someone who is sleeping, by making a noise or movement: *I got undressed in the bathroom to avoid disturbing her.*

3 to get out of bed

get up /ˌget ˈʌp/ [phrasal verb I] to get out of bed, especially in the morning in order to get ready for the day: *Frank gets up at five-thirty every morning.*

get up early *I think we should get up early and leave before breakfast.*

be up /biː ˈʌp/ [phrasal verb I] to be out of bed and doing things: *Is Harry up yet?* | *I was up at six this morning.* | *Jake had been up since dawn.*

4 to stay in bed until late in the morning

get up late /ˌget ʌp ˈleɪt/ to get out of bed later than usual in the morning: *We usually get up late on Sundays.* | *I got up late and missed my nine o'clock class.*

W

have a lie in BRITISH **sleep late** AMER-ICAN /hæv ə 'laɪ ɪn, ˌsliːp 'leɪt/ to stay in bed longer than usual in the morning, because you do not need to get up: *It's Saturday tomorrow, so I can have a lie in.* | *She knows I sleep late on weekends, so she doesn't disturb me.*

stay in bed /ˌsteɪ ɪn 'bed/ to not get out of bed, even though you are awake: *If you're not well, you'd better stay in bed.* | *He's so lazy – he often stays in bed all day!*

oversleep /ˌəʊvəˈsliːp/ [v I] to accidentally sleep longer than you intended to, so that you are late for something: *Sorry I'm late – I overslept.* | *I was worried that we would oversleep and miss the plane.*
oversleeping – overslept – have overslept

WALK

➡ see also **RUN**

W

1 to walk

walk /wɔːk/ [v I] *Anna missed the bus, so she decided to walk.* | *How old was your baby when she learned to walk?*
+ into/out of/along/back etc *He walked out of the station and got into a taxi.* | *I was walking along Main Street when I met Pierre.*
walk home *She hates walking home alone at night.*
walk two miles/100 metres etc *We must have walked about five miles today.*

on foot /ɒn 'fʊt/ if you go somewhere **on foot**, you walk instead of going by car, bus, train etc: *It isn't far. It'll take you about ten minutes on foot.*
go/travel on foot *The bus left us at the bottom of the hill, and we went the rest of the way on foot.*

wander /ˈwɒndəʳ‖ˈwɑːn-/ [v I] to walk without hurrying and without going directly to a particular place, either for pleasure or because you are lost
+ around/about/into etc *I spent the morning wandering around the old part of the city, looking at the buildings.*

stride /straɪd/ [v I] to walk quickly, taking big steps, in an angry or confident way
+ into/out of/towards etc *Brian strode out of the room without speaking.* | *The Principal came striding towards me, and shook my hand.*

stride

striding – strode – have strode

⚠ Use **stride** especially in written stories or descriptions.

march

march /mɑːtʃ/ [v I] if soldiers **march**, they all walk together with regular steps
+ into/through/past etc *Thousands of US soldiers marched through the streets of Paris.*

wade

wade /weɪd/ [v I] to walk through deep water
+ across/towards/through etc *They waded across the river.*

2 to walk for pleasure or for exercise

go for a walk /ˌgəʊ fər ə 'wɔːk/ to walk somewhere for pleasure or for exercise: *It's a lovely evening. Why don't we go for a walk?*

When you see **EC**, go to the **ESSENTIAL COMMUNICATION** section.

stroll/go for a stroll

/strəʊl, ˌɡəʊ fər ə ˈstrəʊl/ [v I] to walk in a slow and relaxed way, especially for pleasure

stroll

+ along/through/across etc They strolled along the riverbank, enjoying the evening sun. | They decided to go for a stroll along the beach.

hiking /ˈhaɪkɪŋ/ [n U] the activity of going for long walks in the countryside

go hiking My parents go hiking a lot.

3 a journey that you make by walking

walk /wɔːk/ [n C] a journey that you make by walking, either for pleasure or exercise, or in order to go somewhere

go for a walk (=walk for pleasure or exercise) I love going for walks in the countryside.

a long/short/ten-minute etc walk (=used to say how long it takes to walk somewhere) It's a long walk from here to the nearest town. | "How far is it to the post office?" "It's not far – just a 5-minute walk."

hike /haɪk/ [n C] a long walk in the countryside

go on a hike We went on lots of great hikes.

4 to walk quietly

tiptoe

tiptoe /ˈtɪptəʊ/ [v I] to walk on your toes because you do not want to make any noise

+ into/out of/past etc He tiptoed out of the room, trying not to wake the baby.

tiptoeing – tiptoed – have tiptoed

creep

creep/sneak /kriːp, sniːk/ [v I] to walk quietly and carefully because you do not want anyone to notice you

+ in/through/across/out etc He unlocked the back door and crept out into the yard. | They must have sneaked in while the guard wasn't looking.

creep up/sneak up behind sb (=in order to surprise them) She crept up behind him and put her hands over his eyes.

creeping – crept – have crept

sneaking – sneaked (also **snuck** AMERICAN) **– have sneaked** (also **have snuck** AMERICAN)

5 to walk slowly and with difficulty

limp /lɪmp/ [v I] to walk with difficulty because you have hurt one of your legs

+ along/over/towards She limped painfully over to a chair and sat down.

a limp [n singular] a limping movement: Josie walked with a slight limp.

stagger /ˈstæɡəʳ/ [v I] if you **stagger**, you do not walk straight and you almost fall over, because you are injured, drunk, or very tired

+ into/out of/along etc Kevin staggered over to our table. | A man came staggering into the building, bleeding from his chest.

trudge /trʌdʒ/ [v I] to walk slowly using a lot of effort, for example because you are going up a hill, carrying heavy bags, or walking through snow

+ back/along/home etc The car broke down and we had to trudge back home through the snow.

6 a single movement you make when you are walking

step /step/ [n C] the single movement that you make when you put one foot in front of the other when you are walking

W

take a step *She walked briskly, taking quick, short steps.*

footstep /'fʊtstep/ [n C usually plural] the sound of someone's feet when they are walking or running: *Suddenly Rachel heard footsteps behind her in the dark street.*

pace /peɪs/ [n C] the distance you go when you take a single step: *He took a couple of paces forward, then stopped.*

7 someone who is walking

pedestrian /pɪ'destrɪən/ [n C] someone who is walking in a town, instead of going by car, bus, bicycle etc: *Banning traffic from the shopping areas has made life much more pleasant for pedestrians.*

walker /'wɔːkəʳ/ [n C] someone who walks in the countryside for pleasure: *There's a rough track through the woods for riders and walkers.*

WANT

W

LIKE/NOT LIKE   DON'T CARE

ENJOY   INTEND

see also

LOVE   EXCITING/ EXCITED

ENTHUSIASTIC/   POPULAR/
UNENTHUSIASTIC   UNPOPULAR

1 to want something or want to do something

want /wɒnt‖wɑːnt, wɔːnt/ [v T]
want to do sth *What do you want to do at the weekend?* | *Stacey wants to be a doctor.*
want sth *Do you want milk in your coffee?* | *My parents moved out of London because they wanted a bigger house.*
want sb to do sth *She wants Tom to come to her party.*
what sb wants is *What we want is a car that's cheap and reliable.*

⚠ Don't say 'I want visit England'. Say **I want to visit England.**

⚠ Don't say 'I want that you do it'. Say **I want you to do it.**

⚠ You can use **want** without an object or infinitive in expressions like 'if you want' or 'if you want to': *You can come with us if you want to.* | *They are free to leave whenever they want.*

would like /wʊd 'laɪk/ ESPECIALLY SPOKEN use this as a polite way of asking for something, offering something, or saying what you want to do
would like to do sth *I'd like to reserve a room for Saturday.* | *Would you like to borrow this book?*
would like sth *We'd like some information about flights to Chicago, please.* | *Would you like some more coffee?*
would like sb to do sth *We would like you to attend an interview at 3:30 on Friday.*

feel like /'fiːl laɪk/ ESPECIALLY SPOKEN to want to have something or do something, because you think you would enjoy it
feel like doing sth *I feel like watching a video tonight.* | *I just didn't feel like going to school.*
feel like sth *Do you feel like a glass of wine?* | *It's a lovely day – do you feel like a walk?*
if you feel like it (=if you want to) *Come and see us tomorrow if you feel like it.*

be interested in /biː 'ɪntrɪstɪd ɪn/ to think that you may want to do something, buy something, or get involved in something
be interested in doing sth *We're interested in buying an apartment downtown.* | *Would you be interested in joining the local drama club?*
be interested in sth *Clare was interested in a career in teaching.*

I wouldn't mind /aɪ ˌwʊdnt 'maɪnd/ SPOKEN say this to tell someone politely that you want to do something or want to have something, especially with them
I wouldn't mind sth *I wouldn't mind another cup of coffee. How about you?*
I wouldn't mind doing sth *It was a really good play. I wouldn't mind seeing it again.*
I wouldn't mind (when answering someone's question) *"Do you want to go out*

for a meal sometime?" "Yes, I wouldn't mind."

⚠ **I wouldn't mind** is less definite than **I want** or **I'd like**.

🔍 **if you like** /ɪf juː 'laɪk/ SPOKEN say this when you are offering to let someone do something if they want to do it: *You can stay here tonight, if you like.* | *If you like, I could check your essay for you.*

by choice /baɪ 'tʃɔɪs/ if you do something **by choice**, you do it because you want to do it, and not because anyone forces you to do it: *Jim lives with his parents by choice – he could rent his own place if he wanted to.*

2 to want something very much

wish /wɪʃ/ [v T not in passive] to want something to happen, when it is unlikely or impossible that it will happen, or when you cannot control what will happen
+ (that) *I wish I had a car like that.* | *Beth wished that she could stay there forever.*
wish sb/sth would do sth *I wish they would turn that music down.*

⚠ Don't confuse **wish** (=want something that is unlikely or impossible) and **hope** (=want something that is likely or possible) *I wish the weather would stay like this forever.* | *I hope the weather stays fine this weekend.*

⚠ Don't say 'I wish I can fly'. Say **I wish I could fly** (=but I can't). Use past tense forms after **wish (that)** *I wish I knew* (=but I don't know). | *I bet you wish you had a ticket!* (=but you don't).

⚠ Don't say 'I wish to be rich'. Say **I want to be rich** (=it is possible) or **I wish I were rich** (=but I am not). **Wish** is used with the infinitive only in very formal or official situations: *The President wishes to thank all his staff for their help.*

🔍 **would love** /wʊd 'lʌv/ ESPECIALLY SPOKEN to want something very much, and feel that you would be happy if you had it
would love sth *I would love a cup of coffee.*

would love to do sth *She would love to have children but she hasn't met the right man.*
would love sb to do sth *My mother would love me to come and live in New York with her.*

🔍 **I can't wait** /aɪ ˌkɑːnt 'weɪt‖-ˌkænt-/ SPOKEN say this when you want something to happen as soon as possible, because you know you will enjoy it and you are very excited about it: *"You're going on holiday soon, aren't you?" "Yes, I can't wait."*
I can't wait to do sth *I can't wait to see Bill again – it's been a long time.*
+ for *I can't wait for Christmas.*

🔍 **be dying** /biː 'daɪ-ɪŋ/ SPOKEN INFORMAL to want something very much, and feel that you must have it or do it immediately
be dying to do sth *I'm dying to meet Lisa's new boyfriend.*
+ for *I'm dying for a drink – let's go to a bar.*

3 to want one thing more than another thing

would prefer /wʊd prɪ'fɜːʳ/ if you **would prefer** something or **would prefer** to do something, you want it or want to do it more than something else: *"Would you like a coffee?" "I'd prefer a cold drink, please."*
would prefer to do sth *Anna would prefer to live in Italy, but she can't find a job there.*
would much prefer (=want something much more than something else) *Jack wants to go out, but I'd much prefer to stay home and watch TV.*

🔍 **I'd rather** /aɪd 'rɑːðəʳ‖-'ræ-/ SPOKEN use this to say that you want something or want to do something more than something else
I'd/she'd rather do sth *Paula said she'd rather go by car.* | *an experience that I'd rather forget* | *Would you rather go swimming or play tennis?*

4 to be willing to do what someone else wants you to do

be willing to do sth /biː ˌwɪlɪŋ tə 'duː (sth)/ if you **are willing to** do something, you will agree to do it because it is necessary or because someone has asked you to do it: *He's willing to tell the police everything he knows.* | *To do well as a journalist, you have to be willing to change jobs very frequently.*

willingly [adv] *I'd willingly pay higher taxes if the money was spent on health and education.*

be ready to do sth /biː ˌredi tə ˈduː (sth)/ to be willing to do something at any time, whenever it needs to be done: *I'm always ready to help if you need me.* | *The Bosnian leaders said they were ready to discuss a peace settlement.*

be glad/happy to do sth /biː ˌglæd, ˌhæpi tə ˈduː (sth)/ to be very willing to do something in order to help someone: *John says he'd be happy to give you a hand with the gardening.* | *The bank will be glad to assist you with a loan.*

5 to not want to do something

not want to do sth /nɒt ˌwɒnt tə ˈduː (sth)‖ˌwɑːnt-/ *She doesn't want to see me anymore.* | *We asked him to come with us, but he said he didn't want to.*

not want sb to do sth *"Why didn't he tell me he was sick?" "He didn't want you to worry."*

○**not feel like doing sth** /nɒt ˌfiːl laɪk ˈduːɪŋ (sth)/ ESPECIALLY SPOKEN to not want to do something, especially because you think you would not enjoy it or because you feel too lazy: *I don't feel like writing that essay today.* | *Some days she just doesn't feel like going to work.*

○**I'd rather not** /aɪd ˈrɑːðər nɒt‖-ˈræ-/ SPOKEN say this when you do not want to do something, especially because you think it may cause problems for you: *I suppose I could lend him the money, but to be honest, I'd rather not.*

I'd rather not do sth *Really, I'd rather not talk about it right now.*

be unwilling to do sth /biː ʌnˈwɪlɪŋ tə duː (sth)/ FORMAL to not want to do something, even though you should do it or someone wants you to do it: *She is unwilling to admit that she was wrong.* | *Most people here are unwilling to give up their cars and use buses and trains instead.*

reluctant /rɪˈlʌktənt/ [adj] unwilling to do something, even though you may agree to do it if someone persuades you

be reluctant to do sth *Some of the older staff were reluctant to use the new equipment.*

reluctantly [adv] *We offered them $500, which they accepted rather reluctantly.*

against your will /əˌgenst jɔːr ˈwɪl/ if you do something **against your will**, you do not want to do it, but someone makes you do it: *The refugees were sent back against their will.* | *Her father can't force her to marry against her will.*

6 a feeling that you want to do something

desire /dɪˈzaɪər/ [n C] ESPECIALLY WRITTEN a strong feeling of wanting to have something or wanting to do something, especially something important, which makes you try very hard to have it or do it

desire to do something *children with a keen desire to learn and succeed*

+ for *After so many years of war, there was a great desire for peace.*

⚠ Don't say 'a desire of doing something'. Say **a desire to do something.**

urge /ɜːrdʒ/ [n C] a sudden strong feeling that you want to do something, especially a feeling that is difficult to control

urge to do sth *I felt a sudden urge to tell him all my problems.* | *Sheena resisted the urge to get in her car and go home.*

wish /wɪʃ/ [n C] FORMAL a feeling that you want something to happen, especially when this is very important to you: *His last wish was that his body should be buried in his home town.*

sb's dearest/greatest wish (=the thing they want most of all) *She always wanted to see her grandchildren again – it was her dearest wish.*

respect sb's wishes (=do what someone wants you to do because it is important to them) *The doctor has to respect the wishes of the patient.*

When you see **EC**, go to the **ESSENTIAL COMMUNICATION** section.

7 something that you want to achieve

ambition /æmˈbɪʃən/ [n C] something which you want to achieve in the future, especially in your work, and which you will try hard to achieve

sb's ambition is to do sth *Her ambition was to go to law school and become an attorney.*

achieve/fulfil your ambition (=finally do what you wanted to do) *Earlier this year, he achieved his ambition of competing in the Olympic Games.*

dream /driːm/ [n C] something very special that you want to do and that you think about a lot, especially something that is not very likely to happen

sb's dream is to do sth *Her dream was to go to Hollywood and become a movie star.*

dream of doing sth *After the accident, Clarke had to give up his dream of becoming a racing driver.*

sb's dream comes true (=they finally do what they want) *Last year her dream came true and she was offered a chance to study in America.*

goal /gəʊl/ [n C] something important that a person, company, or government hopes to achieve in the future, even though it may take a long time

achieve/reach a goal *By 1975, they had achieved their goal of providing free education for every child.*

sb's goal is to do sth *Our goal is to become the biggest-selling brand of coffee in the country.*

short-term goal/long-term goal (=one that you hope to achieve soon/a long time in the future)

target /ˈtɑːrgət/ [n C] a particular amount or total that you want to achieve, for example an amount of products you must sell or produce: *We produced 16,000 cars this year, but our target was 17,500.*

achieve/reach/meet a target *The Government is struggling to reach its target of $23 billion in spending cuts.*

set (sb) a target (=say what the target is) *I set myself a target of learning 20 new words each week.*

8 an offer, opportunity etc that makes you want to do something

attractive /əˈtræktɪv/ [adj] an **attractive** offer, idea, opportunity etc makes you want to do something because you think that you would enjoy it or get advantages from it: *It was an attractive offer, and I accepted the job.* | *Cycling would be an attractive alternative to driving if there were better cycle paths.*

+ to *Low business taxes make the area attractive to foreign investors.*

tempting /ˈtemptɪŋ/ [adj] a **tempting** offer or suggestion makes you want to do something, but you think that you should not do it: *"Why don't you come out with Phil and me tonight?" "It's a very tempting idea, but I have an essay to finish."* | *They made me a tempting offer, but it wasn't quite enough to make me take the job.*

incentive /ɪnˈsentɪv/ [n C] something that makes you want to work harder or do what someone else wants you to do, because you think you will get something good by doing it

incentive to do sth *We need to give young people an incentive to stay at school for longer.*

incentive for sb to do sth *There is no incentive for farmers to grow more food.*

WAR

➡ opposite **PEACE**

see also

ARMY
ATTACK
EXPLODE
DEFEND
DESTROY
WEAPON
KILL
SHOOT
HURT/INJURE

1 fighting between countries or armies

war /wɔːr/ [n C/U] a long period of fighting, when the armies, ships, and planes of two or more countries fight against each other in many different places: *the Vietnam War* | *When the war ended in 1945, Europe was in chaos.*

win/lose a war *Who won the Franco-Prussian War?*

civil war (=war between groups of people from the same country) *More Americans died in the Civil War than in World War II.*

declare war (on) (=make an official statement that you are going to fight another country)

+ against/with *Iran's seven-year war with Iraq*

+ between *the wars between England and Scotland*

war breaks out (=war begins) *In 1874, war broke out in Europe again.*

> ⚠ You can also use **war** before a noun, like an adjective: *a war hero* | *war movies*

battle /'bætl/ [n C] a fight between two armies, or two groups of ships or planes in one place: *a naval battle in the North Sea*

+ of *the Battle of the Somme*

win/lose a battle *The French lost the Battle of Agincourt in 1415.*

conflict /'kɒnflɪkt‖'kɑːn-/ [n C/U] a situation in which two countries or groups are fighting against each other – used especially in newspapers: *the conflict in Somalia* | *a peace settlement that brought an end to years of conflict.*

rebellion /rɪ'beljən/ [n C] an organized attempt to change or destroy the government by fighting against it: *The rebellion spread quickly through the Western Provinces.*

+ against *an armed rebellion against the government*

crush a rebellion (=use force to stop it) *The army was brought in to crush the rebellion.*

fighting /'faɪtɪŋ/ [n U] when soldiers fight against each other during a war or battle: *The UN had failed to stop the fighting in Rwanda.*

heavy/fierce fighting (=a lot of fighting when many people are hurt) *The streets of Kabul are now quiet again after three weeks of heavy fighting.*

warfare /'wɔːrfeər/ [n U] the activity of fighting in a war – use this especially to talk about the methods of fighting that are used in war: *the history of modern warfare*

nuclear/chemical warfare (=fighting with nuclear bombs or poison gas)

guerrilla warfare (=when small unofficial military groups fight against the government)

2 to fight a war or be in a war

fight /faɪt/ [v I/T] to take part in a war or battle: *His grandfather fought on the Republican side in the Spanish Civil War.* | *The Boers were fighting the British at this time.*

+ for *Most of these young soldiers don't even know what they're fighting for.*

fight a war/battle *They were fighting a war of independence against a powerful enemy.*

fighting – fought – have fought

be at war /biː ət 'wɔːr/ if two countries **are at war** with each other, they are fighting a war against each other: *Iran and Iraq had been at war for several years.*

+ with *In 1792, England was at war with America.*

3 during a war

wartime /'wɔːrtaɪm/ [adj only before noun] happening during the time when there is a war: *He died on a wartime bombing mission.* | *Her wartime experiences were still fresh in her memory.*

wartime /'wɔːrtaɪm/ [n U] (=during the time when there is a war)

in wartime *the importance of secrecy in wartime*

in the war /ɪn ðə 'wɔːr/ during the particular war that you are talking about: *What did your father do in the war?*

4 the place where a war is fought

battlefield /'bætlfiːld/ [n C] a place where two armies fight a battle against each other during a war: *Thousands died on the battlefields of northern France.*

the front line/the front /ðə ˌfrʌnt 'laɪn, ðə 'frʌnt/ [n singular] the line along which enemies are fighting each other during a war: *We were now just a few kilometres behind the front line.*

the Western/Eastern/Russian front *Her grandfather had spent four years on the Western Front.*

war zone /'wɔːʳ zəʊn/ [n C] an area which is very dangerous because a war is being fought there: *the latest news from the war zone*

5 the people you are fighting against in a war

enemy /'enəmi/ [n C] someone that you are fighting against in a war: *Even though these soldiers were our enemies, I still felt sorry for them.*

the enemy (=the army or country that your army or country is fighting against in a war) *They accused him of giving secret information to the enemy.*

plural **enemies**

⚠️ You can also use **enemy** before a noun, like an adjective: *an enemy plane | enemy territory*

WARN

➡ see also **TELL, ADVISE**

warn /wɔːʳn/ [v T] to tell someone about something bad or dangerous that might happen, so that they can avoid it or prevent it: *We tried to warn her, but she refused to listen.*

warn sb (that) *Allen warned him that he might be killed if he stayed in Beirut. | The local people were warned that the volcano might erupt at any time.*

warn sb about sth *Parents should warn their children about the dangers of smoking.*

warn sb not to do sth/warn sb against doing sth (=tell someone they should not do something because it is dangerous or risky) *Police are warning drivers not to go out on the roads unless their journey is really necessary. | I tried to warn him against sending Phil any money.*

warning /'wɔːʳnɪŋ/ [n C/U] something that you say or do to warn people about danger or to warn them not to do something: *All cigarette packets carry a government health warning.*

give a warning *The weather report gave a warning of more snow and icy roads.*

+ to *Two of the prisoners were publicly beaten, as a warning to the others.*

without (any) warning (=without giving a warning) *Soldiers began firing into the crowd without any warning.*

⚠️ You can also use **warning** before a noun, like an adjective: *Headaches may be warning signs of a more serious illness.*

beware /bɪ'weəʳ/ [v I only in imperative] used on signs to warn people about something dangerous

+ of *Beware of the bull. | Beware of falling rocks.*

WASH

➡ if you mean 'to make something clean', go to **CLEAN 2**
➡ see also **DIRTY, MARK, SHINE**

1 to wash your hands/ face/body etc

wash /wɒʃ‖wɑːʃ, wɔːʃ/ [v I/T] to clean yourself with soap and water: *Harry went upstairs to wash.*

wash your hands/face/hair *She was washing her hair when the phone rang. | Have you boys washed your hands yet?*

⚠️ Don't say 'I washed myself', 'she washed herself' etc. Say **I washed my hands, she had a wash** etc.

have a wash (also **wash up** AMERICAN) /hæv ə 'wɒʃ, ˌwɒʃ 'ʌp‖-'wɑːʃ/ to wash your hands and face: *You'll feel better once you've had a wash and something to eat. | You kids go wash up now – dinner's nearly ready.*

have a bath BRITISH **take a bath** AMERICAN /ˌhæv ə 'bɑːθ, ˌteɪk ə 'bɑːθ‖-'bæθ/ to wash your whole body while sitting in a bath full of water: *Is there enough hot water for me to have a bath? | All the kids used to take a bath in the same tub.*

have a shower BRITISH **take a shower** AMERICAN /ˌhæv ə ˈʃaʊəʳ, ˌteɪk ə ˈʃaʊəʳ/ to wash your whole body while standing under a shower: *I'll just have a quick shower and get changed.* | *She decided to take a shower before dinner.*

brush your teeth (also **clean your teeth** BRITISH) /ˌbrʌʃ jɔːʳ ˈtiːθ, ˌkliːn jɔːʳ ˈtiːθ/ to clean your teeth by brushing them: *Have you brushed your teeth this morning?*

Ⓠ**freshen up** /ˌfreʃən ˈʌp/ [phrasal verb I] ESPECIALLY SPOKEN to wash your face and hands so that you feel more comfortable, for example when you have been working hard or travelling: *The bathroom's on the right if you'd like to freshen up.* | *She hoped there would be time to freshen up before the interview.*

2 to wash a car/floor/wall/object etc

wash /wɒʃ‖wɑːʃ, wɔːʃ/ [v T] to clean something using a lot of water, and often soap: *He spent all morning washing the car.* | *The spinach leaves should be washed in cold water.*

clean /kliːn/ [v T] to clean something using soap and water or a special liquid or chemical, and usually by rubbing with a cloth or brush: *Nancy cleans the windows once a month.* | *Where's that stuff you use for cleaning the bathtub?*

mop /mɒp‖mɑːp/ [v T] to wash a floor with soap and water, using a special tool with a long handle: *Dan has to mop the floor of the café every night.*
mopping – mopped – have mopped

mop

scrub /skrʌb/ [v T] to make something very clean, using a stiff brush and water, or soap and water
scrub the floor/table/vegetables/your hands *Lou was on her knees, scrubbing the kitchen floor.* | *Scrub the potatoes, then put them in a pan of boiling water.*
scrubbing – scrubbed – have scrubbed

When you see **EC**, go to the **ESSENTIAL COMMUNICATION** section.

⚠ You can also say **give something a wash/a clean/a scrub** (especially in British English), and it means the same: *The oven needs a good clean.* (=needs to be cleaned well)

3 to wash clothes

wash /wɒʃ‖wɑːʃ, wɔːʃ/ [v I/T] to wash clothes, especially in a washing machine: *Could you wash this shirt for me?* | *I seem to spend all my time washing and ironing these days.* | *You ought to wash that sweater by hand.*

dry-clean /ˌdraɪ ˈkliːn/ [v T] to clean clothes using special chemicals instead of soap and water: *Don't put that dress in the washing machine – the label says it should be dry-cleaned.*
dry-cleaner's [n C] a shop where you can get your clothes dry-cleaned: *Could you collect my suit from the dry-cleaner's?*

do the washing BRITISH **do the laundry** AMERICAN /ˌduː ðə ˈwɒʃɪŋ, ˌduː ðə ˈlɔːndri‖-ˈwɑːʃ-/ to wash all the clothes that need to be washed: *Did you do the laundry this morning?*

get sth out /ˌget (sth) ˈaʊt/ [phrasal verb T] to remove a mark from clothes or material: *How can I get this coffee stain out?*

launderette BRITISH **laundromat** AMERICAN /lɔːnˈdret, ˈlɔːndrəmæt/ [n C] a place where you can pay to wash your clothes in a washing machine

4 to wash cups/plates/knives/pans etc

wash the dishes/do the dishes /ˌwɒʃ ðə ˈdɪʃɪz, ˌduː ðə ˈdɪʃɪz‖ˌwɑːʃ-/ to wash all the cups, plates, knives etc that you have used during a meal: *My mom always makes me wash the dishes.* | *Can I help do the dishes?*

do the washing up/wash up BRITISH /ˌduː ðə ˌwɒʃɪŋ ˈʌp, ˌwɒʃ ˈʌp‖-ˌwɑːʃ-/ to wash all the cups, plates, knives etc that you have used during a meal: *If you'll do the cooking tonight, I'll do the washing up.*

⚠ **Wash up** has different meanings in American and British English. In American English it means to wash your hands and face.

5 **to wash with water but without soap**

rinse /rɪns/ [v T] to wash something with water in order to remove soap or dirt: *I'll just rinse the lettuce under the tap.* | *Rosie rinsed her mouth to get rid of the taste.*
rinse out a cup/pan/glass (=quickly clean a container, just using water) *He rinsed out a glass and poured himself a whiskey.*

soak /səʊk/ [v T] to leave something in water for a long time in order to clean it or make it easier to wash later: *You'll have to soak that shirt to get the blood off it.*
leave sth to soak *Just leave that pan to soak overnight.*

WASTE
to use more than you need, or use something in a way that is not useful

➡ see also **RUBBISH, GET RID OF**

1 **to waste something**

waste /weɪst/ [v T] to use time, money, food etc in a way that is not useful or sensible: *I wasted 40 minutes waiting for a bus this morning.* | *Don't leave the light on – you're wasting electricity.*
waste money/time on sth *Bill wastes all his money on beer and cigarettes.* | *Let's not waste any more time on this.*

wasted /ˈweɪstɪd/ [adj] something that is **wasted** is not used in a sensible way, or does not produce a useful result: *I felt as if my education had been wasted when I couldn't get a job.* | *I'm sorry you've had a wasted trip. Mr Newton isn't here at the moment.*

2 **something that wastes time, money etc**

be a waste of sth /biː ə ˈweɪst ɒv (sth)/ if something **is a waste of** time, money, energy etc, it annoys you because it uses time, money etc in a way that has no useful results: *That class was a complete waste of time – I didn't learn anything.* |

My parents think going to football games is a waste of money. | *a pointless war that was a terrible waste of human life*

wasteful /ˈweɪstfəl/ [adj] an activity or method that is **wasteful** uses too much money, food, energy etc, without any useful results: *Vegetarians say that raising animals for food is wasteful and expensive.* | *wasteful packaging*

inefficient /ˌɪnɪˈfɪʃənt◄/ [adj] an organization or system that is **inefficient** does not work well, so it uses more time, money, or energy than it needs to: *an inefficient heating system* | *Local government was corrupt and inefficient.*

WATCH
to look at and pay attention to something that is happening

➡ see also **SEE, LOOK AT**

> ⚠ See, look, or watch? Don't confuse **see** (=notice or experience something with your eyes, though not always deliberately), **look** (=deliberately turn your eyes towards something in order to see it), and **watch** (=look for some time at something that is happening or moving).

1 **to watch someone or something**

watch /wɒtʃ‖wɑːtʃ, wɔːtʃ/ [v I/T] to look for some time at something that is happening or moving, and pay attention to what you see: *A large crowd was watching the football game.* | *Do you want to play with us or just sit and watch?* | *The police were watching the house, but Morgan escaped.* | *Watch me, Dad! I'm going to jump over these boxes.*
watch sb do sth/watch sb doing sth *He watched them slowly climb the hill.* | *I used to love watching my sister riding her horse.*
watch television/a video/a programme etc *You watch too much television.* | *Did you watch 'Roseanne' last night?*

see /siː/ [v T] to watch a television programme, film, play etc – use this especially to say whether you were able to watch a particular programme, film etc or whether you missed it: *I've never seen 'The Sound of Music'.* | *Did you see that programme about pandas last night?*

seeing – saw – have seen

⚠ Don't say 'see television'. Say **watch television**: *I enjoy watching television.*

keep an eye on sb/sth /ˌkiːp ən ˈaɪ ɒn (sb/sth)/ to watch someone or something carefully over a period of time, to make sure that nothing bad happens: *Keep an eye on the baby in case she gets too near the fire.*
+ for *Can you keep an eye on my bag for me? I'm just going to the toilet.*

spy on sb /ˈspaɪ ɒn (sb)/ [phrasal verb T] to watch someone secretly, in order to find out information about them: *The Princess accused some of the reporters of spying on her.*

2 always watching to see what happens

alert /əˈlɜːrt/ [adj] someone who is **alert** is always watching, and notices if anything strange or unusual happens: *Passengers should try to stay alert at all times, and report any suspicious packages to the police immediately.* | *An alert postman noticed some broken glass by the door.*

○**keep your eyes open** /ˌkiːp jɔːr ˈaɪz ˌəʊpən/ SPOKEN say this to tell someone to keep watching carefully so that they will see something that they are hoping or expecting to see: *We might see a dolphin if we're lucky, so keep your eyes open.*
+ for *She kept her eyes open for any bargains.*

3 someone who is watching something

spectator /spekˈteɪtər‖ˈspekteɪtər/ [n C] someone who is watching a game or other sports event: *The stadium holds 50,000 spectators.* | *Some of the spectators began throwing cans and beer bottles.*

audience /ˈɔːdiəns‖-, ˈɑː-/ [n C] all the people who are watching a play, concert, film etc: *The audience clapped and cheered.* | *There were several famous people in the audience.*

⚠ In British English, you can use **audience** with a singular or plural verb: *The audience was/were cheering loudly.* But in American English, use a singular verb.

viewer /ˈvjuːər/ [n C] someone who watches a television programme – used especially in newspapers and news reports: *Many television viewers were upset by the violence in last night's movie.* | *The concert was seen by 500 million viewers around the world.*

WAY

➡ look here for ...
• a way or method of doing something
• the way someone behaves
• the way you go from one place to another

1 a way or method of doing something
➡ see also SYSTEM, ORDER

way /weɪ/ [n C] a way of doing, making, or achieving something: *Potatoes can be cooked in many different ways.*
way to do sth *Visiting a country is a good way to learn its language.*
way of doing sth *Is there any way of controlling the heating in here?* | *Can you think of another way of saying this?*
way (that) sb does sth *I'll show you the way we calculate the cost.*
the best/only way *The only way to lose weight is to eat less.*

○**like this** /laɪk ˈðɪs/ SPOKEN in this way – say this when you are showing someone the way to do something: *You have to fold the corners back, like this.*

how /haʊ/ [adv] use this to say or ask the way that someone does something: *This pizza's delicious! How did you make it?* | *We don't know how she managed to escape.*
how to do sth *My dad's teaching me how to play chess.*

method /ˈmeθəd/ [n C] a planned way of doing something, especially one that is well known and often used: *Newspaper printing methods have changed*

completely in the last twenty years. |
traditional teaching methods

+ of You can choose whichever method
of payment you prefer.

method of doing sth The clinic provides
information about various methods of
preventing pregnancy.

means /miːnz/ [n C] a method, system, or
machine etc that you use to do something
or achieve something that you want

means of doing sth Education and training are the most effective means of
improving the nation's economy.

by means of sth (=using a particular
method or system) Sykes had obtained
the money by means of a trick. | The
enormous political changes in South
Africa were achieved by peaceful means.

**means of communication/transport/
transportation** E-mail has become an
important means of communication.

plural **means**

technique /tekˈniːk/ [n C] a particular way
of doing something, for which you need a
skill that has to be learned and practised:
Our teacher gave us some advice on
improving our exam technique. | man-
agement techniques

technique for doing sth Chapter 6
describes useful techniques for moving
documents about on screen.

strategy /ˈstrætədʒi/ [n C] a set of carefully
planned methods for achieving something
that is difficult and may take a long time:
the company's new marketing strategy

strategy for (doing) sth the government's long-term strategy for reducing
crime

plural **strategies**

tactics /ˈtæktɪks/ [n plural] methods you
use in order to achieve what you want,
especially in a game or competition: The
team was busy discussing tactics for the
game.

2 the way that someone behaves or talks

way /weɪ/ [n C] We try to treat all the
children in the same way. | Losing a job
affects different people in different ways.

the way (that) sb does sth I just love the
way she laughs. | I could tell by the way
he looked at me that he was annoyed.

sb's way of doing sth The younger girls
admired Louise, and tried to copy her
way of dressing.

how /haʊ/ [adv] use this to talk about the
way someone behaves or moves: Watch
how Cantona controls the ball. | I'll ask
her, but I'm not sure how she'll react.

manner /ˈmænər/ [n singular] the way that
someone behaves towards someone else
and talks to them: I didn't like her man-
ner – she seemed very impatient. | The
doctor had a relaxed, friendly manner.

3 the way you go from one place to another

➡ see also **DIRECTION**

way /weɪ/ [n singular] the road, path etc
that you must follow in order to get to a
place: Are you sure this is the way? |
The road was blocked, so we came back
a different way.

+ to/into Is this the way to Grand
Central Station? | I think this is the
quickest way into town.

the right/wrong way I don't recognize
this part of town – I think we've come
the wrong way.

know the way (=know how to get to a
place) Will you come with me? I don't
know the way.

ask/tell sb the way (=ask or tell someone
how to get to a place) He went into a
shop and asked the way to the hospital.

how to get to /ˌhaʊ tə ˈget tuː/ if you ask
or tell someone **how to get to** a place,
you ask or tell them the way to it: Can you
tell me how to get to the Piazza Venezia?
how to get there/back Come with me. I
know how to get there.

route /ruːt‖ruːt, raʊt/ [n C] the way from
one place to another, especially a way that
is used regularly and can be shown on a
map: If you don't enjoy driving on the
big highways, try to find another route.

take a route (=follow a route) There are
two routes we can take – this one along
the coast or this one through the mountains.

+ from/to This is the most direct route
from Baghdad to Damascus.

short cut /ˌʃɔːt ˈkʌt/ [n C] a way of getting
somewhere that is shorter than the usual
way: Taxi-drivers know all the short cuts.

take a short cut (=use a short cut) *Let's take a short cut across the field.*

WEAK

➡ if you mean 'not brave', go to
BRAVE/NOT BRAVE 5
➡ opposite **STRONG**
➡ see also **BREAK**

1 physically weak

weak /wiːk/ [adj] someone who is **weak** is not strong enough to lift heavy things or do a lot of physical work, especially because they are ill: *When you have flu, you feel tired and weak for a long time.* | *weak muscles*
+ from/with *The soldiers were weak from hunger and exhaustion.*
   weakness [n U] *The symptoms of the illness are a sore throat, weakness, and dizziness.*

frail /freɪl/ [adj] someone who is **frail** is thin and weak, especially because they are old: *a frail 85-year-old lady* | *He lay in bed, looking very frail.*

puny /'pjuːni/ [adj] ESPECIALLY WRITTEN a man or boy who is **puny** is small and thin, and looks very weak: *Pete was a puny little lad.* | *His wife was such a big strong woman, she made him look puny.*

weedy /'wiːdi/ [adj] BRITISH INFORMAL a man or boy who is **weedy** is thin and looks weak: *a weedy young man with glasses*

> ⚠ It is rude to describe someone as **weedy**.

2 not powerful

weak /wiːk/ [adj] a **weak** leader, manager, or government does not have clear ideas about what should be done, and is too easily influenced by other people: *Weak management led to the failure of the business.*
   weakness [n U] *The President has often been accused of weakness.*

3 easy to attack or harm

vulnerable /'vʌlnərəbəl/ [adj] someone who is **vulnerable** can easily be harmed

or attacked: *a small vulnerable child in need of protection* | *Wild animals are most vulnerable when they are asleep.*

defenceless BRITISH **defenseless** AMERICAN /dɪ'fensləs/ [adj] not strong enough to protect yourself against an attack: *This was a horrible crime against a defenceless old man.* | *The UN has condemned the latest bombing of defenseless civilians.*

4 to make someone or something weak

weaken /'wiːkən/ [v T] to make someone or something weak: *Her long illness had weakened her.* | *The city's defences had been weakened by enemy shelling.*

WEAPON

something that you use to fight with

ARMY   EXPLODE
WAR   DESTROY
see also
ATTACK   KILL
SHOOT   HURT/INJURE

1 a weapon

weapon /'wepən/ [n C] something that you use to fight with, such as a gun, bomb, or knife: *Drop your weapons and come out with your hands up!* | *Police have not yet found the murder weapon.*
   nuclear/chemical/conventional weapons (=atom bombs, poisonous gases, or ordinary weapons) *a treaty to reduce the number of nuclear weapons*

arms /ɑːrmz/ [n plural] weapons used for fighting wars: *European governments have been supplying arms to the rebels.*

> ⚠ You can also use **arms** before a noun, like an adjective: *a major US arms manufacturer* | *discussions about arms control*

ammunition /ˌæmjʊ'nɪʃən/ [n U] bullets and other things that are fired from large

W

or small guns: *The soldiers kept on firing until they had no more ammunition.* | *Police have found a store of guns, ammunition, and explosives used by the terrorists.*

round of ammunition (=a single bullet or similar object) *Sixteen pistols and 150 rounds of ammunition were stolen.*

2 having weapons

armed /ɑːᵣmd/ [adj] someone who is **armed** is carrying a gun or other weapon: *An armed gang stole jewellery worth £40,000.* | *Do you think that the British police should be armed?* | *armed guards*

3 having no weapons

unarmed /ˌʌnˈɑːᵣmd◄/ [adj] someone who is **unarmed** is not carrying a gun or other weapon: *It was later discovered that the hijacker was unarmed.* | *He had ordered his men to fire on unarmed demonstrators.*

4 to get or provide weapons

arm /ɑːᵣm/ [v T] to provide someone with weapons: *The rebels were trained, armed, and financed by foreign governments.* | *The country does not have sufficient funds to arm its troops.*

arm yourself with sth *We armed ourselves with whatever we could find – sticks, knives, bricks.*

arms race /ˈɑːᵣmz reɪs/ [n singular] when countries keep producing or buying more and more powerful weapons because each one wants to be the most powerful: *The situation is dangerous and could start an arms race in Asia.* | *We have to halt the nuclear arms race.*

WEATHER

HOT   WET

see also

COLD   DRY

ENVIRONMENT

1 weather

weather /ˈweðəᵣ/ [n U] if you talk about the **weather**, you say whether it is hot or cold outside or whether it is raining, snowing, windy etc: *What was the weather like on your vacation?* | *We want to have a picnic on Saturday, but it depends on the weather.*

hot/warm/wet etc weather *a period of warm sunny weather* | *I don't like going to work on my bike in wet weather.*

weather forecast (=a report on television or radio, saying what the weather will be like) *Here is the weather forecast for central Europe.*

it /ɪt/ [pronoun] SPOKEN you can use **it** when you are saying what the weather is like: *What's it like in Spain at this time of year? Is it really hot?*

it's lovely/nice/awful etc *Isn't it nice today?*

it's cold/sunny/cloudy etc *The weather forecast says it's going to be cloudy tomorrow.*

climate /ˈklaɪmɪt/ [n C] the usual weather conditions in a particular country or area: *Queensland has a warm tropical climate.* | *flowers that will not grow in a cold climate*

2 good weather

good weather /ɡʊd ˈweðəᵣ/ [n U] weather that is sunny and warm: *We go to Greece every Easter, and we usually get good weather.*

glorious/beautiful/gorgeous /ˈɡlɔːriəs, ˈbjuːtɪfəl, ˈɡɔːrdʒəs/ [adj] ESPECIALLY SPOKEN very sunny and warm: *a beautiful sunny morning* | *a glorious summer* | *We had three weeks of absolutely gorgeous weather.*

⚠ Don't say 'very glorious', 'very beautiful' etc. Just say **glorious**, **beautiful** etc.

nice/lovely /naɪs, ˈlʌvli/ [adj] ESPECIALLY BRITISH pleasantly warm and sunny: *Morning, Bill. Nice weather, isn't it?*

it's a nice day/it's a lovely morning etc *It's a lovely day – why don't we go for a walk?*

fine /faɪn/ [adj] if the weather is **fine**, it is not raining and the sky is clear: *Next week will be fine but a little cooler.* | *a fine spring evening*

⚠️ Don't say 'very fine'. Just say **fine**.

dry /draɪ/ [adj] if the weather is **dry**, it does not rain: *If it stays dry I'll hang out the washing.* | *The dry weather will continue for several days.* | *the dry season*

dry – drier – driest

sunny /ˈsʌni/ [adj] if the weather is **sunny**, the sun is shining: *a lovely sunny afternoon* | *It's going to be sunny all day.*

sunny – sunnier – sunniest

sunshine /ˈsʌnʃaɪn/ [n U] warm bright light from the sun: *We sat on the patio enjoying the autumn sunshine.* | *Northern regions will start dry with some sunshine.*

in the sunshine *The children ran out to play in the sunshine.*

in the sun /ɪn ðə ˈsʌn/ where the sun is shining down: *I'm just going to lie here in the sun and get a nice tan.*

3 bad weather

bad weather /bæd ˈweðəʳ/ [n U] when it is raining a lot or very cold: *The game was cancelled because of bad weather.*

awful/terrible/horrible /ˈɔːfəl, ˈterɪbəl, ˈhɒrɪbəl‖ˈhɔː-, ˈhɑː-/ [adj] ESPECIALLY SPOKEN very unpleasant, cold, wet etc: *Awful weather, isn't it?* | *It's been absolutely horrible all day.*

⚠️ Don't say 'very awful', 'very terrible' etc. Just say **awful**, **terrible** etc.

4 weather that changes a lot

unsettled /ˌʌnˈsetld/ [adj] if the weather is **unsettled**, it keeps changing and it often rains: *Tomorrow will continue unsettled, with showers in most areas.*

changeable /ˈtʃeɪndʒəbəl/ [adj] likely to change suddenly: *changeable weather with strong winds and some sunshine*

When you see EC, go to the ESSENTIAL COMMUNICATION section.

5 rain

rain /reɪn/ [n U] water falling from the sky in small drops: *The rain was beating against the window.*

in the rain *I like walking in the rain.*

heavy rain (=a lot of rain) *We've had heavy rain and the roads are flooded.*

rain falls (=comes down from the sky)

⚠️ Don't say 'under the rain'. Say **in the rain**: *I've been standing in the rain for an hour.*

it's raining /ɪts ˈreɪnɪŋ/ use this to say that rain is falling: *Look! It's raining again.* | *Is it still raining?* | *It rained all day yesterday.* | *Take a coat in case it rains.*

it's raining hard/heavily (=raining a lot) *It had been raining heavily and the ground was very soft.*

it's pouring /ɪts ˈpɔːrɪŋ/ ESPECIALLY SPOKEN use this to say that it is raining very hard: *As soon as I got outside it started pouring.*

it's pouring with rain *It was pouring with rain, and she had forgotten her umbrella.*

it's drizzling /ɪts ˈdrɪzəlɪŋ/ ESPECIALLY SPOKEN use this to say that it is raining a little, with very small drops of rain: *I think I'll walk to work – it's only drizzling.*

wet/rainy /wet, ˈreɪni/ [adj] if the weather is **wet** or **rainy**, it rains a lot: *It's been wet all week.* | *wet weather* | *a rainy weekend in November*

wet – wetter – wettest

shower /ˈʃaʊəʳ/ [n C] a short period of light rain: *It was just a shower, so we didn't get too wet.*

heavy showers (=when a lot of rain falls during short periods) *Heavy showers are forecast for the weekend.*

the rainy season/the Monsoon /ðə ˈreɪni ˌsiːzən, ðə mɒnˈsuːn‖-ˈmɑːn-/ [n singular] a time when it rains a lot in hot countries

6 snow and ice

snow /snəʊ/ [n U] soft white pieces of frozen water that fall from the sky in cold weather: *The tops of the mountains were still covered in snow.*

snow falls *Some snow is expected to fall on high ground.*

deep snow (=a lot of snow that has fallen on the ground) *Tony and I trudged home through the deep snow.*

it's snowing /ɪts ˈsnəʊɪŋ/ use this to say that snow is falling: *Look! It's snowing! | Do you think it's going to snow tonight?*

it's snowing heavily/hard (=snowing a lot) *It snowed heavily all day long.*

hail /heɪl/ [n U] frozen raindrops that fall as small balls of ice

sleet /sliːt/ [n U] a mixture of snow and rain

frost /frɒst‖frɔːst/ [n U] white powder that covers the ground when it is very cold: *The grass was covered with frost.*

frosty [adj] *frosty winter mornings*

icy /ˈaɪsi/ [adj] covered in ice and very slippery: *Be careful – the roads are icy this morning.*

icy – icier – iciest

7 cloudy

cloudy /ˈklaʊdi/ [adj] if the weather is **cloudy**, there are a lot of clouds in the sky: *a cloudy day*

cloudy – cloudier – cloudiest

dull /dʌl/ [adj] if the weather is **dull**, it is cloudy and there is no sunshine: *It will be dry but dull this morning, with the possibility of showers later in the day.*

grey (also **gray** AMERICAN) /greɪ/ [adj] ESPECIALLY WRITTEN cloudy and not at all bright: *It was a grey winter morning.*

overcast /ˌəʊvərˈkɑːst◀‖-ˈkæst◀/ [adj] if the sky is **overcast**, it is very cloudy and dark, and there will probably be rain: *I think it's going to rain – the sky's very overcast.*

cloud /klaʊd/ [n C/U] a white or grey mass in the sky, which rain falls from: *There wasn't a single cloud in the sky.*

thick/dense cloud (=a lot of cloud) *Dense cloud prevented the rescue helicopter from taking off.*

fog /fɒɡ‖fɑːɡ, fɔːɡ/ [n U] thick cloudy air near the ground, which is very difficult to see through: *Watch out for patches of fog in low-lying areas.*

thick/dense fog (=a lot of fog) *Dense fog is making driving conditions difficult on many roads.*

the fog lifts/clears (=it goes away) *The fog has almost cleared – our plane will be able to take off soon.*

foggy [adj] *a foggy November evening*

mist /mɪst/ [n U] wet light cloud near the ground, which is difficult to see through clearly: *The mist along the valley had gone by 10 o'clock.*

misty [adj] *It may be misty in the east in the morning.*

8 windy

windy /ˈwɪndi/ [adj] if the weather is **windy**, there is a lot of wind: *It was so windy that I could hardly walk straight. | a windy hillside in Northumberland*

wind /wɪnd/ [n C/U] a moving current of air near the ground: *We walked home through the wind and rain.*

the wind blows *A strong wind was blowing from the east.*

in the wind *The flags fluttered gently in the wind.*

strong/high wind *Strong winds caused damage to many buildings.*

gust of wind (=when the wind suddenly blows strongly) *A sudden gust of wind blew the paper out of his hand.*

breeze /briːz/ [n C] a gentle pleasant wind: *A nice cool breeze came in off the sea.*

slight/gentle breeze *A gentle breeze ruffled her hair.*

gale /geɪl/ [n C] a very strong wind: *The fence was blown down in the gale last night.*

9 hot

➡ see also **HOT**

hot /hɒt‖hɑːt/ [adj] *Isn't it hot today? | the hottest summer this century | We had three weeks of very hot weather.*

hot – hotter – hottest

boiling/scorching /ˈbɔɪlɪŋ, ˈskɔːrtʃɪŋ/ [adj] ESPECIALLY SPOKEN extremely hot: *It's boiling in here. | It was scorching on the tennis court.*

boiling hot/scorching hot *a boiling hot day in August*

warm /wɔːrm/ [adj] a little hot but not very hot, in a pleasant way: *It was nice and warm in the sunshine. | I'm looking forward to some warmer weather.*

mild /maɪld/ [adj] **mild** weather is pleasant because it is not as cold as it usually is: *a mild winter* | *It seems quite mild for February.*

humid /ˈhjuːm‚d/ [adj] if the weather is **humid**, the air is hot and wet in a way that makes you feel uncomfortable: *Tokyo is very humid in summer.*

10 cold

➡ see also **COLD**

cold /kəʊld/ [adj] *There was a very cold winter that year.* | *It's so cold. I wish I was back home in Greece.*

　the cold [n singular] the cold weather outside: *Come in out of the cold.*

cool /kuːl/ [adj] pleasantly cold but not very cold: *a cool breeze* | *It gets much cooler in the evenings.*

chilly /ˈtʃɪli/ [adj] rather cold, in a way that makes you feel uncomfortable: *It was getting chilly outside, so we went back into the house.*

　chilly – chillier – chilliest

♀**freezing** /ˈfriːzɪŋ/ [adj] ESPECIALLY SPOKEN extremely cold: *Can't we go inside? It's freezing out here.*

　freezing cold *a freezing cold day in January*

> ⚠ Don't say 'very freezing'. Say **absolutely freezing**.

11 storm

storm /stɔːrm/ [n C] a period of very bad weather, when there is a lot of rain, wind, and sometimes thunder and lightning: *The Spanish ships were wrecked in a storm.*

　rainstorm/snowstorm *Anderson disappeared in a snowstorm while climbing the Alps.*

　　stormy [adj] *stormy weather* | *The sky was starting to look stormy.*

thunderstorm /ˈθʌndərstɔːrm/ [n C] a storm when there is a lot of thunder and lightning: *There was a spectacular thunderstorm that night.*

thunder /ˈθʌndər/ [n U] the loud crashing noise that you hear in a storm: *They could hear thunder rumbling in the distance.*

clap of thunder (=one sudden noise of thunder)

lightning /ˈlaɪtnɪŋ/ [n U] a bright flash of light in the sky during a storm

　flash of lightning *A flash of lightning lit up the whole sky.*

blizzard /ˈblɪzərd/ [n C] a storm with a lot of snow and strong winds: *He had to drive home through the blizzard.*

hurricane/typhoon /ˈhʌr‚kən, taɪˈfuːn‖ ˈhɜːrkeɪn/ [n C] a severe storm with very strong winds that causes a lot of damage: *The hurricane devastated Florida and killed at least 40 people.*

> ⚠ **Hurricanes** happen in the Western Atlantic Ocean. **Typhoons** happen in the Western Pacific Ocean.

tornado /tɔːrˈneɪdəʊ/ [n C] a small but very violent part of a storm, in which a powerful twisting mass of air appears, causing a lot of damage. Tornadoes usually happen in the central area of the US: *A tornado destroyed twelve homes in Ashport, Tennessee yesterday.*

WET

➡ opposite **DRY**
➡ see also **WEATHER**

1 wet

wet /wet/ [adj] if something is **wet**, it has a lot of liquid on it or in it; if someone is **wet**, their clothes and hair are wet: *I can't come out yet – my hair's still wet.* | *You'd better change out of those wet clothes.* | *The grass was wet after the rain.*

　get wet *Hurry up with the umbrella – I'm getting wet!*

♀**soaking wet/wet through** (=very wet) ESPECIALLY SPOKEN *A pipe had burst and the carpet was soaking wet.* | *By the time the bus arrived, we were soaking through.*

♀**all wet** SPOKEN (=very wet) *Oh no! My socks are all wet now!*

　wet – wetter – wettest

drenched/soaked /drentʃt, səʊkt/ [adj] if you are **drenched** or **soaked**, you are

extremely wet, so that drops of water are falling from your clothes: *By the time we got home, we were all drenched. | I'm soaked! I'll have to go and change.*
soaked to the skin (=completely soaked) *I was exhausted, and soaked to the skin.*

damp /dæmp/ [adj] something that is **damp** is slightly wet: *Clean the counter with a damp cloth. | There was a damp spot on the ceiling. | My hair was still damp.*

⚠️ Use **damp** especially to say that something is wet in an unpleasant way: *a dark, damp cellar*

moist /mɔɪst/ [adj] something that is **moist** is slightly wet, and this is the way it should be: *The cake mixture should be slightly moist, but not sticky. | Water the plants regularly to keep the soil moist.*

soggy /ˈsɒgi‖ˈsɑːgi/ [adj] something that is **soggy** is softer than usual and looks or feels unpleasant, because it has become wet: *horrible soggy toast | He always leaves the towels in a soggy heap on the bathroom floor.*

2 when the air feels wet

humid /ˈhjuːmɪd/ [adj] **humid** air or weather is hot and wet in a way that makes you feel uncomfortable: *the humid heat of a tropical rainforest | Summers in Tokyo are hot and humid.*

damp /dæmp/ [adj] **damp** air or weather is slightly wet in an unpleasant way, and makes you feel cold: *It was a cold, damp, windy night. | At first I hated the damp weather in Britain.*

3 to make something or someone wet

🔍**get sth wet** /ˌget (sth) ˈwet/ ESPECIALLY SPOKEN to make something wet, especially by not being careful enough to keep it dry: *Try not to get your feet wet. | How did you manage to get the floor so wet?*

wet /wet/ [v T] to deliberately put water or other liquid on something: *Wet the toothbrush before you put the toothpaste on. | The hairdresser kept wetting my hair so that it was easier to cut.*
wetting – wet (also **wetted** BRITISH) **– have wet** (also **have wetted** BRITISH)

soak /səʊk/ [v T] to leave something in water for a long time in order to make it clean, soft etc: *Soak the lentils overnight before cooking them.*
soak sth in sth *Soak a piece of cotton in water and use it to clean the wound.*

WIDE/NARROW

➡ see also **FAT, THIN, THICK**

1 a long distance from one side to the other

wide

a wide river

wide /waɪd/ [adj] if a road, river, door etc is **wide**, there is a large distance between one side of it and the other: *The doorway isn't wide enough to get the piano through. | a wide straight road | a wide leather belt*
how wide? *How wide is the driveway?*
2 miles wide/1 metre wide (=2 miles, 1 metre etc from one side to the other) *At this point the river is over a mile wide. | Cut a strip of paper 3 cm wide.*
wide – wider – widest

broad /brɔːd/ [adj] wide – use this especially in written descriptions, to describe roads, paths, rivers, or parts of someone's body: *a broad, tree-lined avenue | He was six feet tall with broad shoulders and strong arms.*

width /wɪdθ/ [n C/U] the distance from one side of something to the other: *Calculate the width of the curtain then add six inches. | a pattern of coloured lines of different widths*

When you see **EC**, go to the
ESSENTIAL COMMUNICATION section.

2 not wide

➡ see also **THIN**

narrow

a narrow stream

narrow /ˈnærəʊ/ [*adj*] if something is **narrow**, there is only a small distance between one side of it and the other: *a long narrow bathroom* | *He led me through the narrow streets of the old city.*

WIN

➡ opposite **LOSE**

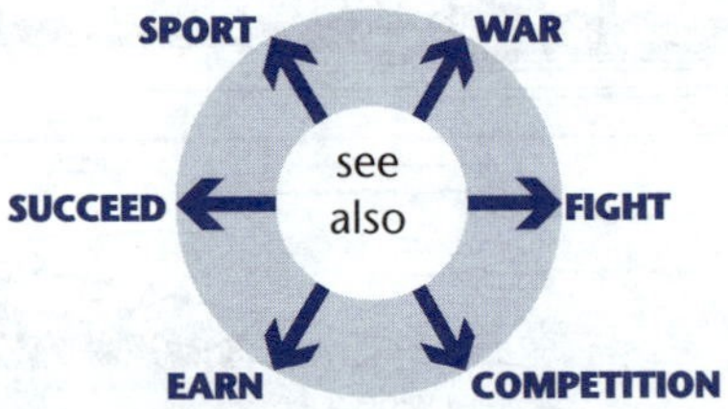

1 to win a race/game/competition/election

win /wɪn/ [*v* I/T] to win a race, competition, election etc, for example by getting more points, votes etc than everyone else or by being the first to finish: *They don't have much chance of winning.*

win a race/game/election etc *Chang won the first set but lost the next two.* | *The competition was won by a Nigerian.*

win a prize/medal etc *His book won the Pulitzer Prize for literature.* | *She won almost $1 million in the lottery.*

win by 6 votes/2 goals etc (=by getting 6 votes etc more than the other person or team) *Bristow won by 50 points.*

win 4–2/20–12 etc (use this to show the final result of a game) *In the European Cup, Barcelona won 3–1.*

winning – won – have won

come first/be first /ˌkʌm ˈfɜːʳst, biː ˈfɜːʳst/ to win a race or competition in which more than two people or teams are competing: *A local team came first, and we were third.*

+ in *An Austrian runner was first in the marathon.*

⚠ Use **come second**, **be third** etc about the teams or players that are the next best, after the winner.

beat/defeat /biːt, dɪˈfiːt/ [*v* T] if you **beat** or **defeat** another team or player, you win a game, race etc against them: *Brazil beat Italy in the final.* | *Since he was defeated by Tyson, Bruno has announced his retirement.*

beat sb 3–1/by 50 points etc *Short beat Redgrave by nearly 200 votes.* | *The Red Sox defeated the Yankees 6–3.*

beating – beat – have beaten

⚠ **Defeat** is more formal than **beat**, and is used especially in written English.

first place /ˌfɜːʳst ˈpleɪs/ [*n* singular] the position of the person or team that wins a race or competition

in first place *Here is the result of the men's 200 metres race: in first place, Michael Johnson, in second place ...*

win first place *Our team won first place.*

⚠ Use **second place**, **third place** etc about the teams or players that are the next best, after the winner: *Gunnell was disappointed to finish in third place.*

2 to win a war/fight/argument

win /wɪn/ [*v* I/T] to be more successful than someone in a war, a fight, or an argument: *The English army won a great victory at Agincourt.* | *I could never win an argument with my big brother.*

winning – won – have won

defeat /dɪˈfiːt/ [*v* T] ESPECIALLY WRITTEN if a leader, army, or country **defeats** another leader, army, or country, they win a war or battle against them: *Wellington's army finally defeated Napoleon.*

defeat [*n* C] *the defeat of the Republican army in Spain*

3 to be winning a game, race etc that has not yet finished

be winning /biː ˈwɪnɪŋ/ to have more points than your opponents in a game, or to be at the front in a race, even though the game or race has not yet finished: *I think Sampras is winning at the moment.*

be in the lead /biː ɪn ðə ˈliːd/ to be in front of everyone else in a race, or to have the most points in a competition, when the race or competition has not yet finished: *Who's in the lead? | Karpov was still in the lead, but only by one point.*

be ahead /biː əˈhed/ to be doing better than someone else in a game, competition, race, or election: *For the first half of the game, the Dodgers were ahead.*

+ of *With over half the votes counted, the Socialists were ahead of all the other parties.*

be 12 points/5 games etc ahead *Damon Hill is now 14 points ahead of his nearest rival.*

4 the person or team that wins

winner /ˈwɪnər/ [n C] someone who has won a game, race, competition, or election: *The winner will receive $50,000 in cash. | Chelsea were the winners with a late goal from Vialli.*

+ of *And the winner of tonight's big prize is ... Peter Lewis!*

champion /ˈtʃæmpiən/ [n C] someone who has won an important sports competition: *Michael Stich, the 1991 Wimbledon men's champion*

world champion (=the winner of the most important competition in a particular sport) *Hill finally achieved his dream of becoming Formula 1 World Champion.*

winning /ˈwɪnɪŋ/ [adj only before noun]
winning team/player/horse etc the team, player etc that wins: *The crowd cheered the winning team. | Traditionally, the winning crew buys drinks for the losers.*

5 an occasion when someone wins

victory /ˈvɪktəri/ [n C/U] when a country, player, team etc wins a battle, game, race etc: *The crowd was celebrating Italy's victory. | Napoleon's victory at Austerlitz | Clinton's second election victory | victory celebrations*

+ over/against *Their 24–3 victory over the Australians was completely unexpected.*

win a victory *Holyfield gained the world title by winning an unexpected victory over Mike Tyson.*

plural **victories**

win /wɪn/ [n C] when a team or player wins in a sport or competition – used especially in news reports: *It was an important win for Manchester United. | celebrating a big lottery win*

+ over/against *a 12–3 win against the French*

6 something that you get when you win

prize /praɪz/ [n C] something that is given to the person who wins a competition, game, or race: *The prize is a 3-week holiday in the Bahamas.*

first/second/third prize *Second prize is a book token.*

win/get a prize *She won the Booker Prize for her novel 'The Ghost Road'.*

cup /kʌp/ [n C] a special silver or gold container, shaped like a large cup with two handles, that is given to the winner of a sports competition: *The Queen presented the cup to the captain of the winning team.*

medal /ˈmedl/ [n C] a round flat piece of metal that is given to someone who has won a race, game, or competition: *The winning team went up to collect their medals.*

gold/silver/bronze medal (=a medal for coming first/second/third) *The gold medal was won by Anna Svensen.*

award /əˈwɔːrd/ [n C] a prize that someone wins for achieving something important or doing something very well

+ for *One of the firefighters was given an award for bravery.*

win an award *Meryl Streep won the best actress award.*

> ⚠ Don't use **award** to talk about sports.

> When you see **EC**, go to the **ESSENTIAL COMMUNICATION** section.

WOMAN

PERSON/PEOPLE   RELATIONSHIP

MAN   see also   MARRY

FATHER   CHILD

MOTHER   GIRLFRIEND/BOYFRIEND

1 a woman

woman /'womən/ [n C] a female adult: *Who's that woman you were talking to just now?* | *Rebecca Stephens was the first British woman to climb Mount Everest.* | *In some African countries, the women do most of the agricultural work.*
plural **women**

> ⚠ **Woman** can also be used before a noun, like an adjective: *Britain's first woman Prime Minister* | *Some companies offer low-cost insurance to women drivers.*

lady /'leɪdi/ [n C] a polite word for a woman, especially a woman who is there when you are speaking about her: *There's a lady here who wants to speak to you about her account.* | *Ladies and gentlemen, I am delighted to welcome you here tonight.*
old lady *Ella is a lovely old lady.*
plural **ladies**

> ⚠ Some women do not like being called 'ladies' and prefer to be called **women**.

female /'fiːmeɪl/ [adj usually before noun] FORMAL a **female** worker, teacher, singer etc is a woman or girl – use this especially to talk about jobs that women do: *The city has a female police chief.* | *Female students tend to get better grades than male students.* | *a company with a mainly female workforce*

girl /ɡɜːʳl/ [n C] a young woman: *He's going out with that girl who works in the library.*

> ⚠ Many young women do not like being called 'girls' and prefer to be called **women**.

2 what you call a woman when you speak to her or write to her

Mrs /'mɪsɨz/ use this before the family name of a woman who is married: *It's Mrs Hawksworth's 70th birthday this weekend.* | *Mrs Thomas, the doctor is ready to see you now.*

Miss /mɪs/ use this before the family name of a woman who has never been married: *He admitted attacking Miss Slater last February.*

Ms /mɪz, məz/ use this before a woman's family name if you do not know whether she is married, or if it is not important to know whether she is married: *We have decided to offer the job to Ms Jacobs.*

> ⚠ Many women prefer to be called **Ms**, instead of **Mrs** or **Miss**, because they do not think it is necessary for people to know whether they are married or not.

madam /'mædəm/ FORMAL use this when writing a formal letter to a woman, or when talking to a customer in a shop, hotel, restaurant etc: *Can I help you, madam?* | *Dear Madam, I am writing in response to your advertisement.*

ma'am /mæm, mɑːm, məm‖mæm/ AMERICAN SPOKEN a polite word used when talking to a woman: *Would you like some help, ma'am?*

3 for women or like women

women's /'wɪmɨnz/ use this about things that are designed for women or done by women, and not designed for or done by men
women's clothes/magazines/football/prison etc *She's the fashion editor for a women's magazine.* | *Why don't they ever show women's football on TV?*

female /'fiːmeɪl/ [adj only before noun] use this about behaviour or personal qualities that are traditionally thought to be typical of women: *Many women reject the traditional female roles of wife and mother.* | *Patience and kindness are often seen as female qualities.*

feminine /ˈfemᵻnᵻn/ [adj] looking attractive in a way that is traditionally thought to be typical of a woman: *The hairstyle is soft and very feminine.* | *Lindsay wears very feminine clothes – pretty dresses with flowers on and things like that.*

effeminate /ɪˈfemᵻnᵻt/ [adj] use this about a man who behaves like a woman or looks like a woman: *He was very young and handsome in a slightly effeminate way.*

WORD/PHRASE/ SENTENCE

➡ see also **LANGUAGE, ANSWER 1, ASK 5**

1 a word or group of words

word /wɜːʳd/ [n C] *Are there any words in this passage that you don't understand?* | *Is 'lunchtime' one word or two?* | *The word 'origami' comes from Japanese.*
word for sth (=word that means something) *'Casa' is the Italian word for 'house'.* | *What's another word for 'way out'?*

phrase/expression /freɪz, ɪkˈspreʃən/ [n C] a combination of two or more words that has a particular meaning: *The students' book has a list of useful phrases at the back.* | *It was Mikhail Gorbachev who first used the expression 'the Iron Lady' about Margaret Thatcher.*

term /tɜːʳm/ [n C] a word or group of words that are used in a technical or scientific subject and have an exact meaning in that subject
technical/medical/legal/scientific term *The medical term for losing your hair is 'alopecia'.*

idiom /ˈɪdiəm/ [n C] a group of words that are used together and have a special meaning that you cannot guess from the meanings of each separate word: *'Full of beans' is an idiom which means lively and energetic.*

cliché /ˈkliːʃeɪ‖kliːˈʃeɪ/ [n C] a phrase that people have used so often that it now seems boring or silly: *It's a cliché I know, but the game isn't over until the final whistle blows.*

2 a sentence or part of a sentence

sentence /ˈsentəns/ [n C] a group of words that begins with a capital letter, ends with a full stop, and includes a verb: *Write a complete sentence for each answer.*

clause /klɔːz/ [n C] a group of words that has a subject and a verb and that is part of a sentence
main clause (=the clause that has the main verb)
subordinate clause/dependent clause (=a clause that depends on the main clause for its meaning) *In the sentence "Can you tell me what time it is?" 'Can you tell me' is the main clause, and 'what time it is' is a subordinate clause.*

3 all the words someone knows or uses

vocabulary /vəˈkæbjᵿləri, vəʊ-‖-leri/ [n C usually singular] someone's **vocabulary** is all the words that they know or use: *These stories are written for students with a vocabulary of about 2000 words.* | *Reading is a good way to increase your vocabulary.*
plural **vocabularies**

4 words that someone has written

writing /ˈraɪtɪŋ/ [n U] words that someone has written or printed: *There's some writing on the back of the photo, but I can't read what it says.*

text /tekst/ [n U] the written part of a book or newspaper, not including pictures, notes at the end etc: *The book consisted mainly of colour photographs and not much text.*

WORK

BUSY/NOT BUSY
JOB   **IN CHARGE OF**
EARN   see also   **MANAGER**
COMPANY   **FREE TIME**
ORGANIZATION   **EXPERIENCE**

1 to do a job

work /wɜːᵣk/ [v I] to do a job that you get paid for: *My dad isn't working at the moment – he lost his job.* | *Susie works in a supermarket on Saturdays.*

work late (=later than normal) *I may have to work late tonight.*

work for (=for a company or organization) *She used to work for the BBC.*

work as a secretary/builder/gardener etc *Russell is working as a software developer for Microsoft.*

> ⚠ **Work** – which preposition? Use **work for** to talk about the company or organization that someone is employed by: *I work for Eriksson International.* | *Pam works for a biotechnology company.* Use **work in** with words like 'school', 'bank', 'hospital', 'factory', 'hotel' etc to talk about the kind of place where someone works: *He used to work in a Chinese restaurant.* | *I've worked in a factory all my life.* Don't use **work in** with the name of a company or organization. You can use **work at** to say the name of the company or organization that someone works for, especially when it is a well-known organization or when the person you are talking to knows it already: *Bill works at McDonald's.* | *During the school vocation, she's working at that bookstore on Ramsey Street.*

be /biː/ [v] if someone **is** a teacher, a doctor etc, that is their job: *She was a journalist for 20 years before she wrote her first novel.* | *"What does your father do?" "He's a dentist."* | *Jill wants to be a professional musician.*

> ⚠ Don't say 'she is nurse/teacher etc'. Say **she is a nurse, she is a teacher** etc.

 do /duː/ [v T] ESPECIALLY SPOKEN use this to ask or talk about the type of job that someone does: *What does her father do?* | *Jess isn't sure yet what she wants to do when she finishes school.*

be employed /biː imˈplɔɪd/ FORMAL to work for a particular organization or in a particular type of work or industry
+ by *She was the first woman pilot to be employed by a commercial airline.*
+ in *The number of people employed in the construction industry has been falling for many years.*

2 to be at the place where you usually work

be at work /biː ət ˈwɜːᵣk/ to be doing your job at the place where you work: *Mark's not at home – he's at work.*

be on duty /biː ɒn ˈdjuːti‖-ˈduːti/ to be at work in a job where there must always be someone working, for example if you are a nurse or a police officer: *Which doctors were on duty on the night of the accident?* | *Will your mother be on duty on Christmas Day?*

on business /ɒn ˈbɪznɪs/ if you go somewhere **on business**, you go there as part of your job: *I had to fly to Tokyo on business.*

3 to do work that is not part of a job

work /wɜːᵣk/ [v I] to do an activity that needs effort and takes time: *I've been working all day in the garden.* | *It's a good school – they really make the students work!*

work on sth (=spend time on a piece of work that will take a long time to finish) *Mary's in the study, working on her history assignment.*

do /duː/ [v T] **do the housework/gardening/cleaning/cooking etc** to do work that must be done regularly in your home, such as cleaning and cooking: *Whose turn is it to do the washing-up?*

4 to work independently, not for someone else

self-employed /ˌself imˈplɔɪd◂/ [adj] someone who is **self-employed** does not have a job with one particular employer, but does work for many different people: *Martin is a self-employed builder.* | *How long have you been self-employed?*

the self-employed (=people who are self-employed) *There are generous tax allowances for the self-employed.*

freelance /ˈfriːlɑːns‖-læns/ [adj only before noun] working for several different organizations instead of being employed by only one – use this especially about people such as writers, designers, and photographers

freelance designer/translator/photographer/journalist *a directory of freelance journalists*

freelance work/translation/photography etc *She works at home, doing freelance work on women's magazines.*

  freelance [*adv*] *Bill works freelance, doing illustrations for children's books.*

5 to work hard

work hard /ˌwɜːʳk ˈhɑːʳd/ to work hard when you are doing your job, your schoolwork, or anything that takes time and effort: *Bruno had been working hard in the kitchen all morning.* | *I wouldn't mind working so hard if they paid us more.*

put a lot of effort into sth /ˌpʊt ə lɒt əv ˈefəʳt ɪntuː (sth)‖-ˈlɑːt-/ to work hard because you think something is important and you want to do it well: *She had obviously put a lot of effort into her assignment.* | *The company puts a great deal of effort into training its staff.*

hardworking /ˌhɑːʳdˈwɜːʳkɪŋ◂/ [*adj*] always working hard in your job or on your schoolwork: *Melissa was a popular and hardworking student.*

dedicated /ˈdedɪkeɪtɪd/ [*adj*] someone who is **dedicated** works very hard at something because they care about it a lot – use this especially about people who do useful work in society, not about people who work in business: *She's a wonderful nurse – completely dedicated.* | *The lifeboat service is run by a team of dedicated volunteers.*

overworked /ˌəʊvəʳˈwɜːʳkt◂/ [*adj*] someone who is **overworked** has too much work to do: *Teachers often complain that they are overworked and underpaid.* | *Nadine was feeling tired and overworked.*

6 work that you do at home, in your job etc

work /wɜːʳk/ [*n U*] the things that you have to do at home or at school or in your job, which need time and effort: *She has a busy job, and she often takes work home with her.* | *I agreed to organize the party, but I didn't realize there would be so much work involved.*

do work *I can't go out tonight, I have a lot of work to do for my biology test tomorrow.*

secretarial/teaching/bar work etc *Have you ever done any secretarial work before?*

effort /ˈefəʳt/ [*n U*] the physical and mental energy that you have to use in order to do something: *Even the slightest effort makes him feel tired.*

take/require effort (=need a lot of work) *Finding the right staff takes a lot of management time and effort.*

job /dʒɒb‖dʒɑːb/ [*n C*] a specific piece of work that you have to do, especially one that you do not get paid for: *My brother's job was to take all the old bottles and newspapers for recycling.* | *Cleaning the bathroom floor is a horrible job.*

do a job *I spent the weekend clearing up and doing various jobs around the house.*

task /tɑːsk‖tæsk/ [*n C*] FORMAL a piece of work – use this especially about a difficult and important job that a politician, manager etc has to do: *Her first task as principal was to improve relations between the teachers and the students' parents.*

have the task of doing sth *The UN has the difficult task of bringing peace to this region.*

duties /ˈdjuːtiz‖ˈduː-/ [*n plural*] FORMAL the various things that you have to do as part of your job: *Your duties will include organizing a monthly departmental meeting.* | *Attending state banquets is one of the Ambassador's official duties.*

housework /ˈhaʊswɜːʳk/ [*n U*] work that needs to be done in your home, for example, cleaning, washing clothes, or keeping rooms tidy: *None of her kids ever helps with the housework.*

do (the) housework *Saturday is the only day I have enough time to do the housework.*

> ⚠ Don't confuse **housework** (=jobs you do to keep your house clean) with **homework** (=schoolwork that you do at home).

homework /ˈhəʊmwɜːʳk/ [*n U*] work that a student has to do at home

do your homework *Have you done all your homework?*

W

for homework *For homework, I'd like you to finish Exercise 3.*

⚠ Don't say 'homeworks'. Say **homework**.

⚠ Don't say 'I made my homework'. Say **I did my homework**.

schoolwork /'skuːlwɜːᵊk/ [n U] all the work that a student has to do, both at home and in class: *Problems at home have affected Laurie's schoolwork.*

7 someone who works for an organization or company

worker /'wɜːᵊkəᵊ/ [n C] someone who works for an organization but is not a manager: *We need better communication between the management and the workers.*

manual worker (=who does physical work, for example in a factory) *The report shows that male manual workers earn twice as much as female workers.*

post office/factory/office worker *Brown was a retired post office worker.*

employee /ɪmˈplɔɪ-iː/ [n C] someone who has a job, especially a permanent job, with a company or organization: *a multinational corporation with 140,000 employees worldwide* | *a bank employee* **+ of** *Employees of American Airlines get generous reductions on the cost of flights.*

⚠ **Employee** is a rather formal word. Don't say 'I am an employee of IBM'. Say **I work for IBM**.

staff /stɑːf‖stæf/ [n U, singular] all the people who work for a company, organization, school etc: *Staff were clearly worried about rumours of job losses.*

library/office/hospital/security staff *The library staff is always available to help you.* | *The company is looking for part-time sales staff.*

member of staff *Training is provided for all members of staff.*

join the staff *In 1992, she joined the President's personal staff in the White House.*

⚠ **Staff** can be used with a singular or plural verb in British or American English: *The staff here are/is very professional.*

⚠ **Staff** can also be used before a noun, like an adjective: *a staff training day* | *staff changes*

workforce /'wɜːᵊkfɔːᵊs/ [n singular] all the people who work in a country, a type of industry, or a large organization: *Women make up 41% of the nation's workforce.* | *The company has had to cut one-third of its workforce.*

8 someone you work with

colleague /'kɒliːg‖'kɑː-/ [n C] someone you work with – use this especially about people who do professional jobs in offices, schools, government etc: *I'd like you to meet a colleague of mine, Jean-Michel Blanc from our Paris office.* | *Jenny is a conscientious manager, very popular with her colleagues.*

workmate /'wɜːᵊkmeɪt/ [n C] someone that you work with, especially someone who works closely with you and who you are friendly with: *Police are questioning neighbours and workmates of the missing woman.*

9 the person or company you work for

➡ see also **MANAGER**

employer /ɪmˈplɔɪəᵊ/ [n C] someone's **employer** is the person, company, or organization that they work for: *We will need a reference from your last employer.*

⚠ **Employer** is a rather formal word. In ordinary conversation, it is more usual to say something like 'the company I work for', instead of 'my employer'.

10 to stop working in order to get more money

strike /straɪk/ [n C] when people deliberately stop working in order to get more money, better working conditions etc: *The strike lasted about two months.*

miners'/teachers'/railworkers' etc strike *The railworkers' strike caused chaos in the city.*

call a strike (=ask workers to join a strike)

call off a strike (=agree to end a strike or not start a strike) *Teachers have called off the strike that was planned for Tuesday.*

on strike /ɒn ˈstraɪk/ if workers go **on strike**, they stop working in order to get more money, better conditions etc

go on strike *Ford workers threatened to go on strike unless the company improved its pay offer.*

be (out) on strike (=not working) *There were frequent power cuts when the electricity workers were out on strike.*

WORKING

when a machine, car etc is working as it should, and is not broken

➡ opposite **BROKEN**

➡ see also **REPAIR**

work /wɜːʳk/ [v I] if a machine or piece of equipment **works** or **is working**, it can be used without any problems because there is nothing wrong with it: *We had to go to the laundromat because the washing-machine wasn't working.* | *I've fixed your heater – it works fine.*

be in working order /biː ɪn ˌwɜːʳkɪŋ ˈɔːʳdəʳ/ if something **is in working order**, it is working well and safely, especially because it has been well cared for: *The mill was built in the 16th century and is still in working order.*

be in good/perfect working order *Your brakes, lights, and steering must be kept in good working order.*

> ⚠ **Be in working order** is more formal than **work**, and is not usually used in ordinary conversation.

go /gəʊ/ [v I] ESPECIALLY SPOKEN to be working properly – use this especially about a car, clock, or watch: *I dropped my watch, but it's still going.* | *I don't mind what kind of car we rent as long as it goes.*

going – went – have gone

> When you see **EC**, go to the **ESSENTIAL COMMUNICATION** section.

be up and running /biː ˌʌp ənd ˈrʌnɪŋ/ to be working well and without any problems – use this about computers or systems, especially new ones: *As soon as the new computer system is up and running, we can transfer our records onto it.*

WORLD

the planet we live on

➡ see also **COUNTRY, ENVIRONMENT, LAND AND SEA**

1 the world

the world /ðə ˈwɜːʳld/ [n singular] the planet we live on, and all the people and places on it: *In some parts of the world, clean drinking water is very scarce.*

all over the world *You can buy Coca-Cola all over the world.*

the whole world (=everyone and everything in the world) *changes that will affect the whole world*

the best, fastest etc in the world/the world's best, fastest etc *It's the tallest building in the world.* | *It's the world's tallest building.*

earth/Earth /ɜːʳθ/ [n singular/U] use this especially when you are comparing our world with the moon, stars, and other places in space: *Light from the stars can take millions of years to reach Earth.*

the earth/the Earth *The earth revolves around the sun.* | *Water is one of the Earth's most important resources.*

to earth *The space shuttle returned safely to earth on December 9th.*

the planet /ðə ˈplænɪt/ [n singular] use this especially when you are talking about problems that affect the environment: *a massive volcanic eruption that could affect the climate of the whole planet* | *Energy conservation is vital for the future of the planet.*

2 things that affect the whole world or happen everywhere in the world

world /wɜːʳld/ [adj only before noun] use this to talk about something that exists everywhere in the world, or affects the whole world, or is the best or most important in the world: *The top 50 multinational companies control about 80% of world trade.* | *At that time Britain was a major world power.* | *Islam is one of the great world religions.*

world champion/record/expert (=the best in the world) *The world champion, Damon Hill, is still in the lead.* | *Jones is a world expert in genetics.*

global /'gləʊbəl/ [adj only before noun] use this especially to talk about political, economic, or scientific problems that affect the whole world: *The fight against AIDS requires a global strategy.* | *Campaigners have called for a global ban on whale hunting.* | *Nuclear war could lead to global catastrophe.*

worldwide /ˌwɜːʳld'waɪd◄/ [adj] existing or happening in every country of the world: *There is a worldwide shortage of oil.* | *The concert attracted a worldwide television audience of over a billion people.*

WORRYING/ WORRIED

RELAX   SAD

see also

PROBLEM   FRIGHTENING/ FRIGHTENED

1 feeling worried

worried /'wʌrid‖'wɜːrid/ [adj] not feeling happy or relaxed, because you keep thinking about a problem or about something bad that might happen: *You look worried – what's the matter?*

+ about *She lay awake worrying about all the work she had to do.*

+ (that) *When I changed schools, I was worried that I wouldn't make any new friends.*

get worried *We began to get worried when she didn't come home on Thursday night.*

a worried look/frown/glance Simon gave me a worried look.

worry /'wʌri‖'wɜːri/ [v I] to keep thinking about a problem or about something bad that might happen, so that you cannot relax or feel happy: *My parents worry when I'm late home from school.* | *You worry too much.*

+ about *He owes the bank a lot of money and he worries about it.*

+ that *I used to worry that I would never get married.*

◯**don't worry** SPOKEN (say this to tell someone not to worry) *Don't worry, I can pay for both of us.*

worrying – worried – have worried

nervous /'nɜːʳvəs/ [adj] worried and slightly frightened about something that is going to happen or something new or difficult that you have to do: *I always get nervous before tests.* | *Bill looked nervous, and I could see that his hands were shaking.*

+ about *Kelly was so nervous about her interview that she couldn't sleep.*

nervously [adv] *Nervously, she twisted her handkerchief in her fingers.*

⚠ Don't confuse **nervous** (=feeling worried and a little frightened) and **annoyed** (=feeling a little angry): *I was very nervous about the test.* | *His stupid questions made me very annoyed.*

anxious /'æŋkʃəs/ [adj] ESPECIALLY WRITTEN very worried because you think that something bad has happened or may happen, and you feel that you have no control over the situation: *She knew it was a simple operation, but she still felt anxious.* | *Anxious relatives waited at the airport for news of the plane crash.*

+ about *Helen is always anxious about travelling alone.*

an anxious face/voice/expression etc *Please come with me, she said in an anxious voice.*

anxiously [adv] *Is he going to be all right? she asked anxiously.*

frightened/scared/afraid /'fraɪtnd, skeəʳd, ə'freɪd/ [adj] worried and frightened because of something bad that might happen

+ (that) *She was frightened that the dog might bite her.* | *I was scared she might never come back.*

+ of *Many people are frightened of losing their jobs.* | *I was afraid of offending her.*

⚠ Scared is more informal than frightened and afraid.

tense /tens/ [adj] so worried about something that you cannot relax, and you easily get angry or upset: *Lesley's problems at work made her tense and irritable.*
tense silence/moment/situation etc *There was a tense silence, then everyone began to laugh.*

stressed out /ˌstrest 'aʊt◂/ [adj] INFORMAL worried and tired all the time, because you have a lot of problems to deal with and too much work to do: *Rob's been really stressed out since he started his new job.*
+ about *She's pretty stressed out about the court case.*

2 to make someone feel worried

worry /'wʌri‖'wɜːri/ [v T] to make someone feel worried: *Recent changes in the climate are beginning to worry environmental scientists.* | *I could tell that something was worrying her.*
it worries sb that *Doesn't it worry you that Stephen spends so much time playing computer games?*
Ꝺ**what worries sb is** ESPECIALLY SPOKEN *What worries me is the cost of all these changes.*
worrying – worried – have worried

worrying /'wʌri-ɪŋ‖'wɜːri-/ [adj] **worrying** events, changes etc make you feel worried: *The increase in homelessness among teenagers is very worrying.*
a worrying time/week/year etc (= a time when you are worried) *It's been a worrying few weeks for all of us since Jan lost her job.*

stressful /'stresfəl/ [adj] a **stressful** job or situation makes you feel worried and tired all the time, for example because you have too many problems or too much work to do: *Looking after small children can be very stressful.*

make sb nervous /ˌmeɪk (sb) 'nɜːʳvəs/ to make someone feel nervous and unable to relax: *Stop watching me when I'm trying to work – you're making me nervous.*

3 a feeling of being worried

anxiety /æŋ'zaɪəti/ [n U] the feeling you have when you are very worried that something bad has happened or is going to happen: *After weeks of anxiety, I finally heard that I would not need an operation.*
+ about *anxiety about the high levels of pollution in the atmosphere*

stress /stres/ [n U] the feeling of being worried all the time, for example about work or personal problems, which can make you ill or very tired: *Her financial problems were causing her a lot of stress.*
stress-related illnesses (=caused by stress)
be under stress (=be feeling stress) *He's been under a lot of stress at work lately.*

concern /kən'sɜːʳn/ [n U] a worried feeling – use this especially when many people are worried about a problem that affects everyone: *The shortage of water is beginning to cause widespread concern.*
+ about/over *Concern over the President's health is increasing.*

4 something that makes you feel worried

worry /'wʌri‖'wɜːri/ [n C] something that makes you feel worried: *It is important to find someone to discuss your worries with.*
sb's main/biggest worry (=the thing someone worries about most) *Her main worry was how the divorce would affect the children.*
plural **worries**

hang-up /'hæŋ ʌp/ [n C] INFORMAL if you have a **hang-up** about something, for example about your appearance or your relationships with other people, you feel worried and embarrassed about it, and this makes you feel less confident: *They wanted their children to grow up without any hang-ups.*
+ about *I don't know why she has such a hang-up about her nose – it looks OK to me.*

When you see **EC**, go to the
ESSENTIAL COMMUNICATION section.

W

5 not worried any more

relieved /rɪˈliːvd/ [adj] feeling relaxed again because you do not need to worry about something that you worried about before: *We were very relieved when they phoned to tell us they were safe.*
+ that *Tim was relieved that the teacher didn't ask him to read out his answer.*
relieved to hear/learn/find/see *I was relieved to hear that I didn't have to have an operation.*

relief /rɪˈliːf/ [n singular/U] the pleasant feeling you have when you no longer have to worry about something
with relief *Everyone smiled with relief as the plane landed safely.*
to sb's relief (=making them feel relieved) *To Sam's relief, nobody asked to check his ticket.*
it is a relief to know/hear/see/find *It was such a relief to know that the children were OK.*
a great relief *The announcement said that no jobs would be lost, which was a great relief to everyone.*

WORSE

➡ opposite **BETTER**
➡ see also **BAD, IMPROVE**

1 worse

worse /wɜːrs/ [adj] more unpleasant, annoying, bad, etc, or of a lower standard or quality than someone or something else
+ than *Conditions in the prison were worse than anything I had seen before.* | *I wish you'd stop complaining – you're worse than my mother!*
even worse (=worse than something that is very bad) *Duncan's handwriting is even worse than his sister's.* | *a terrible script and even worse acting*
a lot worse/much worse *The traffic is a lot worse after five.*
make sth worse *I tried to fix the computer myself, but that just made it worse.*

not as good /ˌnɒt əz ˈɡʊd/ of a lower standard or quality than something else: *Last year's sales figures were excellent but this year's weren't as good.*

+ as *The computing facilities here aren't as good as the ones in my last school.*
not nearly as good (=much less good) *Pop music today isn't nearly as good as in the sixties and seventies.*

> ⚠ **Worse** means 'more bad than something that is bad'. **Not as good** means 'less good than something that is good'. Compare these sentences: *The food was awful, and the service was even worse.* | *It's an enjoyable book, but it's not as good as her last one.*

inferior /ɪnˈfɪəriər/ [adj] FORMAL less well made than something else, or less good at doing something than someone else: *Their furniture is certainly cheaper, but it's of inferior quality.*
+ to *Old Mr Carter was convinced that women doctors were inferior to men.*

worst /wɜːrst/ [adj only before noun] worse than anything else or worse than at any time before: *I think he's the worst teacher in the school.* | *The storms in 1987 were the worst we had ever known.* | *No, don't tell the police about it – that's the worst thing you could do.*
by far the worst (=much worse than any other) *It's by far the worst neighborhood in the whole city.*

2 to become worse

get worse /ˌɡet ˈwɜːrs/ if a situation **gets worse**, it becomes more difficult or more unpleasant: *The situation in Bosnia was getting worse.* | *The pain continued to get worse, so I called a doctor.*
get worse and worse *The traffic on this road is getting worse and worse.*

deteriorate /dɪˈtɪəriəreɪt/ [v I] to gradually become worse: *John's eyesight has deteriorated since his last eye test.* | *All that time, relations between the superpowers were deteriorating.*
deterioration /dɪˌtɪəriəˈreɪʃən/ [n U] when something gradually becomes worse: *the deterioration of the country's road network*

> ⚠ **Deteriorate** is more formal than **get worse.**

go from bad to worse /ˌɡəʊ frəm ˌbæd tə ˈwɜːrs/ if a situation **goes from bad to**

worse, it is already bad and then becomes even worse: *Things then went from bad to worse, and by the end of the year the two countries were at war.*

decline /dɪˈklaɪn/ [v I] FORMAL to become gradually worse – use this especially about standards of work or performance: *Do you think standards of education are declining?* | *Britain's economic performance declined noticeably during the 1970s.*

> **decline** [n singular] *a steady decline in the standard of healthcare provided in our hospitals*

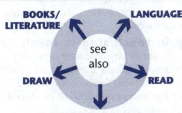

WRITE

BOOKS/LITERATURE

LANGUAGE

see also

DRAW

READ

WORD/PHRASE/SENTENCE

1 to write with a pen or pencil

write /raɪt/ [v I/T] to write words or numbers using a pen or pencil: *By third grade they can all read and write pretty well.* | *At the bottom he wrote: "with sincere love from your oldest friend".*

> **write sth on/in/here etc** *Write your phone number on the back of this envelope.*
> **write down sth/write sth down** (=write information so that you can use it later) *We wrote down everything he told us.* | *I've written the address down for you.*
> **writing – wrote – have written**

○**put** /pʊt/ [v T] ESPECIALLY SPOKEN to write something: *I just put "with best wishes from Mike" on the card.*

> **put sth in/on/at sth** *Put your name at the top of each answer sheet.*
> **putting – put – have put**

make a note of sth /ˌmeɪk ə ˈnəʊt ɒv (sth)/ to write down information that you might need later: *Did you make a note of the times of the trains?* | *"The name of*

that book is 'A Closed Eye'." "Right, I'll make a note of it."

take down/get down /ˌteɪk ˈdaʊn, ˌget ˈdaʊn/ [phrasal verb T] to write down what someone says, at the same time as they are saying it

> **take down sth/get down sth** *A group of reporters was following the Senator trying to get down every word he said.*
> **take sth down/get sth down** *Can I just take your name and address down?*

fill in/fill out /ˌfɪl ˈɪn, ˌfɪl ˈaʊt/ [phrasal verb T] to write information or answer questions on an official document, for example giving your name, address, and age

> **fill in sth** ESPECIALLY BRITISH **fill out sth** ESPECIALLY AMERICAN *Passengers must fill in a short form before boarding the plane.*
> **fill sth in/fill sth out** *You just fill it out and then send it in to the passport office.*

2 to write your name

sign /saɪn/ [v I/T] to write your name at the end of a letter, document etc, in order to prove who you are or show that you wrote it: *Sign here, please.* | *You forgot to sign the credit card slip.*

> **sign your name** *The artist had signed his name in the corner of the painting.*
> **sign for sth** (=to show that you have received it) *Could you sign for this package, please?*

signature /ˈsɪgnətʃər/ [n C] your name written by you, for example on a document or at the end of a letter, in order to prove who you are or show that you wrote it: *Who's it from? I can't read the signature.*

autograph /ˈɔːtəgrɑːf‖-græf/ [n C] the name of a famous person, written by them on a photograph, in a book etc for someone to keep: *She has the autograph of every player in the team.* | *Fans were waiting outside the studio for Neeson's autograph.*

3 to write something quickly or carelessly

jot down /ˌdʒɒt ˈdaʊn‖ˌdʒɑːt-/ [phrasal verb T] to quickly write down ideas, notes, or facts so that you can use them later

jot down sth *Let me jot down the name of that restaurant.*

jot sth down *If anyone has any suggestions, jot them down on a piece of paper and give them to me.*

scribble /'skrɪbəl/ [v T] to write something quickly and untidily: *Andrew scribbled a note and handed it to the chairman.*

4 to write with a computer or typewriter

key in /,kiː 'ɪn/ [phrasal verb T] to write something on a computer, especially something that you are copying from somewhere else

key in sth *I spent all morning keying in the latest sales data.*

key sth in *Find out the name of the file, key it in, and it will appear on the screen.*

type /taɪp/ [v I/T] to write something using a typewriter or computer: *I'm afraid I don't type very fast. | Could you type those letters for me?*

   typing [n U] writing with a typewriter or computer: *We need a secretary with good typing speeds. (=who can type fast)*

enter /'entər/ [v T] to record information in a computer by pressing the keys: *Enter the filename and click 'OK'.*

enter sth in/into sth *The patients' medical records are entered into a database.*

> ⚠ **Enter** is a more technical word than **key in**.

5 to write a letter

write /raɪt/ [v I/T] to write someone a letter: *Sorry, I haven't had time to write.*

write a letter/postcard/note *We wrote about 20 postcards while we were in Greece.*

write sb a letter/postcard/note *Kathleen wrote him dozens of letters but he never replied.*

+ to *You ought to write to your Uncle and thank him for the present.*

write sb AMERICAN (=write a letter to someone) *Steve wrote me about the wedding.*

writing – wrote – have written

> ⚠ In British English, you say **write to someone** (meaning 'write them a letter'), but in American English, you can say either **write to someone** or just **write someone**.

get in touch with sb /,get ɪn 'tʌtʃ wɪð (sb)/ to write to someone, or make a telephone call to them, especially someone you have not seen or written to for a long time: *I'd love to get in touch with Monique again. Do you have her new address?*

contact /'kɒntækt‖'kɑːn-/ [v T] to write to someone that you do not know, or make a telephone call to them, especially in order to ask for help or information: *Elsa contacted several companies to ask if they could offer her part-time work. | If the problem continues, try contacting a software expert.*

keep in touch/stay in touch /,kiːp ɪn 'tʌtʃ, ,steɪ ɪn 'tʌtʃ/ to continue to write to someone or phone them, when you no longer work with them or live near them: *I met Pia in Sweden and we've stayed in touch ever since.*

+ with *Do you keep in touch with any of your friends from school?*

6 to write a story, book etc

write /raɪt/ [v I/T] to write a book, story, newspaper article, piece of schoolwork etc: *I can't come out with you tonight – I have to write an essay. | Who wrote 'Madame Bovary'? | When did he write his first novel?*

+ about *She writes very amusingly about her childhood in Moscow.*

well/badly written *It's a fascinating article, and very well written.*

writing – wrote – have written

writer /'raɪtər/ [n C] someone who writes books, plays, newspaper articles etc as a job: *Terry Pratchett, the science-fiction writer*

+ of *a writer of books about European history*

author /'ɔːθər/ [n C] someone who writes books, or who wrote a particular book: *Jane Austen is one of my favourite authors.*

+ of *Hawking is best known as the author of 'A Brief History of Time'.*

7 to write a song/music

write /raɪt/ [v T] to write music or songs: *Lennon and McCartney wrote over 100 songs.* | *Who wrote the soundtrack for 'The Bodyguard'?*

writing – wrote – have written

compose /kəmˈpəʊz/ [v T] to write a piece of music, especially serious music, not popular music: *Mozart composed his first symphony when he was still a child.*

composer /kəmˈpəʊzəʳ/ [n C] someone who writes music, especially serious music, not popular music: *My favourite composer is Beethoven.*

songwriter /ˈsɒŋˌraɪtəʳ‖ˈsɔːŋ-/ [n C] someone who writes songs, especially modern, popular songs: *songwriter Bernie Taupin*

8 to write the letters of a word

spell /spel/ [v I/T] to write a word using the correct letters in the correct order: *In American English, 'organize' is always spelled with a 'z'.* | *I've never been able to spell very well in English.*

spelling – spelled (also **spelt** BRITISH) – have spelled (also **have spelt** BRITISH)

spelling /ˈspelɪŋ/ [n C/U] the way in which a word is spelled, or someone's ability to spell words correctly: *The dictionary gives both British and American spellings.* | *It's full of spelling mistakes.* | *My spelling isn't very good.*

9 the way someone writes with a pen or pencil etc

writing/handwriting /ˈraɪtɪŋ, ˈhænd-ˌraɪtɪŋ/ [n U] *What beautiful handwriting!* | *Jane's writing's terrible – I can hardly read it.*

10 written, not spoken

written /ˈrɪtn/ [adj] *Some expressions are much more common in written English than in spoken English.*

written statement/agreement/reply/ instructions etc *Don't sign any written agreement until you have read every word of the contract.*

When you see **EC**, go to the **ESSENTIAL COMMUNICATION** section.

---

in writing /ɪn ˈraɪtɪŋ/ if you get or give information **in writing**, it is written down, not spoken, so you can prove later what was actually said: *Apply for tickets in writing to the Adelphi Theatre.* | *Could you confirm in writing the date you intend to leave.*

get it in writing (=ask someone to write something down) ESPECIALLY SPOKEN *"They promised to replace the computer if there are any problems." "Make sure you get it in writing."*

on paper /ɒn ˈpeɪpəʳ/ if you put ideas or suggestions **on paper**, you write them down so that you can remember them or organize them more clearly: *If you have any suggestions for improving the course, put them on paper and we'll discuss them.*

handwritten /ˈhændˌrɪtn/ [adj] written by hand, not using a typewriter or computer: *There was a handwritten note on the desk addressed to Paul.*

WRONG

➡ opposite **RIGHT**

see also

MISTAKE   ACCIDENTALLY

BAD   SUITABLE/ UNSUITABLE

1 wrong

wrong /rɒŋ‖rɔːŋ/ [adj] not right or not correct: *Hank was driving on the wrong side of the road.* | *I tried to telephone her, but she must have given me the wrong number.* | *No, that's wrong – you're supposed to put the flour in first.*

wrong/wrongly [adv] *You've spelled my name wrong.* | *The medicine bottles were wrongly labelled.*

⚠ **Wrong** (adverb) is more informal than **wrongly**. Only use it in spoken English.

incorrect /ˌɪnkəˈrekt◄/ [adj] facts, decisions, answers etc that are **incorrect** are wrong, especially because a mistake has been made, and this can be proved: *The information about current prices was incorrect.* | *incorrect spelling* | *They discovered later that the doctor had made an incorrect diagnosis.*

incorrectly [*adv*] *The article states, incorrectly, that the disease is usually fatal.*

⚠ **Incorrect** is more formal than **wrong.**

inaccurate /ɪnˈækjʊrɪt/ [*adj*] information, numbers etc that are **inaccurate** are not exactly right: *The old maps were usually inaccurate or incomplete.* | *inaccurate measurements*

totally/wildly inaccurate (=very inaccurate) *Figures quoted in the article were wildly inaccurate.*

misleading /mɪsˈliːdɪŋ/ [*adj*] a statement or piece of information that is **misleading** makes people believe something that is wrong, especially because it does not give all the facts: *The article was deliberately misleading, and the newspaper has apologized.*

give a misleading impression/statement etc *Agents often gave a false or misleading description of the properties they were selling.*

2 to believe something that is wrong

➡ see also **MISTAKE**

be wrong /biː ˈrɒŋ‖-ˈrɔːŋ/ if you **are wrong**, you think or say something that is not correct: *I thought a vacation in Greece would be cheap, but I was wrong!* | *Why won't he admit that he was wrong?*

+ about *You were wrong about that train – it left at 10.30.*

be mistaken /biː mɪˈsteɪkən/ FORMAL to have an opinion or belief about something, which is not correct: *Mulder thought he saw an alien spacecraft, but he was almost certainly mistaken.*

you must be mistaken SPOKEN (use this to say politely that someone is wrong) *I think you must be mistaken. He could not have obtained a key to your room.*

3 in the wrong position

wrong /rɒŋ‖rɔːŋ/ [*adj* only before noun]
the wrong direction/way/place/order etc *Someone had moved the road sign so that it was pointing in the wrong direction.* | *The TV antenna is facing the wrong way.* | *The files had been put back in the wrong order.*

the wrong way around (also **the wrong way round** BRITISH) /ðə ˌrɒŋ weɪ (ə)ˈraʊnd‖-ˌrɔːŋ-/ if something is **the wrong way around**, it is pointing or facing in the direction that is opposite to the correct one: *You've got your T-shirt on the wrong way around!* | *Someone's put the battery in the wrong way round.*

inside out /ˌɪnsaɪd ˈaʊt/ if something, especially a piece of clothing, is **inside out**, the inside of it is on the outside and the outside of it is on the inside: *I put my socks on inside out by mistake.* | *The wind blew my umbrella inside out.*

turn sth inside out *Before washing your sweater, turn it inside out.*

upside down /ˌʌpsaɪd ˈdaʊn/ if something is **upside down**, the top of it is at the bottom and the bottom of it is at the top: *One of the pages was upside down.* | *The monkey was hanging upside down from a tree.*

turn sth upside down *Turn the cups upside down and leave them to dry.*

Y

YOUNG

➡ opposite **OLD**

see also

AGE   CHILD
ADULT   BABY
DESCRIBING PEOPLE

1 young

young /jʌŋ/ [adj] *You're too young to smoke.* | *a single mother with two young children* | *When I was younger, I used to play a lot of baseball.* | *Her youngest son works for a television company.*
younger brother/sister *Hannah has two younger brothers.*

○ **little** /'lɪtl/ [adj] ESPECIALLY SPOKEN very young – use this to talk about a young child: *When I was little we used to go camping a lot.*
little brother/sister (=younger brother or sister, who is still a child) *Look after your little sister for a moment, will you?*
little boy/girl (=a young child, or a young son or daughter) *They've been married for ten years and have two little girls.* | *Who's that little boy in the blue sweater?*

2 a young person

teenager /'tiːneɪdʒəʳ/ [n C] someone who is between 13 and 19 years old: *River Phoenix became a famous actor while still a teenager.* | *The survey showed that three out of five teenagers had been offered illegal drugs.*
teenage [adj only before noun] *Jenny has three teenage children.*

youth /juːθ/ [n C] a young man between about 15 and 25 years old – use this especially about young men who behave badly or do something illegal: *A youth pushed her against the wall and took her bag.* | *a gang of youths in leather jackets*

in your teens /ɪn jɔːʳ 'tiːnz/ someone who is **in their teens** is between 13 and 19 years old: *She had run away from home several times in her teens.*
in your early/mid/late teens *Most of the girls at the concert were in their early teens.*

adolescent /ˌædə'lesənt◄/ [n C] someone who is at the age when they change from being a child into a young adult – use this especially when talking about problems that young people have at this age: *John changed from a friendly and cheerful young boy into a confused adolescent.*

> ⚠ You can also use **adolescent** before a noun, like an adjective: *a crowd of screaming adolescent girls*

3 the time when you are young

childhood /'tʃaɪldhʊd/ [n C/U] the time when you are a child: *Nina had happy memories of her childhood on the farm.*
early childhood (=when you are a young child) *His early childhood was spent with his father in Chicago.*

> ⚠ You can also use **childhood** before a noun, like an adjective: *a book about his childhood memories* | *childhood illnesses like measles*

youth /juːθ/ [n U] the time when you are young, especially the time between 15 and 25 when you are no longer a child: *She revisited all the places where she had spent her youth.*
in sb's youth (=when they were young) *Caroline had been a ballet dancer in her youth.*

adolescence /ˌædə'lesəns/ [n U] the time when a young person is changing from being a child into a young adult – use this especially when talking about the problems that young people have at this age: *During adolescence, boys are sometimes very shy and lacking in self-confidence.*

> When you see **EC**, go to the **ESSENTIAL COMMUNICATION** section.

4 connected with things that young people do

youth /juːθ/ [adj only before noun] **youth club/group/organization etc** a club, group etc for young people: *I met her at the local youth club.* | *a concert by the National Youth Orchestra*

teenage /ˈtiːneɪdʒ/ [adj only before noun] **teenage fashions/magazines/pregnancy/drug-taking etc** use this about things produced for teenagers, or things that teenagers do: *There has been a significant increase in teenage pregnancies recently.* | *the teenage music scene*

juvenile /ˈdʒuːvənaɪl‖-nəl, -naɪl/ [adj only before noun] use this about crimes involving young people

juvenile crime/offender (=crime by young people, or a young person who is a criminal)

juvenile court (=a court that deals with crimes by young people)

ESSENTIAL COMMUNICATION

The ESSENTIAL COMMUNICATION section will help you communicate in English. To use it, look up the situation you need to deal with (for example AGREEING or COMPLAINING), and choose the box which best fits what you need to say. The ESSENTIAL COMMUNICATION section has been based especially on the spoken component of the British National Corpus.

ADVICE

| asking for advice | giving advice |

What do you think I should do?

I don't know whether to speak to Bob about it. What do you think I should do?

Can I ask your advice/opinion about something?

Can I ask your advice about something? I'm really worried about my brother.

Do you think I should...?

It's only $10 a month. Do you think I should join?

I'm thinking of... . What do you think?

I'm thinking of dyeing my hair. What do you think?

⚠ Don't say 'Can you give me an advice?' Use one of the phrases above.

You should... /You ought to...

You should phone the police if you're really worried about it.

You shouldn't drink so much.

If I were you,...

use this when you have thought carefully about the situation
If I were you, I'd wait till tomorrow.

If I were you, I wouldn't tell anyone about it.

What you ought to do is...
SPOKEN

What you ought to do is get them to pay in advance.

What you need is... SPOKEN

What you need is a nice long holiday.

Make sure (that) you...

use this to give someone advice that will help them not to make a mistake
Make sure you take enough money for the taxi.

The best thing is to...

The best thing is to drink lots of water.

⚠ In a conversation, don't say 'I advise you to do this' or 'I recommend that you do this'. These are very formal and are mostly used in writing.

SUGGESTIONS

making a suggestion	replying to a suggestion

making a suggestion

Let's...
Let's have a picnic.

We could.../You could...
We could go for a drink before the concert.
You could ask Simon if he wants to come.

Why don't we/you...?
Why don't we go to Spain this summer?
Why don't you paint it white?

What about...?/How about...?
What about going out one night next week?

Do you want to...?
ESPECIALLY AMERICAN
Do you want to see if we can get a room for the night?

Shall I/we...? ESPECIALLY BRITISH
Should I/we...? AMERICAN
Shall I organize the drinks for the party?
Should we go to Becky's then?

YES

Yes/Yeah
How about finding somewhere to eat?
Yes, I'm starving.

OK/Right/All right
Let's go and visit your brother.
OK.

Good idea!
What about a trip to the beach?
Good idea!

That sounds good/great
Shall I organize a barbecue on Saturday?
That sounds good.

Sure! ESPECIALLY AMERICAN
Do you want to try some sushi?
Sure!

NO

⚠ When you say no to a suggestion, it is polite to give a reason, or suggest something else instead.

Sorry, I can't
Let's go out for a pizza on Saturday.
Sorry, I can't. I'm going away for the weekend.

How about ... instead?
Shall I say that we'll come?
How about staying home instead?

I'd rather (do sth)/I'd prefer to (do sth)
Let's stay over till Sunday.
I'd rather come back straight after the party.

CONVERSATION

Kate: *Let's go and see a movie on Saturday.*
Richard: *Sorry, I can't. I'm going to visit my cousins. Why don't we go next week instead?*
Kate: *OK. What about Wednesday?*
Richard: *That sounds good. Shall I meet you at your house?*
Kate: *I have a better idea. How about getting something to eat before the movie?*
Richard: *Good idea! What time? About 7 o'clock?*
Kate: *Right. See you then.*

OFFERS

offering to do something for someone

offering someone a drink, something to eat etc

Would you like me to...?
use this when you want to be polite
Would you like me to help you with your homework?

Do you want me to...?
use this with friends and people you know well
Do you want me to get some tickets for the concert?

Shall I...? BRITISH
Should I...? AMERICAN
Shall I buy the stuff for the picnic?
Should I make the salad?

Would you like...?
use this when you want to be polite
Would you like a drink?

Do you want...?
use this with friends and people you know well
Do you want a cup of coffee?

Can I get you...?
Can I get you a beer or something?

How about...? INFORMAL
How about a quick snack before we leave?

Fancy...?/Do you fancy...? BRITISH INFORMAL
Fancy a drink after work, Annie?

saying yes or no to an offer

YES

Yes, please

Do you want a piece of cake?

Yes, please.

Thanks

Would you like a drink?

Thanks. A glass of white wine, please.

That's very kind of you FORMAL

Would you like a drink?

That's very kind of you. A glass of white wine, please.

NO

No, thanks

Would you like a drink?

No, thanks. I have to leave soon.

No, I'm fine, thanks INFORMAL
use this to say no when someone offers you more food or drink

Do you want another beer?

No, I'm fine, thanks

That's very kind of you, but... FORMAL

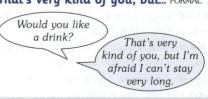

Would you like a drink?

That's very kind of you, but I'm afraid I can't stay very long.

INVITATIONS
asking someone if they would like to do something

asking friends	asking anyone	asking someone you do not know very well

Do you want to...?

Do you want to go to the movies on Saturday?

Would you like to...?

Would you like to go out for dinner sometime?

I was wondering if you'd like to...

I was wondering if you'd like to join us for a drink?

⚠ Don't say 'I invite you...' or 'I'd like to invite you...' Use one of the phrases above.

---

saying yes or no to an invitation

YES	NO

Yes, I'd like that

Would you like to play tennis one night next week?

Yes, I'd like that.

Sorry, (I'm afraid) I can't

Do you want to come swimming on Thursday?

Sorry, I can't. It's my Dad's birthday.

That sounds great! INFORMAL

We're going ice skating. Do you want to come?

That sounds great! Thanks.

Sorry, but I'm going to... on Wednesday/Friday etc

Would you like to come for dinner on Tuesday?

Sorry, but I'm going to aerobics on Tuesday.

Yes, OK

Do you want to join us for a game of basketball?

Yes, OK. What time?

Thanks for asking me, but...

Do you want to come to a party on Friday night?

Thanks for asking me, but I'm going away for the weekend.

REQUESTS
asking someone to do something for you

⚠ Use the polite phrases when you are talking to someone you do not know well, or when you are asking a friend to do something difficult or important.

asking friends	asking anyone	when you want to be polite

Can you...?

Can you lend me $10 till Saturday?

Will you...?

Will you lend me a newspaper while you're out?

Could you...?

Could you give me a ride to work on Monday?

Would you mind... (doing sth)?

Would you mind feeding the cat while I'm away?

Do you think you could...?

Do you think you could check your records again, please?

I wonder if you'd mind... (doing sth)?
FORMAL

I wonder if you'd mind giving this letter to Mr Roberts?

---

saying yes or no to a request

YES	NO

OK/All right

Can you lend me $10 till Saturday?
OK. Here you are.

Yes, sure

Will you buy me a newspaper while you're out?
Yes, sure. Which one?

Certainly FORMAL

Do you think you could check your records again, please?
Certainly. Just one moment.

⚠ It is polite to give a reason if you say no.

Sorry, but...

Can you lend me $10 till Saturday?
Sorry, but I don't really have enough.

I can't really

Could you give me a lift into town?
I can't really. I'm waiting for a phone call.

I'm afraid...

Can you come to my office tomorrow at 10 o'clock?
I'm afraid I'm busy tomorrow morning.

PERMISSION
asking someone to let you do something

⚠️ Use the polite phrases when you are talking to someone you do not know well, or when you are asking a friend if you can do something important, such as borrow their car.

---

asking anyone

Can I...?

Can I borrow your pen?

Is it OK/all right if I...?

Is it OK if I bring a friend to your party?

Do you mind if I...?

Do you mind if I open the window?

when you want to be polite

Would you mind if I...?

Would you mind if I came with you to the concert?

Would it be OK/all right if I...?

Would it be all right if I left early today?

---

saying yes or no to a request

YES	NO
Yes, of course	⚠️ It is polite to give a reason if you say no.
Is it OK if I bring a friend to your party? → *Yes, of course. Bring anyone you like.*	**Sorry, but...**
Yes, sure INFORMAL	*Is it all right if I keep this photo?* → *Sorry, but I only have one copy.*
Can I borrow your pen? → *Yes, sure.*	**No, sorry**
Yes, that's fine	*Can I borrow your pen?* → *No, sorry. I need it.*
Is it all right if I keep this photo? → *Yes, that's fine.*	**I'm afraid...**
No, that's fine	*Can I have a look at the files myself?* → *I'm afraid that's not possible.*
use this to reply to questions which start with *Do/Would you mind if I...?*	**I'd rather you didn't**
Do you mind if I open the window? → *No, that's fine.*	*Do you mind if I open the window?* → *I'd rather you didn't. It gets really noisy with the window open.*

COMPLAINING

complaining to someone you know well	writing a letter to complain about something	complaining in a shop, restaurant, hotel etc

I am writing to complain about...

I am writing to complain about the service I received in your restaurant.

I'm sick of you (doing sth)/ I've had enough of you (doing sth)

use this when you are annoyed at someone's behaviour

I've had enough of you two arguing. Stop it right now!

You're always (doing sth)

use this when someone keeps doing something that annoys you.

You're always flirting with other women.

You're always trying to control what I do.

You never...

use this when someone keeps forgetting to do something or is unwilling to do something

You never listen, do you?

The usual way to complain is just to explain what has happened or what is wrong. For example: *The shower in my room isn't working.* You then expect that the person you are talking to will do something to put it right. Only use the following phrases when you have already done this and you are complaining to someone else because you are still not satisfied.

I'm not satisfied with...

I'm not satisfied with the quality of the repairs that you carried out.

I'd like to make a complaint about...

I'd like to make a complaint about the extra charges on my bill.

APOLOGIZING

when you have made a small mistake, for example if you accidentally stand on someone's foot	if you want to say you are sorry when something bad has happened to someone, go to **SORRY**	when you have done something wrong or upset someone

Sorry

Sorry. I didn't mean to kick you!

Excuse me AMERICAN

Oh, excuse me. That was my fault.

> ⚠ Don't say 'pardon' or 'pardon me' in this situation.

Sorry SPOKEN

Sorry I'm late – the traffic was terrible!
I've forgotten your book. Sorry!
+ about *Sorry about all the mess.*

I'm sorry

I'm sorry I shouted at you.
+ that *I'm sorry that you weren't told about the meeting.*
+ about *I'm sorry about the mix-up. It was my fault.*

I'm really sorry (=very sorry)

I'm really sorry, but I've broken one of your CDs.

I apologize FORMAL SPOKEN

use this in formal spoken situations such as meetings
I apologize for mentioning this again, but we still haven't made a decision.

Apologies for... WRITTEN

Apologies for not replying to your letter sooner.

SAYING THANK YOU

when someone gives you something or when someone says your work is good or that you look good	**when someone has done something for you or has offered to do something**	**when you are writing a letter to thank someone**

Thank you/Thanks

Here, have some gum.

Thanks.

Your report was really good.

Thank you. It took me ages to do.

Thank you very much/Thanks very much

That dress really suits you.

Thanks very much. I got it last year.

⚠ **Thank you** is more formal than **thanks**. Don't say 'very thanks' or 'much thanks'.

Thank you/Thanks

Can I help you with those bags?

Oh, thank you.

+ for doing sth *Thanks for getting the tickets.*

Thank you very much/ Thanks very much

Thanks very much for all your help.

⚠ **Thanks** is more informal than **thank you**.

It's/That's very kind of you.
FORMAL

If the meeting finishes late, I'll drive you back to town.

Thank you. That's very kind of you.

I really appreciate it. SPOKEN
say this when someone has done a lot for you

Thanks for helping out on Sunday. I really appreciated it.

Thank you for...
Thank you for the book you sent me for my birthday.

+ doing sth *Thank you for feeding my cat while I was away.*

Thank you very much for...
Thank you very much for the information about the art course.

Many thanks for... FORMAL
Many thanks for the card and flowers.

---

what to say when someone thanks you for doing something or for giving them something

In American English you usually reply when someone thanks you for doing something or for giving them something. In British English people often do not reply, but this is not rude.

That's OK

Thanks for looking after the kids.

That's OK. I enjoyed having them.

You're welcome
ESPECIALLY AMERICAN

Thanks for letting me stay, Mrs. Parker.

Oh, you're welcome.

No problem INFORMAL

Thanks for coming with me.

No problem.

Don't mention it

Thank you for all your help.

Don't mention it.

Sure AMERICAN

Thanks for the ride.

Sure.

DIRECTIONS

| asking for directions | giving directions |

asking for directions

⚠️ It is polite to say **excuse me**, at the beginning of your question, and **please** at the end. If you use both, you will sound quite formal.

How do I get to...?

Excuse me, how do I get to the post office?

Is there a ... near here?

Excuse me, is there a bank near here, please?

Could/Can you tell me the way to...?

Could you tell me the way to the bus station, please?

Could/Can you tell me where the ... is?

Excuse me, could you tell me where the National Gallery is, please?

⚠️ **Could** is more polite than **can**.

CONVERSATION 1

A *Excuse me, how do I get to the station?*

B *I'm sorry, I don't know.*

CONVERSATION 2

A *Excuse me, could you tell me the way to the library, please?*

B *Yes, sure. Go straight on and keep going until you get to the post office. Then turn left and keep going until you get to the crossroads. Turn right at the crossroads and the library's on your left.*

A *Thanks very much.*

giving directions

Go straight ahead
(also **Go straight on** BRITISH
Go straight AMERICAN)

↑

Turn left (also **Take a left** AMERICAN)

Turn left at the crossroads. ←⌐

Turn right (also **Take a right** AMERICAN)

Take a right at the bank. ⌐→

Go past...
Go past the church. ✝ ——→

Keep going until you get to...

Keep going until you get to the park

PARK

↑
↑

Take the first/second turn on your left/right.

OPINIONS

1. **giving your opinion**
2. **saying what other people think**
3. **asking someone for their opinion**

1. giving your opinion

I think (that)...	this is the most common way of giving your opinion	*I think that we should spend more on education.* *I think it's a waste of time.*
I believe (that)...	use this in formal speech or in writing when you have strong opinions about something	*I believe that abortion is wrong.* *I believe we have made a major financial error.*
In my opinion,...	use this in writing	*In my opinion, less money should be spent on weapons.*
It seems to me (that)...	use this when you are giving your opinion based on things that have happened or on things that you have noticed	*It seems to me that children have too much freedom these days.* *It seems to me you don't have much choice.*
As far as I'm concerned,...	use this to emphasize that you do not care whether people agree with you or not	*As far as I'm concerned, everything's fine the way it is.*
If you ask me,... INFORMAL	use this to say what you think about a particular problem or situation	*If you ask me, they ought to just fire him.*

⚠ Don't say 'according to me' when giving your opinion. Use one of the phrases in the box above.

⚠ Don't talk about 'saying your opinion'. Use **giving your opinion** or **saying what you think**. *We never get a chance to say what we think.*

2. saying what other people think

think (that)	this is the most common way of saying what other people think	*Most students think that getting a job is the most important thing.* *Some people think the laws on drinking are too strict.*
be in favour of BRITISH **be in favor of** AMERICAN	use this in writing before saying what people think is right or good	*Most people are in favour of greater political freedom.* *Only the liberals are in favor of tax reform.*
be against	use this in writing before saying what people think is wrong or bad	*Over 80% of those surveyed are against the use of animals in experiments.*

3. asking someone for their opinion

To ask for someone's opinion you usually ask a direct question. For example:
Do you think the President should resign?
Do you think that Sarah will get the job?
You can also use the following ways of asking:

What do you think about...?	use this to ask for someone's general opinion about something	*What do you think about going to Australia this winter?* *What do you think about the plans to build a new freeway?*
What do you think of...?	use this to ask whether they like someone or something	*What do you think of Sheila's new boyfriend?* *What do you think of the new CD?*

AGREEING

| when you agree strongly | when you agree | when you agree, but not strongly |

when you agree strongly

Absolutely

> Men and women should have equal rights.

> Absolutely!

Exactly

> She shouldn't have come if she didn't want to.

> Exactly!

I couldn't agree more

> Parents are responsible for making sure their children behave well.

> I couldn't agree more.

You're telling me!
INFORMAL

use this to agree with something when you know about it or have personal experience of it

> The buses are always late, aren't they?

> You're telling me! I've been standing here for half an hour.

when you agree

Yes/Yeah

> I think we should get Ann a birthday present.

> Yes. That's a really good idea.

I know

> That meeting was really boring.

> I know. I thought it would never end.

I agree

> It would really help if the bank stayed open later.

> I agree. If the shops can do it, why can't the banks?

Right/That's right/ You're right

> I think we're wasting our time here.

> You're right. Let's go home.

when you agree, but not strongly

I suppose so

> You should tell Jenny how you feel.

> I suppose so, but it's not easy.

I guess so AMERICAN

> It's your first date. Chris will be nervous too.

> I guess so.

DISAGREEING

| when you disagree, but you want to be polite | when you disagree strongly |

when you disagree, but you want to be polite

Yes, but...

> We should buy computers for every class in the school.

>> Yes, but we don't have enough money

I know, but...

> It would be much simpler to meet at the restaurant.

>> I know, but I might get lost. Let's go there together.

I take/see your point, but...

> Famous people can't expect to keep their private lives secret.

>> I take your point, but doesn't everyone have a right to privacy?

But don't you think...?

> We should have the party at a restaurant.

>> But don't you think it might be too expensive?

I'm not so sure...

> Well, it looks as if Greece would be the best choice.

>> I'm not so sure, Larry. It's a long way to go.

when you disagree strongly

⚠ Only use these phrases with people you know well. You will sound rude if you say them to a stranger.

No, it isn't/No, she isn't etc

> The quickest way to get there is to take the train.

>> No, it isn't. It's much faster by car.

That's not true

> Eating meat is bad for you.

>> That's not true. It's a really good source of iron.

You must be joking!/No way!
INFORMAL

> It'll only take 30 minutes to get there.

>> You must be joking! The traffic's really bad at this time of day.

I can't accept that... FORMAL

> I believe we should close the department until next year.

>> I'm sorry, I can't accept that this is the best solution.

Rubbish! BRITISH INFORMAL

> I'm too tired to do the washing up.

>> Rubbish! You haven't done anything all day.

SAYING YES

saying yes to a question

when you want to emphasize that the answer is definitely yes	**when the answer is yes**	**when you think that the answer is yes, but you are not sure**

Definitely!

> *Are you going to Sonya's party?*

> *Definitely! I think it'll be really good.*

Of course!

use this when you are surprised or annoyed that someone has asked you something, or to emphasize your answer

> *Is it OK if Sara stays with us for a few days?*

> *Of course! She's welcome to.*

> *Did you lock the door?*

> *Yes, of course I did!*

Yes

> *Is that ring real gold?*

> *Yes, it is.*

> *Have you bought everything we need?*

> *Yes, I have.*

That's right

use this especially when someone is checking facts

> *You're Ben's sister, aren't you?*

> *That's right.*

Yeah INFORMAL

> *Are you going to the club tonight?*

> *Yeah. Are you?*

I'm afraid so

use this when you think the person asking the question is hoping for a different answer

> *Was she very angry?*

> *I'm afraid so.*

I think so

> *Are you coming to the movies with us?*

> *I think so. It depends what time I finish work.*

Probably

> *Will you be home by six o'clock?*

> *Probably. The class is usually over by five.*

I guess so ESPECIALLY AMERICAN

> *Are you going to take that apartment?*

> *I guess so. It's a little expensive though.*

> *Have they already gone home?*

> *Yes, I guess so.*

➡ **for saying yes to an invitation, go to**  **EC INVITATIONS**
➡ **for saying yes when someone offers you something, go to EC OFFERS**
➡ **for saying yes when someone suggests something, go to EC SUGGESTIONS**
➡ **for saying yes when someone asks you to do something, go to EC REQUESTS**
➡ **for saying yes when someone asks if they can do something, go to EC PERMISSION**
➡ **for saying that you agree with someone's opinion, go to EC AGREEING**

SAYING NO

saying no to a question

when you want to emphasize that the answer is no	when the answer is no	when you think the answer is no, but you are not sure

Definitely not!

So, would you go camping again?

Definitely not! It rained all week.

Of course not!

use this when you are surprised or annoyed that someone has asked you something, or to emphasize your answer

Did he pass any of his exams in the end?

Of course not! He didn't do any work!

Of course I won't/she didn't etc

You won't tell Mike about this, will you? It's supposed to be a secret.

No, of course I won't.

No way!

Are you going to go out with Ron?

No way! He's horrible.

 Use this to emphasize your answer, especially when you are talking to friends or people you know well.

No

Are you Italian?

No, I'm Spanish.

 It often sounds rude or angry if you use **no** on its own. People usually say something else after the word **no**.

Not really

Did you have a good day?

Not really. The car broke down.

I'm afraid not

use this when you think that the person asking the question is hoping for a different answer

Did you find the book I wanted?

I'm afraid not. I looked everywhere.

I don't think so

Will it be ready by tomorrow?

I don't think so. There's a lot to do.

Probably not

Is that enough pasta for four of us?

Probably not. I'd better get some more.

I doubt it

Do you think Sophie will come?

I doubt it. She's very busy at the moment.

➡ for saying no to an invitation, go to **EC** INVITATIONS
➡ for saying no when someone offers you something, go to **EC** OFFERS
➡ for saying no when someone suggests something, go to **EC** SUGGESTIONS
➡ for saying no when someone asks you to do something, go to **EC** REQUESTS
➡ for saying no when someone asks if they can do something, go to **EC** PERMISSION
➡ for saying that you do not agree with someone's opinion, go to **EC** AGREEING

SAYING HELLO

saying hello to friends or to people you already know	saying hello when you have been introduced to someone for the first time	saying hello when you are being very polite because you are in a formal or business situation	when you are introducing someone else	when you are introducing yourself

Hello

Hi

Morning
use this when you see someone at the start of the day, for example when you arrive at work

Hello

Good morning
(=before 12 noon)

Good afternoon
(=12 noon - 6pm)

Good evening
(=after 6pm)

⚠ Only use **Goodnight** when you are saying goodbye in the evening, not when you are saying hello.

Hello, I'm...
Hello, I'm Greg. I'm a friend of Rachel's.

Hello, my name's...
Hello, my name's Lynn. I'll be in the same class as you this year.

Nice to meet you./Pleased to meet you.

Mark:	*Hello, Colin.*
Colin:	*Hello, Mark.*
Mark:	*Have you met my cousin Freddie from Canada?*
Colin:	*No, I haven't.* (they shake hands)
Freddie:	*Hello.*
Colin:	*Hello. Pleased to meet you.*

⚠ **How do you do** is very formal, and is not often used.

This is...
This is my boyfriend, Andy.

Have you met...?
Have you met my brother, Richard?

Do you know...?
Do you know our Sales Manager, Patsy Morris?

I'd like you to meet...
use this in formal situations, for example at work, or when you are talking to a much older person
I'd like you to meet Linda Davis, the new science teacher.

SAYING GOODBYE

when saying goodbye, you usually say
Bye, but you can say these other things

| saying goodbye to a friend you will see again soon | saying goodbye to a friend you may not see very soon | saying goodbye when it's the end of the evening or you are going to bed | saying goodbye when you think it's time to leave – you can say these before you say goodbye | saying goodbye when you want to be formal or very polite |

See you

See you later/See you soon

See you tomorrow/next week etc

See you sometime

See you around

Take care

⚠ You usually give a reason when you tell someone that you have to leave.

I'd better be going INFORMAL

I'd better be going. Jack will wonder where I am.

I must go BRITISH

I must go, or I'll be late for my aerobics class.

I'd better be off BRITISH INFORMAL

Well, I'd better be off. I've got work in the morning.

I've got to go ESPECIALLY BRITISH

I have to go AMERICAN

I have to go or I'll be late.

I'm afraid I have to leave now FORMAL

I'm afraid I have to leave now. My train leaves at nine.

Goodnight

Night

⚠ **Night** is more informal than **Goodnight**.

Goodbye

It was nice meeting you/ talking to you.

HAVING A CONVERSATION

asking someone to repeat what they said	when you want to give yourself more time to think	checking that someone understands or agrees with you	when someone is talking and you want to say something

when you want to start a new subject or go back to the main subject	showing that you are listening to what someone is saying

So...

use this to continue what you were saying before, or to introduce a new subject, especially a question

So, have you decided where you're going to live yet?

So what's the answer – yes or no?

Anyway,...

use this to go back to the main point of what you were saying, especially after talking about other things

Anyway, in the end, I decided to buy the black one.

Um.../Er.../Uh.../Well...

Er... I don't really know.

Well, if there's no-one else, I suppose I'll have to do it

I mean...

It's so far away. And, I mean, if we have to be there by two o'clock...

Do you know what I mean?

I just don't think it's right to treat people like that. Do you know what I mean?

..., you know?

I want to get one of those big leather bags, you know? One with a shoulder strap.

Sorry?/Pardon?

Sorry? Did you say Tuesday?

Could you repeat...

Could you repeat the address, please?

I didn't quite catch...

I didn't quite catch the number. Could you say it again, please?

While someone else is talking, you normally show that you are listening by looking at them, nodding your head, and using these words.

Yes/Yeah/Right/Mm/Uh-huh

A *You know my friend Sam was going to buy a motorcycle...*

B *Yeah...*

A *Well, she went to this place where you get them cheap.*

B *Mm.*

A *...and got a really good one, which she's going to let me borrow.*

B *Oh, right.*

A *So, d'you want to come for a ride sometime?*

When you want to interrupt someone, you usually show this by leaning forward, making a movement, or taking a breath. You can also use these words and phrases.

Um.../Well...

use these to show that you want to interrupt, and then leave a pause to see whether the other person is going to stop or not

A *So, if you come over to my place, then we can all travel there together in my car, and...*

B *Um...*

A *What?*

B *Well, I'm not sure if I can come after all.*

Yes, but.../I know, but...

use these when you want to interrupt in order to disagree

A *It would be great to travel around while we're there, and maybe visit...*

B *Yes, but what if we run out of money?*

Sorry to interrupt, but...

use this when you are interrupting a conversation, which you were not involved in before

Sorry to interrupt, but I have an urgent message for you.

TALKING ON THE PHONE

| when you are making the call | when you are answering the call |

Hello?

In formal or business situations, you usually give your name, or the name of your company. At home, you usually just say *Hello?*

Hello, Gail Block speaking.
Hello, R.W. Motors.

⚠ The person who answers the phone always starts the conversation.

---

asking for the person you want to speak to

when the right person is there

Is... there please?

Hello, is Monica there, please?

⚠ Don't say 'Is there Monica, please?'

Can I speak to..., please?/ May I speak to..., please?

Can I speak to Dr. Chang, please?

⚠ These are more formal than **is ... there, please?**

Is that...?

use this when you think you are speaking to the right person, but you are not sure

Hello, is that Guy?

One moment, please

Hello, can I speak to David Schmidt, please?
One moment please.

Hold on/Hang on* INFORMAL

Hello, is Liz there?
Hold on. I'll see if she's in.

I'll (just) get him/her* INFORMAL

Is Vanessa there, please?
Yes, I'll just get her.

Speaking

say this when you are the person they have asked for

Can I speak to Tom, please?
Speaking.
(=I am Tom)

---

saying who you are

when the right person is not there

It's...

Hello, is Harry there please? It's his sister.

This is...

Can I speak to Catherine Hart, please? This is Grant Davies.

⚠ **This is...** is more formal than **It's...**

Sorry, he's/she's...

Sorry, he's out.
Sorry, she's away for the weekend.

Can I take a message?/ Would you like to leave a message?

Simon's out at the moment. Can I take a message?

Do you want to hold?

(=when someone is already on the phone in an office, but you can wait for them to finish the conversation)
I'm sorry, her line's busy at the moment. Do you want to hold?

---

saying goodbye

At the end of the conversation, it sounds rude if you suddenly say Bye or Goodbye, and put the phone down. People usually say something else first.

A *Well, I'd better go. I have to pick up the kids.*
B *OK, see you soon, then.*
A *Yes, see you on Tuesday. Bye.*
B *Goodbye.*

LINKING WORDS
**use these words and phrases
to link your ideas together**

1. **AND words**
2. **BUT words**
3. **BECAUSE words**
4. **IF words**
5. **THEREFORE words**
6. **IN ORDER TO words**

1.   AND words

and

Use this to join two things, actions, ideas etc in one sentence or in one part of a sentence.

All we had for three days was bread ***and*** water.

Suddenly, she stood up ***and*** started shouting.

Tall ***and*** handsome, *Lionel was very attractive to women.*

I don't know why you think this ***and***, *to be honest,* I really don't care.

⚠ Don't start a sentence with the word **and.**

also

Use this when you are linking one idea, thing, action etc to another one in the previous sentence. Put the word **also** directly before the verb.

*François speaks English. He **also** speaks German.*
*A dog provides friendship and exercise. It can **also** be useful for protecting your house.*

⚠ Don't say 'I also can play the piano.'
Say **I can also play the piano.**

⚠ Don't say 'We also have decided to get a new car.'
Say **We have also decided to get a new car.**

⚠ Don't use **also** with two negative statements. Use **either.**
Don't say 'She doesn't smoke. She also doesn't drink.'
Say **She doesn't smoke. She doesn't drink either.**

too

Use this at the end of a sentence when you are adding something to a list of things that you gave in the previous sentence.

Gary and Sheila and the kids are coming to visit. They're bringing grandmother, **too.**

It's fast and comfortable. It's economical, **too.**

> ⚠ Don't use **too** with negative statements. Use **either.**
> Don't say 'He didn't smoke or drink. He didn't gamble, too'.
> Say **He didn't smoke or drink. He didn't gamble either.**

as well

Use this at the end of a sentence when you are adding something to a list of things that you gave in the previous sentence.

Most of them have a cassette and a radio built in. This one's got a CD player **as well.**

"I'm going to get bread, cheese, tea, and sugar." "Can you get some milk **as well?"**

> ⚠ Don't use **as well** with two negative statements. Use **either.**
> Don't say 'Carlo's not coming to the party. Maria can't come as well.'
> Say **Carlo's not coming to the party. Maria can't come either.**

anyway/besides INFORMAL, ESPECIALLY SPOKEN

Use this at the beginning of a sentence when you have given one reason for doing something and you want to add another.

I hate asking for a pay rise. **Anyway,** *there's no point.*

I don't really need a new car. **Besides,** *I can't afford one.*

furthermore FORMAL, ESPECIALLY WRITTEN

Use this at the beginning of a sentence to add a more important fact than the one that you gave in the previous sentence.

The drug has powerful side effects. **Furthermore,** *it may be addictive.*

2. BUT words

but

Use this to join two words or phrases when the second one has the opposite meaning to the first one, OR when the second one is surprising after the first one, OR when one is negative and one is positive.

The new Skoda is fast **but** *quite cheap to run.*

I called **but** *there was no one there.*

He's short and not really handsome, **but** *women still find him attractive.*

although/even though

Use this before a statement that makes the main statement seem surprising or unlikely.

Although *we are a small company, we still produce over 10,000 cars a year.*
I enjoyed German, **even though** *I wasn't very good at it.*

on the other hand

Use this at the beginning of a sentence when you have just mentioned one side of an argument and you are going to mention the opposite side.

Nuclear power is relatively cheap. **On the other hand**, *you could argue that it's not safe.*

still/then again/mind you SPOKEN

Use this when you have just given one opinion about something and you now want to say something which suggests the opposite, for example when you give an advantage and then a disadvantage.

Teaching must be an interesting job. **Then again**, *it must be stressful too.*
This trip is going to be very expensive. **Still**, *we don't go away very often.*
I'd love to travel around the world. **Mind you**, *I wouldn't want to go on my own.*

however/nevertheless

Use **however** and **nevertheless** in fairly formal writing when giving facts that make your previous sentence seem less true or when giving facts that balance what you said in your previous sentence. Use **nevertheless** at the beginning of a sentence. Use **however** in the middle of a sentence, separated from the rest of the sentence by two commas.

*Young people can be rude and badly-behaved. That is no reason, **however**, for treating them like criminals.*
*The drug may be effective. It's not true, **however,** that it is cheap.*
*It was a terrible accident. **Nevertheless,** air travel is still the safest form of transport.*

in spite of/despite

Use this to introduce a fact in one half of a sentence when this fact makes the rest of the sentence seem surprising.

***In spite of** having lots of money, he was an unhappy man.*
***Despite** his lack of education, Jake became a successful businessman.*
***In spite of** her injuries, Sandra was able to crawl to safety.*

> ⚠ Don't say 'In spite of he had lots of money...' Say **In spite of having lots of money...**
>
> If you put a verb phrase after **in spite of** or after **despite**, it must be in the '-ing' form.

3. BECAUSE words

because

Use this to give the reason for something.

*I can't come **because** my car's broken down.*
*Bring a coat **because** it's very cold outside.*
***Because** you've been so helpful, I'd like to get you all a drink.*

as

Use this mainly when writing stories or descriptions.

***As** he wasn't well, I offered to do the shopping.*
*We left the party early **as** we had school in the morning.*

due to/owing to

Use this in written English or formal spoken English, especially when you are saying what has caused a particular problem.

*The dinner was cancelled, **owing to** the President's ill health.*

> ⚠️ **Owing to** cannot be used after the verb 'to be'.
> Don't say 'The delay was owing to engine failure.'
> Say **The delay was due to engine failure.**

thanks to

Use this when something has been possible because of someone's actions or because something is very good, very effective etc.

***Thanks to** everyone's hard work, the play was a great success.*
***Thanks to** its excellent suspension, the Mercedes feels very comfortable at high speeds.*

because of/as a result of

Use this when saying what made something happen.

*Hundreds of people lost their homes **as a result of** the war.*
***Because of** the increase in street crime, many old people are afraid to go out.*

> ⚠️ **As a result of** is more formal than **because of.**

---

4.   IF words

if

***If** I have the time, I'll come with you.*
***If** the snow doesn't stop, I won't be able to get to work.*
***If** I'd known you were there, I would have phoned.*

even if

Use this when something will still happen if a situation changes or if there is a problem.

*I've got to get a job, **even if** it's not well paid.*
***Even if** we leave now, we'll still be late.*

unless

Use this to say that something will happen if something else does not stop it from happening.

*Let's go now, **unless** you're too tired.* (=if you're not too tired, let's go)
***Unless** you work harder, you'll fail the test.* (=if you don't work harder, you'll fail the test)

in case

Use this to say that you will do something in order to deal with something that might happen.

*Take an umbrella **in case** it rains.* (=if it rains you'll be able to use it)
***In case** I'm late, here's the key to the apartment.* (=if I'm late, you'll be able to get inside)

suppose...?/supposing...? SPOKEN

Use this when you are talking about what the result will be if something happens. You have to make it sound like a 'what if...?' question

***Suppose** you lose your job? What will we do then?*
***Supposing** my Mum finds out we were at the party? She'll kill me.*

or/otherwise

Use this when there will be a bad result if someone does not do something or if something does not happen.

*Don't eat so much chocolate **or** you'll be sick.* (=if you eat so much chocolate you'll be sick)
*I'd better go now, **otherwise** Ann will wonder where I am.* (=if I don't go now, Ann will wonder where I am)

5.   THEREFORE words
use these words to say what the result of something is

so

Use this in spoken English or informal written English to link two ideas in one sentence.

*John's sick, **so** he won't be able to come tonight.*
*My Dad's in a bad mood, **so** there's no point in asking him if I can borrow the car.*

therefore

Use this in formal written English such as essays or reports, to link a result in one sentence with a cause in the previous sentence.

*I would like to spend more time with my family. I have **therefore** decided to resign as chairman.*
*The dollar has gone down against the yen, and **therefore** Japanese goods seem more expensive.*

6.   IN ORDER TO words
use these words to say what the purpose of an action is

to

Use this in spoken or written English.

*I went to the bank **to** get some money.*
***To** lose weight, you should exercise more.*

in order to

Use this in more formal written English.

*Some drug users steal **in order to** buy drugs.*
***In order to** be a doctor, you have to study for six years.*

so (that)

Use this in spoken English or informal written English.

*I'm studying English **so that** I can go to college.*
*I'm saving up **so** I can go to the concert.*

POSITION & DIRECTION

use these words and phrases to say where someone or
something is, or to talk about the direction they are moving in

1. **in a place**
2. **in a room/box etc**
3. **into**
4. **out of**
5. **outside**
6. **to/towards**
7. **(away) from**
8. **on**
9. **next to**
10. **opposite**
11. **in front of**
12. **behind**
13. **between/among**
14. **around**
15. **across/through**
16. **along**
17. **above**
18. **under**
19. **up**
20. **down**
21. **forward**
22. **backwards**
23. **top**
24. **bottom**
25. **front**
26. **back**
27. **side**
28. **corner**

1. in a place

in [*preposition*]

■ use this when you are not saying exactly where someone or
something is within a particular area: *in the garden* | *in the
sky* | *in the city* | *swimming in the lake*

■ use this with names of countries and towns: *My uncle lives
in Canada.* | *I work in Birmingham.*

at [*preposition*]

■ use this when you are saying exactly where someone or something is: *I was waiting at
the bus stop.* | *Let's meet at Bill's house.* | *Turn left at the church.* | *He was sitting
at his desk.* | *They're at the airport.*

■ use this with names of buildings, shops, hotels, theatres, schools etc: *We're staying at
the Holiday Inn.* | *He studied economics at Harvard Business School.*

■ use this with addresses: *The Prime Minister lives at 10 Downing Street.*

on [*preposition*]

on the beach/coast/shore/island *a city on the west coast of Australia* | *He spent the
rest of his life on the island of St Helena.*

on the first/second etc floor *The manager's office is on the third floor.*

on a farm/ranch *She lived with her parents on the farm.*

> ⚠ Don't say 'in our home'. Say **at home**: *We decided to spend a quiet weekend
> at home.*
>
> ⚠ Don't say 'I stayed in my bed.' Say **I stayed in bed.**

2. in a box, room etc

in [preposition/adv]

in a container, room, building, or vehicle: *There were some pink flowers in the vase.* | *He's in the office.* | *There were four people in the car.*

be in/stay in to be in the building where you live or work:
She's never in when I call. | *We're staying in this evening.*

inside [preposition/adv]

■ use this when you are talking about something completely enclosed in a container: *There's a key inside the envelope.*

■ use this when you are outside and thinking about what is happening in a room or building:
The lights were on inside the house. | *It was snowing outside, but inside it was nice and warm.*

indoors [adv]

inside a building, especially someone's home: *I hope you're not going to stay indoors on a sunny day like this.*

indoor [adj only before noun]

used or happening indoors: *indoor tennis* | *an indoor swimming pool*

the inside [n singular]

the part of something that is inside

+ of *The inside of the cupboard had not been painted.*

interior [n singular]

the inside of a building or car: *The all-leather interior and CD player make this new model a truly luxurious car.*

+ of *My eyes gradually became accustomed to the dark interior of the store.*

3. into

into [preposition]

I saw him going into a bar. | *She got back into bed.* | *Pour the milk into a pan.*

⚠ Don't spell this as 'in to'. The correct spelling is **into**.

⚠ After put, **throw**, **drop**, **jump**, and **look** it is more natural to use **in** as a preposition:
Put it in the drawer (not 'into the drawer'). | *My gloves are dirty - I dropped them in the mud.* | *I told him to go and jump in a lake.* | *Look in the cupboard and see if it's there.*

in [adv]

into the place where you are or the place you have just mentioned: *Come in and sit down.* | *Look who's just walked in.* | *All the gates were locked. How did they get in?*

inside [adv preposition]

into an enclosed space such as a cupboard, or into a building from the outside: *Come inside, out of the rain.* | *Jane opened the cupboard and looked inside.* | *Go inside the cave and look around you.*

indoors [adv]

into a building, especially someone's home: *When it got colder, we went back indoors.*

4. out of

out [adv]

moving or looking away from the inside of a building, room, or container: *I sent her out to buy a newspaper.* | *She opened her bag and took out her passport.*

+ of *Sharon sat there, staring out of the window.* | *People came rushing out of the office to see what had happened.*

outside [adv/preposition]

out of a building or room: *Look outside - it's snowing.* | *Why don't we go outside and sit on the patio?* | *As soon as I got outside the room, I wanted to cry.*

5. outside

outside [adv/preposition]

not inside a building, room, or area: *I'm going to sit outside in the sun.* | *Would you wait outside, please* | *When I woke up, it was still dark outside.* | *There's someone outside the door.* | *I'll meet you outside the theatre.*

outside Boston/the US/Europe (=not inside a city/country etc): *Clark Air Base is the largest American military base outside the US.* | *We live just outside the town.*

> ⚠ In American English you can also use **outside of** instead of **outside**.

outdoors/out of doors [adj]

not inside any buildings - use this especially to talk about pleasant or healthy things that you do outside: *We often eat outdoors on summer evenings.* | *I spend my weekends out of doors, playing golf or working in the garden.*

outdoor [adj only before noun] used or happening outdoors: *an outdoor swimming pool* | *outdoor activities such as skiing and climbing*

out [adv]

out in/out on/out there etc somewhere outside a room or building: *We had to stand out in the rain.* "Where's Martin?" | "He's out in the corridor." | *It's cold out there.*

the outside [n singular]

the part of something that you see from outside

+ of *We must paint the outside of the house.*

from the outside *From the outside, it looks like an ordinary townhouse.*

on the outside *I can't eat these hamburgers - they're burnt on the outside and raw in the middle.*

outside [adj only before noun] on the outside of a building: *The outside walls of the school were covered with graffiti.* | *an outside toilet*

---

6. to/towards

on [preposition]

He's gone to Australia. | *She stood up and walked to the door.* | *the road to the airport* | *a trip to Palm Springs*

on your way to (=while going to a place) *We stopped for a drink on our way to the theatre.*

> ⚠ Don't say 'I came in England.' Say **I came to England.**
>
> ⚠ Don't say 'We're going to home. Say **We're going home.**
>
> ⚠ Don't say 'They go to the school/the college'. Say **They go to school/college.**
>
> ⚠ Don't say 'come to here' or 'go to there'. **Say come here** and **go there.**

towards [preposition]

moving, facing, or pointing in a particular direction: *Wright noticed two policemen walking towards him.* | *All the windows face towards the sea.*

in the direction of

going towards a place that you know about but cannot see: *Bramwell rode off in the direction of Foxwood.* | *Guests were starting to move in the direction of the dining room.*

up [adv]

go/come/walk/drive up to go towards someone or something and stop near them: *He drove up in a red Mercedes and parked it in front of the house.*

+ to *An old man came up to me in the street and asked for money.*

7. (away) from

from [preposition]

> You can fly from St Louis to San Francisco. | He broke his leg when he jumped from an upstairs window.

away [adv]

> if you walk **away,** move **away**, run **away** etc you move in a direction that takes you further from someone or something:
> He turned his back on me and walked away.

> **+ from** Keep away from the edge of the cliff - it's dangerous.

off [adv/preposition]

> away from a place

> **go/walk/drive/ride etc off** (=leave a place) Travis got into his car and drove off.

> **off the field/stage/platform etc** The referee sent him off the field. | She bowed to the audience and walked off the stage.

8. on

on [preposition]

> on the surface of something: There was a glass and an empty bottle on the table. | You'll have to sleep on the floor. | Neil Armstrong was the first man to walk on the moon.

> **on the wall/ceiling/door** the pictures on the wall | a fly on the ceiling | You'll see his name on the door.

> **on sb's body/finger/dress etc** the diamond ring on her finger | torture that left no mark on his body | There's lipstick on your collar.

on top of

> on the highest part of something: I found this card on top of the cupboard. | the silver star on top of the Christmas tree

> **one on top of the other** (=in a pile) You'll have to stack the boxes one on top of the other.

onto [preposition]

> moving to a position on the surface of something: Nancy walked onto the stage and took the microphone in her hand.

> ⚠ After **put, throw, drop, land,** and **fall** it is more natural to use **on**: Put the books back on the shelf (not 'onto the shelf').

over [preposition]

> on something and covering it: There was a white sheet over the victim's body. | She wore a coat over her sweater.

> **put/lay/throw sth over sth** She put a blanket over the child's legs to keep him warm.

> **all over** (=on all parts of something) Look, there are pieces of paper all over the floor.

9. next to

next to

closest to the side of another person, room or building - use this especially when there are several people, rooms, buildings etc in a line: *I was sitting next to Mr Gregory.* | *Next to the church was a park.*

right next to (=next to and very close) *I was standing right next to him, but I still couldn't hear what he was saying.*

beside [preposition]

close to the side of something or someone: *Leave the medicine on the table beside her bed.* | *She came and sat down beside me.* | *Harriet was walking beside the river with her dog.*

by [preposition]

beside something: *I'll meet you by the entrance.* | *Relatives are waiting by the phone for more news of the crash.* | *a hotel by the sea*

along [preposition]

continuing or moving close to the side of a river, coast, border etc: *the path along the shore* | *Walk along the canal as far as the bridge.*

all along (=from one end to the other) *There were thousands of tanks and guns all along the border.*

at the side of

next to a road or path: *Richard left his motorcycle at the side of the road and started to walk.*

side by side

if two people are walking, sitting or lying **side by side** they are next to each other: *We walked along slowly side by side.*

next door

next to another building, house, office etc or living in the house next to someone: *The hotel's very noisy at night - there's a night club right next door.*

the house/office/shop etc next door (=next to the place you are in or the place you have mentioned) *The house next door has been sold.*

+ to *There's a bookstore next door to the bank.* | *Mrs Cottrell lived next door to my parents.*

next door neighbour BRITISH **next door neighbor** AMERICAN (=the person who lives next door)

10. opposite

opposite [preposition/adv]

in front of a building, thing or person, and on the other side of a street or table from them: *His wife was sitting opposite me at dinner last night.*

just/right/immediately opposite (=exactly opposite) *There's a bus stop right opposite my house.* | *The Harrisons live just opposite.*

> ⚠ Don't confuse **opposite** and **in front of**. If there is a bus stop **in front of** your house, it is on the same side of the street. If there is a bus stop opposite your house, it is on the other side of the street.

opposite [adj only before noun]
opposite side/end/corner (=the side etc facing you across an area)
I saw him walk past on the opposite side of the street.

facing sth/sb

a person, seat, or building that is **facing** something or someone is opposite them and has its front towards them: *an apartment facing the harbour* | *They sat facing each other across the table.*

across [preposition]

on the opposite side of a road, river, border etc from where you are: *My friend lives across the road.*

just across (=on the opposite side and close to where you are) *Tijuana is just across the border in Mexico.*

11. in front of

in front

further forward than someone or something else: *The car in front started to slow down.* | *She walked in front carrying the baby.*

in front of sb/sth

if something is **in front of** you, you are facing it; if something is **in front of** a building, object etc, the front of the building or object is facing it: *There was a tall man standing in front of me, so I couldn't see what was happening.* | *She parked her car right in front of the main entrance.*

> ⚠ Don't confuse **in front of** (=directly next to the front of a building) and **opposite** (=on the other side of the street).

ahead [adv]

if something or someone is **ahead** of you, they are in front of you, and you are moving in the same direction or towards them: *He knows the way, so let him go on ahead and we'll follow.*

far ahead *I shouted at him to stop, but he was too far ahead and didn't hear me.*

+ of *We could still see their car ahead of us.*

the road/way/path ahead (=the road etc in front of you that you are travelling along) *The road ahead was closed because of an accident.*

12. behind

behind [preposition/adv]

Put your hands behind your back. | *The sun disappeared behind a cloud.* | *I got here first - the others are following on behind.*

at the back ESPECIALLY BRITISH

behind a building: *There's a small garden at the back.*

+ of *The tennis courts were at the back of the main school building.*

in back AMERICAN

behind something, especially a building: *You can park your car in back.*

+ of *The garbage cans are in back of the house*

round the back BRITISH INFORMAL

to or in a place behind a building: *If you go round the back, you can leave your boots next to the door.*

13. between/among

between [preposition/adv]

if something is between two or more things, they are on either side of it: *The ball rolled between the goalkeeper's legs.* | *I was standing between my mother and father.*

halfway between *Nagoya is situated roughly halfway between Tokyo and Kyoto.*

in the middle

if someone or something is **in the middle**, they are in the middle of a group or row, with one or more people or things on either side of them: *Here's a photo of all the family - that's Mario in the middle.* | *My parents sat at either end of the sofa with me in the middle.*

+ of *a seat in the middle of the front row*

among [preposition]

in a group of people or things so that they are all around you: *I saw him standing among a group of students.* | *The house was hidden among the trees.*

surrounded by sth

if you are **surrounded by** people or things, they are all around you on every side: *Jill was sitting on the floor surrounded by boxes.*

14. around

around (also **round** BRITISH) [preposition]

in a circle or moving in a circle, with something or someone in the middle: *The whole family was sitting around the dinner table talking.* | *A small crowd had gathered round us.* | *He had a bandage round his wrist.* | *People used to believe that the sun went around the earth.*

15. across/through

across [preposition/adv]

from one side of something to the other: *The children ran across the road.* | *sailing across the Atlantic* | *We gazed across the valley.* | *The traffic was heavy so it took a long time to get across.*

+ to *He walked across to the window.*

over [preposition]

going from one side of something to the other, especially by flying, jumping, climbing, or using a bridge: *A cat jumped over the fence.* | *the road over the mountains* | *one of the bridges over the Rhine*

through [preposition/adv]

from one side or end of something to the other - use this about going through a town, a forest, or a crowd, or looking through a hole, window etc: *I pushed my way through the crowd.* | *walking through the forest* | *We drove through Baltimore on our way to Washington.* | *I could see her through the window.* | *The trip through the tunnel takes about 40 minutes.* | *We found a gap in the fence and climbed through.*

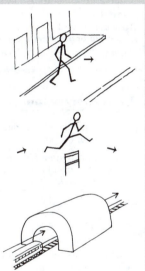

16. along

along/down/up [preposition]

moving or looking from a place on a road, passage, line etc towards the end of it: *walking along the road* | *I could hear him coming along the corridor.* | *I looked down the line of prisoners, but I didn't recognise any of them.* | *Go up Main Street and turn right.*

17. above

above [preposition]

in a higher position than something: *There was a light directly above the table.* | *Mexico City is 2400 metres above sea level.*

the floor/room/apartment above (=above where you are) *We could hear noises in the room above.*

from above *Looking down from above, we could see the whole island spread out like a map.*

over [preposition/adv]

directly above something or moving in the air above it: *Black clouds hung over the valley.* | *As the planes flew over, Selim could see the Russian markings on their wings.* | *Riot police fired over the heads of the demonstrators.*

overhead [adv]

in the sky directly above your head: *Suddenly, they heard the rumble of thunder overhead.* | *The ship moved away slowly with seagulls circling overhead.*

upstairs [adv]

on a higher floor of a building, above where you are: *The bathroom is upstairs.* | *We got a note from the woman who lives upstairs.*

upstairs [adj only before noun] *The burglars got in through an upstairs window.*

up [adv]

up in/up on/up there etc in a higher position than where you are: *The cat's up on the roof again.* | *Is it safe up there?*

18. under/below

⚠ If something is not directly under something else, use **below**: *the path below my bedroom window*

⚠ If something is hidden or covered by something else, or is moving directly under it, use **under**: *The cat was hiding under the table.*

under [preposition]

Wendy hid the box under her bed. | *the first of the boats was already passing under the Golden Gate Bridge.* | *The ruins of the ancient city now lie under the sea.*

■ you can also use this to say that something is covered by clothes, skin, paint etc: *I'm wearing a sweater under my coat.*

below [adv/preposition]

in a lower position than something: *We were standing on top of the mountain, looking down into the valley below.* | *He has a nasty scar just below the left eye.*

the floor/room/apartment below (=below where you are) *I work on the fourth floor and Gerry's office is on the floor below.*

underneath [preposition]

■ directly under another object: *I found your keys on the sofa, underneath a cushion.* | *He got out of the car and looked underneath.*

■ you can also use this to say that something is covered by clothes, skin, paint etc: *a disease caused by a tiny insect that lays its eggs just underneath the skin*

underground [adv]

under the ground: *The explosives are stored underground in concrete bunkers.*

underground [adj only before noun] *An underground passage leads from the castle to a secret cave.*

downstairs [adv]

on a lower floor of a building, below where you are: *I can hear someone moving around downstairs.* | *the people who live downstairs*

downstairs [adj only before noun] *I think it's in the downstairs cupboard.*

19. up

up [adv/preposition]

moving, pointing, or looking up: *Caroline looked up and laughed.*

up a hill/ladder/tree/wall etc *He had climbed up a tree to get a better view.*

+ onto/into/at etc *Don't let the cat jump up onto the table.*

straight up (=directly towards the sky)

upwards (also **upward** AMERICAN) [adv]

towards a higher position, especially towards the sky: *Most plants grow upwards, towards the light.* | *With a loud bang, the rocket shot upward into the night sky.*

upward [adj only before noun] *He signalled with an upward movement of the arm.*

uphill [adv]

going up a slope or hill: *It's hard work biking uphill.* | *The path continues uphill for another mile.*

upstairs [adv]

going up the stairs to a higher level of a building: *They carried her upstairs to the bedroom.*

upstairs [adj only before noun] *There was a slight movement at one of the upstairs windows.*

20. down

> ⚠ If you want to say that something comes onto the ground or a lower place, use **down**: *Come down from that tree!*
>
> ⚠ If you want to say that something is pointing towards a lower place, use the adverb **downwards** or the preposition **down**: *The path continued downwards* | *The path continued down the hill.*

down [adv/preposition]

moving, pointing, or looking down: *I told you not to climb on the table. Get down!* | *Tears ran down his face.*

+ into/at/off/from etc *Dr Morel glanced down at the notepad on his desk.* | *The accident happened as we were coming down off the mountain.*

down a hill/hole/slope etc *We went down some steps into a cellar.*

downwards (also **downward** AMERICAN) [adv]

towards a lower position or place: *a path winding downwards through the woods to the valley below* | *He was gazing downward into the pit.*

downward [adj only before noun] *the downward pull of gravity*

downhill [adv]

going down a slope or hill: *We set off downhill, towards the lake.* | *From here it's downhill all the way to the beach.*

downstairs [adv]

going down the stairs to a lower floor of a building: *She said goodnight to the children and went downstairs.* | *After drinking half a bottle of whisky, he had fallen downstairs.*

21. forward

forward (also **forwards**) [adv]

moving or looking towards a point in front of you: *She leaned forward to speak to the driver.* | *One of the guards stepped forward and raised his rifle.* | *Sit facing forwards with your legs stretched out.*

ahead [adv]

in front of you: *It was impossible to see ahead through the fog.*

straight ahead (=directly ahead) *He was staring straight ahead toward the gates at the end of the road.*

straight on ESPECIALLY BRITISH

if you go **straight on,** you go directly forward, not to the left or right: *When you come to the crossroads, drive straight on.*

22. backwards

back [*adv*]

moving or looking towards a point behind you: *He looked back over his shoulder.* | *I stepped back to let them pass.* | *Police pushed the crowd back, away from the palace gates.*

backwards (also **backward** AMERICAN) [*adv*]

moving back: *She fell backwards onto the bed.* | *Harry took a step backwards, and stood on someone's toe.*

23. top

the top [*n* singular]

the top part or surface of something: *When you get to the top, wait for me.*

+ of *There is a wonderful view from the top of the tower.*

at the top (=on or near the top) *When I'm painting a wall, I always start at the top.* | *He was waiting for me at the top of the stairs.* | *Write your name at the top of the page.*

top [*adj* only before noun]

top shelf/drawer/floor/layer etc *The books are on the top shelf.* | *Our apartment is on the top floor.*

upper [*adj* only before noun]

upper part/teeth/lip/deck etc the part, teeth etc at the top - use this when there is one part or set at the top and one at the bottom: *Several of his upper teeth are missing.* | *As the ship came in, she could see Henry waving from the upper deck.*

24. bottom

the bottom [*n* singular]

the lowest part of something

+ of *There's a crack along the bottom of the wall.* | *The ship sank to the bottom of the ocean.*

at the bottom *Paul was waiting for her at the bottom of the stairs.* | *The answers are at the bottom of Page 51.*

in the bottom (=in the bottom of a container, hole etc) *There's a little paint left in the bottom of the can.*

at the foot of sth

close to the bottom of a mountain, a ladder, a tree, or some stairs:

a hotel situated at the foot of the Lamvern Hills | *Jean stopped at the foot of the stairs and looked back at him.*

> ⚠ Use **at the foot of** in written descriptions.

bottom [*adj* only before noun]

bottom shelf/drawer/layer etc the shelf, drawer etc at the bottom: *She searched through the bottom drawer of her desk.*

lower [*adj* only before noun]

lower part/lip/deck etc the part, lip etc at the bottom - use this when there is one at the top and one at the bottom: *We drove onto the lower deck of the ferry.*

25. front

the front [n singular]

the part of something that is furthest forward, or the part of a moving object that is facing in the direction that it is moving

+ of *The front of the house was painted yellow.* | *You've spilt soup all down the front of your dress.* | *The hijacker walked down to the front of the plane.*

at the front (=at the front of a room, area, or space) *Come and sit at the front - you'll be able to see.*

on the front (=on the front surface or cover of something) *Her picture was on the front of 'Time' magazine.*

front [adj only before noun]

use this about something that is at the front when there are other things of the same kind behind it

front row/seats/page/teeth/legs etc *I don't want to sit in the front row.* | *a story that was on the front page of every newspaper*

front door/garden/room/entrance (=not the one at the back, but the one facing the street) *I walked up to the front door and rang the bell.*

26. back

the back [n singular]

the back part or surface of an object, building, car etc

+ of *I wrote a message on the back of an envelope.* | *We walked past the back of the college.*

at the back (=in the back part of the inside of a room, cupboard, drawer etc) *The students who were sitting at the back could not hear what the teacher was saying.* | *I found your passport. It was right at the back of the drawer.*

in the back (=in the back part of the inside of a car) *Just throw all your bags in the back of the car.*

on the back (=on the back of a piece of paper, clothing etc) *If you turn it over, you'll see the artist's signature on the back.*

back [adj only before noun]

use this about something that is at the back when there are other things of the same kind in front of it

back seat/row/page/teeth/legs etc *the back page of 'The New York Times'* | *There were two children and a large dog on the back seat.*

back door/garden/room (=at the back of the house) *You forgot to lock the back door.*

rear [adj only before noun]

in or on the back part of a building, car, train, or plane - used in official or technical information

rear window/exit/carriage etc *The two rear carriages of the train are reserved for non-smokers.*

27. side

side [n C]

the part of an object, building, car etc that faces left or right, not front or back

+ of *A motorcycle crashed into the side of the car, damaging the door on the driver's side.* | *There's a path along the side of the house.*

side [adj only before noun] at the side: *the side entrance*

sideways [adv]

towards your left or right side, not forward or backwards: *She glanced sideways out of the corner of her eye.* | *Lift your arm sideways and hold that position.*

from side to side

towards the left and then the right, and then towards the left again etc: *The ship swayed from side to side.*

28. corner

in the corner

at the place in a room where two walls meet, or at the place where two sides of an area meet: *The phone's over there, in the corner.*

+ of *He had pitched his tent in the corner of the field.*

on the corner

where two roads meet: *the shop on the corner*

+ of *Ross was standing on the corner of the street, waiting for her.*

around the corner (also round the corner BRITISH)

at or to the other side of a corner, either the outside corner of a building or a corner where two roads meet:
If you go round the corner, you'll see the side entrance. | *I think the gas station is just around the next corner.*

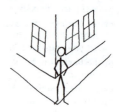

ESSENTIAL GRAMMAR

by David Crystal

The **Essential Grammar** covers the areas of English grammar which most often cause problems for intermediate learners. It has been based on students' needs and analysis of the Longman Learner's Corpus, with natural real-life example sentences taken from the British National Corpus. It provides practical help for students who want to put their grammar to active use when writing or speaking in English.

Contents

1 Statements and questions

STATEMENTS

A 'statement' is a sentence which gives information. If you make a statement, you usually give the sentence a subject, and this must go in front of the verb.

The children are playing in the garden.

NEGATIVE STATEMENTS

Negative statements are made in two main ways:

1. If the statement contains an auxiliary verb, such as **is** or **have,** you usually add **not** or its contracted form **n't.**

She is not leaving. **OR** *She isn't leaving.*

Am and **may** do not allow **n't.** **Will, shall,** and **can** have special contracted forms: **won't, shan't, can't.**

The same rules apply when you make a question negative.

Are they in the garden? Aren't they in the garden?
Will he get the job? Won't he get the job?

2. If the statement has no auxiliary verb, you need to make the negative using a form of **do + not/n't.** Make sure that the main verb is in its basic form.

She likes swimming. She doesn't like swimming. **NOT** *She doesn't likes swimming.*
I saw a ship. I didn't see a ship. **NOT** *I didn't saw a ship.*

QUESTIONS

Questions are sentences which ask for information. They fall into three main types, depending on the kind of reply they expect.

'Yes–no questions' expect a simple **yes** or **no** reply (or a word or phrase which can be used instead of **yes** or **no**). In these cases, you change the order of subject and verb.

Will Jane resign? (Possible answers: *yes, no, don't know, probably, maybe* etc)
Are they ready?

'Wh-questions' begin with a question word, such as **what, why, where,** or **how.** This kind of question can have a wide range of different replies. The answer may be a full sentence, or one which leaves out the words that you can guess from knowing the question. Here too, you need to change the order of subject and verb.

Where are you going? (Possible answers: *I'm going to work, downstairs, the library* etc)

'Alternative questions' give the listener a choice of two possible replies, both of which are mentioned in the question. The two possibilities are connected by the word **or.** Once again, you must change the order of subject and verb.

Will you travel by train or by boat? (Possible answers: *by train, by boat, don't know* etc)

Tag questions

You can change a statement into a question by adding a 'tag question' at the end of it. When you use a tag question, you are asking the listener to agree with the statement you have just made. If you make the statement positive, you expect the answer **yes.** If you make it negative, you expect the answer **no.**

A tag question is a type of 'yes–no question', and shows the same change of word order. You use the same personal pronoun (**she, they** etc) and tense of the verb as in the statement to which the tag question is joined. In the most common kind of tag question, you change from positive to negative, or from negative to positive.

She's outside, isn't she? (Expected answer: *yes*)
They were ready, weren't they? (Expected answer: *yes*)
You aren't going, are you? (Expected answer: *no*)
It isn't difficult, is it? (Expected answer: *no*)

Questions which are not questions

You can also use a sentence which looks like a question, but it is one where you are not actually expecting any reply. Because these sentences are halfway between a question and an exclamation, you will find them sometimes written with a question-mark and sometimes with an exclamation-mark.

In some cases, you already know the answer or you are asking your listener to agree with you. These sentences are called 'exclamatory questions'.

> *Hasn't she grown!*
> *Wasn't the book marvellous?*

In other cases, no answer is possible. (Of course your listener may still give you an answer, whether you like it or not!) These sentences are used when you want to express a strong feeling about something. They are called 'rhetorical questions'.

> *Doesn't everyone know that the whole thing is impossible?*

Polite questions

You can make a question sound more polite by using **please** and by using phrases such as **could I...?** or **may I...?** For more information about this kind of question, go to REQUESTS in the **ESSENTIAL COMMUNICATION** section.

2 Verbs: intransitive and transitive

Most verbs in English belong to either of two types: intransitive verbs or transitive verbs.

INTRANSITIVE VERBS

An intransitive verb does not have an object. You can use it without having to add any more words to the sentence. Here are some examples of intransitive verbs:

> *Something's happening.*
> *I'll wait.*
> *It doesn't matter.*

You can add other words to these sentences in order to show meanings such as time, place, or manner, but these words do not have to be there for the sentence to make sense.

> *Something's happening in the street.*
> *I'll wait for a few minutes.*
> *It doesn't matter at all.*

Other intransitive verbs include **appear, come, go, smile, lie,** and **rise.**

Intransitive verbs cannot be used in the passive.

> ⚠ Don't say 'it was happened' or 'they were died'. Say **it happened** or **they died.**

In this dictionary, intransitive verbs are shown like this: [v I].

TRANSITIVE VERBS

A transitive verb must have an object. Without the object, the sentence does not make sense. The object of the verb is usually a noun, a noun phrase, or a pronoun. Here are some examples of transitive verbs:

> *She bought that dress in Tokyo.* **NOT** *She bought in Tokyo.*
> *Did you find the key?* **NOT** *Did you find?*
> *I really like him.* **NOT** *I really like.*

Sometimes the object is a clause which begins + **(that).** For example:

> *I wish she would stop smoking.* **OR** *I wish that she would stop smoking.*

2: Verbs: intransitive and transitive

Sometimes the object is a whole sentence. For example:

"It's time to go home," he said.

Other transitive verbs include **make, use, need, thank, enjoy, keep,** and **carry.**

In this dictionary, transitive verbs are shown like this: [v T].

VERBS THAT CAN BE TRANSITIVE OR INTRANSITIVE

Several verbs can be used in a transitive or intransitive way. Here are some examples of verbs that can be transitive or intransitive:

There's no need to shout. [v I]
Someone shouted my name. [v T]

Where do you want to meet? [v I]
I'll meet you outside the school. [v T]

I'm sorry. I don't understand. [v I]
She didn't understand his explanation. [v T]

The intransitive uses are very similar to the transitive ones, except that the object has been left out.

In this dictionary, these verbs are shown like this: [v I/T].

OTHER VERBS

Some verbs can be followed by an adjective or adjective phrase. Here are some examples of these verbs:

You seem tired.
It all sounds very interesting.
Was he angry?

In this dictionary, these verbs are shown like this: [v].

3 | Talking about the present

English has two main ways of talking about present time: the simple present and the present progressive.

THE SIMPLE PRESENT

You make the simple present by using the verb in its basic form. You add **-s** or **-es** to the verb in the third person singular.

The simple present is used in the following ways:

1. You use the simple present to talk about something which is happening now, and which will continue to happen in the future. You often use the simple present in this meaning to talk about things that are true about your life, for example where you live, your job, or the kinds of things you like.

Martin lives in Canada.
I work in a hospital.
"What kind of books do you read?" "I mostly read science fiction."

2. You use the simple present when you talk about something which happens again and again, or say that something happens regularly at a particular time. Use words such as **always, often, sometimes, occasionally,** and **never,** or phrases such as **on Tuesdays** or **every day** with the simple present in this meaning.

They often go out to restaurants.
I travel to London twice a month.
He gets up at 6 o'clock.
She goes to church every Sunday.

3. You use the simple present to talk about something which stays the same for ever – such as a scientific fact.

Oil floats on water.
Two and two make four.

4. You use the simple present when you are describing what is happening at the exact moment when you are speaking. This meaning of the simple present is used for example in sports commentaries.

Shearer gets the ball from Gascoigne. He shoots - and scores!

⚠ For descriptions of actions that are happening now, you usually use the present progressive (see below), rather than the present simple. For example:

"What are you doing?" "I'm making a poster." **NOT** *"What do you do?" "I make a poster."*

THE PRESENT PROGRESSIVE

You make the present progressive by using a form of the verb **be** in the present tense, followed by the main verb with an **-ing** ending, for example **I am waiting, she is coming**.

The present progressive is used in the following ways:

1. You use the present progressive to talk about something which is happening now at the time you are speaking or writing. You often use this meaning with words and phrases that express present time, such as **now**, **at the moment**, and **currently**.

"What's Bob doing?" "He's watching television."
It's raining again.
I'm looking for my glasses.

2. You use the present progressive to say that something is happening now, but will only continue for a limited period of time. Compare these pairs of sentences:

We live in France. (=France is our permanent home)
We're living in France. (=we are living there for a limited period of time)

He cooks his own meals. (=he always does it)
He's cooking his own meals. (=he does not usually do it)

If you want to talk about the subjects you are studying at school or university, you usually use the present progressive.

She's studying law at Harvard. **NOT** *She studies law at Harvard.*
I'm studying English. **NOT** *I study English.*

Verbs that cannot be used in the progressive
Verbs which express a situation or process, rather than describing a definite action, are not usually used in the progressive. Do not use the progressive with the following verbs:

be	have	see
believe	like	agree
know	love	disagree
recognize	hate	mean
remember	prefer	need
understand	want	deserve
wish	belong	

I know the answer. **NOT** *I am knowing the answer.*
She understands me. **NOT** *She is understanding me.*

4 Talking about the past

There are several ways of talking about actions that happened in the past. These include the simple past, the past progressive, the present perfect, the past perfect, and the phrase **used to**.

THE SIMPLE PAST

You usually make the simple past by adding -**ed** to the end of the verb. For example:

I walk	→	I walked
we wait	→	we waited
they jump	→	they jumped

Many common verbs have irregular simple past forms, and so you have to use a special ending, or change the verb in some other way. For example:

I go	→	I went
we buy	→	we bought
they see	→	they saw

You use the simple past to talk about an action which happened and finished in the past. There is a space between the time when the action happened, and the time when you are speaking or writing about it.

He kicked the ball into the net.
I went home early because I had a headache.
The police found a dead body in the river.

You often use words or phrases such as **at midnight, on Tuesday, in 1992, yesterday,** and **last year** with the simple past, to draw attention to the time when something happened. For example:

Our visitors arrived yesterday.
Where did you go last week?
The war ended in 1945.

THE PAST PROGRESSIVE

You make the past progressive by using **was** or **were**, followed by the main verb with an -**ing** ending, for example **I was looking, they were laughing.**

The past progressive is used in the following ways:

1. You use the past progressive when you want to talk about something that happened in the past, and continued to happen for only a limited period of time.

We were living in France at that time.
I was trying to get the waiter's attention.
The man was looking at me in a very strange way.

2. You use the past progressive to talk about something which continued to happen for a period of time, during which another thing happened.

I was watching TV when the phone rang.
They met each other while they were staying in London.

> ⚠ Some verbs are not usually used in the progressive. Don't say, 'I was not believing him'.
> Say **I did not believe him.**
> See section **3** for a list of these verbs.

THE PRESENT PERFECT

You make the present perfect by using **has** or **have**, followed by the 'past participle' form of the main verb, for example **I have walked, she has gone, they have seen.**

The present perfect is used in the following ways:

1. You use the present perfect to talk about something that happened in the past and is finished, but which still affects the situation now.

Someone has broken the window. (RESULT NOW: it is still broken, and needs to be mended)
The taxi has arrived. (RESULT NOW: someone needs to go and get into the taxi)
Jane's hurt her hand, so she can't write. (RESULT NOW: Jane can't write)

You often use **just** and **recently** with the present perfect in this meaning.

Jane's just left, but you might catch her in the car park.

In American English, people often use the simple past instead of the present perfect in this sense.

British English	American English
I've just seen Carol.	*I just saw Carol.*
You've already told me that.	*You already told me that.*
Have they come home yet?	*Did they come home yet?*

2. You use the present perfect to say that something started to happen in the past, and has continued to happen up to now. There is a clear difference with the past tense, which you use when the action is finished. Compare these sentences:

present perfect: *I have lived in Chicago for many years.* (=I still live there now)
simple past: *I lived in Chicago for many years.* (=now I live somewhere else)

present perfect: *Jim has worked for us since 1992.* (=he still works for us now)
simple past: *Jim worked for us from 1992 to 1996.* (=he does not work for us any more)

> ⚠ Don't say 'I am living here for 10 years', or 'I live here for 10 years'.
> Say **I have lived here for 10 years.**

3. You use the present perfect to talk about something that happened at some time in the past before now, but it is not important to say when it happened.

She has had several jobs abroad.
There have been problems with this system in the past.

This meaning of the present perfect is often used in news reports.

There has been a big earthquake in Japan, and hundreds of people have been killed.

You can emphasize this meaning by using **ever** in questions, or **never** in negative sentences. For example:

Have you ever visited Scotland?
I've never been in a plane before.

If you give the date, year, or time when something happened, you must use the simple past, not the present perfect. For example:

I spoke to him yesterday. **NOT** *I have spoken to him yesterday.*
They arrived in the US last week. **NOT** *They have arrived in the US last week.*

THE PRESENT PERFECT PROGRESSIVE

You make the present perfect progressive by using **have been/has been**, followed by the main verb with an **-ing** ending, for example **I have been living, she has been studying.** The present perfect progressive has very similar meanings to the present perfect, but draws attention to the period of time during which the action has taken place.

The present perfect progressive is used in the following ways:

1. You use the present perfect progressive to talk about something which has continued to happen for a period of time in the past, and which may still be happening now.
How long have you been learning English?
We've been expecting them to arrive since last Thursday.

2. You use the present progressive to talk about something which has been taking place recently and which affects the situation now.

"You look tired." "I've been working really hard."
It's been raining all week, so the ground's very wet.

4: Talking about the past

> ⚠ Some verbs are not usually used in the progressive.
> Don't say 'I've been knowing John for a long time'. Say **I have known John for a long time**. See section **3** for a list of these verbs.

THE PAST PERFECT

If you want to talk about a past action which took place before another past action, you can use **had**, followed by the past participle of the main verb.

> *After the visitors had left, we watched TV.*
> *They told me that the taxi had already arrived.*

You can also use the past perfect in a 'progressive' form by using **had been**, and putting it in front of a main verb with an **-ing** ending.

> *We had only been driving for an hour when the car ran out of petrol.*

> **Using the right time phrases with the past tense**
>
> If you use words or phrases about time with the simple past, they must have a meaning which shows there has been a space between the time when the action or event happened and the time when you are talking or writing about it. For example:
>
> > *I saw John yesterday/a week ago/last Tuesday.*
>
> If you use other words or phrases about time with the present perfect, they must have a meaning which shows that the action has continued up to the present, and may still be going on. For example:
>
> > *I haven't seen John since Monday/so far/yet.*
>
> ⚠ Don't say 'I've seen him a week ago' or 'I didn't see John since Monday'.

USED TO

You use **used to** when you want to say that something happened in the past over a period of time, but it no longer happens now. It is found only in the past tense. You use **used to** with the basic form of the main verb, for example **used to smoke, used to live, used to be.**

> *I used to play football a lot when I was at school.*
> *She used to smoke 40 cigarettes a day.*
> *The club used to be very fashionable.*
> *They used to live in Los Angeles.*

In negatives, you say **didn't use to**, or **used not to.**

> *I didn't use to like spicy food.* **OR** *I used not to like spicy food.*

In questions, you say **did (you/she/John** etc) **use to ... ?.**

> *Did you use to smoke?*
> *What did she use to call him?*

5 | Talking about the future

There are several ways of talking about the future in English.

THE FUTURE WITH 'WILL'

You put the verb **will** in front of the main verb. This is the most common way of expressing future time. The short form of **will** is **'ll** and the short form of **will not** is **won't**. You usually use these in spoken English instead of **will** or **will not**. The main verb can be either in its 'simple' form or in its 'progressive' form. For example:

> *I will talk to them.*
> *We'll have a break at six o'clock.*
> *I'll talk to them.*

He'll be arriving later.
Don't worry - I won't break it.

You use **will** in this meaning in sentences that begin **I'm sure, I think, I expect, I suppose, I doubt** etc, or with words such as **probably, perhaps, certainly** etc.

"Do you think Carla will pass her test?" "Yes, I'm sure she will."
I expect I'll see him again soon.
They say it'll probably snow tomorrow.
Perhaps things will be better next week.

THE FUTURE WITH 'SHALL'

In British English, you often use **shall** in questions when making suggestions about what to do, or when discussing what to do. This use is rare in American English.

Shall we go now?
What shall I tell Mike?

In formal British English, you can sometimes hear **I shall** used to express future time.

I shall try to persuade them.

This is very rare in American English.

THE FUTURE WITH 'BE GOING TO'

You use a form of **be going to** to say that something will happen soon.

It's going to rain.
Watch out - you're going to hit that tree!
I think I'm going to be sick.

You also use a form of **be going to** to talk about someone's intentions, or what they have decided to do.

I'm going to ask for my money back.
Lucy is going to travel round the world when she leaves school.

THE FUTURE WITH 'BE ABOUT TO'

You use **be about to** to say that something will happen almost immediately.

Take your seats, please. The show is about to begin.
I was about to go out when the phone rang.

THE FUTURE WITH THE PRESENT PROGRESSIVE

You use the present progressive (**he's leaving, they're starting** etc) with a word or phrase expressing future time to talk about something that will happen because you have planned or arranged it.

We're leaving on Saturday morning.
I'm having a party next week - do you want to come?

THE FUTURE WITH THE SIMPLE PRESENT

You use the simple present (**it starts, we arrive** etc) with a word or phrase expressing future time, to say that something will definitely happen at a particular time, especially because it has been officially arranged.

The next plane to Los Angeles leaves at 6:25.
The meeting is on Thursday.
What time does the show start?

You use the simple present in subordinate clauses to talk about the future, for example in clauses that begin with **when, if, unless, before, after,** and **as soon as.** Don't use **will** in this kind of clause.

I'll call you when I get back. **NOT** *I'll call you when I will get back.*
If the bus leaves now, it will get there by 6. **NOT** *If the bus will leave now,*
* it will get there by 6.*

6 Phrasal verbs

WHAT IS A PHRASAL VERB?

A phrasal verb is a verb which consists of more than one word. Most phrasal verbs consist of two words: the first word is a verb, the second word is a preposition or an adverb. Examples of common phrasal verbs are **get up, put off, turn on, object to**, and **apply for**. There are also some three-word phrasal verbs, such as **look forward to** and **get away with**.

You can sometimes guess the meaning of a phrasal verb from the meaning of the words it contains, for example **come in** = come + in. More often, the meaning of the phrasal verb is different - often very different - from the meaning of the verb which forms its first part.

For example **put off** (=arrange to do something at a later time) has a very different meaning from **put** (=put something somewhere), and **look forward to** (=when you feel happy because something is going to happen soon) has a very different meaning from **look** (=look at something).

Like single-word verbs, some phrasal verbs are 'transitive' (they must have an object), and some phrasal verbs are 'intransitive' (they do not have an object). In this dictionary, transitive phrasal verbs are shown as [*phrasal verb* T], and intransitive phrasal verbs are shown as [*phrasal verb* I]. For example:

take off [*phrasal verb* T] (=remove your shirt, coat etc)
She took off her coat and sat down.
get up [*phrasal verb* I] (=leave your bed in the morning)
I usually get up very early.

Some phrasal verbs can be transitive or intransitive. In this dictionary, this kind of phrasal verb is shown as [*phrasal verb* I/T]. For example:

join in [*phrasal verb* I/T] (=start taking part in something that other people are already doing, for example a game or song)
We all joined in the game.
I want you all to join in.

WHERE DO YOU PUT THE OBJECT?

With transitive phrasal verbs, you have to decide where to put the object.

■ If the phrasal verb ends with a preposition, the preposition must come after the verb, and you cannot split up the phrasal verb. For example:

apply for sth (=ask to be considered for a job)
I've applied for a job at the university.
object to sth (=say that you do not agree with something)
Local people are objecting to the plan.

In this dictionary, this kind of phrasal verb is shown with 'sth' or 'sb' at the end, to show you that you cannot split up the phrasal verb and the object must come after the phrasal verb.

■ If the phrasal verb ends with an adverb, there are three possibilities.

1. If you choose a noun phrase as the object, you can put it either before or after the adverb. For example:

call off (=decide that a meeting, party, strike etc should not happen)
They've called off the strike. **OR** *They've called the strike off.*
turn on (=make a light, television, radio etc start working)
Will you turn on the light? **OR** *Will you turn the light on?*

2. If you choose a pronoun (**him, her, it, them** etc) as the object, you have to put it before the adverb. For example:

turn down (=make a television, radio etc less loud)
Can you turn it down? **NOT** *Can you turn down it?*

3. If the object is a long phrase, you usually put it at the end after the phrasal verb. For example:

They've called off the strike that was planned for next week.
Can you turn down the television in the front room?

This dictionary tells you how to move the object with this kind of phrasal verb. Here is an example of the kind of information it gives you:

try on [*phrasal verb* T] to put on a piece of clothing, to see if it fits you and looks nice on you
  try sth on *If you like the shoes, why don't you try them on?*
  try on sth *I tried on a beautiful coat, but it was too big.*

7 Modal verbs

The main 'modal verbs' (or 'modals') are:

can	may	will	shall	must
could	might	would	should	

Ought to, used to, dare and **need** are also used as modal verbs, but they have other uses as well.

WHEN TO USE MODAL VERBS

Modals have several meanings, so you need to think about the meaning of the sentence as a whole to be sure that your choice of modal expresses exactly what you want to say. The main ideas that modals are used to express are shown in the following sections.

Permission

(=allowing someone to do something)

If you want to give or ask for permission, use **can** or **may.** **May** is more polite or formal than **can.**

You can leave when the bell rings.
Customers may purchase extra copies at half price.

Could is a polite way of asking for permission.

Could I leave early today?

Might is a very formal and old-fashioned way of asking for permission.

Might I borrow your umbrella?

➡ see also **LET** and **EC PERMISSION**

Obligation

(=saying what someone must do)

If you want to demand that something happens, or that someone does something (=to express obligation), use **must.** You can also use this idea about yourself, in order to express a sense of duty.

The builders must finish the job today.
We mustn't leave the house before 6 o'clock.
I must remember to bring my notebook.

➡ see also **MUST**

Intention

(=saying what you are going to do)

If you want to say that you intend to do something, use **will** or **shall.** You can emphasize the meaning of intention if you say the modal louder than the surrounding words.

7: Modal verbs

Shall is only used with the first person (**I** or **we**), and is much less common than **will**. It is hardly ever used in American English.

This letter says they will definitely give us our money back.
I shan't stay long.

To express an intention at a time in the past, use **would**.

I tried to explain, but nobody would listen.

Use **would** if there are conditions controlling whether something will take place.

I would leave tomorrow, if I had the money.

➡ see also **INTEND**

Ability

(=saying whether you are able to do something)

If you want to say whether someone is able to carry out an action, use **can**.

Guy can speak Russian.
Can you remember her name?
I can't find my shoes!

When you put these sentences into the past tense, use **could**.

He was late for school because he couldn't find his bag.

Use **could** if there are conditions controlling whether the event will take place.

I could leave tomorrow, if I had the money.

➡ see also **CAN**

Possibility

(=saying whether something is possible)

If you want to say that something is possible, use **can** or **may**. **May** is more polite or formal than **can**.

You can go by bus from London to Liverpool.
You may find the manager is still there, if you go to the office now.

If you want to suggest that the action is less likely to happen, use **could** or **might**. If you use **might**, you mean that the action is especially unlikely.

We could go by bus.
We might go by bus. (=it is possible, but only if there are no problems)

➡ see also **POSSIBLE**

Probability

(=saying whether something is likely)

If you want to suggest that an event is likely to happen, use **should** or **ought to**. It will probably take place, but you are not completely sure.

They should have had our reply by now.
If you take these tablets, you should be all right.
We ought to be there by 6 o'clock.

➡ see also **PROBABLY, SURE/NOT SURE**

Desirability

(=saying that something is the right thing to do)

If you want to say that you think it is a good thing for something to happen, use **should** or **ought to**. If you think that it is a bad thing for something to happen, put these verbs into the negative.

You should get the early flight, if you want to be in good time.
You ought to see the doctor as soon as possible.

You shouldn't say things like that.
You oughtn't to have left the engine running.

➡ see also **SHOULD**

Necessity
(=saying that something is necessary)

If you want to say that it is necessary for something to happen, use **must**.

We really must go now.
I must get my hair cut this weekend.

If you want to express the opposite meaning (=it is unnecessary for something to happen) use **needn't/need not** or **not need to**.

There's plenty of time so you needn't worry.

> ⚠ Don't use **mustn't** because this gives the meaning of obligation.
> (see **Obligation** above)

➡ see also **NEED**

Certainty
(=saying that you are sure about something)

If you want to say that you are sure something is true, use **must**.

You must be tired, after all your hard work.
They must have left by now.

To express the opposite meaning (=you are sure something is not true) use **can't**.

You can't be that tired - you've only been working for an hour!
They can't have left yet.

➡ see also **SURE/NOT SURE**

Prediction
(=saying what you think is going to happen)

If you want to say that something is certain to happen, use either **will** or **shall**. As with the other uses of these words, **shall** tends to be found only with the first person (**I** or **we**), and is much less common than **will**. **Shall** is very rare in American English.

The cars will be there on time, I promise.
There is no doubt that we shall win.

➡ see also **SURE/NOT SURE**

HOW TO USE MODAL VERBS

■ Modal verbs are used with the basic form of the verb (=the infinitive form, without 'to').

You must pay now.   NOT *You must to pay now.*
They can go home if they want.   NOT *They can to go home if they want.*

■ Modal verbs do not have an **-s** ending in the present tense of the third person singular.

He can speak French.   NOT *He cans speak French.*

■ Modal verbs do not use **do** in questions or negatives.

Can you remember her name?   NOT *Do you can remember her name?*
We must not be late.   NOT *We don't must be late.*
Should we lock the door?   NOT *Do we should lock the door?*

■ Modal verbs do not have an infinitive, a past participle, or a present participle.

8: Conditionals

- In spoken English, you often use short forms when you use the modal verb in the negative.

cannot	→	can't
could not	→	couldn't
will not	→	won't
must not	→	mustn't
shall not	→	shan't
might not	→	mightn't
would not	→	wouldn't
should not	→	shouldn't
ought not	→	oughtn't

⚠ **Mustn't, shan't, mightn't,** and **oughtn't** are normal in British English, but American speakers usually say **must not, shall not, might not,** and **ought not.**

8 Conditionals

When you want to say that one situation (described in the main clause) depends on another situation, you use a conditional clause. Conditional clauses usually begin with **if** or (for negative clauses) **unless.**

Jane will pass the exam if she works hard.
Jane will not pass the exam unless she works hard.

They may follow or go in front of the main clause.

If Jane works hard, she will pass her exam.

Conditional clauses are used in two main ways:

- If you see the situation as a real one, and likely to happen, you use the present simple tense in the conditional clause and **will** (**'ll**) or **won't** in the main clause. Don't use **will** in the conditional clause.

If you take a taxi, you will be there in good time. **NOT** *If you will take a taxi...*
If you wear a coat, you won't get cold. **NOT** *If you will wear a coat...*

- If you see the situation as unreal, imaginary, or less likely to happen, you use the simple past tense in the conditional clause and **would** (**'d**), **might**, or **could** in the main clause. Don't use **would** in the conditional clause.

If you saw a ghost, what would you do? **NOT** *If you would see a ghost...*
If I bought a new coat, I might not feel so cold. (=I would possibly not feel so cold)
If I found their address, I could write to them. (=I would be able to write to them)

In sentences of this kind, the past tense of the verb **be** appears as **were** after the first and third persons, in formal speech and writing. Only use **was** in informal speech.

If I were at home, I would be watching television. (informal: *If I was at home...*)
If John were playing today, we'd have a chance of winning. (informal: *If John was playing...*)

- If you want to talk about conditional situations in the past, use **had** (**'d**) in the conditional clause, and **would have** in the main clause.

If I'd seen her, I would have asked her to call. (=I did not see her)
The books wouldn't have been damaged if Mary had moved them. (=Mary didn't move them)

- You can use **when** instead of **if** in sentences of the first type (present simple + **will** etc), but not with those of the second (simple past + **would** etc). **When** is not used in situations that are unlikely or impossible.

What will John do if he goes home? (=John is probably going home)
OR *What will John do when he goes home?* (=John is definitely going home)
What would John do if he went home? (=John is probably not going home)
NOT *What would John do when he went home?*
I would shout if I saw a ghost. **NOT** *I would shout when I saw a ghost.*

I wish

If you want to talk about a situation in the present which you are not happy about, and would like to change, use the simple past tense in the conditional clause.

I wish I had a new bike. (=unfortunately, I don't have a new bike)

If you want to talk about a situation in the past which you are not happy about, and would like to change, use **had** in the conditional clause.

I wish I'd gone by train. (=unfortunately, I didn't go by train)
I wish I hadn't gone by train. (=unfortunately, I did go by train)

9 | Active and passive

In the sentence *The dog chased the cat,* the verb (*chased*) is active. If you turn it around, and say *The cat was chased by the dog,* the verb (*was chased*) is passive. You form the passive by using the verb **be** and the past participle of the main verb. For example, the passive of **attack** is **be attacked**, the passive of **pay** is **be paid**, and the passive of **see** is **be seen.** You can only use the passive with transitive verbs (see section **2**).

WHEN TO USE AN ACTIVE VERB

You use an active verb when you want to say that the subject of a sentence does something. For example:

She opened the window.

WHEN TO USE A PASSIVE VERB

You use a passive verb when you want to say that something happens to the subject of the sentence. For example:

President Kennedy was killed in 1963.

You often use a passive verb when talking about the history of something. For example:

The bridge was built in the 19th century.
The company was established in 1826.

In these cases, it is much more natural to use the passive than to find a vague, active way of expressing the sentence (such as *Someone built this bridge in the 19th century.*).

You often use a passive verb when you are writing about science, or when you are saying how things are made. For example:

Hydrogen and oxygen can be easily mixed in this way.
Paper is made from wood.

If you used an active verb here, you would have to say who does the action – information which is not known or not important.

If you want to say who does the action of the verb in a passive sentence, use **by** and then say who does it.

President Kennedy was killed by Lee Harvey Oswald in 1963.
The bridge was designed by Brunel.

HOW TO CHANGE AN ACTIVE SENTENCE INTO A PASSIVE ONE

There are three things you need to do in order to change an active sentence into a passive one.

1. Move the subject of the active verb to the end of the sentence, and put **by** in front of it.

2. Move the object of the active verb to the front of the sentence, so that it becomes the passive subject.

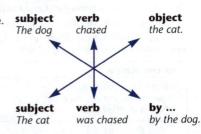

subject	verb	object
The dog	chased	the cat.

subject	verb	by ...
The cat	was chased	by the dog.

3. Change the verb from active to passive. You do this by adding a form of the auxiliary verb **be** and the past participle of the main verb (see section **4**).

THE PASSIVE WITH 'GET'

You can also make a passive using **get** instead of **be**. This kind of passive is very common in conversation. Do not use it in formal writing. You often use this kind of passive to say that something happened suddenly to someone.

I got sacked by my firm.   **OR**   *I was sacked by my firm.*
He got hit by a car.   **OR**   *He was hit by a car.*

You can also use the passive with **get** when you want to suggest that an action is more forceful or more important to you.

I get paid on Thursday.   **OR**   *I am paid on Thursday.*
We often get asked this question.   **OR**   *We are often asked this question.*

10 Nouns: countable and uncountable

COUNTABLE NOUNS

A noun is 'countable' if you can think of it as one of several separate units, for example **book, egg,** or **horse**. As the name suggests, countable nouns can actually be counted. In this dictionary, countable nouns are shown like this: [n C].

UNCOUNTABLE NOUNS

A noun is 'uncountable' if you cannot think of it as one of several separate units, but only as a single idea or substance, for example **butter, music,** or **advice**. These nouns are sometimes called 'mass' nouns. They cannot be counted. In this dictionary, uncountable nouns are shown like this: [n U].

GRAMMATICAL DIFFERENCES

There are some important grammatical differences in the way you use countable and uncountable nouns.

1. You can use a countable noun in the singular or in the plural, for example **book/books, egg/eggs, horse/horses, ticket/tickets, university/universities.** Don't try to use uncountable nouns in the plural. Don't say **butters, musics, advices, informations, furnitures.** It is a common mistake to use an uncountable noun in the plural.

You should listen to his advice.   **NOT**   *You should listen to his advices.*

2. You can use a countable noun with **a** or **an**: for example **a book, an egg, a horse, a ticket, a university.** Don't use **a** or **an** with uncountable nouns. Don't say **a butter, a music, an advice, an information, a furniture.** It is a common mistake to use **a** or **an** with an uncountable noun.

I like listening to music.   **NOT**   *I like listening to a music.*

3. You can use an uncountable noun with quantity words such as **some** and **any: some butter, any music.** If you want to use these words with countable nouns, you must put the nouns into the plural, and say **some tickets, any eggs.**

She bought some books.   **NOT**   *She bought some book.*

4. You can only use the quantity expressions **much, how much,** or **a little** with uncountable nouns. With countable nouns, you have to use **many, how many,** or **a few.**

uncountable	countable
I don't have much money.	He doesn't have many friends.
How much time do you have?	How many records do you have?
There is a little butter in the fridge.	There are a few rooms still available.

5. You can use an uncountable noun on its own without such words as **the, some,** or **any.**

She doesn't eat meat.
If you need advice, don't be afraid to ask.

You cannot use a countable noun in the singular in this way – only in the plural.

I like reading books. **NOT** *I like reading book.*
Computers are always causing problems. **NOT** *Computers are always causing problem.*

NOUNS WHICH CAN BE COUNTABLE OR UNCOUNTABLE

You can use some nouns in either a countable or an uncountable way, depending on their meaning. The following pairs of sentences show how the meaning can change: in each case there is a countable noun in the first sentence, and an uncountable noun in the second.

Would you like a cake? (=one of several cakes which someone can take to eat)
Do you like chocolate cake? (=a type of food)

The lambs were born early this year. (=the animals)
There are several ways of cooking lamb. (=a type of meat)

Most abstract nouns, such as **love, anger, knowledge, intelligence,** or **freedom,** are always uncountable. But some abstract nouns can also be used in a countable way.

uncountable	countable
They did it with difficulty. *Her voice sounded full of doubt.*	*They've had a lot of difficulties.* *I have my doubts about whether he's the right person for the job.*

In this dictionary, nouns which can be countable or uncountable are shown like this: [*n* C/U].

11 Nouns: singular and plural

Most countable nouns (see section **10**) have both a singular and a plural form, showing the difference between 'one' and 'more than one'.

REGULAR PLURALS

The regular way of changing a noun from singular to plural is to add **-s** at the end.

dog – dogs, chair – chairs, difference – differences

For nouns ending in **-y,** you drop the **-y** and add **-ies** to form the plural.

dictionary – dictionaries, opportunity – opportunities

For nouns ending in **-o,** you add **-es** to form the plural.

tomato – tomatoes, potato – potatoes

IRREGULAR PLURALS

There are also several irregular ways of forming a plural. In this dictionary, irregular plurals are shown at the end of the entry, after the definition and examples.

1. With seven nouns you change the vowel. They are:

man – men	*woman – women*
foot – feet	*goose – geese*
mouse – mice	*tooth – teeth*
louse – lice	

2. With a few nouns you change the final **-f** to **-v** before adding the **-s** ending. They include:

knife – knives	*leaf – leaves*
wife – wives	*half – halves*

Some nouns in this group have a regular plural as well: **scarfs** and **scarves, hoofs** and **hooves**. Both possibilities are correct.

3. With three nouns you add **-en**. They are:

ox – oxen, child – children,
brother – brethren (only in the religious sense)

4. A few nouns which have been borrowed from foreign languages have an irregular plural. They include:

stimulus – stimuli, crisis – crises, criterion – criteria, phenomenon – phenomena

Often, these nouns have two plurals: they have developed a regular plural but have also kept their original irregular one. In these cases, the regular form is more informal and popular; the irregular form tends to be used by specialists.

There are no certain formulas for success. (informal)
We have to learn all the relevant chemical formulae. (specialist)

5. A few nouns have no plural ending, but you can still use them in a singular or plural way: they include the names of some animals (such as **sheep, deer, cod**), certain nationalities (such as **Japanese, Swiss**), some nouns expressing quantity (such as **ton, p** (=pence)), and a few others (such as **aircraft, crossroads, kennels, offspring**).

The sheep was making a noise.   *The sheep were making a noise.*

PLURALS FOR COMPOUND NOUNS

Compound nouns combine two or more words into a single unit. You usually make them plural by adding **-s** at the end of the word: **can-openers, grown-ups**. But in a few cases, the first part of the compound takes the **-s** ending, especially when the compound contains a preposition.

runner-up – runners-up
passer-by – passers-by
man-of-war – men-of-war

Sometimes, a regular plural form has developed, which is slowly replacing the irregular one.

spoonfuls (also *spoonsful*)
mother-in-laws (also *mothers-in-law*)

NOUNS WHICH ARE ONLY SINGULAR

Several nouns are used only in the singular. There are three main types:

1. Proper names – names of particular people, places, times, occasions, events, and so on.

John, Robinson, Christmas, Tuesday

You can use these in the plural only if you think of them in a 'countable' way. This is especially common with proper nouns expressing time.

On Tuesdays I go swimming.
Are the Robinsons coming to the party?
We stayed with Mary three Christmasses ago.

2. Most uncountable nouns, such as **music** and **advice**, are only singular (see section **10**).

3. A group of nouns which you use in the singular even though they end in **-s**. These include the names of certain subjects, diseases, and games.

physics, linguistics, mumps, measles, billiards

A common mistake is to think of these as plural, and use them with a plural verb or form a singular noun from them.

Linguistics is fascinating.	**NOT**	*Linguistics are fascinating.*
Billiards is a game.	**NOT**	*Billiards are a game.*
Poor Mike's got measles.	**NOT**	*Poor Mike's got a measle.*

NOUNS WHICH ARE ONLY PLURAL

Several nouns are used only in the plural. There are three main types:

1. A few nouns are related to things consisting of two joined parts. They include **jeans, binoculars, trousers, pliers, scissors.** To talk about these in the singular, you use **a pair of.**

Your jeans are in the wash.	**NOT**	*Your jeans is in the wash.*
I need to buy another pair of jeans.	**NOT**	*I need to buy another jeans.*
	NOT	*I need to buy another jean.*

2. A few nouns ending in **-s** are used only in the plural. They include **congratulations, outskirts, remains, stairs, thanks.**

The stairs were steep and winding.	**NOT**	*The stairs was steep and winding.*
	NOT	*The stair was steep and winding.*

These are not uncountable nouns, because they are used with **how many,** not **how much.**

How many stairs are there?	**NOT**	*How much stairs are there?*

3. A few nouns express the idea of groups of people or animals. They include **people, folk, police, cattle, poultry, livestock.**

The police are outside.	**NOT**	*The police is outside.*
	NOT	*The polices are outside.*

12 Determiners and articles

'Determiners' are used before a noun to 'determine' the character of the noun – in particular, how 'definite' or 'general' a noun it is, and whether it is 'one' or 'more than one'.

When you use a noun, you have the choice of using it in one of three possible states.

1. You can use the noun without any determiner at all.

■ in the singular, if it is a proper noun	*Boston is on the east coast.*
■ in the singular, if it is an uncountable noun	*I can hear music.*
■ in the plural, if it is a countable noun	*Tigers have black stripes.*

When you use a plural countable noun without the article, you are seeing the noun in a general way – 'tigers in general'.

2. You can use the noun with either of the 'articles', **a** or **the:**

■ use **a** with singular, countable nouns	*I can see a car.*
■ use **the** with singular countable nouns	*I can see the car.*
■ use **the** with plural countable nouns	*I can see the cars.*
■ use **the** with uncountable nouns	*I can see the water.*

The articles are the most common determiners in English. Their main job is to say whether the noun is 'definite' or 'indefinite'.

3. You can use the noun with one of the other determiners. This adds a further meaning to the noun. For example:

determiner	adds the meaning of
my book	'possession' (also **your, his, her** etc)
this book	'nearness to the speaker' (also plural **these**)
that book	'distance from the speaker' (also plural **those**)
some books	'quantity' (also **any**)
enough books	'sufficiency'
each book	'item by item' (also **every**)
either book	'one of two' (also **neither**)
no book	'absence'
what book	'unknown item' (also **which, whose** etc)

12: Determiners and articles

> ⚠️ You cannot use two determiners at the same time. Don't say things like 'the this car', 'my an apple', or 'some the cups'.

You can use other words or phrases expressing quantity in front of a determiner to make the meaning of the noun phrase more exact.

NOTE: *(of)* shows that you can leave out the word **of.**

all (of) the people	*both (of) the cats*	*half (of) the gold*
double the amount	*twice the cost*	*a third of the people*
a few of the cars	*half (of) that cake*	*some of those cakes*

You can also add certain quantity words after the determiner. They include the numerals, as well as a few general expressions of quantity.

*The **three** kittens were playing on the floor.*
*I've just taken my **fourth** examination.*
*He bought it on one of his **many** trips abroad.*

If you want to add adjectives to the noun phrase (see section **13**), they always follow any determiners or other quantity expressions.

the three little kittens   my fourth difficult examination   his many interesting trips

WHEN TO USE 'A' AND 'THE'

A and **the** are called 'the articles'. **A** is called 'the indefinite article', and **the** is called 'the definite article'. They are used in the following ways:

1. The main use of **a** and **the** is to say whether you are talking about a noun for the first time, or whether you have mentioned it before. For a first-time mention, use **a**; for later mentions, use **the.**

*Mary bought a car and **a** bike, but she used **the** bike more often.*

2. If you use **the** with a noun that you have not mentioned before, you are actually saying to your listener 'you know which one I mean'. This is usually because there is only one example of the noun in the situation, or you have only one such example in your mind. That is why it is 'definite'.

Have you fed the cat? (=you have only one cat)
There's the hotel. (=that is the hotel we have been looking for)
I met him during the war. (=both you and your listener know which war you mean)
Pass the salt, please.

3. If you want to talk about something of a particular type in an indefinite way, use **a**.

I'm training to be an engineer. **NOT** *I'm training to be engineer.*
I went out to buy a newspaper. **NOT** *I went out to buy newspaper.*

4. Use **a** when you are talking about one of several things or people and it is not important to say which one. Use **the** when it is clear that you are talking about one particular thing or person and there is only one.

A man I work with told me about it. (=you work with several men)
The man I work with told me about it. (=you work with only one man)

5. You must use **the** with singular nouns such as **world, sky**, or **sun**, because there is only one of these things in the situation that you are talking about.

We're going to travel round the world.
Don't look directly at the sun.

6. If you are talking about buildings, places, and organizations as things which you often see or visit, use **the**. For example **the bank, the theatre, the cinema** etc.

I went to the theatre last week.
She's at the gym.

> ⚠️ When **a** is used before a word that begins with a vowel, it changes to **an.**

WHEN NOT TO USE 'A' OR 'THE'

1. If you want to use a countable noun in the plural to talk in general about something, don't use **the**.

Tigers are very fierce animals.
Prices keep going up.

2. If you want to use an uncountable noun to talk in general about something, don't use **the**.

There has been a big increase in crime. **NOT** *There has been a big increase in the crime.*
It takes patience and skill to be a teacher. **NOT** *It takes the patience and the skill to be a teacher.*

3. Most names of places or people that begin with a capital letter do not have **the** before them. Don't use **the** with these names.

They're visiting Belgium and Holland. **NOT** *They're visiting the Belgium and the Holland.*

However, there are some names that always have **the** in them, for example **the United States, the Nile** (=the big river in Egypt) etc. Don't forget to put **the** in these names.

He's from the United States. **NOT** *He's from United States.*

5. There are also many common nouns and phrases which do not use **a** or **the**. This is especially true when talking about meals, illnesses, ways of travelling, times and periods of time.

Will you have lunch with me?	**NOT**	*Will you have the lunch with me?*
Her mother has cancer.	**NOT**	*Her mother has the cancer.*
I travel to work by bus.	**NOT**	*I travel to work by the bus.*
In winter we get a lot of snow.	**NOT**	*In winter we get a lot of the snow.*
It's time to go to bed.	**NOT**	*It's time to go to the bed.*
We got up at dawn.	**NOT**	*We got up at the dawn.*

13 Word order

This section deals with two areas which can cause problems for students: word order with adjectives before a noun, and word order with adverbs after a noun.

WORD ORDER BEFORE THE NOUN

The main way of describing a noun is to use adjectives or words that are like adjectives. You add these words after **a, the, my, her** etc, before the noun. You can add as many as you want, but you sometimes need to be careful about the order in which you use them.

You have a choice of three kinds of word. The largest group consists of adjectives.

*a **lovely** day   a **small round** table   the **best** students*

You may also use a 'participle' before the noun – the **-ing** or **-ed** form of a verb, but here used to describe the noun.

*a **crumbling** wall   her **smiling** face   a **cracked** window   the **stolen** car*

You may also add one noun before another – the first noun is used to describe the second noun, which is the main noun in the phrase.

*the **school** buildings   a **tourist** paradise   a **London** bus*

WHICH ORDER?

As soon as you use two or more describing words, you have to decide which order to put them in.

In many cases, there is no rule: you simply say first what comes into your mind first. But many adjectives, and the other kinds of describing word, are typically used in a particular place before the noun. You should think of these patterns only as a guide to help you, because there are a number of cases which do not follow the rule. But the following patterns are common:

13: Word order

1. Nouns go next to the main noun in the phrase, after any other adjectives.

a big London bus   **NOT** *a London big bus*
the long country road   **NOT** *the country long road*

2. Words which are closely related to nouns, such as the material something is made of or where something is from, also go next to the main noun.

big leather boots   **NOT** *leather big boots*
a serious social problem   **NOT** *a social serious problem*

3. Participles usually go in front of groups (**1**) and (**2**), but after any adjectives.

a broken garden chair   **NOT** *a garden broken chair*
a smiling American tourist   **NOT** *an American smiling tourist*
a happy smiling American tourist   **NOT** *a smiling happy American tourist*

4. Adjectives with an 'intensifying' meaning, for example **entire, whole, same** go near the beginning, close to **a, the, my, her** etc.

the entire local committee   **NOT** *the local entire committee*
the same old battered car   **NOT** *the old battered same car*

5. Other adjectives follow (**4**) and go before (**3**). Those with a more general meaning usually come first, and those which describe properties of the noun which can be clearly seen, such as size and shape, usually come last. There are typical patterns here, too, as the table shows.

those lovely red curtains   **NOT** *those red lovely curtains*
a strange triangular table   **NOT** *a triangular strange table*

your opinion about sth	size	age	shape	colour	where sth is from	material
lovely	big	old	round	black	American	wool
beautiful	little	young	square	red	French	plastic
horrible	small	new	L-shaped	brown	Japanese	leather
etc	etc	etc	etc	etc	etc	etc

WORD ORDER AFTER THE NOUN

Some adverbs of time and frequency usually come immediately after the main verb. These include:

always	almost	just
rarely	nearly	already
ever	never	still

She is always complaining.   **NOT** *Always she is complaining.*
They are still working.   **NOT** *Still they are working.*

Always and **never** are sometimes used at the beginning of a sentence in instructions and warnings, when the verb does not have a subject.

Always keep medicines away from children.
Never look directly at the sun through a telescope.

Adverbs and adverb phrases should not come between the verb and the object.

I like Japanese food very much.   **NOT** *I like very much Japanese food.*

Adverbs and adverb phrases should not come between a main verb and an **-ing** participle, or between a main verb and an infinitive.

Tomorrow we'll go sightseeing.   **NOT** *We'll go tomorrow sightseeing.*
In the evenings she likes to watch television.   **NOT** *She likes in the evenings to watch television.*

Adverbs and adverb phrases should not come between a modal verb (for example **can, must, could**) and a main verb.

> *I can speak Spanish quite well.* **NOT** *I can quite well speak Spanish.*

OTHER WORD ORDER PROBLEMS

The *Essential Activator* also has information about word order with the following words:

all	➡ see **ALL**
both	➡ see **TWO**
each	➡ see **ALL**

14 Comparison

COMPARATIVE AND SUPERLATIVE ADJECTIVES

If you want to compare two things, you use the comparative form of an adjective. For example the comparative form of **big** is **bigger,** and the comparative form of **interesting** is **more interesting.**

> *Your car is bigger than mine.*
> *His new book is more interesting than his last one.*

If you want to say that one thing is bigger, faster, more interesting etc than all the others of a group of things, you use the superlative form of an adjective. For example, the superlative form of **big** is **biggest,** and the superlative form of **interesting** is **the most interesting.**

> *It's the fastest motorcycle in the world.*
> *What's the most delicious food you've ever eaten?*

CHOOSING THE RIGHT FORM OF THE ADJECTIVE

If the adjective is one syllable long, you add **-er** or **-est** to it, sometimes making a change in the spelling.

adjective	comparative	superlative
tall	taller	tallest
big	bigger	biggest
nice	nicer	nicest

If the adjective is three or more syllables long, you add the words **more** or **most** before it.

> *That's a more interesting question.*
> *Kim's question was the most interesting one.*
>
> *The new trains are more comfortable than the old ones.*
> *That's the most comfortable bed I've ever slept in.*

Most adjectives with two syllables use **more** and **most** to form the comparative and superlative, but some two-syllable adjectives have **-er/-est** endings, and some two-syllable adjectives use both methods.

The **-er/-est** endings are possible with adjectives ending in **-y, -ow, -le, -er, -ure.** Don't forget that with adjectives that end in **-y,** the **-y** changes to **-i.**

adjective	comparative	superlative
happy	happier	happiest
gentle	gentler	gentlest
narrow	narrower	narrowest
clever	cleverer	cleverest

14: Comparison

You keep this pattern even in the cases where you can add **un-** to a two-syllable adjective.

unhappier/unhappiest

Proper and **eager** do not follow this rule: you can use only **more/most** with them.

You use **more/most** with all other two-syllable adjectives.

more/most active   *more/most useful*   *more/most recent*

In this dictionary, comparatives and superlatives are shown at the end of the entry if there is anything irregular or unpredictable about them.

ADJECTIVES THAT DO NOT FOLLOW THE NORMAL RULES

Not all adjectives follow the normal rules. Some adjectives have completely irregular forms. The most common ones are:

adjective	comparative	superlative
good	better	best
bad	worse	worst
little	less	least

In this dictionary, we show these irregular forms at the end of the entry.

Words which are formed from a verb, and which end in **-ing, -ed,** or other past forms, always use **more/most,** no matter how many syllables they have.

His latest film is even more boring than his previous ones.
She was more shocked than I was.

COMPARING TWO THINGS WHICH ARE THE SAME

If you want to say that two things are the same size, the same height etc, you can say that one thing is **as big as** the other, **as tall as** the other etc.

She's as tall as her sister.
Do you think this summer will be as hot as last summer?

COMPARING TWO THINGS WHICH ARE NOT THE SAME

If you want to say that two things are not the same size, the same height etc, you can say that one thing is **not as big** as the other, **not as tall** as the other etc.

The meal wasn't as good as the last meal I had there.
I'm not as fat as him.   **OR**   *I'm not as fat as he is.*
London is not as expensive as some other European cities.

You can use **less ... than** to mean the same thing as **not as ... as,** but you usually use it with adjectives that have two or more syllables, for example **less expensive, less important.**

Value for money is less important than quality and reliability.

⚠ Don't use **less** with short adjectives such as **good, old** etc.

You can leave out the second **as** and the noun after it, if you have already mentioned or suggested the second thing that you are comparing.

The material looks like silk, but it's not as expensive. (=not as expensive as silk)

Similarly, you can also leave out the **than** part of the comparison when you are using **less,** if you have already mentioned or suggested the second thing that you are comparing.

I prefer the old Hollywood movies. They're much less violent. (=than modern films)
The buses are less crowded after 10 o'clock. (=than they are before 10 o'clock)

If you want to say that one type of thing is less expensive, less important etc than all other things of the same type, you can say that it is **the least expensive, the least important** etc.

People usually choose the least expensive brand.

⚠ Don't use **least** with short adjectives such as **good, old** etc.

15 Reported speech

REPORTING STATEMENTS

Direct speech

If you want to write what someone has said, the simplest way is to repeat the exact words that they had used in quotation marks ("..."). This is called 'direct speech'.

"I really enjoyed the meal," he said.
She went upstairs and shouted, "Time to get up!"

If you mention the speaker at the end of the sentence, and do not say **he** or **she,** you usually reverse the order of the subject and the verb. For example:

"It's much too cold to swim," said Frank.
"Go back to your room," said her mother.

Indirect speech

You can also report what someone has said without using quotation marks. This is called 'indirect speech'. The usual way of doing this is to use a clause which begins with + **(that).** For example:

"I'm tired!"
He said he was tired. **OR** *He said that he was tired.*

That is more common in written English and in formal spoken English.

Changing from direct to indirect speech

When changing from direct to indirect speech, you need to change the grammar in certain ways.

Verb tense forms usually need to change. In most cases, you change the present tense into the past tense.

She said, "I am staying at the Chelsea Hotel."
She said that she was staying at the Chelsea Hotel.

If the direct speech is already in the past tense, you need to put the verb even further back in time, using **had.** This applies to both past tense and present perfect forms of the verb (see section **4**).

He said, "I came by bus."
He said that he had come by bus.

She said, "I've definitely seen John recently".
She said that she had definitely seen John recently.

However, you do not use this rule if the verb in the direct speech already uses **had.**

She said, "I had given up hope of seeing him again."
She said that she had given up hope of seeing him again.

The correct relationship between the verbs in the reporting clause and the verb in the reported clause is called the 'sequence of tenses'.

If you report something that someone said, which is still true now, you do not need to change the tense of the verb.

"I want to get married."
She said she wants to get married.

"Blue's my favourite colour."
She said that blue's her favourite colour.

If the direct speech contains **will, shall,** or **may** (see section **7**), these also need to change.

will → **would**   **shall** → **should**   **may** → **might**

She said, "I will see you soon."
She said that she would see us soon.

Would, should, could, might, and **must** do not change.

She said, "I could visit him on Thursday."
She said she could visit him on Thursday.

15: Reported speech

You also need to change certain personal pronouns. **I** and **you** have to be changed to **he** and **she**, unless the original people are still taking part in the conversation. Similarly, **my** and **your** need to be changed to **his** and **her.**

Mary said to John, "I saw your cat."
Mary said that she had seen your cat. (if the person who says this is talking to John)
Mary said that she had seen his cat. (if the person who says this is not talking to John)

You also need to change times and places which depend on the speaker's point of view.

He said, "I saw the car here yesterday."
He said that he'd seen the car there the day before.

In this case **here** becomes **there** because you are in a different place, and **yesterday** becomes **the day before** because you are now speaking at a later time.

Similarly, **now** becomes **then, last week** becomes **the week before, two months ago** becomes **two months before, tomorrow** becomes **the next day**, and so on. Of course, if the time phrase does not depend on the speaker's point of view, it can be used without change.

He said, "I bought the car in November 1996."
He said he had bought the car in November 1996.

REPORTING QUESTIONS

When you are changing a question from direct speech into indirect speech, you follow the same kinds of rules as for statements. The only differences are that you need to use a different word to introduce the reported speech, and the word order of the question becomes like that of a statement. You end the sentence with a full stop, not a question mark.

You use **if** or **whether** to introduce a 'yes–no question'.

I asked, "Does he eat meat?"
I asked whether he ate meat. **OR** *I asked if he ate meat.*

You introduce questions where there is a choice in the same way – more usually by using **whether** than by using **if.**

I asked, "Is it Karen's book or Michael's?"
I asked whether it was Karen's book or Michael's.

You introduce questions that begin with **who, why, what, how** etc by using the word which begins the question in direct speech.

Someone asked, "Why doesn't she resign?"
Someone asked why she didn't resign.

She asked, "When will you go back to Japan?"
She asked when he would go back to Japan.

You often mention the person who is being asked the question, by using a pronoun (**him, her, them** etc) or by mentioning their name.

I asked him if he ate meat.
She asked Michael when he would go back to Japan.

REPORTING WHAT SOMEONE HAS TOLD OR ASKED ANOTHER PERSON TO DO

When saying what someone has told or asked another person to do, you usually use an infinitive.

"Go home!"
She told him to go home.

"Can you shut the window?"
She asked him to shut the window.

> ⚠ Don't confuse **say** and **tell.** Don't say 'He said me to go home.' or 'He told, Go home!' Say **He told me to go home.** or **He said, "Go home!"**

INDEX

INDEX

INDEX

When you see **EC**, go to the
ESSENTIAL COMMUNICATION section.

INDEX

INDEX

When you see EC, go to the
ESSENTIAL COMMUNICATION section.

C

When you see ⊠, go to the
ESSENTIAL COMMUNICATION section.

INDEX

INDEX

When you see 🄴, go to the
ESSENTIAL COMMUNICATION section.

When you see **EC**, go to the
ESSENTIAL COMMUNICATION section.

INDEX

INDEX

When you see 🔤, go to the
ESSENTIAL COMMUNICATION section.

　　　　　　　　　　　　　　　　　　　　　energy

E

When you see EC, go to the
ESSENTIAL COMMUNICATION section.

INDEX

When you see EC , go to the
ESSENTIAL COMMUNICATION section.

INDEX

INDEX

When you see ⒠ , go to the
ESSENTIAL COMMUNICATION section.

G

INDEX

When you see **EC**, go to the
ESSENTIAL COMMUNICATION section.

INDEX

When you see **EC**, go to the
ESSENTIAL COMMUNICATION section.

I

INDEX

When you see **EC**, go to the
ESSENTIAL COMMUNICATION section.

INDEX

When you see **▣**, go to the
ESSENTIAL COMMUNICATION section.

INDEX

INDEX

When you see ▣, go to the
ESSENTIAL COMMUNICATION section.

When you see **EC**, go to the
ESSENTIAL COMMUNICATION section.

INDEX

INDEX

N

INDEX

When you see EC, go to the
ESSENTIAL COMMUNICATION section.

When you see **EC**, go to the
ESSENTIAL COMMUNICATION section.

When you see **EC**, go to the
ESSENTIAL COMMUNICATION section.

INDEX

INDEX

When you see EC, go to the
ESSENTIAL COMMUNICATION section.

INDEX

When you see 🗨, go to the
ESSENTIAL COMMUNICATION section.

When you see **🔄**, go to the
ESSENTIAL COMMUNICATION section.

INDEX

INDEX

When you see EC, go to the
ESSENTIAL COMMUNICATION section.

INDEX

When you see 🖪 , go to the
ESSENTIAL COMMUNICATION section.

INDEX

When you see EC, go to the
ESSENTIAL COMMUNICATION section.

INDEX

INDEX

When you see **EC**, go to the
ESSENTIAL COMMUNICATION section.

INDEX

When you see EC, go to the
ESSENTIAL COMMUNICATION section.

When you see 🖪 , go to the
ESSENTIAL COMMUNICATION section.

INDEX

INDEX

When you see **EC**, go to the
ESSENTIAL COMMUNICATION section.

INDEX

Pearson Education Limited
Edinburgh Gate
Harlow
Essex CM20 2JE
England
and associated companies throughout the world

Visit our website: http://www.longman.com/dictionaries

Longman Essential Activator

First published 1997
Thirteenth impression 2003

ISBN
0 582 24741 1 (Cased edition)
0 582 24742 X (Paperback edition)

British Library Cataloguing-in-Publication Data
A catalogue record for this book is available from the British Library.

Typeset by OTS (Typesetting) Limited, Caterham, Surrey
RVC Associates, Hadleigh, Essex

Printed in China
GCC

Short forms

adj	adjective
adv	adverb
C	countable noun
etc	etcetera
I	intransitive verb
n	noun
sb	someone
sth	something
T	transitive verb
U	uncountable noun
US	United States of America
v	verb

Labels

AMERICAN	used in American English, but not in British English
BRITISH	used in British English, but not in American English
ESPECIALLY AMERICAN	used more in American English than in British English
ESPECIALLY BRITISH	used more in British English than in American English
FORMAL	suitable for formal writing or speech, but not normally used in ordinary conversation
INFORMAL	used in normal conversation, but not suitable for more formal situations, such as writing an essay or a business letter
SPOKEN	used mainly in speech, but not often in writing
WRITTEN	used mainly in writing, but not often in speech

Symbols

⚠	help box warning about common mistakes and how to avoid them
◯	word or phrase used mainly in speech